PRINCIPLES OF BUSINESS LAW

THIRTEENTH EDITION

Robert N. Corley
The University of Georgia

Peter J. Shedd
The University of Georgia

Eric M. Holmes
The University of Georgia

Prentice-Hall, Englewood Cliffs, New Jersey 07632

Library of Congress Cataloging-in-Publication Data

CORLEY, ROBERT N.
  Principles of business law.

  Includes index.
    1. Commercial law—United States—Cases.
2. Commercial law-United States. I. Shedd, Peter J.
II. Holmes, Eric M. III. Title.
KF888.C63 1986   346.73'07   85-19321
ISBN 0-13-701186-5   347.3067

Editorial/production supervision and interior design: Sonia Meyer
Chapter Opening Design: Celine Brandes, Photo Plus Art
Art Direction: Janet Schmid
Cover design: Christine Gehring-Wolf
Manufacturing buyer: Ed O'Dougherty

Printed in the United States of America

10 9 8 7 6 5 4 3

ISBN 0-13-701186-5 01

Prentice-Hall International (UK) Limited, *London*
Prentice-Hall of Australia Pty. Limited, *Sydney*
Prentice-Hall Canada Inc., *Toronto*
Prentice-Hall Hispanoamericana, S.A., *Mexico*
Prentice-Hall of India Private Limited, *New Delhi*
Prentice-Hall of Japan, Inc., *Tokyo*
Prentice-Hall of Southeast Asia Pte. Ltd., *Singapore*
Editora Prentice-Hall do Brasil, Ltda., *Rio de Janeiro*
Whitehall Books Limited, *Wellington, New Zealand*

CONTENTS

PART VIII – BUSINESS ORGANIZATIONS

PART IX – GOVERNMENT REGULATION OF BUSINESS

PREFACE

We are pleased to present this thirteenth edition of *Principles of Business Law.* Any book that is fortunate enough to reach a thirteenth edition has a long and rich tradition as a leading text in its field. It is in the spirit of this tradition that we have prepared this new edition. It contains the most up-to-date coverage of business law topics, while continuing to recognize that the students who use this text have needs quite different from those of law students. Whereas law students typically are expected to "search for the law," this text presents the legal principles essential to the businessperson in a straightforward manner.

As in the previous editions, each chapter is divided into several parts. The text should be considered the most important part of each chapter; it is in this material that the basic legal principles are discussed. Chapter summaries are new to this edition; they allow students to review the essential points of each chapter. Except for the first three, each chapter summary is followed by several case excerpts that present additional examples of legal developments using actual cases and decisions. These cases are footnoted in the text and can be read at the point where the footnote appears or after the entire chapter is finished. Following the cases are review questions that highlight key points of the chapter. By the time students have studied text, summary, cases, and review questions, they should be comfortable with the basic principles presented in that chapter.

One suggestion often made by reviewers of this and previous editions is to include forms within the text or in an appendix. After careful consideration, we have decided not to follow this suggestion. It continues to be our philosophy that standardized forms may be perceived as appropriate and usable in situations when such forms need to be tailored specifically for a given transaction. If there is an underlying theme throughout this text, it is that every businessperson needs to have a good working relationship with a competent lawyer. This book is intended to illustrate why such a relationship is necessary in order for the businessperson to succeed in our complex legal-oriented society. The inclusion of forms may encourage the layperson to believe that complex transactions can be completed without a lawyer. Forms such as checks and notes used in simple transactions are readily available, and we encourage professors to make available to students forms for routine transactions used within a particular jurisdiction.

This thirteenth edition consists of forty-nine chapters divided into nine parts.

The parts are designed as independent units, so that the material may be covered in any order. Indeed, even the chapters may be shifted from one part to another if the instructor so desires.

Part I serves as an introduction to various sources of the law and to the court system. Chapter 3 discusses the litigation process in detail. Chapter 4 places special emphasis on the various tort theories used to impose liability, especially on the business community. Problems related to malpractice by professionals such as accountants are highlighted. Chapter 5 is a separate chapter on criminal law because of the increasing importance of white-collar crime and the problems business managers face as a result of the high crime rate. These first five chapters provide an important foundation for the student of business law.

Part II, "Contracts," is designed to give students an understanding of the basic and traditional concepts of contracts, as well as recent developments in the law of "sales" under the Uniform Commercial Code. Chapter 6 is an introduction to this subject matter. Since the UCC and traditional contract law intersect at the offer and acceptance stage, they are treated as a unified body of law in Chapter 7 to avoid duplication. The Uniform Commercial Code is attached to the text as an appendix, and appropriate sections are referred to in brackets within the text for easy reference. The next three chapters (8 to 10) discuss the other essential requirements for every valid contract. Chapter 11 involves issues of form and interpretation of contracts. Chapter 12 includes a discussion of contractual performance, breach, and discharge. Finally, issues created when third parties become involved in contracts are discussed in Chapter 13.

Part III, "Agency," covers the subject in four chapters. Chapter 14 deals with the creation and general principles of the agency relationship. The next two deal with agency and the law of contracts and the law of torts. Chapter 16 on agency and torts also includes a discussion of the law of employment. A new chapter (17) has been added on the termination of the agency relationship. This chapter includes discussions of the declining importance of the "at-will" doctrine and the growth of employment antidiscrimination protections.

Part IV, "Property," has been reorganized, rewritten, and expanded. After an introductory chapter (18), methods of acquiring title to both real and personal property are discussed in Chapter 19. Chapter 20 presents transactions involving the sale of real estate. In Chapter 21, the lease of real estate and the bailment of personal property are discussed. Finally, a new chapter (22) on the use of wills and trusts in estate planning is included.

Without repeating the points emphasized under the law of contracts, Part V, "Sales Transactions," covers the specialized principles related to transactions in movable personal property. Chapters 23 and 24 serve as an overview of the important sections of Article 2 of the UCC which are not discussed in Part II with the contracts material. Chapters 25 and 26 are new chapters covering the subjects of warranties and product liability theories.

Part VI, "Commercial Paper," has also been substantially reorganized and expanded from four to five chapters. Special emphasis continues to be placed on the liability of parties, including banks, in commercial paper transactions.

Part VII, "Creditors' Rights," has been reorganized and rewritten. The first two chapters (32 and 33) of this part are concerned with secured transactions. Basically these chapters address five objectives students should achieve in studying Article 9: gaining an understanding of (1) the scope of Article 9, (2) the creation of a security interest, (3) the perfection of a security interest, (4) the priority issues that arise, and (5) the parties' rights and duties on the debtor's default. Since the 1972 revision of Article 9 has been adopted by most of the states, it receives special attention, with decreased emphasis on the original 1962 version.

Chapter 34 is a logical extension of the preceding discussion on the use of personal property as security. It covers the use of real estate as security for debts. Chapter 35 on other laws assisting creditors has been expanded; its emphasis is on a practical approach to the complex area of suretyship. Chapter 36 gathers in one place much of the recent litigation aimed at protecting debtors and consumers. The material on debtor protection is written from the creditor's perspective as a typical loan transaction develops. Chapter 37 includes an examination of the impact of the Bankruptcy Amendments and Federal Judgeship Act of 1984.

Part VIII discusses business organizations in three stages. In addition to the factors used in selecting the form of organization, these stages are (1) the method of creation of the various forms of organization, (2) the legal aspects of operating the various forms of organization, and (3) the law as it relates to dissolution of business organizations.

Finally, Part IX, "Government Regulation of Business," consists of five chapters that may be omitted if the students have had an introductory course in the legal environment of business which covers these subjects. Chapter 49 on securities regulation can easily be studied with Chapters 42 and 43 concerning corporations' formation and operation.

In addition to the substantial changes made in the text, this edition also reflects a substantial change in the authorship of *Principles of Business Law.* Professor William J. Robert has retired from the faculty of the University of Oregon. His distinguished career as a teacher, scholar, and leader in the business law discipline has meant much to this book. With gratitude for his years of service, we wish Professor Robert well in his retirement. And it is with great pleasure that we welcome Professor Peter J. Shedd as a co-author. Professor Shedd has taught at the University of Georgia for the past seven years. He has been active in both national and regional business law organizations, and has been recognized for his abilities in teaching and research. In 1980, he became the first young faculty member to receive the American Business Law Association's Faculty Award of Excellence.

Professor Barbara George of California State University has written a student workbook to accompany the text. We know that many students will benefit from its use, and we want to express our appreciation to her for its preparation. Professor Andrew Emerson, of East Texas State University, prepared the instructor's manual, and Professor Daphne Dell Sipes of The University of Texas, San Antonio, prepared the test bank. We thank them for their hard work and valuable expertise.

We should also like to acknowledge the assistance of the following professors who reviewed the manuscript and provided many helpful suggestions: Robert V. Nally, College of Commerce and Finance, Villanova, Pennsylvania; John S. Simmons, Nicholls State University, Thibodaux, Louisiana; William L. Yaeger,

Duke University, Durham, North Carolina; Elaine D. Ingulli, Temple University, Philadelphia, Pennsylvania; and Marrell J. McNeal, Auburn University, Auburn, Alabama.

We want to extend our gratitude in particular to Professor Robert L. Black, University of Illinois, who drew upon his thirty years of teaching experience to provide exceptionally detailed comments and suggestions. His contribution was significant to this edition.

We also thank David Boelio, Executive Editor of Business and Economics at Prentice-Hall. His support during the preparation and production of the manuscript was invaluable. Finally, and most important, we thank Sue Hoy of Athens, Georgia. Her assistance with all stages of the manuscript was indispensable. We could not have completed it without her.

Robert N. Corley
Peter J. Shedd
Eric M. Holmes

1 LAW

Each of the nine parts of this book covers a subject of the law that relates to business and the environment in which business operates. We will look at traditional business law subjects, such as contracts and business transactions. In addition, we will examine the legal environment in which business operates.

Part I gives us a background, an understanding of our legal system. We find out where our laws come from, how they are applied, and how they are changed. Our emphasis is on the various methods of resolving conflicts and controversies. Litigation and arbitration as a substitute for litigation are the major areas of study. There is detailed coverage of the law of torts (private wrongs) and criminal law (public wrongs) as they pertain to business. Subsequent parts of the text will consider substantive areas of the law as they relate to business.

Now, more than ever in our nation's history, law controls business decisions. Laws written to solve many of society's problems are directed at business, regulating its activity and its processes. Solutions to many of society's problems are found in laws, especially those regulating business activity.

1. Definitions of Law

Our view of the law will be a broad one, and our first question will be: What is law? In everyday conversation, people use the word *law* in many different ways, but it is a word that is very difficult to define. In its broad context, it expresses a variety of concepts. Law has been defined as rules and regulations established by government and applied to people in order for civilization to exist. Law and legal theory, however, are far too complex for such a simple definition.

1

In attempting to define *law,* it is helpful to look at its purposes or functions. A basic purpose of law in a civilized society is to maintain order. This is the prime function of that body of law known as the *criminal law.* Another role of law is to resolve disputes that arise between individuals and to impose responsibility if one person has a valid, legal claim against another, as in a suit for breach of contract. It is important that we bear in mind that the law is not simply a statement of rules of conduct, but also the means whereby remedies are afforded when one person has wronged another.

In one sense, all issues and disputes in our society—political, social, religious, economic—ultimately become legal issues to be resolved by the courts. Thus it can be said that law is simply what the courts determine it to be as an expression of the public's will in resolving these issues and disputes.

Many legal scholars have defined law in relation to the sovereign. For example, Blackstone, the great legal scholar of the eighteenth century, defined law as "that rule of action which is prescribed by some superior and which the inferior is bound to obey." This concept of law as a command from a superior to an inferior is operative in many areas. For example, the tax laws command that taxes shall be paid to the sovereign.

Another view of law is that it is a method of social control—an instrument of social, political, and economic change. Law is both an instrument of change and a result of changes that take place in our society. The law brings about changes in our society; society brings about changes in the law. The law—responding to the goals, desires, needs, and aspirations of society—is in a constant state of change. Sometimes the law changes more rapidly than the attitudes of the majority. In this event, the law and our legal system provide leadership in bringing about changes. At other times society is ahead of the law in moving in new directions, and changes in the law are brought about by the people. In the field of ecology, for example, various groups have put pressure on legislators to clean up the air and water. As a result, laws have been enacted, requiring devices to be installed to control pollution. Here public pressure resulted in the enactment of laws, and the law was a follower rather than a leader. It is important to note that the law is not static—that it is constantly changing and that the impetus for the changes may come from many different sources.

In still another sense, *law* has been defined as the rules and principles applied by the courts to decide controversies. These rules and principles fall into three categories:

1. Laws, including the federal Constitution and state constitutions, that have been passed by legislative bodies
2. Common law, or case law, derived from cases decided by the courts
3. Procedural rules, which determine how lawsuits are handled in the courts and include matters such as the rules of evidence and related issues

The first two elements provide the rules of substantive law that the courts apply to decide controversies. The third provides the machinery whereby these rules of substantive law are given effect and applied to resolve controversies.

While we are on the subject of definitions, we should point out that the pronoun *he* can mean "he or she," and we intend that inclusive meaning in almost every instance. In order to save the reader from tiresome repetition of the phrase "he or she," we use *he* throughout.

2. Forces That Shape the Law

Throughout history, legal scholars have written about the nature and origin of law, its purposes, and the factors that influence its development. Legal philosophers have generally acknowledged that logic, history, custom, religion, and social utility are among the major influences and forces that have shaped and directed the law. But there has been disagreement as to the relative importance of these forces, and the influence of each has varied throughout history.

Logic. Judicial reasoning often involves the use of prior decisions as precedent. The use of the analogy is of prime importance to the judicial process because of the need for certainty in the law. Logic may involve deductive or inductive reasoning. Deductive reasoning takes the form of a syllogism in which a conclusion concerning a particular circumstance (minor premise) is drawn from a general principle (major premise). Inductive reasoning involves the process of using specific cases to reach a general conclusion. It is often said that application of the doctrine of *stare decisis* by basing a decision on precedent announced in prior cases is inductive in nature, while applying a statute to a given set of facts is an example of deductive reasoning, but these examples are open to some criticism. In addition, the development of the law using logic would require that the law consist of a set of known rules. Since it does not, pure logic cannot always be used to decide cases. Reasoning by example, however, is at the heart of our judicial system.

In any case, "The life of the law has not been logic; it has been experience." In making this statement and in defining law as a prediction of what courts will decide, Justice Oliver Wendell Holmes stressed the empirical and pragmatic aspects of the law, its primary reliance on facts to dictate what the law is. Yet he recognized that law is actually unpredictable and uncertain.

History and Custom. History and custom play a significant role in the development of the law in many areas. The law tends to evolve as we learn from history. As customs and practices gain popular acceptance and approval, they become formalized into rules of conduct. Law was found in the rules, and it evolved from them. Custom results from repeated approved usage, and when such usage by common adoption and acquiescence justifies each member of society in assuming that every member of society will conform, a rule of conduct has been formulated. When such a rule is adopted by a court as controlling in a particular case or is enacted into legislation, law has been made.

Religion. Throughout history, religious principles have played a major role in the development of the law. Many legal theorists have argued that there exists a natural law, based on divine principles established by the Creator, which humans are bound to follow.

This natural law theory softened the rigid common law of England, became the basis of courts of equity, and found its way to America, in the Declaration of Independence: "certain unalienable Rights, . . . Life, Liberty, and the Pursuit of Happiness."

Social Utility. Law was previously defined as a scheme of social control. Social utility is perhaps the most significant force influencing the development of the law today. Social utility involves the use of economic, political, and social considerations as factors in formulating the law. Under the pressure of conflicting interests, legislators and courts make law. Thus law, when enacted by legislatures or pronounced by courts, is the end result of finding an equilibrium between conflicting interests.

Law is not only generalization deduced from a set of facts, a recognized tradition, a prescribed formula for determining natural justice; it is also a set of rules for social control, and it grows out of human experiences. Current social mores, political ideologies, international situations and conditions, and economic and business interests are all elements to be investigated and evaluated in making the law and in determining how it operates.

3. Classifications

Legal subjects may be classified in a variety of ways. Laws and legal principles are sometimes classified as substantive or procedural. The law that is used to decide disputes is *substantive* law. The legal procedures that determine how a lawsuit is begun, how the trial is conducted, how appeals are taken, and how a judgment is enforced are called *procedural* law. Substantive law is the part of the law that defines rights; procedural law establishes the procedures by which rights are enforced and protected. For example, A and B have entered into an agreement, and A claims that B has breached the agreement. The rules that provide for bringing B into court and for the conduct of the trial are rather mechanical, and they constitute procedural law. Whether the agreement was enforceable and whether A is entitled to damages are matters of substance and would be determined on the basis of the substantive law of contracts.

Law is also frequently classified into areas of public and private law. *Public* law includes those bodies of law that affect the public generally. Public law may be further divided into three general categories:

1. *Constitutional law* concerns itself with the rights, powers, and duties of federal and state governments under the U.S. Constitution and the constitutions of the various states.

2. *Administrative law* is concerned with the multitude of administrative agencies, such as the Federal Trade Commission and the National Labor Relations Board.

3. *Criminal law* consists of statutes that forbid certain conduct as being detrimental to the welfare of the state or the people generally and provides punishment for their violation.

Private law is that body of law that pertains to the relationships between individuals in an organized society. Private law encompasses the subjects of contracts, torts, and property. Each of these subjects includes several bodies of law. The law of contracts, for example, may be subdivided into the subjects of sales, commercial paper, agency, and business organizations. The major portion of this text covers these subjects, which constitute the body of law usually referred to as *business* law.

The law of torts is the primary source of litigation in this country and is also a part of the total body of law in areas such as agency and sales. A *tort* is a wrong committed by one person against another or against his property. The law of torts is predicated on the premise that in a civilized society, people who injure other persons or their property should compensate them for their loss. Chapter 4 discusses the law of torts.

The law of property may be thought of as a branch of the law of contracts, but in many ways our concept of private property contains much more than the contract characteristics. Property is the basic ingredient in our economic system, and the subject matter may be subdivided into several areas, such as wills, trusts, estates in land, personal property, bailments, and many more. Part IV of this text is devoted to a study of property.

Any attempt at classification of subject matter, particularly in the area of private law, is difficult because the law is indeed a "seamless web." For example, assume that an agent or a servant acting on behalf of his employer commits a tort. The law of agency, although a subdivision of the law of contracts, must of necessity contain a body of law to resolve the issues of tort liability of employer and employee. Likewise, assume that a person is injured by a product he has purchased. The law of sales, even though a part of the law of contracts, contains several aspects that could best be labeled a branch of the law of torts. Therefore it is apparent that even the general classifications of contract and tort are not accurate in describing the subject matter of various bodies of law.

4. Sources of Law

Our law comes from four basic sources: (1) constitutions, (2) legislation, (3) judicial decisions, and (4) the rules, regulations, and decisions of administrative agencies. Assuming that administrative agencies are part of the executive branch of government, our law comes from all three branches.

A unique characteristic of American law is that a very substantial part of it is found in cases decided by our courts. This concept of decided cases as a source of law comes to us from England and is generally referred to as the *common law*. Our common law system, which relies on case precedent as a source of law, must be contrasted with civil law systems, which developed on the European continent. The civil law countries have codified their laws—reduced them to statutes—so that the main source of law in those countries is to be found in the statutes rather than in the cases. Under the common law system, of course, we have a large number of statutes and ordinances, but these are only a part of our law.

In the United States, common law has been the predominant influence. Since most of the colonists were of English origin, they naturally followed the laws and customs of their mother country. But in Louisiana, and to some extent Texas and California, the civil law has influenced the legal systems, because these states were founded by the French and Spanish. However, much of the law in every state of the United States is statutory, and statutes are becoming increasingly important. Case law, or common law, remains an important source of law because of the extreme difficulty in reducing all law to writing in advance of an issue being raised.

As you read further, remember that the judicial system has established a general priority among the various sources of law. Constitutions prevail over statutes, and statutes prevail over common law principles established in court decisions. Courts will not turn to case decisions for law if a statute is directly in point.

5. Basic Constitutional Principles

In our constitutional system, the Constitution of the United States and the constitutions of the various states provide the basis of our legal system and our supreme law. All other laws must be consistent with them, or they are void. Most state constitutions are modeled after the federal Constitution. They divide state government into executive, legislative, and judicial branches, giving each branch checks and balances on the others. Constitutions also define the powers and functions of the various branches.

The Constitution of the United States and the constitutions of the various states are the fundamental written law in this country. A federal law must not violate the U.S. Constitution. All state laws must conform to, or be in harmony with, the federal Constitution as well as with the constitution of the appropriate state.

Two very important principles of constitutional law are basic to our judicial system. They are closely related to each other and are known as the *doctrine of separation of powers* and the *doctrine of judicial review*.

The doctrine of separation of powers results from the fact that both state and federal constitutions provide for a scheme of government consisting of three branches—legislative, executive, and judicial. Separation of powers ascribes to each branch a separate function and a check and balance on the functions of the other branches. The doctrine of separation of powers implies that each separate branch will not perform the function of the other and that each branch has limited powers. The system of checks and balances may be summarized as follows:

 SENATE: approves key executive and judicial appointments.

BOTH HOUSES: exercise control through power to appropriate funds and to limit or expand authority of the executive branch or the jurisdiction of the judicial branch in most cases.

EXECUTIVE: may veto legislation and appoint judges. (In some states, the judiciary is elected.)

JUDICIARY: reviews actions of the executive and has power to review laws, to determine whether or not they are constitutional.

The doctrine of judicial review is the heart of the concept of separation of powers. This doctrine and the doctrine of supremacy of the Constitution were established at an early date in our country's history in the celebrated case of *Marbury v. Madison.*[1] In this case, Chief Justice Marshall literally created for the court a power the founding fathers had refused to include in the Constitution. This was the power of the judiciary to review the actions of the other branches of government and to set them aside as null and void if in violation of the Constitution. In creating this power to declare laws unconstitutional, Chief Justice Marshall stated:

> Certainly, all those who have framed written constitutions contemplated them as forming the fundamental and paramount law of the nation, and consequently, the theory of every such government must be that an act of the legislature, repugnant to the constitution, is void. This theory is essentially attached to a written constitution and is, consequently, to be considered by this court as one of the fundamental principles of our society.

Justice Marshall then decided that courts have the power to review the action of the legislative and executive branches of government to determine if they are constitutional. This doctrine of judicial review has, to some extent, made the courts the overseers of government and of all aspects of our daily lives.

6. Legislation

Much of our law is legislation. Legislative bodies exist at all levels of government. Legislation is created not only by Congress, but also by state assemblies, city councils, and other local government bodies. The term *legislation* in its broad sense also includes treaties entered into by the executive branch of government and ratified by the Senate.

Legislation enacted by Congress or a state legislature is usually referred to as a *statute.* Laws passed by local governments are frequently called *ordinances.* Compilations of legislation at all levels of government are called *codes.* For example, we have local traffic codes covering all aspects of driving automobiles, and state laws such as the Uniform Commercial Code that cover all aspects of commercial transactions. The statutes of the United States are known as the U.S. Code.

Legislation at all levels contains general rules for human conduct. Legislation is the result of the political process expressing the public will on an issue. Courts also play a significant role in the field of statutory law. In addition to their power of judicial review, courts interpret legislation and apply it to specific facts. Courts interpret legislation by resolving ambiguities and filling the gaps in the statutes. By its very nature, most legislation is general, and interpretation is necessary to find the intent of the legislature when the statute was enacted.

Legislative bodies have procedural rules that must be followed if a law is to be valid. Among the typical procedural rules are those relating to the way

[1] 1 Cranch 137 (1803).

amendments are added to a proposed law, the way proposed statutes are presented for consideration (reading aloud to the members, etc.), and the manner of voting by the members of the legislative body.

7. Interpretation of Legislation

Theoretically, legislation expresses the will or intent of the legislature on a particular subject. In practice, this theory suffers from certain inherent defects. First of all, it is not possible to express the legislative intent in words that will mean the same thing to everyone. Statutes, by their very nature, are written in general language that is frequently ambiguous.

Second, the search for legislative intent is often complicated by the realization that the legislative body in fact had no intent on the issue in question, and the law is incomplete. The matter involved is simply one that was not thought about when the law was passed. Therefore, sometimes the question about legislation is not what did the legislature intend, but what would it have intended had it considered the problem. Both these problems result in an expanded role for courts in our legal system.

One technique of statutory interpretation is to examine the legislative history of an act, to determine the purpose of the legislation or the evil it was designed to correct. Legislative history includes the committee hearings, the debates, and any statement made by the executive in requesting the legislation. Legislative history does not always give a clear understanding of the legislative intent, because the legislature may not have considered many questions of interpretation that confront courts.

Judges use several generally accepted rules of statutory interpretation in determining legislative intent. Many of these rules are based on the type of law being construed. For example, one rule is that criminal statutes and taxing laws should be strictly or narrowly construed. As a result, doubts as to the applicability of criminal and taxing laws will be resolved in favor of the accused or the taxpayer, as the case may be. Another rule of statutory construction is that remedial statutes (those creating a judicial remedy on behalf of one person at the expense of another) are to be liberally construed, in order that the statute will be effective in correcting the condition to be remedied.

There are also rules of construction that aid in finding the meaning of words used in legislation. Words may be given their plain or usual meaning. Technical words are usually given their technical meaning. Others are interpreted by the context in which they are used. For example, if a general word in a statute follows specific words, the general word takes its meaning from the specific words.

Statutory construction is not always based on the type of statute or the words used. For example, if a statute contains both specific and general provisions, the specific provision controls. A frequently cited rule provides: "A thing may be within the letter of the statute and yet not within the statute because not within its spirit nor within the intention of the makers." This rule allows a court to have a great deal of flexibility and to give an interpretation contrary to the plain meaning.

The power of courts to interpret legislation means that in the final analysis, it is what the court says a statute means that determines its effect.

8. Uniform State Laws

Since each state has its own constitution, statutes, and body of case law, there are substantial differences in the law among the various states. It is important to recognize that ours is a federal system in which each state has a substantial degree of autonomy; thus it can be said that there are really fifty-one legal systems—a system for each state plus the federal legal structure. In many legal situations it does not matter that the legal principles are not uniform throughout the country. This is true when the parties to a dispute are *citizens* of the same state; then the controversy is strictly *intrastate* as opposed to one having *interstate* implications. But when citizens of different states are involved in a transaction (perhaps a buyer in one state contracts with a seller in another), many difficult questions can arise from the lack of uniformity in the law. Assume that a contract is valid in one state but not in the other. Which state's law controls? Although a body of law called conflict of laws (see page 12) has been developed to cover such cases, more uniformity is still desirable.

Two methods of achieving uniformity in business law are possible: (1) having federal legislation govern business law, and (2) having uniform laws concerning at least certain phases of business transactions adopted by the legislatures of all states. The latter method has been attempted by a legislative drafting group known as the National Conference of Commissioners on Uniform State Laws. This group of commissioners appointed by the governors of the states endeavors to promote uniformity in state laws on all subjects for which uniformity is desirable and practical. Their goal is accomplished by drafting model acts. When approved by the National Conference, proposed uniform acts are recommended to the state legislatures for adoption.

More than 100 uniform laws concerning such subjects as partnerships, leases, arbitration, warehouse receipts, bills of lading, and stock transfers have been promulgated and presented to the various state legislatures. The response has varied. Very few of the uniform laws have been adopted by all the states. Some states have adopted the uniform law in principle, but have changed some of the provisions to meet local needs or to satisfy lobbying groups, so that the result has often been "nonuniform uniform state laws."

The most significant development for business in the field of uniform state legislation has been the Uniform Commercial Code. It was prepared for the stated purpose of collecting in one body the law that "deals with all the phases which may ordinarily arise in the handling of a commercial transaction from start to finish. . . ." The detailed aspects of the Code, as it is often called, make up a significant portion of this text, and sections of the Code are referred to in brackets throughout this text where appropriate. Its provisions are set forth in Appendix A.

The field of commercial law is not the only area of new uniform statutes. Many states are adopting modern procedures and concepts in criminal codes and other uniform laws dealing with social problems. In addition, the past few years have seen dynamic changes in both state and federal statutes setting forth civil procedures and revising court systems. The future will undoubtedly bring many further developments to improve the administration of justice. The trend, despite some objection, is to cover more areas of the law with statutes and to rely less on precedent in judicial decisions, or common law, as a source of law. Many of these new statutes tend to be uniform throughout the country.

CASE LAW

9. Stare Decisis

Notwithstanding the trend toward reducing law to statutory form, a substantial portion of our law has its source in decided cases. This case law, or common law, is based on the concept of precedent and the doctrine of *stare decisis,* which means "to stand by decisions and not to disturb what is settled." *Stare decisis* tells us that once a case has established a precedent, it should be followed in subsequent cases involving the same issues. Judicial decisions create precedent where there is no legislation, as well as by interpreting legislation.

When a court decides a case, particularly upon an appeal from a lower-court decision, the court writes an opinion setting forth, among other things, the reasons for its decision. From these written opinions rules of law can be deduced, and these make up the body of case law or common law.

Stare decisis gives both certainty and predictability to the law. It is also expedient. Through the reliance upon precedent established in prior cases, the common law has resolved many legal issues and brought stability into many areas of the law, such as the law of contracts. The doctrine of *stare decisis* provides a system so businesspeople may act in a certain way, confident that their actions will have certain legal effects. People can rely on prior decisions and, knowing the legal significance of their action, can act accordingly. There is reasonable certainty as to the results of conduct. Courts usually hesitate to renounce precedent. They generally assume that if a principle or rule of law announced in a former judicial decision is unfair or contrary to public policy, it will be changed by legislation. It is important to note that an unpopular court ruling can usually be changed or overruled by statute. Precedent has more force on trial courts than on courts of review; the latter have the power to make precedent in the first instance.

The doctrine of *stare decisis* must be contrasted with the concept of *res judicata,* which means "the thing has been decided." *Res judicata* applies when, between the parties themselves, the matter is closed at the conclusion of the lawsuit. The losing party cannot again ask a court to decide the dispute. *Stare decisis* means that a court of competent jurisdiction has decided a controversy and has, in a written opinion, set forth the rule or principle that formed the basis for its decision, so that rule or principle will be followed by the court in deciding subsequent cases. Likewise, subordinate courts in the same jurisdiction will be bound by the rule of law set forth in the decision. *Stare decisis,* then, affects persons who are not parties to the lawsuit, but *res judicata* applies only to the parties involved.

10. Problems Inherent in Case Law

The common law system as used in the United States has several inherent difficulties. First of all, the unbelievably large volume of judicial decisions, each possibly creating precedent, places "the law" beyond the actual knowledge of lawyers, let alone laypersons. Large law firms employ lawyers whose major task is to search case reports for "the law" to be used in lawsuits and in advising clients. Today, computers are being used to assist in the search for precedent, because legal research involves examination of cases in hundreds of volumes. Because the total body of ruling case law is so extensive, it is obvious that laypersons who are supposed to know the law and govern their conduct accordingly do not know the law and cannot always follow it, even with the advice of legal counsel.

Another major problem involving case law arises because conflicting precedents are often cited to the court by opposing lawyers. One of the major tasks of the court in such cases is to determine which precedent is applicable to the present case. In addition, even today, many questions of law arise on which there has been no prior decision or in areas where the only authority is by implication. In such situations the judicial process is "legislative" in character and involves the creation of law, not merely its discovery.

It should also be noted that there is a distinction between precedent and mere dicta. As authority for future cases, a judicial decision is coextensive only with the facts upon which it is founded and the rules of law upon which the decision is actually based. Frequently, courts make comments on matters not necessary to the decision reached. Such expressions, called dicta, lack the force of an adjudication and, strictly speaking, are not precedent the court will be required to follow within the rule of *stare decisis.* Dicta or implication in prior cases may be followed if sound and just, however, and dicta that have been repeated frequently are often given the force of precedent.

Finally, our system of each state having its own body of case law creates serious legal problems in matters that have legal implications in more than one state. The problem is discussed in more detail in section 12 of this chapter.

11. Rejection of Precedent

The doctrine of *stare decisis* has not been applied in a fashion that renders the law rigid and inflexible. If a court, especially a reviewing court, finds that the prior decision was "palpably wrong," it may overrule and change it. By the same token, if the court finds that a rule of law established by a prior decision is no longer sound because of changing conditions, it may reverse the precedent. The strength and genius of the common law is that no decision is *stare decisis* when it has lost its usefulness or the reasons for it no longer exist. The doctrine does not require courts to multiply their errors by using former mistakes as authority and support for new errors. Thus, just as legislatures change the law by new legislation, courts change the law from time to time by reversing former precedents. Judges, like legislators, are subject to social forces and changing circumstances. As personnel of courts change, each new generation of judges deems it a responsibility to reexamine precedents and adapt them to the present.

Stare decisis may not be ignored by mere whim or caprice. It must have more impact on trial courts than on reviewing courts. It must be followed rather rigidly in daily affairs. In the whole area of private law, uniformity and continuity are necessary. It is obvious that the same rules of tort and contract law must be applied from day to day. *Stare decisis* must serve to take the capricious element out of law and to give stability to a society and to business.

In the area of public law, however, especially constitutional law, the doctrine is frequently ignored. The Supreme Court recognizes that "it is a constitution which we are expounding, not the gloss which previous courts may have put on it."[2] Constitutional principles are often considered in relation to the times and circumstances in which they are raised. Public law issues are relative to the times, and precedent is often ignored so that we are not governed by the dead. Courts reexamine precedents and adapt them to changing conditions. A doctrine known as *constitutional relativity* means that the meaning of the Constitution is relative to the time in which it is being interpreted. Under this concept great weight is attached to social forces in formulating judicial decisions. As the goals, aspirations, and needs of society change, precedent changes.

12. Conflict of Laws

Certain basic facts about our legal system must be recognized. First of all, statutes and precedents, in all legal areas, vary from state to state. In some states the plaintiff in an automobile accident case must be completely free of fault in order to recover damages; in other states the doctrine of comparative negligence is used, so that a plaintiff found to be 20 percent at fault could recover 80 percent of his or her damages. Second, the doctrine of *stare decisis* does not require that one state recognize the precedent or rules of law of other states. Each state is free to decide for itself questions concerning its common law and interpretation of its own constitution and statutes. (However, courts will often follow decisions of other states if they are found to be sound. They are considered persuasive authority. This is particularly true in cases involving uniform acts, when each state has adopted the same statute.) Third, many legal issues arise out of acts or transactions that have contact with more than one state. A contract may be executed in one state, performed in another, and the parties may live in still others; or an automobile accident may occur in one state involving citizens of different states.

These hypothetical situations raise the following fundamental question: Which state's *substantive* laws are applicable in a multiple-jurisdiction case in which the law differs from one state to the other?

The body of law known as conflict of laws or choice of laws answers this question. It provides the court or forum with the applicable substantive law in the multistate transaction or occurrence. The law applicable to a tort is generally said

---

[2] Chief Justice John Marshall in McCullough v. Maryland, 4 Wheat 316, 407 (1819).

to be the law of the state of place of injury. Thus, a court sitting in state X would follow its own rules or procedure, but it would use the tort law of state Y if the injury occurred in Y. Several rules are used by courts on issues involving the law of contracts:

1. The law of the state where the contract was made
2. The law of the place of performance
3. "Grouping of contacts" or "center of gravity" theory, which uses the law of the state most involved with the contract
4. The law of the state specified in the contract

Many contracts designate the applicable substantive law. A contract provision that provides "This contract shall be governed by the law of the State of New York" will be enforced if New York has at least minimal connection with the contract.

It is not the purpose of this text to teach conflict of laws, but the reader should be aware that such a body of law exists and should recognize those situations in which conflict of laws principles will be used. The trend toward uniform statutes and codes has tended to decrease these conflicts, but many of them still exist. So long as we have a federal system and fifty separate state bodies of substantive law, the area of conflict of laws will continue to be of substantial importance in the application of the doctrine of *stare decisis* and statutory law.

13. Lawyers

English law gave us not only the common law, but also the profession of attorney-at-law. Attorneys-at-law—also known as lawyers, solicitors, or counselors-at-law—are qualified in character and by training to serve as an officer of courts in representing and advising people in regard to the law.

The practice of law may be divided into several categories or types of practice. Some types of practice may be described as trial practice, and trial lawyers as a group are subdivided into plaintiff's counsel and defense counsel because of the different aspects of these activities. Office practice is another type and is concerned with matters such as preparing documents, advising businesses, or settling estates. Many office-practice lawyers never participate in a lawsuit, but leave the trial arena to the specialist in trial work. Large law firms have lawyers practicing in all areas, but small law firms or sole practitioners often refer matters out of their area of expertise to other lawyers. General practitioners, especially in the smaller community, may handle every matter that is brought to their offices. The term *house counsel* is used to describe another large group of attorneys. House counsel is employed by business to assist in the internal operations of the business by preventing and solving legal problems. Unsolved problems that result in litigation are usually referred to outside counsel for trial.

Wherever lawyers practice, they will be engaged in certain activities that are of primary significance to society. First of all, they are advisors. A lawyer's product is advice—advice on an infinite variety of subjects. Much of the advice requested and given is not on legal matters, but may involve business decisions or family affairs.

Second, lawyers are advocates for their clients. Office lawyers negotiating a contract are advocates just as trial lawyers are; their advocacy is directed at other attorneys and their clients, rather than to judges and juries. Third, lawyers are negotiators of compromise. They seek to avoid litigation and to find a mutually satisfactory alternative to the expense and difficulties of litigation. These three roles—advisor, advocate, and negotiator—provide insight into the background required for the practice of law.

Hundreds of thousands of words have been written about the personal qualities required for the practice of law. It is generally conceded that lawyers must be cultured, in the sense of appreciating the historical relevance of our fundamental freedoms and the role of law in our society. They must be keenly aware of the world in which they live, what is right about it and what is wrong, so that they can fulfill their role as instruments of change. They must be compassionate and sensitive to human problems and weaknesses, because the practice of law is a very personal matter.

Lawyers must be courageous and willing to represent unpopular causes, because the right to counsel exists as a necessity. They must be willing not only to defend such causes, but to defend the system that requires such representation. A trial lawyer, as an officer of the court, owes a duty to the court as well as to the client, a duty to aid in the search for truth and the administration of justice.

It is obvious that a lawyer must be fully advised of a client's problems and all matters affecting them. To encourage clients' cooperation, the rules of evidence provide that confidential communications to a lawyer are privileged. The law does not permit a lawyer to reveal such facts and testify against a client. This is called the attorney-client privilege, and it may extend to communications made to employees of the lawyer in certain cases. The privilege extends to corporations as well as to individuals.

SUMMARY

LAW	
Introduction	1. There are many definitions of law depending on the content and subject matter involved.
	2. Many forces shape and give direction to the law as it develops. Among the more important are logic, history, custom, religion, and the attitudes of society.
	3. Logic or reasoning may be inductive, deductive, or a combination of the two.

	4. History and custom are important in shaping the law as it relates to business.
	5. Religion and natural law based on divine principles influence many areas.
	6. Social utility or the mores of the day influence lawmakers.
Classifications	1. Public versus private.
	2. Substance versus procedure.
Sources of Law	1. Constitutional principles provide the foundation of our legal system. The most important constitutional principle is the doctrine of judicial review.
	2. Legislation in the form of statutes, codes, and ordinances provides much of our body of law. Courts have a major role to play in interpreting legislation.
	3. Decided cases provide us with our common-law system. We rely heavily on precedent, but case law is often changed as conditions change.
	4. Conflict of laws principles determine the appropriate statutes and case law to be used in litigation involving more than one jurisdiction.
Lawyers	1. Many lawyers are office lawyers, and they do not engage in litigation.
	2. A lawyer's product is advice.
	3. Lawyers settle most disputes without resorting to a judicial decision.
	4. Communications to one's lawyer are privileged and confidential and cannot be revealed by the lawyer.

REVIEW QUESTIONS

1. Law is defined in a variety of ways. Give three definitions of law, and give an example of the application of each.
2. In what area of the law have history and custom had the greatest influence? Why?
3. Classify the following subjects as public law or private law:
   (a) constitutional law; (b) contract law; (c) administrative law; (d) criminal law; (e) property law; (f) tort law.
4. Compare and contrast the following:
   (a) public law and private law; (b) civil law and common law; (c) torts and crimes; (d) substance and procedure; (e) case law and legislation.

5. Describe three advantages and four disadvantages of the common-law (case law) system.

6. The product of the legislative process is often described by separate terms. List three such terms and distinguish them.

7. Is the judiciary the overseer of government? Explain.

8. Why are there so many uniform state laws?

9. List three rules used by courts to find the meaning of ambiguous statutes.

10. The basic characteristic of the common law is that a case once decided establishes a precedent that will be followed by the courts when similar issues arise later. Yet courts do not always follow precedent. Why?

11. *Stare decisis* is of less significance in public law subjects than in cases dealing with private law subjects. Why?

12. Why is it necessary for each state to have a system of conflict of laws principles?

13. Lawyers serve in three capacities and owe duties and obligations to three groups or institutions. Identify the three capacities and groups.

2 RESOLVING CONTROVERSIES

In our society, a variety of methods can be used to resolve controversies and disputes. The most common is a compromise or settlement agreement between the parties to the dispute. Conflicts and disputes that are not settled by agreement between the parties may be resolved by litigation. A second important method for resolving unsettled conflicts and disputes is known as *arbitration,* submission of a controversy to a nonjudicial body for a binding decision. Litigation has been the traditional method of resolving disputes, but today more and more disputes are being submitted to arbitration because litigation consumes so much time and money. This chapter will discuss our court system and arbitration. The next chapter covers litigation. Before examining the court system and arbitration, we will emphasize the importance of compromise whenever possible and the role of lawyers in settling disputes.

1. Compromises and Settlements

Most disputes are resolved by the parties involved, without resort to litigation or to arbitration. Only a small fraction of the disputes in our society end up in court or even in a lawyer's office. Among the multitude of reasons why compromise is so prevalent a technique for settling disputes, some may be described as personal, others as economic.

The desire to compromise is almost instinctive. Most of us dislike trouble, and many fear going to court. Our moral and ethical values encourage compromise and settlement. Opinions of persons other than the parties to the dispute are often an influential, motivating force in many compromises, adding external forces to the internal ones that encourage people to settle their differences amicably.

Compromise and settlement of disputes is also encouraged by the economics of many situations. Lawsuits are expensive for both parties. As a general rule, both parties must pay their own attorney's fees, and the losing party must pay court costs. As a matter of practical economics, the winning party in a lawsuit is a loser to the extent of the attorney's fees—which are often quite substantial.

At least two additional facts of economic life encourage business to settle disputes out of court. First, business must be concerned with its public image and the goodwill of its customers. Although the motto "The customer is always right" is not universally applicable today, the influence of the philosophy it represents cannot be underestimated. It often is simply not good business to sue a customer. Second, juries are frequently sympathetic to individuals who have suits against large corporations or defendants who are covered by insurance. Close questions of liability, as well as the size of verdicts, are more often than not resolved against business concerns because of their presumed ability to pay. As a result, business seeks to settle many disputes rather than submit them to a jury for decision.

The duty of lawyers to seek and achieve compromise whenever possible is not usually understood by laypersons. In providing services, lawyers will devote a substantial amount of their time, energy, and talent to seeking a compromise solution. Attempts to compromise will be made before resort to the courts in most cases. Of all the disputes that are the subject of legal advice, the great majority are settled without resort to litigation. Of those that do result in litigation, the great majority are settled before the case goes to trial or even during the trial. Literally, the attempt of the lawyers to resolve the dispute never ends. It occurs before suit, before and during the trial, after verdict, during appeal, and even after appeal. As long as there is a controversy, it is the function of lawyers to attempt to resolve it.

Lawyers on both sides of a controversy seek compromise for a variety of reasons. A lawyer may view the client's case as weak, either on the law or on the facts. The amount of money involved, the necessity for a speedy decision, the nature of the contest, the uncertainty of legal remedy, the unfavorable publicity, and the expense entailed are some other reasons for avoiding a court trial. Each attorney must evaluate the client's cause and seek a satisfactory—though not necessarily the most desirable—settlement of the controversy. The settlement of disputes is perhaps the most significant contribution of lawyers to our society.

2. Mediation

The term *mediation* describes the process by which a third person assists the parties to a controversy when they seek a compromise. Although a mediator cannot impose a binding solution on the parties, a disinterested and objective mediator is often able to bring about a compromise that is satisfactory to the parties.

The mediation of labor disputes is the function of the National Mediation and Conciliation Service. This government agency, staffed with skilled negotiators, has assisted in the settlement of countless labor disputes. Mediation is playing an expanding role in the relationship between the business community and the consuming public. Better Business Bureaus and others are serving as mediators of consumer complaints and, on occasion, as arbitrators under arbitration agreements. Their efforts have resolved thousands of consumer complaints, in part because they provide some third parties to whom a consumer can turn.

An amendment to the Federal Trade Commission Act has given added impetus to mediation as a means of resolving consumer complaints. This law provides that if a business adopts an informal dispute-resolution system to handle complaints about its product warranties, then a customer cannot sue the manufacturer or seller for breach of warranty without first going through the informal procedures. This law does not deny consumers the right to sue, nor does it compel a compromise solution. It simply favors mediation by requiring an attempt at settlement before litigation.

3. The Functions

THE COURT SYSTEM

Our system of government has selected courts as the primary means to resolve controversies that cannot be settled by agreement of the parties involved. Courts and litigation are the ultimate method for resolving conflict and disagreements in our society. Whether the issue is the busing of school children, the legality of abortions, the enforceability of a contract, or the liability of a wrongdoer, the dispute, if not otherwise resolved, goes to the courts for a final decision. Courts settle controversies between persons and between persons and the state.

The basic function of the court is to apply the law to the facts. The facts are often determined by a jury. If a jury is not used, the court is the finder of the facts. (Cases in which the parties are entitled to a jury will be noted later.) The rule of law applied to the facts produces a decision that settles the controversy.

The three great powers of the judiciary come into play as it performs its functions of deciding cases and controversies: (1) the power of judicial review, (2) the power to interpret and apply statutes, and (3) the power to create law through precedent. The extent to which these powers are exercised varies from case to case, but all three are frequently involved in a single case.

Of course, not every dispute is capable of resolution by courts. For example, courts would not decide if a Catholic priest should be allowed to marry or the grade to give a college student. Courts are ill-equipped to make such decisions.

Highly technical, the court system must be operated by numerous persons with special training and skills; trial judges, reviewing court justices, and responsible citizens to serve as jurors are required if justice is to be achieved.

4. Judges and Justices

The trial judge, by virtue of the office, owes very high duties to the state, its people, the litigants, the law, the witnesses, and the jury. Since the court is the protector of constitutional limitations and guarantees, a judge should be temperate, attentive, patient, impartial, studious, diligent, and prompt in ascertaining the facts and applying the law. Judges should be courteous and considerate of jurors, witnesses, and others in attendance upon the court, but they should criticize and correct unprofessional conduct of attorneys.

Judges must avoid any appearance of impropriety and should not act in a controversy in which they or near relatives have an interest. They should not be swayed by public clamor or consideration of personal popularity or be apprehensive of unjust criticism.

The trial judge renders decisions at the people's level. It is in the trial courts that the law is made alive and its words are given meaning. Since a trial judge is the only contact that most people have with the law, the ability of such judges is largely responsible for the effective function of the law. Members of reviewing courts are usually called *justices,* to distinguish them from trial court judges, whose role is substantially different. The trial judge has direct contact with the litigation and the litigants, whereas the justice rarely has any contact with litigants.

Justices must do much more than simply decide a case; they usually give written reasons for their decision, so that anyone may examine them and comment on their merits. Each decision becomes precedent to some degree, a part of our body of law. Thus, the legal opinion of the justice—unlike that of the trial judge, whose decision has direct effect only upon the litigants—affects society as a whole. The justice, in deciding a case, must consider not only the result between the parties involved, but the total effect of the decision on the law. In this sense, the justice is a legislator.

Because of this difference in roles, the personal qualities required for a justice are somewhat different from those for a trial judge. The duties of a justice are in the area of legal scholarship. Justices are required to be articulate in presenting ideas in writing and to use the written word as the primary source of their decisions. Whereas trial judges, being a part of the trial arena, observe the witnesses and essentially use knowledge gained from their participation for their decisions, justices spend hours studying briefs, the record of proceedings, and the law, before preparing and handing down their decisions.

5. The Jury

In Anglo-American law, the right of trial by jury, particularly in criminal cases, is traced to the famous Magna Carta issued by King John of England in 1215, wherein it is stated:

> . . . that no freeman shall be taken or imprisoned or disseised or outlawed or exiled . . . without the judgment of his peers or by the law of the land. . . .

In early English legal history, the juror was a witness; that is, he was called to tell what he knew, not to listen to others testify. The word *jury* comes from the French word *juré,* which means "sworn." The jury gradually developed into an institution to determine facts. The function of the jury today is to ascertain the facts, just as the function of the court is to ascertain the law.

The Sixth and Seventh amendments to the United States Constitution guarantee the right of trial by jury both in criminal and civil cases. The Fifth

Amendment provides for indictment by a grand jury for capital offenses and infamous crimes. (*Indictment* is a word used to describe the decision of the grand jury.) A grand jury differs from a petit jury in that the grand jury determines whether the evidence of guilt is sufficient to warrant a trial; the petit jury determines guilt or innocence in criminal cases and decides the winner in civil cases. In civil cases, the right to trial by a jury is preserved in suits at common law when the amount in controversy exceeds $20. State constitutions have like provisions guaranteeing the right of trial by jury in state courts.

Historically, the jury consisted of 12 persons, but many states and some federal courts now have rules of procedure that provide for smaller juries in both criminal and civil cases. Historically, too, a jury's verdict was required to be unanimous. Today, some states authorize less than unanimous verdicts. If fewer than 12 persons serve on the jury, however, the verdict in criminal cases must be unanimous.

The jury system is much criticized by those who contend that many jurors are prejudiced, unqualified to distinguish fact from fiction, and easily swayed by skillful trial lawyers. However, the "right to be tried by a jury of his peers" in criminal cases is felt by most members of the bench and bar to be as fair and effective a method as has been devised for ascertaining the truth and giving an accused his or her "day in court."

The persons who are selected to serve on trial juries are drawn at random from lists of qualified voters in the county or city where the trial court sits. Most states, by statute, exempt from jury duty those who are in certain occupations and professions, such as doctors, dentists, pharmacists, embalmers, the police, firefighters, lawyers, and reporters. Many others attempt to avoid serving because it involves a loss of money or time away from a job; but because of the importance of jury duty, most judges are reluctant to excuse citizens who are able to serve.

When a case is called for trial, those selected appear as the jury panel called the *venire*. Unless excused by the judge for personal reasons, they are available to serve as jurors. Twelve persons, or less if the law so provides, will be selected by drawing, and *voir dire* examination will be conducted to select the jury in a particular case. Serving on the jury is an important civic duty. It is one significant way in which a citizen can take part in government and participate in the administration of justice.

Jury duty in long, complex cases creates a very difficult situation. Because few people can afford to serve for many months, juries in complex antitrust and products liability cases frequently consist of the unemployed and retired. It has therefore been proposed to take long and complex matters out of the jury system.

6. State Court Systems

The judicial system of the United States is a dual system consisting of state courts and federal courts. The courts of the states, although not subject to uniform classification, may be grouped as follows: supreme courts, intermediate courts of review (in the more populous states), and trial courts. Some trial courts have general jurisdiction; others have limited jurisdiction. For example, small claims courts have jurisdiction only if the amount in controversy does not exceed a certain sum.

Lawsuits are instituted in one of the trial courts. Even a court of general jurisdiction has geographical limitations. In many states the trial court of general jurisdiction is called a *circuit court,* because in early times a single judge sitting as a court traveled the circuit from one county to another. In other states the trial court is called the *superior court* or the *district court.* Each area has a trial court of general jurisdiction.

Most states also have trial courts of limited jurisdiction. They may be limited as to subject matter, amount in controversy, or area in which the parties live. Courts with jurisdiction limited to a city are often called *municipal courts.*

Courts may also be named according to the subject matter with which they deal. *Probate* courts deal with wills and the estates of deceased persons; *juvenile* courts with juvenile crime and dependent children; *criminal* and *police* courts with violators of state laws and municipal ordinances; and *traffic* courts with traffic violations. For an accurate classification of the courts of any state, the statutes of that state should be examined. Figure 2-1 illustrates the jurisdiction and organization of reviewing and trial courts in a typical state.

The small-claims court is a court of growing importance. In fact, a popular television program has been created out of this concept. It is an attempt to provide a prompt and inexpensive means of settling thousands of minor disputes that often

FIGURE 2-1

Typical State
Court System

(Figure 2-1: Typical State Court System — flowchart showing: Supreme Court, 5 to 9 Justices; Intermediate Reviewing Courts, 3 to 5 Justices; Trial Court General Jurisdiction — Law / Equity; Inferior Trial Courts; Small Claims Court, Probate Court, Criminal Courts, Municipal Courts, Juvenile Courts; Traffic Court (Magistrates). Labels: Direct Appeal in Limited Cases; Certiorari or Leave to Appeal Certification. Handwritten note: "final decisions")

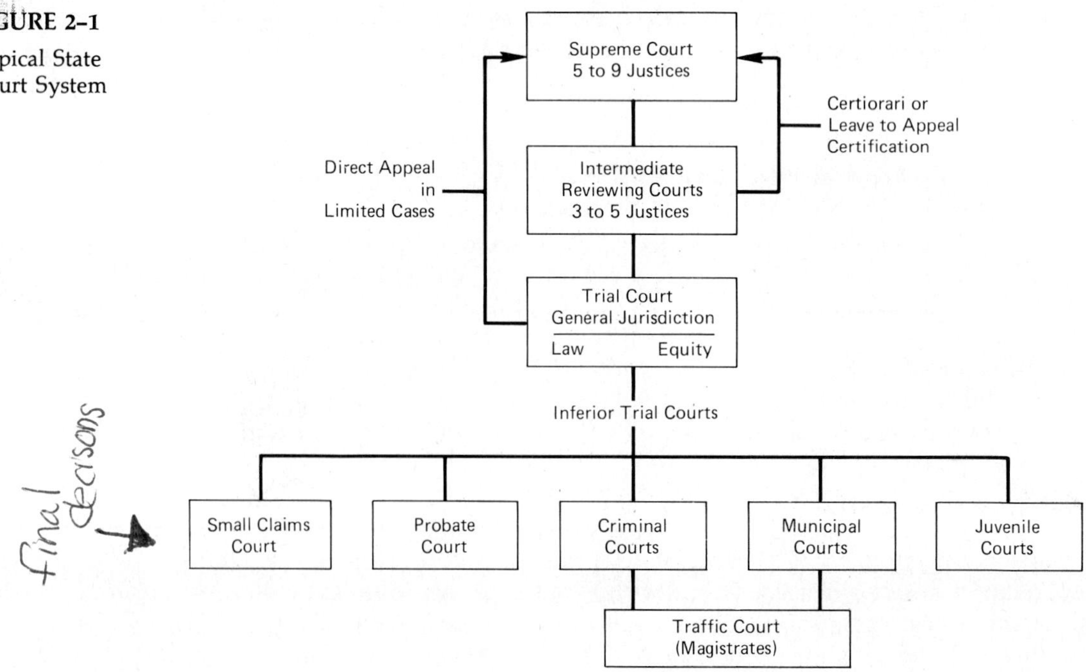

include suits by consumers against merchants for lost or damaged goods or for services poorly performed. Landlord-tenant disputes and collection suits are also quite common in small-claims courts. In these courts, the usual court costs are greatly reduced. The procedures are simplified, so that the services of a lawyer are usually not required. Most of the states have authorized small-claims courts and have imposed a limit on their jurisdiction. Some states keep the amount as low as $500; other exceed $2,500, but $1,500 is a typical limit.

7. The Federal Court System

Congress creates our courts, but the Constitution limits the courts' jurisdiction. The Constitution created the Supreme Court and authorizes Congress to establish inferior courts from time to time. Congress has created 12 United States courts of appeals, plus a special court of appeals for the Federal Circuit. This

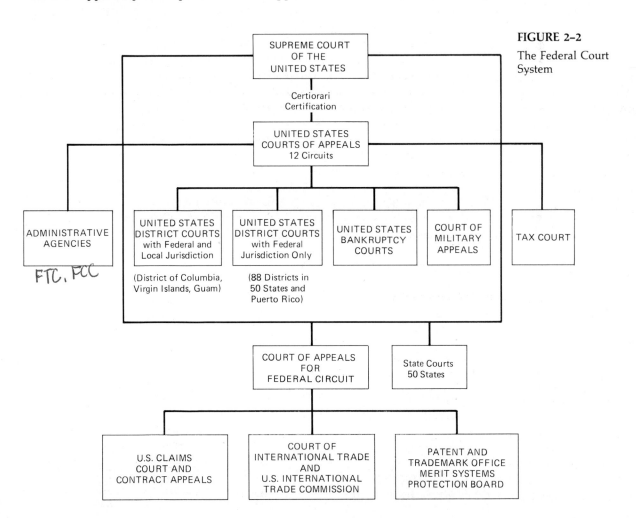

FIGURE 2–2

The Federal Court System

special reviewing court, located in Washington, DC, hears appeals from special courts such as the United States Claims Court and Contract Appeals, as well as from administrative decisions such as those by the Patent and Trademark Office. Congress has also created the United States district courts (at least one in each state), and others to handle special subject matter such as the Court of Military Appeals. Figure 2–2 illustrates the federal court system and shows the relationship of state courts and administrative agencies for review purposes.

8. Federal District Courts

The district courts are the trial courts of the federal judicial system. They have original jurisdiction, exclusive of the courts of the states, over all federal crimes; that is, all offenses against the laws of the United States. The accused is entitled to a trial by jury in the state and district where the crime was committed.

In civil actions, the district courts have jurisdiction only when the matter in controversy is based on either diversity of citizenship or a federal question. Diversity of citizenship exists in suits between (1) citizens of different states, (2) a citizen of a state and a citizen of a foreign country, (3) a state and citizens of another state. For diversity of citizenship to exist, all plaintiffs must be citizens of a state different from the state in which any one of the defendants is a citizen. Diversity of citizenship does not prevent the plaintiff from bringing suit in a state court, but if diversity of citizenship exists, the defendant has the right to have the case removed to a federal court. A defendant, by having the case removed to the federal court, has an opportunity of having a jury selected from an area larger than the county where the cause arose, thus perhaps reducing the possibility of jurors tending to favor the plaintiff.

For the purpose of suit in a federal court, a corporation is considered a "citizen" both of the state where it is incorporated and of the state in which it has its principal place of business. As a result, there is no federal jurisdiction in many cases in which one of the parties is a corporation. If any one of the parties on the other side of the case is a citizen either of the state in which the corporation is chartered or is doing its principal business, there is no diversity of citizenship and thus no federal jurisdiction.

If diversity of citizenship is the basis of federal jurisdiction, the parties must satisfy a jurisdictional amount, which is $10,000. If a case involves multiple plaintiffs with separate and distinct claims, each claim must satisfy the jurisdictional amount. Thus, in a class-action suit, the claim of each plaintiff must exceed the $10,000 minimum, unless changed by statute.

Federal jurisdiction based on a federal question exists if the lawsuit arises out of rights granted by the Constitution, laws, or treaties of the United States. These civil actions may involve matters such as bankruptcy or suits such as those based on patents, copyrights, trademarks, taxes, elections, the rights guaranteed by the Bill of Rights, and those rights secured to individual citizens by the Fourteenth Amendment. In addition, by statute the district courts have original jurisdiction to try tort cases involving citizens who suffer damages caused by officers or agents of the federal government, and they have the power to issue writs of *habeas corpus* and to grant injunctions in a variety of cases. If injunctions are sought, three judges must hear the case.

9. The Law in Federal Courts

Our dual system of federal and state courts creates a unique problem in "conflicts." In all cases, federal courts use their own body of procedural law. In cases involving the U.S. Constitution, treaties, and federal statutes, federal substantive law is used. However, there is no body of federal common law in suits based on diversity of citizenship. Therefore federal courts use the substantive law, including conflict of law principles, of the state in which they are sitting. Thus, just as the state courts are bound by federal precedent in cases involving federal law and federally protected rights, federal courts are bound by state precedent in diversity of citizenship cases.

10. Federal Reviewing Courts

Direct appeals from the decisions of the district courts to the United States Supreme Court may be made in several situations, such as (1) in criminal cases when the decision of the lower court is based upon the invalidity or construction of a statute upon which the indictment or information was founded, (2) when the lower court has held an act of Congress unconstitutional in a case in which an agency of the government is a party; and (3) when the lower court consisting of three judges has either granted or denied an injunction. However, in most cases an appeal is taken from the U.S. district court to the court of appeals. The structure of these appellate courts is discussed in Section 7.

In most cases the decisions of the courts of appeals are final. Cases in the courts of appeals may be reviewed by the Supreme Court, if a *writ of certiorari* is granted upon a petition of any party before or after a decision in the courts of appeals. The writ of certiorari to review a judgment of the courts of appeals is within the discretion of the Supreme Court. The writ will be issued when necessary to secure uniformity of decision or to bring cases of grave public concern to the court of last resort for decision.

Courts of appeals decisions may also be reviewed by the Supreme Court in cases in which a state statute has been held unconstitutional and a federal question is presented. In addition, the courts of appeals may by certification seek instructions from the Supreme Court on any question of law in any civil or criminal case.

The U.S. district courts and the courts of appeals cannot review, retry, or correct the judicial errors charged against a state court. Final judgments or decrees rendered by the highest court of a state are reviewed only by the Supreme Court of the United States. State cases appealed to the U.S. Supreme Court must concern the validity of a treaty or statute of the United States or must present a question involving the validity of a state statute on the grounds that the statute is repugnant to the Constitution, treaties, or laws of the United States and that the state decision is in favor of the statute's validity. When a case involves the constitutionality of a state statute or treaty or when a citizen's rights, privileges, or immunities under a constitution or laws are impaired, the case may be brought to the Supreme

Court by writ of certiorari. In all other cases, the decision of the highest state court is not subject to review.

11. Law and Equity

Historically, trial courts in the United States have been divided into two parts—a court of law and a court of equity or chancery. The term *equity* arose in England because the failure of the law courts to provide adequate remedies often made it impossible to obtain justice in the king's courts of law. The only remedy at law was a suit for money damages.

In order that justice might be done, the person seeking a remedy sought redress from the king in person. Because the appeal was to the king's conscience, he referred such matters to his spiritual adviser, the chancellor, who was usually a church official and, in giving a remedy, usually favored the ecclesiastical law.

By such method, there developed a separate system of procedure and different rules for deciding matters presented to the chancellor. Suits involving these rules were said to be brought "in chancery" or "in equity," in contrast to suits "at law" in the king's courts. Courts of equity were courts of conscience and recognized many rights that were not recognized by common-law courts. For example, trusts in lands were recognized; rescission was allowed on contracts created through fraud; injunction and specific performance were developed as remedies.

In a few states, courts of equity are still separate and distinct from courts of law. In most states, the equity and law courts are organized under a single court with two dockets—one at law, the other in equity. Whether the case is in equity or at law is determined by the remedy desired. Modern civil procedure laws usually have abolished distinction between actions at law and in equity. However, pleadings usually must denote whether the action is legal or equitable because, as a general rule, there is no right to a jury trial of an equitable action. The constitutional guarantee to a trial by jury applies only to actions at law.

12. Equitable Procedures

By statute in some states, a jury may hear the evidence in equity cases, but the determination of the jury in these cases is usually advisory only and is not binding on the court. The judge passes upon questions of both law and fact, and he may decide the case upon the pleadings without the introduction of oral testimony. If the facts are voluminous and complicated, the judge may refer the case to an attorney-at-law, usually called a *master in chancery,* to take the testimony. This is the usual procedure when a complicated accounting is required. The master in chancery hears the evidence, makes findings of fact and conclusions of law, and reports back to the judge.

Courts of equity use maxims instead of strict rules of law to decide cases. There are no *legal* rights in equity, for the decision is based on moral rights and natural justice. Some of the typical maxims of equity are:

- Equity will not suffer a right to exist without a remedy.
- Equity regards as done that which ought to be done.

- Where there is equal equity, the law must prevail.
- He who comes into equity must do so with clean hands.
- He who seeks equity must do equity.
- Equity aids the vigilant.
- Equality is equity.

These maxims guide the chancellor in exercising his discretion. For example, the clean-hands doctrine prohibits a party who is guilty of misconduct in the matter in litigation from receiving the aid of the court.

The decision of the court in equity is called a *decree*. A judgment in a court of law is measured in damages, whereas a decree of a court of equity is said to be *in personam;* that is, it is directed to the defendant, who is to do or not to do some specific thing.

Decrees are either final or interlocutory. A decree is *final* when it disposes of the issues in the case, reserving no question to be decided in the future. A decree quieting title to real estate, granting a divorce, or ordering specific performance is usually final. A decree is *interlocutory* when it reserves some question to be determined in the future. A decree granting a temporary injunction, appointing a receiver, and ordering property to be delivered to such a receiver would be interlocutory.

Failure upon the part of the defendant to obey a decree of a court of equity is contempt of court because the decree is directed not against his property, but against his person. Any person in contempt of court may be placed in jail or fined by order of the court.

Equity jurisprudence plays an ever-increasing role in our legal system. The movement toward social justice requires more reliance on the equitable maxims and less reliance on rigid rules of law.

13. Advantages   ARBITRATION

In arbitration, a person or persons other than the court make a final, binding decision of a controversy. Though rare, the law may require arbitration for certain cases. The right to arbitrate usually arises from a contract; and since the right is based on a contract, the parties are obligated to arbitrate only those issues they have agreed to arbitrate.

There are several advantages to using arbitration as a substitute for litigation. For one thing, it is much quicker and far less expensive. An issue can be submitted to arbitration and decided in less time than it takes to complete the pleading phase of a lawsuit. Then, too, arbitration creates less hostility than litigation, and it allows the parties to continue their business relationship somewhat more peacefully while the dispute is being decided. Arbitration also provides for a decision without resort to a tribunal and allows for a hearing to be conducted without the rigid formality of strict rules of law. Arbitration is favored today because it eases the congestion of court calendars. Finally, under the arbitration process, complex issues can be submitted to an expert for decision. For example, if an issue arises concerning construction of a building, in arbitration it can be submitted to an architect for decision. Lawyers and other specialists frequently serve as arbitrators; physicians decide issues relating to physical disabilities, certified public accountants deal with those regarding the book value of stock, and engineers decide issues relating to industrial production. A substantial amount of arbitration is also conducted by the academic community, especially in the area of labor relations.

For these reasons, arbitration as a substitute for litigation is becoming increasingly useful to business. Commercial arbitration clauses are being added to many business contracts. The American Arbitration Association will furnish experienced arbitrators for parties in a dispute, and many standard contract clauses provide for submission to this group. Since arbitration costs are deductible business expenses, this speedy, inexpensive solution to conflicts should be carefully considered by business and legal counsel in all possible areas of dispute.

14. The Submission

Submission is the act of referring an issue or issues to the arbitration process. The submitted issues may be factual, legal, or both; they may include questions concerning the interpretation of the arbitration agreement. The scope of the arbitrator's powers is controlled by the language of the submission. Doubts concerning the arbitrability of the subject matter of a dispute are usually resolved in favor of arbitration. When a contract leaves it up to the court to determine arbitrability, an order to arbitrate a particular grievance will not be denied unless it may be said with positive assurance that the arbitration clause is not susceptible to interpretation that covers the asserted dispute.

Submission may occur under two circumstances. First, the parties may enter into an agreement to arbitrate an existing dispute. The arbitration agreement serves as the "submission" in this case. Second, the parties may contractually agree to submit to arbitration all issues that *may* arise, or they may agree that either party *may* demand arbitration of any issue that arises. Submission to arbitration under the second circumstance occurs when a demand to arbitrate is served on the other party. This demand may take the form of a notice that a matter is being referred to the arbitrator agreed upon by the parties, or it may be a demand that the matter be referred to arbitration. Merely informing the other party that a controversy exists is not an act of submission or a demand for arbitration.

15. Procedures

In the usual arbitration procedure the parties to the dispute are given notice of the time and place of the hearing. Testimony is given at the hearing; the arbitrator or arbitrators deliberate and render a decision. There are no formal pleadings or motions, and the strict rules of evidence used in trials are frequently not followed. Most often the decision is given without the reasons for it.

The function of the arbitrators is to find a just solution to the controversy; to that end, they have the power to fashion the remedy appropriate to the wrong. Arbitrators are not bound by principles of substantive law or the rules of evidence, unless the submission so provides. As a result, errors of law or fact do not justify a court in setting aside the decision of the arbitration process. The arbitrator is the sole and final judge of the evidence and the weight to be given it.

Once an issue is submitted for arbitration, questions of law are for the arbitrator. They are no longer open to judicial intervention or to judicial review. Arbitrators are obligated to act fairly and impartially and to decide on the basis of the evidence before them. Therefore, it is misconduct for arbitrators to use outside evidence obtained by independent investigation without the consent of the parties.

16. The Award

The decision of the arbitrator, the award, is binding on all issues submitted and may be judicially enforced. Every presumption is in favor of the validity of an arbitration award, and doubts are resolved in its favor. The scope of judicial review of an award is limited in most states by statute as well as by the agreement to arbitrate. Any challenge to an award on the ground that the arbitrator exceeded his powers is properly limited to a comparison of the award with the submission. Once it is decreed that a matter is arbitrable, courts do not decide the issues on the merits.

When the submission does not restrict arbitrators to decide according to principles of law, they may make an award according to their own notion of justice without regard to the law. The scope of judicial review is whether or not the issues contained in the submission have been decided. An allegation that there is insufficient evidence to support an award or that it is contrary to the evidence does not constitute a ground for setting aside an award. Only clear, precise evidence of fraud, misconduct, or other grave irregularity will suffice to vacate an arbitration award. Courts do not reweigh the evidence and make independent findings of fact.

17. Common-Law Arbitration

Arbitration was recognized by the common law. It has been the subject of legislation in many states and by the federal government. Arbitration at common law was not a matter of right, but was based on an agreement to arbitrate. The agreement to arbitrate was revocable until the time of the final award, because it required continued consent of the parties. Thus, a party who felt that the proceeding was not going favorably would frequently withdraw by repudiating the agreement. When this occurred, the other party could sue for breach of contract, but any recovery was limited to the expenses incurred to date in the proceedings.

A distinction existed at common law between an agreement to arbitrate an existing dispute and an agreement to submit future disputes to arbitration. The latter agreement was unenforceable, and a party that refused to arbitrate when a dispute arose had no liability.

18. Types of Arbitration Systems

The various states have taken four distinct approaches to arbitration. A few have not enacted arbitration legislation. In these states, the principles of the common law are applicable. An agreement to arbitrate is revocable, but a final award is enforceable. Other states have enacted statutes that cover only the method of enforcing awards. These states have taken advantage of the cost-savings and time-reduction aspects of arbitration by eliminating the necessity for a suit on an award. In these states, an agreement to arbitrate is revocable, but there is a quick and inexpensive method for enforcing the award, if rendered.

The majority of states fall into a third category. They have enacted comprehensive arbitration statutes that cover all aspects of submission, the award, and its enforcement. They also recognize common-law arbitration. An arbitration agreement is revocable if common-law arbitration is being used, but is not revocable if the statutory method is being used. If a question arises about which method the parties are using, this matter is resolved by reference to the statute. If all the statutory requirements are met in the submission agreement, the arbitration agreement is irrevocable. If any of the statutory requirements for a submission are not met, the arbitration is subject to the common-law principles and the agreement to arbitrate is revocable.

The fourth and final approach to arbitration, legislated by some states, makes the statutory method exclusive. In these states, the statutory requirements for submission must be met, and all proceedings must comply with the statute. Failure to comply with any portion of the statute renders the agreement and the award, if any, a nullity. Statutory compliance makes the agreement irrevocable and the award enforceable.

19. General Aspects of Arbitration Statutes

The Commissioners on Uniform State Laws have prepared a Uniform Arbitration Act. There is also a Federal Arbitration Act, which covers businesses engaged in maritime and interstate commerce. Both statutes authorize voluntary arbitration.

Most statutes authorizing voluntary arbitration require a written agreement to arbitrate. Written agreements are required as a corollary of the provision that makes the agreement to arbitrate irrevocable. It should be remembered, however, that in many states failure to follow the statute is not completely ineffective, because common-law arbitration procedures may be followed as an alternative.

Consistent with the goal of arbitration to obtain a quick resolution of disputes, most statutes require submission within a stated time after the dispute arises—usually six months. These statutes recognize too that arbitration contracts can be rescinded on the same grounds used for any other contract. Fraud, mutual mistake, or lack of capacity would be grounds for voiding arbitration contracts. Revocation by operation of law is provided for also on the death, bankruptcy, or insanity of a party, or by destruction of the subject matter of the agreement.

20. Judicial Procedures in Arbitration

One purpose of arbitration is to avoid the time and expense of litigation. Judicial action may be necessary if either party refuses to submit the dispute to arbitration or refuses to carry out the terms of the award. Statutes usually contemplate the following as the procedures to be followed when a party to an arbitration contract refuses to submit the dispute to arbitration as agreed:

1. The aggrieved party may petition the court for an order directing that the arbitration be carried out according to the terms of the agreement. Upon hearing, if the court finds that making the contract to arbitrate or submission to arbitrate is not an issue, the court directs the parties to proceed to arbitrate according to the terms of the agreement.

2. If there is disagreement over the making of the contract or submission, the court will try that issue, either with or without a jury. If it is found that no contract was made, the petition is dismissed. If it is found that a contract to arbitrate or to submit was made, and there was a default, the court will issue an order directing the parties to proceed with arbitration according to the contract.

If the parties do submit the issues to arbitration as agreed, or if arbitration is conducted pursuant to a court order, certain judicial proceedings may be necessary in order to enforce the award. Most statutes prescribe the following procedures:

1. After the award is made, it is filed with the clerk of the court. After 20 days, if no exceptions are filed, it becomes a judgment upon which a writ of execution may issue in the same manner as if a judgment had been entered in a civil action.

2. A dissatisfied party may file exceptions to the award because, for example, (1) the award covered matters beyond the issues submitted, (2) the arbitrators failed to follow the statutory requirements, and (3) fraud or corruption permeated the decision. The court does *not* review the *merits* of the decision.

3. Appeals from the judgment may be taken as in any legal action, and such appeals cannot be denied by contractual provisions.

4. If it appears that the award should be set aside, the court may refer it back to the arbitrators, with instructions for correction and rehearing.

SUMMARY

METHODS FOR RESOLVING CONTROVERSIES

| Compromises and Settlements | 1. Most disputes in our society are settled without resort to litigation. A major function of lawyers is to negotiate a settlement of controversies. |
| | 2. Mediation is a process by which a third party assists in working out a compromise of a dispute. The National Mediation and Conciliation Service is available to mediate labor disputes. |

THE COURT SYSTEM

Operating the System

1. Judges at the trial court level conduct the trial. They decide questions of procedure and instruct the jury on the law applicable to the issue to be decided by the jury. If a case is tried without a jury, the judge also finds the facts.
2. Justices decide cases on appeal. The questions to be decided are questions of law.
3. The jury function is to decide disputed questions of fact.

State Court System

1. Each state has a trial court of general jurisdiction and inferior courts of limited jurisdiction.
2. The small-claims court is of growing importance because it provides a means of handling small cases without the need for a lawyer.
3. Historically, trial courts were divided into courts of law and courts of equity or chancery.

Federal Court System

1. Federal courts have limited jurisdiction. They hear cases based on federal laws (federal question cases) and cases involving diversity of citizenship.
2. Diversity of citizenship cases have a jurisdictional minimum of more than $10,000.
3. A federal court in a diversity of citizenship case uses the substantive law of the state in which it sits to decide such a case.

Law and Equity

1. Historically, courts of law handled cases involving claims for money damages.
2. Courts of equity or chancery were created where the remedy at law (money damages) was inadequate: for example, suits seeking an injunction or dissolution of a business.
3. Courts of equity use maxims instead of rules of law to decide cases.
4. The right to a jury trial exists only in cases at law.

ARBITRATION	
Advantages	1. Arbitration is the submission to a person or persons other than a court for a final binding decision of a controversy.
	2. Arbitration is less expensive than litigation. It generally takes far less time and allows the parties to remain more amicable than does litigation.
Procedures	1. The term *submission* is used to describe the action of referring an issue to arbitration. The submission governs the duties and powers of the arbitrators.
	2. The decision in arbitration is known as an *award.* Awards may be judicially enforced.
	3. If an award is within the power of the submission, a court will not change it because of errors of fact or errors of law.

REVIEW QUESTIONS

1. Alexander is involved in a dispute related to his business. He is confident that he is right, and he is considering legal action. List the reasons why it may be financially advantageous to Alexander's business to avoid court and to compromise and settle for less money than he claims is owed to him.

2. The trial courts in different states are given different designations. List four names used to describe trial courts and indicate which is used in your state.

3. Why were small-claims courts created? Give three examples of typical cases decided in such courts.

4. Henry, a resident of Nevada, sued Adam, a resident of Utah, in the state court in California. He sought $20,000 damages for personal injuries arising out of an automobile accident which occurred in Los Angeles, California, while both parties were attending the 1984 Olympics. *OVER $10,000 . complete diversity.*
   a. Can Adam have the case transferred to the federal court system? Why? *yes $10,000 . complete diversity.*
   b. What rules of procedure will the California court use? Why? *state rules of producers*
   c. If the case is transferred to the federal district court in California, what rules of procedure will the court use? Why? *federal rules of producers*
   d. If the case is tried in the state court of California, what rules of substantive law will the court use? Why? *state*
   e. If the case is tried in the federal district court, what rules of substantive law will the court use? Why? *state*

5. Wanda, a citizen of Washington, sues Olivia, a citizen of Oregon, for $8,000 in the state court of Oregon. Can Olivia properly have the case removed to a federal court in Oregon? Why? *No under $10,000*

6. Paul, a citizen of Georgia, was crossing a street in New Orleans when he was struck by a car driven by David, a citizen of Texas. The car was owned by David's employer, a Delaware corporation, which has its principal place of business in Atlanta, Georgia. Paul sues both David and the corporation in the federal district court in New Orleans. Paul's complaint alleges damages in the amount of $100,000. Does this court have jurisdiction? Why?

No, because

7. What is the function of a petition for a writ of certiorari or a petition for leave to appeal? Explain.

8. John sues Ivan in a state court, seeking damages for breach of a contract to sell a tennis racquet. The trial court finds for Ivan. John announces that he will appeal "all the way to the Supreme Court of the United States if necessary" to change the decision. Assuming that John has the money to do so, will he be able to obtain review by the Supreme Court of the United States? Explain.

9. Describe three controversies that would be decided in a court of equity or chancery in states that still distinguish between courts of law and courts of equity.

10. Why is arbitration, an alternative to litigation, becoming more popular as a means of resolving disputes?

11. There was a dispute between an automobile insurance company and its insured concerning value in the loss of a truck. The insurance policy required arbitration of disputes. Each party selected an arbitrator and these two, when unable to agree, selected a third party as umpire. The umpire, without consulting anyone or receiving any testimony, fixed the value of the loss. If challenged, will a court set aside this award? Why?

12. A dispute arose between partners on a construction project. The agreement of the parties provided that if the parties were unable to agree on any matter with respect to which a decision was to be made by both parties, the dispute would be submitted to arbitration. One party asked a court to appoint a receiver for the business. The other insisted on arbitration. How will the dispute be resolved? Why?

3 LITIGATION

We have previously noted that law may be classified as *substantive* or *procedural.* Substantive law defines the rights and duties of citizens and is the result of legislative action or judicial action. Procedural law specifies the method and means by which the substantive law is made, enforced, and administered. Procedural rules prescribe the methods by which courts apply substantive law to resolve conflicts. Substantive rights have no value unless there are procedures that provide a means for establishing and enforcing them.

Judicial procedure is concerned with rules by which a lawsuit is conducted. One common method of classifying judicial procedure is to divide it into two parts—criminal and civil. *Criminal procedure* prescribes the rules of law for apprehension, prosecution, and punishment of persons who have committed crimes. *Civil procedure* prescribes rules by which parties to civil lawsuits use the courts to settle their disputes.

In most cases there are three basic questions to be answered: (1) What are the facts? (2) What evidence is relevant and proper to prove the facts? (3) What rules of law apply to the facts? The jury answers the first question; the court answers the second. The court also provides the answer to the third by instructing the jury as to the law applicable to the facts found by the jury.

1. The Parties to Litigation

In a criminal case, *the people* bring the action against the named defendant. Most civil cases use the term *plaintiff* to describe the party bringing the lawsuit, and *defendant* describes the party against whom it is brought; but in some cases, especially in courts of equity, the parties are described as the *petitioner* and the *respondent.*

When the result at the trial court level is appealed, the party appealing is usually referred to as *appellant,* and the successful party in the trial court is called the *appellee.* Many jurisdictions, in publishing the decisions of reviewing courts, list the appellant first and the appellee second, even though the appellant may have been the defendant in the trial court. This is true of the cases appearing later in this text.

In most states and in the federal courts, all persons may join in one lawsuit as plaintiffs if the causes of action arise out of the same transaction or series of transactions and involve common questions of law or fact. In addition, the plaintiffs may join as defendants all persons who are necessary to a complete determination or settlement of the questions. In addition, if a defendant alleges that a complete determination of a controversy cannot be made without other parties, that defendant may bring in new third parties as third-party defendants. This procedure is usually followed when someone is liable to a defendant who, in turn, is liable to the plaintiff.

Two problem areas or issues relating to the parties to a lawsuit frequently arise in litigation. The first of these areas is generally described as standing to sue. The second is class-action suits. These special problems are discussed more fully below.

2. Standing to Sue

The question of *standing to sue* is whether the litigant is entitled to have the court decide the dispute. The issue arises because of the limited role of courts in our society. The constitution requires that a plaintiff must allege a case or controversy between himself and the defendant if the court is to hear the case. A plaintiff must have a personal stake in the outcome of the controversy, and this stake must be based on some threatened or actual injury resulting from the defendant's action. Without the requirement of "standing," courts would be called upon to decide abstract questions of wide public significance. Such questions are best resolved by the political process.

When the asserted harm is a generalized grievance shared in substantially equal measure by all or a large class of citizens, that harm alone normally does not grant standing to sue. For example, a taxpayer filed suit challenging the budget of the CIA. The court held that the taxpayer lacked standing to sue. Likewise, a plaintiff must assert his own legal rights and not those of some third party. A citizen objected to the army's surveillance of civilians, but the case was dismissed without a showing that the plaintiff was one of the civilians under surveillance.

Standing to sue is in no way dependent upon the merits of the plaintiff's contention that particular conduct is illegal. The presence of standing is determined by the nature and source of the plaintiff's claim. As a general rule, standing requires that a complaining party have a personal stake in the outcome of the controversy, a stake that would result in adversity from all aspects of the issues being presented for decision. A complainant must present facts sufficient to show that his or her individual needs require the remedy being sought in suits directed at government. A plaintiff must show that he or she has sustained or is immediately in danger of sustaining a direct injury as a result of some governmental action included in the lawsuit. In civil rights cases and in cases involving threats to the environment, the courts have been rather liberal in finding a personal stake in a plaintiff bringing an action relating to those subjects.

3. Class-Action Suits

A *class-action suit* is one in which a person files suit on his own behalf and on behalf of all other persons who may have a similar claim. A class-action suit may be brought on behalf of all purchasers of a defective product. The number of people who comprise a class is frequently quite large. Class-action suits are popular because they often involve matters in which no one member of the class would have a sufficient financial interest to warrant filing suit. The combined interest of all members of the class not only makes litigation feasible, but often makes it very profitable for the lawyer who handles the suit.

Because many defendants consider class-action suits a form of harassment, courts have tended to discourage the suits. For example, cases have held that all members of the class be given actual notice of the lawsuit. They must be given individual notice, not merely public notice. In addition, plaintiffs who bring the class-action suit must pay all court costs of the action, including the cost of compiling names and addresses of members of the class.

If a class-action suit is in federal court because of diversity of citizenship, the claim of each member of the class must meet the jurisdictional amount of $10,000. This requirement, together with the requirement of notice to each member of the class, has greatly reduced the number of class-action suits in the federal courts. However, the practice of plaintiffs' lawyers combining a single grievance into a lawsuit on behalf of every possible litigant is quite common in state courts. There are numerous state class-action statutes that allow consumers and others to file suit in state courts on behalf of all citizens of that state.

4. Jurisdiction

THE PLACE OF LITIGATION

The first requirement in any lawsuit is that it must be brought before a court that has the power to hear the case. This power to hear the case is known as *jurisdiction,* and it has two aspects: jurisdiction over the subject matter and jurisdiction over the parties. Jurisdiction over the subject matter means that the lawsuit is of the type that the court was created to decide. A probate court would have no jurisdiction to determine questions of law involving a civil suit for damages. A criminal court would have no jurisdiction in a divorce matter. As previously noted courts may also be limited by the amounts of money involved in the case.

Sometimes the subject-matter jurisdiction of a court is exclusive. This means that no other court has the *power* to hear such cases. The Supreme Court of the United States has exclusive jurisdiction in all proceedings affecting ambassadors, public ministers, and consuls, and in all actions in which a state is a party.

A court must also have jurisdiction over the parties—the plaintiff and the defendant. A plaintiff voluntarily submits to the jurisdiction of the court when the suit is filed.

Jurisdiction over the defendant is accomplished by the service of a summons issued by the court. It is delivered to a sheriff or other person, to be served upon the defendant. Jurisdiction over a defendant in a limited number of cases may be obtained by publishing a notice in a newspaper. This method is possible in a suit for divorce or one concerning real estate, something important enough to be written up in a public notice that would be deemed adequate to notify the defendant.

Publication may also be accompanied by proper attachment proceedings. In such cases, service by publication brings under the court's jurisdiction all attached property of a nonresident defendant if it lies within the territorial limits of the court. When this technique is employed, the attached property may be used to satisfy any judgment.

Most cases, however, require the actual service of a summons to the defendant in order to give him notice of the suit. Many states allow a summons to be served upon any member of the family above a specified age, such as 10 years, at the defendant's home. In such cases, a copy is also mailed to the defendant.

5. Long-Arm Statutes

Historically, the jurisdiction of courts to enter judgment against a person required actual personal service of the summons on the defendant in the state in which the suit was brought. This was necessary in order to give the defendant notice of the suit and an opportunity to defend. Because the jurisdiction of courts was limited to geographical areas such as a state, the power to issue and serve a summons beyond the borders of the state did not exist.

Limiting the jurisdiction of courts to persons physically present in the state is no longer accepted. Personal jurisdiction over nonresidents has been expanded because modern transportation and communication facilities have minimized the inconveniences to a nonresident defendant who must defend himself in courts beyond his home state. There is no longer any logical reason to deny a local citizen a remedy in local courts for an injury caused by a nonresident temporarily present in the state.

The first extension of jurisdiction over nonresidents occurred in auto accident cases. This extension was made by creating a legal "fiction" that resulted in the summons being served within the state whose court issued the summons. This legal fiction was created by the enactment of statutes providing that a nonresident, by using the state highways, automatically appointed a designated state official, usually the secretary of state, as his agent to accept service of process. The summons would be served on the secretary of state, who would notify the defendant of the suit, and the defendant was then subject to the power of the court.

These nonresident motorist statutes opened the door for adoption of other statutes called *long-arm statutes,* which further extend the jurisdiction of courts over nonresidents, whether individuals or corporations. Long-arm statutes typically extend the jurisdiction of courts to cases in which a tort injury has been caused by a nonresident temporarily present in the state. They also usually extend jurisdiction to cases arising out of the ownership of property located within the state. Of course, the conduct of business such as entering into contracts confers jurisdiction. Thus, a nonresident individual or a corporation may be subject to a suit for injuries if either has certain "minimal contacts" within the state, so long as the maintenance of the suit does not offend traditional notions of fair play and substantial justice.

What "minimal contacts" and activities are necessary to bring the defendant into a state is a fact question depending upon each particular case. Whatever the basis for the action may be, either in contract or in tort, the court can acquire jurisdiction over the defendant if these minimal contacts are present.

6. Venue

As previously discussed, the term *jurisdiction* defines the power of the court to hear and adjudicate the case. Jurisdiction includes the court's power to inquire into the facts, apply the law to the facts, make a decision, and declare and enforce a judgment. *Venue* relates to, and defines, the particular territorial area within the state, out of all those with jurisdiction in which the case should be filed and tried. Matters of venue are usually determined by statute. In a few states, the subject of venue is covered in the state constitution.

Venue statutes usually provide that actions concerning interests in land must be commenced and tried in the county or district in which the land is located. Actions for the recovery of penalties imposed by statute against public officers must be commenced and tried in the county or district in which the cause of action arose. Suits for divorce must be commenced and tried in the county in which one of the parties resides. All other suits or actions must be commenced and tried in the county in which one or all of the defendants reside or in the county in which the transaction took place or where the wrong was committed. A tort action, for example, may be commenced and tried either in the county or district where the tort was committed or where the defendant resides. If the defendants are nonresidents, and assuming that proper service can be made upon them under a long-arm statute, the suit may be commenced and tried in any county the plaintiff designates in his complaint.

The judge may change the place of trial at the request of either party when it appears from an affidavit of either party that the action was not commenced in the proper venue. A change of venue may be requested also on the ground that the judge has an interest in the suit or is related to any parties to the action or has manifested a prejudice that would interfere with the conduct of a fair and impartial trial. A change of venue is often requested in criminal trials when the inhabitants of the county are allegedly so prejudiced against the defendant that a fair trial is not possible. The convenience of witnesses and the parties may also justify a change of venue.

PROCEEDINGS PRIOR TO TRIALS

7. Pleadings

A *pleading* is a legal document filed with the court that sets forth the position and contentions of a party. The purpose of pleadings in civil actions is to define the issues of the lawsuit. This is accomplished by each party making allegations of fact and the other party either admitting the allegations or denying them. The procedure begins when the plaintiff files with the clerk of the court a pleading usually called a *complaint.* In some types of cases this initial pleading is called a *declaration* or a *petition.* The clerk then issues a summons that, together with a copy of the complaint, is served on the defendant. The summons notifies the defendant of the date by which he is required to file a pleading in answer to the allegations of the complaint or to file some other pleading attacking the complaint.

If the defendant has no legal basis to attack the sufficiency of the complaint, he may simply file an entry of appearance, or he may file an *answer* either admitting or denying each material allegation of the complaint. This answer will put in issue all allegations of the complaint that are denied. A simple entry of appearance is an admission of the truth of all allegations of the complaint.

In addition to admissions and denials, an answer may contain affirmative defenses, which if proved will defeat the plaintiff's claim. The answer may also contain *counterclaims,* causes of action the defendant has against the plaintiff. Upon receipt of the defendant's answer, the plaintiff will, unless the applicable rules of procedure do not so require, file a reply that specifically admits or denies each new allegation in the defendant's answer. These new allegations are those found in the affirmative defenses and counterclaims. Thus the allegations of each party are admitted or denied in the pleadings. Allegations of fact claimed by either party and denied by the other become the issues to be decided at the trial.

A defendant that fails to answer the allegations of the plaintiff is in default, and a court of law may enter a default judgment against him. In effect, the defendant has admitted the allegations of the plaintiff. A court of equity would enter a similar order, known as a decree *pro confesso.* A plaintiff who fails to reply to new matter such as a counterclaim is also subject to a judgment or decree by default.

8. Motions Attacking Pleadings

The first pleading (complaint), in order to be legally sufficient, must allege facts sufficient to set forth a right of action or the plaintiff's right to legal relief. The defendant's attorney, after studying the complaint, may (instead of answering) choose one of several different ways to challenge its legal sufficiency. For example, by motion to the court, the defendant may object to the complaint, pointing out specifically its defects. The defendant, through such motion, admits for purposes of argument all the facts alleged in the complaint. His position is that those facts are not legally sufficient to give the plaintiff the right to what is sought in the complaint. Such motion, called a *demurrer* at common law, raises questions of law, not questions of fact. If the court finds that the complaint does set forth facts sufficient to give the plaintiff what is sought, it will deny the motion. Some states require that the complaint state a cause of action. Others require only that the facts alleged establish a right to the relief sought. In either case, it is reversible error to dismiss a complaint that is legally sufficient.

If the motion is denied, the defendant will then be granted time to answer the complaint. Should he fail to do so within the time limit set by the court, a judgment by default may be entered for the plaintiff. If the court finds, however, that the complaint fails to state facts sufficient to give the plaintiff the relief sought, the court will allow the motion and dismiss the suit, but will give to the plaintiff permission to file an amended complaint. The plaintiff will thus be given an opportunity to restate the allegations so that he may be able to set forth a right to recover from the defendant.

In addition to a motion to dismiss for failure to allege a valid cause of action, a defendant may also move to dismiss the suit for reasons that as a matter of law would prevent the plaintiff from winning his suit. Such matters as a discharge in bankruptcy, a lack of jurisdiction of the court to hear the suit, or an expiration of the time limit during which the defendant is subject to suit may be raised by such a motion. These are technical matters that raise questions of law for the court's decision.

9. Decisions Based on Pleadings

Many lawsuits are decided by use of a procedure known as a *summary judgment,* a procedure created to avoid trials when the facts are not disputed. The only issue before the court is the legal effect of those facts. This issue can be decided by the court on a motion by one of the parties.

Either party may ask the court for a summary judgment by filing a motion, usually with supporting affidavits. The usual procedure is to attach to the motion supporting affidavits that set forth the facts and to supplement these affidavits with depositions taken during the discovery process. The opposing party is also permitted to file affidavits and depositions with the court. These affidavits and depositions in effect supply the court with sworn testimony. The court then examines this sworn testimony to see whether there is a genuine issue as to any material fact. If there is no factual issue, the litigation should be decided on the facts presented to the court. A summary judgment may also be issued if as a matter of law the facts establish an absolute defense to the plaintiff's claim.

If the court finds that there is no genuine issue of fact, it will grant a summary judgment for one party or the other. In most states, it may render a summary judgment on the issue of liability alone and leave the amount of damages to be decided at the trial. Many of the cases set forth in later chapters of this text were decided by the summary judgment procedure. Remember that a summary judgment will not be granted when there is a disputed question of any material fact.

Most states and the federal courts also have procedures known as *motions for judgment on the pleadings,* by which either party may seek a final decision without a trial. In hearings on these motions, the court examines the pleadings on file in the case to see if a genuine material issue of fact remains. If there is no such question of fact, the court will then decide the legal question raised by the facts and find for one party or the other. In such cases, the pleadings establish that there is no reason for a trial, and the issues between the parties are pure questions of law.

10. Discovery Procedures

During the pleading stage and in the interval before the trial, the law provides for procedures called *discovery* procedures. Discovery is designed to take surprise out of litigation and to ensure that the results of lawsuits are based on the merits of the controversy rather than on the ability, skill, or cunning of counsel. Discovery procedures prevent a party or a witness from remaining silent about material facts. They ensure that all potential testimony and other evidence is equally available to both parties. With each side fully aware of the strengths and weaknesses of both sides, the second of the avowed purposes of discovery—to encourage settlement of suits and to avoid actual trial—is facilitated. Modern discovery procedures result in the compromise and settlement of most civil suits.

Discovery practices include deposing (questioning under oath) of other parties and witnesses; written questions answered under oath by the opposite party; compulsory physical examinations by doctors chosen by the other party in personal injury cases; orders requiring the production of statements, exhibits, documents, maps, photographs, and so on; and serving of demands by one party on the other to admit facts under oath. These procedures allow a party to learn not only about matters that may be used as evidence, but also about matters that may lead to the discovery of evidence.

Just prior to the trial, a pretrial conference between the lawyers and the judge will be held in states with modern rules of procedure. At this conference the pleadings, results of the discovery process, and probable evidence are reviewed in an attempt to settle the suit. The issues may be further narrowed, and the judge may even predict the outcome in order to encourage settlement.

THE TRIAL

11. Jury Selection

Not every case can be settled, even under modern procedures. Some must go to trial on the issues of fact raised by pleadings that remain after the pretrial conference. If the only issues are questions of law, the court will decide the case without a trial by ruling on one of the motions previously mentioned. If the case is at law and either party has demanded a jury trial, the case will be set for trial and a jury empaneled. If the case is in equity or if no jury demand has been made, it will be set down for trial before the court. For purposes of the following discussion, we shall assume a trial before a jury.

The first step of the trial is to select the jury. Prior to calling the case, the clerk of the court will have summoned potential jurors, known as the *venire.* They will be selected at random from lists of eligible citizens, and the appropriate number (usually 12) will be called into the jury box for the conduct of *voir dire* examination.

In *voir dire,* the court and attorneys for each party question prospective jurors to determine their fairness and impartiality. Jurors are sworn to answer truthfully and may be challenged or excused for cause, such as bias or relation to one of the parties. A certain number of *peremptory challenges,* for which no cause need be given, may also be exercised to reject potential jurors.

12. Introduction of Proof

After selecting the jurors, the attorneys make opening statements. An opening statement is not evidence. Its purpose is to familiarize the jury with essential facts that each side expects to prove, in order that the jury may understand the overall picture of the case and the relevance of each piece of evidence. After the opening statements, the plaintiff presents his evidence.

Evidence is presented in open court by means of examination of witnesses and the production of documents and other exhibits. The party calling a witness questions him to establish the facts about the case. As a general rule, a party calling a witness is not permitted to ask *leading questions,* questions in which the desired answer is indicated by the form of the question. After the party calling the witness has completed his direct examination, the other party is given the opportunity to cross-examine the witness. Matters inquired into on cross-examination are limited to those matters that were raised on direct examination. After cross-examination, the party calling the witness again has the opportunity of examining the witness, and this examination is called redirect examination. It is limited to the scope of those matters covered on cross-examination and is used to clarify matters raised on cross-examination. After redirect examination, the opposing party is allowed recross-examination, with the corresponding limitation on scope of the questions. Witnesses may be asked to identify exhibits. Expert witnesses may be asked to give their opinion, within certain limitations, about the case, and sometimes experts are allowed to answer hypothetical questions.

In the conduct of a trial, rules of evidence govern admissibility of testimony and exhibits and establish which facts may be presented to the jury. Each rule of evidence is based on some policy consideration and the desire to give each party an opportunity to present his evidence and contentions without unduly taking advantage of the other party. Rules of evidence were not created to serve as a stumbling block to meritorious litigants or to create unwarranted roadblocks to justice. On the contrary, rules of evidence were created and should be applied to ensure fair play and to aid in the goal of having controversies determined on their merits. Modern rules of evidence are liberal in the sense that they allow the introduction of most evidence that may contribute to the search for truth.

For example, with respect to written documents, courts generally have required that the original writing be presented as evidence of that document's contents. This rule, known as the *best evidence rule,* is important for businesspeople to understand and remember. The original of all contracts, promissory notes, and other written documents must be signed by the parties and preserved in case they are needed as evidence to resolve a dispute. However, when the original cannot be located, an authenticated copy generally will be accepted as evidence as an exception to the best evidence requirement.

To illustrate the policy considerations that form the basis of the rules of evidence, an examination of the rules relating to privileged communications is helpful. The policy behind the Fifth Amendment's privilege against self-incrimination is obvious. Other communications—such as between husband and wife, doctor and patient, clergy and penitent, and attorney and client—are also considered privileged by the law, in order that they can be made without fear of their subsequent use against the parties involved. Fair play requires that attorneys not be required to testify on matters told to them in confidence by their clients. The preservation of the home requires that a spouse not be required to testify against the other spouse regarding confidential communications. The existence of insurance coverage for a party is privileged because of the impact that knowledge of the existence of insurance would have on a jury. Jurors might award damages or increase the amount simply because of the ability of an insurance company to pay. By these rules of fair play, privileged matters should not be admitted into evidence. Similar policy considerations support all rules of evidence. Each rule is designed to assist in the search for truth.

13. Motions during Trial

A basic rule of evidence is that a party cannot introduce evidence unless it is competent and relevant to the issues raised by the pleadings. A connection between the pleadings and the trial stage of the lawsuit is also present in certain motions made during the trial. After the plaintiff has presented his evidence, for example, the defendant will usually make a motion for a directed verdict. This motion asks the court to rule as a matter of law that the plaintiff has failed to establish the case against the defendant and that a verdict should be entered for the defendant as a matter of law. The court can direct a verdict for the defendant only if the evidence taken in the light most favorable to the plaintiff establishes as a matter of law that the defendant is entitled to a verdict. The defendant argues that the plaintiff has failed to prove each allegation of his complaint. Just as a plaintiff must allege certain facts or have his complaint dismissed, he must also have some proof of each essential allegation or lose his case on a motion for a directed verdict. If he has some proof of each allegation, the motion will be denied.

In cases tried without a jury, either party may move for a finding in his favor. Such a motion will be allowed during the course of the trial if the result is not in doubt. The judge in ruling on such motions weighs the evidence, but he may end the trial before all the evidence is presented only if there is no room for a fair difference of opinion as to the result.

If the defendant's motion for directed verdict is overruled, the defendant then presents his evidence. After the defendant has presented all his evidence, the plaintiff may bring in rebuttal evidence. When neither party has any additional evidence, the attorneys and the judge retire for a conference to consider the instructions of law to be given the jury.

14. Jury Instructions

The purpose of jury instructions is to acquaint the jury with the law applicable to the case. Since the function of the jury is to find the facts, and the function of the court is to determine the applicable law, court and jury must be brought together in an orderly manner that will result in a decision. This uniting is accomplished by the court's instructing the jury, which acquaints the jury with the law applicable to the case.

In order to prepare instructions, the court confers with attorneys for both sides. At the conference, the attorneys submit to the court the instructions they feel should be given to the jury. The court examines these instructions and allows each side to object to the other's instructions. A party who fails to submit an instruction on a point of law cannot later object to the failure to instruct on that point. Similarly, the failure to object to an instruction is a waiver of the objection. The court then decides which instructions will be given to the jury. A jury instruction tells the jury that if it finds certain facts, then its verdict should be for the plaintiff. If it fails to find these facts, then the verdict should be for the defendant.

In the federal courts and in some state courts, judges may comment on the evidence while giving instructions. They may indicate the importance of certain portions of evidence, the inferences that might be drawn therefrom, the conflicts, what statements are more likely to be true than others, and why. The judge, however, is duty bound to make clear to the jury that it is not obligated to follow the court's evaluation of the evidence and that it is the jury's duty to determine the facts of the case.

15. Burdens of Proof

The term *burden of proof* has two meanings. It may describe the person with the burden of coming forward with evidence on a particular issue. The party alleging the existence of a certain fact usually has the burden of coming forward with evidence to establish that fact. The more common usage of the term, however, is to identify the party with the burden of persuasion. The party with this burden must convince the trier (judge or jury) on the factual issues. If a party with the burden of persuasion fails to do so, that party loses the issue.

The extent of proof required to satisfy the burden of persuasion varies, depending upon the issue and the type of case. There are three distinct levels of proof recognized by the law: (1) beyond a reasonable doubt, (2) manifest weight, and (3) clear and convincing proof. For criminal cases, the burden of proof is described as "beyond a reasonable doubt." This means that the prosecution in a criminal case has the burden of convincing the trier of fact, usually a jury, that the defendant is guilty of the crime charged and that the jury has no reasonable doubt about guilt. This burden of proof does not require evidence beyond any doubt, but only beyond a reasonable doubt. A reasonable doubt is one that a reasonable person viewing the evidence might reasonably entertain.

In civil cases the party with the burden of proof will be subject to one of two standards: the manifest weight of the evidence standard or the clear and convincing proof standard. Manifest weight standard is used most frequently. It requires that a party convince the jury by a preponderance of evidence that the facts are as contended. By *preponderance of evidence* we mean that there is greater weight of evidence in support of the proposition than there is against it.

The clear and convincing proof requirement is used in certain situations in which the law requires more than a simple preponderance of evidence but less than proof beyond a reasonable doubt. In a securities law case, proof of fraud usually requires clear and convincing evidence if a plaintiff is to succeed. A slight preponderance of evidence in favor of the party asserting the truth of a proposition is not enough. Unless the evidence clearly establishes the proposition, the party with the burden of proof fails to sustain it and loses the lawsuit.

16. Verdicts and Judgments

After the conference on jury instructions, the attorneys argue the case before the jury. The party with the burden of proof, usually the plaintiff, is given an opportunity to open the argument and to close it. The defendant's attorney is allowed to argue only after the plaintiff's argument and is allowed to argue only once. After the arguments are completed, the court gives instructions to the jury. The jury then retires to deliberate. In some states the jurors take written instructions with them to the jury room. In others, they must remember the instructions. Whether they are able to do so is very questionable.

Upon reaching a verdict, the jury returns from the jury room and announces its verdict. There are two kinds of verdicts—general and special. A *general verdict* is one in which the jury makes a complete finding and single conclusion on all issues presented to it. First it finds the facts, as proved by the evidence, then applies the law as instructed by the court, and returns a verdict in one conclusion that settles the case. Such verdict is reported as follows: "We the jury find the issues for the plaintiff [or defendant, as the case may be] and assess his damages at One Thousand Dollars." The jury usually does not make separate findings of fact or report what law is applied.

In a *special verdict,* the jury makes findings of fact only. It is the duty of the court to apply the law to the facts as found by the jury. A special verdict is not a decision of the case; it resolves only the questions of fact. Since the jury finds only the facts, the court does not instruct it about the law. The duty of applying the law to the fact is left to the court. The circumstances under which a general or a special verdict may be used are controlled by statute.

PROCEEDINGS AFTER THE TRIAL

17. Post-Trial Motions

After the verdict is announced, the court enters a judgment. Then the losing party starts the procedure of post-trial motions, which raise questions of law concerning the conduct of the lawsuit. These motions seek relief such as a new trial or a judgment, notwithstanding the verdict of the jury. A motion seeking a new trial may be granted if the judge feels that the verdict of the jury is contrary to the manifest weight of the evidence. The court may enter a judgment opposite to that of the verdict of the jury if the judge finds that the verdict is, as a matter of law, erroneous. To reach such a conclusion, the court must find that reasonable men viewing the evidence could not reach the verdict returned. For example, a verdict for the plaintiff based on sympathy instead of evidence could be set aside.

After the judge rules on the post-trial motion, the losing party may appeal. It should be noted that lawsuits usually end by a ruling on a motion, either before trial, during the trial, or after the trial. Motions raise questions of law that are decided by the court. The right to appeal is absolute if perfected within the prescribed time. All litigants are entitled to a trial and a review, provided the proper procedures are followed.

18. Appeals

A dissatisfied party—plaintiff or defendant—has a right to appeal the decision of the trial court to a higher court, provided he proceeds promptly and properly. The cases collected and abstracted in this text are with a few exceptions decisions of a reviewing court.

Appellate procedures are not uniform among the states, and the appellant must comply with the appropriate statute and rules of the particular court. Appeals are usually perfected by the appellant's giving *notice of appeal* to the trial court and opposing parties. This notice of appeal must be filed within a statutory time period (usually 30 days) after the trial court has entered a final judgment or order. Failure to file the notice of appeal on time denies the appellate court jurisdiction.

Most states require that within at least 10 days after giving notice of appeal, the appellant must file an appeal bond, in effect guaranteeing to pay costs that may be charged against him on the appeal. This bond permits the appellee to collect costs if the appellant loses an appeal.

The statutes usually require that within a specified time after an appeal is perfected, the appellant shall file with the clerk of the appellate court a *transcript,* consisting of the record of the testimony, a copy of the judgment, decree, or order appealed from, and other papers required by rules of the court.

The transcript alone, however, is not enough to present the case to the appellate court. The appellant must prepare and file a *brief* that contains a statement of the case, a list of the assignment of errors upon which the appellant has based his appeal, his legal authorities and argument. The brief contains the arguments on both fact and law by which the attorney attempts to show how the lower court committed the errors alleged.

The appellee (respondent) files a brief of like character, setting out his side of the case with points, authorities, and arguments. By such procedure, the case on the issues raised goes to the appellate court for decision.

The appellate court, upon receipt of the appeal, will place it on the calendar for hearing. Attorneys will be notified of the time and will be given an opportunity for oral argument. After the oral argument, the court prepares a written opinion stating the applicable law involved and giving the reasons for its decision. The court, by its decision, may affirm or reverse the court below, or the court may remand (send back) the case for a new trial. At the end of each published opinion found in the reports, a word or a few words will express the court's decision: "affirmed," "reversed," "reversed and remanded," or whatever the case requires.

The appellate courts basically review the legal rulings made by the trial judge. Very seldom will the jury's or judge's factual findings be reversed during the appeals process. Since those at the trial had an opportunity to see and hear the witnesses in person, their determination of the factual situation is presumed to be accurate. In other words, the reviewing court will not disturb the trial court's findings of fact unless such findings are clearly unreasonable.

19. Enforcement of Judgments and Decrees

A decision of a court becomes final when the time provided for a review of the decision has expired. In the trial court, a decision is final at the expiration of time for appeal. In a reviewing court, the decision is final at the expiration of the time to request a rehearing or to request a further review of the case. After the decision has become final, judicial action may be required to enforce the decision. In most cases the losing party will voluntarily comply with the decision and satisfy the judgment or otherwise do what the decree requires, but the assistance of the court is sometimes required to enforce its final decision.

If a judgment for dollar damages is not paid, the judgment creditor may apply for a *writ of execution.* This writ directs the sheriff to seize personal property of the judgment debtor and to sell enough thereof to satisfy the judgment and to cover the costs and expenses of the sale. The writ authorizes the sheriff to seize both tangible and intangible personal property, such as bank accounts. If the judgment debtor's personal property seized and sold by the sheriff does not produce sufficient funds to pay the judgment, the writ of execution is returned to the court with a statement of the extent to which the judgment is unsatisfied. If an execution is returned unsatisfied in whole or in part, the judgment becomes a *lien* on any real estate owned by the debtor if it is within the jurisdiction of the court that issued the writ of execution. An unpaid judgment creditor is entitled to have the real estate sold at a judicial sale and to have the net proceeds of the sale applied on the judgment. A judgment creditor with an unsatisfied writ of execution has not only a lien on real property owned by the judgment debtor at the time the judgment becomes final, but also a judicial lien on any real property acquired by the judgment debtor during the life of judgment.

Garnishment is another important method used by judgment creditors to collect a judgment. A judgment creditor can "garnish" the wages of the judgment debtor or his bank account or any other obligation owing to him from a third party. In the process of garnishment, the person owing the money to a judgment debtor—the employer, bank of deposit, third party—will be directed to pay the money into court rather than to the judgment debtor, and such money will be applied against the judgment debt.

In connection with writs of execution and garnishment proceedings, it is extremely significant that the laws of the various states have statutory provisions that exempt certain property from writs of execution and garnishment. The state laws limit the amount of wages that can be garnished and usually provide for both real-property and personal-property exemptions. This will be discussed with the materials on bankruptcy.

In recent years many states have adopted a *citation proceeding,* which greatly assists the creditor in collecting a judgment. The citation procedure begins with the service of a citation on the judgment debtor to appear in court at a stated time for examination under oath about his financial affairs. It also prohibits the judgment debtor from making any transfer of property until after the examination in court. At the hearing, the judgment creditor or his attorney questions the judgment debtor about his income, property, and affairs. Any nonexempt property that is discovered during the questioning may be ordered sold by the judge, with the proceeds applied to the judgment. The court may also order that weekly or monthly payments be made by the judgment debtor. In states that have adopted the citation proceeding, the difficulties in collecting a judgment have been substantially reduced.

One important method of collecting a judgment is also relevant to the procedures that may be used to commence a lawsuit. The procedure with these dual purposes is known as *attachment.* Attachment (discussed in Section 4) is a method of acquiring *in rem* jurisdiction over property of a nonresident defendant who is not subject to the service of process. Attachment gives jurisdiction over the defendant to the extent of the value of the property attached. Attachment as a means of obtaining *in rem* jurisdiction is used in cases involving the status of a person, such as a divorce, or the status of property, such as in eminent domain (acquisition of private property for public use) proceedings.

Attachment as a method of ensuring collection of a judgment is used by a plaintiff who fears that the defendant will dispose of his property before the court is able to enter a final decision. The plaintiff has the property of the defendant seized, pending the outcome of the lawsuit. It is of vital importance to the success of the attachment that the creditor prove the property being attached is either owed to the debtor or is some of the debtor's property.

Attachment and the procedures controlling its use are governed by statutes that vary among the states. The attaching plaintiff-creditor must put up a bond with the court for the protection of the defendant, and the statutes provide methods whereby the attachment may be set aside by the defendant. If the plaintiff receives a judgment against the defendant, the attached property will be sold to satisfy the judgment.

In spite of the remedies the creditor may use, it frequently develops that the judgment is of little value because of the lack of assets that can be reached or because of other judgments. It must be remembered that a judgment standing alone has little value. In many cases, the debtor may file a voluntary petition in bankruptcy, which will extinguish the judgment debt.

In other cases, the creditor recognizes the futility of attempting to use additional legal process to collect, and the matter simply lies dormant until it dies a natural death by the expiration of the time allowed to collect the claim or judgment. Everyone should be aware that some people are judgment-proof and that in such cases the law has no means of collecting a judgment. Debtors are not sent to prison simply because of their inability to pay debts or judgments.

20. Full Faith and Credit

One further aspect of litigation as it relates to the enforcement of judgment and decrees must be noted. Article IV, Section 1, of the U.S. Constitution provides: "Full faith and credit shall be given in each State to the public acts, records, and judicial proceedings of every other State. . . ." This means the decision in one state is binding in other states, only that the final decisions or judgments rendered in any given state by a court with jurisdiction shall be enforced as between the original parties in other states. "Full faith and credit" is applicable to the result of a specific decision as it affects the rights of the parties, not to the reasons or principles on which it was based.

Full faith and credit requires that a suit be brought to enforce the judgment on decree in the other state. However, the plaintiff need not prove any facts other than the entry of the judgment or decree in the sister state. The doctrine dispenses with the necessity of re-proving one's claim.

SUMMARY

LITIGATION

Parties	1. The names used to describe the parties in litigation vary depending on the type of lawsuit and the stage of the litigation. Cases on appeal are usually titled in the name of the appellant versus the appellee.
	2. A plaintiff must have standing to sue. Standing requires that the plaintiff have an actual stake in the controversy such that all issues will be adequately raised.
	3. Suits are often brought by one person on behalf of a class. Class-action suits require notice to all members of the class, and each member must meet the jurisdictional amount in the federal courts.
Jurisdiction	1. To render a binding decision, a court must have jurisdiction over the subject matter of the litigation and over the parties.
	2. Jurisdiction over the defendant is usually obtained by the service of a summons. In some cases jurisdiction may be obtained by publishing a notice in the newspaper.
	3. A summons may be served beyond the borders of the state if the state has a long-arm statute. Such service is not a denial of due process if the party served has sufficient contact with the state issuing the summons, that requiring the

out-of-state defendant to appear and defend the lawsuit does not offend our traditional notions of fair play and substantial justice.

4. A plaintiff may file a lawsuit in a state without minimum contact, since the plaintiff is voluntarily submitting to the jurisdiction of the court.

5. Jurisdiction is the power to hear a case. The term *venue* is used to describe the appropriate court among all those with jurisdiction to hear the case.

PRETRIAL PROCEEDINGS

Pleadings

1. The term *pleading* is used to describe papers filed with the court by the parties in order to create the issues for trial. The plaintiff makes allegations in a complaint, and the defendant answers the complaint by admitting or denying each allegation of the complaint.

2. The answer may contain counterclaims of the defendant, and in some states the plaintiff must file a reply to all new matters raised in the answer.

3. Many cases are decided on motions attacking pleadings. The law requires certain minimal allegations, and if each of these allegations is not present, a court may dismiss the complaint.

4. Motions may also be filed during the pleading stage that raise technical matters such as bankruptcy, illegality, or other matters which would indicate that a trial was unnecessary.

5. If during the pleading stage it appears that there is no material fact in dispute, then there is no need for a trial. The court will decide the questions of law raised by the pleadings and other documents on file. This decision may be a judgment on the pleadings, or it may be a summary judgment.

Discovery

1. During the pleading stage and thereafter, the law has several techniques which the parties use to discover facts known by the other.

2. These techniques include the taking of depositions, the furnishing of copies of documents and photographs, serving interrogatories, and compulsory physical examinations.
3. The purpose of discovery is to encourage settlement and to take the surprise element out of litigation.
4. At the close of discovery the parties and the judge meet at a pretrial conference to finish narrowing the issues for trial and to settle the case if possible.

TRIAL

Proof of Facts

1. In selecting the jury, each party is entitled to challenge any potential juror for cause. In addition, each party is given a specified number of peremptory challenges to reject potential jurors without giving a reason.
2. The parties attempt to prove their factual contentions by introducing evidence in open court. Evidence is presented through questioning of witnesses, with the opposing party being given the right of cross-examination.
3. Numerous rules restrict the admissibility of evidence which may be presented. These rules are based on policy considerations. For example, the best evidence rule requires that the original document be presented if its content is at issue.
4. At the close of the plaintiff's case, a defendant will ordinarily make a motion for a directed verdict. The court will grant this motion and order the jury to return a verdict for the defendant if the evidence considered in the light most favorable to the plaintiff will not support a verdict for the plaintiff. The motion will be denied if there is any evidence to support each allegation of the complaint.
5. After the parties have introduced all their evidence, the court instructs the jury on the law applicable to the case. Jury instructions tell the jury that if it finds certain facts, then it should reach a certain result.

6. The term *burden of proof* is used to describe the party that is required to come forward with evidence on a certain point. It is also used to describe the party with the burden of persuasion.

7. The law imposes three levels in satisfying the burden of persuasion. In criminal cases, the burden is beyond a reasonable doubt. In most civil cases, the burden is by a preponderance or greater weight of the evidence. In some special situations, there is a burden between these other two which is known as the clear and convincing proof standard.

8. The decision of a jury is known as a verdict. The final decision of the court based on the verdict is known as a judgment. In cases tried in equity, the decision of the court is known as a decree.

PROCEEDINGS AFTER THE TRIAL

Post-Trial Motions

1. The losing party before the trial judge ordinarily files a post-trial motion. In this post-trial motion, the losing party seeks either a new trial or a judgment in its favor notwithstanding the verdict.

2. It is from the ruling on this post-trial motion that the losing party appeals.

Appeals

1. Appeals are costly and time-consuming. The party must obtain a transcript of the proceedings before the trial court and excerpt therefrom the matters to be raised on appeal. A brief must be prepared containing the points to be considered by the reviewing court and a party's legal authorities in support of the appeal.

2. The issues before the reviewing court are essentially questions of law, and great deference is given the findings of fact at the trial level.

Enforcement

1. It is not enough for a party to obtain a judgment against another. If the losing party does not voluntarily satisfy the judgment, then further legal proceedings may be required. These may include judicial sales of property, garnishment of wages, and court orders requiring parties to take certain actions.

Full Faith and Credit	1. A final decision in a legal proceeding in one state is entitled to full faith and credit in all other states.

REVIEW QUESTIONS

1. Match each term in column A with the appropriate statement in column B.

A	B
1. Venue	a. The removal of a prospective juror for which no cause need be given.
2. Long-arm statute	b. The questioning of prospective jurors as to their qualifications to be fair and impartial.
3. Summary judgment	c. The burden of proof standard in criminal cases.
4. Demurrer	d. The usual burden of proof standard in civil cases.
5. Beyond a reasonable doubt	e. A law that authorizes the service of a summons beyond the border of the state.
6. Brief	f. The common-law term for a motion to dismiss a complaint.
7. Venire	g. A document used in the appeal process to set forth the grounds on which the appeal is based.
8. Preponderance of the evidence	h. Potential jurors.
9. Voir dire examination	i. A burden of proof standard used in limited situations where the law requires more proof than usual.
10. Peremptory challenge	j. A final decision without a trial because no facts are in dispute.
11. Clear and convincing proof standard	k. The proper court in which to conduct a trial.

2. The Sierra Club, an organization devoted to the conservation and maintenance of national forests, sued the secretary of the interior to prevent federal approval of an extensive skiing development. The secretary asked the court to dismiss the suit on the ground that the plaintiffs lacked standing to sue. With what result? Why?

3. A paving contractor incorporated in Delaware with its principal place of business in Indiana was hired to oil and chip streets in a mobile home park located in Urbana, Illinois. Heavy winds developed during the spraying of oil on the street, and a light film of oil was sprayed on 36 mobile homes, doing approximately $500 damage to each. A class-action suit was filed in federal court seeking $18,000 damages. Does the court have jurisdiction? Explain.

4. An accounting firm incorporated in Oregon performed accounting services in California in connection with a merger. A dispute arose later and the corporation was sued in California. The summons was served in Oregon as authorized by the California long-arm statute. The accounting firm objected to the jurisdiction of the court. Did the California court have jurisdiction over the defendant? Why?

5. Pauline filed a complaint for divorce against Daniel. The complaint and summons was left with

Daniel's secretary at his office while he was out of town. Was Daniel properly served with these process papers? Why?

6. Munns suffered injuries in an automobile accident while driving his VW beetle in Alaska. He sued Volkswagen and recovered a sizable judgment because of a defective seat belt mechanism. Volkswagen then sued Klippan, a German corporation, which had sold the seat belt mechanism to Volkswagen in Germany. This suit was filed in Alaska. Klippan contended that the court lacked personal jurisdiction over it. Could Alaska's long-arm statute properly be used in this case? Why?

7. Ron sues Walter for personal injuries arising out of an automobile accident. Walter was allegedly driving under the influence of alcohol at the time of the accident. An investigation reveals that the list of prospective jurors includes a relative of Ron and the owner of a package liquor store. Walter does not want his case to be tried by a jury that includes these persons. What can he do? Explain.

8. George enters into a written contract to sell his house to Wally. When Wally fails to pay for the house as agreed, George sells it to Henry for $10,000 less. George sues Wally for the $10,000. At the trial, George took the stand and attempted to testify about the two contracts of sale. Wally's attorney objected and the judge stopped George's testimony. What was the basis of the objection? Explain.

9. Pat sued Vince for breach of contract. Pat testified that Vince had agreed to work as a salesman for a 10 percent commission. Vince testified that the commission was to be 15 percent. There were no witnesses to the conversation that created the oral contract. Assume that the case is tried before a jury.
   a. Which party has the burden of producing evidence as to the terms of the contract? Why?
   b. Which party has the burden of persuasion?
   c. What standard of proof is required? Explain.
   d. Is it possible for the jury to find for Pat without any corroborating evidence? Explain.

10. Explain the difference between a verdict, a judgment, and a decree.

11. Motions are used to raise legal issues at various stages of a trial. Name two motions that are usually made after a trial is complete, and indicate some of the grounds or bases of such motions.

12. Appeals are costly in time and money. Give three examples of procedures used in the review process that increase both costs.

13. Nancy sued John in Maryland and recovered a judgment for $10,000. John moved to Florida. Nancy has not collected the judgment. If she sues John in Florida, will the court relitigate the issues of the first case? Why?

4 THE LAW OF TORTS AND BUSINESS

A *tort* is an omission (failure to act) or a wrongful act (other than a breach of contract) against a person or his property. The term is somewhat difficult to define, but the word *wrongful* in the definition means a violation of one person's legal duty to another. The victim of a tort may recover damages for the injuries received, usually because the other party was "at fault" in causing the injury.

Acts or omissions, to be tortious, need not involve moral turpitude or bad motive or maliciousness. Moreover, an act or an omission that does not invade another's rights is not tortious, even though the actor's motive is bad or malicious.

Torts as private wrongs must be contrasted with *crimes,* which are public wrongs. The purpose of the criminal law is to punish the wrongdoer, while the purpose of the law of torts is to compensate the victim of wrongful conduct. To deter intentional torts, however, the law may impose punitive in addition to actual damages.

The same act may be both a crime and a tort: an assault and battery is both a wrong against society and a wrong against the victim. Society may punish the guilty party, and the victim may sue in tort to recover damages. It must be recognized that the criminal action does not benefit the victim of the crime or compensate him for his injury. Such compensation is left to the civil law of torts.

1. Theories of Tort Liability

Tort liability is predicated on two premises: (1) In a civilized society one person should not intentionally injure another or his property, and (2) all persons should exercise reasonable care and caution in the conduct of their affairs. The first premise has resulted in a group of torts labeled *intentional torts.* The second premise is the basis for the general field of tort liability known as *negligence.* Liability based on negligence is liability based on fault, just as it is in an intentional tort. However, because the wrong in negligence is of a lesser degree than it is in torts, the theory of damages in negligence cases does not include punishment. For simple negligence, a person is entitled to collect only actual damages from the wrongdoer; that is, enough money to make the injured party whole. He is not entitled to collect punitive damages to discourage the wrongdoer from repeating his negligence.

A third theory of tort liability, called *strict liability,* is not based on wrongful conduct in the usual sense, although the party committing the tort usually does something intentionally or negligently. Strict liability is based on peculiar factual situations and the relationship of the parties. To the extent that an activity by one party causes injury, there is liability because of the injury, not because the defendant was at fault in the traditional sense of wrongdoing. Although there is no fault in the sense of wrongdoing, there is fault in that actions caused the injuries. Strict liability is imposed when harm is caused by dangerous or trespassing animals, blasting operations, or fire.

2. Damages

The purpose of tort litigation is to require a wrongdoer or the party at fault to compensate a victim for the injury incurred (*compensatory damages*). The theory of damages is that the victim of a tort should receive a sum of money that will make him "whole." In other words, dollar damages are supposed to place the victim of the tort in as good a position as he would have been in had the tort not been committed. This, of course, is impossible, because no amount of money can replace an arm, a leg, or an eye, let alone a life. Therefore, in very serious cases, especially those that involve substantial pain and suffering, any money damages are probably inadequate.

Compensatory damages in the typical tort case usually include: (1) medical expenses, (2) lost income from earnings, (3) property damage, (4) pain and suffering and (5) loss of life or limb. These losses are those actually sustained in the past and those estimated in the future. As a result of the latter aspect, the calculation of damage awards creates significant problems. Expert witnesses use life expectancy tables and present-value discount tables to help them testify so that a jury may determine the amount of damages to award. But uncertainty about the life expectancy of injured plaintiffs and the impact of inflation makes the use of these tables questionable. Also, awarding damages for pain and suffering may result from jury sympathy as much as for compensation for financial loss.

Compensatory damages are not the only kind of damages. There are also *punitive damages,* which are awarded to punish defendants for committing intentional torts and for negligent behavior considered "gross" or "willful and wanton." For an award of punitive damages, the defendant's motive must be "malicious," "fraudulent," or "evil." Increasingly, punitive damages are also awarded for dangerously negligent conduct that shows a conscious disregard for the interests of others. These damages are used to deter future wrongdoing.

Because they make an example out of the defendant, punitive damages are sometimes called *exemplary damages.* Punitive damages are a windfall to the injured plaintiff who also receives compensatory damages.

To collect damages, most victims must hire an attorney, whose fee is usually contingent on the total amount collected. The contingent fee system means that the attorney is paid a percentage of the recovery, but nothing if the case is lost. Usual contingent fees are 33⅓ percent if a trial is held, and 40 to 50 percent if the case is appealed. Contingent fees make the legal system and the best lawyers available to all, irrespective of ability to pay. However, if the injuries are very substantial and liability is easily established, the fees of the attorney may be viewed as unfair and unreasonable. Assume that a $3 million verdict is given for the loss of two legs. It is difficult to see how the attorney's $1 million could have been earned if the liability is clear. The chance of earning similarly large fees has encouraged "ambulance chasing" of potentially big cases, especially in large cities.

3. Persons Liable

Every person legally responsible is liable for his or her own torts. It is no defense that the wrongdoer is working under the direction of another. That fact may create liability on the part of the other person, but it is no defense to the wrongdoer. The theory of liability by which one person is liable for the torts of another is known as *respondeat superior.* This theory imposes liability on principals or masters for the torts of their agents or servants if the agent or servant is acting within the scope of employment when the tort was committed. This subject is discussed more fully in chapter 16.

If two or more persons jointly commit a tort, all may be held liable for the total injury. The liability is said to be *joint and several.* All are liable, and each is liable for the entire damage.

In general, an infant has tort liability, depending on the age of the infant, the nature of the tort involved, and whether the tort is intentional or based on a theory of negligence. In most states, a child under the age of 7 is conclusively presumed to be incapable of negligence; from ages 7 to 10, a child is still presumed to be incapable, but the presumption may be rebutted. A child older than 10 is treated as any other person insofar as tort liability is concerned. Some states use the age 14 instead of 10 for these rules. A minor above the minimum age is held to the same standard as an adult. A minor driving an automobile owes the same duty of due care that an adult owes.

Another area of substantial misunderstanding of the law is concerned with parents' liability for the torts of their children. As a general rule, a parent is not responsible for such torts. Parents are liable if the child is acting as an agent of the parent, or if the parents are themselves at fault. In addition, some states have adopted the "family-purpose" doctrine, which provides that when an automobile is maintained by a parent for the pleasure and convenience of the family, any member of the family, including an infant, who uses it is presumed the owner's agent, and the owner is responsible for the negligence of the family member. The presumption may be rebutted, however. Other states have gone further and provided that anyone driving a car with the permission of the owner is the owner's agent, and the owner has vicarious liability to persons injured by the driver.

In recent years, courts have been faced with cases in which a person is injured by a product but the person is unable to determine which company manufactured the product. Such cases are common when drugs cause injuries not only to the persons taking the drug, but also to their children. While there are only a few cases to date, the trend is to hold all manufacturers liable and to allocate the loss by market share. A manufacturer can avoid its share of liability only by proving that its products could not have been the cause of the injury. Otherwise, all manufacturers share responsibility for injuries.[1]

4. Introduction

INTENTIONAL TORTS

Several intentional torts often involve the business community as either plaintiffs or defendants. The imposition of liability for these torts provides protection to basic individual interests of people and their property. The torts may involve (1) interference with the personal freedom of an individual, (2) interference with property rights, (3) interference with economic relations, and (4) wrongful communications. Table 4–1 briefly describes each.

5. Interference with Personal Freedom

Assault and *battery* and *false imprisonment* involve business more commonly than they should. If an employee of a business engages in a fight with a customer, a lawsuit on the theory of assault and battery is likely to follow. Similarly, if an employee wrongfully physically restrains a customer, there may be a tort action for false imprisonment. Assume that Pat is suspected of shoplifting and Dot physically restrains him. If Dot is wrong, and Pat is not a shoplifter, a tort has been committed.

Inflicting *mental distress* is a tort very important to the business community. It is an invasion of a person's peace of mind by insults or other indignities or by outrageous conduct. If someone without a privilege to do so, by extreme and outrageous conduct, intentionally or recklessly causes another person severe emotional distress with bodily harm resulting from that distress, the offender is subject to liability for the other's emotional distress and bodily harm. Liability does not exist for every case of hurt feelings or bad manners—only where conduct is so outrageous in character and so extreme in degree that it goes beyond all possible bounds of decency. For liability, the conduct must be regarded as atrocious, utterly intolerable in a civilized community. Liability exists in cases in which the facts, if told to an average person, would lead him to exclaim "Outrageous!" High-pressure tactics of collection agencies, including violent cursing and accusations of dishonesty, have often been held to be outrageous.

[1] Sindell v. Abbott Laboratories, p. 76.

However, a person is not liable where he has done no more than to insist on his legal rights in a permissible way, even though he is aware that such insistence is certain to cause emotional distress. Also, there is no liability for offensive conduct that is not extreme.

TABLE 4–1
Intentional Torts Common to Business

THEORY OF LIABILITY	DESCRIPTION
Interference with Personal Freedom	
Battery	Intentional and unpermitted physical contact with a person's body.
Assault	Causing the apprehension of a harmful or offensive contact with a person's body.
Assault and battery	A combination of assault and battery (some hits and some misses).
False imprisonment	A wrongful restraint of a person's freedom of movement.
Mental distress	Wrongful interference with a person's peace of mind by insults, indignities, or outrageous conduct.
Interference with Property	
Trespass to land	An unauthorized entry upon the land of another.
Trespass to chattels	A direct intentional interference with a chattel in possession of another person, such as taking it or damaging it.
Conversion	Interference with a person's chattels to the extent that the wrongdoer ought to pay for the chattel.
Nuisance	An intentional invasion or disturbance of a person's rights in land or the conduct of an abnormally dangerous activity.
Interference with Economic Relations	
Disparagement	Injurious falsehoods about a person's business or property, damaging prospective advantage.
Contracts	Inducing a party to a contract to breach it, or interfering with its performance.
Prospective advantage	Interfering with an expectancy such as employment or an opportunity to contract.
Wrongful Communications	
Slander	Oral defamation. Holding a person's name or reputation up to hatred, contempt, or ridicule, or causing others to shun him.
Libel	Written defamation.
Invasion of privacy	Interfering with one's right to be let alone by (1) appropriating the name or picture of a person, (2) intruding upon a person's physical solitude, (3) the public disclosure of private facts, and (4) publicity that places a person in a false light in the public eye.
Fraud	An intentional misstatement of a material existing fact relied upon by another, to his injury.

6. Trespass

Interference with property is the basis of several tort theories. The tort of trespass is a common one, and the term is applied both to real and personal property. Trespass to land occurs when there is an unauthorized entry upon the land of another. The person in exclusive possession of land is entitled to enjoy the use of that land free from interference of others. Entry upon the land of another is a trespass even if the one who enters is under the mistaken belief that he is the owner or has a right, license, or privilege to enter.

Trespass to land may be *innocent* or *willful.* An innocent trespass would occur when one goes on another's land by mistake or under the impression that he has a right to be there. It is still an intentional wrong because persons intend the natural and probable consequences of their acts. A trespass is willful if the trespasser knowingly goes on another's land, aware that he or she has no right to do so. In a trespass case, if the trespass is willful, the plaintiff is entitled to exemplary or punitive damages, which may include attorney's fees. It should be kept in mind that except for tort cases involving punitive damages, every litigant pays his or her own attorney's fees in tort cases.

A trespass to personal property—goods and the like—is unlawful interference with the control and possession of the goods of another. One is entitled to have exclusive possession and control of his personal property and may recover for any physical harm to his goods by reason of the wrongful conduct of another. The intent need not be wrongful. If a person mistakenly interferes with the goods of another, a trespass has occurred. A trespass to goods may occur by theft of the goods or by damage to the goods. In such cases, the owner recovers the property and is entitled to be paid for the damage to the property and for its loss of use during the period that the owner lost possession of the property.

7. Conversion

The action of conversion is quite similar to trespass. It differs in that a suit for conversion of goods is used when the interference is so significant that the wrongdoer is compelled to pay the full value of the goods as damages. Conversion, in theory, is a judicial sale of the chattel to the wrongdoer. Using someone else's lumber for building purposes would be a conversion. Among the factors used to determine if the interference is relatively minor (trespass) or serious (conversion) are (1) the extent and duration of the interference, (2) the defendant's motives, (3) the amount of actual damage to the goods, and (4) the inconvenience and other harm suffered by the plaintiff. Conversion results from conduct intended to affect the chattel. The intent required is not conscious wrongdoing but an intent to exercise control over the goods. For example, a purchaser of stolen goods is guilty of conversion even though he does not know the goods are stolen. An act of interference with the rights of the true owner establishes the conversion.

Conversion frequently occurs even though the defendant's original possession of the goods is lawful. It may result from several actions, such as a transfer of the goods to another person or to another location. A laundry that delivers shirts to the wrong person is guilty of a conversion. If the laundry refuses to deliver the shirts to the owner, a conversion has occurred. Destruction, alteration, or misuse of a chattel may also constitute a conversion.

8. Nuisance

Tort liability may also be predicated upon the unreasonable use by a person of his own property. Any improper or indecent activity that causes harm to another person, to his property, or to the public generally is tortious. Such conduct is usually described as a *nuisance,* either private or public. A private nuisance disturbs only the interest of some private individual, whereas the public nuisance disturbs or interferes with the public in general. The legal theory supporting tort liability in these areas is that an owner of property, although conducting a lawful business thereon, is subject to reasonable limitations and must use his property in a way that will not unreasonably interfere with the health and comfort of his neighbors or with their *right to the enjoyment of their property.* The ownership of land includes the right to reasonable comfort and convenience in its occupation. In addition to tort liability, the remedy of an injunction is used to abate a nuisance.[2]

A nuisance may result from intentional conduct or from negligence. Although malice may not be involved, most nuisances are intentional in the sense that the party creating the nuisance did so with the knowledge that harm to the interests of others would follow. A nuisance requires a substantial and unreasonable interference with the rights of others and not a mere annoyance or inconvenience.

A nuisance may exist because of the type of business activity being conducted. Operation of a drag strip or a massage parlor has been held to constitute a private nuisance to the neighbors. Many nuisances result from the manner in which business is conducted. Pollution of the air or water by a business frequently results in tort liability based on the nuisance theory. Most tort litigation dealing with private nuisances is resolved by weighing the conflicting interests of adjoining landowners. If one party is seriously injuring the other, the activity may be enjoined and dollar damages awarded. Even if the courts are unwilling to enjoin an activity, dollar damages may still be awarded because of a nuisance.

9. Interference with Economic Relations

Interference with commercial or economic relations includes three business torts: (1) disparagement, (2) interference with contractual relations, and (3) interference with prospective advantage. *Disparagement* is a communication of an injurious falsehood about a person's property, quality of product, or character and conduct of business in general. Such false statements are regarded as "unfair" competition and are not privileged. The basis of the tort is the false communica-

---

[2] Morgan County Concrete Co. v. Tanner, p. 77.

tions that result in interference with the prospect of sale or some other advantageous business relation. The falsehood must be communicated to a third party and must result in specific pecuniary loss. The loss of specific customers, sales, or business transactions must be demonstrated. Although closely related, slander or personal defamation of one's reputation is another tort, which will be discussed with other wrongful communications.

Interference with contractual relations usually takes the form of inducing a breach of contract. In order to hold someone liable for interference with a contract, a direct causal relation and improper motive must be shown. Mere loss suffered from a broken contract is insufficient. Crucial to the question of liability is the balancing of the conflicting interests of the parties involved. For example, assume that a depositor tells the bank's president that she believes one of the cashiers is dishonest. She suggests that the cashier be discharged. Has the depositor committed a tort? The policy of protecting employees from wrongful interference with the employment contracts must be weighed against the desirability of ensuring that bank employees are honest. The trend of cases is to allow recovery for wrongful interferences with the rights of others. Any intentional invasion or interference with the property or contractual rights of others without just cause is a tort. The economic harm due to the breach of an existing contract is weighed against the motive and the reasonableness of the action. The courts tend to favor the sanctity of existing contracts over other interests such as unrestricted competition.

Interference with prospective or potential advantage is considered a tort, in order to protect the expectancies of future contractual relations, including the prospect of obtaining employment, employees, or customers. It is no tort to use fair business practices to beat a business rival to prospective customers; however, the competitor's motive and means of accomplishment determine liability. Fraud, violence, intimidation, and threats that drive away potential customers from one's market result in liability. As in suits for lost profits, obtaining sufficient proof that losses were actually suffered is sometimes difficult.

Another interference with economic relations tort is the wrongful appropriation of another's goodwill or business value. It is a tort to infringe on another's patent, trademark, or copyright. In addition, a trade name such as Holiday Inn or Coca-Cola is entitled to protection from theft or appropriation by another. Many cases involving the appropriation of another's business values involve words or actions that are deceptively similar to those of another. It is a tort to use a name or take an action that is deceptively similar to the protected interests of another. But what degree of similarity may exist before a wrong is committed? In general, it can be said that whenever the casual observer, as distinct from the careful buyer, tends to be misled into purchasing the wrong article, an injunction as well as a tort action is available to the injured party.

The remedy of injunction is perhaps more important than the tort action where there is infringement of a patent, copyright, or trademark. The injunction that prohibits the continued appropriation protects not only the owner of the right, but the consuming public as well.

Trade secrets are also protected by the law of torts and courts of equity. Information about one's trade, customers, processes, or manufacture is confidential; but if it is not patented or copyrighted, another firm may make the same discoveries fairly—through research, study, or observation—and may use them freely. "Reverse engineering," by which one party studies another's product to come up with a similar product, is permissible. But if the second firm bribes or hires an employee of the first company in order to obtain secrets, the second firm may be enjoined from using them. Novelty and breach of confidential relationships are not necessary before there can be a trade secret. What constitutes a trade secret is a question of fact.

10. Wrongful Communications

Defamation consists of the twin torts of libel and slander. *Libel* is generally written; *slander* is oral. A defamatory communication is one that holds a person up to hatred, contempt, or ridicule or causes a person to be shunned by others. Tort liability for defamation exists in order to protect a person's name and reputation.

As a general rule, a charge of slander requires proof of actual damage; however, four categories of statements justify the awarding of damages without actual proof of damage. These are statements (1) imputing the commission of a crime of moral turpitude; (2) imputing the presence of a loathsome disease; (3) relating to the conduct of a business, trade, profession, or office; and (4) accusing a female of unchastity. All other slanders require proof of special damage.

The law of libel is complicated by the written aspect of defamation. Freedom of the press, for example, is guaranteed by the First Amendment, to which the law must adhere. Furthermore, application of the law of libel depends upon whether or not the person defamed is a public figure, subject to a set of standards different from those governing the rest of society. Celebrities must prove malice in order to collect damages. Businesses are not public figures and they are not required to prove malice.

If a statement is libelous on its face, it is actionable without proof of special damages. If additional facts are necessary to establish that a writing is defamatory, the law for libel is the same as for slander, and—unless the statement falls into one of the four categories previously noted—proof of actual damage is required.

Some defamatory statements are absolutely privileged. Statements made as a part of a judicial proceeding cannot constitute a tort because of the need for all witnesses to be able to testify freely, without fear of a subsequent lawsuit. Legislative proceedings and many executive communications are also absolutely privileged.

Some defamatory statements are subject to a qualified or limited privilege. For example, many communications to public officials are privileged in order to encourage citizens to report matters to officials. In addition, fair comment on matters of public concern cannot result in tort liability.

In recent years, the law has developed a tort known as *invasion of the right of privacy.* The right of privacy is the right to be let alone, but it may be invaded in numerous ways, as set forth in Table 4–1. Many cases involve newspaper or magazine stories about one's private life. A detective magazine that publishes a picture of a family at the funeral of a loved one may be guilty of an invasion of privacy. But this tort must be distinguished from libel and slander. Invasion of privacy does not involve defamation. It involves wrongful intrusion into one's private life in such a manner as to outrage or to cause mental suffering, shame, or humiliation to a person of ordinary sensibilities. The protection is for a mental condition, not a financial one. Invasion of privacy is the equivalent of a battery to one's integrity; actual damage need not be proved. Unjustified invasion of privacy entitles the victim to damages. Punitive damages may be collected if malice is shown.

The intentional tort of fraudulent misrepresentation is the subject of more litigation than any other of the intentional torts. It is used not only as the basis of suits for dollar damages, but to avoid contract liability and as a basis to rescind or cancel otherwise valid contracts. It will be discussed more fully with the materials on contracts.

11. Elements—Duty   NEGLIGENCE

By most definitions, negligence has four basic elements: (1) a duty imposed on a person in favor of others, (2) an act or omission that constitutes a breach of this duty, (3) proximate cause, and (4) an injury to another. In a few states, negligence actions also require proof of freedom from contributory negligence. In most states, a doctrine known as *comparative negligence* is used to determine the amount of damages an injured party that is partially at fault may collect.

Under the doctrine of comparative negligence, liability is assessed in proportion to the fault of each party. In states using comparative negligence, a plaintiff can collect even if partially at fault, but when the degree of fault reaches 50 percent, a plaintiff is barred from recovery. In states which do not follow this doctrine, a plaintiff is required to be free from contributory negligence. The law in these states requires that the defendant be 100 percent at fault and the plaintiff 0 percent at fault before there is liability.

The concept of a legal duty means that a person must meet certain standards of conduct in order to protect others against unreasonable risks. These standards of conduct may vary, depending on the relationship of the parties. An owner of property would owe a higher duty to a business visitor than to a trespasser. The duty owed to a trespasser is only to warn of known dangers, while the duty to business visitors is to protect them against known dangers and dangers that, with reasonable care, the landowner might discover. The duty is to make the premises reasonably safe for business visitors. However, a business is not an insurer of the safety of its customers.

Whenever the law imposes a duty upon a person, another person has a right, and there exists a right-duty relationship. This relationship exists because the law recognizes it. Moral obligation does not impose a duty or create a right. The duty must be owed to the person claiming injury. An airline owes a duty to its passengers, and the passengers have the right to safe transportation. Assume that this duty is breached and the plane crashes, killing all on board. Assume also that one of the passengers was a key employee of a large company. The company has no claim or tort action against the airline, because the right-duty relationship did not exist between the airline and the company. In recent years courts have expanded the duty owed in cases involving physical injury to one person and emotional injury to another. Many of these cases involve bystanders.[3]

12. Due Care

Negligence is sometimes defined as a failure to exercise due care. People are required to exercise due care and caution for the safety of others when the risk of injury to another is present. Failure to do so is negligence. In determining if a person has exercised due care and caution, the law recognizes that some injuries are caused by unavoidable accidents. There is no tort liability for injuries received in unavoidable accidents. It is only when a person is guilty of unreasonable conduct that tort liability is imposed. Some conduct is declared to be unreasonable by statute, while most conduct is judged by case law standards. The basic issue is whether or not the conduct alleged to be negligent was reasonable or unreasonable.

Liability for negligence is sometimes imposed on a defendant based on a presumption of negligence. This presumption is based on a doctrine known as *res ipsa loquitor*—the thing speaks for itself. It is used in cases where injury would not have occurred unless someone was negligent and the defendant is the only logical one who could have responsibility. This latter conclusion is based on exclusive control of the property causing the injury.

Negligence cases may arise out of a breach of contract. A party to a contract owes a duty to perform the contract with due care. Failure to do so is negligence and a tort. Thus, the same act may result in a suit for breach of contract or in a tort suit for damages. It often may make a difference in which theory is used.[4]

13. Proximate Cause

Proximate cause is the element of negligence perhaps most difficult to understand. Proximate cause means that the act or the omission complained of is the cause of injury. There must be a causal connection between the breach of the duty and the injury or damage. Problems in applying the rule of proximate cause arise because events sometimes break the direct sequence between an act and injury. In other words, the chain of events sometimes establishes that the injury is remote from the wrongful act. Assume that a customer slips on the floor of a store

---

[3] Ramirez v. Armstrong, p. 78.

[4] Lewis v. Farmers Ins. Co. Inc., p. 80.

and breaks a leg. While en route to the hospital in an ambulance, there is a collision in which the customer is killed. The store would not be liable for the wrongful death because its negligence was not the proximate cause of the death, although it was one event in the chain of causation of death.

Difficult questions often arise over the issue of intervening cause. If liquor is sold to someone who is intoxicated and that person later causes an accident, is the chain of causation broken? Most modern courts would say "no." Moreover, many courts also find that selling alcoholic beverages to a minor is an act of negligence which is one cause of subsequent auto accidents. Proximate cause is closely linked to foreseeability in these cases.[5]

The issue of proximate cause must be decided on a case-by-case basis. Proximate cause requires that the injury be the natural and probable consequence of the wrong. Proximate cause means that the injury was foreseeable from the wrong; and without the wrong, the injury would not have occurred. Issues of foreseeability are often difficult.

Assume that a plaintiff suffered a heart attack when informed that her daughter and granddaughter were killed in an auto accident. The plaintiff could not collect from the party at fault in the auto accident, because her injury was not foreseeable and predictable. There was no proximate cause.

Proximate cause need not be the sole cause nor the one nearest in time. Where several causes contribute together to an injury, they each may constitute proximate cause. If two autos, each with a negligent driver, collide and injure some third party, both drivers are liable. The negligence of each is a proximate cause of the injury. Their liability is joint and several. Both have liability for the total injury, and they may be sued separately or together. The plaintiff may collect the total damages only once, however.

14. The Reasonable Person

Negligence presumes a uniform standard of behavior. This standard is that of a reasonable, prudent person using ordinary care and skill. The reasonable man or woman is a community ideal of reasonable behavior that varies from situation to situation. Therefore, the standard is applied by asking the question: What would the reasonable person do under these circumstances?

The reasonable person's physical characteristics are those of the actor in the case being tried. If a person is disabled, so is the reasonable person. On the other hand, the actual mental capacity of the actor may be very different from that of a reasonable person. The law cannot allow a person who has bad judgment or a violent temper to injure others without liability simply because of these mental defects. While the mental capacity required ignores temperament, intellect, and education, it does take age into account, as noted previously in section 3.

The reasonable-person test implies that everyone has a minimum level of

---

[5] McClellan v. Tottenhoff, p. 81.

knowledge. A reasonable person is presumed to know that gasoline will burn; that ice is slippery; and that the greater the speed of an automobile, the greater the danger of injury. In addition, if the person in question has knowledge superior to most people, the law requires that he conduct himself according to his actual skill and knowledge. A skilled orthopedic surgeon is held to a higher degree of care than a general practitioner of medicine.

Among the factors that affect the application of the reasonable-person standard are community customs, emergencies, and the conduct of others. If a person conducts himself in the manner customary to the community, then such conduct probably is not negligent. If everyone does it, then it probably is not unreasonable behavior. Custom, however, does not as a matter of law establish due care, because everybody may in fact be negligent. It has been held that following generally accepted accounting principles may still constitute negligence.

The effect of emergencies is obvious. A person in an emergency situation is usually not held to as high a standard as a person who is not confronted with an emergency. The actual effect of the emergency is not to lower the standard, but to qualify it by asking: Is this conduct reasonable under the circumstances?

Negligence actions often involve the conduct of others. An operator of a business may be negligent in the selection of employees or in the failure to anticipate wrongful acts of others. The law requires that we take reasonable precautions to avoid injuries that are foreseeable. If a tavern employs a bartender with violent tendencies and he injures customers, liability based on a theory of negligence may be imposed. Likewise, entrusting an automobile to one incapable of driving would be a negligent act.

15. Degrees of Negligence

Courts sometimes talk about degrees of negligence. These have been created for several reasons, such as (1) defining the extent of the risk involved and (2) determining the legal relationship of the parties.[6] As a general rule, the greater the risk, the higher the duty owed to others. In addition, the fact that a person is being paid to be careful usually increases the duty owed. A common carrier is an insurer of the goods carried and is liable except for acts of God and the public enemy if the goods are damaged. A common carrier is not an insurer of passengers, however. It owes the highest degree of care to them and will be liable to passengers for injuries resulting from even slight negligence. The carrier does not owe this high duty to persons who are on the premises of the carrier but not on board it. If a farmer is traveling on a train with hogs being delivered to market, the train is liable as an insurer for any injury to the hogs. It is liable to the farmer only if it is negligent. (Slight negligence is all that is required.)

The degrees of negligence are sometimes described as *slight negligence,* which is the failure to exercise great care; *ordinary negligence,* which is the failure to use ordinary care; and *gross negligence,* which is the failure to exercise even slight care.

---

[6] Underberg v. Cain, P. 82.

Such distinctions are of special importance when personal property is entrusted by one person to another. The duty owed depends upon the legal relationship. If the duty is to exercise great care, there is liability for slight negligence; and if the duty is to exercise only slight care, there is liability only for gross negligence. Gross negligence is sometimes known as willful and wanton misconduct or a conscious disregard for the safety of others.

16. Negligence by Professional Persons—Malpractice

Among the more significant trends in the law of negligence is the substantial increase in malpractice suits by patients and clients against professional persons such as doctors or accountants. A malpractice suit may be predicated on a theory of breach of contract; but the usual theory is negligence, failure to exercise the degree of care and caution that the professional calling requires. Negligence by professional persons is not subject to the reasonable person standard. Their standard is stated in terms of the knowledge, skill, and judgment usually possessed by members of the profession, because a professional person holds himself out to the public as having the degree of skill common to others in the same profession. However, professional persons do not guarantee infallibility. Although malpractice suits involve standards of professional conduct, the issue of negligence is submitted to a jury as a question of fact for a decision. Such cases usually require the testimony of experts to assist the jury in its findings of negligence.[7] In many cases, juries find that liability exists, even though members of the profession contend and testify that the services performed were all that could reasonably be expected under the circumstances.

Malpractice suits against doctors and hospitals have multiplied so rapidly that they have significantly affected the practice of medicine and the cost of malpractice insurance. They have also been a significant cause of spiraling medical costs, a major factor in inflation. Not only has the number of malpractice suits more than doubled in recent years, but the size of the verdicts has frequently reached astronomical proportions.

Many doctors and some hospitals have been unable to obtain adequate malpractice insurance coverage. More significantly, many doctors have been reluctant to attempt medical procedures that could result in a malpractice suit. Because of the trends in malpractice litigation, most doctors are practicing defensive medicine: prescribing tests that are probably not indicated, requiring longer hospital stays, and consulting with other doctors as a matter of routine. Defensive medicine obviously is more costly.

Malpractice cases against lawyers have also increased significantly; and although their impact on the cost of legal services is not as significant as it is in medical services, their importance is growing. Malpractice litigation against accountants is another area of great significance. Several aspects of this type of negligence action are discussed in the next section.

---

[7] Harris v. Grizzle, p. 83.

17. Malpractice by Accountants

An accountant is liable to a client for breach of contract if the services are not performed as agreed upon. There is liability to the client also if the services are negligently performed. Negligence is present if the accountant fails to exercise the degree of care and caution that the professional calling requires.

Accountants may have liability also to third parties, because the services are frequently performed for the benefits of others as well as the client. When third parties sue an accountant on a theory of negligence, it is necessary to distinguish between third parties that the accountant knew would rely on his work and third parties that may be described as unforeseen. While there is some conflict between various jurisdictions, the majority and better-reasoned rule is that an accountant is liable for negligence in the performance of his services to those persons whose reliance on the financial representations was actually foreseen by the accountant. The Restatement of Torts (second), a legal treatise, extends the liability of the accountant to persons he knows will receive the product of his services, transmitted by his client. If an accountant knows that his financial statements are to be furnished to banks as a part of the process of obtaining a loan, the negligent accountant has liability to a lending bank for negligence in the preparation of the financial statements relied upon by the bank.

The liability of the accountant for negligence is limited to the class of third persons who come within the description "actually foreseen." It is the law in most jurisdictions that an accountant is not liable on a theory of general negligence to "unforeseen" third persons, because there is no contractual connection with the third party. Third persons without a contractual connection can sue for fraudulent acts of accountants, but not for mere negligence. There is no liability to unforeseen third parties for mere negligence, even though the accountant recognizes that some third party may rely on his work.

It should be noted that an accountant may also be liable to third persons under the federal securities laws. This statutory liability, which will be discussed later in chapter 49, may involve issues of negligence. Under the Securities Act of 1933, an accountant is liable to any purchaser of a security upon proof that the portion of a registration statement attributable to the accountant contains an untrue statement of a material fact or omits to state a material fact necessary to prevent the statements made from being misleading.

The accountant's defense, however, may be that he had, after reasonable investigation, reasonable grounds to believe—and did believe—that the statements contained in the registration statement were true and that there was no omission to state a material fact required or necessary to make the statements not misleading. In other words, "due diligence" or "lack of negligence" is a defense to an allegation of a 1933 Securities Act violation. In determining whether or not an accountant has made a reasonable investigation, the law provides that the standard of reasonableness is that required of a prudent man in the management of his own property.

18. Problems of the Fault System

In recent years the fault system has been widely criticized, primarily in automobile accident, product liability, and malpractice litigation, and major changes have been suggested. Among the system's inherent problems are (1) court congestion and delays, (2) overcompensation of minor claims and undercompensation of major claims, (3) the high cost of liability insurance, (4) inaccurate testimony and unreliable evidence, (5) inconsistency of juries, and (6) the high cost of operating the system.

Of the criticisms of litigation, perhaps none is more significant than the high cost of operating under the fault theory, an expense that is readily apparent in liability insurance premiums. There are also substantial additional costs to the victim, to the alleged wrongdoer, and to society as a whole. Even if a victim is able to collect damages, the attorney's fees are usually one-third of the amount collected.

The alleged wrongdoer in most tort litigation is usually defended by an insurance company. A substantial portion of the insurance premium dollar is spent on investigations and in trying to prevent payment to the person seeking the damages. Thus, both parties to the occurrence are spending considerable sums attempting to determine what, if anything, one must pay the other. Moreover, society must operate an extensive court system and pay judges, court personnel, and jurors to try these cases and to settle these controversies. Obviously, the fault system is a very expensive system to operate.

Studies have been conducted attempting to show that the great majority of automobile accident victims are not appropriately compensated. In very serious cases, especially those that involve substantial pain and suffering, any money damages are probably inadequate. In very minor cases, many plaintiffs are overcompensated. A person with little or no personal injury who brings suit will frequently be overcompensated for injuries because of the nuisance value of the case. Because it will cost money to investigate and defend the case and because the amount of jury verdicts is highly unpredictable, insurance companies frequently pay some amount to obtain a settlement of a claim, even though the claimant is probably not entitled to the amount paid.

The theory of fault was developed long before there were automobiles. Now, in many auto accident cases the litigation is quite unrealistic. Witnesses usually do not remember exactly what happened, so they testify to what they thought (sometimes hoped) happened. Witnesses with faulty memories have their memories refreshed and tend not to testify about what actually happened, but about what somebody said happened.

Many factors influence verdicts in these negligence cases. One very important factor is sympathy for the plaintiff or animosity toward the defendant. A very seriously injured person or the next of kin of a deceased is frequently the obvious beneficiary of sympathy. When the testimony is conflicting and the memory of witnesses questionable, sympathy may play a major role. Animosity is frequently just as important. If a teenager runs a stop sign and kills an innocent bystander, a jury is likely to award high damages, especially if the jury believes an insurance company for the teenager will pay.

19. The Trend toward No-Fault

In recent years there have been numerous proposals to eliminate the fault system in auto accident cases. These proposals have taken various forms. Some have recommended that auto accident cases be turned over to an administrative agency for decision. Others have recommended that the fault system be replaced by a no-fault system, or a system of first-party insurance.

Although the approaches to no-fault vary from state to state, most have elements in common. First of all, a party injured in an auto accident collects from his own insurance company just as he would if he were collecting on his own health insurance. Payment is made irrespective of fault. Just as health insurance would pay the hospital bill of a person attempting suicide, so would no-fault insurance pay the hospital bill of a person injured in an automobile accident even if he were at fault. Second, claimants are entitled to collect their medical bills, lost earnings, and out-of-pocket expenses up to a stated amount. Third, most no-fault laws contain a formula for computing the amount to be paid for pain and suffering, which may be an amount equal to patient's medical bills. If the total medical bill is $500, an additional $500 would be paid for pain and suffering. Fourth, tort claims may still be filed in very serious cases. The approach of no-fault has been to keep the fault system for serious cases, such as permanent disability, disfigurement, and death. Only the minor cases are usually covered by no-fault legislation. This is accomplished by the law's setting a threshold above which the fault system is retained. Finally, claimants cannot collect their medical bills under no-fault if the medical bills are paid by another form of health insurance or by worker's compensation. This eliminates duplicate payment of medical expenses.

Critics of no-fault have been able to delay its enactment in many states, have obtained repeal in a few, and have kept the threshold quite low in others. Among the most often cited objections are (1) the victims of automobile accidents are receiving substantially less for their injuries under no-fault than they would receive under the fault system, and (2) the elimination of the jury system from auto accident litigation deprives a plaintiff of the very important fundamental right to trial by jury.

SUMMARY

GENERAL PRINCIPLES

Damages

1. The theory of damages in tort liability is that the victim will be paid a sum of money that will put a person in as good a position as the person would have been in had the tort not occurred.

2. Compensatory damages include out-of-pocket losses plus pain and suffering, decreased life expectancy, and loss of life or limb.

3. Punitive damages are awarded in some cases to punish the wrongdoer and to deter wrongful conduct.

Persons Liable

1. Employers have liability for the torts of their employees if the employee is acting within the scope of his or her employment.

2. If two or more persons commit a tort, they are jointly and severally liable.

3. A child may have tort liability after reaching a certain age.

4. Parents are generally not liable for the torts of their children unless the child is an agent or servant, or there is a special statute imposing liability.

INTENTIONAL TORTS

Interference with Personal Freedom

1. There are intentional torts for which both compensatory and punitive damages may be awarded in most cases.

2. The tort of inflicting mental distress is of growing importance. It is based on "outrageous" conduct.

Interference with Property

1. Trespass may occur as to both real and personal property. A trespass may be innocent or willful.

2. When a conversion of personal property occurs, the wrongdoer has liability for the value of the goods.

	3. A nuisance is the unreasonable use of one's property that causes injury to another. A nuisance may be enjoined or may result in dollar damages to the victim.
Interference with Economic Relations	1. Interference with commercial or economic relations includes three business torts: disparagement, interference with contractual relations, and interference with prospective advantage.
	2. Disparagement is a false communication about a product or business.
	3. Interference with contractual relations usually takes the form of inducing a breach of contract.
	4. Interference with prospective or potential advantage is considered a tort, in order to protect the expectancies of future contractual relations, including the prospect of obtaining employment, employees, or customers.
Wrongful Communications	1. Defamation consists of the twin torts of libel and slander. Libel is generally written; slander is oral. Tort liability for defamation exists in order to protect a person's name and reputation.
	2. The right of privacy is the right to be let alone. It involves wrongful intrusion into one's private life in such a manner as to outrage or to cause mental suffering, shame, or humiliation to a person of ordinary sensibilities.

NEGLIGENCE

Elements	1. The four basic elements of negligence are (1) a duty owed by one person to another, and (2) a breach of that duty (3) that was the proximate cause of (4) an injury.
	2. The duty owed by one person to another varies depending on the relationship of the parties.
	3. Negligence is the failure to exercise due care. Due care is reasonable conduct under the circumstances.

4. The doctrine of *res ipsa loquitor* creates a presumption of negligence.

5. Proximate cause means that there is a connection between the breach of duty and the injury. Proximate cause is often based on foreseeability.

6. The standard for judging whether or not a duty has been breached is to judge the conduct against the standards of the reasonable person.

Degrees of Negligence

1. The greater the risk, the higher the duty owed to others.

2. A common carrier is an insurer of goods and owes passengers the highest degree of care.

3. Slight negligence is the failure to use great care.

4. Ordinary negligence is the failure to use ordinary care.

5. Gross negligence is the failure to use slight care.

Malpractice

1. Malpractice by professional persons is the failure to exercise that degree of care and caution which the profession calls for. It is the failure to meet the standards of the profession.

2. Accountants are liable for malpractice not only to their clients, but to third persons known to them who will rely on their work product.

3. Accountants also have malpractice liability under the securities laws.

Problems of the Fault System

1. The fault system suffers from court congestion, overcompensation of minor claims and undercompensation of major claims, unreliable evidence, inconsistent juries, and the high costs of operation.

2. Automobile insurance, product liability, and malpractice insurance costs are skyrocketing.

3. It is extremely difficult to determine compensation for pain and suffering.

4. Factors such as sympathy often influence verdicts.

The Trend Toward No-Fault	1. No-fault systems are now in place for auto accident cases in most states. 2. No-fault is really first party insurance rather than third party insurance. 3. Most no-fault systems retain the fault system for serious cases.

CASES – The Law of Torts

Sindell v. Abbott Laboratories
607 P.2d 924 (Ca. 1980)

Plaintiff Sindell brought suit against 11 companies which formerly had manufactured the drug diethylstilbestrol (DES). She alleged that she had developed cancer as the result of her mother's use of the drug 20 years earlier to prevent miscarriage. She contended that the defendants knew or should have known that DES was both dangerous and ineffective to prevent miscarriages. The trial court dismissed her suit because she failed to allege which defendant had manufactured the precise prescription taken by her mother. The plaintiff appeals.

MOSK, J. . . . We begin with the proposition that, as a general rule, the imposition of liability depends upon a showing by the plaintiff that his or her injuries were caused by the act of the defendant or by an instrumentality under the defendant's control. The rule applies whether the injury resulted from an accidental event or from the use of a defective product.

There are, however, exceptions to this rule. Plaintiff's complaint suggests several bases upon which defendants may be held liable for her injuries even though she cannot demonstrate the name of the manufacturer which produced the DES actually taken by her mother. The first of these theories places the burden of proof of causation upon tortious defendants in certain circumstances. The second basis of liability emerging from the complaint is that defendants acted in concert to cause injury to plaintiff. There is a third and novel approach to the problem, sometimes called the theory of "enterprise liability," but which we prefer to designate by

the more accurate term of "industry-wide" liability, which might obviate the necessity for identifying the manufacturer of the injury-causing drug. We shall conclude that these doctrines, as previously interpreted, may not be applied to hold defendants liable under the allegations of this complaint. However, we shall propose and adopt a fourth basis for permitting the action to be tried. . . .

In our contemporary complex industrialized society, advances in science and technology create fungible goods which may harm consumers and which cannot be traced to any specific producer. The response of the courts can be either to adhere rigidly to prior doctrine, denying recovery to those injured by such products, or to fashion remedies to meet these changing needs. Just as Justice Traynor in his landmark concurring opinion in *Escola v. Coca Cola Bottling Company* recognized that in an era of mass production and complex marketing methods the traditional standard of negligence was insufficient to govern the obligations of manufacturer to consumer, so should we acknowledge that some adaptation of the rules of causation and liability may be appropriate in these recurring circumstances. . . .

The most persuasive reason for finding plaintiff states a cause of action is . . . : as between an innocent plaintiff and negligent defendants, the latter should bear the cost of the injury. Here, . . . , plaintiff is not at fault in failing to provide evidence of causation, and although the absence of such evidence is not attributable to the defendants either, their conduct in marketing a drug the effects of which are delayed for many years played a significant role in creating the unavailability of proof.

From a broader policy standpoint, defendants

are better able to bear the cost of injury resulting from the manufacture of a defective product. As was said by Justice Traynor in *Escola,* "[t]he cost of an injury and the loss of time or health may be an overwhelming misfortune to the person injured, and a needless one, for the risk of injury can be insured by the manufacturer and distributed among the public as a cost of doing business." . . .

We hold it to be reasonable in the present context to measure the likelihood that any of the defendants supplied the product which allegedly injured plaintiff by the percentage which the DES sold by each of them for the purpose of preventing miscarriage bears to the entire production of the drug sold by all for that purpose. Plaintiff asserts in her briefs that Eli Lilly and Company and 5 or 6 other companies produced 90 percent of the DES marketed. If at trial this is established to be the fact, then there is a corresponding likelihood that this comparative handful of producers manufactured the DES which caused plaintiff's injuries, and only a 10 percent likelihood that the offending producer would escape liability. . . .

The presence in the action of a substantial share of the appropriate market also provides a ready means to apportion damages among the defendants. Each defendant will be held liable for the proportion of the judgment represented by its share of that market unless it demonstrates that it could not have made the product which caused plaintiff's injuries. In the present case, one DES manufacturer was dismissed from the action upon filing a declaration that it had not manufactured DES until after plaintiff was born. Once plaintiff has met her burden of joining the required defendants, they in turn may cross-complaint against other DES manufacturers, not joined in the action, which they can allege might have supplied the injury-causing product. . . .

We are not unmindful of the practical problems involved in defining the market and determining market share, but these are largely matters of proof. . . . Defendants urge that it would be both unfair and contrary to public policy to hold them liable for plaintiff's injuries in the absence of proof that one of them supplied the drug responsible for the damage. Most of their arguments, however, are based upon the assumption that one manufacturer would be held responsible for the products of another or for those of all other manufacturers if plaintiff ultimately prevails. But under the rule we adopt, each manufacturer's liability for an injury would be approximately equivalent to the damages caused by the DES it manufactured. . . .

Reversed.

Morgan County Concrete Co. v. Tanner
374 So.2d 1344 (Ala. 1979)

Ninety-eight homeowners brought action seeking to enjoin as a nuisance, the construction and operation of a ready-mix concrete plant on property adjacent to a residential area. The property is a rectangle about 100 feet long and 300 feet wide bounded by a highway on the east. Plaintiffs live southwest, west, and east across the highway from the plant. The plant is bounded immediately on the north and south by other business concerns: on the north by a farm equipment dealership, a fertilizer mixing plant, and a trucking firm; on the south by a machine shop and a truck rental concern. Also on the east across U.S. 31 in the vicinity of the plant is a manufacturing plant and a junkyard. The area in question has been rezoned from light industrial to general industrial.

The trial court held that owing to noise created by the plant, accumulations of sediments attributable to drainage problems, and inevitable accumulations of dust, the plant constituted a nuisance. The defendants appealed.

TORBERT, J. . . . Appellants contend that the trial court erred in finding that the operation of the plant was a nuisance. Appellants argue that locality is important in determining a nuisance, and here, appellees purchased their homes near a major highway and business zone where commercial activity could be expected to flourish. . . .

"The essence of private nuisance is an interference with the use and enjoyment of land. . . . So long as the interference is substantial and unreasonable, and such as would be offensive or inconvenient to the normal person, virtually any disturbance to the enjoyment of property may amount to a nuisance." Accordingly, this court has often stated that any establishment erected on one's premises, though for the purposes of a lawful trade or business, which, from the situation, the inherent qualities of the business, or the manner in which it is conducted, directly causes substantial injury to the property of another or produces material annoyance or inconvenience to the occupants of adjacent dwellings rendering them physically uncomfortable, is a nuisance. In applying this principle it has been repeatedly held that smoke, offensive odors, noise, or vibrations of such degree or extent as to materially interfere with the ordinary comfort of human existence will constitute a nuisance.

Location is one factor to consider in determining whether a given activity constitutes a nuisance. In considering locality, this court has stated:

> What may be a nuisance in one locality may not in another. Noises may be a nuisance in the country which would not be in a populous city. A person who resides in the center of a large city must not expect to be surrounded by the stillness which prevails in a rural district. He must necessarily bear some of the noise and occasionally feel slight vibrations produced by the movement and labor of its people and by the hum of its mechanical industries.

Thus, locality may be determinative in deciding whether the use of land by defendant unreasonably interferes with plaintiff's use of his land so as to constitute a nuisance. However, the determination of the existence of a nuisance necessarily depends upon the circumstances of each case and is a question of fact for the jury or the judge sitting without a jury.

In this case, although there was conflicting evidence as to the amount of noise and accumulations of dust arising from the plant, there was credible evidence that such noise and dust caused a substantial and unreasonable interference with the use and enjoyment of appellees' property. . . . Accordingly, we cannot say that the character of the area in question was so predominantly industrial that as a matter of law appellants' operation of the plant would not constitute a nuisance in relation to appellees. . . . The trial court found that "when consideration is given to the noises created by the business in excess of the noises created by the business for which the area was zoned, the drainage problem which accumulates sediments daily, the dust which is inevitably created under the best operations together with the occasional breakdown of dust control industrial equipment, which appears unavoidable at times, the operation of the plant is a nuisance in relation to the plaintiffs." We find from the record that the trial court's finding is supported by credible evidence and is not palpably wrong or manifestly unjust. Accordingly, it is due to be upheld.

Affirmed.

Ramirez v. Armstrong
673 P.2d 822 (N.M. 1983)

This is a tort action which seeks damages for the negligent infliction of emotional distress. Santa Ramirez was struck by a car and killed. The plaintiffs are his three children, two of which witnessed the accident. The third was simply told of it. The trial court dismissed the complaint for failure to state a cause of action.

FEDERCI, J. . . . The sole issue before this Court is whether a cause of action exists in New Mexico for negligent infliction of emotional distress to bystanders. We hold that it does, under certain conditions.

Whether a bystander, not in any physical danger, may recover for the consequences resulting from the emotional shock of seeing a person injured through the negligence of another is a controversial question in the law. New Mexico recognizes the tort of *intentional* infliction of emotional distress. However, recovery for negligent infliction of emotional distress is a question which New Mexico courts have addressed only tangentially. . . .

The courts in other jurisdictions have developed three rules in an attempt to define the liability for negligence to a bystander. They are: (1) the "impact" rule; (2) the "zone of danger" rule; and (3) the "negligence theory." . . . Prior to the present case, we had no occasion to determine which, if any, of these rules should be adopted in New Mexico.

In New Mexico, negligence encompasses the concepts of foreseeability of harm to the person injured and of a duty of care toward that person. Jurisdictions adopting the "impact" or "zone of danger" rules argue the lack of these elements when denying recovery to bystanders not themselves in any physical danger.

Duty and foreseeability [are] closely integrated concepts in tort law. . . . If it is found that a plaintiff, and injury to that plaintiff, were foreseeable, then a duty is owed to that plaintiff by the defendant. Dean Prosser defines duty, in negligence cases, as "an obligation to which the law will give recognition and effect, to conform to a particular standard of conduct toward another." The key to Dean Prosser's definition is the requirement that the obligation of the defendant be one to which the law will give recognition and effect. Cases dealing with negligent infliction of emotional distress often couch the issue in terms of foreseeability. More important to the acceptance of this cause of action is a determination of the specific personal interest to be protected. This interest, in turn, establishes the legally recognized obligation of the defendant to the plaintiff.

The interest to be protected in the present case . . . is more than a general interest in emotional tranquility. It is the profound and abiding sentiment of parental love. The knowledge that loved ones are safe and whole is the deepest wellspring of emotional welfare. Against that reassuring background, the flashes of anxiety and disappointment that mar our lives take on softer hues. No loss is greater than the loss of a loved one, and no tragedy is more wrenching than the helpless apprehension of the death or serious injury of one whose very existence is a precious treasure. The law should find more than pity for one who is stricken by seeing that a loved one has been critically injured or killed.

The existence of a marital or intimate familial relationship is the nucleus of the personal interest to be protected. The tort of negligent infliction of emotional distress is a tort against the integrity of the family unit.

In order to insure that the interest to be protected is actually foreseeable, courts, . . . have adopted a number of criteria to be met in any case where such injury is claimed. . . .

The following standards are adopted by this Court to apply to actions for negligent infliction of emotional distress to bystanders .

1. There must be a marital, or intimate familial relationship between the victim and the plaintiff, limited to husband and wife, parent and child, grandparent and grandchild, brother and sister and to those persons who occupy a legitimate position in loco parentis;

2. The shock to the plaintiff must be severe, and result from a direct emotional impact upon the plaintiff caused by the contemporaneous sensory perception of the accident, as contrasted with learning of the accident by means other than contemporaneous sensory perception, or by learning of the accident after its occurrence;

3. There must be some physical manifestation of, or physical injury to the plaintiff resulting from the emotional injury;

4. The accident must result in physical injury or death to the victim.

These criteria do not alter traditional legal principles of the tort of negligence in New Mexico. Proof of the other elements of a cause of action in negligence, as well as proof of damages, are still required. In order for a plaintiff to recover under the tort of negligent infliction of emotional distress, he must not only meet the outlined criteria, but also the other traditional requirements recognized under established principles of tort law. This cause of action imposes no new obligation of conduct on potential defendants. Ordinary care is still required, and use of such ordinary care will relieve potential defendants from liability. . . .

The judgment of the trial court is reversed as to plaintiffs Job Ramirez and Jesus Elena Ramirez (who witnessed the accident), and affirmed as to plaintiff Bertha Alicia Ramirez (who did not.) . . .

It is so ordered.

Lewis v. Farmers Ins. Co., Inc.
681 P.2d 67 (Okl. 1983)

HODGES, J.

The novel question presented is whether the twelve-month statute of limitations . . . contained in the standard fire policy controls the time to bring an action for alleged bad faith refusal to pay a valid insurance claim; or if, because the action sounds in tort, the two-year tort limitation period applies.

The (appellant-homeowner), Floyd Lewis, Jr., purchased a fire insurance policy from Farmers Insurance Company, Inc., (appellee-insurer). On January 15, 1981, while the policy was in full force and effect, the residence sustained substantial fire damage, and afterwards the home was vandalized. The homeowner demanded payment by the insurer under the terms of the policy; on January 16, 1981, he discussed his loss with insurer's independent adjuster; on March 8, 1981, the insured submitted an unnotarized proof of loss; and on May 19, 1981, the insurer's counsel conducted a sworn examination. Because the original proof of loss was incomplete, it was returned by the insurer's counsel to the insured May 28, 1981. Two blank proof of loss forms were enclosed and a sixty-day extension was granted. July 1, 1981, counsel noted that the sworn examination had been returned unclaimed; receipt of the insured's proof of loss and sworn examination was acknowledged July 24, 1981; and the claim was denied August 12, 1981.

An action was filed February 4, 1982, seeking recovery for the damage to the residence and its contents, and punitive damages based on the wrongful refusal of the insurer to pay the claim. The insurer . . . asserted that the claim was barred by the statute of limitations.

[The trial court dismissed the complaint] upon the theory that the one-year contractual limitation was applicable to the homeowner's bad faith claim instead of the two-year tort statute of limitations.

The homeowner contends that the gravamen of his action is the tortious failure of the insurer to deal fairly in good faith and that the two-year statute of limitations is controlling. . . . The insurer counters that: the limitation period set by the contract governs . . . that the crux of the suit is an action ex contractu; . . .

A breach of contract is a material failure of performance of a duty arising under or imposed by agreement. Although torts may be committed by parties to a contract, a tort is a violation of a duty imposed by law independent of contract. If the contract is merely the inducement which creates the occasion for the tort, the tort, not the contract, is the basis of the action. A common law duty to perform with care, skill, reasonable expediency, and faithfulness accompanies every contract. Negligent failure to observe any of these conditions will give rise to an action ex delicto as well as an action ex contractu.

In *Christian* v. *American Home Assur. Co.*, 577 P.2d 899 (Okl. 1978), this court clearly recognized the two causes of action which may be asserted premised on the existence of an insurance contract: an action based on the contract; and an action for breach of the implied duty to deal fairly and in good faith. In this instance, the insured seeks damages for tortious failure of the insurer to deal fairly and in good faith, and for repairs to his home. The homeowner argues that the repaid costs he seeks is one type of consequential damages recognized by *Christian. Christian* established that the insurer is responsible for all consequential damages and in a proper case, punitive damages, which result in failure to deal fairly and in good faith. The obligation of an insurer to its insured upon proper presentation of a valid claim is not limited to the payment of money. The statutory duty imposed upon the insurer to accept or reject the claim within ninety days of the receipt of the proof of loss recognizes that a substantial part of the right purchased by the insured is the right to receive benefits promptly. Unwarranted delay causes the sort of economic hardship which the insured sought to avoid by the purchase of the policy, and results in possible mental stress which may result from the loss.

Tort liability may be imposed only if there is a clear showing that the insurer in bad faith unreasonably withholds payment of the claim. A cause of action in tort arose when the insurer breached the implied duty to deal fairly and in good faith with its insured. We find that the homeowner's alleged cause of action is founded in tort, and that the two-year statute of limitations is applicable. . . .

Reversed.

McClellan v. Tottenhoff
666 P.2d 408 (Wyo. 1983)

Billy W. McClellan, as administrator of the estate of Chad W. McClellan, sued Mary Jane Tottenhoff, individually and doing business as To-dy's Liquors, and Michael Buffington, an employee bartender. The complaint alleged that the defendants had negligently sold liquor to a minor at a drive-in area, that the minor became intoxicated and killed Chad W. McClellan, the child of the plaintiff, in an automobile accident, and that the sale of the liquor was a proximate cause of the accident. There was a state law prohibiting the sale of alcoholic beverages to the minors. The trial court dismissed the suit.

BROWN, J. . . . The sole issue on appeal is whether a complaint against a vendor unlawfully selling liquor to a minor who becomes intoxicated and injures a third party states a claim for relief in Wyoming. . . .

Under the traditional common law a cause of action against a liquor vendor for injuries to a third person by a consumer of alcohol was unknown. The basis for refusing to impose liability usually rested on the theory that it was the drinking of liquor, not the sale, which was the proximate cause of the injury. There may be sales without intoxication, but no intoxication without drinking. . . .

Courts which base their finding of a cause of action against a liquor vendor using the common law of negligence state that a liquor vendor owes the same duty to the whole world as does any other person.

Once the general duty to use reasonable care is acknowledged, then courts focus their attention on the foreseeability of the resulting harm to establish proximate cause. We think this is a sensible and just approach. . . .

Negligence consists of a duty on the part of the defendant and a violation of the duty which proximately causes injury to the plaintiff. The question whether a duty exists is one of law. The Wyoming common law of negligence imposes a duty on the defendants to exercise the degree of care required of a reasonable person in light of all the circumstances.

We agree with the reasoning of the cases acknowledging a cause of action based on common law negligence. We hold that a vendor of liquor owes a duty to exercise the degree of care required of a reasonable person in light of all the circumstances.

The duty of exercising care to protect another person may either exist at common law or be imposed by statute. The pertinent statutes in this case [prohibit the sale of alcoholic beverages to minors].

Appellee argues that these statutes were meant only to protect minors. We disagree. At least fourteen jurisdictions have established a duty toward the general public based on similar statutes. . . .

We see no difference whether the statutes forbid sales to intoxicated persons or to minors. The idea behind both statutes is that these people are more likely to be unable to handle alcohol, that they need protection from themselves, and that society needs protection from them. . . . We hold that [this statute] establishes a duty toward the general public . . . and that the violation of it . . . is evidence of negligence and may be considered by the trier of fact together with other circumstances in determining the issue of negligence.

We have now established a duty based both upon the common law and upon statutes. The question of proximate cause must also be addressed. Proximate cause means that the accident or injury must be the natural and probable consequence of the act of negligence. In determining what constitutes proximate cause, the same principles apply whether the negligence is a violation of a statutory duty or a nonstatutory duty. The question whether proximate cause exists is one for the trier of fact, unless the evidence shows that reasonable persons could not disagree.

We hold that the ultimate test concerning proximate cause will be whether the vendor could foresee injury to a third person. This question will be one of fact based on the circumstances of each particular case. It is, however, not necessary that a specific injury be foreseen.

It is sufficient if a reasonably prudent person would foresee that injury of the same general type would be likely to happen in the absence of such safeguards.

The argument is also made that even if the sale of alcohol does eventually result in injury to a third person, the injury which the consumer of alcohol brings about is an independent intervening cause. An intervening cause is one which occurs after a defendant's negligent act or omission. A defendant is usually relieved of liability by an unforeseeable intervening cause. However, an intervening cause does not relieve an earlier actor of liability if it was reasonably foreseeable. The causal connection is not broken where the original wrongdoer could reasonably have foreseen that injury to another would be a probable consequence of his negligence.

A tortfeasor is generally held answerable for the injuries which result in the ordinary course of events from his negligence and it is generally sufficient if his negligent conduct was a substantial factor in bringing about the injuries. The fact that there were also intervening causes which were foreseeable or were normal incidents of the risk created would not relieve the tortfeasor of liability. Ordinarily these questions of proximate and intervening cause are left to the jury for its factual determination.

When alcoholic beverages are sold by a tavern keeper to a minor or to an intoxicated person, the unreasonable risk of harm not only to the minor or the intoxicated person but also to members of the traveling public may readily be recognized and foreseen; this is particularly evident in current times when traveling by car to and from the tavern is so common-place and accidents resulting from drinking are so frequent. . . .

Refusing to acknowledge a claim for relief against a liquor vendor harms society in two ways. First, it is an unjust doctrine which often limits recovery when an intoxicated minor driver injures someone. Businesses which sell liquor are usually in a more solid financial position than a minor. Second, it is reasonable to assume that the current state of the law places us all at more peril, because there is no effective deterrent to keep liquor vendors from selling liquor to minors or to intoxicated persons. Liquor licenses are seldom revoked. Perhaps the threat of civil liability or increased insurance premiums will serve to make liquor vendors more careful. . . .

Reversed and remanded.

Underberg v. Cain
348 N.W.2d 145 (S.D. 1984)

ANDERST, J. . . . This is an action by a licensee against a landowner for injuries suffered. The jury returned a verdict in favor of the landowner. We affirm.

Barney W. Cain and Barney W. Cain, III, (Cains) own and operate Barney's Auto Salvage. To enlarge their business area, they had excavated into the hillside on which their business was located. This left a drop-off of thirty to fifty feet. No fence or other warning was placed at the top of the excavation.

At 8:30 P.M. on the night of November 30, 1981, Underberg was snowmobiling on the Cain property. Two or three inches of new snow had accumulated that day and the only illumination was that provided by the headlights on the snowmobile. After slowing to three or four miles per hour to make a turn, Underberg went over the embankment caused by the excavation. As a result of this accident, he suffered a shattered left shoulder and a broken left femur.

A jury returned a verdict in favor of the Cains. Underberg raises two issues on appeal: (1) That the trial court erred in instructing the jury regarding the duties of a possessor of land towards a licensee; and (2) That the trial court erred in instructing the jury on assumption of the risk.

South Dakota follows the traditional common law categories of trespasser, licensee, and invitee in defining the duty of care owed by a possessor of land to those who enter upon his land.

It is undisputed that Underberg was a licensee. This court has defined the duty of care owed to a licensee in terms of the principle that permission or license gives leave only to take the property as the visitors find it, and that the owner or occupant undertakes no duty to these visitors who come for their own pleasure or convenience, and not at his invitation or upon inducement, express or implied, from a common advantage, except that, being aware of their presence, he must not injure them willfully or entrap them.

Underberg would have us change this rule and in its place impose upon landowners an affirmative duty to exercise due care with respect to all persons who enter upon land, regardless of their status. This we decline to do. Accordingly the trial court correctly stated the law when it gave the jury South Dakota Pattern Jury Instruction 120.02-B.

To charge a party with assumption of the risk, it must be established that he had knowledge of the danger involved; that he appreciated the risk therefrom; and that he voluntarily accepted the risk. Ordinarily, the question of whether a party has assumed a risk is a determination to be made by the jury. Under the facts of this case, it was proper for the trial court to instruct the jury on the defense of assumption of the risk.

The judgment of the trial court is affirmed.

Harris v. Grizzle
625 P.2d 747 (Wyo. 1981)

On May 22, 1975, Diane Harris was involved in an automobile accident in which she sustained severe brain damage, resulting in her total paralysis. She was hospitalized until September 1975. She was readmitted on May 9, 1976 and was treated on two later dates in the emergency room. She died on August 1, 1976. Suit was filed allegedly against her doctors and the hospital for malpractice, allegedly negligent care, treatment, and diagnosis. The defendants filed a motion for summary judgment, which was allowed. Plaintiffs appealed.

BROWN, J. As background for our analysis of the issues, we note several basic rules of law applicable to medical malpractice actions. The gist of a malpractice action is negligence on the part of defendant. The mere fact of injury or the occurrence of a bad result, standing alone, is no proof of negligence in the ordinary malpractice action. The law does not require that for every injury there must be a recovery of damages, but only imposes liability for a breach of legal duty by a doctor proximately causing injury to the patient. . . . It is now necessary to determine if the evidence contained in the appellant's deposition and the affidavits of appellees was insufficient to establish an issue of material fact.

Appellant stated in his deposition that the deceased was not fed while in the hospital and that a gastrostomy tube was inserted incorrectly, causing a condition that led to the death of Mrs. Harris. Appellant further contends that some appellee expert witnesses stated that the cause of death was pneumonia, while other appellee expert witnesses specified a different cause of death. Appellant contends that statements in his deposition and the doctors' different opinions in their affidavits as to the cause of death establish a question of fact sufficient to defeat appellees' motions for summary judgment. Such an argument ignores, among other things, the fact that appellant has failed to establish a causal connection between appellees' actions and decedent's death. . . .

In order to defeat a motion for summary judgment in a medical malpractice action, a plaintiff has the obligation to establish (1) the accepted standard of medical care or practice, (2) that the doctor's conduct departed from the standard, and (3) that his conduct was the legal cause of the injuries suffered. Appellant has wholly failed to establish these things by admissible medical testimony. . . .

One of appellant's complaints is that the gastrostomy tube was incorrectly inserted. Expert testimony is necessary to support a complaint of this type. Appellant, as a layperson without any special training in the areas complained of, is not competent to show that conduct by appellees in regard to the insertion of gastrostomy tubes, in the schedule of feeding or other treatment and care is so wanting in reasonable medical skill that no expert testimony is needed. . . .

It is well settled that in all but the extraordinary medical malpractice case, the plaintiff has the burden of producing expert testimony to support a prima facie case of negligence. If the origin of the injury is obscure and not readily apparent to a layman, or if there are several equally probable causes of the condition, testimony of a qualified physician is essential to establish a reasonable probability that the physician's negligence caused the injury. This is such a case.

A physician or surgeon is presumed to have carefully and skillfully treated or operated upon a patient. Moreover, there can be no presumption of negligence from the mere fact of an injury or adverse result. Expert testimony is ordinarily required to establish negligence or a lack of reasonable care on the part of a physician in his performance or surgical procedures and in the care and treatment of his patients. . . .

The law of proximate cause in malpractice cases is clear. Malpractice is a form of negligence. Before a physician may be held liable for malpractice, it must be shown that he departed from recognized standards of medical practice. In addition, that departure must be the proximate cause of the incident or occurrence which is the subject of the litigation.

In an action for malpractice, the plaintiff must establish that an act or omission by a physician has breached a standard of care and that the breach was the cause, both in fact and proximately, of the damage suffered by the patient.

Appellant failed to prove that the proximate cause of deceased's death was the negligence of appellees. Appellant has failed to provide the causal link by expert testimony.

The burden of establishing negligence must be met both at trial and in opposition to appellees' motions for summary judgment. A party opposing a motion for summary judgment must show that evidence is available which would justify a trial of that issue. In this case appellant did not come forward with evidence which would justify a trial on the issue of negligence.

Affirmed.

REVIEW QUESTIONS

1. Identify the terms in column A by matching each with the appropriate statement in column B.

A	B
1. Contingent fee	a. Unreasonable use of property.
2. Slander	b. The right to be left alone.
3. Libel	c. A doctrine which may reduce a recovery.
4. Invasion of privacy	d. A presumption of negligence.
5. Nuisance	e. Written defamation.
6. Conversion	f. Closely akin to foreseeability.
7. Comparative negligence	g. Oral defamation.
8. *Res ipsa loquitor.*	h. Liability without wrongful conduct.
9. Proximate cause	i. Major interference with goods.
10. Strict liability	j. Assures equal access to the judicial system.

2. A shopping center operator was in the process of selling the shopping center. One of the tenants informed the potential buyer that it had a long-term lease, which in fact was not true. The buyer asked for a release from the lease. When the seller could not furnish the release, the sale fell through. The seller sues the tenant and seeks punitive damages. Is it entitled to them? Why?

3. Give two examples of conduct that constitutes each of the following:
(a) interference with an individual's personal freedom; (b) interference with property rights; (c) interference with economic relations; (d) wrongful communications.

4. The CAT collection agency, trying to collect fees owed to a physician, called an ex-patient 10 to 20 times daily for several days, using obscene and threatening language. CAT also wrote several threatening letters. The former patient sued CAT for damages, alleging severe emotional distress. Was CAT's conduct tortious? Explain.

5. A law firm sued several of its former associates for damages and to enjoin them from soliciting the firm's clients. These former associates actively encouraged the older firm's clients to terminate that relationship and become clients of the new firm. Was this new firm's conduct tortious? Why?

6. A physician photographed a dying patient in his hospital room. When the doctor lifted his patient's head to place a blue towel under it for color contrast, the dying man raised a clenched fist in protest and turned away from the camera. The patient's wife told the doctor before he entered the room that her husband did not wish to be photographed. As his widow, she is suing the doctor for invading her late husband's privacy. Is the doctor liable? Why?

7. A customer brought suit against the operator of a tavern seeking damages for injuries sustained as the result of an assault by a third party in the tavern's parking lot. The tavern had a history of fighting and other disturbances. The operator had previously had a policy of hiring security personnel to take glasses from patrons as they left the tavern and to patrol the parking lot, but had abandoned the policy. Did the operator breach a duty to the customer? Why?

8. Plaintiff, a customer in the defendant's restaurant, fell when her chair struck the chair of a fellow diner when she attempted to rise. She fell when she caught her leg between the leg of the chair and the leg of the table. Was the defendant guilty of negligence? Why?

9. Plaintiff was traveling in a northerly direction on Belmont Avenue through an intersection, in compliance with the traffic signals, when her car collided with an automobile driven into her path by a customer exiting from the Burger King located on the east side of Belmont Avenue. The traffic signal for the northbound lane could not be seen from the parking lot. When the customer saw the southbound traffic stop, he assumed that the northbound traffic was also stopped. Instead, the lights for northbound traffic remained green as long as a green arrow was showing on the signal for left-turning northbound traffic. Plaintiff sued Burger King for her injuries. Is the defendant liable? Why?

10. Helen toured a townhouse built by Thames. While inspecting the kitchen, she opened a cabinet and the cabinet door fell and struck her on the head. An examination revealed that no screws were affixed to the door to secure it to the cabinet. She filed suit against the cabinetmaker and offered proof of her injury, relying on the doctrine of *res ipsa loquitor*. With what result? Why?

11. Mary witnessed an automobile strike a pedestrian. She wrongfully believed that her daughter was the pedestrian. Mary collapsed and continues to suffer severe mental distress. She sued the driver of the automobile for her injuries. Should she collect? Why?

12. Plaintiff was injured in an automobile accident caused entirely by the defendant. Plaintiff was not wearing his seat belt. He was thrown from his Jeep and sustained a compression-type injury to the lower back when he landed on the pavement. The defendant offered evidence that had the plaintiff been wearing his seat belt, he would not have been thrown from the Jeep. If the doctrine of comparative negligence is followed, will this fact reduce the damages to which the plaintiff is entitled? Explain.

13. A paint manufacturing company sought financing from a local bank. In order to evaluate the company's financial condition, the bank required it to submit certain financial statements. To comply with this request, the company hired an accountant. The prepared statements represented the company to be solvent, when in fact it was insolvent. Relying on these statements, the bank loaned the money. Later, the bank lost a substantial portion of the money loaned. May the bank recover its losses from the accountant? Why?

14. On a rainy day, Nancy entered a grocery store to shop. When she stepped off a cloth mat at the entrance and onto the terrazzo floor, she slipped and fell. Water had accumulated on the floor from other customers' feet and from grocery carts coming back into the store. The store had been mopped and cleaned periodically throughout the morning, and the area in which Nancy fell had been mopped and cleaned 10 minutes prior to the accident. Is the grocery liable to Nancy for her injuries? Why?

5 THE CRIMINAL LAW AND BUSINESS

1. Introduction

Much of the law is concerned with wrongful conduct; if it is wrongful against society, it is a crime. Criminal conduct usually affects individual persons, and as noted in the previous chapter this effect is, by definition, tortious. In this chapter, we will briefly discuss some of the general principles of the criminal law and business.

Since a crime is a public wrong against society, criminal actions are prosecuted by the government on behalf of the people. Historically, upon a person's conviction of a crime, one of the following punishments has been imposed by society: (1) death, (2) imprisonment, (3) fine, (4) removal from office, or (5) disqualification to hold and enjoy any office or to vote. Among the purposes of punishment and of the criminal law are the protection of the public and the deterrence of crime. Punishment is also imposed simply for the sake of punishment, as well as the isolation and suppression of the criminal element of society. Table 5-1 indicates the various crimes and the interest which each was created to protect.

Conduct is criminal because a legislative body has declared it to be wrongful and has authorized punishment if it occurs. Some crimes, such as murder, have always been considered wrongful by a civilized society. They are said to be *malum in se,* or per se wrongful. Other crimes have been created by legislative bodies because of a desire to prevent certain conduct. Such crimes are said to be *malum prohibitum.* For example, gambling is a crime only because a legislature has declared it to be.

TABLE 5-1
Classification of Crimes by Purpose

1. Protection of the person from harm
   Assault and battery
   Kidnapping
   Manslaughter
   Mayhem
   Murder
   Sexual crimes (see 3 below)
2. Protection of property
   Arson
   Blackmail
   Burglary
   Embezzlement
   Extortion
   Forgery
   Larceny
   Robbery
3. Protection from sexual abuse
   Adultery
   Bigamy
   Incest

   Rape
   Sodomy
4. Protection of government
   Bribery of officials
   Sabotage
   Treason
5. Protection of the courts
   Bribery of witnesses, judges, jurors
   Perjury
6. Protecting the public interest
   Antitrust
   Disorderly conduct
   Food and drug laws
   Gambling
   Liquor and drunkenness
   Narcotics
   Obscenity
   Pollution

Some crimes are said to be administrative crimes. Administrative agencies such as the Environmental Protection Agency or the Pure Food and Drug Administration may adopt rules, the violation of which is punishable as a crime. The legislative body by statute declares the violation to be criminal and delegates the power to the agency to adopt the rules and regulations.

In most administrative crimes the statute fixes the penalty for the violation. In a few cases, the statutes not only authorize the agency to create the regulations, but also to fix the penalty. For example, a statute may authorize an agency to issue regulations and to set penalties not to exceed a $500 fine or six months in jail or both. Such statutes may be valid if the punishment is reasonable.

Agencies may not be given the power to conduct the trial, as a general rule. If conduct is criminal, the accused has a right to a trial by jury. Exceptions exist for minor penalties such as revocation or suspension of licenses or levying small fines. Such proceedings may be considered quasi-criminal in the nature of a civil penalty similar to traffic violations and parking meter fines.

2. White-Collar Crime

Historically, the criminal law was concerned with acts of violence and the wrongful application of physical force. Murder, arson, rape, burglary, robbery, and other violent crimes affected the business community, but businesses seldom committed them. Today, businesspeople are guilty of hundreds of new crimes, the so-called white-collar or business crimes. In addition, in a recent case the operators of a business were convicted of murdering an employee who was poisoned by cyanide used on the job.

White-collar or *business* crimes are illegal acts committed by guile, deceit, and concealment, rather than by force and violence. Such crimes usually involve attempts to obtain money, property, or services without paying for them or to secure some other business advantage. Such crimes are not limited to executives; they are committed by employees at all levels. Any employee with access to cash may be guilty of embezzlement or theft of company property. Salespersons may engage in price fixing in violation of the antitrust laws, and marketing persons are frequently charged with false advertising.

Business crime is far more significant than many businesses and law enforcement persons realize. Losses from embezzlement and employee theft, including theft through manipulation of computers, probably exceed losses from burglary and larceny. Theft of technology recently caused an international furor when agents of Japanese firms admitted purchasing secrets stolen from IBM. There is evidence that shoplifting by employees exceeds shoplifting by customers. The cost of crime is added to the cost of doing business; the result: higher prices for consumers. Costs include higher insurance premiums as well as the cost of the property stolen. It has been estimated that the total cost of business crime exceeds $40 billion annually, that 30 percent of all business failures are the result of internal theft, and that many retail outlets lose as much as 50 percent of their profits to unaccountable "inventory shrinkage." Many stores mark up goods an extra 15 percent to cover such losses, which means that the consuming public actually pays the bill for theft.

Fraud in various forms is rampant. The fraudulent use of another's credit card, forgery, obtaining money by false pretenses, and false auto repair bills are everyday occurrences. By statute, all these are crimes. Bribery, kickbacks, and payoffs have become so common that the Securities and Exchange Commission demands that the amounts paid be included in the reports filed by major corporations.

Although business crime does not depend on force or violence, physical injury and even death can be caused by it. Defective products sold in violation of applicable statutes frequently cause injuries. Building code violations may result in fire and injury to persons and property. Some businesses, in order to compete, buy stolen merchandise or employ illegal aliens. The maintenance of a dangerous workplace may be a crime.

One reason for the massive amount of white-collar crime is that, in the past, the risk of being caught and sent to prison was slight. White-collar crime has often been considered a legitimate cost of doing business, especially overseas. A business is usually hesitant to prosecute its employees, because disclosure would have an adverse effect on the image of the business. Even when there have been successful prosecutions, sentences have been minimal in the light of the economic consequences of the crimes.

Now that the relation of crime to business has reached crisis proportions, many people are advocating new approaches in an attempt to alter criminal conduct. Perhaps the most common suggestion is to impose stiff penalties for white-collar crime. Another is to improve the internal controls of businesses, so that internal theft and wrongdoing are more likely to be discovered. Finally, there is a trend toward punishing corporate officials who commit crimes on behalf of their corporations. A corporate official who fixes prices with competitors in violation of the Sherman Antitrust Act is more likely to go to jail now than in the past, and the fine for such conduct has been greatly increased. Knowledge about the criminal law, its enforcement, and crime prevention are key elements in business decision making. This chapter will introduce the student to some of the problems involved in the criminal law and its enforcement.

3. Classifications of Crimes

Crimes are traditionally classified as treason, felonies, and misdemeanors. *Treason* against the United States consists of levying war against it or in adhering to its enemies, giving them aid and comfort. *Felonies* are offenses usually defined by statute to include all crimes punishable by incarceration in a penitentiary. Examples are murder, grand larceny, arson, and rape. Crimes of lesser importance than felonies—such as petty larceny, trespass, and disorderly conduct—are called *misdemeanors.* They are usually defined as any crimes not punishable by long imprisonment, but punishable by fine or confinement in the local jail.

Violation of traffic ordinances, building codes, and similar municipal ordinances, prosecuted before a city magistrate, are sometimes termed *petty offenses* or *public torts* instead of crimes. The distinction is insignificant; because whether they are called crimes or public torts, the result is the same—the party charged may be fined or put in jail or both. Table 5–2 lists typical felonies and misdemeanors.

4. Terminology

The criminal law has developed some terminology separate and distinct from that of civil-law cases. The word *prosecution* is used to describe criminal proceedings, and *prosecutor* is the name usually given to the attorney who represents the people. Although the proceedings are brought on behalf of the people of a given

TYPICAL FELONIES (IMPRISONMENT FOR MORE THAN ONE YEAR AND/OR FINE)	TYPICAL MISDEMEANORS (JAIL FOR LESS THAN ONE YEAR AND/OR FINE)	
Aggravated assault	Battery	**TABLE 5–2**
Arson	Disorderly conduct	Classification
Bribery	Gambling	of Crimes
Burglary	Larceny (petty)	by Punishment
Embezzlement	Prostitution	
Forgery	Public disturbance	
Kidnapping	Simple assault	
Larceny (grand)	Traffic offenses	
Manslaughter	Trespass	
Mayhem		
Murder		
Price fixing		
Rape		
Robbery		

state or of the United States, the people are generally not called the plaintiff, as in a civil case. Rather, the case is entitled *U.S. v. John Doe,* or *State of Ohio v. John Doe.*

In felony cases, the usual procedure is for a court to conduct a preliminary hearing to determine if there is sufficient evidence that the accused committed the crime charged to justify submission of the case to the grand jury. If the court finds this probable cause, the accused is *bound over* to the grand jury. The grand jury examines evidence against the accused and determines if it is sufficient to cause a reasonable person to believe that the accused probably committed the offense. If this *probable cause* exists, the grand jury *indicts* the accused by returning to the court what is called a *true bill.* If it is the opinion of the grand jury that the evidence is insufficient to indict, then a *no true bill* is returned to the court. Indictment by the grand jury will be discussed with the Fifth Amendment, later in this chapter.

If the crime involved is a misdemeanor or if the accused waives the presentment of the case to the grand jury, the prosecution may proceed by filing the charges in a document known as an *information.* Both an indictment and an information serve to notify and to inform the accused of the nature of the charges, so that a defense may be prepared.

The technical aspects of the various crimes are beyond the scope of this text; however, it should be recognized that every crime has elements that distinguish it from other crimes. Larceny, robbery, and burglary are crimes with many common characteristics, yet they are legally distinct. Robbery is theft with force; larceny implies no force. Burglary is breaking and entering with intent to commit a felony (usually larceny). One act may be more than one crime, and it is possible to be convicted of more than one crime for any particular act. Many crimes are actually a part of another crime and are known as *lesser included offenses.* An assault would be a lesser included offense of forcible rape.

Criminal cases differ from civil cases in the amount of proof required to convict. In a civil case, the plaintiff is entitled to a verdict if the evidence preponderates in his favor. In other words, if, when weighing the evidence, the scales tip ever so slightly in favor of a plaintiff, the plaintiff wins. In a criminal case, however, the people or prosecution must prove the defendant's guilt beyond a reasonable doubt. Note that the law does not require proof "beyond the shadow of a doubt" or proof that is susceptible of only one conclusion. It does require such a quantity of proof that a reasonable person viewing the evidence would have no reasonable doubt about the guilt of the defendant.

5. Act and Intent

As a general rule, a crime involves a combination of *act* and *criminal intent.* Criminal intent without an overt act to carry it out is not criminal. If Joe says to himself, "I am going to rob the First National Bank," no crime has been committed. Some act toward carrying out this intent is necessary. But if Joe communicates his desire to Frank, who agrees to assist him, then a crime has been committed. This crime is known as *conspiracy.* The criminal act was the communication between Joe and Frank.

Just as a crime requires an act, most crimes also require criminal intent. A wrongful act committed without the requisite criminal intent is not a crime. Criminal intent may be supplied by negligence to the degree that it equals intent. If a person drives a car so recklessly that another is killed, his criminal intent may be supplied by the negligent act.

Criminal intent is not synonymous with motive. Motive is not an element of a crime. Proof of motive may help in establishing guilt, but it is not an essential element of a prosecution.

Some crimes are known as *specific intent* crimes. When a crime has a specific intent as part of its definition, that specific intent must be proved beyond a reasonable doubt. In a burglary prosecution, there must be proof of intent to commit some felony, such as larceny, rape, or murder. Also, if a crime is defined in part "with intent to defraud," this specific intent must be proved, as any other element of the crime must be.

There is a presumption of intent in crimes that do not require a specific intent. The intent in such crimes may be implied by the facts. In other words, the doing of the criminal act implies the criminal intent. The accused may rebut this presumption, however. The accused is presumed to intend the natural and probable consequences of his acts. Thus, if one performs an act that causes a result the criminal law is designed to prevent, he is legally responsible, even though the actual result was not intended. If a robber dynamites a safe and a passerby is killed in the explosion, the robber is guilty of homicide even though he did not actually intend to kill the passerby; the robber intended the natural and probable consequences of his act.

Criminal liability may be imposed without fault or without criminal intent. Such crimes are often referred to as *strict liability crimes.* The crime consists of conduct, and the law does not require that the actor have any particular intent or mental state. In effect, the crime consists of conduct that brings about a stated result. It is immaterial whether the conduct is intentional, reckless, or negligent. Usually only a misdemeanor, the conduct is declared to be criminal in order to discourage it. For example, most liquor and narcotics laws, pure food and drug laws, and traffic laws impose liability without fault. Under these statutes, proof of the state of mind of the accused is not required. Proof of the sale of alcoholic beverages to a minor is a crime, even though the seller did not intend to commit an unlawful act.

6. Capacity

At common law children under the age of 7 were conclusively presumed to lack sufficient mental capacity to form criminal intent. Those over 14 were treated as fully capable of committing a crime. Children between the ages of 7 and 14 were subject to a rebuttable presumption that they could have criminal capacity, but this presumption could be overcome by proof of lack of mental capacity. Many states have changed these ages by statute, and all states have juvenile courts that provide special procedures for crimes involving minors. Juvenile courts usually handle cases involving persons under 18. They attempt to avoid harsh punishment and seek to rehabilitate the juvenile and prevent further criminal conduct.

However, most states allow the prosecution to elect to try an offender as an adult for certain serious crimes, such as murder or rape.

The criminal law as it pertains to juveniles differs greatly from that applied to adults. While in most cases juveniles are given preferential treatment, juveniles may be subjected to sanctions to which adults may not.[1]

7. Corporate Liability

In the early common law, a corporation could not be held criminally liable, since it was incapable of forming criminal intent. Corporations were not liable for the conduct of others, including agents and employees acting within the scope of their employment on behalf of the corporation. Today a corporation is considered a person as the word is used in most criminal statutes, and a corporation may have criminal liability.

Corporate criminal liability may be imposed under the strict liability theory or under the vicarious liability concept. A vicarious liability crime occurs where one person without personal fault is liable for the conduct of another. Some criminal statutes impose criminal liability on a principal for the criminal conduct of its agents and servants. For example, most states have statutes that impose liability on the employer if an agent sells articles short weight or sells liquor to a minor. This vicarious liability is imposed even though the employer may have instructed the employee not to engage in the illegal conduct. Vicarious liability is often imposed on corporations, especially if the activity is performed in part by the board of directors, an officer, or high managerial agent. Lack of criminal intent on the part of the corporate principal is no defense. Moreover, high corporate officials may have liability because of the high standards of conduct imposed upon them by some statutes. Such crimes exist in order to impose strict standards of performance on certain business activities. The punishment imposed in such cases is a fine and in some cases other sanctions, such as the loss of a license to do business.

The officers and directors of a corporation are ordinarily not personally liable for the crimes of the enterprise or their subordinates. However, a few cases have imposed liability under a theory that the person was accountable for the conduct of others.[2]

8. Defenses to Criminal Prosecutions

A defendant in a criminal case may avail himself of a variety of defenses. He may contend that he did not commit the act of which he is accused. He may present an alibi—proof that he was at another place when the crime was committed. He may also contend that if he did the act, it was not done with the requisite intent. There are also many technical defenses used on behalf of persons accused of crimes. Some of them are described in the following paragraphs.

Entrapment.   This is a defense commonly raised in certain crimes, such as the illegal sale of drugs. Entrapment means that the criminal intent originated with

---

[1] Schall v. Martin, p. 103.
[2] United States v. Park, p. 105.

the police. When a criminal act is committed at the instigation of the police, fundamental fairness seems to dictate that the people should not be able to contend that the accused is guilty of a crime. Assume that a police officer asked Bill to obtain some marijuana. Bill could not be found guilty of illegal possession, because the criminal intent originated with the police officer. Entrapment is sometimes described as a positive defense, because the accused must, as a basis for the defense, admit that the act was committed.

Immunity from Prosecution.   This is another technical defense. The prosecution may grant immunity in order to obtain a "state's witness." When immunity is granted, the person receiving it can no longer be prosecuted, and thus he no longer has the privilege against compulsory self-incrimination. When several persons have committed a crime together, it is common practice for one to be given immunity so that evidence is available against the others. The one granted immunity has a complete defense.

Insanity.   A person cannot be guilty of a crime if he or she lacks the mental capacity to have the required criminal intent. Likewise, a person who is insane cannot properly defend the suit, so insanity at the time of trial is also a defense.

The defense of insanity poses many difficult problems for courts and for juries. Many criminal acts are committed in fits of anger or passion. Others, by their very nature, are committed by persons whose mental state is other than normal. Therefore, a major difficulty exists in defining insanity. In the early criminal law, the usually accepted test of insanity was the "right-from-wrong" test. If the accused understood the nature and consequences of the act and had the ability to distinguish right from wrong at the time of the act involved, the accused was sane. If he or she did not know right from wrong or did not understand the consequences of the act, insanity was a defense.

Subsequently, the courts of some states, feeling that the right-and-wrong test did not go far enough, adopted a test known as "irresistible impulse." Under this test, it was not enough that the accused knew right from wrong. If the accused was possessed of an irresistible impulse to do what was wrong, and this impulse was so strong that it compelled him or her to do what was wrong, insanity was a defense.

As psychiatry and psychology began to play a greater role in the criminal law and in the rehabilitation of criminals, many courts became dissatisfied with both the "right-and-wrong" and "irresistible-impulse" tests of insanity. A new test known as the Durham rule was developed. Under the Durham rule, an accused is not criminally responsible if his act was the product of a mental disease or defect. This new test has not received universal acceptance. Perpetrators of some crimes almost always have some mental abnormality, and the Durham rule makes their conduct unpunishable. Sexual assault on a child is probably committed only by one with some mental depravity, but the Durham rule makes prosecution of such cases more difficult and might result in freeing many who are guilty. Today there is a wide disparity among the states as to which test of insanity will be followed. All three tests have had significant acceptance. In the years ahead, additional developments in the law of insanity are likely.

Intoxication. This defense is quite similar to insanity, but its application is much more restricted. Voluntarily becoming intoxicated is generally no defense to a crime. It is simply no excuse for wrongful conduct. However, if the crime charged is one of specific intent and the accused was so intoxicated that he could not form the specific intent required, then intoxication is a defense of sorts. It can be used to establish lack of the required specific intent. In a prosecution for an assault with intent to rape, intoxication sufficient to negate the intent would be a defense.

Other Defenses. Return of property stolen, payment for damages caused, and forgiveness by the victim of a crime are not defenses. If a person shoplifts and is caught, it is no defense that the goods were returned or that the store owner has forgiven him. Since the wrong is against society as a whole, the attitude of the actual victim is technically immaterial. As a practical matter, however, many prosecutors do not prosecute cases that the victims are willing to abandon.

Ignorance of the law is not a defense to a criminal prosecution. Everyone is presumed to know the law and to follow it. No other system would be workable. The various constitutional protections and guarantees available to a defendant may prohibit or impede prosecution of a case. They may make it impossible for the prosecution to obtain a conviction. If evidence of the crime is illegally obtained, that evidence is inadmissable; and by preventing its admission, the accused may obtain an acquittal. These constitutional and procedural aspects of the criminal law are discussed in the sections that follow.

CRIMINAL LAW AND THE CONSTITUTION

9. General Principles

The Constitution of the United States is a major source of the law as it relates to crimes. Constitutional protections and guarantees govern the procedural aspects of criminal cases. The Bill of Rights—especially the Fourth, Fifth, Sixth, and Eighth amendments—contains these constitutional guarantees. The Fourteenth Amendment "picks up" these constitutional protections and makes them applicable to the states.

As these constitutional guarantees are studied, three aspects of constitutional law should be kept in mind. First, constitutional guarantees are not absolutes. Every one of them is limited in its application. Just as freedom of speech under the First Amendment does not allow one to cry "Fire!" in a crowded theater, the Fourth Amendment's constitutional protection against illegal search and seizure is not absolute. Both are limited protections. Second, in determining the extent of limitations on constitutional guarantees, the courts are balancing the constitutional protections against some other legitimate legal or social policy of society or other constitutional guarantees. A state enacted a so-called hit-and-run statute requiring the driver of a motor vehicle involved in an accident to stop at the scene and give his name and address. His action obviously may be self-incriminating, in that he is admitting the identity of the driver of the vehicle involved. Thus, the law created a conflict between the state's demand for disclosures and the protection of the right against self-incrimination. The Supreme Court, in resolving this conflict, noted that the mere possibility of incrimination is insufficient to defeat the strong policies in favor of a disclosure, and it held that the law did not violate the Constitution. In criminal cases, courts are often required to balance the interest and rights of the accused with those of the victim of crime and of society as a whole. Third, constitutional protections are variable. They change to meet the needs of modern society. The Constitution is often said to be interpreted relative to the times. The criminal law changes as the needs of society change.

10. The Fourth Amendment

Several procedural issues may arise as a result of the Fourth Amendment's protection against illegal search and seizure. Among the more common Fourth Amendment issues in criminal cases are (1) the validity of searches incident to an arrest without a warrant, (2) the validity of search warrants—the presence of probable cause, (3) the validity of consents to searches by persons other than the suspect, and (4) the extent of the protection afforded.

To illustrate the first issue, assume that a student is arrested for speeding. Is it a violation of the Fourth Amendment if the police officer searches the trunk of the car without a search warrant and finds heroin? The answer is yes, and the student could not be convicted of illegal possession of drugs, because the evidence was unconstitutionally obtained.

A search may be illegal even if it is conducted pursuant to a search warrant. The Constitution provides that a search warrant may be issued only if probable cause for its issue is presented to the court.

The validity of a consent to search premises without a search warrant is frequently an issue in a criminal case. A parent may consent to a police search of a child's room in the family home. Is this a valid waiver of the constitutional protection of the Fourth Amendment? The decision depends on many factors, including the age of the child, the extent of emancipation, and the amount of control the parents have over the total premises. Similar issues are raised when a landlord consents to the search of premises leased to a tenant. As a general rule, such consents are not sufficient to eliminate the need for a search warrant.

Fourth Amendment issues frequently have an effect on civil law as well as criminal law. The protection has been extended to prohibit activities such as inspection of premises by a fire inspector without a search warrant. Criminal charges for violating building codes cannot be based on a warrantless inspection of the premises if the owner objects.

In recent years, the protection of the Fourth Amendment has been narrowed somewhat by court decisions and legislation. Electronic surveillance is possible pursuant to a search warrant, and the "bugs" may be installed by covert entry. Moreover, warrants may be issued based on information obtained by electronic means.[3]

One of the more controversial aspects of the Fourth Amendment is the so-called *exclusionary rule.* The exclusionary rule, which was created by the Supreme Court, is a rule of evidence. It provides that evidence illegally obtained by the

---

[3] United States v. Knotts, p. 106.

police and all information flowing from it cannot be used to convict a person accused of crime. Thus, if evidence is obtained without a search warrant, or if the search warrant was not properly issued, a defendant can ask the court to prevent the use of the evidence. This request is usually called a *motion to suppress evidence.*

As a result of the exclusionary rule, many persons who have in fact committed crimes are either not prosecuted or are found to be innocent because the evidence establishing their guilt is not admissible at the trial. In recent years some courts have sought to modify the exclusionary rule and have argued that justice would be better served in certain cases if evidence is admissible notwithstanding the fact that it was improperly or illegally obtained. For example, they argue that evidence illegally obtained by state and local police should nevertheless be admissible in a federal prosecution when the federal authorities were not a party to the illegal search and seizure of evidence.

Another exception was created in a 1984 decision when a warrant was obtained without probable cause, but the police who used it were acting in good faith. This good-faith exception to the exclusionary rule is a further indication of the narrowing of the Fourth Amendment.

11. The Fifth Amendment

Almost everyone understands that a person "pleading the Fifth Amendment" is exercising the right against compulsory self-incrimination. The Fifth Amendment also (1) contains a due process clause, which requires that all court procedures in criminal cases be fundamentally fair; (2) requires indictment by a grand jury for a capital offense or infamous crime; and (3) prohibits double jeopardy.

A grand jury decides if there is sufficient evidence of guilt to justify the accused's standing trial. It is contrasted with a petit jury, which decides guilt or innocence. Grand juries are usually made up of 23 persons, and it takes a majority vote to indict a defendant. It takes less proof to indict a person and to require him to stand trial than it does to convict. The grand-jury provision contains an exception for court-martial proceedings.

The grand-jury provision is limited to capital offenses and infamous crimes. *Infamous crimes* are those that involve moral turpitude. The term indicates that one convicted of such a crime will suffer infamy. Most felonies are infamous crimes.

The prohibition against *double jeopardy* means that a person cannot be tried twice for the same offense. A defendant who is acquitted in a criminal case cannot be retried on the same offense; however, a defendant who, on appeal, obtains a reversal of a conviction may be tried again. The reversal, in effect, means that the defendant was not in jeopardy.

Notwithstanding the foregoing provisions of the Fifth Amendment, the protection against compulsory self-incrimination is still its most important constitutional protection. The prohibition against being compelled to be a witness against oneself extends to oral testimony of an accused before and during his trial, to documents, and to statements before grand juries, legislative investigation committees, and judicial bodies in civil and criminal proceedings.

A statement or a document does not have to be a confession of crime in order to qualify under the privilege. Both are protected if they might serve as a "link in the chain of evidence" that could lead to prosecution. The protection of the Fifth Amendment is the right to remain silent and to suffer no penalty for silence.

To illustrate the extent of the protection provided by the Fifth Amendment, the Supreme Court has held that (1) a prosecutor may not comment on the failure of a defendant to explain evidence within his knowledge; (2) a court may not tell the jury that silence may be evidence of guilt; (3) an attorney may not be disbarred for claiming his privilege at a judicial inquiry into his activities, just as a policeman may not be fired for claiming the privilege before the grand jury; and (4) the privilege protects a state witness against incrimination under federal as well as state law, and a federal witness against incrimination under state law as well as federal law. To illustrate this latter concept, assume that a person is granted immunity from state prosecution in order to compel him to testify. He cannot be compelled to testify if it is possible that his testimony will lead to a conviction under federal law. The granting of immunity must be complete.

Limitations on the protections afforded by the Fifth Amendment are also readily apparent. The drunk driving laws that require a breath or blood test are one example. In a drunk-driving case the prosecution can use as evidence the analysis of a blood sample taken without consent of the accused, or a driver's license can be revoked if a person refuses to submit to a breath test. The evidence is admissible even though the accused objects to the extraction of blood or taking the breath test. The Fifth Amendment reaches an accused's communications, whatever form they might take, but compulsion that makes a suspect the source of "real or voice samples for evidence" does not violate the Fifth Amendment. In addition, the protection is personal and does not prevent the production of incriminating evidence by others.[4]

12. The Sixth Amendment

The Sixth Amendment contains several provisions relating to criminal cases. It guarantees to a defendant the right (1) to a speedy and public trial, (2) to a trial by jury, (3) to be informed of the charge against him, (4) to confront his accuser, (5) to subpoena witnesses in his favor, and (6) to have the assistance of an attorney.

The right to a speedy trial is of great concern today. Most states require that a defendant in jail be tried within a minimum period of time—such as four months. This limits the punishment of those not convicted of a crime.

The right to a jury trial does not extend to state juvenile-court delinquency proceedings, as they are not criminal prosecutions; however, juveniles do have the right to counsel, to confront the witnesses against them, and to cross-examine them. Thus it can be seen that there are many technical aspects to the Sixth Amendment.

The Sixth Amendment gives the right to counsel and involves two funda-

---

[4] Couch v. United States, p. 107.

mental questions: (1) At what stage of the proceedings does the right to counsel attach? and (2) To what types of cases is it applicable?

For many years, it was thought that the right to counsel existed only during the trial and that it did not exist during the investigation of the crime. Today, the right to counsel exists before the trial.

A Constitution that guarantees a defendant the aid of counsel at trial must also protect an indicted defendant or an accused under interrogation by the police. Anything less denies a defendant effective representation by counsel at the only stage when legal aid and advice would help him. The guiding hand of counsel is essential when the police are seeking to obtain a confession from an accused.

This right to counsel must be explained to persons accused of crime. The explanation is commonly referred to as the *Miranda warning* because it arose in a case by that name. It warns the accused that he has the right to remain silent, that anything he says may be used against him in court, that he has the right to the presence of an attorney and to have an attorney appointed before questioning if he cannot afford one. The *Miranda* case recognized that a defendant may waive the right to counsel, provided the waiver is made voluntarily, knowingly, and intelligently.

Other decisions have required that the *Miranda* warning be given to an accused who was not in custody at a police station but on whom the investigation was centering, if the accused was being deprived of his freedom of action in any significant way. Today the right to counsel has been extended to postindictment lineups, because the Sixth Amendment protection extends the right to counsel whenever necessary to ensure a meaningful defense. An accused is guaranteed that he need not stand alone against the state at any stage of the prosecution, formal or informal, in court or out, where counsel's absence might detract from the accused's right to a fair trial.

In recent years the Supreme Court has limited the effect of the *Miranda* decision. It has held that a confession obtained without the requisite warning being given could nevertheless be used to impeach a defendant who denied under oath committing the crime. The courts have also created a public safety exception to the *Miranda* warning.[5]

The courts have also extended the types of cases to which the right to counsel attaches. Historically, the right existed only in felony cases. Today, it extends to any case, felony or misdemeanor, in which the accused may be incarcerated. In addition, the right to counsel extends to juveniles in juvenile proceedings. It also extends to investigations by the Internal Revenue Service. Thus, any person charged with any crime for which he may be put in jail or prison has the right to counsel at all stages of the proceedings, from the time the investigations center upon him as the accused, through his last appeal.

13. The Eighth Amendment

The Eighth Amendment provides that "excessive bail shall not be required, nor excessive fines imposed, nor cruel and unusual punishments inflicted." Bail is excessive if greater than necessary to guarantee the presence of the accused in

---

[5] New York v. Quarles, p. 109.

court at the appointed time. The function of bail is not to restrict the freedom of the accused prior to trial, because of the presumption of innocence. Most states today require that only a small percentage of the actual bail be posted. The law may require that 10 percent of the total bail be deposited with the court. If the defendant fails to appear, the persons signing the bail bond then owe the other 90 percent.

At one time, the Eighth Amendment was used as the basis for declaring the death penalty to be unconstitutional; however, many legislative bodies reinstated the death penalty, and some of these laws were later held to be constitutional.

14. Contemporary Problems

The criminal law system has failed generally to deter crime or to accomplish most of its other assumed goals. An ever-increasing crime rate, especially in larger communities, puts crimes of violence as well as the so-called white-collar crimes constantly in the news. Because our penal system has not found the means to rehabilitate the convicted, a significant portion of all crimes are committed by repeat offenders.

Many people believe that the inadequacy of criminal law results from its failure to provide swift and sure punishment for those committing wrongs against society. Delays in all steps of criminal procedure are quite common, most of them probably the result of defense tactics, as time favors the accused. But court congestion also contributes to delay, and vice versa. Recent decisions such as those expanding the right to counsel have contributed to court congestion too.

One of the more controversial procedures in the criminal law is commonly referred to as *plea bargaining,* by which an accused pleads guilty to a lesser offense than that which is charged, or there is an agreement to less than normal punishment in return for a plea of guilty. Plea bargaining is essential, because the case load is too great to try all cases; however, plea bargaining has many adverse side effects. It allows persons who have committed serious crimes to go almost immediately back on the streets to commit more crimes after only paying a fine or serving a much shorter sentence than would have been imposed if they had been convicted of the crime originally charged.

The increased criminal law case load has had a great impact on the work of reviewing courts. Today, approximately 75 percent of those convicted of crimes appeal their convictions. This increase is largely due to the fact that the indigent defendant is now entitled to a free appeal. We do not have enough judges to handle this case load properly, and delay is inevitable.

Another inherent problem in our criminal law system arises from the fact that many recent law-school graduates join the staff of either the prosecutor or the public defender. Criminal cases are thus frequently tried by lawyers with little experience and a minimum of training. After gaining experience, they leave for private practice. The criminal law has, to a significant degree, become an internship for training lawyers for private practice.

The free legal services provided to indigents also create some problems. Many people close to the situation believe that the free public defender, who is frequently underpaid by the state and overworked because of the volume of cases, often does not do an adequate job in defending clients. In addition, these attorneys are to all intents and purposes on the court payroll, which may affect the vigor of their representation of defendants. As a result, an adequate legal defense is a goal that is yet to be achieved for many defendants.

Many other problems arise as a result of the failures of our criminal-law system. Overcrowded jails, unworkable probation systems, unequal sentences, plea bargaining that tends to favor the wealthy, and the failure of sentencing laws to deter crime are but a few of the obvious ills. Most legal scholars agree that the criminal law system needs a drastic overhaul. In fact, the Supreme Court, in its process of reviewing convictions, is bringing about many changes. It is requiring prompt trials or the dismissal of charges. Other decisions have reduced the number of appeals that are available to a convicted defendant. Finally, the Court is reconsidering many of the highly technical aspects of the Bill of Rights as they affect criminal prosecutions. In many of these cases, the Court is balancing the competing and conflicting policies more heavily in favor of the police and the victims of crimes than in favor of the accused.

Congress is involved in changing our criminal justice system. In 1984, Congress passed a federal anticrime bill designed to give law enforcement the tools to attack organized crime and especially drug pushers. Among the key parts of this law are the following:

1. The federal judiciary was directed to set standard penalties for federal offenses. This attempt to end sentencing inequities increases the penalties for drug violations and for persons who use guns.

2. Federal judges are authorized to deny bail to suspects they believe to be dangerous. This preventive detention is similar to that approved for juveniles.

3. Federal suspects using the insanity defense have the burden of proving insanity. Psychiatrists may testify, but may not give their opinion on sanity.

4. Assets obtained while dealing in drugs are presumed to come from the illegal activity. Such assets may be seized and sold by the government.

5. The unauthorized use of computers is outlawed if the action leads to illegal profits or access to national security information.

The constitutionality of many of the foregoing provisions will undoubtedly be challenged. In the meantime, this law is clear evidence of the public's growing concern with the criminal justice system and its demand for improvement.

SUMMARY

GENERAL PRINCIPLES

Classes of Crimes	1. Crimes may be classified by their purpose, such as the protection of individuals, the protection of property, the protection of

government, or the protection of the public interest.

2. Crimes are defined by the legislature. In addition, the legislature may authorize administrative agencies to adopt rules the violation of which is criminal.

3. White-collar crime is of growing importance to the business community and is a major cause of business failure. There is a trend toward stiffer punishment for white-collar crime.

4. Crimes may also be classified as felonies or misdemeanors.

Basic Concepts

1. There is special terminology used in criminal cases. Such terms as *indictment, information,* and *lesser included offense* have special meanings.

2. A crime is a combination of act and intent. Some crimes require a specific intent, while others require only a general intent. In a few instances conduct is criminal without intent, and doing the act is all that is required.

3. The criminal law has special rules and procedures for handling crimes committed by children. These cases are handled in special courts in order to rehabilitate and deter further criminal conduct by those under age.

4. Corporations may be held criminally liable for the acts of their directors, officers, and important managerial agents. In addition to vicarious liability, corporations may be punished for strict liability crimes.

5. Various defenses may be used by one accused of crime to avoid liability. Some of these defenses, such as insanity, are under challenge and are in the process of change.

CRIMINAL LAW AND THE CONSTITUTION

Fourth Amendment

1. The Fourth Amendment protects those accused of crime from having evidence illegally obtained.

2. If evidence is illegally obtained, the exclusionary rule prevents its use at trial.

3. Evidence may be illegally obtained even though a search warrant is used if the warrant was improperly issued.

4. In recent years the courts have narrowed the meaning of the Fourth Amendment. For example, evidence obtained by electronic surveillance is not an illegal search and seizure.

5. There is a good-faith exception to the exclusionary rule.

Fifth Amendment

1. The Fifth Amendment requires indictment by a grand jury for capital offenses and infamous crimes.

2. The Fifth Amendment provision on double jeopardy protects against a person's being tried twice for the same offense.

3. The Fifth Amendment protection against compulsory self-incrimination is personal to the accused. It does not prevent others from testifying or documents in the hands of others from being used as evidence.

Sixth Amendment

1. The Sixth Amendment contains six rights of a defendant. They are (1) the right to a speedy trial, (2) to a trial by jury, (3) to be informed of the charges, (4) to confront the accuser, (5) to subpoena witnesses, and (6) to have the assistance of an attorney.

2. The right to an attorney exists in any proceeding in which incarceration is a possible penalty.

3. The right to an attorney exists in any stage of the proceeding in which the investigation centers on the accused.

4. Persons suspected of crime are entitled as a general rule to be given the *Miranda* warning, but there are exceptions.

Eighth Amendment

1. The Eighth Amendment prohibits excessive bail and cruel and unusual punishment.

2. The death penalty may be imposed if subject to stringent safeguards by the courts.

Contemporary Problems

1. Our criminal justice system does not provide for swift and sure punishment for those committing crimes.
2. The criminal justice system does not serve as an adequate deterrent and has not been successful in rehabilitating most persons convicted of crime.
3. Persons operating the criminal justice system are frequently less experienced than those operating our civil law system. Criminal cases are frequently used as a means of training trial lawyers, and neither the public nor the accused are frequently satisfied with the quality of the lawyers operating the system.

CASES – Criminal Law and Business

Schall v. Martin
104 S.Ct. 2403 (1984)

The New York Family Court Act authorizes pretrial preventive detention of an accused juvenile delinquent. The detention must be based on a finding that there is a "serious risk" that the child "may . . . commit an act which if committed by an adult would constitute a crime." Juveniles who had been detained under that statute brought suit contending that the statute violates the constitutional guarantee of due process of law.

The lower courts held that the statute is administered not for preventive purposes, but to impose punishment for unadjudicated criminal acts, and that therefore the statute is unconstitutional as to all juveniles.

REHNQUIST, J. . . . We conclude that preventive detention under the Family Court Act serves a legitimate state objective, and that the procedural protections afforded pretrial detainees by the New York statute satisfy the requirements of the Due Process Clause of the Fourteenth Amendment to the United States Constitution. . . .

There is no doubt that the Due Process Clause is applicable in juvenile proceedings. "The problem," we have stressed, "is to ascertain the precise impact of the due process requirement upon such

proceedings." We have held that certain basic constitutional protections enjoyed by adults accused of crimes also apply to juveniles (notice of charges, right to counsel, privilege against self-incrimination, right to confrontation and cross-examination, proof beyond a reasonable doubt, and double jeopardy). But the Constitution does not mandate elimination of all differences in the treatment of juveniles. The State has "a *parens patriae* interest in preserving and promoting the welfare of the child," which makes a juvenile proceeding fundamentally different from an adult criminal trial. We have tried, therefore, to strike a balance— to respect the "informality" and "flexibility" that characterize juvenile proceedings, and yet to ensure that such proceedings comport with the "fundamental fairness" demanded by the Due Process Clause.

The statutory provision at issue in this case permits a brief pretrial detention based on a finding of a "serious risk" that an arrested juvenile may commit a crime before his return date. The question before us is whether preventive detention of juveniles is compatible with the "fundamental fairness" required by due process. Two separate inquiries are necessary to answer this question. First, does preventive detention under the New York statute serve a legitimate state objective? And, second, are the procedural safeguards contained in the Family Court Act adequate to authorize the pretrial detention of at least some juveniles charged with crimes?

Preventive detention under the Family Court Act is purportedly designed to protect the child and society from the potential consequences of his criminal acts. When making any detention decision, the Family Court judge is specifically directed to consider the needs and best interests of the juvenile as well as the need for the protection of the community. As an initial matter, therefore, we must decide whether, in the context of the juvenile system, the combined interest in protecting both the community and the juvenile himself from the consequences of future criminal conduct is sufficient to justify such detention.

The legitimate and compelling state interest in protecting the community from crime cannot be doubted. We have stressed before that crime prevention is a weighty social objective, and this interest persists undiluted in the juvenile context. The harm suffered by the victim of a crime is not dependent upon the age of the perpetrator. And the harm to society generally may even be greater in this context given the high rate of recidivism among juveniles.

The juvenile's countervailing interest in freedom from institutional restraints, even for the brief time involved here, is undoubtedly substantial as well. But that interest must be qualified by the recognition that juveniles, unlike adults, are always in some form of custody. Children, by definition, are not assumed to have the capacity to take care of themselves. They are assumed to be subject to the control of their parents, and if parental control falters, the State must play its part as *parens patriae.* In this respect, the juvenile's liberty interest may, in appropriate circumstances, be subordinated to the State's *parens patriae* interest in preserving and promoting the welfare of the child. . . . Society has a legitimate interest in protecting a juvenile from the consequences of his criminal activity—both from potential physical injury which may be suffered when a victim fights back or a policeman attempts to make an arrest and from the downward spiral of criminal activity into which peer pressure may lead the child. . . .

The substantiality and legitimacy of the state interests underlying this statute are confirmed by the wide-spread use and judicial acceptance of preventive detention for juveniles. Every State, as well as the United States in the District of Columbia, permits preventive detention of juveniles accused of crime. . . .

The fact that a practice is followed by a large number of states is not conclusive in a decision as to whether that practice accords with due process, but it is plainly worth considering in determining whether the practice offends some principle of justice so rooted in the traditions and conscience of our people as to be ranked as fundamental.

In light of the uniform legislative judgment that pretrial detention of juveniles properly promotes the interests both of society and the juvenile, we conclude that the practice serves a legitimate regulatory purpose compatible with the "fundamental fairness" demanded by the Due Process Clause in juvenile proceedings.

Of course, the mere invocation of a legitimate purpose will not justify particular restrictions and conditions of confinement amounting to punishment. It is axiomatic that due process requires that a pretrial detainee not be punished. Even given, therefore, that pretrial detention may serve legitimate regulatory purposes, it is still necessary to determine whether the terms and conditions of confinement are in fact compatible with those purposes. A court must decide whether the disability is imposed for the purpose of punishment or whether it is but an incident of some other legitimate governmental purpose. Absent a showing of an express intent to punish on the part of the State, that determination generally will turn on whether an alternative purpose to which the restriction may rationally be connected is assignable for it, and whether it appears excessive in relation to the alternative purpose assigned to it.

There is no indication in the statute itself that preventive detention is used or intended as a punishment. First of all, the detention is strictly limited in time. The maximum possible detention . . . of a youth accused of a serious crime . . . is seventeen days. The maximum detention for less serious crimes . . . is six days. These time-frames seem suited to the limited purpose of providing the youth with a controlled environment and separating him from improper influences pending the speedy disposition of his case.

The conditions of confinement also appear to reflect the regulatory purposes relied upon by the

State. When a juvenile is remanded after his initial appearance, he cannot, absent exceptional circumstances, be sent to a prison or lockup where he would be exposed to adult criminals. . . . We cannot conclude from this record that the controlled environment briefly imposed by the State on juveniles in secured pretrial detention "is imposed for the purpose of punishment" rather than as "an incident of some other legitimate government purpose."

Reversed.

United States v. Park
95 S.Ct. 1903 (1975)

Acme Markets, Inc., a large national retail food chain, has 874 retail outlets and 16 warehouses. Acme and Park, its chief executive officer, were charged with violating the Federal Food, Drug, and Cosmetic Act for allowing interstate food shipments being held in Acme's Baltimore warehouse to be exposed to contamination by rodents. Acme pleaded guilty, but Park pleaded not guilty.

He testified that although all of Acme's employees were in a sense under his general direction, the company had an "organizational structure for responsibilities for certain functions," according to which different phases of its operations were "assigned to individuals who, in turn, have staff and departments under them." He identified those individuals responsible for sanitation and stated that he had been informed that the Baltimore division's vice-president "was investigating the situation" when it was called to the company's attention by FDA. Park stated that he did not "believe that there was anything [he] could have done more constructively than what [he] found was being done."

On cross-examination, Park conceded that providing sanitary conditions for food offered for sale to the public was something that he was "responsible for in the entire operation of the company," and he stated that it was one of many phases of the company that he assigned to "dependable subordinates."

The trial court instructed the jury that it was not necessary for Park to have participated personally in the situation to be convicted, as long as he had "a responsible relationship to the issue." His conviction was reversed by the Court of Appeals on the ground that the jury instructions should have required a finding of "wrongful action." The Supreme Court granted certiorari.

BURGER, J. The question presented [is] whether "the manager of a corporation, as well as the corporation itself, may be prosecuted under the Federal Food, Drug, and Cosmetic Act of 1938 for the introduction of misbranded and adulterated articles into interstate commerce." In *Dotterweich*, a jury . . . had convicted Dotterweich, the corporation's president and general manager. The Court of Appeals reversed the conviction on the ground that only the drug dealer, whether corporation or individual, was subject to the criminal provisions of the Act, and that where the dealer was a corporation, an individual connected therewith might be held personally only if he was operating the corporation "as his 'alter ego.' "

In reversing the judgment of the Court of Appeals and reinstating Dotterweich's conviction, this Court looked to the purposes of the Act and noted that they "touch phases of the lives and health of the people which, in the circumstances of modern industrialism, are largely beyond self-protection." It observed that the Act is of "a now familiar type" which "dispenses with the conventional requirement for criminal conduct—awareness of some wrongdoing. In the interest of the larger good it puts the burden of acting at hazard upon a person otherwise innocent but standing in responsible relation to a public danger."

Central to the Court's conclusion that individuals other than proprietors are subject to the criminal provisions of the Act was the reality that "the only way in which a corporation can act is through the individuals who act on its behalf." . . .

[T]he cases reveal that in providing sanctions which reach and touch the individuals who execute the corporate mission—and this is by no means necessarily confined to a single corporate agent or employee—the Act imposes not only a positive duty to seek out and remedy violations when they occur but also, and primarily, a duty to implement measures that will insure that violations will not occur. The requirements of foresight and vigilance imposed on responsible corporate agents are beyond question demanding, and perhaps onerous, but they are no more stringent than the public has a right to expect of those who voluntarily assume positions of authority in business enterprises whose services and products affect the health and well-being of the public that supports them. . . .

[The Court then turned to respondent's argument that the instructions to the jury were defective because they suggested that a finding of guilt could be justified solely because of respondent's corporate position.]

Reading the entire charge satisfies us that the jury's attention was adequately focused on the issue of respondent's authority with respect to the conditions that formed the basis of the alleged violations. Viewed as a whole, the charge did not permit the jury to find guilt solely on the basis of respondent's position in the corporation; rather, it fairly advised the jury that to find guilt it must find respondent "had a responsible relation to the situation," and "by virtue of his position . . . had . . . authority and responsibility" to deal with the situation. The situation referred to could only be "food . . . held in unsanitary conditions in a warehouse with the result that it consisted, in part, of filth or . . . may have been contaminated with filth. . . ."

The record in this case reveals that the jury could not have failed to be aware that the main issue for determination was not respondent's position in the corporate hierarchy, but rather his accountability, because of the responsibility and authority of his position, for the conditions which gave rise to the charges against him.

We are satisfied that the Act imposes the highest standard of care and permits conviction of responsible corporate officials who, in light of this standard of care, have the power to prevent or correct violations of its provisions. . . .

Reversed.

United States v. Knotts
103 S.Ct. 1081 (1983)

A chemical manufacturer notified the Minnesota police that a former employee, Armstrong, had been stealing chemicals which could be used in manufacturing illegal drugs. Surveillance revealed that the employee had been purchasing similar chemicals from another chemical company. With the consent of Hawkins Chemical, officers installed a beeper inside a drum of chloroform sold to Armstrong. Officers then followed Armstrong's car, using visual surveillance and a monitor which received the beeper signals. Armstrong transferred the drum to a car driven by Petschen. They ultimately traced the chloroform, by beeper monitoring alone, to a secluded cabin in Wisconsin. After three days of surveillance of the cabin, officers secured a search warrant and discovered a drug laboratory inside the cabin.

Armstrong and others were charged with conspiracy to manufacture controlled substances. They moved to suppress the evidence because of the warrantless monitoring of the beeper. The motion was denied and the defendant was convicted.

REHNQUIST, J. . . . [T]he application of the Fourth Amendment depends on whether the person invoking its protection can claim a justifiable, a reasonable, or a legitimate expectation of privacy that has been invaded by government action. This inquiry, . . . normally embraces two discrete questions. The first is whether the individual, by his conduct, has exhibited an actual (subjective) expectation of privacy—whether . . . the individual has shown that he seeks to preserve [something] as private. The second question is whether the individual's subjective expectation of privacy is one that society is prepared to recognize as reasonable—whether . . . the individual's expectation, viewed objectively, is "justifiable" under the circumstances.

The government surveillance conducted by means of the beeper in this case amounted principally to the following of an automobile on public streets and highways. We have commented more than once on the diminished expectation of privacy in an automobile:

> One has a lesser expectation of privacy in a motor vehicle because its function is transportation and it seldom serves as one's residence or as the repository of personal effects. A car has little capacity for escaping public scrutiny. It travels public thoroughfares where both its occupants and its contents are in plain view.

A person travelling in an automobile on public thoroughfares has no reasonable expectation of privacy in his movements from one place to another. When Petschen travelled over the public streets he voluntarily conveyed to anyone who wanted to look the fact that he was travelling over particular roads in a particular direction, the fact of whatever stops he made, and the fact of his final destination when he exited from public roads onto private property.

Respondent Knotts, as the owner of the cabin and surrounding premises to which Petschen drove, undoubtedly had the traditional expectation of privacy within a dwelling place insofar as the cabin was concerned. . . . But no such expectations of privacy extended to the visual observation of Petschen's automobile arriving on his premises after leaving a public highway, nor to movements of objects such as the drum of chloroform outside the cabin in the "open fields."

Visual surveillance from public places along Petschen's route or adjoining Knotts' premises would have sufficed to reveal all of these facts to the police. The fact that the officers in this case relied not only on visual surveillance, but on the use of the beeper to signal the presence of Petschen's automobile to the police receiver, does not alter the situation. Nothing in the Fourth Amendment prohibited the police from augmenting the sensory faculties bestowed upon them at birth with such enhancement as science and technology afforded them in this case. . . .

Respondent does not actually quarrel with this analysis, though he expresses the generalized view that the result of the holding sought by the government would be that "twenty-four hour surveillance of any citizen of this country will be possible, without judicial knowledge or supervision." . . . Insofar as respondent's complaint appears to be simply that scientific devices such as the beeper enabled the police to be more effective in detecting crime, it simply has no constitutional foundation. We have never equated police efficiency with unconstitutionality, and we decline to do so now. . . .

. . . Admittedly, because of the failure of the visual surveillance, the beeper enabled the law enforcement officials in this case to ascertain the ultimate resting place of the chloroform when they would not have been able to do so had they relied solely on their naked eyes. But scientific enhancement of this sort raises no constitutional issues which visual surveillance would not also raise. A police car following Petschen at a distance throughout his journey could have observed him leaving the public highway and arriving at the cabin owned by respondent, with the drum of chloroform still in the car. This fact, along with others, was used by the government in obtaining a search warrant which led to the discovery of the clandestine drug laboratory. But there is no indication that the beeper was used in any way to reveal information as to the movement of the drum within the cabin, or in any way that would not have been visible to the naked eye from outside the cabin. . . .

We thus return to the question posed at the beginning of our inquiry . . . , did monitoring the beeper signals complained of by respondent invade any legitimate expectation of privacy on his part? For the reasons previously stated, we hold they did not. Since they did not, there was neither a "search" nor a "seizure" within the contemplation of the Fourth Amendment. The judgment of the Court of Appeals is therefore

Reversed.

Couch v. United States
93 S.Ct. 611 (1973)

Petitioner operates a restaurant, and since 1955 she had given her financial records to her accountant, Shafer, for the purpose of preparing her income tax returns. During an IRS audit, the auditor believed that there was a substantial understatement of gross income and reported the matter to the Intelligence Division of the IRS. A special agent of the Intelligence Division contacted Shafer to go over the records, and his request was refused. A summons was then delivered to Shafer who, at petitioner's request, delivered all of the records to petitioner's attorney. An action was then commenced in the District Court to enforce the summons for the records. Petitioner then asserted her Fifth Amendment privilege against compulsory self-incrimination. The lower court held that the records were not privileged and ordered them delivered to the IRS.

POWELL, J. . . . The question is whether the taxpayer may invoke her Fifth Amendment privilege against compulsory self-incrimination to prevent the production of her business and tax records in the possession of her accountant. . . . The importance of preserving inviolate the privilege against compulsory self-incrimination has often been stated by this Court and need not be elaborated. By its very nature, the privilege is an intimate and personal one. It respects a private inner sanctum of individual feeling and thought and proscribes state intrusion to extract self-condemnation. Historically, the privilege sprang from an abhorrence of governmental assault against the single individual accused of crime and the temptation on the part of the State to resort to the expedient of compelling incriminating evidence from one's own mouth.

In *Murphy v. Waterfront Commission of New York Harbor,* 378 U.S. 52, 55 (1964), the Court articulated the policies and purposes of the privilege:

> . . . our unwillingness to subject those suspected of crime to the cruel trilemma of self-accusation, perjury or contempt; our preference for an accusatorial rather than an inquisitorial system of criminal justice; our fear that self-incriminating statements will be elicited by inhumane treatment and abuses; our sense of fair play which dictates "a fair state-individual balance by requiring the government . . . in its contest with the individual to shoulder the entire load," . . . our respect for the inviolability of the human personality and of the right of each individual "to a private enclave where he may lead a private life." . . .

It is important to reiterate that the Fifth Amendment privilege is a *personal* privilege: it adheres basically to the person, not to information which may incriminate him. As Mr. Justice Holmes put it: "A party is privileged from producing the evidence, but not from its production." The Constitution explicitly prohibits compelling an accused to bear witness "against himself": it necessarily did not proscribe incriminating statements elicited from another. Compulsion upon the person asserting it is an important element of the privilege, and "prohibition of compelling a man . . . to be witness against himself is a prohibition of the use of physical or moral compulsion to extort communication from *him.*" It is extortion of information from the accused himself that offends our sense of justice.

In the case before us the ingredient of personal compulsion against an accused is lacking. The summons and the order of the District Court enforcing it are directed against the accountant. He, not the taxpayer, is the only one compelled to do anything. And the accountant makes no claim that he may tend to be incriminated by the production. Inquisitorial pressure or coercion against a potentially accused person, compelling her, against her will, to utter self-condemning words or produce incriminating documents is absent. In the present case, no "shadow of testimonial compulsion upon or enforced communication by the accused" is involved.

The divulgence of potentially incriminating evidence against petitioner is naturally unwelcomed. But petitioner's distress would be no less if the divulgence came not from her accountant but from some other third party with whom she was connected and who possessed substantially equivalent knowledge of her business affairs. The basic complaint of petitioner stems from the fact of divulgence of the possibly incriminating information, not from the manner in which or the person from whom it was extracted. Yet such divulgence, where it did not coerce the accused herself, is a necessary part of the process of law enforcement and tax investigation. . . .

Petitioner further argues that the confidential nature of the accountant-client relationship and her resulting expectation of privacy in delivering the records protect her, under the Fourth and Fifth Amendments, from their production. Although not in itself controlling, we note that no confidential accountant-client privilege exists under federal law, and no State-created privilege has been recognized in federal cases. . . . Nor is there justification for such a privilege where records relevant to income tax returns are involved in a criminal investigation or prosecution. . . . The criterion for Fifth Amendment immunity remains not the ownership of property, but the "physical or moral compulsion exerted." *Perlman, supra,* 247 U.S., at 15, 38 S. Ct., at 420. We hold today that no Fourth or Fifth Amendment claim can prevail where, as in this case, there exists no legitimate expectation of privacy and no semblance of governmental compulsion against the person of the accused. It is important, in applying constitutional principles, to interpret them in light of the fundamental interests of personal liberty they were meant to serve. Respect for these principles is eroded when they leap their proper bounds to interfere with the legitimate interest of society in enforcement of its laws and collection of the revenues. . . .

Judgment affirmed.

New York v. Quarles
104 S.Ct. 2626 (1984)

A policeman investigating a rape spotted Quarles, who matched the rapist's description. When Quarles saw the policeman, he began to run toward the back of a store. After a chase, the policeman cornered the suspect and noticed that he had an empty shoulder holster. The policeman asked where the gun was. Quarles pointed and said: "The gun is over there." The policeman retrieved the gun and then arrested Quarles. At this point, the *Miranda* warning was read to Quarles.

At trial the evidence about the gun and all statements of the accused were excluded because the *Miranda* warning was not given prior to the question about the gun.

REHNQUIST, J. . . . For the reasons which follow, we believe that this case presents a situation where concern for public safety must be paramount to adherence to the literal language of the prophylactic rules enunciated in *Miranda*.

The Fifth Amendment guarantees that "[n]o person . . . shall be compelled in any criminal case to be a witness against himself." In *Miranda* this Court for the first time extended the Fifth Amendment privilege against compulsory self-incrimination to individuals subjected to custodial interrogation by the police. The Fifth Amendment itself does not prohibit all incriminating admissions; [a]bsent some officially coerced self-accusation, the Fifth Amendment privilege is not violated by even the most damning admissions.

The *Miranda* Court, however, presumed that interrogation in certain custodial circumstances is inherently coercive and held that statements made under those circumstances are inadmissible unless the suspect is specifically informed of his *Miranda* rights and freely decides to forgo those rights. The prophylactic *Miranda* warnings therefore are "not themselves rights protected by the Constitution but [are] instead measures to insure that the right against compulsory self-incrimination [is] protected." Requiring *Miranda* warnings before custodial interrogation provides "practical reinforcement" for the Fifth Amendment right.

In this case we have before us no claim that respondent's statements were actually compelled by police conduct which overcame his will to resist.

Thus the only issue before us is whether Officer Kraft was justified in failing to make available to respondent the procedural safeguards associated with the privilege against compulsory self-incrimination since *Miranda*. . . .

We hold that on these facts there is a "public safety" exception to the requirement that *Miranda* warnings be given before a suspect's answers may be admitted into evidence, and that the availability of that exception does not depend upon the motivation of the individual officers involved. In a kaleidoscopic situation such as the one confronting these officers, where spontaneity rather than adherence to a police manual is necessarily the order of the day, the application of the exception which we recognize today should not be made to depend on *post hoc* findings at a suppression hearing concerning the subjective motivation of the arresting officer. Undoubtedly most police officers, if placed in Officer Kraft's position, would act out of a host of different, instinctive, and largely unverifiable motives— their own safety, the safety of others, and perhaps as well the desire to obtain incriminating evidence from the suspect.

Whatever the motivation of individual officers in such a situation, we do not believe that the doctrinal underpinnings of *Miranda* require that it be applied in all its rigor to a situation in which police officers ask questions reasonably prompted by a concern for the public safety. The *Miranda* decision was based in large part on this Court's view that the warnings which it required police to give to suspects in custody would reduce the likelihood that the suspects would fall victim to constitutionally impermissible practices of police interrogation in the presumptively coercive environment of the station house. . . .

The police in this case, in the very act of apprehending a suspect, were confronted with the immediate necessity of ascertaining the whereabouts of a gun which they had every reason to believe the suspect had just removed from his empty holster and discarded in the supermarket. So long as the gun was concealed somewhere in the supermarket, with its actual whereabouts unknown, it obviously posed more than one danger to the public safety: an accomplice might make use of it, a customer or employee might later come upon it.

In such a situation, if the police are required to recite the familiar *Miranda* warnings before asking the whereabouts of the gun, suspects in Quarles' position might well be deterred from responding. Procedural safeguards which deter a suspect from responding were deemed acceptable in *Miranda* in order to protect the Fifth Amendment privilege; when the primary social cost of those added protections is the possibility of fewer convictions, the *Miranda* majority was willing to bear that cost. Here, had *Miranda* warnings deterred Quarles from responding to Officer Kraft's question about the whereabouts of the gun, the cost would have been something more than merely the failure to obtain evidence useful in convicting Quarles. Officer Kraft needed an answer to his question not simply to make his case against Quarles but to insure that further danger to the public did not result from the concealment of the gun in a public area.

We conclude that the need for answers to questions in a situation posing a threat to the public safety outweighs the need for the prophylactic rule protecting the Fifth Amendment's privilege against self-incrimination. We decline to place officers such as Officer Kraft in the untenable position of having to consider, often in a matter of seconds, whether it best serves society for them to ask the necessary questions without the *Miranda* warnings and render whatever probative evidence they uncover inadmissible, or for them to give the warnings in order to preserve the admissibility of evidence they might uncover but possibly damage or destroy their ability to obtain that evidence and neutralize the volatile situation confronting them. . . .

We hold that the Court of Appeals in this case erred in excluding the statement, "the gun is over there," and the gun because of the officer's failure to read respondent his *Miranda* rights before attempting to locate the weapon. . . . We therefore reverse and remand for further proceedings not inconsistent with this opinion.

Reversed.

REVIEW QUESTIONS

1. Match each term in column A with the appropriate statement in column B:

A	B
1. *Malum in se*	**a.** The process by which the prosecution and defense in effect settle a criminal case.
2. True bill	**b.** A defense in criminal cases when the criminal intent originated with the police.
3. Strict liability crime	**c.** A group that has a responsibility to determine if there is probable cause sufficient to warrant a defendant's standing trial.
4. Entrapment	**d.** An act that is historically a crime in any civilized society.
5. Irresistible impulse	**e.** The decision of a grand jury which indicts an accused.

6. Exclusionary rule

7. Grand jury

8. *Miranda* warning

9. Plea bargaining

10. *Malum prohibitum*

f. Something the police must give to inform a person of his or her rights.

g. Criminal conduct that is not inherently wrongful but is declared so by legislative action.

h. An act that is criminal without proof of criminal intent.

i. A test for insanity when the defendant knows right from wrong but is compelled to do what is wrong.

j. A rule of evidence that prevents the use of evidence obtained through illegal search and seizure.

2. Which of the following are generally considered to be white-collar crimes?
   a. Arson
   b. Bribery
   c. Burglary
   d. Embezzlement
   e. Forgery
   f. Obstruction of justice
   g. Price fixing
   h. Rape
   i. Robbery
   j. Securities fraud

3. Compare and contrast the following terms:
   a. Indictment and information
   b. Grand jury and petit jury
   c. Felony and Misdemeanor
   d. General intent and specific intent

4. FBI agents obtained a court order to "bug" the defendant's office. They entered the office in the middle of the night and spent three hours installing an electronic bug. The defendant contended that a covert entry to install a bug is a violation of the Fourth Amendment. Is he correct? Explain.

5. For a crime to be committed, the prosecutor must be able to prove a criminal intent and an overt act to carry out that intent. Jack and Mary previously had agreed to rob a series of banks. Prior to beginning their bank robbery spree, they were arrested and charged with criminal conspiracy. What act did Jack and Mary do that justifies a finding that they committed a crime? Explain.

6. When police entered her room without a warrant, Suzy swallowed two "uppers." Portions of the capsules were recovered by the police with the use of a stomach pump. Was the evidence lawfully obtained? Why?

7. Dan was suspected by customs and immigration officers of having information concerning the smuggling of drugs into the United States. Acting undercover, a customs and immigration official went to Dan and suggested that he bring illegal drugs into this country. Dan refused, but at the official's insistence he later agreed. After the drugs entered this country, Dan was arrested. Does Dan have a valid defense to the charge of smuggling? Explain.

8. Devin was arrested and tried for murder. After deliberating for 3 days, the jury informed the judge that it was hopelessly deadlocked and could not reach a verdict. The judge declared a mistrial and

scheduled a new trial. Devin objected, contending that a second trial constituted double jeopardy. Is he correct? Why?

9. List the protections in the Sixth Amendment that are available to the criminal suspect.

10. What statements must be contained in the *Miranda* warning given to an accused in a criminal case? Give two exceptions to the *Miranda* rule.

11. What are some of the problems inherent in the criminal law system?

6 INTRODUCTION TO CONTRACTS AND REMEDIES

Each of us lives and works in a legal environment. No doubt our greatest participation in this legal environment arises from our freedom to make contracts. Every day we enter into numerous contracts as we purchase goods, hire the services of others, buy a house or rent an apartment, visit the dentist, register for a college course, and so on. Since the legal device of contract is basic to business law, Part II of this text covers the law of contracts in detail.

Among the various meanings of the word *contract* is its technical definition: a promise or several promises under which the law recognizes a duty to perform and for which, if breached, the law gives the aggrieved party a remedy. Realistically, a contract is a legal device to control the future through promises. By definition, a promise is a present commitment, however expressed, that something will or will not be done. Parties are allowed to create rights and duties between themselves, and the state will enforce them through legal machinery. When people make a contract, by their mutual assent they create the terms of their contract, which sets up the bounds of their liability. It is important, then, that you keep two points in mind: (1) a contract contains a present undertaking or commitment concerning future conduct of the parties, and (2) the law sanctions the commitment by putting its legal machinery behind it.

1. Elements of a Contract

There are four basic elements to the formation of a contract:

   1. An agreement that is a manifestation of the parties' mutual assent as found in two legal concepts called offer and acceptance (Chapter 7).

2. Bargained-for consideration or other validation device, which the law uses to validate and make the mutual assent legally operative (Chapter 8).

3. Two or more parties who are legally competent; that is, they have the legal capacity to contract (be of legal age and sane) (Chapter 9).

4. A legal purpose consistent with law and sound public policy (Chapter 10).

These elements of a contract will be considered in detail in the chapters listed above. For the moment, the four elements are useful in giving us a way to think about contract law. As we do so, problems in contract law fall into three groupings: (1) preformation, (2) contract formation, and (3) contract performance. The initial approach to any contract problem is to decide at which of the three stages it arises. In addition to the elements listed above, at the preformation stage we also are concerned about sources of contract law, general contract classifications and terminology, and remedies for breaches of contract. These topics make up the material contained in this chapter. The following seven chapters deal with the contract formation and performance stages. This organization will cause you to ask the following progressive questions:

1. Has an offer been made?

2. Has there been an acceptance?

3. If there has been an offer and acceptance (mutual assent), is there a validation device like consideration to make the offer-acceptance legally operative?

4. Assuming a valid contract has been formed, are there any legal defenses such as incapacity, illegality, fraud, mistake, or the statute of frauds that may nullify the contract?

5. Assuming a valid contract with no defenses to its formation, how is the contract to be performed? (This question concerns performance problems under the general heading of the law of conditions.)

6. Do third parties have rights or duties that may be legally recognized under the contract?

At this introductory point, you are not equipped to answer any of the questions; however, when you have finished the chapters on contracts, come back and consider them. The law of contracts will then be in sharper focus.

2. Sources of Contract Law

The bulk of contract law is judge-made case law and is for the most part uncodified. The basic rules or principles are found in the written opinions of courts. Specialized areas of contract law such as labor law and insurance law have been partially codified, but even in these areas the primary source of applicable legal principles is decided cases.

During the 1940s the Commissioners on Uniform State Laws drafted the Uniform Commercial Code for consideration by the legislatures of the various states. The stated purpose of the Uniform Commercial Code was to collect in one body the law that "deals with all phases which may ordinarily arise in the handling of a commercial transaction from start to finish." The Code was initially enacted in 1952 in Pennsylvania and thereafter over the next several years by every state and territory except Louisiana and Puerto Rico. The detailed aspects of the Code, as it is usually referred to, constitute a significant portion of this text, and sections of the Code are referred to in brackets where appropriate. The references pertain to sections of this law, which are presented as an appendix at the end of the book.

As a result of the enactment of the Uniform Commercial Code, some contracts are subject to its provisions, and some are not. It is essential that you keep in mind the limited applicability of the Code and that you recognize which contracts are covered by the general common law and which are covered by the Code. Most contracts (employment, construction, real property, general business, and the like) follow the common law rules as developed in cases. If a contract concerns the sale of goods (personal property), then it is governed by the Code. When the Code applies to a transaction, courts follow Code rules.

Since most rules concerning contracts are the same under the common law and under the Code, these rules will be considered, whenever possible, at the same time. When the Code has special rules different from the common law, these will be set out carefully in the text of this and the next seven chapters. Rules for sale-of-goods transactions that have nothing to do with the general common law of contracts will be discussed in Part V.

3. Introduction

CONTRACT
CLASSIFICATION
AND
TERMINOLOGY

In the early common law, contracts were formal documents that included a seal. The seal was often a wax impression made by the ring of the contracting party. This impression was later replaced with the word *seal*. Today the requirement of using a seal to have a binding contract has been abolished; formality is no longer required.

In the early law, contracts that were not under seal were called *informal contracts* and were unenforceable. Today, as a general rule, contracts, either written or oral, are enforceable. However, a statute known as the *statute of frauds* does require that certain contracts be evidenced in writing to be enforceable. (This statute of frauds will be discussed in depth in chapter 11.)

In addition to being formal or informal, contracts may be classified in a variety of ways. Among the more common classifications are the following:

1. Form: bilateral or unilateral
2. Expression: express or implied-in-fact or implied-in-law (quasi-contract)
3. Enforcement: valid, void or voidable, and unenforceable
4. Performance: executed or executory

The meaning and significance of these classifications will be discussed in the following sections and throughout the other chapters on contracts.

4. Bilateral and Unilateral Contracts

Contracts are either *bilateral* (a promise exchanged for another promise) or *unilateral* (a promise exchanged for an act of performance). Most contracts are bilateral, based on an exchange of mutual promises. A bilateral contract is formed when the promises are exchanged between the parties. It is immaterial that neither party has rendered any performance, because the law recognizes that each party has a legal duty to perform its contractual duties. In the Figure 6–1, note that there are two promises, two duties, and two correlative rights. This contract is bilateral (two-sided). *Example*: Mary promises to sell her truck to Dan for $2,000, and Dan promises to pay $2,000 for Mary's truck.

FIGURE 6-1

Whereas a bilateral contract is characterized by a promise for a promise, a unilateral contract is characterized by a promise for an act of performance. The *offeror* (person who makes an offer) promises the *offeree* (person to whom the offer is addressed) a benefit *if* the offeree performs some act, such as building a house, mowing the grass, fixing a car, climbing a flagpole, or programming a computer. The offeror does not bargain for a promise, but for performance of an act. In Figure 6–2, note that there is only one promise, one duty, and one right. The contract is unilateral (one-sided). *Example*: April says to Bill: "Bill, I've had enough of your promises. If you paint my house by the end of the month, I promise to pay you $4,000." Bill paints April's house by the end of the month.

FIGURE 6-2

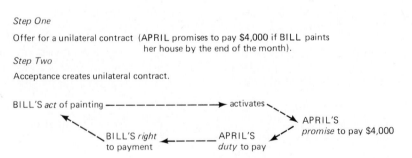

When April made her promise to pay $4,000 to Bill, there was not as yet a unilateral contract, but only an *offer* for a unilateral contract. When Bill did the act of performance bargained for (that is, painting the house), a unilateral contract was formed. Note that prior to Bill's painting there was only an offer for a unilateral contract. This distinction between an offer for a unilateral contract and a unilateral contract will be important in later chapters, especially concerning *part performance* of the act requested in an offer for a unilateral contract.

5. Express and Implied-in-Fact Contracts

An *express* contract occurs when the parties state their agreement orally or in writing. When the parties manifest their agreement by conduct rather than by words, it is said to be *implied-in-fact*.[1] You drive up to a full-service gas station and say, "Fill it up." The station attendant fills it up. Although you've said nothing about paying, it is an implied-in-fact term. The contract then is partly express and partly implied. You are walking down Lexington Avenue and come upon a grocery stand filled with apples under a sign stating 35 cents per apple. You pick one up and take a bite. At that moment, an implied-in-fact contract expressed totally by conduct is formed.

An additional point should be noted. For some time, sellers shipped goods to persons who had not requested them. This technique is used to sell items like religious bookmarks, neckties, records, and books. The seller would then make a contract claim based on acceptance by conduct in keeping the goods (implied-in-fact). To stop this unfair method of selling goods, the U.S. Postal Services Act, 39 U.S.C. §3009 (1970), was enacted. It allows the recipient of unsolicited goods to treat them as a gift and retain, use, discard, or dispose of the goods in any manner without obligation. There are also state statutes relieving the recipient of any duty to pay for unsolicited goods when the goods have been received through the mail or otherwise.

6. Implied-in-Law or Quasi-Contract

Implied-in-law contracts, referred to as quasi-contracts, are not true contracts. Rather, they are legal fictions that courts use to prevent wrongdoing and the unjust enrichment of one person at the expense of another. When one party confers a benefit upon another, the party receiving the benefit may be unjustly enriched if he were not required to pay for the benefit received.[2] Suppose that you mistakenly thought you owned a tract of land. You paid taxes and made improvements on the land. Certainly, the true owner should legally have to reimburse you for the taxes. Regarding the improvements, the true owner likewise should have to pay for the value of those improvements, which were benefits to the owner. To avoid any unjust enrichment, courts permit the party who conferred the benefit to recover the reasonable value of that benefit. Under common law, this legal action was brought in the form of a contract action—hence the name quasi-contract. Nonetheless, there is no real promise, and none of the other elements of a true contract are present. If a contract exists, the remedy of quasi-contract cannot be used.

7. Enforcement Terminology

Contract terminology regarding enforcement involves the following terms: valid, void, voidable, enforceable, and unenforceable. A *valid* contract is one that

---

[1] Newman v. City of Indianola, p. 126.
[2] County of Champaign v. Hanks, p. 127.

is in all respects in accordance with the legal requirements for a contract (that is, offer, acceptance, consideration, legal capacity, and legal purpose). A *void* contract is not a contract in the eyes of the law. For example, an illegal contract is void in the sense that there is no legal machinery to protect the bargain of the parties. A *voidable* contract is one in which one or more parties have the power to end the contract. A voidable contract will be enforced unless one of those parties elects to disaffirm it. A contract executed by one who is under legal age is voidable and can be disaffirmed (set aside) by the underage party.

When one party is entitled to a money judgment or to specific performance because of breach, the contract is *enforceable*. Although legally there may be a contract, a defense to that contract may deny any party any remedy under the contract. Later chapters discuss these defenses to contract formation. Such a contract is said to be *unenforceable*. For example, the law requires that a contract for the sale of land be in writing; if it is oral, then it is unenforceable.

8. Performance Terminology

With respect to performance, contracts often are referred to as executed or executory. An *executed* contract is one that has been fully performed by the contracting parties. An *executory* contract is one that is yet to be performed. The traditional definition of contract, in terms of promises that are commitments regarding the future, stresses the executory nature of most contracts. When Martha offers to sell Walter a beer for $1, and Walter promises to buy, the contract is bilateral and executory. If Martha (rather than promising) hands Walter a beer, and he simultaneously gives her $1, then the contract is executed. Although there is nothing to perform under an executed contract, modern definitions of contract include executed in addition to executory contracts. Note also that an agreement may be mixed; that is, executed by one party and executory on the part of the other.

LEGAL REMEDIES FOR BREACH OF CONTRACT

9. Introduction

When one of the parties to a contract fails to perform as promised, that party may have breached the contract. If a breach occurs, the other party may seek a remedy. This remedy may be classified as legal or equitable. *Legal remedies* or *remedies at law* involve the recovery of money damages. *Equitable remedies* involve a request for something other than money. Some of the equitable remedies available for a breach of contract are discussed in sections 16 through 19.

With respect to legal remedies, four types of money damages can be awarded by the courts: *nominal* damages, *compensatory* (or general) damages, *consequential* (or special) damages, and *punitive* (or exemplary) damages. Additionally, the parties may insert in their contract a provision that attempts to state the amount of money damages to be awarded for contract breach. This *liquidated damages clause,* if fair and not a penalty, will be adopted by the court.

10. Nominal Damages

For every legal wrong, there is a legal remedy. So if there is a contract breach but the nonbreaching party suffers no compensable loss, he can still recover nominal damages. The award (usually $1) symbolizes vindication of the wrong done by the mere breach of contract. Nominal damages thus recognize a technical injury and can be awarded even when the nonbreaching party is in a better position. Suppose that Lamar contracts to buy from Bubba 10,000 pounds of boiled peanuts at 50 cents a pound. Later, Bubba breaches and delivers nothing. If Lamar can buy boiled peanuts for 30 cents per pound on the open market, he can still recover nominal damages, even though he is not harmed by Bubba's breach. Occasionally businesspersons sue for nominal damages so they can establish judicial precedent concerning their rights under contracts that involve continuing, long-term relationships.

11. Compensatory Damages—Theory

When the loss caused by the contract breach is more than nominal, the aggrieved party will sue for compensatory (general) damages designed to compensate for that party's loss of his bargain. Compensatory damages are the primary damages sought in most contract actions. These damages must be a *direct, foreseeable* result of the breach of contract.

The purpose and the theory of damages is to make the injured party whole. As a result of the payment of money, the injured party is in the same position he would have occupied had the breach of contract not occurred. Damages give just compensation for the losses that flowed from the breach. In other words, a person is entitled to the benefits of his bargain. If a purchaser receives less than he bargained for, the difference between the actual value and the contract price constitutes the damages. Unusual and unexpected damages resulting from peculiar facts unknown to the breaching party at the time the agreement was entered into are generally not recoverable. Nor is the injured party entitled to a profit from the breach of the contract; his recovery is limited to an amount that will place him in the same position in which he would have been had the contract been carried out. Likewise, if a contract is terminable at the will of either party, there is no liability if a party terminates it prior to the time the other party anticipated that it would end.[3]

The amount of damages is usually one of fact and therefore presented to the jury. A jury may not speculate on the amount of damage. Damages that are uncertain, contingent, remote, or speculative cannot be used. Loss of profits may be included as an element of recoverable damages if they can be computed with reasonable certainty from tangible and competent evidence.

A party suing for breach of contract is not entitled to recover the amount expended for attorney's fees, unless the contract so provides or special legislation

---

[3] Dalton Properties, Inc. v. Jones, p. 128.

permits it. Litigation is expensive, and the party who wins the lawsuit is still "out of pocket," since the legal expenses will usually substantially reduce the net recovery. Court costs, which include witness fees and filing costs, are usually assessed against the losing party.

12. Compensatory Damages—Rules

The injured party is duty bound to *mitigate* the damages. It is his duty to take reasonable steps to reduce the actual loss to a minimum. He cannot add to his loss or permit the damages to be enhanced when it is reasonably within his power to prevent such occurrence. An employee who has been wrongfully discharged cannot sit idly by and expect to draw his pay. A duty is imposed upon him to seek other work of a substantially similar character in the same community. He is not required to accept employment of a different or an inferior kind.[4]

When a contract is *willfully* and *substantially* breached after partial performance has occurred, there may be some benefit conferred on the nonbreaching party. Furthermore, the benefit may be of such character that the nonbreaching party cannot surrender it to the other. In construction contracts, the benefit received from partial performance cannot be returned. Under these circumstances, the law does not require the person entitled to performance to pay for the benefit conferred upon him if the party conferring it is guilty of a substantial and willful breach. As a result, the party who has refused to complete the job is penalized because of his failure to perform.

A different result occurs when the breach is unintentional—resulting from a mistake or a misunderstanding. In this situation, the party may be required to pay for the net benefit he has received. The court may award damages in the amount necessary to complete the performance, in which event the defaulting party is automatically credited for his partial performance.

In those contracts where partial performance confers benefits of such a nature that they can be returned, the recipient must return the benefits or pay for their reasonable value. This rule is applied to willful breaches as well as unintentional breaches.

13. Consequential Damages

Compensatory damages are general damages that arise directly and naturally from the contract breach. Everyone would expect (or foresee) these damages. Yet, special circumstances surrounding a contract might give rise to special damages that are not normally foreseeable. These damages are called consequential damages. Whereas compensatory damages are presumed and require no special proof, consequential damages are not presumed, since they are caused by special circumstances beyond the contract itself. To recover these special damages, evidence must be submitted that the breaching party knew (or had reason to know) that special circumstances existed and would cause the other party to suffer additional losses if the contract were breached.

---

[4] Parker v. Twentieth Century-Fox Film Corporation, p. 129.

This requirement of actual knowledge (or reason to know) is only fair to prevent a windfall to the nonbreaching party. This rule of a special knowledge of the "consequential" circumstances comes from the famous 1854 English case of *Hadley v. Baxendale.* Plaintiffs, owners of a mill, delivered a broken crankshaft (used in the mill operation) to the defendant, a common carrier, to be delivered to the factory for repair. Defendant delayed an unreasonable time in making the delivery. Since plaintiffs had no other crankshaft, they had to close the mill, and they lost considerable profits. At that time, it was customary (the usual situation) for large mills like theirs to have more than one crankshaft. Plaintiffs' damage recovery was limited by the court to compensatory damages, since the consequential damages (lost profits) were not reasonably foreseeable. The defendant did not have knowledge of the special circumstances—that plaintiffs had only one shaft, which if broken would cause the entire mill to shut down.

Thus, in the usual case, a plaintiff is given compensation only for injuries that one would normally and naturally expect (that is, foresee) as a probable result of the breach of contract. If the injury is beyond that naturally expected, then the plaintiff must prove that the defendant knew (or had reason to know) of these special facts, so that he could foresee the injury.[5] Note that consequential damages are given in addition to compensatory damages.

14. Punitive Damages

The term *punitive damages* or *exemplary damages* refers to money damages awarded one party to punish the other's conduct, as well as to deter others from such conduct in the future. Since punitive damages seek to punish the wrongdoer, they bear no relationship to the actual (compensatory, consequential) damages. Although it is not the purpose of a civil action to punish a party, punitive damages are frequently awarded in tort actions. Ordinarily, under common-law theory, punitive damages were not allowed, since it was not "wrong" to breach a contract. However, today punitive damages can be awarded in a contract case if the contract breach itself constitutes a separate tort. Moreover, the modern trend is to allow punitive damages when the contract breach is fraudulent, oppressive, malicious, or otherwise indicative of the breaching party's intent to harm the other's reasonable expectations under the contract.

15. Liquidated Damages Clause

The parties to a contract may state the money damages applicable when the contract is breached. The term *liquidated damages* describes this situation, and the provision in the contract is called a *liquidated damages clause.* These provisions will be enforced unless the court considers the stipulation to be a penalty for failure to perform rather than compensation for damages. Should the court find that the term was inserted primarily to force actual performance and not to compensate for probable injury, it will be considered to be a penalty and will not

---

[5] Bartinikas v. Clarklift of Chicago North, Inc., p. 130.

be enforced.[6] In order to be valid, the amount of recovery agreed upon must bear a reasonable relation to the probable damage to be sustained by the breach. Recovery is allowed for the amount agreed upon by the parties, although the damages actually suffered may vary somewhat from those agreed on in the contract. In cases of doubt, the courts tend to hold that the stipulated sum is a penalty.

EQUITABLE REMEDIES FOR BREACH OF CONTRACT

16. Introduction

As noted above, equitable remedies involve a request for some remedy other than money damages. These remedies generally will be allowed only if money does not provide adequate relief for the nonbreaching party. Examples of equitable remedies for breach of contracts include *specific performance, rescission,* and *restitution. Specific performance* is a remedy that requires the party in breach to do exactly what he agreed to do under the contract. *Rescission* disaffirms (annuls) the contract and returns the parties to the position each occupied before making the contract. *Restitution* (sometimes called quasi-contract) rectifies unjust enrichment by forcing the party who has been unjustly enriched to return the item unfairly gained or its value if the item cannot be returned. These remedies are discussed in more detail in the following sections.

17. Specific Performance

The legal remedy of dollar damages or the equitable remedy of rescission may not be adequate to provide a proper remedy to a party injured by a breach of contract. The only adequate remedy may be to require the breaching party to perform the contract. This remedy is called *specific performance.* It is used in contracts involving real estate and personal property; it is not available for contracts involving relationships and services.

Specific performance is granted in cases when the court in the exercise of its discretion determines that dollar damages would not be an adequate remedy. Specific performance is not a matter of right but rests in the discretion of the court. To warrant specific performance, the contract must be clear, definite, complete, and free from any suspicion of fraud or unfairness. Dollar damages are considered inadequate and specific performance is the proper remedy when the subject matter of the contract is unique. Since each parcel of real estate differs from every other parcel of real estate, all land is unique, and courts of equity will therefore specifically enforce contracts to sell real estate. Examples of unique personal property are antiques, racehorses, heirlooms, and the stock of a closely held corporation. Such stock is unique because each share has significance in the power to control the corporation. Items readily available in the marketplace are not unique.

The Uniform Commercial Code provides that specific performance may be

---

[6] Southeastern Land Fund v. Real Estate World, p. 130.

decreed when the goods sold are *unique or in other proper circumstances* [2-716]. The Code retains the traditional requirement that the goods be unique and that there be no adequate remedy at law.[7] However, the Code also allows this specific performance remedy "in other proper circumstances," which generally means that the goods cannot be bought elsewhere at a reasonable price. For example, peaches and oranges are not unique. But if an early severe frost destroys most of the peaches and oranges, drastically raising the price of the surviving crop, a court might award specific performance to a buyer in a contract to sell peaches and oranges.

18. Rescission

The equitable remedy of rescission is available in a variety of circumstances. It may be granted by a court of equity when a transaction has been induced by fraud or mistake. Rescission will also be granted to a minor in order that he may exercise his privilege of withdrawing from a contract. It is also used as a remedy if one party's breach of a contract is so substantial that the other party should not be required to perform either. This is covered in detail in chapter 12.

A party who discovers facts that warrant rescission of a contract has a duty to act promptly. If he elects to rescind, he must notify the other party within reasonable time, so that rescission may be accomplished when parties may still be restored, as nearly as possible, to their original positions. A party entitled to rescission may either avoid the contract or affirm it. Once he makes his choice, he may not change it. Failure to rescind within a reasonable time is tantamount to affirming the contract. The party who seeks rescission must return what he has received in substantially as good condition as it was when he received it. Since this remedy is an equitable one, it is subject to the usual maxims of courts of equity.

19. Restitution

In many cases, restitution follows rescission. As stated above, to rescind a contract both parties must make restitution to each other; that is, they must return any benefit received under the contract. Restitution thus prevents any party from being *unjustly enriched* when a contract has been legally anulled. The purpose of restitution is to place the parties in the position they were in prior to making the contract. Goods and property received must be returned if they exist and have not been consumed. Otherwise, each party must pay for the reasonable value of the goods consumed or of the services received so that they will not be enriched unjustly.

Although restitution follows rescission, restitution alone can be a remedy. This occurs when a court imposes a contract (a quasi-contract) to prevent unjust enrichment.Quasi-contracts are discussed earlier in this chapter. Remember that a quasi-contract is not a true contract, but is an implied-in-law contract to prevent unjust enrichment.

---

[7] Beckman v. Vassall-Dillworth Lincoln-Mercury, p. 132.

SUMMARY

Elements of a contract	1. Offer and acceptance.
	2. Consideration.
	3. Legal capacity to contract.
	4. Legal purpose of contract.
Sources of contract law	1. Common-law cases.
	2. Article 2 of the Uniform Commercial Code.

CONTRACT CLASSIFICATIONS AND TERMINOLOGY

Bilateral or unilateral	1. A bilateral contract is an exchange of a promise for a promise.
	2. A promise exchanged for an act of performance creates a unilateral contract when the act is performed.
Express and implied-in-fact	1. A contract formed by words (oral, written, or a combination thereof) is an express contract.
	2. A contract formed by parties' conduct, not by their words, is an implicd-in-fact contract.
Implied-in-law or quasi-contract	1. A court-imposed remedy (a quasi-contract) to prevent unjust enrichment.
	2. It cannot be used if there is a contract.
Enforcement terminology	1. A contract is valid if it contains the requisite legal requirements of offer, acceptance, consideration, legal capacity, and legal purpose.
	2. When the term "void contract" is used, no contract legally exists (for example, illegal contract). The promises exchanged do not create legal obligations.
	3. A contract one party has the option to avoid (set aside) or to enforce is a voidable contract.
	4. An existing contract that cannot be legally enforced due to a legal defense is unenforceable.
Performance terminology	1. A contract is executed when all duties are fully performed by all parties.

2. A contract is executory when duties remain to be performed by the parties.

3. A contract may be partially executed and partially executory.

LEGAL REMEDIES FOR BREACH OF CONTRACT

Nominal damages

1. Nominal damages are an insignificant symbolic money award to acknowledge technical injury when no actual damage from the contract breach can be proved.

Compensatory damages

1. Compensatory damages are a money award for injuries presumed in law to arise normally and naturally from the contract breach.

2. These damages are designed to place the nonbreaching party in the same position as if the contract had been performed.

Consequential damages

1. Consequential damages are a special money award in addition to the award of general compensatory damages.

2. The purpose of consequential damages is to compensate for indirect damage arising from special circumstances the breaching party could reasonably foresee would result from the contract breach.

Punitive damages

1. Punitive damages are awarded to punish the breaching party and to deter others from such conduct in the future.

2. Punitive damages are generally not available in a contract action unless the contract breach itself constitutes an independent tort.

Liquidated damages clause

1. Liquidated damages are awarded in an amount agreed by the parties in their contract (liquidated damages clause) to be reasonable compensation for future contract breach.

2. The agreed amount of liquidated damages cannot be a penalty; it must bear a reasonable relation to the actual damages that will probably occur if the contract is breached.

EQUITABLE REMEDIES FOR BREACH OF CONTRACT

Specific performance	1. Specific performance is a remedy that requires the party in breach to perform the contract.
	2. Specific performance is granted only when money damages are an inadequate remedy. Dollar damages are usually considered inadequate when the subject matter of the contract is unique.
Rescission	1. Rescission is a remedy that cancels the contract and restores the parties to the position they occupied before the contract was formed.
	2. In many cases, to rescind a contract, the parties must make restitution.
Restitution	1. Restitution is a remedy to recapture a benefit conferred to prevent that party from being unjustly enriched.
	2. In restitution, actual goods or property must be returned in specie. But if the goods or property have been consumed, an equivalent amount of money must be given.

CASES

Newman v. City of Indianola
232 N.W.2d 568 (Iowa 1975)

The plaintiff owns and operates a trailer court. The defendant owns and operates the municipal electric utility which serves the mobile home park. The plaintiff requested the defendant to serve three new mobile home spaces. In order to do so, the defendant extended its lines approximately 500 feet at a cost of $473.47. The plaintiff seeks a declaratory judgment that he is not obligated to pay the cost of extending the utility lines.

MASON, J. . . . The trial court's decision requiring Newman to pay the reasonable costs of the extension was based on a theory of a contract because there was a request by plaintiff to extend the services and pay the reasonable cost thereof. . . . Plaintiff contends there is not support in the record for this theory. Although plaintiff concedes he requested an extension of the electrical service he points out that the record is void of any evidence he agreed to pay for the work.

The portion of the stipulation apparently relied upon by the trial court reads as follows: "That on or about the 26th day of August, 1971, at the request of the plaintiff, the defendant extended electrical services . . . for the purpose of serving three (3) additional mobile home units with electrical power. . . ."

As indicated, the factual circumstances leading to this lawsuit were stipulated. There is nothing in the stipulation which would support a finding plaintiff had expressly agreed to pay the reasonable costs for the extension involved. Thus, any agreement in order to serve as a basis for the court's theory must be one implied in fact.

A promise may be stated in words either oral or written, or may be inferred wholly or partly from conduct.

This statement of principle quoted in 1 Corbin on Contracts, section 18, n. 42, is relevant:

Contracts may be express or implied. These terms, however, do not denote different kinds of contracts, but have reference to the evidence by which the agreement between the parties is shown. If the agreement is shown by the direct words of the parties, spoken or written, the contract is said to be an express one. But if such agreement can only be shown by the acts and conduct of the parties, interpreted in the light of the subject matter and of the surrounding circumstances, then the contract is an implied one.

It was stipulated Newman requested the City to extend the service a distance of 500 feet in order to serve additional mobile home spaces. His conduct in making such request was effective as a manifestation of his assent to pay the fair and reasonable cost for such service. There was an implied contract.

The court concludes the trial court was correct in holding Newman was to pay the cost of the extension.

The case is therefore affirmed.

County of Champaign v. Hanks
353 N.E.2d 405 (Ill.App. 1976)

The state's attorney of plaintiff county brought suit against the defendant to recover the value of legal services furnished the defendant by the county public defender. Defendant had been charged with burglary. He executed an affidavit of his assets and liabilities which stated that he was indigent. Based on this affidavit, the public defender was appointed and the defendant was furnished extensive free legal counsel. Later it was discovered that the defendant had a net worth in excess of $50,000.

Plaintiff sued on a theory of quasi-contract and the trial court awarded plaintiff the sum of $2,000. The defendant appeals.

STENGEL, J. . . . A quasi contract, or contract implied in law, is one which reason and justice dictate and is founded on the equitable doctrine of unjust enrichment. A contract implied in law does not depend on the intention of the parties, but exists where there is a plain duty and a consideration. The essential element is the receipt of a benefit by one party under circumstances where it would be inequitable to retain that benefit without compensation.

The county does not officiously confer the benefits of free legal representation, but furnishes legal services to those criminal defendants who qualify by virtue of their indigency. The undisputed facts reveal that defendant received free legal representation when he clearly was not entitled to such representation and that defendant failed to disclose his assets. Under these circumstances the law will imply a promise by defendant to compensate the county and, accordingly, we find that summary judgment was properly granted. . . .

Defendant's final contention concerns the correct measure of damages. The trial court, having heard testimony from private attorneys that the reasonable value in Champaign County for the type of services furnished to defendant was $3,000, awarded damages of $2,000 after considering the experience of the particular attorneys involved and other factors. Defendant has maintained that the correct measure of damages is the cost to plaintiff, which defendant asserts as being that portion of the attorney's salary attributable to his defense, or $181.

The measure of damages for an implied-in-law contract is the amount by which defendant has been unjustly enriched or the value of the actual benefit received by defendant, and recovery is usually measured by the reasonable value of the services performed by plaintiff. In implied-in-law contracts, involving principles of restitution and the avoidance of unjust enrichment, the proper determination of damages may be difficult and often depends on the peculiar facts of the individual case. The Restatement of Restitution, section 152, provides:

Where a person is entitled to restitution from another because the other has obtained his services, or services to which he is entitled, by fraud, duress or undue influence, the measure of recovery for the benefit received by the other is the market value of such services irrespective of their benefit to the recipient.

In the instant case, defendant's assertion regarding the proper amount of damages is patently erroneous. Even if plaintiff's recovery were limited to its costs, as opposed to the benefit received by defendant, computation of such an amount would include many factors other than the applicable portion of the attorneys' salaries. Moreover, such an award would not effect substantial justice between the parties, as it ignores defendant's unjust enrichment.

Defendant, by his misrepresentations, received legal services which were found by the trial court to have a reasonable value of $2,000. The services rendered by three different attorneys from the Public Defender's Office were not only competent but lengthy and most thorough. The record reveals that between March 28, 1972, and July 17, 1972, they appeared in court at least nine days on various matters from preliminary hearing and arraignment to motions to suppress the in-court identification. The jury trial consumed four days from July 17 to July 20, 1972. Motions for mistrial, post-trial motions, probation hearing and finally sentencing hearing were not completed until October 6, 1972. Thus the damage award does not exceed the extent of defendant's unjust enrichment as it is no more than defendant would have paid for such services had he not misrepresented his assets. This damage award more nearly reflects the value of the benefit received by defendant, and a lesser measure of damages would be tantamount to allowing defendant to profit from his wrongful conduct. . . .

Affirmed.

Dalton Properties, Inc. v. Jones
683 P.2d 31 (Nev. 1984)

PER CURIAM. The present appeal questions the appropriateness of an award of monetary damages in an action for the breach of a subcontractor's agreement which is terminable without cause. Under the agreement, Jones was employed as a subcontractor to remove trash and other debris from a HUD housing complex which was in the process of being renovated. The subcontract stated that the prime contractor "reserves the absolute right to terminate this agreement."

From the record it appears that Jones performed under the terms of the agreement for approximately three months until a dispute arose between Jones and Dalton Properties. According to Jones, he and his men were wrongfully accused of stealing appliances out of the apartments that they had been cleaning and as a result were ordered off the job site on February 7, 1980. Five months later, Jones requested and received a hearing before the State Contractor's Board to determine whether an amiable solution could be worked out. . . . [As] a result of the hearing, Jones was allowed to resume work on the project.

A complaint was subsequently filed against Dalton Properties in November, 1980, seeking general damages in excess of $10,000 for the loss of income over the five-month period which otherwise would have been received had Jones not been terminated from the project. Following a trial before the bench, judgment was entered in favor of Jones. The lower court specifically found that Jones had been "wrongfully terminated" from the project from February to August, 1980. As a result, the court awarded Jones $8,000 plus interest from February, 1980.

In the present appeal, Dalton Properties contends that damages for lost profits may not be recovered for the breach of a contract that is terminable at will or without cause. We agree.

The courts have long recognized the validity of contracts that provide either party the option of terminating the contract at will. Where a contract provides that either party may terminate the agreement at will, the party so terminated may not recover damages for those profits that he purportedly could have gained over the maximum life of the contract. The object of compensatory damages in an action for breach of contract is merely to place the injured party in the position that he would have been in had the contract not been breached.

Since a party to a contract which is terminable at the will of another cannot rely on duration of the contract, if damages for lost profits were permitted, the injured party would be in a better position than the terms of the contract allowed. . . .

Reversed.

Parker v. Twentieth Century-Fox Film Corporation
89 Cal. Rptr. 737 (1970)

Plaintiff, a well-known actress, was engaged by defendant corporation to act in a musical motion picture entitled *Bloomer Girl,* her compensation to be $750,000. Prior to the date upon which production was to begin, defendant notified plaintiff that production of *Bloomer Girl* had been canceled. The actress was offered a role in a dramatic Western, to be titled *Big Country, Big Man. Bloomer Girl* was to have been filmed in California; *Big Country* was to be produced in Australia at the same compensation. Plaintiff did not accept the new role, but sued instead for payment on the *Bloomer Girl* contract. Defendant asserted as an affirmative defense plaintiff's allegedly deliberate failure to mitigate damages, asserting that her refusal to accept the other role was unreasonable. The lower court found for plaintiff, and defendant appealed.

BURKE, J. . . . The general rule is that the measure of recovery by a wrongfully discharged employee is the amount of salary agreed upon for the period of service, less the amount which the employer affirmatively proves the employee has earned or with reasonable effort might have earned from other employment. However, before projected earnings from other employment opportunities not sought or accepted by the discharged employee can be applied in mitigation, the employer must show that the other employment was comparable, or substantially similar, to that of which the employee has been deprived; the employee's rejection of or failure to seek other available employment of a different or inferior kind may not be resorted to in order to mitigate damages.

In the present case defendant has raised no issue of *reasonableness of efforts* by plaintiff to obtain other employment, the sole issue is whether plaintiff's refusal of defendant's substitute offer of *Big Country* may be used in mitigation. Nor, if the *Big Country* offer was of employment different or inferior when compared with the original *Bloomer Girl* employment, is there an issue as to whether or not plaintiff acted reasonably in refusing the substitute offer. Despite defendant's arguments to the contrary, no case cited or which our research has discovered holds or suggests that reasonableness is an element of a wrongfully discharged employee's option to reject, or fail to seek, different or inferior employment lest the possible earnings therefrom be charged against him in mitigation of damages.

Applying the foregoing rules to the record in the present case, with all intendments in favor of the party opposing the summary judgment motion—here, defendant—it is clear that the trial court correctly ruled that plaintiff's failure to accept defendant's tendered substitute employment could not be applied in mitigation of damages because the offer of the *Big Country* lead was of employment both different and inferior, and that no factual dispute was presented on that issue. The mere circumstances that *Bloomer Girl* was to be a musical review calling upon plaintiff's talents as a dancer as well as an actress, and was to be produced in the City of Los Angeles, whereas *Big Country* was a straight dramatic role in a "Western Type" story taking place in an opal mine in Australia, demonstrates the difference in kind between the two employments; the female lead as a dramatic actress in a western style motion picture can by no stretch of imagination be considered the equivalent of or substantially similar to the lead in a song-and-dance production.

Additionally, the substitute *Big Country* offer proposed to eliminate or impair the director and screenplay approvals accorded to plaintiff under the original *Bloomer Girl* contract and thus constituted an offer of inferior employment. No expertise or judicial notice is required in order to hold that the deprivation or infringement of an employee's rights held under an original employment contract converts the available "other employment" relied upon by the employer to mitigate damages, into inferior employment which the employee need not seek or accept. . . .

The judgment is affirmed.

Bartinikas v. Clarklift of Chicago North, Inc.
508 F. Supp. 959 (Ill. 1981)

Bartinikas was employed by Clarklift from September 1976 until Bartinikas resigned his position as a commissioned salesman in September 1978. In October 1978, Clarklift sent Bartinikas a commission statement detailing his outstanding commissions. On several occasions after receiving the statement, Bartinikas told Clarklift that he had not been credited with all commissions due him and that he needed payment of these commissions to make a down payment on a home in Florida. Clarklift refused to pay the commissions. Bartinikas sued Clarklift, alleging that because Clarklift refused to pay the commissions he was unable to purchase certain real estate in Florida. Thus, he claims that he suffered damages measured by the "profits" he would have earned had he been able to invest the commissions in the property. Clarklift moves for summary judgment to dismiss Bartinikas's complaint.

ASPEN, J. . . . Since *Hadley v. Baxendale,* 9 Ct. of Exch. 341 (1854), it has been established that damages for breach of contract are limited to those that "may reasonably be supposed to have been in the contemplation of the parties, at the time they made the contract, as the probable result of the breach of it."

Recent Illinois decisions continue to follow this doctrine:

When the profits which are sought are those arising out of the breached contract, those profits are considered one of the elements of the contract, and are presumed to have been within the contemplation of the defaulting party at the time he entered into the contract; they are recoverable if proved with reasonable certainty. However, when the profits sought are those which would have arisen only out of a collateral transaction, not only must these profits be proved with reasonable certainty, but also it must be shown that they were reasonably made within the contemplation of the defaulting party when the contract was made. Notice of the possible existence of collateral profits, given after execution of the contract, will not satisfy this requirement.

It is undisputed that Bartinikas did not inform Clarklift of his investment opportunity until well after the making of the contract. Indeed, Clarklift did not learn of plaintiff's alleged opportunity until after he had left its employ. Since Bartinikas has failed to show that his investment opportunity was within the contemplation of the parties when the contract was made, Bartinikas cannot base a cause of action upon these alleged damages. Accordingly, Clarklift's motion for summary judgment on plaintiff's complaint is granted.

It is so ordered.

Southeastern Land Fund
v. Real Estate World
227 S.E.2d 340 (Ga 1976)

The plaintiff and the defendant entered into a contract for the sale of real estate. The defendant-buyer paid $5,000 as earnest money when the contract was signed. He also signed a promissory note for $45,000 representing additional earnest money. When the buyer defaulted at the closing, the seller sued to collect the $45,000 note.

The trial court gave the plaintiff-seller a judgment for $45,000 but this was reversed by the Court of Appeals on the grounds that the earnest money provisions of the contract amounted to a penalty. The contract had provided that the seller could retain the earnest money as liquidated damages and had further barred the remedy of specific performance.

INGRAM, J. . . . If, as the Court of Appeals found, this provision in the contract was a penalty, or is unenforceable as a liquidated damages provision, then the buyer can prevail in asserting a defense to the enforcement of the $45,000 note. If, on the other hand, this is a proper provision for liquidated damages, then the seller can prevail in enforcing the note. Of course, whether a provision represents liquidated damages or a penalty does not depend upon the label the parties place on the payment but rather depends on the effect it was intended to have and whether it was reasonable. Where the parties do not undertake to estimate damages in advance of the breach and instead provide for both a forfeiture [penalty] plus actual damages, the amount, even though called liquidated damages, is instead an unenforceable penalty. . . .

Depending on the language used in the contract and the discernable intent of the parties, the existence of an earnest money provision in a real estate sales contract can have one of three effects in the case of a breach by the buyer. First, the money could be considered as partial payment of any actual damages which can be proven as the result of the buyer's breach. Second, the money could be applied as part payment of the purchase price in the enforcement of the contract in a suit for specific performance by the seller. Third, the money could be liquidated damages for breach of the contract by the buyer. A provision for earnest money cannot, however, under Georgia law, be used for all three results as we shall see.

Of course, if the real estate sales contract is silent on the remedy to be provided, the nonbreaching seller is entitled to his proven actual damages. The ordinary measure of damages is the difference between the contract price and the market value of the property at the time of the buyer's breach. If the non-breaching seller sues for actual damages, the earnest money then becomes a fund out of which those damages are partially paid if the proven damages exceed the amount of the earnest money.

Even if the real estate contract is silent as to the remedy of specific performance, it is still available as a remedy unless it is specifically excluded as a remedy. In the cases in which rescission has been used as a remedy the parties are put as nearly as is possible back to the status quo ante.

Of course, Georgia law also recognizes that the parties may agree in their contract to a sum to liquidate their damages. . . .

In deciding whether a contract provision is enforceable as liquidated damages, the court makes a tripartite inquiry to determine if the following factors are present:

First, the injury caused by the breach must be difficult or impossible of accurate estimation; second, the parties must intend to provide for damages rather than for a penalty; and third, the sum stipulated must be a reasonable pre-estimate of the probable loss.

Another feature implicit in the concept of liquidated damages in addition to the above factors is that both parties are bound by their agreement. A non-breaching party who has agreed to accept liquidated damages cannot elect after a breach to take actual damages should they prove greater than the sum specified. The breaching party cannot complain that the actual damages are less than those specified as liquidated damages. The liquidated damages become the "maximum as well as the minimum sum that can be collected. . . ."

The contract provision that included the retention of the right to elect specific performance as an alternative remedy to damages poses no problem in our analysis as it does not render a valid liquidated damages provision unenforceable. "The law is now well settled that a liquidated damages provision will not in and of itself be construed as barring the remedy of specific performance." To bar specific performance there should be explicit language in the liquidated damages provision that it is to be the sole remedy. Thus the retention of the right to elect specific performance in this contract does not render the purported liquidated damages provision invalid. The answer must be found elsewhere in the construction of these contract provisions.

We think a correct resolution of this issue must be found in the doctrine that "in cases of doubt the courts favor the construction which holds the stipulated sum to be a penalty, and limits the recovery to the amount of damages actually shown, rather than a liquidation of the damages." If the parties intended for the $5,000 and the $45,000 to represent the "maximum as well as the minimum sum that can be collected," from the buyer's breach, the contract should have made it clear that this was the effect intended by these provisions. It is the lingering ambiguity inherent in these provisions of the contract that persuades us to affirm the result reached by the Court of Appeals in construing the contract.

In summary, we hold that these contract provisions are not enforceable under Georgia law as proper liquidated damages provisions in this real estate sales contract. . . .

Affirmed.

Beckman v. Vassall-Dillworth Lincoln-Mercury
468 A.2d 784 (Pa. Super. 1983)

On December 14, 1978, Beckman signed a contract with the automobile dealership of Vassall-Dillworth Lincoln-Mercury for the purchase of a 1979 Lincoln Continental. Four weeks later Beckman inquired about the car. The dealership said the purchase order agreement was lost, so no car was ordered. The dealership offered to order a 1979 Lincoln Continental but at a price higher than the price originally agreed upon. Beckman sued the dealership for specific performance which the trial court denied.

MONTGOMERY, J. . . . Beckman contends the trial court incorrectly held he was not entitled to specific performance because he failed to show that he had no adequate remedy at law. It is clear that an order for specific performance is inappropriate where the moving party has an adequate remedy at law. Our Court has held that specific performance is a proper remedy when the subject matter of an agreement is an asset that is unique or one such that its equivalent cannot be purchased on the open market. In this case, the record shows that the Appellant was given an opportunity by the dealer to purchase the automobile he wanted, but at a higher price. It may not be ignored that the Appellant could also have sought to purchase the same vehicle from another source. His remedy in such circumstances was to seek damages for any difference between the original order price and the actual purchase price he paid. Because the subject matter of the contract was not unique, and because it is obvious that an adequate remedy at law was available, we agree with the lower court's rejection of the Appellant's demand for specific performance.

Affirmed.

REVIEW QUESTIONS

1. Identify the types of contracts in column A by matching each with the appropriate statement(s) in column B.

A	B
1. Express contract	a. Contract duties completely performed
2. Implied-in-fact contract	b. Formed by parties' conduct
3. Implied-in-law contract	c. Contract exists but cannot be enforced in court
4. Executed contract	d. Formed either by oral or written words or both
5. Executory contract	e. Imposed by law to prevent unjust enrichment
6. Void contract	f. One party has option of avoiding or enforcing contract
7. Voidable contract	g. Contract duties have not been performed
8. Unenforceable contract	h. Illegal contract

2. What are the basic elements of a contract?
3. What are the four judicial remedies for breach of contract?

4. Peters and Wallach made an agreement whereby Peters was to receive one-third of the stock in a closely held corporation upon payment of $45,000 to Wallach. Later Wallach refused to transfer the stock. Is Peters entitled to the remedy of specific performance? Explain.

5. After buying a home and lot from Pyburn, Hutchison later discovered that the home site had not been approved by the health board because it lacked enough topsoil to sustain a septic tank and overflow field for sewage disposal. Hutchison charged that Pyburn knew of this condition and that there was no practical means of correcting it. If Hutchison's charge is true, is he entitled to rescission? Could punitive damages also be awarded?

6. Fay and John made a contract for the sale of land that Fay intended to develop into a housing project. It was agreed that Fay would pay in installments. Before taking possession of the land, Fay drafted plans for the housing project. Shortly thereafter, she realized that the land was 4 acres smaller than John had said. Because of this difference, Fay had to hire a surveyor to replot the housing project. When Fay refused to make further payments on the land, John filed suit. What type of damages can Fay claim in defending the suit? Explain.

7. J.R. Drilling Co. of Houston, Texas, ordered a replacement drilling shaft to substitute for a broken one. The shaft was to be shipped from Chicago to Texas via Whitlock Truck Company. J.R. told Whitlock that he (J.R.) owned only one oil well drilling rig and that he needed the replacement shaft immediately. Whitlock delayed 10 days in transporting the shaft from Chicago to Houston. Is J.R. entitled to recover the profits he lost from the lack of a prompt delivery? Explain.

8. Johnson was fired from his job with the Empire State Building Company for "no good reason." Although his employment contract was not for a definite term, Johnson sues to be reinstated in his job. Did he win? Why or why not?

9. After driving your new car for a few weeks, you discover that it was actually used. Its odometer had been set back. Are you entitled to punitive damages from the dealership? Why or why not?

10. Suppose you have made reservations through American Express with the Plaza Hotel. Your reservations were confirmed by the hotel and guaranteed by American Express. Upon your arrival, the Plaza refused you a room, stating there was none available. In addition to your out-of-pocket expenses for contract breach, are you entitled to recover punitive damages? Why or why not?

11. Cleaver installed a coin-operated phonograph in Mel's restaurant. The contract provided that the damages for Mel's breach would be the amount of revenue Cleaver would have received for the balance of the contract period. Mel breached. Cleaver sued under the contract provision, which Mel claimed was unenforceable. Was Mel right? Why or why not?

12. Pierre leased a restaurant and lounge from Scott. Pierre, with Scott's knowledge and consent, extensively remodeled the premises. One year later Pierre failed to pay the rent and was evicted. He sued for the amount spent in remodeling. Scott claims he is not liable because he had never agreed to pay for the work. Should Pierre succeed? Why or why not?

13. Nursing Company assumed the operation of a nursing home. The previous owner had a contract with Linen Supply. Linen Supply continued to furnish services after Nursing Company assumed ownership. Nursing Company argues that it does not have to pay for the linen services because it had no express contract with Linen Supply. Can Linen Supply recover based on breach of an express contract? Why or why not?

7 THE AGREEMENT: OFFER AND ACCEPTANCE

The first requirement of a valid contract is an agreement between the parties. An agreement is typically reached when one party (the *offeror*) makes an offer to another party (the *offeree*) who accepts the offer. Offer and acceptance are the acts by which the parties come to a "meeting of the minds." They reach an accord on the terms of their agreement. This accord is referred to as a *manifestation of mutual assent*.

1. Objective Theory of Contracts

Mutual assent, then, is the first ingredient of a contract. Classical common-law rules required that the assent of both parties exactly match at the same point in time; that is, that there be a subjective meeting of the minds. Since nobody can actually know the inner thoughts of another, this requirement proved unworkable. Rather than dealing with subjective thoughts, modern contract law follows an objective theory based on the manifestation of mutual assent. Assent to the formation of a contract is legally operative only if it is objectively manifested.

Unless there is an *objective* "meeting of the minds" of the parties on the subject matter and terms of the agreement, no contract is formed. To determine whether the minds have met, both offer and acceptance must be analyzed. The offeror may have had something in mind quite different from that of the offeree. Notwithstanding, the intention of the parties is determined not by what they think, but by their outward conduct; that is, by what each leads the other reasonably to believe.

The minds of the parties are also said to have met when they sign a written agreement. Each person possessing legal capacity to contract who signs a written document with the idea of entering into a contract is presumed to know the contents thereof. Where one who can read signs a contract without reading it, he is bound by the terms thereof unless he can show (1) that an emergency existed at the time of signing that would excuse his failure to read it, (2) that the opposite party misled him by artifice or device, which prevented him from reading it; or (3) that a fiduciary or confidential relationship existed between parties upon which he relied in not reading the contract. Because the act of signing indicates a person's intention to be bound by the terms contained in the writing, he is in no position at a later date to contend effectively that he did not mean to enter into the particular agreement. All contracts should, therefore, be read carefully before they are signed.

Offers clearly made in jest or under the strain or stress of great excitement are usually not enforced because one is not reasonably justified in relying on them. Whether an offer is made in jest can be determined by applying the objective standard. If the jest is not apparent and a reasonable bearer would believe that an offer was being made, a contract is formed.[1]

2. Definition of Offer

OFFERS

An offer is a conditional promise made by the offeror to the offeree. It is conditional because the offeror will not be bound by his promise unless the offeree responds to it in the manner sought by the offeror. This may be that the offeree (1) does something (perform an act), (2) refrains from doing something (forbearance), or (3) promises to do something or to refrain from doing something. If the offeree complies with the terms of the offer within the proper time, there is an agreement. The offeror's manifestation must create a reasonable expectation in the offeree that the offeror is willing to contract. This expectation arises when the offeror's promise demonstrates a *present commitment* in exchange for one of the three responses by the offeree listed above. The first task is to determine if an offer has been made.

3. Test of Offer's Existence

The test for determining if an offer has been made is as follows: What would a reasonable person in the position of the offeree think the manifestation from the offeror meant? In our legal system, the reasonable person is the jury; the test asks the jury to make that factual determination. The jury looks at all the surrounding circumstances to determine what the offeree ought to have understood. It makes no difference what the offeror actually intended, because the test looks to the presumed intent of the offeror. In making the analysis of the offeror's presumed intent, juries weigh the answers to these three questions:

> **1.** Did the offeror's manifestation demonstrate a present commitment or only an intent to bargain? (Language of present commitment is necessary for an offer.)

---

[1] Barnes v. Treece, p. 152.

2. How definite were the terms as communicated? (The more definite, the more likely it was an offer.)

3. To whom was the manifestation addressed? (If addressed to a specific person rather than the public generally, then probably it was an offer.)

4. Language Used

To decide if an offer was made, the first step is to evaluate the language used. If there are no words of present commitment or undertaking, then probably the manifestation was only a preliminary negotiation or an invitation to the other party to make an offer. The following is preliminary negotiation language: "I am asking," "I would consider," "I am going to sell," etc. Such language is generally construed as inviting offers, because there is no present commitment. Consider the following:

> *Problem*: In reply to Ronald McDonald's inquiry if Griese would sell his business for $30,000 (Bob Griese Fried Chicken), Griese said: "It would not be possible for me to sell unless I got $45,000 in cash." Ronald hands Griese $45,000. Was there an offer by Griese? No. Griese was only saying that he would consider offers that were at least $45,000. He made no commitment to sell.
>
> *Problem*: "I quote you $20 per hockey puck for immediate acceptance." Is this communication an offer? Probably. In general, price quotations are not considered offers, because there is no present commitment. Here there is promissory language "for immediate acceptance," which would lead a reasonable person in the offeree's position to think an offer was made.

5. Definiteness of Offer

Many transactions involve lengthy negotiations between the parties, often with an exchange of numerous letters, proposals, and conversations. It is frequently difficult to establish the point at which the parties have concluded the negotiation stage and have entered into a binding contract. The key question in such situations is whether a definite offer was made and accepted *or* whether the letters, communications, and proposals were simply part of continuing negotiations. The courts must examine the facts of each case, and to those facts they must apply the basic contract rules concerning the requirements of an offer. An offer must be definite and must be made under such circumstances that the person receiving it has reason to believe that the other party (offeror) is willing to deal on the terms indicated.

One of the reasons for the requirement of definiteness is that courts may have to determine at a later date whether or not the performance is in compliance with the terms. Consequently, if the terms are vague or impossible to measure with some precision, or if major terms are absent, no contract results. Therefore, before a proposal can ripen into a contract, the offer must be sufficiently definite (when coupled with the acceptance) so a court can be reasonably certain regarding both the *nature* and *extent* of the assumed duties. Otherwise, a court has no basis for adjudicating liability. The more certain and definite the communications, the more reasonable it is to conclude that an offer is intended. But the issue remains: How definite must an offer be?

If the parties have intended to make a contract, uncertainty concerning incidental or collateral matters is not fatal to the contract's existence. For example, assume that the parties agree that certain performances shall be mutually rendered by them "immediately" or "promptly" or "as soon as possible" or "in about a month." Although these promises are indefinite, modern contract law would view them as sufficiently definite to form a contract. It should be noted, however, that the more terms the parties leave open, the less likely it is that they have intended to create a binding agreement.

In essence, the existence of a contract is determined by three rules. (1) The parties must intend (under the objective theory) to make a contract. (2) One or more material terms can be omitted from the agreement without the contract failing for indefiniteness. (3) A contract must have enough terms so a court can determine when the contract has been breached and then can fashion an appropriate remedy.

6. Gap-Filling

Courts should be willing to fill gaps or missing terms under an agreement, especially if the parties intend to contract but are silent regarding some terms. The trend of the Code and modern case law is to supply reasonable terms—even material terms. Time for performance and the price to be paid, for example, are important terms and usually are included in the contract. If no time clause is included, a court in most contracts will supply a reasonable time for performances [2-309(1)]. If no price is specified, a court will rule that a reasonable price was intended [2-305].[2] Gap-filling the price term also applies when the parties have agreed that the price is to be fixed by a market or other standard and that standard fails. In a non-Code case, however, if the contract is totally executory (neither party has performed), the contract with an unspecified price term may not be enforced. *Note*: A court can gap-fill a missing term but cannot rewrite the contract. Courts follow the presumption that the parties intend reasonable terms; that presumption applies only to omitted terms. If a term is vague, gap-filling is not allowed. Thus, when parties express their intention on a matter, the court cannot supply an external, reasonable term. To do so would be inconsistent with the express intention of the parties.

Although the Code allows material terms to be supplied by the court, the contract must contain sufficient terms so that the court can fashion an appropriate remedy [2-204(3)]. Quite naturally, the question arises: What term or terms are absolutely necessary before a court can state a proper remedy? The one term that must be in every contract is the *quantity* term. Without it, a court has no basis to figure damages.

---

[2] Arrowhead Constr. Co. v. Essex Corp., p. 153.

7. To Whom Addressed

In addition to the language used and the definiteness of the communication, another factor to consider is the person addressed. Since an offer creates in someone the power to accept, the communication must sufficiently identify the offeree or the class from whom the offeree may emerge. The usual rule is that if the addressee is an indefinite group, as in the case of advertisements, then there is no offer.[3] Reward offers illustrate an exception to this rule. Although the offeree is unidentified and unknown at the time a reward offer is made, the performance of the act requested in the reward is an acceptance that also identifies the offeree.

In general, advertisements, estimates, quotes, catalogs, circulars, proposals, and the like are not offers, for several reasons. There is no quantity term or language of present commitment; the goods are seldom adequately described. Practically speaking, advertisers do not intend the communication to be an offer that can ripen into a contract on the basis of the terms expressed. While it is possible for an ad or quote to constitute an offer, most do not.

8. An Offer Must Be Communicated

An offer is not effective until it has been communicated to the offeree by the offeror. It can be effectively communicated only by the offeror or his duly authorized agent. If the offeree learns of the offeror's intention to make an offer from some outside source, no offer results. Also, to be effective, the offer must be communicated through the medium or channel selected by the offeror. Thus, if Terry was in Margaret's office and noticed on the desk a letter directed to Terry and containing an offer, the offer would not have been communicated to Terry. Terry would not be in a position to accept the offer.

An offer to the public may be made through newspapers or posted notices. As far as a particular individual is concerned, it is not effective until he learns that the offer has been made. As a result, a person without actual knowledge cannot accept the offer. If a reward is offered for the arrest of a fugitive and a person makes the arrest without actual knowledge of the offer of the reward, there is no contract.

An offer is effective when received even though it is delayed in reaching the offeree. Because the delay normally results from the negligence of the offeror or his chosen means of communication (for example, a telegraph company), he should bear the loss resulting from the delay. If the delay is apparent to the offeree, the acceptance will be effective only if it is communicated to the offeror within a reasonable time after the offer would normally have been received. If the offeree knows that there has been a delay in communicating the offer, he cannot take advantage of the delay.

It should be noted that printed material often found on the back of contract forms and occasionally on letterheads, unless embodied in the contract by reference to it, is not generally considered part of any contract set forth on the

---

[3] Rhen Marshall, Inc. v. Purolator Filter Div., p. 153.

form or letterhead. It is not a part of the contract because it has not been communicated by the offeror to the offeree.

9. Auctions

Auctions are either with reserve or without reserve. An auction is considered to be "with reserve" unless it is specifically announced to be "without reserve." In a "with reserve" auction, the bidders are the offerors, and the acceptance occurs with the fall of the hammer. Thus, the auctioneer may withdraw the property at any time, and the owner or his agents may bid. In a "without reserve" auction, the auctioneer makes the offer, and each bid is an acceptance subject to there being no higher bid. In either auction, the bidder can withdraw the bid freely before the fall of the hammer.

The Code has a separate section that covers sales of goods by auction [2-328]. In an auction sale, the sale is completed when the auctioneer strikes his hammer. At the point when the hammer falls, the person making the highest bid is entitled to the article and must pay for it. It sometimes happens that while the auctioneer's hammer is falling, but before it has struck the table, another bid is made. In this case, the Code provides that the auctioneer can reopen the bidding or declare the goods sold under the bid on which the hammer was falling [2-328(2)].

One who is selling goods at auction cannot bid at his own sale unless notice has been given that he retains this privilege. The Code provides that if the auctioneer knowingly receives a bid that has been made by the seller or on his behalf, and no notice has been given that the seller has the privilege of bidding at his own sale, the buyer has a choice of remedies. If the seller's wrongful bidding has bid up the price, the bidder can refuse to be bound by the sale. If he wishes to do so, he could demand that the goods be sold to him at the price of the last good-faith bid prior to the completion of the sale [2-328(4)]. The Code provisions are designed to protect people who bid at auction sales and to prevent them from being defrauded.

10. Introduction

DURATION OF OFFERS

Assuming that an offer has been made, you must consider the next legal issue, the duration of that offer; that is, how long does the offeree have the power to accept? The offeree has the power to accept until the offer is terminated. An offer that has been properly communicated continues in existence until it (1) lapses or expires, (2) is terminated by operation of law (illegality and incapacity), (3) is rejected by the offeree, or (4) is revoked (directly or indirectly) by the offeror.

11. Lapse of Time

An offer does not remain open indefinitely, even though the offeror fails to revoke it. If an offer does not stipulate the period during which it is to continue, it remains open for a reasonable time, a period that a reasonable person might conclude was intended. Whether an offer has lapsed because of the passage of time is usually a question of fact for the jury after it has given proper weight to all related circumstances, one of which is the nature of the property. An offer involving property that is constantly fluctuating in price remains open a relatively short time in comparison with property that has a more stable price. Other facts that should be considered are the circumstances under which the offer is made, the relation of the parties, and the means used in transmitting the offer. An offer made orally usually lapses when the conversation ends, unless the offeror clearly indicates that the proposal may be considered further by the offeree.

If the offer stipulates the period during which it may be accepted, it automatically lapses at the end of that period. How do you measure the time period? Assume the offer is in a letter that states it will remain open for 5 days. The letter is dated May 1 and received by the offeree on May 7. One might argue that the offer lapsed on May 6, since the letter is dated May 1. Since an offer is not an offer until communicated, however, and if there is no contrary intent, the time will be measured from the time the offeree *receives* the offer. The rationale is to protect the offeree unless he has some reason to know that time should be measured from some earlier date.

12. Termination of an Offer by Operation of Law

Several events will terminate an offer as a matter of law. Notice of their occurrence need not be given or communicated to the offeree or the offeror, as the offer ends instantaneously upon the occurrence of the event. Such events include the death or adjudicated insanity of either party or the destruction of the subject matter of the offer or illegality that occurs after the offer is made. The occurrence of any one of these events eliminates one of the requisites for a contract, thereby destroying the effectiveness of the acceptance of the offer to create a contract. Thus, if the offeror dies before the acceptance is effective, the offer is terminated and there is no contract. The offer terminates at the moment of death or on the date a legal guardian is appointed. Another event is the enactment of a statute or ordinance making illegal the performance of any contract that would result from acceptance of the offer. Supervening illegality of the proposed contract legally terminates the offer.

There is a distinct difference between the termination of an offer and the termination of a contract. It should be emphasized that death, for example, terminates an offer but not a contract. As a general rule, death of either party does not excuse performance of contracts, although it would excuse performance in contracts for personal service. To illustrate the effect of the death of one of the parties to an offer, assume that Jeffrey offers to sell to Clint a certain electronic computer for $15,000. After Jeffrey's death, Clint, without knowledge of the death, mails his acceptance to Jeffrey and immediately enters into a contract to resell the computer to West for $17,000. Jeffrey's estate has no duty to deliver the machine, even though West may have a claim against Clint for breach of contract if the latter failed to deliver the computer. Had Clint's acceptance become effective before Jeffrey's death, the executor of the estate would have been obligated to deliver the computer.

13. Rejection by Offeree

An offeree's power of acceptance terminates if the offeree rejects the offer. An offeree who rejects cannot later bind the offeror by tendering an acceptance. A rejection terminates an offer even though the offeror had promised to keep the offer open for a specified time. Rejection of an offer is not effective in terminating the offer until the rejection has been received by the offeror or his authorized agent. Thus, a rejection that has been sent may be withdrawn at any time prior to delivery to the offeror. Such action does not bar a later acceptance.

It is often difficult to determine whether a communication by an offeree is a rejection or merely an expression of a desire to negotiate further on the terms of the agreement. Thus, it is possible to suggest a counterproposal in a way that clearly indicates the offer is still being considered and is not being rejected. The offeree wishes a reaction from the offeror to the suggested changes. Also, the offeree may, in his acceptance, set forth terms not included in the offer, but only those that would be implied as normally included in such an agreement. The inclusion of such terms will not prevent formation of a contract.

A request for further information by an offeree who indicates that he still has the offer under consideration will not constitute a rejection of the offer. As discussed later under the law of acceptances, a counteroffer usually is a rejection that terminates an offer.

14. Actual Revocation by Offeror

If the offer is not irrevocable, an offeror may revoke at any time before it is accepted by the offeree. As stated, the offeror may revoke even though he has promised to hold the offer open for a definite period. So long as it remains a revocable offer, it can be legally withdrawn, although morally or ethically such action may be unjustified. However, the next section discusses the three ways the law may recognize that an offer is irrevocable.

The offeror, possessing the power to revoke, can terminate the offer by communicating the revocation to the offeree. This communication can be direct or indirect. A directly communicated revocation to the offeree is effective only when received. Merely sending a notice of revocation is insufficient. It must be received by the offeree or reach a destination where it would be available to him. Nonetheless, the communication of the revocation is effective when actually received, regardless of how or by whom it is conveyed. Just as the offer is not an offer until received, a revocation is not effective until receipt.

Although most revocations are made directly, the law recognizes that the revocation can occur indirectly through some third party not associated with the offeror. Indirect revocation occurs when the offeree secures reliable information from a third party that the offeror has engaged in conduct that indicates to a reasonable person that the offeror no longer wishes to make the offer. An effective indirect revocation requires that (1) the third party give correct information, (2) the offeror's conduct would indicate to a reasonable person that the offeror no longer recognizes the offer, and (3) the third party is a reliable source.

15. Option Contract

The offeror, as master of the offer, retains the power to revoke his offer. Although most offers are thus revocable, the law acknowledges that an offer may be irrevocable. The power to revoke may be lost by: (1) contract (2) legislation, and (3) conduct of the offeree. All three ways are based on option contract principles.

The offeror can sell away his power to revoke. Recall that an offeror can revoke the offer even if he says he will not or that the offer will remain open for a specified time. For a consideration, however, the offeror can sell away his power to revoke, thereby creating an option contract.

An *option* is a contract based upon some consideration, whereby the offeror binds himself to hold an offer open for an agreed period of time. It gives the holder of the option the right to accept the continuing offer within the specified time. Quite often the offeree pays or promises to pay money in order to have the option (the continuing offer) remain open. The consideration need not be money. It may be anything that the law recognizes as legal value. The significant fact is that the offer has been transformed into a contract of option because of consideration supplied by the offeree. The offer becomes irrevocable for the period of the option. Of course, the offeree in an option contract is under no obligation to accept the offer; he simply has the right to do so.

Frequently, an option is part of another contract. A lease may contain a clause that gives to the tenant the right to purchase the property within a given period at a stated price;[4] a sale of merchandise may include a provision that obligates the seller to supply an additional amount at the same price if ordered by the purchaser within a specified time. Such options are enforceable because the initial promise to pay rent serves as consideration for both the lease and the right to buy. The original purchase price of goods serves as consideration for the goods purchased and the option to buy additional goods.

16. Legislation: Firm Offers

Several states have statutes that make certain types of offers irrevocable. The most significant statute is found in the Code [Sec. 2-205], which operates to make a merchant's offer irrevocable *without consideration*. A *merchant* is a business person dealing in goods [2-104(1)]. The requisites of this so-called firm offer under the Code are: (1) assurance given in a signed writing that the offer will be held open, (2) offeror is a merchant, and (3) the transaction involves the sale of goods. The offer is then irrevocable for the time stated in the offer (but no longer than 3 months) or for a reasonable time not to exceed 3 months if the offer has no stated time period. If the writing assuring the offer will remain open is on a form supplied by the offeree, it must be separately signed by the offeror. The offeree in a firm offer can rely upon the continuing legal obligation of the offeror and make other

---

[4] Northwestern Bell Telephone Co. v. Cowger, p. 154.

commitments on the strength of it. In effect, the firm offer by a merchant is the equivalent of an option without consideration.

17. Conduct of the Offeree

The third irrevocable offer springs from a situation analogous to an option contract. When the offeree starts to perform or relies on the offer, the law protects the offeree by holding that the offeror has lost the power to revoke. Analytically, the offeree has done something that the law sees as legal value. This legal value buys away the power to revoke, just as actual consideration does in a true option contract. The legal value consists of either part performance in the unilateral contract situation or reliance (substantial change of position) by the offeree.

Suppose Lucy says to Shirley: "I will pay you $50 to sew the letter L on four of my sweaters." When Shirley finishes sewing the Ls (the act requested), that is acceptance. At that moment, a contract springs into existence. It is a unilateral contract with only one duty—to pay $50; however, problems can arise prior to complete performance. After Shirley starts to perform, can Lucy revoke her offer for a unilateral contract? In the early common law, the offer could be revoked anytime prior to *complete* performance. The offeree who had partly performed was relegated to a quasi-contract action for the reasonable value of the services bestowed upon the offeror. Since this action could cause unfair results, modern law favors the proposition that the offeree should be given a reasonable time to perform fully, once she starts to perform. The majority of courts hold that the offer is irrevocable for that reasonable time.

Sometimes it is difficult to decide if an offeree is partly performing or merely preparing to perform. Let's take the classic example. I offer to pay you $100 if you walk across the Brooklyn Bridge. You start to walk and get about halfway across the bridge, and I run up beside you and shout: "I revoke." You respond: "You cannot revoke, because my part performance has made your offer irrevocable, like an option contract." You are legally correct. But decide if any of the following are part performances or merely preparing to perform: (1) You buy a pair of running shoes to use in crossing the bridge. (2) You start on a daily exercise routine to get in shape for the walk. (3) You catch a cab that delivers you to the Brooklyn Bridge. These are only preparatory acts and do not make the offer irrevocable.

Reliance by an offeree on either a bilateral or unilateral offer can create an "option" contract. For example, assume that an offer is made which the offeror should reasonably expect will induce substantial reliance by the offeree and that such reliance happens. In such a case, the offer is binding to the extent necessary to avoid injustice, as if an option contract existed. Note that the reliance must be substantial as well as reasonably foreseeable by the offeror. In some instances, it is foreseeable that the offeree must incur substantial expense, or undertake substantial commitments, or forgo alternatives, to put himself in a position to accept by either a promise or performance. The offeree may have to borrow money, or undertake special training, or refuse other offers before he can accept. In such cases, to avoid injustice the offer is irrevocable, like an option contract.

THE LAW OF ACCEPTANCES

18. Introduction

A contract consists of an offer by one party (offeror) and its acceptance by the person (offeree) to whom it is made. An acceptance is an indication by the offeree of his willingness to be bound by the terms of the offer. Figuratively speaking, an offer hangs like a suspended question. The acceptance must be a positive answer to that question. For example, the offeror says: "I will sell you this article for $200. Will you buy it?" The offeree now has the legal power to accept this offer, and if he does so in proper fashion, a contract will result. A contract therefore results when the offeree (promisee) answers the question in the affirmative.

Acceptance may, if the offer permits, take the form of an act (unilateral offer), a return promise communicated to the offeror (bilateral offer), or the signing and delivery of a written instrument. The last-named method is the most common in transactions of considerable importance and in those that are more formal.

Only the person to whom the offer is made can accept the offer. Offers to the public may be accepted by any member of the public who is aware of the offer. In general, an offeree cannot assign the offer to a third party. For example, if goods are ordered from a firm that has discontinued business, that firm cannot transfer the order to another firm. If the goods are shipped by its successor, the offeror (the purchaser) is under no duty to accept the goods. If he does accept them, knowing that they were shipped by the successor, then by implication he agrees to pay the new concern for the goods at the contract price. If he does not know of the change of ownership when he accepts the goods, he is not liable for the contract price. His only liability is in quasi-contract for the reasonable value of the goods. In the alternative, the purchaser could return them to the seller if he so elected.

Despite the general rule just discussed, option contracts may be transferred by the holder of the option to another person. Such a transfer is called an *assignment*. The reason an option is transferable is that the option is a completed contract, and its offer is not considered personal.

19. Accepting a Bilateral Offer

An offer for a bilateral contract is accepted by the offeree making a promise in response to the promise of the offeror. The offeree's promise is to perform in the manner required by the offer. The promise of the offeree (acceptance) must be communicated to the offeror or his agent and may consist of any conduct on the part of the offeree that clearly shows an intention to be bound by the conditions prescribed in the offer.

The acceptance may take the form of a signature to a written agreement or even a nod of the head or any other indication of a willingness to perform as required by the offer. No formal procedure is generally required. If the offer is made to two or more persons, the acceptance is not complete until each of the parties has indicated acceptance. Until all have responded and accepted, the offeror is at liberty to withdraw the offer.

When it is understood that the agreement will be set forth in a written instrument, the acceptance is effective only when the document has been signed and delivered (unless it was clearly the intention of the parties that the earlier verbal agreement be binding and that the writing act merely as a memorandum or evidence of the oral contract that was already effective and binding upon the parties).

20. Counteroffers under the Mirror-Image Rule

In forming a bilateral contract, an attempted acceptance may have terms new or different from those stated in the offer. Under common law, this variance between the offer and acceptance is the *mirror image* or *matching acceptance* rule. It requires that the acceptance be absolute and unconditional. To be effective, an acceptance must conform exactly to the terms of the offer. *Any* deviation from the terms of the offer and the acceptance will be held to be a counteroffer, which constitutes a rejection terminating the original offer. *Note*: Once a counteroffer is made (that is, the acceptance is not a mirror image of the offer), then the attempted acceptance becomes a *new* offer and the original offer terminates.[5]

It may at times be difficult to decide if the acceptance is a counteroffer or merely a counterinquiry. The original offer does not terminate if the offeree merely suggests or requests new or different terms or makes a counterinquiry. Monty offers to sell one antique cabinet to Brian for $3,500. Brian replies, "Will you take $3,000?" This is only a counterinquiry. Suppose Brian wires, "Please send lowest cash price for cabinet." This is not a counteroffer but only a request for different terms. But in the usual case, Brian would say: "I'll pay only $2,500." This is a counteroffer under the mirror image rule and a rejection.

21. Variance under the Code

The Code rejects the mirror-image rule. Under the Code, a definite expression of acceptance of a written confirmation operates as an acceptance. This is true even though the acceptance states terms additional to, or different from, those offered or agreed upon, unless acceptance is made conditional upon agreement to the additional or different terms [2-207(1)]. This means that the additional or different terms do not prevent the formation of a contract, unless they are expressed in the form of a counterproposal.

Assuming that there is acceptance, what is the status of the additional or different terms? The different terms do not become part of the contract; they are eliminated. Regarding the additional terms, the impact of these terms depends on whether either party to the contract is a merchant. If at least one party is not a merchant, the additional terms become proposals for addition to the contract. Such proposals may be accepted or rejected by the offeror. But if the contract is *between merchants,* the additional terms become part of the contract unless (a) the offer expressly limits acceptance to the terms of the offer; (b) the added terms

---

[5] Benya v. Stevens and Thompson Paper Co., p. 155.

materially alter the offer; or (c) notification of objection to them has already been given or is given within a reasonable time after notice of them is received.

The problem of variance arises in three similar situations: (1) an acceptance states terms additional to, or different from, those offered, (2) a written confirmation of an informal or oral agreement sets forth terms additional to, or different from, those previously agreed upon, and (3) the printed forms used by the parties are in conflict, especially in the "fine print." The Code takes the position that in all three situations "a proposed deal which in commercial understanding has in fact been closed is recognized as a contract" [2-207][6].

22. Silence as Assent

As a general rule, the offeror cannot force the offeree to reply to the offer. In most cases, therefore, mere silence by the offeree does not amount to acceptance, even though the offeror in his offer may have stated that a failure to reply would constitute an acceptance. However, a previous course of dealing between the parties or the receipt of goods by the offeree under certain circumstances could impose a duty on the offeree to speak in order to avoid a contractual relationship. This duty to speak arises when the offeree has led the offeror to believe that silence or inaction is intended as a manifestation of intent to accept and the offeree believes that it is. In other words, silence where a duty exists to communicate either an acceptance or rejection is an acceptance.

Under the Code, a buyer has accepted goods when he fails to make an effective rejection or does any act inconsistent with the seller's ownership. However, failure to reject will not be construed as an acceptance unless the buyer has had a reasonable opportunity to examine the goods.

23. Communication of Acceptances

The offeror is the master of the offer. As such, the offeror has the power to control both the *manner* (promise or performance) and *mode* or *medium* of acceptance (phone, telegram, mail). If the offeror specifically seeks only a promise, then the offeree can accept only by promising (bilateral contract). Likewise, the offeror may authorize only one medium of acceptance, and that is the only medium the offeree can use in communicating the acceptance. *Example*: Tom mails a letter to Ralph stating the terms of a proposed contract. At the end Tom writes: "You can accept this offer only by signing on the dotted line below my signature and returning the contract by express mail." Ralph immediately sends a telegram saying: "I accept your offer." There is no contract because a telegram was not an authorized medium of acceptance.

In the early common law, unless the offeror stated otherwise, the only authorized medium of communication was the medium used by the offeror in communicating the offer. Assuming the offeree uses the authorized medium to accept, this question arises: When does the acceptance take effect? (1) Upon

[6] Rangen, Inc. v. Valley Trout Farms, Inc., p. 156.

receipt by the offeror? Or (2) upon dispatch (such as mailing a letter) by the offeree?

The law generally adopted a rule that protects the offeree by making the acceptance effective at the time it is dispatched. This is known as the *deposited acceptance* or *mailbox rule.* If mail is the authorized medium, the acceptance letter is effective the moment it is mailed, even if the offeror never receives the letter of acceptance. Note that the offeror can change the mailbox rule by simply stating in the offer that the acceptance is not effective until actually received by the offeror, but few offerors so provide. The deposited acceptance rule could be applied harshly, especially when the offeree accepted by a reasonable medium other than the one used by the offeror. In response, modern law recognizes that some offerors may be indifferent to how the offeree accepts. Some cases have held that an offer invites acceptance in any manner and by any medium reasonable under the circumstances. The Code has a provision which adopts this approach [2-206(1)(a)]. In cases under the Code, the offeror can insist on the manner and medium of acceptance. But if the offeror does not exercise his power to limit the manner or mode of acceptance, the offeree may accept in any *reasonable manner* and by any *reasonable medium.* Such acceptances are effective when deposited. What is reasonable depends on all the circumstances surrounding each situation.[7] For example, an offer to sell certain stock is telephoned to you and nothing is said about the medium of acceptance. In a highly speculative market, a quicker medium than mail (telegram, telex, or telephone) may be the *reasonable* medium for acceptance.

24. Accepting a Unilateral Offer

As indicated previously, an offer may be either unilateral or bilateral. Most offers are bilateral; when there is doubt as to whether they are unilateral or bilateral, the courts tend to construe them as bilateral. When an offer is unilateral, the offeror does not desire a *promise* of performance; he insists on substantial completion of the act or forbearance requested. As a general rule, substantial performance of the act requested constitutes an acceptance of a unilateral offer. If the offeree ceases performance short of substantial performance, there is no acceptance and no contract.

A difficult question arises when an offeror seeks to withdraw a unilateral offer during the course of the offeree's attempted performance of the act requested. Today, the generally accepted view is that an offeror of a unilateral offer cannot withdraw during the performance by the offeree. The offeror becomes bound when performance is commenced or tendered, and the offeree has a duty to complete performance. It is part performance by the offeree that legally "buys away" the offeror's power to revoke.

The Code makes some changes in the law of acceptance of unilateral offers. Basically, the Code provides that an order for goods may be accepted either by a shipment of the goods or by a prompt promise to ship the goods [2-206(1)(b)]. To

---

[7] Prince Enterprises, Inc. v. Griffith Oil Co., p. 157.

illustrate: A merchant who desperately needs several items of merchandise mails a letter to a manufacturer asking for immediate shipment of the articles listed. This unilateral offer could be accepted by the act of shipment, even though the offeror (the buyer) had no actual knowledge of the acceptance. The buyer, however, could withdraw her offer at any time before the seller's delivery to the carrier. This revocation could harm a seller who has incurred expense by procuring, assembling, or packing the goods for shipment. Under the Code, such an offer may be treated either as a unilateral offer and accepted by shipment, or it may be treated as a bilateral offer and accepted by a promise to ship. The seller, under the Code, is thus afforded an opportunity to bind the bargain prior to the time of shipment if he wants to do so.

SUMMARY

Objective theory of contracts	1. The formation of a contract requires a bargain in which there is a manifestation of mutual assent.
	2. Manifestation of mutual assent to an exchange requires that each party either make a promise or begin to render a performance.

OFFERS

Definition	1. An offer is a promise to do or refrain from doing some specified thing in the future.
Tests for offer	1. The language used must indicate a promise (present commitment), rather than bargaining language.
	2. The language of an offer must be reasonably certain so that a court can determine if a breach has occurred and fashion an appropriate remedy.
	3. Assuming that an offer has been made, a court can gap-fill reasonable terms like time and place of performance, price, and the like.
	4. An offer *must* contain a subject matter, a quantity term and indicate the parties' intent to be contractually bound.

	5. An offer must sufficiently identify the offeree or the class from whom the offeree may emerge.
Auctions	**1.** Auctions may be with or without reserve.
	2. In auctions with reserve, the fall of the gavel is the acceptance, and all bids may be rejected.
	3. Sellers cannot bid at auctions under the Code unless notice of that fact is given.

DURATION OF OFFERS

Lapse of time	**1.** If a time period for acceptance is stated in the offer, the offer lapses at the end of that time.
	2. If no time period for acceptance is stated, the offer lapses at the end of a reasonable period of time.
Termination of an offer by operation of law	**1.** Death or insanity of either the offeror or offeree terminates an offer from that moment. Communication to the other party is not required.
	2. Supervening illegality terminates an offer.
	3. Destruction of the subject matter of the offer terminates the offer.
Rejection by offeree	**1.** Rejection by the offeree terminates an offer.
	2. Rejection requires words or conduct by the offeree that demonstrate a clear intent not to accept the offer. Inquiries or suggestions about the offer are not rejections.
	3. A rejection is not effective until actually communicated to the offeror or his agent.
	4. A counteroffer is both a rejection of the offer and a new offer.
Revocation by offeror	**1.** Unless the offer is irrevocable, the offer can be revoked at *any time* without liability.
	2. The revocation of an offer must be communicated, directly or indirectly, to be effective.
	3. Indirect revocation occurs when a *reliable* source gives *reliable* information that

would cause a *reasonable* person to think the offer had been revoked.

IRREVOCABLE OFFERS

Option contracts	1. Offerors can always sell their power to revoke, which creates an option contract.
	2. An option contract is based on consideration that binds the offeror to keep the offer open for a stated time period.
	3. Option contracts must be strictly performed by the offeree.
Legislation: Firm offers	1. The UCC makes a merchant's written offer irrevocable without consideration. This is called a firm offer.
	2. The *merchant's* offer to sell *goods* must be in *writing* and state that it will be firm. The firm offer is irrevocable for the time stated or a reasonable time, but in no event beyond 3 months.
Conduct of the offeree	1. Part performance of the contract by the offeree makes the offer for a unilateral contract irrevocable.
	2. Substantial reliance on the offer by the offeree that is foreseeable by the offeror makes the offer irrevocable, like an option contract.

LAW OF ACCEPTANCES

Introduction	1. Acceptance of an offer is a manifestation of assent to the proffered terms made by the offeree in a manner required or invited by the offeror.
	2. Offers cannot be transferred unless they are part of an option contract.
Accepting of a bilateral offer	1. The offeree accepts a bilateral offer by making a promise.
	2. The offeree's promise must be communicated to the offeror.
	3. There are no formal procedures required for this communication. Written or verbal statements or conduct indicating a willingness to be bound may act as acceptance.

Counteroffers under the mirror-image rule	**1.** Under the mirror-image rule at common law, the acceptance must be absolute, unconditional, and conform exactly to the terms of the offer. Otherwise it would be a counteroffer.
Variance under the Code	**1.** Under the Code, a variant acceptance *operates* as an acceptance even if it has terms *additional to* or *different from* the offer.
	2. Different terms do not become part of the contract.
	3. When one party is a nonmerchant, the additional terms are proposals for addition to the contract which may be accepted.
	4. Between merchants, the additional terms become part of the contract unless (*a*) the offer limits acceptance to the terms of the offer, or (*b*) the new terms materially alter the contract, or (*c*) the new terms are rejected by reasonable notice.
Silence as assent	**1.** Silence in the absence of a duty to speak does not amount to an acceptance.
	2. Under the Code, a buyer accepts goods if he fails to make an effective rejection.
Communication of acceptances	**1.** In cases not under the Code, acceptance of an offer for a bilateral contract is effective at the time it is deposited in the offeror's medium of communication.
	2. Under the Code, an acceptance is effective when deposited in the authorized medium, or any other medium reasonable under the circumstances.
	3. Modern cases adopt the Code approach for all contracts.
Accepting unilateral offers	**1.** A unilateral offer is accepted by substantial performance of the act requested.
	2. Under the Code, an order for goods may be treated as either bilateral or unilateral.

CASES

Barnes v. Treece
549 P.2d 1152 (Wash. App. 1976)

The defendant, Vend-A-Win, Inc., is a corporation engaged in the distribution of punchboards. Treece as vice president of the corporation, when speaking before the state gambling commission stated, "I'll pay $100,000 to anyone that finds a crooked punchboard; if they find it, I'll pay it." The audience laughed. The next morning the plaintiff heard a television (news) report of Treece's statement; he also read about it in the newspaper.

A number of years earlier while employed as a bartender, plaintiff had bought two fraudulent punchboards. After locating his two punchboards, the plaintiff contacted the defendant and inquired if the statement about the $100,000 had been made seriously. The defendant informed the plaintiff that it had and asked him to bring the punchboards to the company office. The plaintiff took a board to the office and was given a receipt for it. Both Treece and the company refused to pay the $100,000 even though the board was admittedly fraudulent.

The trial court found a contract existed but only with Treece individually since he lacked authority to bind the corporation.

CALLOW, J. . . . The first issue is whether the statement of Treece was the manifestation of an offer which could be accepted to bind the offeror to performance of the promise. Treece contends that no contract was formed. He maintains that his statement was made in jest and lacks the necessary manifestation of a serious contractual intent.

When expressions are intended as a joke and are understood or would be understood by a reasonable person as being so intended, they cannot be construed as an offer and accepted to form a contract. However, if the jest is not apparent and a reasonable hearer would believe that an offer was being made, then the speaker risks the formation of a contract which was not intended. It is the objective manifestations of the offeror that count and not secret, unexpressed intentions.

If a party's words or acts, judged by a reasonable standard, manifest an intention to agree in regard to the matter in question, that agreement is established, and it is immaterial what may be the real but unexpressed state of the party's mind on the subject.

The trial court found that there was an objective manifestation of mutual assent to form a contract. This was a matter to be evaluated by the trier of fact. The record includes substantial evidence of the required mutual assent to support the finding of the trial court. Although the original statement of Treece drew laughter from the audience, the subsequent statements, conduct, and the circumstances show an intent to lead any hearer to believe the statements were made seriously. There was testimony, though contradicted, that Treece specifically restated the offer over the telephone in response to an inquiry concerning whether the offer was serious. Treece, when given the opportunity to state that an offer was not intended, not only reaffirmed the offer but also asserted that $100,000 had been placed in escrow and directed Barnes to bring the punchboard to Seattle for inspection. The parties met, Barnes was given a receipt for the board, and he was told that the board would be taken to Chicago for inspection. In present day society it is known that gambling generates a great deal of income and that large sums are spent on its advertising and promotion. In that prevailing atmosphere, it was a credible statement that $100,000 would be paid to promote punchboards. The statements of the defendant and the surrounding circumstances reflect an objective manifestation of a contractual intent by Treece and support the finding of the trial court.

The trial court properly categorized Treece's promise of $100,000 as a valid offer for a unilateral contract. The offer made promised that a contract would result upon performance of the act requested. Performance of the act with the intent to accept the offer constituted acceptance. The trial judge entered a specific finding that Barnes performed the requested act of acceptance when he produced a rigged and fraudulent punchboard. We concur with the trial court's holding that a binding unilateral contract was formed between Barnes and Treece

and uphold the conclusions of the trial court in that regard. . . .

Affirmed.

Arrowhead Constr. Co. v. Essex Corp.
662 P.2d 1195 (Kan. 1983)

Arrowhead Construction Company had a contract for the construction of a low-income housing project. Arrowhead wanted to subcontract the rough-framing carpentry work to Crotts, a subcontractor. They discussed the project and considered a "ballpark" figure of $1.25 per square foot for the carpentry work. However, no agreement was made regarding the price to be paid. Crotts began work and later received a written contract from Arrowhead specifying payment at $1.25 per square foot. Crotts refused to sign the contract and told Arrowhead that he would require $1.35. When Crotts finished the carpentry work, he was not paid, so he sued. The trial court awarded Crotts $1.35 per square foot, and Arrowhead appealed.

HERD, J. . . . Arrowhead argues that there was no contract since the parties had not agreed on the essential term of price. Certainly nothing was ever settled regarding the price for Crotts' work. The Restatement (Second) of Contracts §33 (1981), offers some guidance:

> (1) Even though a manifestation of intention is intended to be understood as an offer, it cannot be accepted so as to form a contract unless the terms of the contract are reasonably certain.
> (2) The terms of a contract are reasonably certain if they provide a basis for determining the existence of a breach and for giving an appropriate remedy.

> (3) The fact that one or more terms of a proposed bargain are left open or uncertain may show that a manifestation of intention is not intended to be understood as an offer or as an acceptance.

Comment a to this section makes clear the omission of a single term is not always fatal to the contract:

> [T]he actions of the parties may show conclusively that they have intended to conclude a binding agreement, even though one or more terms are missing or are left to be agreed upon. In such cases courts endeavor, if possible, to attach a sufficiently definite meaning to the bargain.
> An offer which appears to be indefinite may be given precision by usage of trade or by course of dealing between the parties. Terms may be supplied by factual implication, and in recurring situations the law often supplies a term in the absence of agreement to the contrary.

Here the evidence clearly shows the parties intended to be bound by a contract. They discussed the particulars of the project beforehand, Crotts began work, a representative of Arrowhead visited with them at the project site where Crotts informed him of their requested price, and Crotts continued working with no objection from Arrowhead. Further, the reasonableness of the price term supplied by the trial court is clear. At trial Arrowhead's principal, Wayne Hunter, testified "for the amount of work they had to do and under the circumstances $1.35 would have been extremely reasonable."

Judgment for Crotts affirmed.

Rhen Marshall, Inc.
v. Purolator Filter Div.
318 N.W.2d 284 (Neb. 1982)

In the fall of 1977, Rhen received in the mail an advertising brochure from Purolator. The brochure stated that with an order of 100,000 pounds of Purolator products, the customer would receive a 1978 Buick Electra car as a free gift. Rhen ordered

over 100,000 pounds of Purolator oil filters and demanded delivery of the car. Purolator refused to fill the order, and Rhen sued for breach of contract. Purolator denied that there was a contract.

STUART, J. . . . Rhen Marshall's suit was brought on the theory that the circular received by it was an offer and the order placed by it was an acceptance of that offer and that damages resulted from the nonfulfillment of such contract.

This general subject has been covered in text form by Professor Williston as follows:

> Frequently negotiations for a contract are begun between parties by general expressions of willingness to enter into a bargain upon stated terms and yet the natural construction of the words and conduct of the parties is rather that they are inviting offers, or suggesting the terms of a possible future bargain, than making positive offers. Especially is this likely to be true where the words in question are in the form of an advertisement. Thus, if goods are advertised for sale at a certain price, it is not an offer, and no contract is formed by the statement of an intending purchaser that he will take a specified quantity of the goods at that price. The construction is rather favored that such an advertisement is a mere invitation to enter into a bargain rather than an offer. So a published price list is not an offer to sell the goods listed at the published prices. Even where the parties are dealing exclusively with one another by private letters or telegrams, or by oral conversation, the same question may arise; and language that at first sight may seem an offer may be found merely preliminary in its character.

In *Nebraska Seed Co. v. Harsh*, 98 Neb. 89, (1915), the defendant sent a letter to plaintiff in which he stated he had about 1,800 bushels of millet seed, of which he was mailing them a sample. He further stated: "I want $2.25 per cwt. for this seed f.o.b. Lowell." Upon receipt of the letter the plaintiff replied in part: "Sample and letter received. Accept your offer." The defendant refused to deliver and the plaintiff brought suit for such nondelivery. We ruled therein that the letter was not an offer but was an invitation for offers, quoting in part: "If a proposal is nothing more than an invitation to the person to whom it is made to make an offer to the proposer, it is not such an offer as can be turned into an agreement by acceptance. Proposals of this kind, although made to definite persons and not to the public generally, are merely invitations to trade; they go no further than what occurs when one asks another what he will give or take for certain goods. Such inquiries may lead to bargains, but do not make them. They ask for offers which the proposer has a right to accept or reject as he pleases.' ". . .

We hold that the brochure was not an offer by Purolator, but that Rhen Marshall's order was itself an offer which Purolator did not accept. The judgment of the trial court is correct and is

Affirmed.

Northwestern Bell Telephone Co.
v. Cowger
303 N.W.2d 791 (N.D. 1981)

The Cowgers leased certain real property to Northwestern Bell. The lease contained an option under which Northwestern Bell had the exclusive right to buy the property, provided it gave 60 days prior notice of its intention to purchase. Northwestern Bell gave the required 60 days notice, but the Cowgers refused to sell, claiming that Northwestern Bell did not tender the purchase price at the time it gave notice. Northwestern Bell sued for specific performance, which the trial court granted. The Cowgers appealed on the basis that the option had not been properly exercised.

PAULSON, J. . . . The issue is whether or not the option to purchase had been exercised by Northwestern Bell. Paragraph 12 of the lease provides that the lessee (Northwestern Bell) had the exclusive right to purchase the property during the term of the lease, which extended for a period of ten years from the date the building was completed. . . . It is undisputed that Northwestern Bell exercised its option to purchase in the time period specified in the lease and that Northwestern Bell had the exclusive right to purchase the property. The dispute centers upon whether or not Northwestern Bell complied with the terms of the lease regarding the exercise of the option to purchase.

One method by which an offer is rendered irrevocable is by the acceptance of consideration by the offeror in exchange for his promise to keep the offer open. This type of offer is commonly referred to as an option contract. Options must be accepted unequivocally and in accordance with the terms of the option. Under the provisions of paragraph 12 of the lease, Northwestern Bell was required to give sixty days' notice of its intention to purchase the property and Northwestern Bell did send letters to this effect to the Cowgers as early as September 30, 1974. Upon receipt of the notice of election to exercise the option, the Cowgers were to deliver a satisfactory abstract of title to Northwestern Bell. Upon receipt of the abstract and the subsequent examination of title, Northwestern Bell was to deliver the purchase price to the Cowgers and would in turn receive a warranty deed to the property. . . .

Where the exercise of the option to purchase does not provide for payment of the purchase price coincident with the optionee's exercise of the option, the payment of the purchase price is merely an incident of performance of the bilateral contract created by the exercise of the option.

. . .[A]cceptance of an option which results in a contract of purchase and the performance of the contract itself are distinct. . . . [T]he payment of the purchase price for the property was not a condition precedent to the exercise of the option and was an incident of performance of the contract to purchase, as distinct from its formation. The Cowgers were not entitled to reject Northwestern Bell's option to purchase because Northwestern Bell had the exclusive right to purchase the property and they exercised this right as early as September 30, 1974. The Cowgers also failed to comply with the terms of the option because no abstract of title was delivered to Northwestern Bell. Therefore, the district court properly entered judgment in favor of Northwestern Bell.

Affirmed.

Benya v. Stevens and Thompson Paper Co.
468 A.2d 929 (Vt. 1983)

Benya wanted to buy 5,000 acres of timber land from Stevens and Thompson. On September 24, 1979, Benya prepared and sent to Stevens and Thompson a detailed purchase and sales agreement. Stevens and Thompson made a number of additions and modifications concerning the amount of deposit required, cash at closing, and the rate of interest charged. After making these changes, Stevens and Thompson signed the agreement and returned it to Benya. Benya disagreed with these changes and prepared a new purchase and sales agreement which reduced the deposit and postponed the due date of the first payment. In early November 1979 Benya sent the new agreement to Stevens and Thompson, who refused to sign it. Benya then sued Stevens and Thompson for breach of the September 24, 1979, agreement.

BILLINGS, J. . . . The trial court found that the September 24, 1979 purchase and sales agreement constituted a binding contract for the sale of the woodlot between plaintiff and defendant, as both parties had signed it. The court concluded that the changes made by defendant to plaintiff's purchase and sales agreement were minor since the purchase price, closing date and deposit were substantially the same, and therefore did not constitute a counteroffer. The court found that the changes

involving mortgage details were separate and distinct from the offer to purchase and did not, therefore, affect the existence of a contract between the parties.

The law relative to contract formation has long been well settled in Vermont and elsewhere. For an acceptance of an offer to be valid, it must substantially comply with the terms of the offer. An acceptance that modifies or includes new terms is not an acceptance of the original offer; it is a counteroffer by the offeree that must be accepted or rejected by the original offeror. . . .

On the record before us it is clear that the September 24th purchase and sales agreement was an offer from plaintiff to defendant that defendant never accepted. Instead, defendant significantly altered the terms of plaintiff's offer: the amount of the deposit was increased from $5,000 to $10,000; cash at closing was reduced by $5,000; the rate of interest was increased from 9% to 10%; payments were to be made quarterly rather than annually; the type of deed was changed from a warranty to a special warranty deed. These changes were not, as characterized by the trial court, minor and therefore of no effect on plaintiff's offer. Taken together, they constitute defendant's proposal for a new deal, or, more precisely, a counteroffer. Also clear from the record is that plaintiff never accepted, either expressly or otherwise, defendant's counteroffer. After plaintiff considered defendant's counteroffer, the decision was made to draft a third proposal, which in turn altered the deposit and time of payment terms of defendant's counteroffer. Defendant never signed or in any other way expressed its assent to this proposal. Additionally, the conduct of the parties demonstrates their understanding that agreement had not yet been reached.

Reversed.

Rangen, Inc. v. Valley Trout Farms, Inc. 658 P.2d 955 (Idaho 1983)

For several years Valley Trout Farms bought fish food from Rangen. In making its purchases, Valley Trout would send a purchase order to Rangen requesting feed. Rangen would send the feed, together with an invoice which provided for a 1 percent per month late charge. Valley Trout's purchase form did not mention late charges. When Valley Trout got seriously behind in paying its bills, Rangen sued for monies past due and for late charges. The trial court found that the "late charge" language in Rangen's acceptance invoice was an additional term that materially altered the contract and therefore was not part of the contract terms.

McFADDEN, J. . . . Under the provisions of Code section 2-207(1), Rangen's shipments of the food was an acceptance of the purchase orders. The invoice accompanying the shipment from Rangen provided an additional term, beyond that contained in the purchase order, the late charge. Under UCC 2-207(1) the shipment acted as an acceptance because "a definite and seasonable expression of acceptance or a written confirmation which is sent within a reasonable time operates as an acceptance even though it states terms additional to or different from those offered or agreed upon. . . ."

Whether the additional term becomes part of the contract is determined by UCC 2-207(2). There is no question that Rangen and Valley Trout are "merchants" within the meaning of UCC 2-104 and therefore the additional terms become part of the contract unless one of the enumerated exceptions, U C C 207(2)(a), (b) and (c) is present. The trial court decided the issue under subsection (b). There is no language in Valley Trout's purchase orders which indicate that the offers were expressly limited to their terms, therefore subsection (a) is inapplicable. The president of Valley Trout testified that he was aware that a finance charge was being assessed on the account for late payments and yet no written objection was made to these charges until after this action was instituted by Rangen to collect on the account. Valley Trout had adequate notice of the late charge. Consequently, as "between merchants", the additional term will become part of a contract unless "it materially alters the contract" or notification has been given or is given within a reasonable time.

The trial court concluded that this additional term was a material alteration of the contract. However, it is our interpretation that the trial court erred in its application of UCC 207(2)(b) and therefore we reverse the judgment in this regard.

The trial court compared the amount of interest Rangen would have received if the term did not become part of the contract, and the interest Rangen would receive if the term were incorporated. The former figure was $1,400 and the latter amounted to approximately $27,000. The court therefore concluded that this was a "material alteration in anyone's view." This view might seem logical except for comment 5 to 2-207 which provides,

> Examples of clauses which involve no element of unreasonable surprise and which therefore are to be incorporated in the contract unless notice of objection is seasonably given are . . . a *clause providing for interest on overdue invoices or fixing the seller's standard credit terms where they are within the range of trade practice and do not limit any credit bargained for. . . .*" (Emphasis added.)

It is the view of the drafters of the code that this type of term, which adds a finance charge for past due accounts, is not a material alteration under the code. Courts of other jurisdictions which have dealt with this issue are in accord.

Reversed.

Prince Enterprises, Inc. v. Griffith Oil Co. 664 P.2d 877 (Kan.App. 1983)

Griffith Oil Co. leased two lots in Manhattan, Kansas, from Prince Enterprises. The lease began on January 1, 1960, and expired on January 1, 1980. Rent was $442 per month. The lease provided it could be extended for 5 years if Griffith Oil gave notice to Prince 30 days prior to the expiration of the lease (January 1, 1980). Griffith Oil wanted to extend the lease for 5 years but forgot to give the required notice. On January 29, 1980, Griffith sent a letter to Prince stating that Griffith wanted to extend the lease. Griffith enclosed a $442 check in payment of the January rent under the extended lease. Although Prince cashed the check, it replied that Griffith had not extended the lease correctly because Griffith did not give notice 30 days prior to January 1, 1980. Prince then raised the rent to $600 per month. Griffith asserted that Prince had accepted his offer to extend the lease for 5 years.

MEYER, J. . . . The trial court concluded that plaintiff's (Prince) act of depositing the rent check which accompanied defendant's (Griffith) letter constituted an acceptance of the offer contained in that letter. We would note here that in addition to the reference to renewal in its letter, defendant's check also contained the statement, "Jan. 80 Rent Renewal." Plaintiff argues that the cashing of the check was simply a receipt by it of the monthly rental payment to which it was entitled, due to defendant's continued possession of the property. Plaintiff argues that defendant became a tenant from year to year after the expiration of the term of the original lease. It cites cases holding that the mere acceptance of holdover rents does not operate as a renewal of the original lease.

The facts of the instant case are such that plaintiff's act of cashing defendant's check was more than merely accepting a regular monthly payment. Defendant's letter made it clear that defendant intended to renew the lease for five years. There is no indication that plaintiff did anything which would lead defendant to believe that the lease had not in fact been renewed. Thus, plaintiff's act could be construed as an acceptance of defendant's offer; this construction is especially convincing when one considers that plaintiff continued to accept and deposit defendant's checks, in the amount specified in the original lease, for some 23 months after that original lease would otherwise have expired, without ever objecting to or contradicting defendant's expressed intention to renew the lease, contained in its letter of January 30, 1980.

Authority for this proposition is found in *Crouch v. Marrs,* 199 Kan. 387 (1967). In that case it was held that the endorsing and depositing of a check constituted an acceptance of the offer to purchase certain property which accompanied that check. That case stands for the proposition that the acceptance of an offer may be manifested by the performance of an act, such as the exercise of dominion over a thing, as well as by an affirmative answer. We agree with the trial court's conclusion that the conduct of the parties herein constitutes an offer to renew the lease for five years and an acceptance of that offer.

Affirmed.

REVIEW QUESTIONS

1. Identify the terms in column A by matching each with the appropriate statement(s) in column B.

A	B
1. Irrevocable offer by offeree's conduct	**a.** UCC written merchant's offer
2. Offer terminated by operation of law	**b.** Offer without a time limit for acceptance

3. Counteroffer

4. Offer terminated after reasonable time

5. Irrevocable firm offer

6. Rejection

7. Option contract

8. Indirect revocation

c. Reliable person gives reliable information that offer is revoked

d. Part performance or reliance

e. Words or conduct by offeree that reasonably shows offer is not accepted

f. Both a rejection and a new offer

g. Death or insanity of offeror or supervening illegality

h. For consideration offeror sells power to revoke

2. Lucy and Carter were drinking at their favorite watering hole. During their conversation, the subject of Carter's farm came up. Lucy said, "I bet you wouldn't take $100,000 cash for that farm of yours." Carter replied that he would, for cash only. Lucy countered, "I bet you won't put that in writing." Carter did. Later Lucy sued to enforce the contract. Carter's defense is that it was all a joke: "I was as high as a Georgia pine. We were just two doggoned drunks bluffing to see who could talk the biggest and say the most." Is Lucy entitled to specific performance? Explain why or why not.

3. Suppose I invite you over next Saturday to a catfish and hush puppy dinner, and you agree to come. You arrive next Saturday, only to find I've left town. (a) Do you have a contract action against me? (b) Would it make any difference if we signed a contract stating, "We intend to make this a binding obligation"? (c) Would it make any difference if you had to drive 325 miles to my house?

4. Seller and buyer execute a contract for 500 jogging shoes. The contract has all the basic terms, except the parties "agree to agree" on the price per shoe at a later date. (a) Is there a contract? Consult Code 2-305(1). (b) If so, what happens if they later fail to agree? (c) Would your answer change if seller says, "I need at *least* $10 per set of shoes," and buyer accepts? Explain.

5. Seller wires buyer that she will sell between 5,000 and 7,000 tons of steel at $80 per ton. Buyer replies that he agrees to buy 6,000 tons. Is a contract formed? Why or why not?

6. Seller wrote a general circular to 10 buyers asking, "Do you want to buy 240 good 1,000-pound cattle at $8.25? Must be sold by Friday. Phone me at Wichita, Kans." One buyer telegraphs an immediate acceptance for all 240 cattle. Is there a contract? Why or why not?

7. The following ad appeared in your local newspaper: "1 black lapin stole, beautiful, worth $139.50. $1.00. FIRST COME, FIRST SERVED." You are the first to appear at the store and tender $1. Is a contract formed? Why or why not?

8. Jimmy offers to sell Margaret a parcel of land for $5,000, stating that the offer will remain open for 30 days. Margaret replies, "I will pay $4,700 for the parcel," and on Jimmy's declining that, Margaret writes, within the 30-day period, "I accept your offer to sell for $5,000." Is there a contract? Explain.

9. Jimmy makes the same offer to Margaret as that stated in the previous question, and Margaret replies, "Won't you take $4,700?" Jimmy answers "no." Would an acceptance thereafter by Margaret within the 30-day period be effective? Explain.

10. Dairy mails Grocery Store an offer to sell 200 quarts of milk at a stated price. Grocery Store immediately replies, "Please send immediately 200 quarts of milk in one-quart plastic containers." Dairy ignores Grocery Store's reply. If the milk is not sent, has Dairy breached a contract? Explain.

11. Utility offers a promotional allowance to anyone who uses electricity as the primary home-heating method. The allowance is based on complying with Utility's approval standards. HomeBuilder changed his construction plans from oil heating to electricity. After his homes were 90 percent complete, HomeBuilder, to avoid taxes, sold the homes. At the time of sale, HomeBuilder had not completely complied with Utility's approval standards, although the homes were completed in full compliance with the standards. Explain how a contract was formed between HomeBuilder and Utility prior to HomeBuilder's sale of the homes.

12. Elmina mails Mickey an offer. Mickey drafts an acceptance but then decides not to accept. Later, Mickey accidentally mails the letter of acceptance together with other letters. Is there a contract? Would your original answer change if Mickey accidentally dropped his letter on the street and a passerby later saw and mailed the letter? Explain your answers.

13. Contractor agreed to build a building for Brooke within a specified time. Owing to extremely bad weather, contractor asked for a time extension. Brooke sent the request to his architect, but ultimately ignored it. If the building was not completed within the specified time, should the lack of disapproval of the request for an extension be held to be an acceptance of the extension? That is, should silence be deemed an acceptance? Explain.

8 BARGAINED-FOR CONSIDERATION

To have a valid contract, the offer and acceptance (mutual assent) must be validated by bargained-for consideration. Not every agreement (offer and acceptance) will be legally enforced. In the validation process, promises that will be enforced are separated from those that should not be. If an agreement is based on a *bargain,* then the promises are legally enforceable. Something is said to be *bargained for* if it is sought by the promisor in exchange for his promise and is given by the promisee in exchange for that promise.

Consideration, then, is defined as a *bargained-for exchange.* The exchange can be a promise exchanged for a promise, a promise exchanged for an act of performance, or a promise exchanged for a forebearance to act. The doctrine of consideration requires that the promises or performance of *both* parties be legally valid. If mutuality of consideration is not present, there is no contract.

1. Bargain Theory of Consideration

To have consideration, all contracting parties typically will receive a *legal benefit* and incur a *legal detriment.* Legal benefit occurs when a party receives something which he had no prior legal right to receive. Legal detriment is a little more difficult to define. It is either (1) a promise to perform (or act of performance) which one had no prior legal obligation to perform, *or* (2) a promise not to do something (or actually refraining from doing something) that one could legally do and had no prior legal obligation not to do.[1]

---

[1] Dickinson v. Auto Center Mfg. Co. p. 172.

Example: Al promises to sell Mary his car for $2,000. Mary promises to pay Al $2,000 for his car. Al incurs *legal detriment* (sells his car which he had no prior obligation to do) and receives *legal benefit* (payment of $2,000 which he had no prior legal right to obtain). Mary likewise incurs *legal detriment* (must pay $2,000 which she had no prior legal obligation to do) and receives *legal benefit* (legal right, which she did not previously have, to receive Al's car). Since both promises induced one another, a true bargain occurred. Therefore, this bilateral contract is validated by bargained-for consideration.

2. Three Elements of a Bargain

A bargain results when there is causation between the legal detriment and the legal benefit. For a promise to be supported by bargained-for consideration, the following three elements must be present:

1. The promisee must suffer *legal detriment.*
2. The promise in question must *induce* the legal detriment.
3. The legal detriment must *induce* the making of the promise.

Legal detriment is not necessarily synonymous with real detriment or loss. For example, uncle tells niece that if she stops smoking for one month, then uncle will give her $500. If niece refrains from smoking for a month, she incurs legal detriment. Since quitting smoking may actually be a benefit, no real detriment may be present. But because she has a legal right to smoke, she incurs legal detriment by giving up that right.

The promisor must have made the promise at least in part to exchange it for the detriment incurred by the promisee. The detriment must be the price paid for the promise. Sometimes factual situations require one to decide if the detriment was merely a condition for a gift or was bargained for, in that it induced the promise. If the detriment is not a legal benefit to the promisor, it probably did not induce the promise. For example, suppose that you say to a tramp: "If you go around the corner to the clothing store, you may purchase an overcoat on my credit." It is a detriment to the tramp to make the walk, but the walk is not consideration, because (on a reasonable construction) the walk was not requested as the price to be paid for the promise. It was merely a condition for a gratuitous promise. On the other hand, assume that Dotty writes to her sister-in-law: "If you will come down and take care of me, I promise you a place to raise your family." If the sister-in-law moves down to live with Dotty, then the sister-in-law has incurred legal detriment, which is a legal benefit to Dotty. The sister-in-law's move was thus bargained for as a trade for Dotty's promise.

3. Adequacy of Consideration

Historically, it has not been a function of law to make value judgments or economic judgments concerning contracts voluntarily entered into by the parties. As a general rule, courts have not attempted to weigh the consideration received by each party to determine if it is fair in the light of that which the other party gave. It has been sufficient in law if a party received something of legal value for which he bargained. The law is concerned only with the existence of consideration, not with its value. It does not inquire into the question of whether the bargain was a good one or bad one for either party. In the absence of fraud, oppression, undue influence, illegality, or statutory limitation, parties have been free to make any contract they please. The fact that it is onerous or burdensome for one or the other has been immaterial.

Today, this philosophy is changed. The Code provides that contracts which are so one-sided as to be unconscionable may be unenforceable [2-302]. Courts as well as legislative bodies have attempted to protect consumers by changing the historical view of consideration. These matters will be discussed further in subsequent chapters dealing with consumer protection and illegal contracts.

4. Recitals of Consideration

Many written contracts have a provision reciting that there is consideration. The contract may state "For, and in consideration of, the mutual promises exchanged, the parties agree as follows." If the recital takes this form, "For, and in consideration of, $1 in hand paid," an issue may be raised related to the presence of consideration. Nominal consideration will generally validate a promise especially if it is paid. However, *sham* consideration will not. The recital of $1, even if it is paid, may be a sham (pretense). A *sham* is a recital of fact contrary to fact. The recital of consideration may be a sham—not because $1 is economically inadequate—but because it is not a material inducing factor. Although consideration does not have to be the sole inducement, it must be one inducement to making a promise. If out of friendship I sell you my valuable horse for $30, my promise is supported by consideration. Your detriment (paying $30) need not be the sole inducement, but it must at least be some inducement to my promise to sell. This requirement establishes the bargain.

There is an exception for option contracts, because the business community customarily expects them to be valid. Consequently, the law does accept a recital of $1 if there is a signed writing in a business context involving either an option contract or a guarantee of credit. An exception also exists in many states regarding recitals of consideration in *deeds* conveying real estate.

MUTUALITY OF OBLIGATION

5. Introduction

This doctrine of mutuality of consideration applies only to bilateral contracts. In a bilateral contract, each party must be bound, or neither party is bound. The problem of mutuality arises when one party tries to show that a promise is defective in that it does not promise anything. Since it is defective, it cannot provide consideration to support the other promise. When a promise is not supported by consideration, one party is not legally bound. Thus, since one party is not bound, no one is contractually bound. One party tries to prove that a promise is invalid because it fails under one of the following:

- The promise is *illusory* (sections 6–7).
- The promisor is already bound (*preexisting duty*) to do what he now promises to do (sections 8–12).

• The promise is to forbear from suing, but the promisor has an *invalid claim*—that is no legal right to sue (section 13).

The sections that follow discuss these special problems of mutuality of obligation.

6. Illusory Promises

An illusory promise is not a promise at all. What purports to be a promise is not one because the promisor need not perform it. There must be some restriction on the promisor's ability to avoid the promise; otherwise, the promise cannot be construed as providing consideration. Courts require that there be a *possibility* that the promisor will incure legal detriment, otherwise the promisor's promise is illusory. In a typical illusory promise, the promisor's promise is conditional. The first step is to analyze the nature of the condition and determine if the condition is based on something beyond the promisor's control or within his control.

When the promise is conditioned on a fortuitous event (something beyond either party's control), the promise is not illusory. *Example*: I promise to buy your car for $2,500 if it rains tomorrow or if I am hired by the TNT Corporation or if the Atlanta Braves win the next World Series. Since it is possible that it will rain or that I will get the job or Atlanta may win, there is a possibility that I will have to buy your car (legal detriment).

If the condition is within the control of the promisor, then the promise may be illusory.[2] Example: "If I decide to buy a car, I'll buy yours" or "I'll buy your car if I am fully satisfied with its performance" or "I'll buy your car, but I can cancel at anytime." Since the condition in each example is within the promisor's control, the promise is illusory. Many promises are partially within the control of one party or the other. Such promises are not illusory if there are duties implied on the promisor or the condition is met.

If the condition is one of personal satisfaction, for instance, courts will usually restrict the promisor's free will by imposing a promise that any dissatisfaction must be in good faith. Thus, a promise to buy goods if satisfied is not illusory, since the promisor cannot refuse the goods unless actually dissatisfied. Another example is the implied promise to use best efforts regarding the condition. If I promise to buy your car only if I get a bank loan, courts will imply that I promised to use reasonable diligence to get a loan. I must take affirmative action (detriment) to attempt to satisfy the condition.

7. Requirement and Output Contracts

Requirement contracts ("I'll buy all the widgits I need from you this year") and output contracts ("I'll sell you all the widgits I manufacture") are not illusory. Courts find them enforceable because the seller of output or buyer of requirements has incurred legal detriment in that he has given up the right to sell to, or buy from, others. The Code explicitly enforces these contracts with a rule against unreasonably disproportionate quantities [2-306]. Both parties must act in good

---

[2] De Los Santos v. Great Western Sugar Co., p. 173.

faith in their outputs or requirements. Moreover, the fact that a party to either contract might go out of business does not make the contract illusory. The Code provides protection by requiring "that no quantity unreasonably disproportionate to any stated estimate or in the absence of a stated estimate to any normal or otherwise comparable prior output or requirements may be tendered or demanded" [2-306](1)]. Therefore, the promisor must conduct his business in good faith and pursuant to commercially reasonable standards, so that his output or requirements will approximate a reasonably foreseeable figure.

8. Preexisting Duty

The preexisting duty rule is a second way in which a party may claim no mutuality of obligation. When one promises to do what he is already legally obligated to do or promises to refrain from what he legally cannot do, then the promisor incurs no legal detriment. Therefore, it is traditionally stated that a promise to perform or the performance of an existing duty is not consideration. The preexisting duty may be either a duty imposed by law or a contractual duty.[3]

The problem of preexisting obligations has arisen in various circumstances. It is possible to categorize these cases under three headings: (1) modification of non-Code contracts, (2) modification of Code contracts, and (3) discharge of debts.

9. Modification of Non-Code Contracts

Since an agreement to do that which one is already obliged to do does not constitute consideration, a subsequent agreement modifying an existing contract must be supported by new consideration independent of the consideration contained in the original agreement. Assume that one party to a contract refuses to continue performance unless and until the terms of the contract are modified. To ensure performance, the other party may assent to the demands and agree to terms that are more burdensome than those provided in the agreement. He may agree to pay more or accept less, but as a general rule the new promise is not supported by consideration. An employee may seek more money for the work he is already contractually bound to do, or a contractor may want more pay for the same work and materials specified in the original contract. In either case, the employee and contractor do not incur legal detriment to support the promise to modify.

Although some modifications are in bad faith or even extortionate, many are in good faith and should be validated. Assuming good-faith dealings, courts will find exceptions to the preexisting duty rule by using any of these rationales: (1) new or different duties, (2) unforeseeable difficulties, and (3) rescission.

If the promisor agrees to assume a new duty, give something in addition, or vary the preexisting duty (e.g., accelerating performance) the promise supplies consideration to support the promised modification. Usually an owner who promises a contractor an additional sum to complete a job under contract is not legally bound to pay the additional sum. If, however, the promisee (contractor)

---

[3] Slattery v. Wells Fargo Armored Service Corp., p. 174.

agrees to do anything other than, or different from, that which the original contract required, consideration is provided. The contractor who agrees to complete his work at an earlier date or in a different manner may recover on a promise by the owner to pay an additional amount.

The parties to a contract often make provisions for contingencies that may arise during the course of the performance of the contract. Wisely, they recognize that problems may arise and make performance more difficult. Frequently, however, they do not provide for contingencies, or they do not encompass all the difficulties that may render performance by either party more burdensome than anticipated. In the absence of an appropriate contract clause, two questions are raised when unanticipated difficulties arise during the course of performance: (1) Will the party whose performance is rendered more difficult be required to complete performance without any adjustment in compensation? (2) Will a promise to pay an additional sum because of the difficulty be enforceable?

Excuses for breach of contract are discussed in chapter 12. For purposes of this discussion, it must be recognized that additional hardship is not an excuse for breach of contract as a general rule. Thus, the answer to the first question is usually "yes." Difficulties do not excuse performance.

The second question assumes that a promisor, although not required to do so, has promised to pay an additional sum because of the difficulty. Courts hold that where a truly unforeseen difficulty arises, and because of it a promise to pay an additional sum is made, the promise is legally valid and will be enforced.[4]

Unforeseen difficulties are those that seldom occur and are extraordinary in nature. Price changes, strikes, inclement weather, and shortage of material occur frequently and are not considered unforeseen. Thus, it may be that a person who has contracted to build a building finds that the cost of materials has risen since he entered the contract, or he may be faced with a carpenters' strike. Nevertheless, he must perform at the original price unless he has made provisions in the contract that some relief shall be given when such things occur.

If the contract is rescinded, there is no longer a preexisting duty problem. The parties are now free to make a new contract on whatever terms they desire. Note that there are three contracts involved: (1) the original contract, (2) the rescission contract, and (3) the new contract. Further, note that rescission is generally not presumed, so the facts must show an actual rescission, such as tearing up the original contract.

10. Modification of Code Contracts

The Code has made substantial inroads into the validation element of a contract, especially regarding alteration or modification of contracts by not requiring consideration to support the changes. Under the Code, parties to a binding contract for the sale of goods may change the terms; and if the change is mutually agreeable, no consideration is required to make it binding [2-209(1)]. This means that if a buyer agrees with the seller to pay more than the contract

---

[4] Angel v. Murray, p. 175.

price for goods purchased, he will be held to the higher price. To illustrate: A car manufacturer entered into a contract with a tire dealer to purchase a certain number of tires at a stated price. Thereafter, the dealer told the manufacturer that because of higher production and labor costs, he would need to be paid $5 more per tire in order to carry on with the contract. If the auto maker agrees to pay the additional sum, his promise to do so will be binding even though there is no consideration present for the new promise.

The Code section that sustains modifications of a contract without any additional consideration could, if not limited in some way, permit a party with a superior bargaining position to take advantage of the other party to a contract. Accordingly, the Code provides that the parties must act in good faith, and the exercise of bad faith in order to escape the duty to perform under the original terms is not permitted. The "extortion" of a modification without a legitimate reason therefore is ineffective, because it violates the good-faith requirement.

To safeguard against false allegations that oral modifications have been made, it is permissible to include in the contract a provision that modifications are not effective unless they are set forth in a signed writing [2-209(2)]. If a consumer enters into such a contract, in addition to signing the contract he must sign the restrictive provision, to assure that he is aware of the limitation. Otherwise, it is not effective. If the restrictive provision is not signed, a consumer is entitled to rely upon oral modifications. The provision is apparently designed to protect the unwary consumer against reliance upon statements made to him that certain provisions of the contract do not apply to him or that others are subject to oral change. He is entitled to be forewarned not to rely upon anything but the printed word, and it is expected that the double signing will bring this message to his attention.

The Code allows necessary and desirable modifications of sales contracts without regard to technicalities that hamper such adjustments under traditional contract law. The safeguards against improper and unfair use of this freedom are found in the requirements of good faith and the "observance of reasonable commercial standards of fair dealing in the trade." There is recognition of the fact that changes and adjustments in sales contracts are daily occurrences and that the parties do not cancel their old contract and execute an entirely new one each time a change or modification is required.

11. Discharge of Liquidated Debts and Claims

As previously noted, if the consideration on each side of an agreement involves money, the consideration must be equal. Because of this rule, a debtor and creditor cannot make an enforceable agreement to have a liquidated debt of a fixed amount discharged upon payment of less than the amount agreed to be owing. In other words, there is no consideration for the agreement to accept less than the full amount owed. In most states the unpaid portion is collectible even though the lesser sum has been paid. If there is no dispute as to the amount owed, a debtor who sends in a check for less than the amount of the indebtedness and marks on the check "paid in full" will still be liable for the balance due.

Payment of a lesser sum is only performance of an existing duty; it cannot serve as consideration for a release of the balance. However, if there is sufficient evidence that the creditor intended a gift of the balance to the debtor, then the creditor may not recover the balance. A paid-in-full receipt given to the debtor by the creditor is usually regarded as evidence (though not conclusive) that a gift was intended. Likewise, where the debt is evidenced by a note, the cancellation and return of the note upon receipt of part payment is evidence that a gift of the balance was intended.

Just as a promise to pay an additional sum for the completion of an existing contract is enforceable if the promisee does something other than, or in addition to, the required performance, a debtor may obtain a discharge of the debt by paying a lesser sum than the amount owing if he gives the creditor something in addition to the money. The settlement at the lower figure will then be binding on the creditor. Since the value of consideration is ordinarily unimportant, the added consideration may take any form. Payment in advance of the due date, payment at a place other than that agreed upon, surrender of the privilege of bankruptcy, and substitution of a secured note for less than the face of the debt have all been found sufficient to discharge a larger amount than that paid. The mere giving of an unsecured note for a lesser sum than the entire debt will not release the debtor of his duty to pay the balance. The note is only a promise to pay; consequently, the promise to pay less than is due will not discharge the debt.

12. Discharge of Unliquidated Debts and Claims

Whereas a liquidated debt involves no question that the debt is due and payable, an unliquidated debt is a disputed debt. The dispute may involve the amount owed, the time or manner of payment, or related matters. An unliquidated debt may be subject to a compromise settlement. For example, when one party has a claim against another party and the amount due is disputed, a compromise settlement at a figure between the amount claimed or demanded and the amount admitted to be owing is binding on the parties. Payment of money that one party claims is not owed is consideration for the other party's loss of the right to litigate the dispute.

It does not matter whether the claim is one arising from a dispute that is contractual in nature, such as one involving damaged merchandise, or is tortious in character, such as one rising from an automobile accident. The compromise figure agreed to by both parties operates as a contract to discharge the claim. This kind of settlement contract is known legally as an *accord and satisfaction.*

An accord and satisfaction is a fully executed contract between a debtor and a creditor to settle a disputed claim. The accord consists of an agreement whereby one of the parties is to do something different by way of performance than that called for by the contract. This accord is satisfied when the substituted performance is completed and accepted by the other party. Both must be established. The cashing of a check marked "paid in full" when it is tendered to settle a *disputed* claim is a typical example of an accord and satisfaction.[5]

---

[5] A. G. King Tree Surgeons v. Deeb, p. 176.

An accord may be either oral or written. For an accord and satisfaction to discharge a claim, the claim must be disputed between the parties. If the creditor is not aware of the dispute, the cashing of a check tendered in the usual course of business with a "full payment" notation will not operate as an accord and satisfaction. An accord, like any other agreement, requires a meeting of the minds. An accord will not be implied from ambiguous language. In other words, the intent to settle the dispute must be clear.

13. Forbearance

Consideration, which usually takes the form of a promise or an action, may take the opposite form: forbearance from acting or a promise to forbear from taking some action. The law also considers the waiver of a right or the forbearance to exercise a right to be sufficient consideration for a contract. The right that is waived or not exercised may be one that exists either at law or in equity. It may be a waiver of a right that one has against someone other than the promisor who bargains for such a waiver.

There are numerous other examples of forbearances that may constitute consideration. Relinquishment of alleged rights in an estate will furnish consideration to support a return promise to pay money. An agreement by the seller of a business not to compete with the person who has bought a business from him is another example of forbearance. Mutual promises to forbear are sufficient to support each other. They are commonly used as a part of a settlement of a dispute.[6] Each party agrees not to sue the other.

Although forbearances generally constitute consideration, a problem can arise when the forbearance is a promise not to bring a lawsuit. Clearly, a promise to forbear from suing is a legal detriment and, if bargained for is valid consideration. The problem arises when the underlying claim is invalid. Arguably, a promise not to sue on an invalid claim really promises nothing, since the promisor has no claim on which to sue. Older cases held that the promise regarding the invalid claim was not legal detriment. Modern courts hold that a promise to surrender or forbear from suing on an invalid claim is consideration, provided two matters are proved: (1) The promisor thought the claim was valid (subjective honesty); and (2) the claim had some reasonable basis in law and in fact (objective test). The general rule now is that surrender of or forbearance to assert an invalid claim is detriment if the claim is asserted in good faith and is not unreasonable.

CONTRACTS VALID WITHOUT CONSIDERATION

14. Promissory Estoppel

When bargained-for consideration is not present, a court may nonetheless validate a promise based on *promissory estoppel*. A good way to view promissory estoppel (sometimes called *detrimental reliance*) is to see it as unbargained-for detriment. When a promisor's promise induces a promisee's detriment, this validation device estops the promisor from denying contractual duties because of a lack of consideration. Promissory estoppel forces the promisor to live up to his promise.

---

[6] Veilleux v. Merrill Lynch Relocation Mgt., p. 177.

The doctrine of promissory estoppel is equitable in nature in that it compensates for harm which is caused by a promise when the harm is reasonably foreseeable by the promisor. Promissory estoppel involves as a promise which the promisor should reasonably expect [foresee] to induce a detrimental change of position by the promisee. There is reliance on the promise and a change of position. The promise is binding if injustice can be avoided only by enforcement of the promise. And the remedy granted may be as limited as justice requires. A classic example demonstrates the main elements of promissory estoppel. Uncle, knowing that nephew is going to college, promises nephew that he will give him $5,000 to buy a car on completion of his degree. Nephew goes to college and borrows $4,000 to buy a car. When nephew has nearly completed his degree, uncle notifies him that he revokes his promise. Promissory estoppel makes the uncle's promise legally binding. First, the uncle should have reasonably expected the nephew to buy a car, since the nephew knows that he will soon receive $5,000. Second, the nephew did in fact rely on the promise by borrowing $4,000 to buy a car. Third, justice under these facts requires the promise to be binding. Finally, the nephew should receive only $4,000 because the remedy should be limited to the change of position, as justice requires.

The doctrine of promissory estoppel is limited in its application and provides only a limited means of enforcing promises that fail to pass the test of consideration. Although the modern tendency is to apply the doctrine to a wide variety of situations, it has been used frequently in the following situations:

1. Bidding on construction projects. The cases hold that a subcontractor's bid is irrevocable if used by the general contractor in submitting his bid for the primary contract.

2. Promised pensions and other employee benefits. Notwithstanding the fact that the employee continues to work (preexisting duty and hence no consideration), courts validate employer promises of benefits by using promissory estoppel.

3. Promises of dealer franchises. The doctrine of promissory estoppel has been used to permit recovery when there has been justifiable reliance upon preliminary negotiations, wherein a franchise was promised.

15. Moral Obligation

A promisor may from time to time make a promise based on his or her individual view of ethics and morality. The promisor feels some moral obligation to make a promise and to perform that promise. As a general rule, such promises are not supported by consideration, and an obligation arising out of ethics and morality alone is not enforceable.[7]

Notwithstanding the general rule illustrated by the preceding case, moral obligation is sometimes used to validate a promise lacking consideration. Moral obligation in such cases may be seen as arising from an unbargained-for benefit. Some benefit previously received by the promisor is said to induce the later promise. The promise then becomes enforceable because of the moral obligation

---

[7] Matter of Estate of Voight, p. 178.

resulting from the benefit previously received. This theory is used to validate a subsequent promise only when the past benefit is a material one. Examples of such benefits conferred: someone rescues and repairs another's boat; medical services are rendered to an unconscious person; a person is injured in saving another's life. Then there is a subsequent promise by the other to pay the person who gave the benefit. These examples illustrate that the *material benefit rule* only applies to circumstances in which a reasonable promisee would expect compensation.

Obligations discharged by law may later be the subject matter of a new promise. Such promises also may be enforceable under the moral obligation theory. For example, a new promise to pay a debt may be enforceable without consideration even though it has been discharged in bankruptcy or barred by a statute of limitations (a statute that cuts off a claim if no suit is brought within a stated time period). Some courts state that the past debt, together with the moral obligation to pay, is sufficient to validate the new promise to pay the debt. There are different rules for debts discharged in bankruptcy and debts barred by a statute of limitations. A court can infer a new promise from part payment of a debt barred by the statute of limitations, but an express written promise is required for debts discharged in bankruptcy. There are some other special rules on reaffirming debts discharged in bankruptcy. These are covered by federal law and discussed later in chapter 35.

16. Firm Offers and Renunciations

As noted in the last chapter, firm offers are irrevocable without consideration. More specifically, under the Code a written offer by a merchant to buy or sell goods is not revocable for lack of consideration during the time for it to remain open (but not to exceed 3 months). If no time is stated, it is irrevocable for a reasonable time, but again not to exceed 3 months.

Either party may voluntarily renounce or waive any right or claim arising out of a breach of contract. Such a renunciation or waiver is valid without consideration, provided it is in writing. A renunciation or waiver is recognized by both the Code and the common law.

SUMMARY

BARGAIN THEORY OF CONSIDERATION

Elements of consideration (bargain requirement)	1. Promisee must suffer legal detriment.
	2. The promise must induce the detriment.
	3. The detriment must induce the promise.
Adequacy of consideration	1. Courts will not normally inquire into the adequacy of consideration.

Recitals of consideration	**2.** Exception: Inadequacy may be evidence of fraud, duress, or undue influence.
	1. Sham consideration: Failure to pay the recited amount renders the contract unenforceable.
	2. Nominal consideration: The recited amount, even if nominal, is sufficient if bargained for.

MUTUALITY OF OBLIGATION

Illusory promises	**1.** A promise is illusory if there is no restriction on a party's freedom of action.
	2. A promise is not illusory if based upon the occurrence of conditions.
Requirements and output contracts	**1.** Requirements and output contracts generally are not illusory and thus are enforceable.
Preexisting duty	**1.** If a promisor is already legally bound to do the thing promised, there is no consideration present to support the promise made.
Modification of non-Code contracts	**1.** In general, non-Code modifications must be supported by consideration.
	2. Non-Code modifications are valid if new duties are assumed, unforeseeable difficulties occur, or a rescission of the original contract occurs.
Modification of Code contracts	**1.** In general, modifications of Code contracts are enforceable even though consideration is lacking.
	2. Modifications of Code contracts are valid if the modifications are made in good faith (i.e., made for a legitimate commercial reason).
Discharge of debts	**1.** The payment of a lesser sum than a liquidated debt or claim cannot serve as consideration for a release of the balance.
	2. A promise to forbear from suing on an unliquidated debt or claim is sufficient consideration, and a binding compromise results.
	3. An accord and satisfaction is one example of how unliquidated debts are discharged.

Forbearance	1. Refraining from doing something that a party has a right to do is called forbearance.
	2. In general, forbearance is consideration to validate another's promise.
	3. A promise not to sue on valid claim is consideration.
	4. A promise not to sue on invalid claim is consideration if promisor in good faith thinks the claim is valid and the claim is reasonable in law and fact.

CONTRACTS VALID WITHOUT CONSIDERATION

Promissory estoppel	1. A promise induces promisee to rely detrimentally on promise.
	2. Elements: (a) Promisor should reasonably expect promisee to rely; (b) promisee relies to his detriment; (c) injustice can be avoided only by enforcing promise; and (d) remedy may be as limited as justice requires.
Moral obligation	1. Moral obligation will validate a subsequent promise when the moral duty was previously a legal duty.
	2. Moral obligation may validate a promise to pay for material benefits previously received.
Firm offers and renunciation	1. Firm offers are irrevocable even though they are not supported by consideration.
	2. A renunciation is a written waiver of a right or claim arising under a contract.
	3. A renunciation is enforceable without supporting consideration if it is in writing.

CASES

Dickinson v. Auto Center Mfg. Co.
639 F.2d 250 (Fla. 1981)

Dickinson entered into an oral employment contract on March 27, 1973, with his employer, Auto Center. The agreement in part provided that Dickinson would receive 2,500 shares or 25 percent of the employer's stock for a price of $25,000, to be paid by Dickinson on September 30, 1973. Auto Center also promised to supply Dickinson with the $25,000, but it later refused to make the loan and refused to deliver the stock, which was valued at almost $700,000. When Dickinson sued for breach of contract, the lower court ruled against him because of lack of consideration. It held that he did not obligate himself in any way other than to continue his existing employment with Auto Center or give up anything to benefit the Auto Center in return for its obligation to supply the $25,000 to pay for the stock. Dickinson had requested that the jury be instructed that a promise to do some act or to refrain from some act is sufficient to support a contract. The lower court refused to do so, and Dickinson appealed.

PER CURIAM: . . . It is clear that in Florida the primary element of consideration essential to formation of a contract is satisfied when any act of a plaintiff from which a defendant derives benefit, or by any labor, detriment, or inconvenience sustained by a plaintiff at either defendant's express or implied consent is present. Moreover, the detriment which may be found to constitute adequate consideration for a promise need not be an actual loss to the promisor and may be based on either the express or implied consent of the promisee.

The Florida Courts' applications of these principles have been broad and have often been utilized to interpret employment contracts. Indeed, particularly where employment was a continuing contract terminable at the will of either the employer or employee, the Florida Courts have held continued employment constitutes adequate consideration to support a contract.

Inasmuch as Dickinson's employment was a continuing contract terminable at the will of either Auto Center or himself, his continued employment and continued guaranties for the financing of Auto Center could, if credited, constitute sufficient consideration for the promise of Auto Center to issue stock to him. . . .

Reversed.

De Los Santos v. Great Western Sugar Co.
348 N.W.2d 842 (Neb. 1984)

CAMBRIDGE, J. This is an appeal by the plaintiff of a summary judgment entered by the trial court in favor of the defendant in an action for breach of contract. . . .

This appeal centers around the following provision contained in the "Hauling Contract" executed by the plaintiff and the defendant in October 1980:

> The Contractor [i.e., plaintiff] shall transport in the Contractor's trucks *such tonnage of beets as may be loaded by the Company* [i.e., defendant] from piles at the beet receiving stations of the Company, and unload said beets at such factory or factories as may be designated by the Company. The term of this contract shall be from October 1, 1980, until February 15, 1981.

(Emphasis supplied.) The plaintiff, as an independent contractor, was obligated under the "Hauling Contract" to furnish certain insurance, suitable trucks and equipment, and all necessary labor, maintenance, fuel, and licenses required for his operations thereunder, and the compensation which he was to receive for his services was based solely upon the amount of beets which he transported, the rate per ton varying with the length of the haul.

It is undisputed that upon executing the hauling contract the plaintiff knew that the defendant had executed identical such contracts with other independent truckers who would also be hauling the defendant's beets and that the plaintiff would therefore transport on his trucks only "such tonnage of beets as may be loaded by" the defendant upon the plaintiff's trucks, not all of the beets "as may be loaded by" the defendant from piles at the defendant's beet receiving stations. The plaintiff had been transporting beets under the contract for approximately 2 months when, in early December 1980, the defendant informed the plaintiff that his services would no longer be needed. The plaintiff does not claim that he was entitled to transport all of the beets, but he does contend that he was entitled to continue to haul until all of the beets had been transported to the factory, that the defendant did not allow him to do so, and that the defendant thereby wrongfully terminated the hauling contract, causing the plaintiff loss of profits, forced sale of his trucks at a loss, and other damages to be proved on trial. In his petition the plaintiff predicated his action against the defendant upon the hauling contract. The defendant in its amended answer thereto alleged that the defendant was not obligated under the contract to allow the plaintiff to haul any particular amount of tonnage and that its determination that it would no longer require the plaintiff's services was a determination which was within the defendant's discretion under the terms of the contract. . . . The plaintiff was paid in full for all beets which were in fact hauled by him, and there is no issue in this case in that regard.

Considering the words contained therein together with the aforesaid undisputed facts known to both the plaintiff and the defendant when they executed the hauling contract, it is clear that neither the plaintiff nor the defendant intended to or did, either in fact or law, promise to transport a specific quantity of beets or promise to transport beets during a specific period of time. The term of the contract set forth therein, i.e., October 1, 1980, until February 15, 1981, did not constitute a promise, but merely established the period of time during which the promises which were contained in the contract would be in effect. Although the plaintiff made a number of promises in the hauling contract, all centered around the plaintiff's promise to transport beets as loaded by the defendant on the plaintiff's trucks during the period of October 1, 1980, through February 15, 1981. The defendant made no promises at all other than the promise to pay for the transportation of those beets which were in fact loaded by the defendant onto the trucks of the plaintiff during that period. An agreement which depends upon the wish, will, or pleasure of one of the parties is unenforceable. . . .

Where a promisor agrees to purchase services from the promisee on a per unit basis, but the agreement specifies no quantity and the parties did not intend that the promisor should take all of his needs from the promisee, there is no enforceable agreement, and the promisor is not obligated to accept any services from the promisee and may terminate the relationship at any time without liability other than to pay for the services accepted. The fact that the promisor has accepted services from the promisee in the past under such an agreement does not furnish the consideration necessary to require the promisor to accept such services in the future under the agreement. Nor does the specification in such an agreement of the period of time during which it will be operative impose an obligation that is not already present under the agreement. Applying the foregoing to this case, it is apparent that the right of the defendant to control the amount of beets loaded onto the plaintiff's trucks was in effect a right to terminate the contract at any time, and this rendered the contract as to its unexecuted portions void for want of mutuality. In the absence of a specification of quantity, the defendant had no obligation to use any of the plaintiff's service, and the defendant's decision to cease using those services after a certain point is not actionable. . . .

Affirmed.

Slattery v. Wells Fargo Armored Service Corp.
366 So.2d 157 (Fla. 1979)

Wells Fargo offered a $25,000 reward for information leading to the arrest and conviction of the person or persons who shot a Wells Fargo agent. Slattery, a licensed polygraph operator, is employed by the government to interrogate persons suspected by law enforcement agencies. During a polygraph exam on an unrelated matter, a suspect (on the second day of questioning) admitted to Slattery that he shot and killed the Wells Fargo agent. Slattery furnished the information and sued to recover the $25,000 reward, The court gave summary judgment for Wells Fargo. Slattery appealed.

PER CURIAM: . . . Appellant argues that, but for his expertise in interrogation and the operation of a polygraph, the authorities would not have linked the perpetrator to the crime. Thus, appellant contends, he is entitled to the reward offered by appellee. . . . Initially, it must be kept in mind that a reward is contractual in nature, requiring the acceptance of an offer supported by consideration.

The record, reveals the following facts which do support the entrance of summary judgment. . . . While appellant was an independent contractor, during the polygraph interrogation he was employed by either the office of the State Attorney or the Dade County Public Safety Department and was paid for his services on an hourly rate. Further, while so employed, appellant was under a duty to provide his employers with any and all information ascertained by him through interrogation which might be of aid to the State Attorney or Public Safety Department in their capacity as law enforcement agencies.

We . . . uphold the summary judgment on the ground that appellant was under a pre-existing duty to furnish his employers with all useful information revealed to him through interrogation of the perpetrator. Thus, when appellant "accepted" the offer of reward by furnishing information to the authorities, he was doing no more than he was already bound to do as part of his employment. The performance of a pre-existing duty does not amount to the consideration necessary to support a contract. As such, no contract was formed.

Further, as a corollary to the above and as a matter of public policy, it is our opinion that to allow appellant to recover a reward for the furnishing of information to the authorities, when he was under a duty to furnish such information as part of his employment, would be tantamount to undermining the integrity and the efforts of those involved in law enforcement.

Accordingly, as no genuine issues of material fact were left unresolved, and as it affirmatively appears that appellee was entitled to judgment as a matter of law, the summary final judgment entered in favor of appellee is hereby affirmed.

Affirmed.

Angel v. Murray
322 A.2d 630 (R. I. 1974)

James Maher executed a contract with John Murray, director of finance for the city of Newport, under which Maher promised to collect all the trash in the city for five years for a stated compensation. When the number of required collections increased substantially after three years, the city, via Murray, agreed to pay an additional $10,000 per year. Angel and other interested citizens of Newport objected to the increased payments and sought to recover $20,000 paid over a two-year period. When the trial court ordered Maher to repay $20,000 to the city, he appealed.

ROBERTS, J. . . . We are confronted with the question of whether the additional payments were illegal because they were not supported by consideration.

It is generally held that a modification of a contract is itself a contract, which is unenforceable unless supported by consideration. In *Rose v. Daniels,* 8 R.I. 381 (1866), this court held that an agreement by a debtor with a creditor to discharge a debt for a sum of money less than the amount due is unenforceable because it was not supported by consideration.

Rose is a perfect example of the preexisting duty rule. Under this rule an agreement modifying a contract is not supported by consideration if one of the parties to the agreement does or promises to do something that he is legally obligated to do or refrains or promises to refrain from doing something he is not legally privileged to do.

The primary purpose of the preexisting duty rule is to prevent what has been referred to as the "hold-up game." A classic example of the "hold-up game" is found in *Alaska Packers' Ass'n v. Domenico,* 117 F.99 (9th Cir. 1902). There 21 seamen entered into a written contract with Domenico to sail from San Francisco to Pyramid Harbor, Alaska. They were to work as sailors and fishermen out of Pyramid Harbor during the fishing season of 1900. The contract specified that each man would be paid $50 plus two cents for each red salmon he caught. Subsequent to their arrival at Pyramid Harbor, the men stopped work and demanded an additional $50. They threatened to return to San Francisco if Domenico did not agree to their demand. Since it was impossible for Domenico to find other men, he agreed to pay the men an additional $50. After they returned to San Francisco, Domenico refused to pay the men an additional $50. The court found that the subsequent agreement to pay the men an additional $50 was not supported by consideration because the men had a preexisting duty to work on the ship under the original contract, and thus the subsequent agreement was unenforceable.

Another example of the "hold-up game" is found in the area of construction contracts. Frequently, a contractor will refuse to complete work under an unprofitable contract unless he is awarded additional compensation. The courts have generally held that a subsequent agreement to award additional compensation is unenforceable if the contractor is only performing work which would have been required of him under the original contract.

. . . The modern trend appears to recognize the necessity that courts should enforce agreements

modifying contracts when unexpected or unanticipated difficulties arise during the course of the
performance of a contract, even though there is no
consideration for the modification, as long as the
parties agree voluntarily.

The modern trend away from a rigid application of the preexisting duty rule is reflected by
§89D(a) of the American Law Institute's Restatement Second of the Law of Contracts, which provides: "A promise modifying a duty under a contract not fully performed on either side is binding
(a) if the modification is fair and equitable in view
of circumstances not anticipated by the parties
when the contract was made. . . ." Section 89D(a),
of course, does not compel a modification of an
unprofitable or unfair contract; it only enforces a
modification if the parties voluntarily agree and if
(1) the promise modifying the original contract was
made before the contract was fully performed on
either side, (2) the underlying circumstances which
prompted the modification were unanticipated by
the parties, and (3) the modification is fair and
equitable.

The evidence, which is uncontradicted, reveals
that in June of 1968 Maher requested the city
council to pay him an additional $10,000 for the
year beginning on July 1, 1968, and ending on June
30, 1969. This request was made at a public meeting
of the city council, where Maher explained in detail
his reasons for making the request. Thereafter, the
city council voted to authorize the Mayor to sign an
amendment to the 1964 contract which provided
that Maher would receive an additional $10,000 per
year for the duration of the contract. Under such
circumstances we have no doubt that the city voluntarily agreed to modify the 1964 contract.

Having determined the voluntariness of this
agreement, we turn our attention to the three criteria delineated above. First, the modification was
made in June of 1968 at a time when the five-year
contract which was made in 1964 had not been fully
performed by either party. Second, although the
1964 contract provided that Maher collect all refuse
generated within the city, it appears this contract
was premised on Maher's past experience that the
number of refuse-generating units would increase at
a rate of 20 to 25 per year. Furthermore, the evidence is uncontradicted that the 1967–1968 increase
of 400 units "went beyond any previous expectation." Clearly, the circumstances which prompted
the city council to modify the 1964 contract were
unanticipated. Third, although the evidence does
not indicate what proportion of the total this increase comprised, the evidence does indicate that it
was a "substantial" increase. In light of this, we
cannot say that the council's agreement to pay
Maher the $10,000 increase was not fair and equita-
ble in the circumstances.

Judgment reversed.

A. G. King Tree Surgeons v. Deeb
356 A.2d 87 (N.J. 1976)

DALTON, J. . . . This is a contract action
brought by A. G. King Tree Surgeons for the
contract price of $480, plus tax and interest, for tree
pruning work performed at the home of defendant
George Deeb on or about May 30, 1975.

Plaintiff alleges the work was performed pursuant to an oral contract made by telephone, after
an estimate of $480 had been transmitted orally,
also by phone, to defendant. The work agreed on
and actually performed was, according to plaintiff,
the pruning of 15 trees on defendant's propety.

Defendant states by way of affirmative defense that . . . an accord and satisfaction was
reached before the filing of this lawsuit. . . .

First, it is undisputed that defendant, upon
receipt of the invoice for $504 (representing the
$480 contract price plus $24 tax), protested to
plaintiff by telephone that he had never entered into
a contract for this amount and had only authorized
an estimate from plaintiff, nor did he ever sign a
contract or an acknowledgement of work performed. This is not, therefore, a case of a liquidated
sum which is due and owing but rather a genuine
dispute between the parties as to what liability, if
any, defendant owes to plaintiff for the work performed.

Second, it is undisputed that shortly after this
controversy arose defendant's attorney forwarded
to plaintiff defendant's check in the amount of $100
with a notation typed on the reverse side (above the
space for the indorser's signature) to the effect that
this $100 was in full and final settlement of all
claims of A. G. King against defendant for work

performed in May 1975. Along with the check defendant's attorney sent a letter of transmittal which stated in no uncertain terms that although defendant denied that authorization was ever given to plaintiff to perform work for defendant, nevertheless the $100 check was submitted in good faith in an attempt to amicably settle the claim, and that if plaintiff wished to settle for this amount, he should deposit the check. Plaintiff corporation, through its president A. G. King, did deposit the check but only after he obliterated the notation placed on it by the drawer and substituted in its place a notation that the check was only in partial payment of the amount due. Based on this set of facts defendant argues that an accord and satisfaction was reached between the parties at the time the check was deposited, notwithstanding the fact that the president of plaintiff corporation altered the notation on the reverse side of the check. This court agrees.

The traditional elements of an accord and satisfaction are the following: (1) a dispute as to the amount of money owed; (2) a clear manifestation of intent by the debtor to the creditor that payment is in satisfaction of the disputed amount; (3) acceptance of satisfaction by the creditor.

The president of plaintiff corporation alleges, of course, that there could be no acceptance of any offer of settlement since he deliberately altered the check before depositing it, making it clear that he considered the $100 only a partial payment and not a full settlement of the matter. However, it is clear that plaintiff had no right to alter the check. If the check was unacceptable as a final settlement, plaintiff's remedy was to return the check to defendant and sue for the full amount claimed due. Plaintiff chose rather to alter the check, accept the $100 "in partial payment" and sue for the difference.

In this case, however, the check did not stand alone; it was accompanied by a letter from defendant's attorney which made it clear that (1) there was a genuine dispute between the parties as to what amount of money, if any, was due plaintiff; (2) defendant intended that the $100 check was to be in full satisfaction of the dispute between the parties, and (3) if, and only if, plaintiff agreed to settle the dispute for this amount, the check was to be deposited.

It is the opinion of this court that the check and letter can, and indeed must, be read together as constituting an offer to settle this dispute for $100, and that the depositing of the check constituted the acceptance of this offer. Once the check was deposited by plaintiff, no matter what alterations the corporation's president personally made on its reverse side, an accord and satisfaction was reached. . . .

The letter of transmittal . . . recites the basis of the genuine dispute between the parties and the intent of defendant to have the enclosed payment totally satisfy the dispute, and this satisfies the first two requirements of an accord and satisfaction. The third requirement of an accord and satisfaction is the acceptance of the offer and, in this case, the deposit of the check by plaintiff operated *ipso facto* as such an acceptance. . . .

Judgment for defendant.

Veilleux v. Merrill Lynch Relocation Mgt.
309 S.E.2d 595 (Va. 1983)

Mary Veilleux signed a contract to purchase a house, but before the closing she discovered the house had a leaky basement. She attended the closing but said she would not pay until the seller (Merrill Lynch) promised to repair the basement. When Merrill Lynch promised to repair it, she paid the purchase price. Merrill Lynch then hired someone to repair the basement, but after the work was done, the basement still leaked. Mary hired another company to fix the leak and presented the repair bill to Merrill Lynch, which refused to pay. She sued to collect the repair bill. Merrill Lynch contended that there was no consideration to support its promise to repair the basement.

THOMAS, J. . . . The trial court struck the evidence of an oral promise to repair the basement because it found, as a matter of law, that there was no consideration for the promise. At the time the trial court ruled, it did not have the benefit of our decision in *Pierce* v. *Plogger,* 223 Va. 116, 286 S.E.2d 207 (1982). *Pierce* is on all fours with the present case and controls its disposition.

In *Pierce,* Plogger was a builder-developer.

Pierce signed a contract to purchase one of Plogger's houses. After the contract was signed, but prior to the scheduled closing, Pierce discovered that there was a leak in the basement and that the air conditioning did not work. Pierce notified the realtor who contacted Plogger. Pierce refused to close until after Plogger had executed a written warranty regarding the leaking basement and the air conditioning, and had given a one-year oral warranty covering unknown defects in the entire house.

Plogger fixed the air conditioning and contracted to have the leak fixed. It is not clear from *Pierce* whether the leak was ever fixed. However, Pierce detected a defect in one of the foundation walls of the house. He had that repaired and paid $3,385.00. Plogger refused to reimburse Pierce. Pierce sued. A jury returned a verdict for Plogger on which judgment was entered. Pierce appealed. We reversed and remanded the case.

In disposing of *Pierce,* we addressed the question whether Pierce's forbearance to sue provided adequate consideration for the oral and written warranties. We held it did and wrote as follows:

> The evidence reveals that, before contracting with Plogger, Pierce inspected the basement during a dry period. After signing the contract, but before closing, he discovered a cracked basement wall and a severe leakage. Plogger agreed, but failed, to correct the defects before closing. *On condition that Plogger give the express oral and written warranties, Pierce agreed to close and not pursue his remedy in rescission. Pierce's agreement to forego suit constitutes valuable consideration for the warranties.*

The facts in this appeal do not, in our opinion, differ materially from those in *Pierce.* Veilleux refused to close until she received the oral promise to repair the basement. She did not say the words "I refuse to close until you promise to fix the basement." But her actions establish that refusal. Only after she received the promise did she sign the settlement papers. Prior to that time she made unmistakably clear that because of the leaky basement she did not want the house. . . .

On cross-examination, Merrill Lynch's counsel read from a deposition of Veilleux where she had testified as follows:

> It was my understanding before I signed the settlement papers that the leak problem would be fixed, that the pool would be in A-1 condition, and that I would not have to worry about anything. That Long & Foster would get the work done and that Merrill Lynch would pay the price.

While still on cross-examination, she testified further as follows:

> [I]f I had not been assured that the conditions on that house would have been put in order, I would have not [sic] signed the settlement papers. I would have gone, at that point, to get a lawyer who would protect me. . . .

She could hardly have made her position any clearer. We have no doubt that had she not received the oral promise to repair the basement there would have been no settlement and she would have pursued her legal remedies against Merrill Lynch.

When she settled, she forbore to sue. She gave up a valuable right. *Pierce* establishes that she could have maintained a claim for rescission. *Pierce* also teaches that whether consideration is adequate is a question of law. In light of these authorities and upon our consideration of the facts we hold, as a matter of law, that there was consideration to support Merrill Lynch's promise to repair Veilleux's basement.

Reversed.

Matter of Estate of Voight
624 P.2d 1022 (N.M. 1981)

When Mrs. Voight died, she owed her sons money for certain property sales. Although Mr. Voight had no obligation to pay the money owed by his wife to his stepsons, a few months before his death he signed two notes for $13,500 each to the stepsons. The notes were signed in the State of Illinois. They now seek to enforce these promissory notes against Mr. Voight's estate. The trial court concluded that the notes were signed without any legal consideration and thus were not valid. The stepsons appealed.

LOPEZ, J. . . . After Mrs. Voight's death, the claims could have been made against her estate for any interest in the proceeds of the property sales.

Considering that the debt was Mrs. Voight's alone, the court could properly find that Mr. Voight undertook to pay it out of a moral obligation.

The issue has become whether a moral obligation constitutes legal consideration. The stepsons assert that under Illinois case law, a moral obligation constitutes consideration. . . .

Under Illinois law, a person has no legal obligation to assume the debt of his deceased spouse, and a moral obligation alone is not valid consideration for a promise to pay. This is consistent with the law in most other states. A moral obligation will support a subsequent promise in Illinois only when the moral duty was once a legal one. As Mr. Voight never had a legal duty to pay the [sons] the money his wife owed them, the only consideration for the promissory notes was the moral duty he felt. This is not sufficient to make the notes valid and enforceable in Illinois.

The judgment is affirmed.

REVIEW QUESTIONS

1. Identify the terms in column A by matching each with the appropriate statement(s) in column B.

A

1. Accord and satisfaction
2. Adequacy of consideration
3. Sham consideration
4. Written waiver of contract right
5. Illusory promise
6. Preexisting duty
7. Mutuality of obligation
8. Promissory estoppel
9. Moral obligation
10. Promise not to sue on invalid claim

B

a. Renunciation
b. Validation device (unbargained-for benefit to promisor)
c. No possibility promisor will incur legal detriment
d. Fully executed contract between debtor and creditor to settle disputed claim
e. Promisor is already bound to do matter promised
f. Courts will not inquire into this
g. Failure to pay consideration recited
h. Both parties are bound or nobody is bound
i. Promise valid if good-faith claim that is reasonable in fact and law
j. Validation device (unbargained-for detriment to promisee)

2. Jack, a golf course architect, agrees with Sneed to direct a current construction project for a fixed fee of $5,000. During the course of the project, Jack, without excuse, takes away his plans and refuses to continue, and Sneed promises him an extra fee of $2,000 if Jack will resume work. Is Jack's resumption of work consideration for Sneed's promise of the extra fee? Explain.

3. Libby owned a gold mine in Alaska. She told Duke that if Duke would give her $55, so she could go to Alaska, she would pay Duke $10,000 if the mine produced gold. Sure enough, the mine later produced a half-million dollars in gold. Is Duke entitled to $10,000? Why or why not?

4. Burt pays 25 cents in return for a 30-day option to purchase real estate from Reynold for $100,000. The next day Reynold tries to revoke the option. Can Reynold revoke? Why or why not?

5. Humphrey pays Doug $250 for a 60-day option to buy Doug's farm. Near the end of the option period, Humphrey asks for and gets a 15-day extension. No money was paid for the extension. After the original 60-day period but within the 15-day extension, Doug withdraws the offer. Can Doug legally revoke the offer? Why or why not?

6. Buyer agreed with seller that buyer would buy 1,500,000 gallons of a particular grade of oil. The agreement stated: "Seller may cancel any unshipped portion of this order if for any reason it should discontinue making this grade of oil." Was this a valid agreement? Why or why not?

7. Widgit, a manufacturer of widgits, agreed to supply Midgit all the widgits that Midgit needed in his gidgit business. For several years prior to this agreement, Midgit used between 2,500 to 3,000 Widgit widgits per month. On the sixth month, Midgit ordered 10,000 widgits. Widgit said it would not honor the order. (a) Is this a valid agreement? (b) Is Widgit liable to Midgit for breach of contract? Why or why not?

8. Baillie sold lumber to Kincaid, who agreed to pay $5,000. Later, having financial problems, Kincaid offered to pay 35 percent of the $5,000 in full satisfaction. Kincaid paid the 35 percent in two checks, which Baillie cashed. On the second and last check, Kincaid marked "Final Installment." Can Baillie now legally recover the 65 percent of the original amount due? Why or why not?

9. Burgess made a contract to furnish material and labor for plumbing modifications in Davis's house. A dispute developed over the amount Davis owed Burgess. Davis drafted a check on which he wrote "Payment of account IN FULL." When Burgess received the check, he crossed out what Davis had written, wrote in "Paid on Account," and deposited it. Was there an accord and satisfaction? Explain.

10. Hoffman wanted to acquire a franchise from Red Owl Stores. Red Owl told Hoffman that if he would sell his bakery and buy a certain tract of land, he would be given a franchise. Hoffman did these things, but was not given the promised franchise. Hoffman sued and Red Owl defended on the ground that there is no consideration to support the contract. Who won? Why?

11. Tom employs Leslie to repair a vacant house. By mistake, Leslie repairs the house next door, which belongs to George. George later promises to pay Leslie the value of the repairs. Is George's promise binding? What results if the reasonable value of the repairs is $400 and George promises to pay $600, but later refuses to pay anything? Explain.

9 CONTRACTUAL CAPACITY AND GENUINE ASSENT

In Chapter 6, it was noted that a contract has four elements:

1. Offer and acceptance
2. Consideration
3. Legal capacity
4. Legal purpose

The first two have been explained in the previous two chapters. This chapter explores the third element, and the next chapter considers the fourth. Some contracts are legally required to be evidenced by a writing. The requirement is discussed in Chapter 11. Assuming that an offer, acceptance and consideration are present, the agreement still may not be legally enforceable. This chapter and the two that follow (chapters 10 and 11) consider the policing process whereby courts decide which valid expressions of mutual assent are legally "operative" and which are "inoperative." This process can generally be classified under one of these headings:

1. Avoidance and reformation (this chapter): incapacity, mistake, fraud, misrepresentation, duress, and undue influence
2. Public policy (chapter 10): illegality and unconscionability
3. Form of the agreement (chapter 11): statute of frauds

A valid contract may be rendered inoperative through the equitable remedy of *rescission.* When a party has the right to disaffirm or rescind a contract, that contract is said to be *voidable*. All parties must have the legal capacity to give their consent. Some parties, such as infants, insane persons, and intoxicated persons, do not have the legal capacity to assent to contract terms, and they can undo (rescind) their contracts. Even if a party has the legal ability to assent or consent, that consent may not be *genuine*. Genuine consent is not present when a contracting party promises because of a mistake, fraud, duress, or undue influence. In such cases, the contract is avoidable by rescission because the consent given was not real or genuine.

INCAPACITY TO CONTRACT

1. Types of Incapacity

Incapacity refers to the mental state of a party to a contract. A party lacks capacity to contract if he fails to have a full understanding of his rights and fails to have sufficient mental capacity to understand the nature, purpose and legal effect of the contract. Capacity-to-contract issues generally involve infants, mental incompetents, intoxicated persons, and drug addicts. Incapacity that makes a contract voidable may be permanent or temporary.

A party without mental capacity to contract (if he has not been adjudicated insane) can avoid the contract or defend on lack of mental capacity. The contract is voidable because the incapacitated party may choose to avoid it. No other party may raise the issue. If a person has been judged insane or is totally without understanding, then the contract is void, not merely voidable. If a contract is disaffirmed by an insane person, he must return all the consideration or benefit received, assuming the other party has treated him in good faith. But if the contract is unconscionable or the other party has unfairly overreached, the incapacitated party can rescind by returning whatever he has left of the consideration received.

Minors and insane persons are presumed to lack the requisite capacity to contract. The test of insanity for avoiding a contract is different from the test of insanity for matters involving criminal intent, making a will, commitment to a mental institution, or other purposes. In contract law, the test is whether the party was capable of understanding the nature, purpose, and consequences of his acts at the time of contract formation.[1] A party is incompetent if he is unable to act in a reasonable manner in relation to the transaction, and the other party has reason to know of this condition.

2. Minors' Contracts

The age of majority and capacity to contract has been lowered to 18 in most states; however, the statutory law of each state must be examined to determine the age of majority for contracts.

A person below the age of capacity is called *an infant* or *a minor*. Minors have the right to avoid contracts. The law grants minors this right in order to promote justice and to protect them from their presumed immaturity, lack of judgment and experience, limited will power, and imprudence. An adult deals with

---

[1] Gallagher v. Central Indiana Bank, N.A., p. 194.

a minor at his own peril. A contract between an infant and an adult is voidable only by the infant. The right to disaffirm exists, irrespective of the fairness of the contract and whether or not the adult knew he was dealing with a minor. It even extends to contracts involving two minors.

Legislation in many states has, in a limited way, altered the right of minors to avoid their contracts. Purchase of life insurance or contracts with colleges or universities are binding, and some statutes take away the minor's right to avoid contracts after marriage. A few give the courts the right to approve contracts made by emancipated minors.

3. Avoiding Contracts by Minors

A minor has the right to disaffirm contracts; but until steps are taken to avoid the contract, the minor remains liable. A minor can disaffirm a purely executory contract by directly informing the adult of the disaffirmance or by any conduct that clearly indicates an intent to disaffirm. If the contract has been fully or partially performed, the infant also can avoid it and obtain a return of his consideration. If the infant is in possession of consideration that is passed to him, he must return it to the other party. He cannot disaffirm the contract and at the same time retain the benefits.

The courts of various states are in conflict when an infant cannot return the property in the same condition in which he purchased it. The majority of the states hold that the infant may disaffirm the contract and demand the return of the consideration with which he has parted even though he cannot return the property received.[2] A few courts, however, hold that if the contract is advantageous to the infant and if the adult has been fair in every respect, the contract cannot be disaffirmed unless the infant returns all the consideration received. These courts take into account the depreciation of the property while in the possession of the infant.

The minor may avoid both executed and executory contracts at any time during the minority and for a reasonable period of time after majority. What constitutes a reasonable time depends on the nature of the property involved and the specific circumstances.[3] Many states establish a maximum period, such as one or two years.

4. Ratification

Ratification means "to approve and sanction, to make valid, or to confirm." It applies to the approval of a voidable transaction by one who previously had the right to disaffirm. Applied to contracts entered into by infants, it refers to conduct of a former minor after majority, conduct that indicates approval of, or satisfaction with, a contract. It eliminates the right to disaffirm.

Generally, an executed contract is ratified if the consideration is retained for an unreasonable time after majority. Ratification also results from acceptance of

---

[2] Halbman v. Lemke, p. 194.
[3] Bobby Floars Toyota, Inc. v. Smith, p. 195.

the benefits incidental to ownership, such as rents, dividends, or interest. A sale of the property received or any other act that clearly indicates satisfaction with the bargain made during minority will constitute a ratification. In general, a contract that is fully executory is disaffirmed by continued silence or inaction after the minor reaches legal age. Ratification is not possible until the infant reaches legal age, because prior to that date the contract can always be avoided.

5. Liability for Necessaries

The law recognizes that certain transactions are clearly for the benefit of minors and hence are binding upon them. The term *necessaries* is used to describe the subject matter of such contracts. A minor is not liable in contract for necessaries; the liability is in quasi-contract. The fact that the liability is quasi-contractual has two significant features: (1) the liability is not for the contract price of necessaries furnished, but rather for the reasonable value of the necessaries; (2) there is no liability on executory contracts, but only for necessaries actually furnished.

What are necessaries? In general, the term includes whatever is needed for a minor's subsistence as measured by his age, station in life, and all his surrounding circumstances. Food and lodging, medical services, education, and clothing are the general classifications of *necessaries*. It is often a close question as to whether a particular item or service is to be regarded as a necessary.

6. Third-Party Rights

If an infant sells goods to an adult, the adult obtains only a voidable title to the goods. The infant can disaffirm and recover possession from the adult buyer. At common law, even a good-faith purchaser of property formerly belonging to a minor could not retain the property if the minor elected to rescind. This rule has been changed under the Code. It provides that a person with voidable title has "power to transfer a good title to a good-faith purchaser for value" [2-403]. The common-law rule, however, is still applicable to sales of real property by minors. If Minor sells his farm to Major, who in turn sells the farm to Good-Faith Purchaser, Minor may avoid against Good-Faith Purchaser and regain the farm. You may think that's unfair, but remember that Minor's name appears in the record books and is in the chain of title. Minor must return all remaining consideration to Major. Major, in turn, is liable on the warranty deed to Good-Faith Purchaser for failing to convey clear title.

MISTAKE

7. Introduction

Mistake is some unintended act, omission, or error that arises from ignorance, surprise, imposition, or misplaced confidence. A variety of mistakes may occur in forming a contract. They may involve errors in arithmetic, errors in transmitting the offer or acceptance, errors in drafting the written contract, or errors about existing facts. A court may or may not grant relief because of a mistake. A court may grant relief if the mistake shows that there is no real or genuine assent. The mistake must be a *material* one. The relief granted may be *contract reformation* (court changes contract to correct a mistake) or *contract avoidance* (court allows any party adversely affected by the mistake to avoid his contract). Courts may grant relief when there has been a bilateral mistake of material fact.

8. Bilateral Mistake

The word *bilateral* in the law of mistakes means a mutual mistake. To have a bilateral mistake, all parties must have the same (identical) mistake. Before making a contract, a party usually evaluates the proposed bargain based on various assumptions regarding existing facts. Many of these assumptions are shared by the other party. A bilateral mistake occurs when both parties are mistaken as to the same assumption. Relief is appropriate where a mistake of both parties has a material effect on the agreed exchange of performances. Two examples may help illustrate when relief is appropriate.

1. Al contracts to sell and Bob agrees to buy a tract of land, the value of which has depended primarily on the timber on it. Both Al and Bob believe the timber is on the land, but unknown to them a fire destroyed the timber the day before they contracted. The contract is voidable by Bob, since he is adversely affected by the material bilateral mistake. Note that the court could not reform the contract to correct the mistake.

2. Al contracts to sell and Bob agrees to buy a tract of land for $500,000 which they believe contains 200 acres. In fact, the tract contains 205 acres. The contract is not voidable by either Al or Bob unless additional facts show that the effect on the agreed exchange is material.

In the transaction of business, it is customary in many situations to dispose of property about which the contracting parties willingly admit that all the facts are not known. In such instances, the property is sold without regard to its quality or characteristics. Such agreements may not be rescinded if later the property appears to have characteristics that neither of the parties had reason to suspect or if it otherwise differs from their expectations. Under such conditions, the property forms the subject matter of the agreement, regardless of its nature. If shortly after a farm is sold a valuable deposit of ore is discovered on it, the agreement could not be rescinded by the seller on the grounds of bilateral mistake.

To illustrate and compare cases in which mutual mistake may be a ground for rescission, consider the two problems that follow.

Problem: A woman finds a yellow stone about the size of a bird's egg and thinks it might be a gem. She takes it to a jeweler who honestly states that he is not sure what the stone is. Nonetheless, he offers her $15 for the stone, and she sells it. The stone is later discovered to be an uncut diamond worth $3,000. *Result:* No relief will be granted. There was no mistake of fact, only of value. Both parties bargained with the knowledge that they were consciously ignorant, both thereby assuming the risk that the stone might be worth nothing or might be a valuable gem. *Rule:* When parties are uncertain or consciously ignorant of facts about the thing sold, there is no avoidance for mistake.

Problem: A buyer and seller both mistakenly believed a cow of excellent breeding stock to be sterile. In fact, the cow could breed and was already pregnant. The cow was sold for beef at a price far below what she would otherwise have brought for breeding purposes. *Result*: When the mistake became apparent, the seller wanted to rescind. The parties were not negligent in being mistaken, nor were they consciously ignorant. Both parties thought they knew what they were buying and selling. But what they brought and sold was in fact not what they contemplated buying and selling. A sterile cow is substantially different from a breeding cow. There is as much difference between them as between an ox and a cow. Since there is no good basis to place the risk of the mistake on either party, the contract is voidable for mutual mistake. *Rule*: A mutual mistake regarding the quality of the item sold, a quality that goes to its very essence, is grounds for avoiding a contract.

9. Unilateral Mistake

When only one party is laboring under a mistake, it is said to be a unilateral (one-sided) mistake. Generally, a contract entered into because of some mistake or error by only one party affords no relief to that party. The majority of such mistakes result from carelessness or lack of diligence by the mistaken party and therefore should not affect the rights of the other party.[4]

This general rule is subject to certain exceptions. An offeree who has reason to know of a unilateral mistake is not permitted to "snap up" such an offer and profit thereby. For example, if a mistake in a bid on a contract is clearly apparent to the offeree, it cannot be accepted by the offeree. Sometimes the mistake is discovered prior to the bid opening and the offeror seeks to withdraw the bid. Bids are often accompanied by bid bonds, which have the effect of making them irrevocable. Most courts will allow the bidder to withdraw the bid containing the error (1) if the bidder acted in good faith, (2) if he acted without gross negligence, (3) if he was reasonably prompt in giving notice of the error in the bid to the other party, (4) if the bidder will suffer substantial detriment by forfeiture, and (5) if the other party's status has not greatly changed, and relief from forfeiture will work no substantial hardship on him. Courts clearly scrutinize the facts to make sure that all these requirements are met. It should be difficult for low bidders to claim an error in computation as the basis for escaping from a bid noticeably lower than the competition's. This is the "bad-faith" element of the test stated above.

The only remedy in cases of unilateral mistake apparent to the other party is rescission. Reformation is not an available remedy, since it can be used only to correct the written contract to reflect the actual intentions of both parties. Reformation is available only for a case of mutual mistake.

10. Reformation of Written Contracts

In most instances a written contract is preceded by negotiations between the parties who agree orally upon the terms to be set forth in the final written contract. This is certainly the case when the parties contemplate a written statement signed

---

[4] Home Ins. Co. v. Honaker, p. 196.

by both as necessary to a binding agreement; that is, the oral agreement was not itself to have binding effect. Of course, the parties could intend otherwise. They could regard the oral agreement as binding without any writing, or they could regard the writing as simply a subsequent memorial of their oral agreement.

Suppose the written agreement that is finally executed by the parties contains a mistake. The signed writing does not conform to what the parties agreed to orally. Frequently, the draftsman or typist may make an error that is not discovered prior to the signing of the contract, and the party benefiting from the error seeks to hold the other party to the agreement as written. For such situations, courts of equity provide a remedy known as *reformation*; the court corrects (reforms) the contract.

11. Introduction

A contract is voidable if one party has been induced and injured by reliance on the other's misrepresentation of a material fact. The misrepresentation may be intentional, in which case the law considers the misrepresentation to be *fraudulent*. It may be unintentional, in which case there has been no fraud, but only *innocent misrepresentation*. In both cases, the victim of the misrepresentation may rescind the contract. In fraudulent misrepresentation, the victim is given the choice of the additional remedy of a suit for dollar damages.

While the elements of actionable fraud are stated differently from state to state, the following are those generally required:

1. *Scienter,* or intention to mislead. *Scienter* means knowledge of the falsity, or statements made with such utter recklessness and disregard for the truth that knowledge is inferred.
2. A false representation or the concealment of a material fact.
3. Justifiable reliance on the false statement or concealment.
4. Damages as a consequence of the reliance.

Innocent misrepresentation does not require proof of *scienter* but does require proof of all the other elements of fraud. The absence of *scienter* is the reason that a suit for dollar damages cannot be based on an innocent misrepresentation.

Rescission is permitted only in case the defrauded party acts with reasonable promptness after he learns of the falsity of the representation. Undue delay on his part waives his right to rescind, thus limiting the defrauded party to an action for recovery of damages. A victim of fraud loses his right to rescind if, after having acquired knowledge of the fraud, he indicates an intention to affirm the contract. These principles result from the fact that rescission is an equitable remedy.

12. Scienter

The requirement of intent to mislead is often referred to as *scienter,* a Latin word meaning "knowingly." *Scienter* may be present in circumstances other than the typical false statement made with actual intent to deceive. *Scienter* may be found when there has been a concealment of a material fact. Moreover, a

FRAUD AND MISREPRESEN- TATION

statement that is partially or even literally true may be fraudulent in law if it is made in order to create a substantially false impression. Intention to mislead may also be established by showing that a statement was made with reckless disregard for the truth. An accountant who certifies that financial statements accurately reflect the financial condition of a company may be guilty of fraud if he has no basis for the statement. Perhaps he does not intend to mislead, but his statement is so reckless that the intention is inferred from the lack of actual knowledge.

13. False Representation

To establish fraud, there must be an actual or implied misrepresentation of a fact.[5] The misstatement of fact must be material or significant to the extent that it has a moving influence upon a contracting party, but it need not be the sole inducing cause for entering into the contract.

False statements in matters of opinion, such as the value of property, are not factual and are usually not considered actionable. An intentional misstatement even with regard to value may be fraudulent if the person making the statement has another opinion and knowingly states a false opinion. This concept is sometimes used when the person who is allegedly fraudulent is an expert, such as a physician, or when the parties stand in a fiduciary relationship (a position of trust) to each other. Assume that a doctor, after examining a patient for an insurance company physical, states he is of the opinion that the person has no physical disability. If his actual opinion is that the patient has cancer, the doctor is guilty of fraud. He has misstated a fact (his professional opinion). The same is true if a partner sells property to the firm of which he is a member. His false statement of opinion concerning the value of the property will supply the misstatement-of-fact element. Each partner is a fiduciary toward his other partners and the firm, and he must give honest opinions.

The misstatement may be oral and may in fact be partly true. A half-truth (or partial truth) that has the net effect of misleading may form the basis of fraud, just as if it were entirely false. A partial truth in response to a request for information becomes an untruth whenever it creates a false impression and is designed to do so.

An intentional misrepresentation of existing local or state law affords no basis for rescission, because it is not a statement of fact in the technical sense. Statements of law are traditionally seen as assertions of opinion.

A misrepresentation may be made by conduct as well as by language. Any physical act that attempts to hide vital facts relating to property involved in the contract is, in effect, a misstatement. One who turns back the odometer on a car, fills a motor with heavy grease to keep it from knocking, or paints over an apparent defect asserts an untruth as effectively as if he were speaking. Such conduct, if it misleads the other party, amounts to fraud and makes rescission or an action for damages possible.

---

[5] Sellers v. Looper, p. 197.

14. Silence as Fraud

Historically, the law of contracts has followed *caveat emptor* (let the buyer beware), especially in real estate transactions. The parties to a contract are required to exercise ordinary business sense in their dealings. As a result, the general rule is that silence in the absence of a duty to speak does not constitute fraud.

In at least three situations there is a duty to speak the truth, and failure to do so will constitute actionable fraud. First of all, there is a duty to speak when the parties stand in a fiduciary relationship (the trust that should exist among partners in a partnership, between a director and a corporation, or between an agent and a principal). Because such parties do not deal "at arm's length," there is the duty to speak and to make a full disclosure of all facts.

The second duty is based on justice, equity and fair dealing. This duty typically arises when a material fact is known by one party but not by the other who reasonably could not discover the fact; had the other party known the fact, there would have been no contract. For example, when there is a latent defect in property (such as termites in a home) which could not be reasonably discovered by a buyer, a seller who knows of the defect has a duty to inform the buyer. Failure to do so is fraudulent.[6]

The third duty is that of a person who has misstated an important fact on some previous occasion and is obligated to correct the statement when negotiations are renewed or as soon as he learns about his misstatement. This is not a true exception to the silence rule, because there is in fact a positive misstatement.

The gist of these exceptions is that one of the parties has the erroneous impression that certain things are true, whereas the other party is aware that they are not true and also knows of the misunderstanding. It therefore becomes his duty to disclose the truth. Unless he does so, most courts would hold that fraud exists. This does not mean that a potential seller or buyer has to disclose all the facts about the value of property he is selling or buying. The duty to speak arises only when he knows that the other party to the agreement is harboring a misunderstanding on some vital matter.

15. Justifiable Reliance

Before a false statement can be considered fraudulent, the party to whom it has been made must reasonably believe it to be true and must act on it, to his damage. If he investigates before he acts upon it, and the falsity is revealed, no action can be brought for fraud. The cases are in conflict concerning the need to investigate. Some courts have indicated that if all the information is readily available for ascertaining the truth of the statements, blind reliance upon the misrepresentation is not justified. In such a case, the party is said to be negligent in not taking advantage of the facilities available for confirming the statement.

If a party inspects property or has an opportunity to do so, and if a reasonable investigation would have revealed that the property was not as it had

---

[6] State Dept. of Environ. Protect. v. Ventron, p. 199.

been represented, he cannot be considered misled. On the other hand, some courts deny that there is any need to investigate. They hold that one who has misrepresented facts cannot avoid the legal consequences by saying in effect: "You should not have believed me. You should have checked whether what I told you was true." Generally, reliance is justified when substantial effort or expense is required to determine the actual facts. The standard of justified reliance is not whether a reasonably prudent man would be justified in relying, but whether the particular individual involved had a right to rely. In any case, the issue of whether or not the reliance is justified is for the jury.

16. Injury or Damage

In order to prevail, the party relying upon the misstatement must offer proof of resulting damage. Normally, resulting damage is proved by evidence that the property in question would have been more valuable had the statements been true. Injury results when the party is not in as good a position as he would have been had the statements been true.

In an action for damages for fraud, the plaintiff may seek to recover damages on either of two theories. He may use the "benefit of the bargain" theory and seek the difference between the actual market value of what he received and the value if he had received what was represented. A plaintiff may also use the "out-of-pocket" theory and collect the difference between the actual value of what was received and its purchase price.

Perhaps the most significant aspect of a suit for dollar damages is that the victim of fraud may be entitled to punitive damages in addition to compensatory damages. If the fraudulent representations are made maliciously, willfully, wantonly, or so recklessly that they imply a disregard of social obligations, punitive damages as determined by a jury may be awarded.

OTHER GROUNDS FOR RESCISSION

17. Undue Influence and Duress

Equity allows a party to rescind an agreement that was not entered into voluntarily. The lack of free will may take the form of duress or undue influence. A person who has obtained property under such circumstances should not in good conscience be allowed to keep it. A person may lose his free will because of duress—some threat to his person, his family, or property.[7] The loss may come from the more subtle pressure of undue influence, whereby one person overpowers the will of another by use of moral, social, or domestic force as contrasted with physical or economic force. Cases of undue influence frequently arise in situations involving the elderly. In those cases where free will is lacking, some courts hold that the minds of the parties did not meet.

Under early common law, duress would not be present when a courageous man would have possessed a free will in spite of a threat, but modern courts do not require this standard of courage or firmness as a prerequisite for the equitable remedy. If the wrongful pressure applied in fact affected the individual involved to

---

[7] Aurora Bank v. Hamlin, p. 199.

the extent that the contract was not voluntary, there is duress. If a person has a free choice, there is no duress even though some pressure may have been exerted upon him. A threat of a lawsuit made in good faith is not duress that will allow rescission. Economic pressure may constitute duress if it is wrongful and oppressive.

SUMMARY

INCAPACITY TO CONTRACT

Types of incapacity	1. A party is declared to lack capacity to contract if he cannot understand his rights, the purpose of the agreement, or the legal effect of the contract.
	2. Examples of parties who may be temporarily or permanently incapacitated include minors, mental incompetents, intoxicated persons, and drug addicts.
	3. Contracts made before a person is adjudged incompetent are voidable. Contracts entered into after one of the parties is declared incompetent generally are void.
	4. If the competent party is unaware of the other party's incompetency, the incompetent party must make restitution before the contract is voidable.
Minors' contracts	1. In most states, everyone below the age of 18 is considered to be a minor or an infant.
	2. Minors' contracts generally may be disaffirmed by the minor, but not by the competent adult party.
Avoiding contracts by minors	1. In order to disaffirm, a minor must communicate his desire to avoid contractual liability.
	2. This communication must be made to the competent adult party in writing or by spoken words or by the minor's conduct.
	3. In order to void a contract, the minor must return all the consideration received that he still has.

Ratification	1. Ratification of a contract occurs when the party who was incompetent becomes competent and affirms or approves of the contract.
	2. Ratification can be by a manifestation of intent to be bound or by retaining the consideration for an unreasonable time after majority.
	3. After reaching majority, a minor must disaffirm within a reasonable time or be held to have ratified the contract.
Liability for necessaries	1. If a contract is for "necessaries," the minor is bound to pay for the reasonable value of these items instead of the contract price. (Of course, in many situations, the contract price is a very good indication of the reasonable value of the items involved.)
	2. What is a necessary often must be determined from the facts of each case.
Third-party rights	1. A minor cannot avoid a contract if the personal property involved has been transferred by the competent adult party to a good-faith purchaser for value.
	2. This rule does not apply to real property. In other words, a minor can always rescind a contract involving land even when a third party is involved.

MISTAKE

Bilateral mistake	1. Bilateral mistake occurs when all parties have the identical misconception of a material fact or of the contract terms.
	2. Bilateral mistake negates the element of mutuality of contract and allows either party to rescind or reform the contract.
Unilateral mistake	1. Unilateral mistake is not grounds for rescission unless the other party knew or should have known of the mistake.
Reformation	1. Reformation is not an available remedy for unilateral mistake.

FRAUD AND MISREPRESENTATION

| Elements | 1. *Scienter.* |
| | 2. False material representation. |

Scienter	**3.** Justifiable reliance on the representation.
	4. Injury caused by such reliance.
	1. *Scienter* is the intent to mislead. It is supplied by proof of knowledge of the falsity.
	2. *Scienter* is also established by proof that the statement was made with a reckless disregard for the truth.
False misrepresentation	**1.** There must be a misstatement of a material existing fact.
	2. Statements of opinion are not factual unless made by an expert or unless the actual opinion is not as stated.
	3. Misstatements of applicable laws are not statements of fact.
	4. Misstatements may be by conduct as well as language.
Silence as fraud	**1.** In the absence of a duty to speak, silence is not fraud.
	2. Duty to speak arises (a) from a fiduciary relationship, or (b) when equity and justice so demand, or (c) to correct a prior misrepresentation.
Justifiable reliance	**1.** A party must reasonably believe the statement to be true and must act on it.
	2. There is no duty to take extraordinary steps to investigate the accuracy of statements.
Damages	**1.** A plaintiff is entitled to the benefit of the bargain theory in some cases and to use the out-of-pocket theory in others.
	2. Punitive damages may be awarded in addition to compensatory damages.

OTHER GROUNDS FOR RESCISSION

Undue influence and duress	**1.** One party exerts undue influence upon another to compel a contract.
	2. Undue influence normally occurs when a fiduciary or close family relationship exists.
	3. Duress is compulsion or constraint that deprives another of the ability to exercise free will in making a contract.
	4. Physical threats are generally required. But economic duress is recognized in a

few states, especially when a party is responsible for the economic necessity of the other party.

CASES

Gallagher v. Central Indiana Bank, N.A.
448 N.E.2d 304 (Ind.App. 1983)

In 1978 David Gallagher borrowed $165,000. He signed a note secured by his father (Victor) giving a mortgage to the bank. When David defaulted on the note, the bank sued to foreclose on the mortgage. Victor defended on the ground that he did not have the requisite mental capacity to sign the mortgage. Victor had suffered a stroke in 1974. At trial, Victor's doctors testified that Victor could not understand a mortgage transaction. A local judge testified that Victor was incompetent in 1978, when he signed the mortgage. However, the bank introduced evidence of Victor's participation in complex business transactions prior to and after 1978. In 1979 Victor executed his will and sold his farm. The trial court found that Victor had the required mental capacity to execute the mortgage agreement. The Gallaghers appealed.

ROBERTSON, J. . . . The entire basis for Gallaghers' argument is that Victor suffered permanent damage from his stroke in 1974 which prevented his participation in normal business. However, the Bank introduced evidence of Victor's participation in relatively complex business transactions both prior to and subsequent to November 3,

1978. In August, 1979, Victor participated in selling the farm on contract to his son, Paul Robert Gallagher. At trial, Victor displayed an understanding of this transaction. From early 1976 to March, 1978, Victor acted as a co-maker and guarantor of several notes for David's benefit. Evidence was also presented that Victor discussed the mortgage with David prior to executing it, that Victor and Opal initially discussed a loan for David with the Federal Land Bank on September 28, 1978, and that Victor executed a will after his stroke.

The test for determining a person's mental capacity to contract is whether the person was able to understand in a reasonable manner the nature and effect of his act. In order to avoid a contract, the party must not only have been of unsound mind, but also must have had no reasonable understanding of the contract's terms due to his instability. In light of the evidence showing Victor's participation in business transactions after his stroke, it can be inferred that Victor understood the nature of these transactions and also that Victor understood the mortgage he signed on November 3, 1978. These inferences are sufficient to support the trial court's conclusions under our standard of review. We cannot reverse a conclusion merely because experts' testimony contradicted it. It was the trial court's function to weigh the experts' testimony. . . .

Affirmed.

Halbman v. Lemke
298 N.W.2d 562 (Wis. 1980)

On July 13, 1973, Halbman (a minor) bought a 1968 Oldsmobile from defendant Lemke (an adult). About five weeks after the purchase and after Halbman had paid $1,100 of the $1,250 purchase price, the car's connecting rod in the engine broke. The car was repaired, but the repair bill of

$637.40 remains unpaid. On October 15, 1973, Halbman disaffirmed the purchase contract and demanded all of the money he had paid defendant.

CALLOW, J. . . . The sole issue before us is whether a minor, having disaffirmed a contract for the purchase of an item which is not a necessity and having tendered the property back to the vendor, must make restitution to the vendor for damage to the property prior to the disaffirmance. Lemke argues that he should be entitled to recover for the damage to the vehicle up to the time of disaffirmance, which he claims equals the amount of the repair bill.

Neither party challenges the absolute right of a minor to disaffirm a contract for the purchase of items which are not necessities. That right, variously known as the doctrine of incapacity or the "infancy doctrine," is one of the oldest and most venerable of our common law traditions. Although the origins of the doctrine are somewhat obscure, it is generally recognized that its purpose is the protection of minors from foolishly squandering their wealth through improvident contracts with crafty adults who would take advantage of them in the marketplace. Thus it is settled law in this state that a contract of a minor for items which are not necessities is void or voidable at the minor's option.

Once there has been a disaffirmance, however, as in this case between a minor vendee and an adult vendor, unresolved problems arise regarding the rights and responsibilities of the parties relative to the disposition of the consideration exchanged on the contract. As a general rule, a minor who disaffirms a contract is entitled to recover all consideration he has conferred incident to the transaction. In return, the minor is expected to restore as much of the consideration as, at the time of disaffirmance, remains in the minor's possession. The minor's right to disaffirm is not contingent upon the return of the property, however, as disaffirmance is permitted even where such return cannot be made.

The return of property remaining in the hands of the minor is not the issue presented here. In this case we have a situation where the property cannot be returned to the vendor in its entirety because it has been damaged and therefore diminished in value, and the vendor seeks to recover the depreciation. Although this court has been cognizant of this issue on previous occasions, we have not heretofore resolved it.

Here Lemke seeks restitution of the value of the depreciation by virtue of the damage to the vehicle prior to disaffirmance. Such a recovery would require Halbman to return more than that remaining in his possession. It seeks compensatory value for that which he cannot return. Where there is misrepresentation by a minor or willful destruction of property, the vendor may be able to recover damages in tort. But absent these factors, as in the present case, we believe that to require a disaffirming minor to make restitution for diminished value is, in effect, to bind the minor to a part of the obligation which by law he is privileged to avoid.

As we noted, modification of the rules governing the capacity of infants to contract are best left to the legislature. Until such changes are forthcoming, however, we hold that, absent misrepresentation or tortious damage to the property, a minor who disaffirms a contract for the purchase of an item which is not a necessity may recover his purchase price without liability for use, depreciation, damage, or other diminution in value.

Judgment for plaintiff affirmed.

Bobby Floars Toyota, Inc. v. Smith
269 S.E.2d 320 (N.C.App. 1980)

Charles Smith, a minor, bought a car from Bobby Floars Toyota, and agreed to make 30 installment payments of $100. After making 11 payments, Smith was financially unable to continue his payments, so he voluntarily returned the car to Floars. At that time, he had been an adult for 10 months. When Floars sued Smith for the unpaid installments, Smith defended on the ground that he had disaffirmed the contract upon his becoming an adult. Floars asserted that Smith had not disaffirmed within a reasonable time after becoming an adult.

MORRIS, C.J. . . . The only question posed

for review is whether defendant Charles Smith's voluntarily relinquishing the automobile ten months after attaining the age of majority constitutes a timely disaffirmance of his contract with plaintiff.

The rule in North Carolina regarding a minor's contract liability is as follows:

> It is well settled that the conventional contracts of an infant, except those for necessities and those authorized by statute, are voidable at the election of the infant and may be disaffirmed by the infant during minority or within a reasonable time after reaching majority. "[W]hat is a reasonable time depends upon the circumstances of each case, no hard-and-fast rule regarding precise time limits being capable of definition."

This concept of "reasonable time" is more

fully explained in *Weeks v. Wilkins,* 47 S.E. 24, 26 (1904), where the Court quoted from Devlin on Deeds, Vol. I, sec. 91:

> The most reasonable rule seems to be that the right of disaffirmance should be exercised within a reasonable time after the infant attains his majority, or else his neglect to avail himself of this privilege should be deemed an acquiescence and affirmation on his part of his conveyance. The law considers his contract a voidable one, on account of its tender solicitude for his rights and the fear that he may be imposed upon in his bargain. But he is certainly afforded ample protection by allowing him a reasonable time after he reaches his majority to determine whether he will abide by his conveyance, executed while he was a minor, or will disaffirm it. And it is no more than just and reasonable that if he silently acquiesces in his deed and makes no effort to express his dissatisfaction with his act, he should, after the lapse of a reasonable time, dependent upon circumstances, be considered as fully ratifying it.

Applying the general rule in an action involving a contract concerning personalty, the Court in *Hight v. Harris,* 124 S.E. 623 (1924), for example, held that an infant may avoid such a contract on account of his infancy during his minority or on coming of age, "if he acts promptly in the matter." In *Insurance Co. v. Chantos,* 214 S.E.2d 438 (1975), this Court stated that "the defendant's silence or acquiescence for eight months after reaching majority may work as an implied ratification, that determination depending upon whether his failure to disaffirm within that eight-month period was within a reasonable time. . . ." In the instant case, we believe that ten months is an unreasonable time within which to elect between disaffirmance and ratification, in that this case involves an automobile, an item of personal property which is constantly depreciating in value. Modern commercial transactions require that both buyers and sellers be responsible and prompt.

Reversed and remanded.

Home Ins. Co. v. Honaker
480 A.2d 652 (Del. Supr. 1984)

On November 3, 1979, Honaker was injured in a rear-end collision while a passenger in an automobile owned by Helen Cliver. The Home Insurance Co. (Home) insured Cliver's automobile and was liable for Honaker's medical and living expenses up to the limits of its policy under Delaware's no-fault statute.

Under the personal injury protection ("PIP") provisions of Cliver's policy, Home paid a total of $24,907 to Honaker over a period of two years, believing that the coverage limit was $25,000. In fact, the policy limit was $10,000. The payments made by Home were spent for Honaker's living and medical expenses, and for the living expenses of his child. Subsequently, Home discovered its error and demanded repayment. The parties concede that the overpayment to Honaker was Home's unilateral mistake. Honaker had no actual knowledge of the policy's limits, nor access to such information.

Home filed suit for restitution of the $14,907 overpayment and damages. Thereafter, Honaker settled his claim for personal injuries against the driver of the car which had caused the accident. The settlement was for $20,000.

The trial court granted summary judgment for Honaker, and Home appeals.

MOORE, J. . . . This [case] presents a question of first impression for this Court: whether an insurer, acting under a unilateral mistake of coverage, may regain overpayments made to a nonpolicyholder unaware of the mistake. . . .

As a general rule, money paid due to a mistake of law is not recoverable, while money paid under a mistake of fact may be recovered in equity under an unjust enrichment theory. The negligence of the payor in mistakenly compensating the payee, alone, is no bar to restitution of the sum paid. However, where the mistake of fact was not shared by the payee, i.e., in cases of unilateral mistake on the payor's part, equitable principles may bar restitution of the sum paid. Thus, while mutuality of mistake is usually required for restitution, unilateral mistake does not in every case bar recovery.

Regaining of money paid under a mistake of fact is barred where recovery would be inequitable, such as when the payee has changed his position. In such circumstances, while the payee has been enriched mistakenly at the expense of the paying party, equity will not unfairly force the payee to disgorge any profit to his or her detriment. The burden of proving a change of circumstances or other inequities sufficient to bar restitution is upon the payee.

Thus, our analysis begins with a determination of whether the mistake is one of law or fact. We then consider the circumstances under which it was made, the conduct of the payee and payor, and any other factors bearing on whether it would be unjust to permit the retention of the benefit or to order its restitution.

First, we note Home's admission that it was under a unilateral mistake regarding the limits of the "PIP" coverage provided in this policy. Second, Honaker was not the policyholder here, only a passenger in a car insured by Home. Thus, it is undisputed that Honaker had no actual knowledge of Home's error. It is also clear that Honaker had no access to any information which would provide that knowledge. Hence, Honaker could not have misled Home, either directly or indirectly, through nondisclosure of the overpayments he received. In fact he was unaware of the error until after Home had completed its payments, which had been made over a period of two years. Thus, Honaker appears before this Court with clean hands. What remains is that Home acted under a mistake of fact, due to its own negligence, which continued for two years. There is no mistake of law present here.

It is undisputed that but for the $20,000 tort settlement, Honaker lacks sufficient funds from which the $14,907 overpayment could be returned to the insurer. Thus, it is clear that Honaker has not retained the value originally represented by the overpayment. For this reason, we conclude that Honaker has in fact and in equity changed his position in reliance on the insurer's payment.

Home, however, claims that Honaker can return the $14,907 overpayment using this personal injury settlement recovered from the driver of the car causing the accident. Home contends that such use of the settlement award is not inequitable, because it leaves Honaker with the same dollar amount which he would have received absent Home's error.

We disagree. Acceptance of the insurer's argument would in effect force Honaker to disgorge a benefit received from a separate source for entirely different reasons. Second, while a payor's negligence is not a *per se* bar to recovery, here the insurer made its erroneous payments to Honaker and other third parties for a period of two years, rather than in one lump sum. Under these circumstances, an insurer must be charged with knowledge of the provisions of the policies which it writes. It alone must bear the burden of its unilateral mistake, particularly where the error was prolonged over a two year period. There are no factors meriting any other conclusion.

Affirmed.

Sellers v. Looper
503 P.2d 692 (Or. 1972)

BRYSON, J. . . . This is an action for damages based on fraudulent misrepresentations pertaining to the well on property plaintiffs purchased from defendants. The jury returned a verdict in favor of plaintiffs. On motion, the trial court granted judgment in favor of defendants notwithstanding the verdict, and the plaintiffs have appealed. . . .

Defendants argue here that the plaintiffs had not submitted evidence sufficient to establish fraudulent representations on the part of defendants to induce plaintiffs to enter into the contract to purchase the property.

The plaintiffs . . . contend: "Statements regarding quality, value or the like may be considered misrepresentations of fact where the parties are not on an equal footing and do not have equal knowledge or means of knowledge" and the "[d]ecision of whether a representation is of fact or of 'opinion' is always left to the jury and therefore the order setting aside the jury's verdict should not have been entered."

Interwoven with defendants' contention that the evidence was insufficient to justify the plaintiffs' verdict is their argument that the representation of a "good well" was "mere inclusion of adjectival words of commendation" or "opinion" and, therefore, not actionable.

In Holland v. Lentz, 239 Or. 332, 345, 397, P.2d 787, 794 (1964), we held:

> . . . It is recognized, however, that statements of opinion regarding quality, value, or the like, may be considered as misrepresentations of fact, that is, of the speaker's state of mind, if a fiduciary

relation exists between the parties as, for example, representations of value made by a real estate broker to his principal: or where the parties are not on an equal footing and do not have equal knowledge or means of knowledge.

Prosser treats the matter by stating:

A statement of opinion is one which either indicates some doubt as to the speaker's belief in the existence of a state of facts, as where he says, "I think this is true, but I am not sure," or merely expresses his judgment on some matter of judgment connected with the facts, such as quality, value, authenticity and the like, as where he says, "This is a very fine picture." It is not, however, the form of the statement which is important or controlling, but the sense in which it is reasonably understood. . . .
It is stated very often as a fundamental rule in connection with all of the various remedies for misrepresentation, that they will not lie for misstatements of opinion, as distinguished from those of fact. . . .
But this explanation is scarcely adequate, since an expression of opinion is itself always a statement of at least one fact—the fact of the belief, the existing state of mind, of the one who asserts it. . . . [Prosser, Torts (4th ed.) 720-721.]

The evidence discloses that defendants owned a home and acreage located in Illinois Valley near the city of Cave Junction, Josephine County, Oregon. In May of 1969 defendants executed a listing, or employment, agreement to sell their property with Mrs. McLean, a real estate broker. This agreement included information given to realtor by the defendants. Mrs. McLean testified:

I asked the Loopers, "Do you have a good well?" and the comment came back, "Yes, we have a good well. . . ."

On July 28, 1969, plaintiffs contacted Mrs. McLean. They desired to buy a house large enough for plaintiffs and their six children. Mrs. McLean further testified:

Q. . . . At the time you told them that there was a good well on the property, did you tell them that for the purpose of inducing them to buy the Loopers' property?
A. A good well on any property is a tremendous

inducement. If you have a good well, that's a selling point. . . .
Q. . . . At the time you represented to Mr. and Mrs. Sellers that there was a, quote, good well on the property, what did you mean to convey by that, what meaning did you mean to get across to prospective buyers?
A. The meaning I've always inferred before, and I inferred at that time, was that it was an adequate well, there was plenty of water.
Q. Plenty of water for what?
A. Well, I told them at the time that you couldn't go out and irrigate the pasture, if they wanted to irrigate pasture they would perhaps have to put down an irrigation well, but there was a good well, and this was understood to be adequate for household, and usually that includes a modest garden. . . .

In the early evening of July 28, 1969, the plaintiffs, with the realtor, met the defendants and inspected the house and "looked at the well and pumphouse." No specifications as to the depth of the well or how many gallons it would pump per hour were given the plaintiffs and the realtor did not have this information. They returned to the realtor's office; she prepared the earnest money agreement; defendants signed the agreement that evening, the plaintiffs signed it and made the down payment. . . .

On August 15, 1969, plaintiffs moved onto the property and on August 22, 1969, the well went dry. Plaintiffs drilled two additional wells but found no water.

We conclude that there was sufficient evidence to submit the case to the jury. A reasonable person, in this day of modern household conveniences, could believe that a "good well" meant a well with adequate water for family household use and the plaintiffs relied on this representation. The evidence shows that defendants knew the water in the well got low in the fall of the year and they had to be careful in flushing the indoor toilet or the well would probably go dry. The plaintiffs were not on equal footing with the defendants and did not have equal knowledge of the adequacy or lack of adequacy of the water in the well. The jury returned a verdict for the plaintiffs and these matters are ordinarily for the determination of the jury. . . .

Reversed with instructions to reinstate the jury's verdict.

State Dept. of Environ. Protect. v. Ventron
468 A.2d 150 (N.J. 1983)

Ventron buried mercury on its land, which it later sold to the Wolfs without telling them about the mercury. The New Jersey Department of Environmental Protection sued Ventron and the Wolfs for mercury pollution of a state waterway. The Wolfs seek to rescind its land sale contract with Ventron, which would leave Ventron solely liable for any damage caused by the mercury. The trial court found that Ventron knew of the mercury pollution in the soil, but intentionally failed to disclose that fact to the Wolfs.

POUND, J. . . . We now consider the issue raised by the Wolfs' claim against Ventron, in which the Wolfs alleged fraudulent nondisclosure in the sale of realty. As noted by the trial court, the elements necessary to prove fraudulent concealment on the part of a seller in a real estate action are: the deliberate concealment or nondisclosure by the seller of a material fact or defect not readily observable to the purchaser, with the buyer relying upon the seller to his detriment. The trial court found that Ventron knew of a latent defect, gross mercury pollution in the soil, but intentionally failed to disclose that fact to the Wolfs. Furthermore, the court found that the contamination was not readily observable by the Wolfs and that the Wolfs relied upon the nondisclosure to their detriment. The Appellate Division determined that those findings were supported by credible evidence.

Affirmed.

Aurora Bank v. Hamlin
609 S.W.2d 486 (Mo. 1980)

The Hamlins owed the Aurora Bank several unpaid loans. The bank decided to ask the Hamlins to sign two renewal notes as well as a deed of trust on the farm. When Mrs. Hamlin refused to sign, she was told she was responsible for her husband's debts and that the bank would foreclose on the farm if she did not sign. In this suit by the bank on the two promissory renewal notes, the trial court found that Mrs. Hamlin's signature was secured by threats and coercion by the bank employees. As a result, she was allowed to disaffirm the notes. Thereafter, the bank appealed.

PREWITT, J. . . . Duress can avoid a contract if the contract was obtained by threats of the person claiming the benefit of it which caused the victim "to be bereft of the quality of mind essential to the making of a contract." Duress is to be tested, not by the nature of the threats, but by the state of mind induced thereby in the victim. The ultimate fact in issue is whether the victim was bereft of the free exercise of his will power; "and of which, the means used to produce such state of mind, the age, sex, capacity, situation, and relation of the parties, are all evidentiary."

There was evidence of a threat to sue Mrs. Hamlin along with her husband and then to levy on defendants' farm. The bank officers, while denying they made such a statement, acknowledged that when they went to the Hamlin residence the bank had no basis for bringing a suit against Mrs. Hamlin nor any basis to levy upon the farm. Threats to take legal action with knowledge of the falsity of the claim can amount to duress. A claim of duress cannot generally be sustained where there is knowledge of the facts and opportunity for investigation, deliberation and reflection. We cannot say as a matter of law that Mrs. Hamlin had "knowledge of the facts". There was evidence she thought that the bank would sue her and could have the farm sold.

The Hamlins and the bank officers testified that Mrs. Hamlin was very upset and cried during the discussions at the Hamlin residence. She was described by the loan officer as a "mild mannered person", and not "strong willed". The trial court, after hearing the evidence and observing her, found that Mrs. Hamlin's "will could have been easily overcome by other persons and particularly, in this instance, by anyone in a position of authority." She refused to sign the notes when first asked but testified she signed them after the threats to sue her and to sell the farm because they convinced her that she was liable and she didn't want to lose the farm.

We believe that there was sufficient evidence for the trial court to find that the duress was present when Mrs. Hamlin signed the notes.
Affirmed.

REVIEW QUESTIONS

1. Identify the terms in column A by matching each with the appropriate statement(s) in column B.

A	B
1. Ratification	**a.** Minor must pay their reasonable value
2. *Scienter*	**b.** Rescission not allowed unless other party has knowledge of it
3. Concealment	**c.** A fiduciary or someone in close family relationship exerts pressure
4. Bilateral mistake	**d.** What minor may choose to do upon reaching majority
5. Necessaries	**e.** Upon reaching majority, minor retains consideration without doing more
6. Undue influence	**f.** Rescission granted if a duty to speak is not performed
7. Unilateral mistake	**g.** Physical threats usually required
8. Duress	**h.** Misconception of material fact by all contracting parties
9. Disaffirmance	**i.** Intent to defraud
10. Reformation	**j.** Court rewrites contract so it conforms with parties' intent

2. Jones, a minor, contracted to use Dressel's recreational sky-diving facilities. The contract released Dressel from any liability. Ten months later, Jones (then an adult) suffered serious injury when the airplane rented by Dressel crashed. Can Jones now successfully sue Dressel for damages? Explain.

3. Bill, under guardianship by reason of mental illness, buys an old car from Larry for $700, giving a promissory note for that amount. Subsequently, Bill abandons the car. Is Bill liable on the note? Would it make any difference if the car was a necessary? Explain your answers.

4. Beachcomer, a coin dealer, sues to rescind a purchase by Boskett, who paid $50 for a dime both parties thought was minted in San Francisco. In fact, it was a very valuable dime minted in Denver. Beachcomer asserted a mutual mistake of fact regarding the genuineness of the coin as San Francisco-minted. Boskett contends any mistake was about value only. Explain who should win.

5. Libby bought a used car from Alice. The bill of sale showed that the car was a 1986 Buick Skylark, when in fact the car was actually a 1985 Buick Skylark. Alice knew that the car was a 1985 model. Can Libby rescind the contract? Explain.

6. In the previous question, if Alice had turned the mileage on the car's odometer from 11,496 to 100 at the time of sale, should Libby be entitled to punitive damages in addition to rescission? Explain.

7. Four oral surgeons appeal an order suspending their licenses to practice because they submitted false

claims to Blue Shield. Blue Shield excluded coverage for oral surgery for extraction of teeth not fully or partially impacted. The surgeons submitted claims to Blue Shield for the removal of impacted teeth when X rays indicated that the teeth extracted were not impacted. The surgeons claim that the *scienter* element is not met because if false claims were filed, they were the responsibility of clerical help. Were the surgeons guilty of fraud? Explain.

8. Purchasers of a residence sue the realtor for fraud. They allege that the realtor failed to reveal his knowledge of the extensive termite damage to the beams which supported the floors in the house. The realtor did inform them that there was termite insurance, that the house had been treated for termites, and that a one-year guarantee against reinfestation went with the house. Is the realtor guilty of fraudulent concealment? Explain.

9. A minor sold a painting for $200. Upon reaching majority, he discovered that the painting he sold was worth $2,000. He sued to recover the painting. What was the result? Explain. Would the result change if he waited 2 months after reaching majority? Two years? Explain.

10. Leon, an infant, signed a contract with Step-Up Employment Agency, in which Leon promised to pay a fee if Step-Up secured him a job as a pianist. Step-Up did find suitable employment, but Leon refused to pay the $500 fee, since he was a minor. Can Step-Up recover the fee? Why or why not?

11. Barron, to no avail, had long sought Jackson's Stradivarius violin. One night Barron plied Jackson with food and drink and persuaded him to agree to sell the violin for a reasonable price. Sober now, Jackson wants to disaffirm. Can he? Explain.

12. A representative for a data-processing firm bought a computer after the computer salesperson assured her that the computer would be more than adequate for her particular purposes. Later she discovers that the computer printout is too slow for her company's needs. She seeks to rescind the sales contract on the basis of misrepresentation. With what result? Explain.

13. Big Electric Power Company formulated a plan to acquire a large area of land for a hydroelectric project. Harion owned 138 acres of land in the area. Burroughs, an undisclosed agent of the power company, offered to buy Harion's land. To Harion's inquiry about why Burroughs wanted the land, Burroughs falsely replied he had just come into a large sum of money that he wanted to invest in land. They then executed a buy-sell contract with a purchase price of $4,100. Alleging that he would have asked $27,000 if he had known the power company to be the real buyer, Harion sues to rescind. Does he win? Explain.

14. Phoenix Co. was awarded a $6 million contract by the navy for the production of radar sets. It was a severe contract that imposed substantial penalties for late deliveries and gave the navy the right to cancel for any default by Phoenix Co. Phoenix then made a contract with Logan, Inc., whereby Logan agreed to furnish many of the component parts. After making a few deliveries, Logan refused to deliver any more unless the price was increased. Being unable to get the components elsewhere, Phoenix acceded to the demand. Later, Phoenix sued to have the price increase set aside. Was Phoenix successful? Explain.

10 ILLEGALITY AND PUBLIC POLICY

An additional requirement for a valid contract is that it have a lawful purpose or object. Contracts that do not have a lawful object are illegal and therefore unenforceable. A contract or provision of a contract may be declared to be illegal if it is specifically prohibited by statute, contravenes the rule of the common law, or is contrary to public policy. It may be illegal in either its subject matter, its formation, or its performance. It is axiomatic that a contract that violates a statute or an ordinance is illegal and void. A contract provision is contrary to public policy if it is injurious to the interests of the public, contravenes some established interest of society, violates the policy or purpose of some statute, or tends to interfere with the public health, safety, morals, or general welfare.[1] Although all agreements are subject to the paramount power of the sovereign and to the judicial power to declare contracts illegal, contracts are not to be lightly set aside on the grounds of public policy, and doubts will usually be resolved in favor of legality. An endless variety of agreements have been held to be illegal: wagering agreements, agreements to affect the administration of justice (concealing evidence or suppressing a criminal investigation), agreements to influence legislation or executive action by bribery or undue influence, and agreements to interfere with public service. Other examples of illegal agreements are discussed throughout this chapter.

The term *public policy* is vague and variable and changes as our social, economic, and political climates change. As society becomes more complex, courts

---

[1] Laos v. Soble, p. 211.

turn more and more to statutory enactments in search of current public policy. A court's own concept of right and wrong, as well as its total philosophy, will frequently come into play in answering complex questions of public policy.[2] Cases involving public policy are often in conflict from jurisdiction to jurisdiction. The economic interests of a state may play a major role in the development of public policy. As the law on illegal contracts is studied, care should be taken to ascertain the reason behind each rule or decision, and the major emphasis should be on indicated trends in the law. Keep in mind that matters of illegality will be discussed throughout the text.

1. Status of Illegal Contracts

As a general rule, the status of an illegal contract is that a court will not allow litigation involving it. This means that if the illegal contract is executory, neither party may enforce performance by the other. If it is executed, the court will not order rescission—it will not allow recovery of what was given in performance. An illegal contract cannot be ratified by either party, and the parties can do nothing to make it enforceable. Stated simply, in an illegal-contract situation, the court literally "leaves the parties where it finds them." A party to an illegal contract cannot recover damages for breach of such contract. If one party has performed, he cannot generally recover either the value of his performance or any property or goods transferred to the other. As a result of the rule, one wrongdoer may be enriched at the expense of the other wrongdoer, but the courts will not intercede to rectify this because the purpose is to deter illegal bargains.

There are three basic exceptions to the rule that precludes the granting of any relief to a party to an illegal contract. First, if a person falls in the category of those for whose protection the contract was made illegal, he may obtain restitution of what he has paid or parted with or may even obtain enforcement. For example, both federal and state statutes require that a corporation follow certain procedures before securities (stocks and bonds) may be offered for sale to the public. It is illegal to sell such securities without having complied with the legal requirements. Nevertheless, a purchaser is allowed to obtain a refund of the purchase price if he desires to do so. The act of one party (the seller) is more illegal than that of the other party (the buyer). Many statutes are designed to protect one party in an illegal transaction, and when this is the case, the protected party is allowed a legal remedy.

A second exception applies when a person is induced by fraud or duress to enter into an illegal agreement. In such cases, the courts do not regard the defrauded or coerced party as being an actual participant in the wrong, and will, therefore, allow restitution of what he has rendered by way of performance. It has been suggested that the same result would obtain if the party were induced by strong economic pressure to enter into an illegal agreement.

Third, there is a doctrine called *locus poenitentiae* that may provide the remedy of restitution to one who has become a party to an illegal contract.

---

[2] Strickland v. Gulf Life Ins. Co., p. 212.

Literally, the phrase means "a place for repentance," by extension, "an opportunity for changing one's mind." As applied to an illegal contract, it means that within very strict limits, a person who repents before actually having performed any illegal part of the contract may rescind it and obtain restitution of his part performance. Thus, wagers are illegal transactions except under certain circumstances. Suppose that A and B wager on the outcome of an election, and each places $100 with C, the stakeholder, who agrees to turn $200 over to the winner. Prior to the election, either A or B could recover his $100 from C by legal action, since the execution of the illegal agreement would not yet have occurred. Actually, the loser could obtain a judgment against C if he gives notice of his demand prior to the time that the stake has been turned over to the winner.

2. Violations of License Requirements

Some contracts are void and unenforceable because they involve a purpose that violates a statute. Most personal service contracts do not involve an unlawful purpose. However, personal service agreements may be unenforceable if the party performing the service is not legally entitled to do so. For example, doctors, dentists, pharmacists, architects, lawyers, accountants, surveyors, real estate brokers, and others who perform professional services must be licensed by the appropriate body before they are allowed to contract with the general public.

As a general rule, if the service rendered requires a license, the party receiving the benefit of the service can successfully refuse to pay an unlicensed plaintiff on the ground that the contract is illegal.[3] This is true even if the person is licensed in another jurisdiction, but not the one in which the services were rendered. A real estate broker licensed in one state cannot perform services in another state. If he does so, he cannot collect for the services.

The practice of law by unauthorized persons is a significant problem. A person who practices law without a license is not only denied the right to a fee, but also subject to criminal prosecution in many states, and such activity may also be enjoined. Since the practice of law primarily entails giving advice, difficult questions are presented when advice is given by business specialists such as certified public accountants, insurance brokers, bankers, and real estate brokers. Although the line between permissible and impermissible activities of these business specialists is often difficult to draw, some activities and services performed by various business specialists clearly constitute unauthorized practice of law. An accountant's handling of a complicated tax case has been held to constitute unauthorized practice of law, and a real estate broker's preparation of a real estate deed is illegal in most states. Business specialists should be aware that giving legal advice and preparing legal documents are illegal performances by one not licensed to practice law. A major danger in doing these things is the loss of the right to compensation.

---

[3] Kazmer-Standish v. Schoeffel Instrument, p. 213.

3. Usury

State statutes limit the amount of interest that may be charged upon borrowed money. Any contract by which the lender is to receive more than the maximum interest allowed by the statute is usurious and illegal. In most states, the civil penalty for usury is that the lender is denied the right to collect any interest. There are also criminal penalties for charging illegal interest.

Difficult issues often arise over what actually constitutes interest. Creditors develop ingenious schemes to charge more than the maximum legal rate of interest.[4] For example, the calculation of interest on the basis of 360 days was held to be illegal if the computation produced in a single year more interest than would be produced by applying the maximum legal rate to a calendar year of 365 days.

The law against usury is generally not violated if the seller sets a cash price different from a credit price, but he cannot disguise interest by calling it something else, like a finder's fee or broker's fee. If the buyer is charged for making a loan, it is interest, regardless of the terminology used in many states. As long as one lends the money of others, he may then charge a commission in addition to the maximum rate. A commission may not be legally charged when one is lending his own funds, even though he has to borrow the money with which to make the loan and expects to sell the paper shortly thereafter.

The laws on usury are not violated by collection of the legal maximum interest in advance or by adding a service fee that is no larger than reasonably necessary to cover the incidental costs of making the loan (inspection, legal, and recording fees). A seller can also add a finance or carrying charge on long-term credit transactions. Some statutes allow special lenders such as pawnshops, small loan companies, or credit unions to charge in excess of the otherwise legal limit. In fact, the exceptions to the maximum interest rate in most states far exceed the situations in which the general rule is applicable. The laws relating to usury were designed to protect debtors from excessive interest. This goal has been thwarted by these exceptions, so only modest protection is actually available.

The purchase of a note at a discount greater than the maximum interest is not usurious unless the maker of the note is the person who is discounting it. Thus if A, who is in need of funds, sells B a $500 note made by C, payable in six months for $100, the sale is not usurious, although the gain to B could be very large. A note is considered the same as any other personal property and may be sold for whatever it will bring on the market.

Today, in most states there is no maximum legal rate of interest when the borrower is a business, whether or not it is incorporated. Some states limit this exception to a fixed sum, such as $10,000, but little protection is afforded by such laws. Loans to corporations usually are exempt in most states, regardless of the amount of the loan.

---

[4] Standard Leasing Corporation v. Schmidt Aviation, Inc., p. 214.

4. Agreements Not to Compete

Several federal laws declare that agreements in restraint of trade are illegal. These laws are discussed in chapter 47 with other aspects of government regulation of business. In the meantime, it should be recognized that price-fixing and other agreements that tend to eliminate competition are generally illegal. For example, an agreement among lawyers that they would not represent each other's clients for five years is illegal. However, some agreements, such as those between a franchiser and its franchisees, are usually found to be legal. They are legal because their effect on competition is minimal compared with the interests of the franchiser in having similarity in all of its franchised operations. Thus, certain exclusive dealing contracts are legal.

Another form of agreement that may be legal even though it is in partial restraint of trade is an agreement not to compete. An agreement by one person not to compete with another is frequently contained in a contract for the sale of a going business. The seller, by such a provision, agrees not to compete with the buyer. Agreements not to compete are also commonly found in contracts creating a business or a professional practice. Each partner or shareholder in the closely held corporation agrees not to compete with the firm or practice, should he leave the business or professional activity. In addition, as a part of their employment contract, many employees agree that they will not compete with their employer upon termination of their employment. Such agreements will be enforced if they are reasonably necessary for the protection of a purchaser, the remaining members of a business, or an employer, provided the covenant (1) is reasonable in point of time, (2) is reasonable in the area of restraint,[5] (3) is necessary to protect goodwill, (4) does not place an undue burden on the covenantor, and (5) does not violate the public interest. Each covenant is examined by the court to see if it is reasonable to both parties and to the general public. Factors such as uniqueness of product, patents, trade secrets, type of service, employee's contract with customers, and other goodwill factors are significant on the reasonableness issue. In the employment situation, whether or not the employee will become a burden on society and whether or not the public is being deprived of his skill are factors.

The law will look with more favor on these covenants if they involve the sale of a business interest rather than employment. In fact, an agreement not to compete may even be presumed in the case of a sale of business and its goodwill, and the seller must not thereafter directly or indirectly solicit business from his old customers, although he may advertise generally. Agreements between a buyer and seller or between partners are more likely to be held valid than are employer-employee contracts, because there is more equality of bargaining power in the first two situations than in the last. A seller or a former partner could readily refuse to sign an agreement not to compete, whereas an employee seeking a job might feel obligated to sign almost anything in order to gain employment.

Comparable to the employee's agreement not to compete is a restrictive provision in a contract for the sale or lease of real property. The landowner may wish to prevent the use of his land for any purpose that would be competitive with

---

[5] Egnell v. Weniger, p. 215.

his own business. In a lease, the landowner may provide that the lessee cannot operate an appliance store on the leased property. In that case, the landowner (who owns an appliance store) wants to avoid competition, and he does so by the restrictive provision. Although on its face the provision does restrict trade, it is binding because other property in the community can be used for competitive purposes.

Agreements not to compete must be a part of another contract to be legal. A bare agreement by one party not to compete with another is against public policy. If Lori threatens to open a business to compete with Elaine, and Elaine offers Lori $1,000 to agree not to do so, the contract is illegal.

5. Unconscionability

Unconscionability allows a judge to strike any portion of a contract or to strike the entire contract or to limit the application of a clause, in order to avoid any unconscionable result. Unconscionability is a question of law for the judge, and not the jury. Although no precise meaning is given, its purpose is to prevent oppression and unfair surprise.[6] The concept of unconscionability is an important part of the Code [2–302] and is applicable to transactions in goods.

For a contract to be conscionable, its material terms need to be conspicuous, to be understandable by an ordinary person, and to result from a true bargain. It is not a contract of bargain, but one in which one party imposes terms on another party. Thus, a party must be able to *find* and to *understand* all material terms, as well as have the right to *bargain* over them. The contract cannot be oppressively imposed.

Unconscionability has been used to excise substantially offensive provisions like disclaimer-of-warranties and limitation-of-remedies clauses, exculpatory clauses, and confession of judgment clauses. It has been applied in cases concerning real estate brokerage contracts, home improvement contracts, apartment leases, equipment leases, filling station leases, contracts to open a checking account, construction contracts, and so on. In modern contract law, unconscionability may be applied to any contract of adhesion, to any contract oppressively imposed by a superior party, or to any contract term that causes unfair surprise to an inferior party. These examples are discussed in the following sections.

Since unconscionability involves questions of public policy, it is difficult to predict when a court will or will not find a particular contract or contract provision unconscionable. As noted earlier, a court's own concept of right and wrong as well as its total philosophy will often come into play in answering complex questions of public policy.

6. Contracts of Adhesion

The term *contract of adhesion* was developed in French civil law. It has been widely used in international law, and in recent years has become important in our law of contracts. An adhesion contract is a standardized contract entirely prepared

---

[6] In re Friedman, p. 216.

by one party. As a result of the disparity or inequality of bargaining power between the drafter and the second party, the terms are submitted on a take-it-or-leave-it basis. The standardized provisions are such that they are merely "adhered to," with little choice as a practical matter on the part of the "adherer." If the terms are viewed as unsatisfactory, the party cannot obtain the desired service or product.

The term *contract of adhesion* was first used in the United States in 1919 in a case involving an insurance contract. For several decades it was almost exclusively applied to insurance contracts. However, many contracts today are standardized form contracts entered into by parties who are unequal in knowledge and unequal in bargaining power. The common law ignored this inequality and applied a doctrine of *caveat emptor.* In the 1960s, courts began to police contractual abuses by superior parties using contracts of adhesion. To do that, they used the equitable principle of *unconscionability.* This principle is discussed more fully in the sections that follow.

Contracts of adhesion are not illegal but are strictly construed against the drafting party. Courts police these contracts carefully to ensure that they are conscionable, and the courts will excise clauses that are oppressive or cause unfair surprise. Employment contracts, insurance policies, and leases are frequently held to be contracts of adhesion.

7. Contracts Disclaiming Liability

A party to a contract frequently includes a clause that provides that the party has no tort liability even if at fault. Such a clause is commonly called an *exculpatory clause.* These disclaimers of liability are not favored by the law and are strictly construed against the party relying on them. While some are valid, many disclaimers are frequently declared to be illegal by courts as contrary to public policy.[7] Some states have by statute declared these clauses, in certain types of contracts such as leases, to be illegal and void.

The reasoning behind these statutes and judicial decisions is clear. Absolute freedom of contract exists in a barter situation because of the equal bargaining position of the parties. At the other extreme are the contracts with public utilities, in which there is no equality of bargaining power between the parties because of the existence of a virtual monopoly. The law therefore denies freedom of contract in the monopoly situation. The difficulty is that many contracts involve parties and circumstances that fall between these extremes. Many contracts are entered into between parties with substantially unequal bargaining power. When the subject matter of the contracts involves items of everyday necessity, courts frequently hold that one of the parties is a quasi-public institution and that such institutions are not entitled to complete freedom of contract because freedom of contract is not in the public interest. Thus, contracts or parts of the contracts of such institutions may be held illegal whenever the quasi-public institution has taken advantage of its superior bargaining power and drawn a contract, or included a provision in a

---

[7] Hy-Grade Oil Co. v. New Jersey Bank, p. 217.

contract, that in the eyes of the court excessively favors the quasi-public institution to the detriment of the other party and the public. This is especially true when the contract provision is an exculpatory clause.

Not every exculpatory clause is unconscionable just as not every printed contract is one of adhesion. Many businesses are allowed to contract away liability when the bargaining power is essentially equal and the contract is basically a fair one.

8. Tickets Disclaiming Liability

Tickets purchased for entrance into places of amusement, for evidence of a contract for transportation, or for a service often contain provisions that attempt to limit or to define the rights of the holder of the ticket. It is generally held that the printed matter on the ticket is a part of an offer that is accepted by the holder of the ticket if he is aware of the printed matter, even though he does not read it. Some cases hold that the purchaser is presumed to know about the printed matter, even though his attention is not called to it at the time the ticket is delivered.

If a ticket is received merely as evidence of ownership and is to be presented later as a means of identification, the provisions on the ticket are not a part of the contract unless the recipient is aware of them or his attention is specifically directed to them. Tickets given at checkrooms or repair shops are usually received as a means of identifying the article to be returned, rather than as setting forth the terms of a contract. Thus, the fine print on such tickets is usually not a part of the offer and acceptance unless communicated.

Many terms on tickets may be unconscionable and will not be enforced in any event. The terms are unconscionable when public policy, as previously noted, would declare such a provision in a formal contract to be unconscionable. The quality of the bargaining power of the parties and the nature of the product or service are major factors to be considered in determining unconscionableness.

SUMMARY

Status of illegal contracts	**1.** An illegal agreement is legally void and courts will not provide a remedy for any party.
	2. If a party is protected by statute, he can rescind and recover any consideration given.
	3. If a party has been defrauded or unduly influenced, he can rescind and seek restitution.

	4. Under the doctrine of *locus poenitentiae*, a person who repents before performing may rescind and seek restitution.
Violation of license requirements	**1.** An unlicensed person providing a service that requires a license is not entitled to compensation.
	2. An unlicensed person practicing law cannot recover a fee and may be subject to criminal prosecution.
Usury	**1.** Any contract by which a lender receives more interest than allowed by statute is usurious and illegal.
	2. There are many exceptions to usury laws.
Agreements not to compete	**1.** Agreements not to compete which are unreasonable restraints of trade are illegal.
	2. Reasonableness of covenants not to compete is determined by (a) length of time, (b) geographic area restrained, and (c) the need for such protection.
	3. To be legal, covenants not to compete must be part of another contract, such as a sale of business or employment contract.
	4. In the sale of a business, an agreement not to operate a competing business is enforceable if reasonable.
	5. In employment contracts covenants not to compete are enforceable if reasonable in time and territorial effect, considering the business interest protected and the effect on the employee.
Unconscionability	**1.** Unconscionability is an equitable doctrine used by courts to prevent oppression and unfair surprise in contracts.
	2. To be conscionable, material terms of a contract must be conspicuous, understandable, and the result of a true bargain.
	3. The doctrine of unconscionability allows a judge to strike contract terms or eliminate the entire contract or limit the unconscionable effect of a term.
Contracts of adhesion	**1.** A contract of adhesion is a form contract offered on a take-it-or-leave-it basis to one with little or no bargaining power.

Contracts disclaiming liability	**2.** These contracts may be enforceable, but they may be found to be unconscionable if they are oppressive.
	1. An exculpatory clause is a provision that attempts to relieve a party of all tort liability.
	2. An exculpatory clause may or may not be unconscionable depending on the bargaining power of the parties.
Tickets disclaiming liability	**1.** Provisions printed on tickets that disclaim liability are binding if the ticket is purchased as admission to a business establishment or for a service.
	2. Similar disclaimer provisions are not part of the contract and thus not enforceable if the ticket is merely evidence of ownership.

CASES

Laos v. Soble
503 P.2d 978 (Ariz. 1972)

HOWARD, J. . . . This is an appeal from a judgment in favor of defendants in a lawsuit to recover from them a fee purportedly due and owing to the plaintiff.

The plaintiff's claim was predicated upon the following document, written in longhand and signed by attorney Soble:

7–24–70

Paul Laos

Your fee is $1500.00 for appraisal fees for $200,000 or below & $2500.00 for anything over $200,000.

Joseph H. Soble

The case was tried to the court, both Laos and Soble testifying as to the circumstances which gave rise to this writing. The trial court, in ruling in defendants' favor, apparently believed Sobel's version, i.e., that the agreed-upon compensation was for Laos' services as an appraisal witness in an impending condemnation trial. Since, according to

him, he did not avail himself of such services, the obligation to pay Laos did not arise.

On appeal, Laos, contends that the document upon which he relied reflects that he was entitled to judgment as a matter of law. We believe that the document reflects the contrary—that, as a matter of public policy, the contract is illegal and therefore void. Although illegality was neither asserted in the trial court nor on appeal, we have a duty to raise such questions *sua sponte* when the face of the record reflects illegality.

An agreement to pay a witness a fee contingent on the success of the litigation is against public policy and void.

Professor Corbin points out that the use of "expert" testimony has been subject to grave abuses and that bargains for obtaining same should be under close supervision by the court. A similar concern was expressed in *Belfonte* v. *Miller:*

. . . The difficulties and dangers which surround so-called expert testimony are well understood by the profession and it is the manifest duty of our courts to carefully scan all special contracts relating to the employment of experts, providing for the payment of special compensation in addition to the witness fees allowed by the law. . . . The rule applied to such contracts is not to be affected by proof that the behavior of the parties was in fact exemplary, for it is the tendency of such contracts which serves to generate their undesirability. Improper conduct or bias can be predicted easily when the compensation of the witness is directly related to the absolute amount of an award which may in turn be dependent to a great degree on the testimony of that same witness. . . .

We are of the opinion, and so hold, that a contract providing for compensation of a witness contingent on the success of the litigation is subversive of public justice for the reason that his evidence may be improperly influenced. Public policy considerations brand such contract illegal.

Although the trial court's denial of plaintiff's claim was correct, but for a different reason,
We affirm.

Strickland v. Gulf Life Ins. Co.
242 S.E.2d 148 (Ga. 1978)

Strickland, an insured under a Gulf Life disability policy, injured his right leg. Doctors worked unsuccessfully for 118 days to save his leg. The insurance policy provided that Gulf Life would pay disability benefits if an insured lost a leg through "dismemberment by severance" within 90 days after an accident. Gulf Life denied liability because severance of Strickland's leg was not within the 90-day limitation. Strickland sued, but the court dismissed the lawsuit, stating: "The policy is a contract, and we cannot rewrite it. Nor do we feel that we can declare it void as against public policy. The limb was not severed within the specified ninety days, and the loss is therefore not covered." Strickland appealed.

UNDERCOFLER, J. . . . Where loss of a limb is involved at an arbitrary point in time, here 90 days, the insured under these cases is confronted with the ugly choice whether to continue treatment and retain hope of regaining the use of his leg or to amputate his leg in order to be eligible for insurance benefits which he would forgo if amputation became necessary at a later time. We find an insurance limitation forcing such a gruesome choice may be unreasonable and thus may be void as against public policy.

Finding such a limitation unreasonable is not without precedent. In *Burne v. Franklin Life Ins. Co.,* 451 Pa. 218, 301 A.2d 799, 801 (1973), a pedestrian had been struck by an automobile and had lain in a vegetative state for 4 1/2 years. The insurance company paid the life policy, but refused to pay the double indemnity accidental death benefits which were "payable only if '. . . such death

occurred . . . within ninety days from the date of the accident.'"

As stated in *Burne:*

[t]here are strong public policy reasons which militate against the enforceability of the ninety day limitation. The provision has its origins at a much earlier stage of medicine. Accordingly, the leading [Pennsylvania] case construing the provision predates three decades of progress in the field of curative medicine. Advancements made during that period have enabled the medical profession to become startlingly adept at delaying death for indeterminate periods. Physicians and surgeons now stand at the very citadel of death, possessing the awesome responsibility of sometimes deciding whether and what measure should be used to prolong, even though momentarily, an individual's life. The legal and ethical issues attending such deliberations are gravely complex. The result reached by the trial court presents a gruesome paradox indeed—it would permit double indemnity recovery for the death of an accident victim who dies instantly or within ninety days of an accident, but would deny such recovery for the death of an accident victim who endures the agony of prolonged illness, suffers longer, and necessitates greater expense by his family in hopes of sustaining life even momentarily beyond the ninety-day period. To predicate liability under a life insurance policy upon death occurring only on or prior to a specific date, while denying policy recovery if death occurs after that fixed date, offends the basic concepts and fundamental objectives of life insurance and [is] contrary to public policy. Hence, the ninety-day limitation is unenforceable.

In *INA Insurance Co. v. Commonwealth Ins. Dept.,* 376 A.2d 670 (Pa.Cmwlth.1977), the insurance company also argued that the causation problem was the main reason for these time limitations.

That court rejected the argument, observing that the burden was on the claimant to establish the causative relationship, and held that causation was not a weighty enough problem to deny benefits arbitrarily to those surviving beyond the time limitation set out in the policy, but who had died as a result of the accident. Following *Burne,* the court upheld the insurance commissioner's ruling that all similar time limitations in accident policies are arbitrary and unreasonable and thus against public policy.

> [I]t may be pointed out that "liberty of contract" as that term is used by its admirers includes two very different elements. These are the privilege of doing the acts constituting the transaction and the power to make it legally operative. One does not have "liberty of contract" unless organized society both forbears and enforces, forbears to penalize him for making his bargain and enforces it for him after it is made.
>
> This is the "liberty of contract" that has so often been extolled as one of the great boons of modern democratic civilization, as one of the principal causes of prosperity and comfort. And yet the very fact that a chapter on "legality" of contract must be written shows that we have never had and never shall have unlimited liberty of contract, either in its phase of societal forbearance or in its phase of societal enforcement. There are many contract transactions that are definitely forbidden

by the law, forbidden under pains and penalties assessed for crime and tort; and there are many more such transactions that are denied judicial enforcement, even though their makers are not subjected to affirmative pains and penalties.

Corbin, in his treatise on contracts, also observes that the declaration of public policy is the proper function of the courts, as well as of the legislature. "Constitutions and statutes are declarations of public policy by bodies of men authorized to legislate. It is the function of the courts to interpret and apply these, so far as they go and so far as they are understandable. Some judges have thought that they must look solely to constitutions and statutes and to earlier decisions interpreting and applying them as the sources from which they may determine what public policy requires. This is far from true, even though these are the sources that are first to be considered and that often may be conclusive.

"In determining what public policy requires, there is no limit whatever to the 'sources' to which the court is permitted to go; and there is no limit to the 'evidence' that the court may cause to be produced, ..." Then, the validity of the contract in question is one of law for the court.

Judgment reversed.

Kazmer-Standish v. Schoeffel Instrument 426 A.2d 1061 (N.J. 1981)

Kazmer-Standish, management consultants on mergers and acquisitions, found a buyer (Kratos) for a New Jersey corporation (Schoeffel). Schoeffel sold its entire assets, including its plant and land, to Kratos for $2.7 million, but the parties refused to pay Kazmer-Standish a $100,000 business broker's or finder's fee for finding the buyer for the Schoeffel business. Kazmer-Standish filed suit to collect the fee. Kratos and Schoeffel asserted that Kazmer-Standish could not recover a broker's commission on the sale, which included real estate because the plaintiff did not have the license. Defendants were granted a summary judgment.

KING, J. . . . Our Real Estate Broker's Act states, in pertinent part:

No person shall engage either directly or in-

directly in the business of a real estate broker or salesman, temporarily or otherwise, and no person shall advertise or represent himself as being authorized to act as a real estate broker or salesman, or to engage in any of the activities described in section 45:15–3 of the Revised Statutes, without being licensed so to do as hereinafter provided.

Any single act, transaction or sale shall constitute engaging in business within the meaning of this article.

No person, firm, partnership, association or corporation shall bring or maintain any action in the courts of this State for the collection of compensation for the performance of any of the acts mentioned in this article without alleging and proving that he was a duly licensed real estate broker at the time the alleged cause of action arose.

An unbroken line of New Jersey cases, beginning with *Kenney v. Paterson Milk & Cream Co.,* 110 *N.J.L.* 141, 164 *A.* 274 (E. & A. 1933), supports the Law Division judge's ruling that plaintiff is barred from recovery as a matter of law by these provisions of the Real Estate Broker's Act. In *Kenney* plaintiff provided defendant with a ready, willing and able buyer for defendant's dairy business pursuant to a written brokerage agreement. The broker agreement listed all the dairy's assets, including the real property, improvements and fixtures thereon. The value of the real estate was admittedly about one-third of the sale price. Our then highest court held that the transaction was not divisible or severable and the unlicensed plaintiff could recover no commissions, even on the portion of the transaction unrelated to real estate. The holding in *Kenney* has been followed consistently over the years with no signs of erosion. . . .

Kenney has spawned the nationwide majority rule which "has consistently held that if any real estate at all is involved in the transaction, the business broker must be licensed under the appropriate real estate licensing code" before any commission may be collected.

We are bound by the holding in *Kenney* and do not feel free to reexamine the problem in light of modern economic conditions which have proliferated national and multinational corporate mergers, acquisitions, divestitures, transfers of assets and spinoffs which have fostered the business broker's profession.

Affirmed.

Standard Leasing Corporation v. Schmidt Aviation, Inc.
576 S.W.2d 181 (Ark. 1979)

SMITH, J. This case is similar to *Bel v. Itek Leasing Corporation,* where we held . . . that an instrument which purported to be a lease of printing equipment was in fact a financing transaction that was void for usury. In the present case the circuit judge, sitting as a jury, found as a fact that the "lease" sued upon in this case is usurious and void. Several points for reversal are argued, but the validity of the contract is the essential issue.

We state the facts most favorably to the trial court's judgment. Standard Leasing brought this suit to recover all future installments under the lease, which it had declared immediately due and payable. Standard Leasing is engaged in what its principal witness, John Coppedge, described as the leasing of all types of general equipment. Standard Leasing does not have possession of the property that it leases. Instead, it supplies sellers of equipment with its forms and instructs the vendors how to fill out a form when equipment is sold. The form, with the purchaser's credit references, is then submitted to Standard Leasing for approval. If Standard Leasing approves the transaction, it pays the seller for the equipment and executed the "lease." The trial judge could have found that the papers are then transferred to a bank or other lender. That is, Coppedge testified that its business was "funded through certain banks and funding associates that we have." He also said that the original documents

in this case were in the possession of the Dekalb County Bank. The lease itself contains detailed provisions for its assignment and ironclad restrictions against the possibility that either Standard Leasing or its assignee can be held liable for breach of warranty or for other claims that might be asserted by the purchaser of the equipment.

In this case two representatives of Grimes Oil Company, of Memphis, Tennessee, came to Jonesboro, Arkansas, in 1976 and sold an air compressor to the appellee Schmidt Aviation. The purchaser was offered the option of buying the compressor for cash or leasing it. The purchaser elected, for tax purposes, to lease rather than to buy. One of the sales representatives stated that at the expiration of the lease Schmidt Aviation could buy the compressor for 10% of the price.

The sellers used a Standard Leasing form in writing up the transaction. In most respects it is similar to the lease in Bell, supra. That is, the document sets forth a "price" of $2,895.00, plus sales tax (at the Arkansas rate) of $86.85, making a total of $2,981.85. The instrument then provides for 36 monthly rental payments of $107.65, with the first and last to be paid in advance—apparently as a down payment. The monthly payments seem, mathematically, to have been arrived at by adding 30% to the total purchase price, which of course would amount to about 15% interest upon a transaction payable in 36 monthly installments.

The document, as in Bell, puts all the risk upon the lessee and provides the same remedies upon the lessee's default that would be available to a conditional seller . . . upon a similar delinquency. The lessee also waives trial by jury and the right to interpose any counterclaim or offset against the lessor in litigation with respect to the lease or the repossession of the property. The lessee authorizes the lessor to file a financing statement where necessary to perfect a security interest in the equipment.

In Bell the lease was silent with regard to the purchase of the property at the expiration of the lease, but there was oral testimony that it could be bought for 10% of the price. Here the lease, contrary to the salesmen's representations, recites that there is no option to purchase. Coppedge testified, however, that in a number of cases Standard Leasing does not get the property back, from which the trial judge could infer that in those instances the purchaser becomes the owner of the equipment when all payments have been made. To say the least, after the defendants below had made a prima facie showing that the lease was a sham Standard Leasing made no effort to go forward with the proof by showing that it is actually engaged in good faith in the leasing of equipment, not as acting as a broker or middleman in financing its sale. . . .

More than 10 years ago we gave explicit warning that agreement purporting to be leases would be examined closely to be certain that they were not being used as a cloak for usurious charges. In the case at bar we hold that the testimony presented an issue of fact about whether the transaction was in truth an instance of financing rather than of leasing. We refuse to take the view that the entire transaction was purged of the possibility of usury by the insertion of a sentence declaring that the lessee had no option to purchase the property. It goes without saying that, despite that sentence, the lessor could simply permit the lessee to retain the property after he had paid the 36 monthly installments on the price. Coppedge's testimony may be taken to imply that is what actually happens.. . .

Judgment affirmed.

Egnell, Inc. v. Weniger
418 N.E.2d 916 (Ill.App. 1981)

Egnell sued Weniger, seeking injunctive relief and damages based on his alleged breach of contract. On August 22, 1980, Weniger quit as president of Egnell and commenced working for a competitor of Egnell. Weniger's original employment contract (1975) contained the following provision: "Weniger hereby agrees that throughout the two-year period commencing on the termination of his employment hereunder for whatever reason he will not, directly or indirectly, be or become engaged or financially interested in, or an officer or director, employee, consultant or advisor of or to, any business, firm or corporation which engaged anywhere in the United States or Canada in any business which competes in any way with Egnell." When the trial court enjoined Weniger based on this provision, he appealed.

GOLDBERG, J. . . . The trial court found defendant Weniger bound by the restrictive covenant in his 1975 employment agreement with plaintiff. Thus, we must first consider the validity of the covenant. It is an accepted principle of law that the enforceability of a restrictive covenant "in restraint of competition is conditioned upon its reasonableness in terms of its effect upon the parties to the contract and the public. Illinois courts, through recent decisions, have encouraged fair competition in business while exhibiting an abhorrence of restraint of trade." For this reason covenants not to compete are carefully scrutinized by the courts.

The restrictive covenant in this case may be held enforceable only if its time limit and geographical scope are reasonable, trade secrets or confidential information are involved, and the restriction is reasonably necessary to protect a legitimate business interest. Whether [the] restrictive covenant is enforceable is a question of law.

We find the restrictive covenant at issue to be unreasonably broad. As written, the covenant contains no actual geographic limitation, as it would prohibit Weniger from working for two years for any company which had competed with plaintiff in the United States or Canada during the five years of Weniger's employment with plaintiff. Pursuant to this restriction, Weniger would not be able to work anywhere in the world for a firm which had competed in any manner with plaintiff in the United States or Canada for the past five years. Plaintiff has not demonstrated any compelling reason for such a broad restriction. The burden placed on Weniger far exceeds what would have been necessary for the protection of plaintiff's interests. We therefore conclude the restrictive covenant to be an unreasonable restraint of trade and therefore void and unenforceable as a matter of law.

Order reversed.

In Re Friedman
407 N.Y.S.2d 999 (1978)

When the artist Arnold Friedman died, his widow "sold" over 300 works of art to Charles Egan, a New York art dealer. Under the terms of the "agreement of sale," Egan obtained title to the art collection and the right to resell the works as he chose. According to the agreement, the consideration to be received by Mrs. Friedman consisted of one-half the purchase price of the art works which Egan resold. In fourteen years Egan resold only one painting. After her death, Mrs. Friedman's estate sued to recover the remaining art works. The trial court held the sale to be in effect a consignment. It ordered the art works returned to Mrs. Friedman's estate. On appeal the New York Supreme Court addressed the issue of whether or not the passing of title to Egan under such an agreement was unconscionable.

MARGETT, J. . . . To the extent that the "agreement" purports to transfer ownership of the paintings to Egan, it is unconscionable on its face.

The doctrine of unconscionability has been discussed by the courts and the commentators at great length and we therefore limit our observations on the subject. The doctrine appears in Section 2–302 of the Uniform Commercial Code (which became effective after the instant contract was executed), but the conclusion is inescapable that the Uniform Commercial Code simply codified the doctrine, which was used by the common-law courts to invalidate contracts under certain circumstances. The classic definition was a broad one. An unconscionable contract was one "such as no man in his senses and not under delusion would make on the one hand, and as no honest and fair man would accept on the other." A contractual clause would not be enforced where it is "so monstrous and extravagant that it would be a reproach to the administration of justice to countenance or uphold it."

The concept of unconscionability must necessarily be applied in a flexible manner depending upon all the facts and circumstances of a particular case. The courts have identified various elements of the unconscionable contract that may be characterized as substantive and procedural. Substantive elements of unconscionability appear in the content of the contract per se; procedural elements must be identified by resort to evidence on the contract formation process. Inflated prices (i.e., grossly inadequate consideration given by the seller), unfair disclaimers of warranty and termination clauses have been deemed substantively unconscionable. High pressure sales tactics, misrepresentation and unequal bargaining position have been recognized as procedurally unconscionable. The foregoing examples of unconscionable elements are by no means exhaustive; nor would we attempt to define a hierarchy of importance for any particular element in all cases. The weight to be given to each factor is as variable as the facts of each individual case. Where the disparity in the consideration exchanged by the parties is overwhelming, that factor alone "may be sufficient to sustain [a finding that the contract is unconscionable]," since such disparity "itself leads inevitably to the felt conclusion that knowing advantage was taken of [one party]."

At bar, the contract of the parties qua "sale" is grossly unconscionable in the substantive sense. In return for the stated conveyance of more than 300 works of art, Mrs. Friedman received neither the payment of a purchase price at the time of the "agreement" nor the right to receive a fixed price within a definite time in the future. Instead, she obtained only the uncertainty of payment to be made if and when sales were effected. Complete control over the timing of these "future sales" was placed in the hands of the dealer.

The "consideration" given by the dealer actually resulted in a situation where his interests were potentially adverse to the widow's. By holding out for a price far in excess of the fair market for the art works, the dealer could deny Mrs. Friedman any payment whatsoever. The dealer would, however, still retain title to the paintings. The incentive for the dealer to make any sales was therefore questionable. If he made no sales, he owned the collection outright. If he made sales, he would have to part with 50 percent of the purchase price.

This conflict of interest is reflected by the actual course of events over the last 15 years. From the date the contract was signed until Mrs. Friedman's death, Egan held only one exhibition of the Friedman paintings and made only one sale. Although the expert testimony established that dealers ordinarily seek to promote an artist's reputation through exhibits, catalogs and other efforts, Egan's own testimony was that he "protected," "watched" and "nursed" the paintings (at least during the period 1963–1969). It was certainly in his own self-interest to do that—and nothing more.

Viewed as a sale, the contract gave Egan similar latitude in the opposite direction. He could "dump" the paintings at a minimal price in order to raise immediate cash. While there is no indication that he did so, the opportunity for such abuse was present.

In sum, the "consideration" given for this "sale" was so contingent and so dependent upon the discretion of one who had a "built-in" conflict of interest as to be grossly inadequate. This patent inadequacy so permeates the "agreement" as to render it unconscionable. . . .

Furthermore, although the substantive unconscionability here present predominates, there are elements of procedural unconscionability attendant upon the execution of this contract which negate the possibility of any salvation for this "agreement." At the time the "agreement" was entered into Mrs. Friedman was about 75 years of age. Her only formal education had been at a convent in France. There was testimony at the hearing to the effect that she had no real business experience and that she displayed "an unworldly attitude" towards business matters. She did not have her own lawyer and professed that she could not afford one.

In contrast, when the agreement was executed, Charles Egan had been in business nearly 30 years and had spent 18 years as the owner of his own gallery. He was represented by his own attorney who had participated in previous transactions between Egan and other artists. His attorney drafted the agreement and "explained" it to the widow. . . .

After 15 years of exile, Arnold Friedman's legacy should be returned to his family.

Judgment affirmed.

Hy-Grade Oil Co. v. New Jersey Bank
350 A.2d 279 (N.J. 1975)

Plaintiff, a customer of the defendant bank, brought suit against the bank when it refused to credit his account with funds allegedly deposited in a night depository box. The plaintiff had signed an agreement with the bank covering such losses. Based upon this agreement, the lower court dismissed plaintiff's complaint.

BISHOFF, J. . . . The resolution of this appeal requires us to determine whether a clause in a "night depository agreement" between a bank and a customer, providing that "the use of the night depository facilities shall be at the sole risk of the customer," is valid and enforceable. . . .

Where they do not adversely affect the public interest, exculpatory clauses in private agreement are generally sustained.

It is clear that where a party to the agreement is under a public duty entailing the exercise of care he may not relieve himself of liability for negligence and unequal bargaining power or the existence of a public interest may call for the rejection of such clauses.

Turning to the factual situation before us, it involves the relationship between a national bank and a depositor. We have held that a "bank has been entrusted with an important franchise to serve the public and has, from time to time, received broad legislative protection."

The Uniform Commercial Code, "Bank Deposits and Collections," contains many provisions protecting banks in their daily operations. We find it significant that the Legislature provided in the same statute, that a bank may not, by agreement, disclaim responsibility for "its own lack of good faith or failure to exercise ordinary care" in the discharge of the duty imposed upon it by that statute.

A review of the cases in other states considering the validity of similar exculpatory clauses in night depository contracts indicates that the majority rule is to give full force and effect to the clauses.

The basic theory underlying these and other similar cases is that the absence of an agent of the bank when the night depository facilities are used creates the possibility of dishonest claims being presented by customers. In New Jersey we have rejected such a thesis in other situations and have held that the possibility of fraudulent or collusive litigation does not justify immunity from liability for negligence.

Other courts have refused to recognize the validity of such clauses. In holding such a clause inimical to the public interest, a [Pennsylvania] court said:

> We find the public need for professional and competent banking services too great and the legitimate and justifiable reliance upon the integrity and safety of financial institutions too strong to permit a bank to contract away its liability for its failure to provide the service and protections its customers justifiably expect, that is, for its failure to exercise due care and good faith. . . .

Banks perform an important and necessary public service. It cannot be seriously argued that they are not affected with a public interest. That this is so obvious from only a cursory examination of the extensive statutory regulations covering every phase of the banking business, including organization, merger, establishment of branches, investments, insurance of deposits, and others. . . .

We therefore hold that a bank cannot, by contract, exculpate itself from liability of responsibility for negligence in the performance of its functions as they concern the night depository service.

We should not be understood as implying that a bank and a customer may not, by negotiation and agreement, determine the standards by which the responsibility of the bank is to be governed so long as those standards are not unreasonable. The burden of proof of a violation of such a standard and proximate causation would remain on the depositor. However, an agreement such as the one now before us, which exculpates the bank from all responsibility without reference to any standard of care, we hold to be contrary to public policy and invalid.

It follows from what we have said that plaintiff's right to recover herein is based on the usual principles of negligence and proximate cause as they are applied between bailor and bailee.. . .

Reversed and rewarded.

REVIEW QUESTIONS

1. Identify the terms in column A by matching each with the appropriate statement(s) in column B.

A	B
1. Usury	**a.** Agreement in violation of a statute or public policy.
2. Agreement in restraint of trade	**b.** Equitable doctrine to prevent unfair surprise or oppression in contracts
3. Covenant not to compete	**c.** To be legal, it must be reasonable in time and geographic scope
4. Illegal agreement	**d.** Contract terms are imposed on adhering party
5. *Locus poenitentiae*	**e.** Clause that disclaims liability
6. Contract of adhesion	**f.** Lender receives more interest than allowed by law
7. Unconscionability	**g.** Person who repents before performing can rescind and seek restitution
8. Exculpatory clause	**h.** Price fixing or other agreement that limits competition

9. Effect of illegality

i. Since agreement is legally void, no remedy is available

10. Unlicensed practice of law

j. Cannot recover fee for services rendered and may violate criminal law

2. Aztec borrowed $50,000 from Union Bank and signed a promissory note in which Aztec promised to pay Union Bank $50,000 plus 10 percent per annum plus an "indexed principal." The note had a complicated inflation adjustment formula which yielded an additional $500 as the "indexed principal" when the note became due. The legal rate of interest is 10 percent per annum. Is this promissory note usurious? Explain.

3. Baker rented a golf cart at the Jackson Municipal Golf Course. While he was returning the cart, the brakes failed and it overturned, resulting in personal injuries to Baker. When Baker sued, the golf course defended by pointing to a disclaimer of liability clause located on the back of a Golf Cart Rental Agreement signed by Baker. Is the defense valid? Explain.

4. A landlord brought an action to evict a tenant who had refused to pay rent for several months, claiming that the premises were uninhabitable and in violation of the Housing Code regulations. Was the tenant right? Explain.

5. A real estate broker prepared a contract for the sale of land for a seller and a buyer. A state statute makes it illegal for brokers to prepare such agreements. What two legal dangers does the broker face?

6. Assume that you want to open a retail wine and cheese specialty shop in a shopping mall that is being developed. How might you reduce competition by the terms of your lease with the mall? Explain fully.

7. An experienced dentist with an established practice engaged the services of an associate dentist. The contract provided that if the associate left, she could not practice her profession for a period of 5 years within the radius of 30 miles from the town where the two had their practice. The agreement is later terminated, and the associate claims that the provision is unenforceable. Is she right? Why or why not?

8. Ketchum sold his plant, which manufactures window frames, to Cheatham. As part of the sales contract, Ketchum agreed to refrain from manufacturing or selling window frames within a 150-miles radius of Cheatham's plant for as long as Cheatham was engaged in that business. Thereafter, Ketchum does manufacture window frames, and Cheatham sues for an injunction. Does Cheatham carry the day and romp home? Why or why not?

9. Laudisio leased two gas stations from Amoco. Under the lease agreement, Amoco promised to provide proper gas storage tanks and pumps. When the tanks and pumps later malfunctioned, Laudisio sued for $25,000 lost profits. Amoco defended using two clauses in the lease: an exculpatory clause and a disclaimer of all warranties clause that would bar Laudisio from recovering anything. Laudisio claims the agreement was executed under duress and that the terms were nonnegotiable. Should Laudisio win? Explain.

10. An action is brought against Macy's Department Store because it charges a 1½ percent service charge per month on all revolving charge accounts. The usury law allows a maximum of 12 percent interest per annum. Is the charge usurious? Explain.

11. Lou, the owner of a newspaper, promises Grant, a politician, that he will publish a statement about Woodward, a rival politician, if Grant pays Lou $25,000. Both Lou and Grant know the statement is false and defamatory. Grant pays Lou $25,000. Is Lou's promise unenforceable on the grounds of public policy? Why or why not?

12 Willis, an owner of a restaurant business for 13 years, sued Southwestern Bell to recover damages caused by the omission of his ad from the Yellow Pages of the telephone directory. The contract contained a provision limiting the telephone company's liability to the cost of the ad. Willis claimed the clause was unconscionable. Was it? Explain.

11 FORM AND INTERPRETATION OF CONTRACTS

In the preceding five chapters, the elements of a valid, enforceable contract were explained (offer, acceptance, consideration, legal capacity, and legal purpose). Even if an *oral* contract has the required five elements, it may nonetheless be unenforceable because it is not evidenced by a writing.

As a general rule, an oral contract is just as valid and enforceable as a written contract. But some oral contracts are unenforceable under a law known as the *statute of frauds.* The statute of frauds recognizes that some contracts are subject to fraudulent proofs and perjured testimony; therefore, it requires written proof of the contract for the contract to be enforceable. Numerous exceptions to the statute of frauds have been recognized by courts. This chapter considers those contracts within the statute of frauds, the exceptions to the statute, and the nature of the writing that will satisfy the statute.

The term "within the statute" is used throughout this chapter. If a contract requires written proof, it is "within the statute." If a writing is not required, the contract is "outside" the statute.

When parties dispute the meaning of their contract, a court will be asked to decide what the contract terms mean. The process of discovering the meaning of a contract is called *interpretation.* For example, a court frequently must determine if a written contract is the sole evidence of the parties' agreement, or if other evidence may be considered. Certain statements or promises that occur prior to the written contract may not be considered because of a rule of procedure called the *parol evidence rule.* This rule and standards of contract interpretation are covered in this chapter.

1. The Approach

Of English origin, the statute of frauds was enacted in 1677. It is designed to prevent fraud by excluding from the courts legal actions on certain important contracts unless there is written evidence of the contract signed by the defendant. The statute of frauds makes some contracts unenforceable unless evidenced by a writing signed by the party sought to be bound. The statute attempts to prevent perjury by requiring written evidence in proving certain contracts. It also places restraints on the jury, which might not perceive that a party is lying about an oral contract. Yet the statute, rather than deterring fraud, has often promoted fraud or injustice by voiding socially useful contracts. Consequently, courts have recognized numerous exceptions and have narrowly construed the language of the statute.

Generally, the statute is used as a defense, even though there is no factual dispute over the existence of the contract or its terms. A contract that requires a writing may come into existence at the time of the oral agreement, but it is not enforceable until written evidence of the agreement is available. The agreement is valid in every respect except for the lack of proper evidence of its existence. The statute creates a defense in suits for the breach of executory oral contracts if they are covered by its provisions.

Study of the statute of frauds involves three questions: (1) Is the contract at issue within the statute? (2) If the contract is within the statute, is there written evidence of the contract which satisfies the statute? (3) If there is not sufficient written evidence, does an exception to the statute make the oral agreement legally enforceable?

2. Contracts within the Statute

Under state law, the following contracts are within the statute of frauds and must have written evidence to be enforceable. They are discussed in the next five sections.

1. Special promise of a surety to pay the debt of another, commonly known as a guaranty contract

2. Agreements for the sale of land or an interest in land

3. Agreements that cannot be performed within one year

4. Under the Code, contracts for the sale of goods with a price of $500 or more

5. Contracts for the sale of personal property other than goods

3. Guaranty Contracts

A person may seek to help another by guaranteeing his debt. In such a case, the debtor is primarily liable and the guarantor or surety is secondarily liable. A guarantor is not liable to pay until it is shown that the debtor has not or cannot pay the debt. The statute of frauds requires a guarantor's promise to be in writing. An oral promise to be primarily liable is not within the statute. The statute protects only persons who assume a secondary liability—that is, a promise to pay another's debt only if the other person does not pay.

In some cases, it is difficult to determine whether a party has made a promise to be secondarily liable or has incurred a direct, primary obligation to pay.[1] A person can make a direct obligation to pay for someone else. For example, Father says to auto dealer: "Deliver the car to my son, and I'll pay for it." This primary, direct promise is not within the statute of frauds. But if someone assumes a secondary obligation to pay, that promise is a guarantee and is within the statute. For example, Father says to auto dealer: "Deliver the car to my son. If he does not pay for it, then I promise to pay." The father is secondarily liable and his promise must be in writing to be enforceable.

At times a guarantor may intend primarily to benefit himself and not the debtor. For example, a person with a substantial financial interest in a corporation may promise orally to pay a debt of the corporation if it cannot pay. The law does not extend the protection of the statute of frauds to this type of guarantor. It analyzes the *main purpose* or *leading object* of the promisor in making the promise. When the leading object is to become a guarantor of another's debt primarily to benefit that person, the promise is secondary and within the statute. When the leading object of the promisor is to serve some interest or purpose of his own, even though he guarantees another's debt, the promise is direct and primary; it is not within the statute. Under the leading object rule, a court must determine whether the promisor intended primarily to benefit himself or the debtor.

4. Contracts Involving Interests in Land

Since the law has always placed importance on contracts involving land, it is logical that the statute of frauds should require a writing for a contract creating or transferring any interest in land. In addition to contracts involving a sale of an entire interest, the statute is applicable to contracts involving interests for a person's lifetime (called life estates), to mortgages, to easements, and to leases for a period in excess of one year.

One problem under the statute is to determine what is real property. Generally, it is land and all things affixed to the land. What is the status of things such as standing timber or minerals? Is an oral contract to sell oil and gas a contract involving real estate? The general rule is that these items are real property if the title to them is to pass to the buyer before they are severed from the land; they are personal property if title to them passes subsequently. The Code provides that a contract to sell minerals, oil, and the like, or a contract for a structure or its materials to be removed from realty, is a contract for the sale of goods if they are to be severed by the seller. If the buyer is to sever them, the contract affects and involves land and is subject to the real estate provisions of the statute of frauds. The Code also provides that a contract for the sale of growing crops is a contract for the sale of goods, whether they are to be severed by the buyer or by the seller.

Note that one of the exceptions to the statute (discussed in more detail later)

---

[1] Otto Contracting Co. v. S. Schinella & Son, p. 234.

is the doctrine of part performance. This exception frequently applies to oral contracts granting an interest in land. For example, courts will enforce an oral contract for the sale of land if, with the seller's consent, the buyer takes possession of the land, and makes a partial payment and valuable improvements on it.

5. Contracts That Cannot Be Performed within One Year

A contract is within the statute if, by its terms, it cannot be performed within one year from the time it is made. The period is measured from the time an oral contract is made to the time when the promised performance is to be completed. Thus, an oral agreement to hire a person for two years or to form and carry on a partnership for ten years would not be enforceable.

The decisive factor in determining whether a long-term contract comes within the statute is whether performance is possible within a year from the date of making. If a contract, according to the intentions of the parties as shown by its terms, may be fully performed within a year from the time it is made, it is not within the statute of frauds, even though the time of its performance is uncertain and may probably extend—and in fact does extend—beyond the year. If one party has fully performed, the contract is then not within the statute of frauds.

Even though it is most unlikely that performance could be rendered within one year, the statute does not apply if there is even a remote possibility that it could. This rule is one of possibility and not probability. Thus, assuming all elements of a valid contract, a promise to pay $10,000 "when cars are no longer polluting the air" would be enforceable even though given orally. Moreover, if a contract, otherwise to continue for more than a year, is by its own terms subject to termination within a year, it is not within the prohibition of the statute of frauds.

Thus, the question is not how long performance will *probably* run, but can the contract *possibly be performed* within one year from the making of the contract.[2] To put the matter in sharper focus, the rule should be stated: An oral contract that by its terms has no possibility of being performed within one year from the date of formation must be evidenced by a writing.

6. Contracts for the Sale of Goods

The Code contains several provisions regarding the statute of frauds. The provision applicable to the sale of goods stipulates that a contract for the sale of goods for the price of $500 or more is not enforceable unless there is some writing sufficient to indicate that a contract for sale has been made. The writing must be signed by the defendant or his authorized agent or broker. The Code further states that a writing is not insufficient if it omits or incorrectly states a term agreed on, but the agreement will not be enforced beyond the quantity of goods mentioned in the writing.

The Code favors contract formation and performance. Given that philosophy, the Code has four exceptions to the statute of frauds provision. These exceptions are explained later in this chapter.

---

[2] Hardin Associates, Inc. v. Brummett, p. 235.

7. Contracts for the Sale of Personal Property Other than Goods

The Code has several additional sections that require a writing. A contract for the sale of securities such as stocks and bonds is not enforceable unless (1) there is a signed writing setting forth a stated quantity of described securities at a defined or stated price, or (2) delivery of the security has been accepted or payment has been made, or (3) within a reasonable time a writing in confirmation of the sale or purchase has been sent and received and the party receiving it has failed to object to it within ten days after receipt, or (4) the party against whom enforcement is sought admits in court that such a contract was made. Note that this relates only to contracts for the sale of securities [8-319].

Another section concerns contracts for the sale of personal property other than goods or securities. For these contracts, which involve matters such as royalty rights, patent rights, and rights under a bilateral contract, a writing is required if the amount involved exceeds $5,000 [1-206].

In the article on secured transactions, discussed in Chapter 32 and 33, the Code usually requires a signed security agreement. Therefore, when a person borrows money and gives the lender an interest in his property as security, the debtor (borrower) must sign a security agreement [9-203].

8. Writing Required by the Statute of Frauds

If a contract is within the statute of frauds, there must be a signed writing sufficient to satisfy the statute of frauds. Generally, the common law requires more terms to be in the writing than does the Code. The general common law will be explained in this section, and the Code requirements will be covered in the next.

The statute of frauds does not require a formal written contract signed by both parties. All that is required is a note or memorandum that provides written evidence of the transaction. It must be signed by the party sought to be bound by the agreement (the defendant). The memorandum need contain only the names of the parties, a description of the subject matter, the price, and the general terms of the agreement. A memorandum of sale of real property must describe the real estate with such certainty that a court may order its conveyance.[3]

Under the statute, one party may be bound by an agreement even though the other party is not. Only the party who resists performance need have signed. Such a result is predicated on the theory that the agreement is legal in all respects, but proper evidence of such an agreement is lacking. This is furnished when the person sought to be charged with the contract has signed a writing.

The note or memorandum may consist of several writings, even though the writing containing the requisite terms is unsigned. However, it must appear from an examination of all the writings that the writing signed by the party to be charged was signed with the intention that it refer to the unsigned writing. In effect, the writings must be connected by internal reference in the signed memorandum to the unsigned one, so that they may be said to constitute one paper relating to the contract.

[3] Pick v. Bartel, p. 236.

The unsigned document is part of the memorandum if the documents by internal reference refer to the same subject matter or transaction. But if the documents do not refer to the same subject matter, they may not be read together. Oral evidence is not admissible to connect them.

As to the signature of the party sought to be charged, it may be quite informal and need not necessarily be placed at the close of the document. It may be in the body of the writing or elsewhere, as long as it identifies the writing with the signature of the person sought to be held.

9. Writing Required for Code Contracts

The Code has three minimal requirements for the writing to satisfy its statute of frauds provision. First, there must be some writing sufficient to indicate that a contract for the sale of certain goods has been made between the parties. Second, the writing must contain a quantity term, which need not be accurately stated. But a contract will not be enforced beyond the quantity term stated in the writing. Third, the writing must be signed by the party against whom the contract is being enforced. Thus, a plaintiff who is seeking to enforce the contract is not required to have signed the writing. Beyond these three requirements, the writing need not contain the material terms of the contract.

10. Introduction

The statute of frauds is not applicable to executed contracts. A party who has, for example, purchased or sold land under an oral contract cannot obtain a refund of his money or cannot obtain a return deed to his land. The statute of frauds does not allow rescission; it serves only as a defense to a suit for breach of an executory contract. Likewise, a contract that cannot be performed within one year which is fully executed cannot be rescinded.

If an agreement is within the statute of frauds and no written evidence of the contract exists, the contract will still be enforced and the defense ineffectual if one of the exceptions to the statute applies. Two exceptions are applicable to all types of contracts: (1) partial performance, and (2) promissory estoppel. These exceptions will be considered first; then the special Code exceptions will be explained. The Code has four exceptions: (1) confirmation between merchants, (2) specially manufactured goods, (3) judicial admissions, and (4) part performance.

EXCEPTIONS TO THE STATUTE OF FRAUDS

11. Part Performance

When a party has partly or fully performed his oral promise or has detrimentally relied on another's oral promise, it would be inequitable in most cases to deny that party relief because of the statute of frauds. Consequently, courts have made equitable exceptions to the statute. One exception is commonly called the *doctrine of part performance.* When one party to an oral contract partly or fully performs, then the other party is equitably estopped from using the statute as a defense. Another name for this doctrine is *equitable estoppel.* It is used primarily in oral contracts for the sale of real property, because many oral contracts involving real estate become partially executed as a result of part payment by the buyer or surrender of possession to the buyer by the seller or both. Since the statute of frauds is a complete defense to an executory oral contract involving real estate and it is no defense to a fully executed contract, what is the status if the contract is partially performed?

Performance to satisfy the statute of frauds has two aspects. First, the performance must establish and point unmistakably and exclusively to the existence of an oral contract. Performance eliminates the statute as a defense in such cases because it eliminates any doubt that a contract was made. Thus, the reason for the defense of the statute does not exist. Second, the performance must be substantial enough to warrant judicial relief, such as specific performance of the oral contract. In other words, it must be such that returning the parties to the status quo is unreasonable. To illustrate, assume that a buyer of real property under an oral contract has paid part of the purchase price. The money can be returned, and the statute of frauds would be a defense because even if it were admitted that the oral contract was entered into, there would be no equitable reason to enforce the oral agreement. However, when the seller under an oral contract also delivers possession to the buyer, the defense of the statute of frauds becomes more tenuous, because returning the parties to the status quo becomes somewhat difficult. When improvements are made by one in possession, a return to the status quo becomes quite difficult, if not impossible.

It is clear that the transaction is taken out of the statute if the buyer has taken possession, paid all or part of the price, and made valuable improvements. Less part performance may also take the contract out of the statute if the buyer takes possession and pays part of the price, giving good evidence of a contract. If he also pays taxes and mortgage payments while in possession, specific performance may be warranted. Payment of the price, standing alone, is not a basis for specific performance and will not satisfy the statute; but if the buyer enters into possession and makes valuable improvements, there is sufficient part performance to make the contract enforceable and to satisfy the statute.

12. Promissory Estoppel

Chapter 8, explained promissory estoppel as a doctrine for validating contracts as an alternative to consideration. That same concept is sometimes used by courts to prevent a party to an oral contract from using the statute of frauds as a defense. When a party relies to his detriment on an oral promise, the oral promise may be enforceable, notwithstanding the statute of frauds. The reliance must be foreseeable by the promisor, and enforcement of the promise must be necessary to avoid injustice. The remedy may be limited as justice requires.

Like the part performance exception, courts may use promissory estoppel to achieve fairness and prevent an unfair result. Promissory estoppel is used whenever the plaintiff's equities are so great that any contrary decision would be inequitable. In many cases, parties will rely on oral promises. In such cases, to allow the statute of frauds to be used as a defense would itself constitute a type of fraud on the relying party. The trend of decisions is to use promissory estoppel to prevent an unfair use of the statute.[4]

13. Code Exceptions

Written Confirmation Between Merchants. The Code provisions relating to the sale of goods contain four exceptions to the rule that requires a writing if the contract involves $500 or more. One exception is limited to transactions between "merchants." It arises from the business practice of negotiating contracts orally, often by telephone. A merchant who contracts orally with another merchant can satisfy the statute of frauds requirement by sending a confirming writing to the other merchant [2-201(2)]. This confirmation will satisfy the statute, *even though it is not signed by the party to be charged,* unless written notice of objection to its contents is given within 10 days after it is received. This means that a merchant who has dealt orally with another merchant will have an enforceable contract unless the merchant receiving the writing objects within the 10-day period.

Specially Manufactured Goods   A second exception to the writing requirement under the Code relates to conduct that clearly shows a contract has been made. The Code explicitly excludes from the statute transactions that involve goods to be specially manufactured. To fit within this exception, three requirements must be met [2-201(3)(a)].

1. The goods are to be specially manufactured for the particular buyer and are not suitable for sale to others.[5]
2. The seller has made a substantial beginning to manufacture or commitments to obtain the goods.
3. The circumstances reasonably indicate that the goods are for the buyer.

Judicial Admissions   Another substitute for writing is based upon recognition that the required writing is simply a formality and that a contract may very well exist. The oral contract is unenforceable without proof of its existence; but when proper proof is available, the contract becomes enforceable. If the party who is resisting the contract admits its existence in the proper circumstances and surroundings, such admission will substitute for a writing.[6] Thus, the Code provides that an oral contract for the sale of goods is enforceable if (when legal action is brought to enforce it) the defendant admits in the court proceedings that a contract for sale was made. It is quite possible that the admission will be made in the pleadings, during discovery, or as testimony during a trial. That judicial admission satisfies the Code statutory requirement of a writing [2-201(3) (b)].

Performance   The final exception is part performance. The Code excepts oral contracts for the sale of goods that have been paid for or received and

---

[4] Potter v. Hatter Farms, Inc., p. 236.
[5] Colorado Carpet Installation v. Palermo, p. 237.
[6] Farmers Elevator Co. of Reserve v. Anderson, p. 238.

accepted [2-201(3)(c)]. In the sale of goods, the Code takes the contract out of the statute only to the extent of the part performance. In other words, these contracts are enforceable to the extent the buyer has made payment for goods or to the extent the seller has shipped goods which the buyer has accepted. Any unperformed part of the contract is still within the statute, and some writing is required unless one of the other exceptions is applicable.

PAROL EVIDENCE RULE

14. The Theory

Courts are often asked to interpret the meaning of a contract. If the contract is written, courts may face the question of whether or not they can consider oral or other evidence that is not in the written document. The law seeks to protect the sanctity of written contracts. Therefore, it is generally held that statements, promises, guarantees, and representations made by the parties prior to signing a written contract may not be considered if the written contract represents the entire agreement of the parties. This law is called the *parol evidence rule.*

The parol evidence rule prevents the introduction of prior or contemporaneous oral or written agreements that might vary or contradict the final written contract. When parties to a contract embody the terms of their agreement in a writing intended to be the final and exclusive expression of their agreement, the written contract cannot be contradicted, explained, varied, or supplemented by previous or contemporaneous oral or written agreements. Everything that happens prior to or contemporaneously with the execution of the written contract is assumed to be integrated into it. The written contract is deemed the only permissible evidence of the agreement. All earlier negotiations, understandings, representations, and agreements are said to have merged in the written contract. Therefore, *parol* (extrinsic) evidence is not admissible to supplement, subtract from, alter, vary, or contradict the agreement as written.[7]

15. Exceptions to the Parol Evidence Rule

But most legal rules have exceptions based on notions of equity, good conscience, and common sense. The parol evidence rule has several such exceptions. First, since the rule presumes all prior negotiations are merged into the written contract, it obviously cannot apply to agreements made after the written contract. Thus, the rule does not prevent the use of oral evidence to establish modifications agreed upon subsequent to the execution of the written contract. Likewise, the rule is inapplicable to evidence of a cancellation of the agreement. Other exceptions include evidence of fraudulent misrepresentations, lack of delivery of an instrument when delivery is required to give it effect, and errors in drafting or reducing the contract to writing. Moreover, oral evidence is always allowed to clarify the terms of an ambiguous contract.

Perhaps the most important exception is the *partial integration rule.* This exception requires the judge to determine if the written contract is totally or merely partially integrated. A total integration occurs when the parties intend the

---

[7] Snow v. Winn, p. 239.

written contract to be the *final* and *complete* statement of their agreement. If they do, evidence of prior agreements is not permitted for any reason. A partial integration occurs when the parties intend the writing to be final on the terms as written but not necessarily complete on all terms of their agreement. Although the contract cannot be *contradicted* under the partial integration rule, it can be *supplemented* or *explained* by prior agreements between the parties.

To decide if the contract is a total or partial integration, the judge uses a reasonable person test. He looks to the evidence of the prior agreement. If reasonable persons would have *normally* and *naturally* included the prior agreement in the written contract, then the writing is totally integrated. If they would not, then the contract is partially integrated, and the evidence is allowed in to explain or supplement the written contract. In most cases, the written contract will be viewed as totally integrated unless the additional terms are the kind that might naturally be agreed upon and not included in the writing by reasonable persons situated as were the original parties. In that event, consistent additional terms are admissible.

16. Parol Evidence and the Code

The Code recognizes that the parol evidence rule prevents the use of oral evidence to contradict or vary the terms of a written memorandum or of a contract that is intended to be the final expression of the parties. The impact of the rule is greatly reduced, however, by the Code's provision that a written contract may be explained or supplemented by a prior course of dealing between buyer and seller, by usage of trade, or by the course of performance. The Code also allows evidence of consistent additional terms to be introduced, based on the partial integration rule [2-202]. The provisions allowing such evidence are designed to ascertain the true understanding of the parties concerning the agreement and to place the agreement in its proper perspective. The assumption is that prior dealings between the parties and the usages of the trade were taken for granted when the contract was worded. Often a contract for sale involves repetitive performance by both parties over a period of time. The course of performance is indicative of the meaning that the parties, by practical construction, have given to their agreement. It is relevant to interpretation of the agreement and thus is admissible evidence.

When oral evidence of a course of dealing, trade usage, or course of performance is introduced under the Code's exceptions to the parol evidence rule, the law recognizes an order of preference in the event of inconsistencies. Express terms will prevail over an interpretation based on the course of performance, and the course of performance will prevail over an interpretation predicated upon either the course of dealing or the usage of trade [2-208].

17. Construction and Interpretation of Contracts

Courts are often called upon to construe or interpret contracts. Although there is a technical distinction between *construction* (courts construe a contract's legal effect) and *interpretation* (juries interpret the parties' intentions), these words are generally interchangeable. The basic purpose of construing a contract is to determine the intention of the parties. If the language is clear and unambiguous, construction is not required, and the intent expressed in the agreement will be followed. When the language of a contract is ambiguous or obscure, courts apply certain established rules of construction in order to ascertain the supposed intent of the parties. These rules will not be used to make a new contract for the parties or to rewrite the old one. They are applied by the court merely to resolve doubts and ambiguities within the framework of the agreement.

The general standard of interpretation is to use the meaning the contract language would convey to a reasonably intelligent person who is familiar with the circumstances in which the language was used. Thus, language is judged objectively rather than subjectively, and is given a reasonable meaning. What one party says he meant or thought he was saying or writing is immaterial, since words are given effect in accordance with their meaning to a reasonable person in the circumstances of the parties. In determining the intention of the parties, it is the expressed intention that controls, and this will be given effect unless it conflicts with some rule of law, good morals, or public policy.

The language is judged with reference to the subject matter of the contract, its nature, objects, and purposes. Language is usually given its ordinary meaning, but technical words are given their technical meaning. Words with an established legal meaning are given that legal meaning. The law of the place where the contract was made is considered a part of the contract. Isolated words or clauses are not considered; instead, the contract is considered as a whole to ascertain the intent of the parties. If one party has prepared the agreement, an ambiguity in the contract language will be construed against him, since he had the chance to eliminate the ambiguity.[8] As an aid to the court in determining the intention of the parties, business custom, usage, and prior dealings between the parties are considered.

In the interpretation of contracts, the construction the parties have themselves placed on the agreement is often the most significant source of the intention of the parties. The parties themselves know best what they meant by their words of agreement, and their action under that agreement is the best indication of what that meaning was.

---

[8] Grove v. Charbonneau Buick-Pontiac, Inc., p. 240.

SUMMARY

STATUTE OF FRAUDS

The approach	1. Contracts within the statute of frauds are unenforceable unless evidenced by a writing.

	2.	The statute of frauds results in an affirmative defense which must be pleaded.
Guaranty contracts	1.	A direct, primary promise to pay another's debt is not within the statute.
	2.	A secondary promise to pay another's debt if the debtor does not pay is within the statute and must be evidenced by a writing.
	3.	If the promisor's leading object or main purpose is to serve his own interests, the promise is not within the statute.
Contracts involving interests in land	1.	Any contract that creates or transfers any interest in land must be evidenced by a writing and signed by the party to be charged.
	2.	Sale of realty, leases for 1 year or more, liens, mortgages, and easements are within the statute.
	3.	Promises to transfer timber, minerals, oil and gas, and structures are within the statute *unless* the seller is to sever them from the realty.
	4.	Growing crops are goods, not interests in land, and are not within the statute regardless of who severs them.
Contracts that cannot be performed within one year	1.	Any contract which, by its terms, is impossible to perform within 1 year is within the statute.
	2.	If there is *any possibility* a contract can be performed in 1 year, it is not within the statute.
Contracts for the sale of goods	1.	Contracts for the sale of goods having a *price* of $500 or more is within the statute.
	2.	The Code has four exceptions: written confirmation between merchants, specially manufactured goods, judicial admissions, and performance.
Writing required for non-Code contracts	1.	A writing satisfies the statute if it states with *reasonable* certainty the identity of the parties, the subject matter, the essential terms and conditions, and is signed by the party to be charged.
	2.	If there is more than one writing and one writing is signed, the unsigned writing is

	part of the signed writing if the writings by internal reference refer to the same subject matter or transaction.
Writing required for Code contracts	1. A writing satisfies the statute if it (a) indicates a sale of certain goods between the parties, (b) has a quantity term, and (c) is signed by the party to be charged.
	2. Omission of any term other than quantity does not make writing insufficient. The quantity term may be supplied by any means such as outputs and requirements.
	3. The contract will not be enforced beyond the quantity stated in the writing.

EXCEPTIONS TO THE STATUTE OF FRAUDS

Part performance	1. If an oral contract was fully performed by both parties, the statute is not applicable.
	2. Performance must establish and point unmistakably and exclusively to the existence of an oral contract.
	3. Performance must be so substantial that it would be inequitable not to grant judicial relief.
	4. If it is reasonable to return the parties to the status quo, a court will rescind the transaction. A buyer who has only paid the price will have his money returned.
	5. If a buyer has paid the price and taken other actions (such as making valuable improvements to land), courts will recognize an exception to the statute.
	6. In contracts of long duration, full performance by one party makes the agreement enforceable.
Promissory estoppel	1. If a party detrimentally relies on an oral promise, some courts will enforce the promise.
	2. The reliance must be foreseeable by the promisor, enforcement of the promise is necessary to avoid injustice, and the remedy may be as limited as justice requires.
Code exceptions	1. *Between merchants,* a signed confirmation of an oral contract sent within a

reasonable time satisfies the statute if the merchant who actually receives it does not object by written notice within 10 days.

2. At a minimum, the confirmation must be written, signed by the sender, evidence an actual contract between the parties, and contain a quantity term.

3. Contracts involving goods specially manufactured for the buyer are enforceable even though the contracts are not evidenced by signed writings.

4. If the party to be charged admits in his pleadings, testimony, or otherwise in court that a contract of sale was made, the statute is satisfied.

5. Part or full payment or part or complete acceptance of goods satisfies the statute. The contract is enforced only to the extent of the part performance.

THE PAROL EVIDENCE RULE

Theory

1. Evidence of prior or contemporaneous agreements (whether written or oral) is inadmissible to vary, contradict, or modify an unambiguous written contract.

2. Parol evidence will be excluded only if the court finds that the writing was intended as a *final and complete* agreement (totally integrated).

3. A merger or integration clause ("This is the final and complete agreement.") is generally given effect.

Exceptions

1. Parol evidence may be used to (a) show that writing was not the final and complete agreement, (b) show defects in formation, (c) show and explain ambiguity, and (d) show subsequent agreements.

The Code

1. Under the Code, agreements may be explained by evidence of course of dealing, usage of trade, or course of performance.

RULES OF CONTRACT INTERPRETATION

General rules

1. Words are given their plain and ordinary meanings.
2. Ambiguities are construed against the party who drafted or used the ambiguous language.
3. Writings are to be interpreted as a whole and language is not to be taken out of context.
4. Special circumstances under which a contract was made may be used to show the actual understanding of the parties.
5. Specific provisions control general provisions.
6. Handwritten provisions prevail over typed provisions, and typed provisions prevail over printed provisions.
7. The Code supplies (gap-fills) terms omitted by the parties. Code-implied terms are applicable unless the parties provide otherwise in their agreement.

CASES

Otto Contracting Co. v. S. Schinella & Son
427 A.2d 856 (Conn. 1980)

Camarda, a medical doctor, and Schinella, a general contractor, entered into a partnership to develop an office building called Stevanton Plaza. In the course of that development, plumbing work was required, for which Otto was the successful bidder. Because Otto had doubts about the financial responsibility of Schinella, he refused to execute a subcontract for the plumbing work unless Camarda would personally guarantee payment. Although a separate contract of guaranty was not executed by Camarda, he did personally sign the subcontract.

When Otto was not paid for his work, he sued, and the issue at trial narrowed to the personal liability of the defendant Camarda. The trial court concluded that Camarda was liable because his assurance of payment was an original undertaking not within the statute of frauds. Camarda appealed.

PETERS, J. . . . The defendant's attack on the trial court's conclusion relies on the provision of the statute of frauds, General Statutes §52-550, that bars action "upon any agreement . . . against any person upon any special promise to answer for the debt, default or miscarriage of another . . . unless such agreement, or some memorandum thereof, is made in writing and signed by the party to be charged therewith or his agent." The defendant claims that the contract he signed does not sufficiently memorialize the terms of his obligations, and that therefore the requirements of the statute have not been met and the plaintiff's action cannot be maintained. The trial court did not address the merits of this claim, but ruled instead that no memorandum was required because the undertaking of Camarda . . . under the contract was an original undertaking and not within the statute of frauds. The issue before us then is whether the defendant's commitment was a collateral undertaking within the statute of frauds, and hence presumably unenforceable, or whether it was an original undertaking to which the statute of frauds does not apply. We agree with the trial court's conclusion.

A contract that all or part of a duty of a third person to the promisee shall be satisfied is not within the Statute of Frauds as a promise to answer for the duty of another if the consideration for the promise is in fact or apparently desired by the promisor mainly for his own economic advantage, rather than in order to benefit the third person. The "main purpose" or "leading object" rule, which defines when an undertaking is original rather than collateral, is an exception of long standing to the statute of frauds' guaranty provision.

The test established by our cases is: "If . . . there is a benefit to the promisor which he did not before and would not otherwise enjoy, and in addition the act is done upon his request and credit, there ordinarily arises an original undertaking not within the statute." "The question as to whom credit was given, which is determinative of whether the agreement was an original undertaking not within the statute, is one of fact." On the basis of the evidence and the record before it, the trial court could readily have inferred that the defendant, as owner, stood to benefit from the work done to complete Stevanton Plaza. Moreover, there was ample evidence that the plaintiff Otto gave credit, not to the nominal contractor, S. Schinella & Son, Inc., but rather to the owners Schinella and Camarda personally. The plaintiff never agreed to perform any part of the subcontract until it had received assurance of their personal liability; the payments that were made were payments by the partnership and not by the corporation. . . . Under these circumstances, the trial court correctly concluded that the defendant Camarda had made a commitment as an original undertaking not within the statute of frauds.

There is no error.

Hardin Associates, Inc. v. Brummett
613 S.W.2d 4 (Tex. 1981)

Hardin Associates was in the business of developing shopping centers, and it hired Brummett to head a new division called the development division. Brummett was hired on an oral contract of employment for an indefinite time. In February 1978, Hardin eliminated the development division, and Brummett went to work for another company. When Hardin refused to pay Brummett certain fees earned under the terms of the employment contract, Brummett sued. Hardin claims that the oral indefinite employment contract is void because it was within the statute of frauds. The trial court found for Brummett.

CORNELIUS, J. . . . Hardin asserts that Brummett's contract was in violation of our Statute of Frauds, which provides that an agreement which is not to be performed within one year is unenforceable unless it is in writing. We disagree. Indefinite term employment contracts are considered performable within one year and do not come within the purview of the Statute of Frauds. Even if it be considered that the contract was for the definite time needed to complete the Commerce Square project, the rule is that, where the time for performance is indefinite in that the agreement merely provides for the performance of a particular act or acts which can conceivably be performed within one year, the Statute of Frauds is inapplicable, however improbable performance within one year might be.

The judgment of the trial court is affirmed.

Pick v. Bartel
659 S.W.2d 636 (Tex. 1983)

Truebenbach owned two adjacent tracts of land, one containing 165 acres and the other 25 acres. He sold the 165-acre tract to Pick. The deed stated: "Grantors also guarantee Pick a right-of-way across the 25-acre tract sold to Walter Bartel." Five days later, Truebenbach sold the 25-acre tract to Bartel and the deed provided for the easement to Pick. When Pick sued Bartel to enforce his easement, the court held that Pick's deed was not a sufficient writing to satisfy the statute of frauds because the land subject to the easement was not adequately described. Pick appealed.

ROBERTSON, J. . . . An easement is an interest in land which is subject to the Statute of Frauds. It is well settled that in order for a conveyance or contract of sale to meet the requirements of the Statute of Frauds, it must, insofar as the property description is concerned, furnish within itself or by reference to other identified writings then in existence, the means or data by which the particular land to be conveyed may be identified with specific certainty. . . .

The writing required by the Statute of Frauds, which identifies the servient estate of an easement, must contain the essential terms of a contract, expressed with such certainty and clarity that it may be understood without recourse to parol evidence to show the intention of the parties. No part of the instrument is more essential than that which identifies the subject matter of the agreement. The words in the Pick deed "sold to Walter Bartel" does not identify the alleged servient estate with sufficient certainty to satisfy the Statute of Frauds, nor does it refer to some other existing writing, by which the alleged servient estate may be identified with sufficient certainty.

This Court has held that a description in a writing which states "my property," "my land," or "owned by me" is a sufficient description when it is shown by extrinsic evidence that the party to be charged owns a tract and only one tract of land which satisfies the description. . . .

In the instant case, we cannot infer that the "25-acre tract sold to Walter Bartel" refers to the alleged servient estate. The owner of the property referred to in the Pick deed is not stated. Moreover, since the Pick and Bartel deeds were dated five days apart, the 25-acre tract had *not* been sold to Bartel at the time the Pick deed was executed. No city, county or state is mentioned in connection with its location. No lot or block number is given, nor is there any indication as to the amount of land. No description by any particular name appears. In fact, every essential element of the description is left to inference or to be supplied by parol. To permit the Picks to show by parol evidence what land was under consideration would be, in effect, to abrogate the rule requiring contracts or the conveyance of land to be in writing. We need not reach the issue of whether the words "we guarantee" in the Pick deed are sufficient words of grant to convey an easement. We hold that, as a matter of law, the description of the land subject to the alleged easement will not support a suit to establish a roadway easement.

Affirmed.

Potter v. Hatter Farms, Inc.
641 P.2d 628 (Or.App. 1982)

Potter operates a turkey hatchery in Oregon. Hatter raises turkeys in Oklahoma for sale to food processors. In 1979 Potter and Hatter orally agreed to a buy-sell contract for young turkeys. Shortly thereafter, they discovered a problem in transporting the young turkeys from Oregon to Oklahoma, since the turkeys are not fed while being transported. In late 1979, Hatter assured Potter that he would find a solution to the transportation problem. In reliance on this assurance, Potter turned down an offer to sell his young turkeys to a California buyer, Kent. Two months later, Hatter said he would be unable to buy the turkeys and Potter sued. The statute of frauds was raised as a defense.

GILLETTE, J. . . . The issue in the present case is whether promissory estoppel should be allowed as an exception to the UCC statute of frauds. Allowing promissory estoppel as an exception to the Statute of Frauds is consistent with the obligation of good faith. Exclusion of promissory estoppel, on the other hand, would allow a party to enter into an oral contract, induce the other party to rely to its detriment and yet completely escape liability under the contract. We do not believe the legislature intended such a result.

Defendant argues that allowing promissory estoppel to defeat the Statute of Frauds would render the statute meaningless. It is true that any exception to such a writing requirement increases the possibility of fraud through perjury. Despite that fact, the Supreme Court has created exceptions to the general Statute of Frauds for both promissory estoppel and for part performance, and the Code's Statute of Frauds contains some express exceptions. Neither the Oregon court nor the legislature apparently believed that creating exceptions to the statute render it a nullity. A promissory estoppel exception essentially enhances the Statute of Frauds by preventing its use as an instrument of fraud. Neither do we believe that a promissory estoppel exception eliminates the incentive for merchants to memorialize their agreements in writing. Those who would comply with the statute to avoid unenforceability of their agreements would likewise comply to avoid the uncertainty and difficulty of having to prove the elements of promissory estoppel at trial.

To avoid a Statute of Frauds defense through promissory estoppel, it is necessary to prove 1) actual reliance on a promise, 2) a definite and substantial change of position occasioned by the promise and 3) foreseeability to the promisor, as a reasonable person, that the promise would induce conduct of the kind that occurred. The difficulty of meeting that burden of proof should both encourage merchants to put agreements into writing and decrease the likelihood of a proponent of a contract being able to prove its existence through perjury. . . .

Finally, we must decide whether there was substantial evidence to satisfy the requirements of promissory estoppel. As we pointed out above, Potter's testimony provides substantial evidence that a promise was made. Potter's testimony that he turned down offers to sell the poults to buyers in California in reliance on defendant's promise satisfies the actual reliance and substantial change of position requirements. His testimony that he reached an agreement with Gil Kent in January, 1979, that in June of that year he told defendant of the offers he had from other buyers and that Hatter Farms did not indicate to him that it was no longer interested in the poults satisfies the reasonable foreseeability requirement.

There was substantial evidence of the existence of an oral contract between plaintiff and defendant. Although the contract would otherwise be unenforceable for violating the Statute of Frauds, there was substantial evidence here of promissory estoppel barring defendants' assertion of that defense.

Affirmed.

Colorado Carpet Installation v. Palermo 647 P.2d 686 (Colo.App. 1982)

COYTE, J. . . . Defendants appeal from a judgment entered against them for damages for breach of contract. We reverse.

The evidence revealed that plaintiff and defendants negotiated for plaintiff to furnish and install carpeting and tile in the defendants' home. Plaintiff submitted several bids to defendants one of which defendant Zuma Palermo orally accepted. Plaintiff then ordered the carpeting and tile from various companies. When the tile arrived, plaintiff delivered it to defendants' home and left it there until the house was ready for it to be laid. When plaintiff's employee arrived to install the tile, a dispute developed and defendant Zuma refused to let plaintiff proceed with the job. Plaintiff removed the tile. Subsequent negotiations proved futile and plaintiff instituted this action.

Defendants contend that plaintiff's claim is barred by the application of §2–201, (the statute of frauds), in that the contract was for the sale of goods with a value in excess of $500 and was not signed by the party to be charged. We agree.

The trial court found that the contract came under the specially manufactured goods exception to the statute of frauds and was therefore enforceable notwithstanding the lack of a signed writing. However, the specially manufactured goods exception applies only when goods are not a stock item and are unsuitable for sale to others in the ordinary course of business.

Here, the carpeting was a standard item carried by a number of carpeting distributors. It was not specially cut to fit the particular dimensions of defendants' rooms, but rather, was taken off a full roll of carpeting. The plaintiff was able to resell two of the rugs which fact further indicates that it was suitable for sale to others in the ordinary course of business.

Thus, the trial court erred when it found the carpeting came within the specially manufactured goods exception to the statute of frauds.

Plaintiff argues that the trial court's judgment may also be upheld under the part performance exception to the statute of frauds. We disagree.

While part performance can be sufficient to remove the bar of the statute of frauds, it will remove only that portion of the contract which relates to goods which have actually been received and accepted.

Here, the tile was the only item which was delivered to and initially accepted by the defendants. However, plaintiff removed the tile, and payment for the tile forms no part of plaintiff's present claim. As the carpeting was neither received nor accepted by the defendant, the part performance exception cannot apply to validate that portion of the contract.

Judgment reversed.

Farmers Elevator Co. of Reserve v. Anderson
552 P.2d 63 (Mont. 1976)

HARRISON, J. . . . This appeal is taken from a judgment entered August 25, 1975, in the district court, Sheridan County. Farmers Elevator Co. of Reserve, a cooperative enterprise, successfully sought damages for breach of a contract made with Dale Anderson, a local farmer in the Dagmar area. . . .

On October 28, 1972, Anderson contracted with the Farmers Elevator Co. for the sale of 18,000 bushels of durum wheat at a price stipulated in the record to be $1.80 per bushel. . . .

The contract was strictly oral, the only written evidence of the agreement being an unsigned notation in a small "book" used by Farmers Elevator Co. to record its purchases in the ordinary course of its business. Testimony and a confirmatory memorandum established that the approximate delivery date contemplated by the parties was February 1973.

Although the contract was oral in nature, we note Anderson has at no time denied the existence of the contract, the quantity contracted for, or the stipulated price. Farmers Elevator Co. normally contracts orally with its patrons and pays by check upon delivery, whether in full or partial satisfaction of its purchase contracts.

Pursuant to his contract, Anderson delivered 8,802 bushels of durum wheat in approximately 36 truckloads between March 27, 1973, and May 30, 1973. . . .

On September 27, 1973, the Board Chairman learned by telephone of Anderson's refusal to deliver further on his contract. The next day plaintiff was forced to cover for the undelivered wheat, and purchased 9,198 bushels at the then current market price, which by that time had risen to $6.50 per bushel. It was established at trial that Anderson sold his wheat to another elevator in North Dakota for $5.35 per bushel. Anderson raised and harvested more wheat in August and September 1973, but he never tendered any of this to plaintiff or made any further effort to honor his contract with it.

Is enforcement of the oral agreement . . . barred by the Statute of Frauds?

In a commercial setting such as here, Montana law provides that no contract for the sale of goods, for the price of $500 or more, is enforceable unless some writing exists sufficient to establish that an agreement between the parties was reached. However, several exceptions are listed in the statute; one is:

> A contract which does not satisfy the requirements of subsection (1) but which is valid in other respects is enforceable. . . . (b) if the party against whom enforcement is sought admits in his pleading, testimony or otherwise in court that a contract for sale was made but the contract is not enforceable under this provision beyond the quantity of goods admitted. . . .

That the agreement, but for the lack of writing, is "valid in other respects" is not contested by the parties. There can be no doubt of Anderson's admissions, in his deposition and at trial, as to the existence of the contract. At trial he testified:

> Q. So your testimony is that there was an agreement for you to sell eighteen thousand bushels of durum? A. Yes.

Q. And that agreement was made in October, October 28th, of 1972, is that correct? A. Yes.

The so-called "judicial admission" exception to the Statute of Frauds . . . prevents a litigant from simultaneously admitting the existence of a contract and claiming the benefits of the statute. . . .
Affirmed.

Snow v. Winn
607 P.2d 678 (Okla. 1980)

OPALA, J. . . . Plaintiff (Landlord) brought this suit to terminate a commercial lease with defendant (tenant). The leased premises consists of a filling station with car wash facilities in the City of Weatherford. Landlord claimed that tenant breached the lease agreement by his impermissible use of the premises for a convenience grocery store contrary to the "purpose clause" of the agreement. The lower court found for the landlord, and the tenant appealed. . . .

The purpose clause of the lease in suit is as follows:

> . . . [tenant] will use said premises for a gasoline service station, car wash and *associated activities* [emphasis added]

For proof of tenant's breach of this covenant landlord relies on tenant's use of the premises as convenience store and asserts it is impermissible as an "associated" activity. Landlord's evidence showed he had allegedly had an oral understanding with the tenant, before the lease was signed, that the premises would not be used for a convenience store.

Before the tenant moved upon the leased premises, landlord knew that "Tank and Tummy" would be the name of tenant's establishment and that the store would be selling convenience store items, such as bread, milk, candies and various snack items. Tenant had in fact been selling at the filling station over 30 items in that category ever since it first opened for business in 1972. Since the

station facility neither had a wash-and-lube bay nor was used to market tires or car accessories, it seemed to be suitable mainly for "quick stop" gas and convenience food sales.

Absent a lease provision expressly prohibiting the sales shown to have been made, a reasonable interpretation of the phrase "associated activities" in the purpose clause of the lease does not rule out a convenience store.

Unless fraud is involved, precontract negotiations and oral discussions are merged into, and superseded by, the terms of an executed written agreement. The written instrument cannot be varied, modified or changed by parol testimony. When proof of an oral promise is essential to one's claim and the testimonial evidence proffered as to its existence, though unobjected to, is violative of the parol evidence rule, it is entirely proper for the court to rule as a matter of law that the claim is without legal support. This is so because the parol evidence rule is part of the substantive rather than adjective law.

Under the terms of the lease agreement tenant is not expressly prohibited from operating a convenience store. The oral promise landlord relied upon, if one in fact existed, is unenforceable in law and without binding force. If the lease phrase "associated activities" may be viewed as a latent ambiguity, there is ample support for the . . . view that retail gasoline operations are, in the light of present-day merchandising methods, commonly associated with convenience store facilities and that the parties intended to have food items sold on the premises.
Reversed.

Grove v. Charbonneau Buick-Pontiac, Inc.
240 N.W.2d 853 (N.D. 1976)

As a part of a golf tournament a new 1974 automobile was offered "to the first entry to shoot a hole-in-one on hole No. 8." The golf course on which the golf tournament was played had only nine holes and players played the course twice to complete 18 holes. The first nine holes were marked with blue tee markers, and the second nine holes were marked with red tee markers. As a result, both hole number 8 and Hole number 17 were played on the same portion of the golf course. Hole 17 was actually 60 yards longer than hole number eight because of the placement of the tee markers.

The plaintiff scored a hole-in-one while playing from the 17th tee on the eighth hole of the golf course. Plaintiff claimed this satisfied the requirements of the offer but the defendant refused to deliver contending that the hole-in-one had been scored on the wrong hole. The lower court gave the plaintiff damages in the amount of $5,800 and the defendant appealed.

SAND, J. . . . The offer made by Charbonneau Buick stated that a 1974 Pontiac Catalina would be awarded to the "first entry who shoots a hole-in-one on hole No. 8." Grove claims that his performance was an acceptance of this offer and created a binding contract.

Rewards and prizes are governed by the general rules of contract. There must be a genuine offer and an acceptance. To collect a prize, the person must perform all of the requirements of the offer in accordance with the published terms in order to create a valid and binding contract under which he may be entitled to the promised award. . . .

The acceptance or performance may not be a modification of the offer.

Substantial compliance, however, is sufficient.

The general rule of the law of contracts which provides that where an offer or promise for an act is made, the only acceptance of the offer that is necessary is the performance of the act, applies to prizewinning contests. . . .

The . . . burden is upon the contestant in such a case to establish, by a preponderance of the evidence, that the promoter's offer was accepted by

substantial performance under (and) in accordance with the terms and conditions of the offer, i.e., the rules of the contest. . . .

If the language of a contract leaves an uncertainty as to its meaning, the legislature has provided for another test to be applied by the court in Section 9-07-19, NDCC, which states:

> In cases of uncertainty not removed by the preceding rules, the language of a contract should be interpreted most strongly against the party who caused the uncertainty to exist. The promisor is presumed to be such party, except in a contract between a public officer or body, as such, and a private party, and in such case it is presumed that all uncertainty was caused by the private party.

Where a contract contains ambiguous terms which are in dispute it is the duty of the court to construe them. The ambiguous terms of a contract will be interpreted most strongly against the party who caused the ambiguity.

In *Schreiner v. Weil Furniture Co.*, 68 So. 2d 149 (La. App. 1953), the court stated it is a well settled proposition of law that where there is a dispute over what the terms of a contract are or what the stipulations mean, the document must be interpreted against the one who has prepared it, and applied such rule to an offer of a prize made to the public. The *Schreiner* case involved a "count-the-dots" contest where certificates worth money-off on the purchase of a television were awarded. The plaintiff won and a dispute developed as to what prizes were to be awarded under the rules of the contest. The court held that it was the duty of the defendant to explain the contest so that the public would not be misled.

We believe the rule on ambiguous contracts applies to this case, and therefore any language of this contract which is not clear and definite or in which an uncertainty exists as to its meaning must be interpreted most strongly against Charbonneau.

The offer does not contain any qualifications, restrictions, or limitations as to what is meant by the phrase "on hole No. 8." Neither does the award or offer make any statement restricting or qualifying that the hole-in-one on hole No. 8 may be accomplished only from tee No. 8. If Charbonneau had in mind to impose limitations, restrictions, or qualifications he could have made this in the offer so that a person with ordinary intelligence would have been fully apprised of the offer in every respect. . . .

. . . [W]hen good arguments can be made for either of two contrary positions as to the meaning of a term in a document an ambiguity exists. . . . [W]e are satisfied that the language in question, "hole-in-one on Hole No. 8," in the offer, under this setting is ambiguous.

Having concluded as a matter of law that the offer in this setting is ambiguous, the rule of law providing that the ambiguous terms will be construed and interpreted most strongly against the party who caused the ambiguity applies. . . .

If this rule of law were not applied it would permit the promoter who is so inclined, where there has been a performance, to keep adding require-ments or conditions which were not stated in the offer. An example, such as, "must use a certain club; the ball must be of a certain brand; the play must be accomplished by a person playing left-handed," to name only a few.

By interpreting and construing the ambiguous provisions of the offer most strongly against the party who caused them . . . , and as announced in case law developed on this subject, we construe it to mean that an entrant in the golf tournament who had paid the fee and who during regular tournament play drives the ball in one stroke into hole No. 8 from either the 8th or 17th tee has made a hole-in-one on hole No. 8, and has met the conditions of the offer and is entitled to the award or the equivalent in money damages.

Affirmed.

REVIEW QUESTIONS

1. Match each term in column A with the appropriate statement in column B.

A		B	
1.	Guarantor of another's debt primarily wants to benefit himself	**a.**	Party detrimentally relies on oral promise
2.	Contract that cannot be performed within one year	**b.**	Indicates a contract between the parties, indicates quantity, and is signed by party to be charged
3.	Promissory estoppel exception	**c.**	Promise to pay another's debt, grant of an interest in land, cannot be performed in one year, and sale of goods
4.	Equitable estoppel exception	**d.**	Writing that satisfies statute but is not signed by the party to be charged
5.	Sufficient writing required by the Code	**e.**	Written contract is final, but not the complete agreement
6.	Confirmation between merchants	**f.**	Confirmation between merchants, specifically manufactured goods, judicial admissions, performance
7.	Parol evidence rule	**g.**	Leading object rule
8.	Partial integration	**h.**	Eliminates prior or contemporaneous evidence which varies, contradicts, or modifies written contract
9.	Contracts granting interests in land	**i.**	Part or full performance by one party
10.	Merger or integration clause	**j.**	Two-year employment contract
11.	Code exceptions to the statute of frauds	**k.**	"This is the parties' entire agreement"
12.	Contracts within the statute of frauds	**l.**	Easement, mortgage, lease for more than a year

2. Holman sued Louron Industries for specific performance of an oral contract to sell land. Holman had originally leased the land from Louron and then signed a written contract of purchase. Believing that Louron had also signed the agreement, Holman made substantial improvements to the land beyond those permitted by the lease. Can Louron successfully use the statute of frauds as a defense? Explain.

3. Paul and Sherry orally agree on the sale of a farm by Paul to Sherry for $155 an acre. Paul signs and dates the following memorandum: "Received from Sherry $100 as payment on my 64-acre farm, [at $155 an acre]. Balance to be paid when deed and abstract are presented." Would the memorandum satisfy the statute of frauds if the bracketed words are omitted? Explain.

4. Kodak and Owens made an oral contract that gave Owens the exclusive right to do Kodak commercials for as long as Owens wished. Is this oral contract within the statute of frauds? Explain.

5. Libby made an oral contract to buy land from Elmina. In reliance on the contract, Libby passed up an opportunity to buy other land that would have suited her needs. When Elmina later refused to sell, Libby sued. Is the statute of frauds a proper defense in this case? Why or why not?

6. A butcher sold meat on credit to Helen's Restaurant. When Helen's was late in paying its bills, the butcher contacted Jim, who orally promised to pay any bill that the restaurant failed to pay. Is this oral promise admissible in court? Why or why not? Would your answer change if Jim said: "The restaurant is on hard times. Send the bills to me, and I'll pay." In the original case, would it make any difference if Jim had some financial interest in the restaurant? Why or why not?

7. Chisholm had a written option to purchase 1.862 acres of land out of a 10-acre tract owned by the Cartwrights. The exact piece of property covered by the option was not specified. If Chisholm sues for specific performance of the option, will the statute of frauds be a valid defense? Explain.

8. Roper bought a triplewide mobile home from Flamingo Home Sales. The written installment sale contract disclaimed any warranty obligation of the seller. Roper experienced several problems with the mobile home, which Flamingo refused to repair. Roper sued on Flamingo's oral promise that if problems did arise, Flamingo would "take care of them." Is this oral promise admissible in court? Explain why or why not. Would it make any difference if this oral contract were made contemporaneously with the signing of the sale contract? Explain. Would it make any difference if the oral promise were made three days after the signing? Explain.

9. Yabby agreed in writing to sell certain property to Mollenhoff. When Mollenhoff failed to pay the installments due, they made a new long-term agreement. Just before he signed, Mollenhoff orally promised to pay interest on all past and future late payments. Is this oral promise admissible in court? Explain why or why not.

10. Farmer made an oral contract with grain operator for the sale of soybeans for future delivery. Five days later, in confirmation of the oral contract, grain operator sent farmer a written contract for his signature. Farmer refused to sign. When sued, farmer claimed that he was not liable for breach of contract, since the contract was not in writing. At the trial it was proven that farmer had been farming for 34 years, had 150 acres of soybeans, and had sold his crop to grain operators in "cash sales" and "future contracts" for at least five years. Is farmer liable? Why or why not?

11. Ben, a printer, sued The Tuggle Company to recover the price of printing services. After several negotiations over the telephone, Ben printed business cards, letterheads and envelopes, invoices and purchase order forms, and prepared an etching and rubber stamp—all with Tuggle's corporate name. Should the court dismiss this action since the contract is oral? Explain.

12. Grayson made an oral contract with Jesse's Drilling Company to buy a large drilling machine. Grayson sent a check payable in full to Jesse, which Jesse retained for 30 days, but did not deliver the machine. Since there is no writing to satisfy the statute of frauds, should Grayson sue Jesse? Explain.

13. Alex signed an order form to purchase a car from Baker's Better Cars Company for $2,500. Neither Baker nor anyone else from his company signed the form. Alex made a $50 down payment. Later, Baker tells Alex that there was a mistake; the price is $2,675. Alex sues, and Baker defends on the ground that the company had not signed the form. Is the defense valid? Why or why not? Would your answer change if Alex had bought two cars rather than one? Explain.

12 CONTRACT PERFORMANCE, BREACH, AND DISCHARGE

We have now encountered most of the basic issues in contract law. First, there has to be an agreement consisting of offer and acceptance. Second, the agreement must be validated by bargained-for consideration. Finally, the valid contract may be legally unenforceable because of defenses like incapacity, illegality, public policy, or form. Assuming that a valid contract exists without any defense to its formation, the next grouping of contract issues concerns performance, breach (nonperformance), excuses for nonperformance, and discharge of contracts.

The focus of this chapter is on the problems that arise during the period of the performance of a contract. Such problems come up in a variety of ways. One of the parties may refuse to perform or may perform in an unsatisfactory manner; he may not render complete performance; he may be unable to perform because of circumstances beyond his control; or he may contend that, because of changed conditions, he should be excused from performing. Questions arise as to the order of performance—who must perform first in a bilateral contract? Usually, a default or breach of a contract will occur at or after the time when performance was due, but as will be noted, a contract can be breached prior to the date for performance.

1. Definition

CONDITIONS

A *condition* is an act or event (other than the lapse of time) that, unless excused, must occur before performance under a contract becomes due. A condition is an act or event that limits or qualifies a promise. The condition must occur before the promisor has a present duty to perform. Assume that you promise to sell me your car for $3,000 and I promise to buy your car for $3,000 if I can obtain a loan of $2,000. I have no present duty to pay you $3,000. When and if I obtain a loan of $2,000, my promise to pay you is activated. My promise to pay is a conditional promise.

There is no exclusive or conclusive test to determine whether a particular contractual provision is a promise or a condition. Although no particular words are necessary for the existence of a condition, terms such as *if, provided that, on condition that,* and others that condition a party's performance usually connote an intent for a condition rather than a promise. In the absence of a clause expressly creating a condition, whether a certain contractual provision is a condition rather than a promise must be gathered from the contract as a whole and from the intent of the parties.

Conditions determine when a party has to perform. However, many promises are unconditional and absolute. The party who makes an unconditional promise has an immediate duty to perform, regardless of the other party's duties. The failure to perform such a promise is a breach of contract unless the duty is excused. Where a promise is conditional, the duty to perform it is dormant or unactivated until the condition occurs. A duty to perform is conditional if some event must occur before the duty becomes absolute.

2. Types of Conditions

Conditions may be classified by time—*when* the conditioning event must occur in relation to the promise. Under this classification, conditions are labeled as *conditions precedent, concurrent conditions,* and *conditions subsequent.*

A condition precedent is an act or event that, unless excused, must exist or occur before a duty of immediate performance of a promise arises. It usually takes the form of performance by the other party. Contracts often expressly provide that one party must perform before there is a right to performance by the other party. The first party's performance is a *condition precedent* to the duty of the other party to perform. Since one party must perform before the other is under a duty to do so, the failure of the first party to perform permits the other to refuse to perform and to cancel the contract and sue for damages.[1]

Not all the terms that impose a duty of performance on a person are of sufficient importance to constitute conditions precedent. As a general rule, if a provision is relatively insignificant, its performance is not required before recovery may be obtained from the other party. In such cases, the party who was to receive performance merely deducts the damages caused by the breach. Determining whether the breach of a particular provision is so material that it justifies rescission is a problem of construction. If the damage caused by the breach can be readily measured in money, or if the nature of the contract has not been so altered that it defeats the justifiable expectations of the party entitled to performance, the clause breached is generally not considered a condition precedent.

For example, a contractor substantially follows all the plans and specifications in building a house, but completes the work 10 days late. Rescission is not

---

[1] Whiteley v. O'Dell, p. 263.

justified. Such a breach is of minor importance. The purchaser would have been required to pay the contract price less any damages sustained because of the delay. It is often difficult to judge whether the breach of a particular provision is so material that it justifies rescission. If the damage caused by the breach can be readily measured in money, and if the other party receives basically what he was entitled to under the contract, the clause breached is not considered a condition precedent.

If parties are to exhange performances at the same time, their performances are concurrently conditioned. "I promise to sell you my car for $700 on April 1." Tender of $700 and tender of the car are concurrent conditions of exchange. Since a contract seldom states that performances are simultaneously conditioned on one another, courts will generally find concurrent conditions if both parties can perform simultaneously. Suppose, in the example above, no date for performance was set. In that case, neither party could demand that the other perform until he or she has performed or tendered performance. Each party's performance is conditioned on concurrent performance by the other party.

A condition subsequent stated in the contract is an event that discharges a duty of performance that has become absolute. In an insurance contract you might find the following example: "In the event of accident or loss, written notice containing all particulars shall be given by the insured to the Insurer as soon as practicable. No action shall be brought after the expiration of 12 months from the occurrence of any loss." The insurance company's duty to pay under the policy does not arise (become absolute) until the insured gives notice. The requirement of notice is an express condition precedent. Failure to bring suit within 12 months will discharge the absolute duty. This requirement is an express condition subsequent. Note that conditions subsequent are rare.

Conditions may also be classified according to the way they are created. This method of classification recognizes two types of conditions: (1) express conditions specifically set out in the contract, and (2) constructive conditions which the parties did not consider but the court imposes to achieve fundamental fairness between the parties. These two types of conditions are discussed in the sections that follow.

3. Express Conditions

An express condition is included in a contract and designated as a condition that must be strictly performed before the other party's duty to perform arises. The penalty for failure to perform an express condition properly may be the loss of the right to receive payment or otherwise to obtain the return performance. The parties may stipulate that something is a condition precedent, even though it would not ordinarily be considered so. If that stipulation is made, failure to perform exactly as specified is ground for rescission, unless the court construes the clause to be a penalty provision and therefore unenforceable.

A contract may provide that "time is of the essence of this agreement."[2] This means that performance on or before the date specified is a condition precedent to

---

[2] Bell v. Coots, p. 264.

the duty of the other party to pay or to perform. Another common express condition precedent, found in many construction contracts, provides that the duty of the owner to make the final payment on completion of the building is conditioned upon the builder's securing an architect's certificate. This is certification by the owner's architect that the construction is satisfactory and in accordance with the plans and specifications. Thus, the condition is, to a large degree, outside the control of both parties and within the exclusive control of a third party, the architect.

4. Conditions of Personal Satisfaction

A common provision in many contracts expressly conditions a party's performance on personal satisfaction with the other party's performance. Suppose that Wyeth agrees to paint your portrait to your personal satisfaction for $20,000. When he is finished, you say that you are not satisfied with it and refuse to pay the $20,000. The condition precedent of your personal satisfaction, you argue, has not happened to activate your duty to pay. Would it make any difference if 50 art experts state that the portrait is a masterpiece? To answer that question and to avoid unfair forfeitures, the law has adopted rules involving two categories of satisfaction cases: (1) situations involving personal taste, fancy, or judgment (subjective dissatisfaction); and (2) situations involving mechanical fitness, utility, or marketability (objective dissatisfaction).

When the satisfaction condition concerns your individual taste or judgment, as in the case of Wyeth's painting, the law requires that you genuinely be dissatisfied. Your dissatisfaction must be honest and in good faith, which is a subjective fact question. If you are dissatisfied with the bargain (paying $20,000), however, then you are refusing to pay in bad faith. The condition in that case is excused. The testimony of the art experts can therefore be used as circumstantial evidence of bad faith. This fact issue is given to the jury to determine.

When the satisfaction condition concerns something like construction or repair that can be measured objectively, the law requires reasonable rather than personal satisfaction. If the average person would be satisfied (reasonable, objective satisfaction), then you must pay, despite the fact that you personally might be dissatisfied. Thus, performance that is objectively satisfactory must be paid for, notwithstanding personal (subjective) dissatisfaction.[3]

5. Constructive Conditions

A constructive condition is one not expressed by the parties, but is read into the contract to serve justice (that is, an implied-in-law condition). In a bilateral contract, one party can perform, regardless of what the other party does. But in most cases it would be inequitable to require one party to perform without requiring the other to perform. In the interest of fairness, courts make performances of bilateral promises constructively conditional on one another. In an

---

[3] Forman v. Benson, p. 265.

employment contract, for example, one must work before getting paid. Working is a constructive condition precedent, which must occur to activate the duty to pay an employee.

When parties understand that one performance must occur before the other (or such is understood by custom), the former is a constructive condition precedent to the latter. When a contractor promises to build a house for an owner who will pay him $200,000, a court will construe the builder's performance as a condition that must happen to activate the owner's duty to pay.

If both performances can be performed simultaneously, the promises are constructively concurrent. To activate the other's duty to perform, a party must tender his performances. Most contracts for the sale of goods under the Code are examples of constructive concurrent conditions of exchange. *Note:* The express contract terms or custom, usage of trade, course of dealing, and the like can change the rule. A passenger, by custom, pays for an airline ticket before the airline's duty to provide transportation is activated.

6. Tender of Performance

A *tender* in the law of contracts is an offer to perform. When a person makes a tender, it means that he is ready, willing, and able to perform. The tender is especially significant in contracts requiring both parties to perform at the same time. One party can place the other party in default by making a tender of performance without having actually rendered the performance.

The concept of tender is applied not only to concurrent condition situations, but also to contract performance in general. In most contracts, one party or the other is required to tender payment. Such a tender requires that there be a bona fide, unconditional offer of payment of the amount of money due, coupled with an actual production of the money or its equivalent. A tender of payment by check is not a valid tender when an objection is made to this medium of payment. When a tender is refused for other reasons, one may not later complain about the use of a check as the medium of tender. A person to whom a tender is made must specify any objection to it or waive it, so that the debtor may know and comply with the creditor's demands.

Tenders of payment are often refused for one reason or another. A party may contend that the tender was too late. The creditor may refuse to accept the offer to pay because he believes that the amount tendered is less than the amount of the debt. If it turns out that the tender was proper, the valid tender will have three important legal effects.

1. It stops interest from accruing after the date of the tender.
2. In case the creditor later brings legal action recovering no more than the amount tendered, he must pay the court costs.
3. If the debt were secured by a security interest in property belonging to the debtor, this security interest would be extinguished.

Thus a tender of payment, although it does not discharge the debt, has important advantages to the person making it.

PERFORMANCE OF CONDITIONS

The Code article that deals with the sale of goods has two provisions relating to tender. Unless the buyer and the seller have otherwise agreed, *tender of payment* by the buyer is a condition to the seller's duty to deliver the goods sold [2-511(1)]. Unless the seller demands payment in legal tender, the buyer is authorized to make payment by check [2-511(2)]. The Code also provides for the manner of a seller's tender of delivery of the goods involved in the contract. The Code requires that the seller make the goods available to the buyer and that he give the buyer reasonable notification that the goods are available for him [2-503(1)]. If the seller gives notice that the goods are available for the buyer and the buyer does not tender payment, then the buyer would be placed in default. Tender of delivery is a condition to the buyer's duty to accept the goods [2-507(1)].

7. Substantial Performance

Express conditions must be strictly met, or there is a material breach of contract. Constructive conditions need be only substantially performed to avoid a material breach. Because constructive conditions are imposed in the interest of good faith and fair dealing, it naturally follows that substantial performance of a constructive condition satisfies the condition. Thus, the other party's duty to perform is activated by substantial performance.[4] Note that substantial performance is not complete performance, so there has been an immaterial breach and dollar damages may be awarded. Although the nonbreaching party can sue for damages for this immaterial breach, the suing party must still perform, because the constructive condition precedent has been fulfilled. Thus, an immaterial breach does not excuse the nonbreaching party of the duty of performance under the contract.

The consequences of a material breach are more severe. Normally, a material breach gives the nonbreaching party an option. He can opt to treat the contract as rescinded, or choose to continue under the contract by treating it as only a partial breach. A partial breach, in effect, continues the contract, and all parties must continue to perform. The nonbreaching party can sue for damages that accrued from the breach, and the contract is not rescinded. If a total breach is elected, the contract is at an end, and there is an immediate right to all remedies for breach of the entire contract.

8. Divisibility—Installment Contracts

Whereas many contracts require a single performance by each party and are completely performed at one point of time, others require or permit performance by one or both parties in installments over a period of time. The rights and obligations of parties during the period when the contract is being performed frequently depend upon whether the contract is entire or divisible. A contract is said to be *divisible* if performance by each party is divided into two or more parts *and* performance of each part by one party is the agreed exchange for the

---

[4] Alaska State Housing Auth. v. Walsh & Co., Inc., p. 266.

corresponding part by the other party. It is to be noted that a contract is not divisible simply by virtue of the fact that it is to be performed in installments.

The parties may specify whether a contract is divisible or entire. Thus, a contract may contain a clause stipulating that each delivery is a separate contract, or other language may be used to show the intention of the parties that their agreement is to be treated as if it were a series of contracts. Some contracts are obviously divisible. Assume Sam promises to sell and Dave to buy a car for $5,000 and a boat for $3,000. This contract is legally divisible into two parts, a sale of a car and a sale of a boat. If Sam tenders the car, he is entitled to $5,000 even though he has not performed the entire contract since he has not tendered the boat. Sam is liable for not tendering the boat, but he can still recover for the sale of the car.

The concept of divisibility is applicable to a variety of contracts, including insurance contracts, employment contracts, construction contracts, and sales contracts. As a general proposition, employment contracts are interpreted to be divisible, but construction contracts are usually deemed to be entire. The divisibility of contracts for the sale of goods is the subject of several Code provisions discussed below.

If a contract is divisible, the second party is under a duty to perform in part after the first party performs an installment. For example, the employer owes a duty to pay wages at the end of the pay period. In addition, a material breach of an installment justifies a rescission of the balance of the agreement. Assume that a party is to write five songs each month for a year. Only one song is written the first month. While the failure to deliver the other four would not be a substantial breach of the entire agreement, it would be a substantial breach of the installment. If the contract were treated as divisible, such a material breach would justify rescission of the contract. Likewise, if a party substantially performs an installment of a divisible contract, he may nevertheless recover the value of that installment less damages caused by any breach of the contract without rendering performance of the balance of the agreement.

There have been numerous cases involving the question of whether or not a contract is divisible. No general test can be derived from these cases. Courts are called upon to determine in any given case whether the parties intended that (1) each would accept part performance of the other in return for his own without regard to subsequent events or (2) the divisions of the contract were made merely for the purpose of requiring periodic payments as the work progresses. In any event, the party who breaches is liable for damages resulting from his breach.

Under the Code, unless the parties have otherwise agreed, a sales contract is *entire;* all the goods called for by the contract must be tendered in a single delivery, and payment in full is due upon such tender [2-307]. If the contract permits installment deliveries, the seller can demand a proportionate share of the price for each delivery as it is made, provided the price can be apportioned, as for goods sold at a certain price per item. If there is a substantial default on an installment (the goods tendered or delivered may not conform to the contract), the buyer may reject the installment [2-612(2)]. When an installment breached indicates that the seller will not satisfactorily perform the balance of the contract or that he is unreliable, the buyer can rescind the entire contract [2-612(3)]. Should the buyer accept a nonconforming installment without giving notice of cancellation or demanding that the seller deliver goods that conform, he may not use the breach as a basis for rescission.

9. Anticipatory Repudiation

Before the time specified for performance, there can be no actual breach, but there may be a breach by *anticipatory repudiation.* The expression explains itself: Repudiation occurs before performance is due; one of the parties to a bilateral contract repudiates the contract. The repudiation may be express or implied. An express repudiation is a clear, positive, unequivocal refusal to perform. An implied repudiation results from conduct in which the promisor puts it out of his power to perform, making substantial performance of his promise impossible. In either case, the repudiation must be *positive* and *unequivocal.*

When a promisor repudiates his prospective duty to perform, the nonrepudiating party has an election of remedies. He can treat the repudiation as an anticipatory breach and immediately seek damages for breach of contract, rather than having to wait until the time set for the repudiating party's performance. Thus, the doctrine excuses any express or constructive condition to the repudiating party's duty and thereby permits an immediate lawsuit. Rather than suing, the injured party can treat the repudiation as an empty threat, wait until the time for performance arrives, and exercise his remedies for actual breach if a breach does in fact occur. If the injured party disregards the repudiation and treats the contract as still in force, the repudiation is nullified, and the injured party is left with his remedies, if any, invocable at the time of performance.

The doctrine of anticipatory breach does not apply to promises to pay money on or before a specified date. If a promissory note matures on June 1, 1990, and in 1983 the maker states that he will not pay it when the maturity date arrives, that would not give rise to a present cause of action by the holder.

The Code provides that after a breach including anticipatory repudiation, the buyer may "cover" by making in good faith and without unreasonable delay any reasonable purchase of, or contract to purchase, goods in substitution for those due from the seller [2-712]. The difference between the cost of cover and the contract price, together with any incidental or consequential damages, may be recovered by the buyer from the seller. Failure of the buyer to effect cover does not bar him from recovering damages for nondelivery, but damages will be limited to those that could not have been prevented by proper cover.

A party may retract his repudiation, provided he does so prior to any material change of position by the other party in reliance upon it. The retraction would simply be a notice that he will perform the contract, after all. The Code allows a retraction of anticipatory repudiation until the repudiating party's next performance is due unless the aggrieved party has, since the repudiation, canceled or materially changed his position or otherwise indicated that he considers the repudiation final [2-611]. Retraction may be by any method that clearly indicates to the aggrieved party that the repudiating party intends to perform, but it must include adequate assurance that he will in fact perform if the other party demands it [2-609]. Retraction reinstates the repudiating party's rights under the contract, with due excuse and allowance to the aggrieved party for any delay caused by the repudiation.

10. Introduction

A party to a contract may be relieved from the duty to perform or from his liability for breach if he is legally excused from contract performance. Moreover, a duty under a conditional promise may be activated not only by performance of the condition, but also if the condition is excused. Actual failure of an express or a constructive condition may be legally excused in any of the following five ways: (1) hindrance, prevention, or noncooperation; (2) waiver, estoppel, or election; (3) impossibility; (4) frustration of purpose; and (5) commercial impracticability.

11. Hindrance, Prevention, and Noncooperation

In every contract there is an implied duty of good faith and fair dealing requiring each party not to prevent or substantially hinder the other party's performance. If a party whose promise is conditional wrongfully prevents the condition from occurring, then the condition is excused. The dependent duty is immediately activated. Although the cases vary, the wrongful conduct can be characterized as either hindrance, wrongful prevention, or noncooperation.

The conduct must be *wrongful,* which usually means that no party reasonably contemplated or assumed the risk of the kind of conduct that occurred. Seller agrees to sell buyer 3,000 tons of railroad rails for $50 per ton. The rails are in short supply. Seller fails to deliver, because buyer has been buying rails from seller's only sources. A court held that although buyer did substantially hinder seller's performance, it was not wrongful. Seller assumed the risk of such market conditions.

The wrongful prevention of performance by one party to a contract will excuse nonperformance by the other party. It is obvious that a person may not recover for nonperformance of a contract if he is responsible for the nonperformance. If a party creates a situation that makes it impossible for the other party to perform, the other party is excused. To illustrate: Barrow had leased a building to Calhoun for the operation of an ice cream store. The rent was to be a percentage of the gross income. Thereafter, Calhoun established another ice cream store a block away and did very little business in the building rented to her by Barrow. Calhoun has prevented the normal performance of the contract by carrying on another business that detracted from the profits. Barrow may cancel the lease without liability because Calhoun has prevented the performance of the contract.

As a part of the good-faith requirement, the law implies that the parties will reasonably cooperate with each other. If as the result of one party's failure to cooperate and to in effect act in good faith the other party breaches the contract, then the noncooperating party is not entitled to the usual contract remedies. In fact, the other party may rescind the agreement because the implied condition of good faith has been breached.[5]

---

[5] Fernandez v. Vazquez, p. 267.

12. Waiver

Waiver has been defined as the passing by of an occasion to enforce a legal right, whereby the legal right is lost. As applied to contract law, it means (1) a promise to forego the benefit of a condition to the promisor's duty, or (2) an election to continue under a contract after the other party has breached. The essence of waiver is conduct that indicates an intention not to enforce certain provisions of the agreement. The waiver may be made either before or after a breach. If it is made before, it constitutes an assurance that performance of the condition will not be insisted upon. For example, a building contract provides for completion on a certain date. If the owner grants an extension of 6 months, he has waived his right to insist upon completion at the earlier date. The waiver may be retracted unless it is supported by consideration or the promisee has made a substantial change of position in reliance upon it. One who has waived the time for performance may withdraw the waiver if he gives the other party a reasonable opportunity to perform the condition waived.

The Code allows a party who has waived a provision of an executory contract to retract it upon giving reasonable notice that he will require strict performance of it, "unless the retraction would be unjust in view of a material change of position in reliance on the waiver" [2-209[5]]. Under the Code, the retention or acceptance of defective goods may constitute a waiver of the defect. A buyer who fails to particularize defects in goods may in fact be waiving his objections based on these defects [2-605].

13. Impossibility of Performance

Actual impossibility of performance is a valid excuse for breach of contract and releases a party from duty to perform. Impossibility is much more than mere "additional hardship." As a general rule, in the absence of an appropriate contract provision, circumstances that impose additional hardship on one party do not constitute an excuse for breach of contract. The fact that the promised performance may be more difficult or expensive does not discharge the promisor from his duty to perform, especially when the risk of such problems was anticipated or reasonably foreseeable.[6] Therefore, many contracts provide that manufacturers, suppliers, or builders shall be relieved from performance in case of fire, strikes, difficulty in obtaining raw materials, or other incidents imposing hardship over which they have no control. Without such a provision there would be no excuse, as they do not constitute impossibility of performance.

To have the effect of releasing a party from duty to perform, the impossibility must render performance "physically and objectively impossible." If objective impossibility is present, the discharge is mutual; that is, the promisor is discharged, and the promisee is also discharged from his corresponding obligation. Many cases state that in order for impossibility to exist, there must be a fortuitous or unavoidable occurrence that was not reasonably foreseeable. The fact that an act of God is involved does not necessarily create an excuse. If a house under

---

[6] Marcovich Land Corp. v. J.J. Newberry Co., p. 268.

construction is destroyed by fire caused by lightning, the contractor is not excused from his obligation to complete the house. The contractor takes the risk of fire unless he protects himself by expressly contracting that he shall not be held liable for an act of God or other untoward circumstance against which he is not willing to be bound.

Likewise, if the situation is caused by the promisor or by developments that he could have prevented, avoided, or remedied by corrective measures, there is no excuse. For this reason, the failure of a third party, such as a supplier, to make proper delivery does not create impossibility. Impossibility will not be allowed as a defense when the obstacle was created by promisor or was within his power to eliminate. It must not exist merely because of the inability or incapacity of the promisor to do it; that is, subjective impossibility is no excuse.

14. Specific Cases of Impossibility

There are four basic situations in which impossibility of performance is frequently offered as an excuse for nonperformance. In the first of these, performance becomes illegal because of the enactment of some law or governmental action. A manufacturer or supplier may be prevented from making delivery of merchandise because of government allocations, as in the mandatory allocation of fuel oil and gasoline. Government action that merely makes an agreement more burdensome than was anticipated does not afford a basis for relief.

The second situation is the death or incapacitating illness of one of the contracting parties. This is not deemed to be a form of impossibility unless the contract demands the personal services of the disabled or deceased person. Ordinary contracts of production, processing, and sale of property are unaffected by the death or illness of one or both of the parties. In the event of death, it is assumed that the contract will be carried out by the estate of the deceased. If a contract is for personal services or it clearly implies that the continued services of the contracting party are essential to performance, death or illness will excuse nonperformance. In contracts for personal services, the death of the employer also terminates the relation. The estate of the employer in prematurely terminating the contract is not liable for damages to the employee.

Many agreements involve the continued existence of certain subject matter essential to completion of the contract. The third rule is that destruction of any subject matter essential to the completion of the contract will operate to relieve the parties of the obligations assumed by their agreement. A different situation arises where property that only one of the parties expected to use in his performance is destroyed. If a factory from which the owner expected to deliver certain shoes is destroyed by fire, performance is not excused, inasmuch as performance is still possible, even though an undue hardship may result. The shoes needed to fill the order can be obtained from another source. Had the contract stipulated that the shoes were to be delivered from this particular factory, however, its destruction would have operated to excuse a failure to perform. In recent years, there has been a trend toward holding that where both parties understood that delivery was to be made from a certain source, even though it was not expressly agreed, destruction of the source of supply will relieve the obligor from performing.

The last form of impossibility arises when there is an essential element lacking. This situation has never been satisfactorily defined, but apparently the agreement may be rescinded when some element or property is lacking, although the parties assumed it existed or would exist. Some courts would hold that no contract, in fact, existed because of mutual mistake. This is said to be a form of impossibility at the time of making the contract, and courts have tended to act as if there had been no meeting of the minds. It must be definitely proved that performance is substantially impossible because of the missing element. Davis contracts to build an office building at a certain location. Because of the nature of the soil, it is utterly impossible to build the type of building provided for in the agreement; the agreement must therefore be terminated. The missing element is the proper condition of the soil. In other words, from the very beginning, the contract terms could not possibly have been complied with, and in such cases the courts are prone to excuse the parties if nobody is at fault.

15. Commercial Frustration

Since the notion of *absolute* impossibility may create harsh results in certain cases, courts may excuse performance using the *doctrine of commercial frustration*. The doctrine excuses performance when the essential purpose and value of the contract have been frustrated. Typically, something happens to prevent achievement of the object or purpose of the contract. If so, the courts may find an implied condition that the unforeseen development will excuse performance.

Commercial frustration arises whenever there is an intervening event or change of circumstances so fundamental it is entirely beyond that which was contemplated by the parties. Frustration is not impossibility, but it is more than mere hardship. It is an excuse created by law to eliminate liability when a fortuitous occurrence has defeated the reasonable expectations of the parties. It will not be used when the supervening event was foreseeable or assumed as a part of the agreement.[7]

16. Commercial Impracticability Under the Code

The Code uses the term *commercial impracticability* in a manner similar to *commercial frustration*. The Code recognizes that without the fault of either party, unexpected developments or government action may cause the promised performance to become impracticable. In some cases, the Code authorizes substituted performance. If the loading or unloading facilities of the agreed-upon carrier are unusable, a commercially reasonable substitute must be tendered and accepted if it is available [2-614].

The Code also provides that commercial impracticability is often an excuse for a seller who fails to deliver goods or is delayed in making the delivery. The excuse is limited to cases in which unforeseen supervening circumstances not within the contemplation of the parties arise [2-615(a)]. The law does not specify all the contingencies that may justify the application of the doctrine of commercial

---

[7] No. Ill. Gas Co. v. Energy Co-Op, Inc., p. 269.

impracticability. Increased costs will not excuse the seller unless they are due to some unforeseen contingency that alters the basic nature of the contract.

Neither increased costs, a rise in the market, nor dramatic fluctuations in currencies[8] excuse performance. But a severe shortage of raw materials or of supplies due to a contingency such as war, an unforeseen shutdown of major sources of supply, a local crop failure, or the like, which increases costs or prevents a seller from securing necessary supplies, does constitute commercial impracticability.

In order to use the excuse, the seller is required to notify customers seasonally of any delay or nondelivery. This notification is to allow the buyers to take prompt action to find another source of supply. The notice must include an estimate of the buyer's allocation when the seller is able to perform partially [2-615(c)] and is subject to the Code's allocation requirement [2-615(b)].

Upon receipt of a notice of a substantial or indefinite delay in delivery or of an allocation, the buyer has two alternative courses of action. The buyer may terminate the contract insofar as that delivery is concerned. He may also terminate and discharge the whole contract if the deficiency substantially impairs the value of the whole contract [2-616(1)]. The buyer may also modify the contract by agreeing to take his available quota in substitution. If the buyer fails to modify the contract within a reasonable time not exceeding 30 days, the contract lapses with respect to the deliveries covered by the seller's notice [2-616(2)].

17. Introduction

DISCHARGE
OF
CONTRACTS

The rights and duties created by a contract continue in force until the contract is discharged. The term *discharge* is used to describe the cancellation of a contract and the acts by which the enforcement of its provisions are terminated. The usual and intended method of discharge is the complete performance by both parties of their obligations under the agreement. A valid excuse is a discharge in the sense that the excused party has no liability for failure to perform. The same may be said of grounds for rescission. A rescinded contract is in effect discharged.

Although no particular form is required for an agreement to discharge a contract duty, the term *release* has traditionally been reserved for a formal written statement by one party that the other's duty is discharged. In chapter 8, the word *renunciation* is introduced. It is equivalent to a release. Either party may voluntarily renounce or waive any right or claim arising under a contract. A renunciation is valid without consideration provided it is in writing.

A cancellation of a written contract and the surrender of it by one party to the other will usually discharge the agreement. Such a discharge requires consideration or proof of a gift. If both parties have obligations, there is consideration on the mutual surrender of the rights to performance. If only one party has an obligation, the necessary intent to make a gift and delivery of it may be found in the delivery of the written cancelled contract. However, such evidence is not conclusive, and a jury may find that a gift was not in fact made.

---

[8] Bernina Distributors, Inc. v. Bernina Sewing Mach., p. 270.

The law makes a distinction between a writing that is merely the *evidence* of the obligation and one that *is* the obligation, such as a promissory note. There is no particular sanctity in the law to the physical evidence of an ordinary contract, and the destruction of this evidence does not destroy the contract. However, if the actual obligation such as a negotiable instrument is surrendered or intentionally destroyed by the holder of it, the obligation is discharged.

There are other methods of discharge, such as a novation. The term *novation* has two meanings. First of all, it is used to describe the situation in which the parties to a contract substitute a new debt or obligation for an existing one. The substitution of the new agreement operates to release or discharge the old one. *Novation* is also used to describe an agreement whereby an original party to a contract is replaced by a new party. The concept of novation is discussed further at the end of the next chapter.

The legal concept of *accord and satisfaction* allows discharge of a contract by a performance different from that agreed upon in the agreement. Laws sometimes have the effect of discharging obligation by prohibiting lawsuits to enforce them. For example, passage of time without litigation to enforce one's rights will operate to discharge an obligation. A discharge in bankruptcy has the same effect. (This is the subject matter of chapter 37.)

18. Payment

The obligation of one party to a contract is usually to pay the other for goods sold or services rendered. There are three especially significant issues about payment that affect the matter of discharge: What constitutes payment? What is good evidence that payment has been made and that the obligation has been discharged? When a debtor has several obligations to a creditor, how will a payment be applied?

Certainly, the transfer of money constitutes payment, but this is not necessarily the case when the payment is by a negotiable instrument such as a check or a promissory note. Generally, payment by delivery of a negotiable instrument drawn or indorsed by the debtor to the creditor is a conditional payment and not an absolute discharge of the obligation. If the instrument is paid at maturity, the debt is discharged; if it is not so paid, the debt then exists as it did prior to the conditional payment. In the latter situation, the creditor can either bring an action to recover on the defaulted instrument or pursue his rights under the original agreement.

The parties may agree that payment by a negotiable instrument is an absolute discharge, in which event, if the instrument is not paid at maturity, the only recourse of the creditor is to bring action on the instrument—the original contract is discharged. A similar situation exists when accounts receivable are assigned by a debtor to his creditor. An assignment of accounts is a conditional payment only. If the accounts are not collected, the debtor is still obligated to pay his indebtedness. If the parties intend that the receipt of negotiable instruments or accounts receivable be treated as a discharge of the obligation, they must so specify.

As to what constitutes acceptable evidence of payment and discharge, a receipt given by the creditor will usually suffice. Such receipt should clearly indicate the amount paid and specify the transaction to which it relates. However, the creditor may be able to rebut the receipt by evidence that it was in error or that it was given under mistake. A cancelled check is also evidence of payment, but the evidence is more conclusive when the purpose for which it is given is stated on the check. The drawer of a check may specify on the instrument that the payee by indorsing or cashing it acknowledges full satisfaction of an obligation of the drawer. Mutual debts do not extinguish each other, and in order for one to constitute payment of another, in whole or in part, there must be agreement between the creditor and the debtor that the one shall be applied in satisfaction of the other.

Where a debtor owes several obligations to one creditor, the debtor may direct how any payment is to be applied. The creditor who receives such payment is obligated to follow the debtor's instructions. In the absence of any instructions, the creditor may apply the payment against any one of several obligations that are due, or may credit a portion of the payment against each of several obligations. The creditor may apply a payment against a claim that has been outlawed by the statute of limitations, but this will not cause the outlawed claim to revive as to the balance.

If the source of a payment is someone other than the debtor and this fact is known to the creditor, the payment must be applied in such a manner as to protect the third party who makes the payment. Hence, if the money for the payment is supplied by a surety who has guaranteed that a particular obligation will be paid by the debtor, and the creditor knows it, he is bound to apply the payment on the obligation for which the surety was secondarily liable. Finally, if the creditor fails to make a particular application, the payment will be applied by the courts to the obligation oldest in point of time. However, where the creditor holds both secured and unsecured obligations, the courts of most states are inclined to apply it on an unsecured obligation. Similarly, if both principal and interest are due, the court considers the interest to be paid first, any balance being credited on the principal.

19. Accord and Satisfaction

An *accord* is an agreement whereby one of the parties undertakes to give or to perform and the other to accept something different from that which he is or considers himself entitled to. An accord may arise from a disputed claim in either tort or contract. The term *satisfaction* means that the substituted performance is completed.

The doctrine of accord and satisfaction requires that there be a dispute or uncertainty as to amount due and that the parties enter into an agreement that debtor will pay, and the creditor will accept, a stated amount as a compromise of their differences and in satisfaction of the debt. It must clearly appear that the parties so understood and entered into a new and substitute contract. The surrender of the legal right to litigate the dispute or the settlement agreement often serves as consideration.

The usual accord and satisfaction case involves a debtor's sending a creditor a check for less than the amount claimed by the creditor to be due. This check is usually marked "Paid in full." The courts of a few states hold that the cashing of the check constitutes an accord and satisfaction without additional proof. Most states, however, require that the party asserting the accord and satisfaction also prove (1) that the debt or claim was in fact the subject of a bona fide dispute, (2) that the creditor was aware of the dispute, and (3) that the creditor was aware that the check was tendered as full payment. If the creditor cashes the check, this act constitutes the satisfaction of the accord and completes the discharge. The creditor cannot change the language of the check, deposit it, or cash it and still contend that there was no accord and satisfaction.

20. Statute of Limitations

The statute of limitations prescribes a time limit within which suit must be started after a cause of action arises. Failure to file suit within the time prescribed is a complete defense to the suit.

The purpose of a statute of limitations is to prevent actions from being brought long after evidence is lost or important witnesses have died or moved away. An action for breach of any contract for sale of personal property under the Code must be commenced within four years [2-725]. The Code further provides that the parties in their agreement may reduce the period of limitation to not less than one year but may not extend it. Contracts that are not controlled by the Code are covered by a variety of limitation periods. Some states distinguish between oral and written contracts, making the period longer for the latter.

Any voluntary part payment made on a money obligation by the debtor with intent to pay the balance tolls the statute, starting it to run anew. Similarly, any voluntary part payment, new promise, or clear acknowledgment of the indebtedness made after the claim has been outlawed reinstates the obligation, and the statute commences to run again. A payment or part payment by a third person or a joint debtor does not operate to interrupt the running of the statute as to other debtors not participating in the payment. No new consideration is required to support the reinstatement promise. If the old obligation has been outlawed, a new promise may be either partial or conditional. Since there is no *duty* to pay the debt, the debtor may attach such conditions to his new promise as he sees fit or may promise to pay only part of the debt. A few states require the new promise or acknowledgement to be in writing. The Code does not alter the law on tolling of the statute of limitations (2-725[4]).

A problem exists when a party is incapacitated by minority or insanity. Most jurisdictions hold that lack of capacity stops the running of the statute and extends the period of filing suit. A minor or an insane person usually has a specified time in which to bring an action—after the minor reaches his majority or the insane person regains capacity—although the full period set by statute has expired earlier.

SUMMARY

CONDITIONS

Definition	1. A condition is an act or event that limits or qualifies a promise.
	2. A duty to perform is conditional if something other than the passage of time must occur before performance is due.
	3. Conditions set the order of performance and prevent lawsuits by establishing defenses if conditions do not occur.
	4. Failure of a promise gives rise to a remedy for breach; a failure of condition only excuses performance.
Types of conditions	1. Conditions may be classified in terms of time (conditions precedent, concurrent, and subsequent) and manner of creation (express or constructive).
	2. A condition precedent is an act or event that, unless excused, must occur before a duty to perform is activated.
	3. Concurrent conditions require the parties to exchange performances at the same time.
	4. A condition subsequent is an act or event that discharges a duty which had previously become absolute.
Express conditions	1. An express condition is specifically stated by the parties' agreement as activating or discharging duties.
	2. Express conditions must be strictly satisfied.
Conditions of personal satisfaction	1. If a condition involves personal taste or judgment, dissatisfaction is judged by a subjective standard. If good-faith dissatisfaction exists, the condition is not met.
	2. If a condition involves mechanical fitness, utility, or marketability, an objective standard of dissatisfaction is used to decide if the condition has been met.
Constructive conditions	1. A court-created condition imposed to serve justice.

2. Substantial performance of constructive conditions will make the other party's duty to perform absolute.

PERFORMANCE OF CONDITIONS

Tender of performance	1. Tender is an offer to perform. The party making the tender indicates he is ready, willing, and able to perform.
	2. Tender of payment by the buyer is a condition to the seller's duty to deliver the goods.
	3. Tender by the seller occurs when the goods are available to the buyer. The seller must give reasonable notice that the goods are available.
Substantial performance	1. Substantial performance of a constructive condition is required in order to make the other party's duty absolute.
	2. Substantial performance is not full performance and is an immaterial breach.
	3. Failure to perform at the proper time is not substantial performance if time was of the essence.
Divisibility-installment contracts	1. A party can recover for performance of divisible portions of a contract.
	2. Breach of one part of a divisible contract does not allow the other party to refuse to pay for the part performed.
Anticipatory repudiation	1. Before the time for performance, a party may expressly or implicitly repudiate his duty to perform. If he does so, it is an anticipatory repudiation.
	2. The repudiation is not favored and must be shown to be clear, positive, and unequivocal.
	3. A repudiation may be withdrawn unless it is relied on by the other party.

EXCUSES FOR NONPERFORMANCE

Hindrance, prevention, and noncooperation	1. Wrongful conduct by a party which prevents or unduly hinders the other party's performance will excuse performance.

	2. Wrongful conduct is conduct which was not reasonably contemplated or the risk of which was not assumed by the nonperforming party.
Waiver	**1.** Waiver is a voluntary and intentional relinquishment of an express or constructive condition.
	2. A waiver may be retracted unless it is supported by consideration or the other party has relied on the waiver.
	3. A waiver may be made prior to or after a party has breached the agreement.
Impossibility of performance	**1.** When an unforeseen event makes performance impossible, all duties to perform are excused.
	2. Occurrence of reasonably foreseeable events will not excuse duties to perform.
	3. Change in market price, strikes, accidents, unavailability of materials, and governmental regulations are normally foreseeable.
	4. Acts of God, supervening illegalities, war, and death of a party or destruction of the contract's subject matter are normally unforeseeable.
Commercial frustration	**1.** An intervening event or change of circumstances that was not foreseeable which prevents achievement of the object or purpose of the contract.
	2. The purpose or object frustrated must have been the *basic* purpose or object of the contract from the time the contract was made.
Impracticability under the Code	**1.** If the contract can be performed but performance is *unduly* burdensome, impracticability may excuse performance.
	2. No excuse for change in market price but more likelihood of an excuse for foreseeable events such as strikes, government regulations, unavailable materials, and the like.

DISCHARGE OF CONTRACTS

Introduction	**1.** The term *discharge* describes the cancellation of a contract and the acts by which enforcement of its provisions is terminated.

	2. The usual method of discharge is performance.
	3. A contract may also be discharged as the result of excuses for nonperformance, a mutual release of terms, rescission either by agreement of the parties or operation of law, novation, accord and satisfaction, and the expiration of the period of the statute of limitations.
	4. The intentional destruction of a negotiable instrument is by a form of cancellation.
Payment	1. A check constitutes only conditional payment.
	2. If a debtor owes several obligations, the debtor may specify which is being paid.
	3. If the debtor fails to specify, the creditor may apply it to any debt.
	4. If the payment is by a third party, it must be applied to the debt on which the third party is obligated.
Accord and satisfaction	1. An accord is an agreement to change a contract, and the satisfaction is the performance of the accord.
	2. If the parties agree to settle a dispute either in contract or tort, there is an accord and satisfaction. The consideration is the agreement not to litigate the dispute.
Statute of limitations	1. The statute of limitations prescribes a time limit beyond which a suit cannot be brought on a claim.
	2. There are various time periods for contracts and torts, and these vary from state to state.
	3. The Code period is 4 years.
	4. Various events may toll the running of the statute and commence the period over again. These include payment, part payment, and a new promise to pay.

CASES

Whiteley v. O'Dell
548 P.2d 798 (Kan. 1976)

OWSLEY, J. . . . This is an action brought to recover damages for a breach of a real estate purchase contract. Plaintiffs appeal from the trial court's entry of judgment generally in favor of defendant contractor.

On April 16, 1973, plaintiffs Roy L. and Evelyn L. Whiteley entered into a written contract with defendant Clinton E. O'Dell for the purchase of a house in Wichita, Kansas. Under the terms of the contract, O'Dell, doing business as the O'Dell Construction Company, agreed to construct and convey to plaintiffs a house similar to another built by O'Dell. The contract price was listed at $31,040, with $1,000 to be paid as earnest money and the balance due upon closing. The closing date was designated as September 1, 1973, or a "reasonable time thereafter." On the back of the contract, and incorporated therein, were listed certain specifications to be followed by the contractor.

The Whiteleys . . . paid O'Dell $1,000 in earnest money. Shortly thereafter, O'Dell commenced construction of the house, but he did not comply with certain contract specifications hereinafter noted. . . .

In ruling in favor of defendant O'Dell on the plaintiffs' petition, the trial court concluded that "time not being of the essence," the contractor had a reasonable time to complete the house according to specifications, but plaintiffs never gave him an opportunity to do so. The court reasoned that the variances noted by plaintiffs in June could easily have been rectified prior to the completion date of the contract. As a result, the court ruled that plaintiffs were premature in assuming the house had not been built according to specifications. . . .

Plaintiffs contend the trial court erred in finding defendant had not breached the contract. The record reveals that at the time plaintiffs inspected the house in June, 1973, there were variances from the contract specifications in at least three respects. First, the bathroom fixtures were not the color specified in the contract. The trial court

determined this was an insignificant difference which could have been resolved rather simply. The fixtures had not been installed at that time. Although O'Dell made no offer to cure the defect we cannot say this alone would entitle the purchaser to rescind the contract. It is not every breach which gives rise to the right to rescind a contract. In order to warrant rescission of a contract the breach must be material and the failure to perform so substantial as to defeat the object of the parties in making the agreement. Obviously, the variance in the appearance of the bathroom fixtures is not so substantial that it would constitute a material breach of contract.

The variances in the shingles and the brick veneer are entirely different matters. While the sealdown shingles used by the builder differed only in appearance from those specified, the contract disclosed that plaintiffs specifically ordered T-lock shingles. Defendant offered no excuse for the variance, nor did he offer to replace them with the proper shingles. From the testimony it is apparent to this court that defendant had no intention of curing this defect. . . .

An even more serious variance of the contract specifications was discovered by plaintiffs when they saw that brick veneer was added only to the front of the house. The contract specified the house was to be all brick. The normal method of adding brick veneer to a house is to extend the foundation so a ledge is formed to support the brick veneer. O'Dell testified his employees had omitted the ledge on three sides of the house by mistake. When plaintiffs discovered the error they immediately notified defendant they were no longer going to buy the house. After learning of the plaintiffs' repudiation of the contract, defendant attempted to remedy the situation by laying cement blocks where the ledge should have been extended. . . . There was considerable testimony indicating it was neither the normal nor the desired method for construction of a brick veneer. . . .

In addition to these defects in construction of the house, O'Dell admitted on cross-examination that he discovered a bow of almost two inches in the foundation. O'Dell attempted to correct the bow by building out the cement blocks at one end of the house. In spite of his efforts there was testimony from other witnesses that by so doing he only increased the amount of weight off center which the footings would have to support.

On the basis of this evidence we are inclined to agree with plaintiffs that there was a material breach of the contract at the time the defects were discovered. If it is clear that one party to a contract is going to be unable to perform it, the other party need not wait for the date when performance is due. He is entitled to treat the contract at an end and pursue his remedies.

Even though O'Dell negotiated with plaintiffs and offered to build them another house, he never offered to correct these variances. . . . As a practical matter, we realize replacement of the shingles and proper construction of the ledge at this stage would be excessively expensive, if not impossible. There is nothing in the record to support the conclusion of the trial court that plaintiffs were premature in their determination that the contract had been breached. After examining the whole of the contract and the expert testimony we are convinced that construction of the house in compliance with the named specifications was of importance to plaintiffs. Substantial variations such as shown herein obviously should entitle the purchaser to rescind the contract. In our opinion, the failure to include a ledge on three sides of the house and the use of the wrong shingles constituted a present material breach of the contract, and the trial court erred in its finding to the contrary. . . .

Reversed.

Bell v. Coots
451 So.2d 268 (Ala. 1984)

ADAMS, J. . . . On February 11, 1980, Coots and her husband, now deceased, entered into a written contract to sell certain real property to the Bells. Among other things, the sale contract required the Bells to pay the total purchase price in monthly intallments beginning on February 5, 1980, with a thirty-day grace period for payments. It also contained provisions for Coots' immediate recovery of possession in the event of the Bells's default in making the monthly payments, even if she had not strictly enforced payment within the grace period.

From February 1980, until July 1982, the Bells made the monthly installments required under the contract of sale in a timely fashion. However, they failed to remit the installment due in August 1982 within thirty days of the 5th of that month. Coots immediately filed a lawsuit to recover possession of the property. The Bells then paid their August installment, and Coots dismissed the suit. Then, the Bells did not send Coots the installments due on October 5, 1982, until sometime in December 1982.

Continuing in this pattern, the Bells failed to make their installments for November and December of 1982 within the respective grace periods. Coots did not receive the payments for those months until January 11, 1983. Hence, this action to recover possession was filed.

It is a general rule in equity that time is not of the essence of a contract. However, the parties to a contract may make time of its essence by a clear manifestation of their intent to do so in the terms of their agreement.

We think the terms of the contract at issue in this case clearly manifest an intention of the parties that time be of its essence. In addition to including a provision for the seller's declaration of a forfeiture upon the purchasers' default in paying the monthly installments on the purchase price, which generally has been held to make time essential, the parties specifically agreed to an acceptable leeway in the Bell's remittance of payments, namely, a thirty-day grace period.

Our conclusion that time is of the essence of the contract is reinforced by the parties' testimony concerning their conduct under the agreement. The Bells compliantly made *all* payments prior to the dates when due or within the thirty-day grace period until August 1982. Moreover, Coots unequivocally indicated her intention to strictly enforce the terms of the contract by filing suit for recovery of possession on the two occasions that the Bells failed to make their payments by the end of the grace period. There should be no serious doubt that the words and actions of the parties indicate that time is of the essence of this contract.

Next we consider the Bells's assertion that they were entitled to be called upon to perform and given a reasonable time in which to do so. For this proposition, they rely upon the case of *Wilson v. Thompson,* 255 Ala. 165, 51 So.2d 20 (1951), in which this court stated:

> It is well settled that to rescind a land sale contract for the failure of the other party, the party complaining of such failure must call upon the other to perform and give him a reasonable time after notice in which to comply or be foreclosed.

We think their reliance is misplaced. The above-quoted rule is applicable to contracts requiring performance within a reasonable time. It does not pertain to contracts when time is of the essence. Consequently, absent Coots's waiver of the time requirement in the contract, she was entitled to the strict enforcement of the terms of the agreement, including the forfeiture provision, without giving prior notice to the Bells.

The lower court decision that the plaintiff recover the property and treat all payments as rent is

Affirmed.

Forman v. Benson
446 N.E.2d 535 (Ill.App. 1983)

Forman contracted to buy land from Benson for $125,000 to be paid over a ten-year period. The contract stated: "Subject to Benson's approving Forman's credit report." The credit report showed Forman had liabilities of $80,000 and liquid assets of $24,000. Forman's tax return showed a $2,000 loss for the tax year. When Benson refused to proceed with the sale of his land, Forman sued for specific performance. At the trial, a bank official testified that Forman had an excellent credit rating. The trial court found that Benson was held to a standard of reasonableness in his rejection of Forman's credit report, and found his rejection was unreasonable. Benson appealed.

HOFF, J. . . . We have discovered no case dealing with the interpretation of the specific clause in question. However, there is some Illinois case law regarding the interpretation of "satisfaction" clauses in general. In *Reeves & Co. v. Chandler* (1903), 113 Ill. App. 167, 170, the court found that satisfaction clauses generally fall into one of two classes. In one class, the decision as to whether a party is satisfied is completely reserved to the party for whose benefit the clause is inserted, and the reasons for his decision may not be inquired into and overhauled by either the other party or the courts. Cases falling into this class generally involve matters which are dependent upon the feelings,

taste, or judgment of the party making the decision. The second class of cases are those in which the party to be satisfied is to base his determination on grounds which are just and reasonable. . . . These cases generally involve matters which are capable of objective evaluation, or which involve considerations of operative fitness or mechanical utility. Matters of financial concern generally fall into this second category of cases.

In *Stribling v. Ailion* (1967), 223 Ga. 662, 157 S.E.2d 427, the supreme court of Georgia also interpreted a similar provision in a real estate sales contract as a matter of personal opinion and judgment. In that case, the vendor included the following stipulation in the contract:

> Seller * * * reserves the right to run a credit investigation on purchaser and if in seller's opinion purchaser's credit is not sufficient, then the terms of this contract are null and void.

The court held that the stipulation reserved the right in the seller not only to run a credit investigation, but also to determine in his sole discretion whether the buyer's credit was to his satisfaction.

Although these . . . cases seem to stand for the proposition that personal judgment is involved when the evaluation of a credit rating is at issue, a different conclusion was reached in *Weisz Trucking Co., Inc. v. Emil R. Wohl Construction* (1970), 13 Cal.App.3d 256, 91 Cal.Rptr. 489. In that case a contract between a contractor and a subcontractor provided that "[t]he subcontractor shall furnish, if requested, a corporate surety contract bond * * * written * * * by a company acceptable to the contractor * * *." The subcontractor thereafter submitted a surety bond in the amount of $168,000 which was written by a company with a Treasury rating of only $61,000. The contractor rejected the bond, stating that it wanted a company with a Treasury rating of $500,000. The contractor cancelled the contract and the subcontractors sued for breach. The appellate court held that the sufficiency of the performance bond should be determined by the application of an objective test of reasonableness. In reaching this conclusion, the court relied upon numerous decisions dealing with satisfaction clauses in which it was generally found that "where the contract calls for satisfaction as to commercial value or quality or sufficiency which can be evaluated objectively, the standard of a reasonable person should be used in determining whether or not satisfaction has been received." . . .

It seems clear from the foregoing cases that a reasonableness standard is favored by the law when the contract concerns matters capable of objective evaluation. However, where the circumstances are such that it is clear the provision was added as a personal concession to one of the contracting parties, the subjective, rather than the objective standard, should be applied. . . .

In the present case, it is uncontroverted that the clause in question was inserted as a concession to the defendant and as an inducement to him to sign the contract, which he subsequently did. Ken Burnell testified that the addition of the provision indeed eased defendant's mind about the plaintiff's credit worthiness. In light of the fact that the relationship between the parties was to endure over a ten-year period of time, we think it is a reasonable construction of the provision that it was intended to allow defendant the freedom of making a personal and subjective evaluation of plaintiff's credit worthiness. We, therefore, conclude that the trial court erred in applying a reasonableness standard to the instant case.

Reversed.

Alaska State Housing Auth. v. Walsh & Co., Inc.
625 P.2d 831 (Alaska 1980)

On July 28, 1972, Walsh & Company made a contract with ASHA to construct a gravel surface road. The road was to be constructed of 12 inches of crushed rock surfacing and a 12-inch layer of compacted wood chips to be placed below the gravel surface. Instead, the wood-chip layer after the project was completed averaged 9 inches, with a 2,000 foot section averaging only 5 inches. The insufficient layer of wood-chip insulation caused increased rutting along the road, necessitating frequent maintenance. When ASHA failed to pay Walsh $138,000 as per the contract, Walsh sued. ASHA defended and counterclaimed for damages incurred by reason of Walsh's failure to perform properly. The trial court found that Walsh could recover, since the company had substantially performed the contract. The court also awarded ASHA $65,250 (the value of the wood chips that had been omitted). ASHA appealed.

CONNOR, J. . . . The doctrine of substantial performance permits recovery by a contractor who has substantially, though imperfectly, performed his contractual undertaking. In such circumstances the contractor is entitled to recover the contract price, less the reasonable costs of remedying the defects in the work or materials. The initial burden of proving substantial performance is on the contractor. If his evidence shows substantial performance, the burden is then upon the owner to prove that certain deficiencies in the work require a recoupment or set-off. As it applies here, the burden should be on ASHA to establish any set-off for deficiencies in performance of the work. Substantial performance is determined by considering such factors as the character of the performance that was promised, the purpose that the contract was meant to serve, and the extent to which any nonperformance by the contractor has defeated the purposes or ends which were meant to be achieved. This means that in many cases substantial performance becomes a matter of degree, to be determined by weighing a number of factors together.

In the case at bar the trial court stated:

In reaching the conclusion that Walsh did substantially perform its obligations I especially considered the extent of Walsh's performance, the lack of any willful noncompliance with the technical specifications, and the fact that the roadway as constructed has not required any inordinate or special maintenance by ASHA. . . .

ASHA's argument is that the departures from the contract specifications were so grave that the owner was deprived of what it bargained for in that the road it received in its entirety averaged only 75% of the specified insulation depth, with a 2,000 foot section averaging only 40% of the design insulation depth.

However, the court had before it evidence that the road was substantially serving its intended purpose and did not require rebuilding. The evidence on this point consisted of both oral testimony and documentary evidence, from which inferences could be drawn both for and against a finding that Walsh had substantially performed. We conclude that the trial court did not err in deciding that substantial performance had been rendered.

We do agree with ASHA, however, that the court, after it found that there was substantial performance, applied an improper measure of damages for deficiencies in the work. . . .

In cases of substantial performance, recoupment for defects in construction should be measured either by the cost of correcting the deficiency or, if this would involve unreasonable economic waste, the difference in value between the project as contracted for and as received.

The aim in assessing damages for deficiencies in performance should be to put the injured party in substantially as good a position as performance in accordance with the contract. The law recognizes, however, that sometimes actual reconstruction in compliance with the plans and specifications of the contract may be possible only at a cost that would be imprudent and unreasonable. In such cases, the court should consider alternative measures of recoupment which will substantially compensate the injured party for the deficiency in a less economically wasteful manner. For example, it may be possible to remedy the defect in the construction without having to tear down and rebuild. Although controverted, evidence was presented that the road as constructed by Walsh could be brought up to design function without rebuilding by placing crushed gravel over the under-insulated areas of the road. If so, the cost of repairing the defect in this manner could provide the appropriate measure of damages. Alternatively, recovery could be measured by the reasonable maintenance costs for foreseeable additional repair made necessary by the wood chip shortage. If, in the last analysis, the court is convinced that the defect cannot be remedied without economic waste, it must award ASHA the diminished value of the road due to the defect.

Since it is apparent from the court's award of the bare cost of the omitted wood chips that it did not apply the proper measure of damages, we remand to the superior court for a redetermination of the amount of recoupment owed to ASHA as a result of the wood chip deficiency.

Remanded.

Fernandez v. Vazquez
397 So.2d 1171 (Fla. 1981)

FERGUSON, J. Lessees, Jose Fernandez and Hialeah Bakery, Inc., appeal from an order of summary judgment dismissing their counterclaim against lessors, Oscar Vazquez and Filiberto Portales, doing business as Job Development. The issue on appeal is whether a lessor may arbitrarily refuse consent to an assignment of a lease which provides that the lessee shall not assign or sublease the premises without written consent of the lessor. We have been unable to find any case in Florida where this issue has been squarely presented to the court. The very able trial judge granted the summary judgment based on what the state of the law was assumed to be.

The law generally favors free alienation of property and under common law a tenant has the right to assign his leasehold interest without the consent of the lessor. In order to protect the landlord from this common law right of assignment, many leases expressly provide that the property cannot be assigned without the written consent of the landlord. A decreasing majority of jurisdictions hold that when such written consent is required, a landlord may arbitrarily and capriciously refuse to approve a subtenant or assignee.

The arbitrary and capricious rule is undergoing continued erosion. An increasing number of jurisdictions hold that when a lease requires written consent prior to assignment or subleasing, but does not contain any language limiting the withholding of that consent, such consent may not be arbitrarily or unreasonably refused.

Underlying the cases abolishing the arbitrary and capricious rule is the now well-accepted concept that a lease is a contract and, as such, should be governed by the general contract principles of good faith and commercial reasonableness. One established contract principle is that a party's good faith cooperation is an implied condition precedent to performance of a contract. Where that cooperation is unreasonably withheld, the recalcitrant party is estopped from availing herself of her own wrongdoing.

Accordingly, we hold that a lessor may not arbitrarily refuse consent to an assignment of a commercial lease which provides, even without limiting language, that a lessee shall not assign or sublease the premises without the written consent of the lessor. A withholding of consent to assign a lease, which fails the tests for good faith and commercial reasonableness, constitutes a breach of the lease agreement. Whether a landlord breached the lease by acting unreasonably in withholding consent of a commercial tenant is to be determined by a jury according to the facts of that case. The following factors are among those which a jury may properly consider in applying the standards of good faith and commercial reasonableness: (a) financial responsibility of the proposed subtenant (b) the "identity" or "business character" of the subtenant, i.e., suitability for the particular building, (c) the need for alteration of the premises, (d) the legality of the proposed use, and (e) the nature of the occupancy, i.e., office, factory, clinic, etc. . . . Denying consent solely on the basis of personal taste, convenience or sensibility or in order that the landlord may charge a higher rent than originally contracted for have been held arbitrary reasons failing the tests of good faith and reasonableness under commercial leases.

Reversed and remanded.

Marcovich Land Corp. v. J.J. Newberry Co.
413 N.E.2d 935 (Ind. 1980)

J.J. Newberry Company, a tenant, sued its landlord, Marcovich Land Corporation, to recover profits allegedly lost because the landlord refused to rebuild the leased building as required by a fire clause in the lease. On grounds of impossibility because of inadequate proceeds from insurance, the blighted condition of the area, the short time (6 years) remaining on the 25-year lease, and the alleged difficulty in obtaining financing, Marcovich defended its failure to rebuild as the lease required. When the trial court granted tenant $117,000, an appeal was taken.

MILLER, J. . . . The law in Indiana in regard to impossibility of performance as a defense to a contract action is well stated in *Krause v. Board, etc.* (1904), 162 Ind. 278, at 283–84, 70 N.E. 264, at 265:

> We regard it as thoroughly settled that the words of a mere general covenant will not be construed as an undertaking to answer for a subsequent event, happening without the fault of the covenantor, which renders performance of the covenant itself *not merely difficult or relatively impossible, but absolutely impossible*, owing to the act of God, the act of the law, or the loss or destruction of the subject-matter of the contract. Where performance is thus rendered impossible, the inquiry naturally arises as to whether there was a purpose to covenant against such an extraordinary and therefore presumably unapprehended event, the happening of which it was not within the power of the covenantor to prevent.

Significantly it does not appear that it was absolutely impossible to rebuild the structure rented by Newberry at the time of the fire. Indeed, the only evidence presented at trial which was arguably intended to show such absolute impossibility of performance concerned the purported inability of the [defendant] to obtain financing under the existing lease terms with Newberry. . . .

The defendant maintains, however, that apart from any issue of "absolute" impossibility, the essential question raised by this appeal is whether in Indiana impossibility of performance should include the defense that performance is "impractical" where it involves "excessive and unreasonable cost." They concede such issue is unanswered in any Indiana precedent, but contend their position should be adopted in light of the practice in other jurisdictions, *citing Transatlantic Financing Corp. v. United States,* a case in which Judge Wright acknowledged such a defense but concluded it was not "commercially impractical" under a contract to require a ship carrying wheat to travel 3,000 additional miles on an original 10,000-mile trip, at an alleged cost of almost $44,000, because of the closing of the Suez Canal.

Turning to the evidence relied on by [defendant] we note the uncontroverted (though challenged by objection) testimony of [defendant's] expert, Richard J. Kestle, that it would cost at least $452,000 in 1972 to construct a building on the site in accordance with certain rough plans prepared by Newberry. Additionally, [defendant] presented evidence they received only $200,000 in insurance proceeds, such lesser figure presumably being attributable to the fact that defendant chose not to insure the structure for its replacement cost. [Defendant] also presented evidence in this regard, however, in the form of testimony from a real estate appraiser using the $452,000 reconstruction figure and a six-year lease, that rebuilding would not be economically or commercially "feasible," a conclusion which he explained in an offer to prove, took into account what return a prudent investor would want for his money invested in a new building in 1972, assuming such an investor "would want at least 8% on his money and we said that the recapture or depreciation rate would be 2½% or a total capitalization rate of 10½%." The same expert observed the property in question was in an "urban renewal" area in 1974 or 1975 (though not in 1972),

and concluded, "I would advise my client that this is a very poor deal to get into."

In viewing such evidence we are cognizant that even under the standard advocated by defendant, the test is not simply whether a particular performance would be a bad business risk or even a "very poor deal" for a prudent investor, but rather whether there was "*extreme . . .* difficulty, expense, injury, or loss" which goes well beyond the normal range of what might have been expected, Comment d to the proposed Restatement (Second) of Contracts, and whether the parties failed to allocate such risk. We believe the trial court could properly have concluded the evidence in the instant case, involving regrettable but unextraordinary rebuilding considerations, did not rise to such a level, but that the risk was unanticipated by the parties, and thus not expected, and that such risk was, moreover, intended to be allocated between them by the "fire clause" itself. As was observed in *Transatlantic Financing Corp. v. United States,*

> While it may be an overstatement to say that increased cost and difficulty of performance never constitute impracticability, to justify relief there must be more of a variation between expected cost and the cost of performing . . . than is present in this case, where the promise can legitimately be presumed to have accepted some degree of abnormal risk, . . .

Like the Court in *Kruse,* which similarly reflected a defense of impossibility of performance, we believe the trial court did not err in its ultimate determination. . . .

Affirmed.

No. Ill. Gas Co. v. Energy Co-op, Inc. 461 N.E.2d 1049 (Ill.App. 1984)

HEIPLE, J. An action was brought in the Circuit Court of Grundy County by Northern Illinois Gas Company (hereinafter NI-Gas), seeking a declaratory judgment that it had properly ceased performance under a long-term supply contract with Energy Cooperative Inc. (hereinafter ECI). ECI counterclaimed for breach of contract and the jury returned a verdict for $305.5 million on ECI's counterclaim. . . .

NI-Gas is a public utility which distributes

natural gas to customers throughout the northern third of Illinois (excluding Chicago). . . .

NI-Gas argues that the trial court erred in granting ECI's motion for summary judgment on NI-Gas' frustration of purpose defense. In its reply to ECI's counterclaim, NI-Gas alleged as an affirmative defense that its non-performance was justified by circumstances beyond its control that frustrated the purpose for which it had entered the contract.

Frustration of purpose or commercial frustration as the doctrine has been called in Illinois, is a viable defense but is not to be applied liberally.

(*Smith v. Roberts* (1977), 54 Ill.App.3d 910, 12 Ill.Dec. 648, 370 N.E.2d 271.) The *Smith* decision sets out a rigorous two-part test which requires a party to show that: (1) the frustrating event was not reasonably foreseeable; and (2) the value of counterperformance has been totally or nearly totally destroyed by the frustrating event.

NI-Gas argues that due to increases in natural gas supplies, its need for the naphtha produced by ECI was reduced. This factor, coupled with increased naphtha prices caused by rising crude oil prices plus the ICC rate order and other regulatory restraints destroyed the value of ECI's counterperformance. NI-Gas also contends that these events were unforeseeable and beyond its control.

First and foremost, as any trader knows, the only certainty of the market is that prices will change. Changing and shifting markets and prices from multitudinous causes is endemic to the economy in which we live. Market forecasts by supposed experts are sometimes right, often wrong, and usually mixed. If changed prices, standing alone, constitute a frustrating event sufficient to excuse performance of a contract, then the law binding contractual parties to their agreements is no more.

Moreover, we do not regard the events complained of by NI-Gas as unforeseeable. As early as 1972, NI-Gas executives were aware that demand for natural gas was being reduced due to consumer conservation caused by the OPEC oil embargo. Despite the fact that NI-Gas could not reasonably predict the future supply and demand of natural gas beyond two or three years, NI-Gas entered into an agreement which required it to take 56 million barrels of naphtha over a period of at least 10 years. Furthermore, as a regulated public utility, NI-Gas should have known that the ICC might not grant all of its future requests for rate increases to cover costs generated by its performance of the contract with ARCO.

In 1976, NI-Gas and ECI negotiated the terms under which ECI would assume ARCO's rights and obligations under the naphtha supply contract. At this time, the nation was recovering from a crippling oil embargo by OPEC nations. Fully aware of how oil prices had behaved in the past, NI-Gas agreed to an amended price escalation formula which specified that the contract price for naphtha would increase at a rate 1.4 times any increase in crude oil costs. NI-Gas agreed to this amendment despite the fact that in 1974, the chairman of the board of NI-Gas was publically predicting that by the mid-1980's, crude oil prices would be in the range of $32 to $35 a barrel. As predicted, crude oil prices rose to about $31 per barrel by late 1979.

Thus, in 1973 when the contract was formed and in 1976 when the contract was assigned to ECI, NI-Gas was aware of the potential for adverse market shifts which now form the basis for its defenses based on impracticability and frustration of purpose. At either time, NI-Gas could have included specific terms in the contract to provide relief when these events came to pass. NI-Gas failed to do so.

The facts which constitute the frustrating events complained of by NI-Gas are not in dispute and the record clearly demonstrates that these events were, to a large degree, foreseeable to NI-Gas and in some cases predicted by NI-Gas. Applying these facts to the test set out in the *Smith* decision, there is no room for a difference of opinion. As a matter of law, NI-Gas was unable to show that the supposed frustrating events were not reasonably foreseeable. Therefore, the defense of commercial frustration was not available to NI-Gas and summary judgment was properly entered in favor of ECI.

Affirmed.

Bernina Distributors, Inc. v. Bernina Sewing Mach.
646 F.2d 434 (Utah 1981)

A distributor of sewing machines brought an action against an importer of sewing machines for interpretation of their contract, which was for 7 years commencing in 1971. The contract provided that the exchange rate between dollars and Swiss francs would be treated as an increase in invoice costs to the importer. With the precipitous decline of the dollar in relation to the Swiss francs, the importer began to surcharge the distributor 10 percent above the increased cost of purchasing Swiss francs, so it "could retain sufficient profit margin to justify sales." The trial court, however, determined that the importer could exact no profit on the additional costs incurred from the exchange rate fluctuations, and the importer now claims the contract does not have to be performed, owing to the commercial impracticability doctrine of the Uniform Commercial Code.

LOGAN, J. . . . Importer asserts that the court's interpretation makes the contract impracticable under Utah Code Ann. §70A–2–615 (1980). That U.C.C. section excuses performance under the contract "[e]xcept so far as a seller may have assumed a greater obligation" when performance "has been made impracticable by the occurrence of a contingency the nonoccurrence of which was a basic assumption on which the contract was made. . . ." In our view the instant contract is not one made "impracticable" by the contingency of the devalued dollar. The contract, as interpreted by the trial court, always allows a gross profit margin, although the return on capital investment has been reduced considerably because of the devaluation of the dollar. Moreover, there is considerable evidence that Importer assumed this particular risk. The contract lumps all the shipping and invoice costs in one provision which allows price increases only to the extent of the cost increases to Importer. Importer's letter to Distributor concerning a 7% devaluation of the dollar in relation to the franc, sent three weeks prior to the contract execution, shows clear foreknowledge of the possibility of currency fluctuations and, thus, supports the finding that section 2-615 is inapplicable. Uniform Commercial Code 2-615, Comment 8 states:

> [T]he exemptions of this section do not apply when the contingency in question is sufficiently foreshadowed at the time of contracting to be included among the business risks which are fairly to be regarded as part of the dickered terms, either consciously or as a matter of reasonable, commercial interpretation from the circumstances.

Finally, cost increases alone, though great in extent, do not render a contract impracticable. UCC §2-615, Comment 4. The Third Circuit held that the doctrine of impracticability was not available unless the party seeking to excuse performance could show he could perform only at a loss, and that the loss would be especially severe and unreasonable. We hold the defense of impracticability is unavailable in the instant case. . . .

Affirmed.

REVIEW QUESTIONS

1. Match each term in column A with the appropriate statement in column B.

A		B
1. Condition	**a.**	Condition that discharges duty.
2. Condition precedent	**b.**	Condition created by the court to achieve justice.
3. Condition subsequent	**c.**	Party clearly indicates that he will not perform in the future.
4. Express condition	**d.**	An unforeseen event that makes performance impossible.
5. Constructive condition	**e.**	An act or event that limits or qualifies a contract duty.
6. Substantial performance	**f.**	An immaterial breach.
7. Divisibility	**g.**	A voluntary, intentional relinquishment of a condition.

8. Waiver

9. Anticipatory repudiation

10. Commercial frustration

11. Impossibility

12. Discharge by party's agreement

13. Discharge by operation of law

14. Commercial impracticability

h. A condition created expressly by the parties' agreement.

i. Code's version of commercial frustration.

j. Contract can be apportioned into several contracts.

k. Condition that activates a contract duty.

l. Unforeseeable, intervening event that prevents fulfillment of contract's main purpose.

m. Contract avoidance, bankruptcy, and statute of limitations.

n. Rescission, release, novation, and accord and satisfaction.

2. Merv and Harold contract to merge their corporate holdings into a single new company. It is agreed that the project is not to be operative unless they raise $800,000 additional capital. Is the raising of additional capital a condition? What happens if they cannot raise an additional $800,000?

3. Elmina contracts with Mickey to build a house for $60,000, payable on condition that Elmina present a certificate from Libby, Mickey's architect, showing that the construction work has been properly completed. Elmina properly completes the work, but Libby refuses to give the certificate because of collusion with Mickey. Is the nonoccurrence of the condition therefore excused? Explain.

4. John contracts with Fay to install a heating system in Fay's factory for a price of $30,000 to be paid "on condition of satisfactory completion." John installs the heating system, but Fay states that she is not satisfied with it and refuses to pay the $30,000. Fay gives no reason except that she does not approve of the heating system. According to experts, the heating system as installed is entirely satisfactory. May John successfully recover $30,000 from Fay? Explain why or why not.

5. Bob contracts with Elizabeth to paint a portrait of Elizabeth's daughter Della, for which Elizabeth promises to pay $6,000 "if entirely satisfied." Bob paints Della's portrait, but Elizabeth states that she is not satisfied with it and refuses to pay the $6,000. Elizabeth gives no reason except that the portrait does not please her. According to experts in the art field, the portrait is an admirable work of art. Will a court require Elizabeth to pay Bob $6,000? Explain.

6. Schmidt, a citizen of Germany, contracts with Brown to sell Brown the output of Schmidt's mill for one year. War breaks out, and Germany orders Schmidt to sell the output of his mill to Germany instead. Schmidt complies with the order and fails to deliver to Brown. May Brown successfully sue Schmidt? Explain.

7. Harte contracted with Connolly to install a new roof on Connolly's house. It was agreed that the roofing shingles were to be "Russet glow," a shade of brown. The roof was installed, and many of the shingles were discolored, showing streaks of yellow. Harte replaced some of the shingles, but the new shingles did not match the others. The overall appearance of the roof is that it has been patched with nonblending colors. The roof is functional and is guaranteed to last 15 years. Must Connolly pay? Why or why not? Would your answer change if Harte were building a house for Connolly and on the scheduled completion date had done everything required by the contract except grading and paving? Why or why not?

8. Johnson agreed to erect 6 signs on a highway near Clark's Place. Four small signs are to read: "4 miles to Clark's Place, 3 miles to Clark's Place," etc. One large sign is to read: "STOP! You're at Clark's Place." The sixth sign reads: "Turn around, You've just missed Clark's Place." Clark agreed to pay $30 each for the 5 small signs and $50 for the large sign. Johnson erected only 3 small signs and sues for $90. May he recover? Why or why not?

9. Wells contracted with the state to erect a building according to the state's specifications and to lease it to the state. Time was made of the essence in the contract. Wells completed the building two months late. The state canceled the contract and leased space elsewhere. Wells sued and proved at trial that the delay was caused by the state's failure to indicate locations for electrical fixtures, outlets, and other details as required by the contract. Did Wells win? Why or why not?

10. Stacey, a pro football quarterback, signed a 7-year contract with the Professional Football League for $875,000. Stacey was to receive $50,000 upon signing and another $50,000 at the end of the first year. Although he received the $50,000 upon signing, the league could pay but $20,000 at the end of the year. At that time, the league was in financial difficulties to the tune of $1,600,000 indebtedness and an overdraft at the bank for $67,000. Should Stacey treat the contract as rescinded? Why or why not?

11. Rick agreed to buy two campers from McMahon and made a deposit of $1,000 as partial payment. Rick then wired McMahon not to ship the campers and explained his reasons for delaying shipment. Later, Rick decided not to buy the campers and demanded a return of his $1,000. Was Rick's instruction not to ship an anticipatory repudiation that will justify McMahon's retention of the $1,000? Explain.

12. Ferd agreed to take dancing lessons from Muffy for a specified period at a predetermined price. After only part of the lessons were completed, Ferd broke his leg. Should he be released from the contract? Why or why not?

13. John Henry Mining Company was hired to drill a coal mine. The mine failed because tunneling became too difficult. Is John Henry excused for discontinuing? Why or why not?

14. Union agreed to supply Publicker with a petroleum product for three years starting in 1972. The contract had a complicated pricing formula that allowed Union to adjust prices as costs increased, but there was a fixed ceiling on the amount of any increase. When the Arabs dramatically increased oil prices following the 1973 Middle East war, Union's costs more than doubled. Since the ceiling on price increases in the contract would not allow Union to raise prices in proportion to the Arab increase, Union refused to perform. Is Union excused from delivering the petroleum product in the future? Explain.

15. Pate, a contractor, agreed with the city of Kiteville to construct a golf course for $230,329.88. After Pate had completed all the clearing and dirt work, a torrential rainfall of 12.47 inches occurred in a 10-hour period. It will cost $60,000 to restore the golf course to its condition prior to the rain. Is Pate relieved from the contract by the doctrine of commercial frustration? Explain why or why not.

13 CONTRACT RIGHTS OF THIRD PARTIES

The discussion of contracts up to this point has dealt with the law of contracts as applied to the contracting parties. Frequently, persons who are not in privity of contract (not parties to the contract) may have rights and even duties under the contract. The rights and duties of third parties may come into play when there is: (1) a *third-party beneficiary* contract—which a party contracts with another party for the purpose of conferring a benefit upon a third party (beneficiary); or (2) an *assignment* of the contract—a party to a contract (assignor) transfers to a third party (assignee) his rights under the contract; or (3) a *novation*—a new party (third party) becomes a party to an existing contract as he is substituted for one of the original parties.

CONTRACTS FOR BENEFIT OF THIRD PARTIES

1. Nature of Such Contracts

Contracts are often made for the express purpose of benefitting some third party. Such contracts, called *third-party beneficiary contracts,* are of two types— *donee-beneficiary* and *creditor-beneficiary.*[1] Both types of third-party beneficiaries are entitled to enforce a contract made in their behalf because the promisee has provided that the performance shall go to the beneficiary rather than to himself.

If the promise was purchased by the promisee in order to make a gift to the third party, such party is a donee-beneficiary. The most typical example of such an agreement is the contract for life insurance in which the beneficiary is someone

---

[1] Keel v. Titan Construction Corp., p. 286.

other than the insured. The insured has made a contract with the life insurance company for the purpose of conferring a benefit upon a third party, namely, the beneficiary named in the policy.

If the promisee has contracted for a promise to pay a debt that he owes to a third party, such third party is a creditor-beneficiary—the debtor has arranged to pay the debt by purchasing the promise of the other contracting party to satisfy his obligation. The promisee obtains a benefit because his obligation to the creditor will presumably be satisfied. To illustrate: A operates a department store. He sells his furniture, fixtures, and inventory to B, who, as part of the bargain, agrees to pay all of A's business debts. A's purpose for making this contract was to have his debts paid, and he obtained B's promise to pay them in order to confer a benefit on his creditors. A's creditors are creditor-beneficiaries and can enforce their claims directly against B. Of course, to the extent that B does not pay them, the creditors still have recourse against A.

2. Legal Requirements

A third-party beneficiary is not entitled to enforce a contract unless he can establish that the parties actually intended to benefit the third party, who must be something more than a mere incidental beneficiary.[2] The intent to benefit the third party must clearly appear from the terms of the contract.

The intent is more easily inferred in creditor-beneficiary situations than in donee-beneficiary ones. The third party need not be named as an individual in the contract if he can show that he is a member of a group for whose direct benefit the contract was made. A third-party beneficiary need not have had knowledge of the contract at the time it was made. The fact that the actual contracting party could also sue to enforce the agreement will not bar a suit by the beneficiary if he was intended to benefit directly from the contract. A third-party beneficiary need not be the exclusive beneficiary of the promise.

If the benefit to the third party is only incidental, the beneficiary cannot sue. Contracts of guaranty assuring the owner of property that contractors performing construction contracts for him will properly complete the project and pay all bills have been held in many states to benefit the materialmen and laborers. A few states have held otherwise, indicating their belief that the agreement was made primarily to protect the owner and benefits others only incidentally.

In most states, a contract made for the express purpose of benefitting a third party may not be rescinded without the consent of the beneficiary after its terms have been accepted by the beneficiary. The latter has a vested interest in the agreement from the moment it is made and accepted. For example, an insurance company has no right to change the named beneficiary in a life insurance policy without the consent of the beneficiary, unless the contract gives the insured the right to make this change. Until the third-party beneficiary has either accepted or acted upon provisions of a contract for his benefit, the parties to the contract may abrogate the provisions for the third party's benefit and divest him of the benefits

---

[2] Jackson, Lewis, Schnitzler v. Local 100, p. 286.

that would otherwise have accrued to him under contract. Minors, however, are presumed to accept a favorable contract upon its execution, and such contract may not be changed so as to deprive the minor of its benefits.

One who seeks to take advantage of a contract made for his benefit takes it subject to all legal defenses arising out of contract. Thus, if one party has not performed or satisfied the conditions precedent to the other party's obligation, the third party would be denied recovery.

ASSIGNMENTS

3. General Principles

A bilateral contract creates *rights* for each party and imposes on each corresponding *duties*. Each party is an obligor (has an obligation to perform the duties), and each is an obligee (is entitled to receive the performance of the other). Either party may desire to transfer to another his rights or his rights and duties. A party *assigns* rights and *delegates* duties. The term *assignment* may mean a transfer of one's rights under a contract, or it may mean a transfer both of rights and duties. The person making the transfer is called the *assignor*, and the one receiving the transfer is called the *assignee*.

A person who has duties under a contract cannot relieve himself of those duties by transferring the contract or delegating the duties to another person.[3] An obligor that delegates duties as well as assigns rights is not thereby relieved of liability for proper performance if the assignee fails to perform. An assignor continues to be responsible for the ultimate performance.

No particular formality is essential to an assignment. Consideration, although usually present, is not required. As a general proposition, an assignment may be oral or written, although it is of course desirable to have a written assignment. Some statutes require a writing in certain assignment situations. An assignment of an interest in real property must be in writing in most states.

The main feature of an assignment is a *present transfer* of a contract right. An assignment is a *completed* transaction. After the assignment, the assignor has no interest in the contract right. The assignor's right belongs exclusively to the assignee. If the assignor retains any portion of the right, there is no valid assignment and the assignee cannot sue to enforce the right.[4]

4. Consent Required

The rights under most contracts may be assigned if both parties to the agreement are willing to let this be done. Public policy prevents the assignment of some contract rights, however. For example, many states by statute prohibit or severely limit the assignment of wages under an employment contract. In addition, rights created by the law, such as the right to collect for personal injuries, cannot be assigned in most states.

As a general rule, contract rights may be assigned by one party without the consent of the other party. In most contracts, it is immaterial to the party

[3] Ryder Truck Rental v. Transp. Equipment Co., p. 287.
[4] Kelly Health Care v. Prudential Ins. Co., p. 288.

performing who receives the performance. A party has no right to object to most assignments.

There are certain exceptions to these general rules. Some contracts cannot be assigned without consent of the other party. Of the several classes of contracts that may not be transferred without the consent of the other party, the most important are contracts involving personal rights or personal duties. A personal right or duty is one in which personal trust and confidences are involved, or one in which skill, knowledge, or experience of one of the parties is important. In such cases, the personal acts and qualities of one or both of the parties form a material and integral part of the contract. For example, a lease contract where the rent is a percentage of sales is based on the ability of the lessee and would be unassignable without the consent of the lessor. Likewise, an exclusive agency contract would be unassignable.

If a contract involves multiple rights and duties, those that are not personal may be assigned. It is only the personal rights and duties that may not be transferred.

Some duties that might appear to be personal in nature are not considered so by the courts. For example, unless the contract provides to the contrary, a building contractor may delegate responsibility for certain portions of the structure to a subcontractor without consent. Since construction is usually to be done according to specifications, the duties are delegable. It is presumed that all contractors are able to follow specifications. Of course, the delegatee must substantially complete the building according to the plans and specifications. The obligor will not be obligated to pay for it if it is not, and the assignor will be liable in event of default by the assignee.

Another example of a contract that is unassignable without consent is one in which an assignment would place an additional burden or risk upon a party—one not contemplated at the time of the agreement. Such appears to be true of an assignment of the right to purchase real estate on credit.

Most states also hold that one who has agreed to purchase goods on credit, and has been given the right to do so, may not assign his right to purchase the goods to a third party (assignee), since the latter's credit may not be as good as that of the original contracting party—the assignor.

This reasoning is questionable because the seller could hold both the assignor and the assignee responsible. However, the inconvenience to the seller in connection with collecting has influenced most courts to this result. But in contracts where the seller has security for payment such as retention of title to the goods, a mortgage on the goods, or a security interest in the goods, the seller has such substantial protection that the courts have held that the right to purchase on credit is assignable.

5. Consent under the Code

The Code contains provisions that generally approve the assignment of rights and delegation of duties by buyers and sellers of goods. The duties of either party may be delegated *unless* the parties have agreed otherwise or the nondelegating party has ". . . a substantial interest in having his original promisor perform or control the acts required by the contract" (2-210[1]). Accordingly, a seller can ordinarily delegate to someone else the duty to perform the seller's obligations under the contract. This would occur when no substantial reason exists why the delegated performance would be less satisfactory than the personal performance of the assignor.

The Code does provide that rights cannot be assigned where the assignment would materially change the duty of the other party, or increase materially the burden or risk imposed on him by his contract, or impair materially his chance of obtaining return performance (2-210[2]). These Code provisions in effect incorporate the personal rights and duties exception previously discussed.

6. Anti-assignment Clauses

Some contracts contain a clause stating that the contract cannot be assigned without the consent of the other party. Older cases held these clauses to be against public policy and unenforceable, an unlawful restraint on alienation (right to sell one's property). Recognizing freedom of contract, modern courts uphold the clause prohibiting assignment and find it legally operative. Nonetheless, looking to the *language* of the clause in non-Code cases, courts have reached three different results. (1) The clause *prohibits* assignment; for example, "This contract cannot be assigned without the other party's consent." Courts hold that this creates a promise (*duty* in the assignor) not to assign, but the assignor still has the *power* to assign. Thus, the assignment is effective, but the obligor has a legal claim against the assignor for breach of his *promise* (duty) not to assign.[5] (2) The clause *invalidates* the contract; for example, "In the event of an assignment, this contract is void." Although the assignment is still effective, courts give the obligor an option to avoid the contract for breach of the condition. (3) The only way to prohibit an assignment is to *make it void;* for example, "Any purported assignment is void."

Unless the nonassigning party (obligor) consents, courts hold that such a clear stipulation obviously contemplates that the assignment itself is ineffective. Rather than merely creating a *duty* (promise) not to assign, this invalidation clause deprives any party of the power to assign. Thus, the outcome in a given case depends on whether the clause (1) prohibits assignment, (2) invalidates the contract if assigned, or (3) invalidates an assignment.

The Code has effected significant changes regarding anti-assignment clauses. First, in Article 2 it notes the progressive undermining of the original rule invalidating these clauses, as shown by the preceding discussion. The Code observes that the courts have already construed the heart out of anti-assignment clauses. Second, in Article 9 it acknowledges the economic need of freedom of contract rights in modern commercial society. Thus an anti-assignment clause is ineffective to prohibit the assignment of an account or contract right [9-318(4)]. In a sale of business, typically both the rights are assigned and the duties are

---

[5] Hanigan v. Wheeler, p. 288.

delegated. Lacking a release, the delegating party is still liable on the duties delegated. Consequently, Article 2 of the Code provides that in a sales situation, a clause prohibiting assignment should be construed as barring only the delegation of duties [2-210(3)]. Therefore, a generally phrased anti-assignment clause is to be read as allowing an assignment of rights but forbidding delegation of duties. Despite the use of the term *anti-assignment,* the drafters of the Code took notice that in a sales situation the parties were usually more concerned with delegation than with assignment. Moreover, they saw great commercial need for free assignability of rights and struck the compromise of allowing assignment but prohibiting delegation when confronted with an anti-assignment clause.

7. Claims for Money

As a general rule, claims for money due or to become due under existing contracts may be assigned. An automobile dealer may assign to a bank the right to receive money due under contracts for the sale of automobiles on installment contracts. Although the law tends toward greatly reducing or eliminating the right of employees to assign wages, an employee may assign a portion of his pay to a creditor, in order to obtain credit or to satisfy an obligation. The Uniform Consumer Credit Code (adopted in several states) provides that a seller cannot take an assignment of earnings for payment of a debt arising out of a consumer credit sale. Lenders are not allowed to take an assignment of earnings for payment of a debt arising out of a consumer loan. The Consumer Credit Code is a part of the trend toward greater consumer and debtor protection.

When a claim for money is assigned, an issue that frequently arises is the liability of the assignor in case the assignee is unable to collect from the debtor-obligor. If the assignee takes the assignment merely as *security* for a debt owed to him by the assignor, it is clear that if the claim is not collected the assignor still has to pay the debt to the assignee. But if someone *purchases* a claim against a third party, generally he has no recourse against the seller (assignor) if the third party (debtor-obligor) defaults. If the claim is *invalid* or sold expressly "with recourse," the assignor would be required to reimburse the assignee if the debtor-obligor did not pay.

In all cases, an assignor *warrants* that the claim he assigns is a valid, legal claim, that the debtor-obligor is really obligated to pay, and that there are no valid defenses to the assigned claim. If this warranty is breached (that is, if there are valid defenses or the claim is otherwise invalid), the assignee has recourse against the assignor.

8. Rights of the Assignee

An assignment is more than a mere authorization or request to pay or to perform for the assignee rather than the assignor. The obligor-debtor *must* pay or perform for the assignee, who now, in effect, owns the rights under the contract. If there is a valid assignment, the assignee owns the rights and is entitled to receive them. Performance for the original party will not discharge the contract. Unless the contract provides otherwise, the assignee receives the identical rights of the assignor. Since the rights of the assignee are neither better nor worse than those of the assignor, any defense the third party (obligor) has against the assignor is available against the assignee. Part payment, fraud, duress, or incapacity can be used as a defense by the third party (obligor) if an action is brought against him by the assignee, just as the same defense could have been asserted against the assignor had he been the plaintiff. A common expression defining the status of the assignee is that he "stands in the shoes" of the assignor.

Some contracts contain a provision to the effect that "if the seller assigns the contract to a finance company or bank, the buyer agrees that he will not assert against such assignee any defense that he has against the seller-assignor." This "waiver of defense" clause is an attempt to give the contract a quality usually described as negotiability, a concept that will be discussed in detail in chapter 28. It is a legal rule that cuts off defenses by giving one party a protected status. If a negotiable instrument is properly negotiated to a party, that party may have a protected status called a *holder in due course*. Thus, most defenses of the original party (the buyer above) cannot be asserted against the holder in due course (the finance company or bank above). The purpose of the concept of negotiability is to encourage the free flow of commercial paper. Adding a provision to a contract that gives it the same effect obviously places the assignee in a favored position and makes contracts with such clauses quite marketable.

As a part of the growing movement toward greater consumer protection, the Federal Trade Commission has ruled that such clauses cutting off defenses of consumers against delinquent sellers when a contract is assigned constitute an unfair method of competition. They are therefore illegal. The commission has also prohibited the use of the holder in due course concept against consumers. This 1976 action by the Federal Trade Commission will be discussed further in chapter 30.

9. Duties of the Parties

As previously noted, an assignor is not relieved of his obligations by a delegation of them to the assignee. The assignor is still liable if the assignee fails to perform as agreed, in which case the assignor would have a cause of action against the assignee. If a party upon the transfer of a contract to a third person wishes to be released of liability, a legal arrangement known as a novation is required. The requirements for a valid novation are discussed in section 11.

The liability of the assignee to third persons is a much more complicated issue. The liability of the assignee is determined by a careful examination of the transactions to see whether it is an assignment of only the rights under the agreement or whether the duty has also been delegated. This is often difficult to determine when the language used refers only to an "assignment of the contract."

As a general rule, the *mere assignment* of a contract calling for the perform- ance of affirmative duties by the assignor, with nothing more, does not impose those duties upon the assignee. However, there is a decided trend in such cases to hold that an assignment of an entire contract carries an implied assumption of the liabilities. When the assignee undertakes and agrees to perform the duties as a condition precedent to enforcement of the rights, or has assumed the obligation to perform as part of the contract of assignment, he has liability for failure to perform. To illustrate: If a tenant assigns a lease, the assignee is not liable for future rents if he vacates the property prior to expiration of the period of the lease, unless he expressly assumes the burdens of the lease at the time of the assignment. He is obligated simply to pay the rent for the period of his actual occupancy. To the extent that an assignee accepts the benefits of a contract, he becomes obligated to perform the duties that are related to such benefits.

If an "entire contract" has been assigned—that is, if duties have been delegated to the assignee as well as the assignment of the rights—a failure by the assignee to render the required performance gives rise to a cause of action in favor of the third party (obligee). The obligee can elect to sue either the assignor or the assignee.

Under the Code, an assignment of "the contract" or of "all my rights under the contract" or an assignment in similar general terms is an assignment of rights, and unless the language or the circumstances (as in an assignment for security) indicate the contrary,[6] it is also a delegation of performance of the duties of the assignor and an assumption of those duties by the assignee. Its acceptance by the assignee constitutes a promise by him to perform those duties. This promise is enforceable by either the assignor or the other party to the original contract (2-210[4]).

When the assignor delegates his duties, although the assignor remains liable, the obligee may feel insecure as to the ability of the assignee to perform the delegated duties. The obligee may demand that the assignor furnish him with adequate assurance that the assignee will in fact render proper performance (2-210[5]).

10. Notice of Assignment

Immediately after the assignment, the assignee should notify the obligor or debtor of his newly acquired right. This notification is essential for two reasons.

1. In the absence of any notice of the assignment, the debtor is at liberty to perform (pay the debt or do whatever else the contract demands) for the original contracting party, the assignor.[7] In fact, he would not know that anyone else had the right to require performance or payment. Thus, the right of the assignee to demand performance can be defeated by his failure to give this notice. The assignor who receives performance under such circumstances becomes a trustee of funds or property received from the obligor and can be compelled to turn them over to the assignee. Upon receipt of notice of assignment, the third party *must perform* for the assignee, and his payment or performance to the assignor would not relieve him of his obligation to the assignee.

2. The notice of assignment is also for the protection of innocent third parties. The assignor has the *power*, although not the *right*, to make a second

---

[6] Cuchine v. H. O. Bell, Inc., p. 290.
[7] Equilease Corp. v. State Federal S & L Ass'n, p. 291.

assignment of the same subject matter. If notice of the assignment has been given to the obligor, it has much the same effect as the recording of a mortgage. It furnishes protection for a party who may later consider taking an assignment of the same right. A person considering an assignment should therefore always communicate with the debtor to confirm that the right has not previously been assigned. If the debtor has not been notified of a previous assignment, and if the prospective assignee is aware of none, in many states the latter can feel free to take the assignment. He should immediately give notice to the debtor. In other words, the first assignee to give notice to the debtor, provided such assignee has no knowledge of a prior assignment, will prevail over a prior assignee in most states.

In some states, it is held that the first party to receive an assignment has a prior claim, regardless of which assignee gave notice first. In these states, the courts act on the theory that the assignor has parted with all his interest by virtue of the original assignment and has nothing left to transfer to the second assignee. In all states, however, the party who is injured by reason of the second assignment has a cause of action against the assignor, to recover the damages he has sustained. The assignor has committed a wrongful and dishonest act by making a double assignment.

NOVATION

11. Requirements

Novation (*novo* = new) describes an agreement whereby one of the original parties to a contract is replaced by a new party. The word *novation* originated in Roman law to refer to the *substitution* of a new contract. Thus, when a *new* person becomes a party to a *new* contract by *substitution* to the same rights and duties of an original party, a novation occurs and discharges the original contract. For example, Tommy, who is indebted to Nancy on an earlier contract, agrees with Nancy and Jesse that in consideration of Nancy's discharging Tommy, Jesse promises to do what Tommy was originally obligated to do. Jesse is thus substituted for Tommy, and a new contract exists between Nancy and Jesse.

A distinction must be made between an assignment-delegation and a novation. In a novation, one party is completely dismissed from the contract as another is substituted. The dismissed party is no longer liable on the original contract. In an assignment-delegation, the original party (assignor) remains liable.

For a novation to be effective, it must be agreed to by all the parties. The remaining contracting party must agree to accept the new party and simultaneously specifically agree to release the withdrawing party.[8] The latter must consent to withdraw and to permit the new party to take his place. The new party must agree to assume the burdens and duties of the retiring party. The agreement to release a former party and the agreement to assume the duties supplies bargained-for consideration to support the new or substituted contract. Note that a novation is never presumed. The burden of proving all the elements is on the party who claims a novation.

---

[8] Jacobson v. Stern, p. 291.

SUMMARY

THIRD-PARTY BENEFICIARY CONTRACTS

Nature of such contracts	1. A noncontracting party may have enforceable contract rights if a party to the contract intended to confer a benefit on the third party.
	2. Creditor and donee beneficiaries are intended beneficiaries.
	3. If performance by the promisor will satisfy a duty owed to the beneficiary by the promisee, the beneficiary is a creditor beneficiary.
	4. If the promisee purchased a promise in order to make a gift to a third party, the party is a donee beneficiary.
Legal requirements	1. If a third party is not an intended beneficiary, he is an incidental beneficiary with no right to enforce the agreement.
	2. Original parties can modify or rescind their contract until the third party's rights vest.
	3. A third party's rights vest when he either relies on the contract to his detriment or manifests assent to the rights.
	4. A third party beneficiary is subject to all defenses arising out of the contract.

ASSIGNMENT

General principles	1. An assignment is a transfer of rights arising from an earlier contract.
	2. A delegation is a transfer of duties arising from an earlier contract.
	3. When A assigns his rights against B to C, A is the assignor, B is the promisor-obligor, and C is the assignee.
	4. When A delegates his duties owed B to C, A is the delegator, B is the promisee-obligee, and C is the delegatee.

5. "Assignment of the contract" is usually held to be both an assignment and a delegation.

6. An effective assignment requires the assignor to transfer those rights irrevocably to the assignee.

7. Neither consideration nor, generally, a writing is required.

8. An assignor is not relieved of his duties by delegating them to an assignee.

Consent required

1. Most rights are assignable unless the assignment would (a) materially change the other party's duty, (b) materially increase the burden or risk imposed by the contract, or (c) materially impair the other party's chance of obtaining return performance.

2. The duties under contracts for personal services generally may not be delegated.

3. The right to purchase on credit cannot be assigned without consent in most states.

Consent under the Code

1. The Code generally approves the assignment of rights and the delegation of duties.

2. Unless the buyer has a substantial interest in having the seller perform, the seller may delegate the duty to deliver goods.

Anti-assignment clauses

1. Contractual limitations on assignments are strictly construed in most cases to prevent only a delegation of duties.

2. An assignment in violation of such clause may be interpreted as (a) breaching the promise not to make an assignment, (b) invalidating the contract, or (c) void.

Claims for money

1. As a general rule, claims for money may be assigned, but there are statutory exceptions.

2. If the assignment is security for a debt, the assignor still owes the debt if it remains unpaid by the obligor.

3. If the assignor sells the debt, there is no recourse against the assignor if the obligor defaults.

	4. An assignor warrants the genuineness of the money claims assigned.
Rights of the assignee	**1.** The assignee may enforce all the rights of his assignor.
	2. The obligor may raise all defenses against the assignee which the obligor had against the assignor prior to the assignment.
	3. Failure of assignor to fulfill his duties to the obligor will be a defense against the assignee.
	4. Contract provisions cutting off defenses of consumers are illegal under a FTC rule.
Duties of the parties	**1.** An assignor is not relieved of duties by a delegation of those duties.
	2. The mere assignment of rights does not include the delegation of duties.
	3. Under the Code, the assignment of the contract generally includes the assignment of rights and the delegation of duties.
	4. If an assignor delegates duties to an assignee, the assignee thereby becomes primarily liable to perform for the obligee.
Notice of assignment	**1.** Notice of the assignment must be given by the assignee to the obligor if the assignee is to receive performance.
	2. In a case of multiple assignments of the same right, the first to give notice in good faith to the obligor has priority to receive performance.

NOVATION

Requirements	**1.** A novation means a new contract. It involves the substitution with the express consent of all parties of a third party for one of the original parties.
	2. A novation requires a prior valid contract, agreement for substitution of a third party, an express release of one party, and a new valid contract.

CASES

Keel v. Titan Construction Corp.
639 P.2d 1228 (Okla. 1982)

Keel contracted with Titan Construction Corporation to build a house with an auxiliary solar energy system. The plans and specifications for the house were to be provided by Titan. Titan subsequently contracted with Anderson to draw plans for an auxiliary solar energy system for the house. When the solar energy system later failed to function properly, Keel sued Anderson for breach of the contract with Titan to design a proper system. Anderson contended that since Keel was not a party to the contract, Keel could not sue for breach of the contract.

LAVENDER, J. . . . Keel maintains that he is a third party beneficiary to the contract between Titan and Anderson.

By express statute, "A contract, made expressly for the benefit of a third person, may be enforced by him at any time before the parties thereto rescind it." It is not necessary that the party be specifically named as a beneficiary but only that the contract be made "expressly for the benefit of a third person" and "expressly" simply means "in an express manner; in direct or unmistakeable terms; explicitly; definitely; directly." A third party beneficiary of a contract may avail himself of its benefits and maintain an action thereon notwithstanding he was a stranger thereto, had no knowledge of the contract, and was not identified therein when it was made if it appears the parties intended to recognize him as a beneficiary. It is the intention of the parties to the contract as reflected in the contract which must provide the answer to the question of whether the contracting parties intended that a third person should receive a benefit which might be enforced in the courts.

Here, the contract between Titan and Anderson is one whereby Titan engaged Anderson to design house plans including an auxiliary solar heat system. Titan was a primary beneficiary of the contract, likewise the owner of the premises under construction was also a primary beneficiary of the contract, whose existence although not identified must have been known to Anderson. We therefore hold that under the allegations . . . a third party beneficiary contract cause of action is stated.

Affirmed.

Jackson, Lewis, Schnitzler v. Local 100
437 N.Y.S.2d 895 (N.Y. 1981)

On April 1, 1980, in violation of an injunction, the members of the defendants' unions commenced a strike, halting all mass transit in the city of New York and paralyzing its life and commerce. In contracts with the public employers, the unions had agreed not to strike. The plaintiff, a New York law firm, brought a class action suit against the transit unions and certain of their officers, seeking damages for the mass transit strike.

KASSOFF, J. . . . Plaintiffs seek recovery as a third-party beneficiary of the collective bargaining agreement between defendant unions and the public employers. Plaintiffs particularly claim the benefit of the no-strike clauses contained in those agreements. Historically, New York has been in the vanguard of the development of the third-party beneficiary doctrine. The doctrine itself had its American genesis in *Lawrence v. Fox,* 20 N.Y. 268 [1859]. Subsequent cases have applied this principle to contracts where one of the parties was a governmental entity. Extensive research by the court has failed to disclose any New York case where a public sector union breached an explicit no-strike clause of a contract which explicitly referred to protecting the interests of those who utilize the public service. In this regard, the facts before the court are highly unusual.

The critical inquiry in third-party beneficiary

claims is whether the contracting parties intended their contract to benefit third parties. The best evidence of such intent is language in the agreement to that effect. The TWU'S agreement states one of its purposes is "[t]o assure to the people of the State of New York efficient, economic, sufficient and dependable transportation service . . . and to protect the interests of the public" (Agreement, Article 1A). The TWU has also agreed "to cooperate with the authorities in a joint effort to place and keep the transit system on a safe, efficient, economical operating basis" (Agreement, Article 4).

As a member of the public which depends on the public transit system and which employs dozens of persons who need the public transit system to get to and from work, plaintiffs argue that they are within the class of persons for whose benefit the TWU has promised to provide "dependable transportation service."

A person not a party to a contract may sue for damages resulting from non-performance if the contract demonstrates that its primary intent was to benefit that person. Such cannot be said to be the case here. Where, as here, the government agency contracts for services which it bears no obligation to provide to the public, no duty can be found against the promissor on behalf of the member of the public unless the contract clearly makes the promisor answerable to that person for the breach. This, the court does not find. All other "consequential" damages could not be recovered under any theory of breach of contract since the contract did not permit enforcement by any member of the public. Therefore, no cause of action lies in breach of contract.

[*In the remainder of the opinion, the court held that defendants could be held liable under either a prima facie tort or public nuisance theory.*]

Ryder Truck Rental v. Transp. Equipment Co.
339 N.W.2d 283 (Neb. 1983)

In 1977 Ryder rented a truck to Transportation Equipment. In 1978 Transportation, with the approval of Ryder, assigned the truck rental contract to Williams Transfer. A few months later, the truck was damaged and Ryder delivered a substitute truck to Williams Transfer. When Williams subsequently refused to pay the rent for the truck, Ryder sued Transportation Equipment for the balance due on the truck rental contract. Transportation Equipment asserted that it was released from the contract when Ryder approved the assignment.

BOSLAUGH, J. . . . The trial court found generally for the plaintiff and awarded judgment in the amount of $7,901.17. The defendant has appealed and has assigned as error the finding that the defendant was liable for rental charges for the substituted vehicle. The agreement contained the following provision: "Ryder will, at the request of Customer, rent Customer a replacement vehicle, if available from Ryder's rental fleet,

at a rental rate equal to the charges applicable to the inoperable vehicle."

The defendant contends that it is not liable because it did not request the substitute vehicle, was not notified that a substitute vehicle had been requested by Heifner, and Heifner was not empowered to request a substitute. None of these arguments has merit.

The assignment of the agreement to Williams Transfer provided: "Assignor does hereby assign to Assignee all of its right, title and interest in and to the above described Lease Agreement and the use of the vehicles covered thereby."

By this assignment, the assignee Williams acquired all of the rights and interests of the assignor, Transportation Equipment Co. Generally, an assignor retains only those rights which have not passed to the assignee by the assignment. The assignor loses all right to control or enforce an assigned right against the obligor. In this case the defendant transferred its right to request a substitute vehicle to Williams Transfer, and it cannot now claim that its failure to request a substitute vehicle or Ryder's failure to notify it of Heifner's request precludes its liability.

Affirmed.

Kelly Health Care v. Prudential Ins. Co. 309 S.E.2d 305 (Va. 1983)

Green was insured under a Prudential health insurance policy. Green incurred medical expenses while a patient in a facility operated by Kelly Health Care, Inc. When Green entered the facility, she signed an authorization which stated: "I hereby authorize payment directly to Kelly Health Care of the nursing service benefits otherwise payable by me." Kelly submitted Green's nursing bills to Prudential, which Prudential refused to pay. Kelly sued Prudential, claiming to be an assignee of Green's contract rights under the insurance contract. Prudential contended that Kelly had no rights to sue on the contract as an assignee thereunder.

POFF, J. . . . The trial court ruled, and we agree, that there was no assignment, legal or equitable, in this case. An assignment is a transfer, but a transfer is not necessarily an assignment. If the transfer is less than absolute, it is not an assignment; the obligee must have intended, at the time of the transfer, to dispossess himself of an identified interest, or some part thereof, and to vest indefeasible title in the transferee. The intention of the assignor is the controlling consideration. The intent to transfer a present ownership of the subject matter of the assignment to the assignee must be manifested by some word, written or oral, or by some act inconsistent with the assignor's remaining as owner. This has sometimes been called a "*present appropriation.*" *The assignor must not retain any control over the fund or property assigned, any authority to collect, or any form of revocation.*

Under this definition, the appointment of an agent or the grant of a power of attorney cannot qualify as an assignment. Both are revocable, and the latter expires at the grantor's death. One of the documents upon which Kelly relies does no more than appoint Kelly as Green's special agent with authority to collect payments from Prudential as Green's entitlement falls due. The other document granted Prudential authority in the nature of a power of attorney to make such payments.

[A] mere communication to holder of the fund (the obligor), containing no words of present assignment and merely authorizing and directing him to pay to a third party, may properly bear the interpretation that it is a mere power of attorney to the obligor himself, empowering him to effectuate a transfer by his own subsequent act. With this interpretation, the communication to the obligor is not an assignment; and, like most other powers of attorney, it is revocable by its creator and it is terminated by its creator's death.

Affirmed.

Hanigan v. Wheeler 504 P.2d 972 (Ariz. 1972)

In August 1962, Hanigan entered into a "Dairy Queen Store Agreement" with LeMoine. The agreement provided that "Second Party shall not assign or transfer this Agreement without the written approval of First Party." On March 7, 1972, LeMoine entered into a contract to sell the Dairy Queen franchise and all its assets to Wheeler. Hanigan refused to approve the sale because he felt that the price ($90,000) was too high and that an inflated sales price was detrimental to the Dairy Queen business. Hanigan also stated that Wheeler was too inexperienced in business and too young to run the business properly. Plaintiff Wheeler then sued Hanigan for a declaratory judgment that the contract provision disallowing the assignment of the franchise was unenforceable as against public policy. The trial court found for plaintiff, and defendant appealed.

HOWARD, J. . . . The primary question dispositive of this appeal is whether the trial court erred in determining that the contract provision precluding the franchise transfer without the area franchise holder's approval is unenforceable as against public policy. A review of the record and the relevant law leads us to answer this question in the affirmative. Given the instant fact situation, the law in this area does not warrant the trial court's order requiring Hanigan to consent to the subject transaction:

> As a general rule, a contract is not assignable where the nature or terms of the contract make it nonassignable, unless such provision is waived. . . . The parties may in terms, by a provision in the contract, prohibit an assignment thereof. . . .
> Provisions in bilateral contracts which forbid or restrict assignment of the contract without the consent of the obligor have generally been upheld as valid and enforceable when called into question, although the meaning of such terms becomes a matter of interpretation. . . . 6 Am.Jur.2d Assignments §22 (1963).

These general statements are in accord with the Restatement of the Law of Contracts §151, which reads as follows:

> A right may be the subject of effective assignment unless . . . (c) the assignment is prohibited by the contract creating the right.

The treatises on this subject are likewise in accord.

A leading case, *Allhusen v. Caristo Construction Corporation,* 303 N.Y. 446, stated the law as follows:

> . . . we think it is reasonably clear that, while the courts have striven to uphold freedom of assignability, they have not failed to recognize the concept of freedom to contract. In large measure they agree that, where appropriate language is used, assignments of money due under contracts may be prohibited. When "clear language" is used, and the "plainest words . . . have been chosen," parties may "limit the freedom of alienation of rights and prohibit the assignment."

> Such a holding is not violative of public policy. Professor Williston, in his treatise on Contracts, states (Vol. 2 §422, p. 1214): "The question of the free alienation of property does not seem to be involved."

In opposition to the above principles, appellees contend that more than a contract right is involved in the case at bench in that the subject clause restricting assignment without Hanigan's approval serves as an unreasonable and unlawful restraint on the right of alienation of property, since the Store Agreement provides no guidelines by which the area franchise holder is to base his approval or disapproval of potential buyers, and that hypothetically, through the whim or arbitrariness of the holder, the LeMoines could be prevented from ever selling their franchise and the property associated with the franchise.

We accept the fundamental principle that one of the primary incidents inherent in the ownership of property is the right of alienation or disposition. However, this right is not limitless. The right to make an assignment of property can be defeated where there is a clear stipulation to that effect. The current state of the law in this area appears to be that a restraint on the alienation of property may be sustained when the restraint is reasonably designed to attain or encourage accepted social or economic ends. . . .

We also perceive that despite the restriction on assignment of the store agreement, the LeMoines are not entirely powerless. Where a contract contains a *promise* to refrain from assigning, an assignment which violates it would not be ineffective. "The promise creates a *duty* in the promisor not to assign. It does not deprive the assignor of the *power* to assign and its breach, therefore, would simply subject the promisor to an action for damages while the assignment would be effective. . . .

In summary, we hold that the law as set forth above demonstrates that the contract limitation against assignment of the Store Agreement without the approval of the area franchise holder is proper and valid. The trial court erred in concluding that the provision limiting assignability was unenforceable as against public policy. The court also erred in ruling that defendants had a duty to consent to the franchise sale, for this is contrary to the manifested intention of the parties to the contract. The general proposition is that "a covenantor is not to be held beyond his undertaking and he may make that as narrow as he likes." . . .

Reversed and remanded.

Cuchine v. H. O. Bell, Inc.
682 P.2d 723 (Mont. 1984)

On October 15, 1980, Timothy Cuchine purchased a pickup from H.O. Bell, Inc. under a retail installment sales contract which was subsequently assigned to Ford Motor Credit Company. Cuchine later began experiencing difficulties with the pickup and returned it to H.O. Bell to be repaired. When it became apparent that the truck could not be adequately repaired, Cuchine left the truck with H.O. Bell and filed a suit against H.O. Bell and the credit company for rescission of the installment contract due to breach of warranty and to recover his payments.

Cuchine contends that the credit company assumed full contract liability when the assignment was accepted.

Cuchine predicates the credit company's liability under the contract upon the following language which appears in the contract in bold, capital letters:

> NOTICE—ANY HOLDER OF THIS CONSUMER CREDIT CONTRACT IS SUBJECT TO ALL CLAIMS AND DEFENSES WHICH THE DEBTOR COULD ASSERT AGAINST THE SELLER OF GOODS OR SERVICES OBTAINED PURSUANT HERETO OR WITH THE PROCEEDS HEREOF. RECOVERY HEREUNDER BY THE DEBTOR SHALL NOT EXCEED AMOUNTS PAID BY THE DEBTOR HEREUNDER.

The District Court granted the credit company's motion for summary judgment and Cuchine appealed.

SHEEHY, J. . . . The issue presented on appeal is whether the assignment of a retail installment sales contract imposes full contract liability on the assignee of certain rights under the contract.

Section 9-318 of the Uniform Commercial Code reads in pertinent part:

> Unless an account debtor has made an enforceable agreement not to assert defenses or claims arising out of a sale as provided in 30-9-206, the rights of an assignee are subject to:
> (a) all the terms of the contract between the account debtor and assignor and any defense or claim arising therefrom; . . .

At common law, it is a well established rule that a party to a contract cannot relieve himself of the obligations which the contract imposed upon him merely by assigning the contract to a third person. Therefore, we must determine whether, under the Uniform Commercial Code, the assignment of the contract to the credit company imposed full contract liability on the credit company as assignee.

The case law as to the effect of section 9–318 of the UCC on the liabilities of an assignee of contract rights is scant, but conclusive. In *Michelin Tires v. First National Bank of Boston* (1st Cir.1981), 666 F.2d 673, the court examined section 9–318 and determined that:

> The key statutory language is ambiguous. That 'the rights of an assignee are *subject* to . . . (a) all the terms of the contract' connotes only that the assignee's rights to recover are limited by the obligor's rights to assert contractual defenses as a set-off, implying that affirmative recovery against the assignee is not intended.

The court also noted that:

> The words 'subject to,' used in their ordinary sense, mean 'subordinate to,' 'subservient to,' or 'limited by.' There is nothing in the use of the words 'subject to,' in their ordinary use, which would even hint at the creation of affirmative rights.

Such a conclusion is buttressed by the official comment to section 9-318. Official Comment 1 provides in pertinent part:

> Subsection (1) makes no substantial change in prior law. An assignee has traditionally been subject to defenses or set-offs existing before an account debtor is notified of the assignment.

Under prior law, the assignee of a contract was generally not held liable for the assignor's breach of contract. This rule has been carried into current law as well; where it is not clearly shown that the assignee under a contract expressly or impliedly assumed the assignor's liability under the contract the assignee is not subject to the contract liability imposed by the contract on the assignor.

We believe that the intent of section 9–318 of the Uniform Commercial Code was to allow an account debtor to assert contractual defenses as a set-off; the provisions were not intended, generally, to place the assignee of a contract in the position of being held a guarantor of a product in place of the assignor. Therefore, the summary judgment of the District Court is

Affirmed.

Equilease Corp. v. State Federal S&L Ass'n.
647 F.2d 1069 (Okla. law) 1981

On October 31, 1973, Equilease leased 7 trucks to Henry Oil Co. The lease was secured by 6 savings certificates issued by State Federal to Henry Oil, who pledged and delivered these certificates to Equilease on November 12, 1973. Henry Oil later encountered financial difficulties and on December 13, 1974 it notified State Federal that the 6 certificates had been lost and that Henry Oil desired to withdraw the funds. On December 16, 1974, State Federal paid the funds to Henry Oil. On May 27, 1975, Henry Oil defaulted on one of its leases with Equilease, and it was then that Equilease discovered for the first time that Henry Oil had withdrawn the funds. State Federal had not been notified of the pledge agreement at any time prior to May, 1975. When Equilease sued State Federal for negligence in allowing Henry Oil to withdraw the funds without first presenting the certificates, the trial court granted State Federal's motion for summary judgment.

BARRETT, J. . . . It is generally agreed that prior to notification of an assignment, a debtor may pay the creditor the funds owing and such payment constitutes a complete defense against an action brought by the undisclosed assignee against the debtor.

The general rule is that, as between the assignor and his assignee and the assignor's creditors or those who merely succeed to the rights of and stand in his shoes, notice of the assignment to the debtor or holder of the fund is not a prerequisite to the protection of the assignee. However, the requirement as to notice applies to the assignment of obligations represented by the savings certificates involved in the instant case, in order to create a liability flowing from the debtor to the assignee who failed to give notice. Oklahoma has followed the general rule that an assignee must notify the debtor prior to debtor's payment to the assignor in order to bind the debtor to the obligation asserted by the assignee.

. . . [A]n assignment of a chose in action, made in good faith, for a sufficient consideration, and without intent to defraud creditors, or subsequent purchasers, is complete upon the mutual assent of the assignor and assignee, and does not gain an additional validity, as against third persons, by notice to the debtor . . . Notice is, indeed, needful, in order to charge the debtor with the duty of payment to the assignee, so that if, without notice, he pay the debt to the assignor or to a subsequent assignee, or on a garnishee process, he will be discharged from the debt.

Equilease's fourth cause of action alleged a breach of contract theory. The predicate was that because Equilease became the owner of the savings certificates following their pledge from Henry Oil, Equilease was entitled to rely upon the express terms of the savings certificates that no withdrawals could be expected without presentation of the passbooks issued by State Federal. In light of its failure to give notice, we hold that Equilease is not entitled to invoke a contractual obligation against State Federal.

We affirm.

Jacobson v. Stern
605 P.2d 198 (Nev. 1980)

Martin Stern sued for his architectural services rendered to Jacobson in Jacobson's development of a hotel and casino, known as King's Castle, on the north shore of Lake Tahoe, Nevada. In April of 1969, Jacobson contracted with Stern for the architect's services and the fee. On May 1, 1969, Jacobson acquired all the stock of A.L.W., Inc., a corporation that had previously operated a casino on the site of the new development. On May 9, 1969, A.L.W. began to operate the King's Castle, but it went bankrupt in 1972. Stern did not file a claim in the bankruptcy proceeding but rather, brought this suit directly against Jacobson. When Stern was awarded $132,590.37 by the trial court, Jacobson appealed on the ground that his obligations were adopted by A.L.W., which constituted a novation.

PER CURIAM: . . . Under Nevada law, if a pre-incorporation contract made by a promoter is within the corporate powers, the corporation may, when organized, expressly or impliedly ratify the contract and, thus, make it a valid obligation of the corporation. If the corporation accepts the benefits of the contract, it will be required to perform the contractual obligations. The evidence supports a finding that the A.L.W. corporation accepted the benefits of the contract for architectural services, and in fact adopted the contractual obligations and made partial payments on the obligation. However, liability of the corporation by adoption does not, absent a novation, end the liability of the promoter to the third party.

Appellant argues that there was, in fact, a novation by A.L.W., Inc. in its adoption of all agreements as its corporate liabilities. Where there is a valid express or implied novation, the corporation is substituted for the promoter as a party to the contract in all respects, and the promoter is divested of his rights and released of his liabilities. In order to constitute a valid novation, however, the creditor must assent to the substitution of a new obligor, but this assent may be inferred from his acceptance of part performance by the new obligor, if the performance is made with the understanding that a complete novation is proposed.

Appellant contends that, because the evidence shows that after May 1, 1969, Stern probably knew, or should have known, that he was performing for the benefit of A.L.W., Inc., and was paid by A.L.W., Inc., he impliedly consented to a novation. There is no evidence, however, showing that Stern agreed to the substitution of A.L.W., Inc. for Jacobson in the contract, or that he performed with the knowledge or understanding that a novation was proposed. In fact he maintained throughout that he had contracted with Jacobson and felt that Jacobson was personally liable on the contract. The intent of the parties to cause a novation must be clear. The trial court found there was no novation and that Stern never agreed to release Jacobson from his obligations. We agree with this finding.

Affirmed.

REVIEW QUESTIONS

1. Match each term in column A with the appropriate statement in column B.

A		B	
1. Intended third-party beneficiary		**a.**	Performance will satisfy a duty the promisee owes the beneficiary.
2. Incidental third-party beneficiary		**b.**	A present transfer of rights arising from an earlier contract.
3. Main purpose and direct obligation tests		**c.**	Transfer of rights would materially change the other party's duty, increase the risk imposed by the contract, or impair return performance.
4. Creditor beneficiary		**d.**	Third party who has no legally enforceable rights under a contract.
5. Donee beneficiary		**e.**	Usually both an assignment and a delegation.
6. When beneficiary's rights vest		**f.**	Rights vest based on reliance or consent of third party.

7. Assignment

g. A new contract with the substitution of a third party for an original party.

8. Delegation

h. Third party who has legally enforceable rights under a contract.

9. Nonassignable rights

i. Duties of personal service or duties that may materially vary the performance given to the obligee.

10. Nondelegable duties

j. Tests for determining if a third party is an intended beneficiary.

11. Novation

k. Transfer of duties arising from an earlier contract.

12. "Assignment of the contract"

l. Promisee buys a promise to make a gift to a third party.

2. Crane is a troublesome person who is annoying Al. Al dislikes Crane but, believing the best way to obtain freedom from annoyance is to make a present, secures a promise from Bill to give Crane a handsome box of cigars. Is Crane an intended third-party beneficiary? Explain.

3. Boyce contracts to build a house for Anne. Pursuant to the contract, Boyce and his surety Travelers execute a payment bond to Anne by which they promise Anne that all of Boyce's debts for labor and materials on the house will be paid. Boyce later employs Sam as a carpenter and buys lumber from Larry's Lumber Company. Are Sam and Larry's Lumber Company intended beneficiaries of Travelers' promise to Anne? Explain.

4. Rhodes is employed by Mack Company, and designates his infant son Will as beneficiary of a death benefit under a plan set up by Mack Company. No provision is made for a power to change the beneficiary. Later Rhodes notifies Mack Company that the designation of Will is revoked and that the death benefit is to be paid to Alice, to whom Rhodes is newly married. What are Will's rights, if any? Explain.

5. Wichita State University leased an airplane to fly its football team. The lease provided that the university would secure liability insurance to cover any deaths or injuries from the operation of the plane. No liability insurance was bought. The plane later crashed, killing all on board. Can the estates of the deceased football players sue the university as intended beneficiaries? Explain why or why not.

6. Gaither entered into a contract with a nonprofit corporation whereby Gaither would receive $700 per month while in medical school, provided that he return to his small home town, Chester, to practice medicine for 10 years after becoming a licensed physician. The residents of Chester voted approval of bonds to construct a medical clinic. Gaither practiced medicine in Chester for about 5 weeks but then left for Mt. Clement. Do the representatives of the medical clinic and the citizens of Chester have a right to sue Gaither? Explain.

7. General Greer had an insurance policy with the Good Insurance Company. Upon being injured in a car accident, he was treated, free of personal cost, at a governmental medical facility. The policy required Good to pay all reasonable medical expenses and provided that it would pay any person or organization rendering the services for the insured. Should the government sue for reimbursement of the reasonable medical expenses rendered to Greer? Explain.

8. Hunt, an employee of the Marie Reading School, was injured when the elevator he was operating fell. The school had a contract with Shaft Elevator, Inc., whereby Shaft was to inspect and service the elevator on a regular basis. Hunt contended that Shaft had not properly inspected the elevator and that its omission caused the accident. Can Hunt maintain an action against Shaft? Why or why not?

9. Athens Lie Detector company, for good consideration, gave Yarbrough an exclusive license to operate certain lie detector machines. As part of the agreement, the company agreed to tell him how the manufacturing process works. Yarbrough assigned his rights and delegated his duties under the contract to Travers. Are the rights assignable? Are the duties delegable? Explain.

10. Corey sold his property to Greer, who assigned the contract right to Bob. The original contract of sale (earnest money contract) provided for an extension of credit by Corey to Greer and did not require a total cash payment at the time of closing. Is a contract for the sale of real estate assignable by the buyer if it provides for credit from the seller to the buyer? Explain.

11. Suppose a contract for the sale of goods contains this clause: "Under no circumstances may any rights under this contract be assigned." After the seller delivers goods to the buyer, may the seller assign the buyer's unpaid account to a third party? Explain.

12. Debtor owed money to worker for work performed. Worker assigned his claim to bank and notified debtor of the assignment. Bank then demanded payment from debtor, but debtor refused and paid worker instead. Can bank now collect from debtor? Why or why not? Suppose debtor was not notified of the assignment to bank. Subsequently, worker assigned his claim to Dewey and debtor was informed of this assignment. To whom should debtor make payment? Explain.

13. Brown purchased a car from Morgan, who falsely told him that the car was in good condition when she knew that it needed extensive repairs. Morgan assigned the installment sale contract to Friendly Finance Company, which then sued Brown for nonpayment. Brown claims the right to set aside the contract for fraud. Can he use that defense against the finance company? Explain.

14. Andrews entered into a five-year employment contract with Arnold as president of its subsidiary. Then Andrews decided to sell the subsidiary to Long, Inc. The contract of sale provided for assignment of Arnold's contract of employment, but Arnold was unaware of the assignment and sale. Is he obligated to work for Long, Inc.?

14 THE PRINCIPAL-AGENT RELATIONSHIP

The term *agency* is used to describe the fiduciary relationship that exists when one person acts on behalf, and under the control, of another person. The person who acts for another is called an *agent.* The person for whom he acts, and who controls the agent, is called a *principal.* Traditionally, issues of agency law arise when the agent has attempted to enter into a contract on behalf of his principal; however, the law of agency includes several aspects of the law of torts. Although tort litigation usually uses the terms *master* and *servant,* rather than principal and agent, both relationships are encompassed within the broad legal classification of agency law.

The principles of agency law are essential for the conduct of business transactions. A corporation, as a legal entity, can function only through agents. The law of partnership is, to a large degree, agency principles specially applied to that particular form of business organization.

Case law, as contrasted with statutory law, has developed most of the principles applicable to the law of agency. Agency issues are usually discussed within a framework of three parties: the principal (P), the agent (A), and the third party (T), with whom A contracts or against whom A commits a tort while in P's service. The following examples illustrate the problems and issues involved in the law of agency.

> **P v. A:** Principal sues agent for a loss caused by A's breach of a fiduciary duty, such as to obey instructions.

P v. T: Principal sues third party for breach of a contract that T negotiated with A while A was acting on P's behalf.

A v. P: Agent sues principal for injuries suffered in the course of employment, for wrongful discharge, or for compensation owed for services rendered.

A v. T: Agent sues third party for a loss suffered by A, such as the loss of a commission due to T's interference with contractual obligations.

T v. P: Third party sues principal for breach of a contract that T negotiated with A or for damages caused by a tort committed by A.

T v. A: Third party sues agent personally for breach of a contract signed by A or for damages caused by a tort committed by A.

1. Types of Principals

From the third party's perspective, an agent may act for one of three types of principals. First, an agent who reveals that he is working for another and who reveals the principal's identity is an agent of a *disclosed principal.* The existence of a disclosed principal will be found in most agency relationships, particularly employment situations.

At the other extreme, a principal is *undisclosed* whenever a third party reasonably believes that the agent acts only on his or her own behalf. In essence, when an undisclosed principal is involved, the third party does not realize that any agency relationship exists. A well-known or wealthy principal may not want a third party to know he is interested in buying that third party's land, business, or merchandise. Therefore, the principal hires an agent to deal with the third party. This agent would be instructed by the principal to keep that principal's existence a secret from the third party.

A third situation falls in between the disclosed and undisclosed principals' circumstances. A third party may know an agent represents a principal, but that third party may not know the identity of the principal. When a third party learns of the principal's existence but not his identity, a *partially disclosed principal* is present. For the most part, legal issues treat undisclosed and partially disclosed principals in a similar manner.

2. Types of Agents

Some agents have special terms to identify them. For example, some agents are known as *brokers* and others as *factors.* A *broker* is an agent with special, limited authority to procure a customer in order that the owner can effect a sale or exchange of property. A real estate broker has authority to find a buyer for another's real estate, but the real estate remains under the control of the owner. A *factor* is a person who has possession and control of another's personal property, such as goods, and is authorized to sell that property. A factor has a property interest and may sell the property in his own name, whereas a broker may not.

Although the term is seldom used today, a retail merchant who has a manufacturer's goods on consignment is a factor.

Agents are also classified as *general* or *special* agents. A *general* agent has much broader authority than a special agent. Some cases define a general agent as one authorized to conduct a series of transactions involving a continuity of service, whereas a *special* agent conducts a single transaction or a series of transactions without continuity of service. Most agents usually are considered to be general agents of the employer as long as they stay within the scope of their employment. However, an athlete's agent assisting in contract negotiations likely would be a special agent and generally would not be authorized to make investments or purchase property.

Some persons who perform services for others are known as *independent contractors.* A person may contract for the services of another in a way that gives him full and complete control over the details and manner in which the work will be conducted, or he may simply contract for a certain end result. If the agreement provides merely that the second party is to accomplish a certain result and that party has full control over the manner and methods to be pursued in bringing about the result, such a party is deemed an independent contractor. The person contracting with an independent contractor and receiving the benefit of his service is usually called a *proprietor.* A proprietor is generally not responsible to third parties for the independent contractor's actions, either in contract or in tort. On the other hand, if the second party places his services at the disposal of the first in such a manner that the action of the second is generally controlled by the former, a principal-agent relationship is established. The liabilities of these parties are discussed in the next two chapters.

3. Capacity of Parties

It is generally stated that anyone who may act for himself may act through an agent. For example, a minor may enter into a contract, and so long as he does not disaffirm it, the agreement is binding. Likewise, the majority of states have held that a contract of an agent on behalf of a minor principal is voidable. Therefore, such an agreement is subject to rescission or ratification by the minor, the same as if the minor personally had entered into the contract. To this general rule concerning an infant's capacity as a principal some states recognize an exception. In other words, there is some authority to the effect that any appointment of an agent by an infant is void, not merely voidable. Under this view, any agreement entered into by an infant's agent would be ineffective, and an attempted disaffirmance by the principal would be unnecessary.

A minor may act as an agent for an adult, and agreements he makes for his principal while acting within his authority are binding on the principal. Although the infant agent has a right to terminate his contract of agency at his will, as long as he continues in the employment, his acts within the scope of the authority conferred upon him become those of his principal.

4. Formal Requirements

As a general rule, agency relationships are based on the consent of the parties involved. No particular formalities are required to create a principal-agent relationship. A principal may appoint an agent either in writing or orally. The agency may be either expressed or implied.

Despite the general lack of formal requirements, most states require that the appointment of an agent be evidenced by a writing when the agent is to negotiate a contract under the statute of frauds. Recall from chapter 11 that these written contracts include those involving (1) title to real estate,[1] (2) guaranty contracts, (3) performance that cannot be completed within 1 year of the date of making, and (4) sales of goods priced over $500.

When a formal instrument is used for conferring authority upon an agent, it is known as a *power of attorney*. Generally, this written document is signed by the principal in the presence of a notary public. The agent named in a power of attorney is called an *attorney in fact*. The term distinguishes this formally appointed agent from an *attorney at law,* who is a licensed lawyer.

A power of attorney may be general, which gives the agent authority to act in all respects for the principal. Sometimes an elderly person signs a power of attorney appointing a general attorney in fact to handle all the necessary matters that may arise. On the other hand, a power of attorney may be narrowly written. For example, a seller of land may need to be out of town on the date set to close the sales transaction. This seller can sign a special power of attorney that grants the agent the limited authority to act on the seller's behalf by signing the deed and other necessary papers required to complete the closing.

Section 13, below, discusses real estate listing agreements. Although these documents are used to authorize a real estate agent to find a ready, willing and able buyer, most states do not require these agreements to be in writing. Technically the agent cannot create a binding sales contract between the buyer and seller. In other words, the real estate agent is not authorized to sign a contract on the seller's behalf. That agent's responsibility is to bring the buyer and seller together so that these parties may sign a contract. Despite oral listing agreements being enforceable, agents generally insist upon a written one to ease the burden of proof required to establish when a commission is owed. Furthermore, a number of states do require that listing agreements be evidenced by a writing.

DUTIES OF AGENTS

5. Introduction

The nature and extent of the duties imposed upon agents and servants are governed largely by the contract of employment. In addition to the duties expressly designated, certain others are implied by the fiduciary nature of the relationship and by the legal effects on the principal of actions or omissions by the agent. The usual implied duties are (1) to be loyal to the principal; (2) to protect confidential information; (3) to obey all reasonable instructions; (4) to inform the

[1] Cady v. Johnson, p. 308.

principal of material facts that affect the relationship; (5) to refrain from being negligent; and (6) to account for all money or property received for the benefit of the principal. The sections that follow will discuss how these implied duties are essential to the principal-agent relationship.

6. Duty of Loyalty

At the foundation of any fiduciary relationship is the duty of loyalty each party owes to the other. Since an agent is in a position of trust and confidence, the agent owes an obligation of undivided loyalty to the principal. While employed, an agent should not undertake a business venture that competes or interferes in any manner with the principal's business, nor should the agent make any contract for himself that should have been made for the principal. A breach of this fundamental duty can result in the principal's enjoining the agent's new business or recovering money damages, or both.[2]

This duty of loyalty also prevents an agent from entering into an agreement on the principal's behalf if the agent himself is the other contracting party. In order to create a binding agreement with the principal, the agent first must obtain the principal's approval. Since a contract between the agent and the principal is not a deal "at arm's length," the circumstances demand the utmost good faith from the agent. Indeed, an agent must disclose fully all facts that might materially influence the principal's decision-making process.

Likewise, an agent usually cannot represent two principals in the same transactions if the principals have differing interests. To act as a dual agent often leads the agent to an unavoidable breach of the duty of loyalty to one, if not both, principals. In order to prevent the breach of this basic duty in this situation, the agent should inform both principals of all the facts in the transaction, including that he (the agent) is working for both principals. If these principals agree to continue negotiations, the agent in effect becomes a "go-between" or messenger. Then the agent is acting on behalf of both principals while avoiding active negotiation. Due to the nature of their business, real estate agents particularly must be aware of the hazards of dual agencies.

Transactions violating the duty of loyalty may always be rescinded by the principal, despite the fact that the agent acted for the best interests of his principal and the contract was as favorable as could be obtained elsewhere. The general rule is applied without favor, in order that every possible motive or incentive for unfaithfulness may be removed.

In addition to the remedy of rescission, a principal is entitled to treat any profit realized by the agent in violation of this duty as belonging to the principal. Such profits may include rebates, bonuses, commissions, or divisions of profits received by an agent for dealing with a particular third party. Here again the contracts may have been favorable to the employer, but the result is once again in favor of the principal, because the agent should not be tempted to abuse the confidence placed in him.

---

[2] Chelsea Industries, Inc. v. Gaffney, p. 309.

7. Duty to Protect Confidential Information

The duty of loyalty demands that information of a confidential character acquired while in the service of the principal shall not be used by the agent to advance his interests in opposition to those of the principal. In other words, an agent has a duty to protect the principal's confidential information. This confidential information is usually called a *trade secret*. Trade secrets include plans, processes, tools, mechanisms, compounds, and information used in business operations. They are known only to the owner of the business and to a limited number of other persons in whom it may be necessary to confide. An employer seeking to prevent the disclosure or use of trade secrets or information must demonstrate that he pursued an active course of conduct designed to inform his employees that such secrets and information were to remain confidential. An issue to be determined in all cases involving trade secrets is whether the information sought to be protected is, in fact and in law, confidential. The result in each case depends on the conduct of the parties and the nature of the information.[3]

An employee who learns of secret processes or formulas or comes into possession of lists of customers may not use this information to the detriment of his employer. Former employees may not use such information in a competing business, regardless of whether the trade secrets were copied or memorized. The fact that a trade secret is spied out does not make it any less a secret, nor does the fact that a product is on the market amount to a divulgence or abandonment of the secrets connected with the product. The employer may obtain an injunction to prevent their use. Such use is a form of unfair competition. The rule relating to trade secrets is applied with equal severity whether the agent acts before or after he severs his connection with the principal.

Knowledge that is important but not a trade secret may be used, although its use injures the agent's former employer. That information which by experience has become a part of a former employee's general knowledge should not and cannot be enjoined from further and different uses. For this reason, there usually is nothing to hinder a person who has made the acquaintance of his employer's customers from later contacting those he can remember. His acquaintances are part of his acquired skill. The employer may protect himself by a clause in the employment agreement to the effect that the employee will not compete with the employer or work for a competitor for a limited period of time after his employment is terminated. (See chapter 10 for a further discussion on the proper use of agreements not to compete.)

8. Duty to Obey Instructions

It is the duty of an agent to obey all instructions issued by his principal as long as they refer to duties contemplated by the contract of employment. Burdens not required by the agreement cannot be indiscriminately imposed by the employer, and any material change in an employee's duties may constitute a breach of the employment contract.

---

[3] J & K Computer Systems, Inc. v. Parish, p. 310.

An instruction may not be regarded lightly merely because it departs from the usual procedure and seems fanciful and impractical to the agent. It is not the agent's business to question the procedure outlined by a superior. Any loss that results while an agent is pursuing any other course makes that agent absolutely liable to the principal for any resulting loss.

Furthermore, an instruction of the principal does not become improper merely because the motive is bad, unless it is illegal or immoral. The principal may be well aware of the agent's distaste for certain tasks; yet, if those tasks are called for under the employment agreement, it becomes the agent's duty to perform them. Failure to perform often results in proper grounds for discharge.[4]

Closely allied to the duty to follow instructions is the duty to remain within the scope of the authority conferred. Because it often becomes possible for an agent to exceed his authority and still bind his principal, the agent has a duty not to exceed the authority granted. In case the agent does so, the employee or agent becomes responsible for any resulting loss.

Occasionally, circumstances arise that nullify instructions previously given. Because of the new conditions, the old instructions would, if followed, practically destroy the purpose of the agency. Whenever such an emergency arises, it becomes the duty of the agent, provided the principal is not available, to exercise his best judgment in meeting the situation.

9. Duty to Inform

In the next chapter we will see that knowledge acquired by an agent within the scope of his authority binds the principal. More succinctly, the law states that an agent's knowledge is imputed as notice to the principal. Therefore, the law requires that the agent inform his principal of all facts that affect the subject matter of the agency and that are obtained within the scope of the employment. The rule requiring full disclosure of all material facts that might affect the principal is equally applicable to gratuitous and to compensated agents.

This rule extends beyond the duty to inform the principal of conflicting interests of third parties or possible violations of the duty of loyalty in a particular transaction. It imposes upon the agent a duty to give his principal all information that materially affects the interest of the principal. Knowledge of facts that may have greatly advanced the value of property placed with an agent for sale must be communicated before property is sold at a price previously established by the principal.

10. Duty Not to Be Negligent

As we discuss more fully in chapter 16, the doctrine of *respondeat superior* imposes liability upon a principal or master for the torts of an agent or servant acting within the scope of his employment. The agent or servant is primarily liable, and the principal or master is vicariously or secondarily liable.

It is an implied condition of employment contracts, if not otherwise

---

[4] Central Alaska Broadcasting, Inc. v. Bracale, p. 311.

expressed, that the employee has a duty to act in good faith and to exercise reasonable care and diligence in performing his tasks. Failure to do so is a breach of the employment contract. Therefore, if the employer has liability to third persons because of the employee's acts or negligent omissions, the employer may recover his loss from the employee. This right may be transferred by the doctrine of subrogation to the liability insurance carrier of the employer. For example, assume that a bakery company is held liable for damages to an injured child who was struck by a company delivery truck as the result of the employee-driver's negligence. After the company's insurance company pays the total coverage to the injured party, any unpaid damages can be collected from the company. The company in turn can sue the employee for breach of the duty not to be negligent. In some states, the insurance company could also collect from the employee. However, there are some reasons to keep liability from being passed ultimately to the careless employee; these reasons are discussed in the chapter on agency and tort responsibility.

11. Duty to Account

Money or property entrusted to the agent must be accounted for to the principal. Because of this fact, the agent is required to keep proper records showing receipts and expenditures, in order that a complete accounting may be rendered. Any money collected by an agent for his principal should not be mingled with funds of the agent. If they are deposited in a bank, they should be kept in a separate account. Otherwise, any loss resulting must be borne by the agent. The duty to account can also arise out of the agent's breach of another fiduciary duty.

An agent who receives money from third parties for the benefit of the principal owes no duty to account to the third parties. The only duty to account is owed to the principal. On the other hand, money paid to an agent who has no authority to collect it, and who does not turn it over to the principal, may be recovered from the agent in an action by the third party.

A different problem is presented when money is paid in error to an agent, as in the overpayment of an account. If the agent has passed the money on to his principal before the mistake is discovered, it is clear that only the principal is liable. Nevertheless, money that is still in the possession of the agent when he is notified of the error should be returned to the third party. The agent does not relieve himself of this burden by subsequently making payment to his principal.

Any payment made in error to an agent and caused by the agent's mistake or misconduct may always be recovered from him, even if he has surrendered it to his principal. Also, any overpayment may be recovered from the agent of an undisclosed principal, because the party dealing with the agent was unaware of the existence of the principal.

DUTIES OF PRINCIPALS

12. Introduction

The principal-agent relationship is a fiduciary one. Like agents, principals have fiduciary duties. The trust and confidence of a fiduciary relationship is a two-way obligation. Thus the law requires that the principal be loyal and honest in dealing with the agent. In addition, the agent is entitled to be compensated for his services in accordance with the terms of his contract of employment. If no definite compensation has been agreed upon, there arises a duty to pay the reasonable value of such services—the customary rate in the community. Furthermore, the principal owes duties to reimburse agents for their reasonable expenses and to hold the agents harmless for liability that may be incurred while the agent is within the scope of employment.

13. Duty to Compensate in General

Many employment contracts include provisions for paying a percentage of profits to a key employee. If the employment contract does not include a detailed enumeration of the items to be considered in determining net income, it will be computed in accordance with generally accepted accounting principles, taking into consideration past custom and practice in the operation of the employer's business. It is assumed that the methods of determining net income will be consistent and that no substantial changes will be made in the methods of accounting without the mutual agreement of the parties. The employer cannot unilaterally change the accounting methods, nor can the employee require a change in order to effect an increase in his earnings.

The right of a real estate broker or agent to a commission is frequently the subject of litigation. In the absence of an express agreement, the real estate broker earns a commission (1) if he finds a buyer who is ready, willing, and able to meet the terms outlined by the seller in the listing agreement; or (2) if the owner contracts with the purchaser (whether or not the price is less than the listed price), even though it later develops that the buyer is unable to meet the terms of the contract. The contract is conclusive evidence that the broker found a ready, willing, and able buyer. If a prospective purchaser conditions his obligation to purchase on an approval of credit or approval of a loan, he is not a ready, willing, and able buyer until such approval. If the purchaser is unable to obtain a loan, the broker is not entitled to a commission.

The duty to pay a real estate commission is dependent upon which type of listing has been agreed upon. An owner who lists property with several brokers is obligated to pay the first one who finds a satisfactory purchaser, at which time the agency of other brokers is automatically terminated, assuming a simple *open listing*. In an open listing, the owner is free to sell on his own behalf without a commission. The second type of listing is called an *exclusive agency listing*. For an agreed period of time, it gives the broker the exclusive right to find a buyer. In this arrangement, the seller is not free to list the property with other brokers, and a sale through other brokers would be a violation of the contract of listing, although the seller himself is free to find a buyer of his own. With the third type of listing, called an *exclusive right to sell*, even the seller is not free to find a buyer of his own choosing. If the seller does sell on his own behalf, he still is obliged to pay a commission to the broker.

Multiple listing is a method of listing property with several brokers simultaneously. These brokers belong to an organization, the members of which share listings and divide the commissions. A typical commission could be split 60 percent to the selling broker, 30 percent to the listing broker, and 10 percent to the organization for operating expenses. These multiple-listing groups give homeowners the advantage of increased exposure to potential buyers. In return for this advantage, most multiple-listing agreements are of the exclusive right-to-sell type.

The right to a real estate commission is subject to statutory limitations in several states. Some require a written contract, and most require a person engaged in this activity to be licensed by a state real estate commission. Chapter 20 discusses the real estate sales transaction in further detail.

14. Duty to Compensate Sales Representatives

Sales representatives who sell merchandise on a commission basis are confronted by problems similar to those of the broker, unless their employment contract is specific in its details. Let us assume that Low Cal Pies, Inc., appoints Albert, on a commission basis, as its exclusive sales representative in a certain territory. A grocery chain in the area involved sends a large order for pies directly to the home office of Low Cal Pies. Is Albert entitled to a commission on the sale? It is generally held that such a salesman is entitled to a commission only on sales solicited and induced by him, unless his contract of employment gives him greater rights.

The sales representative usually earns a commission as soon as an order from a responsible buyer is obtained, unless the contract of employment makes payment contingent upon delivery of the goods or collection of the sale's price. If payment is made dependent upon performance by the purchaser, the employer cannot deny the sales representative's commission by terminating the agency prior to collection of the account. When the buyer ultimately pays for the goods, the seller is obligated to pay the commission.

An agent who receives a weekly or monthly advance against future commissions is not obligated to return the advance if commissions equal thereto are not earned. The advance, in the absence of a specific agreement, is considered by the courts as a minimum salary.[5]

15. Duty to Reimburse

An agent has a general right to reimbursement for money properly expended on behalf of his principal. It must appear that the money was reasonably spent and that its expenditure was not necessitated by the misconduct or negligence of the agent. Travel-related expenses, such as air fares, mileage, lodging, and meals are typical examples of items a principal must reimburse an agent for unless those parties agree otherwise.

An agent also is entitled to be reimbursed for the costs of completing an agreement when the performance was intended to benefit the principal. This is especially true when the agent has performed on behalf of an undisclosed principal. That principal must protect his agent by making funds available to

---

[5] M & D Simon Company v. Blanchard, p. 312.

perform the contract as agreed. Suppose that McDonald's Hamburgers is seeking prime locations for its franchises. Not wanting to pay an additional premium just because it is the buyer, McDonald's may hire a local real estate agent to purchase a site in his own name. McDonald's must reimburse this agent for any money the agent may have used to complete the performance of any contract signed.

16. Duty to Indemnify

Whereas to *reimburse* someone means to repay him for funds already spent, to *indemnify* means to hold a person harmless or free from liability. An employee is entitled to indemnity for certain losses. The duty to indemnify usually arises in factual situations in which the employee is not at fault and his liability results from following the instructions of the employer.[6] An agent or a servant is justified in presuming that a principal has a lawful right to give his instructions and that performance resulting from his instructions will not injure third parties. When this is not the case, and the agent incurs a liability to some third party because of trespass or conversion, the principal must indemnify the agent against loss. There will ordinarily be no indemnification for losses incurred in negligence actions because the servant's own conduct is involved. The indemnification is usually of the master by the servant in tort situations. If the agent or servant is sued for actions within the course of employment, the agent or servant is entitled to be reimbursed for attorney's fees and court costs incurred if the principal does not furnish them in the first instance.

---

[6] Machinists Automotive Trade District Lodge No. 190 of Northern California v. Utility Trailer Sales Company, p. 312.

SUMMARY

Types of principals	**1.** A *disclosed* principal is one whose existence and identity are known by third parties.
	2. A *partially disclosed* principal is one whose existence is known but whose identity is unknown by third parties.
	3. An *undisclosed* principal is one whose identity and existence are unknown by third parties.
Types of agents	**1.** A *general* agent has broad authority to conduct a series of transactions with continuity of service.
	2. A *special* agent has narrower authority and conducts a single transaction or lacks continuity of service.

	3. A *broker* has limited authority to find a customer in order that a sale of property may be completed.
	4. A *factor* has possession and control of another person's property and is authorized to sell that property.
	5. An *independent contractor* retains control over the details of how work is to be accomplished. The person hiring an independent contractor contracts for a certain end result.
Capacity of parties	1. In general, a minor may act as a principal. Actions by an adult agent on behalf of a minor principal generally are voidable by the minor.
	2. In general, a minor may act as an agent. Actions by a minor agent on behalf of an adult principal generally are binding on the principal.
Formality requirements	1. Usually, no particular requirements need be followed to create an agency.
	2. Agency may be expressed or implied. Expressed relationships may be created orally or in writing.
	3. The appointment of an agent must be in writing when the agent is to negotiate a contract required to be in writing under the statute of frauds.
	4. A *power of attorney* is the written document used to formally appoint an agent.

DUTIES OF AGENTS

Duty of loyalty	1. Foundation of every agency relationship.
	2. Duty is breached if agent takes for himself an opportunity intended to benefit the principal.
	3. Duty is breached if agent secretly contracts with himself on behalf of the principal.
	4. Duty is breached if agent attempts to represent two principals in the same

	transaction. This is known as the dual agency situation.
Duty to protect confidential information	**1.** Agent must protect principal's trade secrets and not use them for personal profit.
	2. Trade secrets might include plans, processes, tools, compounds, customer lists, and other information used in business operations.
	3. Principals often have agents sign agreements not to compete in order to reinforce this duty.
Duty to obey instructions	**1.** An agent must follow all reasonable instructions given by the principal.
	2. An agent also must not exceed the authority granted by the principal.
	3. If an emergency prevents the agent from obeying the instructions given, that agent must seek additional directions. If the principal is not available, the agent must use his best judgment.
Duty to inform	**1.** Agents have the duty to give their principals all the information that materially affects the principals' interest.
Duty not to be negligent	**1.** A principal (master) may be liable for the personal injuries caused by agents (servants) within the scope of authority (employment).
	2. Because agents (servants) can create this liability by negligence, these parties have the legal duty to refrain from negligent acts.
Duty to account	**1.** An agent always must account to the principal for any money the agent has received from or for the principal.
	2. In general, an agent's duty to account is owed only to the principal, not to third parties.
	3. However, an agent must account to third parties (a) if too much money is collected innocently and the agent still has the money, (b) if too much money is collected on purpose regardless of whether the agent has the money, and (c) if too much money is collected on behalf of an undisclosed principal.

DUTIES OF PRINCIPALS

Duty to compensate in general	1. Compensation of agents must be reasonable if an amount is not stated in an agreement. 2. A percentage of profits is calculated using generally accepted accounting principles. 3. Real estate agents are compensated in accordance with the type of listing agreement signed.
Duty to compensate sales representatives	1. Unless the agreement states otherwise, a sales representative receives a commission only on sales solicited and induced directly. 2. The commission generally is earned as soon as an order is placed. 3. In general, an advance against commissions is considered a minimum salary, and the sales representative does not have to return an excess advance.
Duty to reimburse	1. A principal must reimburse agents who have expended reasonable amounts on behalf of the principal. 2. Expenses such as transportation costs, lodging, and meals are common reimbursable expenses.
Duty to indemnify	1. To indemnify means to hold a person harmless or free from liability. 2. An agent is entitled to be indemnified when the agent becomes liable to third parties while that agent was following the principal's instructions.

CASES

Cady v. Johnson
671 P.2d 149 (Utah 1983)

HOWE, J. This appeal arises from a suit brought by plaintiffs Jon and Carolyn Cady, husband and wife, Telford Realty and Rich Edwards. On July 8, 1980, the Cadys received a written offer from defendants, Jared and Reta May Johnson, to purchase their home in Kaysville, Utah. At that time the home was being advertised for sale by Telford Realty under a listing agreement. Rich Edwards, a salesman for All Seasons Realty, prepared the offer which was signed "Reta May Johnson by Jared Johnson, son" as purchaser. Jared also gave Edwards a $500 check drawn on his mother's bank account as earnest money. The Cadys accepted the offer.

On August 19, 1980, the Cadys vacated their home. A closing date on the sale was set for August 25. Financing arrangements had been submitted and approved. On August 25, the defendants did not appear for closing. One week later, Edwards received a letter from defendants indicating their desire not to purchase the home and requesting the return of their $500 earnest money deposit. Plaintiffs refused, retained the earnest money deposit, and brought suit for additional damages for breach of contract or, in the alternative, for equitable relief for failure to perform the contract. . . .

In their answer, defendants alleged that Jared Johnson was not properly authorized to enter into the agreement in behalf of Reta May Johnson, his mother. They also alleged that plaintiffs holding real estate licenses knew or should have known that the statute of frauds requires written authorization

from one to allow another to bind him to a contract for the purchase of real property. Utah law is clear that only a written power of attorney will authorize one to bind another to a contract for the sale of real property.

> No estate or interest in real property . . . shall be created . . . otherwise than by deed or conveyance in writing subscribed by the party creating . . . or by his lawful agent thereunto authorized by writing.

In the instant case, there was no dispute as to the absence of the written power of attorney. Therefore, no authorization was ever established. There being no authorization, there could be no contract; there being no contract, there could be no right to recover. . . . Therefore, the trial court correctly dismissed the plaintiffs' . . . cause of action.

Affirmed.

Chelsea Industries, Inc. v. Gaffney
449 N.E.2d 320 (Mass. 1983)

Gaffney and McElroy were employed as executives of Ideal Tape Company, a manufacturer of tapes used in the shoe industry. Ideal Tape Company was owned by Chelsea Industries, Inc. During 1976 and 1977, while still employed, these men planned to form a business to compete with Ideal and Chelsea. They consulted with a lawyer about creating a corporation. They hired persons to locate a suitable site for a factory and to find equipment similar to that used by Ideal. During this time, these men purchased equipment for their future business instead of buying the equipment for Ideal. They made plans to solicit customers of Ideal for their new business. They also encouraged two other employees of Ideal, named Graff and Wormwood, to participate in the competing firm. All these actions occurred while the four men were being paid by Ideal. When officers of Chelsea discovered these plans, the four men resigned. Chelsea sued Gaffney and McElroy and asked for money damages resulting from the breach of duties owed. A hearing was held before a master who found in Chelsea's favor. Gaffney and McElroy appealed.

ABRAMS, J. . . . The master found . . . that

the defendants . . . acted in violation of their fiduciary duties. . . . The record is replete with acts of disloyalty by these defendants toward Ideal.

Employees occupying a position of trust and confidence owe a duty of loyalty to their employer and must protect the interests of the employer.

The master found that although none of the four joint venturers was an officer or director of Chelsea, they were trusted executives composing virtually all of Ideal's management. As such, they owed a fiduciary duty to Chelsea. Because he is bound to act solely for his employer's benefit in all matters within the scope of his employment, an executive employee is "barred from actively competing with his employer *during* the tenure of his employment, even in the absence of an express covenant so providing." The master's findings amply support the conclusion that the defendants violated their fiduciary duty of loyalty to Chelsea.

Gaffney and McElroy contend that the judge erroneously awarded damages to the plaintiff equal to the entire compensation paid the defendants during the period they participated in a joint venture to compete with Chelsea. . . . They urge us, however, to conclude that their services were worth the total compensation they received.

Thus, the defendants urge us to follow those cases in which we have ordered a disloyal employee, after proving the value of his services, to repay only that portion of his compensation, if any, that was in excess of the worth of his services to his employer. Gaffney and McElroy urge that the judgment requiring them to forfeit all compensation was a "penalty disproportionately harsh under all the circumstances," and resulted in Chelsea's retaining the benefit of their valuable services without paying the agreed compensation for them.

The defendants argue that as business executives managing Ideal, their job was to produce profits for the plaintiff, and over a five year period, during most of which they were in control of Ideal, it was a profitable company. Relying solely on Ideal's growth in sales and profits for this five year period, the defendants contend that they are entitled to retain the entire compensation they received while engaging in conduct disloyal to Chelsea. The defendants' contention misconstrues the equitable nature of the remedy of restoration of compensation for employee breaches of the fiduciary duties of loyalty and diligence. For such breaches, the defendants can be required to forfeit the right of compensation even absent a showing of actual injury to the employer. Further, the fact that Ideal made profits during the period in question "is no answer to the established violation of duty. The fact that the division may have made money does not prove that no breach took place." . . .

Affirmed.

J & K Computer Systems, Inc., v. Parrish 642 P.2d 732 (Utah 1982)

HOWE, J. Plaintiff, J & K Computer Systems, Inc., brought this action seeking to recover damages from and enjoin its former employees Douglas T. Parrish and A. Chris Chlarson, and a corporation formed by them, Dynamic Software Corporation, from using or disclosing certain of plaintiff's confidential computer programs. . . .

The trial court found for the plaintiff, awarded it $7,500 damages and enjoined the defendants and all persons associated with them from further use of the computer programs. . . . Defendants appeal.

J & K was originally formed . . . by John Robertson and Keith Blake in 1976 to develop, market and install computer software. In March 1978, they hired Parrish as a computer programmer.

In the months that followed, Parrish developed an open-item/balance forward accounts receivable program which would be usable on the IBM System 34. After the program was developed, it was installed by Parrish at the Arnold Machinery Company in Salt Lake City. . . .

In May 1979, Parrish's brother-in-law, Chlarson, was hired as a trainee by J & K and was assigned to work under his direction. Chlarson also entered into an employment agreement similar to the contract between Parrish and J & K prohibiting the disclosure of J & K's computer programs. Two months later, in May 1979, Parrish voluntarily left the employ of J & K and entered into an agreement with Arnold Machinery Company whereby Parrish would provide Arnold Machinery with programming services. . . .

In June 1979, Chlarson voluntarily left J & K and began working with Parrish. Later that month, they formed Dynamic Software Corporation with Parrish as president and Chlarson as secretary-treasurer. The record shows that in July 1979, Parrish made an electronic copy of the accounts receivable program which J & K had installed at Arnold Machinery Company. This copy was made on a magnetic disk which Parrish then gave to Chlarson so that Chlarson could become familiar with it. Chlarson took the disk to the IBM 34 Computer workroom in the IBM building in Salt Lake City, and there began to work with the programs contained thereon. While Chlarson was working with the disk, an employee of J & K saw one of its programs displayed on the screen of the computer terminal. The employee then advised his employer who thereafter, upon advice of legal counsel, went back to the computer room at IBM. Plaintiff retrieved from the garbage can two printouts of the programs which had been displayed and discarded by Chlarson. Those programs were similar to the J & K accounts receivable program and serve as the basis for this lawsuit.

Defendants assail the judgment of the trial court awarding the plaintiffs damages and injunctive relief claiming that the accounts receivable programs were not confidential or trade secrets. There is no dispute that the plaintiff regarded the programs which it developed and used in its business as proprietary. The employment contracts which Parrish and Chlarson signed specified that the computer programs were "valuable, special and unique assets" of plaintiff's business. An expert witness . . . gave testimony which supports the finding that the programs are trade secrets. . . .

A trade secret includes any formula, patent, device, plan or compilation of information which is used in one's business and which gives him an opportunity to obtain an advantage over competitors who do not know it.

It is a well recognized principle that our law will afford protection to the inventor of a special process or trade secret. With the evidence recited above before it, the trial court could have reasonably determined that J & K's accounts receivable program was secret and worthy of protection by the law. Defendants assert that the accounts receivable program was revealed to certain customers and therefore not protectable. The record, however, shows that the plaintiff endeavored to keep its accounts receivable program secret. Plaintiff's em-

ployees and customers were informed of the secret nature of the program. The program was marked with the following legend: "Program Products Proprietary To–J & K Computer Systems, Inc., Salt Lake City, Utah. Authorized Use By License Agreement Only." That a few of the plaintiff's customers had access to the program does not prevent the program from being classified as a trade secret where the plaintiff was attempting to keep the secret and the program is still unavailable to the computer trade as a whole.

Defendants next contend that it is unlawful to enjoin them from using their skills, training and experience which they have gained in the computer programming business. . . . Defendants were not enjoined by the order of the trial court from using their general knowledge, skills, memory or experience. They were, however, enjoined from using the proprietary accounts receivable program which the plaintiff had developed. . . .

Affirmed.

Central Alaska Broadcasting, Inc. v. Bracale
637 P.2d 711 (Alas. 1981)

Carl Bracale was employed as the general manager of an Anchorage television station owned by the Central Alaska Broadcasting Company (CAB). In his position, Bracale exercised all management authority over programming, personnel, and business operations, subject to the supervision and control of CAB's directors. Bracale hired Sam Stewart as the station's advertising sales manager. Despite increases in advertising sold, CAB's directors recommended that Stewart's employment be terminated. This recommendation was based on the embarrassment Stewart's heavy drinking had caused the station. When Bracale refused to fire Stewart, the directors discharged Bracale for refusing to follow directives. Bracale then filed a suit against CAB on the basis that he was wrongfully discharged. He argued his refusal to fire Stewart was only a minor breach of his responsibilities. The trial court ruled in favor of Bracale, and CAB appealed.

COMPTON, J. . . . CAB argues that the

board's order to fire Stewart was reasonable as a matter of law because it was consistent with the contractual duty owed by Bracale. It is undisputed that Bracale's refusal to follow the board's directive was willful. From this, CAB concludes that Bracale's refusal to obey its order is a material breach of contract as a matter of law. . . .

"[U]nless otherwise agreed, an agent is subject to a duty to obey all reasonable directions in regard to the manner of performing a service that he has contracted to perform." Bracale acknowledges this general rule, but he argues that a willful failure to obey a reasonable order may not be a material breach of contract when the harm from the breach is small. Bracale further argues that the reasonableness of the board's directive was for the jury to decide. He argues that CAB's order to fire Stewart was unreasonable and Bracale's refusal to follow the board's directive was proper. . . .

We find Bracale's arguments to be without merit. The general rule that an employee's willful refusal to obey the reasonable instructions of his employer is grounds for discharge is unquestioned. Equally well established is the general rule that only a material breach of contract justifies termination.

In the context of employment contracts, it is axiomatic that within the limits set by the contract the duty of obedience by the employee to the employer is central to the agreement.

Whether the relationship created by an employment contract is that of principal and agent or master and servant, there is a right of control by the employer over the employee set by the terms of the contract. In this sense, any willful refusal to obey a reasonable directive is an act that strikes at the very heart of the contractual relationship existing between an employer and his employee. . . . Thus, when an order given is reasonable and consistent with the contract, the failure to obey it is always a material breach as a matter of law.

Bracale admits that the order given was consistent with his employment contract. The employment contract gave the Board of Directors direct control of his management functions, including

matters relating to personnel. The board had the authority to terminate an employee for any reason. The board also had the authority to order Bracale to fire any employee. There is no evidence to show that the board's reasons for ordering the firing of Stewart were arbitrary or merely a screen to accomplish an illegitimate purpose, such as the forced removal of Bracale. Bracale failed to show any change of circumstances following the board's order of November 17, 1975, that might have justified his refusal to fire Stewart or cast his refusal in a less defiant light. Thus, there is no dispute as to the continuing propriety of the board's order to fire Stewart and its authority under the contract to do so. . . .

[W]e conclude that it was reasonable as a matter of law for the board to order Bracale to fire Stewart.

Reversed.

M & D Simon Company v. Blanchard
389 So.2d 401 (La. App. 1980)

SCHOTT, J. Defendant Jody Blanchard was employed as a salesman by plaintiff, M & D Simon Company, from December, 1976, until March 15, 1977. Plaintiff brought this suit against Blanchard for $722.55 as the value of clothing samples issued to Blanchard for his use as a salesman. Blanchard reconvened for unpaid compensation. . . . From a judgment in favor of plaintiff on the main demand and dismissing the reconventional demand Blanchard has appealed.

The issues are whether Blanchard, who was employed on the basis of a draw against a commission, is entitled to a draw, even though previous draws had exceeded the commission earned. . . .

Defendant's employment was on the basis of an oral contract in which he was to receive a 5% commission, against which he would draw $550 per week, of which half would be treated as salary and

the other half as an allowance for travel and other expenses. On Wednesday, March 15, Blanchard was notified that the company's efforts to sell out had been unsuccessful and it was being liquidated so that Blanchard's employment was terminated. The last payment for his draw was made on Saturday, February 26, paying him through that date, so that he was due $1267 for the last two weeks and two days of his employment. Plaintiff took the position that Blanchard's previous draws exceeded his 5% commission by an amount in excess of the $1267, so that Blanchard was not entitled to the final draw.

Plaintiff's position is contrary to the law. . . . In the absence of an agreement to the contrary a drawing account is in the nature of a guaranteed minimum compensation for the employee's services and not a loan against commissions or profits to be earned. Therefore, Blanchard is entitled to a judgment on his reconventional demand in the amount of $1267.

Reversed.

Machinists Automative Trades District Lodge No. 190 of Northern California v. Utility Trailer Sales Company
190 Cal. Rptr. 98 (App. 1983)

FEINBERG, J. . . . The facts were not in dispute and were found as follows by the court:

Bowers, a refrigeration mechanic, pursuant to the custom of the industry, furnished the tools necessary to do his assigned work. Bowers' tools were very heavy and were kept in two toolboxes. Three men were needed to move one toolbox; the other could be moved only by forklift.

Bowers' tools were kept inside the inner building of the Employer's shop. Before the Thanksgiving weekend of 1977, Bowers locked his tools in the inner office provided by the employer by welding a steel bar across the inner door. The tools were stolen in a burglary over that weekend. Bowers' tools were valued at over $8,000. The Employer refused to reimburse him. The parties submitted the question of whether Bowers had a right to reimbursement to arbitration under their collective bargaining agreement. After the arbitrator rendered a decision in favor of the Employer, Bowers . . . [appealed].

Section 2802 [of the California Code] in pertinent part, provides: "An *employer shall indemnify his employee for all that the employee* necessarily expends or *loses in direct consequence of the discharge of his duties* as such. . . ." The question here is whether the loss occurred in *direct consequence* of the employment. . . .

While Bowers was required to provide the tools necessary for his work pursuant to the custom of the industry, he was not required to leave the tools on the Employer's premises nights and weekends. Given their weight and the equipment and men required to move them, carrying the tools back and forth from the Employer's premises would have been practically impossible. In addition, the Employer required employees to submit to an inspection and inventory whenever tools were brought to and taken from its premises. The trial court found that the Employer's inspection and inventory procedures were for the purpose of safeguarding the tools for the benefit of the employees and not to permit the Employer control of the use and availability of the tools. . . .

[W]e are faced with construing sections 2800 and 2802. . . . Section 2800 provides: "An employer shall in all cases indemnify his employee for losses caused by the employer's want of ordinary care;" section 2802, as indicated above, provides for indemnity for losses in direct consequences of the discharge of the employee's duties.

Here admittedly Bowers' tools were so heavy that he had no option but to leave them in the inner room on the premises provided by the Employer. Further, by its inspection requirements and security provisions the Employer exercised a substantial amount of control over Bowers' tools. Our Supreme Court has indicated that "legal duties are not discoverable facts of nature, but merely conclusory expressions, that, in cases of a particular type, liability should be imposed for damage done."

We hold that section 2802 applies where, as here, the custom of the trade requires the employee to supply his own tools for the performance of his duties, and while the employer does not require the employee to leave his tools on the employer's premises, the tools are too heavy to be transported routinely to and from the place of employment. Bowers' tools were left locked on the premises in the inner room provided by the Employer. The loss therefore was incurred in direct consequence of the discharge of the employee's duties, and was therefore incidental to his employment.

Reversed.

REVIEW QUESTIONS

1. Identify the terms in column A by matching each with the appropriate statement in column B.

A	B
1. Disclosed principal	**a.** Principal whose identity and existence are unknown by third parties.
2. Undisclosed principal	**b.** Agent must protect these and not use them for personal profit.
3. Broker	**c.** Type of agent who retains control over the details of how work is to be accomplished.
4. Independent contractor	**d.** Type of agent who has limited authority to find a customer in order to complete a sale of property.
5. Power of attorney	**e.** A principal whose existence and identity are known by third parties.

6. Duty of loyalty

7. Trade secrets

8. Duty to account

9. Indemnification

f. A duty generally owed only to principals, but in certain situations also to third parties.

g. Means to hold a person harmless or free from liability—a duty owed by principals to agents.

h. The written document used to formally appoint an agent.

i. The foundation of every agency relationship.

2. Define the following terms: (a) agency, (b) undisclosed principal, (c) disclosed principal, (d) factor, (e) independent contractor, (f) attorney in fact.

3. The Pedestrian Shoe Company hired Angela, age 16, to work during the summer. Angela was to solicit orders from shoe stores in her hometown. She was to be paid $1 for each pair of shoes ordered. Angela was so successful that she hired Beth, age 25, to help, and she promised to pay Beth 50 cents for each pair of shoes ordered. Can Angela properly be an agent for Pedestrian? Can Beth properly treat as void her appointment as an agent of Angela and submit her orders to Pedestrian for the larger compensation? Explain.

4. Ethel and Gladys, retired schoolteachers, wanted to buy an apartment house in the $80,000 to $90,000 price range. Since they were inexperienced in real estate transactions, they contacted Mr. Bunger, a salesperson in the Dooright Realty firm. These women told Mr. Bunger that they were totally dependent upon his advice. Bunger did not tell Ethel and Gladys that Dooright Realty was an agent for Johnson, a builder of apartment houses. Nevertheless, through Mr. Bunger, the women were encouraged to sign a contract with Johnson to have an apartment house built for a price of $120,000. When Ethel and Gladys learned of Dooright's "dual representation," they sued. Is Dooright liable? If so, liable for what?

5. The St. Paul's Insurance Company instructed its agent, Albert, to notify Thomas that his insurance policy had been canceled. Albert failed to give this notice, and three weeks later a tornado destroyed the insured property owned by Thomas. The company was forced to pay the claim. Can it recover its loss from Albert? Why?

6. Peterson's Florist Company hired Alex to deliver floral arrangements. One day while on a delivery, Alex fell asleep and hit a telephone pole. The delivery van was damaged to the extent of $1,600. Can Peterson's Florist Company recover this amount from Alex? Explain.

7. Perry hired the Creditor's Collection Agency to collect overdue accounts. Perry informed the agency that Terry owed $500 for merchandise received. In fact, Terry owed only $400. However, the agency did collect $500, because Terry also was mistaken about the amount. Later, Terry discovered the overpayment. Under what circumstances does the agency owe an accounting to Terry? Explain.

8. New World Fashions provides guidance to persons interested in entering the retail clothing business. Anderson was hired as a sales representative of New World. After several months of working for New World, Anderson decided to start a competing business. However, prior to resigning, Anderson encouraged one of New World's prospective clients to contract with Anderson personally. He then provided to this client services typically furnished by New World. Upon discovery of these facts, New World fired Anderson and sued him to recover lost profits. Must Anderson account to New World for the financial gain he obtained in this transaction? Explain.

9. Patricia listed her house for sale with Rex, a real estate broker, under a listing contract that gave Rex the exclusive right to sell this house for 3 months. During this time, Patricia sold her house to a friend who did not know Rex. Patricia refused to pay Rex any commission because Rex was not the procuring cause of the ready, willing, and able buyer. Is Rex entitled to a commission? Why?

10. Douglas, a newspaper reporter, sued his former employer, a newspaper publisher. Douglas sought to recover the attorney's fees and court costs incurred in his defense of a libel action. Douglas had been sued as the result of an article written for his employer's newspaper. Douglas had won the libel case. Is the employer obligated to indemnify Douglas for his legal expenses? Explain.

15 AGENCY AND THE LAW OF CONTRACTS

The law of agency is essentially concerned with issues of contractual liability. Because corporations act only through agents, and because partners in a partnership are agents of the partnership, a substantial portion of all contracts entered into by businesses are entered into by agents on behalf of principals.

One ultimate goal of these transactions is to establish a relationship that binds the principal and third party contractually. In other words, although the agent negotiates with the third party, the principal is substituted for the agent in the contract with the third party. Despite this objective, whenever a contract is entered into by an agent, issues as to the liability of the various parties may arise. Is the agent personally liable on the contract? Is the principal bound? Can the principal enforce the agreement against the third party? This chapter will discuss these issues and others that frequently arise out of contracts entered into by agents on behalf of principals.

However, prior to addressing these questions, in the next three sections we examine the fundamental legal concept of *authority*. Before an agent can create a binding contract between the principal and third party, that agent must have authority from the principal, or his unauthorized actions must have been ratified by the principal. As we will see, authority may actually be granted to the agent by the principal, or it may be apparent to the third party from the principal's actions or inactions.

1. Actual Authority

AUTHORITY

A principal may confer actual authority upon the agent or may unintentionally, by want of ordinary care, allow the agent to believe himself to possess it. Actual authority includes express authority and implied authority. The term *express authority* describes authority explicitly given to the agent through the principal's written or oral instructions. *Implied authority* is used to describe authority that is necessarily incidental to the express authority or that arises because of business custom and usage or prior practices of the parties. Implied authority is sometimes referred to as *incidental authority*; it is required or reasonably necessary in order to carry out the purpose for which the agency was created. Implied authority may be established by deductions or inferences from other facts and circumstances in the case, including prior habits or dealings of a similar nature between the parties.

Implied authority based on custom and usage varies from one locality to another and among different kinds of businesses. Perfection Fashions, Inc., appoints Andrea as its agent to sell its casual wear to retail stores. As a part of this relationship, Andrea has express authority to enter into written contracts with the purchasers and to sign Perfection Fashions' name to such agreements. Whether Andrea has implied or incidental authority to consign the merchandise, thereby allowing the purchaser to return items not sold, may depend on local custom and past dealings. Likewise, whether Andrea may sell on credit instead of cash may be determined by similar standards. If it is customary for other agents of fashion companies in this locality to sell on consignment or on credit, Andrea and the purchasers with whom she deals may assume she possesses such authority. Customs, in effect, create a presumption of authority. Of course, actual knowledge that contradicts customs or past dealings destroys implied authority. In other words, express authority that is stated clearly can limit the existence of implied or incidental authority.[1]

Implied authority cannot be derived from the words or conduct of the agent. A third person dealing with a known agent may not act negligently in regard to the extent of the agent's authority or blindly trust his statements. The third party must use reasonable diligence and prudence in ascertaining whether the agent is acting within the scope of his authority. Similarly, if persons who deal with a purported agent desire to hold the principal liable on the contract, they must ascertain not only the fact of the agency, but the nature and extent of the agent's authority. Should either the existence of the agency or the nature and extent of the authority be disputed, the burden of proof regarding these matters is upon the third party.

All agents, even presidents of corporations, have limitations on their authority. Authority is not readily implied. Possession of goods by one not engaged in the business of selling such goods does not create the implication of authority to sell. Authority to sell does not necessarily include the authority to extend credit, although custom may create such authority. The officers of a corporation must have actual authority to enter into transactions that are not in the ordinary course of the business of the corporation. For this reason, persons purchasing real estate from a corporation usually require a resolution of the board of directors specifically authorizing the sale.

2. Apparent or Ostensible Authority

To be distinguished from implied authority is *apparent* or *ostensible authority*, terms that are synonymous. These terms describe the authority a principal,

---

[1] Kasselder v. Kapperman, p. 332.

intentionally or by want of ordinary care, causes or allows a third person to believe the agent possesses. Liability of the principal for the ostensible agent's acts rests on the doctrine of estoppel. The estoppel is created by some conduct of the principal that leads the third party to believe that a person is his agent or that an actual agent possesses the requisite authority. The third party must know about this conduct and must be injured or damaged by his reliance upon it. The injury or damage may be a change of position, and the facts relied upon must be such that a reasonably prudent person would believe that the authority of the agency existed. Thus, three usual essential elements of an estoppel—conduct, reliance, and injury—are required to create apparent authority.

The theory of apparent or ostensible authority is that if a principal's words or conduct leads others to believe that he has conferred authority upon an agent, he cannot deny his words or actions to third persons who have relied on them in good faith. The acts may include words, oral or written, or may be limited to conduct that reasonably interpreted by a third person causes that person to believe that the principal consents to have the act done on his behalf by the purported agent. Apparent authority requires more than the mere appearance of authority. The facts must be such that a person exercising ordinary prudence, acting in good faith, and conversant with business practices would be misled.

Apparent authority may be the basis for liability when the purported agent is, in fact, not an agent. It also may be the legal basis for finding that an actual agent possesses authority beyond that actually conferred. In other words, apparent authority may exist in one not an agent or it may expand the authority of an actual agent. However, an agent's apparent authority to do an act for a principal must be based on the principal's words or conduct and cannot be based on anything the agent himself has said or done. An agent cannot unilaterally create his own apparent authority.

An agency by estoppel or additional authority by estoppel may arise from the agent's dealings being constantly ratified by the principal, or it may result from a person's acting the part of an agent without any dissent from the purported principal, even though it was the principal's duty to speak.[2] Perhaps the most common situation in which apparent authority is found to exist occurs when the actual authority is terminated, but notice of this fact is not given to those entitled to receive it. Cancellation of actual authority does not automatically terminate the apparent authority created by prior transactions. The ramification of apparent authority's surviving the termination of an agency relationship requires the principal to give notice of termination to third parties. The legal aspects of this notification are discussed in chapter 17.

3. Ratification

If there is no binding contract, a purported principal may nevertheless become bound by ratification. Having knowledge of all material matters, he may express or imply adoption or confirmation of a contract entered into on his behalf by someone who had no authority to do so. Ratification is implied by conduct of the principal, which is inconsistent with the intent to repudiate the agent's action. It is similar to ratification by an adult of a contract entered while a minor.

---

[2] Goldstein v. Hanna, p. 333.

Ratification relates back to, and is the equivalent of authority at the commencement of the act or time of the contract. It is the affirmation of a contract already made. It cures the defect of lack of authority and creates the relation of principal and agent.

Capacity required.   Various conditions must exist before a ratification will be effective in bringing about a contractual relation between the principal and the third party. First, because ratification relates back to the time of the contract, ratification can be effective only when both the principal and the agent were capable of contracting at the time the contract was executed and are still capable at the time of ratification. For this reason, a corporation may not ratify contracts made by its promoters on the corporation's behalf before the corporation was formed. For the corporation to be bound by such agreements, a novation or an assumption of liability by the corporation must occur.

Acting as agent.   Second, an agent's act may be ratified only when he holds himself out as acting for the one who is alleged to have approved the unauthorized agreement. In other words, the agent must have professed to act as an agent. A person who professes to act for himself and who makes a contract in his own name does nothing that can be ratified, even though he intends at the time to let another have the benefit of his agreement.

Full knowledge.   Third, as a general rule, ratification does not bind the principal unless he acts with full knowledge of all the material facts related to the negotiation and execution of the contract. Of course, when there is express ratification and the principal acts without any apparent desire to know or to learn the facts, he may not later defend himself on the ground that he was unaware of all the material facts. When, however, ratification is to be implied from the conduct of the principal, he must act with knowledge of all important details.[3]

Conduct constituting ratification.   Ratification may be either express or implied. Any conduct that definitely indicates an intention on the part of the principal to adopt the transaction will constitute ratification. It may take the form of words of approval to the agent, a promise to perform, or actual performance, such as delivery of the product called for in the agreement. Accepting the benefits of the contract or basing a suit on the validity of an agreement clearly amounts to ratification. Knowing what the agent has done, if the principal makes no objection for an unreasonable time, ratification results by operation of law. Generally, the question of what is an unreasonable time is for the jury.

The issue of whether or not ratification has occurred is also a question to be decided by the jury. Among the facts to be considered by the jury are the relationship of the parties, prior conduct, circumstances pertaining to the transaction, and the action or inaction of the alleged principal upon learning of the contract. Inaction or silence by the principal creates difficulty in determining if ratification has occurred. Failure to speak may mislead the third party, and courts frequently find that a duty to speak exists where silence will mislead. Silence and

[3] Perkins v. Philbrick, p. 334.

inaction by the party to be charged as a principal, or failure to dissent and speak up when ordinary human conduct and fair play would normally call for some negative assertion within a reasonable time, tends to justify the inference that the principal acquiesced in the course of events and accepted the contract as his own. Acceptance and retention of the fruits of the contract with full knowledge of the material facts of the transaction is probably the most certain evidence of implied ratification. As soon as a principal learns of an unauthorized act by his agent, he should promptly repudiate it if he is to avoid liability on the theory of ratification.

An unauthorized act may not be ratified in part and rejected in part. The principal cannot accept the benefits of the contract and refuse to assume its obligations. Because of this rule, a principal, by accepting the benefits of an authorized agreement, ratifies the means used in procuring the agreement, unless within a reasonable time after learning the actual facts he takes steps to return, as far as possible, the benefits he has received. Therefore, if an unauthorized agent commits fraud in procuring a contract, acceptance of the benefits ratifies not only the contract, but the fraudulent acts as well, and the principal is liable for the fraud.

4. Introduction

LIABILITY OF
PRINCIPALS—
IN GENERAL

With respect to contractual matters, a principal may become liable to its agents and third parties. The answers to when and why such liability is created depends in part on the type of principal involved. As mentioned in the previous chapter, there are three possible choices concerning the types of principals. From the third party's perspective, a principal may be *disclosed, partially disclosed,* or *undisclosed.* When studying the rest of this chapter, you must keep the distinctions between these categories in mind. For the most part, the law treats disclosed principals differently from other types of principals. In general, the law views the liability of partially disclosed and undisclosed principals as being the same. Therefore, in the following sections, any mention of an undisclosed principal's liability includes the liability of a partially disclosed principal unless the text states otherwise.

5. Disclosed Principal's Liability to Agents

Generally a disclosed principal's liability to its agents is based on the fiduciary duties discussed in chapter 14. From a contractual perspective, a disclosed principal implicitly agrees to protect its agents from any liability as long as these agents act within the scope of authority granted. In other words, when a disclosed principal is involved, agency principles are applied in such a way that the third party must look to the principal for contractual performance if the agent acted within the authority given. If the third party seeks to hold the agent personally liable, that agent may insist the disclosed principal hold him harmless for liability purposes. A similar result of the principal holding the agent harmless for contractual performance occurs if a disclosed principal ratifies an unauthorized agent's actions.

However, if an agent for a disclosed principal exceeds the authority granted, the principal is not liable to the agent and is not required to protect the agent from liability. In general, the agent who exceeds authority becomes personally liable to the third party and cannot rely on the principal as a substitute for liability or indemnification. The one exception to this general rule is when the disclosed principal ratifies the unauthorized actions of an agent. When ratification does occur, the liability of the parties is the same as if the agent's acts were authorized prior to their happening.

6. Disclosed Principal's Liability to Third Parties

Because of the concept of the principal holding the agent harmless, generally a disclosed principal becomes liable to third parties who negotiate and enter into contracts with authorized agents. With respect to transactions involving disclosed principals, the agent's authority may be either actual or apparent.

Furthermore, disclosed principals become liable to third parties if the unauthorized actions of an agent are ratified. With respect to such ratification, the laws of agency state that the act of ratification must occur before the third party withdraws from the contract. The reason for protecting the third party in this way is the constant legal concern with mutuality of obligations. One party should not be bound to a contract if the other party is not also bound. Therefore, the law recognizes that the third party may withdraw from an unauthorized contract entered into by an agent at any time before it is ratified by the principal. If the third party were not allowed to withdraw, the unique situation in which one party is bound and the other is not would exist. Remember, though, that ratification does not require notice to the third party. As soon as conduct constituting ratification has been indulged in by the principal, the third party loses his right to withdraw.

Remember that the burden of proving the requisite authority or ratification is on the party asserting the agency relationship's existence. The principal does not have the burden of proving lack of authority or lack of ratification. The agent's authority can come only from the principal. An agent, by words or conduct, cannot create authority unless those words or actions are consented to, or ratified by, the principal. A third party who deals with an agent, knowing that the agent has exceeded its authority, does so at his peril, since the disclosed principal does not become liable for the contract's nonperformance. However, if the third party proves authority exists or ratification has occurred, the principal is liable to the third party.[4]

7. Undisclosed Principal's Liability to Agents

The fact that a principal's identity or even existence is hidden from third parties does not change the principal-agent relationship. Therefore, undisclosed principals may become liable for breach of a fiduciary duty owed to agents. Furthermore, undisclosed principals are liable to agents who negotiate and enter into contracts within their actual authority. Since a third party may hold an agent

---

[4] Pfliger v. Peavey Company, p. 335.

of an undisclosed principal personally liable, the authorized agent may recover the amount of its liability from the undisclosed principal.

It is important to understand why the rule of law set forth in the previous paragraph limits the undisclosed principal's liability to contracts entered pursuant to the agent's *actual* authority. When a principal is undisclosed, neither apparent authority nor ratification can occur, since these arise as a result of the principal–third party relationship. Of course, when the principal's identity or existence is unknown to the third party, there cannot be a principal–third party relationship. In other words, an undisclosed principal has no liability to an agent who exceeds the actual authority granted by the principal.

8. Undisclosed Principal's Liability to Third Parties

The liability of undisclosed principals to third parties is limited by two important principles. First, undisclosed principals are liable to third parties only when the agent acted within the scope of actual authority. Remember, apparent authority and ratification cannot occur when the principal is undisclosed. However, an undisclosed principal who retains the benefits of a contract is liable to the third party in a quasi-contract for the value of such benefits. To allow this principal to keep the benefits would be an unacceptable form of unjust enrichment at the third party's expense.

Second, the contract entered into by an actually authorized agent must be of a type that can be assigned to the undisclosed principal. For example, an employment contract requiring the personal services of the agent would not bind the undisclosed principal and the third party. Suppose a group of young engineers form an architectural design firm. Wishing to be hired to design a new 50-story building that will serve as Exxon's headquarters, these engineers decide to submit a bid. However, being fearful that their lack of reputation will harm their chances of being employed, they hire Phillip Johnson, a renowned designer-architect, to present the bid. Mr. Johnson is instructed not to reveal the new firm's identity. In other words, the bid is to be submitted in Phillip Johnson's name alone. If Exxon awarded the design job to Mr. Johnson, it is very unlikely that the new firm and Exxon would be contractually bound. This result would occur because of Exxon's belief that it was hiring the unique personal talents of Mr. Johnson. That is, the contract between the agent (Phillip Johnson) and the third party (Exxon) is not assignable to the undisclosed principal (young engineering firm) without the third party's consent. The vast majority of contracts negotiated by agents for undisclosed principals will not involve those agents' personal services. Most of these contracts will thus be freely assignable.

In addition to the requirements that the agent be actually authorized and that the contract be assignable, there are two further items to consider concerning the undisclosed principal's liability to third parties. These additional legal concepts are called (1) election and (2) settlement, and they are applicable to undisclosed principals only. Recall that up until now, undisclosed and partially disclosed principals have been treated the same way. The following discussions of elections and settlements do not apply to partially disclosed principals—only to those who are entirely undisclosed.

9. Effect of Election

When the existence and identity of the principal become known to the third party, the third party may look to either the agent or the principal for performance. If the third party elects to hold the principal liable, the agent is released. Similarly, if the third party elects to hold the agent liable, the previously undisclosed but now disclosed principal is released. An election to hold one party releases the other from liability.

It is sometimes difficult to know when an election has occured. Clearly, conduct by the third party preceding the disclosure of the principal cannot constitute an election. Because of this rule, it has been held that an unsatisfied judgment obtained against the agent before disclosure of the principal will not bar a later action against the principal. After disclosure, the third party may evidence an election by making an express declaration of his intention to hold one party and not the other liable. Most states also hold that the mere receipt, without collection, of a negotiable instrument from either principal or agent does not constitute an election. Furthermore, it is clear that merely starting a lawsuit is not an election. However, there has been some controversy among the states about whether obtaining a judgment against the principal or agent is an election if that judgment remains uncollected. Whereas all states agree that a third party is entitled to only one satisfaction, the predominant theory is that obtaining a judgment, even if it remains uncollected, amounts to an election. This theory has been called the *judgment theory* of elections.[5]

10. Effect of Settlement

Suppose the undisclosed principal supplied the agent with money to purchase merchandise, but the agent purchased on credit and appropriated the money. In such cases, the principal has been relieved of all responsibilities. The same result may occur when the undisclosed principal *settles* with the agent after the contract is made and the goods are received, but before disclosure is made to the third party. A majority of states have held that a bona fide settlement between principal and agent before disclosure occurs releases the principal. A settlement cannot have this effect, however, when it is made after the third party has learned of the existence of the principal. This *settlement rule,* adopted by most states, is based on equitable principles. It is fair to the third party in that it gives him all the protection he originally bargained for, and it is fair to the principal in that it protects him against a second demand for payment.

LIABILITY OF PRINCIPALS— SPECIAL SITUATIONS

11. Introduction

Many special problems arise in the law of agency as it relates to contractual liability and authority of agents. Some of these problems are founded on the relationship of the parties. A spouse is generally liable for the contracts of the other spouse when the contracts involve family necessities. In most states this liability is statutory. Others involve special factual situations. An existing

---

[5] Sherrill v. Bruce Advertising, p. 336.

emergency that necessitates immediate action adds sufficiently to the agent's powers to enable him to meet the situation. If time permits and the principal is available, any proposed remedy for the difficulty must be submitted to the principal for approval. It is only when the principal is not available that the powers of the agent are extended. Furthermore, the agent receives no power greater than that sufficient to solve the difficulty.

Frequently, the liability of the principal is dependent upon whether the agent is, as a matter of fact, a general agent or a special agent. If the agency is general, limitations imposed upon the usual and ordinary powers of the general agent do not prevent the principal from being liable to third parties when the agent acts in violation of such limitations, unless the attention of the third parties has been drawn to them. In other words, the third party, having established that a general agency exists and having determined in a general way the limits of the authority, is not bound to explore for unexpected and unusual restrictions. He is justified in assuming, in the absence of contrary information, that the agent possesses the powers such agents customarily have. On the other hand, if the proof is only of a special or limited agency, any action in excess of the actual authority would not bind the principal. The authority for a special agent is strictly construed; if the agent exceeds his authority, the principal is not bound.

To illustrate, assume an instruction to a sales agent not to sell to a certain individual or not to sell to him on credit, although credit sales are customary. Such a limitation cannot affect the validity of a contract made with this individual, unless the latter was aware of the limitation at the time the contract was made. The principal, by appointing an agent normally possessed of certain authority, is estopped to set up the limitation as a defense unless the limitation is made known to the third party prior to the making of the contract.

12. Notice to Agents

There are other issues directly related to the authority possessed by an agent. A common problem involves whether or not notice to an agent or knowledge possessed by him is imputed to the principal. Some of these questions are covered by statutes. Civil practice statutes contain provisions on service of a summons on an agent. They specify who may be an agent for the service of process and, in effect, provide that notice to such agents constitutes notice to the principal.

Notice to, or knowledge acquired by, an agent while acting within the scope of his authority binds the principal. This rule is based on the theory that the agent is the principal's other self; therefore, what the agent knows, the principal knows. While *knowledge* possessed by an agent is *notice* to the principal, the principal may not have actual knowledge of the particular fact at all. Knowledge acquired by an agent acting outside the scope of his authority is not effective notice unless the party relying thereon has reasonable ground to believe that the agent is acting within the scope of his authority (similar to apparent authority). An agent who is acquiring property for his principal may have knowledge of certain unrecorded liens against the property. The principal purchases the property subject to those liens. Equal knowledge possessed by another agent who did not represent the principal in the particular transaction, and who did not obtain the knowledge on behalf of his principal, is not imputed to the principal.

A question exists as to whether or not knowledge acquired by an agent before he became an agent can bind the principal. The majority view is that knowledge acquired by an agent before commencement of the relationship of principal and agent is imputable to the principal if the knowledge is present and in the mind of the agent while acting for the principal in the transaction to which the information is material. There are some court decisions to the contrary which have stated the agent must acquire the knowledge during the agency relationship before the principal is presumed to have notice of that information.

Notice or knowledge received by an agent under circumstances in which the agent would not be presumed to communicate the information to the principal does not bind the principal. This is an exception to the general rule that will be observed when the agent is acting in his own behalf and adversely to the principal or when the agent is under a duty to some third party not to disclose the information. Furthermore, notice to the agent, combined with collusion or fraud between him and the third party that would defeat the purpose of the notice, would not bind the principal.

As a general rule, an agent or person ostensibly in charge of a place of business has apparent authority to accept notices in relation to the business. An employee in charge of the receipt of mail may accept written notifications.

13. Agent's Power to Appoint Subagents

Agents are usually selected because of their personal qualifications. Owing to these elements of trust and confidence, a general rule has developed that an agent may not delegate his duty to someone else and clothe the latter with authority to bind the principal. An exception has arisen to this rule in cases in which the acts of the agent are purely ministerial or mechanical. An act that requires no discretion and is purely mechanical may be delegated by the agent to a third party. Such a delegation does not make the third party the agent of the principal or give him any action against the principal for compensation unless the agent was impliedly authorized to obtain this assistance. The acts of such a third party become in reality the acts of the agent. They bind the principal if they are within the authority given to the agent. Acts that involve the exercise of skill, discretion, or judgment may not be delegated without permission from the principal.

An agent may, under certain circumstances, have the actual or implied authority to appoint other agents for the principal, in which case they become true employees of the principal and are entitled to be compensated by him. This power on the part of the agent is not often implied; but if the major power conferred cannot be exercised without the aid of other agents, the agent is authorized to hire whatever help is required. Thus, a manager placed in charge of a branch store may be presumed to possess authority to hire the necessary personnel.

14. Agent's Financial Powers

An agent who delivers goods sold for cash has the implied authority to collect all payments due at the time of delivery. A salesperson taking orders calling for a down payment has implied authority to accept the down payment. By the very nature of their jobs, salespeople have no implied authority to receive payments on account, and any authority to do so must be expressly given or be implied from custom. Thus, a salesperson in a store has authority to collect payments made at the time of sale, but no authority to receive payments on account. If payment to a sales agent who has no authority to collect is not delivered to the principal, it may be collected by the principal from the agent or from the party who paid the agent.

Possession of a statement of account on the billhead of the principal or in the principal's handwriting does not create implied or apparent authority to collect a debt. Payment to an agent without authority to collect does not discharge the debt.

Authority to collect gives the agent no authority to accept anything other than money in payment. Unless expressly authorized, the agent is not empowered to accept negotiable notes or property in settlement of an indebtedness. It is customary for an agent to accept checks as conditional payment. Under those circumstances, the debt is not paid unless the check is honored. If the check is not paid, the creditor principal is free to bring suit on the contract that gave rise to the indebtedness or to sue on the check, at his option.

A general agent placed in charge of a business has implied or apparent authority to purchase for cash or on credit. The implied authority is based on the nature of his position and on the fact that the public rightly concludes that a corporation or an individual acting through another person has given him the power and authority that naturally and properly belong to the character in which the agent is held out.

Authority to borrow money is not easily implied. It must be expressly granted or must qualify as incidental authority to the express authority, or the principal will not be bound. The authority to borrow should always be confirmed with the principal.

15. Introduction

Sections 4 through 10 of this chapter discuss the general rules of the principal's liability. The following sections address the corresponding issues of when agents and third parties are liable. In essence, the legal principles attempt to make sure that if one party is bound to a contract, so is another party. For example, if a disclosed principal is liable to a third party, that third party must be liable to the disclosed principal. The law always attempts to find that parties are mutually obligated for contractual performances.

16. Agent's Liability to Principals

As long as the agent acts within the scope of authority actually granted, the agent has no liability to the principal. The one exception occurs when an undisclosed principal has settled with the agent prior to the principal's being disclosed to the third party. In that situation, the agent is liable to the principal to perform the contract as instructed.

If the agent of a disclosed principal exceeds the actual authority granted but binds the principal to the third party due to the existence of apparent authority,

LIABILITY OF AGENTS AND THIRD PARTIES

that agent is liable to the principal for the damages caused. The basis of holding the agent liable in this situation is that the agent has breached the duty to obey instructions. Of course, if the disclosed principal ratifies an agent's unauthorized actions, the agent does not become liable to the principal.

17. Agent's Liability to Third Parties

Agents generally do not become contractually bound to third parties, because the principal usually takes the agent's place for liability purposes. However, an agent of an undisclosed principal may become liable to the third party in one of two situations. First, if the principal settles with that agent before becoming disclosed, the agent and third party are contractually bound. Second, the third party may elect to hold the agent liable instead of the principal after the latter's identity is disclosed.

With respect to contractual matters in general, an agent may become bound to the third party by the way the agent signs the agreement or due to the language of the actual contract; that is, the agent may be liable because of the contractual document. An agent can become liable to a third party if that agent exceeds actual and apparent authority and no ratification by the principal occurs. In other words, based on a breach of an implied promise that the agent is representing a principal, the agent and third party legally are bound to one another. Further details of these two methods of binding the agent to the third party follow.

Based on the contract. Three situations may arise that make the agent liable to the third party due to the contract itself. First, if the agent carelessly executes a written agreement, he may fail to bind his principal and may incur personal liability. For example, when an agent signs a simple contract or commercial paper, he should execute it in a way that clearly indicates his representative capacity. If the signature fails to indicate the actual relationship of the parties and fails to identify the party intended to be bound, the agent may be personally liable on the instrument. Many states permit the use of oral evidence to show the intention of the agent and the third party when the signature is ambiguous—the agent is allowed to offer proof that it was not intended that he assume personal responsibility. The Code contains express provisions on the liability of an agent who signs commercial paper. These are discussed in chapter 31.

Second, if the agent does not disclose his agency or name his principal, he binds himself and becomes subject to all liabilities, express and implied, created by the contract and transaction, in the same manner as if he were the principal. If an agent wishes to avoid personal liability, the duty is upon the agent to disclose the agency. There is no duty on the third party to discover the agency.

An agent who purports to be a principal is liable as a principal. The fact that the agent is known to be a commission merchant, auctioneer, or other professional agent is immaterial. He must disclose not only that he is an agent, but the identity of his principal if the agent is not to have personal liability. Any agent for an undisclosed or partially disclosed principal assumes personal liability on the contract into which he enters.[6]

---

[6] Como v. Rhines, p. 337.

Third, the third party may request the agent to be bound personally on the contract. This request may be due to lack of confidence in the financial ability of the principal, because the agent's credit rating is superior to that of the principal, or some personal reason. When the agent voluntarily assumes the burden of performance in his personal capacity, he is liable in the event of nonperformance by his principal.

Based on breach of warranty.   An agent's liability may be implied from the circumstances as well as being the direct result of the contract. Liability in such situations is usually said to be implied and to arise from the breach of an implied warranty. Two basic warranties are used to imply liability: the warranty of authority and the warranty that the principal is competent.

As a general rule, an agent impliedly warrants to third parties that he possesses power to effect the contractual relations of his principal. If in any particular transaction the agent fails to possess this power, the agent violates this implied warranty, and he is liable to third parties for the damages resulting from his failure to bind the principal. The agent may or may not be aware of this lack of authority, and he may honestly believe that he possesses the requisite authority. Awareness of lack of authority and honesty is immaterial. If an agent exceeds his authority, he is liable to the third parties for the breach of the warranty of authority.

The agent may escape liability for damages arising from lack of authority by a full disclosure to a third party of all facts relating to the source of the agent's authority. Where all the facts are available, the third party is as capable of judging the limits of the agent's powers as is the agent.

Every agent who deals with third parties warrants that his principal is capable of being bound. Consequently, an agent who acts for a minor or a corporation not yet formed may find himself liable for the nonperformance of his principal. The same rule enables the third party to recover from the agent when his principal is an unincorporated association, such as a club, lodge, or other informal group. An unincorporated association is not a legal entity separate and apart from its members. In most states it cannot sue or be sued in the name it uses, but all members must be joined in a suit involving the unincorporated group. When an agent purports to bind such an organization, a breach of the warranty results because there is no entity capable of being bound. If the third party is fully informed that the principal is an unincorporated organization and he agrees to look entirely to it for performance, the agent is not liable.

The warranty that an agent has a competent principal must be qualified in one respect. An agent is not liable when, unknown to him, his agency has been cut short by the death of the principal. Death of the principal terminates an agency. Because death is usually accompanied by sufficient publicity to reach third parties, the facts are equally available to both parties, and no breach of warranty arises.

18. Third Party's Liability to Principals

A disclosed principal may enforce any contract made by an authorized agent for the former's benefit. This right applies to all contracts in which the principal is the real party in interest, including contracts made in the agent's name. Furthermore, if a contract is made for the benefit of a disclosed principal by an agent acting outside the scope of his authority, the principal is still entitled to performance, provided the contract is properly ratified before withdrawal by the third party.

An undisclosed principal is entitled to performance by third parties of all assignable contracts made for his benefit by an authorized agent. It is no defense for the third party to say that he had not entered into a contract with the principal.

If a contract is one that involves the skill or confidence of the agent and is one that would not have been entered into without this skill or confidence, its performance may not be demanded by the undisclosed principal. This rule applies because the contract would not be assignable, since personal rights and duties are not transferable without consent of the other party.

In cases other than those involving commercial paper, the undisclosed principal takes over the contract subject to all defenses that the third party could have established against the agent. If the third party contracts to buy from such an agent and has a right of setoff against the agent, he has this same right to setoff against the undisclosed principal. The third party may also pay the agent prior to discovery of the principal and thus discharge his liability.

19. Third Party's Liability to Agents

Normally, the agent possesses no right to bring suit on contracts made by him for the benefit of his principal, because he has no interest in the cause of action. The agent who binds himself to the third party, either intentionally or ineptly by a failure properly to express himself, may, however, maintain an action. An agent of an undisclosed principal is liable on the contract and may sue in his own name in the event of nonperformance by the third party. Thus, either the agent or the undisclosed principal may bring suit, but in case of a dispute, the right of the previously undisclosed principal is superior.

Custom has long sanctioned an action by the agent based upon a contract in which he is interested because of anticipated commissions. As a result, a factor may institute an action in his own name to recover for goods sold. He may also recover against a railroad for delay in the shipment of goods sold or to be sold.

Similarly, an agent who has been vested with title to commercial paper may sue the maker of the paper. The same is true of any claim held by the principal that he definitely places with the agent for collection and suit, where necessary. In all cases of this character, the agent retains the proceeds as a trust fund for his principal.

SUMMARY

AUTHORITY

Actual authority	1. Actual authority is transmitted directly by the principal to the agent.

	2. Such authority may be expressed by the principal in written or spoken form.
	3. Actual authority may be implied from the actions of the principal and agent or from the nature of either party's position (such as a corporate officer).
Apparent authority	1. When actual authority is missing, the doctrine of estoppel may create apparent authority.
	2. The basis of apparent authority is the indication of an agency relationship by the principal to third parties. This authority is possible only with fully disclosed principals.
	3. Apparent authority is most likely to exist when an agent is terminated and the principal fails to give notice to third parties of this event.
Ratification	1. If neither actual nor apparent authority can be found, ratification by the principal may still bind the principal and third party contractually.
	2. Ratification of an unauthorized agent's acts can occur only when the principal is fully disclosed.
	3. Furthermore, principal must have full knowledge of all material facts and give a clear indication (expressed or implied) of ratification.

LIABILITY OF PRINCIPALS

Disclosed principal's liability to agents	1. As long as agents act in an authorized manner, principals must indemnify agents.
	2. When an agent exceeds the actual authority, the principal is not liable to the agent unless the unauthorized acts were ratified.
Disclosed principal's liability to third parties	1. If an agent negotiates a contract within either actual or apparent authority, the principal is legally bound to the third party.
	2. If an agent exceeds the authority, the principal is bound to the third party only if ratification occurs before the third party withdraws.

Undisclosed principal's liability to agents	1. These rules apply to partially disclosed and undisclosed principals alike.
	2. A principal is liable to hold an agent harmless if the agent acted within actual authority granted. (There is no apparent authority in these situations.)
	3. A principal has no liability to an agent who exceeds actual authority. (Ratification is not possible.)
Undisclosed principal's liability to third parties	1. These rules apply to partially disclosed and undisclosed principals alike.
	2. A principal is contractually bound to third parties if the agent acted within actual authority, and the contract can be assigned to the principal without the third parties' consent.
Election	1. These rules apply only to fully undisclosed principals.
	2. Third parties must elect to hold either the agent or the previously undisclosed (now revealed) principal liable on the contract.
	3. What constitutes an election is not clear. Most states follow the judgment theory of elections.
Settlement	1. This rule applies only to fully undisclosed principals.
	2. A principal is not contractually bound to a third party if that principal settles with the agent after the contract is negotiated, but before the principal becomes disclosed.
Special situations	1. Principals are liable for the knowledge possessed by the agent unless the third party has requested that the agent keep the information confidential.
	2. In general, principals are liable only for the agent's actions. Agents must be given clear authority to appoint subagents.
	3. Principals generally are not liable for an agent's abuse of financial powers. Such powers are very limited and must be explicitly granted by the principal to the agent.

LIABILITY OF AGENTS AND THIRD PARTIES

Agent's liability to principals	1. In general, an agent is not liable to the principal if that agent followed

instructions and did not breach any fiduciary duties.

2. An agent of an undisclosed principal becomes liable to perform the contract if that principal has settled with the agent.

3. An agent is liable to the principal if the agent exceeded the actual authority granted, unless the disclosed principal ratified the unauthorized actions.

Agent's liability to third parties

1. Generally, an agent does not become contractually bound to third parties.

2. An agent of an undisclosed principal does become contractually bound to the third party if that principal settles with the agent or if the third party elects to hold the agent liable.

3. An agent becomes bound to the third party if that agent fails to indicate his representative capacity.

4. An agent becomes bound to the third party when that agent breaches the implied warranty that the agent is acting within the authority granted by a competent principal.

Third party's liability to principals

1. A third party is contractually liable to a disclosed principal when the agent acts within the authority granted or when the principal ratifies the unauthorized acts prior to the third party withdrawing from the contract.

2. A third party is bound to a partially disclosed or undisclosed principal if the contract is assignable by the agent without the third party's consent.

Third party's liability to agents

1. A third party is contractually liable to an agent when that agent is liable to the third party.

2. Examples of these situations might include the application of the concepts of settlement or election when an undisclosed principal is involved, the agent failing to sign in a representative capacity, and the agent breaching the warranty of authority.

CASES

Kasselder v. Kapperman
316 N.W.2d 628 (S.D. 1982)

DUNN, J. . . . Kapperman owns a Galion road grader which had a defective engine. Appellant James Schladweiler (Schladweiler) offered to purchase the grader for the sum of $8,500.00, if the grader was in running condition. Kapperman said he would pay up to $3,000.00 to have the engine repaired and Schladweiler said he could have it repaired for less than that sum at Truck Repair in Mitchell, South Dakota. Kapperman shipped the grader from Minnesota to Schladweiler's residence in Mitchell.

At the request of Schladweiler, Truck Repairs' mechanics took the engine apart and discovered that it was not repairable. They suggested to Schladweiler that a new engine be purchased for $7,000.00. Schladweiler informed Kapperman of this information and Kapperman said he was not interested in spending that much money. Kapperman tried to locate a used engine that could be rebuilt, but was unsuccessful. The mechanics located a used engine in Omaha, Nebraska, and told Schladweiler the cost of repairs would be $1,000.00 to purchase the engine, $1,300.00 for labor, and the cost of oil and gaskets. Schladweiler informed Kapperman of this estimate and Kapperman approved the purchase of the engine but specified that he would not pay more than $3,000.00 in repair costs.

A short time later, the mechanics contacted their supplier in Sioux Falls, South Dakota and were informed that the supplier had repaired a similar engine for $5,000.00, which did not include repairing the cylinder head. The Omaha engine had a cracked cylinder head. Truck Repair relayed this estimate to Schladweiler. Schladweiler authorized the repairs, but did not inform Kapperman of this increased bid. The repairs to the engine took several months and Schladweiler periodically followed the progress of the repairs. At no time did Truck Repair discuss the cost of repairs with Kapperman. When the repairs were finally completed, the total cost was $6,441.06. Neither Kapperman nor Schladweiler would pay the bill.

The trial court found for Truck Repair and entered an order and judgment against Schladweiler in the amount of $3,441.06 plus interest and against Kapperman in the amount of $3,000.00 plus interest. Schladweiler moved for a new trial, alleging insufficiency of the evidence to support the judgment. This motion was denied.

Schladweiler's only contention is that the evidence presented at trial was insufficient to support the trial court's finding that he was liable for $3,441.06, plus interest, of the Truck Repair bill. He alleges that his agency relationship with Kapperman should have precluded his liability. We disagree. In reviewing this matter, we must give due regard to the opportunity of the trial court to judge the credibility of the witnesses. We cannot set aside the trial court's findings unless they are clearly erroneous.

An agency relationship is defined as "the representation of one called the principal by another called the agent in dealing with third persons." . . .

To determine whether an agency relationship has in fact been created, we examine the relations of the parties as they exist under their agreement or acts. Agency "is a legal concept which depends upon the existence of required factual elements: The manifestation by the principal that the agent shall act for him, the agent's acceptance of the undertaking, and the understanding of the parties that the principal is to be in control of the undertaking." . . .

The evidence indicates that an actual agency relationship did exist between Kapperman and Schladweiler but only to the extent of $3,000.00. Kapperman allowed Schladweiler to act for him regarding repair of the grader but specified that he would not pay more than $3,000.00 for repair costs. Schladweiler agreed to represent Kapperman in the transaction with Truck Repair. However, Schladweiler exceeded the scope of his agency authority when he authorized repairs exceeding $3,000.00 and failed to consult with Kapperman regarding the increased expenditures. . . . "When an agent exceeds his authority, his principal is bound by his authorized acts so far only as they can be plainly separated from those which are unauthorized." We hold that the trial court was correct in its determination that Schladweiler was liable for $3,441.06, plus interest, of the Truck Repair bill, because this sum represented the portion of the bill resulting from his unauthorized acts as agent.

Affirmed.

Goldstein v. Hanna
635 P.2d 290 (Nev. 1981)

GUNDERSON, J. Appellants, Ronald and Mary Goldstein, sued respondent, Fuad Hanna, to compel specific performance of an option to purchase Hanna's condominium. The district court entered judgment in favor of Hanna. We reverse and remand.

On or about December 10, 1977, the parties entered into a lease relating to Hanna's condominium in Clark County, Nevada. The lease granted the Goldsteins an option to purchase the condominium, and declared "the option may be exercised at any time after December 1, 1977 and shall expire at midnight December 9, 1978 unless exercised prior thereto." Callahan Realty conducted all negotiations on behalf of respondent Hanna, and was designated in the agreement as his authorized agent. The Goldsteins dealt exclusively with Callahan Realty, both as tenants and prospective purchasers. They had no direct dealings with Hanna until after August 1978.

In the summer of 1978, the Goldsteins chose to exercise their option to purchase. They contemplated a purchase from Hanna, with a simultaneous sale from themselves to another purchaser. To effectuate this double sale, Callahan Realty established two escrows, both with closing dates of August 29, 1978. Shortly before the escrows were to close, however, the ultimate purchaser declined to perform.

Three days before their escrow with Hanna was due to close, the Goldsteins contacted Mr. Callahan, and specifically advised him that they intended to complete the purchase. They advised Callahan they would purchase the condominium themselves, rather than find another purchaser. Callahan informed the Goldsteins that they need not consummate the purchase by August 29, because their option would continue to be valid under the terms of the lease until December 9, 1978. To insure that respondent Hanna shared this understanding of the option terms, Mr. Goldstein requested Callahan call Hanna, in his presence, and confirm the agent's representations.

Callahan called Hanna and advised him that the ultimate purchaser would not close escrow as planned. Callahan also told Hanna that the Goldsteins' option to purchase would still be in effect until expiration of the lease term. Although Hanna testified at trial that he never authorized Callahan Realty to extend the escrow, the record indicates he never asserted that the option would not remain viable following termination of the pending escrow. On this issue, it appears he remained silent, and thus permitted the Goldsteins to rely on Callahan's representations. Callahan Realty, as Hanna's agent, thereafter accepted the Goldsteins' check for payments on the lease through October. Callahan Realty deposited the money in a trust account and issued a check to Hanna for the lease payments, less commission. . . .

[In October, the Goldsteins attempted to exercise their option. Hanna refused to sell on the grounds that the option expired when the Goldsteins failed to complete the transaction in August.]

Where there is a duty to speak, silence can raise an estoppel quite as effectively as can words. A duty to speak arises when another is or may come under a misapprehension regarding the authority of the principal's agent. Under such circumstances, the principal is obligated to exercise due care, and to conduct himself as a reasonably prudent business person with normal regard for the interests of others. Thus, "a person remaining silent when he ought, in the exercise of good faith, to have spoken, will not be allowed to speak when he ought, in the exercise of good faith, remain silent." Similarly, silence or failure to repudiate an agent's representations can give rise to an inference of affirmation. . . .

In the instant case, during his telephone conversation with Callahan, Hanna made no effort to assure that the Goldsteins were not misled or lulled by his agent's representations. Hanna knew the Goldsteins might not hasten to complete the August escrow while assuming they still had several months to exercise the option. Consequently, Hanna's silence and acquiescence in his agent's representations manifestly caused the Goldsteins to do what they otherwise would not have done, *i.e.* to permit, at least arguably, a lapse of their valuable option rights. . . .

The doctrine of equitable estoppel is properly invoked whenever "unconscionable injury would result from denying enforcement of the contract after one party has been induced by the other seriously to change his position in reliance on the contract." In the case at bar, the detriment suffered by the Goldsteins involves the loss of the benefit of their bargain: the right to purchase the property for a specified sum.

Thus, we need not decide whether or not Callahan Realty would have had actual authority, acting alone, to extend the Goldsteins' right to exercise the option or to interpret the contract's meaning. In effect, Hanna imbued his agent, Callahan, with apparent authority to make the representations upon which the Goldsteins relied. "Apparent authority (when in excess of actual authority) proceeds on the theory of equitable estoppel; it is in effect an estoppel against the owner to deny agency when by his conduct he has clothed the agent with apparent authority to act."

We therefore conclude that the doctrine of equitable estoppel precludes Hanna from claiming a forfeiture of the Goldsteins' option rights.

Reversed.

Perkins v. Philbrick
443 A.2d 73 (Me. 1982)

WATHEN, J. . . . The issue raised by this appeal is whether defendant's forged signature on settlement drafts and a release form can effectuate a settlement and bar defendant's underlying tort claim against plaintiff. We hold that it cannot and deny the appeal.

In 1976 the parties were involved in an automobile accident in which defendant was injured. He hired an attorney to press his claim against plaintiff, and the attorney entered into communications with plaintiff's insurer. In late 1976, in a conversation with the attorney, the insurer's claims adjuster offered to settle defendant's claim for $26,000. The attorney replied that he would have to discuss the offer with his client. In January 1977 without prior discussion with his client the attorney told the adjuster that the settlement was acceptable. The insurer prepared drafts together with a release and inadvertently mailed them to the defendant. Two of the drafts received by the defendant were payable jointly to him and his attorney and one was payable to him and Blue Cross/Blue Shield. Defendant gave the unsigned documents to his attorney explaining that he did not want to settle for that amount. Defendant neither signed nor authorized the endorsement of any draft or the release. The two drafts payable jointly to defendant and his attorney were subsequently presented for payment bearing defendant's purported endorsement. The release form was not immediately returned to the insurer.

When, after numerous calls, the claims adjuster visited the attorney's office, he was given the release purportedly signed by defendant. Sometime in February or March of 1977 the attorney gave defendant between $7,000 and $7,800 which he claimed was part of a $10,000 advance by the insurer. Throughout this period defendant took an active interest in the progress of his claim without learning that the drafts and release had been signed and presented.

In 1979 defendant, represented by his present attorney, commenced suit against plaintiff in Superior Court, seeking damages for his injury in the 1976 accident. Plaintiff then filed this action seeking a declaratory judgment that her obligation to defendant had been discharged when the drafts issued by her insurance company were paid by the bank and the executed release form was received by the insurer. The presiding justice did not issue a declaratory judgment but instead denied plaintiff's request. He based his order on his findings that defendant had neither accepted the settlement nor authorized anyone including his attorney to do so for him by signing the release. These factual findings are undisputed, and we find no settlement has been effectuated under these circumstances. . . .

The parties' briefs focus solely upon the legal principles of authority and ratification applicable to defendant's endorsement forged by his attorney. Dealing with the issue as thus framed, we find a long established principle in Maine and many other jurisdictions that "an attorney clothed with no other authority than that arising from his employment in that capacity has no power to compromise and settle or release and discharge his client's claim." In the absence of authority, the mere fact that the release was signed with defendant's name does not constitute a bar to defendant's tort action.

Neither does the payment of the settlement draft over defendant's forged endorsement effect a settlement of the underlying claim. "Any unauthorized signature is wholly inoperative as that of the person whose name is signed, unless he ratifies it or is precluded from denying it." Thus, the forgery of defendant's name, even if accomplished by his attorney, was not an acceptance of the draft according to its terms as "a release of all claims for damages."

Plaintiff argues that even if the forgeries cannot effectuate a settlement, defendant is bound by them because he ratified the purported settlement by accepting what he thought was an advance. We conclude, as did the Superior Court, that no ratification occurred which would bar defendant's underlying tort action.

For ratification of an agent's actions to occur, it is necessary that all material facts be known by the principal. . . . The record in this case plainly shows that defendant did not have knowledge of the forgery when he accepted the advance from the attorney; therefore the court correctly concluded that ratification had not occurred.

Affirmed.

Pfliger v. Peavey Company
310 N.W.2d 742 (N.D. 1981)

PAULSON, J. Peavey Company ["Peavey"] appeals from a judgment . . . which found Peavey liable for the negligent construction of a farm building on the principle of an ostensible agency and awarded Richard Pfliger ["Pfliger"] the sum of $6,057. . . .

In the early summer of 1978, Arnold Krein, a Peavey sales representative, contacted Pfliger at his farm after learning that Pfliger was interested in purchasing a steel farm building. They had a conversation about steel buildings and Krein showed Pfliger a brochure for a Circle Steel building. Pfliger asked for a bid for such a building as he needed one to present to the Agriculture Stabilization & Conservation Service in order to obtain financing. . . .

To prepare his bid Krein contacted a contractor, Miller Construction Co. ["Miller"], for estimated labor costs. Krein also contacted a concrete supplier for an estimated cost of the concrete. These contacts were made without any direction or endorsement by Pfliger.

On July 11, 1978, Pfliger ordered the building materials from Peavey and signed a customer order for the purchase. The order involved the materials for the physical structure of the proposed building, but not for concrete or labor costs. On July 28, 1978, the day before the construction of the building began, Mr. James Miller, of Miller Construction, met Pfliger at the Pfliger farm. Pfliger signed a "proposal" presented by Miller for the erection of

the building. This proposal provided that Miller Construction was to furnish labor for pouring and forming the concrete and for erecting the structure. Miller told Pfliger that before he begins construction on any job he asks for half of his money down, and, at that time, Pfliger paid Miller $1,889.40, one-half of the labor costs.

The next day the concrete was delivered and poured. Pfliger paid Atlas, Inc., the concrete supplier, $3,542.72. . . .

Pfliger did not supervise the construction of the building. When problems arose during the course of construction, Pfliger would contact Krein, who in turn, would contact Miller. Problems arose from side walls which were improperly bolted together, resulting in gaps through which daylight could be seen; the roof was improperly installed and leaked; and there were problems with doors not fitting or operating properly. The building was not suitable for Pfliger to use for grain storage. Peavey admitted that the building was negligently constructed. . . .

The issues presented on appeal for our determination [is]: Whether the trial court's finding that an ostensible agency relationship existed between Peavey Company as principal and Miller Construction as agent was clearly erroneous. . . .

An agency relationship must be found by clear and convincing evidence, and the burden of proof when an agency is denied is upon the one who asserts that an agency exists. An agency is ostensible "when the principal intentionally or by want of ordinary care causes a third person to believe another to be his agent, who really is not employed by him." "Ostensible authority is such as the principal intentionally or by want of ordinary care causes or allows a third person to believe the agent to possess." There must have been some conduct on the part of the principal reasonably resulting in the belief in the mind of the third party, that an agency existed together with a reliance thereon. . . . Peavey did nothing to keep Pfliger from continuing to believe that Miller was the agent for Peavey. . . .

After reviewing the record we are satisfied that the trial court's determination that an ostensible agency existed between Peavey and Miller is supported by substantial evidence. From the initial contact of Mr. Pfliger, initiated by Mr. Krein of Peavey Company, it was understood that Pfliger was seeking a completed building and that he wanted no part in supervising or constructing it.

Consistent with Pfliger's desire, Krein prepared a written bid containing the estimated costs for the building materials, the labor, and the concrete. Krein was aware that this bid was to be used by Pfliger to obtain financing for the proposed building. The bids for the work to be performed by Miller and for the concrete were obtained by contacts made by Krein. After the materials for the building were obtained by Peavey, Peavey's representative directly contacted Miller to perform his services.

Pfliger had never met James Miller prior to July 28, 1978, the day before construction of the building was to begin. The concrete supplier was unknown to Pfliger until the date of delivery of the materials.

Peavey supplied the plans for the building for Miller. When problems arose during the course of the building's construction, Pfliger directed his complaints to Krein, the Peavey sales representative, who responded by contacting Miller Construction. . . .

The evidence shows that Peavey gave the impression that it was in control of the building process from its first contact with Mr. Pfliger to its responses to Pfliger's complaints about the construction of the building. These actions created and perpetuated the appearance of a principal and agent relationship between Peavey and Miller throughout and after the period of construction.

Peavey created this appearance of principal and agent relationship and stood to gain by it by the sale of a building. Pfliger relied on Peavey to provide him with a completed building. By want of ordinary care, Peavey caused Pfliger to believe that Miller was Peavey's ostensible agent for the erection of the building.

From the outset, Pfliger made it clear that he wanted no part of the building's construction. Krein secured bids from Miller and a concrete supplier and presented his bid for the total cost of the building to Pfliger. Pfliger relied on it by choosing to do business with Peavey rather than with the other parties from whom he had received bids.

. . . [A]fter allowing or permitting the creation of an ostensible agency relationship, the principal is required to correct the erroneous impression left by means equal to, or greater than that which permitted or allowed the impression to be created. If a principal fails to correct an erroneous impression of an ostensible agency relationship, he will be liable to third parties which acted thereunder in good faith. . . .

. . . Rather than correcting the impression of a principal-agency relationship with Miller, Peavey, through Krein, perpetuated this impression by Krein's further contacts with Miller to remedy defects in the construction of the building.

Affirmed.

Sherrill v. Bruce Advertising, Inc.
538 S.W.2d 865 (Tex. 1976)

COULSON, J. . . . This is an appeal from a suit on a contract for services rendered. Bruce Advertising, Inc. sued M. A. Sherrill, Trustee of the William W. Sherrill Trust and Crane-Maier and Associates, Inc. for services rendered in connection with the development of real property owned by the Sherrill Trust. The trial court entered judgment for

Bruce Advertising. . . . The judgment against Crane-Maier has not been appealed and has become final. This appeal relates only to the judgment entered against M. A. Sherrill, Trustee of the William W. Sherrill Trust. We reverse.

In 1970, an agreement was entered between Crane-Maier and the Sherrill Trust whereby the Trust's real property located in Galveston County would be subdivided, developed and sold by Crane-Maier. Bruce Advertising dealt with Crane-Maier by supplying services to them on a contractual basis for development of the realty. Bruce Advertising was not aware that the Sherrill Trust owned the property which Crane-Maier was developing. Suit was brought against Crane-Maier for the services rendered by Bruce Advertising when payment was not forthcoming. After suit was instituted, Crane-Maier by way of its pleadings informed Bruce Advertising that the Sherrill Trust was owner of the property which Crane-Maier was developing. The trial court sitting without a jury entered judgment against both Crane-Maier and the Sherrill Trust holding them jointly and severally liable for the services rendered by Bruce Advertising. . . . The court stated that the association of an agreement between Crane-Maier and the Sherrill Trust constituted a joint venture for the development of the property. The Sherrill Trust has appealed the judgment claiming that as a matter of law there is no joint venture between it and Crane-Maier. We agree. . . .

However, we must consider whether the findings of fact will support the judgment against the Sherrill Trust on any other theory of law. The findings of fact show that Crane-Maier agreed with Bruce Advertising to handle the advertising requirements of the property belonging to the Sherrill Trust. They further show that an agreement was entered into between the Sherrill Trust and Crane-Maier for development and sale of the lots of the Sherrill Trust's property and that Crane-Maier was to be compensated for its services of promotion, development and sales of the project by a percent-age of the sales price of each lot sold. These findings contain elements supporting the theory that Crane-Maier was the agent acting for the principal, the Sherrill Trust, in ordering advertising services from Bruce Advertising.

Whether Bruce Advertising may recover a judgment on a joint and several basis against both a principal and agent is the question presented. . . .

We may imply from the findings of fact that a principal and agent relationship existed between the Sherrill Trust and Crane-Maier, which theory is supported by Bruce Advertising's pleadings. Bruce Advertising did not know that Crane-Maier was acting for anyone other than itself. The Sherrill Trust is in the position of an undisclosed principal. An undisclosed principal is discharged from liability upon a contract if, with knowledge of the identity of the principal, the other party recovers judgment against the agent who made the contract, for the breach of the contract. While this rule has received some discredit, the Texas courts have consistently followed it. Here, the judgment against the agent Crane-Maier has become final. On the theory of principal and agent, the principal, Sherrill Trust, cannot now be held liable since there is a final judgment had against its agent for breach of the contract.

The judgment against Crane-Maier having been entered and now final, there is no theory which can support joint and several liability against the Sherrill Trust. . . .

Reversed.

Como v. Rhines
645 P.2d 948 (Mont. 1982)

This case arises out of the breach of an employment contract. Sound West, Inc., is a Montana corporation which owns a chain of stores. Jim Rhines is the president and a shareholder of Sound West. Gary Como, who has worked as an accountant and with computers, sought employment in Montana. Through an employment agency's reference, Como met with Rhines about possible employment. After a series of interviews in April 1978, Rhines agreed to hire Como and to pay his moving expenses. They agreed Como would begin working for Sound West in June. After Como moved and settled his family, he contacted Rhines about begin-ning his employment. Rhines was noncommittal. Following several more requests by Como for a starting date, Rhines told Como there was no job for him at Sound West. Como secured employment elsewhere and sued Rhines individually for lost wages and moving expenses. Rhines argued he was acting as an agent for Sound West, Inc.; therefore, he was not personally liable to Como. The District Court found for the plaintiff, and the defendant appealed.

DALY, J. . . . Appellants raise . . . [the following issue]: Did the District Court err by holding appellant Jim Rhines liable for respondent's damages? . . .

The District Court concluded as a matter of

law that "Jim Rhines as the president and manager of Sound West, Inc., did offer employment to Gary Como for an accounting position with express terms." . . . The District Court then went on to conclude that Jim Rhines and Sound West, Inc., breached the employment contract and that both Rhines and Sound West were liable for the damages arising out of this breach.

This Court has recognized the general rule that an agent is not personally liable on a contract entered into by him on behalf of his principal if it appears, in fact, that he disclosed the identity of his principal and made the engagement for him. This Court has [also] recognized that the existence of the agency must be disclosed in appropriate terms, including the name of the principal for whom the agent is acting. Moreover, merely because the agent, in making the contract for his principal, uses the trade name under which his principal transacts business is not of itself a sufficient identification of the principal to protect the agent from liability.

This general rule of agency also applies to the corporate setting:

The rule that where an agent enters into a contract in his own name for an undisclosed principal, the other party to the contract may hold the agent personally liable, applies equally well to corporate officers or agents. It has been held that the managing officer of a corporation, even though acting for the company, becomes liable as a principal where he deals with one ignorant of the company's existence and of his relation to it, and fails to inform the latter of the facts. . . .

Here, the record does not indicate that Rhines told respondent he would be working for Sound West, Inc. In fact, this lawsuit was initiated by respondent against "Jim Rhines, d/b/a (doing business as) Sound West." While the agency was disclosed during the course of this litigation, the disclosure of the principal after the contract is executed will not relieve the agent from liability.

In the absence of a showing by appellants that respondent understood Rhines was acting as an agent for the corporation, Sound West, Inc., and not as an individual doing business as Sound West, it cannot be said the District Court erred by holding Rhines personally liable on the contract.

Affirmed.

REVIEW QUESTIONS

1. Identify the terms in column A by matching each with the appropriate statement in column B.

A	B
1. Actual authority	**a.** The required step to bind a disclosed principal and third party to a contract, if the agent's actions are unauthorized.
2. Apparent authority	**b.** An event that constitutes an election.
3. Ratification	**c.** Because of the personal nature of the principal-agent relationship, an agent must be given clear authority to do this.
4. Election	**d.** Breach of this is one example of how an agent becomes contractually liable to a third party.
5. Judgment	**e.** Its existence is possible only when the principal is fully disclosed.
6. Settlement	**f.** The process whereby a third party chooses to hold the agent or a previously undisclosed principal liable on a contract.
7. Appointment of subagents	**g.** This type of authority may be conveyed by a principal to an agent by written or spoken words, or by the parties' conduct.

8. Warranty of authority

    h. Method whereby an undisclosed principal is relieved of liability to a third party prior to the principal becoming disclosed.

2. Pat, the owner of a grocery store chain, hires Amy to manage one store. Pat tells Amy to stock the store. Pat also tells Amy: (a) "Be sure to buy soup," (b) "Don't buy soup," (c) nothing about soup. Amy then proceeds to buy 40 cases of soup from Tom. In which situations, if any, is Pat liable to Tom? Why?

3. A buyer sued the Farm Corporation for specific performance of a contract for the sale of farmland. The contract had been signed by the president of the corporation. The board of directors had authorized the president to discuss the sale of land, but had not authorized the sale. The land described in the contract was 35 percent of the corporation's assets. Is the Farm Corporation bound to perform the contract signed by its president?

4. Barney purchased a new car and called the Friendly Insurance Company's home office to transfer the insurance from his old car to his new one and to obtain collision coverage. He talked to two employees before being switched to Ann, who replied, "O.K., you are covered." Ann had no authority to give additional insurance coverage. Barney had an accident the day after he talked to Ann. Barney is suing Friendly for damage to his car. Should he succeed? Explain.

5. Jerry, the managing agent of Pet Shop, Inc., borrowed $3,500 from Turner on the shop's behalf for use in the business. The company had not authorized Jerry to borrow the money, but it did repay $500 of the amount to Turner. Is Turner entitled to collect the balance due from the shop? Why?

6. Oxford operates a janitorial service and cleans commercial buildings. Oxford contracted with Gresham to clean several buildings on a regular basis, not knowing that Gresham was only an agent hired to manage these buildings. Gresham failed to make several payments owed to Oxford. When Oxford sued Gresham for the money owed, Gresham argued he was not liable, since he was merely an agent. Is Gresham correct? Why?

7. Ann worked for Perry's Grocery as purchasing agent for poultry and farm produce. In all transactions with farmers, Ann acted as the principal and purchased on the strength of her own credit. Ann failed to pay for some of the produce purchased. The farmers, having ascertained that Perry's Grocery was the true principal, seek to hold it responsible. May they do so? Suppose Perry's had previously settled with Ann. Explain.

8. Alice was hired by Petro Chemical, Inc., as a member of the land acquisitions department. While investigating the possible purchase of a large tract of land, Alice learned that there was neither oil nor gas under the land. Trion, the owner of this land, was dismayed by Alice's findings. Trion persuaded Alice not to tell her employer of her knowledge. Indeed, if Petro Chemical purchased his land, Trion agreed to pay Alice $25,000. Trion was able to convince Petro Chemical to buy his land, since it had the possibility of containing oil and gas. After this purchase, Petro Chemical discovered it had been defrauded. It sued Trion, but he claimed he could not be liable, since Alice's knowledge of the barren land was imputed to Petro Chemical. Was this agent's knowledge notice to her principal? Explain.

9. Patricia owned a retail clothing store. As her agent, Patricia's father did business in the store's name. Indeed, a power of attorney signed by Patricia gave her father the authority "to sign and endorse all checks and drafts and to transact all business." Patricia's father borrowed money from a bank for the store's benefit. Did the power of attorney give her father the authority to approve this loan?

10. Alfred is the president and part owner of Ross Production Company. Ross ordered $3,000 worth of pipe from the Tri-Pipe Corporation. Due to Ross's poor payment record, Tri-Pipe decided it could not sell to Ross on credit. Alfred signed an undated check payable to Tri-Pipe for the amount of $3,000. There was no name or address on this check. This check was not honored, and Tri-Pipe sued Alfred personally. Is Alfred, as Ross's agent, personally liable? Why?

11. Alex, thinking he had authority to do so, signed a promissory note as an agent of Patterson's Paint Corporation. Later Alex and the payee learned that Patterson's was not bound, owing to Alex's lack of authority to borrow money. Is Alex liable if the note was signed "Patterson's Paint Corporation, by Alex Ander, as agent"? Why?

16 AGENCY, TORTS, AND EMPLOYMENT

The fundamental principles of tort liability in the law of agency, which are discussed in this chapter, can be summarized as follows:

1. Agents, servants, and independent contractors are personally liable for their own torts.
2. Agents, servants, and independent contractors are not liable for the torts of their employers.
3. A master is liable under a doctrine known as *respondeat superior* for the torts of his servant if the servant is acting within the scope of his employment.
4. A principal, proprietor, employer, or contractee (each of these terms is sometimes used) is not, as a general rule, liable for the torts of an independent contractor.
5. Injured employees may have rights against their employers as well as against third parties who cause their injuries.

The terms *master* and *servant* are technically more accurate than the terms *principal* and *agent* in describing the parties when tort liability is discussed. Courts, nevertheless, frequently describe the parties as *principal* and *agent*. A principal, however, is liable for torts of only those agents who are subject to the kind of control that establishes the master-servant relationship. For the purpose of tort liability, a *servant* is a person who is employed with or without pay to perform personal services for another in his affairs, and who, in respect to the physical movements in the performance of such service, is subject to the master's right or power of control. A person who renders services for another but retains control over the manner of rendering such services is not a servant, but an independent contractor.

In addition to the tort liability that may arise from an agency relationship, this chapter also includes material on other aspects of the employer-employee relationship which are related to tort liability. Among the other aspects of employment are issues relating to workers' injuries and diseases, the Occupational Safety and Health Act, third parties' interference with the master-servant relationship, and discrimination in employment.

1. Tort Liability of Agents, Servants, and Independent Contractors

Every person who commits a tort is personally liable to the individual whose body or property is injured or damaged by the wrongful act. An agent or officer of a corporation who commits or participates in the commission of a tort, whether or not he acts on behalf of his corporation, is liable to third persons injured. One is not relieved of tort liability by establishing that the tortious act was committed under the direction of someone else or in the course of employment of another. The fact that the employer or principal may be held liable does not in any way relieve the servant or agent from liability. The agent's or servant's liability is joint and several with the liability of the principal. Of course, the converse is not true. An agent, servant, or independent contractor is not liable for the torts of the principal, master, or employer.

Suppose that Matthews hires Stewart to drive a truck. While driving within the scope of Matthew's instructions, Stewart carelessly runs through a stop sign and collides with a car driven by Trevor. Trevor may bring an action against Stewart or Matthews as individual defendants, or he may sue them jointly as co-defendants, as is typically the case. Assume that Trevor sues and collects from Matthews, since the employer's financial standing usually is better than the employee's. Can Matthews, upon paying the judgment, recover this loss from Stewart? Yes, if there was no contributing fault of Matthews. A servant is liable for his own misconduct either to others or to his employer.

Suits by masters against servants for indemnity are not common, for several reasons. First, the servant's financial condition frequently does not warrant suit. Second, the employer knows of the risk of negligence by his employees and covers this risk with insurance. If indemnity were a common occurrence, the ultimate loss would almost always fall on employees or workers. If this situation developed, it would have an adverse effect on employee morale and would make labor-management relations much more difficult. Therefore, few employers seek to enforce the right to collect losses from employees.

Just as a master may have a right to collect from the servant, under certain situations the servant may maintain a successful action for reimbursement and indemnity against the master. Such a case would occur when the servant commits a tort by following the master's instructions if that servant did not know his conduct was tortious. *Example:* Matthews, a retail appliance dealer, instructs Stewart to repossess a TV set from Trevor, who had purchased it on an installment contract. Matthews informs Stewart that Trevor is in arrears in his payments. Actually, Trevor is current in his payments. A bookkeeping error had been made by Matthews. Despite Trevor's protests, Stewart repossesses the TV set pursuant to Matthew's instructions. Stewart has committed the torts of trespass and wrongful conversion. Matthews must idemnify Stewart and satisfy Trevor's claim if Trevor elects to collect from Stewart.

TORT
LIABILITY
OF MASTERS

2. Respondeat Superior

A master is liable to third persons for the torts committed by his servants *within the scope of their employment* and in prosecution of the master's business. This concept, frequently known as *respondeat superior* (let the master respond), imposes vicarious liability on employers as a matter of public policy. Although negligence of the servant is the usual basis of liability, the doctrine of *respondeat superior* is also applicable to intentional torts, such as trespass, assault, libel, and fraud, which are committed by a servant acting within the scope of his employment. It is applicable even though the master did not direct the willful act or assent to it.

This vicarious liability imposed on masters, which makes them pay for wrongs they have not actually committed, is not based on logic and reason, but on business and social policy. The theory is that the master is in a better position to pay for the wrong than is the servant. This concept is sometimes referred to as the "deep pocket" theory. The business policy theory is that injuries to persons and property are hazards of doing business, the cost of which the business should bear, rather than have the loss borne by the innocent victim of the tort or society as a whole.

There is universal agreement that a master is vicariously liable for the actual damages caused by a servant acting within the scope of employment. However, there is disagreement about when the master is liable for punitive damages that may be awarded to punish the servant's wrong. One theory that has been widely adopted by courts in some states is called the *vicarious liability rule*. This rule states that the master is always liable for punitive damages awarded against the servant if the wrong committed occurred within the scope of the servant's employment. The logic behind this rule involves the belief that making the master liable for punitive damages will help deter reckless or intentional torts. The more modern view of punitive damages that has been adopted by a growing number of states has been called the *complicity rule*. The advantage of this rule is that it allows for a determination of whether a master is actually blameworthy before making that master liable for punitive damages.[1] In essence, under this second principle, in order to collect punitive damages from the master, an injured third party must be able to prove that (1) the master had authorized the servant to commit the tort; or (2) the master was reckless in employing or retaining the servant; or (3) the servant was employed in a managerial position; or (4) the master had ratified the servant's tortious conduct.

---

[1] Mercury Motors Express, Inc. v. Smith, p. 357.

The application of the doctrine of *respondeat superior* usually involves the issue of whether the servant was *acting within the scope of his employment* at the time of the commission of the tort. The law imposes liability on the master only if the tort occurs while the servant is carrying on the master's business or if the master authorizes or ratifies the servant's actions. The master's liability does not arise when the servant steps aside from his employment to commit the tort or when the servant does a wrongful act to accomplish a personal purpose.

Not every deviation from the strict course of duty is a departure that will relieve a master of liability for the acts of a servant. The fact that a servant, while performing his duty to his master, incidentally does something for himself or a third person does not automatically relieve the master from liability for negligence that causes injury to another. To sever the servant from the scope of his employment, the act complained of must be such a divergence from his regular duties that its very character severs the relationship of master and servant.

It is not possible to state a simple test to determine if the tort is committed within the scope of the employment. Factors to be considered include the nature of the employment, the right of control "not only as to the result to be accomplished but also as to the means to be used," the ownership of the instrumentality such as an automobile, whether the instrumentality was furnished by the employer, whether the use was authorized, and the time of the occurrence. Most courts inquire into the intent of the servant and the extent of deviation from expected conduct involved in the tort.

As a general rule, the master cannot avoid liability by showing that he has instructed the servant not to do the particular act complained of. When a servant disobeys the instructions of his master, the fact of disobedience alone does not insulate the master from liability. In addition, the master is not released by evidence that the servant was not doing the work his master had instructed him to do, when the servant had misunderstood the instruction. As long as the servant is attempting to further his master's business, the master is liable, because the servant is acting within the scope of his employment.

The issue of whether a servant is acting within the scope of employment usually is one of fact. Therefore, this issue typically must be resolved by a jury. Seldom will a judge be able to make a ruling involving the doctrine of *respondeat superior* as a matter of law. One of the most difficult situations to resolve occurs when an accident happens while an employee is going to or coming from work. Although general statements could be made, the peculiar facts of each case are crucial in determining whether an employer is liable for the employee's acts.

3. Expanding Vicarious Liability

In recent years, the law has been expanding the concept of vicarious liability to acts of persons who are not employees. A person engaged in some endeavor gratuitously may still be a "servant" within scope of the master-servant doctrine. The two key elements for determination of whether a gratuitous undertaking is a part of master-servant relationship are (1) whether the actor has submitted himself to the directions and to the control of the one for whom the service is done, and (2) whether the primary purpose of the underlying act was to serve another. If these elements are satisfied, the "master" is liable for the torts of the unpaid "servant."

Most of the expansion of the application of *respondeat superior* and vicarious liability has been by statute. Liability for automobile accidents has been a major area of expansion. Some states have adopted what is known as the "family car doctrine." Under it, if the car is generally made available for family use, any member of the family is presumed to be an agent of the parent-owner when using the family car for his or her convenience or pleasure. The presumption may be rebutted, however. Other states have gone further and provided that anyone driving a car with the permission of the owner is the owner's agent, and the owner has vicarious liability to persons injured by the driver. The family purpose doctrine may extend to nonfamily members under some circumstances.

4. Exceptions—Frolics and Detours

Although it often is difficult to know with certainty whether a servant is or is not within the scope of employment, the law has recognized that the master is *not* liable when the servant is on a frolic or when the servant has detoured in a substantial manner from the master's instructions. A *frolic* exists whenever a servant pursues his personal interests while neglecting the master's business. For example, a route salesman who leaves his route to accomplish a personal errand is on a frolic. If an accident occurs while this salesman is on the frolic, his master would not be liable for the third party's injuries. A very hard question to answer is this: When does a frolic or detour end so that the servant is again within the scope of employment?

Another difficult situation is presented when the servant combines his own business with that of his master. As a general rule, this fact does not relieve the master of liability. Furthermore, the doctrine of *respondeat superior* has been extended to create the master's liability for the negligence of strangers while assisting a servant in carrying out the master's business if the authority to obtain assistance is given or required, as in an emergency.

5. Intentional Torts

Intentional or willful torts are not as likely to occur within the scope of the servant's employment as are those predicated upon a negligence theory. If the willful misconduct of the servant has nothing to do with his master's business and is animated entirely by hatred or a feeling of ill will toward the third party, the master is not liable. Nor is the master liable if the employee's act has no reasonable connection with his employment. However, the injured third party generally does not have to prove that the master actually instructed the servant to commit the intentional tort. Once again, the key issue for determining the master's liability is whether the servant was within the scope of employment.[2]

---

[2] Condict v. Condict, p. 358.

6. Tort Suits—Procedures

As previously noted, the law of torts in most states, unlike the law of contracts, allows joinder of the master and servant as defendants in one cause of action or permits them to be sued separately. Although the plaintiff is limited to one recovery, the master and servant are jointly and severally liable. The party may collect from either or both in any proportion until the judgment is paid in full. If the servant is sued first and a judgment is obtained that is not satisfied, the suit is not a bar to a subsequent suit against the master, but the amount of the judgment against the servant fixes the maximum limit of potential liability against the master.

If the servant is found to be free of liability, either in a separate suit or as a codefendant with the master, then the suit against the master on the basis of *respondeat superior* will fail. The master's liability is predicated upon the fault of the servant; if the servant is found to be free of fault, the master has no liability as a matter of law.

7. Control over Independent Contractors

An *independent contractor* has power to control the details of the work he performs for his employer. Because the performance is within his control, he is not a servant, and his only responsibility is to accomplish the result contracted for. For example, Rush contracts to build a boat for Ski-King at a cost of $40,000, according to certain specifications. It is clear that Rush is an independent contractor; the completed boat is the result. Had Ski-King engaged Rush by the day to assist in building the boat under Ski-King's supervision and direction, the master-servant relationship would have resulted. Keep in mind that an agent with authority to represent his principal contractually will, at the same time, be either a servant or an independent contractor for the purpose of tort liability.

The hallmark of a master-servant relationship is that the master not only controls the result of the work, but also has the right to direct the manner in which the work will be accomplished. The distinguishing feature of a proprietor–independent contractor relationship is that the person engaged to do the work has exclusive control of the manner of performing it, being responsible only to produce the desired result. In ascertaining whether a person is a servant or an independent contractor, the basic inquiry is whether such person is subject to the alleged employer's control or right to control his physical conduct in the performance of services for which he was engaged. Whether the relationship is master-servant or proprietor–independent contractor is usually a question of fact for the jury.

Without changing the relationship from that of proprietor and independent contractor or the duties arising from that relationship, an employer of an independent contractor may retain a broad general power of supervision of the work to ensure satisfactory performance of the contract. He may inspect, stop the work, make suggestions or recommendations about details of the work, or prescribe alterations or deviations.

8. General Rule—No Liability

The distinction between servants and independent contractors is important because, as a general rule, the doctrine of *respondeat superior* and the concept of vicarious liability in tort are not applicable to independent contractors. There is no tort liability, as a general rule, because the theories that justify liability of the master for the servant's tort are not present when the person engaged to do the work is not a servant. Nor is any liability imputed to one who controls certain activities of persons not employed by him.

The application of the doctrine of *respondeat superior* and the tests for determining if the wrongdoer is an independent contractor are quite difficult to apply to professional and technically skilled personnel. It can be argued that a physician's profession requires such high skill and learning that others, especially laymen, cannot as a matter of law be in control of the physician's activities. That argument, if accepted, would eliminate the liability of hospitals for acts of medical employees.

Notwithstanding the logic of this argument, courts usually hold that *respondeat superior* may be applied to professional persons and that such persons may be servants. Of course, some professional and technical persons are independent contractors. Hospitals and others who render professional service through skilled employees have the same legal responsibilities as everyone else. If the person who commits a tort is an employee acting on the employer's behalf, the employer is liable, even though no one actually "controls" the employee in the performance of his art or skill. These concepts are applicable to doctors, chemists, airline pilots, lawyers, and other highly trained specialists.

Since it is generally understood that one is not liable for the torts of an independent contractor, contracts frequently provide that the relationship is that of proprietor–independent contractor, not master-servant. Such a provision is not binding on third parties, and the contract cannot be used to protect the contracting parties from the actual relationship as shown by the facts.

9. Exceptions—Liability Created

The rule of insulation from liability in the independent contractor situation is subject to several well-recognized exceptions. The most common of these is related to work inherently dangerous to the public, such as blasting with dynamite. The basis of this exception is that it would be contrary to public policy to allow one engaged in such an activity to avoid his liability by selecting an independent contractor rather than a servant to do the work.

Another exception to insulation from vicarious liability applies to illegal work. An employer cannot insulate himself from liability by hiring an independent contractor to perform a task that is illegal. Still another common exception involves employees' duties considered to be duties that cannot be delegated. In discussing the law of contracts, we noted that personal rights and personal duties could not be transferred without consent of the other party. Many statutes impose strict duties on parties such as common carriers and innkeepers. If an attempt is made to delegate these duties to an independent contractor, it is clear that the employer upon whom the duty is imposed has liability for the torts of the independent contractor. In a contract to perform a service or supply a product, liability for negligence cannot be avoided by engaging an independent contractor to perform the duty. Finally, an employer is liable for the torts of an independent contractor if the tort is ratified. If an independent contractor wrongfully repossesses an automobile, and the one hiring him refuses to return it on demand, the tort has been ratified, and both parties have liability.

Tort liability is also imposed on the employer who is himself at fault, as he is when he negligently selects the employee. This is true whether the party performing the work is a servant or an independent contractor.[3]

10. Common Law Principles

TORT LIABILITY
OF EMPLOYERS

An employer owes certain nondelegable duties to his employees. These include the duty to (1) warn employees of the hazards of their employment, (2) supervise their activities, (3) furnish a reasonably safe place to work, and (4) furnish reasonably safe instrumentalities with which to work. As part of the obligation to provide a safe place to work, the employer must instruct his employees in the safe use and handling of the products and equipment used in and around the employer's plant or facilities. What is reasonable for the purposes of these rules depends on all the facts and circumstances of each case, including the age and ability of the worker, as well as the condition of the premises. It might be negligent to put a minor in charge of a particular instrument without supervision, although it would not be negligent to assign an adult or experienced employee to the same equipment.

Under common law, the employer who breached these duties to his employees was liable in tort for injuries received by the employees. The employer was not an insurer of his employee's safety, but liability was based on negligence. In turn, the employee in his tort action was confronted with overcoming three defenses available to the employer, one or more of which frequently barred recovery. The first of these defenses was that the employee was *contributorily negligent.* If the employee was even partially at fault, this defense was successful, even though the majority of the fault was the employer's. Second, if the injury was caused by some other employee, the *fellow-servant* doctrine excused the employer and limited recovery to a suit against the other employee who was at fault. Finally, in many jobs that by their very nature involved some risk of injury, the doctrine of *assumption of risk* would allow the employer to avoid liability.

The common law rules resulted for the most part in imposing on employees the burdens that resulted from accidental injuries, occupational diseases, and even death. Through the legislative process, all states have determined that this result is undesirable as a matter of public policy. Statutes known as *worker's compensation* have been enacted in all the states. These laws impose liability without fault (by eliminating the common-law defenses) on most employers for injuries, occupational diseases, and deaths of employees.

---

[3] Pontiacs v. K.M.S. Investments, p. 359.

11. Workers' Compensation—In General

Workers' compensation laws vary a great deal from state to state in their coverage of industries and employees, the nature of the injuries or diseases that are compensable, and the rates and source of compensation. In spite of these wide variances, certain general observations can be made.

State laws for workers' compensation provide a system of paying for death, illness, or injury that arises out of, and in the course of, the employment. The three defenses the employer had under common law are eliminated. The employers are strictly liable without fault. Furthermore, states have begun to hold employers liable even though an employee cannot prove the employer solely responsible for the damages done. This legal principle is applied especially when occupational diseases, as opposed to accidental injuries, are involved.[4]

Most state statutes exclude certain types of employment from their coverage. Generally, domestic and agricultural employees are not covered. In the majority of states, the statutes are compulsory. In some states, employers may elect to be subject to lawsuits by their employees or their survivors. In such cases, the plaintiff must prove that the death or injury resulted proximately from the negligence of the employer. But the plaintiff is not subject to the common-law defenses. In addition, there is no statutory limit to the amount of damages recoverable. Thus, few employers elect to avoid workers' compensation coverage.

12. Workers' Compensation—Benefits

The workers' compensation acts give covered employees the right to certain cash payments for their loss of income. A weekly benefit is payable during periods of disability. In the event of an employee's death, benefits are provided for the spouse and minor children. The amount of such awards is usually subject to a stated maximum and is calculated by using a percentage of the wages of the employee. If the employee suffers permanent partial disability, most states provide compensation for injuries that are scheduled in the statute and those that are nonscheduled. As an example of the former, a worker who loses a hand might be awarded 100 weeks of compensation at $90 per week. Besides scheduling specific compensation for certain specific injuries, most acts also provide compensation for nonscheduled ones, such as back injuries, based upon the earning power the employee lost owing to his injury. In addition to the payments above, all statutes provide for medical benefits and funeral expenses.

In some states, employers have a choice of covering their workers' compensation risk with insurance or being self-insured (i.e., paying all claims directly) if they can demonstrate their capability to do so. In other states, employers pay into a state fund used to compensate workers entitled to benefits. In these states, the amounts of the payments are based on the size of the payroll and the claim experience of the employer.

---

[4] Tavares v. A.C. & S., Inc., p. 360.

13. Workers' Compensation—Burden of Proof

Although the right to workers' compensation benefits is given without regard to fault of either the employer or the employee, employers are not always liable. The tests for determining whether an employee is entitled to workers' compensation are simply: (1) Was the injury accidental? and (2) Did the injury arise out of and in the course of the employment? Since workers' compensation laws are remedial in nature, they have been very liberally construed. In recent years, the courts have tended to expand coverage and scope of the employer's liability. It has been held that heart attacks and other common ailments are compensable as "accidental injuries," even though the employee had either a preexisting disease or a physical condition likely to lead to the disease. Likewise, the courts have been more and more liberal in upholding awards that have been challenged on the ground that the injury did not arise out of and in the course of the employment.[5]

The system of separate and varying state laws for workers' compensation has been subject to much criticism. The laws have been attacked as inadequate because of their restrictive coverage and limited benefits. Not all types of employment or occupational risks are covered. Many states exempt businesses that do not employ a certain minimum number of workers. Criticism has also been leveled at the quality of administration of most workers' compensation programs. The weaknesses in the present laws and the wide variations in workers' compensation acts (as well as case law) from state to state have led to suggestions that workers' compensation be modernized to meet the social needs of today and that it be made uniform from state to state. Some have proposed a Federal Worker's Compensation Act to replace the state laws.

14. Federal Legislation—Liability Issues

Several federal statutes pertain to the liability of certain kinds of employers for injuries, diseases, and deaths arising out of the course of employment. Railroad workers are covered by the Federal Employers' Liability Act. This statute does not provide for liability without fault, as in the case of workers' compensation, but it greatly increases the chances of a worker's winning a lawsuit against his or her employer by eliminating or reducing the defenses the latter would have had at common law. While fault of the carrier must be proved for an employee to recover for injuries under the FELA, and a regular lawsuit must be filed in court, the act provides the worker with a distinct advantage over many workers' compensation systems. There is no limit or ceiling to the amount an employee can recover for injuries. The Jones Act gives maritime employees the same rights against their employers as railway workers have against theirs under the FELA.

Other federal statutes require that awards for on-the-job injuries or deaths of certain employees be made in the manner of state laws for workers' compensation: without regard to the fault of the employer. These federal laws provide formulas to

---

[5] Chung v. Animal Clinic, Inc., p. 361.

use in computing the amounts of the awards for various kinds and degrees of disability, along with upper and lower limits for such awards. One such statute is the Longshoremen's and Harbor Workers' Compensation Act. The coverage of this statute was extended to workers for private employers on United States defense bases by the Defense Bases Act.

15. Federal Legislation—OSHA

Because workers' compensation statutes and similar federal laws had not reduced or eliminated accidental injuries, diseases, and deaths connected with employment, in 1970 Congress passed the Occupational Safety and Health Act (OSHA). Its purpose is to assure safe and healthful working conditions for virtually every employee in the United States. The law requires that employers furnish to each employee a place of employment free from recognized hazards that are causing or are likely to cause death or serious physical harm to the employee. It also requires that the employer comply with occupational safety and health standards promulgated under the act by the secretary of labor. In order to accomplish the foregoing, Labor Department investigators conduct unannounced inspections to determine if violations exist. Employers are required to make and preserve certain records relating to accidents and injuries and to conduct periodic inspections to ensure compliance with the standards.

There are civil and criminal penalties for violating OSHA rules and regulations. Most OSHA inspections have resulted in at least some fines. As a result, in the late 1970s, Congress prohibited imposing fines on a business if only 10 or fewer nonserious violations of OSHA standards are cited during a first-time inspection. Today, OSHA is less concerned with safety problems than with health hazards, such as chemicals that cause cancer.

16. Tort Liability of Third Parties

Irrespective of other legal relationships, any person injured by the commission of a tort has a cause of action against the wrongdoer. An employee who is injured by the wrongful conduct of the third person may recover from the third person. If the employee has been compensated for his injuries by his employer under the applicable worker's compensation law, the employer is entitled to recover any worker's compensation payments from the sum that the employee recovers from the wrongful third party.

Three rather unusual tort situations have a direct relation to the employment contract. First, any third party who maliciously or wrongfully influences a principal to terminate an agent's employment thereby commits a tort. The wrongful third party must compensate the agent for any damages that result from such conduct. Second, any third person who wrongfully interferes with the prospective economic advantage of an agent has liability to the agent for the loss sustained.[6] Third, any person who influences another to breach a contract in which

---

[6] Hangar One, Inc. v. Davis Associates, Inc., p. 362.

the agent is interested renders himself liable to that agent as well as to the principal. These three torts by third parties are discussed in further detail in chapter 4.

17. Equal Employment Opportunity

The basic federal law on equal employment opportunity was enacted in 1964. The Civil Rights Act of 1964, as now amended, covers all employers with 15 or more employees, labor unions with 15 or more members, labor unions that operate a hiring hall, and employment agencies. The 1972 amendment extended coverage to state and local governments and to educational institutions.

A federal administrative agency known as the Equal Employment Opportunity Commission has the primary responsibility for enforcing the act. In the course of its investigations, the commission has broad authority to examine and copy evidence, require the production of documentary evidence, hold hearings, and subpoena and examine witnesses under oath.

By a 1972 amendment, the EEOC has the power to file a civil suit in court and to represent a person charging a violation of the act; however, it must first exhaust efforts to concilate the claim. The remedies available in such an action include reinstatement with back pay for the victim of an illegal discrimination and injunctions against future violations of the law.

The federal law seeks to preserve state and local employment practice laws. Where an alleged violation of federal law, if true, is violative of a state or local law, the commission may not act until 60 days after the proceedings, if any, have been commenced under that law. Similarly, the commission must notify the appropriate officials and defer all action until the local authority has had, in general, at least 60 days to resolve the matter.

18. Discrimination on Basis of Race, Color, National Origin, and Religion

Practices involving recruiting, hiring, and promotion of employees are often charged as being discriminatory on the basis of race, color, or national origin. Though a company's standards or policies for selecting or promoting may appear neutral, if they have the effect of discriminating against blacks or other minorities and have no substantial, demonstrable relationship to qualification for the job in question, they are illegal. Under this rule several hiring policies have been found illegal: denying employment to unwed mothers in a locale where the rate of illegitimate births was higher among blacks than among whites; refusing to hire persons because of their poor credit rating; refusing to hire those with an arrest record; and giving priority to relatives of present employees in hiring when there was a very low percentage of minority workers among these employees.

The practice of using personnel tests also has been challenged under this rule. The Civil Rights Act states that it is not unlawful for an employer to hire or promote employees on the basis of the results of professionally developed ability tests, provided they are not designed or used to discriminate illegally. The courts, however, have held that the use of a standardized general intelligence test in selecting and placing personnel is prohibited, being discriminatory on the basis of race. Tests, neutral on their face and even neutral in terms of intent, cannot be maintained if they operate to "freeze" the status quo of prior discriminatory employment practices. If an employment practice cannot be shown to be related to job performance, the practice is prohibited. The Civil Rights Act proscribes not only overt discrimination, but also practices that are fair in form but discriminatory in operation. As a result, job tests have been dropped by many companies because of the difficulty of proving that all questions are validly related to job performance.

Religious corporations, associations, or societies can discriminate in all their employment practices on the basis of religion, but not on the basis of race, color, sex, or national origin. Other employers cannot discriminate on the basis of religion in employment practices, and they must make reasonable accommodation to the religious needs of their employees if it does not result in undue hardship to the employers.

19. Sex Discrimination

Discrimination based on sex is a major area of equal employment opportunity litigation. A federal law requires that women and men be paid equivalent wages for equivalent work, although executive personnel are exempt from the Equal Pay Act. Many state laws have long protected women from employment in certain occupations (such as those requiring lifting heavy objects) and from working at night or working an excessive number of hours per week or day. Under EEOC guidelines and court decisions, the state laws are unconstitutional and not a defense to a charge of illegal sex discrimination. Other EEOC guidelines forbid (1) employers' classifying jobs as male or female, (2) advertising in help-wanted columns that are designated male or female, unless sex is a bona fide job qualification; and (3) separate male and female seniority lists or lines of progression. For sex to be a valid job qualification, it must be demonstrably relevant to job performance. Very few jobs meet this test.

20. Age Discrimination

In 1967 Congress passed the Age Discrimination in Employment Act, which protects persons between 40 and 65 years of age from job discrimination because of age. This law is enforced by the EEOC and is of great importance today.

A 1978 amendment to the law prohibits mandatory retirement before age 70 of most workers employed by private businesses with over 19 employees. With the exception of the police and firemen, almost all local and state employees are protected by the act, and most federal employees cannot be forced to retire at *any* age because of their years. "Bona fide executives" and "high policy makers" of private companies who will have pensions of at least $27,000 per year, however, can be forced into early retirement. The statute invalidates retirement plans and labor contracts that call for retirement before age 70, even if they were in force at the time the law became effective in January 1979.

21. Discrimination on Basis of Handicaps

In order to promote and expand employment opportunities for handicapped persons, both in the public and private sectors, Congress enacted the Rehabilitation Act of 1973. This statute requires each department and agency in the executive branch of the federal government to have an approved affirmative action plan for the hiring, placement, and advancement of qualified handicapped people. It also requires every employer with a federal government contract for over $2,500 to take *affirmative action* to hire and advance qualified handicapped persons at all levels, including executive. This affirmative action requirement applies also to job assignments, promotions, training, transfers, accessibility, working conditions, and termination. The federal contracts and subcontracts covered include those for the procurement of personal property and nonpersonal sources.

A handicapped person is anyone who has or has had a physical or mental impairment that substantially limits a major life activity. To be hired, however, that person must be "qualified," or capable of performing a particular job, with reasonable accommodation to his or her handicap. The term *handicapped individual* does not include an alcoholic or drug abuser whose current use of alcohol or drugs prevents him from performing the duties of the job in question or whose current alcohol or drug abuse would constitute a direct threat to the property or safety of others.

Federal contractors covered not only must take affirmative action themselves, but also must include a clause in all their contracts or subcontracts or purchase orders of over $2,500 by which the subcontractor agrees not to discriminate against any qualified handicapped person and also agrees to take affirmative action to hire and advance them. The subcontractor must also agree to post affirmative action notices in conspicuous places around its plant.

22. Affirmative Action Programs

The desire to eliminate the adverse effects of past discrimination prompted most governmental bodies and many private employers to adopt policies and practices described as affirmative action programs. These programs usually established goals for hiring and promoting members of minority groups, to be accomplished by active recruitment programs and by giving priority to minorities. Members of minorities were to be given priority when fewer of them were working in a given job category than one would reasonably expect there should be, considering their availability.

Affirmative action programs and similar efforts have led white males to charge reverse discrimination. They argue that it is just as wrong to discriminate in favor of minorities as it is to discriminate against them. In 1980, the Supreme Court held that voluntary affirmative action programs may be constitutional and companies that adopt them are not in violation of the law.

SUMMARY

General principles	1. Agents, servants, and independent contractors are personally liable for their own torts.
	2. Agents, servants, and independent contractors are not liable for the torts of their employers.
	3. A master is liable under the *respondeat superior* doctrine for the torts of his servant if the servant is acting within the scope of employment.
	4. A principal, proprietor, employer, or contractee (each of these terms is sometimes used) is not, as a general rule, liable for the torts of an independent contractor.
	5. Injured employees may have rights against their employers as well as against third parties who cause their injuries.

TORT LIABILITY OF MASTERS

Respondeat superior	1. Literally means "let the master respond."
	2. Legal doctrine that places liability as a matter of public policy on employers for the torts of their employees.
	3. This doctrine allows injured persons to recover from the party with the "deeper pocket."
	4. The basic issue is whether the servant was acting within the scope of employment at the time the tort occurred.
	5. This issue is a factual one that usually must be decided by a jury.
Expanding vicarious liability	1. A person who is not paid may be a gratuitous "servant" and may make the "master" liable.
	2. The family car doctrine is an expansion of vicarious liability beyond the traditional master-servant relationship.
Exceptions to master's liability	1. Typically a servant is outside the scope of employment if the servant is on a frolic or detour.

2. A frolic exists when a servant pursues his personal interests instead of the master's business.

3. A detour may occur when a servant fails to follow the master's instructions.

4. Intentional or willful torts are less likely to occur within the servant's scope of employment than are torts caused by negligence. Thus masters generally are not liable for harm intentionally caused by servants.

INDEPENDENT CONTRACTORS' TORTS

General rule

1. The doctrine of *respondeat superior* and the concept of vicarious liability are not applicable to torts caused by independent contractors.

2. Therefore, proprietors generally are not personally liable to third parties who are injured by independent contractors.

Exceptions

Proprietors are liable if:

1. The work of the independent contractor is inherently dangerous.

2. The independent contractor's work is illegal.

3. The work to be done by the independent contractor is nondelegable.

4. The proprietor ratifies the independent contractor's tort.

5. The independent contractor is negligently selected by the proprietor.

TORT LIABILITY OF EMPLOYERS

Worker's compensation laws

1. State statutes passed to ensure that injured employees do not bear the loss caused by the injury.

2. Because employees no longer have to sue, employers no longer are protected by common-law defenses of contributory negligence, assumption of risk, and fellow-servant rule.

	3. Employees' benefits include payment of medical bills, loss of income, and rehabilitation income for disabilities suffered.
	4. Employees must prove that their injuries, illnesses, or deaths arose out of and in the course of employment.
Federal legislation	1. The Federal Employers' Liability Act and the Jones Act protect injured railroad and maritime employees, respectively.
	2. The Occupational Safety and Health Act requires employers to furnish every employee a place of employment free from safety and health hazards.
Third party's liability	Third parties who interfere with the employer-employee relationship may become liable for damages to either the employer or the employee or both.

DISCRIMINATION IN EMPLOYMENT

Equal employment opportunity	1. The federal legislation governing this area is the Civil Rights Act of 1964 and the Equal Employment Opportunity amendments of 1972.
	2. These laws prohibit discrimination in the recruiting, hiring, promoting, and firing of employees based on race, color, national origin, religion, and sex.
	3. The Age Discrimination in Employment Act protects workers in the age range of 40 to 70 years old.
	4. The Rehabilitation Act of 1973 prohibits discrimination within the executive branch of the federal government on the basis of mental or physical handicaps of otherwise qualified persons.
	5. This area of preventing discrimination in order to ensure equal employment opportunities has created affirmative action programs and resulting controversy.

CASES

Mercury Motor Express, Inc. v. Smith
393 So.2d 545 (Fla. 1981)

ALDERMAN, J. . . . Richard Welch, an employee of the petitioner, Mercury Motors Express, while driving a tractor-trailer for his employer, lost control of the vehicle, drove off the road, and hit David J. Faircloth, Jr., causing his death. Respondent, the personal representative of the decedent's estate and the plaintiff in the trial court, alleged that Welch, "while acting in the scope of his employment with the Defendant, MERCURY MOTORS EXPRESS, INC.," was "driving and operating the said vehicle while under the influence of alcohol to the extent that his ability to drive was impaired and did so in a reckless and negligent manner and at an excessive rate of speed, with a willful and wanton disregard for the life and safety of others. . . ." Mercury Motors does not dispute these factual allegations, and for the purpose of our review, we accept them as true. When the case was tried, the jury awarded the plaintiff $400,000 compensatory and $250,000 punitive damages. Mercury Motors paid the compensatory damage award and appealed only the punitive damage judgment. In a brief opinion, the district court said that the legal issue presented "is whether a corporate employer and Interstate Commerce Commission permit holder can be liable in punitive damages for the willful and wanton misconduct of its employee while acting within the scope of his employment and operating a tractor and trailer leased by the corporate employer and operated under its permit." The district court, concluding that "a jury may assess punitive damages against a corporate employer when its employee, acting within the scope of his employment, has been guilty of willful and wanton misconduct, such as in this case," affirmed the award of punitive damages. We quash the decision of the district court and hold that, in the absence of some fault on the part of the corporate employer, it is not punitively liable for the willful and wanton misconduct of its employees.

We begin our analysis of this case by affirming the long-established Florida rule that "the liability of a corporate master for punitive or exemplary damages for wanton or malicious torts committed by an agent or servant is no different from the liability of an individual master under the same circumstances." The fact that the employer in this case is a corporation rather than a natural person is not legally significant. . . .

Plaintiff effectually argues that under the doctrine of respondeat superior, an employer without fault on his part will always be vicariously liable for punitive damages for the willful and wanton misconduct committed by his employees within the scope of their employment. We reject this argument. . . .

We conclude that the principles of law which should be applied in this and in other similar respondeat superior cases are as follows: (1) An employer is vicariously liable for *compensatory* damages resulting from the negligent acts of employees committed within the scope of their employment even if the employer is without fault. This is based upon the long-recognized public policy that victims injured by the negligence of employees acting within the scope of their employment should be compensated even though it means placing vicarious liability on an innocent employer. (2) Punitive damages, however, go beyond the actual damages suffered by an injured party and are imposed only as a punishment of the defendant and as a deterrent to others. (3) Before an employer may be held vicariously liable for punitive damages under the doctrine of respondeat superior, there must be some fault on his part. (4) Although the misconduct of the employee, upon which the vicarious liability of the employer for punitive damages is based, must be willful and wanton, it is not necessary that the fault of the employer, independent of his employee's conduct, also be willful and wanton. It is sufficient that the plaintiff allege and prove some fault on the part of the employer which foreseeably contributed to the plaintiff's injury to make him vicariously liable for punitive damages.

Applying these principles, we hold that there

is no basis for the punitive damage award against the defendant employer. The plaintiff alleges no fault on the part of the employer and relies entirely upon the master-servant relationship to make the employer vicariously liable for punitive damages. The district court should have reversed the punitive damage judgment.

Reversed and remanded.

Condict v. Condict
664 P.2d 131 (Wyom. 1983)

ROSE, J. . . . Appellant Wynn Condict is the nephew of appellee Alden Condict who, with his brother, Winthrop Condict, operates a ranch in Carbon County, Wyoming. . . .

Appellant's claim arises from an incident in which he was involved with Ted Jenkins, an employee of Alden Condict. There is an area on the Condict ranch where gas pumps are located close to a bridge, and, because of its weakened condition, this bridge had been designated for use by lighter-weight vehicles only. On the morning in question, Wynn Condict was at the gas pumps assigning his father's employees their various tasks for the day. At the same time, Ted Jenkins and another employee of Alden Condict were gassing two vehicles, one of which was a heavy army-surplus six-by-six truck utilized in haying operations. An altercation occurred between Jenkins and Wynn Condict when Jenkins made known his intent to drive the large army truck over the bridge, it being Wynn Condict's position that this was one of the heavy vehicles for which the bridge was not to be used. Wynn Condict became alarmed because his new pickup truck was blocking the bridge and he proceeded to back his pickup across the bridge. In the meantime, Jenkins had commandeered the army-surplus vehicle, crashed it through a gate and headed toward Wynn's vehicle. Somewhere near the end of the bridge or just off the other side, Jenkins rammed the pickup with the six-by-six truck.

As a result of this impact, appellant claims that he suffered severe injury to his back, which resulted in his bringing a personal-injury action against Alden Condict, as Jenkins' employer, in which he sought both compensatory and punitive damages.

In directing a verdict for Alden Condict, the trial judge held that plaintiff had failed to prove that Jenkins was acting in the scope of his employment at the time of the incident. In reaching this decision, the judge commented:

. . . What I'm saying is simply this: that if—you say that Ted Jenkins was engaged in the scope of his employment, and in going to the hayfields, then I think that it is certainly demonstrated by this evidence that he had to deviate from that scope when he took control of the six by six and did something that the evidence indicates to me Alden Condict didn't even know about at that time, much less thereby be presented with the opportunity to say, "fine, do it. Go ahead. I recognize that you have done this and I condone your actions." And that simply hasn't been demonstrated through the evidence at all. . . .

Appellant argues that, by holding that the evidence must show that Alden Condict specifically authorized Ted Jenkins to commit the alleged tortious act, the trial judge erroneously applied the rules announced by this court in *Sage Club v. Hunt*, Wyo. 638 P.2d 161 (1981). He also urges that the evidence introduced at trial was sufficient to make out a prima facie case under that decision. We agree with the appellant's contentions. . . .

Stated succinctly, in *Sage Club v. Hunt*, we embraced a rule of law which holds an employer liable for the intentional torts of his employee committed while the employee is acting, at least in part, in furtherance of the employer's interests. We also noted in that case that an important factor in deciding the principal's liability for his agent's intentional torts is whether the "use of force is not unexpectable by the master." However, in order for a jury to assess liability, the plaintiff need not prove that the employer foresaw the precise act or exact manner of injury as long as the general type of conduct may have been reasonably expected.

Applying these rules to this litigation, we are led to the conclusion that the trial judge erroneously found that appellant Condict had failed to discharge his burden of proof. According to *Sage Club v. Hunt*, the appellant was obliged to establish that a question of fact existed as to whether Jenkins was acting within the scope of his employment at the time of the incident in question. It was not his obligation to produce evidence, either direct or circumstantial, to the effect that Alden Condict authorized Jenkins to ram the six-by-six truck into Wynn Condict's vehicle. Appellant's burden was to show that when Jenkins intentionally rammed the pickup he, Jenkins, was then engaged, at least in part, in furthering Alden Condict's interests and that Jenkins' acts were not outside the realm of foreseeability. Appellant, under *Sage Club v. Hunt*, was not required to show Alden's authorization and consent in the specific tortious activity, or that Jenkins' specific conduct was foreseeable, but only that Jenkins committed the tort while at least

partially engaged in a task for which he was employed and with respect to which Alden Condict could foresee that force might be used by Jenkins. According to the record, which shows that Jenkins was on his way to perform haying operations when the incident occurred, we find that appellant established a fact issue for the jury as to scope of employment and Alden Condict's liability for the intentional acts of Jenkins. Under applicable rules, it was error for the trial court to take the case from the jury.

Reversed and remanded.

Pontiacs v. K.M.S. Investments
331 N.W.2d 907 (Minn. 1983)

K.M.S. Investments, owners of a large apartment complex, rented an apartment to Jorge and Stephanie Pontiac in May, 1978. In August, K.M.S. hired Dennis Graffice as the complex' resident manager. Graffice was hired despite having a criminal record which indicated he had been convicted of four felonies in two different states. K.M.S. made no attempt to conduct a first-hand investigation of Graffice's background. They relied solely on the completed application and a personal interview. In September, 1978, while Jorge was out of town, Stephanie Pontiac was raped at knife point by a person she recognized as Dennis Graffice. He had entered the Pontiacs' apartment with his passkey. After Graffice was convicted of this sexual assault, the Pontiacs sued K.M.S. for damages.

KELLEY, J. . . . At the outset, we must determine whether, in a tort action, a person may recover from an employer if the person was injured by a negligently hired employee. We have recognized that a person injured by a negligently retained employee may recover damages from the employer. The origin of the doctrine making an employer liable for negligent hiring, as well as negligent retention, arose out of the common law fellow-servant law which imposed a duty on employers to select employees who would not endanger fellow employees by their presence on the job. The concept of direct employer liability arising as a result of negligent hiring was later expanded to include a duty to "exercise reasonable care for the safety of members of the general public" so today it is

recognized as the rule in the majority of the jurisdictions. . . .

Liability is predicated on the negligence of an employer in placing a person with known propensities, or propensities which should have been discovered by reasonable investigation, in an employment position in which, because of the circumstances of the employment, it should have been foreseeable that the hired individual posed a threat of injury to others.

The connection between the employment relationship and the plaintiff has been found sufficient by courts of other jurisdictions to impose upon a landlord a duty to use reasonable care in the hiring of an employee who may pose a threat of injury to tenants. The rationale employed in those cases, as well as in similar cases involving deliverymen or others who gain access to a dwelling by virtue of their employment, is that since plaintiff comes in contact with the employee as the direct result of the employment, and since the employer receives some benefit, even if only a potential or indirect benefit, by the contact between the plaintiff and the employee, there exists a duty on the employer to exercise reasonable care for the protection of the dwelling occupant to retain in such employment only those who, so far as can be reasonably ascertained, pose no threat to such occupant.

We can ascertain no substantial difference in imposing a duty on an employer to use reasonable care in the initial hiring from his duty to use that care in the retention of an employee. We therefore align ourselves with the majority of those jurisdictions which recognize a claim by an injured third party for negligent hiring . . . and hold that an employer has the duty to exercise reasonable care in view of all the circumstances in hiring individuals who, because of the employment, may pose a threat of injury to members of the public. Here, the respondent Stephanie Pontiac met Graffice as a direct result of his employment as apartment manager, and appellants received a benefit from Graffice's employment in having a caretaker for upkeep of the property and to aid tenants with complaints of property malfunction. Therefore, we hold that these appellants owed to the tenants of the Driftwood Apartments, including these respondents, the duty of exercising reasonable care in hiring a resident manager.

We next address the question of whether there was sufficient evidence to support the jury's verdict that appellants had breached their duty. . . . This is generally a jury question. Here, the jury could have found that appellants made slight effort to determine whether it was safe to hire Graffice and give him access into the living quarters of the tenants of the apartments. . . .

Affirmed.

Tavares v. A.C. & S. Inc.
462 A.2d 977 (R.I. 1983)

Frank Tavares began his employment career as an insulation worker in 1953. During his career, he worked for many different companies, always as an insulation worker. During 1977, Tavares worked for A.C. & S., Inc. In January, 1978, Tavares became ill. After consulting several doctors, it was determined that Tavares suffered from pulmonary asbestosis, which was caused by his exposure to asbestos dust found in insulation. Tavares filed for workers' compensation benefits from A.C. & S. Inc. The company argued it was not liable since Tavares could not prove his disease was caused during his employment with the company during 1977. The Workers' Compensation Commission awarded benefits, and the company appealed.

BEVILACQUA, J. . . . The Legislature enacted [the Rhode Island Workers' Compensation Law] in order to protect the worker who was exposed to conditions that resulted in disability because of an occupational disease. Evidently the Legislature recognized that an occupational disease is set apart from accidental injuries in that it is not unexpected—because it is incident to a particular employment—and it is gradual in development.

[The law] defines the term "occupational disease" as "a disease which is due to causes and conditions which are characteristic of and peculiar to a particular trade, occupation, process or employment." . . . Moreover, a disabled employee is entitled to compensation if the occupational disease is due to the nature of the employment and was contracted within that employment. Furthermore, when a worker has contracted an occupational disease from being exposed to a harmful substance over a period of years and in the course of successive employment, the employer who last exposed the worker to the harmful substance is liable to pay the entire compensation.

An occupational disease, unlike an accidental-injury disability, is commonly characterized by a long history of injurious exposure without actual disability. Because the date of actual contraction is difficult or not susceptible of positive determination, most state statutes specify that the date of disability is controlling, rather than the actual time of contraction, for fixing the rights and liabilities of the employee and employer. We therefore are of the opinion that in cases of this type involving disability because of occupational diseases incurred while working for multiple employers, "the last employer is liable either if (a) the employee's work with the last employer caused an aggravation of the prior condition or (b) the last employment (no matter how brief) was of the same nature and type in which the disease was first contracted, regardless of whether the last employment aggravated the prior condition." . . . After examining the record, it is our opinion that the employee has met his burden. The facts are not in dispute. The evidence sufficiently establishes that the employee was exposed to asbestos dust for a period of time for successive employers. Moreover, the evidence indicates that he worked for his last employer for over a year and that during this time he was exposed to asbestos. The medical testimony was uncontradicted and confirmed the fact that the employee's disability resulted from a history of exposure to asbestos and that the disease manifested itself during the employee's employment with his last employer. . . .

Affirmed.

Chung v. Animal Clinic, Inc.
636 P.2d 721 (Haw. 1981)

LUM, J. This is an appeal brought by appellants Animal Clinic, Inc., and its insurance company from a decision of the Labor and Industrial Relations Appeals Board (Board) granting appellee Dr. Nam Y. Chung compensation benefits under Hawaii's Workers' Compensation Law.

On December 23, 1974, Dr. Chung suffered a heart attack after office hours while jogging around the Kalani High School track. At the time of his heart attack, Dr. Chung was employed as the president of Animal Clinic, Inc. He was also the sole director and sole stockholder of the corporation.

Appellants' first argument is that Dr. Chung was not an "employee" of Animal Clinic, Inc. . . . at the time he suffered his heart attack.

The essential prerequisite for coverage under Hawaii's Workers' Compensation Law is the existence of an employer-employee relationship. An "employee" is "any individual in the employment of another person" except where such employment is solely for personal, family, or household purposes. . . . The fact that Dr. Chung was the sole director, sole stockholder and president of the corporation violates no requirements of our statutory law. . . . The corporate entity was valid and could properly enter into a contractual relationship with Dr. Chung as an employee. We conclude that Dr. Chung was an employee of Animal Clinic, Inc., on the date of his heart attack.

Appellants' second argument is that the Board applied an improper legal standard in determining whether Dr. Chung's heart attack arose out of and in the course of his employment with Animal Clinic, Inc. In its finding that Dr. Chung's heart attack was a covered injury, the Board, interpreting the statutory language, defined the test for whether an injury is covered as whether there was "a sufficient work connection to bring the accident within the Law. . . ." Appellants contend that the correct test consists of two steps in which the elements "arising out of" and "in the course of" employment must both be separately established.

Courts have developed two approaches for determining whether injuries arise out of and in the course of employment. Under the traditional view, to which this court adhered in its early workers' compensation decisions, a claimant is required to establish that his injury arose both "out of" and "in the course of" his employment. The words "out of"

are deemed to signify a causal connection between the injury and the claimant's employment, while the words "in the course of" point to the injury's proximity in time, place and circumstances to the employment. Both components of the statutory formula must be separately established before compensation will be awarded.

. . . [H]owever, this court moved towards adoption of the liberal, unitary concept of work-connection for interpreting the statutory requirement. The work-connection approach rejects the necessity of establishing temporal, spatial, and circumstantial proximity between the injury and employment. Instead, focusing on the injury's origin rather than the time and place of its manifestation, the work-connection approach simply requires the finding of a casual connection between the injury and any incidents or conditions of employment.

We now conclude that the unitary work-connection approach is the correct one for interpreting and applying [Hawaii's workers' compensation law] in a way which fairly carries out the purposes of Hawaii's workers' compensation laws. As we have previously observed, "the legislature has decided that work injuries are among the costs of production which industry is required to bear. . . ." Inequity would easily result from a rule which denied compensation for injuries having their inception at work but not becoming manifest until the employee had left the employer's premises. We therefore hold that the Board properly utilized the work-connection test in deciding whether Dr. Chung's heart attack arose out of and in the course of his employment.

Applying this standard to the present case, we cannot conclude that the Board erred in deciding that Dr. Chung's heart attack was work-connected. The testimony of the two doctors directly conflicted on the issue of the heart attack's causal connection to Dr. Chung's employment activity. In such cases, . . . the legislature has decided that the conflict should be resolved in the claimant's favor. This is so especially in view of the special weight accorded the statutory presumption in the cases of heart disease, where the precise causes of the disease are particularly difficult to ascertain. . . .

We are satisfied that the Board's conclusion that Dr. Chung's heart attack was in fact causally related to his employment is supported by the applicable law and the record.

Affirmed.

Hangar One, Inc. v. Davis Associates, Inc.
431 A.2d 792 (N.H. 1981)

GRIMES, J. This is an action to recover a broker's commission on the sale of a helicopter. The plaintiff brought suit against the seller, Davis Associates, Inc. (Davis Associates), and its president, James L. Davis (Davis). . . . The Trial Court ruled that both Davis and Davis Associates were liable for the plaintiff's commission in the amount of $1,500. . . . Davis appealed that portion of the ruling holding him personally liable. . . .

The plaintiff is an aircraft broker. In December 1978, the plaintiff contracted with Davis to sell a helicopter owned by Davis Associates. It was the parties' understanding that the plaintiff would receive a ten per cent commission if it produced a buyer for the aircraft at a price acceptable to the seller. The helicopter was transported to the plaintiff's facilities in Laconia, and the plaintiff began seeking prospective purchasers in January 1979.

In June 1979, the plaintiff produced a buyer, John Kilburn, who offered to purchase the aircraft, but no sale was consummated while the brokerage agreement was in effect. After the brokerage agreement expired, Davis made arrangements to pick up the helicopter. The plaintiff was under the impression that Davis Associates had rejected the offer made by Kilburn and was going to attempt to sell the helicopter without the assistance of a broker. On July 28, 1979, Davis arrived at the plaintiff's business office, paid the plaintiff the cost of insuring the helicopter during the term of the brokerage agreement and obtained a release from the plaintiff of "all obligations." The trial court found that this release "did not release liability for commissions on the sale of the aircraft but only such liability as might exist with respect to storage fees, insurance . . . [and] maintenance." Thereafter, on the same day, Davis sold the helicopter to Kilburn for $15,000, the price at which Kilburn, through the plaintiff, had previously offered to buy the helicopter. . . .

The principal issue on appeal is whether the plaintiff is entitled to recover a commission on the sale of the helicopter from . . . the defendants.

It is well established that "[a] broker earns a commission when he is the effective cause of the sale of property which he is authorized to sell. . . . It is not necessary that the broker participate in the final negotiations leading to the sale."

The trial court found that the "plaintiff produced a buyer ready, willing and able to purchase defendant's helicopter at the price at which defendant sold the helicopter to the same buyer immediately following [the] expiration of plaintiff's exclusive sales contract. . . ." In these circumstances, the plaintiff clearly has a right to its commission on the sale of the helicopter.

Defendant Davis concedes that Davis Associates, as the actual owner and seller of the aircraft, is liable to the plaintiff for its commission. Davis contends, however, that he cannot be held personally liable for the corporation's debt. . . .

A broker may be entitled to recover damages from one who wrongfully prevents the broker's obtaining a commission, providing all essential elements of an actionable wrong exist. The actionable wrong on which Davis' liability is based is interference with contractual relations. . . .

Our review of the record compels us to conclude that Davis contrived to sell the helicopter to enable Davis Associates to avoid having to pay the plaintiff a commission on the sale. One who intentionally and improperly interferes with the performance of a contract . . . between another and a third person by inducing or otherwise causing the third person not to perform the contract, is subject to liability to the other for the pecuniary loss resulting to the other from the failure of the third person to perform the contract. Because Davis was responsible for the failure of Davis Associates to fulfill its contractual obligations to pay the plaintiff the commission it had earned by producing the buyer to whom Davis Associates sold the helicopter, Davis is liable to the plaintiff for the amount of that commission. . . .

Affirmed.

REVIEW QUESTIONS

1. Identify the terms in column A by matching each with the appropriate statement in column B.

A		B
1. Respondeat superior	a.	Example of when a proprietor becomes liable for torts of an independent contractor.
2. Family car doctrine	b.	Burden of proof that an employee must meet in order to recover under workers' compensation laws.
3. Frolic	c.	Type of tort for which a third party is liable for money damages.
4. Inherently dangerous work	d.	An expansion of vicarious liability which makes the owner of a vehicle liable for the torts of a family member.
5. Workers' compensation	e.	Exists when a servant pursues his personal interests instead of the master's business.
6. Arising out of and in the course of employment	f.	State statutes passed to ensure that injured employees receive benefits from employers.
7. Interference with economic relationships	g.	Controversial attempt to ensure that past employment discrimination is overcome.
8. Affirmative action programs	h.	Doctrine that allows injured persons to recover from the party with the "deeper pocket."

2. Which party, the master or the servant, has the ultimate liability for torts that are the servant's rather than the master's fault? How would your answer change if the tort by a servant was caused by the master's improper instructions?

3. Steve was employed by Greta as a trainee photographer. Late one night after photographing a wedding, Steve was returning the camera equipment to the studio (he was not required to return the equipment that night) when his auto collided with Tim's auto, and Tim was killed. Tim's estate sues Greta and Steve. What should be the result? Why?

4. Overton was shot in a barbershop by Henderson. Henderson apparently was upset by a letter sent by Overton to Cole. Overton claimed Cole owed him money for work done for Cole's hotel. Henderson was a desk clerk for the hotel and was also Cole's brother. Overton claimed that Cole was liable for the assault upon the principle of *respondeat superior,* since Cole employed Henderson. Is an employer liable for an assault by his employee that takes place off the premises? Explain.

5. Stanfield brought this action for damages arising out of an accident in which Roy's truck collided with an automobile in which Stanfield was a passenger. Roy was returning from a trip where he had performed several errands for his parents, who owned and operated several businesses. Did the accident occur while Roy was within the scope of employment, so as to place liability on Roy's parents under the doctrine of *respondeat superior?* Why or why not?

6. Anthony was an employee of the Trojan Fireworks Company. On December 21, Trojan held a Christmas party at its factory from noon until 4:00 P.M. The employees were not required to perform

their regular duties that afternoon. Instead they were encouraged to attend the party and to enjoy the alcoholic beverages provided. Anthony attended the party and drank heavily. He then attempted to drive home. Anthony was involved in a wreck that killed James Harris and injured two others. Suits were filed against Trojan asserting that the company was liable for Anthony's actions, since he was within the scope of employment. Is the company liable? Explain.

7. White, an employee of Inter-City Auto Freight, Inc., was driving a large tractor-trailer truck. In attempting to pass Mr. Kuehn, a motorist, White swerved his truck toward Kuehn. After Kuehn had moved to the next lane, he stepped on the gas, caught up with the truck, and motioned with his fist for White to pull over. White again forced Kuehn into another lane. After Kuehn regained control of his car, both parties stopped on the highway's shoulder. White got out of his cab carrying a two-foot-long metal pipe. As he approached Kuehn, White swung the pipe. It grazed the side of Kuehn's face and knocked Kuehn's glasses to the ground. As Kuehn bent over to pick up his glasses, White hit him two more times. Prior to this incident, White's record as a driver had been very good. Kuehn sued both White and his employer, Inter-City. Should Inter-City be liable for Kuehn's injuries? Why?

8. Dr. Keldene was employed at a regular salary by the QRS shipping lines to serve aboard ship and treat passengers. Keldene treated Barry, a passenger, who died as a result of Keldene's negligence. May Barry's heirs recover from QRS? Explain.

9. While a guest at the Marshview Inn, Tom was severely beaten by Seth, a night watchman for the inn. Tom sued the inn and Seth, as an agent for the inn. Because Marshview Inn was not the proper company name, Tom's suit against the inn was dismissed. Tom's suit against Seth was dismissed since Seth was not technically an agent for the inn. (He was an agent for the inn's corporate owner.) Tom appealed the dismissal of his claim against Seth. What is the basis for this appeal? Should Tom be allowed to continue his claim against Seth? Why or why not?

10. Joiner employed an independent contractor to spray pesticide on his crops. During the application process, the spray damaged a nearby fishing lake owned by Boroughs. When Boroughs sued, the trial court held that Joiner was not liable as a matter of law, since the injury was inflicted by an independent contractor. Boroughs contends that Joiner is liable because the work done was inherently or intrinsically dangerous. On appeal, does Boroughs' argument have merit? Why or why not?

11. Everson, a Lockheed employee, was assigned to work out of town for 1 week. After dinner following the third day of this job, Everson and three friends decided to "go out on the town." They drove to a bar and dance hall where they had some drinks, listened to the music, and talked about the work to be done. About 12:30 A.M., Everson left to drive back to the motel. On the way, he failed to round a curve and died as a result of the accident. Can Everson's spouse collect workers' compensation benefits? Explain.

12. John H. Roberts, an engineer for Southern Railway Company, was injured when the train he was operating derailed. The track slopes downhill at that point and curves sharply. A seven-foot section of broken rail was found at the site of the accident. Whether the rail was cause or effect of the accident was an issue at trial. Southern Railway was found to be negligent by the jury, and Roberts was awarded $100,000. Will a jury's verdict in a FELA case be overturned on appeal where there is some evidence to support it? Why or why not?

13. Describe the three situations in which a third party may be liable for interfering with the employer-employee relationship.

14. Artie, the owner of a lounge, hired women bartenders, contrary to a state statute that prohibited women from tending bar except when the woman was the holder of a liquor license. The state revoked Artie's liquor license and he brought suit, claiming that the state statute violated the 1964 Civil Rights Act. In defense, the state contended that a bartender must be physically strong enough to protect himself against inebriated customers and to maintain order in the bar and that women as a class are unable to do so. Is the state law invalid? Why or why not?

17 TERMINATION OF THE AGENCY RELATIONSHIP

Two issues are basic to termination of an agency relationship. First, what acts or facts are sufficient to terminate the authority of the agent insofar as the immediate parties are concerned? Second, what is required to terminate the agent's authority insofar as third parties are concerned? The latter question recognizes that an agent may continue to have the *power* to bind the principal, but not the *right* to do so. The first part (sections 1 through 4) of this chapter is concerned with how an agency relationship is terminated. Sections 5 through 12 examine exceptions to the general rules on termination. The last part of this chapter answers how termination may affect the third parties who have dealt with an agent. In other words, the answer to the first question asked above is the subject matter of the bulk of this chapter. The second question is answered in sections 13 and 14.

With respect to the actual termination of the relationship between a principal and an agent, two methods are crucial. The next section contains information on how an agency can be terminated by operation of law. The other method—termination by the acts of the principal or agent—is discussed later.

1. Termination by Operation of Law

The occurrence of certain events is viewed as automatically terminating the agency. As a legal principle, any one of four happenings may end the principal-agent relationship. These events are as follows: (1) the death of either party, (2) the insanity of either party, (3) the bankruptcy of either party under specific conditions, and (4) the destruction or illegality of the agency's subject matter.

The death of an individual acting as a principal or agent immediately terminates the agency[1] even if the other party is unaware of the death. Once the time of death is established, there should not be any controversy about an agency ceasing to exist. Insanity of a party does not always provide such a distinctive time of termination. For example, if the principal has not been adjudged insane publicly, courts have held that an agent's contracts are binding on the principal unless the third party was aware of the principal's mental illness. This ruling has occurred especially when the contract has been beneficial to the insane principal's estate.

The timing of the termination of an agency due to bankruptcy also is not always clear. Bankruptcy has the effect of termination only when it affects the subject matter of the agency. Suppose that a business organization, which is either a principal or an agent, files for the court's protection via a chapter 11 petition. Since the court's order of relief will allow this organization to continue its business activity, its agency relationships will not be terminated. However, if the debtor's petition sought chapter 7 liquidation, the organization's bankruptcy would terminate all its agencies. This result occurs because the organization will cease to exist as a viable principal. When a bankruptcy case will act to terminate an agency, its impact happens at the time the court grants an order of relief. At that time, a trustee typically is appointed to hold the debtor's assets. (See chapter 37 on bankruptcy.)

Events that destroy the agency's subject matter may be things other than bankruptcy. For example, if the purpose of the agency relationship becomes illegal or impossible to perform, termination occurs automatically. Whereas it may be unlikely for the purpose of most business relationships to become illegal, the purpose may become impossible to perform whenever the agency's subject matter is destroyed. Suppose that an owner of real estate hires a real estate agent to find a ready, willing and able buyer for his four-bedroom, two-bathroom house. If that house is destroyed by fire or wind or other causes, the agent's appointment would be terminated, since the house could not now be sold in its former condition.

TERMINATION BY PARTIES' ACTIONS

2. Mutual Agreement

Termination of an agency may occur due to the terms of the principal-agent agreement. For example, an agency may be created to continue for a definite period of time. If so, it ceases, by virtue of the terms of the agreement, at the expiration of the stipulated period. If the parties consent to the continuation of the relationship beyond the period, the courts imply the formation of a new contract of employment. The new agreement contains the same terms as the old one and continues for a like period of time, except that no implied contract can run longer than 1 year because of the statute of frauds.

Another example is an agency created to accomplish a certain purpose, which ends automatically with the completion of the task assigned. Furthermore, when it is possible for one of several agents to perform the task, such as selling

---

[1] Sturgill v. Virginia Citizens Bank, p. 376.

certain real estate, it is held that performance by the first party terminates the authority of the other agents without notice of termination being required.

An agency may always be terminated by the mutual agreement of the principal and agent. Even if their original agreement does not provide for a time period of duration, the parties may agree to cancel their relationship. Since the agency is, in essence, based on a consensual agreement, the principal and agent can agree to end their association.

3. Unilateral Action

In addition to the principal and agent's mutually agreeing to end their relationship, the law generally allows either one of these parties to act independently in terminating an agency unilaterally. As a general rule, either party to an agency agreement has full *power* to terminate the agreement whenever he desires, even though he possesses no *right* to do so. For example, if the Paulson Company agreed to employ Alicia for 1 year, an agency for a definite stated period has been created. That is, these parties have agreed to be principal and agent, respectively, for a 1-year period. Despite this agreement, the courts are hesitant to force either an employer or employee to remain in an unhappy situation. Therefore, these parties generally do have the power to terminate this employment contract. A premature breach of the agreement is considered to be a wrongful termination, and the breaching party becomes liable for damages suffered by the other party. Of course, if an agent is discharged for cause, such as for failing to follow instructions, he may not recover damages from the employer.

4. Traditional Notions of Termination at Will

Many, and perhaps most, agency contracts do not provide for the duration of the agreement. When an agency is to last for an unspecified or indefinite time period, the relationship may be terminated at the will of either the principal or the agent. There is some controversy about whether a contract for permanent employment is terminable at the employer's will. Many courts have followed the traditional view that a promise for permanent employment, not supported by any consideration other than the performance of duties and payment of wages, is a contract for an indefinite period and terminable at the will of either party at any time. However, there is an opposing view that requires the employer to prove good cause or reason to dismiss an employee who has been promised permanent employment.[2]

As a general rule, when an agency agreement is terminable at the will of either party, both principal and agent have the legal *right* as well as the power to terminate the relationship. When a party has the right to do so, a termination is not a breach of contract, and no liability is incurred. In other words, both principal and agent have had the ability to end an agency at any time for any reason, as long as the relationship was not to last for a definite time. For a number

---

[2] Eales v. Tanana Valley Medical-Surgical Group, Inc., p. 377.

of reasons, in recent years courts have established many exceptions to this "terminable at will" notion. The following sections (5 through 8) examine some of the more prominent exceptions.

**PUBLIC POLICY
EXCEPTIONS TO
TERMINATION
AT WILL**

5. Introduction

The vast majority of employees are not covered by a collective bargaining agreement, and they are not employed for a specified time. At first glance, these employees would seem to be terminable at the employer's will without any reason being given for the dismissal. However, there is growing acceptance of theories which require that an employee's discharge be supported by a reasonable basis. Courts throughout this country have ruled that an employment relationship cannot be terminated by the employer without that party's proving there is a justifiable reason for the discharge. The decisions usually state that employees must be protected as a matter of public policy. The theories used to support these exceptions to "termination at will" include (1) breach of an implied duty or agreement, (2) denial of a protected right, and (3) violation of a constitutional or statutory provision prohibiting discrimination.

6. Breach of an Implied Duty or Agreement

There has been a strong trend to imply upon an employer a duty to act in good faith. Inclusive in this responsibility is the commitment that all employees will be terminated only for good cause. In other words, termination of the agency at the whim of the employer is becoming less acceptable. Especially relevant to this exception are those employees who are given a handbook or similar information by the employer. Many of these handbooks contain a statement that the employee will be terminated only if cause is proved. The handbook's language reinforces the court's inclination to find that the employer is bound to an implied promise which makes the concept of termination at will inapplicable.[3]

Discharged employees have been successful in arguing that the employer's violation of this implied duty or promise to act in good faith is either a tort or a breach of a contract. Either theory, if accepted and applied, would allow the wronged employee to recover actual damages, such as accrued back pay. Courts that have used a tort theory in order to hold the employer liable are more likely to award the employee punitive damages in addition to compensatory damages.

7. Denial of Protected Rights

There are numerous examples of employees challenging their discharge on the grounds that the employers' actions were in retaliation for their exercise of protected rights. Employers in this situation have argued that the employment relationship is terminable at will at any time. To illustrate: Suppose Aaron is employed by the Pencil Manufacturing Company. While lifting heavy boxes, Aaron strains his back. He files a workers' compensation claim to recover his

---

[3] Weiner v. McGraw-Hill, Inc., p. 377.

medical costs and lost wages. A week later, Aaron is fired and no reason is given. What impact could this firing have on other employees filing compensation claims? It is obvious that the discharge of Aaron could inhibit the filing of other compensation claims. Indeed, this may be the desired result for the Pencil Manufacturing Company.

Because of this adverse impact of allowing employment agreements to be terminable at will, courts have created this second exception to the traditional notion of termination at will. Whenever an employee exercises a right protected by statute or common law, public policy protects that employee from being discharged without good cause. In addition to filing a workers' compensation claim, other protected rights have included (1) serving on a jury, (2) resisting sexual harassment, (3) refusing to give perjured testimony, (4) refusing to commit an illegal or unethical act, and (5) aiding in the investigation of another's wrongful actions. This last example has been called *whistleblowing.* Although the employer's justified firing of an employee is limited by this second public policy exception, the courts have not given absolute protection to all whistleblowers. Indeed, whether an employee who has reported a violation by the employer is protected from being terminated at will depends on the employee's position with the employer and the wrong committed.[4] The public policy to protect the employee must be weighed against the employer's expectation of loyalty from the employee. As a general rule, the less serious the employer's wrong is, the less the public needs to know of this wrong, and thus the protection given to the whistleblowing employee is diminished.

8. Discrimination

An employer may be required to justify discharging an employee if that employee claims that he or she is being discriminated against. As noted in chapter 16, many cities, almost every state, and the federal government have enacted statutes designed to prevent discrimination on the basis of race, color, religion, sex, national origin, age, and physical handicaps in the hiring, promoting, and paying of employees. In addition, these laws also prohibit discrimination on the bases stated when laying off or firing employees. These statutes serve collectively as a third exception to the traditional common-law concept that an employer may discharge an employee for no apparent reason. *Note:* A review of sections 17 through 22 of chapter 16 may be helpful in understanding the laws preventing discrimination.

9. Rights of Wronged Employees

The employee whose employment has been wrongfully cut short is entitled to recover compensation for work done before his dismissal and an additional sum for damages. Most states permit him to bring an action either immediately following the breach, in which event he recovers prospective damages, or after the period has expired, in which event he recovers the damages actually sustained. In

---

[4] Palmateer v. International Harvester Co., p. 378.

the latter case, as a general rule, he is compelled to deduct from the compensation called for in the agreement the amount that he has been able to earn during the interim.

Under such circumstances, a wrongfully discharged employee is under a duty to exercise reasonable diligence in finding other work of like character. Idleness is not encouraged by the law. Apparently, this rule does not require him to seek employment in a new locality or to accept work of a different kind or more menial character. The duty is to find work of like kind, provided it is available in the particular locality.[5] One way that damages for wrongful discharge may be mitigated is for the employer to rehire the employee. A discharged employee often seeks this remedy in addition to accrued back pay.

GENERAL EXCEPTIONS TO TERMINATION

10. Introduction

In addition to the public policy reasons for not making employment relationships terminable at will, there are two other exceptions to the general rules on how agency relationships are terminated. Whereas the principle of and exceptions to "termination at will" usually are related to employment situations, these general exceptions may be applicable to any principal-agent relationship. These two general exceptions are known as an agency coupled with either an interest or an obligation.

While reading the next two sections, keep in mind that agencies may be terminated by operation of law or by the parties' actions. Also keep asking why these general exceptions are necessary. That is, look for the answer to the question: What is so important about the agency discussed to justify making it not subject to termination?

11. Agency Coupled with an Interest

The first general exception to how and when an agency is terminated is the factual situation described as an agency *coupled with an interest.* This term describes the relationship that exists when the agent has an actual beneficial interest in the property that is the subject matter of the agency. A mortgage or a security agreement usually contains a provision naming the lender as the agent to sell the described property in the event of a default. Thus, this lender becomes an agent with a security interest in the subject matter of the principal-agent relationship. In other words, these documents do create an agency coupled with an interest. A more modern phrase used to describe this situation is a *power given as security.* Mortgages and security agreements usually give the lender the power to sell the collateral as security for repayment.

An agency coupled with an interest in property cannot be terminated unilaterally by the principal and is not terminated by events (such as death or bankruptcy of the principal) that otherwise terminate agencies by operation of law.[6] The net effect is that an agency coupled with an interest in property cannot be terminated without the consent of the agent.

---

[5] Vieira v. Robert's Hawaii Tours, Inc., p. 380.

[6] Matter of Estate of Head, p. 380.

12. Agency Coupled with an Obligation

An agency coupled with an interest in property must be distinguished from an agency *coupled with an obligation,* an agency created as a source of reimbursement to the agent. For example, an agent who is given the right to sell a certain automobile and to apply the proceeds on a claim against the principal is an agency coupled with an obligation. Such an agency is a hybrid between the usual agency and the agency coupled with an interest in property. The agency coupled with an obligation cannot unilaterally be terminated by the principal, but death or bankruptcy of the principal will terminate the agency by operation of law.

Under either type of agency, it should be clear that the interest in the subject matter must be greater than the mere expectation of profits to be realized or in the proceeds to be derived from the sale of the property. The interest must be in the property itself. A real estate broker is not an agent coupled with an interest, even though he expects a commission from the proceeds of the sale. Likewise a principal who has appointed an agent to sell certain goods on commission has the power to terminate the agency at any time, although such conduct might constitute a breach of the agreement.

13. Problems with Apparent Authority

ISSUES INVOLVING THIRD PARTIES

As this chapter has explained to this point, issues involving the termination of agencies concern both principal and agent. Indeed, subject to some exceptions, termination of an agency occurs by operation of law or by the actions of the principal or agent. Whereas these parties, by the nature of the relationship, will learn of the termination, the third parties who know of the agency may not be aware that a particular relationship is terminated. Whenever a third party has been induced by the principal to believe an agency exists, there is an opportunity for the principal to become bound to the third party due to apparent authority. Recall that the existence of apparent or ostensible authority was discussed in chapter 15.

In order to prevent the existence of apparent authority, the law requires the principal to give notice of termination to all third parties who have learned of the agency. How and when this required notice is to be given to third parties involves whether these parties had dealt personally with the agent or had just known of the agency's existence. Also important is whether the notice required be personally delivered or constructively given.

14. Notice Required

Notice of an agency's termination may be delivered in one of two ways. First, the notice may be personally or privately given. Examples of this type of notice include oral communication, face to face or over the phone. Sending a notice through the mail also is considered to be personally delivered when it is properly addressed and stamped. The second type of notice is public or constructive notice. Such notices include an announcement in a newspaper or other periodical. Notice can also be given constructively over radio, television, or other media of communication.

The type of notice of termination required to cut off an agent's apparent authority depends on the third party's relationship to the agent. When the agency is terminated by the acts of the principal or agent, the principal has the duty to give personal notice of the termination to those third parties who have dealt with the agent. When a third party has not previously dealt with the agent, the principal satisfies his duty to give notice by providing for public notice. If the principal fails to give the type of notice required, that principal is allowing the agent's apparent authority to exist.[7]

By fulfilling the duty to give notice of termination to third parties according to the factual situation and the legal requirements, the principal prevents apparent authority from existing. A third party who has not dealt with the agent may not learn of the notice given publicly. If that third party relies upon the continuation of the agency, he does so to his own detriment. In other words, the principal does not become liable to the third party in such a situation. If a third party who did deal with the agent has not received direct personal notice from the principal, but has learned indirectly of the agency's termination or of facts sufficient to place him on inquiry, he is no longer justified in dealing as if the agent represents the principal. In other words, a third party who has dealt with the agent cannot rely on apparent authority to bind the principal when that third party learns of the agency's termination via public rather than personal notice.

When the agency is terminated by action of law, such as death, insanity, or bankruptcy, no duty to notify third parties is placed upon the principal. Such matters receive publicity through newspapers, official records, or other means. Third parties normally become aware of the termination without the necessity for additional notification. If the death of the principal occurs before an agent contracts with a third party, the third party has no cause of action against either the agent or the estate of the principal unless the agent is acting for an undisclosed principal. In the latter case, since the agent makes the contract in his own name, he is liable to the third party. Otherwise, the third party is in as good a position to know of the death of the principal as is the agent.

A special problem exists in regard to notice in cases of special agents as distinguished from general agents. Ordinarily, notice is not required to revoke the authority of a special agent, since the agent possesses no continuing authority, and no one will be in the habit of dealing with him. Only if the principal has directly indicated that the agent has authority in a certain matter or at a certain time will notice be required, to prevent reliance on the principal's conduct by a party dealing with the agent. This is especially true if the agent is acting under a special power of attorney. Actual notice of termination is required in these cases.

---

[7]Moore v. Puget Sound Plywood, Inc., p. 381.

SUMMARY

Termination by operation of law	**1.** Death of either principal or agent ends the relationship.

2. Insanity of either principal or agent ends the relationship.

3. Bankruptcy of principal or agent may end the relationship if subject matter of relationship is affected.

4. Destruction or illegality of the agency's subject matter ends the relationship.

TERMINATION BY PARTIES' ACTIONS

Mutual agreement

1. Due to its contractual nature, an agency relationship can be terminated by the principal's and the agent's consent at any time.

2. Such consent may be reflected in an original agreement that is to last for a stated time period.

3. Consent to terminate also occurs if the purpose of relationship is accomplished or if the parties agree to end the relationship prior to the stated date of termination.

Unilateral action

1. In general, even if the agency is to last for a stated time, either principal or agent can end the relationship at any time.

2. The parties have the power of termination even if they lack the legal right.

3. If a party exercises the power of termination while lacking the right, that party is liable for money damages that the premature termination causes.

Termination at will

1. Traditionally, if there was no stated period of duration, both principal and agent had the right and power to terminate the relationship at their desire or will.

2. If the agency is terminable at will, the party terminating the relationship has no liability for damages.

PUBLIC POLICY EXCEPTIONS TO TERMINATION AT WILL

In general

1. There is a growing trend to require that employers support their decisions to fire employees on a reasonable basis.

	2. In essence, this trend is a move away from traditional notions of agency relationships being terminable at will when they are not to last for a stated period.
Breach of an implied duty or agreement	**1.** Courts have found that employers have an implied duty or have implicitly agreed not to fire an employee without good cause.
	2. Language taken from employees' handbooks have been used to justify these rulings.
	3. Employees who have been wrongfully fired may sue on the basis of a tort theory or a breach of contract theory.
	4. Punitive damages may be recovered under a tort theory, but not under a breach of contract theory.
Denial of protected rights	**1.** This is another reason employees have used to argue successfully that employers cannot unilaterally terminate the agency relationship.
	2. Protected rights include (1) filing a workers' compensation claim, (2) serving on a jury, (3) resisting sexual harassment, (4) refusing to give perjured statements, (5) refusing to commit an illegal or unethical act, and (6) engaging in a whistleblowing activity.
	3. In order to end the relationship, an employer should have a good reason to fire an employee, especially when an employee has been engaged in one of these protected activities.
	4. Employers are denied the use of claiming termination at will if a firing may be a possible method of illegally discriminating against an employee.

GENERAL EXCEPTIONS TO TERMINATION

Agency coupled with an interest	**1.** This relationship occurs when an agent has an actual beneficial interest in the property that is the subject matter of the agency.

	2. This also is described as a power given as security.
	3. This type of agency cannot be terminated by operation of law or by the unilateral acts of the principal.
Agency coupled with an obligation	1. A relationship created as a source of reimbursement to the agent.
	2. This relationship cannot be terminated by the unilateral acts of the principal. However, it can be terminated by operation of law.

ISSUES INVOLVING THIRD PARTIES

Cutting off apparent authority	1. Although an agent's actual authority is removed when the agency is terminated, apparent authority may still exist from the third parties' perspective.
	2. The principal is required to give notice of termination to third parties in order to cut off the agent's apparent authority.
Notice required	1. Notice of termination may be personally or publicly given.
	2. Personal notice includes that given face to face, over the phone, or by mail.
	3. Public notice is that given constructively through newspaper, radio, television, or other means of public communication.
	4. When termination occurs by the acts of the parties, personal notice must be given to the third parties who have dealt with the agent. Public notice is sufficient to cut off an agent's apparent authority when a prospective third party has not previously dealt with the agent.
	5. When termination occurs by operation of law, generally no notice needs to be given by the principal to third parties.

CASES

Sturgill v. Virginia Citizens Bank
291 S.E.2d 207 (Va. 1982)

PER CURIAM. In a motion for judgment, Rose Mary McCoy Sturgill, Administratrix (Administratrix), attempted to recover from Virginia Citizens Bank (Bank) the $13,748.58 balance of R. V. McCoy, Jr.'s bank account which the Bank, after McCoy's death, had transferred to a third party. In a bench trial, the trial court struck the Administratrix's evidence and granted summary judgment for the Bank.

On March 28, 1975, McCoy opened an individual checking account with the Bank. Eighteen months later, McCoy telephoned Jimmy Vanover, the Bank president, stating that he had remarried and desired to change his account to a joint account. On October 11, 1976, he and "Kaye Stanley McCoy" appeared at the Bank. [Actually these persons were not legally married.] They added "Kaye McCoy's" signature to the account card and requested new checks issued bearing both their names. . . .

On the reverse side of the account card, there is this notation: "Kaye McCoy's signature added Oct. 11, 1976." Vanover admitted that in another trial he testified that the Bank's practice was to note the word "joint" on joint account cards. This notation did not appear on McCoy's account card.

Vanover's office lies next door to the apartment complex where McCoy lived. On December 4, 1976, Vanover was working in his office when he noticed an ambulance. Upon investigation, he learned of McCoy's death: The Administratrix received McCoy's personal effects and discovered the account's existence. She testified that she called Vanover on December 6, 1976, between 9:00 and 9:05 A. M. and instructed him not to honor any checks drawn on McCoy's account. According to Vanover, the Administratrix did not call him until 10:30 A.M., after "Kaye McCoy" had cashed a check for $13,748.58. The Administratrix offered into evidence a cancelled check in the amount of $13,748.58, dated December 6, 1976, and drawn by "Kaye McCoy" on McCoy's account payable to the Bank to close the account. . . .

We first must determine what rights McCoy and Kaye Stanley had in the account. The account's signature card is a contract between a depositor and the Bank. . . . This account began as an individual account and remained unchanged. The account card, dated March 28, 1975, designates the account as an individual account in the name of R. V. McCoy, Jr., and lists only his social security number. The only change occurred 18 months later, when McCoy added "Kaye McCoy" as an authorized signature and the Bank made a notation on the card's reverse side of the transaction date. If McCoy intended to convert the individual account to a joint account, he failed. He merely added a new authorized signature, but did not create a new account or amend the existing account.

Our next inquiry is whether the Bank properly paid a check issued after McCoy's death and signed by "Kaye McCoy." McCoy added the "Kaye McCoy" signature for his personal convenience, thus establishing an agency relationship between himself and his girlfriend. Because death of a principal terminates an agent's authority, . . . "Kaye McCoy" had no authority to write checks on the account after December 4, 1976. Simply put, "a power ceases with the life of the person who gives it." Of course, a customer's death will not revoke a bank's authority to pay a check until the bank knows of the death and has had a reasonable opportunity to act on it. In this case, the Bank had immediate, actual knowledge of McCoy's death and a reasonable opportunity to act on this knowledge. It could have refused payment easily on the December 6 check.

We conclude that "Kaye McCoy" had the authority to sign checks on McCoy's account, that her authority ended at his death, and that the Bank knew of McCoy's death within a reasonable time to act on such knowledge. We reverse the judgment of the trial court and enter final judgment for the Administratrix in the amount of $13,748.58. . . .

Reversed.

Eales v. Tanana Valley Medical-Surgical Group, Inc.
663 P.2d 958 (Alas. 1983)

MATTHEWS, J. James Eales, who had been a physician's assistant at the Tanana Valley Medical-Surgical Group (Tanana Clinic) since 1974, was fired from his job on April 2, 1980. Eales sued the Tanana Clinic for wrongful discharge.

Tanana Clinic's motion for summary judgment was granted. For purposes of the motion, the Clinic conceded that Eales had been offered a job that would last until he reached retirement age and that he was fired without cause. In addition Eales filed an affidavit stating that he would not have given up his previous job if Tanana Clinic's offer had not been for permanent employment. The trial court held that the contract created was for an indefinite term, terminable at the will of either party. Eales has appealed.

An employee who has been hired for some definite period of time is not an employee at will. Here, Eales' normal retirement age as an employee of the clinic is capable of being determined. Since, for the purposes of the summary judgment motion, Tanana Clinic conceded that Eales' contract was for employment until retirement, the contract should be considered to be one for a definite period. As employment contracts for a definite period can be terminated early only for good cause a remand is necessary. . . .

Implicit in the foregoing conclusions is our rejection of those authorities which hold that employment contracts until retirement, or for permanent employment, or for life are necessarily terminable at the will of the employer, where the employee furnishes no consideration in addition to the services incident to the employment. We have never so held. Those authorities which have are generally based on the lack of mutuality of obligation which exists in such cases; since an employee cannot be bound to work permanently for a particular employer, the employer is not bound to engage the employee permanently. . . .

As a matter of contract doctrine we regard this rationale as unsound. There is no requirement of mutuality of obligation with respect to contracts formed by an exchange of a promise for performance. "If the requirement of consideration is met, there is no additional requirement of . . . (c) 'mutuality of obligation.' " . . .

While there are many cases supporting the rule that contracts for permanent employment are necessarily terminable at will by the employer unless supported by independent consideration, there is a substantial body of authority which recognizes, correctly in our view, the unsound foundation of that rule.

Reversed.

Weiner v. McGraw-Hill, Inc.
443 N.E.2d 441 (N.Y. 1982)

FUCHSBERG, J. In a matter raising an issue of wide concern to employers and employees, we must decide whether, in the circumstances of this case, the plaintiff, though not engaged for a fixed term of employment, pleaded a good cause of action for breach of contract against his employer because, allegedly, he was discharged without the "just and sufficient cause" or the rehabilitative efforts specified in the employer's personnel handbook and allegedly promised at the time he accepted the employment.

The facts deserve emphasis. . . . They show that, in 1969, the plaintiff, Walton Lewis Weiner, a young man who four years earlier had entered upon a career in book publishing with another employer, Prentice-Hall, was invited to engage in discussions looking towards his joining the staff of the defendant, McGraw-Hill, Inc. In the course of these talks, McGraw's representative, aware of Weiner's position with Prentice-Hall, assured his prospect that, since his company's firm policy was not to terminate employees without "just cause," employment by it would, among other things, bring him the advantage of job security.

The application Weiner thereafter signed and submitted, on a printed McGraw form, specified that his employment would be subject to the provisions of McGraw's "handbook on personnel policies and procedures." This reference as relevant here, represented that "[t]he company will resort to dismissal for just and sufficient cause only, and only after all practical steps toward rehabilitation or salvage of the employee have been taken and failed. However, if the welfare of the company indicates that dismissal is necessary, then that decision is arrived at and is carried out forthrightly."

These undertakings were important to Weiner, who alleges not only that he placed "good faith reliance" on them in leaving his existing employer, but in the process forfeited all his accrued fringe benefits and a salary increase proffered by Prentice-Hall to induce him to remain in its employ.

Following written approval, affixed at the foot of the application form by two members of the defendant's staff, one the interviewer and the other a supervisor, McGraw engaged Weiner's services. For the next eight years, so far as escalation in rank (to director of promotion services) and periodic raises in his level of compensation would seem to indicate, Weiner had every reason to believe he had, if anything, more than met the reasonable requirements of his new post. Other offers of employment he routinely rejected. Nevertheless, in February, 1977, he suddenly found himself discharged for "lack of application."

There ensued this litigation, by which, in a complaint speaking broadly in the language of breach of contract, the plaintiff seeks damages for his wrongful termination. To support its motion to dismiss, defendant's argument was, and is, that there existed no contract of employment under which McGraw-Hill's evaluation of Weiner's job performance could be challenged in a court of law.

In its view, the form signed by the parties was just an application for employment and nothing more. Defendant further contends that its oral promise of job security was in no way binding on it. . . .

[The trial court overruled the defendant's motion to dismiss. However, on appeal, the appellate court reversed the trial court and dismissed the plaintiff's complaint.]

For the reasons which follow, we believe the plaintiff stated a cause of action.

. . . [W]e find in the record, inclusive of plaintiff's own affidavit, sufficient evidence of a contract and a breach to sustain a cause of action. First, plaintiff was induced to leave Prentice-Hall with the assurance that McGraw-Hill would not discharge him without cause. Second, this assurance was incorporated into the employment application. Third, plaintiff rejected other offers of employment in reliance on the assurance. Fourth, appellant alleged that, on several occasions when he had recommended that certain of his subordinates be dismissed, he was instructed by his supervisors to proceed in strict compliance with the handbook and policy manuals because employees could be discharged only for just cause. He also claims that he was told that, if he did not proceed in accordance with the strict procedures set forth in the handbook, McGraw-Hill would be liable for legal action. In our view, these factors combine to present a question for trial: Was defendant bound to a promise not to discharge plaintiff without just and sufficient cause and an opportunity for rehabilitation?

Consequently, the order of the Appellate Division should be reversed and the order of Special Term reinstated.

Reversed.

Palmateer v. International Harvester Co. 421 N.E.2d 876 (Ill. 1981)

SIMON, J. The plaintiff, Ray Palmateer, complains of his discharge by International Harvester Company (IH). He had worked for IH for 16 years, rising from a unionized job at an hourly rate to a managerial position on a fixed salary. Following his discharge, Palmateer filed a . . . complaint against IH, alleging . . . that he had suffered a retaliatory discharge. According to the complaint, Palmateer was fired both for supplying information to local law-enforcement authorities that an IH employee might be involved in a violation of the Criminal Code and for agreeing to assist in the investigation and trial of the employee if requested. The circuit court of Rock Island County ruled the complaint failed to state a cause of action and dismissed it; the appellate court affirmed . . . We granted Palmateer leave to appeal to determine the contours of the tort of retaliatory discharge. . . .

Illinois has joined the growing number of States recognizing the tort of retaliatory discharge. The tort is an exception to the general rule that an "at-will" employment is terminable at any time for any or no cause. . . .

Recognition of the tort of retaliatory discharge acknowledges the common law principle that parties to a contract may not incorporate in it rights and obligations which are clearly injurious to the public. This principle is expressed forcefully in cases which insist that an employer is in contempt for discharging an employee who exercises the civic right and duty of serving on a jury. . . . But the Achilles heel of the principle lies in the definition of public policy. When a discharge contravenes public policy in any way the employer has committed a legal wrong. However, the employer retains the right to fire workers at will in cases "where no clear mandate of public policy is involved." But what constitutes clearly mandated public policy?

There is no precise definition of the term. In general, it can be said that public policy concerns what is right and just and what affects the citizens of the State collectively. It is to be found in the State's constitution and statutes and, when they are silent, in its judicial decisions. Although there is no precise line of demarcation dividing matters that are the subject of public policies from matters purely personal, a survey of cases in other States involving retaliatory discharges shows that a matter must strike at the heart of a citizen's social rights, duties, and responsibilities before the tort will be allowed. Thus, actions for retaliatory discharge have been allowed where the employee was fired for refusing to violate a statute. It has also been allowed where the employee was fired for refusing to evade jury duty, for engaging in statutorily protected union activities, and for filing a claim under a worker's compensation statute.

The action has not been allowed where the worker was discharged in a dispute over a company's internal management system, where the worker took too much sick leave, where the worker tried to examine the company's books in his capacity as a shareholder, where the worker impugned the company's integrity, where the worker refused to be examined by a psychological-stress evaluator, where the worker was attending night school, or where the worker improperly used the employer's Christmas fund.

The cause of action is allowed where the public policy is clear, but is denied where it is equally clear that only private interests are at stake.

Where the nature of the interest at stake is muddled, the courts have given conflicting answers as to whether the protection of the tort action is available. . . .

It is clear that Palmateer has here alleged that he was fired in violation of an established public policy. The claim is that he was discharged for supplying information to a local law-enforcement agency that an IH employee might be violating the Criminal Code, for agreeing to gather further evidence implicating the employee, and for intending to testify at the employee's trial, if it came to that. . . . There is no public policy more basic, nothing more implicit in the concept of ordered liberty than the enforcement of a State's criminal code. There is no public policy more important or more fundamental than the one favoring the effective protection of the lives and property of citizens.

No specific constitutional or statutory provision requires a citizen to take an active part in the ferreting out and prosecution of crime, but public policy nevertheless favors citizen crime-fighters. Public policy favors the exposure of crime, and the cooperation of citizens possessing knowledge thereof is essential to effective implementation of that policy. Persons acting in good faith who have probable cause to believe crimes have been committed should not be deterred from reporting them by the fear of unfounded suits by those accused.

Public policy favors Palmateer's conduct in volunteering information to the law-enforcement agency. Once the possibility of crime was reported, Palmateer was under a statutory duty to further assist officials when requested to do so. Public policy thus also favors Palmateer's agreement to assist in the investigation and prosecution of the suspected crime.

The foundation of the tort of retaliatory discharge lies in the protection of public policy, and there is a clear public policy favoring investigation and prosecution of criminal offenses. Palmateer has stated a cause of action for retaliatory discharge. . . . The law is feeble indeed if it permits IH to take matters into its own hands by retaliating against its employees who cooperate in enforcing the law. . . .

The cause of action expressed in . . . Palmateer's complaint was improperly dismissed, and the cause should be returned to the circuit court for further proceedings.

Reversed.

Vieira v. Robert's Hawaii Tours, Inc.
630 P.2d 120 (Haw. App. 1981)

PER CURIAM. In this case we review the trial court's determination that Robert's Hawaii Tours, the employer, breached its employment contract with Wayne R. Vieira, the employee, and its findings with respect to damages for the breach. . . .

Robert's, a tour coordinating business, and Vieira, a person with experience in that business, entered into an Employment Agreement . . . whereby Robert's hired Vieira as "a Vice President of Sales" for five years, commencing July 1, 1975. . . .

On February 21, 1976, Robert's terminated Vieira's employment and thereafter Vieira sued for all amounts due under the agreement. . . .

. . . [T]he lower court determined that Robert's . . . wrongfully terminated the agreement without cause.

The lower court found that through February 1978 Vieira reasonably sought other employment and earned $5,645.57 gross but that he failed to act in mitigation of his damages subsequent to February 1978. . . .

On its appeal, Robert's contends that the trial court erred in . . . finding that through February 1978 Vieira made a reasonable attempt to mitigate damages. . . .

The measure of recovery by a wrongfully discharged employee is the amount of compensation agreed upon for the remaining period of service, less the amount which the employer affirmatively proves the employee has earned or with reasonable effort might have earned from other employment. . . .

. . . [T]he mitigation . . . rule is:

[B]efore projected earnings from other employment opportunities not sought or accepted by the discharged employee can be applied in mitigation, the employer must show that the other employment was comparable, or substantially similar, to that of which the employee has been deprived; the employee's rejection of or failure to seek other available employment of a different or inferior kind may not be resorted to in order to mitigate damages.

The only evidence of Vieira's failure to mitigate was Vieira's testimony that the first week after he was terminated at Robert's he was offered two or three sales positions at $400 per month plus a commission receivable after the completion of the tours sold. In Vieira's view, this was too little compensation and it was payable too late. He also testified that some of the offers came from companies which were financially unstable. . . .

The trial court found that Vieira's efforts to mitigate through February 1978 were reasonable but that he "failed to act in mitigation of damages subsequent to February 1978." Vieira's uncontradicted testimony was that he accepted employment as a life insurance solicitor commencing May 1977; that he was still so employed at the time of trial in May 1978; that through February 1978 he had earned $5,645.47 in commissions; that he earned "around $900" in March 1978; that he did not know how much commissions he earned in April 1978. Since he had the same employment at the time of trial in May of 1978 as he had since May of 1977, it is clear error to say that he "failed to act in mitigation of damages subsequent to February 1978." . . .

. . . [W]e reverse the trial court's entire decision on damages and remand for a new trial on that issue only.

Reversed and remanded.

Matter of Estate of Head
615 P.2d 271 (N.M. App. 1980)

While of sound mind, William Grady Head signed a general power of attorney in March, 1976. This document appointed his wife, Emma, to act on his behalf in all matters. Also while he was mentally competent, Mr. Head along with Mrs. Head created a revocable trust for the benefit of their two natural daughters and a third woman (Esther Taute) they had raised. Each daughter's interest in the trust assets was 40 percent, and Esther Taute's interest was 20 percent. Six days after the trust agreement was signed, Mr. Head signed a document called a First Amendment, which removed Taute's 20 percent interest. It was established that Mr. Head was not mentally competent when this amendment was signed. Three weeks later, Mrs. Head, acting for herself and as Mr. Head's attorney-in-fact, ratified the amended trust document. After both Mr. and Mrs. Head had died, the beneficiaries of this trust sought a declaration of their respective interests. The trial court ruled that the trust was valid as originally written. The natural daughters appealed, arguing their mother's ratification of the amendment removed Esther Taute's interest.

SUTIN, J. . . . A power of attorney is revoked by operation of law upon an adjudication of insanity. If the agent's authority is "coupled with an interest" the principal's insanity does not terminate the agency. . . .

"Coupled with an interest" means that the agent must have a present interest in the property upon which the power is to operate. There must be a beneficial interest in the thing itself which is the subject of the power.

As a trustor, Mrs. Head had a present existing interest in the trust estate and in the distribution of the property held in trust. It was independent of the power conferred. It was of primary importance that she determine the beneficiaries of the trust. If she desired to restore her . . . property interest, she could have revoked the trust. She had an interest in the subject upon which the power was to be exercised. She had a power of attorney coupled with an interest.

Mrs. Head sought to exercise her power of attorney with reference to the Trust Agreement. A "trust" is the beneficial ownership of property of which the legal title is in another. Mr. and Mrs. Head were the joint beneficial owners of the trust property. Mrs. Head was a trustor along with her husband. She had the right at any time during his lifetime to amend or revoke the trust. Her Power of Attorney was "coupled with an interest" in the trust estate and was irrevocable.

The Trust Agreement was validly ratified regardless of the mental competency of Mr. Head. . . . [T]his cause is reversed and remanded to the district court to enter judgment that the First Amendment . . . is valid and that Esther Taute take nothing under her claim.

Reversed and remanded.

Moore v. Puget Sound Plywood, Inc. 332 N.W.2d 212 (Neb. 1983)

In the early 1970s, the Moores purchased siding during the construction of their home. This siding, which was manufactured by Puget Sound Plywood, Inc., began to come apart during 1977. The problem became so severe in 1979 that the Moores attempted to contact their source of the siding. They discovered that company no longer existed. However, they learned that Rehcon, Inc., represented Puget Sound concerning the defective siding. Thereafter, in March, 1980, Rehcon quit in its representative capacity of Puget Sound because of a lack of cooperation. No efforts were made by Puget Sound to notify the public that Rehcon was no longer its agent. On June 24, 1980, Mr. Moore notified Rehcon of his defective siding. Subsequently, the Moores sued Puget Sound for $4,550, which was the cost of replacing the siding. The basis of this suit was a breach of warranty concerning the siding. Puget Sound defended by asserting that it had not been notified, as required, of the Moores' problem with the siding. The trial court dismissed the Moores' complaint, and they appealed.

CAPORALE, J. . . . The Moores' . . . assignment of error relates to the lower courts' holdings that they failed to prove proper notice to Puget Sound. . . . [T]he buyer must, within a reasonable time after he discovers or should have discovered any breach, notify the seller of the breach or be barred from any recovery. We have held that a purchaser must plead that he gave timely notice of the breach. The Moores did so plead. The question is, then, whether the evidence supports that allegation. The June 24, 1980, written complaint to Rehcon was given within a reasonable time of the initial discovery in 1977 and the determination in 1979 that the problem was severe enough to warrant action. It is true that by the time of that complaint Rehcon no longer had any relationship with Puget Sound. However, that fact is not in and of itself determinative.

. . . [A]pparent authority may exist beyond termination of the principal-agency relationship when notice of the termination has not been given. . . . Where a principal has, by his voluntary act, placed an agent in such a situation that a person of ordinary prudence, conversant with business usages and the nature of the particular business, is justified in presuming that such agent has authority to perform a particular act, and therefore deals with the agent, the principal is estopped as against such third person from denying the agent's authority.

Whether or not an act is within the scope of an agent's apparent authority is to be determined under the foregoing rule as a question of fact from all the circumstances of the transaction and the business. . . . [A]pparent or ostensible authority to act as an agent may be conferred if the alleged

principal affirmatively, intentionally, or by lack of ordinary care causes third persons to act upon the apparent agency. Under the facts and circumstances of this case, Mr. Moore's notice to Rehcon was notice to Puget Sound. The Moores' assignments of error are meritorious. The judgment of the District Court is reversed and the matter remanded with directions that judgment be entered in favor of the Moores in the sum of $4,550.

Reversed and remanded.

REVIEW QUESTIONS

1. Identify the terms in column A by matching each with the appropriate statement in column B.

A	B
1. Operation of law	a. Generally present even though the legal right of termination is lacking.
2. Power of termination	b. One example of an employee's protected right.
3. Termination at will	c. Often used as a basis for proving that an employer breached an implied duty or agreement.
4. Employees' handbook	d. A relationship created as a source of reimbursement to the agent.
5. Jury service	e. Termination by death, insanity, bankruptcy, destruction, or illegality.
6. Agency coupled with an interest	f. Given constructively through the newspaper, radio, or television.
7. Agency coupled with an obligation	g. Also known as a power given as security.
8. Public notice	h. A traditional legal concept whereby the terminating party has the right and power to end a relationship.

2. As a matter of law, the occurrence of any one of four events operates to terminate a principal-agent relationship. List these four events.
3. In addition to termination by operation of law, an agency may be terminated by the mutual agreement of principal and agent. Describe three factual situations wherein the parties' agreement ends their relationship.
4. When agency relationships are terminated by the actions of the parties involved, the concepts of the *power* to terminate and *right* to terminate become important. Explain the distinction between and the legal significance of these terms.
5. The Dixie Company offered Papageorge a contract of employment as a regional manager. Dixie's offers contained a proposed annual salary of $35,000. Papageorge accepted this offer, but he was not allowed to come to work. Dixie canceled the contract. When Papageorge sued, Dixie denied liability and contended that without an agreed-upon duration, this employment was terminable at will.

Papageorge argued that the stated annual salary implied a contract to last at least a year. Which party is correct? Why?

6. Patty, an employee of David's Cafe, was called for jury duty. David wrote a letter to the court asking that Patty be excused from serving as a juror. However, Patty told a court clerk that she would like to serve. After sitting on a jury for 3 days, Patty received a notice from David that her employment was terminated. Patty sued David for wrongful termination. David contended Patty's employment was terminable at his will. Should Patty recover? Explain.

7. Suppose in the preceding factual situation that Patty was discharged when she refused actively to support David's brother in his bid to be elected to the county commission. Assume that there is no other legitimate reason for terminating Patty's employment. If Patty sued, should she recover for being wrongfully discharged? Why?

8. Anil Shah was employed as a chemical engineer by the American Synthetic Rubber Corporation (ASRC). Although Shah's employment contract was for an indefinite time period, Shah was told his relationship would be governed by the personnel policies and procedures established by ASRC. Despite these policies and procedures stating that an employee will be discharged only for good cause, Shah was fired for no stated reason. ASRC claimed the employment agreement was terminable at the will of either party. Shah sued, arguing that he was wrongfully discharged. Was Shah's employment agreement terminable at ASRC's will? Explain.

9. Employees who have been discharged may challenge their dismissals as wrongful. Courts have utilized either a tort or a breach of contract theory to support a decision in favor of a wronged employee. Why is it important to distinguish between these two theories?

10. Ann, a real estate agent, was authorized by Peter to sell several lots at specified prices. Ann was to receive an 8 percent commission on each lot sold. Before any lots were sold, Peter revoked the authorization granted. Since Ann had spent her own money advertising these lots, she claimed that her authority was irrevocable as an agency coupled with either an interest or obligation. Is Ann correct? Why?

11. Dr. Thompson's malpractice insurance was obtained through the Duncan Insurance Agency. During 1979 and 1980, Thompson's insurance was with Aetna Casualty & Surety Company. In 1981, the Duncan Agency ceased being an agent for Aetna, and it became an agent for St. Paul Insurance Company. Duncan changed Dr. Thompson's coverage to St. Paul without explaining why the change occurred. In 1981, Dr. Thompson was sued for an alleged act of malpractice which occurred in July, 1979. Dr. Thompson immediately notified the Duncan Agency, which mistakenly notified St. Paul. St. Paul began defending Dr. Thompson, but it then discovered it was not the doctor's insurer in 1979. Aetna was notified, but it refused to defend the malpractice, since it was not promptly and timely notified of the filed suit as the insurance policy required. Dr. Thompson sued Aetna, relying on the immediate notice given to the Duncan Agency. Is Aetna liable for not defending the malpractice case against Dr. Thompson? Why?

12. Alicia, a buyer for Patterson's Department Store, was discharged. Although Turner Manufacturers knew of Alicia's position with Patterson's, it had never sold merchandise to Alicia. After Alicia was discharged, an article about her changing jobs appeared in the local newspapers, but Turner did not read it. If Alicia now purchases goods on credit from Turner and charges them to Patterson's, is Patterson's liable to Turner? Explain.

18 GENERAL PRINCIPLES OF THE LAW OF PROPERTY

The term *property* is meaningless unless it is associated with people or with legal entities that qualify as persons. Some of the terms frequently used in expressing this association are *ownership, title,* and *possession.* The word *owner* usually describes someone who possesses all of the rights or interests associated with the thing involved. The word *title* is often used synonymously with *ownership. Title* is also used to signify the method by which ownership is acquired, as by a transfer of title. It may also be used to indicate the evidence by which ownership is established—a written instrument called a title, as a car title. Thus the word *title* has a variety of meanings, depending upon the context.

The word *possession* is equally difficult to define accurately. Its meaning is also dependent somewhat on the context in which it is used. Possession implies the concept of physical control by a person over property and the personal and mental relationship to it. While it is physically possible to possess a watch or a ring, it is obviously physically impossible to possess one thousand acres of land in the same manner. Yet the word *possession* as a legal term is used in both instances. Possession describes not only physical control, but the power to obtain physical control by legal sanctions, if necessary. In general, the concepts of possession and title should be kept separate and distinct. In other words, having possession of property does not mean the possessor also has title. The reverse is also true—a person who has title to property does not always have possession of that property. For example, a landlord of an apartment building owns (has title to) each unit; the tenants have physical control (possession) of the premises.

Part IV includes materials on a variety of topics related to property. The subsequent chapters concentrate on various transactions involving property; this chapter is concerned with some introductory principles of property. In particular, this chapter discusses the distinction among categories of property, the property status of fixtures, and the variety of ownership interests that may be held in land.

1. Real versus Personal Property

From the standpoint of its physical characteristics, property is classified as either *real property* or *personal property.* When describing property, the adjective *real* refers to land and things attached to the land. Therefore, land as part of the earth's surface, buildings, fences, and trees are examples of things classified as real property. *Personal property* consists of all other things that are not real property. By definition, all items of property are classified either as real or personal property.

2. Real Property

The legal terms real property and real estate are very similar and frequently confused. In fact, these terms are often used interchangeably. However, there is a technical distinction between real property and real estate. The term *real estate* refers to the physical aspects of land and its attachments. For example, the dirt on the land is real estate, as are any actual improvements, such as buildings, roads, fences, and landscaping. Also included in the definition of real estate are the spaces above and below the land's surface. Included in these spaces are mineral, water, and air rights. Historically, real estate included unlimited subsurface and air rights. Today, these rights are limited to a reasonable distance. Despite this limitation, these rights still have great value to the landowner. Indeed, interference with subsurface and air rights is treated similarly to trespass on the land's surface.[1]

The term *real property* is used to describe the legal rights that a person can have in real estate. For instance, the ownership interest a person may have in land and its improvements is classified as a real property interest. Because the distinction between real property and real estate is a subtle one, the text and cases included in this book use the terms as synonyms.

The three most important areas of the law of real property concern (1) ownership interests, (2) methods of acquiring title, and (3) transactions. The various ownership interests that can be created in land are discussed in this chapter. The next chapter includes a discussion of the methods used to acquire real property. Also important to this discussion is chapter 22 on estate planning, wills, and trusts. Sales transactions involving real property interests are reviewed in chapter 20, and lease transactions are discussed in chapter 21.

3. Personal Property

Personal property may be classified as tangible or intangible. The term *tangible personal property* includes objects such as goods. The term *intangible personal property* refers to things such as accounts receivable, good will, patents, and trademarks. Intangible personal property has value, as tangible property has, and each can be transferred.

CLASSIFICA-
TIONS OF
PROPERTY

---

[1] United States v. Causby, p. 399.

The term *chattel* is used to describe personal property generally, but chattels may also be classified as *chattels real* and *chattels personal.* Chattels real describes an interest in land, such as a leasehold; chattels personal is applied to movable personal property. When the term *chattel* is used in connection with intangible personal property, the property is referred to as *chattels personal in action.* A chattel personal in action—or *chose in action,* as it is frequently called—is something to which one has a right to possession, but concerning which he may be required to bring some legal action in order ultimately to enjoy possession. A contract right may be said to be a chose in action because a lawsuit may be necessary to obtain the rights under the contract. A negotiable instrument is a common form of chose in action. Although the instrument itself may be said to be property, in reality it is simply evidence of a right to money, and it may be necessary to maintain an action to reduce the money to possession.

In this text, three aspects of personal property are considered most important. First, what happens if an item of personal property becomes permanently attached to real estate? This question is answered in sections 6 through 10 of this chapter. Second, how does a person acquire or transfer ownership of personal property? This issue is discussed in both the next chapter and in chapter 22. Third, what transactions involving personal property are most important? Chapter 21 concentrates on personal property transactions, especially the legal aspects of bailments.

4. Reasons for Distinguishing between Real and Personal Property

The distinction between real and personal property, significant in a variety of situations, is important in determining the law applicable to a transaction that has contact with more than one state. Such issues are known as *conflict of laws* problems.

As a general rule, conflict of laws principles provide that the law of the situs—the law of the state where real property is located—determines all legal questions concerning real property. Legal issues concerning conflict of laws relating to personal property are not so easily resolved. Conflict of laws rules may refer to the law of the owner's domicile to resolve some questions and to the law of the state with the most significant contacts with the property to resolve others. The law of the situs of the property is also used to resolve some legal issues. Therefore, the description of property as real or personal has a significant impact on the determination of the body of substantive law used to decide legal issues concerning the property.

In most states, real and personal property are handled under different rules of law and procedures when their owner dies. Insofar as inheritance is concerned, however, many modern statutes abolish any distinction between the two. The law as it relates to the passing of property on the death of the owner is discussed later in chapter 22.

During the lifetime of the owner, the distinction between real and personal property is significant, since the methods of transferring them are substantially different. Formal instruments such as deeds are required to transfer an interest in land, whereas few formalities are required in the case of personal property. A bill of sale may be used in selling personal property; but it is not generally required, and it does not, in any event, involve the technicalities of a deed. The transfer of personal property is, as a rule, quite simply accomplished (a motor vehicle transfer may require the delivery of a certificate of title), whereas formality is required to transfer real property.

Systems for taxing real estate are different from those for taxing personal property in many states. Property taxes on real estate are significant in every state, while personal property taxes often are less significant. Typical of the issues that may arise are those relating to mobile homes. Is a mobile home that is placed on a foundation real estate and thus subject to real estate taxation, or is it personal property? Similar questions make it apparent that parties to various transactions and courts are frequently called upon to label property as real or personal. If the issue is likely to arise, it should always be covered in agreements.

5. What Is a Fixture?

FIXTURES

The classification of property as real or personal may be very difficult at times, and it may change from time to time. For example, when a dishwasher is purchased at an appliance store, it is clearly personal property. However, what is its status if it is built into your kitchen cabinets? Does this dishwasher remain an item of personal property, or has it become a part of the real estate? The answers to these questions are determined by the law of *fixtures*. A fixture is personal property that has become a part of real estate.

To understand better what a fixture is, it is helpful to examine the reasons for distinguishing between personal and real property. Also important is being able to know when personal property is likely to have become a fixture. There are three tests, discussed below, that courts have used to determine fixture status. These are often called the intention, annexation, and adaptation tests. As you read the following sections, keep in mind that once personal property becomes a fixture, it is treated as a part of the real estate. The tests are not cumulative and their use depends on the factual situation.

6. Reasons for Determining Fixture Status

The question of whether or not an item is a fixture and thus part of the real estate arises in determining: (1) the value of real estate for tax purposes; (2) whether or not a sale of the real estate includes the item of property in question; (3) whether or not the item of property is a part of the security given by a mortgagor of the real estate to a mortgagee; and (4) whether the item belongs to the owner of the building or to the tenant on termination of a lease. Fixture issues also arise under Article 9 of the Uniform Commercial Code in disputes between secured creditors and persons with an interest in the land. The UCC provides that no security interest exists in "goods incorporated into a structure in the manner of lumber, bricks, tile, cement, glass, metal work and the like." A party with a security interest in such goods loses it when the goods are incorporated into the real estate.

If property is a fixture: (1) it is included in the value of real estate for tax purposes; (2) it is sold, and title to it passes with the real estate; (3) it is a part of the security covered by a mortgage; and (4) it belongs to the landlord owner, not to the tenant on termination of a lease.

7. Annexation Test

The degree of attachment of personal property to the real estate is the essence of the annexation test. Furthermore, whether the article can be removed without material injury to the article, building, and land are important considerations in determining whether the article is a fixture.

The common law required the chattel to be "let into" or "united" to the land. The test of annexation alone is inadequate, for many things attached to the soil or buildings are not fixtures, and many things not physically attached to the soil or buildings are considered fixtures. Articles of furniture substantially fastened but easily removed are not necessarily fixtures. Physical annexation may be only for the purpose of more convenient use. On the other hand, machinery that has been annexed but detached for repairs or other temporary reasons may still be considered a fixture, although severed.

Doors, windows, screens, storm windows, and the like, although readily detachable, are generally considered fixtures because they are an integral part of the building and pertain to its function. Electric ranges connected to a building by a plug or vent pipe generally are not fixtures, but the removal of wainscoting, wood siding, fireplace mantels, and water systems would cause a material injury to the building and land; therefore, these items usually are fixtures.

8. Adaptation Test

Because the annexation test alone is inadequate to determine what is a fixture, the adaptation test has been developed. Adaptation means that the article is used in promoting the purpose for which the land is used. Thus, if an article is placed upon, or annexed to, land to improve it, make it more valuable, and extend its use, it is a fixture. Pipes, pumps, and electric motors for an irrigation system are chattels that may be adapted to become fixtures. This test alone is not adequate, because rarely is an article attached or placed upon land except to advance the purpose for which the land is to be used.

9. Intention Test

Because of the inherent weaknesses with the annexation and adaptation tests, it is always best for parties to specify their intentions concerning the issue of fixtures. However, when the parties' intent is not clear, in addition to annexation and adaptation, the following situations and circumstances may be useful in determining the parties' intent: (1) the kind and character of the article affixed; (2) the purpose and use for which the annexation has been made; and (3) the relation and situation of the parties making the annexation. The relation of landlord and tenant suggests that items such as showcases, acquired and used by the tenant, are not intended to become permanently part of the real property. Such property, called *trade fixtures,* is an exception to the general rule of fixtures because they are generally intended to be removed by the tenant at the end of the lease. Trade fixtures continue to be classified as personal property.

The most important factor to consider in determining whether personal property has become a fixture is the intent of the parties. In other words, as between a buyer and seller of real estate, those parties may clearly state in their contract that an attached ceiling fan will be removed by the seller. Likewise, mortgage documents, security agreements, and leases should all be written in a way to indicate whether the parties intend the property to be treated as personal property or as a fixture. If the parties neglect to state their intentions, courts have turned to the annexation and adaptation tests as a way to predict what the parties' intent really was. However, when the parties' intent is clear, courts have used this factor as the controlling one in determining fixture status.[2]

10. Introduction

In the early law, property was thought of as a thing that could be touched, possessed, and delivered. As the law of property developed, courts began to recognize that property was more accurately described as the *bundle of rights* a person had in respect to a thing. Today, property is thought of as an object or a thing over which someone exercises legal rights.

Defining property as a bundle of rights enables courts and the law to develop a variety of interests in property. A person may possess all of the bundle of rights in relation to a thing, in which case he is the only owner. On the other hand, the bundle of rights may be divided among several people, in which case there is incomplete ownership by any one person. For example, the owner of a tract of land may authorize the local public utility companies to install power and telephone lines through his land. The utility companies are granted what is called an *easement,* which is a property right. As a result, the owner has less than the full bundle of rights, and the title is subject to an *encumbrance.*

Furthermore, this bundle of rights concept allows owners of real property to create a variety of ownership interests. In essence, the type of real property ownership interest is determined by the rights of an owner to possess, use, and transfer the land. In order to understand the possible variations of ownership interests, keep in mind that the complete bundle of rights has to be accounted for at all times. In addition, realize that every ownership interest may be held by one person as an individual, or by two or more persons jointly. A discussion of multiple ownership interest is presented in chapter 22.

11. Fee Simple Estates

When used in connection with land, the legal term *estate* is synonymous with ownership interests. *Fee simple estates* are those interests classified as either absolute or qualified present interests. *Present interests* are those that allow the owner to possess the land now. In the alternative, the owner of a present interest may transfer the right of possession to another party. A *fee simple absolute* is the

REAL PROPERTY OWNERSHIP INTERESTS

---

[2] Pacific Metal Company v. Northwestern Bank of Helena, p. 400.

most complete ownership interest possible. It contains the largest bundle of rights of any estate in land. The fee simple absolute is the interest usually received by the grantee in a real estate sales transaction. The language used to create this unlimited interest does not contain words of limitation.

A fee simple interest that may be defeated in the future by the occurrence or nonoccurrence of a stated event or condition is called a qualified or conditional fee simple. The possible variations of these fee simple estates are complex and beyond the scope of this text. It is sufficient for you to keep two points in mind about qualified fee simple estates. First, these interests do not contain the complete bundle of rights that exists with every piece of land. Therefore, there is a future ownership interest that may become possessory, causing the holder of this future interest to gain superior title relative to the owner of the qualified fee simple interest. Second, these qualified interests usually are less valuable when compared to a fee simple absolute interest. Thus, you should always be aware of the ownership interest involved in a real estate transaction. Generally you would not be willing to pay as much for a qualified fee simple as you would for a fee simple absolute interest.

12. Life Estates

One of the most widely used ownership interests in estate planning is the *life estate.* When properly used, the life estate enables landowners to provide for those they desire, while reducing both income and estate taxes. The life estate interest may be created either by will or by deed. A life estate may be for the life of the grantee, or it may be created for the duration of the life of some other designated person. It may be conditional upon the happening of an event, such as the marriage of the life tenant. A husband may convey property to his wife for life or until she remarries. Unless the instrument that creates the life estate places limitations upon it, the interest can be sold or mortgaged like any other interest in real estate. The buyer or mortgagee must, of course, take into consideration the fact that the life estate may be terminated at any time by the death of the person for whose life it was created.

The life tenant is obligated to use reasonable care to maintain the property in the condition in which it was received, ordinary wear and tear excepted. There is a duty to repair, to pay taxes, and, out of the income received, to pay interest on any mortgage that may have been outstanding at the time the life estate was created. The life tenant has no right to waste the property or to do anything that tends to deplete the value of the property. A life tenant would have no right to drill for oil, mine coal, or cut timber from the land, unless those operations were being conducted at the time the life estate was created. Likewise, a life tenant has no duty to make lasting improvements to the property.

13. Remainders and Reversions

Because a life estate represents less than the complete bundle of rights, there must be a future interest accompanying every life estate. After the termination of a life estate, the remaining estate may be given to someone else, or it may go back to the original owner or to his heirs. If the estate is to be given to someone else upon the termination of a life estate, it is called an *estate in remainder.* If it is to go back to the original owner, it is called a *reversion.* When a reversion exists and the original owner of that interest is dead, the property reverts to the heirs of that original owner. Regardless of whether a remainder or a reversion follows a life estate, these future interests may be sold, mortgaged, or otherwise transferred as if they were any other real property interest. This right to transfer these interests exists even before the life estate ends and the remainder or reversion become present possessory interests. Upon the death of the life tenant, the remainder or reversion generally converts into a fee simple absolute interest once again.

Since the owners of remainders and reversions have a valuable real property interest, they have the right to enforce the life tenant's duty not to waste the land's value. The timing for filing a suit to recover damages for or to enjoin waste depends on the type of waste occurring. For example, the holder of a life estate may actively destroy an improvement on the real estate or neglect an improvement, allowing it to deteriorate. In general, the statute of limitations for filing an action against waste begins to run when active waste occurs on the one hand and when the life tenant dies if the neglect type of waste has occurred.[3] While the owners of the remainder or reversion can sue to prevent the life tenant from wasting the property's value, these owners of the future interest generally cannot be required to contribute to the cost of improvements made by the life tenant.[4]

14. Condominiums and Cooperatives

A *condominium* is an individually owned apartment or town house in a multiunit structure such as an apartment building or in a complex. A method of owning and transferring property, it possesses some of the characteristics of individual ownership and some of multiple ownership. In addition to the individual units, the owner has an undivided interest in the common areas of the building and land, such as hallways, entrances, yard, and recreation areas. Thus the deed to a condominium covers the housing unit involved and an undivided fractional interest in the common areas. Taxes, expenses, and liabilities arising from these common areas are usually divided on a proportional basis, using each owner's fractional interests in the undivided common areas.

Condominiums are of growing importance in commercial as well as residential uses. Due to its structural nature, a determination of an owner's full rights and duties requires an understanding not only of the law of property, but also of the law of business organizations. In a condominium complex there is an organization created to operate the common areas, to make repairs, and to make improvements. Each owner of a unit has one vote in an election of a board of directors or governors. This board of the owners' association operates the development subject to the owners' approval.

There is a distinction between a *condominium* and a *cooperative* insofar as the ownership of real estate is concerned. A cooperative venture may involve an

---

[3] Moore v. Phillips, p. 401.
[4] Harris v. Audubon Society of Rhode Island, p. 402.

activity such as a retail store, or it may involve the ownership and operation of a residential development. If a person buys an interest in a cooperative, he is purchasing a share of a not-for-profit corporation. Strictly speaking, the owner of an interest in a cooperative does not own real estate. He owns personal property—his share of the cooperative. The cooperative would pay taxes and upkeep out of the assessments to its members. A condominium contains multiple units for taxing purposes; the cooperative is a single unit. The same may be said for the financing. Each owner of a condominium may mortgage his or her own portion. In a cooperative, if there is financing, there will be only one mortgage. In both the condominium and the cooperative there is a special form of business organization to coordinate the operation of the property.

RESTRICTIONS ON OWNERSHIP INTERESTS

15. Introduction

One other fact of life must be recognized when studying the law of real property ownership interests. There can be no property rights without a government and a legal system to create and enforce them. Private property rights cannot exist without some method of keeping the bundle of rights for the true owner and for restoring these rights to him if he is deprived of them. It should also be recognized that no one person has a complete bundle of rights. To some extent, the law limits private property rights and the use of private property in order to protect the public's interest.

Actually, there are two basic methods of restricting ownership interests in land. First, governing bodies at the federal, state, and local levels may require an owner to sell his or her land so that it may be utilized for a public purpose. These governing bodies may also regulate the use of land through statutes and ordinances. For example, there are many environmental protection laws designed to control the use of land. Furthermore, zoning regulations are typical of the ordinances intended as land use controls. Collectively, governmental regulations of an ownership interest are called *public restrictions.*

The second method of restricting ownership interests is that referred to as *private restrictions.* By private, we mean that nongovernmental parties limit an owner's use and enjoyment of the land. Examples of private restrictions, discussed below, include easements, licenses, conditions, and covenants. Although these items may be considered to be interests in the hands of those that can enforce them, they are restrictions on the ownership interests on which they exist.

16. Public Restrictions—Eminent Domain

One of the inherent rights our forefathers recognized was the right of individuals to own property. Indeed, the United States Constitution, in the Fifth Amendment, states that property shall not be taken from any person for a public use without just compensation. This language has been interpreted to be applicable to all levels of government. In essence, the Constitution not only protects the property owner, it also gives the governing body the power to buy private property when two conditions are satisfied. First, the property being acquired must be needed for the public's use and benefit. Second, the property owner must be justly compensated. This constitutional power is known as the power of *eminent domain.* In other words, the government may terminate an owner's interest by acquiring it for a public purpose upon payment of the fair market value.

Without question, the public use requirement is satisfied when land is needed for the construction of a public highway, park, hospital, school, or airport. Indeed, in similar cases, the issue of public use for the condemned land is seldom litigated. However, more recently there has been an expansion of the public use doctrine. For example, the exercise of the eminent domain power has been justified even when the property taken was not to be used by the public.[5]

Today, the more difficult issue to resolve when property is being condemned is how much is just compensation. Indeed, the question of property's fair market value usually is the basic factual issue to be answered by the court in eminent domain cases. Expert appraisers are called to testify, and the final determination of what is just compensation frequently is left to a jury. With respect to the concept of just compensation, you should realize it is not equal to full compensation. Although some statutes have been adopted by legislatures defining the items a property owner must be paid for, the Constitution does not require that the owner be reimbursed for attorneys' fees, expert witnesses' fees, costs of relocating, or loss of business goodwill.

17. Public Restrictions—Zoning Regulations

The primary method local governments use to restrict a landowner's interest is the adoption of a *zoning ordinance.* These ordinances typically divide a community into zones and regulate the use of land within each zone. The type and intensity of the land's use in these zones can be classified as open space, residential, commercial, or industrial. Within each classification there can be several categories that further regulate the owner's use of his or her land. For example, property zoned R-1 might be reserved for single-family residences with lot sizes of not under 1/2 acre. R-5 could represent that zone wherein multiple-family residences (apartments or condominiums) were permitted.

A community's comprehensive zoning plan also restricts the use of land regarding the density of development allowed. Restrictions on buildings' height and bulk are not uncommon. Height limitations usually restrict the maximum height of buildings in feet or stories. Bulk regulations control the percentage of the lot the building may occupy. Setback and lot size requirements are examples of typical bulk restrictions.

The overall purpose of zoning ordinances is to provide a more esthetically pleasing environment for all citizens of the community. Few people want their residence located in or near the site of a major industrial facility. Although it is a restriction on ownership interests, properly designed and implemented zoning regulations can enhance property values. Despite these benefits, you should know that there are methods for changing zoning classifications when they become unreasonable. In other words, in most communities the local zoning ordinances are subject to a continuous review process.

---

[5] Poletown Neighborhood Council v. City of Detroit, p. 403.

18. Private Restrictions—Easements and Licenses

An *easement* is a right granted for the use of real property. The grantor may convey to the grantee a right of way over his land, the right to erect a building that may shut off light or air, the right to lay drain tile under the land, or the right to extend utilities over the land. If these rights of easement are reserved in the deed conveying the property or granted by a separate deed, they pass along with the property to the next grantee and are burdens upon the land. An easement made by separate contract is binding only on the immediate parties to the agreement. If a right to use another's land is given orally, it is not an easement but a *license.* The owner of the land may revoke a license at any time unless it has become irrevocable by conduct constituting estoppel. An easement given by grant cannot be revoked except by deed, as such a right of way is considered a right in real property; nor can it be modified without the consent of the owner of the easement.

An owner of land may create an easement for the benefit of another by deed. Usually, a party desiring an easement purchases it from the owner of the servient land. Or a seller of real estate may reserve an easement in his favor when deeding the property to someone else, a situation that will occur when a party sells only part of his land, and the portion retained requires the easement. Assume that Farmer Brown sells half of his farm to a neighbor. Since the half sold borders on the only road touching the farm, Farmer Brown will need to reserve an easement for ingress and egress.

Easements may be obtained by adverse possession, just like any other interest in land. Such easements are known as easements *by prescription.*[6] Easements may also be obtained through judicial proceedings in certain cases. Since the law takes the position that an owner of land should be entitled to access to that land, owners of land that would otherwise be landlocked may be entitled to an easement *by necessity.* Such an easement is, in effect, granted by the owner of the servient land to the owner of the other land by implication. Government bodies and public utilities may obtain easements by condemnation proceedings without the consent of the owner. Of course, the owner of the land is entitled to just compensation in such cases.

19. Private Restrictions—Conditions and Covenants

An ownership interest in land may be restricted by *conditions* or *covenants.* In section 11 above, qualified fee simple estates were discussed. In essence, these interests are conditioned on the occurrence of a stated event. For example, land may be conveyed to a grantee, Albert, on the condition that he marry before his twenty-fifth birthday. If Albert does not satisfy the condition of marriage, he loses all ownership interest in the property conveyed. In other words, a breach of a stated condition may result in termination of all interests previously held.

Quite often a grantor of land may wish to restrict the use of the land conveyed, but not wish to use the harshness of stated conditions. Restrictive covenants give such a grantor an alternative. These restrictions may be contained

---

[6] Bull v. Salsman, p. 405.

in the deed, or they may be made applicable to several tracts of land by attaching them to a plat of a subdivision. A *plat* is a diagram of the lot lines contained in a subdivision. This plat often is recorded in the public records so that reference can be made to it. Where such restrictions are contained in a plat, they are binding on all subsequent purchasers, and they supplement the applicable zoning laws.

The typical restrictions contained in a plat or a deed may provide that the land shall be used exclusively for residential purposes,[7] that the style and cost of the residence must meet certain specifications, and that certain restrictions inserted in the deed are covenants or promises on the part of the grantee to observe them and are said to run with the land. Even though the grantee fails to include them in a subsequent deed made by him, any new owner is nevertheless subject to them. They remain indefinitely as restrictions against the use of the land, although they may not be enforced if conditions change substantially after the inception of the covenants.

Most of these covenants are inserted for the benefit of surrounding property. They may be enforced by surrounding owners, particularly when the owner of a subdivision inserts similar restrictions in each deed or in the plat. The owner of any lot subject to the restrictions is permitted to enforce the restrictions against other lot owners in the same subdivision. Restrictions in a deed, however, are strictly construed against the party seeking to enforce them. Doubts about restrictions are resolved in favor of freedom of the land from servitude, as a matter of public policy.

Occasionally, a covenant is inserted for the personal benefit of the grantor and will not run with the land. If a grantee, as part of the consideration, covenants to repair a dam on land owned by the grantor, the covenant will not run with the land and will not place a duty upon a subsequent grantee. The promise neither touches nor concerns the land; it is only a personal convenant for the benefit of the grantor.

It should be emphasized that covenants and conditions that discriminate on the grounds of race, creed, color, or national origin are unconstitutional as a denial of equal protection of the laws. Such covenants were common at one time, and many are still incorporated in restrictions that accompany plats. When challenged, they have been held to be unconstitutional. They should be considered void.

---

[7] Sandy Point Improvement Co. v. Huber, p. 406.

SUMMARY

Terminology	1. *Ownership* is synonymous with *title*. 2. *Title* means the right or legal interest in a property item. 3. *Possession* represents the physical control a person may exert over property.

CLASSIFICATIONS OF PROPERTY

Real property	1. The legal interests a person may have in land and things attached to or growing upon the land.
	2. These interests may include the right to the use and benefit of the land's surface, air space, subsurface area, or any combination of these.
Personal property	1. The legal interests in all property other than real property.
	2. Personal property may be tangible, such as a car or book.
	3. Personal property also includes intangible items, such as accounts receivables, goodwill, and rights to enforce contracts.
	4. A name for personal property in general is *chattel*.
Reasons for distinguishing between real and personal property	1. Conflict of laws principles apply differently depending on the type of property.
	2. Real and personal property may be treated differently when the owner dies.
	3. Transactions involving real property generally are more formal than personal property transactions.
	4. These types of property are treated differently from the standpoint of taxation.

FIXTURES

Definition	1. A fixture is an item of personal property that has become part of the land.
Reasons for determining fixture status	1. Fixtures increase the value of real estate.
	2. Fixtures generally are included in the sale of real property—personal property can be retained by the seller.
	3. Fixtures generally are part of the security given to the creditor taking real property as security. Personal property items are excluded from this security.

4. Fixtures usually remain as the landlord's property at the end of a lease, whereas personal property often can be taken by the tenant.

Tests for determining fixture status

1. The annexation test states that the more firmly personal property is attached to real estate, the more likely it is to be a fixture.

2. The adaptation test states that the more the personal property item is used to promote the use and enjoyment of the land, the more likely it is to be a fixture.

3. The intention test, which is the most important, relies on the parties involved to agree whether an item is a fixture or whether it remains as personal property.

REAL PROPERTY OWNERSHIP INTERESTS

Bundle of rights

1. A theoretical approach to the various ownership interests that may be created in real property.

2. These rights may be held by one person, or they may be divided among two or more people.

3. How these rights are divided determines the ownership interests that may be created. Regardless of how many interests are created, the entire bundle of rights must be accountable with respect to each piece of land.

Fee simple estates

1. The basic types of interests presently held by the owner.

2. A fee simple absolute represents the most complete bundle of rights possible.

3. Qualified or conditional fee simple ownership interests may be defeated by the future occurrence of a stated event.

Life estates

1. The life estate is an important tool in estate planning.

2. This type of ownership interest will terminate upon the death of a designated person.

3. The life tenant has a duty to preserve the value of the real property and not to waste the land's resources or improvements.

4. A life estate must be followed by a future interest known as a remainder or reversion.

5. A remainder is held by a third party, and a reversion is held by the grantor of the life estate.

Condominiums and cooperatives

1. A condominium is an individually owned apartment or townhouse in a multiunit complex.

2. In addition to the individual unit, a condominium owner has an undivided interest in the common areas.

3. A person with an interest in a cooperative owns at least one share in a corporation that owns the real property. This personal property interest allows the owner to lease a portion of the real estate.

RESTRICTIONS ON OWNERSHIP INTERESTS

Public restrictions

1. The power of eminent domain allows a government body to take private property for the public use upon the payment of just compensation.

2. Through its zoning regulations, a local community can restrict the use of land. Typically the zones include open space, residential, commercial, and industrial uses.

Private restrictions

1. An easement is the right of one person to use the land owned by another person. Usually an easement is thought of as a permanent restriction that passes from one owner to the next.

2. A license is a less permanent grant of use of land as compared to an easement.

3. Restrictive covenants are commonly seen in subdivisions. Their purpose is to enhance the value of neighboring property by having all owners agree not to use their land in destructive or unpleasing ways.

> **4.** These covenants must be distinguished from conditions. A breach of a covenant may make the owner liable for damages. However, a breach of a condition usually causes the loss of the ownership interest.

CASES

United States v. Causby
328 U.S. 256 (1946)

DOUGLAS, J. This is a case of first impression. The problem presented is whether respondent's [Causby's] property was taken within the meaning of the Fifth Amendment by frequent and regular flights of army and navy aircraft over respondents' land at low altitudes. The Court of Claims held that there was a taking and entered judgment for respondent. . . .

Respondents own 2.8 acres near an airport outside of Greensboro, North Carolina. It has on it a dwelling house, and also various outbuildings which were mainly used for raising chickens. The end of the airport's northwest-southeast runway is 2,220 feet from respondents' barn and 2,275 feet from their house. The path of glide to this runway passes directly over the property—which is 100 feet wide and 1,200 feet long. The thirty to one safe glide angle approved by the Civil Aeronautics Authority passes over this property at eight-three feet, which is sixty-seven feet above the house, sixty-three feet above the barn and 18 feet above the highest tree. . . .

Since the United States began operations in May, 1942, its four-motored heavy bombers, other planes of the heavier type, and its fighter planes have frequently passed over respondents' land and buildings in considerable numbers and rather close together. They come close enough at times to appear barely to miss the tops of the trees and at times so close to the tops of the trees as to blow the old leaves off. The noise is startling. As a result of the noise, respondents had to give up their chicken business. As many as six to ten of their chickens were killed in one day by flying into the walls from fright. The total chickens lost in that manner was

about 150. Production also fell off. The result was the destruction of the use of the property as a commercial chicken farm. Respondents are frequently deprived of their sleep and the family has become nervous and frightened. . . . These are the essential facts found by the Court of Claims. On the basis of these facts, it found that respondents' property had depreciated in value. It held that the United States had taken an easement over the property on June 1, 1942, and that the value of the property destroyed and the easement taken was $2,000.

It is ancient doctrine that at common law ownership of the land extended to the periphery of the universe. . . . But that doctrine has no place in the modern world. The air is a public highway, as Congress has declared. Were that not true, every transcontinental flight would subject the operator to countless trespass suits. Common sense revolts at the idea. To recognize such private claims to the airspace would clog these highways, seriously interfere with their control and development in the public interest, and transfer into private ownership that to which only the public has a just claim. . . .

We have said that the airspace is a public highway. Yet it is obvious that if the landowner is to have full enjoyment of the land, he must have exclusive control of the immediate reaches of the enveloping atmosphere. Otherwise buildings could not be erected, trees could not be planted, and even fences could not be run. The principle is recognized when the law gives a remedy in case overhanging structures are erected on adjoining land. The landowner owns at least as much of the space above the ground as he can occupy or use in connection with the land. . . . The fact that he does not occupy it in a physical sense—by the erection of buildings and the like—is not material. As we have said, the flight of airplanes, which skim the surface but do not touch it, is as much an appropriation of the use of the land as a more conventional entry upon it. We would not doubt that if the United States erected an elevated railway over respondents' land at the precise altitude where its planes now fly, there would be a partial taking, even though none of the supports of the structure rested on the land. The reason is that there would be an intrusion so immediate and direct as to subtract from the owner's full enjoyment of the property and to limit his exploitation of it. While the owner does not in any physical manner occupy that stratum of airspace or make use of it in the conventional sense, he does use it in somewhat the same sense that space left between buildings for the purpose of light and air is used. The superadjacent airspace at this low altitude is so close to the land that continuous invasions of it affect the use of the surface of the land itself. We think that the landowner, as an incident to his ownership, has a claim to it and that invasions of it are in the same category as invasions of the surface. . . .

The airplane is part of the modern environment of life, and the inconveniences which it causes are normally not compensable under the Fifth Amendment. The airspace, apart from the immediate reaches above the land, is part of the public domain. We need not determine at this time what those precise limits are. Flights over private land are not a taking, unless they are so low and so frequent as to be a direct and immediate interference with the enjoyment and use of the land. We need not speculate on that phase of the present case. For the findings of the Court of Claims plainly established that there was a diminution in value of the property and that the frequent, low-level flights were the direct and immediate cause. We agree with the Court of Claims that a servitude has been imposed upon the land. . . .

[The Court then decided that the easement taken by these overflights had not been adequately described.]

Since on this record it is not clear whether the easement taken is a permanent or a temporary one, it would be premature for us to consider whether the amount of the award made by the Court of Claims was proper.

The judgment is reversed and the cause is remanded to the Court of Claims so that it may make the necessary findings in conformity with this opinion.

Reversed.

Pacific Metal Company v. Northwestern Bank of Helena
667 P.2d 958 (Mont. 1983)

Burlington Northern, Inc., leased a part of its right-of-way to Carson Company. This lease allowed Carson Company to construct a building on the leased land, but the lease required Carson Company to remove the building at the lease's termination. Carson Company was obligated to restore the land to its former state. Carson Company built a large warehouse and office building which was affixed to the land by a cement foundation and abutted by cement loading docks.

Through a series of loan transactions, Northwestern Bank obtained a security interest in Carson Company's personal property. This bank perfected its interest in Carson Company's warehouse by proper filings on January 1, 1981. On June 1, 1981, Pacific Metal obtained a judgment against Carson Company. This judgment became a lien against all the real property owned by Carson Company.

WEBER, J. . . . The issue is whether a building that was constructed on leased real property, pursuant to a lease which required the lessee to remove the building upon termination of the lease, is real or personal property. . . .

On June 11, 1982, Pacific Metal initiated a declaratory judgment action against Northwestern Bank seeking a district court judgment declaring that the Carson Company building was real property.

The District Court determined that the building was personal property and that Pacific Metal had no property interest in the building since its judgment lien attached only to real property owned by Carson Company.

Montana law defines real property as:

"(1) land;
(2) that which is affixed to land;
(3) that which is incidental or appurtenant to land;
(4) that which is immovable by law."

A fixture is a thing affixed to the land when it is:

> "(1) attached to it by roots, as in the case of trees, vines, or shrubs;
> (2) imbedded in it, as in the case of walls;
> (3) permanently resting upon it, as in the case of buildings; or
> (4) permanently attached to what is thus permanent as by means of cement, plaster, nails, bolts, or screws."

While these two statutes appear to define all buildings resting upon land as fixtures, it is possible for parties to agree that a building is personal property even though it is attached to and resting upon land. . . .

When additions are affixed to property by a tenant without an agreement allowing him to remove those additions or fixtures, they may not be removed if their removal will damage the premises. . . . Here, an agreement exists specifically authorizing the tenant to construct a warehouse and office building on the premises, and requiring removal of "all structures upon termination of the lease." The terms of the agreement are clear and unambiguous. . . .

The statutory definition of fixtures is "merely a rule for general guidance concerning itself more with ultimate than with probative facts."

This Court has set forth a three-pronged test to determine the status of structures such as the Carson Company building. The character of the structure and the manner in which it is annexed to the realty are factors of lesser weight than evidence of the parties' intent. . . .

In landlord-tenant situations, whether an improvement is personal property or part of the realty is to be determined by the intention of the parties, as expressed in the lease. Rights between a landlord and tenant with respect to fixtures may be modified, restricted or extended by agreement.

. . . [T]he lease agreement constitutes probative evidence that the parties intended the warehouse to retain its character as personalty belonging to the lessee. . . .

We hold that the building was intended by the parties to be personal property, that the building remained personal property, and that the judgment lien did not constitute a lien upon that property.
Affirmed.

Moore v. Phillips
627 P.2d 831 (Kan. App. 1981)

At her husband's death in 1962, Ada Brannan was given a life estate of some farmland that contained a house. The remainder interests were left to Dorothy Moore and Kent Reinhardt. Ada lived in or rented the farmhouse until 1965. From then until her death in 1976, the house was unoccupied, and as a result, it slowly deteriorated. Due to poor family relationships, the remaindermen were estranged from Ada. Although they inspected the house from time to time, the remaindermen took no official action to stop the ongoing waste. However, Dorothy (Ada's daughter) did mention to her mother many times the need to fix up the farmhouse. At Ada's death, Dorothy and Kent filed a claim against Ada's estate for $16,159, the amount of damage done to the house during the life estate. The representative of Ada's estate did not deny that waste had occurred. Instead she asserted the defense that the remaindermen are barred from filing a claim, since they unreasonably delayed taking action to prevent Ada's waste.

PRAGER J. . . . In order to place this case in proper perspective, it would be helpful to summarize some of the basic principles of law applicable where a remainderman asserts a claim of waste against a life tenant. They are as follows:

(1) A life tenant . . . occupies a fiduciary relation to the remaindermen. The life tenant . . . cannot injure or dispose of the property to the injury of the rights of the remaindermen, but he . . . may use the property for his exclusive benefit and take all the income and profits.

(2) It is the duty of a life tenant to keep the property subject to the life estate in repair so as to preserve the property and to prevent decay or waste. Stated in another way, the law imposes upon a tenant the obligation to return the premises to the . . . remaindermen at the end of the term unimpaired by the negligence of the tenant.

(3) The term "waste" implies neglect or misconduct resulting in material damages to or loss of property, but does not include ordinary depreciation of property due to age and normal use over a comparatively short period of time.

(4) Waste may be either voluntary or permis-

sive. Voluntary waste, sometimes spoken of as commissive waste, consists of the commission of some deliberate or voluntary destructive act. Permissive waste is the failure of the tenant to exercise the ordinary care of a prudent man for the preservation and protection of the estate.

(5) The owner of a reversion or remainder in fee has a number of remedies available to him against a life tenant who commits waste. He may recover compensatory damages for the injuries sustained. He may have injunctive relief in equity. . . .

(6) By statute in Kansas, "[a] person seized of an estate in remainder or reversion may maintain an action for waste or trespass for injury to the inheritance, notwithstanding an intervening estate for life or years." Thus a remainderman does not have to wait until the life tenant dies in order to bring an appropriate action for waste.

(7) Where the right of action of the remainderman or landlord is based upon permissive waste, it is generally held that the injury is continuing in nature and that the statute of limitations does not commence to run in favor of the tenant until the expiration of the tenancy. . . .

(8) There is authority which holds that an action for waste may be lost by laches. Likewise, estoppel may be asserted as a defense in an action for waste. The doctrine of laches and estoppel are closely related, especially where there is complaint of delay which has placed another at a disadvantage. Laches is sometimes spoken of as a species of estoppel. Laches is a wholly negative thing, the result of a failure to act; estoppel on the other hand may involve an affirmative act on the part of some party of the lawsuit. The mere passage of time is not enough to invoke the doctrine of laches. Each case

must be governed by its own facts, and what might be considered a lapse of sufficient time to defeat an action in one case might be insufficient in another. Laches, in legal significance, is not mere delay, but delay that works a disadvantage to another.

The basic question for our determination is whether the district court erred in holding that the defense of laches or estoppel should not be applied in this case. We have concluded that the district court did not commit error in its rejection of the defense of laches or estoppel under the circumstances of this case. . . . The evidence is clear that the life tenant, Ada Brannan, failed to carry out her duty as life tenant . . . to keep the property in reasonable repair. The claim of waste does not arise out of any act on the part of the remaindermen. Preservation of the property was the responsibility of the life tenant. . . . The fact that permissive waste occurred was proved beyond question. If the life tenant had been alive, she could not very well have disputed the fact that the property has been allowed to deteriorate. Hence, any delay in filing the action until after Ada's death could not have resulted in prejudice to her executrix. There is no evidence in the record to support the defense of estoppel.

Furthermore, the evidence was undisputed that the life tenant was an elderly woman who died in August of 1976 at the age of 83. The position of Dorothy Moore was that she did not wish to file an action which would aggravate her mother and take funds which her mother might need during her lifetime. Even though Dorothy Moore was estranged from her mother, the law should not require her to sue her mother during her lifetime under these circumstances. . . .

Affirmed.

Harris v. Audubon Society of Rhode Island
468 A.2d 258 (R.I. 1983)

Ralph W. Harris died on December 28, 1976. In his will, he devised a sixty-acre parcel, to his wife, Helen G. Harris, for the duration of her life. On her death, the remainder was to pass to the Audubon Society to be used as "a wildlife refuge and bird sanctuary to be known as 'The Alice O.

Harris Memorial Wildlife Refuge.'" Alice O. Harris was the testator's first wife.

On a small section of the property there is a commercially operated kennel for cats and dogs. The testator had operated the kennel at one time and later leased it to a third party. [T]he life tenant, and [the] executor under the will, have continued to lease the kennel to a third party. This lease produces about $3,600 a year in rental income for the life tenant.

In 1977, less than a year after the testator's death, the Rhode Island Department of Health inspected the kennel and ordered improvements to the kennel facility as a condition of license renewal. The cost of these improvements is estimated at $28,570.

SHEA, J. . . . The issue presented . . . concerns the responsibility, if any, of the remainderman for the cost of improvements to the property ordered by the Department of Health of the State of Rhode Island.

In his decision, the trial justice held that the life tenant and the estate of the testator should bear the full financial responsibility for the improvements ordered by the Department of Health. . . .

It is well settled that a life tenant who makes permanent improvements to property does not acquire a lien that is enforceable against the remainderman. The life tenant should not be permitted to make improvements for the benefit of the life estate at the remainderman's expense which the remainderman does not desire.

There are, however, exceptions to this general rule which are equally well settled. Section 127 of 1 *Restatement of the Law of Property* (1936) provides:

> (1) The owner of an estate for life has a power to impose a lien upon the interests subsequent to the estate for life, for the portion of the cost of such improvement ascertained under the rule stated in Subsection (2), when such improvement is of a permanent character and . . . (b) the owner of the estate for life was compelled by governmental authority to make it. . . .

The plaintiffs argue . . . that the facts of this case fall within the exception set forth in section 127(1)(b) of the restatement having to do with improvements mandated by the government. After examination of the cited cases that apply this exception, we conclude that plaintiffs are in error. That exception has been applied principally when the property has only one practical use, generally as a residence, and the modifications to the property, such as indoor plumbing and structural rehabilitation, are required by municipal regulations in order to obtain an occupancy permit. Two other facts common to those cases are that the property was received by the life tenant in an untenantable condition and that the improvements were found to benefit the remainderman. . . .

In this case, the trial justice found as a fact that the proposed improvements, although permanent in nature, applied only to the kennel, which was a discretionary use by the life tenant. The kennel operation could not be carried on by the remainderman since its use of the property was limited to that of a wildlife refuge. This court has held many times that a trial justice's findings sitting without a jury are entitled to great weight and will not be overturned unless clearly wrong.

The findings of the trial justice in this case were not clearly wrong. The kennel use was forbidden to the remainderman, and the improvements therefore were not necessary to preserve the remainder interest, nor would the improvements benefit the remainder. This case does not come within the governmentally mandated improvements exception.

Consequently, the trial justice below was correct when he determined that the life tenant was not entitled to reimbursement for the proposed improvements to the kennel. . . .

Affirmed.

Poletown Neighborhood Council v. City of Detroit
304 N.W.2d 455 (Mich. 1981)

PER CURIAM. This case arises out of a plan by the Detroit Economic Development Corporation to acquire, by condemnation if necessary, a large tract of land to be conveyed to General Motors Corporation as a site for construction of an assembly plant. The plaintiffs, a neighborhood association and several individual residents of the affected area, brought suit . . . to challenge the project. . . .

Defendants' motions for summary judgment were denied pending trial on a single question of fact: whether the city abused its discretion in determining that condemnation of plaintiffs' property was necessary to complete the project.

The trial lasted 10 days and resulted in a judgment for defendants and an order on December 9, 1980, dismissing plaintiffs' complaint. The plaintiffs file a claim of appeal. . . .

This case raises a question of paramount

importance to the future welfare of this state and its residents: Can a municipality use the power of eminent domain . . . to condemn property for transfer to a private corporation to build a plant to promote industry and commerce, thereby adding jobs and taxes to the economic base of the municipality and state? . . .

The term "public use" has not received a narrow or inelastic definition by this Court in prior cases. Indeed, this Court has stated that " '[a] public use changes with changing conditions of society' " and that " '[t]he right of the public to receive and enjoy the benefit of the use determines whether the use is public or private.' " . . .

[T]he legislature has authorized municipalities to acquire property by condemnation in order to provide industrial and commercial sites and the means of transfer from the municipality to private users.

Plaintiffs-appellants do not challenge the declaration of the legislature that programs to alleviate and prevent conditions of unemployment and to preserve and develop industry and commerce are essential public purposes. Nor do they challenge the proposition that legislation to accomplish this purpose falls within the Constitutional grant of general legislative power to the legislature. . . .

What plaintiffs-appellants do challenge is the constitutionality of using the power of eminent domain to condemn one person's property to convey it to another private person in order to bolster the economy. They argue that whatever incidental benefit may accrue to the public, assembling land to General Motors' specifications for conveyance to General Motors for its uncontrolled use in profit making is really a taking for private use and not a public use because General Motors is the primary beneficiary of the condemnation.

The defendants-appellees contend, on the other hand, that the controlling public purpose in taking this land is to create an industrial site which will be used to alleviate and prevent conditions of unemployment and fiscal distress. The fact that it will be conveyed to and ultimately used by a private manufacturer does not defeat this predominant public purpose.

There is no dispute about the law. All agree that condemnation for a public use or purpose is permitted. All agree that condemnation for a private use or purpose is forbidden. Similarly, condem-

nation for a private use cannot be authorized whatever its incidental public benefit and condemnation for a public purpose cannot be forbidden whatever the incidental private gain. The heart of this dispute is whether the proposed condemnation is for the primary benefit of the public or the private user. . . .

In the court below, the plaintiffs-appellants challenged the necessity for the taking of the land for the proposed project. In this regard the city presented substantial evidence of the severe economic conditions facing the residents of the city and state, the need for new industrial development to revitalize local industries, the economic boost the proposed project would provide, and the lack of other adequate available sites to implement the project.

When there is such public need, "[t]he abstract right [of an individual] to make use of his own property in his own way is compelled to yield to the general comfort and protection of community, and to a proper regard to relative rights in others." Eminent domain is an inherent power of the sovereign of the same nature as, albeit more severe than, the power to regulate the use of land through zoning or the prohibition of public nuisances.

In the instant case the benefit to be received by the municipality invoking the power of eminent domain is a clear and significant one and is sufficient to satisfy this Court that such a project was an intended and a legitimate object of the Legislature when it allowed municipalities to exercise condemnation powers even though a private party will also, ultimately, receive a benefit as an incident thereto.

The power of eminent domain is to be used in this instance primarily to accomplish the essential public purposes of alleviating unemployment and revitalizing the economic base of the community. The benefit to a private interest is merely incidental.

Our determination that this project falls within the public purpose, as stated by the Legislature, does not mean that every condemnation proposed by an economic development corporation will meet with similar acceptance simply because it may provide some jobs or add to the industrial or commercial base. If the public benefit was not so clear and significant, we would hesitate to sanction approval of such a project. The power of eminent domain is restricted to furthering public uses and purposes and is not to be exercised without substantial proof that the public is primarily to be benefited. Where, as here, the condemnation power is exercised in a way that benefits specific and identifiable private interests, a court inspects with heightened scrutiny the claim that the public interest is the predominant interest being advanced. Such public benefit cannot be speculative or mar-

ginal but must be clear and significant if it is to be within the legitimate purpose as stated by the Legislature. We hold this project is warranted on the basis that its significance for the people of Detroit and the state has been demonstrated.

Affirmed.

Bull v. Salsman
435 So.2d 27 (Ala. 1983)

ALMON, J. . . . Defendant J.C. Bull owns approximately 183 acres of land in Winston County, fronting on Alabama Highway # 195. He purchased this property in 1976 or 1977 from the heirs of Jodie M. Lee. Plaintiff Erin Harper Salsman owns forty acres of land to the north and east of Mr. Bull's property. She and her son Fred Salsman, III, brought this suit to have the court "establish and declare the old roadway which traverses the defendant's property from Alabama Highway 195 to the plaintiffs' property a permanent right-of-way or easement. . . ." The complaint alleged that "the said easement, right-of-way or roadway is theirs by prescription. . . .

The trial court held that an easement by prescription has been established.

Mr. Bull appeals, arguing that the Salsmans have not proved facts which would entitle them to either an easement by prescription. . . . He cites authorities for the propositions that an easement by prescription can be established only by use for a period of twenty years or more, adverse to the owner of the premises, under claim of right, exclusive, continuous, and uninterrupted, with actual or presumptive knowledge of the owner. . . .

To establish an easement by prescription, the claimant must use the premises over which the easement is claimed for a period of twenty years or more, adversely to the owner of the premises, under claim of right, exclusive, continuous, and uninterrupted, with actual or presumptive knowledge of the owner. The presumption is that the use is permissive, and the claimant has the burden of proving that the use was adverse to the owner.

To determine whether the Salsmans have established an easement by prescription, it will be necessary to set out the facts in more detail.

In 1933, Mrs. Salsman's parents, the Harpers, set out to build a vacation cabin on the piece of land to which the Salsmans are now seeking access. A stream known as Clifty Creek runs across the land which is now owned by Mr. Bull and which was previously owned by the Lees. The road used by the Harpers at the time, and now claimed by Mrs. Salsman, crossed this creek on the Lees' land. Mr. Harper hired Homer Noblett to replace an old bridge across Clifty Creek in 1933. The Harpers substantially completed their cabin, but their son, Mrs. Salsman's brother, was killed in an accident with a firearm on Clifty Creek in 1934. They did not use their cabin after the accident, and vandals stole the doors and windows from it. Mr. Harper disassembled the cabin and sold the logs to a neighbor.

The bridge built by Mr. Noblett washed away some time in the late forties or early fifties. Mrs. Salsman testified that it was still standing in 1954 when she sold timber off of her land and used the road in question to haul the timber out. She testified that she and her family had visited the land four or five times a year since the thirties, and that since the bridge had washed away they had parked the car when they reached the creek bank. She testified that they had gone to the land by way of this road every winter to cut a Christmas tree for their home. Her son testified that he had gone on the land every year to hunt and fish.

The Lees' land was largely wooded, but had a large field which the road in question skirted for the first portion . . . of the Lees' property. The Lee family home was directly across Highway # 195 from this field, and the testimony was that the Lees could see the field and the road from their house. About seven years before he died, Jodie Lee put a gate on the road where it met the highway, but the evidence is unclear whether the Salsmans merely opened the gate or drove around it. Sam Lee, Jodie Lee's brother, testified that he had heard that the Harpers "slipped in" and hunted on their land. After Mr. Bull bought the land, he put up a better gate and locked it, but the Salsmans drove around it.

The above evidence and other evidence of record supports the trial court's judgment that the Salsmans have an easement for private roadway purposes. There was evidence that the Lees were aware of the Harpers' and the Salsmans' use of the property and that they did not give them permission to use the road. The use of the road was not frequent after the Harper boy died in 1933, but the evidence that it was used several times every year suffices, under the circumstances, to meet the test that it was continuous and uninterrupted. The facts that Mr. Harper built a bridge on the road and that they used the road in spite of the Lees' gate indicate that they used the road under claim of right. The requirement that the use be exclusive does not mean that it be to the exclusion of the Lees, but that the Harpers' claim was independent of any other claim. The Harpers have been using the road since the 1920's, when they acquired the land.

Thus, all of the requirements for an easement by prescription have been met, and the trial court did not err in determining that the Salsmans have an easement across Mr. Bull's land. . . .

Affirmed.

Sandy Point Improvement Co. v. Huber 613 P.2d 160 (Wash.App. 1980)

JAMES, J. Plaintiff Sandy Point Improvement Company was granted a permanent injunction enjoining defendants Leonard and Delores Huber from constructing a building on the Hubers' property. We affirm.

The Hubers purchased two adjoining lots within the Sandy Point Heights development in Whatcom County. On one of the lots they started construction of a storage building to store their boats, car, tractor, camper, 32-foot travel-trailer, washer and dryer, rock-cutting equipment and canned goods. The Declaration of Restrictions, Easements and Reservations of Sandy Point Heights reads in relevant part:

> Except for portions of the real property as may be used for recreational purposes or common service facilities by Sandy Point Improvement Company, a Washington Corporation, no lot in the plat of Sandy Point Heights shall be used for any purpose other than for residential purposes. . . .

The trial judge found that the storage building was not for residential purposes and enjoined further construction. . . . The trial judge found that "[t]he Defendants' building plan, given its size and purpose, is not consistent with any reasonable interpretation of residential use." We conclude the finding is supported by substantial evidence.

It is well settled in this jurisdiction that words in a deed of conveyance or any instrument restricting the use of real property by the grantee are to be construed strictly against the grantor and those claiming the benefit of the restriction. Restrictive covenants upon the use of real property will not be extended beyond the clear meaning of the language. In *Beros* v. *Cape George Colony Club,* the court stated:

> The intent of the parties to the covenant is the key factor in determination of the effect to be given restrictions.

> When meaning is doubtful, surrounding circumstances must be considered to determine proper meaning. Doubts must be resolved in favor of free use of land, but intended necessary implications from the writing may be enforced. Intent is preeminently a question of fact.

However, unambiguous language in a covenant will be given its plain and reasonable meaning; the courts will not apply a rule of construction when it will defeat the obvious purpose of the restriction.

A private garage is a proper appurtenance necessary to the enjoyment of a dwelling house and does not violate a "for residence purposes only" covenant. However, if the garage is placed on an adjoining lot, it is no longer deemed to be appurtenant and does violate such a restriction even though used in connection with a residence on an adjoining lot.

Affirmed.

REVIEW QUESTIONS

1. Identify the terms in column A by matching each to the appropriate statement in column B.

A	B
1. Title	**a.** The legal interests a person may have in land and things attached to or growing upon the land.
2. Possession	**b.** This power allows the government to take private property for public use upon the payment of just compensation.
3. Real property	**c.** An item of personal property that has become attached to land and is treated as real property.
4. Chattel	**d.** The legal interest in property, synonymous with ownership.
5. Fixture	**e.** The most important method for determining fixture status.
6. Intention test	**f.** Another name for personal property.
7. Fee simple absolute	**g.** The most complete ownership interest in real property.
8. Remainder	**h.** A permanent right of one person to use the land of another person.
9. Eminent domain	**i.** The right to physical control of the use and enjoyment of property.
10. Easement	**j.** The future interest that follows a life estate and is held by a third party.

2. Why is it important to make a legal distinction between personal property and real property? Explain.

3. List the three tests for determining if personal property has become a fixture.

4. The state of New Jersey sought to tax as real property cranes used in the loading and unloading of ships designed to carry freight in containers. These large cranes were mounted and movable on tracks at the pier. Each crane weighed 1,000,000 pounds and required special concrete piles for the base of the piers. Each crane was 50 feet wide and stood 170 feet above the rail. The boom could be raised to 245 feet. Complex electrical systems were required for operation of the cranes. The cranes were movable by barge. Were the cranes fixtures and thus taxable as part of the real estate? Explain.

5. Turner owned and operated a comprehensive cable television system that contained about 630 miles of feeder cable. The cable was annexed to telephone poles owned by the telephone company, under a lease that required removal if the telephone company should need the space for its own service needs. The county assessed the television cable system as real property, contending that the cable is a fixture under common law principles. Should the television cable be classified as a fixture? Why?

6. What is the advantage of describing ownership interests in real property as a bundle of rights?

7. A husband willed certain land to his wife for life, with the remainder to their children. After the husband's death, his wife leased the property to a coal company, which strip-mined the land. Is it legal for a holder of a life estate to transfer her interest? Do the children have a good cause of action against the coal company? Why?

8. What are the two requirements that must be satisfied in order for the government properly to exercise the power of eminent domain?

9. List the four basic classifications zoning ordinances use in regulating the use of land.

10. Marguerite sold land to Joe, reserving her right of free egress and ingress over the private road. Joe sold the land to Kim, but the deed did not mention that Kim was taking the land subject to the easement contained in the conveyance by Marguerite to Joe. Is the easement effective against Kim? Why?

11. Edgell filed suit against Divver to cancel or modify private driveway easements. The easements gave Divver the right to drive across Edgell's land. The easements were granted by Edgell's predecessor in title and were a matter of record. At the time the easements were granted, both the dominant parcel and the servient parcel were used for residential purposes, but the servient parcel is now zoned for commercial uses. Is Edgell entitled to cancel or modify these easements? Why?

12. Alan owned land in a subdivision and planned to construct two apartment buildings on the land. Some residents of the subdivision brought suit for an injunction, contending that the construction would violate the covenants contained in the subdivision plat, which restricted buildings to single-family residences. Alan claimed that the covenant was no longer effective because the land had been rezoned for multifamily buildings. Should the restrictive covenant remain enforceable? Why?

13. Terry planned to construct an apartment building on land he owned in a subdivision. The plat of the subdivision contained a restrictive covenant prohibiting use of its land for business purposes. Some residents of the subdivision contended this covenant prohibited Terry's plan. Terry sought a court decision determining the impact of the covenant on his proposal. Should the covenant be interpreted to prevent the construction of an apartment building? Explain.

19 ACQUIRING TITLE TO PROPERTY

In addition to the general legal principles of property discussed in chapter 18, it is important to understand how title to both personal and real property is acquired. The legal requirements for obtaining an ownership interest differ greatly, depending on whether the property involved is personal or real. Therefore, this chapter first examines the methods of acquiring title to personal property. It then concentrates on both voluntary and involuntary transfers of real property. An understanding of acquiring title to property will allow us to examine transactions involving property in the following chapters.

1. Methods

Title to personal property may be acquired through any of the following methods: *original possession, transfer, accession,* or *confusion.* Original possession is a method of extremely limited applicability. It may be used to obtain title over wild animals and fish or things that are available for appropriation by individuals. Property that is in its native state and over which no one as yet has taken full and complete control belongs to the first person who reduces such property to his exclusive possession. Property once reduced to ownership, but later abandoned, belongs to the first party next taking possession.

In addition to the above, it might be said that property created through mental or physical labor belongs to the creator unless he has agreed to create it for someone else for compensation. Books, inventions, and trademarks would be included under this heading. This kind of property is usually protected by the government through means of copyrights, patents, and trademarks.

2. Title by Transfer—In General

As a general rule, a transferee receives the rights of the transferor, and a transferee takes no better title than the transferor had. If the transferor of the personal property did not have title to the property, the transferee would not have title, either, even though the transferee believes that his transferor had a good title. Suppose Pastor Jones purchases a new stereo set for a church from parishioner Tithe. Unknown to Pastor Jones, Tithe had stolen the stereo from the Bulldog Music Store. The stereo set still belongs to Bulldog Music, and the church has no title to it. An innocent purchaser from a thief obtains no title to the property purchased, and no subsequent purchaser stands in any better position. Because the thief had no title or ownership, persons who acquired the property from or through the thief have no title or ownership. If the transferor of the property has a voidable title, and he sells property to an innocent purchaser, the transferee may obtain good title to the property. Assume that through fraudulent representations, Fred acquires title to Sam's property. Sam could avoid the transaction with Fred and obtain return of his property. If Fred sells the property to Ann, and she does not know about his fraudulent representations, Sam cannot disaffirm against Ann. Ann has good title to the property, since she is a good-faith purchaser for value.

Title to personal property may be transferred by sale, gift, will, or operation of law. Since it is probably most relevant in business transactions, the law relating to transfer by sale is discussed in chapters 23 and 24 on Article 2 of the Uniform Commercial Code. Transfers of title by gift are taken up in the next section. Wills and intestate succession are discussed in chapter 22. Finally, transfer of title to personal property may occur at a judicial sale or lien foreclosure. Chapter 33 on the secured party's rights under a security agreement upon default by the debtor is an example of how the law operates to transfer title to personal property.

3. Transfer by *Inter Vivos* Gift

The phrase *inter vivos* refers to gifts made voluntarily during the life of the party transferring title. A *testamentary* gift is one which is effective only at the owner's death.

Generally there are just two people required to accomplish an *inter vivos* gift. The *donor* is the party making the gift of property. The *donee* is the one receiving or acquiring title to the property. The law requires that three elements be satisfied in order to have a valid *inter vivos* gift. These elements are (1) the donor's intent to make a gift, (2) delivery of possession by the donor, and (3) acceptance of the gift by the donee. From a legal standpoint, the element of delivery usually is most important. Unless a contrary intent is clear and obvious, the physical change of possession of personal property creates a presumption that both donor and donee consent to a gift. However, in the event there is a dispute over the true ownership of personal property, all three elements must be established in order to have a valid gift.[1]

---

[1] Barham v. Jones, p. 422.

The delivery can be actual or constructive or symbolic, if the situation demands. Thus, if the property is in storage, the donor could make a delivery by giving the donee the warehouse receipt. A donor may also accomplish delivery by giving the donee something that is a token representing the donee's dominion and control. A delivery of the keys to an automobile may be a valid symbolic delivery, although a symbolic or constructive delivery will not suffice if actual delivery is reasonably possible.

In general, an executory promise to make a gift is not enforceable, since the donee typically has not given consideration to support the donor's promise. However, subject to one exception, an executed or completed gift cannot be rescinded by the donor. Gifts *causa mortis* constitute an exception to the general rule on the finality of completed gifts. A gift *causa mortis* is in contemplation of death and refers to the situation in which a person who is, or who believes he is, facing death makes a gift on the assumption that death is imminent. A person about to embark on a perilous trip or to undergo a serious operation or one who has an apparently incurable and fatal illness might make a gift and deliver the item to the donee on the assumption that he may soon die. If he returns safely or does not die, the donor is allowed to revoke the gift and recover the property from the donee.

4. Title by Accession

Accession literally means "adding to." In the law of personal property, accession has two basic meanings. First of all, it refers to an owner's right to all that his property produces. The owner of a cow is also the owner of each calf born, and the owner of lumber is the owner of a table made from the lumber by another. *Accession* is also the legal term used to signify the acquisition of title to personal property when it is incorporated into other property or joined with other property.

When accession occurs, who has title is frequently in issue. The general rule is that when the goods of two different owners are united without the willful misconduct of either party, the title to the resulting product goes to the owner of the major portion of the goods. This rule is based on the principle that personal property permanently added to other property and forming a minor portion of the finished product becomes part of the larger unit. Since title can be in only one party, it is in the owner of the major portion. The owner of the minor portion might recover damages if his portion were wrongfully taken from him. The law of accession simply prevents the owner of the minor portion from recovering the property itself.

The law of accession distinguishes between the rights of innocent and willful trespassers, although both are wrongful. An *innocent* trespasser to personal property is one who acts through mistake or conduct that is not intentionally wrongful. A *willful* trespasser cannot obtain title against the original owner under any circumstances.

Suppose that Garrod owns some raw materials, and that Durham inadvertently uses these materials to manufacture a product. The product belongs to Garrod. If Durham also adds some raw materials of his own, the manufactured product belongs to Garrod. If Durham becomes the owner, Garrod is entitled to recover her damages. If Garrod is the owner, Durham is not entitled to anything, since he used Garrod's materials without authority to do so. If Durham had knowingly used Garrod's raw materials, Durham could not recover the completed product under any circumstances due to his willful misconduct.

In order to make this example an even clearer illustration of the law of accession, suppose that each of the labels on the following chart (Fig. 19–1) describes actions by Durham. The owner of the finished product is indicated in each box. As you can see, the real distinction occurs when Durham makes a major addition to Garrod's raw materials. It is under these circumstances that the innocent or intentional nature of Durham's trespass becomes most important.

FIGURE 19–1

	NO ADDITION	MINOR ADDITION	MAJOR ADDITION
Innocent Wrongdoer	Garrod	Garrod	Durham
Intentional Wrongdoer	Garrod	Garrod	Garrod

Similar issues arise when unauthorized repairs are made to an owner's personal property and when property subject to an accession is sold. In general, the owner is entitled to goods as repaired, irrespective of the repair's value, unless the parts added during the repair can be severed without damaging the original goods. If the property that is the subject of accession is sold to a good-faith purchaser, the rights and liabilities of the third party are the same as those of the original trespasser. A willful trespasser has no title and can convey none. The owner can recover the property without any liability to the third party. If the third party makes improvements or repairs, he has the right to remove his additions if they can be removed without damaging the original goods.

5. Title by Confusion

Property of such a character that one unit may not be distinguished from another unit and that is usually sold by weight or measure is known as *fungible property*. Grain, hay, logs, wine, oil, and similar property are of this nature. When it belongs to various parties, it may be mixed by intention, accident, mistake, or wrongful misconduct of an owner of some of the goods. Confusion of fungible property belonging to various owners, assuming that no misconduct (confusion by consent, accident, or mistake) is involved, results in an undivided ownership of the total mass. To illustrate: Grain is stored in a public warehouse by many parties. Each owner holds an undivided interest in the total mass, his particular interest being dependent upon the amount stored by him. Should there be a partial destruction of the total mass, the loss would be divided proportionately.

Confusion of goods that results from the wrongful conduct of one of the parties causes the title to the total mass to pass to the innocent party. If the mixture is divisible, an exception exists. The wrongdoer, if he is able to show that the resultant mass is equal in value per unit to that of the innocent party, is able to recover his share. If the new mixture is worth no less per unit than that formerly belonging to the innocent party, the wrongdoer may claim his portion of the new mass by presenting convincing evidence of the amount added by him. If two masses are added together and the wrongdoer can only establish his proportion of one mass, he is only entitled to that proportion of the combined mass.

For example, Farmers Smith and Jones grow corn on adjoining property. Farmer Smith agrees to store Jones's corn in return for 25 percent of the corn stored. Without measuring the amount of corn stored for Jones, Smith adds this corn to a silo containing corn grown by Smith. Since there is no certainty as to how much corn belongs to Jones, a court would probably award him 75 percent of all the corn stored. Smith is limited to a one-fourth interest of even his corn, since he wrongfully commingled a fungible product. This result is necessary in order to ensure that Jones recovers at least his share of the corn.

6. Abandoned, Lost, and Mislaid Property

Property is said to be *abandoned* whenever it is discarded by the true owner who, at that time, has no intention of reclaiming it. The property belongs to the first individual again reducing it to possession.

Property is *lost* whenever, as a result of negligence, accident, or some other cause, it is found at some place other than that chosen by the owner. Title to lost property continues to rest with the true owner, but until he has been ascertained, the finder may keep it. The finder's title is good against everyone except the true owner. The rights of the finder are superior to those of the person in charge of the property upon which the lost article is found unless the finder is a trespasser. Occasionally, state statutes provide for newspaper publicity concerning articles that have been found. If the owner cannot be located, the found property or a portion of it reverts to the state or county if the property's value exceeds an established minimum.

Property is *mislaid* or *misplaced* if its owner has intentionally placed it at a certain spot, but the manner of placement indicates that he has forgotten to pick it up. The presumption is that he will eventually remember where he left it and return for it. The finder must turn it over to the owner of the premises, who may hold it until the owner is located. The distinctions between abandoned, lost, and mislaid property are subtle and frequently litigated.[2]

7. Introduction

Title to real property may be acquired (1) by original entry, called title by occupancy; (2) by a deed from the owner; (3) by judicial sale; (4) by benefit of the period of the statute of limitations, called adverse possession; (5) by accretion, which may happen when a river, lake, or other body of water creates new land by depositing soil; and (6) by will or descent under intestacy statutes.

Original entry refers to a title obtained from the sovereign. Except in those portions of the United States where the original title to the land was derived from

ACQUIRING TITLE TO REAL PROPERTY— VOLUNTARY TRANSFERS

---

[2] Narum v. City of Billings, p. 424.

grants that were issued by the king of England and other sovereigns who took possession of the land by conquest, title to all the land in the United States was derived from the United States government. Private individuals who occupied land for the period of time prescribed by federal statute and met other conditions established by law acquired title by patent from the federal government.

Delivery of a valid deed is the most common method of voluntarily transferring real property ownership interests. Sections 8 through 14 examine the essential requirements and types of deeds frequently used. The final part of this chapter discusses some of the ways in which title to land may be lost by the owner involuntarily. These topics include transfers by judicial sales, adverse possession, and accretion.

8. Essential Requirements of All Deeds—Describing Real Estate

A *deed* is the legal document that represents the ownership interest in or title to land. Although there are other essential elements of deeds, one of the most important parts of any deed is the legal description of the land involved. By reference to the deed, people must be able to get the information that allows them to determine the exact location of the land described. This description is based on one of the following acceptable systems: (1) the metes and bounds system, (2) the rectangular survey system, or (3) the plat system. The *metes and bounds* system establishes boundary lines by reference to natural or artificial monuments; that is, to fixed points, such as roads, streams, fences, trees. A metes and bounds description starts with a monument, determines the angle of the line and the distance to the next monument, and so forth, until the tract is fully enclosed and described. Because surveyors may not always agree, the law of metes and bounds creates an order of precedence. Reference to monuments controls over courses (angles), and courses control over distances. In general, the least important factor to consider is the amount of acres contained in a description.[3]

The term *rectangular survey* refers to a system of describing land by using a known base line and principal meridians. The base line runs from east to west, and principal meridians run from north to south. Townships are thus located in relation to these lines. For example a township may be described as 7 North, Range 3 East of the third Principal Meridian. This township is seven townships north of the base line and three east of the third principal meridian. The townships, then, would be divided into 36 sections, each section being one square mile. (There will be fractional sections, owing to the convergence of the meridians.) With the exception of the fractional sections, each section consists of 640 acres. Parts of the section are described by their locations within it, as Fig. 19–2 illustrates.

A *plat* is a recorded document dividing a tract described by metes and bounds or congressional survey into streets, blocks, and lots. The land may thereafter be described in relation to the recorded plat simply by giving the lot number, block, and subdivision name. Lot 8 in Block 7 of Ben Johnson's

---

[3] Brown v. Rines, p. 425.

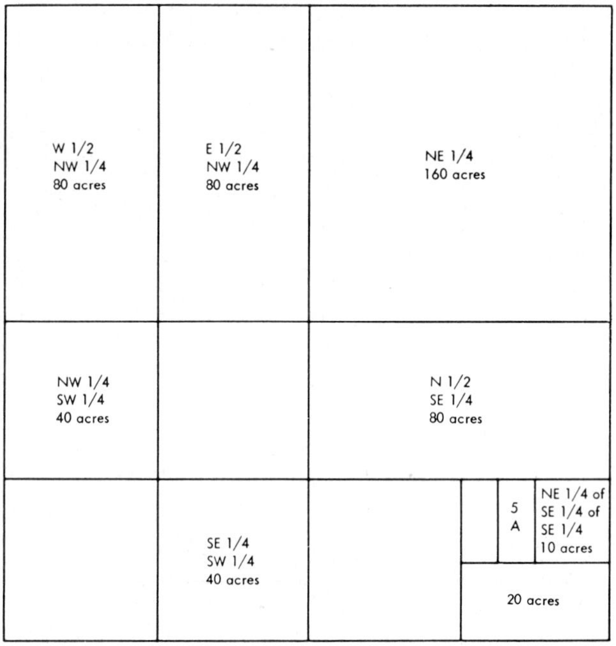

FIGURE 19–2

W 1/2 NW 1/4 80 acres	E 1/2 NW 1/4 80 acres	NE 1/4 160 acres
NW 1/4 SW 1/4 40 acres		N 1/2 SE 1/4 80 acres
	SE 1/4 SW 1/4 40 acres	5 A · NE 1/4 of SE 1/4 of SE 1/4 10 acres / 20 acres

Subdivision in the City of Emporia, Kansas, might describe real property located in that municipality.

9. Other Essential Requirements of All Deeds

The statutes of the various states provide the necessary form, language, and execution requirements of deeds. For example, these statutes usually require that the parties involved be identified at the beginning of the deed. Often these parties are referred to as the grantor and grantee. All deeds must contain language that indicates the type of ownership interest being conveyed. Also the deed must state clearly that this interest is being transferred to the grantee. A properly drafted deed needs to be signed by the grantor, and in some states sealed, witnessed, or acknowledged in the presence of a notary public. Finally, the deed must be delivered.

A deed is not effective until it is delivered—that is, placed entirely out of the control of the grantor. This delivery usually occurs by the handing of the instrument to the grantee or to some third party known as an escrow agent. The delivery by the grantor must occur during the lifetime of the grantor. It cannot be delivered by someone else after the grantor's death, even if the grantor has ordered the delivery.

In order that the owner of real estate may notify all persons of the change in title to the property, the statutes of the various states provide that deeds shall be recorded in the recording office of the county in which the land is located. Failure to record a deed by a new owner makes it possible for the former owner to convey and pass good title to the property to an innocent third party, although the former owner has no right to do so and would be liable to his first grantee in such a case.

10. Optional Elements of Deeds

In addition to the essential requirements of all deeds, a deed may contain all, some, or none of the optional elements referred to as covenants or warranties. These covenants or warranties are promises or guarantees made by the grantor pertaining to the land and the grantor's bundle of rights with respect to it. These covenants may include a promise that (1) at the time of making the deed, the grantor has fee simple title and the right and power to convey it (*covenant of seizin*); (2) the property is free from all encumbrances except those noted in the deed (*covenant against encumbrances*); (3) the grantee and his successors will have the quiet and peaceful enjoyment of the property (*covenant of quiet enjoyment*); and (4) the grantor will defend the title of the grantee if anyone else should claim the property (*covenant of further assurances*).

Many different kinds of deeds are used throughout the country, the statutes of each state providing for the various types. The common types are the *warranty deed,* the *grant deed,* the *bargain and sale deed,* and the *quitclaim deed.* There are also special types of deeds used when the grantor holds a special legal position at the time of conveyance. Special deeds are used by the executors and administrators of estates, by guardians, and by sheriffs or other court officials executing deeds in their official capacity. The major distinction among types of deeds relates to the covenants or warranties the grantor of the deed makes to the grantee. A deed may contain several warranties or none at all, depending upon the type of deed and the language used.

11. Warranty Deed

From the grantee's perspective, the warranty deed provides the broadest protection that the grantor is conveying clear title to the land described in the deed. This protection is provided because the warranty deed contains all four of the covenants mentioned above. Therefore, the warranty deed is the type of deed grantees usually insist upon in traditional real estate sales transactions.

The covenant of seizin is breached when the grantor's title is inferior to another person's ownership interest. The warranty against encumbrances is the one that is most likely to be breached. All real estate is encumbered at least to the extent of taxes that are a lien. Moreover, unsatisfied judgments[4] against the owners constitute an encumbrance in most states, as do both visible and recorded easements. Whether public restrictions on ownership interests, such as zoning ordinances, constitute an encumbrance has created some controversy. In general, the mere existence of a public restriction on the use of real estate does not constitute an encumbrance. However, an existing violation of a public restriction is an encumbrance within the meaning of the covenant against encumbrances.

---

[4]Northeast Petroleum Corporation of New Hampshire, Inc. v. Agency of Transportation, p. 427.

The lawyer drafting a deed must ascertain which encumbrances actually exist and except them in the deed. A typical deed might provide that the conveyance is "subject to accrued general taxes, visible easements, and easements and restrictions of record." If there is an outstanding mortgage, it would also be included as an exception to the warranty against encumbrances. The warranty of quiet enjoyment and the covenant of further assurances are promises by the grantor to defend the title in legal proceedings if someone else claims it. Such defense includes paying court costs and attorneys' fees.

12. Grant Deed

In some states—California being one—a deed known as a grant deed is in more common use than is the warranty deed. In a grant deed, the grantor covenants that no interest in the property has been conveyed to another party, that the property has not been encumbered except as noted, and that any title to the property the grantor might receive in the future will be transferred to the grantee. A grantor under a grant deed has liability only as a result of encumbrances or claims that arose while the property was owned by the grantor. A grant deed does not protect the grantee against encumbrances that existed prior to the grantor taking title. As a result, the grant deed is much narrower than the warranty deed in the promises made to the grantee.

13. Bargain and Sale Deed

A bargain and sale deed warrants that the grantor has title to the property and the right to convey, but it does not contain any express covenants as to the title's validity. This deed also is sometimes called a warranty deed without covenants. The bargain and sale deed simply states that the grantor "does hereby grant, bargain, sell, and convey" his interest in the real property to the grantee. In states that authorize a bargain and sale deed, a grantee who desires the covenants and warranties of a warranty deed must require that the sales contract state that a warranty deed will be delivered by the grantor. If the sales contract is silent about the type of deed, the grantor is obligated only to sign and deliver a bargain and sale deed.

14. Quitclaim Deed

A grantor who does not wish to make warranties with respect to the title may execute a quitclaim deed, merely transferring all the "right, title, and interest" of the grantor to the grantee. Whatever title the grantor has, the grantee receives, but the grantor makes no warranties. A quitclaim deed is used when the interest of the grantor is not clear; for example, where a deed will clear a defective title. It is also used to eliminate possible conflicting interests or when, in fact, there may be no interest in the grantor.

The grantee who takes property under a quitclaim deed must understand that he may be receiving nothing at all. A person could give a quitclaim deed to the Brooklyn Bridge to anyone willing to pay for it. The grantee obviously is not given anything at all by such a deed. The grantor simply conveyed all of his interest in the bridge, without assurances that any rights of ownership did, in fact, exist. To transfer all of a person's rights in someone else's property is to transfer nothing at all.

The amount of protection each deed gives to the grantee is the most important distinction to remember. The order in which these types of deeds was discussed is also the order of the amount of protection provided. The warranty deed contains the greatest protection for the grantee. The grant deed protects the grantee from encumbrances placed on the land's title by the grantor but not by others. The bargain and sale deed simply states that the grantor has the right to convey the title involved, but all other covenants and warranties are missing. Finally, the grantor who gives a quitclaim deed does not even promise that he or she has any rights in the land at all.

ACQUIRING TITLE TO REAL PROPERTY— INVOLUNTARY TRANSFERS

15. Transfer by Judicial Sale

Title to land may be acquired by a purchaser at a sale conducted by a sheriff or other proper official and made under the jurisdiction of a court having competent authority to order the sale. In order to raise money to pay a judgment secured against an owner, a *judicial sale* of the defendant's property may be necessary. To collect unpaid taxes, land owned by a delinquent taxpayer is sold at a public *tax sale*. The purchaser at a tax sale acquires a tax title. A mortgage foreclosure sale is a proceeding in equity by which a mortgagee obtains, by judicial sale, money to pay the obligation secured by the mortgage. The word *foreclosure* is also applied to the proceedings for enforcing other types of liens, such as mechanics' liens, assessments against realty to pay public improvements, and other statutory liens. The character of title acquired by a purchaser at a judicial sale is determined by state statute.

16. Title by Adverse Possession

Although the concepts of title and possession usually are treated as separate and distinct, physical control of land may result in the possessor's acquiring title under the principle known as *adverse possession*. A person who enters into actual possession of land and remains thereon openly and notoriously for the period of time prescribed in the statute of limitations, claiming title in denial of, and adversely to, the superior title of another, will at the end of the statutory period acquire legal title.

The owner's knowledge that his land is occupied adversely is not essential to the claim, but possession must be of a nature that would charge a reasonably diligent legal owner with knowledge of the adverse claim. In other words, the possessor must not try to hide his present use of the land. Indeed, any time the legal owner or anyone else asserts his rights to the land, the possessor must deny his claim and be steadfast in his right to the property's use.

The possessor's claim to be the owner of land must be based on some legal right. Obviously, some mistake leads to the application of the principles of adverse possession. The possessor must be more than a squatter. He must believe that he has a claim of right as the true owner of the property. *Color of title* is an expression that refers to a title that has a defect but is otherwise good. A mistake in a deed does not convey clear title, but does convey color of title. In many states adverse possession by one with color of title who pays real estate taxes will ripen into title in a much shorter period than is required for adverse possession without color of title. For example, a state with a 20-year requirement may require only 10 years if there is color of title and payment of the taxes. This use of adverse possession is very important in clearing defective titles. Errors can be ignored after the statutory period if there is adverse possession, color of title, and payment of taxes.

Adverse possession may still be one method by which a landowner of a large tract involuntarily "transfers" an ownership interest in that tract. However, today the bulk of reported adverse-possession cases deal with boundary disputes involving strips of land just a few feet wide. This factual situation frequently arises when neighbors discover that a fence or hedge has been located on their common boundary for a number of years.[5]

In our mobile society, it is a fact that residential property typically is transferred every few years. Therefore, the issue of how the statutory period of adverse possession is satisfied often arises. The answer to this issue is found in the principle of *tacking*. Tacking allows successive owners to add their time periods of ownership together to satisfy the long statutory period required for adverse possession. In order for tacking to occur, successive owners must claim under the same chain of title. In other words, a buyer may be able to tack to the seller's period of ownership. Likewise, an heir may tack to his or her ancestor's ownership period.

Although adverse possession does occur among private owners of land, it has been held that a municipal corporation or other governmental body cannot lose their interests in land to one claiming to be the owner, regardless of how long that person has possessed the land. In other words, governmental land cannot be adversely possessed.

17. Title by Accretion

Soil added to land by action of water is an *accretion*. If a shore or bank is extended by gradual addition of matter deposited by water, the extension is called an *alluvion*. If water recedes and exposes more land, the increase in the shore or bank is a *reliction*. A sudden deposit of land such as that caused by a flood does not make a change in ownership or boundary lines; but, if the change is slow and gradual by alluvion or reliction, the newly formed land belongs to the owner of the bed of the stream in which the new land was formed. If opposite banks of a private stream belong to different persons, it is a general rule that each owns the bed to the middle of the stream; however, title to lands created by accretion may be acquired by adverse possession. In public waters, such as navigable streams, lakes, and the sea, the title of the bed of water, in the absence of special circumstances,

---

[5] Doenz v. Garber, p. 428.

is in the United States. Accretion to the land belongs to the riparian owner; islands created belong to the government.

SUMMARY

ACQUIRING TITLE TO PERSONAL PROPERTY

Title by transfer	1. The most common way title to personal property is transferred is by an Article 2 sales transaction (see chapters 23–24.)
	2. Title to personal property may also be transferred by will at the owner's death (see chapter 22).
	3. Title to personal property may also be transferred as a gift or by operation of law.
Title by gift	1. An *inter vivos* gift is one made voluntarily during the life of the giver.
	2. The giver of a gift is called a *donor*. The *donee* is the person receiving the gift.
	3. In order to have a valid *inter vivos* gift, there must be donative intent, delivery, and acceptance.
	4. In general, a promise to make a gift is not enforceable. However, once the gift is made, it generally cannot be revoked. A gift *causa mortis* is an exception to the irrevocability of completed gifts.
Title by accession	1. Accession literally means "adding to."
	2. This concept governs the acquisition of title to personal property when it is incorporated into or joined with other property.
	3. The principles of accession depend on whether the wrongdoer was an innocent or willful trespasser.
Title by confusion	1. Fungible property usually is sold by weight or measure. One unit of this type of property cannot be distinguished from another unit.
	2. Confusion or commingling of fungible property may cause title to all or some

	portion of the property to pass from a wrongdoer to an innocent party.
Abandoned, lost, and mislaid property	1. Abandoned property is discarded by the true owner who has no intent to reclaim it. The first person to take possession of abandoned property is considered the new owner.
	2. Lost property is that found in some place other than that chosen by the owner. The person who finds lost property has superior rights to everyone except for the true owner.
	3. Mislaid property are those items the owner has forgotten to pick up. The owner of the real estate on which the mislaid property is discovered holds the property subject to the claims of the true owner.

ACQUIRING TITLE TO REAL PROPERTY—VOLUNTARY TRANSFERS

Original entry	1. Title originally obtained from the government by patent. It is seldom applicable today.
Transfer by deed	1. A deed is the legal document that represents title to land.
	2. A valid deed must contain an accurate legal description based on the metes and bounds, the rectangular survey, or the plats system of describing land boundaries.
	3. A valid deed must also identify the parties involved, contain language transferring an ownership interest, be signed by the grantor, and be delivered during the grantor's lifetime.
Types of deeds	1. By including or deleting optional covenants or warranties, various types of deeds can be created.
	2. Deeds vary in the amount of protection they give to the grantee. From the most to least protection provided, these deeds include the warranty deed, the grant deed, the bargain and sale deed, and the quitclaim deed.

ACQUIRING TITLE TO REAL PROPERTY— INVOLUNTARY TRANSFERS

Transfer by judicial sale

1. A court with proper jurisdiction may order that real property be sold in order to satisfy the owner's creditors.
2. Examples of judicial sales include tax sales and foreclosures of mortgages, mechanics' liens, assessment for public improvements, and other statutory liens.

Title by adverse possession

1. An example of when possession may result in legal title.
2. The essential elements of adverse possession are satisfied if a person possesses land openly, notoriously, hostilely, and continuously for the statutory period under a claim of right.
3. In essence, the record owner is prevented from claiming title if possession has adversely continued for the statutory time period.

Title by accretion

1. Soil added to land by the action of a body of water.
2. The gradual extension of a shoreline by matter being deposited by water is called *alluvion.*
3. If more land is exposed by the water receding, *reliction* occurs.
4. The gradual increase in land belongs to the owner of the streambed in which the new land was formed.

CASES

Barham v. Jones
647 P.2d 397 (N.M. 1982)

RIORDAN, J. Rayford A. Barham, special administrator (Administrator) of the estate of his mother, Leona C. Barham (Decedent), brought an action to recover certain personal property from Rhena Jones (Jones), the sister of the Decedent, which the Administrator claims belongs to the estate of the Decedent. The Administrator specifically alleged that after his making proper demand, Jones wrongfully retained possession of a set of diamond rings, a house trailer and its contents, $328.98 from the Decedent's bank accounts and a grandfather clock. The Administrator denies Jones' claim that she owns the property as a result of valid and completed gifts by the Decedent. The trial court found in favor of Jones. We affirm the trial court except as to the disposition of the clock.

I. *Diamond Rings*

The evidence indicates that sometime before the Decedent's death she gave Jones her two diamond rings. At the time of delivery, the Decedent was emotionally upset. She told Jones that if Jones did not want the rings she could flush them down the commode. Jones testified that the day after receiving the rings, she handed them back to the Decedent and told her to put them back on because "you [the Decedent] are just not you without them." The Administrator argues that Jones never accepted the rings; therefore, there was not a completed gift. We disagree.

There is substantial evidence in the record to support the trial court's finding that there was a completed gift of the rings. . . . To have a completed gift there must be delivery of the gift to the donee, and the donee must accept the gift. The fact that the day after the rings were given to Jones she returned them to the Decedent to wear does not defeat a valid acceptance by Jones.

II. *House Trailer*

The Administrator claims that there was no valid gift to Jones of the house trailer and its contents because the Decedent intended these items to be gifts only after her death. He claims this is a transaction in violation of the laws on testamentary transfer. We disagree.

There is substantial evidence to support the trial court's finding that the Decedent made a valid inter vivos gift of the trailer and its contents (excepting only family pictures). The record contains testimony that the Decedent intended Jones to have the house trailer and all of its contents. After purchasing the house trailer and before it was registered, the Decedent, during her lifetime, had the seller change the seller's affidavit of title from her name to that of Jones and her husband. The Joneses then duly registered the house trailer in their names and obtained title. The record also contains evidence that before the Decedent's death, Jones had access to the house trailer and used it on occasion for personal use. These facts support a

finding that the Decedent fulfilled the requirements for making a completed gift.

III. *Bank Accounts*

The Administrator argues that even though Jones was a joint party to the Decedent's two checking accounts and one savings account, Jones was only an authorized signatory for the limited purpose of writing checks for the Decedent and paying her bills after she died. The Administrator claims that the Decedent never intended to give Jones the funds from her accounts. He contends that the lack of intent defeats a valid gift to Jones of the balance of funds. We disagree.

Jones testified that when she signed the signature card, the Decedent told her to sign it so that Jones could get the money out of the bank "just as quick as possible" because the Decedent wanted her bills and funeral expenses paid and "Ray [the Administrator] was never known to pay bills."

After the Decedent's death, Jones paid all of the Decedent's bills (including the $271.53 balance due on the grandfather clock on layaway) leaving $328.98 in the account. We find that the $328.98 belongs to Jones.

The Decedent's bank accounts were joint accounts with Jones. A "joint account" is an account "*payable on request* to one or more of two or more parties whether or not mention is made of any right of survivorship." It is undisputed that because Jones signed the signature card the funds were payable to Jones "on request."

With a joint account, the law presumes a right of survivorship in the surviving party. . . .

Jones is the "surviving party." . . . Although Jones admits that the Decedent never actually said she was giving the funds in the accounts to Jones, there is no clear and convincing evidence to the contrary; therefore, the presumption under the statute controls.

IV. *Grandfather Clock*

We find that the $271.53 owed on the grandfather clock was a debt of the Decedent and properly paid by Jones from the joint account. We also find that there was no completed gift of the clock. The uncontradicted testimony by Jones is that the Decedent intended to give Jones the grandfather clock in the *future*. At the time of the Decedent's death, the clock was on layaway and had not been delivered to Jones. Therefore, there was no delivery as is required for a completed gift. We, therefore, reverse the trial court on this point.

So Ordered.

Narum v. City of Billings
673 P.2d 1253 (Mont. 1983)

Larry Narum was hired by the City of Billings to paint a building in one of the city's parks. Narum's employee completed the painting and left the equipment near the curb, as instructed, so that Narum could pick up the equipment later that evening. On his way home, Barry Beringer saw the equipment. Beringer called the police to report the equipment's location. When the police arrived, Beringer indicated he would like to have the equipment if no one claimed it. The police told Beringer that he could have the equipment if no one claimed it within ninety days.

Four days after these events, Narum telephoned the Billings police to report that his equipment had been stolen. Narum was told to submit a written report of this fact. Due to an error by one of his employees, Narum's written report about the stolen equipment was not filed with the police until 7 weeks later.

The property officer searched the department's computer twice during the initial 30-day period for a written report concerning the theft of the paint equipment. Despite retaining the property an additional 60 days, no other search of the stolen property reports was ever made. Thus, the property officer was unaware that the equipment had been reported as stolen. Therefore, when Beringer inquired about the equipment after 90 days had past, the police released the equipment to Beringer. Although the equipment was valued at $1,843.70, Beringer sold it to Richard Wagner for only $800.

Upon learning that the paint equipment he had purchased from Beringer was equipment previously reported stolen by Narum, Richard Wagner contacted Beringer and a meeting between a representative of the police department, Beringer, Narum, and Wagner followed. However, the participants were unable to reach a mutually satisfying solution and this action was commenced.

MORRISON, J. Following a trial . . . Beringer was ordered to pay Narum the $800 by which he was unjustly enriched and the City was ordered to pay Narum the remaining $1,043.70. . . . A notice of appeal was filed by Narum. Beringer and the City of Billings have filed cross appeals. . . .

At trial, Assistant Police Chief Sampson testified that it is the duty of the investigating officer to follow-up on stolen property reports and the duty of the property officer to check the computer for any reported thefts of property meeting the description of that in his possession. Neither officer fulfilled his responsibilities regarding this property. . . .

Barry Beringer became the statutory finder of the paint equipment by discovering the property and exerting control over it. If control was not exercised in reporting to the police it was exercised when Beringer ultimately obtained the subject equipment and sold it. Although Beringer may well have acted in good faith he became obligated to follow the statutory procedures for locating the true owner of the property. Since Beringer failed to follow those procedures and chose instead to treat the property as his own by selling it to an innocent third party, he became liable to the true owner of the property for its value.

In addition [the Montana law] penalizes finders for failing to follow the statutory mandated procedures by holding them liable to the true owner for double the value of the lost property. Therefore, since the value of the paint equipment was $1,843.70, Barry Beringer is liable to Larry Narum for $3,687.40.

However, the evidence presented at trial supports the conclusions of the District Court that (1) "The City of Billings knew the true owner of the property as a result of information provided to the City by Narum on December 21st, 1979, and therefore had a duty to use reasonable diligence" to return the property to the owner; (2) the City of Billings negligently dealt with the property while it was in its possession, and "such negligence was the proximate cause of the damages sustained by Plaintiff Narum"; and (3) Beringer justifiably relied on representations made to him by the City of Billings indicating that the property was his. These conclusions support a finding for Beringer on his cross-claim against the City of Billings, which asserts that the City's negligence was the primary cause of Narum's loss. . . .

We therefore remand this case to the District Court for a determination of damages in favor of Beringer on his cross-claim against the City of Billings. The District Court may consider any damages legally caused by the negligence of the City of Billings including attorneys fees and costs.

Remanded.

Brown v. Rines
464 A.2d 283 (N.H. 1983)

DOUGLAS, J. The issue in this boundary dispute appeal is whether the court below properly determined the location of the common boundary separating the properties of the plaintiffs, Henry and Eleanor Brown, and the defendants John E. and E. Janice T. Rines in Nottingham. . . .

The source of the controversy in this case can be traced back to common grantors through the chains of title to the two properties. In 1962, Henri H. and Georgette A. Cote conveyed by deed to Richard B. Allen, the Rines' predecessor in title, a parcel of land described as [per the] . . . See diagram attached to this opinion. This description of the property remained identical in each subsequent deed in the Rines' chain of title.

Sixteen days after the conveyance to Richard Allen, the Cotes conveyed a contiguous parcel to the plaintiffs' predecessors in title, Kenneth J. and Ruth L. Jacobson. . . .

. . . Sometime within the next two years, the plaintiffs and the owners of the other three lots in the subdivision contacted the surveyor who had prepared the subdivision plan to advise him that there appeared to be an error. He agreed with the lot owners to resurvey the entire subdivision and to stake out the correct boundaries.

A new subdivision plan was prepared based upon the results of the new survey and apparently accepted by the four lot owners. As depicted on the new subdivision plan, the Rines' lot was reduced in size from 7.45 acres to 4.84 acres. This reduction was due to a shortening of the westerly boundary from 640 feet to 527 feet, based on the surveyor's determination that the boundary ended at a stone wall which ran easterly across the land. This stone wall was shown to be the Rines' northerly boundary.

In December 1980, the plaintiffs filed a petition to quiet title. . . . At a hearing before a Master on the plaintiffs' petition, two expert witnesses testified that, in their opinion, the northerly boundary of the Rines' property was the stone wall as depicted on the new subdivision plan. . . .

The master recommended that the stone wall be fixed as the northerly boundary of the Rines' property, thereby making their westerly boundary 527 feet from Gebig Road to the stone wall. Citing the rule of construction that monuments prevail over courses and distances, the master rejected the Rines' assertion that their westerly and northerly boundaries should be determined by reference to "640 feet" in both chains of title rather than by reference to the stone wall described in the parties' chains of title. The Superior Court approved the master's report and entered a decree accordingly, reforming the plaintiffs' deed from Kristy.

On appeal, the Rines concede that the master's ruling with regard to their westerly boundary is correct. They contend, however, that the master erred in finding the location of their northerly boundary. The Rines claim that a stone wall located to the northeast of the stone wall found by the master to be the northern boundary was actually intended to determine the northerly boundary of the property. The area in dispute is approximately 1.3 acres. (See diagram.)

The Rines urge this court to reverse the superior court's decree for a number of reasons. First, they argue that if their northerly boundary was located where they suggest, the length of that boundary would be 510 feet. This length would be closer to the 500-foot length specified in both deeds given by the Cotes, the common grantors, than is the 586-foot length of the boundary as found by the master. This argument ignores the underlying rationale for the rule regarding the superiority of monuments that "objects which are visible and permanent" are considered more reliable than courses and distances.

Second, the Rines cite the fact that if their contention as to the proper boundary were accepted, their lot would contain 6.1 acres, which is closer to the reference in their chain of title to "six

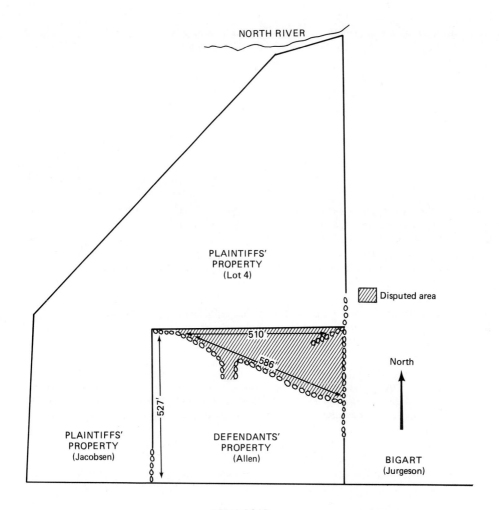

NORTH RIVER

PLAINTIFFS'
PROPERTY
(Lot 4)

Disputed area

510'

586'

527'

North

PLAINTIFFS'
PROPERTY
(Jacobsen)

DEFENDANTS'
PROPERTY
(Allen)

BIGART
(Jurgeson)

GEBIG ROAD

acres, more or less" than is the 4.84 acres which results from the northerly boundary found by the master. This argument disregards the fact that, as one of the experts testified, area is the least reliable criterion for resolving ambiguities in deed descriptions. . . .

The master's report shows that he correctly recognized that the deeds should be interpreted in light of the parties' intentions. He also was correct in applying the rule that, in construing an ambiguous boundary description, monuments prevail over courses and distances. Determination of the loca-

tion of a boundary is a question of fact, which will not be disturbed on appeal when supported by the evidence.

In this case, two experts testified that, in their opinion, the stone wall depicted on the new subdivision plan as being the northerly boundary of the Rines' property was, in fact, the common boundary between the plaintiffs' and the Rines' properties. This, in itself, was sufficient evidence for the master to find that the stone wall was the Rines' northerly boundary.

Affirmed.

Northeast Petroleum Corporation of New Hampshire, Inc. v. Agency of Transportation
466 A.2d 1164 (Vt. 1983)

UNDERWOOD, J. On November 2, 1980, plaintiff obtained a judgment and judgment lien in Washington Superior Court for $27,488.17 against Twin City Fuels, Inc., and John E. Hallihan. Thereafter, plaintiff brought suit in the same court to foreclose its judgment lien against property in Berlin, Vermont, owned jointly by the defendants, Hallihan and Valsangiacomo. . . . [This property was leased to the State's Agency of Transportation.]

On January 12, 1981, prior to the January 21, 1981, recording of plaintiff's judgment lien, defendants Hallihan and Valsangiacomo granted the State an option to purchase the demised property. Pursuant to the terms of the option agreement, defendant State had to exercise its option before August 1, 1981. In the event that defendant State did elect to exercise its option, defendants Hallihan and Valsangiacomo agreed to convey title by a warranty deed free and clear of all liens and encumbrances.

In its suit to foreclose its judgment lien against the property, plaintiff moved for summary judgment. The State filed a cross-claim against Hallihan and Valsangiacomo. Valsangiacomo moved to dismiss the State's cross-claim against him. The trial court granted the plaintiff's motion for summary judgment, entered a decree of foreclosure, and ordered a public sale. It also granted Valsangiacomo's motion to dismiss the State's cross-claim against him. The State appeals this dismissal. . . .

Although there was no evidentiary hearing and therefore no findings, it is plainly evident from the admitted pleadings that Hallihan and Valsangiacomo bought the property in question in connection with a joint commercial venture. They erected buildings and other structures on it and subsequently leased it to the State. During the pendency of the lease they granted an option to the State. . . .

Hallihan and Valsangiacomo, by each signing this option agreement jointly obligated themselves to convey title to *all* the land described in the option agreement by warranty deed, free and clear of all liens and encumbrances, should the State timely exercise its option. Neither cotenant contracted with the State to convey an interest in only half of the demised premises.

When the State did exercise its option in a timely manner, and Hallihan and Valsangiacomo executed a warranty deed of the property to the State, neither grantor purported to limit the extent of his conveyance to one-half of the property conveyed; rather, each conveyed title to all of the property. Simultaneously each cotenant covenanted with the State to warrant and defend the title to the entire parcel, and each further covenanted that the entire parcel was free and clear of liens and encumbrances. . . .

There was a judgment lien against the property, duly recorded on January 21, 1981, in the land records of the Town of Berlin. This constituted a valid lien or encumbrance on the property when Hallihan and Valsangiacomo conveyed it by warranty deed to the State. As such this conveyance constituted a breach of warranty, as well as a breach of the option agreement.

Valsangiacomo maintains innocence arguing that he should be absolved from liability to the State, and that the court's order dismissing the State's cross-claim against him should be affirmed. He states that he had no notice of the judgment lien when he signed the option agreement and the warranty deed, because he was not a party to the original action in which plaintiff obtained its judgment lien, and because the judgment lien did not attach to his undivided one-half interest in the property. . . .

Notwithstanding that Hallihan and Valsangiacomo held title as tenants in common, they had a common purpose in jointly granting an option to the State to purchase *all* of the property they owned. When the State exercised its option, they were carrying out that common purpose when, by a single warranty deed, they jointly conveyed to the State *all* the property they owned. This is exactly what they contracted to do under their option agreement with the State and this is exactly what they intended to do by their warranty deed. Thus, they jointly and severally committed themselves to convey the entire parcel free and clear of all liens and encumbrances, despite the fact that the judgment lien attached only to the undivided [half] of Hallihan.

Valsangiacomo contracted in the option agreement to join with his cotenant Hallihan in conveying, by warranty deed, title to all of the land they held as tenants in common, free and clear of all liens and encumbrances. He further covenanted

when he executed the warranty deed that there was no encumbrance against the property. The judgment lien was such an encumbrance, and therefore the State's cause of action for the breach of warranty accrued at that time.

The trial court erred when it dismissed the State's cross-claim against the defendant Valsangiacomo.

Reversed.

Doenz v. Garber
665 P.2d 932 (Wyom. 1983)

On March 19, 1971, Victor and Phyllis Garber acquired 80 acres adjacent to land owned by William and Herbert Doenz. The Garbers recorded their deed in December, 1971. About 10 years later, the Doenzes had this land surveyed. They discovered that the fence separating their property from the Garbers' was 20 to 30 feet from the boundary described in their deed. The fence encroached upon the Doenzes' land, giving the Garbers use of 3.01 acres not described in their deed. A sketch of the fence location and disputed ground follows to help describe this situation.

The Doenzes began building a new fence on the deed line in September 1981. In March 1982,

after this new fence was completed, the Garbers sued to quiet title to the disputed land. They argued they now owned that property because they had adversely possessed it over the 10-year period required by Wyoming statutes. The trial court entered a judgment in favor of the Garbers, and the Doenzes appealed.

RAPER, J. The issues . . . are. . . .

1. "Whether the trial court correctly held that the Garbers [appellees] established the necessary elements of adverse possession to the tract of land in dispute."

2. "Whether the trial court properly held that the Garbers [appellees] possessed the disputed tract for the statutory period of ten years."

3. "Whether the movement of fences by Doenz

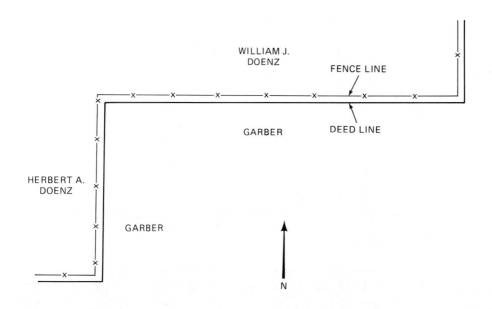

[appellants] onto the adversely possessed tract held by Garbers [appellees] defeated the adverse possession claim." . . .

I. Were the necessary elements of adverse possession present? The elements of adverse possession consist of actual, open, notorious, exclusive and continuous possession of another's real property for the statutory period of ten years under a claim of right or color of title. . . .

There is no question but that appellees actually, openly, notoriously and exclusively occupied the land between the fence line and the deed line. They used it to graze cattle and for hay which was cut. It had never been so used by appellants, nor had any question about the boundary ever before been raised. . . .

II. Did the appellees possess the disputed area for ten years? The appellants contend that while appellees received a deed to the lands on March 19, 1971, it was not recorded until December 30, 1971; so, therefore, adverse possession could not start until the latter date. Prior to the expiration of ten years after the recording, appellants had built their new fence on the east-west deed line, had downed the old fence, and the new posts were up on the north-south line. The survey was undertaken prior to March 1981. Appellants were informed of the discrepancy by the surveyor in March 1981. Appellants started new fence construction in September 1981, less than ten years after the deed was recorded. Appellants add to that the further fact that the court action, appellees' first recognizable objection, was not started until April 1982, after appellants claim they had stopped the ten-year continuity of appellees' possession by reentry. Appellants' position is that there must be some notice to the owner that adverse possession has begun.

[T]his court [has] held that where the land under dispute was within the fence line of the adverse possession claimants who had exercised dominion over it . . . and who believed they possessed the land to the fence line for more than ten years, all the essential elements of adverse possession were present. . . .

The appellants have overlooked the language of the rule [of adverse possession] as being in the alternative, "color of title *or* claim or right." Appellants look only at the "color of title" . . . situation. . . . However, a claim of right is sufficient in

this state for the purpose of initiating adverse possession. . . .

The deed to appellees coupled to the presence of the old fence plus use to the fence gave them a claim of right. . . . The presence of the fence and the continuous farming operations by appellees on the enclosed land put appellants on notice to make inquiry. Failure to record a deed does not render it void where prior to the conveyance subsequent purchasers are put on due inquiry and with reasonable investigation the existence of the deed could have been determined. . . .

III. Did the construction of the new fence and removal of the old fence by appellants defeat the adverse possession claim? The appellees' first notice that appellants were asserting a claim to land south of the old fence was in September 1981, when they noticed fence posts along the deed line. Appellants never advised appellees what they were doing but had instructed the surveyor to advise appellees of the property line he had established. The surveyor did not do that until David Garber, appellees' son, went to the surveyor's office in Sheridan with considerable concern to inquire about what was going on and then found out. Appellees consulted with their attorney. He advised moving with caution and watching developments until the matter could be adequately investigated and a position taken. On December 14, 1981, appellees met with one of the appellants, William Doenz, to object to movement of the fence to the deed line and attempt a peaceable settlement. Settlement efforts were tried again in January 1982, but failed; appellees were advised by appellants to go to court. By March 1982, appellees were fenced out of the disputed land. This litigation was initiated by filing of the complaint on April 23, 1982. . . .

The movement of the fences such that for a short period of time the old fence was down and the new fence was in place on the deed line did not defeat the adverse possession claim on the ground that possession was not continuous to the time of filing of the complaint. This court approved the rule that a temporary break or interruption, not of an unreasonable duration, does not destroy the continuity of the adverse claimant's possession, depending somewhat upon the intention of the adverse possessor as shown by the circumstances of the case.

There was, as one of the surrounding circumstances, only about a month between the time of completion of the new fence and the filing of an action. The other facts and circumstances here show no intention to give up their adverse possession claim. This was adequately demonstrated by the remonstrances of appellees, and their attempts to negotiate a settlement. They entered in litigation as a last resort within a very short time.

Affirmed.

REVIEW QUESTIONS

1. Identify the terms in column A by matching each to the appropriate statement in column B:

A		B	
1. *Inter vivos* gift		a.	Discarded by the owner with no intent to reclaim it.
2. Accession		b.	An example of when possession of real property may result in legal title.
3. Fungible property		c.	Legal documents that represent title to real property.
4. Abandoned property		d.	Usually sold by weight or measure. Subject to confusion.
5. Mislaid property		e.	The deed that assures the grantee of the most protection possible.
6. Deeds		f.	This concept governs the acquisition of title to personal property when it is incorporated into or joined with other property.
7. Rectangular survey system		g.	Made voluntarily during the life of the donor.
8. Warranty deed		h.	Occurs when land is exposed by water receding.
9. Adverse possession		i.	A method used to describe accurately the boundaries of real estate.
10. Reliction		j.	Held by the owner of the real estate on which it is found subject to the true owner's claims.

2. Aunt Bee bought 10 lottery tickets, each representing a chance to win an automobile. She wrote her minor niece's name on the back of one of these tickets and mailed it to her niece's mother. The niece was never informed that this ticket was received. At the drawing for the car, the niece's ticket was selected. Aunt Bee claimed the car belonged to her, since the niece had not accepted the gift. Is Aunt Bee correct? Explain.

3. Vivian lived with and cared for her uncle, Mr. Evans, throughout the last years of his life. One month before he died, Mr. Evans went to his bank and examined the contents of his safe deposit box. He asked for both keys to this box. Upon arriving home, he gave Vivian one of these keys and told her that the contents belonged to her when he died. The safe deposit box contained stocks, bonds, and other items worth approximately $800,000. Although Vivian had a key, she could not have obtained access to its contents, since the box remained registered in Mr. Evans's name alone. When Mr. Evans died, some of his heirs claimed the contents of his deposit box. Vivian argued she was the donee of an *inter vivos* gift of the box's contents. Have all the elements of a valid *inter vivos* gift been proved? Explain.

4. Troop, who is in the oil business, is the sole owner of a well named Gusher. Troop also is in partnership with Wright, and together they have equal interests in Spindletop. These parties have agreed that Troop will store the oil produced by Spindletop and will make monthly reports to Wright. After several months passed without a report, Wright discovered that Troop was storing oil produced from Gusher and Spindletop in the same holding tank. If Troop has not kept accurate records of both wells' production, how much of the stored oil is Wright entitled to, if any? Explain.

5. Bernice rented a safe deposit box from the Old Orchard Bank. While examining the contents of her own box, Bernice discovered $6,325 in cash on a chair which was pushed under an examination table. Bernice turned this money over to the bank, which sent a notice to its safe deposit box customers that property had been discovered in the safety vault. No one responded to this ad, and Bernice claimed she was entitled to this lost property. The bank refused to give her the money, since it argued the money had been mislaid. Who is entitled to the $6,325? Why?

6. While swimming in a pond on Cutter's property, several children discovered some money in a watertight container on the bottom of the pond. Cutter admits it is not his money. Who has title to the money? Who has the right to possession? Explain.

7. List the essential elements of a valid deed.

8. Campbell entered into a sales contract to buy real estate from Storer. To complete this transaction, a warranty deed was delivered to Campbell in 1965. Although he received it, Campbell failed to record this deed. In 1970, Storer conveyed by deed the same land to a third person. When he discovered he no longer was the record owner, Campbell sued Storer for damages. Storer defended his second conveyance on the grounds that Campbell's failure to record his deed prevented him from acquiring legal title to the real estate. Did Campbell acquire legal title in 1965? Why or why not?

9. Name four types of deeds and distinguish the legal significance of each.

10. Bryan and Linda contracted to have Pioneer Homes build a house. In return for $52,000, Pioneer Homes deeded a house and lot to them. The deed delivered specifically stated the title conveyed was good, marketable, and free of all encumbrances. Later, Bryan and Linda decided to sell this house and lot. It was then that they discovered their house was only 3.5 feet from the side boundary. This location of the house violated the local minimum side-lot requirement of 15 feet. To resolve this violation, Bryan and Linda purchased a strip of land for $1,500. They then sued Pioneer Homes for breach of the covenant against encumbrances. Did Pioneer Homes breach this covenant? Why or why not?

11. In 1947, J. G. Head's Farms, Inc., conveyed Lot 12, Block 8 of Unit A to Lottie Morrison. Lottie failed to record and then lost her deed. In 1960, J. G. Head's Farms, Inc., signed and delivered a quitclaim deed covering all the land it owned in Unit A to the Miami Holding Corporation. In 1963, J. G. Head's Farms, Inc., conveyed Lot 12 of Block 8 to Lottie Morrison by quitclaim deed. This deed, which replaced the 1947 warranty deed that had been lost, was recorded on March 4, 1963. Lottie Morrison conveyed Lot 12 to Matthews in 1970. Thereafter, a dispute arose between Matthews and the Miami Holding Corporation as to who had superior title to Lot 12. Who does have superior title to Lot 12? Explain.

12. Dick and Dan owned adjoining property. By an honest mistake, Dick built a fence that was 5 feet onto Dan's property. Both owners recognized the fence as the boundary. Twenty-five years after the fence was built, Dan had his property surveyed. The survey revealed the fence's improper location. Dan sought to have the fence removed, but Dick sued, claiming he now owned the disputed 5-foot strip through adverse possession. Should Dick be declared to own this land? Why? (Assume a 20-year statutory period.)

20 REAL ESTATE SALES TRANSACTIONS

As was mentioned in a previous chapter, interests in real estate can be divided into surface rights, air rights, and subsurface (such as minerals) rights. Any of these rights may be bought, sold, or leased without affecting the others. However, all three interests typically are included in a sale or lease. Only when the documents transferring the real estate clearly separate these interests does the law make a distinction as to which rights are involved.

Many topics in this text concerning contracts are applicable to real estate transactions. For example, an understanding of the law of offer and acceptance (chapter 7), consideration (chapter 8), voidable contracts (chapter 9), and the statute of frauds (chapter 11) is important background to the material that follows.

In this chapter, we first present the basic process that makes up the typical or traditional real estate sales transaction. The focus is on residential sales; however, the same process is followed in selling commercial real estate. The second part of the chapter discusses some alternatives to the traditional sales contract.

TRADITIONAL SALES TRANSACTIONS

1. In General

The ultimate purpose of any sale is to transfer title or legal ownership from the seller to the buyer. The sale of personal property items usually is fairly simple. The buyer offers the purchase price; the seller accepts the money and gives the buyer a receipt; and the buyer leaves with the merchandise and receipt. The real estate sales transaction is much more complex. This complexity has developed in an attempt to protect the ownership of real estate, which often is a person's most valuable asset. This desire to provide protection is one reason real estate sales contracts must be in writing and why there are official records of land sales.

In a real estate sales transaction, the seller and buyer may utilize the assistance of a real estate agent, albeit for different purposes. Other important steps in this transaction include negotiating the sales contract, securing financing, examining the title, inspecting the property, and closing the transaction. In the following sections we examine each of these steps.

2. Use of Real Estate Agents

A seller of real estate may employ a real estate agent to help locate a ready, willing, and able buyer. Prospective buyers often rely on the assistance of real estate agents to help locate real estate suitable for the buyer's needs. These agents may be a *broker* or a *salesperson*. Both must be licensed in the state in which the real estate is located. Generally a salesperson's license is held by a broker. Therefore, sellers and buyers frequently deal with salespeople who are representatives of the real estate broker.

Typically a seller-agent relationship is created through a formal listing agreement. In essence, the listing agreement authorizes the agent to find buyers and to represent the seller in the negotiations with the buyer. However, listing agreements generally do not give the agent the authority to sign a contract binding the seller. In other words, the agent must present the buyer's offer to the seller for his consideration.[1]

A major purpose of a listing agreement is to provide provisions governing when a seller must compensate the agent. It is these provisions that determine which type of listing is utilized in a particular transaction. An *open listing,* for example, provides that the agent who locates a ready, willing, and able buyer is the agent paid. In other words, the seller may have several agents working to find a buyer. Furthermore, if the seller sells the real estate without any agent's assistance, no commission is payable. An *exclusive agency listing* contains language that makes one agent the only agent the seller hires. In essence, the listing agent will be entitled to a commission if he or any other agent locates a buyer. However, if the seller sells the real estate without any agent's assistance, again no commission is payable.

The type of listing most preferred by real estate agents is called the *exclusive-right-to-sell listing.* This listing makes one agent the exclusive agent for the seller. Under this listing, the agent must be paid if a buyer is located, regardless of whether the listing agent, some other agent, the seller, or any other person finds the ready, willing, and able buyer.[2]

Any one of these listing agreements may require that the agent share the information about the real estate for sale with all the other real estate agents who belong to the community's multiple-listing service (MLS). A listing passed through the MLS usually is known as a *multiple listing.* This type of listing agreement

---

[1] Virginia Real Estate Commission v. Bias, p. 447.

[2] Kerry-Rand and Associates v. Peddicord, p. 448.

actually makes all the MLS members subagents representing the seller. Therefore, any prospective buyer of residential property who is looking with an agent should realize that this agent owes a duty of loyalty to the seller, and not to this buyer. Of course, one advantage of this system is that the buyer does not pay any direct cash compensation to the agent. *Note*: For further discussion on the general principles of real estate agents, see sections 4, 6, and 13 of chapter 14 on the principal-agent relationship.

3. Negotiating the Sales Contract

The typical contract for the sale of real estate originates with the buyer making a written *offer to purchase.* This offer to purchase may be presented to the seller by the buyer or by a real estate agent. In most states, an offer to purchase may be prepared by a real estate agent without that agent's being guilty of unauthorized practice of law. The offer is submitted to the seller for acceptance or rejection. If accepted, this offer often becomes a contract between the parties. The informal offer and acceptance may be taken to the buyer's or the seller's attorney for preparation of a formal written contract.

It is important not only that an attorney prepare a contract of sale after the offer and acceptance are complete, but that the other party's attorney review the contract. Each party to a real estate contract needs the advice of legal counsel for several reasons. First of all, buyers must make sure that the contract gives them all the benefits they have agreed to pay for. If there is to be a warranty that the premises are free of termites, the contract should so provide. Second, the interests of the seller and the interests of the buyer are in conflict. A seller is best served by a contract requiring delivery of a quitclaim deed, while a buyer's interests are best served by a contract calling for a warranty deed. Because of these conflicts of interest, it is neither wise nor ethical for one attorney to represent both parties to a transaction. Third, essential provisions may be omitted from offers to purchase. Among the provisions that may not be found in offers to purchase are those relating to how the purchase price will be paid, the type of deed required to be delivered by the seller, the proration of certain costs, the terms of escrow, what happens if improvements are destroyed, and the sellers' warranties. These and other provisions of a sales contract are discussed below.

4. Terms of the Sales Contract

Generally there is a span of time between when the buyer and seller agree to the sale of real estate and when they actually transfer the title and possession. The sales contract is necessary to govern the parties' relationship during this time period. The provisions discussed below are used to help the parties know their rights and duties prior to the transaction's being completed.

In order to be enforceable, the sales contract must specify the names of the parties, and it must be signed by these parties. Additionally, the contract has to contain a complete and accurate description of the real estate involved. This legal description will usually follow the format of a metes and bounds, a rectangular survey, or a reference to a plat type of description. Section 9 of chapter 18 will provide a review of how real estate is properly described.

As a general rule, a buyer will want to make certain that his performance is contingent upon his ability to obtain the needed financing. Failure to include this contingency provision would make the buyer liable to pay the purchase price in cash even if financing is not available.

The sales contract should contain specific language about what type of deed the seller must have prepared, signed, and delivered to the buyer. Sections 12 through 15 of chapter 19 discuss the various types of deeds and the protection each provides for the buyer. The responsibilities of the parties concerning the validity of the seller's title should be stated in the contract. For instance, a provision should state whether proof of title will be made by a lawyer's title search or by the seller furnishing either a title abstract or a title insurance policy. Section 6 discusses these requirements in more detail.

A properly drafted sales contract should contain a clause specifying when closing is to occur. At the very least, this clause needs to state within what time period the closing will occur. For a residential sales transaction, the closing usually occurs within 60 days after the contract is signed. Whether possession of the real estate is to be transferred at closing or at some other time should be specified. Many items (such as real property taxes, insurance premiums, and monthly payments) may need to be prorated between the parties. When and how these prorations are to be calculated should be included in the contract.

Because there is a gap in time between the contract being signed and the title being transferred, improvements may be damaged or destroyed in this interim period. A good sales contract specifies that in the event improvements are damaged, the buyer may choose to rescind the contract or perform as agreed while receiving the proceeds from the seller's insurance policy. In addition to harm that may occur to the improvements, unexpected happenings may befall the buyer or seller. Inclusion of an escrow clause can facilitate the smooth completion of the transaction in the event of a party's death, incapacity, marriage, or insolvency. Section 10 describes the benefits of an escrow arrangement more thoroughly.

This entire discussion on contractual terms is intended to emphasize that the parties involved have a great deal of freedom to write the contract to meet their individual as well as mutual needs. For example, if the buyer is purchasing personal property such as appliances along with the real estate, that buyer can insist on the seller's warranting that these appliances will be in good working order on the date of the closing. Furthermore, in many areas of the country where pest infestation may cause problems, the buyer may want the seller to be bound to present a certificate that the improvements are free from such infestations. Finally, the parties can include provisions governing their rights in the event the other party defaults. A liquidated damage clause illustrates one such possible provision.

5. Financing the Sales Transaction

A buyer may face a real predicament if he cannot obtain the financing needed to complete the purchase, if he is not otherwise excused from his contractual performance. However, let's assume that the sales contract contains a properly drafted contingency clause relieving the buyer of liability if financing is not obtained. What does this clause require of the buyer? After the offer to purchase is accepted and the sales contract becomes binding, one of the first responsibilities the buyer has is to attempt to obtain the necessary financing. Legally, the buyer must make this attempt in good faith. In other words, the buyer must honestly try to get the financing described in the contract. In order to satisfy this good-faith standard, the buyer may have to apply for a loan from several different lenders.

The loan application process must be done promptly so that the time involved in the lender's review process will not prevent the closing from occurring when contractually required. The lender uses the application as a means of gathering information about the buyer/borrower and about the real estate being purchased. In addition to the actual application, the lender will study credit reports, a verification of employment, and appraisals. When the lender feels that the applicant is creditworthy and that the real estate's value represents adequate security, a commitment to finance will be sent to the applicant. This commitment letter describes the terms and conditions of the loan.

A discussion of the further documentation of the financing transaction is presented in chapter 34. If the purchase being financed is residential real estate, the lender will have to comply with the Real Estate Settlement Procedures Act. RESPA is discussed in chapter 36. Although obtaining the necessary financing is an important and essential duty placed on the buyer, it is by no means the buyer's only responsibility after the sales contract is signed. This next section discusses another item of concern in the sales transaction.

6. Evidence of Title

Ownership of real estate is a matter of public record. Every deed, mortgage, judgment, lien, or other transaction that affects the title to real estate must be made a matter of public record in the county in which the real estate is located. Deeds and other documents are usually recorded in the county recorder's office. The records of the probate court furnish the public documents necessary to prove title by will or descent. Divorce proceedings and other judicial proceedings that affect the title to real estate are also part of the public record.

In order to establish title to real estate, it is necessary to examine all the public records that may affect the title. In a few states, lawyers actually examine all the public records to establish the title to real estate. Because it is extremely difficult for an individual or his attorney to examine all the records, in most states businesses have been formed for the express purpose of furnishing the appropriate records for any given parcel of real estate. These *abstract companies* are usually well-established firms that have maintained tract indexes for many years and keep them current on a daily basis. Upon request, an abstract company prepares an abstract of the records that sets forth the history of the parcel in question and all matters that may affect the title. The abstract of title is examined by an attorney, who writes his opinion concerning the title, setting forth any defects in the title as well as encumbrances against it. The abstract of title must be brought up to date each time the property is transferred or proof of title is required, in order that the chain of title will be complete. The opinion on title will be useless unless all court proceedings, such as foreclosures, partitions, transfers by deed, and probate proceedings, are shown. It should be noted that an attorney's opinion on title is just that—an opinion. If the attorney makes a mistake—his opinion states that his client has title to Blackacre, when in fact he does not have title to Blackacre—the client does not have title. His only recourse would be a malpractice suit against the attorney.

Because of limited resources, many lawyers are unable to respond in damages to pay losses caused by their mistakes. Therefore, the abstract of title and attorney's opinion as a means of protecting owners is often not satisfactory. There may be title defects that do not appear in the record and that the attorney does not cover in his title opinion. An illegitimate child may be an unknown heir with an interest in property, as may a spouse in a secret marriage. To protect owners against such hidden claims and to offset the limited resources of most lawyers, *title insurance* has developed.

Title insurance is, in effect, an opinion of the title company instead of the lawyer. The opinion of the title company is backed up to the extent of the face value of the title insurance policy. If the purported owner loses his property, he collects the insurance just as if it were life insurance and the insured had died. Title insurance can cover matters beyond those in a title opinion. It has the financial backing of the issuing company, which is financially more secure than any law firm. Modern real estate practice uses title policies rather than abstracts and title opinions. Title insurance companies usually maintain their own tract records, thus eliminating the cost of bringing the abstract up to date. Generally, title insurance companies issue a *title commitment letter* at the seller's request. This commitment becomes the basis of the title insurance policy issued to protect the buyer. Title insurance companies that are negligent in searching a title become liable for the damages such negligence causes.[3]

Another method used to prove ownership in some localities is known as the *Torrens system,* based on a registered title that can be transferred only upon the official registration records. The original registration of any title usually requires a judicial determination as to the current owner, and then all subsequent transfers merely involve the surrender of the registered title, in much the same way that an automobile title is transferred. The Torrens system is a much simpler system to use after a title has once been registered, but the high cost of obtaining the original registration has prevented it from replacing abstracts and title policies as proof of title in most areas.

7. Housing Warranties

Due to the nature of the transaction, the buyer normally will have had very little opportunity to inspect the real estate and its improvements prior to the signing of a contract. Therefore, during the time prior to the closing, the buyer should make an effort to inspect the property thoroughly. A smart buyer would seek the assistance of experts to inspect, when applicable, the roof, the air

---

[3] Malinak v. Safeco Title Insurance Company of Idaho, p. 449.

conditioning and heating unit, the plumbing, the electrical wiring, and other major appliances and utilities. Even after such inspections, the buyer may not discover some substantial defect that adversely affects the property's value.

Buyers have been allowed to rescind purchases on the ground of fraud or misrepresentation, but historically warranties were found to exist only when specifically included in the contract. In other words, the seller of housing was not held responsible for the habitability of the structure or the quality of workmanship and materials. In recent years, most states have changed the law as it relates to the sale of housing, but have retained the doctrine of caveat emptor for vacant real estate. The courts in these states have imposed liability on sellers and builders of housing by use of a variety of theories. Some courts have held that there is an implied warranty against structural defects, similar to the implied warranty of fitness in the sale of personal property, and that there is no rational basis for differentiating between the sale of a newly constructed house by the builder-vendor and the sale of any other manufactured product. These courts usually have not extended the warranty against structural defects to the individual who builds a house himself and later decides to sell it. Casual sales and resales are not included because the warranty arises when the seller is in the business of selling housing. Furthermore, warranties of habitability usually are not implied in the sale of vacant land.[4]

Other courts have created an implied warranty that a home is built and constructed in a reasonably workmanlike manner and that it is fit for its intended purpose—habitation. In one case, there was no water supply, and the subdivider-seller was held liable for breach of this warranty. In another case, the air conditioning system did not work properly, and the seller was held to have breached an implied warranty. In some cases, the buyer is entitled to damages. If the breach is so great that the home is unfit for habitation, rescission is an available remedy. However, the theory of implied warranty does not impose on the builder an obligation to build a perfect house.

The issue of whether the builder's liability is limited to the first purchaser or extends to subsequent purchasers has caused courts a great deal of difficulty. Some courts have held that subsequent purchasers are protected by the builder's implied warranty. Other courts have ruled that the subsequent purchaser can recover when it is proved the builder was negligent. The distinctions between implied warranty and negligence theories are subtle and at times confusing.[5]

This issue of how to protect subsequent purchasers may be of less importance today because of the variety of builder-supported programs that give the buyers of new homes an express warranty for a stated period. These warranties require the builder or an insurance company to repair major defects discovered within the period of coverage. Actually these warranties can be positive selling points for the property, since they can be transferred during the time provided. Express warranty programs as well as court-adopted remedies involving implied warranties and negligence make it clear that consumer protection has been extended to housing.

---

[4] Witty v. Schramm, p. 450.

[5] Cosmopolitan Homes, Inc. v. Weller, p. 451.

8. Closing the Transaction

The real estate sales transaction is completed at the *closing*. In some areas of the country, this event is known as the *settlement*. Whereas many inexperienced or uninformed parties to a sales transaction may believe that the sales contract and the closing are the only steps in a successful transaction, in fact the parties have many responsibilities during the interim between the contract's being signed and the closing.

In its essence, the closing is the opportunity to tie up all the loose ends. Typically, the buyer's, seller's, and lender's lawyer will conduct the closing. The buyer will be asked to review and sign all the loan-related documents. Of particular importance are the promissory note and the mortgage. In addition, these loan-related documents can include required truth-in-lending papers and the closing statement. The seller must sign the deed, if that has not already been done, and deliver it to the buyer. Either the buyer or his lawyer will want to take this deed to the appropriate office for recording.

At closing, the purchase price must be distributed among the parties in accordance with the closing statement. Figure 20–1 illustrates a typical closing statement based on the following facts. First, John and Ethel Bagby have contracted to buy Richard and Janet Stevenson's house for $64,900. The Bagbys are to assume the Stevenson's mortgage, which has a principal amount still due of $47,749.38. The property taxes, hazard insurance premium, and monthly interest payment are to be prorated as of December 17, 1985, which is the date of closing. Assume that the taxes for 1985 and the insurance premium through November 20, 1986, have been paid by the sellers prior to the closing. Also assume that the Bagbys will purchase the Stevensons' escrow account for taxes and insurance dollar for dollar. Finally, the Stevensons are obligated to pay the Century 21 Realtors a real estate commission equal to 7 percent of the contract price. This closing statement indicates that the Bagbys need $16,590.74 in cash to close this transaction. The Stevensons will receive $11,785.54 at the closing. *Note:* On a closing statement similar to the one in Figure 20–1, the amount at the bottom of part III must equal the amount at the bottom of part I. In other words, the total distributed and the net amount due from the buyers must be the same to have an accurate closing statement.

9. Introduction

Because there really is no such thing as a "typical" real estate sales transaction, understanding the traditional sales contract is not enough. Since you have the legal flexibility to structure the sales transaction however you wish, you should consider possible alternatives to the agreement discussed above. For example, knowing how the escrow arrangement can protect both buyer and seller is important. An understanding of the contract for a deed, the option contract, and the right of first refusal is essential in order to transact business in the most beneficial manner, given the particular circumstances. Each of these alternatives or supplements to the traditional sales contract is discussed below.

ALTERNATIVES TO TRADITIONAL SALES CONTRACTS

FIGURE 20-1

Closing statement

PROPERTY: 173 O'Farrell Street, High Point Subdivision, Smith County, Anywhere, U.S.A.

SELLERS: Richard and Janet Stevenson

BUYERS: John and Ethel Bagby

I. Summary of Buyers' Transaction

A. Gross Amount Due from Buyers

1. Contract Sales Price	$64,900.00	
2. Adjustment of items paid by seller in advance of closing:		
a. 1985 Property Taxes (12/17 to 12/31/85)	14.75	
b. Escrow Account	138.45	
c. Hazard Insurance (12/17/85 to 11/20/86)	296.84	
3. Recording Fees (warranty deed)	5.00	
4. Transfer Fee to Mortgagee (1st Mortgage Co.)	65.00	
5. Attorney's Fees to Ralph Dodge (Title Search and Closing)	150.00	
GROSS AMOUNT DUE FROM BUYERS		$65,570.04

B. Amount Paid by or on Buyers' Behalf

1. Earnest Money	$ 1,000.00	
2. Amount of Loan Assumed	47,749.38	
3. Adjustment of items paid by buyers after closing:		
a. Interest due on January 1, 1986 (for 12/1 to 12/17/85)	229.92	
TOTAL PAID BY/FOR BUYERS		$48,979.30
NET AMOUNT DUE FROM BUYERS		$16,590.74

10. Escrow Arrangements

An escrow provision is desirable because to be effective, a deed must be delivered during the lifetime of the grantor. Because it is always possible for the grantor to die or otherwise become incapacitated between the time of executing the contract and the date of delivery of possession and final payment, the deed should be executed concurrently with the contract. The deed is then delivered to a third person known as the *escrowee* or *escrow agent,* to be delivered to the grantee upon final payment. If the seller-grantor dies in the meantime, the transaction can be closed without delay.

The escrow arrangement also prevents a claim of a creditor or the rights of a new spouse from interfering with the rights of the buyers if the creditor's claim arose or the marriage occurred after a contract was signed but before the closing. The escrow in effect removes title from the seller. In essence, the law presumes at

FIGURE 20-1
(Continued)

II.   Summary of Sellers' Transaction
   A. Gross Amount Due to Sellers
      1. Contract Sales Price $64,900.00
      2. Adjustment of items paid by sellers
         in advance of closing:
         a. 1985 Property Taxes (12/17 to 12/31/85)   14.75
         b. Escrow Account   138.45
         c. Hazard Insurance (12/17/85 to 11/20/86)   296.84

GROSS AMOUNT DUE TO SELLERS $65,350.04
   B. Reductions in Amount Due Sellers
      1. Earnest Money Received   1,000.00
      2. Amount of Loan Assumed   47,749.38
      3. Adjustment of items paid by buyers
         after closing:
         a. Interest due on January 1, 1986
           (for 12/1 to 12/17/85)   229.92
      4. State Transfer Tax   17.20
      5. Real Estate Commission to Century
         21 Realtors   4,543.00
      6. Attorney's Fees to Jeff Thicke
         (warranty deed)   25.00

TOTAL REDUCTIONS   53,564.50
NET AMOUNT DUE TO SELLERS $11,785.54

III.   Distribution of Net Due from Buyers
   A. Net Due To Sellers $11,785.54
   B. Real Estate Commission to Century 21 Realtors   4,543.00
   C. Transfer Fee to 1st Mortgage Co.   65.00
   D. Clerk, Smith County Court
      1. Recording Fee (warranty deed)   5.00
      2. State Transfer Tax   17.20
   E. Attorney's Fees to Ralph Dodge   150.00
   F. Attorney's Fees to Jeff Thicke   25.00

TOTAL DISTRIBUTED $16,590.74

The undersigned parties agree to the accuracy and to the receipt of this closing statement. This 17th day of December, 1985.

_____   _____
Richard Stevenson, Seller   John Bagby, Buyer

_____   _____
Janet Stevenson, Seller   Ethel Bagby, Buyer

the actual closing that the transfer of title relates back to the time the escrow was established. Although an escrow arrangement may be created as a separate contract, it is often included as part of the sales contract, especially when the time period until closing is long.

11. Contract for a Deed

A special type of real estate sales contract that simplifies the need for institutional financing and the formal closing is a *contract for a deed.* It is actually a conditional sale of real estate in which the seller retains title to the land and the buyer makes payments for an extended period of time. In essence, the seller finances the sales transaction. A contract for a deed providing for payments over 5, 10, or 20 years is not unusual. The buyer's right to a deed to the property is conditioned on all payments being made. The seller is protected against nonpayment, since he retains legal ownership of the property until all payments are made.

Sometimes this type of sales agreement is known as an *installment land contract.* Regardless of its name, this contract contains many of the usual provisions found in the traditional sales contract. In addition, the purchaser has the risk of loss if improvements are destroyed during the period of the contract, unless there is an agreement or state statute to the contrary. The escrow provision is essential in contracts for a deed because several years usually intervene between execution of the contract and delivery of the deed. The buyer usually makes payments to the escrow agent, who must at all times be aware of the status of the contract.

Two additional clauses in most installment land contracts are of particular significance. One of them is known as the *acceleration clause;* the other is known as the *forteiture clause.* The acceleration clause allows the seller to declare the full amount of the contract due and payable in the event the buyer fails to make any of the payments or fails to perform any other of the contract's provisions as agreed. The default or forfeiture clause allows the seller, when the buyer is in default, to terminate the contract and to get the deed back from the escrow agent. The net effect of this clause is to allow the seller to keep all payments and improvements made as liquidated damages for breach of contract and to regain possession of the premises even if leased to a third party.

After a buyer has made substantial payments or has a substantial equity in the land, forfeiture of a contract for a deed might be inequitable. The principles discussed in chapter 6 that apply to liquidated damages and forfeitures are also applicable to these contracts because courts of equity abhor forfeitures. When the buyer's equity is substantial and forfeiture would be inequitable, a court, upon proper application, may prohibit the forfeiture. The court orders the property to be sold and the proceeds distributed to the seller, to the extent necessary to pay off the contract. The balance is paid to the buyer. No general rule can be stated to describe cases in which a forfeiture will be allowed or not. As a part of its equitable jurisdiction, the court will examine all the facts. If the buyer has paid only a small amount, forfeiture usually will be permitted. If the buyer has made only a slight default with regard to the amount and time of payment, or the amount of the unpaid purchase price is much less than the value of the property involved, forfeiture will be denied.[6] Forfeiture clauses are easily waived, but usually a buyer must be notified if the clause is to be reinstated after he has defaulted without having been required to forfeit.

12. The Doctrine of Equitable Conversion

In contracts for the sale of real estate and in contracts for a deed, there is frequently a substantial time lag between the execution of the contract and its performance. During this period, one or more of the parties may die, the property may be destroyed, or the original parties may enter into other transactions, such as an assignment of the contract. The legal effect of these events and transactions is frequently affected by whether or not the interest of a party is real estate or personal property. In community property states, for example, a husband may transfer personal property without his wife's joining in the transfer; whereas if the interest is real estate, the wife must join in conveyance.

The interest of a party to a contract involving real estate is not determined by legal title to the property involved. Rather, the interest is determined by equitable principles and a doctrine known as the *doctrine of equitable conversion.* The doctrine of equitable conversion operates on the execution of a contract involving real estate and converts the interest of the seller who has legal title to real property to an interest in personal property, and it converts the interest of the buyer who owes money to an interest in real estate. In other words, after the execution of a contract, the law considers that the seller's interest in the transaction is personal property and that the buyer's interest is real estate. This result comes from the concept that equity regards the transaction as being completed.

To illustrate the foregoing, assume that your Aunt Agatha, in her will, leaves all her real estate to you and all her personal property to me. Aunt Agatha then enters into a contract to sell her house for $50,000 but dies before receiving the money. Although Aunt Agatha has legal title to the real estate at the time of her death, the doctrine of equitable conversion converts that to personal property, and the $50,000 would be paid to me, not you, under Agatha's will.

13. Option Contracts

As was explained in chapter 7 on offers and acceptances, an option is the irrevocable commitment of an offeror to keep an offer open for acceptance for a stated time. In order to be valid an option must be supported by consideration. In an option to buy, the seller makes the promise to keep the offer to sell open and the buyer can decide whether to accept or reject the offer. An option to sell may be created when the buyer is the offeror and the seller is the offeree.

The consideration needed to create an option contract often is very small, particularly when the option period is short. For example, a buyer may pay the seller $50 in return for the seller's promise to sell certain real estate at any time

---

[6] Huckins v. Ritter, p. 452.

before the end of the month. Frequently option contracts are made a part of a lease wherein the tenant has the right to buy the real estate being rented during the term of the lease. Another typical example of the option's use is in the sales transaction when the seller wishes to retain the ability and opportunity to repurchase the land being sold. A portion of the tenant's rent or a part of the seller's willingness to sell can be interpreted as consideration to support the options in the lease or repurchase situations.

With every option contract involving real estate, it is essential that there be a sufficient legal description of the property and a specified sales price. Although no one can force the option holder to exercise the option, once it is exercised, a binding sales contract is created. In other words, a valid option contract standing alone or associated with another transaction may lead to a traditional sales contract or a contract for a deed.

14. Right of First Refusal

Another important type of contract related to real estate is the *right of first refusal*. Although many people confuse this agreement with an option, there are important differences. First, under a right of first refusal, a seller of real estate promises to give a potential buyer the first opportunity to purchase the described real estate. The holder of a right of first refusal cannot force the seller to enter into a binding sales agreement if the seller refuses to sell the property.

Second, a right of first refusal does not have to contain a specific price for the real estate. However, the parties' conduct must be in good faith at all times. A seller cannot propose an unreasonably high price to the potential buyer in order to defeat the right of first refusal. Indeed, the property typically must be priced at a level that some other prospective buyer has offered and that is acceptable to the seller.

Like the option, a right of first refusal is often included in a lease or sales transaction. Also, the holder of a right of first refusal cannot be forced to buy the property. In other words, this holder can always say that he has no interest in purchasing the real estate at the offered price. But the exercise of a right of first refusal leads to a binding sales contract.

SUMMARY

TRADITIONAL SALES TRANSACTIONS

Use of real estate agents	1. A seller hires a real estate agent through a listing agreement.
	2. The listing agreement may be one of several types, including an open listing, an exclusive agency listing, an exclusive right-to-sell listing, or a multiple listing.

	3. The type of listing determines when the seller owes a commission to the agent.
Negotiating the sales contract	1. Generally, negotiations between buyer and seller take place in writing so that when an agreement is reached, the statute of frauds is satisfied.
	2. If negotiations are oral, the parties' agreement must be drafted into a written contract by a lawyer.
	3. The provisions of the contract should reflect the parties' negotiations.
Terms of the sales contract	1. The contractual terms govern the parties' relationship after their agreement and before the title is transferred at closing.
	2. A sales contract should include provisions concerning the buyer's performance being conditioned on securing financing and the seller being able to convey marketable title.
	3. Other important terms include the type of deed the seller is to deliver, the method of prorating taxes and insurance, who has the risk of loss, and when closing is to occur.
Financing the sales transaction	1. The buyer must make good-faith efforts to secure the required financing.
	2. This process involves the buyer's applying, the lender's reviewing the buyer's creditworthiness, and the lender's making a loan commitment.
Evidence of title	1. The seller typically is required to transfer marketable title.
	2. In order to establish the marketability of the seller's title, a lawyer's title opinion letter or a title insurance policy should be obtained.
	3. A few states allow a title registration, known as the Torrens system, as an alternative method of showing marketable title.
Housing warranties	1. Prior to closing, the buyer should inspect the real property thoroughly for possible problems.
	2. To protect buyers from the hard-to-discover defects, courts have held that builders implicitly warrant that a residence is habitable.

Closing the transaction	**3.** Many builders have begun to give express warranties that houses are free from structural defects.
	1. The closing event is when title is actually transferred from the seller to the buyer.
	2. The closing often involves many documents that must be properly signed and filed.

ALTERNATIVES TO TRADITIONAL SALES CONTRACTS

Escrow arrangements	**1.** The escrow may be a part of the sales contract or a separate agreement.
	2. This arrangement involves the constructive delivery of a deed from the seller to the buyer.
	3. The deed is delivered to a disinterested third party who holds it until closing.
	4. The delivery to the buyer relates back to the time of delivery to the escrow. This concept avoids many problems that arise with respect to either party's death or the claims of the seller's creditors.
Contract for a deed	**1.** A type of conditional sales contract.
	2. The seller finances the transaction and retains title as security.
	3. Payments are made over a substantial time period.
	4. An escrow arrangement is essential in such contracts.
	5. During the extended time of performance, the doctrine of equitable conversion shifts the seller's and buyer's legal interests.
Option contract	**1.** An agreement supported by consideration whereby one party makes an offer and agrees that it will not be revoked for a stated time period.
	2. This agreement may be an option to buy (seller has made the offer) or an option to sell (buyer has made the offer).
	3. The agreement must state a specific purchase price.
Right of first refusal	**1.** A seller's promise to give a potential buyer the first opportunity to purchase the described real estate.

> **2.** This agreement does not allow a buyer to force a sale.
>
> **3.** The right of first refusal does not have to contain a specific purchase price, but the seller must act in good faith at all times.

CASES

Virginia Real Estate Commission v. Bias
308 S.E.2d 123 (Va. 1983)

RUSSELL, J. The controlling question in this appeal is whether there was substantial evidence in the record of proceedings before an administrative agency to support its findings.

The Virginia Real Estate Commission, acting upon a complaint against Dorsey V. Bias, a broker, found that Bias had violated its Regulation, which requires a broker or salesman "to promptly tender to the seller every written offer to purchase obtained on the property involved." The commission suspended Bias' license for one year and fined him $1,000.00. Bias appealed the ruling to the Circuit Court of Albemarle County, which reviewed the record and heard arguments of counsel. The court held that the commission's ruling was based upon an "error of law" and that the commission had "improperly admitted" certain evidence. The court vacated the commission's order and remanded the case. The commission appeals.

The essential facts are undisputed. Dorsey Bias is a licensed broker in Charlottesville, trading as Cavalier Realty Company. In 1977, Dr. John Staige Davis was the owner of a tract of 125 acres in Buckingham County. He agreed to sell ten acres to a Mrs. Rathbone for $15,000.00 to settle a debt, but died before the sale could be effected. His widow, Tolly E. Davis, was aware of the proposed sale to Mrs. Rathbone and intended to honor it. Mrs. Davis was in need of funds, however, and on September 18, 1977, listed the remaining 115 acres with Bias for sale at a price of $75,000. A prospective purchaser, Thomas Wetzel, had visited the farm before the death of Dr. Davis and knew that it contained 125 acres. He discussed the property with

John Bias, a son of Dorsey Bias and also a broker with Cavalier Realty Company. Neither John Bias nor Wetzel was aware of the reduction in the acreage offered for sale. At John Bias' suggestion, Wetzel and his wife signed a written offer to purchase the entire 125-acre tract for $60,000. They deposited the written offer in the mailbox of Cavalier Realty on the evening of September 20, 1977. John Bias found the offer the next morning and acknowledged it by letter to Wetzel. He testified that he did not remember what he did with the offer, but his normal practice would have been to place it on his father's desk.

Wetzel inquired about his offer at Cavalier Realty on September 24 or 25. He was informed that it had been rejected. Mrs. Davis never received any offer from Wetzel.

Dorsey Bias was in West Virginia on September 19, 20, and 21. On the morning of September 22, he returned to Cavalier Realty and called Mrs. Davis on the telephone, offering to purchase in his own name, for $50,000, the 115 acres listed with him for sale. When Mrs. Davis indicated her agreement, he prepared contracts . . . for his purchase . . . and mailed them to Mrs. Davis for her signature. He testified that he was then unaware of the Wetzel offer.

Dorsey Bias talked with Mrs. Davis by telephone again on September 24. Mrs. Davis indicated a desire for a higher price, and Bias increased his offer to $53,000. Mrs. Davis agreed to this and promised to alter the price in the written contract, sign it, and return it to him.

Bias testified that he first became aware of the Wetzel offer on September 24, after the telephone conversation with Mrs. Davis, but that he made no effort to communicate it to her because he considered himself to be the contract purchaser and regarded his responsibilities as a broker to be at an end.

Bias received the signed contracts from Mrs. Davis by mail on September 26 or 27. . . .

The commission found as facts that Bias "reasonably should have known" of Wetzel's first offer on September 22, that he did know of it on September 24, and that in failing to communicate it, he "represented his personal interests to the detriment of the seller and . . . of the prospective buyers.". . .

It is clear that Wetzel's offer was in the office of Cavalier Realty on September 21 and that Dorsey Bias was present there on the morning of September 22 and during the next five days. Bias admitted having knowledge of the offer on September 24. The commission reasonably could have concluded that he knew of the offer as early as the morning of September 22.

The commission's Regulation required Bias to tender "promptly" to the seller any offer obtained. A broker has at all times a duty to act with entire good faith toward his principal. This includes an obligation to disclose to the principal all facts within his knowledge which are or may be material,

or which might influence the principal in deciding upon a course of action. The commission properly could have found that Bias, acting in his own interest, remained silent about the Wetzel offer for five or six days after he had knowledge of it, even though he could not have known he was a contract purchaser until he received the signed contracts on September 26 or 27. Thus there was ample and substantial evidence to support the commission's finding that he had violated his duty under the regulation. A reviewing court need inquire no further.

The presence or absence of "detriment" to the seller, caused by Bias' non-disclosure, is irrelevant. A broker's duty to communicate an offer promptly to the seller is absolute. It does not depend upon the broker's evaluation of the offer as advantageous or otherwise. That decision is the seller's alone. The seller might have preferred to deal with Wetzel for reasons unknown to Bias. Further, the forwarding of an offer is merely the opening of what may become an extended course of negotiations. The final price might have borne little resemblance to the initial offer.

Reversed.

Kerry-Rand and Associates v. Peddicord
340 N.W.2d 880 (Neb. 1983)

COLWELL, J. This is a suit by Kerry-Rand and Associates, plaintiff, to recover a real estate broker's commission from Tom Peddicord, defendant. Summary judgment was entered in favor of plaintiff for $99,925.73. Defendant appeals. . . .

The petition alleges the parties executed an exclusive "Farm Listing Contract" (Listing) on April 23, 1981, for the sale of a ranch and that defendant sold the ranch himself during the term of the Listing, which obligated him to pay a broker's commission under the express "fees" terms of the Listing. Defendant denied that plaintiff either found a buyer or expended any reasonable effort to find a buyer, or that defendant sold the ranch to anyone due to plaintiff's efforts.

On April 23, 1981, plaintiff and defendant executed a printed form farm listing contract. The first two paragraphs are material here:

IN CONSIDERATION of your agreement to list,

and to offer for sale the property hereinafter described and to use your efforts to find a purchaser, I (we) hereby give you the sole and exclusive right until November 1, 1981, to sell. . . .

See Attached Addendum 9,954 acres more or less . . . for the sum of Two Million Four Hundred Eighty Eight Thousand Five Hundred & no/100 ($2,488,500.00) dollars. . . ."

I (We) agree to pay you for professional services a cash fee of 5% of the gross sale price, or $_____, said fee to be payable on the happening of any one or more of the following events, to wit:

If a sale is made, or a purchaser found, who is ready, willing and able to purchase the property before the expiration of this listing, by you, myself, or any other person, at the above price and terms I (we) may agree to accept, . . .

In early 1981 both Marvin Metzger, a neighboring rancher, and Richard Satterlee, a real estate broker in Martin, South Dakota, discussed the sale of the ranch with defendant. In June 1981 Metzger, acting through Satterlee, made an offer to buy, which was refused by defendant. A second offer was accepted and a written contract executed on July 21, 1981, providing for defendant's sale of the ranch to Cross Heart Ranch Company and Robert A. Metzger for $2,194,000; vendees made a $100,000 down-payment; possession was to be given about July 26, 1981; final settlement was to be November 15, 1981. The contract provided that a $75,000 commission was to be paid by seller to Richard Satterlee, listing broker, and Thomas Metzger, selling broker. . . . The contract was performed on November 27, 1981, when defendant conveyed the Nebraska land for $1,998,514.06. The $75,000 commission was paid.

During the period from April 23 to November 1, 1981, no agent of plaintiff brought a prospective purchaser to the ranch. Upon execution of the Listing, plaintiff included the ranch in its inventory of land for sale available to its agents; advertising data was prepared, followed by advertising in newspapers, professional publications, and other shoppers' media. The first advertising was on May 4, 1981; the next began October 2, 1981. Agents of plaintiff also circulated brochures at seminars attended in four major cities.

. . . [D]efendant claims as error that the Listing agreement alone entitled plaintiff to a commission as a matter of law; he argues . . . that plaintiff was required to make some reasonable effort to find a buyer. . . .

Here, the issue relates to a special provision in the Listing purporting to obligate the owner to pay a broker's commission if the owner sells the land during the Listing term. . . . Is the "fees" agreement in the Listing enforceable?

The general rule is stated: "A broker is entitled to a commission on a sale by the principal, where, in addition to language indicating an exclusive agency, there is a special contractual provision giving a right to a commission on a sale by the owner." In *Dial Realty, Inc. v. Cudahy Co.*, we considered a similar "fees" provision, and we said that "even if the defendant had not admitted its liability, under the plain and unambiguous terms of the listing agreement, the defendant was clearly liable to the plaintiff. . . ." . . .

The "fees" provision in the Listing obligated defendant to pay plaintiff a commission if he sold the ranch during the Listing term. . . . Plaintiff was entitled to a finding that defendant sold the ranch himself on July 21, 1981, during the Listing term. . . .

Plaintiff met its burden of proof by a prima facie showing that there was no genuine issue as to any material fact and that it was entitled to judgment as a matter of law . . .

Affirmed.

Malinak v. Safeco Title Insurance Company of Idaho
661 P.2d 12 (Mont. 1983)

Paul Malinak owned 640 acres of land in Montana. During his ownership, St. Regis Paper Company acquired rights to timber on this land. Malinak mistakenly believed these rights expired in 1974. During early 1975, Malinak agreed to sell his land, and he requested a title insurance commitment from Safeco Title Insurance Company. This commitment deleted any mention of possible rights of St. Regis. Although that sale of the land fell through, Malinak sold his land to Lowell Novy in late 1975. Relying on the title commitment previously received, Malinak warranted the title to Novy without timber reservations. Safeco issued a title insurance policy to Novy which also made no mention of St. Regis's timber rights. Shortly after the sales transaction was closed, St. Regis notified Novy of its plans to cut timber. Novy sued Safeco under the title policy. Safeco notified Malinak that it would seek to recover from him if the company was liable to Novy. Malinak argued that Safeco was liable to him for his expenses in defending the title transferred to Novy. Malinak asserted that his warranty of clear title was based on Safeco's title commitment.

SHEEHY, J. . . . Malinak appeals from a summary judgment granted by the District Court, determining in effect that he had no right to recovery. . . .

Malinak contends . . . the . . . title insurance company is [liable] to the vendor or seller of the land, for providing to the seller a title commitment which fails to disclose to the seller defects in the seller's title, where the seller relies on the title commitment to warrant the title he is selling.

Title insurance is a contract to indemnify the insured against loss through defects in the insured title or against liens or encumbrances that may affect the insured title at the time the policy is issued. Undoubtedly the named insured in a policy may enforce the terms of the contract of title insurance for defects in the title conveyed and insured.

A title commitment is in a somewhat different category from the title policy that follows it. Ordinarily a commitment is ordered by the seller for the purpose of exhibiting it to the buyer as a representation of the quality of the title seller expects to sell to the buyer. A title commitment naturally contemplates a search by the title insurer of the chain of title, an opinion by an expert of what the search reveals, a guaranty that the search was accurate and that the title commitment expresses the quality of the title of the seller as shown by the record. The person who seeks a title insurance commitment expects to obtain a professional title search, as well as a professional legal opinion as to the condition of the title and a guaranty that the title expressed in

the commitment will be insured to the extent of the policy coverage. A title commitment does not propose that the title company will insure the property; rather that the title company will insure the title. The title insurer, of course, does not agree to clear the title; rather by its commitment, the title company agrees to afford coverage in a title policy later to be issued insuring the title according to its commitment. . . .

It is within the expectations of the parties, the seller ordering the title commitment and the title insurer inspecting the public records, that the title commitment will accurately reflect the insurability of the title, or the condition of the public record, as the case may be, with respect to that title. We find a duty on the part of the title insurer when it issues a title commitment which later forms the basis for a title insurance policy, particularly where the seller relies on the title commitment, to base its title commitment and report upon a reasonably diligent title search of the public records. A breach of that duty would constitute negligence. . . .

Accordingly, the summary judgment entered by the District Court against Malinak is reversed and this cause is remanded.

Reversed and remanded.

Witty v. Schramm
379 N.E.2d 333 (Ill. App. 1978)

SCOTT, J. . . . The plaintiffs brought an action against the defendants for both damages and rescission of a contract for the purchase of an unimproved parcel of land upon which the plaintiffs intended to erect a home. The plaintiffs alleged in their complaint as amended that after purchasing the property they excavated for a basement and footings for the intended home and that shortly thereafter water began bubbling and percolating to such an extent and in such a manner as to fill the entire excavated area. The plaintiffs alleged that the defendants as vendors of the parcel of land breached an implied warranty of fitness and habitability and that they were therefore entitled to damages and rescission of the contract which they entered into for the purchase of the land.

The defendants filed a motion to dismiss . . . on the grounds . . . that there is no implied warranty of habitability as a matter of law as far as vacant

lots are concerned. The trial court granted defendants' motion to dismiss and this appeal ensued. . . .

We know of no cases which have determined the question as to whether an implied warranty of habitability exists as to vacant lots. The parties to this appeal have conceded that the question is one of first impression in our state. In order to determine the question we find helpful the reasoning set forth in the case of *Conyers v. Molloy* (1977), 50 Ill.App.3d 17. In the case of *Conyers* the reviewing court stated:

> Some of the reasons for the recognition of the warranty are set out in *Wawak v. Stewart* (1970), 247 Ark. 1093. That court stated that the contrast between the law of personal property and the law of real property is so great as to be indefensible. Why should a $10 iron have a warranty of fitness while the biggest purchase ever made by a majority of families, their home, is unprotected? The relationship of a mass producer-builder-seller and the purchaser is vastly different from the relationships from which the rule of *caveat emptor* arose.

In the early days of the common law, the main concern of the parties was the land, and whatever structures were on it could be easily repaired by the new landholder. Today, the purpose is to buy a dwelling, rather than land per se, and most purchasers are not equipped to undertake major repairs. Like the buyer of an automobile, the purchaser of a house generally has neither the bargaining power to insist on a warranty nor the expertise to detect what could be wrong. Finally, but certainly not least, it seems only fair to put the burden of repairing defects in construction on the person who is (1) responsible for the defects, (2) is in a position to repair them and (3) is in a position to spread the costs of the repair. This is especially true since a significant amount of the defects can be so buried in the construction that it could be impossible to find them before buying, no matter how careful or thorough the inspection. In fact, the consensus is that there is no defensible reason why the warranty should not be recognized, save the argument that such change should be for the legislature. In view of the inequities created by the judge-made rule of *caveat emptor,* that hardly seems an answer. . . . Consequently, we hold that an implied warranty of habitability in this context does exist and that a breach thereof is actionable.

In examining the foregoing language as set forth in the *Conyers* case we note that in determining whether or not an implied warranty of habitability is to exist you determine whether someone is at "fault," you determine whether someone is "responsible" for the complained of defect, and you further determine if someone is in the position to "repair" the defect. In the instant case that subsurface water was under the vacant lot purchased by the plaintiffs cannot be attributed as being the fault of anyone. Stated in another manner, it cannot be said that anyone is responsible for the presence of the subsurface water and it follows that the vendors not being at fault or responsible for the natural condition of subsurface water being present then they have no special knowledge of the complained of defect that would make it incumbent on them to repair or correct it.

It is abundantly clear to us that there is not and should not be applicable to a vacant lot of land an implied warrant of habitability. To hold otherwise could well lead to the opening of Pandora's box and the escape of the evils contained therein. Should a vendor of a vacant lot by implication be charged with warranting that there is no subsurface water, or that there is a certain amount of subsurface water, or that the soil is of a certain texture or consistency? We believe not, for what may be a defect in one instance may be a desirable feature or benefit in another.

The plaintiffs have made no allegations of fraud or misrepresentation. They purchased a lot in a subdivision, they made plans to build a home, they excavated dirt for a basement and encountered troublesome subsurface water. The problems encountered by the plaintiffs are not unique to them. The presence of water undoubtedly will result in additional expense to the plaintiffs, however, the defendants should not be placed in the position of having warranted to the plaintiffs that they would be able to erect and maintain a home free and immune from all problems.

We believe that there are compelling reasons why an implied warranty of habitability should not be applicable to a vacant lot of land and therefore the trial court's dismissal of Count 1 of the plaintiffs' amended complaint is

Affirmed.

Cosmopolitan Homes, Inc. v. Weller
663 P.2d 1041 (Colo. 1983)

DUBOFSKY, J. We granted certiorari to review the Court of Appeals' holding in *Weller v. Cosmopolitan Homes, Inc.,* which allowed subsequent purchasers of a home to assert a claim for property damage to the structure allegedly caused by the negligence of the homebuilder. We affirm the judgment of the Court of Appeals but limit the negligence claim to latent defects which the purchaser was unable to discover prior to purchase.

The plaintiffs, Shirley Mae Weller and William S. Weller, are the fourth owners of a house designed, built and sold in 1973 by the defendants Cosmopolitan Homes, Inc., Hutchinson Construction Company, and Builders' Research Engineering Company (the builders). Although the Wellers seek to recover for deficiencies in workmanship, design and materials in the house attributable to negligent design and construction by the defendants, the facts alleged in the complaint relate to cracking in the foundation from movement or settling of the house which had not occurred at the time the Wellers made their purchase on January 4, 1977.

The district court dismissed the Wellers' complaint on the ground that there was no privity of contract between the defendants and the Wellers because the Wellers were not the first purchasers or users of the house, and therefore the defendants did not owe the Wellers a duty of reasonable care. The Court of Appeals reversed the district court ruling, holding that regardless of lack of privity of contract, the purchaser of a used home may recover for property damage caused by the negligence of the builder.

On certiorari review, the defendants argue that a claim for negligence against a builder is indistinguishable as a matter of proof from a claim of breach of implied warranty of habitability. The defendants therefore assert that the builder should not be held liable in a negligence action brought by a subsequent purchaser because case law in Colorado has limited an implied warranty's protection to first purchasers. We disagree with the defendants' assertion. An obligation to act without negligence in the construction of a home is independent of contractual obligations such as an implied warranty of habitability. . . .

The policy supporting the extension of the negligence remedy to a subsequent purchaser is based on many of the reasons for implying a warranty of habitability to the first purchaser. . . .

[G]iven the mobility of most potential home owners, it is foreseeable that a house will be sold to subsequent purchasers, and any structural defects are as certain to harm the subsequent purchaser as the first. We see no reason for disallowing a subsequent purchaser to state a claim in negligence.

Although some states have allowed both a claim for negligence against a builder and a claim for implied warranty to be brought by subsequent purchasers, and despite the claim of the builder here that the two claims are indistinguishable as a matter of proof, we conclude that there are a number of differences between the two claims and therefore they should be treated differently. Some overlap in elements of proof of such actions may occur, but the scope of duty differs and the basis for liability is distinguishable. The implied warranty of habitability and fitness arises from the contractual relation between the builder and the purchaser. Proof of a defect due to improper construction, design, or preparation is sufficient to establish liability in the builder-vendor. Negligence, however, requires that a builder or contractor be held to a standard of reasonable care in the conduct of its duties to the foreseeable users of the property. Negligence in tort must establish defects in workmanship, supervision, or design as a responsibility of the individual defendant. Proof of defect alone is not enough to establish the claim. Foreseeability limits the scope of the duty, and the passage of time following construction makes causation difficult to prove. Moreover, in the context of the purchase of a used home, the owner must demonstrate that the defect is latent or hidden, and must show that the defect was caused by the builder.

The reason for allowing recovery only for latent or hidden defects, which have been defined as "those manifesting themselves after purchase and which are not discoverable through reasonable inspection," is to prevent an action where mere deterioration or loss of a bargain is claimed. Often a buyer is willing to accept certain deficiencies in a house in exchange for a lower purchase price. However, a buyer cannot be expected to discover structural defects which remain latent at the time of purchase.

Affirmed.

Huckins v. Ritter
661 P.2d 52 (N.M. 1983)

FEDERICI, J. . . . On July 28, 1981, plaintiffs Huckins and defendant Ritter entered into a real estate contract for the purchase and sale of residential property situated in Ruidoso, New Mexico. The purchase price of the house was $155,000. Plaintiffs agreed to a down payment on the home in the amount of $45,000 and assumed an underlying real estate note in the amount of $40,725.73. The remaining outstanding balance on the house, $69,274.67, was due and payable on October 15, 1981. Plaintiffs were unable to meet the payment due on October 15, 1981. On October 30, 1981, defendant's attorney notified plaintiffs that if the amount due was not paid within fifteen days of the date of the letter, then the defendant intended to exercise her right to retain all sums paid under the real estate contract. On November 30, 1981, plaintiffs filed an action to enjoin defendant from terminating the real estate contract or alternatively providing for return of a portion of the down payment. The trial court granted temporary injunctive relief restraining defendant from terminating the real estate contract. At a subsequent hearing on December 2, 1981, the parties, by stipulation, agreed to an extension of time until January 10, 1982 to correct the default and to make the payment. Plaintiffs were not able to arrange payment by that due date and attempted to arrange a partial payment by that date, to no avail. On February 25, 1982, defendant terminated the real estate contract and proceeded to obtain the closing documents from the escrow agent. On June 29, 1982, the trial court entered its order in favor of defendant. . . .

The rule is well settled in New Mexico that in general, the type of real estate contract involved is enforceable. Thus, upon default by the purchaser, the vendor is entitled to terminate the real estate contract, regain possession of the property and retain the payments made as rental. But this Court has also recognized that there are exceptions to the rule under appropriate circumstances.

An exception is recognized when the enforcement of the literal terms of the contract would result in a forfeiture or in unfairness which shocks the conscience of the court. This exception should be applied in this case. The record shows that on July 28, 1981, plaintiffs made a down payment in the amount of $45,000. This is almost one-third of the purchase price of the house. Plaintiffs were in possession of the property only from July 28, 1981 until February 25, 1982. The property still has a market value equal to the original sale price. . . .

To permit defendants to retain the $45,000 down payment and in addition to regain possession of the house would, in our opinion, constitute an unwarranted forfeiture.

Plaintiffs are entitled to a return of the $45,000 down payment, less reasonable rental to be assessed during plaintiffs' occupancy of the house, and the diminution, if any, to the property during plaintiffs' occupancy. . . .

Reversed.

REVIEW QUESTIONS

1. Identify the terms in column A by matching each to the appropriate statement in column B:

A	B
1. Listing agreement	**a.** When title is actually transferred by the seller to the buyer.
2. Contractual terms	**b.** Determines when the seller owes a commission to an agent.
3. Application and commitment	**c.** A seller's promise to give a potential buyer the first opportunity to purchase described real estate.
4. Title insurance policy	**d.** Governs the parties' relationship after their agreement and before the closing.
5. Closing event	**e.** A popular method of proving the marketability of real estate titles.
6. Escrow arrangement	**f.** A type of conditional sales contract.
7. Contract for a deed	**g.** Seller's irrevocable offer to sell the described real estate.

8. Equitable conversion

9. Option to buy

10. Right of first refusal

h. A constructive delivery of a deed from the seller to the buyer.

i. Changes the view of the seller's and buyer's legal interests prior to the transaction's completion.

j. Part of the process involved in financing the sales transaction.

2. Define and distinguish the following types of listing agreements:
  a. Open listing
  b. Exclusive-agency listing
  c. Exclusive-right-to-sell listing

3. Why is it desirable to have a provision in the sales contract specifying which party has the risk of loss in the event improvements are substantially damaged or destroyed prior to the closing?

4. Pauline Patrick, a purchaser, signed a real estate sales contract that conditioned her performance on her ability to obtain adequate financing. Pauline never applied for a loan. Therefore, Pauline did not obtain the money required to complete her performance. At closing, will Pauline be excused from performing her duties under this contract? Explain.

5. Describe the advantages of a title insurance policy over a lawyer's title opinion letter.

6. In 1982, Solid Construction Company built and sold a house to Proffitt. Proffitt sold the house to Laser in 1985. After moving into the house, Laser discovered that the basement leaked and that there was a large crack around three of the basement walls. Should Solid Construction be liable to Laser for the cost of repairs, which amounted to $3,500? Why?

7. James and Bessie Egan had a life estate in a tract of land, and Melford Egan owned the remainder. An agreement between these parties provided for a fifty-fifty division of the proceeds of any sale of the property. Under a threat of condemnation, these parties signed a contract and a deed to the state of Missouri. On October 5, this contract and deed were placed in escrow to be held until a check for the purchase price was received. On October 25, James and Bessie were killed in an accident. On November 9, the state delivered its check to the escrow agent. A dispute arose concerning who was entitled to the sales proceeds. Was the delivery of the signed deed to an escrow agent on October 5 effective to pass title to the state, so that James and Bessie were entitled to half the proceeds? Why?

8. How does a contract for a deed differ from a traditional sales contract? What other names are synonymous with a contract for a deed?

9. Neil executed a contract for the purchase of a commercial building from Butler. The contract contained a provision stating that if the payments by Neil were more than 30 days overdue, Butler could declare a default and obtain the deed back from the escrowee. After 12 years of the 20-year contract, Neil has fallen on hard times and has made no payments for almost a year. Should a court allow Butler to default the contract, cancel the deed, and reacquire possession of the property? Explain.

10. The Overland Park Credit Union sold some vacant land to Marley. On the date this sale was completed, Marley agreed to lease this land and an office building to be built to the Credit Union for a 12-year period. This lease granted the Credit Union the option to buy the building and land before the lease expired. This option clause stated the following:

> The Lessee is hereby given the option to purchase the property described in the paragraph next following and all buildings thereon, of which the leased premises is a part, at the end of the original term of this lease at a price of $93,000.00. Such option shall be exercised by the Lessee delivering written notice to the Lessor, not less than sixty (60) days prior to the end of the original term of this lease, of Lessee's intention to exercise said option. If said

option is exercised, the Lessor and Lessee shall, within ten days after such exercise, execute and acknowledge in duplicate a Contract of Sale the terms thereof to be for cash upon expiration of the original lease term or upon such other conditions and terms as the parties might mutually agree.

Prior to the end of the lease, within the allowable time, the Credit Union gave notice it was exercising the option. The landlord-seller objected and claimed the option was unenforceable because it was not definite concerning the rights of the parties. Is this option clause sufficiently specific and complete to be enforceable? Explain.

21 OTHER PROPERTY TRANSACTIONS: LEASES AND BAILMENTS

There are many ways to classify transactions involving property interests. One way is to look at real property versus personal property transactions. Another way is to examine the interest transferred. It is this latter method we have chosen to utilize. For example, in the previous chapter, the subject matter was real estate *sales* transactions. Chapters 23 through 25 discuss Article 2's coverage of the *sale* of movable personal property. In these transactions, the seller transfers both ownership and possession of the property to the buyer.

In this chapter, our principal consideration is those transactions involving real and personal property in which possession but not ownership is transferred. In particular, the following sections are concerned with leases of real estate and bailments of personal property.

LEASE TRANSACTIONS

1. In General

A *lease* is a transfer of possession of real estate from a landlord (lessor) to a tenant (lessee) for a consideration called *rent*. A lease may be oral or written, expressed or simply implied from the facts and circumstances. A lease differs from a mere license, which is a privilege granted by one person to another to use land for some particular purpose. A license is not an interest in the land. A license to the licensee is personal and not assignable.

2. Classification of Leases

A lease may be a tenancy (1) for a stated period, (2) from period to period, (3) at will, or (4) at sufferance. As its name implies, a tenancy for a stated period lasts for the specific time stated in the lease. The statute of frauds requires a written lease if the period exceeds one year. The lease for a stated period terminates without notice at the end of the period. It is not affected by the death of either party during the period. A lease of land for a stated period is not terminated by destruction of the improvements during the period unless the lease so provides. If a lease covers *only* the improvements on land, destruction of them creates impossibility of performance.

A tenancy from period to period may be created by the terms of the lease. A lease may run from January 1, 1986 to December 31, 1987, and from year to year thereafter unless terminated by the parties. Many leases from period to period arise when the tenant, with the consent of the landlord, holds over after the end of a lease for a stated period. When a *holdover* occurs, the landlord may object and evict the former tenant as a trespasser. Or he may continue to treat the tenant as a tenant; in which case the lease continues from period to period, with the period being identical to that of the original lease, not to exceed one year. The one-year limitation results from the language of the statute of frauds. The amount of rent is identical to that of the original lease.

Leases from year to year or from month to month can be terminated only upon giving proper notice. The length of the notice is usually prescribed by state statute—usually 30 days for a month-to-month lease, 60 to 90 days for one that is year-to-year. Statutes usually provide the time of the notice, such as on the day the rent is due. Farm leases usually have a special notice period, so that the tenant will have notice before planting the next year's crops.

A tenancy at will, by definition, has no fixed period and can be terminated by either party at any time upon giving the prescribed statutory notice. A few states do not require notice, but if legal action is necessary to obtain possession for the lessor, a time lag will be automatically imposed. A tenancy at sufferance occurs when a tenant holds over without the consent of the landlord. Until the landlord decides to evict him or to allow him to stay, he is a tenant at sufferance.

3. Tenants—Rights and Duties

The rights and duties of the parties to the lease are determined by the lease itself and by the statutes of the state in which the property is located. Several rights of tenants are frequently misunderstood. For example, the tenant is entitled to exclusive possession and control of the premises unless the lease provides to the contrary. The landlord has no right to go upon the premises except to collect rent. This means that the owner of an apartment building cannot go into the leased apartments and inspect them unless the lease specifically reserves the right to do so. At the end of the lease, the landlord may retake possession of the premises and inspect for damage. A landlord may also retake possession for purposes of protecting the property if the tenant abandons the premises.

Unless the lease so provides, a tenant has no duty to make improvements or substantial repairs. A tenant is not obligated to replace a worn-out heating or air conditioning system, but it is his duty to make minor repairs such as replacing a broken window. Because of the difficulty in classifying repairs, the lease should spell out the exact obligations of both parties. If the lease obligates the tenant to make repairs, the obligation includes significant items such as replacing a rotten floor or a defective furnace. The duty to repair usually does not extend to replacing the whole structure if it is destroyed.

An important right in many leases of commercial property is the tenant's right to remove trade fixtures that he has installed during the lease period. Remember the distinction between fixtures and trade fixtures. The former become a part of the real estate and belong to the owner of the land. The latter remain personalty and belong to the tenant. The right of removal terminates with the lease, and unremoved trade fixtures become the property of the lessor.

Another important right of the tenant relates to his corresponding duty to pay rent. The duty to pay rent is subject to setoffs for violations of the provisions of the lease by the landlord. The duty to pay rent is released in the event of an eviction, actual or constructive. *Constructive* eviction occurs when the premises become untenantable, not because of any fault of the tenant, or when some act of the landlord deprives the tenant of quiet enjoyment of the premises. (One example of such an act involves the landlords' breach of an implied warranty of habitability, which is discussed in section 5 below.) Assume that Joe College rents a basement apartment on campus. A spring rain floods the apartment and makes it uninhabitable. Joe has been constructively evicted. He may move out, and his duty to pay rent is released. Failure to vacate the premises is a waiver of constructive eviction grounds, however. A tenant who continues in possession despite grounds for constructive eviction must continue to pay rent unless this duty is relieved by statute. Some states and cities in recent years have enacted such laws in an attempt to force landlords to maintain their property in a tenantable condition. These laws allow tenants to withhold rent where the premises are in such disrepair that the health and safety of the tenant is jeopardized. Such laws protect low-income tenants from slum landlords.

Unless prohibited by the lease, a tenant may assign the lease or sublet the premises without the consent of the landlord. In an *assignment,* the assignee becomes liable to the landlord for the rent (of course, the assignor remains liable also). In a *sublease,* the sublessee is liable to the tenant, and the tenant is liable to the landlord. An assignment transfers the original leasehold to the assignee. A sublease creates a new leasehold estate. Ordinarily, an assignment is for the balance of the original lease, whereas a sublease is only for part of the term.

If a lease prohibits assignment, it does not necessarily prevent a sublease; if a lease prohibits subleasing, it does not necessarily prevent assignment; if both are to be prohibited, the lease should so provide. Most leases provide that any assignment or sublease must have the approval of the landlord. Whether the landlord can withhold consent arbitrarily is an issue that has frequently arisen. Historically, the landlord's consent to a proposed assignment or sublease could be withheld without any reason. However, the trend now is to require that the landlord's lack of consent be reasonable under the factual circumstances.[1]

4. Landlords—Rights and Duties

The landlord's foremost right is to collect payment of rent. In many states and by the express terms of many leases, the landlord has a lien for unpaid rent on

---

[1] Funk v. Funk, p. 473.

the personal property of the tenant physically located on the premises. This lien right is exercised in a statutory proceeding known as *distress for rent.* By following the prescribed procedures, the landlord is able to distrain or physically hold personalty on the premises until the rent is paid. If not paid, the tenant's personal property may be sold pursuant to court order. The proceeds of the sale, after deducting court costs, are applied to the rent.

A second basic right belonging to the landlord is to have the tenant vacate the premises upon termination of the tenancy. If the tenancy is terminated lawfully, the landlord's right to possession is absolute. The tenant may not deny the landlord's title. Furthermore, tenants have a duty to redeliver physical control of the premises in the same condition as received, ordinary wear and tear excepted. The motive of the landlord in terminating the lease usually is immaterial. However, as the result of federal and state statutes, a landlord may not discriminate in leasing or terminating a lease on the basis of race, color, religion, sex, or national origin.

A landlord also is entitled to recover from either the tenant or third parties for injuries to or waste of the property. Tenants may not make any material changes to improvements without the landlord's permission. They may not move walls, install new ones, or do anything else that would constitute a material change in the premises without permission.

Tenants sometimes vacate the premises and refuse to pay any further rent prior to the expiration of the lease's full term. This is especially true in long-term commercial leases. What are the rights and duties of the parties when the tenant breaches the lease contract by abandoning the premises? Does the landlord have a duty to seek a new tenant? The answer to these questions depends on state law. In some states a landlord need not seek a new tenant and the full obligation of the tenant remains. In these states, the tenant can look for someone to take over the lease, but the lessor need not. The modern view is that the landlord has a duty to mitigate the tenant's damages. If the landlord fails to attempt to mitigate the damages, the tenant's liability is eliminated.

It is common practice for a landlord to require that the tenant deposit a stated sum of money, such as one month's rent, as security for the lease. This security deposit covers nonpayment of rent and possible damage to the premises. Many landlords have been reluctant to return these security deposits, contending in most cases that damages were present, requiring repairs. As a result, many tenants have refused to pay the last month's rent, demanding that the security deposit be applied. Such practices by landlords and tenants have created a great deal of animosity and litigation. To alleviate this problem, the legislatures of many states have passed laws governing lease security deposits. Such laws usually require that the landlord pay interest on the deposits and itemize the cost of any repairs that were made from the deposit. They further require the landlord to return the deposit promptly and prohibit the landlord from using it to repair conditions caused by normal wear and tear. In the event a tenant is required to sue the landlord to recover the deposit, the tenant is entitled to collect attorney's fees. Finally, under these statutes, the tenant usually is not allowed to set off the deposit against the last month's rent.

5. Warranty of Habitability

In recent years, courts have been called upon to decide if there is an implied warranty of habitability in a lease of residential property. (This is similar to the issue of warranties on the sale of new housing and is part of the broadened protection given the consuming public.) Some courts have held in all housing leases that there is an implied warranty of habitability. One court held that the fact that a tenant knew of a substantial number of defects when he rented the premises and that rent was accordingly reduced did not remove the tenant from protection of the warranty. The court reasoned that permitting that type of bargaining would be contrary to public policy and the purpose of the doctrine of implied warranty of habitability. In determining the kinds of defects that will be deemed to constitute a breach of warranty of habitability, several factors are considered. Among the common factors are (1) the violation of any applicable housing code or building or sanitary regulations; (2) whether the nature of the deficiency affects a vital facility; (3) the potential or actual effect upon safety and sanitation; and (4) whether the tenant was in any way responsible for the defect. A breach of this warranty may allow a tenant to terminate the lease. It may serve as a defense to a suit for rent and as a means to obtain a rent reduction.

Defects in vital portions of the premises that may affect health are more important than defects in extras such as swimming pools or recreational facilities, which are not likely to render the premises uninhabitable. It should be kept in mind that not all states recognize an implied warranty of habitability in residential leases. Also, most states have not extended implied warranties to commercial leases. In general, implied warranties of habitability are created either by courts on a case-by-case basis or by statutory enactment.[2]

6. Liability to Third Parties

Difficult legal questions arise in cases involving the landlord's and tenant's liability for injuries to persons on the premises. As a general rule, a landlord makes no warranty that the premises are safe or suitable for the intended use by the tenant, and third persons are on the premises at their own peril. A landlord owes no greater duty to a tenant's guests than is owed to the tenant. A landlord does have a duty to give notice of latent defects of which he has knowledge, and some states add unknown defects of which he *should* have knowledge in the exercise of ordinary care. In recent years, the liability of landlords under this view has expanded, but there still must be a duty that is breached before there is liability.

Knowing that business invitees of the tenant will be constantly entering the premises to transact business, the owner of business property has an increased responsibility known as the *public use* exception to the general rule. The basis of the exception is that the landlord leases premises on which he knows or should know that there are conditions likely to cause injury to persons, that the purpose for which the premises are leased involve the fact that people will be invited upon the premises as patrons of the tenant, and that the landlord knows or should know

---

[2] Mansur v. Eubanks, p. 474.

that the tenant cannot reasonably be expected to remedy or guard against injury from the defect. Thus a landlord of a business owes a higher duty than does the landlord of essentially private premises.[3] Moreover, landlords of business premises often undertake to care for the common areas. In such cases, they have a duty to inspect, repair, and maintain common areas in a reasonably safe condition.

Many suits against lessors by third persons result from falls on the premises, often associated with ice, snow, or waxed floors. Historically, a landlord had no duty to remove ice and snow. In recent years, many courts have changed this rule as it is applied to multiple-family dwellings and businesses. Many tenants are simply unequipped to perform the task of snow and ice removal. They sometimes lack the physical wherewithal, capability, or the equipment (and storage space) necessary to the task.

Even in those states that do not require removal of ice and snow, if the landlord does undertake to remove snow and ice, he must do so with ordinary care, taking into account dangerous conditions caused by subsequent thawing and freezing of snow placed near the walkway.

7. Uniform Residential Landlord and Tenant Act

The National Conference of Commissioners on Uniform State Laws has proposed that state legislatures adopt the Uniform Residential Landlord and Tenant Act (URLTA). To date, at least 17 states have followed this recommendation. The URLTA or a substantially similar version has been adopted and is law in Alaska, Arizona, Connecticut, Florida, Hawaii, Iowa, Kansas, Kentucky, Michigan, Montana, Nebraska, New Mexico, Oklahoma, Oregon, Tennessee, Virginia, and Washington.

In addition to making the laws governing residential lease transactions simpler, clearer, and more uniform, URLTA attempts to assure equal bargaining power between landlord and tenant. Many of the rights and duties already discussed are part of URLTA. For example, the landlord cannot collect a security deposit that exceeds one month's rent. Failure to return this deposit without justification makes the landlord liable for twice the amount of the deposit, plus the tenant's attorney's fees. The landlord must deliver possession of the premises at the beginning of the lease term, and the landlord must maintain the premises in a habitable condition.

A tenant's basic responsibilities are to pay rent, to keep the dwelling safe and clean, and to allow the landlord to enter the premises under reasonable circumstances. Examples of when the landlord must be allowed to enter would include the making of periodic inspections, repairs, or improvements. The tenant also must cooperate in showing the premises to potential buyers or tenants. Of course, URLTA provides the landlord with the right to enter in all emergency situations.

URLTA also contains an article on the remedies available to either tenant or landlord when the other party breaches the lease agreement. For the most part, URLTA adopts the common-law remedies and defenses, such as constructive and

---

[3] Stewart v. 104 Wallace Street, Inc., p. 475.

retaliatory eviction, previously discussed. Furthermore, provisions allow the tenant to make minor repairs and deduct the cost from the rent if the landlord fails to make the repair after being notified of the defect. A minor repair is defined as one costing less than $100 or one-half the periodic rent, whichever amount is greater. The common-law remedy available to the landlord known as distress for rent (see section 5) is abolished. However, if the tenant holds over in bad faith after the lease expires, the landlord can sue for possession and three times the actual damages suffered or three months' rent, whichever is greater.

BAILMENTS

8. Introduction

Possession of personal property is often temporarily surrendered by the owner to another person. The person to whom the goods are delivered may perform some service pertaining to the goods, such as a repair, after which the goods are returned to the owner. Or someone may borrow or lease an article from its owner. Another temporary transfer of possession occurs when the owner causes the goods to be stored in a warehouse. In general, the provisions of the Uniform Commercial Code are applicable to these transactions involving the temporary transfer of possession of personal property.

An agreement whereby possession of personal property is surrendered by the owner with provision for its return at a later time is known as a *bailment*. The owner of the goods is called the *bailor*. The one receiving possession is called the *bailee*. There are three distinct requirements for a bailment: (1) retention of title by the bailor, (2) possession and temporary control of the property by the bailee, and (3) ultimate possession to revert to the bailor or to someone designated by the bailor.

9. Types of Bailments

Bailments can be categorized naturally into three classes: bailments for the benefit of the bailor, bailments for the benefit of the bailee, and bailments for the mutual benefit of bailor and bailee. Typical of the first group are those cases in which the bailor leaves goods in the safekeeping of the bailee without any provision for paying the bailee for caring for the article. Because the bailee is not to use the goods or to be paid in any manner, the bailment is for the exclusive benefit of the bailor.

A bailment for the benefit of the bailee is best illustrated by a loan of some article by the bailor to the bailee without any compensation to the bailor. Assume a student borrows a professor's automobile for a weekend date. The bailment is one for the sole benefit of the student, the bailee.

The most common type of bailment is the one in which both parties are to benefit. Contracts for repair, carriage, storage, or pledge of property fall within this class. The bailor receives the benefit of some service; the bailee benefits by the receipt of certain agreed compensation. Thus, both parties benefit as a result of the bailment.

To constitute a bailment for mutual benefit, it is not essential that the bailee actually receive compensation in money or tangible property. If the bailment is an incident of the business in which the bailee makes a profit, or it was accepted because of benefits expected to accrue, it is a mutual benefit bailment.

10. Degree of Care Owed by Bailor

Property leased by a bailor to a bailee (a mutual benefit bailment) must be reasonably fit for the intended purpose. For this reason, it is the duty of the bailor to notify the bailee of all defects in the property leased of which the bailor might reasonably have been aware. The bailor is responsible for any damage suffered by the bailee as the result of such defects, unless the notice is given. This rule holds even though the bailor is not aware of the defect if, by the exercise of reasonable diligence, the defect could have been discovered.

If, on the other hand, an article is merely loaned to a bailee—a bailment for the benefit of the bailee—the bailor's duty is to notify the bailee only of known defects. A bailor who fails to give the required notice of a known defect is liable to any person who might be expected to use the defective article as a result of the bailment. Employees of the bailee and members of the bailee's family may recover from the bailor for injuries received as a consequence of known defects.

11. Degree of Care Owed by Bailees

BAILEES: RIGHTS AND DUTIES

Provided that proper care has been exercised by the bailee, any loss or damage to the property bailed falls on the bailor. Each type of bailment requires a different degree of care by the bailee. In a bailment for the benefit of the bailor, the bailee is required to exercise only slight care.[4] In a bailment for the benefit of the bailee, extraordinary care is required. A bailment for the mutual benefit of the parties demands ordinary care on the part of the bailee. *Ordinary care* is defined as care that the average individual usually exercises over his own property.

The amount of care demanded of a bailee varies with the nature and value of the article bailed. The care found to be sufficient in the case of a carpenter's tool chest would probably not be ample for a diamond ring worth $10,000. A higher standard of protection is required for valuable articles. Moreover, when damages are assessed against a bailee, they are based on retail replacement value, not the wholesale cost to a bailee.

In addition to the duty to exercise due care, the bailee promises to return the property to the bailor undamaged upon termination of the bailment. This promise can be used to create a prima facie case of negligence. A bailor who proves that property delivered in good condition was returned from the bailee in bad condition establishes a presumption of negligence, and that bailor is entitled to recover from the bailee unless the presumption is rebutted. If there is no other evidence, the bailor will win the suit. The bailee may rebut this prima facie case by introducing evidence to establish that there was no negligence on its part, but the bailee has the burden of proving that it has used reasonable care and caution after the prima facie case has been established.[5] This prima facie case of negligence

---

[4] Morris v. Hamilton, p. 477.

[5] Knight v. H&H Chevrolet, p. 478.

exists only if all elements of a bailment are present. If there is no bailment, there is no prima facie case upon nondelivery or damage to the goods.

12. Disclaimers of Liability by Bailees

Bailees frequently attempt to disclaim liability for damage to property while it is in their possession. Such a clause in a contract is known as an *exculpatory clause.* Dry cleaners' tickets often bear statements disclaiming liability for damage to property delivered to them for cleaning. An exculpatory clause disclaiming liability for negligence is illegal if the bailee is a quasi-public institution, because such contracts are against public policy. This was discussed in chapter 10.

More and more bailees are being classified as quasi-public businesses because of the inequality of bargaining power between many bailors and their bailees. Not all exculpatory clauses seek to eliminate liability completely; some seek to limit the amount of damages. Contracts limiting the amount of damages are looked upon more favorably than absolute disclaimers because it is fair for both parties to know the value of the property and the risk present. In accordance with this theory, the Uniform Commercial Code provides that the warehouse receipt or storage agreement may limit the amount of liability in case of loss or damage to the covered property, but the agreement cannot disclaim the obligation of reasonable care.

Carriers also attempt to limit their liability. A carrier may not contract away its liability for goods damaged in shipment, but it may limit the liability to a stated amount. A carrier may also, where lower rates are granted, relieve itself from the consequences of causes or conduct over which it has no control.

Because a carrier may limit liability to an agreed valuation, the shipper is limited in recovery to the value asserted in the bill of lading. The rate charged for transportation will vary with the value of the property shipped. For this reason, the agreed valuation is binding.

13. Other Rights and Duties of Bailees

The bailment agreement governs the rights and duties of the bailee. If the bailee treats the property in a different manner or uses it for some purpose other than that contemplated by the bailment contract, the bailee becomes liable for any loss or damage to the property, even though the damage can in no sense be attributed to the conduct of the bailee. Let us assume that Murray stores a car for the winter in Plante's public garage. Because of a crowded condition, Plante has the car temporarily moved to another garage without Murray's consent. As the result of a tornado, the car is destroyed while at the second location. The loss falls upon Plante, who breached the terms of the bailment contract. In a restricted sense, the bailee is guilty of conversion of the bailor's property during the period in which the contract terms are being violated.

The bailee has no right to deny the title of the bailor unless the bailee has yielded possession to one having a better title than the bailor. The bailee has no right to retain possession of the property merely because he is able to prove that the bailor does not have legal title to the goods. In order to defeat the bailor's right to possession, the bailee must show that the property has been turned over to someone having better title or that he is holding the property under an agreement with the true owner.

14. Common Carriers as Bailees

The contract for carriage of goods constitutes a mutual benefit bailment, but the care required of the carrier greatly exceeds that of the ordinary bailee. A common carrier is an absolute insurer of the safe delivery of the goods to their destination. Proof of delivery to a carrier of a shipment in good condition and its arrival at the destination in a damaged condition creates a prima facie case against the carrier.

This absolute liability of a common carrier is subject to only five exceptions. Any loss or damage must fall upon the shipper if it results from (1) an act of God, (2) action of an alien enemy, (3) order of public authority, (4) inherent nature of the goods, or (5) misconduct of the shipper. Thus, any loss that results from an accident or the willful misconduct of some third party must be borne by the carrier. A person who wanted to injure a certain railway company set fire to several boxcars loaded with freight. Losses due to damage to the goods fell upon the carrier. On the other hand, if lightning, an act of God, had set fire to the cars, the loss would have fallen upon the shipper. However, the defense of an act of God is narrowly construed to include only events that were not foreseeable.

The shipper must suffer any damage to goods in shipment if damage results from the very nature of the goods, improper crating, or failure to protect the property. Thus, if a dog dies because his crate was poorly ventilated, the shipper is unable to recover from the carrier. Remember, though, that the carrier has the burden of proving that it was free from negligence and that the damage falls within one of the exceptions to the rule establishing the carrier's liability as an insurer of the shipment.

The burden is on the shipper to prove that the goods were in good condition at the time and place of shipment. Although proof that the goods were in good condition when delivered to the carrier and that they were damaged when delivered by the carrier creates a prima facie case of liability, there is no presumption that the goods were in good condition when delivered to the carrier. Actual proof is required.

The liability of the carrier attaches as soon as the goods are delivered. The extreme degree of care required of the carrier may be terminated before the goods are actually delivered to the consignee. Three views in this country determine when the relationship of the carrier ceases. Some states hold that the duties of the carrier end, and those of a warehouseman begin, as soon as the local shipment is unloaded from the car into the freight house. Others hold the carrier to strict liability until the consignee has had a reasonable time in which to inspect and remove the shipment. Still other states hold that the consignee is entitled to notice—and that he has reasonable time after notice—in which to remove the goods before the liability of the carrier as a carrier is terminated. For example, assume that goods arrive at their destination and are unloaded and placed in the freight house. Before the consignee has had time to take them away, the goods are destroyed by fire, although the carrier has exercised ordinary care. Under the first of these views, the loss would fall upon the shipper because at the time of the fire, the railway was no longer a carrier but a warehouseman. Under the other two views, the loss would fall on the carrier, whose extreme liability had not yet terminated because no time had been given for delivery.

A common carrier, while not an insurer of its passengers' safety, owes the highest degree of care to them. In other words, a common carrier will be liable to passengers for injuries caused by even the slightest negligence.[6] This high duty is not owed to persons who are on the premises of the carrier, but not on board the carrier. To these people, the carrier owes only ordinary care. Passengers who are in the process of boarding or exiting are considered to be on board and are protected by the carrier's duty to exercise extraordinary care.

15. Innkeepers as Bailees

Issues similar to those involved with common carriers frequently arise in suits against hotel and motel operators. Under common law, an innkeeper was an insurer of the safety of the goods of its guests. The law imposed liability as a matter of public policy because the innkeeper and his employees had easy access to the guests' rooms. Exceptions to this general rule relieved the inkeeper from liability for loss caused by an act of God, a public enemy, an act of public authority, the inherent nature of the property, or the fault of the guest.

Most states have enacted statutes pertaining to hotel or motel operators' liability. These statutes usually provide that if the operator appropriately notifies guests that a safe or lockbox is maintained for their use, there is no liability if guests' property is stolen from their rooms. Such laws usually cover property of "small compass," which includes money, negotiable instruments, jewelry, and precious stones. The requirement that notice of the availability of the safe be given with notice of the liability limitation is usually strictly enforced.

Some states also have laws that limit the maximum liability of hotel and motel operators to a stated amount, such as $500. Others have changed the liability from that of an insurer to that of a bailee of a mutual benefit bailment (ordinary care as the duty). In all states, the liability of the innkeeper is limited to the value of the property. There is no liability for consequential damages that may flow from the loss of the property.

DOCUMENTS OF TITLE

16. General Concepts and Definitions

A *document of title* is broadly defined as any "document which in the regular course of business or financing is treated as adequately evidencing that the person in possession of it is entitled to receive, hold and dispose of the document *and the goods it covers*" (1-201[15]). Such a document must indicate that it was issued by a bailee or directed to a bailee and that it covers goods in the bailee's possession. The term primarily covers bills of lading and warehouse receipts.

---

[6] Carey v. Jack Rabbit Lines, Inc., p. 479.

Documents of title are covered by Article 7 of the Code. Numerous other statutes, both state and federal, also regulate the business of carriers and warehousemen. The federal Bills of Lading Act, for example, controls bills of lading covering foreign exports and interstate shipments of goods. The Code does not displace such statutes. Article 7 deals only with rights related to documents of title, not to the regulation of the services rendered by carriers or warehousemen.

Documents of title can serve a dual function. They may serve as receipts for goods stored or shipped, and they may be representative of the goods. In the representative capacity, they are most useful in financing commercial transactions.

Some other common terms may be defined as follows:

- *Warehouse receipt*: An acknowledgment issued by a person engaged in the business of storing goods for hire [1-201(45)].
- *Bill of lading*: A document evidencing receipt of goods for shipment.
- *Issuer*: A bailee who prepares the document of title.
- *Consignor*: The person named in a bill of lading as the person from whom the goods have been received for shipment.
- *Consignee*: The person named in a bill of lading as the one to whom delivery is to be made.

Documents of title may be negotiable or nonnegotiable. The concept of negotiability for a document of title is similar to that of negotiability discussed in connection with commercial paper. The holder of a negotiable document is in a much more favorable position than he would be with a nonnegotiable document. The holder of a negotiable document obtains the direct obligation of the issuer to hold or deliver the goods free from most defenses and claims. In essence, the holder is so well protected that he can almost regard the document as the equivalent of the goods it represents.

17. Negotiation and Transfer

A warehouse receipt, bill of lading, or other document is negotiable if, by its terms, the goods are to be delivered to the bearer or to the "order of" a named person. A document not containing these "words of negotiability" is not negotiable. Thus, a bill of lading which states that goods are consigned to John Doe would not be negotiable.

Both negotiable and nonnegotiable documents can be transferred, but the method of transfer is different. A nonnegotiable document can be *assigned*; then the assignee acquires only the rights of the assignor and is subject to all defenses that are available against the assignor. The assignee is burdened with all defects in the assignor's title. *Negotiation* of a negotiable document places the transferee in a much more favorable position. If there is "due negotiation," the transferee is free from the defects of the transferor's title and the claims of third persons.

The method of negotiating a document of title depends upon whether it is an order document or a bearer document. The *order* document is negotiated by indorsement and delivery; the *bearer* document, by delivery alone. The effects of blank and special indorsements are the same as those for commercial paper, and the last indorsement controls. See chapter 29 for a further discussion of indorsements.

In order for the holder of a negotiable document of title to have the preferred status, there must have been a due negotiation. This means not only any necessary indorsement and delivery, but also that the holder must satisfy certain requirements similar to those of a holder in due course of commercial paper. He must have purchased the document in good faith, without notice of a defense against it or claim to it on the part of any person. He must have paid value for it, and the negotiation must have been in the regular course of business or financing. One to whom a document is negotiated in satisfaction or payment of a prior debt has not paid value.

If there has been due negotiation, the holder acquires title to the document, title to the goods, and the direct obligation of the issuer to hold or deliver the goods according to the terms of the document. The holder's rights cannot be defeated by any stoppage of the goods or surrender of them by the bailee. His rights are not impaired even if the negotiation or any prior negotiation constituted a breach of duty; even if any person has been deprived of possession of the document by misrepresentation, fraud, accident, mistake, duress, loss, theft, or conversion; and even if a previous sale or other transfer of the goods or document has been made to a third person (7-502[2]).

18. Liability of Indorsers and Transferors

The *indorser* or *transferor* of a document of title makes three warranties to the immediate purchaser. He warrants that

1. The document is genuine. One who purchases a forged document of title may, upon discovery of the forgery, recover from the person who sold it to him.

2. He has no knowledge of any facts that would impair its validity or worth.

3. His sale of the document is rightful and fully effective with respect to the title to the document and the goods it represents. However, unless he has also sold the goods, he does not make any additional warranties concerning the goods. If he is also the seller of the goods, he makes the usual seller's warranties. The indorser of a document of title does not warrant performance by the bailee.

The warranties are satisfied when the purchaser obtains a good right against the warehouseman or carrier. If the bailee has misappropriated the goods or refuses to surrender them, the holder of the document has as his only recourse an action against the bailee who issued the document.

If a bank or other person has been authorized to deliver a document of title, acting as an agent for this purpose, the delivery of the document creates no warranty by the agent as to the document itself. Thus, no liability would be assumed by any such agent if the document were not genuine.

19. Obligations of Bailees under Documents of Title

A public warehouse that issues a negotiable receipt is not at liberty to surrender the goods to the original bailor unless he surrenders the receipt for cancellation. The receipt represents the goods and must be surrendered before the goods may be obtained. A warehouse that surrenders goods without the return of the receipt may be called upon for the goods by someone who has purchased the document. The goods should be delivered only to the person who possesses the receipt, and then only if the receipt has been properly indorsed when such indorsement is required.

A bailee can refuse to deliver the goods called for by the document until payment of his just charges has been made. Applicable law may actually prohibit delivery without payment.

If a receipt was complete when issued but was later altered without authority, the warehouse's liability is determined by the original terms of the document. If a receipt was issued with blanks, a good-faith purchaser of the completed receipt may recover from the warehouse that issued the incomplete receipt.

A warehouse receipt, even though it has been properly negotiated, will in one situation be inferior to the rights of a buyer of the goods represented by the receipt. When a buyer in the ordinary course of business buys fungible goods from a warehouseman who is also engaged in the business of buying and selling such fungible goods, he takes the goods free of any claim under the receipt. A typical case might involve the purchase of grain from an elevator. The holder of a receipt for grain stored would have no claim to grain purchased by a person from the owner of the elevator if the owner became insolvent and unable to deliver to the receipt holder.

SUMMARY

LEASE TRANSACTIONS

Classification of leases	1. A tenancy for a stated period lasts for the time specified in the lease.
	2. A tenancy from period to period may run from month to month or year to year. Such a lease often is created when a tenant holds over, with the landlord's consent, after a lease for a stated period.
	3. A tenancy at will has no definite duration and can be terminated by either landlord or tenant after proper notice is given.

	4. A tenancy at sufferance occurs when a tenant holds over without the landlord's consent.
Tenants—rights and duties	**1.** In general, the tenant has the right to exclusive possession free from interference.
	2. Tenant has the right to have the premises suitable for the intended use.
	3. Unless the lease provides otherwise, the tenant is free to assign or sublease his interest to a third party. (Note that leases frequently require the landlord's approval prior to such transfer.)
	4. The tenant's basic duty is to pay the rent and to return possession at the end of the lease term.
Landlords—rights and duties	**1.** The landlord has the right to expect the tenant to pay rent.
	2. The landlord has legal remedies such as distress for rent and eviction powers to encourage the tenant's performance.
	3. The landlord generally has the duty to maintain the premises. Although tenants may be liable for damages caused, the landlord cannot unreasonably retain a security deposit.
Warranty of habitability	**1.** Many courts have held that landlords implicitly warrant that residence property is habitable.
	2. A breach of this warranty allows the tenant to reduce rental payments or to terminate the lease without further liability.
Liability to third parties	**1.** In general, a landlord has no greater duty to protect third parties from injuries than is owed to the tenants.
	2. The "public use" exception means that a landlord of a business owes a higher duty to third parties than does a landlord of private premises.
Uniform Residential Landlord and Tenant Act	**1.** This act is an attempt to make all state laws uniform in the area of residential leases.
	2. At least 17 states have adopted substantial portions of this act.

BAILMENTS

Required elements	**1.** A bailment involves the temporary transfer of possession of personal property with the understanding that possession must be returned. There is no transfer of ownership.
	2. A bailor is the owner who transfers physical possession to another person. A bailee is the person receiving possession who understands that the possession will be returned to the bailor or a designated party.
Types of bailments	**1.** A bailment for the sole benefit of the bailor usually occurs when a bailee is not compensated.
	2. A bailment for the sole benefit of the bailee is illustrated by a bailee borrowing some item of personal property.
	3. A bailment for the mutual benefit of the parties is the most common in commercial transactions. Rental agreements, warehouse arrangements, and shipping contracts are examples of this third type of bailment.
Bailor's degree of care	**1.** This duty of care depends on the type of bailment.
	2. In bailments for the sole benefit of the bailee, bailor must give notice of any defects of which he is aware.
	3. In other types of bailment, the bailor must inspect the personal property and give notice of those defects known or those that should have been discovered.

BAILEES: RIGHTS AND DUTIES

Degree of care owed	**1.** Again this degree of care depends on the type of bailment.
	2. In bailments for the sole benefit of the bailor, the bailee owes only slight care.
	3. In bailments for the sole benefit of the bailee, the bailee owes extraordinary care.

	4. In bailments for the mutual benefit of the parties, bailees owe ordinary reasonable care.
	5. Regardless of type of bailment, the bailee must return possession to the bailor or there is a presumption of negligence.
Disclaimers of liability	1. Courts tend to declare disclaimers of liability, known as exculpatory clauses, invalid as against public policy.
	2. Clauses limiting a bailee's liability are viewed more favorably and often enforced.
Common carriers	1. As a bailee, a common carrier owes a duty of absolute assurance of the property's safe delivery.
	2. A common carrier's liability is limited by five exceptions. These are damage to the property being caused by (a) an act of God, (b) an action of an alien enemy, (c) an order of public authority, (d) the inherent nature of the property, and (e) the misconduct of the shipper.
Innkeepers	1. Originally, innkeepers were considered absolute insurers of the safety of guests and the guests' belongings.
	2. Today, most states have statutes that limit the innkeeper's liability with respect to guests' personal property.

DOCUMENTS OF TITLE

Concepts and definitions	1. A document of title evidences the right to possess the personal property described in the document.
	2. Typical examples are bills of lading and warehouse receipts.
	3. These documents facilitate the sale and financing of personal property.
	4. Documents may be negotiable or nonnegotiable in form, with negotiable documents generally being preferable.
Negotiation and transfer	1. A negotiable document of title may be an order document or a bearer document.
	2. Order documents are negotiated by proper indorsement and delivery.

Obligations of bailees	**3.** Bearer documents are negotiated by delivery alone. **1.** A bailee that issued a negotiable document of title can properly deliver the goods only to the person who holds a properly negotiated document. **2.** A bailee may require full payment of charges prior to honoring the document of title.

CASES

Funk v. Funk
633 P.2d 586 (Idaho 1981)

SHEPARD, J. . . . In November of 1969, plaintiff-appellants Ewald and Pearl Funk [hereinafter lessors] leased certain farm land to Melvin and Diane Funk [hereinafter lessees] for a ten year period commencing January 1, 1970 and ending December 31, 1979. Semi-annual rental payments were required on or before March 1 and December 1 of each year. The written lease provided in pertinent part: "(e) That the Lessee shall have the right and privilege of sub-leasing or assigning this instrument provided that the consent of the Lessor is first obtained."

During early 1978 the lessees were desirous of subleasing the property for the 1978 crop year. In January, the then attorney for the lessees wrote a letter expressing the lessees' desire to sublet the property and indicated that the lessees would make both 1978 lease payments on March 1 to ensure that the entire 1978 rent was paid in advance. They also promised to supervise the subtenant's operations to assure that the land was farmed in a good and husbandrylike manner and that proper weed control was practiced. They also offered to provide any additional information concerning the sub-tenant that might be requested by the lessors.

In February, lessors responded ". . . that we cannot allow a sublease of any type" and declared ". . . that we do not intend to allow a sublease of this property." In response to further correspondence from lessees' attorney, the lessors in February expressed their belief that the rental fee was below the fair rental value and again emphasized their refusal to allow a sublease, stating: ". . . we do not now or in the future wish to honor any subleasing of this property. We already have more information concerning the proposed sublessees than you can possibly assemble." Thereafter, an additional letter was written on behalf of lessors indicating that a sublease would be allowed if the lessees would assign one-half of the sublease proceeds to the lessors, if the lessees would pay the 1978 property taxes and if the lessees would agree to terminate the underlying lease on December 31, 1978. Thereafter, the lessees indicated they would farm the property themselves and would not sublease it.

Lessees did, however sublet at least a portion of the premises for the 1978 crop year. When lessors learned of that sublease in September of 1978 they served notice of termination of the lease agreement. When lessees refused to quit the premises, this action was commenced. In March, 1979, summary judgment was entered in favor of the lessees declaring the lease agreement to be in full force and effect. The lessees continued to farm the property through the final year of the lease, 1979, and lessors accepted semi-annual rental payments in March and December of both 1978 and 1979. . . .

We now turn to the principal question presented here, i.e., whether a lessor has an absolute right to withhold consent to a proposed sublease when the underlying lease grants to the lessee a right of assigning or subleasing upon the consent of a lessor.

A tenant holding under a lease for a definite period may sublet the premises in whole or in part in the absence of restrictions placed thereon by the parties or by statute. That common law right is limited to the extent that a lessee may not sublet premises to be used in a manner which is injurious to the property or inconsistent with the terms of the original lease.

In the case at bar the lessees' right to assign or sublet existed by virtue of the parties' written agreement, as well as by virtue of common law, but was also subject to a contractual restriction.

The appellant-lessors correctly argue that the traditional majority position is that unless the lease provides that the lessors' consent shall not be unreasonably withheld, a provision against assignment or subletting without the lessors' consent authorizes the lessor to arbitrarily withhold consent for any reason or for no reason.

We find, however, an increasing number of jurisdictions departing from that traditional position and an increasing volume of authority that the consent of a lessor may not be *unreasonably* withheld. . . .

We deem the principal enunciated in the minority position to be based on more solid policy rationale than is the traditional orthodox majority's position. A landlord may and should be concerned about the personal qualities of a proposed subtenant. A landlord should be able to reject a proposed subtenant when such rejection reflects a concern for the legitimate interest of the landlord, such as assurances of rent receipt, proper care of the property and in many cases the use of the property by the subtenant in a manner reasonably consistent with the usage of the original lessee. Such concerns by the landlord should result in the upholding of a withholding of consent by a landlord. However, no desirable public policy is served by upholding a landlord's arbitrary refusal of consent merely because of whim or caprice or where, as here, it is apparent that the refusal to consent was withheld for purely financial reasons and that the landlord wanted the lessees to enter into an entirely new lease agreement with substantial increased financial benefits to the landlord. If the lessor is allowed to arbitrarily refuse consent to a sublease for what is in effect no reason at all, such would virtually nullify the right of a lessee to sublet. The imposition of a reasonableness standard also gives greater credence to the doctrine that restraints on alienation of leased property are looked upon with disfavor and are strictly construed against the lessor. . . .

In the instant case, the proper standard by which to review the lessors' refusal to consent to the proposed sublease is one of a reasonable person in the position of a landlord owning and leasing commercial farm land. Criteria to be utilized in application of that standard would include, but would not necessarily be limited to, assurances of proper farming practices and financial responsibility. In the instant case the record discloses no contentions by the landlord of the absence of these or any other criteria and hence we hold that the arbitrary refusal of the appellant-lessors in the instant case to grant their consent to the sublease was unreasonable. . . .

Affirmed.

Mansur v. Eubanks
401 So.2d 1328 (Fla. 1981)

BOYD, J. . . . Sometime in mid-July, 1976, Marie Grigsby paid a deposit of $25 to Jean M. Barnett in order to reserve an apartment owned by Mrs. Barnett and Mary G. Eubanks. By their informal oral agreement, the apartment was to be available for occupancy, and the term of lease would commence, on August 1, 1976. On July 31, Grigsby began moving her possessions into the apartment. Michael Mansur, who lived in an adjacent apartment also owned by Barnett and Eubanks, helped Grigsby move in. In an effort to get the gas-fueled appliances (stove and water heater) operational, Grigsby and Mansur opened the gas line from outside the apartment. Then they attempted to light the stove and smelled gas in the process. Then they proceeded to try to light the water heater. Mansur struck a match and an explosion occurred. According to his complaint, he was seriously injured. . . .

[Mansur sued the landlords but lost on the theory that the landlord is not liable for injuries caused by the condition of the leased premises.

Mansur appealed. The court of appeals affirmed the trial court's decision, and Mansur sought review by the Supreme Court.]

The court [of appeals] quoted from *Brooks v. Peters,* where this Court said:

> It is established law that when a landlord delivers to the tenant possession and control of the demised premises, including the plumbing, drains, and appliances for heating, lighting, and power, the landlord is not liable for an injury to the property or person of the tenant or those on the premises in the right of the tenant, although such injuries are attributable to defects in such apparatus, appliances or fixtures. Thus a tenant may not hold a landlord liable for injuries caused by explosion of plumbing, or heating apparatus on premises, the possession and control of which have been surrendered to him in the absence of fraud or concealment.

> The landlord's liability is based on his right of control over the appliances and he is not liable for injuries for defects in appliances located on the leased premises if he does not reserve control thereof, and accordingly it has been held that he is not liable for defects in water pipes in an apartment when the only purpose of such pipes is to supply and distribute water for the apartment. On the other hand, he is liable for defects in pipes on the leased premises if he retains control thereof. Where the landlord surrenders possession and control of the leased premises to the tenant, in the absence of fraud or concealment the tenant assumes the risk as to the condition of the premises, including the heating, lighting apparatus, plumbing, water pipes, sewers, etc. In other words, the rule of caveat emptor applies, hence the landlord is not liable for any personal injuries or sickness of tenants, although attributable to the defects in the fixtures.

. . . We hold that the owner of a residential dwelling unit, who leases it to a tenant for residential purposes, has a duty to reasonably inspect the premises before allowing the tenant to take possession, and to make the repairs necessary to transfer a reasonably safe dwelling unit to the tenant unless defects are waived by the tenant. This duty may be modified by agreement of the parties.

After the tenant takes possession, the landlord has a continuing duty to exercise reasonable care to repair dangerous defective conditions upon notice of their existence by the tenant, unless waived by the tenant. This latter duty corresponds to the statutory warranty of habitability. . . .

We do not believe there are sufficient reasons to continue to completely insulate the landlord from liability. We live in an age when the complexities of housing construction place the landlord in much better position than the tenant to guard against dangerous conditions.

In rendering summary judgment the trial court recited that there were no genuine issues of material fact but did not indicate what principle of law entitled the defendants to judgment in their favor.

The district court concluded that the pleadings and depositions showed that Grigsby had taken possession of the apartment by leave of the owners and that therefore the lease and the relationship of landlord and tenant had commenced by the time of the accident. The record shows, however, that there was a factual dispute as to this matter.

The district court also concluded that the explosion was caused by gas that escaped through a gap where the stove had been disconnected from the gas line. The actual cause of the explosion, however, and the questions of knowledge of and responsibility for the disconnected line were disputed matters which were never litigated due to the summary judgment.

The decision of the district court of appeal, affirming summary judgment, is quashed. We direct that the cause be remanded to the trial court for further proceedings consistent with this opinion.

So ordered.

Stewart v. 104 Wallace Street, Inc.
432 A.2d 881 (N.J. 1981)

PASHMAN, J. In this case we are called upon . . . to review this State's law of sidewalk negligence.

In particular, we must decide whether an abutting commercial landowner is liable for a pedestrian's injuries caused by a dilapidated sidewalk. Today, for the reasons stated below, we . . . hold that a plaintiff has a cause of action against a commercial property owner for injuries sustained on a deteriorated sidewalk abutting that commercial property when that owner negligently fails to maintain the sidewalk in reasonably good condition.

> In the afternoon of May 30, 1976 plaintiff, Harold Stewart, went to Ernie's Tavern . . . where he had one glass of beer. Ernie's Tavern was owned by defendant, 104 Wallace Street, Inc., and the property on which the tavern was located was owned by defendant Jay-Nan Corporation.

> After having the beer, Stewart remained at Ernie's for a time, watching people play pool. Upon leaving the tavern, Stewart walked a short distance from the tavern entrance and then fell on the sidewalk abutting a vacant boarded lot adjacent to Ernie's Tavern. This lot, like the property on which Ernie's was located, was owned by defendant Jay-Nan.

> Stewart's fall was allegedly caused by the seriously dilapidated condition of the sidewalk abutting Jay-Nan's lot. As a result of the fall, Stewart was apparently seriously injured, and underwent surgery and prolonged hospitalization.

> Plaintiff brought an action for damages against defendants, 104 Wallace Street, Inc., and Jay-Nan Corp. . . . [The trial court dismissed the plaintiff's complaint, and he appealed.]

> Sidewalks are an essential feature of our urban landscapes. Consistent with their function, it has long been the law of this State that "[a] sidewalk is intended primarily for pedestrians" and that "the primary function of the sidewalk [is] the public's right of travel on it. . . ."

Until today, our courts have not extended the liability of owners of abutting property, commercial or residential, to include injuries to pedestrians caused by the evident and dangerous deterioration or dilapidation of sidewalks because of neglect. . . .

The "no liability" rule is a product of early English common law, which provided that "the parish at large is prima facie bound to repair all highways lying within it." The consequence in New Jersey was that in early cases the primary responsibility for the maintenance of sidewalks was placed on the government. . . .

The general rule of non-liability undermines basic goals of tort law in two critical ways. First, as this Court has recognized, it has "left without recourse many innocent parties who suffered serious injuries because of sidewalk defects." Second,

the present law gives abutting property owners no incentive to repair deteriorated sidewalks and thereby prevent injuries. Indeed, it actually provides a disincentive since an owner, presently not liable for failure to repair, will be liable for repairs voluntarily undertaken but negligently performed. . . .

We hold today that commercial landowners are responsible for maintaining in reasonably good condition the sidewalks abutting their property and are liable to pedestrians injured as a result of their negligent failure to do so. . . .

This new rule responds to many of the weaknesses of the no liability rule. It will provide a remedy to many innocent plaintiffs for injuries caused by improper maintenance of sidewalks. As a corollary, it will give owners of abutting commercial property an incentive to keep their sidewalks in proper repair, a duty already created in many cases by municipal ordinances. It will also eliminate much of the arbitrariness of the old rule. In addition, injured persons will be able to recover for injuries sustained just outside a store as well as those sustained within it. . . .

We do not believe that the duty we are imposing on abutting property owners will be an onerous one. The standard of care, after all, will be *reasonableness*. We do not contemplate liability "for injuries caused by minor flaws and stretches of unevenness." Nor are we creating an entirely new field of liability with respect to sidewalks, but are merely adding to duties of abutting owners that already exist.

The duty to maintain abutting sidewalks that we impose today is confined to owners of commercial property. While we acknowledge that whether the ownership of the property abutting the sidewalk is commercial or residential matters little to the injured pedestrian, we believe that the case for imposing a duty to maintain sidewalks is particularly compelling with respect to abutting commercial property owners.

We recognize that the rule adopted today will increase the expenses of many businesses, and will be proportionately more burdensome to small firms than to large ones. However, we anticipate that appropriate insurance will become available and that the cost of such insurance will be treated as one of the necessary costs of doing business. . . .

Consistent with the rule adopted today, we

reverse the judgment of the trial court dismissing plaintiff's complaint against defendant Jay-Nan Corp., the owner of the commercial property abutting the sidewalk where plaintiff's injury allegedly occurred, and remand for a full trial. The judgment dismissing plaintiff's complaint against defendant 104 Wallace Street, Inc., lessee of an adjacent property, is affirmed.

So ordered.

Morris v. Hamilton
302 S.E.2d 51 (Va. 1983)

STEPHENSON, J. In this appeal involving a bailment, we must decide what standard of care is imposed upon the bailee by the relationship.

. . . Marsha Hamilton and Andrea Morris were guests at a dinner party attended by approximately 25 people. The party began about 7:00 p.m. and ended approximately 1:00 a.m. the following morning. Alcoholic beverages were served throughout the evening.

Approximately 11:30, while working in the kitchen, Hamilton removed her wristwatch and placed it on a counter. About midnight, the water in the house "went off," and Hamilton left the kitchen. Since she intended to resume her work when the water came on again, she left her watch on the counter. Hamilton went outside, where she had an after-dinner drink with several other guests. After 10 to 15 minutes, she became ill and fled to a bathroom.

Shortly after Hamilton left the kitchen, Morris saw the watch on the counter. Fearing for its safety, she picked it up and carried it in her hand as she looked for Hamilton. Morris was unable to find Hamilton and cannot recall what she did with the watch. She thought she either gave it to Hamilton's fiance or put it somewhere in the house for safekeeping. . . .

The following day, Hamilton discovered she did not have her watch and returned to the house to retrieve it. A maid who was in the kitchen when Hamilton arrived told her she had not seen the watch. Although the house was searched thoroughly, the watch was never recovered.

Hamilton sued Morris alleging Morris was the bailee of the watch and that she negligently lost it while it was in her possession. Morris concedes she was a bailee. She contends, however, she acted gratuitously and therefore owed Hamilton a duty of only slight care. The trial court, sitting without a jury rejected the bailment theory, instead finding for Hamilton on a pure negligence theory. The court ruled Morris had violated her duty to exercise ordinary or reasonable care of the watch, and that her negligence was the proximate cause of its loss.

Acting upon Morris' concession that she was a bailee, we decide the case with reference to bailment principles. Ordinarily, in order to establish a bailment, there must be a delivery by the bailor and an acceptance by the bailee. However, no formal contract or actual meeting of the minds is necessary. Indeed, "it is the element of lawful possession, however created, and duty to account for the thing as the property of another that creates the bailment, regardless of whether or not such possession is based on contract in the ordinary sense." For an alleged bailee to have possession, he must have both physical control over the property and an intent to exercise that control.

When, as here, one comes into possession of a chattel and exercises physical control over it, a bailment is created by operation of law. It is known as a constructive or quasi-bailment.

The evidence shows that Morris acted solely for the benefit of Hamilton. She therefore was a gratuitous bailee. . . .

A bailee who acts gratuitously is not held to the same standard of care as one who enters upon the same undertaking for pay. The latter owes a duty of reasonable or ordinary care, while a gratuitous bailee owes only a duty of slight care. Thus, in order for a bailor to recover from a gratuitous bailee, he must prove the bailee was guilty of gross negligence.

We hold, therefore, the trial court erred in ruling no bailment existed and in holding Morris to a standard of ordinary or reasonable care. Morris is liable for the loss of the watch only if she was guilty of gross negligence.

"[G]ross negligence is that degree of negligence which shows indifference to others as constitutes an utter disregard of prudence. . . . It must be such a degree of negligence as would shock fair minded persons. . . ." Ordinarily, gross negligence is an issue for decision by the factfinder. It becomes a question of law only when reasonable minds cannot differ about the conclusion to be reached from the evidence.

Viewing the evidence and all reasonable infer-ences in the light most favorable to Hamilton, we hold as a matter of law that Morris' conduct was not sufficient to constitute gross negligence. There-fore, we will reverse the judgment of the trial court and enter final judgment for the appellant.

Reversed.

Knight v. H&H Chevrolet
337 N.W.2d 742 (Neb. 1983)

McCOWN, J. This is a bailment action brought by the plaintiff bailor to recover for the loss of his automobile while it was in the possession of the defendant bailee for purposes of repair. The jury returned a verdict in favor of the defendant and the plaintiff has appealed.

On Wednesday, May 28, 1980, the plaintiff, Ronald W. Knight, delivered his 1980 Corvette automobile to the premises of the defendant, H & H Chevrolet, to have some warranty repair work done. Plaintiff talked to the defendant's service adviser, who had the plaintiff fill out a service order for the repair work and told plaintiff that the repairs should be completed by Friday, May 30. The plain-tiff left his automobile and keys with the service adviser.

On Friday, May 30, the service adviser tele-phoned the plaintiff and told him that it was neces-sary to order parts and that the repair work would be delayed. The service adviser also told plaintiff that the car was drivable and that plaintiff could pick up the car while the parts were on order. The plaintiff did not pick up his car and the car was moved into a fenced lot located alongside the defendant's garage.

On Saturday, May 31, the service adviser observed plaintiff's car parked in the fenced lot. He searched the car to make sure that the keys were not in it and that the doors were locked. It was the defendant's practice to keep keys either in the car or in the "tower" inside the garage.

The service adviser knew that a Corvette was a "high risk" automobile susceptible to theft and vandalism, and testified at trial that he intended to move the automobile into the garage for safekeep-ing over the Memorial Day weekend but became busy with other customers and forgot to move the car.

The open lot in which plaintiff's automobile was placed was surrounded by a Cyclone fence topped with barbed wire and had two gates, each of which was chained and padlocked when the garage was closed. . . .

Plaintiff's automobile was apparently stolen from the defendant's lot on Sunday morning, June 1, 1980. A witness dining at a restaurant located across the street from the lot observed a young man walk up to the Corvette, hesitate at the door, enter the car, and, after a short time, drive the car around the garage and out of sight.

On Monday morning, June 2, the defendant's employees discovered that a chain securing one of the gates to the fenced lot had been cut. A visual inventory by the employees failed to disclose that plaintiff's automobile was missing.

On Wednesday, June 4, 1980, the service adviser was ready to commence repairing the plain-tiff's automobile but was unable to find the car. The service adviser assumed that plaintiff had picked up his automobile and telephoned the plaintiff to have him return the car, only to learn that plaintiff had not picked up his car.

A thorough search of the garage premises failed to locate either the car or the keys, and neither the vehicle nor the keys have ever been found. The police were contacted, and on Saturday, June 7, 1980, the service adviser notified the plain-tiff that his car had been stolen and could not be found.

Following demand and refusal, this bailment action was commenced. . . . The . . . [complaint] alleged that plaintiff had delivered the Corvette to the defendant, that the defendant had impliedly promised to return the car after completing the repair work, and that the defendant had breached its implied promise by failing to timely redeliver the car. The defendant's answer alleged that the loss of the plaintiff's automobile was proximately caused by the intervening independent acts of an unknown thief and that defendant was not negligent. . . .

[At the trial, the jury was instructed that the plaintiff had the burden of proving the defendant's negligence.]

The jury brought in a verdict for the defendant and the plaintiff has appealed.

The issue on this appeal is whether or not the instruction placing upon the plaintiff the burden of proving the defendant's negligence was correct.

A great many courts and legal writers have considered the policy issues involved, and a substantial number of states have adopted a rule as to the burden of proof in bailment cases.

[W]here the property is in the sole possession of the bailee, the bailee may well be the only party in a position to explain the circumstances under which the property was lost or damaged; in such circumstances it would be unfair to require the bailor to prove negligence on the part of the bailee.

We therefore hold that in a bailment for hire or a mutually reciprocal bailment case, in the absence of statutory or contractual provisions to the contrary, once bailor proves delivery of property to bailee in good condition and failure to redeliver upon timely demand, the burden is irrevocably fixed upon bailee to prove by a preponderance of the evidence that he has exercised due care to prevent the loss, damage, or destruction of the property.

This principle applies to all bailment for hire cases . . . in which bailee has exclusive control over the property at the time it was lost, destroyed, or damaged.

In the present case the jury was instructed that the burden of proving negligence on the part of the bailee was upon the bailor and that the bailor could not recover without sustaining that burden of proof. In view of the foregoing discussion that instruction was erroneous, and the judgment must be reversed and the cause remanded for further proceedings.

Reversed and remanded.

Carey v. Jack Rabbit Lines, Inc.
309 N.W.2d 824 (S.D. 1981)

WOLLMAN, J. This case involves an action for personal injuries sustained by Isabel Carey (appellee) when she fell while alighting from a bus owned and operated by Jack Rabbit Lines, Inc. (appellant). The case was tried to the court, which entered judgment for appellee. . . .

Appellant is a common carrier transporting passengers for hire. On July 13, 1978, appellee boarded one of appellant's buses in Aberdeen, South Dakota. The bus arrived in Mobridge at approximately 10:30 p. m. The bus driver parked the bus twelve to eighteen inches from the curb, whereupon he left the vehicle and began unloading the baggage compartment. The curb in the area of the bus stop was eight inches high. The area was dimly lighted, the nearest street light being located approximately ninety-four feet from the bus stop area. The lights inside the bus did not adequately illuminate the curb at the point where passengers stepped off the bus.

Appellee proceeded to alight from the bus utilizing the handrail. As she stepped from the last step of the bus she unexpectedly stepped down into the gutter instead of onto the sidewalk, lost her balance, and fell to the ground. Appellee, who was seventy-nine years old at the time, suffered a fractured left shoulder and also injured her wrist, resulting in some permanent physical impairment.

The bus driver admitted that he could have parked the bus within two or three inches of the curb but testified that he had stopped twelve to eighteen inches from the curb because to do so made it more convenient to unload the baggage compartment. He neither warned the passengers of the potential danger nor helped them to alight from the bus.

The trial court held that the accident was the result of appellant's negligence and awarded appellee $7,000 for pain and suffering and temporary and permanent physical injury and disability, $1,290.70 for medical and other expenses, and $359.55 for costs.

Appellant contends that the place for alighting was reasonably safe for that purpose and that appellee failed to prove that appellant's employee knew, or should have known, that the place for alighting was dangerous. We do not agree.

The applicable standard of care required of appellant is as follows:

> A carrier of persons for reward must use the utmost care and diligence and a reasonable degree of skill and provide everything necessary for their safe carriage.

Although this statute did not make appellant an insurer of appellee's safety, it did require appellant to exercise the highest care that could reasonably have been exercised. This duty extended to passengers who were in the process of alighting from the bus. . . .

What our holding might have been had this accident occurred in broad daylight, we need not speculate. Here, however, the accident occurred late at night at a poorly lighted area. Under these circumstances, we hold that the failure of appellant's driver to park the bus close enough to the curb to permit appellee and the other passengers to step safely onto the sidewalk and his failure to warn them of the possible danger or to assist them in alighting constituted negligence that supports the trial court's award of damages.

Appellant contends that appellee did not exercise ordinary care for her own safety. This contention is belied by the record, which shows that appellee held onto the stair railing as she proceeded to alight from the bus. Because of her short, stocky figure, appellee, who testified that she "couldn't hardly see outside," apparently had to release her hold on the railing to make the step to what she thought was the sidewalk but in reality was the gutter. It appears that there was little more that appellee could have done in the way of exercising care for her safety. Having been left to fend for herself by the driver, whose principal concerns apparently lay elsewhere, appellee did the best she could under the circumstances. It was for the trier of fact to determine whether appellee was guilty of contributory negligence, and we cannot say that the trial court erred in its finding on this issue.

Affirmed.

REVIEW QUESTIONS

1. Identify the terms in column A by matching each to the appropriate statement in column B.

A	B
1. Tenancy for a stated period	**a.** Occurs when a tenant holds over without the landlord's consent.
2. Tenancy at will	**b.** The transfer of possession but not ownership of personal property.
3. Tenancy at sufferance	**c.** Proper negotiation is by indorsement and delivery.
4. Distress for rent	**d.** A lease for a specific period of time.
5. Bailment	**e.** One of the landlord's legal remedies when a tenant refuses to pay rent.
6. Bailor	**f.** The owner of personal property who transfers possession to a bailee.
7. Ordinary care	**g.** A lease with no stated duration that can be terminated by either landlord or tenant after proper notice is given.
8. Document of title	**h.** Evidences the right to possess the described personal property.

9. Order document

    i. The degree of care owed by the bailee in a bailment for the mutual benefit of the parties.

2. List four types of legal classifications of leasehold interests and describe the distinctions among each.

3. The Kroger Company opened a supermarket as one of the original tenants of a shopping center owned by Developer's Unlimited. Kroger signed a 10-year lease. However, due to declining sales, Kroger subleased the store space to Thomas, who operated a discount department store. Thomas agreed to assume all of Kroger's obligations under the original lease. Developer's claims that Kroger's sublease to Thomas is inconsistent with the terms of the original lease. Assuming there is no clause in the lease concerning Kroger's right to assign or sublease, does Developer's have any basis for denying Thomas the right to use the store space? Explain.

4. Jeff and four friends leased a house owned by Amanda Hogg. At the commencement of the lease, each tenant gave Ms. Hogg $100 as a security deposit. When the lease term legally expired, these tenants asked that their deposits be returned to Jeff. Ms. Hogg was given Jeff's forwarding address. Ms. Hogg failed to send a list of damages with itemized repair costs within 30 days after the premises were vacated. Ms. Hogg also refused to refund any of the tenants' security deposits. Are these tenants entitled to receive their deposits plus damages? Why?

5. Alice Sorrells and her husband leased a single-family house from the Pole Realty Company. After several years of this lease relationship, Pole filed suit to recover possession on the grounds that the tenants had not paid rent and had not heated the premises as they were required to do. Mrs. Sorrells defended this suit by alleging that Pole had breached the implied warranty that the house would remain habitable. She stated that she was unable to heat the house because the windows, doors, and roof were defective. Pole sought to have this defense set aside since the implied warranty of habitability applies only to multiple-family residential complexes. Should the landlord's implied warranty of habitability be applicable to single-family residences? Why?

6. Miller's car was parked in a large self-service parking garage owned by the Central Parking System. The parking garage is the type where a machine automatically gives a ticket to a driver before he enters the garage. The driver then parks in a place of his choice, leaves his car, and takes his keys with him. The only employee on duty is the attendant who collects the money from the driver upon exiting. Miller parked his car in the garage following this procedure. The wheels were stolen from his car. Is the garage company liable for the stolen wheels without a showing of negligence? Why?

7. Patrick left some of his clothes at the Douglas Dry Cleaners, Inc. Through no negligence of Douglas, an arsonist started a fire that destroyed the company's building and its contents. Patrick sues to recover the value of his clothes. Should he recover? Why?

8. Lloyd Groat was licensed as a common carrier. Arnold Albrecht, a logger, hired Groat to transport a 45-ton crawler log loader from one job site to another. Some of Albrecht's employees accompanied Groat during this transfer. While the equipment was being moved, the truck carrying the loader bogged down on a steep, freshly graveled logging road. Groat and Albrecht's employees used a Caterpillar bulldozer to extract the truck from the mire. While the truck was being pulled free, the log loader came loose from the trailer. The loader cascaded down an embankment, where it came to rest in a damaged condition. Albrecht filed suit, claiming Groat was strictly liable for the damage to the log loader, since he was a common carrier. Groat contended he should be able to reduce his liability due to the negligence of Albrecht's employees, which contributed to the damaging of the loader. Is strict liability the proper standard of liability of a common carrier? Explain.

9. The McLean Trucking Company, duly licensed by the ICC as a motor carrier, delivered some wood shipped by Jergen to Haas. The wood was water-soaked, although there was no evidence that this resulted from McLean's fault or negligence. May Jergen recover from McLean? What assumption have you made? Why?

10. Walls was a paying guest at the Dumler Hotel. He left his $3,500 Rolex watch on the nightstand, locked the door, and went out to dinner. When Walls returned, the watch was gone. He discovered that the door lock had not been functioning properly, and anyone could have entered his room easily. Walls claimed that the hotel's lack of maintenance amounted to willful and wanton misconduct. The hotel contended that a state statute exempted innkeepers from any liability for whatever reason if the guest fails to deposit small, valuable objects in the hotel's safe. Will this statute protect the hotel from liability even though the loss is the result of willful and wanton misconduct instead of simple negligence? Why?

11. Bob Baylor stored 10 valuable Oriental rugs with the Bailey Warehouse Corporation. Bob received a negotiable warehouse receipt at the time the rugs were stored. Bob then transferred this receipt to Nancy by properly indorsing it. To whom is Bailey now obligated to return the rugs? Why?

22 ESTATE PLANNING, WILLS, AND TRUSTS

Perhaps no aspect of the ownership of property is of greater significance than the various methods available for disposing of that property on death. This significance is due in part to transfer taxes imposed by both federal and state governments. As a result of transfer taxes, income tax problems, and other related concerns, specialists are actively engaged in estate planning.

Estate planning involves much more than the transfer of property at the owner's death. Proper planning includes the creation of an estate, as well as the distribution of estate assets. For example, a young couple with small children may be very concerned about providing for their children's college education. How this goal is achieved is one part of estate planning. Acquisition of a principal residence, a vacation home, or other assets may play a major part in planning an estate. How one provides for loved ones in the event of death or disability should be considered. Retirement plans also are an important part in estate planning.

Estate planning is a lifelong, ever-changing process; it is not a one-time transaction. This chapter presents material on some of the legal principles involved in the estate planning process. For instance, a valid will often is considered the cornerstone or foundation of a well-planned estate. However, substitutes for wills may be useful in particular circumstances. Furthermore, trusts can be utilized separate from or in conjunction with a will. Wills, substitutes for wills, and trusts are discussed in the following sections.

1. Terminology
WILLS

A *will* is a document that expresses a person's intention as to the disposition of his or her property on death. It also serves several additional functions. It designates the personal representative who is to be responsible for settling the affairs of the deceased. A will may make provision for the appointment of guardians of the person and the estate of a minor child. Indeed, for young parents who have not yet amassed much financial wealth, the appointment of a guardian for their minor children usually is the most important reason to have a will. Many wills also provide for payment of taxes that may be due on the death of the deceased and for matters such as whether or not the personal representative should be required to have sureties on the official bond.

A person who dies leaving a valid will is said to die *testate.* This person, upon signing a will, generally is referred to as the *testator.* The personal representative of a testator is an *executor.* A person who dies without leaving a valid will dies *intestate.* The personal representative of a person who dies intestate is called an *administrator.* This personal representative (whether an executor or an administrator) is in charge of gathering the deceased's assets, paying the lawful debts, and distributing the assets to the appropriate persons. A *guardian* is the personal representative in charge of the well-being of a person's body or property or both. A guardian may be appointed when the care of minor children or mentally incompetent adults is involved.

A gift by will of real estate usually is called a *devise;* a gift of personal property other than money is called a *bequest;* and a gift of money is referred to as a *legacy.* Devises, bequests, and legacies are further classified as specific, general, or residuary. A *specific* gift (devise, bequest, or legacy) is a gift of particular property described to identify and distinguish it from all other parts of the deceased's property. If property described in a specific gift is not owned by the testator at death, the gift fails or is said to be *adeemed.* A *general* gift is one that does not describe any particular property, and it may be satisfied by delivery of any property of the general kind described. A gift of a specified sum of money is a general legacy. A *residuary* gift is one that includes all the property not included in the specific or general devises, bequests, or legacies. All of these terms are important in the payment and distribution of the shares of an estate and in determining which party actually receives a specific item of property.

2. Testamentary Capacity

Testamentary capacity does not require a perfect mind or average intelligence. Testamentary capacity first of all requires a minimum age, such as 18 years. The person executing the will must have sufficient mental capacity to comprehend and remember who are the natural objects of his affection, to comprehend the kind and character of his property, and to understand that he or she is engaged in making a will. Less mental capacity is required to execute a will than is required to execute ordinary business transactions and contracts. Since many people at the time of making a will are in poor health, the law recognizes that many testators will not be of perfect mind, and all that is required is a minimum capacity to understand the nature and extent of one's property and to formulate the plan involved in making the will.[1]

---

[1] Hellams v. Ross, p. 498.

3. Formalities of Execution

In general, the testator must sign the will. In the alternative, since many people who are physically incapacitated will not be able to sign, the will may be signed by someone else in the testator's presence and at his direction. It will not be set aside simply by proving that the signature on it is not that of the deceased.

In most states, the testator need not sign in the presence of witnesses if he acknowledges to them that the instrument is his own and that it bears his signature. The witnesses need not be informed that the document is a will, but only that it is the testator's instrument. The signature aspect of attestation occurs when the testator watches the witnesses sign. In most states, it is essential that the witnesses testify that the testator watched them sign as attesting witnesses.

A *credible* witness is one who is competent to testify in support of the will. If the witness is an interested party because he takes something under the will, in most states, the witness will not be allowed to receive any more property as a result of the will than he would have received had there been no will. In other words, a witness to the will cannot profit or gain any property as a result of the will. He will be required to testify and will lose whatever the will gives him in excess of his intestate share of the deceased's estate.

The most important thing to remember about executing a will is that the number of credible witnesses and the formalities required vary from state to state. Consultation with a lawyer licensed in the state involved is always recommended.

4. Grounds for Challenging a Will's Validity

Very often a disinherited or disappointed party will challenge the validity of a will by proving that a testator lacked the mental capacity to make that will. Another challenge might be that the formal requirements of signing and witnessing the will were not met. In addition, the validity of a testator's will may be challenged on the grounds that the testator was unduly influenced to make a will which provides for a distribution scheme contrary to that testator's expected wishes and desires. This ground for challenging a will is defined as influence that overpowers the mind of the testator and deprives him of his free agency in the execution of the will. It is the equivalent of saying, "This is not my wish, but I must do it." It is more than mere persuasion, for here there is an exercise of independent judgment and deliberation. A presumption of undue influence is often found to exist where there is a fiduciary relationship between a testator and a beneficiary who takes substantial benefits from the will. This is especially true if the beneficiary is a nonrelated dominant party and the testator a dependent party and the will is written, or its preparation procured, by the beneficiary.

5. Revocation, Republication, Revival, and Renunciation

A will is said to be *ambulatory,* or not effective, until the death of the testator. It may be revoked at any time. Among the common methods of revoking a will are physical destruction, making a will declaring the revocation, a later will that is inconsistent with the prior will, marriage, and divorce. In many states, divorce revokes the will only to the extent of bequests or devises to the former spouse. Marriage revokes a will because it is presumed that the testator would want a different plan of distribution as the result of the marriage. It is therefore important that whenever there is a marriage or a divorce, the law of the state of the domicile be consulted to determine its effect on a prior will.

State laws usually prohibit partial revocation of a will except by a duly signed and attested instrument. Additions, alterations, substitutions, interlineations, and deletions on the face of a will are therefore ineffective, and the will stands as originally executed. The law prohibits partial revocation because of the ease with which such minor changes could be made by third parties even after the death of the person whose will is involved.

Unless a provision is made for a child born after the execution of the will, or unless the will by clear and convincing language indicates that after-born children are to be disinherited, the after-born child in most states takes from the estate whatever he or she would have received had there been no will. A legal adoption has the same effect. This stipulation is based on the assumption that the testator at the time of the execution of the original will would not have considered the after-born child and that a provision would have been intended had the child been considered.

In most states, a will that is in any manner totally revoked can be revived only by the republication of the will or by an instrument in writing declaring the revival and executed in the same manner as a new will. This process commonly is referred to as republication. To illustrate, assume that a person during her lifetime has executed four wills, each specifically revoking the former. None of these wills had been destroyed until the testator, shortly before her death, physically destroyed will number 4. Is number 3 then valid? In most states, the answer is no. Wills are not stacked one on the other so that the revocation of the latest will revives the earlier will. In the situation described, the person would die without a will.

Some states have recognized an exception to the general rule that a revoked will is ineffective unless the testator's intent indicates otherwise. This exception is known as the *doctrine of dependent relative revocation*. In essence, this doctrine applies when the testator intends to revoke one will and substitute a new will in its place. If the new will is not made or is not valid for some reason, this doctrine allows the previously revoked will to remain valid. In order for the doctrine to apply, it must be proved that the testator intended the revocation of an old will to be conditioned on the validity of a new will. Usually the nature of a deceased person's intent is very difficult to prove. Therefore, the doctrine of dependent relative revocation will be applied to a very narrow factual situation. As a practical matter, an old will should not be destroyed prior to the execution of a new one.[2]

A similar issue as to a will's validity arises when a person executes a codicil or a minor change to a will. When a codicil is executed and it specifically refers to a former will, it has the effect of bringing the former will down to the date of the

---

[2] Larrick v. Larrick, p. 499.

codicil, and the will is then construed as of the date of the codicil. A codicil can validate a previously invalid will. It can also validate a will that has been revoked by marriage or divorce.

The law in most states gives a spouse certain rights that cannot be denied by will. These rights include support during the period of administration, with a statutory minimum usually provided. The court will determine the exact amount, based on the size of the estate and the standard of living of the surviving spouse. A spouse may also *renounce* a will and take a statutory share in lieu of provisions made by the will. In other words, one spouse cannot completely prevent his or her property from passing to a surviving spouse by making different provisions in the will. In many states, a spouse receives half the estate upon renunciation, irrespective of the provisions of the will. It should be recognized that the right to renounce usually exists for spouses only—children can be completely disinherited.

6. Introduction

ALTERNATIVES TO WILLS

Numerous methods, legal devices, and techniques can serve as a valid substitute for a will. In one sense, the law of intestacy is a substitute for a will because it is, in effect, a state-made will for people who have not taken the trouble to execute one for themselves. Among the more common substitutes for wills are contracts, including life insurance contracts, trusts, and joint tenancy property.

Life insurance policies name a beneficiary to receive the proceeds on the death of the insured. This beneficiary may be the estate of the insured, in which case the proceeds will pass under the will of the deceased; or if the insured dies without a will, the proceeds will be distributed according to the laws of intestacy. The usual arrangement is to name an individual beneficiary and successive beneficiaries in the event the primary beneficiary predeceases the insured. In that case, the provisions of the will are immaterial, and the life insurance will be paid in accordance with the terms of the policy, even if the will purports to cover life insurance.

Individuals enter into numerous contracts that have the effect of disposing of property on death. Some contracts stipulate the terms of a will or surrender rights to renounce a will or take an intestate share. Such contracts known as *antenuptial agreements,* are often entered into by parties contemplating marriage, especially when one or both have children by a prior marriage.

In part VIII, "Business Organizations," reference is made to *buy and sell* agreements between partners and between the shareholders of closely held corporations. These contracts, in effect, dispose of the interests of partners and shareholders on death. The contractual agreement will dispose of the property, irrespective of any provision in a will, in much the same manner as does life insurance. Other contracts, including employment contracts and leases, may have a similar effect.

A living trust is another substitute for a will when it contains provisions for the disposition of property on the death of a life tenant. Since this device is so important and so commonly used, it is discussed more fully in sections 13 through 18 starting on page 492.

Finally, some methods of joint ownership are used as substitutes for wills because ownership automatically passes to the surviving owner on the death of the other. In particular, joint tenancies and tenancies by the entirety are used to accomplish this purpose.

Prior to examining the various forms of multiple ownership, we discuss what happens when a person dies without leaving a valid will.

7. Intestate Succession

As stated previously, a person who dies without leaving a valid will is said to die *intestate.* When a person dies intestate, state law provides how the deceased's property will be distributed. In this sense, a state's intestate succession law acts as an alternative to a will. Although all the states attempt to provide a scheme of distribution that a reasonable person likely would have intended, statutes of intestacy do vary from state to state. To complicate matters, the intestate laws of two or more states may have to be used in settling the estate of a person who dies without a will. For example, when real estate is a part of the deceased's estate, the appropriate intestate statute is that of the state in which the land is located. When personal property is to be distributed, the law of the deceased's domicile generally controls.

The typical intestate succession statute provides that the deceased's assets are to be inherited by that deceased's closest living relative. However, the intestate succession statute in one state may provide that a spouse of the deceased receives the entire estate if there are no surviving children. In another state, under similar circumstances the intestate statute may require that the property be divided between the deceased's spouse and parents. If a person is survived by a spouse and children, most states provide that the estate is divided among the spouse and children. Often this is an undesirable result, because of the unmarketability of property owned by minors. This problem arises due to the fact that minors generally can void contractual transactions prior to reaching the age of majority.

Everyone over the legal age of testamentary capacity should be aware of his or her state's scheme of intestate succession. If that scheme contradicts a person's desires for distributing assets, that person should have a valid will prepared and executed. Indeed, as an alternative to a valid will which can be personalized to the testator's specific needs, the intestate succession scheme is considered inferior as an estate planning tool.

8. Multiple Ownership

There are three distinct methods by which two or more people may own property at the same time. These are the (1) tenancy in common, (2) joint tenancy, and (3) tenancy by the entirety. These first two types of co-ownership are applicable to every kind of property, real or personal. However, tenancy by the entirety is a type of joint tenancy held by spouses in real estate only. Several states have modified the common-law characteristics of these forms of ownership, so it is essential that each state's law be consulted for the technicalities of these tenancies.

A basic distinction between a tenancy in common and a joint tenancy is the effect of death on the tenancy. In the event of the death of a tenant in common, his or her share in the property passes to the executor named in the will or to the administrator of the deceased's estate. If property is held in joint tenancy, the interest of a deceased owner automatically passes to the surviving joint owner. Such property is not subject to probate or to the debts of the deceased joint tenant. Thus joint tenancy with the right of survivorship passes the title of the deceased by operation of law to the survivor or survivors, free of the claims of anyone else except for taxes that may be due.

Both joint tenancy and tenancy in common ownership may include two or more persons who may or may not be related. In tenancy in common, the share of the tenants may differ. One may own an undivided two-thirds; the other an undivided one-third. In joint tenancy, the interests must not only be equal, but they must be created at the same time. These requirements and others are discussed in the following section.

Eight states (Arizona, California, Idaho, Louisiana, Nevada, New Mexico, Texas, and Washington) have what is known as *community property,* having inherited it in part from their French and Spanish ancestors. In these states, most property acquired after marriage other than by devise, bequest, or from the proceeds of noncommunity property becomes the joint property of husband and wife. Upon the death of one of the parties, title to at least half the community property passes to the survivor. In most of the states, the disposition of the remainder may be by will or under the rules of descent.

9. Joint Tenancy

In order to establish a valid joint tenancy, certain requirements must be satisfied. These requirements are known as the four unities of time, title, interest, and possession. The *unity of time* requires that the joint tenants' ownership be created in the same conveyance. To have the *unity of title,* each owner must have the same estate, such as a fee simple absolute, a remainder, or any other estate, which is created by the same conveyance. The *unity of interest* exists when each owner has the same percentage interest subject to the other owners' interest. For example, two joint tenants must each own 50 percent of the undivided property, three own 33 percent each, four own 25 percent each, and so forth. Finally, the *unity of possession* is present when each joint tenant has the right to possess all of the real estate subject to the other owners' rights of possession.

When there is a question about which form of ownership exists in any specific case, the law usually favors property passing by will or intestacy, rather than its passing by right of survivorship. Courts do not find that property is held in joint tenancy with the right of survivorship unless there is a contract between the two co-owners clearly stating that such is the case and that the right of survivorship is to apply. Bank signature cards and stock certificates that use the term *joint tenancy* or "with the right of survivorship" create such a contract, as does the language "as joint tenants and not as tenants in common." In most states, the contract must be signed by both parties to be effective. Failure to use the proper language or have a properly executed contract results in a tenancy in common.

Several additional aspects of holding property in joint tenancy frequently result in litigation. First of all, joint tenancy is often used as a substitute for a will. A party wishing to leave property to another on death sometimes puts the property in joint tenancy. Is a present gift intended? Does the new joint tenant have the right to share in the income of the property prior to the death of the original owner? Such issues are frequently litigated.

A similar issue arises when one person in ill health or incapacitated adds another person's name to a savings or a checking account in order to allow the latter to pay bills and handle the former's business transactions. The signature card often provides for a joint tenancy. Was a joint tenancy or mere agency intended? Joint tenancy arrangements are frequently challenged successfully on the ground that the right of survivorship was not intended.[3]

Another difficulty involves describing the property held in joint tenancy. Frequently, a contract covering a safety deposit box will provide that it be held in joint tenancy. Does such a contract cover the contents of the box as well? If two people hold a safety deposit box in joint tenancy, and the box contains $20,000 in cash, most courts would hold that the cash was not held in joint tenancy.

Another disadvantage of the joint tenancy arrangement is the ease with which it may be severed or terminated. Each joint tenant has the power to terminate the right of survivorship by a simple transfer or conveyance of his interest to a third party. The severance of the unities of time, title, interest, or possession converts the joint tenancy to a tenancy in common. This severance may occur either by one of the co-owner's actions or by order of a court in a suit for partition of the owners' interests.[4]

10. Tenancy by the Entirety

If the owners are related by marriage and the state law so provides, a conveyance to a husband and wife creates a specialized joint tenancy, which is called *tenancy by the entireties*. A tenancy by the entirety in states that authorize such common ownership of real estate can exist only between husband and wife. A conveyance of real estate to a husband and wife in these states is automatically a tenancy by the entirety if all four unities, discussed above, are present. Neither tenant can unilaterally sever or end the tenancy. It may be terminated only by divorce, a joint transfer to a third party, or a conveyance by one spouse to the other. The inability of either spouse to terminate the tenancy unilaterally is the primary difference between a joint tenancy and a tenancy by the entireties, as the basic characteristic of each is the right of survivorship. In most states that authorize tenancy by the entireties, not only is there a prohibition on one tenant making a voluntary transfer of his or her share, but there are also severe

---

[3] Sly v. Barnett, p. 500.

[4] Hall v. Hamilton, p. 501.

restrictions on the rights of creditors to collect an individual debt from one tenant of the property. Suppose a husband and wife own their home as tenants by the entireties. A creditor has a judgment for $10,000 against the husband alone. In most states, the creditor could not cause a sale of the house to collect the debt. Of course, if the creditor had a judgment against both husband and wife, he could collect from a judicial sale of the property.

11. Probate and Administration

The statutes of each state specify the steps the executor or the administrator must take to settle an estate. The law usually requires that a petition be filed informing the court of the death of the deceased, together with a copy of the will, if any, requesting the court to hold a hearing, at which time the will will be presented for probate. If the person dies without a will, the petition will be signed by someone entitled under the law to be administrator of the estate. This person is usually the closest relative. In either case, every person interested in the estate as a beneficiary under the will or as an heir or next of kin of the deceased is entitled to notice of the time and place of the hearing. This notice may be waived by a written document filed with the court.

At the time of the hearing, there will be testimony about the death of the deceased, and the attesting witnesses will be called upon to testify about the execution of the will. The evidence offered will be for the purpose of establishing that at the time of the execution the deceased possessed the requisite mental capacity, that the instrument was signed either by the deceased or by someone in his presence and at his direction, and that it was properly attested to by the required number of witnesses. There will also be a report to the court on the approximate value of the estate, so that the personal representative may be properly bonded. If it appears to the court that the will was properly executed, it will be admitted to probate, and an executor named by the testator will be appointed. If there was no will and the person entitled to administer has so requested, an administrator will be appointed. The executor or the administrator will then file an oath of office and an appropriate bond to guarantee the faithful discharge of the duties of personal representative. In the case of an administrator, sureties on the bond will be required. In the case of an executor, sureties will be required unless these are waived by the will.

After the executor or the administrator is appointed, there will usually be a notice of publication in an appropriate newspaper, informing all creditors that they may file their claims against the estate. In addition, the executor or the administrator will gather up the personal property of the deceased, inventory it, and file an inventory with the court. The inventory will include all real estate and all personal property owned by the deceased. It will not include joint tenancy property. Should there be any disputed claims, the court will hold an appropriate hearing and determine which claims, if any, will be paid.

During the period of administration, the personal representative will file the deceased's final income tax returns, the necessary income tax returns for the estate, the federal estate tax return if one is required, and the appropriate state death-tax returns. The personal representative will also attempt to collect any sums due the deceased and compromise any claims owing to, or debts owned by, the deceased. At the end of the period of administration, the property remaining after the payment of all debts and taxes will be distributed by the personal representative to the persons entitled to it. If the deceased died intestate, these will be the persons who are determined by the court to be the legal heirs of the deceased as of the date of death. In most states, if the deceased leaves a spouse and children, they will constitute the heirs. If there are no spouse and no children, then the court will determine which blood relatives are next in line to receive the property.

12. Uniform Probate Code

As the previous sections of this chapter have indicated, there is a great deal of variety in state laws concerning elements of a valid will, intestate succession distribution plans, probate procedures, and administration of estates. In an attempt to reduce some of this confusion, the National Conference of Commissioners on Uniform State Laws has prepared the Uniform Probate Code (UPC). The UPC has been proposed for adoption by state legislatures, and by 1983 it had been adopted in fourteen states. They include Alaska, Arizona, Colorado, Idaho, Maine, Michigan, Minnesota, Montana, Nebraska, New Jersey, New Mexico, North Dakota, Pennsylvania, and Utah.

The stated purpose of the UPC is to clarify, simplify, and make uniform laws that should provide an efficient system of liquidating a deceased person's estate, paying debts, and distributing assets to the proper parties. The UPC establishes the requirements for a will and for the administration of a decedent's estate. It also describes who can elect to take a share that is not provided in the will, and under what circumstances this election may occur. This UPC also provides a plan of intestate succession in case a person dies without leaving a valid will. For example, a surviving spouse will receive at least one-half of the intestate estate, and an even larger interest if there are no surviving descendants or parents of the decedent. In lieu of an executor managing a testator's estate and an administrator handling an intestate estate, the UPC adopts the concept of a personal representative who assists in the gathering and distribution of a decedent's estate.

In our increasingly mobile society, there are obvious advantages in having uniform laws throughout the country for the distribution of a decedent's property. Since these benefits of uniformity exceed the need of each state to have its own peculiar laws, the UPC is likely to be more widely adopted in the future.

TRUSTS

13. Introduction

The word *trust* is generally used to describe an express private trust. An *express private trust* is a fiduciary relationship with respect to property, which subjects the person with legal title to property (the trustee) to equitable duties to deal with the property for the benefit of another (the beneficiary). In other words, a *trust* is a fiduciary relationship under which one person, the trustee, holds title to property and deals with it for the benefit of another person known as the *beneficiary*. The most important single aspect of the relationship is its fiduciary character. The trustee is under an absolute obligation to act solely for the benefit of the beneficiary in every aspect of the relationship. Both real and personal property may be held in trust.

A trust may be created by a transfer of property during one's lifetime (a *living*, or *inter vivos, trust*), or it may be created by a transfer on death (a *testamentary trust*). The person creating the trust is usually called the *settlor*, although he is sometimes referred to as the *creator* or the *trustor* in estate planning literature. The settlor may create the trust by a transfer of property to the trustee, or the settlor may declare himself to be trustee of described property for the benefit of designated beneficiaries.

Consideration is not required to create a trust. Although consideration may support the creation of an *inter vivos* trust, it is rarely present in a testamentary trust. A trust involving real estate requires written evidence of the intention to create the trust and an exact description of the property held in trust. This writing requirement must be satisfied, since the statute of frauds is applicable to trusts containing real estate. In general, personal property may be held in a trust that is created orally. Although it is preferable to state clearly that a trust is being created, not all trusts are created by a formally drafted trust agreement.[5]

A trust may have several beneficiaries, and their rights may be dependent upon several variable factors. The trustee may be authorized to determine which beneficiaries shall receive the income of the trust and how much each shall receive. The right of a trustee to allocate the income of the trust among the beneficiaries is sometimes referred to as a *sprinkling trust* provision. It has the advantage of allowing the trustee with actual knowledge of the needs of the beneficiaries to take those needs into account in the distribution of income. A trust may also have successive beneficiaries. A trust could provide that the income would go to the deceased's spouse for life; and on the death of the spouse, to their children for life; on the children's death, to grandchildren.

A settlor may be a trustee as well as one of the beneficiaries of a trust. A trustee may be one of the beneficiaries of a trust, but the sole trustee cannot be the sole beneficiary. If the sole trustee is the sole beneficiary of a trust, there is a merger of the legal and equitable interests, causing a termination of the trust by operation of law.

When the settlor is also the trustee and life beneficiary, the trust operates in effect as a will. It is nevertheless valid in most states, even though it is not executed with the formality required of a will. In such case, it is used to avoid probate proceedings and to save the costs involved in such proceedings.

14. Types of Trusts

In addition to the express private trust, the law recognizes trusts created by operation of law: constructive trusts, resulting trusts, and charitable trusts. A court of equity may create a *constructive trust* in order to prevent unjust enrichment, as in a transfer of property procured by fraud or violation of some

---

[5] Sundquist v. Sundquist, p. 502.

fiduciary duty. Courts of equity also create *resulting trusts,* which result when the person with legal title is not intended to have it. For example, if a child purchases property in the name of a parent, there is no presumption of a gift, and the child may establish that the parent holds title in trust for the child.

The *charitable trust* is a valuable estate-planning tool. It differs from a private trust in that it can benefit an indefinite group and can have perpetual existence. Among typical charitable purposes for which a trust can be created are the promotion of religion, education, health, public comfort, and the relief of poverty.

Perhaps the single most important principle in the law of charitable trusts is the doctrine of *cy pres,* which provides that if a particular charitable purpose cannot be carried out in the manner directed by the settlor, the court can direct the application of the trust property to another charitable purpose consistent with the general charitable intention. The words *cy pres* mean "as nearly as," and the courts simply choose another charitable purpose that is as nearly as possible like the one designated by the settlor.[6]

15. Administration of Trusts

Since a trust is a fiduciary relationship, the trustee owes a high duty of loyalty to the beneficiary. The trustee is not allowed to enter individually into transactions with the trust. Such contracts or transactions are voidable without regard to fairness, and good faith is no defense. A trustee also has a duty not to delegate his responsibility to another.

Perhaps the most important duty of the trustee is in regard to investments. The trustee has a duty not to commingle trust funds with his individual funds and a duty to earmark and segregate trust property. The trustee has a duty to diversify investments. This diversity is sometimes horizontal, sometimes vertical. *Horizontal diversity* means that the trustee should diversify his investments geographically and in various industries throughout the country. *Vertical diversity* means that he should diversify by investing in different companies within the same industry.

It is frequently stated that trustees, in the selection of trust investments, must exercise a degree of care that men of prudence and intelligence exercise in the management of their own affairs, not in regard to speculation, but in regard to the permanent disposition of these funds, considering probable income as well as the probable safety of the investment. This is generally known as the *prudent man rule.*

To obtain the requisite diversification, especially in trusts with relatively small amounts of assets, *common trust funds* have developed. They allow a trustee, such as a bank or a trust company that holds several trusts, to invest the trust funds together. The duty not to commingle is not violated, because each trust fund has its stated proportion of the total investment.

The trustee has all necessary powers to carry out the appropriate duties. These generally include the power to sell if necessary, to lease, to incur necessary expenses, to settle claims, and to retain investments. A trustee generally has no

---

[6] Estate of Puckett, p. 503.

power to borrow money or to mortgage the trust assets. A trustee is liable to the beneficiary for any loss caused by a breach of trust and for any personal profit made in breach of his duty of loyalty. A trustee who makes improper investments cannot set off the gains on one against the losses on the other. Any gain in an improper investment remains in the trust, and the trustee is required to make up the losses created by making improper investments.

16. Termination of Trusts

In the absence of fraud or mistake, a settlor cannot revoke a trust unless he has specifically reserved the power to do so. The same principle applies to modifications of the trust. A trust may be terminated when its purposes have been accomplished or if the trust purpose becomes illegal. A trust may be terminated by the consent of all beneficiaries, provided they are all of legal age and all consent, and provided also that termination will not defeat the purpose for which the trust was created. This last provision is especially important in the so-called *spendthrift trust*. If the purpose of the settlor was to conserve the estate of a spendthrift, it cannot be terminated even with the consent of the beneficiaries.

In regard to spendthrift trusts, it should be noted that all trusts are spendthrift trusts to a certain extent. That is, as a general rule, a creditor cannot collect a debt of the beneficiary directly from the trust estate if the trust was created by someone other than the beneficiary. One of the purposes of a trust is to protect the beneficiary from the claims of his creditors, and allowing a creditor to collect directly from the trust estate would defeat this purpose. Therefore, with the exception of a few claims, such as alimony, child support, and taxes, the trustee is not obligated to pay over the income or principal of the trust estate to anyone other than the beneficiary. Of course, after the beneficiary has received the income, a creditor may use legal process to collect a claim. The fact that all trusts are spendthrift regarding involuntary transfers is a major reason for use of the trust device.

SUMMARY

WILLS	
Terminology	1. A person who leaves a valid will dies testate. This person is known as a testator.
	2. An executor is the manager of a testator's estate. An administrator is in charge of the estate of a person who died without leaving a valid will. A guardian is a personal representative in charge of the

	well-being of another's body or property or both.
	3. A gift of real property as a term of the will is a devise. A bequest is a gift of personal property in general under a will. A legacy is a gift of a specific amount of money.
Testamentary capacity	**1.** An essential element to make a valid will.
	2. A testator must be the minimum statutory age and must be able to know the natural objects of his bounty and the scheme of distribution provided in the will.
Formalities of execution	**1.** Another essential element of a valid will.
	2. The testator must sign the will and must ask witnesses to sign in his presence. States require either two or three disinterested, competent witnesses.
Challenging a will's validity	**1.** The lack of the testator's capacity to make a will and the lack of proper execution are two grounds for having a will declared void.
	2. Proof that the testator was unduly influenced, which means his true desires were not followed, is another important method for challenging a will.
Ambulatory nature of wills	**1.** A testator retains complete control over his will during his lifetime.
	2. A will may be revoked and made ineffective.
	3. Once a will is revoked, it cannot be revived automatically. In order to be valid, a revoked will must be republished.
	4. A spouse may renounce a will and claim a statutory interest against the estate.

ALTERNATIVES TO WILLS

Intestate succession	**1.** A person who dies without leaving a valid will is said to die intestate.
	2. In such a case, the deceased person's property is distributed according to the scheme of distribution provided by state statute.
Multiple ownership	**1.** Tenancy in common is the type of multiple ownership generally most favored by

courts. There is no right of survivorship, and the deceased co-owner's interest passes by will or by intestate succession.

2. A joint tenancy is characterized by the right of survivorship. However, the right may be severed by one of the co-owners conveying his interest to a third party.

3. A tenancy by the entirety is a special type of joint tenancy. This method of co-ownership is limited to real property interests jointly held by a husband and wife. Generally, this right of survivorship cannot be severed without the consent of both spouses.

TRUSTS

Creation

1. A trust is used by one person to transfer legal title to real or personal property to another person for the benefit of a third person.

2. These parties are known as the settlor, trustee, and beneficiary, respectively.

3. An *inter vivos* trust is created during the lifetime of the settlor. A *testamentary* trust is created in a settlor's will.

Types

1. An express private trust is created by a settlor for the benefit of an individual or a noncharitable organization.

2. A constructive trust can be created by a court of equity in order to prevent unjust enrichment.

3. A resulting trust also can be created by a court of equity when a person who actually has legal title to property is supposed to hold that property for the benefit of another party.

4. A charitable trust occurs when the beneficiary is a charitable organization. This trust is an important estate planning tool, since it can be used to reduce estate taxes. The doctrine of *cy pres* often is applied to accomplish the settlor's charitable intent.

Administration

1. All trustees are in the fiduciary position of trust and confidence.

	2. Trustees must use the trust property only for the beneficiary.
	3. Trustees must handle and invest the trust property as a reasonably prudent person would.
Termination	1. Generally, a settlor cannot revoke an established trust unless the right of revocation is reserved.
	2. Trusts usually are terminated when their purpose has been accomplished or when all the beneficiaries (assuming that they are competent) agree to the termination.

CASES

Hellams v. Ross
233 S.E.2d 98 (S.C. 1977)

LEWIS, J. The issues involve the validity of the will of the late Marvin Robert Bass and, particularly, his testamentary capacity at the time he executed the instrument.

The testator died in Laurens County on March 9, 1975, leaving a will dated May 2, 1974, under which he devised all of his property to the Rabon Creek Baptist Church to the exclusion of his wife, the respondent herein. He had no children.

The respondent-widow objected to the probate of the will upon the ground that the testator lacked testamentary capacity to make it. . . . The Probate Court subsequently overruled the attack upon the validity of the will and admitted it to probate. However, upon appeal to the Circuit Court, a jury found that . . . the deceased . . . did not have sufficient mental capacity to make a will on May 2, 1974, the date upon which he signed the instrument offered for probate.

The executor (appellant) took the position at the trial that there was no evidence to sustain the conclusion that the deceased was mentally incompetent . . . at the time of the execution of the will and, accordingly, moved for a directed verdict in favor of the will upon that ground. . . . This appeal by the executor . . . presents the sole issue of whether there was any evidence to support the finding of the jury that the testator lacked mental capacity to make a will. . . .

It is conceded that the will was properly executed. The charge of testamentary incapacity was based upon allegations that the excessive use of alcohol and drugs had affected the testator's mental faculties. The testimony showed that the testator had been a heavy consumer of alcoholic beverages for a number of years. In fact, it is inferable that his consumption of intoxicating beverages had reached a point that he was an habitual drunkard; but the testimony shows conclusively that the testator was not under the influence of intoxicants on the date of execution of the will. The issue then is whether there was any evidence from which a reasonable inference could be drawn that the testator's intemperance had so affected his mental faculties as to render him incompetent to make a will even though he was not actually intoxicated at the time he executed it.

The burden of proof was upon respondent, as the contestant, to show a lack of mental capacity. . . .

The general principles governing the determination of testamentary capacity apply in cases where it is charged that the testator was affected by the use of alcohol or drugs. Therefore, the capacity of the testator to make a will is tested by whether he knew (1) his estate, (2) the objects of his affections, and (3) to whom he wished to give his property.

Since intoxication is a temporary condition, even an habitual drunkard is presumed to be competent, when sober, to make a will; and the person, who asserts that the excessive use of intoxicants rendered a testator incompetent to make a valid will, must affirmatively show either (1) that at the time the will was made the testator's use of intoxicants had so impaired or deranged his mind that he lacked testamentary capacity even when he was not under the immediate influence of intoxicants or (2) that he was in fact incompetent due to intoxication existing at the time of the making and execution of the will.

A careful review of the record convinces us that the evidence failed to show mental incapacity of the testator at the time the will was made. Although the testimony is undisputed that the testator was a heavy drinker and would sometimes, when on one of his frequent drinking sprees, fire his gun into the ceiling of the house and through the windows, there was no evidence of probative value that his drinking had produced a derangement of his mental faculties when he was not under the influence of intoxicants.

One of the witnesses to the will was dead, but the other two testified. One was the attorney who prepared and supervised the execution of the will and the other was the attorney's secretary. Both certified that the testator came to the attorney's office and requested that the will be prepared, giving directions as to the disposition to be made of his estate. These witnesses were positive in their testimony that the testator was sober, normal in his actions, and possessed of testamentary capacity when he signed the will.

We find no evidence of probative value to counter the positive testimony of the attesting witnesses that the testator was possessed of testamentary capacity when he signed the instrument. The lower court was therefore in error refusing to grant appellant's motion for a directed verdict. . . .

The fact alone that the testator disposed of property contrary to what others usually consider fair is not sufficient to declare his will void. . . . The right to make a will carries with it the right to disregard what the world considers a fair disposition of property. . . . That a will is unjust to one's relations is no legal reason that it should be considered an irrational act. The law puts no restrictions upon a man's right to dispose of his property in any way his partialities, or pride, or caprice may prompt him.

There was also testimony that the testator bought two trailers for considerably more than they were worth; took the sink and some furniture from his home and put it in a rental house; and that about five (5) years before his death he expressed a belief that, if he gave his money to the church, he would go to Heaven. Respondent argues that the bad business deal, using articles from his home to fix rental property, and the belief that by giving his property to the church he would go to Heaven constituted some evidence that the testator was of unsound mind. The belief that the giving of his property to the church would, within itself, get him into Heaven might have been inaccurate, but we are not prepared to say that it was evidence of an unsound mind. Neither does the bad business deal nor using his household articles to furnish his rental property reach, under this record, probative value on the question of testamentary capacity. . . .

Reversed in favor of the validity of the will.

Larrick v. Larrick
607 S.W.2d 92 (Ark. App. 1980)

PENIX, J. Woodrow Larrick died June 27, 1979. His widow Verna Larrick, the appellant, petitioned to be appointed administratrix of Woodrow Larrick's estate, stating Woodrow Larrick died intestate. On July 23, 1979 the Probate Court of Cleburne County appointed Verna administratrix. On September 4, 1979, Arthur Larrick, brother of Woodrow Larrick, petitioned for the admission to Probate of the Last Will and Testament of Woodrow Larrick. Verna Larrick responded to the petition stating the Last Will and Testament had been destroyed thereby rendering it null and void. On February 29, 1980 the Probate Court found that Woodrow Larrick personally destroyed the original will by tearing and burning it and that at the time of the destruction his intent was to immediately make a new will. However, he died suddenly. The Court found further the destruction was a revocation conditioned upon his making a new will and that he would prefer the terms of the destroyed will to intestacy. The Court applied the doctrine of dependent relative revocation and ordered the will admitted to probate. The widow Verna Larrick appeals. . . .

The widow Verna testified she observed Woodrow tear up the will and set fire to it about a week before his death. She further testified she was the one who went to Hoyt Thomas' office, the lawyer who had prepared it, and took it home to Woodrow. She said he kept it two or three days before tearing it up. She said also Woodrow was planning to make a new will which he said would be quite a bit different from the destroyed will. . . .

Arthur Larrick, appellee, testified as to how close he and Woodrow had been as brothers down to 1974 when Verna and Woodrow married. He said Woodrow told him he had a will under which he, Arthur, would receive $30,000. Woodrow told Arthur ". . . I have made a will and I have left you $30,000 and the rest goes to Verna, and I want you to be sure that you get this." This conversation occurred March 20, 1979, three months prior to Woodrow's death. He testified seeing Woodrow twice again between March 20 and his death and Woodrow did not mention he was going to destroy his will or make any changes in it. He said he called Verna on August 10, after receiving notice in a letter . . . [that] Woodrow had died intestate, and was told Woodrow had destroyed his will. . . .

It is the contention of Verna, the appellant, Woodrow intended to destroy the will and there is clear, cogent and convincing evidence he intended to destroy the will. . . .

The testimony of Verna Larrick was that Woodrow Larrick destroyed his will because of conversations he had had with members of his family during his last trip to Kansas which indicated Verna was to get nothing. . . . The Court found as a matter of fact Woodrow destroyed his will. We find substantial evidence to support this.

Verna further contends the Court's application of the doctrine of dependent relative revocation is in error. Verna contends the doctrine is not the law in Arkansas.

The Probate Judge, having found the will was destroyed, then applied the doctrine of dependent relative revocation. This is defined as:

The doctrine which regards as mutually dependent the acts of one destroying a will and thereupon substituting another instrument for distribution of estate, when both acts are result of one plan, so that, if second act, through incompleteness or other defect, fails to accomplish its intended purpose, and it thereby becomes evident that testator was misled when he destroyed his will, act of destruction is regarded as bereft of intent of revocation and way for probate of destroyed will is opened. . . .

The Probate Judge found as a matter of fact that a few days before his death Woodrow Larrick personally destroyed the original of said will by tearing and burning it. The Judge further found it was Woodrow Larrick's intent to make a new will as a substitute for the will he was destroying; however, he died from a sudden attack before he made a new will. We, as appellate court, find substantial evidence to support the Probate Court's findings of fact. However, we disagree with the Court's application of the law to those findings of fact.

The intentional physical destruction of the . . . will, in the manner required by law, left the testator without an existing will. Everyone is presumed to possess knowledge of the legal consequences of his acts or omissions. Whatever reason the decedent had, he failed to re-execute either of his known wills or publish a new one. Therefore, he died intestate.

We find the Probate Judge erred as a matter of law in applying the doctrine of dependent relative revocation. Since we hold the doctrine cannot be applied to these findings of fact, the presumption Woodrow Larrick intended to revoke his will has not been overcome nor rebutted. We find it to be error to admit to probate the copy of the revoked will. We therefore reverse and remand to the Probate Court for proceeding with the administration of Woodrow Larrick's estate which we find to be intestate.

Reversed and remanded.

Sly v. Barnett
637 P.2d 527 (Nev. 1981)

SPRINGER, J. This appeal is from a summary judgment entered in favor of respondent Barnett, executrix of the estate of Carolyn Howe, and defendant below.

The issue in this case is whether a joint tenancy relationship existed between appellant Sly and decedent Howe so as to entitle appellant to traceable bank account funds even though the balance of the accounts had been withdrawn by Howe prior to her death.

The matter was submitted to the trial court on cross-motions for summary judgment with an accompanying stipulation of facts; there is, accordingly, no material issue of fact.

From the stipulated facts it appears that Sly and Howe together opened two bank accounts and that by the terms of the bank signature cards, they agreed to be "joint depositors," owning the money "jointly with the right of survivorship." At the time the accounts were opened, NRS 663.015 was in effect. Section 1 of the statute states that where the signatory forms at the bank so provide, joint tenancy is presumed to have been created. The parties agree the presumption is rebuttable. There is thus, under the circumstances of this case, only a prima facie showing of joint tenancy, which then "open[s] the door to competent evidence" that something other than a joint tenancy was actually intended.

It is reasonable that the joint tenancy presumption may be rebutted. Courts have acknowledged the hardship which a contrary view might impose on parties having "convenience" accounts, as where an incapacitated person might have a joint account for the sole purpose of financial management. . . .

In the instant case, the following evidence supports a finding that Carolyn Howe did not intend to create a joint tenancy: Howe was the sole contributor to both accounts; Howe maintained at all times exclusive dominion and control over the savings account passbook and the checking account checks, deposit slips and deposit book; Howe withdrew all funds and thus closed both accounts without the consent of appellant and Howe redeposited the funds in individual accounts on which appellant was not a signatory. . . .

Although it is generally held that a withdrawal of all funds does not of itself terminate a joint tenancy, withdrawal is evidence that a joint tenancy was never intended. It is also true that appellant's lack of contribution to the accounts does not preclude the possibility of survivorship. It is, however, evidence of lack of intent. In addition, one party's exclusive control of the account passbooks is competent evidence against the presumption of joint tenancy. Based on these uncontroverted facts, the court could properly have concluded that the presumption of joint tenancy was rebutted. We therefore affirm the summary judgment entered by the court below.

Affirmed.

Hall v. Hamilton
667 P.2d 350 (Kan. 1983)

MILLER, J. This is an action for the partition of real property, the title to which is held in joint tenancy. The plaintiffs are Robert and James Hall, and James's wife, Nina. The defendant is Beverly J. Hamilton, sister of Robert and James. Robert, James and Beverly are the owners as joint tenants of the property which is the subject of this action, a lot in Prairie Village, Kansas, upon which there is a single family dwelling. The defendant, who occupies the residence, opposed partition. . . .

The real property in question was originally owned by Newton and Maurine Hall, parents of the parties to this action. Mr. and Mrs. Hall conveyed the property by warranty deed to their three children, Robert, James and Beverly, as joint tenants with the right of survivorship and not as tenants in common, in 1969. Mr. and Mrs. Hall continued to live in the home. Mr. Hall died in January, 1973. Shortly thereafter, and at the request of Mrs. Hall,

Beverly moved into the home. She resided with and cared for her mother until the mother died in December, 1980. Beverly continues to reside in the home; she refuses to consent or agree to the sale of the property, and as a result her brothers have been unable to either rent or sell it. The brothers commenced this action for partition of the property in May, 1981.

Both sides moved for summary judgment. The trial court overruled defendant's motion and granted plaintiffs' motion for summary judgment. . . .

The . . . issue . . . is simply whether real property held in joint tenancy may be the subject of involuntary partition. . . .

In our unanimous opinion in *Miller,* we said:

Partition provides a method whereby two or more persons who own property together may put an end to the multiple ownership, so that each may own a separate portion of the property or, if a division in kind is not feasible, the property may be sold and each owner given an appropriate share of the proceeds. It is said to be a right much favored in the law because it secures peace, promotes industry and enterprise, and avoids compelling unwilling persons to use their property in common. The right of partition is said to be an incident of common ownership. . . .

The right of a joint tenant . . . to sever his interest, to dispose of his share by conveying it to a third person, or to seek partition under the appropriate statutes, is widely recognized. . . . In the case at hand, there is no indication that the instrument creating the joint tenancy contained any provisions restricting the rights of the joint tenants to seek partition of the property. . . .

Appellant asserts that a holding that a joint tenant may force partition upon unwilling cotenants will be responsible for all sorts of rifts in the social fabric, but appellant cites no authority to support that argument. On the contrary, given the facts presented at bar, it is clear that partition represents the only equitable solution. Partition in this case accomplishes the goal of avoiding "compelling unwilling persons to use their property in common." It also prevents one joint tenant from enjoying the benefit of the property to the practical exclusion or detriment of the others.

It is undisputed that any joint tenant may sever his or her joint tenancy interest in real property by conveying the interest to a third person, or by mortgaging the joint tenancy interest, or—in some jurisdictions—by leasing that interest. Once the joint tenancy interest is severed, a tenancy in common results. Requiring a joint tenant to sever the joint tenancy interest before bringing an action in partition would serve no useful purpose, and it is often said that the law will not require the doing of a useless act. Severance is accomplished in the partition action by the court's order of partition; we see no need to require a prior severance. We . . . hold that joint tenancy interests in real property are subject to involuntary partition, and conclude that the trial court did not err in ordering partition of the jointly held real estate.

Affirmed.

Sundquist v. Sundquist
639 P.2d 181 (Utah 1981)

Donald and Mary Alice Sundquist were husband and wife. As a result of their divorce and property settlement agreement in 1973, the parties agreed as follows:

That income derived from the interest held by the parties in the real estate syndicate known as the Big Bear Property in San Bernardino County, California, should be established as a family trust . . . with the Plaintiff and Defendant as Trustees with the restriction and requirement that said funds be accumulated for the education of the minor children of the parties. . . .

Throughout the next several years, these parties had the income from their Big Bear Property deposited into an account at a local bank. In 1980, Mary Alice sought to have this account closed and one-half of the $5,914.28 on deposit given to her. After her former husband objected, Mary Alice filed suit and argued that a formal trust was never created. The trial court agreed that a trust had not been created, and Donald appealed.

OAKS, J. . . . The principles governing the creation of a trust are well settled. An inter vivos trust is created when a settlor, with intent to create a trust, transfers property to a trustee in trust for, or declares that he or she (the settlor) holds specific property in trust for, a named beneficiary. The settlor need not sign a formal trust instrument or employ any particular form of words. But the settlor must have an intent to create a presently enforceable trust, the trust property must be clearly specified and set aside, and the essential terms of the trust must be clear enough for the court to enforce the equitable duties that are the *sine qua non* of a trust relationship.

This requirement of clarity is met if the beneficiaries are identified and the nature of their beneficial interests and the duties of the trustee are specified orally, or in writing (as is more common), or are clearly ascertainable from the circumstances. To be enforceable against objections, a trust in real property must be created by a writing signed by the settlor or his agent. But trusts other than those involving real property can be created without the formality of a writing, so long as they are proven by clear and convincing evidence. . . .

As to the $5,914.28 balance of the trust account on deposit in the bank on February 8, 1980, the district court's conclusion that no trust was created was erroneous in law and contrary to the clear preponderance of the evidence. Here two parties signed an enforceable agreement to create a trust for the education of their children, of which they were to be trustees and to which they were to deposit the income derived from specified property. The agreement designated the purpose and beneficiaries of the trust: to provide education for the parties' children with a remainder interest in the parties themselves. . . .

When the parties signed their Property Settlement Agreement in 1973, they fulfilled all the requirements for the creation of a trust except the existence of the trust property. Even the property requirement would have been fulfilled if the parties had transferred or declared a trust of the interest they owned in the Big Bear Property. But the agreement evidences no intent to do this. Instead, the parties agreed "that income derived from the interest held by the parties in the . . . Big Bear Property . . . should be established as a family trust. . . ." By this reference to "income derived" and this use of "should" in the sense of duty, the parties made clear that they were not creating a present trust but only imposing an obligation to create a trust thereafter, and that the subject matter of the trust was not to be the property then owned but the income installments to be received in the future. The installments of income were future property in 1973 and thus could not have been the subject matter of a present creation of trust. Viewing the matter just after the October, 1973, agreement, the parties had an enforceable agreement to create a trust, but no trust had been created. Consequently, as to the Big Bear Property and as to future income installments, we agree with the district court's conclusion that no trust was created.

However, as the parties received each installment of income from the Big Bear Property, the trust automatically came into existence as to that installment. This is a consequence of the fact that the parties had made an enforceable agreement to create a trust in those installments of income, and the fact that equity would therefore treat the trust as having been perfected when the income was received. . . . The parties' deposit of these income installments in the properly labeled trust account in the bank is further confirmation of their performance of their agreement to create a trust and of the existence and validity of the trust as to those deposits. . . .

For reasons set out above, a valid trust was created and exists as to the $5,914.28 balance of the bank account. . . .

Reversed.

Estate of Puckett
168 Cal. Rptr. 311 (App. 1980)

Leta Puckett's will established a trust to be funded by the residue of her estate after specific bequests were completed. The trust was established in order to provide two annual one-year scholarships for students going to college. One scholarship was to benefit a student studying science, chemistry, or pre-medicine. The other scholarship was to benefit a student studying religion. The trust provided that after expenses were paid for the trust's administration, all the net income was to be divided equally among these two scholarships. Lena Lee Myers, a first cousin of Leta Puckett, challenged this testamentary trust on the grounds that the trust property would produce net income far in excess of that needed to establish the two scholarships. Ms. Myers sued and argued that she was entitled to this excess property as the deceased's closest intestate heir. The trial court found there was no intestate property, and Ms. Myers appealed.

PIERSON, J. . . . The validity of appellant's case rests upon the applicability of the doctrine of *cy pres* to the testator's will. The doctrine of *cy pres* has been described as follows:

> "[C]y pres is an equitable power which makes it possible for a court to carry out a testamentary trust established for a particular charitable purpose if the testator has expressed a general charitable intent, and for some reason his purpose cannot be accomplished in the manner specified in the will, the court, to meet unexpected contingencies, directs the disposition of the property to some related charitable purpose in order to carry out the testator's intention as nearly as possible." . . .

Appellant does not dispute that the property in the present case was given in trust to be applied to a particular charitable purpose. Appellant contends that *cy pres* does not apply because (1) it has not become impossible, impracticable or illegal to carry out the charitable purpose, and (2) the settlor did not manifest a general charitable intent.

. . . [A]n essential ingredient of the *cy pres* doctrine is the requirement that the specific charitable purpose of the trust has become either impossible or impractical of fulfillment and interpreted this to mean permanent impossibility or impracticality.

Bogert on Trusts & Trustees views facts such as those presented by the instant case as a type of "impossibility";

> If the income of the charitable trust is or becomes more than sufficient to achieve all the charitable objectives named by the donor in the manner prescribed by him, cy pres is generally applied to the surplus income, in the discretion of the court, since there is an impossibility of using the income to advance any of the charitable purposes of the settlor.

The specific intention of the testator that the trust income be used for the two scholarships becomes impossible to carry out if the net income of the trust exceeds the amount of money granted for the two scholarships. Whether the scholarships will utilize all of the income in a particular year will depend upon the amount of income and the financial needs of the students in light of the costs of receiving an education. The yearly costs of a college education for a physically handicapped person might exceed one-half of the net income of the trust. . . .

A proper construction of the will supports the trial court's finding that the testatrix had a general charitable purpose. Trusts for the advancement of education are charitable in nature.

A testator is said to have had a "general charitable intent" when the particular gift is of a generally charitable nature rather than to benefit a specific charitable entity. The bulk of the testatrix' estate . . . was intended to provide scholarships in the sciences and religion to two students a year on a continuing basis. If one or both of the scholarships should terminate in a given year because of poor grades, the balance of the funds allotted to that scholarship was to be added to the next scholarship selected for the following year. The testatrix further provided that in the event that any of her gifts to charity should fail for any reason, then the portion that failed was to be distributed to the Regents of the University of California. . . . [T]his provision . . . is some indication that the testatrix intended that the bulk of her trust estate should be applied for charitable purposes, i.e., education. . . .

The objects and purposes of the trust are purely charitable. The elements necessary to invoke the doctrine of *cy pres* are present. The testatrix had a general charitable intent to benefit young people in obtaining a college education. . . .

There is authority for the proposition that where the testator has provided certain sums shall be paid to a certain number of persons, and the income is or becomes more than sufficient for the purpose, the court may direct that larger sums be paid to the same number of persons. On the other hand, in an English case where the income was such that there was more than sufficient funds to pay the designated sums to the designated number of recipients, the court allowed an increase in the number of beneficiaries.

. . . [I]n fulfillment of the duty of the trustee to carry out the intentions of the testator as manifested in the will, when surplus income exists greater than that designated to the one student beneficiary, the surplus may be used to support a second student.

There is no intestate property under the will in the instant case. The trial court, upon proper application, will determine the use of the surplus income applying the *cy pres* doctrine.

Affirmed.

REVIEW QUESTIONS

1. Identify the terms in column A by matching each to the appropriate statement in column B.

A	B
1. Testator	**a.** Created during the lifetime of the settlor.
2. Executor	**b.** Dying without leaving a valid will.

3. Bequest

4. Undue influence

5. Intestate

6. Joint tenancy

7. Tenancy by the entirety

8. Settlor

9. *Inter vivos* trust

10. *Cy pres*

c. A person who dies and leaves a valid will.

d. A special method whereby spouses can own real property with a right of survivorship.

e. A gift of personal property under the terms of a will.

f. A method whereby two or more people may own either real or personal property.

g. The personal representative who manages the estate of a testator.

h. An equitable principle used to accomplish a settlor's charitable intent.

i. A ground for challenging a will's validity requiring proof that the testator lacked freedom of choice.

j. The creator of a trust.

2. Define the following terms as each relates to the law of wills: (a) testator, (b) executor, (c) devise, (d) bequest, (e) legacy.

3. Ted died January 12, 1982. His widow presented for probate a will dated October 18, 1981. Betsy, one of the witnesses on the will, testified that she did not see Ted sign this will and that Ted was not present when she signed as a witness. Was this will properly executed? Why?

4. An undertaker has served as a confidential adviser to a woman who died at the age of 80. When her mind was failing, the undertaker had his attorney draw a will for her, leaving virtually all her estate to the undertaker. The will was contested on the grounds that the undertaker exercised undue influence over this woman. Should the court find that undue influence existed? Why?

5. Compare tenancy in common, joint tenancy, and community property as concurrent ownership interests that may have substantial impact on the transfer of property at the owner's death. Describe the impact of each.

6. A mother deposited $10,000 of her money in a joint account with her son in a savings and loan association. Both signatures were required for withdrawal, and the signature card contained the following: "Any funds placed in, or added to, the account by any one of the parties is and shall be conclusively intended to be a gift to the other party to the extent of his pro rata share." The mother retained possession of the passbook and subsequently brought suit, claiming that she is the sole owner of the funds. Is the mother correct? Why?

7. After Henry married Wilma, he transferred a house he owned to himself and Wilma as joint tenants. Later, Henry filed a declaration to sever the survivorship right of the joint tenancy. He then executed a will devising his interest in the house to his daughter by a previous marriage. Upon Henry's death, Wilma claimed ownership of the property. Should Wilma receive the property as the surviving joint tenant? Why?

8. Would your answer to the above question change if a tenancy by the entirety had been created instead of a joint tenancy? Explain.

9. Theresa established a trust of certain farmland in which she was both trustee and income beneficiary during her lifetime. The trust agreement provided that upon Theresa's death, the earnings were to go to her brother for his life. Theresa died intestate. Her nieces claimed that the trust arrangement, though an attempted substitution for a will, was void since it was not executed formally, as a will must be. Is the trust valid? Explain.

10. Marcia, a trustee, was given broad authority by the trust instrument in the administration of the trust. Using trust funds, she made a personal profit from a real estate investment. Valerie, a beneficiary to the trust, sued to recover the profits for the estate. Has Marcia breached her fiduciary duty? Explain.

23 INTRODUCTION TO SALES CONTRACTS

As we learned in the chapters on contracts, the Code has changed many older, classical contract rules to conform with business realities and the reasonable expectations of the contracting parties. Many common-law contract rules also have been changed or modified by Article 2 of the Code to achieve a more commercially desirable result, since some basic contract rules concerning employment, construction, and real property contracts are simply inappropriate in a sale-of-goods context. The important Code modifications or changes are listed in Table 23–1. These Code rules have already been discussed in the chapters on contracts and will not be discussed further. They are summarized for review purposes.

This chapter explores the sales contract, the transfer of title to goods, and the risk of loss when goods are destroyed, damaged, or stolen. The next chapter will cover the remedies available to the parties when the other is in breach.

1. Scope

A sales transaction can relate to real property, goods, and other forms of personal property. This chapter is limited to sales transactions in goods under Article 2 of the Uniform Commercial Code. Article 2 of the Code does not define *transaction*. Although a few sections are limited either explicitly or implicitly to the sale of goods [2-204, 2-314, 2-402, 2-703], courts have extended Article 2 to transactions such as leases and bailments of goods in some cases.

When you lease a car or rent a golf cart, does Article 2 apply if problems arise? The answer is not clear. Some courts have applied the Code to all commercial leases of goods. These courts emphasize that Article 2 governs "transactions" in goods, and a lease of goods is such a transaction. On the other

CODE SECTION 2	RULE	**TABLE 23–1** Special rules for contracts for the sale of goods

Offer and Acceptance

204	All terms need not be included in negotiations in order for a contract to result.
205	Firm, written offers by merchants are irrevocable for a maximum of 3 months.
206(1)(a)	An acceptance may be made by any reasonable means of communication and is effective when deposited.
206(1)(b)	Unilateral offers may be accepted by a promise to ship or by shipment.
206(2)	Acceptance by performance requires notice within a reasonable time, or the offer may be treated as lapsed.
207	Variance in terms between offer and acceptance may not be a rejection and may be an acceptance.
305	The price need not be included in a contract.
311(1)	Particulars of performance may be left open.

Consideration

203	Adding a seal is of no effect.
209(1)	Consideration is not required to support a modification of a contract for the sale of goods.

Voidable Contracts

403	A minor may not disaffirm against an innocent third party.
721	Rescission is not a bar to a suit for dollar damages.

Illegality

302	Unconscionable bargains will not be enforced.

Form of the Agreement

201	Statute of frauds $500 price for goods. Written confirmation between merchants. Memorandum need not include all terms of agreement. Payment, acceptance, and receipt limited to quantity specified in writing. Specially manufactured goods. Admission pleadings or court proceedings that a contract for sale was made.

Rights of Third Parties

210(4)	An assignment of "the contract" or of "rights under the contract" includes a delegation of duties.

Performance of Contracts

209	Claims and rights may be waived without consideration.
307, 612	Rules on divisible contracts.
511	Tender of payment is a condition precedent (rather than a condition concurrent) to a tender of delivery.
610, 611	Anticipatory breach may not be withdrawn if the other party gives notice that it is final.
614	Impracticability of performance in certain cases is an excuse for nonperformance.

Discharge

725	The statute of limitations is 4 years, but parties can reduce it by mutual agreement to not less than 1 year.

hand, a few courts emphasize the word *sales* in the Code and will extend Article 2 only to transactions in goods that are analogous to a sale of goods. Some leases, for example, contain an option to buy; if exercised, it will cause the lease payments (rent) to be applied toward the purchase price. Cars, TVs, stereos, and many other things are frequently leased with an option to buy. Most courts have applied Article 2 to these leases, since they have attributes (option to buy) that make the transactions like a sale of goods.

Article 2 will not apply if the subject matter of the contract is service. But many contracts are "mixed" contracts in that they involve both a sale of services and goods. You hire a painter to paint your house or a contractor to install a heating and air conditioning system in an apartment complex, or a hairdresser to apply a special shampoo. In addition to providing services, these persons have also sold goods (the paint, heating and air unit, and shampoo). These contracts present borderline transactions, and the law is in a state of flux regarding the applicability of Article 2. Most courts tend to apply Article 2 only if the goods aspect of the deal is predominant. Their approach is to ask which part of the transaction is the predominant feature—sale of goods or sale of services?[1]

Some problem areas have definite answers. Article 2 applies to specially manufactured goods [2-105(1)] and to "the serving for value of food or drink to be consumed either on the premises or elsewhere" [2-314(1)]. By statute in many states, Article 2 is inapplicable to blood transfusions, bone transfers, or organ transplants. These are considered medical services.

2. Definitions

Goods. The precise meaning of the term *goods* has long posed a difficult problem for the courts. In general, the term *goods* encompasses things that are movable; that is, items of personal property (chattels) that are of a tangible, physical nature [2-105(1)]. Although broadly interpreted to include even electricity, the definition of goods excludes investment securities (covered by Article 8 of the Code) and negotiable instruments (covered by Article 3 of the Code).

Being limited to *goods,* Article 2 necessarily excludes contracts for personal service, construction, intangible personal property, and the sale of real estate. Goods "associated" with real estate *may* be within Article 2 in sales of "structures," "minerals," and the "like" *if severance is to be made by the seller.* If severance is to be made by the buyer, the contract involves a sale of an interest in land. Growing crops, including timber, fall within Article 2, regardless of who severs them.

Another term used in Article 2 is *future goods,* goods that are not in existence at the time of the agreement or that have not been "identified"; that is, designated as the specific goods that will be utilized in the transaction [2-105(2)].

Sale. The sales transaction involves an exchange of title to the goods for the price. The basic obligation of the seller is to tender the goods, while that of the buyer is to accept the goods and pay the price. Both responsibilities are measured

---

[1] Osterholt v. St. Charles Drilling Co., p. 522.

by the contract [2-301]. In general, the parties to a contract for sale can agree upon any terms and conditions that are mutually acceptable.

Merchant. Special provisions of Article 2 relate to transactions involving a *merchant,* a professional businessperson who "holds himself out as having knowledge or skill peculiar to the practices or goods involved in the transaction" [2-104(1)]. This designation is of great importance and is recognition of a professional status for a businessperson, justifying standards of conduct different from those of "nonprofessionals." The courts of some states have held that farmers are merchants when selling grain and other items raised by them. Other courts have held that farmers are not merchants, so from state to state there is variation in whether or not Code provisions relating to merchants apply also to farmers.

Good Faith. The Code provisions on the sale of goods are based on two assumptions: (1) that the parties should be given the maximum latitude in fixing their own terms and (2) that the parties will act in "good faith." Good faith means honesty in fact in the conduct or transaction [1-201(19)]. In the case of a merchant, "good faith" also includes the observance of reasonable commercial standards of fair dealing in the trade [2-103(1)(b)].

Returned Goods. The buyer and seller may agree that the buyer has the privilege of returning the goods that have been delivered to him. If the goods are delivered primarily for use, as in a consumer purchase, the transaction is called a *sale on approval.* If the goods are delivered primarily for resale, it is called a *sale or return* [2-326(1)]. The distinction is an important one, because goods delivered "on approval" are not subject to the claims of the buyer's creditors until the buyer has indicated his acceptance of the goods; goods delivered on "sale or return," however, are subject to the claims of the buyer's creditors while they are in his possession [2-326(2)]. Delivery of goods on consignment, such as a transaction in which a manufacturer or a wholesaler delivers goods to a retailer who has the privilege of returning any unsold goods, is a "sale or return."

The distinction is also important if the goods are lost, stolen, damaged, or destroyed. This issue is discussed with other aspects of risk of loss later in this chapter.

3. Abbreviations

As a matter of convenience, a number of contract terms are generally expressed as abbreviations. *F.O.B* (free on board) is the most commonly used. *F.O.B. the place of shipment* means that the seller is obligated to place the goods in possession of a carrier, so that they may be shipped to the buyer. *F.O.B. the place of destination* means that the seller is obligated to cause the goods to be delivered to the buyer [2-319(1)(b)]. Thus, if Athens, Georgia is the seller's place of business, "F.O.B. Athens, Georgia" is a *shipment contract.* "F.O.B. Champaign, Illinois," Champaign being the place where the buyer is to receive the goods, is a *destination contract,* and the seller must provide transportation to that place at his own risk and expense. He is responsible for seeing to it that the goods are made available to the buyer at the designated place.

If the terms of the contract also specify *F.O.B. vessel, car, or other vehicle,* the seller must at his own expense and risk load the goods on board. *F.A.S. vessel* (free alongside) at a named port requires the seller at his own expense and risk to deliver the goods alongside the vessel in the manner usual in the port or on a dock designated and provided by the buyer [2-319(2)].

C.I.F. means that the price includes, in a lump sum, the cost of the goods and of the insurance and freight to the named destination [2-320]. The seller's obligation is to load the goods, to make provision for payment of the freight, and to obtain an insurance policy in favor of the buyer. Generally, *C.I.F.* means that the parties will deal in terms of the documents that represent the goods; the seller performs his obligation by tendering to the buyer the proper documents, including a negotiable bill of lading and an invoice of the goods. The buyer is required to make payment against the tender of the required documents [2-320(4)].

THE SALES CONTRACT

4. Express Agreement

The terms of a sales contract are supplied by three sources: (1) the express agreement of the parties; (2) course of dealing, usage of trade, course of performance; and (3) the Code and other applicable statutes.

The general rule in sales law is that the parties are free to make their own contract. The parties are privileged to contract expressly regarding most basic terms—quality, quantity, price, delivery, payment, and the like. In general, their agreement is sufficient to displace any otherwise applicable Code section. But the principle of freedom of contract under the Code is not without exceptions. The parties cannot "disclaim" their Code obligations of good faith, diligence, and due care. Parties may provide a liquidated damages clause, but it cannot be a penalty [2-718(1)]. Consequential damages may be limited, but the limitation cannot be unconscionable [2-719(3)].

The buyer's duty in a sales contract is to pay for the goods. In the absence of a contrary agreement, payment is due at the time and place at which the buyer is to receive the goods [2-310(a)]. The basic obligations of the parties are concurrent conditions of exchange. Accordingly, a buyer who wants credit (to get the goods before he pays in full) must specifically negotiate for it in the contract. Between merchants, most domestic sales transactions are handled on "open account" (the seller ships the goods on the buyer's simple promise to pay for them in 30, 60, or 90 days). The buyer is not required to sign a note evidencing obligation to pay or to grant the seller a security interest in the goods to cover his obligation.

5. Documentary Transactions

When the parties are separated by distance and the seller is unwilling to extend credit to the buyer, they may employ a documentary exchange. As the procedure is sometimes called, the buyer is to pay "cash against documents." In this procedure, the seller utilizes documents of title to control the goods until he is paid. The document of title may be a bill of lading issued by a railroad or steamship company, a warehouse receipt, or any other document which is evidence that the person in possession of it is entitled to the goods it covers [1-201(15)].

Documents of title are multipurpose commercial instruments. They not only act as a receipt for the goods, but also state the terms of the shipment or storage contract between the seller and the transit or warehouse company.

In a typical documentary exchange, the seller may ship the goods by rail to the buyer and receive from the railroad a *negotiable* bill of lading made to the order of the seller. The railroad thereby obligates itself to deliver the goods to the holder of the bill of lading [7-403(4)]. At this point, the seller has shipped "under reservation." His procurement of the negotiable bill reserves a security interest in the goods for their price, which the buyer owes him [2-205]. The seller will indorse the bill of lading and send it to his bank. He will attach to it a sight draft or demand for immediate payment of the purchase price by the buyer. The seller's bank will forward the documents to a bank in the city of the buyer. It is the obligation of that bank to release the bill of lading to the buyer only after he has paid the draft for the purchase price [4-503(a)]. Without the bill of lading, the buyer will not be able to get the goods from the railroad; only when he is in possession under a regular chain of indorsements is the buyer the holder to whom the carrier is obligated to deliver.

This is only one common type of documentary transaction. There are many variations. Similar protections can be obtained if the seller ships under a nonnegotiable bill of lading, taking care to consign the goods to himself or his agent. The railroad is now obligated to deliver to the consignee or to the person specified by his written instructions [7-403(4)]. The seller will withhold any instructions to deliver to the buyer until he has been paid. Under this procedure, possession of the document of title is not required to take delivery from the carrier. But note that the seller should not name the buyer as consignee in the bill of lading; if he does, control over the shipment is lost.

6. Course of Dealing, Usage of Trade, Course of Performance

The agreement of the parties includes in their bargain any previous course of dealing between the parties, general trade custom and usage, and any past course of performance on the present agreement. These three sources are not only relevant in interpreting express contract terms, but also may constitute contract terms. A *course of dealing* is a sequence of prior conduct between the parties, which gives a common basis of understanding for interpreting their communications and conduct between themselves [1-205(1)]. A *usage of trade* is a practice or custom in the particular trade, used so frequently it justifies the expectation that it will be followed in the transaction in question [1-205(2)]. *Course of performance* concerns a contract that requires repeated performances. When an earlier performance has been accepted by the other party, that performance can be used to give meaning to the agreement regarding future performance [2-208(1)]. When any of these sources is conflicting, the Code [2-208(2)] adopts the following initial hierarchy of presumed probative values:

1. Express terms
2. Course of performance

3. Course of dealing

4. Usage of trade

But the last three do more than interpret the first. They may supplement, cut down, even subtract whole terms from the express agreement of the parties. More important, course of performance, course of dealing, and usage of trade may directly override express terms, so that an express contract term like "7 white goods" is changed to "10 black goods." This results from the fact that courts are looking for the intent of the parties and this intent may be best found in what the parties have done rather than in what they said.

7. Gap-Filling under the Code

Written contracts have gaps in them when the parties either intentionally or inadvertently leave out basic terms. Article 2 of the Code has a number of gap-filler provisions which, taken together, comprise a type of standardized statutory contract. As stated earlier, the parties can expressly vary the effect of these provisions by their agreement (including course of dealing, trade usage, and course of performance). The most important gap-filler provisions involve price, quantity, quality, delivery, and payment.

Price. The price term of the contract can be left open, with the price to be fixed by later agreement of the parties, or some agreed market standard [2-305]. It may even be agreed that the buyer or the seller shall fix the price, in which event there is an obligation to exercise good faith in doing so. If the contract is silent on price, or if for some reason the price is not set in accordance with the method agreed upon, it will be determined as a reasonable price at the time of delivery. Thus, if it appears that it is their intention to do so, parties can bind themselves even though the price is not actually agreed upon.[2]

Quantity. The Code also allows flexibility in the quantity term of a sales contract. There may be an agreement to purchase the entire output of the seller, or the quantity may be specified as all that is required by the buyer. To ensure fair dealing between the parties in "output" and "requirements" contracts, the Code provides that if parties estimate the quantity involved, no quantity that is unreasonably disproportionate to the estimate will be enforced [2-306]. If the parties have not agreed upon an estimate, a quantity that is in keeping with normal or other comparable prior output or requirements is implied.

Delivery. The term *delivery* signifies a transfer of possession of the goods from the seller to the buyer. A seller makes delivery when he physically transfers into the possession of the buyer the actual goods that conform to the requirements of the contract. He satisfies the requirement that he "transfer and deliver" when he "tenders delivery" [2-507].

A proper tender of delivery requires the seller to make available conforming goods at the buyer's disposition and to give the buyer any notification reasonably

---

[2] Landrum v. Devenport, p. 523.

necessary to take delivery [2-503(1)]. The seller's tender must be at a reasonable hour, and he must keep the goods available for a reasonable time to enable the buyer to take possession.

Unless the contract provides to the contrary, the place for delivery is the seller's place of business. If the seller has no place of business, it is his residence [2-308(a)]. In a contract for the sale of identified goods that are known to both parties to be at some other place, that place is the place for their delivery [2-308(a)(b)].

Goods are frequently in the possession of a bailee such as a warehouseman. In this event, in order to make delivery, the seller is obligated to (1) tender a negotiable document of title (warehouse receipt) representing the goods, or (2) procure acknowledgment by the bailee (warehouseman) that the buyer is entitled to the goods [2-503(4)(a)].

Unless otherwise agreed, the seller is required to tender the goods in a single delivery rather than in installments over a period of time. The buyer's obligation to pay is not due until such a tender is made [2-307]. In some situations, the seller may not be able to deliver all the goods at once, or the buyer may not be able to receive the entire quantity at one time, in which event more than a single delivery is allowed.

Time of Performance.   The time of delivery is often left out of contracts. Such contracts may be nevertheless generally enforceable. However, if the parties intended the written agreement to be complete and an exclusive statement of the contract and the time of performance is omitted, the contract is unenforceable. In the usual case, the time may be supplied by parol evidence if it was agreed upon. If it was not agreed upon, a reasonable time is perceived [2-309(1)].

Determining what is a reasonable time depends on what constitutes acceptable commercial conduct under all the circumstances, including the obligation of good faith and reasonable commercial standards of fair dealing in the trade. A definite time may be implied from a usage of the trade or course of dealing or performance or from the circumstances of the contract as previously noted.

Payment is due at the time when and place where the buyer is to receive the goods [2-310]. *Receipt of goods* means taking physical possession of them. The buyer is given the opportunity to inspect the goods before paying for them [2-513(1)]. However, when the shipment is C.O.D., the buyer is not entitled to inspect the goods before payment of the price [2-513(3)(a)].

The parties may enter into an open-ended contract that calls for successive performances, such as 1,000 barrels of flour per week. If the contract does not state the duration, it will be valid for a reasonable time. Unless otherwise agreed, either party can terminate it any time.

8. Transfer of Title to Goods   TITLE

The concept of title to goods is somewhat nebulous, but it is generally equated with ownership. Issues related to the passage of title are important in the field of taxation and in areas of the law such as wills, trusts, and estates. The Code has deemphasized the importance of title, and the location of title at any given time is usually not the controlling factor in determining the rights of the parties on a contract of sale. As a general rule, the rights, obligations, and remedies of the seller, the buyer, and the third parties are determined without regard to title [2-401]. However, the concept of title is still basic to the sales transaction, since by definition a sale involves the passing of title from the seller to the buyer.

The parties can, with few restrictions, determine by their contract the manner in which title to goods passes from the seller to the buyer. They can specify any conditions that must be fulfilled in order for title to pass. Since they seldom specify, however, the Code contains specific provisions as to when title shall pass if the location of title becomes an issue. As a general rule, it provides that title passes to the buyer at the time and place at which the seller completes his performance with reference to the physical delivery of the goods.

For purposes of title, some goods are classified as future goods. These goods are not in existence at the time of the agreement, or they are not designated as the specific goods involved in the transaction [2-105(2)]. Title to future goods does not pass at the time of the contract, as is explained further in the next section.

9. Identification to the Contract

Title to goods cannot pass until the goods have been *identified* to the contract [2-401(1)]. Identification requires that the seller specify the particular goods involved in the transaction [2-501(1)]. Carson may contract with Boyd to purchase 100 mahogany desks of a certain style. Boyd may have several hundred of these desks in the warehouse. Identification takes place when Carson or Boyd specifies the particular 100 desks that will be sold to Carson. There could not, of course, be a present identification of future goods (those not yet in existence or not owned by the seller). However, there can be identification of goods that are not in a deliverable state because the seller must do something to the goods prior to delivery.[3]

When goods are identified to a contract, the buyer acquires a special property interest in the goods. This special interest is an insurable one, and it may be created before the passing of title or delivery of possession of the goods.

Present Goods. Although identification can be made at any time and in any manner "explicitly agreed to" by the parties [2-501(1)], they usually do not make provision for identification—in which event the Code rules determine when it has occurred. If goods that are the subject of a contract are in existence and identified at the time the parties enter into the contract, identification occurs and title passes at the time and place of contracting [2-501(1)(a)]. This is true even if the seller has duties to perform in respect to the goods. If the goods are in a warehouse and the seller delivers the warehouse receipt to the buyer, identification occurs and title passes at the time and place the document of title (warehouse receipt) is delivered [2-401(3)(a)].

Future Goods. Contracts to sell future goods and agricultural items raise more difficult identification problems. For future goods, the seller provides

---

[3] Holstein v. Greenwich Yacht Sales, Inc., p. 523.

identification when he ships the goods or marks them as the goods to which the contract refers [2-501(1)(b)]. The requirement is that the seller makes an appropriate designation of the specific goods.

There are special provisions for agricultural items—crops and animals—because of their nature. When there is a sale of a crop to be grown, identification occurs when the crop is planted. If the sale is of the unborn young of animals, identification takes place when they are conceived [2-501(1)(c)].

Identification occurs, and title passes insofar as the specific goods are concerned, when the seller completes his performance with respect to the physical delivery of the goods. When a shipment contract specifies that a seller is to send the goods to the buyer but is not required to deliver them at the destination, title passes at the time and place of shipment [2-401(2)]. If the contract requires that the seller deliver at the destination, title will not pass until the seller has tendered the goods to the buyer at that point.

If the buyer rejects the goods when tendered to him, title will be revested in the seller. Upon the buyer's refusal to receive or retain the goods, the title automatically returns to the seller, whether or not the buyer was justified in his action. The same result obtains if the buyer has accepted the goods but subsequently revokes his acceptance for a justifiable reason [2-401(4)].

As a means of assurance that the price will be paid before the buyer can obtain title to the goods, a seller may ship or deliver goods to the buyer and reserve title in himself. Under the Code, such an attempted reservation of title does not prevent the title from passing to the buyer. It is limited to the reservation of a security interest in the goods [2-401(1)]. To give protection to the seller, the security interest must be perfected under the provisions of Article 9. This will be discussed in chapters 32 and 33. Accordingly, a seller who simply reserves a security interest will not have availed himself of protection against the claims of third parties against the property sold unless the seller complies with the law relating to secured transactions.

10. Good-Faith Purchasers

A purchaser of goods acquires the title his transferor had or had the power to transfer. If the seller has no title, the purchaser receives no title. A purchaser from a thief has no property interest in the goods because the thief had none. The original owner still has title and may recover the goods.[4]

A purchaser of a limited interest in goods has property rights only to the extent of the limited interest. If a person buys a one-half interest in a golf cart with his neighbor, his rights are limited to the one-half interest.

A purchaser of goods may acquire more rights and better title than the seller had. Such a purchaser must qualify as a good-faith purchaser for value. In addition, the seller's title must be at least voidable and not void [2-403].

Assume that Spenser obtains goods by fraud or pays for them with a check that is later dishonored. Spenser has voidable title to the goods. If he should sell

---

[4] First Nat. Bank & Trust v. Ohio Cas. Inc. Co., p. 524.

the goods to Jackson, who does not know that Spenser's title was voidable, Jackson has clear title. Thus a good-faith purchaser for value has better title than did the seller.

Voidable title issues also arise when the same goods are sold to more than one buyer. For example, Franklin sells goods to Talmadge, who leaves them at Franklin's store with the intention of picking them up later. Before Talmadge takes possession, Franklin sells them to Bell, a good-faith purchaser. Bell has title to the goods. Because if possession of goods is entrusted to a merchant who deals in goods of that kind, the merchant has the power to transfer all right of the entrusting owner to a buyer in the ordinary course of business [2-403(2)(3)]. A good-faith purchaser buying from a merchant in the ordinary course of business acquires good title.[5] This rule is applicable to any delivery of possession to a merchant with the understanding that the merchant is to have possession. Thus the rule applies to consignments and bailments as well as to cash sale, but the facts of each case must be examined to ensure that the buyer qualified as a good-faith purchaser for value.

RISK OF LOSS

11. In Breach of Contract Cases

The Code sets forth a number of rules for determining which party to a sales contract must bear the risk of loss in the event of theft, destruction, or damage to the goods during the period of the performance of the contract. The approach is contractual rather than title oriented and covers two basic situations: (1) no breach of contract cases and (2) cases in which one of the parties is in breach. Of course, the provisions are applicable only if the contract has not allocated the risk of loss [2-303].

If the contract has been breached, the loss will be borne by the party who has breached [2-510(1)]. Thus, if the seller has tendered or delivered goods that are "nonconforming," the seller bears the risk of loss. He remains responsible until he rectifies the nonconformity or the buyer accepts the goods despite their defects.

A buyer has the privilege of revoking his acceptance of the goods under proper circumstances (discussed in the next chapter). If the buyer rightfully revokes his acceptance, the risk of loss is back on the seller to the extent that the buyer's insurance does not cover the loss. In this situation, the seller has the benefit of any insurance carried by the buyer (the party most likely to have applicable insurance), but any uninsured loss is on the breaching seller.

Loss may occur while goods are in the seller's control, before the risk of loss has passed to the buyer. If the buyer repudiates the sale (breaches the contract) at a time when the seller has identified proper goods to the contract, the seller can impose the risk of loss upon the buyer for a reasonable time. The basic concept of the Code is that the burden of losses should be that of the party who has failed to perform as required by contract.

---

[5] American Lease Plans, Inc. v. Jacobs Plumbing, Heating & Air Conditioning, Inc., p. 525.

12. If No Breach Exists

Three situations may arise in no breach risk of loss cases. When neither party is in breach: (1) the contract may call for shipment of the goods; (2) the goods may be the subject of a bailment; and (3) the contract may be silent on shipment, and no bailment exists.

Shipment. A shipment contract requires only that the seller make necessary arrangements for transport; a destination contract imposes upon the seller the obligation to deliver at a destination. If a contract between buyer and seller provides for shipment by carrier under a shipment contract (F.O.B. shipping point), the risk of loss passes to the buyer when the goods are delivered to the carrier. If shipment is made under a destination contract (F.O.B. destination), risk of loss does not pass to the buyer until goods arrive at the destination and are available to the buyer for delivery [2-509(1)]. When the parties do not use symbols such as C.I.F., F.A.S., or F.O.B. or otherwise make provision for risk of loss, it is necessary to determine whether a contract does or does not require the seller to deliver at a destination. The presumption is that a contract is one of shipment, not destination, and that the buyer should bear the risk of loss until arrival, unless the seller has either specifically agreed to do so, or the circumstances indicate such an obligation.[6]

Bailments. Often, the goods will be in the possession of a bailee, such as a warehouse, and the arrangement is for the buyer to take delivery at the warehouse. If the goods are represented by a negotiable document of title—a warehouse receipt, for instance—when the seller tenders the document to the buyer, the risk of loss passes to the buyer. Likewise, risk passes to the buyer upon acknowledgment by the bailee that the buyer is entitled to the goods [2-509(2)]. In this situation, it is proper that the buyer assume the risk, as the seller has done all that could be expected to make the goods available to the buyer. It should be noted that if a nonnegotiable document of title is tendered to the buyer, risk of loss does not pass until the buyer has had a reasonable time to present the document to the bailee [2-503(4)(b)]. A refusal by the bailee to honor the document defeats the tender, and the risk of loss remains with the seller.

Other Cases. In cases other than shipment and bailments mentioned above, the passage of risk of loss to the buyer depends upon the status of the seller. If the seller is a merchant, risk of loss will not pass to the buyer until he receives the goods [2-509(3)]. The risk of loss remains with the merchant seller even though the buyer has paid for the goods in full and the buyer has been notified that the goods are at his disposal. Continuation of the risk in this case is justified on the basis that the merchant would be likely to carry insurance on goods within his control, whereas a buyer would not likely do so until he had actually received the goods.

A nonmerchant seller transfers the risk of loss by tendering the goods [2-

---

[6] Pestana v. Karinol Corp., p. 526.

509(3)]. A *tender* of delivery occurs when the seller makes conforming goods available to the buyer and gives him reasonable notice so that he may take delivery. Both parties are in the same position insofar as the likelihood of insurance is concerned, so the risk of loss passes to the buyer in cases where it would not do so if the seller were a merchant.

Sales on approval and sales with the right to return the goods are often involved in risk of loss cases. A characteristic of the sale on approval is that risk of loss in the event of theft or destruction of the goods does not pass to the buyer until he accepts the goods. Failure seasonably to notify the seller of his decision to return the goods will be treated as an acceptance. After notification of election to return, the seller must pay the expenses of the return and bear the risk of loss. In contrast, the buyer in a sale or return transaction has the risk of loss in the event of theft or destruction of the goods [2-327(2)] until the goods are delivered back to the seller.

SUMMARY

ARTICLE 2—UCC	
Contract changes	1. See Table 23–1.
	2. Article 2 covers the sale of goods. It does not cover the sale of real estate or service contracts.
	3. In mixed contracts, the Code is applicable if the sale of goods is the dominant part of the transaction.
Definitions	1. The term *goods* encompasses things that are movable; that is, items of personal property (chattels) that are of a tangible, physical nature.
	2. A sale consists of the passing of title to goods from the seller to the buyer for a price.
	3. A merchant is a professional businessperson who "holds himself out as having knowledge or skill peculiar to the practices or goods involved in the transaction."
	4. Good faith is honesty in fact in the transaction. In the case of a merchant, it also includes the observance of reasonable commercial standards of fair dealing in the trade.

5. A sale on approval gives the buyer a reasonable time to decide if the sale shall take place. It is used in consumer purchases.
6. A sale and return is a present sale which the buyer can cancel and return the goods.

Abbreviations

1. F.O.B.—free on board.
2. F.A.S.—free along side.
3. C.I.F.—cash, insurance, and freight.

THE SALES CONTRACT

The express agreement

1. The general rule in sales law is that the parties are free to make their own contract.
2. Parties cannot disclaim their Code obligations of good faith, diligence, and care, and unconscionable provisions will not be enforced.
3. In the absence of a contrary agreement, payment is due at the time and place at which the buyer is to receive the goods. A buyer who wants credit must specifically negotiate it in the contract.
4. If a seller is unwilling to extend credit to the buyer, they may use a documentary exchange or cash against documents.

Factors affecting contract terms

1. A course of dealing is a sequence of prior conduct between the parties that gives a firm basis for interpreting their communications and conduct between themselves.
2. A usage of trade is a practice or custom in the particular trade used so frequently it justifies the expectation that it will be followed in the transaction in question.
3. Course of performance concerns a contract that requires repeated performances. When an earlier performance has been accepted by the other party, that performance can be used to give meaning to the agreement regarding future performance.

Gap-Filling

1. The price term of the contract can be left open, with the price to be fixed by later

agreement of the parties, or by some agreed market standard.

2. If the contract is silent on price, it will be a reasonable one.

3. The Code also allows flexibility in the quantity term of a sales contract. There may be an agreement to purchase the entire output of the seller, or the quantity may be specified as all that is required by the buyer.

4. If no time of delivery is stated in the contract, it may be supplied by parol evidence of the agreement. If not agreed upon, a reasonable time is assumed.

5. Unless the contract provides to the contrary, the place for delivery is the seller's place of business. If the seller has no place of business, it is his residence.

6. If the time for performance has not been agreed upon by the parties, the time for shipment or delivery or any other action under a contract shall be a reasonable time.

TITLE

Transfer

1. The Code has deemphasized the importance of title, and the location of title at any given time is usually not the controlling factor in determining the rights of the parties in a contract of sale.

2. The parties can specify when title passes. If there is no provision, title passes to the buyer at the time and place at which the seller completes his performance with reference to the physical delivery of the goods.

3. Title to goods cannot pass until the goods have been identified to the contract. Identification requires that the seller specify the particular goods involved in the transaction.

4. If goods that are the subject of a contract are in existence and identified at the time the parties enter into the contract, identification occurs and title passes at the time and place of contracting.

5. In a contract to sell future goods, the seller provides identification when he ships the goods or marks them as the goods to which the contract refers.

6. Identification occurs, and title passes insofar as the specific goods are concerned, when the seller completes his performance with respect to the physical delivery of the goods.

7. In a shipment contract, title passes at the time and place of shipment.

8. If the contract requires that the seller deliver at the destination, title will not pass until the seller has tendered the goods to the buyer at that point.

Good-faith purchasers

1. A purchaser of goods usually acquires at least as good a title as the seller possessed.

2. A good-faith purchaser for value may acquire a better title than the seller had if the seller's title was voidable.

RISK OF LOSS

Breach of contract cases

1. If the contract has been breached, the loss will be borne by the party who has breached. Thus, if the seller has tendered or delivered goods that are "non-conforming," the seller bears the risk of loss.

2. If the buyer breaches the contract at a time when the seller has identified proper goods to the contract, the risk of loss is on the buyer for a reasonable time.

No breach cases

1. If a contract between buyer and seller provides for shipment by carrier under a shipment contract (F.O.B. shipping point), the risk of loss passes to the buyer when the goods are delivered to the carrier.

2. If shipment is made under a destination contract (F.O.B. destination), risk of loss does not pass to the buyer until the goods arrive at the destination and are available to the buyer for delivery.

3. It is presumed that a contract is one of shipment, not destination, and that the buyer should bear the risk of loss until arrival, unless the seller has specifically agreed to do so or the circumstances indicate such an obligation.

4. If the goods are represented by a negotiable document of title, risk of loss passes to the buyer when the document is tendered.

5. In all cases other than shipment and bailment contracts, the passage of risk of loss to the buyer depends upon the status of the seller. If the seller is a merchant, risk of loss will not pass to the buyer until he receives the goods, which means "takes physical possession of them."

6. A nonmerchant seller transfers the risk of loss by tendering the goods.

CASES

Osterholt v. St. Charles Drilling Co.
500 F. Supp. 529 (Ill. law 1980)

Osterholt, a property owner, sued St. Charles Drilling Co. for breach of contract to install a well and water system.

FILIPPINE, J . . . The parties have not addressed the possibility that the Uniform Commercial Code, as adopted by Illinois, governs this case. The Court has given strong consideration to that possibility, but has concluded that the contract at issue was primarily a service contract, with a sale of goods incidental thereto, rather than vice versa.

At least one Illinois appellate court has adopted a "predominant factor in the contract" test, developed in *Bonebrake v. Cox*, 499 F.2d 951 (8th Cir. 1974), to determine the applicability of the U.C.C. *Bonebrake v. Cox* involved a contract to sell and install specified items of used equipment in a bowling alley that had been damaged by fire. The Court held that the contract fell within the (Iowa) Uniform Commercial Code, rejecting the decision below that because the contract was "mixed" (for goods and services), the U.C.C. did not govern. The Court held that the U.C.C. did apply because the

items to be installed fell within the U.C.C.'s definition of "goods" and because the language of the contract was essentially that of a sales contract. The Court formulated the following general test of the U.C.C.'s applicability: "The test for inclusion or exclusion is not whether [contracts] are mixed, but, granting that they are mixed, whether their predominant factor, their thrust, their purpose, reasonably stated, is the rendition of service, with goods incidentally involved (e.g., contract with artist for painting) or is a transaction of sale, with labor incidentally involved (e.g., installation of a water heater in a bathroom)." The Seventh Circuit, in a case governed by Illinois law, approved the *Bonebrake* test and held that a contract for the construction of a one-million-gallon water tank fell within the U.C.C.

This court finds that the transaction between the parties in the instant case falls on the "service" side of the *Bonebrake* test, for two reasons: . . . (First), the parties had no agreement specifying the various component parts of the "water system" which were to be installed. The defendant was not bound to use specified items of "goods" in the water system. . . . Essentially, defendant undertook to install a "water system" of indefinite description but with a certain warranted capacity, rather than to install a detailed list of specific "goods." Therefore, not only was the contract essentially for defendant's services, but the component parts did not become identified to the contract until they were actually installed on plaintiff's property, and thus it is doubtful that they fell within the definition of "goods."

Secondly, the language of the instant contract is unmistakably that of service rather than of sale. Defendant is identified as the "contractor," and the contract acknowledges "an express mechanics lien . . . to secure the amount of contract or repairs."

Thus, the Court concludes that the U.C.C. does not, strictly speaking, govern this case.

So ordered.

Landrum v. Devenport
616 S.W.2d 359 (Tex. 1981)

Landrum, a collector of automobiles, was interested in buying a limited edition Chevrolet Corvette from Devenport. Devenport told him that the price would be the sticker price, $14,000 to $18,000. The car arrived in May of 1978 and carried a sticker price of $14,688.21. By the time it was delivered, the demand for the car had increased to the point where the market price exceeded the sticker price. Devenport demanded $22,000, but Landrum offered to pay the sticker price. Landrum sued, but the trial court ruled that he take nothing. He appealed.

CORNELIUS, J. . . . The evidence at least raised a fact issue on the existence of a valid contract. Joe Devenport testified that the agreed price was to be the market value of the car at the time of delivery, but Jimmy Landrum testified that the agreed price was to be the car's sticker price,

and the jury could reasonably have found that to be the fact. If both parties agreed on a price, the failure to insert that agreed price in the written contract did not invalidate the agreement under the circumstances present here.

Neither did the parol evidence or integration rule prohibit proof of the actual price. When a writing appears obviously incomplete, as when it is silent on a point which would normally be expressed, it may be completed by extrinsic proof of the omitted term. Even if the price was not agreed upon the agreement may still constitute a valid and binding contract if both parties intended to be bound and there is a reasonably certain basis for giving an appropriate remedy. The fact that both parties here signed the agreement, which was complete in all respects except specification of the price, is some evidence that they intended to be bound. The question of price then, whether a specific figure or a reasonable price, was a question for the jury upon the evidence.

Reversed and remanded.

Holstein v. Greenwich Yacht Sales, Inc.
404 A.2d 842 (R.I. 1979)

This is a civil action to determine who has the superior claim to a 27-foot sailless sailboat. The claimants are Holstein and Gladych. Greenwich is in the business of selling boats. Holstein, a specialist in marine financing, agreed to floor plan boats for Greenwich. Among the boats financed was a "1976 Newport 27, Hull No. 551, Serial No. CPY27551M77A, complete with sails and appurtenances."

Greenwich executed a promissory note and a security agreement covering this boat as collateral. A financing statement was duly recorded on September 29, 1976. However, the day before the filing,

on September 28, Gladych and Greenwich had signed a purchase-and-sale agreement which specifically identified the boat as the "Newport 27 #551." Gladych signed the contract without knowledge of the financing agreement between Holstein and Greenwich. Gladych paid for the boat.

The agreement called for the supplying of "optional equipment," which included such items as sails, a bow pulpit, lifelines, a stern rail, winches, a head, and a bilge pump. Also listed as optional extras were "commissioning in spring" and "winter storage."

On February 3, 1977, Greenwich was in default on a series of promissory notes held by Holstein. Upon learning that Greenwich was selling boats in violation of their security agreements, Holstein instituted this civil action seeking to repossess the security. At that time Hull No. 551 was still in Greenwich's yard.

KELLEHER, J. . . . The trial justice ruled that Gladych was not a buyer in the ordinary course of business because "there was no sale and no passage of title." Consequently, the trial justice ruled that Holstein could repossess. We disagree.

The Code provides in its pertinent part: "A buyer in ordinary course of business . . . takes free of a security interest created by his seller even though the security interest is perfected and even though the buyer knows of its existence." . . . Holstein contended before us, . . . that Gladych could not be classified as a buyer because . . . "Title to goods cannot pass under a contract for sale prior to their identification to the contract. . . .

In arguing no identification, Holstein places great emphasis on the undisputed fact that at the time Gladych and Greenwich executed the purchase agreement, none of the optional equipment had been installed on or within the hull. The trial justice, in relying on the lack of identification, observed that "[o]ther things had to be done by the seller in order to put this boat in a condition whereby delivery would be made and title would pass and those things have not been done even to this day. Therefore, I am satisfied that Gladych's contract to purchase the vessel involved did not ripen into a sale. . . ." We disagree with the trial justice's conclusion.

Section 6A–2–501 recognizes that from the moment when goods are identified to a contract of sale, the buyer has a "special property . . . interest" which may arise before the passage of title or the seller's delivery of the goods. This section makes it clear that if the contract is for a sale of goods already existing and identified, identification occurs when the contract is made, or if the contract relates to the sale of future goods, the goods are identifiable when they are shipped, marked, or otherwise designated by the seller as goods to which the contract refers.

In clear and unmistakable language, the drafters of the Code have stated that there is no necessity that goods, to be identifiable, have to be in a deliverable state. Specifically, comment 4 to §6A–2–501 reads:

> In view of the limited function of identification there is no requirement in this section that the goods be in deliverable state or that all of the seller's duties with respect to the processing of the goods be completed in order that identification occur.

We believe that the evidence indicates that the 27-foot boat was identified to the contract at the time the purchase-and-sale agreement was executed on September 28, 1976. The sales contract between Gladych and Greenwich clearly specified the existing "Newport-27 #551." The fact that the boat was not outfitted with all its extras does not bar its identification to the contract. . . .

Gladych viewed the Newport-27 at Greenwich's yard, and the parties specifically referred to it as hull "#551" in the sales contract. This evidence, in our opinion, is sufficient to identify the specific boat to the contract at the time the contract was made. Consequently, . . . Gladych on September 28 obtained a special property interest in and to Hull No. 551 that was superior to the security interest held by Holstein.

Holstein, . . . also argues that . . . Gladych's claim must fail because there was no passage of title since the boat had not been delivered. The Code makes it possible for an individual to become a buyer at the time of identification rather than at the time of delivery. A buyer need not take possession to be a buyer in the ordinary course. . . .

Reversed.

First Nat. Bank & Trust v. Ohio Cas. Ins. Co.
244 N.W.2d 209 (Neb. 1976)

Fernandez owned a 1973 Cadillac insured by the defendant insurance company. On December 10, 1972 it was stolen, and on January 9, 1973 the company paid Fernandez $8,400 for the loss of the car. Fernandez assigned his title to the insurance company who obtained a new certificate in its name.

On December 26, 1972 a Nebraska certificate of title to the car was issued, based upon a forged Arizona certificate of title. The plaintiff bank loaned money on the car and had its lien (security interest) shown on the Nebraska certificate of title. Having obtained information from the F.B.I., the defendant on January 24, 1974, by using self-help repossession, removed the vehicle to California and sold it for $5,500. Plaintiff bank sued the defendant insurance company for the $5,500 and the trial court found for the plaintiff.

BRODKEY, J. . . . The sole issue in this case is whether First National, having noted its lien on the Nebraska certificate of title, acquired rights superior to Ohio Casualty, in view of the fact First National's chain of title originated in a thief. The District Court answered this question in the affirmative. We disagree and reverse. . . .

[A certificate of title] does not . . . create title where none exists, nor does it give a transferee greater title than that of his transferor. . . . A thief with a certificate of title to a stolen automobile does not divest the owner of his right to take it wherever he can find it. A certificate of title is essential to convey the title of an automobile, but it is not conclusive of ownership. It is simply the exclusive method provided by statute for the transfer of title to a motor vehicle. It conveys no greater interest than the grantor actually possesses. . . .

When the property underlying the certificate of title has been obtained by illegal means, a distinction has been made between stolen property and that acquired by fraud. . . . One obtaining property by larceny cannot convey good title even to an innocent purchaser for value, but one obtaining property by fraud has a voidable title, and may convey that title to a bona fide purchaser who is then protected from claims of others. On the other hand, the right of an owner or an assignee of the owner to recover his stolen automobile remains open to him. . . .

In *Hardware Mut. Cas. Co. v. Gall,* 15 Ohio St.2d 261 (1968), the court held that a thief could not convey a valid title to a stolen motor vehicle to a bona fide purchaser for value without notice, although the certificate of title used in the purported transfer appeared valid on its face. . . . We agree with the Ohio Supreme Court. . . . That court in making its ruling stated "[W]e apparently must again dispel the erroneous notion that whoever first obtains an apparently valid Ohio certificate of title will be entitled to retain possession of the automobile regardless of whether he is the real owner or a bona fide purchaser without notice, whose title derives from a thief. . . .

We hold that the true owner, and his lawful successors in interest, have rights paramount to those of a subsequent bona fide purchaser of a stolen automobile holding a Nebraska certificate of title on the vehicle based upon a chain of ownership originating with the thief of the car. . . .

Reversed and remanded.

American Lease Plans, Inc. v. Jacobs Plumbing, Heating & Air Conditioning, Inc.
260 S.E.2d 712 (S.C. 1979)

R. C. Jacobs Plumbing, Heating & Air Conditioning, Inc., . . . purchased a 1977 Dodge pickup truck from Imperial Motors, Inc. (Imperial). . . . Imperial had possession of the truck by virtue of a lease agreement with American Lease Plans, Inc., (respondent) a corporation, primarily engaged in the business of leasing automobiles, aircraft and equipment.

At the time of purchase, title to the truck was held by respondent. Some time after the sale, Imperial went out of business and appellant never received the title certificate to the vehicle. It is not disputed that appellant paid full value for the truck. The lower court awarded possession of the truck to respondent.

GREGORY, J. . . . The primary question on this appeal is whether appellant qualifies as a buyer in the ordinary course of business and is thereby entitled to the protective cloak of Section 36–2–403, subsections (2) and (3), Code of Laws of South Carolina (1976).

That section affords an innocent purchaser protection against the claim of an original owner who entrusts goods to a merchant who in turn transfers the goods by sale to the innocent purchaser. The operative subsections of Sections 36–2–403 provide:

(2) Any entrusting of possession of goods to a merchant who deals in goods of that kind gives

him power to transfer all rights of the entruster to a buyer in ordinary course of business.

(3) "Entrusting" includes any delivery and any acquiescence in retention of possession regardless of any condition expressed between the parties to the delivery or acquiescence and regardless of whether the procurement of the entrusting or the possesser's disposition of the goods have been such as to be larcenous under the criminal law.

Respondent contends that appellant is not a "buyer in the ordinary course of business.". . . §36–1–201(9) "*Buyer in ordinary course of business*" means a person who in good faith and without knowledge that the sale to him is in violation of the ownership rights or security interest of a third party in the goods buys in ordinary course from a person in the business of selling goods of that kind.

The lower court found that appellant's business experience and extensive dealings in buying and selling vehicles disqualified it as a buyer in the ordinary course. This was error. Such a ruling places a burden of inquiry upon appellant which is not required by either the statutory definition of "buyer in ordinary course of business" or Section 36–2–403. Nor do the circumstances warrant imposing such a duty.

Appellant purchased a Chrysler-manufactured product from a Chrysler Motors dealer from whom it had on a prior occasion purchased another used Dodge truck. The instant truck was displayed by Imperial on its lot adorned with sale indicia and in a fashion that would reasonably indicate that Imperial both dealt in goods of this kind and was fully empowered to sell the truck to a buyer in the ordinary course of Imperial's business.

The salesman offered the truck for purchase, and appellant instructed him to forward the title certificate to the bank with which appellant did business.

Under these circumstances, appellant's inquiry into the salability of the 1977 Dodge pickup was reasonable, as it could rightfully have presumed that Imperial was the true owner by virtue of its possession of the truck.

The fact that appellant did not demand to see the title certificate at the time of sale does not mean that appellant purchased with lack of good faith. Good faith is defined as honesty in fact in the conduct or transaction concerned. Appellant's failure to investigate proved unwise, but it does not amount to dishonesty.

Respondent argues that Imperial was to use the truck exclusively as a "shop truck," rather than as an item for sale. Thus, respondent had no knowledge of the sale of the truck to appellant. We are not persuaded that any arrangement that may have existed between respondent and Imperial is significant. . . . Imperial had the power to transfer respondent's ownership rights to appellant regardless of any condition expressed between respondent and Imperial to the delivery or acquiescence. . . .

Reversed.

Pestana v. Karinol Corp.
367 So. 2d 1096 (Fla. App. 1979)

HUBBART, J. . . . This is an action for damages based on a contract for sale of goods. The defendant seller . . . prevailed in this action. . . . The plaintiff buyer appeals.

The central issue presented for review is whether a contract for the sale of goods, which stipulates the place where the goods sold are to be sent by carrier but contains (a) no explicit provisions allocating the risk of loss while the goods are in the possession of the carrier and (b) no delivery terms such as F.O.B. place of destination, is a shipment contract or a destination contract under the Uniform Commercial Code. We hold that such a contract, without more, constitutes a shipment contract wherein the risk of loss passes to the buyer when the seller duly delivers the goods to the carrier under a reasonable contract of carriage for shipment to the buyer. Accordingly, we affirm.

The critical facts of this case are substantially undisputed. On March 4, 1975, the plaintiff . . . who was a resident of Mexico entered into a contract with the Karinol Corporation [the defendant herein]. . . . The terms of this contract were embodied in a one page invoice written in Spanish and prepared by the defendant Karinol. By the terms of this contract, the plaintiff . . . agreed to purchase 64 electronic watches from the defendant Karinol for $6,006. A notation was printed at the bottom of the contract which, translated into English, reads as follows: "Please send the merchandise in cardboard boxes duly strapped with metal bands via air parcel post to Chetumal. Documents to Banco de Commercio De Quintano Roo S.A.". . . .

(The seller delivered the watches to an airline for shipment. When the cartons arrived the watches were missing and plaintiff buyer sued for a refund of the purchase price.)

There are two types of sales contracts under Florida's Uniform Commercial Code wherein a carrier is used to transport the goods sold: a shipment contract and a destination contract. A shipment contract is considered the normal contract in which the seller is required to send the subject goods by carrier to the buyer but is not required to guarantee delivery thereof at a particular destination. Under a shipment contract, the seller, unless otherwise agreed, must: (1) put the goods sold in the possession of a carrier and make a contract for their transportation as may be reasonable having regard for the nature of the goods and other attendant circumstances, (2) obtain and promptly deliver or tender in due form any document necessary to enable the buyer to obtain possession of the goods or otherwise required by the agreement or by usage of the trade, and (3) promptly notify the buyer of the shipment. On a shipment contract, the risk of loss passes to the buyer when the goods sold are duly delivered to the carrier for shipment to the buyer.

A destination contract, on the other hand, is considered the variant contract in which the seller specifically agrees to deliver the goods sold to the buyer at a particular destination and to bear the risk of loss of the goods until tender of delivery. This can be accomplished by express provision in the sales contract to that effect or by the use of delivery terms such as F.O.B. (place of destination). Under a destination contract, the seller is required to tender delivery of the goods sold to the buyer at the place of destination. The risk of loss under such a contract passes to the buyer when the goods sold are duly tendered to the buyer at the place of destination while in the possession of the carrier so as to enable the buyer to take delivery. The parties must explicitly agree to a destination contract; otherwise the contract will be considered a shipment contract.

Where the risk of loss falls on the seller at the time the goods sold are lost or destroyed, the seller is liable in damages to the buyer for non-delivery unless the seller tenders a performance in replacement for the lost or destroyed goods. On the other hand, where the risk of loss falls on the buyer at the time the goods sold are lost or destroyed, the buyer is liable to the seller for the purchase price of the goods sold.

In the instant case, we deal with the normal shipment contract involving the sale of goods. . . . There was no specific provision in the contract between the parties which allocated the risk of loss on the goods sold while in transit. In addition, there were no delivery terms such as F.O.B. Chetumal contained in the contract.

All agree that . . . Karinol performed its obligations as a seller under the Uniform Commercial Code if this contract is considered a shipment contract. Karinol put the goods sold in the possession of a carrier and made a contract for the goods safe transportation to the plaintiff's decedent; Karinol also promptly notified the plaintiff's decedent of the shipment and tendered to said party the necessary documents to obtain possession of the goods sold.

The plaintiff . . . contends, however, that the contract herein is a destination contract in which the risk of loss on the goods sold did not pass until delivery on such goods had been tendered to him at Chetumal, Mexico—an event which never occurred. He relies for this position on the notation at the bottom of the contract between the parties which provides that the goods were to be sent to Chetumal, Mexico. We cannot agree. A "send to" or "ship to" term is a part of every contract involving the sale of goods where carriage is contemplated and has no significance in determining whether the contract is a shipment or destination contract for risk of loss purposes. As such, the "send to" term contained in this contract cannot, without more, convert this into a destination contract.

It therefore follows that the risk of loss in this case shifted to the plaintiff . . . as buyer when the defendant Karinol as seller duly delivered the goods . . . for shipment. . . .

Affirmed.

REVIEW QUESTIONS

1. Identify the terms in column A by matching each with the appropriate statement in column B.

A	B
1. Merchant	**a.** Sale on consignment.
2. C.I.F.	**b.** A term used in shipment by merchant vessel.
3. Bill of lading	**c.** Buyer has the risk of loss if the goods are destroyed.
4. Sale or return	**d.** A requirement for title to pass.
5. Shipment contract	**e.** A farmer in many states.
6. F.A.S.	**f.** The buyer pays the cost of insuring the goods.
7. Sale on approval	**g.** Contract of shipment by a common carrier.
8. Identification	**h.** May acquire a better title than his transferor had.
9. Good-faith purchaser	**i.** This is not covered by Article 2 of the Code.
10. Organ transplant	**j.** Buyer's creditors have no claim on the goods in this transaction.

2. A seller of goods sued the buyer for the purchase price. The contract contained no F.O.B. terms. After the goods were delivered to the carrier for shipment, they were destroyed. The contract was silent on the risk of loss. Who has the risk of loss? Explain.

3. Paschal was the owner of an automobile and advertised it for sale. A prospective buyer made an offer that was accepted. The buyer gave a check to Paschal in exchange for the car and title. Subsequently the check was dishonored. The car was resold to a good-faith purchaser. Is Paschal entitled to recover the car? Why?

4. A package liquor store operator was in the practice of paying for large quantities of liquor in advance in order to take advantage of quantity discounts. He would then order the liquor as needed. A supplier was having financial difficulties, and the operator seized a large amount of undelivered liquor. The supplier went into bankruptcy, and the trustee in bankruptcy claimed the liquor. He contended that the operator did not have title to the liquor. Was the trustee in bankruptcy correct? Explain.

5. Royster agreed to buy at least 31,000 tons of phosphate for 3 years from Columbia. When market conditions changed, Royster ordered only a fraction of the minimum and sought to renegotiate the deal. Columbia refused and sued. At trial, Royster wanted to introduce two forms of proof: (1) a usage of trade that express price and quantity terms in such contracts were never considered in the trade as more than mere projections, to be adjusted according to market forces; (2) course of dealing over a 6-year period, which showed repeated and substantial deviations from the stated quantities or prices in other written contracts between the parties. Is the evidence admissable? Explain.

6. Pam sued an oil company to recover personal property obtained by the oil company under an alleged option contract. The purported contract gave the buyer the right to purchase the property at Pam's cost, less depreciation to be mutually agreed upon. The parties failed to agree on the amount of depreciation, and Pam claimed that, as a result, there was no valid agreement. Is she correct? Why?

7. Adams delivered stereo tapes, cartridges, and stereo equipment to a service station operator for resale. Adams' salesman had written on the invoice, "Terms 30-60-90. This equipment will be picked up if not sold in 90 days." The service station was burglarized about two weeks later, and the stereo equipment was stolen. Who must bear the loss resulting from the burglary? Explain.

8. Peter, a seller of a mobile home, sued David, the buyer, for the price of the home. After they had executed the contract of sale, the mobile home was stolen from Peter's lot. What is the result? Why?

9. Tom entered into a contract to sell Jack 20 acres of sod for $1,000 per acre. Jack was allowed to remove it any time during the next 12-month period. Is the contract governed by the Uniform Commercial Code? Explain.

10. A contract required a subcontractor to supply labor, materials, and equipment for constructing and finishing concrete structures. Is this contract subject to the Uniform Commercial Code? Explain.

11. The Macon Whoopies, a newly formed hockey club, contracts to buy 150 hockey pucks from a wholesaler in Youngstown, Ohio. What are the wholesaler's delivery obligations if the agreement states: (a) F.O.B. Macon? (b) F.O.B. Youngstown? (c) C.I.F. Macon? (d) Ship to Macon Whoopies, Macon, Georgia?

12. A sporting goods manufacturer contracts to sell 200 basketballs to a pro team. The contract does not contain any terms regarding delivery. What are the manufacturer's delivery obligations?

13. On February 11, plaintiff entered into a written contract to buy three sprinkler systems from the defendant. The seller orally agreed to deliver by the middle of May. The written contract contained no designated delivery date. The seller did not deliver by May 15, and plaintiff claimed a crop loss of $75,000 because of the late delivery. Is oral evidence admissible to show the agreed-upon date of delivery? Explain.

24 BREACH AND REMEDIES

The law recognizes that each party to a contract for the sale of goods has certain rights and obligations unless the contract legally eliminates them. In addition, the Code has several provisions relating to the remedies of buyer and seller in the event of a breach of the contract by the other party. There is one provision applicable to both parties. This is known as *adequate assurance.*

As a general rule, a seller is obligated to deliver or tender delivery of goods that measure up to the requirements of the contract and to do so at the proper time and at the proper place. The goods and other performance of the seller must "conform" to the contract [2-106(2)].

The seller is required to tender delivery as a condition to the buyer's duty to accept the goods and pay for them [2-507(1)]. Thus, the seller has performed when he has made the goods available to the buyer. The buyer, in turn, must render his performance, which means he must accept the goods and pay for them.

The parties may, in their agreement, limit or modify the remedies available to each other. The measure of damages may be limited or altered. The agreement may limit the buyer's remedies to return of the goods for refund or replacement of the goods or parts.

The parties may limit or exclude consequential damages, and such limitations and exclusions will be enforced if they are not unconscionable [2-719(3)]. A limitation of consequential damages for injury to the person in the case of *consumer goods* is prima facie unconscionable, but limitations where the loss is commercial are not presumed to be unfair.

These rights and remedies are examined in the sections that follow. Keep in mind that these sections cover sales contracts that are silent on the matter under discussion.

1. Adequate Assurance

A concept applicable to both parties in a sales transaction is known as adequate assurance. Under certain circumstances, either party may be concerned about the other's future performance. If a buyer is in arrears on other payments, the seller will naturally be concerned about making further deliveries. Or a buyer may discover that the seller has been delivering faulty goods to other customers and will be fearful that the goods that he is to receive may also be defective. The law recognizes that no one wants to buy a lawsuit and that merely having the right to sue for breach of contract is a somewhat "hollow" remedy. There is a need to protect the party whose reasonable expectation of due performance is jeopardized.

The Code grants this protection by providing that the contract for sale imposes an obligation on each party that the other's expectation of receiving due performances will not be impaired [2-609]. A party who has reasonable grounds for insecurity about the other's performance can demand in writing that the other offer convincing proof that he will, in fact, perform. Having made the demand, he may then suspend his own performance until he receives assurance. If none is forthcoming within a reasonable time, not to exceed 30 days, he may treat the contract as repudiated [2-609(2)].

Two factual problems are presented. What are reasonable grounds for insecurity? What constitutes an adequate assurance of performance? The Code does not particularize but does provide that between merchants, commercial standards shall be applied to answer these questions [2-609(2)]. In the event of a dispute, these are questions of fact for a jury.

2. Checklist of Code Remedies

Two sections of the Code [2-703 and 2-711] list the remedies of the seller and the remedies of the buyer. Each section provides both parties with four remedies, which are exact counterparts. Table 24–1 shows their significant correlation.

TABLE 24–1

Comparison of code remedies

SELLER'S REMEDIES [2-703]	BUYER'S REMEDIES [2-711]
1. Resell the goods and recover damages [2-706].	1. Cover (buy same goods elsewhere) and recover damages [2-712].
2. Cancel the contract.	2. Reject the contract.
3. Recover damages for nonacceptance [2-708].	3. Recover damages for nondelivery [2-713].
4. Sue for the actual price of the goods [2-709].	4. Sue to get the goods (specific performance or replevin) [2-716].

The four remedies are listed in the Code not only as equivalent actions, but also as equivalent in order of importance. The Code assumes that upon a breach by the buyer, the seller will resell the goods and sue the buyer for any difference between the resale price and the original contract price. When the seller breaches, the Code assumes that the buyer will cover by buying substitute goods and sue the seller for any difference between the cover price and the original contract price.

Obviously, before either party has one of the four remedies, the other party must have breached the contract. There are at least four possible situations in which either party may be in breach of contract.

   1. *Anticipatory repudiation* by the buyer or by the seller.

   2. *Failure of performance* (buyer fails to pay or seller fails to deliver).

   3. A rightful or wrongful *rejection* by the buyer.

   4. A rightful or wrongful *revocation of acceptance* by the buyer.

Anticipatory repudiation and failure to perform are discussed in chapter 12. This chapter will consider the buyer's right to reject and right to revoke acceptance. If these rights are exercised properly by the buyer, the seller has breached the sales contract. If the rejection or revocation of acceptance are wrongfully exercised, the buyer has breached the contract.

BUYER'S RIGHTS AND REMEDIES

3. Right to Inspect

The buyer has a right before payment or acceptance to inspect the goods at any reasonable time and place and in any reasonable manner [2-513(1)].[1] The place for the inspection is determined by the nature of the contract. If the seller is to send the goods to the buyer, the inspection may be postponed until after arrival of the goods.

If the contract provides for delivery C.O.D., the buyer must pay prior to inspection. Likewise, payment must be made prior to inspection if the contract calls for payment against documents of title [2-513(3)]. When the buyer is required to make payment prior to inspection, the payment does not impair his right to pursue remedies if subsequent inspection reveals defects [2-512].

The buyer must pay the expenses of inspection, but he can recover his expenses from the seller if the inspection reveals that the goods are nonconforming and he therefore rejects them [2-513(2)].

4. Right to Reject

If the goods or the tender of delivery fails to conform to the contract, the buyer has the right to reject them. Several options are available. The buyer may reject the whole, or he may accept either the whole or any commercial unit or units and reject the rest [2-601]. A *commercial unit* is one that is generally regarded as a single whole for purposes of sale, one that would be impaired in value if divided [2-105(6)]. When the buyer accepts nonconforming goods, he does not impair his right of recourse against the seller. Provided that he notifies the seller of the breach within a reasonable time, he may still pursue his remedy for damages for breach of contract, even though he accepts the goods.

5. Notice of Rejection

The right to reject defective or nonconforming goods is dependent on the buyer's taking action within a reasonable time after the goods are tendered or delivered to him. If the buyer rejects, he must seasonably notify the seller of this fact. Failing to do so would render the rejection ineffective and constitute an acceptance [2-602(1)]. If the buyer continues in possession of defective goods for an unreasonable time, he forfeits his right to reject them.[2]

---

[1] G&H Land & Cattle Co. v. Heitzman & Nelson, Inc., p. 542.

[2] Conn. Inv. Casting Corp. v. Made-Rite Tool Co., Inc., p. 543.

The requirement of seasonable notice of rejection is very important. Without such notice, the rejection is ineffective [2-602(1)]. As a general rule, a notice of rejection may simply state that the goods are not conforming, without particular specification of the defects relied upon by the buyer. If, however, the defect could have been corrected by the seller had he been given particularized notice, then the failure to particularize will take away from the buyer the right to rely upon that defect as a breach justifying a rejection [2-605(1)(a)]. Therefore, a buyer should always give detailed information relative to the reason for the rejection.

In transactions between merchants, the merchant seller is entitled to demand a full and final written statement of all the defects. If the statement is not forthcoming after a written request for it, the buyer may not rely upon these defects to justify his rejection or to establish that a breach has occurred [2-605(1)(b)].

6. Rights and Duties on Rejection

A buyer who rejects the goods after taking physical possession of them is required to hold the goods with reasonable care long enough for the seller to remove them [2-602(2)(b)]. Somewhat greater obligations are imposed upon a merchant buyer who rejects goods that have been delivered to him [2-603]. The merchant is under a duty to follow the seller's reasonable instructions as to the disposition of the goods. If the seller does not furnish instructions as to the disposition of the rejected goods, the merchant buyer must make reasonable efforts to sell them for the seller's account if they are perishable or if they threaten to decline in value speedily. If a sale is not mandatory for the reasons just stated, the buyer has three options. He may store the rejected goods for the seller's account, reship them to the seller, or resell them for the seller's account [2-604].

Code section 2-711(3) gives a buyer a security interest in the goods in his possession and the right to resell them. Thus, a buyer of defective goods can reject and resell the goods, deduct all expenses regarding care, custody, resale, and other matters (such as the down payment), and then remit any money left over to the seller [2-604 and 2-711(3)].

7. Right to Revoke Acceptance

The buyer has *accepted* goods if (1) after a reasonable opportunity to inspect them, he indicates to the seller that the goods are conforming or that he will take or retain them in spite of their nonconformity, (2) he has failed to make an effective rejection of the goods, or (3) he does any act inconsistent with the seller's ownership [2-606].

The buyer may revoke his acceptance under certain circumstances. In many instances, the buyer will have accepted nonconforming goods because the defect was not immediately discoverable or he reasonably assumed that the seller would correct by substituting goods that did conform. In either case, the buyer has the privilege of "revoking" his acceptance by notifying the seller if but only if the nonconformity "substantially impairs the value to him"[2-608(1)].

Revocation must take place within a reasonable time after the buyer has discovered, or should have discovered, the reason for revocation [2-608(2)].[3] If a

---

[3] Newmaster v. Southeast Equipment, Inc., p. 544.

buyer revokes his acceptance, he is then placed in the same position with reference to the goods as if he had rejected them in the first instance [2-608(3)]. He has a security interest in the goods for the payments made and is entitled to damages, as if no acceptance had occurred.

8. Right to Cover

The buyer who has not received the goods he bargained for may *cover*— arrange to purchase the goods he needs from some other source in substitution for those due from the seller [2-712]. This is a practical remedy, as the buyer must often proceed without delay in order to obtain goods needed for his own use or for resale. The buyer must act reasonably and in good faith in arranging for the cover [2-712(1)]. A rental is not a reasonable substitute for a purchase.[4]

A buyer may collect from a seller the difference between what he paid for the substitute goods and the contract price [2-712(2)]. He may also collect any incidental and consequential damages. *Incidental* damages are defined as those that are reasonably incurred while handling rejected goods. These damages include "commercially reasonable charges, expenses or commissions in connection with effecting cover and any other reasonable expense incident to the delay or other breach" [2-715(1)]. *Consequential* damages include "any loss resulting from general or particular requirements and needs of which the seller at the time of contracting had reason to know and which could not reasonably be prevented by cover or otherwise" [2-715(2)]. The buyer is obligated to keep his damages to a minimum by making an appropriate cover insofar as his right to any consequential damages is concerned.

The cover remedy has the advantage of providing certainty as to the amount of the buyer's damages. The difference between the contract price and the price paid by the buyer for substitute goods can be readily determined. Although the buyer must act reasonably and in good faith, he need not prove that he obtained the goods at the cheapest price available.

9. Rights to Damages for Nondelivery

The aggrieved buyer who did not receive any goods from the seller or who received nonconforming goods is not required to cover; instead, he may bring an action for damages [2-712(3)]. The measure of damages for nondelivery or repudiation is the difference between the contract price and the market price when the buyer learned of the breach [2-713]. The buyer is also entitled to any incidental or consequential damages sustained. Damages to which a buyer is entitled consist of "the loss resulting in the ordinary course of events from the seller's breach as determined in any manner which is reasonable" [2-714(1)]. In a purchase for resale, it would be appropriate to measure the buyer's damage upon nondelivery as the difference between the contract price and the price at which the goods were to be resold. In other words, the damages equal the difference between the contract price and the fair market value of the goods.

---

[4] McGinnis v. Wentworth Chevrolet Co., p. 545.

Another recourse open to the buyer is the right to deduct damages from any part of the price still due under the same contract [2-717]. The buyer determines what his damages are and withholds this amount when he pays the seller. He is required to give notice to the seller of his intention to deduct. When the buyer's damages are established by the cover price, the amount is clear-cut. In other instances, the seller might question the amount of the deduction, and this dispute would have to be resolved between the parties or by a court.

Damages may be deducted only from the price due under the same contract. A buyer could not deduct damages for goods under one contract from the price due under other contracts from the same seller.

10. Right to the Goods

Under proper circumstances, a buyer has rights in, and to, the actual goods purchased. The remedy of specific performance is available (1) when the goods are unique and (2) when other circumstances make it equitable that the seller render the required performance [2-716(1)]. To obtain specific performance, the buyer must have been unable to cover. The Code does not define "unique," but it is fair to assume that it would encompass output and requirement contracts in which the goods were not readily or practically available from other sources. Even if the goods are not unique, the Code provides that the buyer may recover them under "proper circumstances." When a buyer cannot practically buy the goods elsewhere, a proper circumstance for specific performance probably exists.

Another remedy that enables the buyer to reach the goods in the hands of the seller is the statutory remedy of replevin. *Replevin* is an action to recover the goods that one person wrongfully withholds from another. A buyer has the right to replevin goods from the seller if the goods have been *identified* to the contract and the buyer is unable to effect cover after making a reasonable effort to do so [2-716(3)].

A related remedy that also reaches the goods in the hands of the seller is the buyer's right to recover them if the seller becomes insolvent [2-502]. The right exists only if (1) the buyer has a "special property" in the goods (that is, existing goods have been identified to the contract), and (2) the seller becomes insolvent within 10 days after he received the first installment payment from the buyer. Without these circumstances, the buyer is relegated to the position of a general creditor of the seller. It is apparent that if the buyer can recover the goods, he is in a much better position than he would be as a general creditor, particularly if he had paid a substantial amount of the purchase price. To exercise this remedy, the buyer must make and keep good a tender of any unpaid portion of the price.

11. Introduction

SELLER'S RIGHTS AND REMEDIES

The Code establishes certain rights and remedies for sellers just as it does for buyers. A seller has several alternative courses of action when a buyer breaches the contract. One of the most significant rights is to "cure" a defective performance. The seller may cancel the contract if the buyer's breach is material. Under certain circumstances, a seller may withhold delivery or stop delivery if the goods are in transit. A seller also has the right to resell the goods and recover damages or simply to recover damages for the buyer's failure to accept the goods. Finally, the seller may, under certain circumstances, file suit to recover the price of the goods. The remedies of the seller are cumulative and not exclusive. The technical aspects of "cure" and of these remedies are discussed in the sections that follow.

12. Cure

Upon inspecting the goods, if the buyer finds that they do not conform to the contract, he may reject them, providing he acts fairly in doing so. If the rejection is for a relatively minor deviation from the contract requirements, the seller must be given an opportunity to correct the defective performance. This is called *cure*. The seller may accomplish this by notifying the buyer of his intention to cure, then tendering proper or conforming goods if the time for performance has not expired. If the time for performance has expired, the seller—if he has reasonable grounds to believe that the goods will be acceptable in spite of the nonconformity—will be granted further time to substitute goods that are in accordance with the contract. The main purpose of this rule allowing cure is to protect the seller from being forced into a breach by a surprise rejection at the last moment by the buyer. The seller, in order to take advantage of this privilege, must notify the buyer of his intention to cure.

13. Right to Reclaim from an Insolvent Buyer

If a seller discovers that a buyer who has been extended credit is insolvent, the seller will want to withhold delivery before it is completed. An insolvent buyer is one "who either has ceased to pay his debts in the ordinary course of business or cannot pay his debts as they become due or is insolvent within the meaning of the federal bankruptcy law" [1-201(23)].

A seller, upon discovering that a buyer is insolvent, may refuse to make any further deliveries except for cash, and he may demand that payment be made for all goods previously delivered under the contract [2-702(1)]. If goods are en route to the buyer, they may be stopped in transit and recovered from the carrier [2-705]. If they are in a warehouse or other place of storage awaiting delivery to the buyer, the seller may stop delivery by the bailee. Thus, the seller can protect his interests by retaining or reclaiming the goods prior to the time they come into the possession of the insolvent buyer.

This right to reclaim the goods on the buyer's insolvency includes situations in which the goods have come into the buyer's possession. If the buyer has received goods on credit while he is insolvent, the seller can reclaim the goods by making a demand for them within 10 days after their receipt by the buyer [2-702(2)]. By receiving the goods, the buyer has, in effect, made a representation that he is solvent and able to pay for them. If the buyer has made a written misrepresentation of solvency within the 3-month period before the goods were delivered to him, and the seller has justifiably relied on the writing, the 10-day limitation period during which the seller can reclaim the goods from the insolvent buyer does not restrict the seller's right of reclamation.[5] [2-702(2)].

---

[5] In Re Bel Air Carpets, Inc., p. 546.

The importance to a seller of the privilege of reclaiming goods or stopping them in transit should be obvious. If the insolvent buyer is adjudicated a bankrupt, the goods will become a part of the debtor's estate and will be sold by the trustee in bankruptcy for the benefit of *all* the creditors of the buyer. If the seller is able to reclaim the goods, his loss will be kept to a minimum.

14. Right to Reclaim Goods from a Solvent Buyer

The right to stop goods in transit or to withhold delivery is not restricted to the insolvency situation. If the buyer has (1) wrongfully rejected a tender of goods, (2) revoked his acceptance, (3) failed to make a payment due on or before delivery, or (4) repudiated with respect to either a part of the goods or the whole contract, the seller can also reclaim the goods. This right extends to any goods directly affected by the breach.

To stop delivery by a carrier, the seller must give proper and timely notice to the carrier, so that there is reasonable time to follow the instructions [2-705(3)]. Once the goods have been received by the buyer, or a bailee has acknowledged that he holds the goods for the buyer, the right of stoppage is at an end. Only in the case of insolvency [2-705(2)] can the seller reclaim the goods after they are in the buyer's possession.

The right to stop delivery to a solvent buyer is restricted to carload, truckload, planeload, or larger shipments. This restriction is designed to ease the burden on carriers that could develop if the right to stop for reasons other than insolvency applied to all small shipments. The seller who is shipping to a buyer of doubtful credit can always send the goods C.O.D., and thus preclude the necessity for stopping in transit. Of course, the seller must exercise care in availing himself of this remedy, as improper stoppage is a breach by the seller and would subject him to an action for damages by the buyer.

15. Right to Resell Goods

The seller who is in possession of goods at the time of the buyer's breach has the right to resell the goods [2-706]. If part of the goods has been delivered, he can resell the undelivered portion. In this way the seller can quickly realize at least some of the amount due from the buyer. He also has a claim against the buyer for the difference between the resale price and the price the buyer had agreed to pay. The resale remedy thus affords a practical method and course of action for the seller who has possession of goods that were intended for a breaching buyer. Any person in the position of a seller of goods has the right to resell the goods when a buyer defaults.

Frequently, a buyer will breach or repudiate the contract prior to the time that goods have been identified to the contract. This occurs when goods are in the process of manufacture. This does not defeat the seller's right to resell the goods. The seller may proceed to identify goods to the contract [2-704(1)(a)] and then use his remedy of resale. When the goods are unfinished, the seller may also use his remedy of resale if he can show that the unfinished goods were intended for the particular contract [2-704(1)(b)]. The seller may also resell the unfinished goods for scrap or salvage value, or take any other reasonable action in connection with the goods [2-704(2)]. The only requirement is that the seller use reasonable commercial judgment in determining which course of action he will take in order to mitigate his damages. Presumably he would take into consideration factors such as the extent to which the manufacture had been completed and the resalability of the goods if he elected to complete the manufacture. Thus, the law allows the seller to proceed in a commercially reasonable manner in order to protect his interests.

When the seller elects to use his remedy of resale, the resale may be either a private sale or a public (auction) sale [2-706(2)]. The resale must be identified as one relating to the broken contract. If the resale is private, the seller must give the buyer reasonable notification of his intention to resell [2-706(3)]. If the resale is public, the seller must give the buyer reasonable notice of the time and place, so that the buyer can bid or can obtain the attendance of other bidders. With goods that are perishable or threaten to decline speedily in value, the notice is not required. The seller is permitted to buy at a public sale. The prime requirement is that the sale be conducted in a commercially reasonable manner [2-706(2)]. If the resale brings a higher price than that provided for in the contract, the seller is not accountable to the buyer for any profit [2-706(6)].

16. Right to Collect Damages—In General

In many situations, a resale would not be an appropriate or sufficient remedy. The seller may elect to bring an action for damages if the buyer refuses to accept the goods or repudiates the contract [2-708]. The measure of damages is the difference between the market price at the place for tender and the unpaid contract price, plus incidental damages [2-708]. Incidental damages include expenses reasonably incurred as a result of the buyer's breach [2-710].

Usually, this measure of damages will not put the seller in as good a position as he would have had if the buyer had performed and the seller had not lost the sale. Under such circumstances, the measure of damages includes the profit the seller would have made from full performance by the buyer [2-708(2)], as well as incidental damages. In computing profit, the reasonable overhead of the seller may be taken into account. The measure of damages recognizes that a seller suffers a loss, even though he may ultimately resell for the same amount that he would have received from the buyer. He has lost a sale and the profit on that sale.

17. Right to Collect the Purchase Price

When the buyer fails to pay the price as it becomes due, the seller may sue for the contract price of the goods if the buyer has accepted the goods; the goods were destroyed after risk of loss passed to the buyer; or the resale remedy is not practical. If goods are specially manufactured for a buyer and there is no market for the special goods, the seller may collect the purchase price, since his right to resell is not available.[6]

If the seller sues for the price, the goods are held by the seller on behalf of the buyer. In effect, the goods are to be treated as if they belong to the buyer. After the seller obtains a judgment against the buyer, the seller may still resell the goods at

---

[6] Plateq Corp. of North Haven v. Machlett Lab., p. 547.

any time prior to collection of the judgment, but he must apply the proceeds toward satisfaction of the judgment. Payment of the balance due on the judgment entitles the buyer to any goods not resold [2-709(2)].

SUMMARY

Adequate assurance	**1.** This is the one remedy available to both buyers and sellers.
	2. The Code provides that either party may demand in writing that the other give assurance that performance will be forthcoming.
	3. If assurance of performance is not given, the party who requested such assurance may treat the contract as breached.

BUYER'S RIGHTS AND REMEDIES

Right to inspect	**1.** A buyer has a right before payment or acceptance to inspect the goods at any reasonable time and place.
	2. If the contract is C.O.D. or calls for payment against documents, a buyer must pay before he can inspect. Payment, however, is not acceptance, and rejection still is permitted.
Right to reject	**1.** If the goods fail in any respect to conform to the contract, a buyer can reject.
	2. A buyer can reject the whole or accept any commercial unit and reject the rest.
	3. Rejection must be within a reasonable time and notice of rejection must be timely. Failure to do either will result in an acceptance.
	4. After rejection, a buyer who takes possession of the goods must protect them and follow any reasonable instructions from the seller.
	5. A buyer has a security interest in the goods and can resell them to recover his expenses in taking possession and caring for the goods.

Buyer's acceptance	1. A buyer accepts if (1) after a reasonable opportunity to inspect, he indicates he accepts despite any nonconformity, (2) he fails to make an effective rejection, or (3) he does any act inconsistent with the seller's ownership.
Right to revoke acceptance	1. A buyer can revoke his acceptance of nonconforming goods that substantially impair its value if the buyer accepted the goods while thinking the seller would cure or if the nonconformity was very difficult to discover.
	2. Revocation must be within a reasonable time, and the buyer has the same rights and duties as if he had rejected.
Right to damages when a buyer covers	1. A buyer covers when he buys the goods elsewhere and cover is a buyer's primary remedy.
	2. After covering, a buyer can sue the seller for the difference between the cover price and the contract price plus any incidental and consequential damages.
	3. A buyer is not required to cover. If the buyer decides to cover, it must be in good faith.
Right to damages for nondelivery	1. If a buyer does not cover, he can sue for the difference between the contract price and the market price, plus any incidental and consequential damages.
Right to the goods	1. When the goods are unique, or in other proper circumstances, a buyer can get specific performance. The Code remedy is more flexible than the traditional remedy of specific performance in equity.
	2. "Other proper circumstances" occur when the buyer simply cannot reasonably buy the goods elsewhere.

SELLER'S RIGHTS AND REMEDIES

Right to cure	1. If the time for performance has not expired, a seller has an absolute right to cure (correct) his previous nonconforming tender of goods.
	2. If the time for performance has expired, the seller can cure only if the seller had

	reasonable gounds to think his nonconforming tender would have been accepted by the buyer.
Right to reclaim goods on buyer's insolvency	1. When a seller discovers a buyer received goods while insolvent, the seller can reclaim them upon demand within 10 days after receipt. If the buyer in writing 3 months before delivery misrepresented his solvency, the 10-day limitation does not apply.
	2. The seller can also refuse to make further deliveries except for cash and can stop any goods en route to the buyer.
Right to reclaim goods from a solvent buyer	1. If the buyer has improperly rejected, wrongfully revoked acceptance, failed to pay, or repudiated the contract, the seller can reclaim the goods.
	2. The seller can stop goods in transit upon timely notice to the carrier. This right is limited to carload, truckload, or other large shipments.
Right to resell goods	1. Resale is the seller's primary remedy.
	2. A seller can resell the goods and sue for the difference between the resale price and the contract price plus any incidental and consequential damages.
Right to collect damages—in general	1. If the seller does not resell, he can sue for the difference between the market price at the place of tender and the contract price, plus any incidental and consequential damages.
Right to collect the purchase price	1. A seller can collect the contract price if the buyer accepted the goods.
	2. A seller can collect the contract price if the goods were lost or damaged within a reasonable time after the risk of loss passed to the buyer.
	3. A seller can collect the contract price if the goods were identified to the contract and the seller cannot resell them, or the facts indicate the goods cannot be resold.

CASES

G&H Land & Cattle Co. v. Heitzman & Nelson, Inc.
628 P.2d 1038 (Idaho 1981)

McFADDEN, J. On May 23, 1974, Heitzman Produce agreed to purchase from G & H Land & Cattle Company all potatoes to be grown by G & H on its acreage in Jerome County. Heitzman Produce's obligation to purchase was contingent upon the potatoes meeting the size specification set forth in the contract. The potatoes grown did not meet the size specification, and Heitzman Produce refused to accept and pay for the potatoes. G & H brought an action alleging breach of contract. The trial court entered judgment in favor of Heitzman Produce. . . .

On appeal, G & H contends that . . . Heitzman Produce did not act reasonably in rejecting the nonconforming potatoes tendered to it by G & H. . . .

A review of the UCC provisions applicable to the instant case necessarily begins with I.C. §28-2-606(1), which provides for three modes of acceptance by a buyer.

28-2-606. What constitutes acceptance of goods— (1) Acceptance of goods occurs when the buyer (a) after a reasonable opportunity to inspect the goods signifies to the seller that the goods are conforming or that he will take or retain them in spite of their nonconformity; or (b) fails to make an effective rejection (subsection (1) of section 28-2-602), but such acceptance does not occur until the buyer has had a reasonable opportunity to inspect them; or (c) does any act inconsistent with the seller's ownership; but if such act is wrongful as against the seller it is an acceptance only if ratified by him.

In connection with this provision, I.C. §28-2-602(1) provides: "rejection of goods must be within a reasonable time after their delivery or tender. It is ineffective unless the buyer seasonably notifies the seller."

The concepts of a reasonable time period for rejection and a reasonable opportunity to inspect

necessarily overlap. That is, if inspection indicates the goods are nonconforming, there remains the obligation to reject within a reasonable time. But where the buyer does not avail himself of his right to a reasonable opportunity to inspect, he thereby fails to reject within a reasonable time. The thrust of appellant's argument is directed toward this latter situation, and we will accordingly first direct our attention to that issue.

A buyer's right to inspect the goods is defined in I.C. §28-2-513(1), which provides that buyer has a right before payment or acceptance to inspect the goods tendered or delivered at any reasonable place and time and in any reasonable manner. However, the method and manner of inspection may be fixed by the parties, and such a contractual provision is presumed to be exclusive. . . .

In the instant case, the undisputed facts and the language of the contract lead to only one conclusion: the respondent exercised his right of inspection promptly and with due diligence. The parties agreed that the potatoes were to be inspected for size by government inspectors, the decision of the inspectors would be binding, and the inspection was to be "taken at delivery."

The contract contemplated delivery over the course of several months, and payment in the month following each delivery. Likewise, there can be no question that delivery was to be made when the potatoes came out of storage, for the price is conditioned on their weight at such time. The first potatoes came out of storage sometime after November 6, 1974, the government inspector was present at this time, and his inspection showing that only 39.2 percent of the potatoes were six ounces or larger was dated November 15, 1974. Under these circumstances, respondent exercised his right of inspection promptly and in accordance with the applicable provisions of the contract.

The conclusion that respondent acted reasonably is not lessened by the fact that its employees had several opportunities to inspect the potatoes prior to the delivery date. The parties expressly contracted for inspection at delivery, and the method and manner of the inspection contracted for is presumed to be exclusive. This being the case, the respondent had no duty to have the potatoes inspected prior to delivery, and it is irrelevant that they could have been inspected earlier.

We affirm.

Conn. Inv. Casting Corp. v. Made-Rite Tool Co., Inc.
416 N.E.2d 966 (Mass. 1981)

HENNESSEY, J. Connecticut Investment Casting Corporation (Casting) brought an action . . . to recover the contract price of $5,170.81 for barrel latches sold and delivered to Made-Rite Tool Co., Inc. (Made-Rite). Made-Rite filed a counterclaim for $50,000, alleging that it had been damaged by Casting's breach of contract. The District Court judge found for Made-Rite on Casting's complaint and for Casting on Made-Rite's counterclaim. . . .

Casting and Made-Rite had an agreement under which Casting was to supply 1,600 barrel latches by January 27, 1976. Casting shipped seventy-four parts on January 21, 1976, 228 parts on February 27, 1976, 623 parts on March 9, 1976, 629 parts on April 8, 1976, and seventy parts on May 14, 1976. Made-Rite introduced evidence that it needed the parts for a contract with the United States government. There was conflicting evidence of Casting's awareness of the government contract. Made-Rite produced evidence that on January 28, 1976, the day after the due date of the contract with Casting, Made-Rite telephoned Casting and stated that Casting had breached the contract but that Made-Rite would make every effort to obtain an extension on its contract with the government. Made-Rite managed to obtain several extensions on the latter contract but did not meet the final deadline of June 28, 1976. During the same period, Made-Rite had approximately forty other government contracts, six or seven of which were priority contracts. When Made-Rite missed the deadline of June 28, 1976, the government cancelled that contract, as a result of which Made-Rite lost the contract price and certain administrative expenses, and was assessed a penalty. Made-Rite was not able to resell the latches to the government or to use them itself. At the time of trial, all the latches were still in Made-Rite's possession.

The contract between Casting and Made-Rite is for the sale of goods and is governed by Art. 2 of the Uniform Commercial Code. Casting contends that Made-Rite, both by retaining the goods in spite of any nonconformity and by failing to make a proper rejection under §2-602(1), accepted the goods. Under §2-602(1), a buyer who does not intend to accept the goods delivered must give the seller timely notice of his rejection. Failure to do so constitutes acceptance of the goods by the buyer, as long as he has had a reasonable opportunity to inspect them. §2-606(1)(b).

There is no evidence that Made-Rite ever notified Casting of any intention to reject the barrel latches. Made-Rite had a reasonable opportunity to inspect, and in fact did inspect, the latches in its possession in early April. Rather than rejecting them, however, Made-Rite sent back to Casting only those latches found to be nonconforming, which Casting reworked and redelivered. After Made-Rite inspected additional latches on April 26, it decided to rework any nonconforming parts itself. These actions by Made-Rite do not constitute rejection of the barrel latches. Nor can we accept Made-Rite's contention that the "numerous conversations" with Casting constituted proper notice of rejection. On the contrary, the report of the District Court judge states that "[t]he substance of these conversations was that Defendant [Made-Rite] was pressuring Plaintiff [Casting] to deliver and Plaintiff was responding that it was encountering unanticipated difficulties." By pressuring a seller to deliver, a buyer does not reject the goods delivered. . . .

We conclude that Made-Rite failed to make an effective rejection and thus accepted the goods, §2-606(1)(b).

Reversed.

Newmaster v. Southeast Equipment, Inc.
646 P.2d 488 (Kan. 1982)

Newmaster bought a John Deere power seeder from Southeast Equipment. The machine was designed to break soil and crop seed in one operation. When the seeder was delivered on May 15, 1978, Newmaster used it to sow grass seed on three acres. Inspecting the field, Newmaster concluded that there was an insufficient number of seeds deposited by the machine per foot to produce a proper crop. He called Southeast Equipment, told them the seeder did not function properly, and was assured that someone would come to fix it. The defective nature of the machine was difficult, if not impossible, to discover without attempting to use it. When no one came to repair the machine, Newmaster over the next several weeks made 14 telephone calls to Southeast Equipment. None of these calls resulted in the power seeder's being fixed. On July 31, 1978, Newmaster revoked his acceptance, returned the machine, and demanded a refund of the purchase price. When his payment was not returned, Newmaster sued. Southeast Equipment defended by alleging that Newmaster could not revoke acceptance because it was not made within a reasonable time. The trial court decreed revocation of acceptance and entered judgment for the plaintiff.

FROMME, J. . . . K.S.A. 84-2-608 reads:

(1) The buyer may revoke his acceptance of a *lot or commercial unit* whose nonconformity substantially impairs its value to him if he has accepted it

(a) on the reasonable assumption that its nonconformity would be cured and it has not been seasonably cured; or

(b) without discovery of such nonconformity if his acceptance was reasonably induced either by the difficulty of discovery before acceptance or by the seller's assurances.

(2) Revocation of acceptance must occur within a reasonable time after the buyer discovers or should have discovered the ground for it and before any substantial change in condition of the goods which is not caused by their own defects. It is not effective until the buyer notifies the seller of it.

(3) A buyer who so revokes has the same rights and duties with regard to the goods involved as if he had rejected them.

Revocation of acceptance is a remedy which allows a buyer to get rid of defective goods by returning them to the seller. . . .

. . . [R]evocation of acceptance is possible only when the nonconformity substantially impairs the value of the machine to the buyer.

Notification of revocation of acceptance must be accomplished within a reasonable time after discovery of the grounds for such revocation, and the buyer may not revoke his acceptance if the machine has materially deteriorated while in the hands of the buyer except when deterioration has occurred by reason of defects inherent in the machine. . . . The buyer must also have accepted the goods under circumstances which bring him within either paragraph (1)(a), reasonable assumption of cure, or paragraph (1)(b), difficulty of discovery.

In other words the purchaser of a machine who seeks revocation of acceptance must establish (1) the nonconformity of the machine to the needs and circumstances of the purchaser when purchase was made, (2) that such nonconformity in fact substantially impaired the value of the machine to the purchaser, and (3) that the purchaser accepted the machine under circumstances which bring him within either paragraph (1)(a), reasonable assumption of cure, or paragraph (1)(b), difficulty of discovery.

One policy of the UCC is to encourage the parties to work out their differences in order to minimize losses resulting from defective performance. When a tender has been accepted the buyer must, within a reasonable time after he discovers or should have discovered any breach, notify the seller of breach or be barred from any remedy. This notice requirement of the code fits in with 84-2-608(2) which requires notification of revocation of acceptance within a reasonable time.

. . . The first and most important reason for requiring notice is to enable the seller to make adjustments or replacements or to suggest opportunities for care to the end of minimizing the buyer's loss and reducing the seller's own liability to the buyer. . . .

The code provides:

Every contract or duty within this act imposes an obligation of good faith in its performance or enforcement.

What is a reasonable time for taking any action depends on the nature, purpose and circumstances of such action.

So, it appears any attempt to repair defects should be allowed, if attempted within a reasonable time after notice of nonconformity. . . .

In our present case two and one-half months was surely a reasonable time in which to allow a cure or repair of defects.

Summarizing the present case, plaintiff gave notice of nonconformity three days after tender had been accepted. This was within a reasonable time as

required by K.S.A. 84-2-607(3)(a). The defects could not have been discovered without using the machine. Buyer mitigated his damages by using another implement to sow the sudan grass seed. He notified seller and allowed a reasonable time for seller to effect repairs. There was substantial impairment in the value to the buyer. When no repairs were made by the seller for a period of over two months the time for sowing sudan grass seed had passed. Buyer then gave notice of revocation of acceptance. Buyer appears to have justifiably revoked acceptance and was therefore entitled to recover the purchase price.

Judgment affirmed.

McGinnis v. Wentworth Chevrolet Co. 668 P.2d 365 (Or. 1983)

The question presented is the scope of damages recoverable by a disappointed automobile buyer upon her justifiable revocation of acceptance. Plaintiff purchased a new 1978 Chevrolet El Camino automobile for $5,923 from defendant. She alleged and the court agreed that it was a lemon. The trial court ruled that plaintiff was entitled to a refund of the purchase price, less the value of her use of the automobile (which the court set at $1,000). She appealed and the Court of Appeals held that she was entitled to damages for storage, insurance, and the renting of a substitute automobile (as incident to "cover.")

CARSON, J. . . . The issue before us is whether, given Plaintiff's justifiable revocation of her acceptance of the automobile, she is entitled to recompense for her automobile rental fees.

Resolution of this case is governed by the (following) sales provisions of the Uniform Commercial Code (UCC):

A buyer who . . . revokes has the same rights and duties with regard to the goods involved as if he had rejected them. . . .

Where . . . the buyer rightfully rejects or justifiably revokes acceptance then with respect to any goods involved . . . the buyer may cancel and whether or not he has done so may in addition to recovering so much of the price as has been paid:

(a) 'Cover' and have damages . . . as to all the goods affected whether or not they have been identified to the contract: . . .

Thus, a buyer in Plaintiff's position is not relegated merely to cancellation of the contract and recovery of the price paid thereunder (as apparently held by the trial court); rather, she also potentially is entitled to a catalog of other remedies, one of which is "cover." ORS 72.7120 provides:

(1) After a breach . . . the buyer may "cover" by making in good faith and without unreasonable delay *any reasonable purchase of* or contract to purchase *goods in substitution* for those due from the seller.

(2) The buyer may recover from the seller as damages the difference between the cost of cover and the contract price together with any *incidental or consequential damages* . . ., but less expenses saved in consequence of the seller's breach.

(3) Failure of the buyer to effect cover within this section does not bar him from any other remedy. . . .

A buyer who justifiably revokes acceptance of nonconforming goods purchased from a seller is entitled under the UCC to the following remedies:

1. The right to "cancel" the contract; and

2. Recovery of so much of the price as has been paid (including a security interest in goods in her possession and certain expenses incurred incident thereto); and

3. "Cover" damages; or

4. "Nondelivery" damages; and

5. "Incidental" and "consequential" damages under either "3." or "4." above.

The question presented is whether Plaintiff's claim for rental recompense falls within one of the classes outlined above. The Court of Appeals concluded that the renting of a replacement automobile was a reasonable way for Plaintiff to cover and thus the rental costs, as a cost in effecting cover, were recoverable as "incidental" damages. . . .

The Court of Appeals' opinion evinces a misconception as to the purpose and function of the UCC's "cover" remedy. Where a seller breaches a contract for the sale of goods by failing to deliver the agreed-upon goods, the buyer's traditional pre-code contract remedy was to seek "loss-of-bargain" damages. The measure of damages was calculated as the difference between the contract price and the fair market value of the goods. . . .

The UCC's "cover" alternative was intended to enable the buyer to "obtain the goods he needs" by allowing the disappointed buyer to reenter the market place and make a reasonable purchase of substitute goods. . . . When a buyer makes a reasonable "cover," the measure of damages is the difference between the actual "cover" purchased and the contract price. This formula results in a substantial departure from pre-code law where there was no assurance at what time or place the court would measure the market were the buyer to purchase

substitute goods. . . . If the buyer does not "cover," her loss-of-bargain damages, if any, will be computed under the market price provision.

We now focus on the question of whether the renting of a substitute automobile can be "cover" in these circumstances. ORS 72.7120(1) only describes "cover" as "any reasonable purchase of or contract to purchase goods in substitution for those due from the seller." A clear example of "cover" would be if Plaintiff had purchased another 1978 El Camino or even a comparable automobile from another dealer. . . .

Given the "cover" remedy's purpose in providing certainty for the calculation of the buyer's loss-of-bargain, while also allowing the buyer to obtain the needed goods, we conclude that the UCC's "cover" remedy generally is not intended to apply to a rental. Rather, the remedy is limited only to those situations where the buyer has purchased or contracted to purchase goods as an actual replacement for the agreed-upon goods. Rental costs are not readily translatable into a comparable value figure for computation of the loss-of-bargain and, therefore, viewing temporary rentals as "cover" would defeat the remedy's intended purpose. As the rental automobile did not constitute a "cover" in the circumstances, the Court of Appeals erred in awarding Plaintiff her rental fees as a cost "incidental" to "cover.". . .

Reversed and remanded.

In Re Bel Air Carpets, Inc.
452 F.2d 1210 (1971)

Mand Carpet Mills sold carpeting to Bel Air Carpets. To obtain credit, Bel Air had furnished a year-old financial statement which was false. Six weeks after this credit sales transaction, Bel Air was insolvent. As the result of the insolvency, Mand reclaimed the carpeting. An involuntary petition in bankruptcy was filed, and the trustee in bankruptcy sought to recover the carpeting on the ground that the seller had not acted within the time limits for reclaiming goods from an insolvent buyer. He contended that the date of the financial statement determined the rights of the parties. The referee found, however, that Mand's entire claim fell within the 3-month exception and denied the claim.

CHOY, J. . . . Mand's right to the carpets was fixed on August 19, when it made its formal declaration of rescission. The "transfer" here occurred on August 19, prior to the date of bankruptcy and we must determine Mand's legal rights as of that date.

Since the Trustee does not contest the Referee's finding that the Bankrupt was insolvent long before his formal declaration of insolvency, this appeal turns upon a construction of §2702(2) of the California Commercial Code, which provides:

> Where the seller discovers that the buyer has received goods on credit while insolvent he may reclaim the goods upon demand made within 10 days after the receipt, but *if misrepresentation of solvency has been made to the particular seller in writing within three months before delivery the 10-day limitation does not apply.*

The statute is straightforward and, on its face, requires (1) a written (2) misrepresentation of solvency (3) made within three months of delivery (4) to the particular creditor who is attempting to rescind the contract. The Official California Code Comment notes, "A seller could recover goods from an insolvent buyer only . . . if a written misrepresentation of solvency has been made to the particular seller within three months before delivery." It would seem clear that the three month period refers to the time at which the written misrepresentation is presented rather than the actual date the writing bears. . . .

We hold that the policy behind §2702(2) requires that the written misrepresentation be presented, not dated, within the three-month period. Section 2702(2) was written to extend the protection the common law provided to the seller who unwittingly sells goods on credit to an insolvent buyer. Section 2702(2) provides a conclusive presumption of fraud for deliveries made within 10 days of insolvency. Section 2702(2) is similarly aimed at fraud perpetrated within three months of delivery. The protection afforded the seller would be severely limited by allowing the loophole the Trustee would have us create. Reliance upon a financial statement such as that delivered to Mand takes place on the date the statement is delivered, not on the date in the past on which it was purportedly prepared. As the Referee said below,

It would be overly restrictive to hold that the statement speaks only as of the date of the financial statement and has no continuing voice. The credit grantor would normally infer that the statement continues to represent the facts beyond the date on the writing, subject of course to some variation, but not subject to any radical departure, and the credit seeker intends that the credit grantor shall so rely.

The Bankrupt presented a 1968 financial statement which was false as of 1968 and as of 1969. Its president assured Mand that the statement was accurate and that the 1969 statement would be substantially the same. It was primarily on this misrepresentation embodied in the 1968 statement which was presented within three months of delivery that Mand relied when it extended credit. There would be little doubt that, had the Bankrupt sent Mand the 1968 financial statement with a current cover letter incorporating the enclosed statement, §2702(2) would be fully operative. There is no reason for a different result in this case. The misrepresentation of solvency was "made" when the fraudulent statement was given within three months of the delivery of the carpets. Whatever the reason behind the arbitrary time requirement, it was not designed to achieve such an anomalous result as the Trustee espouses which is patently contrary to common sense and to the intent of the Code. Mand was entitled to rescind its contract with the Bankrupt and to retain the entire sum it recovered.

Affirmed.

Plateq Corp. of North Haven v. Machlett Lab.
456 A.2d 786 (Conn. 1983)

On July 9, 1976, the defendant ordered from the plaintiff two lead-covered steel tanks to be constructed by the plaintiff according to specifications supplied by the defendant. The tanks were designed for the special purpose of testing X-ray tubes and were required to be radiation-proof within certain federal standards. Accordingly, the contract provided that the tanks would be tested for radiation leaks after their installation on the defendant's premises. The plaintiff had not previously constructed such tanks, nor had the defendant previously designed tanks for this purpose.

Although the plaintiff encountered difficulties both in performing according to the contract specifications and in completing performance within the time required, the defendant did no more than call these deficiencies to the plaintiff's attention during various inspections in September and early October, 1976. By October 11, 1976, performance was belatedly but substantially completed. On that date, Yannello, the defendant's engineer, noted some remaining deficiencies which the plaintiff promised to remedy by the next day, so that the goods would then be ready for delivery. Yannello gave no indication to the plaintiff that this arrangement was in any way unsatisfactory to the defendant. Not only did Yannello communicate general acquiescence in the plaintiff's proposed tender but he specifically led the plaintiff to believe that the defendant's truck would pick up the tanks within a day or two. Instead of sending its truck, the defendant sent a notice of total cancellation which the plaintiff received on October 14, 1976. That notice failed to particularize the grounds upon which cancellation was based.

The plaintiff sued to recover damages, measured by the contract price and incidental damages, arising out of the defendant's allegedly wrongful cancellation of it.

The trial court found for the plaintiff.

PETERS, J. . . . On this factual basis, the trial court, having concluded that the transaction was a contract for the sale of goods falling within the Uniform Commercial Code, considered whether the defendant had accepted the goods. The court determined that the defendant had accepted the tanks, primarily by signifying its willingness to take them despite their nonconformities, . . . and secondarily by failing to make an effective rejection. . . . Once the tanks had been accepted, the defendant could rightfully revoke its acceptance . . . only by showing substantial impairment of their value to the defendant. In part because the defendant's conduct had foreclosed any post-installation inspection, the court concluded that such impairment had not been proved. Since the tanks were not readily resaleable on the open market, the plaintiff was entitled, upon the defendant's wrongful revocation of acceptance, to recover their contract price, minus salvage value, plus interest. . . .

On the trial court's finding of facts, it was warranted in concluding, that the defendant had accepted the goods it had ordered from the plaintiff. Under the provisions of the Uniform Commercial Code, "[a]cceptance of goods occurs when the buyer (a) after a reasonable opportunity to inspect the goods signifies to the seller . . . that he will take . . . them in spite of their nonconformity; or (b) fails to make an effective rejection."

In concluding that the defendant had "signified" to the plaintiff its willingness to "take" the tanks despite possible remaining minor defects, the trial court necessarily found that the defendant had had a reasonable opportunity to inspect the goods. The defendant does not maintain that its engineer, or the other inspectors on previous visits, had inadequate access to the tanks, or inadequate expe-

rience to conduct a reasonable examination. It recognizes that inspection of goods when the buyer undertakes to pick up the goods is ordinarily at the seller's place of tender. . . . After acceptance, a buyer may still, in appropriate cases, revoke its acceptance, or recover damages for breach of warranty. The trial court reasonably concluded that a post-installation test was intended to safeguard these rights of the defendant as well as to afford the plaintiff a final opportunity to make needed adjustments. The court was therefore justified in concluding that there had been an acceptance. A buyer may be found to have accepted goods despite their known nonconformity.

The trial court's alternate ground for concluding that the tanks had been accepted was the defendant's failure to make an effective rejection. . . . An acceptance occurs when, after a reasonable opportunity to inspect, a buyer has failed to make "an effective rejection. . . . A rejection (is) "ineffective unless the buyer seasonably notifies the seller." . . . A buyer is precluded from relying, as a basis for rejection, upon unparticularized defects in his notice of rejection, if the defects were such that, with seasonable notice, the seller could have cured by making a substituted, conforming tender. The defendant does not question the trial court's determination that its telegram of cancellation failed to comply with the requirement of particularization contained in §42a-2-605(1). . . . The trial court . . . found that the defendant's unparticularized telegram of cancellation wrongfully interfered with the plaintiff's contractual right to cure any remaining post-installation defects. In these circumstances, the telegram of cancellation constituted both a wrongful and an ineffective rejection on the part of the defendant.

Once the conclusion is reached that the defendant accepted the tanks, its further rights of cancellation under the contract are limited by the governing provisions of the Uniform Commercial Code. . . . After acceptance, the buyer must pay for the goods at the contract rate; and bears the burden of establishing their nonconformity. After acceptance, the buyer may only avoid liability for the contract price by invoking the provision which permits revocation of acceptance. That provision requires proof that the "nonconformity [of the goods] substantially impairs [their] value to him." On this question, which is an issue of fact, the trial court again found against the defendant. Since the defendant has provided no basis for any argument that the trial court was clearly erroneous in finding that the defendant had not met its burden of proof to show that the goods were substantially noncon- forming, we can find no error in the conclusion that the defendant's cancellation constituted an unauthorized and hence wrongful revocation of acceptance.

Affirmed.

REVIEW QUESTIONS

1. Match each term in column A with the appropriate statement in column B.

A	B
1. Adequate assurance	a. Buyer's remedy for undoing his acceptance.
2. Inspection	b. Seller's primary remedy.
3. Rejection	c. If buyer is insolvent, seller may be able to do this.
4. Acceptance	d. Buyer's right before he has to pay or accept.
5. Revocation of acceptance	e. Seller's right to correct a nonforming tender.
6. Cover	f. Seller's right to collect the purchase price.
7. Specific performance	g. Buyer fails to make an effective rejection.
8. Cure	h. Buyer's primary remedy.
9. Resale	i. Buyer may do this if the tender of goods fails in any way to conform to the contract.
10. Seller's specific performance	j. Buyer's remedy if goods are unique.
11. Reclaim goods	k. A remedy available to both parties.

2. Amy orders three white slips from a department store. They arrive C.O.D., and Amy pays the delivery person. She opens the box and discovers that black slips were sent. If she does not want these slips, what are her rights? Explain.

3. Newman bought a mobile home from Moses. On February 9, Moses delivered it to Newman's rented lot, blocked and leveled it, and connected the sewer and water pipes. Later that day, Newman's fiancee cleaned the interior of the mobile home and moved some kitchen utensils and dishes into the mobile home. She notices a broken window and water pipe. Newman called Moses and told him about these conditions, as well as having no door keys. On February 10, a windstorm totally destroyed the mobile home. Moses sued Newman for the purchase price. With what result? Why?

4. Plaintiff purchased a mobile home from the defendant. The salesperson told the plaintiff that it was 14 feet wide and 70 feet long. When the home fell from its footings, plaintiff measured it and found that it was only 64 feet long. May the plaintiff rescind the contract of purchase? Why?

5. Paul, a cash buyer of a mobile home, sued the seller for damages for breach of contract. The home was delivered on June 7, but Paul was not given the keys for three weeks. When Paul finally gained access, he found that the windows and doors would not shut tightly, the floors were buckled, and the rafters were warped. When it rained the floors flooded, and the water caused an electrical failure. Paul occupied the mobile home for 3 months before moving out. The seller claimed that the right to cure the defects still existed. Is Paul entitled to revoke the acceptance? Why?

6. Maria buys a new stove from Stove Store. After using it several times, she discovers that its temperature readings are not quite correct. These slight deviations would be significant only to a gourmet cook, which Maria is. May she reject? May she revoke acceptance? Explain.

7. Plaintiff, a used car dealer, brought a car to the defendant, another dealer, for inspection in the hope that a sales agreement could be reached. Two of the defendant's employees examined the car and test drove it. Defendant thereafter agreed to buy the car without reserving any further right to inspect. In fact, the car had several defects that were readily discernible. Can the buyer revoke his acceptance? Why?

8. Chadwell made a contract with English wherein Chadwell was given an option to purchase all of English's shares in an Oklahoma bank. On two occasions, Chadwell attempted to exercise the option, but English refused to convey the shares. Chadwell sued to recover the shares. What result? Why?

9. A country music festival promoter contracted to buy 2,000 kegs of beer at $50 per keg. When the beer that arrived was found to be flat, the promoter rejected it. He could not buy that brand from any other source in time for the festival, so he bought 2,000 kegs of another beer at $55 per keg. What are the promoter's Article 2 damages? Explain.

10. Plaintiff entered into a contract to purchase 4,000 tons of cryolite, a chemical used in the production of aluminum, from defendant. When the chemical was not delivered, plaintiff brought a suit for specific performance. He contended that cryolite was not readily available from any other source. Is plaintiff entitled to the remedy of specific performance? Why?

11. Ray ordered a color TV from a local store. When it was delivered, he saw that the picture had a reddish tint. The man who installed the set offered to take it back to the shop to repair it, but Ray objected. "I don't want a repaired TV. I want a refund." The store maintained it would repair the set but not refund Ray's money. Later, Ray sued to recover his payments. With what result? Why?

12. Pinson purchased a new Oldsmobile automobile from the defendant for $9,720.33. A few days after the purchase, Pinson noticed approximately four small indentations on the hood of the automobile and some paint overspray on the left rear quarter panel of the automobile. He notified the defendant of his discovery, and it offered to correct the defects without charge under the new car warranty. The cost to repair the warranty defects was estimated to be from $75 to $100. Pinson refused to allow Freeman Oldsmobile to correct the defects and instituted suit to obtain a refund of the purchase price. With what result? Why?

13. The city of Louisville executed a requirements contract with plaintiff to provide the city with all its requirements of parking meters for seven months at $54.20 per meter. Two days later, a new mayor took office, repudiated the contract, and entered into a contract with Duncan to supply meters at $46.92. Plaintiff sues for the price of 1,000 meters manufactured pursuant to the city's order and for the lost profits based on the number of meters the city bought from Duncan. Is plaintiff entitled to the purchase price? Why?

14. Slacks, Inc., sells tank tops to a fashionable boutique. Upon receipt, the store inspects them, discovers defects, and seasonably rejects them. Slacks instructs the store to sell the tank tops or return them. The boutique does neither. Is it liable for anything? Explain.

25 WARRANTIES

In the law of sales of goods, the word *warranty* describes the obligation of the seller with respect to goods that have been sold. As a general rule, a seller is responsible for transferring to the buyer a good title and goods that are of the proper quality, free from defects. He may also be responsible for the proper functioning of the article sold and for its suitability to the needs of the buyer. Thus, a warranty may extend not only to the present condition of goods, but also to the performance that is to be expected of them.

A warranty made by a seller is an integral part of the contract. If the warranty is breached and the buyer notifies the seller of the breach within a reasonable time, the buyer may bring an action for damages caused by the breach of warranty. Such damages may include the purchase price of the goods and other damages that resulted from the breach of warranty. A breach of warranty may also result in injuries to the buyer or to third persons. Suits may be brought to recover damages for these injuries as well. The law takes the position that if the goods are defective, the seller should be held responsible. Various tort and contract theories impose liability on manufacturers, packers, producers, and sellers for injuries caused by defective products. This chapter discusses the breach of warranty theories. Other theories are discussed in the next chapter under the general heading of products liability. Keep in mind that the material in this chapter is also a part of products liability.

The Code has several provisions relating to warranties. It draws a distinction between express warranties made by a seller and those implied as a matter of law from the transaction. If the seller guarantees the product directly, it is an *express warranty.* If the warranty arises out of the transaction and its circumstances, it is called an *implied warranty.* When the seller is a merchant, special treatment is sometimes afforded to warranties.

1. Express Warranties

An express warranty is one that is made as a part of the contract for sale and becomes a part of the basis of the bargain between the buyer and the seller [2-313(1)(a)]. An express warranty, as distinguished from an implied warranty, is part of the contract because it has been included as part of the individual bargain. To create an express warranty, the seller does not have to use formal words such as "warrant" or "guarantee," nor must he have the specific intention to make a warranty [2-313(3)].

A seller may make a variety of statements about the goods. It is necessary to evaluate these to determine which statements are warranties and which do not impose legal responsibility because they are merely sales talk. Any positive statement by a seller of the condition of personal property made during the negotiations for its sale which indicates an intention to be bound by the truth thereof, and which was so understood and relied upon by the other party, is an express warranty. A label on a bag of insecticide stated that it was developed especially to control rootworms. This was an express warranty that the insecticide was effective to control the rootworm. The word *guarantee* is often used to give an express warranty. A contract of sale of automobile tires stated that the tires were guaranteed for 36,000 miles against all road hazards, including blowouts. This constituted an express warranty that the tires would not blow out during the first 36,000 miles of use.

When a statement of fact or promise about the goods is made by the seller to the buyer, an express warranty is created [2-313(1)(a)]. The express warranty is that the goods will conform to the statement of fact or promise. Any statement of fact or even of opinion, if it becomes a part of the basis of the bargain, is an express warranty.[1]

Most statements of opinion, such as those concerning the value of the goods, do not give rise to an express warranty. As a general rule, a buyer is not justified in relying upon mere opinions, and they are not usually a part of the basis of the bargain. However, the opinion of an expert, such as a jeweler, with regard to the value of a gem may justify the reliance of the buyer, and such an opinion becomes part of the basis of the bargain and a warranty. When a seller merely states his opinion or his judgment on a matter of which the seller has no special knowledge, or on which the buyer may be expected to have an opinion and exercise his judgment, then the seller's statement does not constitute an express warranty.

An express warranty may be made in a variety of ways. The seller may specifically make a factual statement about the goods. These factual statements may be on labels or in a catalog or other sales promotion material. A direct

[1] Hauter v. Zogarts, p. 563.

promise may state "This grass seed is free from weeds." Generally, words that are descriptive of the product are warranties that the goods will conform to the description [2-313(1)(b)]. Descriptions may also be in the form of diagrams, pictures, blueprints, and the like. Technical specifications of the product would constitute warranties if they were part of the basis for the bargain. An express warranty can also be based on the instructions of the seller regarding use of the product.

Just as the seller may describe the goods, he may also inform the buyer by showing him a model or a sample of what is being sold. Fabrics or clothing might be purchased on the basis of samples shown to the buyer, or a seller might display a working model of an engine. In either event, there would be an express warranty that the goods will conform to the sample or model if the parties have made this a part of their bargain [2-313(1)(c)].

2. The Warranty of Title

IMPLIED
WARRANTIES

A seller may expressly warrant the title to goods, but usually does not do so. Therefore, the law imposes a warranty of title in order to protect buyers that may overlook this aspect of the sale and those that simply assume the seller has good title to the goods. The warranty of title is treated as a separate warranty under the Code.

A seller warrants that he is conveying good title to the buyer and that he has the right to sell the goods. He further warrants that there are no encumbrances or liens against the property sold and that no other person can claim a security interest in them [2-312]. In effect, the seller implicitly guarantees to the buyer that he will be able to enjoy the use of the goods free from the claims of any third party. Of course, property may be sold to a buyer who has full knowledge of liens or encumbrances, and he may buy the property subject to these claims. In this event, there would not be a breach of warranty of title. The purchase price would, however, reflect that he was obtaining less than complete title.

In chapter 23, it was noted that a good-faith purchaser from a seller with voidable title obtains good title. A purchaser from a thief does not. Is there a breach of the warranty of title in such a sale? While there are cases answering the question both ways, most courts would find a breach of warranty even if the buyer actually receives clear title. This results from Code language which requires that the conveyance of title be rightful and free from the difficulties of establishing clear title in such cases. The good-faith purchaser thus has a choice. He may claim the goods by use of the good-faith purchase concept, or he may recover the purchase price or any payments made by electing to sue for breach of the implied warranty of title.[2]

Warranty of title can be excluded or modified only by specific language or by circumstances making clear that the seller is not vouching for the title [2-312(2)]. Judicial sales and sales by executors of estates would not imply that the seller

---

[2] Sumner v. Fel-Air, Inc., p. 564.

guarantees the title. Also a seller could directly inform the buyer that he is selling only the interest that he has and that the buyer takes it subject to all encumbrances.

A seller who is a merchant, regularly dealing in goods of the kind that are the subject of the sale, makes an additional warranty. He warrants that the goods are free of the rightful claim of any third person by way of infringement of the third person's interests—that the goods sold do not, for example, infringe upon a patent. But a buyer may furnish to the seller specifications for the construction of an article, and this may result in the infringement of a patent. Not only does the seller not warrant against such infringement, but the buyer must also protect the seller from any claims arising out of such infringement [2-312(3)].

3. The Implied Warranty of Merchantability

Implied warranties come into being as a matter of law, without any bargaining. As an integral part of the normal sales transaction, implied warranties are legally present unless clearly disclaimed or negated. Implied warranties exist even if a seller is unable to discover the defect involved or unable to cure it if it can be ascertained. Liability for breach of an implied warranty is not based on fault, but on the public policy of protecting the buyer of goods.

A warranty that the goods shall be of merchantable quality is implied in a contract for sale if the seller is a merchant who deals in goods of the kind involved in the contract.[3] It is not enough that the defendant sold the goods. The seller-defendant must have been a merchant dealing in the goods. A person making an isolated sale is not a merchant. For example, a bank selling a repossessed car is not a merchant, and there is no implied warranty of merchantability in such a sale.

The warranty extends to all sales of goods by merchants. It applies to new goods and to used goods in most states, unless the warranty is excluded.[4] In order for a consumer to prevail in an action for damages for breach of an implied warranty of merchantability, he must demonstrate that the commodity was not reasonably suitable for the ordinary uses for which goods of that kind and description are sold, and that such defect or breach existed at the time of sale and proximately caused the damages complained of.

For goods to be merchantable, they must at least be the kind of goods that

1. Pass without objection in the trade under the contract description.
2. In the case of fungible goods, are of fair average quality within the description.
3. Are fit for the ordinary purposes for which such goods are used.
4. Run, within the variations permitted by the agreement, of even kind, quality, and quantity within each unit and among all units involved.
5. Are adequately contained, packaged, and labeled as the agreement may require.

---

[3] Smith v. Stewart, p. 565.

[4] Roupp v. Acor, p. 566.

6. Conform to the promises or affirmations of fact made on the container or label if any [2-314].

These standards provide the basic acceptable standards of merchantability. Fungible goods (2) are those usually sold by weight or measure, such as grain or flour. The term "fair average quality" generally relates to agricultural bulk commodities and means that they are within the middle range of quality under the description. Fitness for ordinary purposes (3) is not limited to use by the immediate buyer. If a person is buying for resale, the buyer is entitled to protection, and the goods must be honestly resalable by him. They must be acceptable in the ordinary market without objection. Subsection (5) is applicable only if the nature of the goods and of the transaction require a certain type of container, package, or label. Where there is a container or label and a representation thereon, the buyer is entitled to protection under subsection (6), so that he will not be in the position of reselling or using goods delivered under false representations appearing on the package or container. He obtains this protection even though the contract did not require either the labeling or the representation.

The implied warranty of merchantability imposes a very broad responsibility upon the merchant seller to furnish goods that are at least of average quality. In any line of business, the word *merchantable* may have a meaning somewhat different from the Code definition, and the parties by their course of dealing may indicate a special meaning for the term.

One purpose of this warranty is to require sellers to provide goods that are reasonably safe for their ordinary intended use. Although the law does not require accident-proof products, it does require products that are reasonably safe for the purposes for which they were intended when they are placed in the stream of commerce.

Liability for breach of the warranty of merchantability extends to direct economic loss as well as to personal injuries and to property damage. Direct economic loss includes damages based on insufficient product value. In other words, the buyer is entitled to collect the difference in value between what was received and what the product would have had if it had been of merchantable quality. Direct economic loss also includes the cost of replacements and the cost of repairs. These damages need not be established with mathematical certainty, but reasonable degrees of certainty and accuracy are required so that the damages are not based on speculation.

4. The Implied Warranty of Fitness for a Particular Purpose

Under the warranty of merchantability, the goods must be fit for the *ordinary purposes* for which such goods are used. An implied warranty of fitness for a *particular purpose* is narrower, more specific, and more precise.[5] It is created if, at the time of contracting, the seller has reason to know any particular purpose for which the buyer requires the goods and is relying on the seller's skill or judgment

---

[5] Smith v. Stewart, p. 565.

to select or furnish suitable goods [2-315]. In these circumstances, the seller must select goods that will accomplish the purpose for which they are being purchased.

The implied warranty of fitness applies both to merchants and nonmerchants, but normally pertains only to merchants, since a nonmerchant does not ordinarily possess the required skills or judgment. The buyer need not specifically state that he has a particular purpose in mind or that he is placing reliance upon the seller's judgment if the circumstances are such that the seller has reason to realize the purpose intended or that the buyer is relying on him. For the warranty to apply, however, the buyer must actually rely upon the seller's skill or judgment in selecting or furnishing suitable goods. If the buyer's knowledge or skill are equal to or greater than the seller's, there can be no justifiable reliance and no warranty.[6] Both issues are questions of fact for a jury.

The difference between the implied warranty of merchantability and the implied warranty of fitness for a particular purpose is very significant. While many cases allege a breach of both warranties, the decisions often only find a breach of one or the other, but not both. The implied warranty of fitness for a particular purpose does not exist nearly as often as the implied warranty of merchantability. Particular purpose involves a specific use by the buyer; ordinary use, as expressed in the concept of merchantability, means the customary function of the goods. Thus, a household dishwasher would be of merchantable quality because it could ordinarily be used to wash dishes; but it might not be fit for a restaurant's particular purpose because it would not be suited for its dishwashing needs. Goods that are of merchantable quality may not be fit for a particular purpose. Goods fit for a particular purpose will almost always be of merchantable quality. Goods that are not of merchantable quality usually will not be fit for a particular purpose.

Breach of the warranty of fitness for a particular purpose may result in disaffirmance of the contract. If the product causes an injury, including economic loss, it may also result in a suit for dollar damages.

5. Limitations of Express Warranties

A seller will often seek to avoid or restrict warranty liability. The Code has provisions on exclusion or modification of warranties which are designed to protect the buyer from unexpected and unfair disclaimers of both express and implied warranties. Sometimes there are statements or conduct which create an express warranty and also statements or conduct which tend to negate or limit such warranties. To the extent that it is reasonable, the two different kinds of statements or conduct are construed as consistent with each other [2-316(1)]. However, negation of limitation of an express warranty is inoperative when such a construction is unreasonable. In other words, if the express warranty and the attempt to negate it cannot be construed as consistent, the warranty predominates. If a seller gives the buyer an express warranty and then includes in the contract a

---

[6] Beam v. Cullett, p. 567.

provision that purports to exclude "all warranties express or implied," that disclaimer will not be given effect. The express warranty will be enforceable.

6. Written Exclusion of Implied Warranties

Implied warranties can be excluded if the seller makes it clear that the buyer is not to have the benefit of them. In general, to exclude or modify the implied warranty of merchantability, the word *merchantability* must be used [2-316(2)]. The warranty of merchantability also may be excluded by oral agreement or by the parties' course of performance. However, if the disclaimer is included in a written contract, it must be set forth in a conspicuous manner. The disclaimer clause of the contract should be in larger type or a different color of ink or indented, so that it will be brought to the buyer's attention. A disclaimer will not be effective if it is set forth in the same type and color as the rest of the contract.

To exclude or modify any implied warranty of fitness for a particular purpose, the exclusion must be conspicuously written. The statement, "there are no warranties which extend beyond the description on the face hereof" is sufficient to exclude the implied warranty of fitness for a particular purpose [2-316(2)]. An exclusionary clause should be printed in type that will set it apart from the balance of the contract.[7]

7. Other Exclusion of Implied Warranties

The Code also provides for other circumstances in which implied warranties may be wholly or partially excluded. The seller may inform the buyer that he is selling goods "as is," "with all faults." Or other language may call the buyer's attention to the exclusion and make it plain that the sale involves no implied warranty [2-316(3)(a)]. The implied warranty of merchantability may be excluded by oral agreement or by the parties' course of performance. The Code does not guarantee every buyer a good deal.

The buyer's examination of the goods or a sample or a model is also significant in determining the existence of implied warranties. If, before entering into the contract, the buyer has examined the goods, sample, or model as fully as he desired, there is no implied warranty on defects that an examination ought to have revealed [2-316(3)(b)]. If the seller demands that the buyer examine the goods fully, but the buyer refuses to do so, there is no implied warranty on those defects that a careful examination would have revealed. By making the demand, the seller is giving notice to the buyer that the buyer is assuming the risk with regard to defects an examination ought to reveal. However, the seller will not be protected if a demand has not been made and the buyer fails to examine the goods [2-316(3)(a)].

A course of dealing between the parties, course of performance, or usage of trade can also be the basis for exclusion or modification of implied warranties.

---

[7] Anderson v. Farmers Hybrid Companies, Inc., p. 568.

These factors can be important in determining the nature and extent of implied warranties in any given transaction [2-316(3)(c)].

8. Limitations on Remedies

The Code also allows the parties to limit the remedies available in the event of a breach of warranty [2-719]. The agreement may provide for remedies in addition to, or in substitution of, those provided by the Code. The parties may also limit or alter the measure of damages. These provisions usually limit a buyer's damages to the repayment of the price upon return of the goods. Contracts often allow a seller to repair defective goods or replace nonconforming parts, without further liability. These provisions in effect eliminate a seller's liability for consequential damages and allow a seller to "cure" a defect or cancel a transaction by refunding the purchase price, without further liability.

Clauses limiting the liability of a seller are subject to the Code requirement on unconscionability [2-719]. Limitations of consequential damages for personal injury related to consumer goods are prima facie unconscionable. Limitations of damages for commercial loss are presumed to be valid.

Disclaimers of implied warranties are greatly limited by federal law today. As a part of the law relating to consumer protection, Congress passed the Magnuson-Moss warranty law. This law and the Federal Trade Commission rules adopted to carry out its purposes prohibit the disclaimer of implied warranties where an express warranty is given. This law is discussed further in chapter 49.

9. Notice

The Code requires a buyer to give notice of any alleged breach of express and implied warranties [2-607(3)(a)]. This notice must be given within a reasonable time after the facts constituting the breach are discovered or should have been discovered using reasonable care. Failure to give the required notice bars all remedies. The giving of notice within a reasonable time to a seller is a condition precedent to filing a suit for damages for breach of express or implied warranties.

There are three policies behind the notice requirement. First, notice is required in order for the seller to exercise its right to cure. The seller should be given the opportunity to make adjustments to or replacement of defective products. Notice allows sellers to minimize their losses and the buyer's damages. For example, the purchaser of a computer with a defective part should not be allowed to wait several months and then sue for loss of use of the computer.

The second policy behind the notice requirement is to provide the seller an opportunity to arm itself for negotiation and litigation. The seller needs an opportunity to examine the product promptly so that it can defend itself against possible false allegations of breach of warranty. If a delay operates to deprive seller of a reasonable opportunity to discover facts that might provide a defense or lessen his liability, the notice probably has not been given within a reasonable time.

The third policy is to provide some psychological protection for sellers. They need to believe that their risk will end after a reasonable amount of time. The notice requirement is somewhat similar to a statute of limitations. Sellers know that after a time they can stop worrying about potential liability.

The notice may be oral or in writing. Written notice is far preferable because it serves as its own proof. The notice need not be a claim for damages or a threat to file suit. All that is required is that the buyer notify the seller of the defect in the product. As a general rule, filing a lawsuit is not notice of breach of warranty, and lawsuits without prior notice are usually dismissed for failure to give the required notice. The notice of the breach of warranty requirement does not contemplate the buyer delivering a summons and complaint to the seller as notice. The Code provides no remedy for a breach of warranty until the buyer has given notice. Therefore, starting suit cannot constitute notice.

The requirement that notice be given within a reasonable time is interpreted flexibly. The comments to the Code encourage courts not to close the door too quickly on "retail consumers" and especially those injured by defective products. The implication is that merchant-buyers are bound by a stricter notice requirement. A "reasonable time" for notification from retail consumer is to be judged by different standards so that in cases involving consumers it will be extended. The rule of requiring notification is not designed to deprive a good-faith consumer of his remedy.

Courts seem not to favor the lack-of-notice defense when invoked against an injured consumer. The defendant's lawyer whose client is sued not by a merchant-buyer but by a consumer, especially by a consumer who suffered personal injury or property damage, should not rely heavily on the lack-of-notice defense. In such cases, the notice policies collide with a countervailing policy that unsophisticated consumers who suffer real and perhaps grievous injury at the hands of the defendant-seller ought to have an easy road to recovery. The rule of requiring notification is designed to defeat commercial bad faith, not to deprive a good-faith consumer of his remedy.

10. Warranties and Third Parties

Historically, suits for breach of warranty required *privity of contract,* a contractual connection between the parties. Lack of privity of contract was a complete defense to a suit for breach of express warranty or for breach of the implied warranties. Two aspects of privity of contract requirements are sometimes described as *horizontal* and *vertical.* The *horizontal* privity issue is: To whom does the warranty extend? Does it run only in favor of the purchaser, or does it extend to others who may use or be affected by the product? The *vertical* privity issue is: Against whom can action be brought for breach of warranty? Can the party sue only the seller, or will direct action lie against wholesalers, manufacturers, producers, and growers?

When privity of contract is required, only the buyer can collect for breach of warranty, and he can collect only from the seller. A seller who is liable may recover from the person who sold to him. Thus the requirement of privity of contract not only prevented many suits for breach of warranty where privity did not exist, but also encouraged multiple lawsuits over the same product.

It is not surprising that the law has generally abandoned strict privity of contract requirements. It has done so by statute and also case by case. The abandonment has occurred in cases involving express warranties, as well as in cases involving implied warranties. Both horizontal and vertical privity have been general eliminated[8] or significantly reduced.

The drafters of the Code prepared three alternative provisions that states could adopt on horizontal privity [2-318]. Alternative A has been adopted by 30 jurisdictions. It provides that a warranty extends to any person in the family or household of the buyer or a guest in the home, if it is reasonable to expect that such a person may consume, or be affected by, the goods and is injured by them.

Alternative B has been adopted in 8 jurisdictions, and alternative C is the law in 4 states. The remaining states have either omitted the section entirely or have drafted their own version on the extent of the warranties. Alternatives B and C extend warranties to any natural person who may be reasonably expected to use, consume, or be affected by the goods and who is injured by them.

These Code provisions on horizontal privity do not attempt to deal with the vertical privity issue. The Code is neutral on it and leaves the development of the law to the courts, case by case. The courts of most states have abandoned the privity of contract requirement, and persons injured by products are allowed to sue all businesses in the chain of distribution without regard to the presence of privity of contract. Some states have retained privity in suits seeking damages for economic loss even though they have abandoned it in suits for personal injuries.

---

[8] Old Albany Estates v. Highland Carpet Mills, p. 568.

SUMMARY

WARRANTIES

Express warranty	1. An express warranty is a statement of fact or promise that is made as a part of the contract for sale and becomes a part of the basis of the bargain between the buyer and the seller.
	2. Most statements of opinion, such as those concerning the value of the goods, do not give rise to an express warranty.
	3. Express warranties may be statements about the goods in sales material or they may arise from a sale by sample or model.
Warranty of title	1. A seller of goods makes a warranty that he has title to the goods and the right to sell them.

	2. The warranty of title includes a warranty that there are no encumbrances and the buyer's use of the goods will be free from the claims of others.
Implied warranty of merchantability	**1.** A warranty that the goods shall be merchantable is implied in a contract for sale if the seller is a merchant who deals in goods of the kind involved in the contract.
	2. For goods to be merchantable, they must at least be the kind of goods that are fit for the ordinary purposes for which such goods are used.
	3. Liability for breach of the warranty of merchantability extends to direct economic loss, as well as to personal injuries and property damage.
Implied warranty of fitness for a particular purpose	**1.** An implied warranty of fitness for a particular purpose is created if, at the time of contracting, the seller has reason to know any particular purpose for which the buyer requires the goods and is relying on the seller's skill or judgment to select or furnish suitable goods.
	2. The buyer need not specifically state that he has a particular purpose in mind or that he is placing reliance upon the seller's judgment if the circumstances are such that the seller has reason to realize the purpose intended or that the buyer is relying on him.
	3. Breach of the warranty of fitness for a particular purpose may result in disaffirmance of the contract. If the product causes an injury including economic loss, it may also result in a suit for dollar damages.
Limitations on warranties	**1.** If there is an express warranty and an attempt to limit warranties, both will be given effect if possible. If not, the warranty will prevail.
	2. To exclude or modify the implied warranty of merchantability, the word *merchantability* must be used. If the disclaimer is included in a written contract, it must be set forth in a conspicuous manner.

3. To exclude or modify any implied warranty of fitness for a particular purpose, the exclusion must be conspicuously written.

4. The Code also provides for other circumstances in which implied warranties may be wholly or partially excluded. The seller may inform the buyer that he is selling goods "as is," "with all faults." Other language may call the buyer's attention to the exclusion and make it plain that the sale involves no implied warranty.

5. If, before entering into the contract, the buyer has examined the goods, sample, or model, there is no implied warranty on defects that an examination ought to have revealed to him [2-316(3)(b)].

6. Disclaimers of warranties are subject to the Magnuson-Moss warranty law.

Notice of breach

1. A buyer must give notice of any breach of warranty within a reasonable time.

2. Failure to give notice prevents a suit for breach of warranty.

3. Filing suit is not notice.

Third-party beneficiaries of warranties

1. The horizontal privity issue is: To whom does the warranty extend? In most states it extends to any person in the family or household of the buyer or a guest in the home, if it is reasonable to expect that such person may consume, or be affected by, the goods and is injured by them.

2. The vertical privity issue is: Against whom can action be brought for breach of warranty? The Code leaves the development of the law to the courts, case by case. The courts of most states have abandoned the vertical privity of contract requirement, and persons injured by products are allowed to sue all businesses in the chain of distribution without regard to the presence of privity of contract.

CASES

Hauter v. Zogarts
534 P.2d 377 (Cal. 1975)

Plaintiff sued the manufacturer of a product, a "Golfing Gizmo," for personal injuries. Plaintiff was hit on the head by a golf ball following a practice swing with the golf-training device. Defendant's catalog stated that the device was a "completely equipped backyard driving range." The label on the shipping carton urged players to "drive the ball with full power" and further stated in bold type: "COMPLETELY SAFE BALL WILL NOT HIT PLAYER." Following a unanimous jury verdict for plaintiff on breach of express warranty, defendant appealed.

TOBRINER, J. . . . We first treat the claim for breach of express warranty, which is governed by California Commercial Code section 2313. The key under this section is that the seller's statements—whether fact or opinion—must become "part of the basis of the bargain." The basis of the bargain requirement represents a significant change in the law of warranties. Whereas plaintiffs in the past have had to prove their reliance upon specific promises made by the seller the Uniform Commercial Code requires no such proof. According to official comment 3 to the Uniform Commercial Code following section 2313, "no particular reliance . . . need be shown in order to weave [the seller's affirmations of fact] into the fabric of agreement.

We are not called upon in this case to resolve the reliance issue. The parties do not discuss the changes wrought by the Uniform Commercial Code, and plaintiffs are fully able to meet their burden regardless of which test we employ. Fred Hauter's testimony shows that he read and relied upon defendants' representation; he was impressed by "something on the cover dealing with the safety of the item." More importantly, defendants presented no evidence which could remove their assurance of safety from the basis of the bargain. . . .

If defendants' assertion of safety is merely a statement of opinion—mere "puffing"—they cannot be held liable for its falsity. The assertion that the Gizmo is completely safe, that the ball will not hit the player, does not indicate the seller's subjective opinion about the merits of his product but rather factually describes an important characteristic of the product. Courts have consistently held similar promises of safety to be representations of fact.

These decisions evidence the trend toward narrowing the scope of "puffing" and expanding the liability that flows from broad statements of manufacturers as to the quality of their products. Courts have come to construe unqualified statements such as the instant one liberally in favor of injured consumers. Furthermore, the assertion "COMPLETELY SAFE BALL WILL NOT HIT PLAYER" constitutes a factual representation. Defendants' statement parallels that of an automobile dealer who asserts that the windshield of a car is "shatterproof," or that of a manufacturer who guarantees his product is "safe" if used as directed.

Moreover, the materiality of defendants' representation can hardly be questioned; anyone learning to play golf naturally searches for a product that enables him to learn safely. Fred Hauter's testimony that he was impressed with the safety of the item demonstrates the importance of defendants' statement. That Fred's injury occurred while he used the Gizmo as instructed proves the inaccuracy of the assertion on the carton. . . .

Although defendants claim they did not intend their statement to cover situations such as the one at bar, subjective intent is irrelevant. The question is not what a seller intended, but what the consumer reasonably believed.

The trial court properly concluded, therefore, that defendants expressly warranted the safety of their product and are liable for Fred Hauter's injuries which resulted from a breach of that warranty.

Affirmed.

Sumner v. Fel-Air, Inc.
680 P.2d 1109 (Alaska 1984)

Sumner, an Anchorage commercial aircraft dealer, sold a Piper Navajo airplane to Fel-Air, Inc., a Barrow Air taxi operator, for $105,000. The title to the airplane was actually in Century Aircraft, Inc., which has leased it to Sumner with an option to purchase.

Fel-Air had taken possession of the plane and paid the down payment. Mechanical difficulties arose and the plane was taken to Seattle Flight Service (Seattle) for repairs. Seattle filed a lien against the plane. Sumner paid off Seattle and took possession of the plane. Fel-Air then sued Sumner for breach of the warranty of title. The trial court found for the plaintiff and awarded damages in the amount of the payments made on the airplane.

RABINOWITZ, J. . . . Title 45 of the Alaska Statutes adopts Article 2 of the Uniform Commercial Code. . . . Under AS 45.02.312, an implied warranty of title accompanies the sale of goods in Alaska. It may expressly be disclaimed.

The superior court specifically found that Sumner did not inform Fel-Air prior to the sale that he had neither title to the Navajo nor the right to sell it, and that the circumstances surrounding the transaction did not give Fel-Air any reason to know that Sumner did not claim title to the plane in himself. The court concluded that Sumner had therefore breached the warranty of title. . . .

Sumner concedes that the superior court's conclusion that there was no express or implied disclaimer of the . . . warranty was a finding of fact which may be reversed only if clearly erroneous. In the case at bar, the superior court's factual finding . . . that an implied warranty of title accompanied the sale of the Navajo must be upheld. The question now becomes whether or not Sumner breached that warranty.

Since Sumner did not have good title to the plane when he purported to convey it to Fel-Air, the answer to this question may seem obvious. Yet both parties agree that Century "entrusted" the plane to Sumner within the meaning of AS 45.02.-403. Under the UCC a merchant to whom goods have been entrusted may give a buyer a better title than the merchant himself possessed. To quote AS

45.02.403(b):

> An entrusting of possession of goods to a merchant who deals in goods of that kind gives him power to transfer all rights of the entruster to a buyer in ordinary course of business.

Because Sumner had possession of the Navajo and was a dealer in airplanes, he had the power to transfer all of Century's rights, including its good title to the airplane. Given the facts as the parties have presented them, Fel-Air could have defeated any attempt by Century to regain possession of the Navajo.

It does not follow from the fact that the parties now agree that Fel-Air's title was good that Sumner did not breach the implied warranty of title. This question has divided the commentators. *Compare* 1 Anderson, Uniform Commercial Code §2–312:36 (3d ed. 1982) (warranty not breached) with 1 Alderman, A Transactional Guide to the Uniform Commercial Code §1.53–52 (2d ed. 1983) (warranty breached, seller should have chance to cure). Alderman emphasizes the full text of UCC 2–312(a)(1), which provides:

> (a) Subject to (b) of this section there is in a contract for sale a warranty by the seller that
>
> (1) the title conveyed shall be good, *and its transfer rightful.*

As Alderman states, the entrustee's "wrongfulness (lack of right) in making the conveyance . . . is unquestionable, for the transfer of title [is] not made pursuant to any 'right'." Here Sumner's lease-purchase arrangement with Century did not authorize him to transfer title to Fel-Air. The transfer he made to Fel-Air was wrongful, and thus we conclude that the warranty UCC 2–312(a)(1) establishes was breached.

Wright v. Vickaryous, 611 P.2d 20 (Alaska 1980), supports this conclusion. *Wright* suggests that a court attempting to determine whether or not a warranty of title was breached must consider the facts as they appeared to the buyer at the time title was called into question. If a reasonable buyer would conclude that "marketable title" had not been conveyed to him, the seller—assuming that he does not save the transaction by showing that the facts are not what the buyer believes them to be—has breached the warranty of title. A "substantial shadow" on title is enough to justify the buyer's refusal to proceed with his contractual performance. Similarly in the instant case the revelation of Century's interest in the Piper Navajo cast such a shadow on the transaction between Sumner and Fel-Air.

To dispel a similar shadow, the buyer in *Wright* would have had to call all the people he believed to be lienholders; had he done so, he would have discovered that their liens had been released. To dispel the shadow of Century Aircraft, Fel-Air would have had to become an expert on the UCC and would then have had to determine that Sumner had not stolen or borrowed the Navajo from Century, that Sumner was indeed a "merchant who

deals in [airplanes]" as the UCC defines "merchant," and that Fel-Air itself qualified as a "buyer in ordinary course of business." The parties' present agreement on these matters does not mean that these things were obvious at the time the transaction between Sumner and Fel-Air began to break down. Even if we decided to ignore AS 45.02.312's intimation that a "wrongful" transfer of title breaches the warranty which that section contains, we would be loath to conclude that a breach did not occur in this case. The superior court correctly decided that Sumner breached the implied warranty of title. . . .

Affirmed.

Smith v. Stewart
667 P.2d 358 (Kan. 1983)

In the fall of 1980 Stewart advertised for sale his 1968 42-foot Trojan yacht known as the "Janice Marie II." Plaintiff Smith saw the advertisement and inspected the boat on the Lake of the Ozarks. Plaintiff was experienced in the operation of boats. He owned a 32-foot boat but had a space problem inasmuch as his family consisted of himself, his wife, and eight children. Plaintiff operated the boat on the lake on a trial run. Ultimately, plaintiff on November 21, 1980, paid $52,000 for the boat. Defendant expressly warranted the vessel was free from dry rot and that he would be responsible for any dry rot discovered within 6 months of date of delivery. Delivery occurred the last weekend in February or the first weekend in March 1981.

Three days after delivery plaintiff notified defendant one of the boat's fuel tanks was leaking and requested the condition be remedied at defendant's expense.

On August 27, 1981, plaintiff removed the boat from the water and dry rot was discovered on the hull below the waterline. On September 22, 1981, this action was filed seeking recovery for repair of the fuel tank on theories of breach of an implied warranty of merchantability and fitness for a particular purpose and for recovery and for repair of the dry rot on the theory of breach of an express warranty.

McFARLAND, J. . . . The first issue before us is whether the district court erred in concluding plaintiff had failed to state a cause of action for breach of implied warranty of merchantability. The applicable statute . . . provides in relevant part:

> (1) . . . a warranty that the goods shall be merchantable is implied in a contract for their sale *if the seller is a merchant with respect to goods of that kind.* . . .
>
> (2) Goods to be merchantable must be at least such as. . . .
>
> (c) are fit for the ordinary purposes for which such goods are used. . . .

As noted in the Kansas Comment following the statute:

> The obligations of this section are imposed upon merchant-sellers, including manufacturers or growers of goods. A person making a casual sale would not be a merchant and no warranty of merchantability would apply.

K.S.A. 84–2–104 defines merchant as follows:

> (1) "Merchant" means a person who deals in goods of the kind or otherwise by his occupation holds himself out as having knowledge or skill peculiar to the practices or goods involved in the transaction or to whom such knowledge or skill may be attributed by his employment of an agent or broker or other intermediary who by his occupation holds himself out as having such knowledge or skill.

Defendant-seller is a dentist practicing in Overland Park, Kansas. There is no allegation defendant was in the boat-selling business at the time of the sale or any other time. The transaction herein involved the casual sale of seller's personal pleasure craft. Clearly the district court did not err in holding "the seller [defendant] does not meet the requirement of being a merchant in respect to boats."

The second issue is whether the district court erred in entering summary judgment in favor of defendant on plaintiff's claim of breach of implied warranty of fitness for a particular purpose. . . . we believe plaintiff has failed to state a cause of action based on breach of implied warranty of fitness for a particular purpose. This implied warranty is . . . as follows:

> Where the seller at the time of contracting has reason to know any particular purpose for which the goods are required and that the buyer is relying on the seller's skill or judgment to select or furnish suitable goods, there is unless excluded or modified under the next section an implied warranty that the goods shall be fit for such purpose.

The Official UCC Comment following said statute states in pertinent part:

> 2. A "particular purpose" differs from the ordinary purpose for which the goods are used in that it envisages a specific use by the buyer which is peculiar to the nature of his business whereas the ordinary purposes for which goods are used are those envisaged in the concept of merchantability and go to uses which are customarily made of the goods in question. For example, shoes are gener-

ally used for the purpose of walking upon ordinary ground, but a seller may know that a particular pair was selected to be used for climbing mountains.

The provisions . . . covering the warranty of fitness for a *particular purpose* are frequently confused with the implied warranty of merchantability which covers fitness for *ordinary purposes*. The warranty of fitness for a *particular purpose* is narrower, more specific, and more precise. . . . When goods are acquired for the *ordinary purposes* for which such goods are generally used, no implied warranty of fitness for a *particular purpose* arises. A use for ordinary purposes falls within the concept of merchantability. So under the facts of the present case no implied warranty of fitness for a particular purpose arises.

Defendant-seller operated the boat as a personal pleasure craft on an inland lake. Plaintiff-buyer purchased the boat for like use. Such usage is well within the ordinary purpose of such goods. There is no allegation that plaintiff's intended usage of the boat was for a particular purpose as opposed to an ordinary purpose. . . . Taking plaintiff's allegations relative to the dangerous conditions resulting from the leaky fuel tank as true, the defect rendered the boat unfit for ordinary purposes as opposed to unfit for a particular purpose.

Under the uncontroverted facts herein, we conclude plaintiff has failed to state a claim of breach of implied warranty of fitness for a particular purpose. This district court's entry of summary judgment on this claim is . . .

Affirmed.

Roupp v. Acor
384 A.2d 968 (Pa. Super. 1978)

On August 15, 1974, plaintiff purchased a 1967 Diamond Reo truck from appellant for the sum of $8,699.42. Prior to purchase Acor informed Roupp he was seeking a truck that had enough power to use in his timber hauling business. He further advised appellant that he wanted a rebuilt truck which would be dependable for three years. The 1967 Diamond Reo was specifically represented to have a completely rebuilt engine. On January 24, 1975, while appellee was transporting a load of timber, the truck lost virtually all of its power and it was left in the middle of a steep

highway until it could be towed. A subsequent examination of the engine, which had been in use for only 6,100 miles since purchased by appellee, revealed that the bearings had seized fast to the crankshaft, rendering the engine permanently useless. Testimony established that this damage was due to a lack of oil in the bearings. As a result of the engine's breakdown, appellee suffered certain damages, including more than $3,000 for the purchase of a new engine.

CERCONE, J. . . . This appeal challenges the lower court's finding that appellant breached the implied warranties of merchantability and fitness for a particular purpose. . . .

Appellant's sole contention is that no implied warranties arose when appellee purchased the truck. . . .

Section 2–314 of the Uniform Commercial Code provides that a warranty of merchantability is implied in a contract of sale (unless excluded or modified) "if the seller is a merchant with respect to goods of that kind." Moreover, to be merchantable, the goods "must be at least such as . . . are fit for the ordinary purposes for which such goods are used. . . ." It is significant that the U.C.C. draws no distinction between new and used articles in either of the implied warranty sections at issue. The official comments to §2–314 simply state in Para-

graph 3 that: "A contract for the sale of second-hand goods, however, involves only such obligation as is appropriate to such goods for that is their contract description." Therefore, we hold that an implied warranty of merchantability may apply to the sale of a used motor vehicle. A similar result has been reached in several other jurisdictions. Instantly, we are in accord with the conclusion of the lower court that when appellant, a dealer in new and used trucks, sold appellee a used truck represented to have a completely rebuilt engine, an appropriate implied warranty of merchantability was created. . . .

Affirmed.

Beam v. Cullett
615 P.2d 1196 (Or. 1980)

Plaintiff brought this action for breach of an implied warranty of fitness for a particular purpose. Plaintiff was in the business of hauling scrap automobile bodies from southern Oregon to a steel plant in McMinnville. Plaintiff learned of defendant's 1969 Ford diesel truck being for sale from one of his employees. Plaintiff had had some experience with trucks, including driving, although usually not diesel trucks. He inspected the truck and drove it for a short distance. He bought the truck from defendant for $10,000. The truck has been used by defendant for approximately two and one-half years until the engine "blew up." Defendant had the engine rebuilt by a diesel engine mechanic whose name was given to the plaintiff. There were no written warranties. After the truck was used for a brief period of time, the engine lost a rod bearing and the intake manifold was broken.

Defendant leases trucks, but does not drive them. He operates a well-drilling business and owns drilling rigs. He does not have any particular expertise concerning diesel trucks. The trial court found for the plaintiff.

JOSEPH, J. . . . ORS 72.3150 provides for an implied warranty of fitness:

> Where the seller at the time of contracting has reason to know any particular purpose for which the goods are required and that the buyer is relying on the seller's skill or judgment to select or furnish suitable goods, there is unless excluded or

modified under ORS 72.3160 an implied warranty that the goods shall be fit for such purpose.

An implied warranty of fitness for a particular purpose arises then when two conditions are met: (1) the buyer relies on the seller's skill and judgment to select or furnish suitable goods; and (2) the seller at the time of contracting has reason to know of the buyer's purpose and that the buyer is relying on his skill and judgment.

The trial court found that defendant was advised that plaintiff intended to use the truck to haul scrap auto bodies. There was evidence to support that finding. . . .

There was no evidence that plaintiff relied on defendant's judgment in selecting the truck he purchased. Defendant merely answered plaintiff's inquiries concerning the mechanic's work on the engine. While the needs of plaintiff were known to defendant, there was no showing that defendant offered to fulfill those needs, that plaintiff in fact relied on defendant's judgment or that defendant had reason to know of plaintiff's reliance, if any.

The existence of a warranty of fitness for a particular purpose depends in part on the comparative knowledge and skills of the parties. There can be no justifiable reliance by a buyer who has equal or superior knowledge and skill with respect to the product purchased by him.

In the instant case, both parties had limited knowledge of diesel trucks. Absent evidence that plaintiff justifiably relied on defendant's judgment in selecting the truck to fulfill his hauling needs, there was no implied warranty of fitness for a particular purpose.

Reversed.

Anderson v. Farmers Hybrid Companies, Inc.
408 N.E.2d 1194 (Ill. 1980)

ALLOY, J. . . . Counts II and III sought recovery on the contract for breach of warranties, specifically for breaches of the warranty of merchantability and of the warranty of fitness for a particular purpose. The trial court dismissed those counts, holding that these warranties had been disclaimed in the contract, the order confirmation slip, between the parties. The Illinois Commercial Code does permit the parties to modify or alter these implied warranties, but it requires that any such disclaimer be in writing and that it be conspicuous. The court found these requirements to be satisfied in the instant case. We do not. The Code defines "conspicuous" as follows:

> A term or clause is conspicuous when it is so written that a reasonable person against whom it is to operate ought to have noticed it. A printed heading in capitals (as: NONNEGOTIABLE BILL OF LADING) is conspicuous. Language in the body of a form is "conspicuous" if it is larger or other contrasting type or color. But in a telegram any stated term is "conspicuous." Whether a term or clause is "conspicuous" or not is for decision by the court.

The disclaimer of warranties in this case was in capital letters under a paragraph heading "Warranties and Limit of Liability," also in capitals. However, the clause itself was on the back of the order confirmation slip sent by the defendants after the oral order had been placed. The front side of the slip, a 4 x 7 piece of paper, contained handwritten information concerning the buyer, his address, directions for delivery and dates for breeding and delivery. That side gave the appearance of being merely a standard order form without more. In small print, in the middle of the slip, was the following sentence: "This order subject to conditions on reverse side hereof and subject to acceptance by the company." This language was not conspicuous in any manner and, in fact, was in smaller print than other on the front side of the order slip. The language in capitals which sought to disclaim warranties was contained only on the reverse side of the order slip. We find little on the front side, under the circumstances, to bring to a reasonable person's attention and notice the existence of express disclaimers on the reverse side of the slip. Not only was the language in reference to conditions on the reverse side in small print, as noted, but also the general format and size of the order confirmation slip was of such an appearance that a person might reasonably conclude that there was little to the document, other than the statement of the order and delivery dates. In short, while the type used for disclaiming the warranties was conspicuous, in the sense of being larger than other type in the paragraph, the presence of that paragraph on the reverse side of the order slip was not at all conspicuous, either from the general appearance of the slip or from any conspicuous language on the front side of the slip. We find that the disclaimer of warranties on the reverse side of the order slip was not conspicuous so as to be valid under the Commercial Code. The trial court erred in dismissing the Count based upon an implied warranty of merchantability.

Reversed.

Old Albany Estates v. Highland Carpet Mills
604 P.2d 849 (Okl. 1980)

Plaintiff purchased carpet for an apartment complex through an interior decorator, Lehman. Lehman in turn contracted with defendant for the purchase specifying details such as color and quality.

Sometime after the carpet was installed, it became apparent the carpet was defective. Defendant refused to make any adjustment and when plaintiff sued for breach of implied warranty, the defendant moved to dismiss because of lack of privity of contract between the defendant and the plaintiff as the ultimate purchaser. The Trial court found for the defendant.

DOOLIN, J. . . . Plaintiff's suit is based on allegations of breach of implied warranties provided for in the Uniform Commercial Code. . . . It is defendant's initial argument that under §2–318, only certain parties other than the immediate buyer may benefit from an implied warranty by the manufacturer. Because plaintiff neither qualifies under this section nor is in privity with defendant he is not entitled to the protection of any implied warranty that might be given. . . .

§2–318 limits warranty protection to persons named in that section, i.e. "any natural person who is in the family or household of his buyer or who is a guest in his home." . . . Plaintiff here however, is a *purchaser* of the goods, not a third party beneficiary of the warranties.

Section 2–318 comes into play only after a final sale has been made and reflects the Legislature's intent to limit warranties applicable to parties with *no contractual* relationship to any person within the distributive chain of ownership through purchase. It has no application to plaintiff here who was the ultimate purchaser of the carpet and in the "vertical" chain of distribution.

The issue of horizontal privity raises the question whether *persons other than buyer* of defective goods can recover from the buyer's immediate seller on a warranty theory. The question of vertical privity is whether parties in the distributive chain prior to the immediate seller, can be held liable to ultimate purchaser for loss caused by the defective product.

In the present case there was no direct con-tract and thus no vertical privity between manufacturer and plaintiff. The code however is silent and strictly neutral as to the necessity of vertical privity in applying implied warranties. It is up to this court to decide to what extent vertical privity of contract will be required.

Recently . . . we held the warranty of merchantability as to *packaged food products* extended directly from bottler to buyer at a retail supermarket, not withstanding the lack of vertical privity. . . .

We believe the same policy reasons . . . also underly cases involving defective nonedibles. To require vertical privity results in perpetuating a needless chain of actions whereby each buyer must seek redress from his immediate seller until the actual manufacturer is eventually reached.

. . . Section 2–318's horizontal application and cases relying thereon have no application to vertical privity. This section relates to third party beneficiaries of warranties and is not intended to set any limits on necessity of vertical privity.

We hold a manufacturer may be held liable for breach of implied warranty of merchantability or fitness for particular purpose under the Uniform Commercial Code without regard to privity of contract between the manufacturer and the ultimate buyer. Plaintiff, being in the chain of distribution, may maintain a direct action against defendant to recover the benefit of his bargain in replacement of the carpet. . . .

Reversed and remanded.

REVIEW QUESTIONS

1. Identify the terms in column A by matching each with the appropriate statement in column B.

A	B
1. Express warranty	a. Made only by a merchant.
2. Warranty of merchantability	b. Arises because of special skill of the seller.
3. Fungible goods	c. To whom does the warranty extend?
4. Warranty of fitness for a particular purpose	d. A guarantee.
5. Horizontal privity	e. A condition precedent to a suit for breach of warranty.
6. Vertical privity	f. Sold by weight or measure.
7. Notice	g. Against whom can suit be brought.

2. Pat, the buyer of a tractor and backhoe, sued the seller for breach of the implied warranty of merchantability. The sales contract contained the following:

> The equipment covered hereby is sold subject only to the applicable manufacturer's standard printed warranty and no other warranties, express or implied, including the implied warranty of merchantability, shall apply.

The type size of the foregoing was slightly larger than the rest of the contract, but it was not boldface. Was the disclaimer effective to negate the implied warranty? Explain.

3. A farmer contracted to grow sweet corn for processing and freezing by a canning company. Before planting, he consulted with the defendant, who sold herbicides. The defendant recommended a product and the farmer applied it. Thereafter, his corn crop was stunted, twisted, and infested with parasites. Is the defendant liable for breach of any warranty?

4. Plaintiff sued the manufacturer for breach of implied warranty allegedly resulting from the use and application of a herbicide. The plaintiff did not purchase the herbicide or take possession of it. He did not see the package container of the product. He merely had defendant's distributor apply it to his farmland. The container had a disclaimer of warranty printed in bold letters on its side. The herbicide severely damaged plaintiff's corn crop. Is the disclaimer of warranty effective? Why?

5. Plaintiff purchased a used combine from a local dealer. During the first few months after purchase, buyer experienced numerous breakdowns in the machine. Because of the breakdowns, buyer claimed to have lost several crops that year. Buyer brought suit against the dealer and the manufacturer for breach of implied warranty. With what result? Why?

6. The purchaser of a tractor brought action against the manufacturer to recover damages that allegedly arose from breach of an express warranty. The warranty was contained in the owner's manual. The defendant contended it had no liability because of lack of privity of contract. With what result? Why?

7. A seller makes the following statements about goods to the buyer. Which are puffing and which are express warranties?
   a. The jukebox is a good machine and will probably not get out of order.
   b. October is not too late to plant this grass seed.
   c. This car is supposed to last a lifetime. It's in perfect condition.
   d. This dredge pipe has expandable ends that will seal upon the spill going through.
   e. This feed additive will increase your milk production and will not harm your dairy herd.
   f. These filter tanks should be able to remove iron and manganese from the water.
   g. This used car has never been wrecked.

8. The purchase agreement for a mobile home stated "Standard Manufacturer Warranty—OTHERWISE SOLD AS IS." The buyer subsequently discovered defects and sued for breach of the implied warranty of merchantability. He contended that the disclaimer was ineffective because it did not contain the word *merchantability* and was not conspicuous. Was the buyer correct? Why or why not?

9. The seller of a grain drying bin directly promised the purchasers that it would dry 5,000 bushels of corn in 24 hours. The written contract disclaimed all warranties. Is the disclaimer a valid defense? Why?

10. A truck salesman told the buyer that the truck would be just right for plowing snow. In fact, the truck was incapable of pushing a snowplow. The buyer sued for breach of express warranty. With what result? Why?

11. Plaintiff purchased a 5,000 gallon polyethylene tank from defendant for the purpose of storing liquid fertilizer. The tank was filled with fertilizer, and a few days later seepage was noted. Plaintiff sued for breach of the implied warranty of fitness for a particular purpose. Is this the correct theory? Explain.

12. Crew members of a fishing vessel sued manufacturers for losses allegedly caused by manufacturers' constructing and selling a vessel with a defective rudder and component parts, resulting in the vessel's returning to shore for repairs. They sued for breach of express warranty. The seller moved to dismiss for lack of privity of contract. With what result? Why?

13. O'Neill purchased a used diesel tractor and trailer from the defendants. The contract provided:

> Each USED motor vehicle covered by this contract is sold AS IS WITHOUT WAR-
> RANTY OF ANY CHARACTER expressed or implied, unless purchaser has received
> from seller a separate written warranty executed by seller.

No written warranties were received by O'Neill. He admitted to reading the contract. O'Neill had many serious problems with the truck and returned it to the defendant, who refused to rescind the sale. He sues for breach of warranty. With what result? Why?

26 PRODUCTS LIABILITY

Products liability is a legal term that describes the liability of sellers and manufacturers of goods. One of the consequences of manufacturing or selling a product is responsibility to a consumer or user if the product is defective and causes injury to a person or to property. Someone sues because of injury due to a defect in the product. Although most suits involve personal injury claims, the term is also used to cover injuries to property. Injuries to property include damage to the product itself, economic losses due to the inadequate performance of the product, and injuries to the property of others. Products liability thus concerns injuries or losses caused by products that are defectively manufactured, processed, or distributed.

The subject of products liability involves several legal theories. A suit for dollar damages for injuries caused by a product may be predicated on the theory of (1) negligence; (2) misrepresentation; (3) breach of warranty, either express or implied; or (4) strict liability. The legal principles relating to breach of warranty were discussed in the prior chapter in detail. You should keep that discussion clearly in mind as a major portion of the law on products liability. The other theories and the reasons for product liability are discussed in this chapter.

1. Basic Principles

The basic principle of products liability is that a manufacturer, distributor, or seller of a product is liable to compensate a person injured by a defective product. The mere occurrence of an injury due to a product does not automatically impose liability. A manufacturer or seller is not an insurer of the safety of persons using products. They do not guarantee the safety of the consumer of their product. Products liability is not absolute liability. It is present only if there has been a violation of a legal duty to the consumer or user, and that duty is to keep a defective product out of the stream of commerce.

Products liability cases may arise out of defective design of products, defective manufacture, or the defective marketing of products. Suit may be brought against manufacturers of component parts, raw material suppliers, anyone who provides supportive services (such as certifying, applying, or installing a product), wholesalers, and jobbers. They may be brought by the buyer, by another user of the product, or by some third party whose only connection with the product is an injury caused by it.

In most products liability cases, the injured party sues all those in the channel of distribution, including the manufacturer, the wholesaler, the distributor, and the retailer. In cases involving multiple defendants, the burden of tracing fault is on the defendant dealers and manufacturer, so that a plaintiff may be compensated while leaving it to the defendants to settle the question of responsibility among themselves. Anyone who had a hand in putting the defective product in the stream of commerce, whether technically innocent or not, may have liability to the injured party.

The trend of the law on products liability is clearly in the direction of expanding liability. A manufacturer has an obligation to the public to market a safe product, free from defects. A producer is presumed to know of defects in its products and is therefore in bad faith in selling defective products. Morever, there is a growing philosophy that the losses caused by products must be shared by business. This shift of responsibility is premised on the notion that manufacturers and sellers best understand their products and are better able to spread the loss as a cost of production and sale. When loss is written into the cost of the product, it is shared by all buyers and users of the product. The philosophy of *shared loss*—together with the increased complexity of many products and the increased chance of errors in design, manufacturing, and marketing—has dramatically enlarged the number of products liability cases in the last two decades.

The potential liability is usually covered by products liability insurance. In recent years, the cost of this insurance has skyrocketed. It has become a significant cost item in many products with a high exposure to products liability suits. To understand products liability law and to predict its future, we turn first to its historical development.

2. History of Products Liability

Although it cannot be precisely stated when products liability law began, it seems to have evolved through these five stages:

1. Trespass (strict tort liability)
2. Privity (*caveat emptor*)
3. Negligence (tort liability)

4. Warranty (contract liability)

5. Strict liability in tort (§402A)

As you can see, the law has come full circle from its origins in strict liability, since it is now based on strict liability for defective products that cause harm.

Prior to 1800, there were few manufactured products and little commerce. Times were simple, and the law reflected the values of small, interdependent communities. Injuries to persons or property were compensated by law through the tort doctrine of trespass. The trespass doctrine imposed strict liability; that is, the fact that defendant was not at fault was irrelevant. But in the 1800s, small village life underwent dramatic changes. Population mushroomed, social and economic life grew complex, and the Industrial Revolution was born. As society's values changed, so did the law. Apparently premised on the notion that infant industries needed protection from widespread liability, the law replaced strict liability in trespass with negligence law. Product manufacturers were liable only if they failed to use "reasonable care" in the manufacture and sale of their products. But eliminating strict liability in tort apparently was not enough protection for these industries. The potential for products liability at that time was great, owing to the numerous sweatshops, factories with unguarded machinery tended by little children, and food products unregulated by government. Privity was born in 1842 to limit further products liability actions.

In 1842 the English court in *Winterbottom* v. *Wright* imposed the privity barrier, lest the courts be faced with "an infinity of actions." The English court held that the injured driver of a defective mail coach could not maintain an action against the supplier of the coach, because no "privity of contract" existed between the driver and the supplier. Nineteenth-century American courts, with a similar reluctance to inhibit the free scope of industrial enterprise, generally followed the privity doctrine of *Winterbottom.*

The privity requirement limits the negligence action, since sellers owe the "reasonable person" duty only to parties with whom they had actually dealt; that is, to parties with whom they had contracted. If an injured person was not the buyer of the product or had bought the product from a retailer, then the manufacturer was not liable, since no privity would exist. Moreover, the retailer who was in privity could be liable only for negligence. However, the defective product was seldom the fault of the retailer who had not designed, manufactured, labeled, or packaged the product. Thus, the privity rule in most cases puts the risk of harm on the injured party. The period was characterized by the rule of *caveat emptor,* which means "Let the buyer beware."

With the advent of the twentieth century, infant industries matured, our country became more prosperous, and the number and complexity of products expanded. The policy of protecting industry more than society became inapplicable, and the barrier of privity was soon dismantled first in tort,[1] then in contract. The death knell of the privity doctrine in tort was sounded in the famous 1916 case of *MacPherson* v. *Buick Motor Company.* MacPherson was driving a Buick

---

[1] Donnelly Const. Co. v. Oberg/Hunt/Gilleland, p. 587.

automobile when a wooden wheel collapsed, injuring him. (Note the factual similarity to *Winterbottom.*) The defendant was the manufacturer who had sold the car to the retailer who sold the car to MacPherson. In the nineteenth century, American courts had recognized exceptions to the privity rule when products— such as drugs, foods, guns, and explosives—were "inherently" or "imminently" dangerous to life or health. The New York court in *MacPherson* found that the category of inherently dangerous products "is not limited to poisons, explosives, and things which in their normal operation are implements of destruction." Rather, it held that if "the nature of a thing is such that it is reasonably certain to place life and limb in peril when negligently made, it is then a thing of danger." The privity doctrine of *Winterbottom* was effectively overruled when the court stated: "If to the element of danger there is added knowledge that the thing will be used by persons other than the purchaser, and used without new tests, then, irrespective of contract, the manufacturer of this thing of danger is under a duty to make it carefully." *MacPherson* has been universally followed.

The demise of privity in contract law was not so easily accomplished, because the claim in contract was based on a theory of breach of warranty. The problem was that since the warranty theory seemed to be more in the nature of a contract right, only parties to the contract could supposedly enforce contract rights. But over time, courts were forced to adapt legal doctrine to the realities of modern marketing. The breakthrough came in the famous 1960 case of *Henningsen* v. *Bloomfield Motors, Inc.*, which is factually similar to *Winterbottom* and *MacPherson.* Mrs. Henningsen was injured when the new family car (a 1955 Plymouth 10 days old with 488 odometer miles) uncontrollably left the road, owing to a defective steering wheel. The New Jersey supreme court said that "where the commodities sold are such that if defectively manufactured they will be dangerous to life or limb, then society's interests can only be protected by eliminating the requirement of privity between the maker and his dealers and the reasonably expected ultimate consumer." In *Henningsen,* the injured plaintiff was not the buyer of the car and therefore was not "in the distributive chain." In addition to eliminating the necessity of establishing privity between the buyer and seller, the court also held that Mrs. Henningsen, whose husband had bought the car, could maintain an action against the remote manufacturer.

The significance of the *Henningsen* principle is recognized in the Uniform Commercial Code. As noted in Chapter 25, the UCC extends the seller's warranties to parties who are not buyers of the products. But procedural problems with warranty liability, like notice of breach, caused many plaintiffs to be denied recovery. Thus one final dismantling stage remained before the law of products liability came full circle to strict tort liability.

The year 1963 is generally regarded as the decisive date in the evolution of products liability law. Prior to that date, actions for injuries caused by defective products were based on negligence or breach of warranty. In 1963 the California supreme court adopted a theory of strict liability in tort.[2] As a result of *Greenman,* tort law is now evolving with a theory of strict liability steadfastly independent of

---

[2] Greenman v. Yuba Power Products, Inc., p. 588.

warranty. In 1965, Section 402A of the Restatement (Second) of Torts was promulgated. Section 402A, adopted by the majority of American courts, follows the strict tort liability theory of Greenman.

3. Theories of Liability

As previously noted, both tort and contract theories are used in products liability cases. A defendant may be held liable under the contract theories of breach of express or implied warranty. The implied warranty may be either the implied warranty of merchantability or the implied warranty of fitness for a particular purpose. Most cases involve the warranty of merchantability. As noted in chapter 25, an action can be maintained for breach of both express and implied warranty without privity of contract in most cases. An action based upon such breach, being a contract action, does not require proof of negligence on the part of manufacturer or seller. A defendant in a products liability case may be found to have breached its warranty of merchantability without having been negligent.

As Table 26–1 explains, products liability cases may be based upon: (1) conduct of the defendant, (2) quality of the product, or (3) performance of the product against the seller's promises or express representations. These may apply to both contract and tort actions.

A plaintiff in bringing a products liability lawsuit does not have to choose between these tort and contract theories, since all the theories may be joined into one lawsuit. Nonetheless, most plaintiffs prefer strict tort because it is usually the simplest remedy, as will be explained later. At trial, a plaintiff may be forced to choose which theories are to be submitted to the jury. Some states have been unwilling to follow strict tort, which in these states leaves breach of warranty as the usual theory of liability. Also, damages incurred are sometimes not recoverable under strict tort, owing either to their nature or the running of the tort statute of limitations. The statute of limitations for tort actions is generally a much shorter time period than it is for contract actions. However, the rights afforded by express and implied warranties may be more difficult to assert because of the contractual rules of notice of breach and disclaimers of warranties. Thus, all theories are important, and each has advantages and disadvantages in comparison with the others.

TABLE 26–1

Theories of products liability

	DEFENDANT'S CONDUCT	QUALITY OF PRODUCT	SELLER'S REPRESENTATIONS
Tort	Negligence	Strict liability for product defects (§402A Rest. of Torts)	Strict liability for public misrepresentations (§402B Rest. of Torts)
Contract	None	Implied warranty of merchantability (UCC §2-314) and fitness (UCC §2-315)	Express warranty (UCC §2-313)

4. Negligence

Negligence is of course a tort theory. In order to recover on a negligence theory, a plaintiff has to establish the negligence of the defendant, its failure to exercise reasonable care. Contributory negligence on the part of the plaintiff in some states is a bar to recovery. In others, which follow comparative negligence, it will reduce the amount of recovery by the percentage of the plaintiff's fault. The mere fact that an injury occurs from the consumption or use of a product does not ordinarily raise a presumption that the manufacturer was negligent. Negligence actions question the reasonableness of the defendant's conduct, since all human activity involves an element of risk. The defendant's conduct is deemed negligent only when it is inferior to what a "reasonable" person would have done under similar circumstances. Negligence involves conduct that falls below the standard set by law for the protection of others against the unreasonably great risk of harm. Since privity of contract is not required, a negligence suit can be brought not only by the person who purchased the defective product, but also by any person who suffered an injury on account of a defect in the product if the defect was the proximate cause of the injury.

The Restatement of Torts (Second), Section 395, states the rule as follows:

> A manufacturer who fails to exercise reasonable care in the manufacture of a chattel which, unless carefully made, he should recognize as involving an unreasonable risk of causing physical harm to those who use it for a purpose for which the manufacturer should expect it to be used and to those whom he should expect to be endangered by its probable use, is subject to liability for physical harm caused to them by its lawful use in a manner and for a purpose for which it is supplied.

The plaintiff, of course, must by appropriate evidence prove that the manufacturer was negligent—failed to exercise reasonable care. He may be able to rely on the doctrine of *res ipsa loquitur,* "the thing speaks for itself," if (1) the instrumentality involved was within the exclusive control of the defendant at the time of the act of negligence, both as to operation and inspection; (2) the injury was not the result of any voluntary action or contribution on the part of the plaintiff; and (3) the accident ordinarily would not have occurred had the defendant used due care. If an elevator falls, killing an occupant, the manufacturer has liability, because the very happening of the accident creates a presumption of negligence.

Another method of establishing negligence is to prove that the manufacturer violated some statutory regulation in the production and distribution of the product. Some industries are subject to regulation under state or federal laws on product quality, testing, advertising, and other aspects of production and distribution. Proof of a violation of a statute may be sufficient to establish negligence of a manufacturer in such industries. Negligence established by proof of violation of a statute is called *negligence per se.*

Negligence is frequently based on failure of a manufacturer to warn of a known danger related to the product. A manufacturer who knows, or should know, his product to be dangerous has a duty to exercise reasonable care and foresight in preventing it from injuring or endangering people. Reasonable care includes the duty to warn of the danger. Negligence is also often based on a design defect. In determining whether a manufacturer exercised reasonable skill and knowledge concerning the design of its product, factors include the cost of safety devices, their use by competitors, their effect on function, and the extent to which the manufacturer conducted tests and kept abreast of scientific development. A manufacturer is not an insurer, nor is he required to supply accident-proof merchandise; nonetheless the responsibilities for injuries often rest with whoever is in the best position to eliminate the danger inherent in the use of the product. A manufacturer of a rotary power lawnmower may be liable for negligent design if a user is able to put his hands or feet in contact with the moving blades of the mower.

5. Public Misrepresentation

Another tort theory used in product liability cases is known as *misrepresentation.* If the seller has advertised the product through newspapers, magazines, television, or otherwise and has made misrepresentations with regard to the character or quality of the product, tort liability for personal injury may be imposed on him. The Restatement of Torts (Second), Section 402B, summarizes the liability of a seller for personal injuries resulting from misrepresentation:

> One engaged in the business of selling chattels who, by advertising, labels, or otherwise, makes to the public a misrepresentation of a material fact concerning the character or quality of a chattel sold by him is subject to liability for physical harm to a consumer of the chattel caused by justifiable reliance upon the misrepresentation, even though
>
> (a) it is not made fraudulently or negligently, and
>
> (b) the consumer has not bought the chattel from or entered into any contractual relation with the seller.

The rationale of the Restatement position is that a great deal of what the consumer knows about a product comes to him through the various media, and sellers should be held responsible for injuries caused by misrepresentations made to the public. In our complex society, where sellers offer apparently similar but in reality fundamentally different products, the rationale behind the rule is most persuasive. A manufacturing seller knows the capabilities of his products, for he is the one who has designed and tested them. The consumer, on the other hand, knows only the information he has been able to glean from the seller's marketing material. Logic dictates that the seller should bear the responsibility for his misrepresentation because of his superior knowledge.[3]

Liability under §402B does not depend upon the factors giving rise to the misrepresentation, nor does it require contractual privity. It is a rule of strict liability which, even in the absence of bad faith or negligence, makes sellers liable

---

[3] Winkler v. Am. Safety Equipment Corp., p. 590.

if a consumer of their product suffers physical harm as a result of justifiable reliance on the seller's misrepresentation. A manufacturer may advertise that a certain shampoo contains no harmful ingredients and is perfectly safe to use even by people with tender skin. If someone uses the shampoo and suffers a skin ailment as a result thereof, he would be entitled to recover.

6. Theory

STRICT LIABILITY

The latest development in products liability is the tort theory, known as *strict liability*. This development imposes liability wherever damage or injury is caused by a defective product that is unreasonably dangerous to the user or consumer. It is the logical result of the elimination of the need to prove negligence and of the demise of the privity requirement in breach of warranty actions. The strict tort action is often preferable to the warranty action because disclaimers of warranty and notice of breach are not problems. As a result, in states that have adopted the strict liability theory, the theories of negligence and breach of warranty are becoming less significant in personal injury cases.

The theory of strict tort liability was developed by legal scholars as a part of the Restatement of the Law of Torts. Section 402A of the Restatement (Second) provides the following:

> 402A. Special Liability of Seller of Product for Physical Harm to User or Consumer.
>
> (1) One who sells any product in a defective condition unreasonably dangerous to the user or consumer, or to his property, is subject to liability for physical harm thereby caused to the ultimate user or consumer, or to his property, if
>
> > (a) the seller is engaged in the business of selling such a product, and
> >
> > (b) it is expected to and does reach the user or consumer without substantial change in the condition in which it is sold.
>
> (2) The rule stated in Subsection (1) applies although
>
> > (a) the seller has exercised all possible care in the preparation and sale of his product, and
> >
> > (b) the user or consumer has not bought the product from or entered into any contractual relation with the seller.

The courts have relied heavily upon these rules in developing the law of strict tort liability. Today, it is the law in most states.

Strict liability is imposed on manufacturers and designers, as well as on the seller of the goods, but in most states it is not applicable to the sale of used goods. But there is now a definite trend toward applying it to used goods. In almost every state, the liability extends not only to users and consumers, but also to bystanders such as pedestrians. Strict liability has been applied both to personal injuries and to damage to the property of the user or consumer. Some courts have refused to extend it to property damage, and most courts have refused to extend it to economic loss.

The theory of strict liability has been applied to leases of goods as well as to sales.[4] The potential liability extends to all commercial suppliers of goods.

7. Product Defined

The question of the scope and substance of the term *product* as used in strict liability cases has received considerable discussion in recent decisions. Originally, product was confined to chattels (tangible personal property), such as food for human consumption or other products intended for intimate bodily use. Using the chattel concept, many courts have had no trouble in finding many items to be products: a can of Drano, baseball sunglasses, a carpenter's hammer, and a Corvair. But with the progress of technology and changing notions of justice and strict liability, case law has progressed so that terms like *defect* and *product* remain open-ended. Recently, blood,[5] electricity, hot water drawn from a faucet, X-radiation, a house, a rental apartment, and a lot "manufactured" by considerable earthmoving have been held to be products—at least in the sense that the theory of strict liability has been applied to them. Courts now focus on the public policy reasons underlying strict products liability, and they label the transaction as the sale of a product when those policies apply.

Public policy considerations advanced to support strict products liability include: (1) public interest in human life and health; (2) the special responsibility of one who markets a defective product that causes harm; (3) invitations and solicitations by the manufacturer to purchase the product and representations that it is safe and suitable for use; and (4) the justice of imposing the loss on the party who created the risk and reaped the benefit by placing the item in the stream of commerce.

Note that *product* also includes its container, whether or not sold with the product. A restaurant was held strictly liable for the injuries to a customer's hand when a wine glass shattered. Moreover, a gas company that furnished a gas tank incidental to the sale of gas had to assume responsibility for injuries caused by the defective tank.

8. Defect

For the product to be considered defective, the plaintiff must establish that it was substandard. In all cases, plaintiff must prove all three of the following:

1. The product was defective.
2. The defect existed at the time the product left the defendant's control.
3. The defect caused plaintiff's injury.

Although any attempt to define *defect* in generalized terms can be misleading, many courts adopt a *consumer expectations test*. If a product meets all demands and expectations of society but someone is nonetheless injured, then we can hardly

---

[4] Dewberry v. La Follette, p. 592.
[5] Belle Bonfils Memorial Blood Bank v. Hansen, p. 592.

blame the manufacturer. A manufacturer is not absolutely liable. It is not an insurer. As consumers, we know and expect some products to be dangerous. Cars kill pedestrians; knives cut fingers; cigarettes cause cancer. These products are considered dangerous, but that fact does not make them defective. A product is defective when it does not meet the standards of safety consumers expect. A self-propelled power lawnmower can slice a user's foot. If that injury could have been prevented by a safety guard or other safety design, the mower without the safety feature may be defective.

Section 402A, in part, provides: "One who sells any product in a defective condition *unreasonably dangerous* to the user or consumer or to his property is subject to liability for physical harm thereby caused to the ultimate user or consumer, or to his property." The majority of courts regard the idea of "unreasonably dangerous" as inseparable from the definition of defect.

Under the comments to Section 402A, a product is defective when "it is in a condition not contemplated by the ultimate consumer, which will be unreasonably dangerous to him." A product is to be found to be unreasonably dangerous when it is "dangerous to the extent beyond that which would be contemplated by the ordinary consumer." We expect that real butter, fatty meat, and good whiskey may be dangerous, but not unreasonably so. The term *defective* as interpreted by courts is applied to an almost endless variety of product design, function, and performance contexts.[6]

9. Proof Required

A product is *unreasonably dangerous* when it has a propensity for causing physical harm beyond that which would be contemplated by the ordinary user who purchases it, with the ordinary knowledge common to the foreseeable class of users as to its characteristics. A *defective condition* of a product is a condition causing injury which was not contemplated by the ultimate user and which presented a hazard he did not expect. Unreasonably defective really means unexpectedly defective.

The crucial difference between strict liability and negligence is that the existence of due care, whether on the part of seller or consumer, is irrelevant to the former. The seller is responsible for injury caused by his defective product, even if he has exercised all possible care in the preparation and sale of the product. The duty of a seller is not fulfilled by taking all reasonable measures to make his product safe. The strict liability issue focuses on whether the product was defective and unreasonably dangerous and not on the conduct of the seller.

Product defects arise from three sources. The first and most basic is the *production defect,* arising from an error during the manufacture of the product. Production defects generally are easy to recognize. The classic example is the soda-pop bottle that explodes because of an imperfection in the glass of the bottle or inadvertent overcarbonization. A production defect, thus, occurs when the product does not meet the manufacturer's own standards.

---

[6] Spencer v. Nelson Sales Co., Inc., p. 593.

The second source of product defect is *design defect.* In contrast to the production defect, the product meets the standard the manufacturer intended. In a design case, the injured plaintiff will allege that the design or the manufacturer's standards were inferior and should be judged defective. The plaintiff, in order to prove that a particular product is defective in design, must show that there was some practical way in which the product could have been made safer.

Finally, there is the product that is made as intended according to a design that could not be improved, but that has some characteristic not brought to the attention of the user or consumer. There has been a failure to warn. A *failure to warn (marketing defect)* is the third source of product defect. The duty of the manufacturer to provide adequate warnings and directions for use is a prolific source of litigation today.[7] To be "adequate," the warning must have two characteristics. First, it must be in such a *form* that it could reasonably be expected to catch the attention of a reasonable person in the context of its use. Second, the *content* of the warning must be comprehensible to the average user and must convey with a degree of *intensity* that would cause a prudent person to exercise caution commensurate with the potential danger. In sum, a warning may be inadequate in factual context, inadequate in expression of facts, or inadequate in the method by which it is conveyed. But note that a manufacturer or seller is not required to warn of dangers that are known or should be known by the user of the product.

A cause of action in strict liability also usually requires proof that the defective product reached the plaintiff without a change of condition, and that the product caused an injury to the plaintiff. For a manufacturer to have liability, the product must be defective at the time it left the manufacturer's possession. A manufacturer may introduce evidence that the product was substantially altered after leaving its possession, which evidence may rebut or overcome plaintiff's showing that his injuries were the result of the product's defect. However, before a manufacturer is put to the trouble and expense of establishing that its product was altered, the plaintiff in most cases must first establish that the product was defective when it left the manufacturer's possession.

There are a few exceptions where such proof would be impossible. For example, a victim of a propane gas explosion was not required to prove the condition of the propane gas when it left the manufacturer. The court in that case held that a plaintiff's burden on the issue of defect is limited to proof that the defect which rendered the product unreasonably dangerous to the user or consumer occurred in the course of the distribution process and before the plaintiff purchased the product. In the case of a product sold in bulk, such as propane, this burden is satisfied by evidence showing that the product was defective and unreasonably dangerous when purchased or when put to use within a reasonable time after purchase.

In strict liability cases there are no issues on disclaimer or warranties, there is no problem of inconsistency with express warranties, and knowledge of the seller of the defect need not be proved. Of course, privity of contract is not required, and neither is reliance on a warranty by the injured party.

Even if a plaintiff proves injury from a product, he cannot recover without

---

[7] Ilosky v. Michelin Tire Corp., p. 594.

proving causation between that defect and the injury. As previously noted, the defect must have existed when the product left the seller's hands. A seller is not liable if a safe product is made unsafe by subsequent changes. All of a plaintiff's proof may be made by circumstantial evidence.

10. Defenses

Strict liability is not synonymous with *absolute liability.* There must be proof that some dangerous defect caused the injury, despite the fact that the product was being used in the manner reasonably anticipated by the seller or the manufacturer. In addition, there are defenses which may be asserted to avoid liability. It is often said that contributory negligence is not a defense to a suit based on the theory of strict liability. This is somewhat of an oversimplification, however, because misuse of a product is a defense. Moreover, a person who voluntarily encounters a known unreasonable danger is not entitled to recover. A seller of a product is entitled to have his due warnings and instructions followed; when they are disregarded and injury results, the seller is not liable. Moreover, when a user unreasonably proceeds to use a product he knows to be defective or dangerous, he relinquishes the protection of the law. There is no duty on the part of manufacturers to create products that will insure against injury to the most indifferent, adventurous, or foolhardy people.

In recent years, a doctrine known as *comparative negligence* has replaced contributory negligence in tort cases based on negligence. Under comparative negligence, an injured person's recovery is reduced by his share of fault. For example, if a plaintiff is 20 percent at fault and the defendant is 80 percent at fault, a plaintiff is entitled to recover only 80 percent of the damages sustained. Today, some courts are applying comparative negligence to suits based on strict liability.[8]

For purposes of comparative negligence, negligence of the plaintiff is not a defense when such negligence consists merely in a failure to discover the defect in the product, or to guard against the possibility of its existence. A consumer's unobservant, inattentive, ignorant, or awkward failure to discover or guard against a defect is not a damage-reducing factor. The consumer or user is entitled to believe that the product will do the job for which it was built.

When comparative negligence is used, the defenses of misuse and assumption of the risk do not bar recovery. Instead, such misconduct is compared in the apportionment of damages. Once a defendant's liability is established, and where both the defective product and plaintiff's misconduct contribute to cause the damages, the comparative fault principle operates to reduce the plaintiff's recovery by that amount which the trier of fact finds him at fault.

Failure to heed a warning with regard to a product will bar a recovery. This, in effect, means that "assumption of the risk" is a defense to a strict liability action. Misuse and abnormal use of a product is a defense because the manufacturer or seller could not have reasonably foreseen the misuse. If a backwoodsman uses a sharp hunting and fishing knife to shave and he cuts his throat, it is conceivable that the manufacturer would be entitled to a defense of misuse of the instrument.

---

[8] Coney v. J. L. G. Industries, Inc. p. 596.

TABLE 26–2

Comparison between strict tort and warranty

	WARRANTY OF MERCHANTABILITY UCC §2-314	STRICT TORT LIABILITY RESTATEMENT (SECOND) TORTS §402A
Condition of goods giving rise to liability	Not merchantable; that is, not fit for ordinary purpose. §2-314(1), (2)(c).	Defective condition unreasonably dangerous. §402A(1).
Character of defendant	Must be seller who is a merchant with respect to goods of that kind. §§2-314(1), 2-104(1).	Must be seller who is engaged in the business of selling such a product. §402A(1)(a).
Reliance	No explicit requirement. Such warranty "taken for granted." §2-314; see however, §2-316(3)(b).	No requirement of "any reliance on the part of the consumer upon the reputation, skill or judgment of the seller." §402A Comment m.
Disclaimer	Limitation of consequential damages for injury to the person in the case of consumer goods is prima facie unconscionable. §§2-316(4), 2-719(3), 2-302.	Cause of action not affected by any disclaimer or any other agreement. §402A Comment m.
Notice	Buyer must within a reasonable time after he discovers, or should have discovered, any breach notify seller of breach or be barred from any remedy. Reason of rule: to defeat commercial bad faith, not to deprive a good-faith consumer of his remedy. §2-607(3)(a).	Consumer not required to give notice to seller of his injury within a reasonable time after it occurs. §402A Comment m.
Causation	Buyer may recover consequential damages *resulting* from seller's breach including injury to person or property *proximately resulting* from any breach of warranty. §§2-714, 2-715(2)(b), §2-314; see §2-316(3)(b).	Seller subject to liability for physical harm *caused.* §402A(1); see Comment n. *Contributory negligence* is not a defense.
Protected persons	The third persons protected depend on the alternative of §2-318 adopted.	Ultimate user or consumer. §402A(1), (2)(b) and Comment l.
Protected injuries	Injuries to person or his property. §2-318.	Physical harm to ultimate user or consumer or to his property. §402A(1).
Statute of limitations	Four years from tender of delivery. §2-725(1), (2).	State law varies (from 1 to 3 years from injury).

11. Comparison of Strict Tort and Warranty

Table 26–2, on the previous page, demonstrates a basic similarity between strict tort liability and the warranty of merchantability. For instance, "defective condition unreasonably dangerous" and "fit for ordinary purposes" seem to be similar tests under the notion of "defect." But strict tort may prove the simplest remedy. In a breach of warranty case, the plaintiff may have to overcome contract defenses such as disclaimers of liability, the requirement of notice of breach, limitation of remedies, and lack of privity. Where there is only economic loss (no physical harm to person or property), then most courts will not allow a recovery in strict tort. Warranty liability for economic loss, however, is available. Moreover, the UCC provides a longer statute of limitations in which to bring the action. Practical considerations such as the availability or solvency of a particular defendant may also affect the choice of theory.

SUMMARY

PRODUCTS LIABILITY THEORIES

Negligence

1. Negligence evaluates the reasonableness of the defendant's conduct. The defendant's conduct is deemed negligent only when it is inferior to what a "reasonable" person would have done under similar circumstances.
2. A negligence suit can be brought not only by the person who purchased the defective product, but also by any person who suffered an injury due to a defective product.
3. The doctrine of *res ipsa loquitur* may be used to prove negligence.
4. Negligence may be established by proof that the manufacturer violated some statutory regulation in the production and distribution of the product.
5. Negligence is frequently based on failure of a manufacturer to warn of a known danger related to the product. A manufacturer who knows, or should know, his product to be dangerous has a duty to exercise reasonable care and foresight in preventing it from injuring or endangering people.

Misrepresentation	1. If the seller has advertised the product through newspapers, magazines, television, or otherwise and has made misrepresentations regarding the character or quality of the product, strict tort liability may be imposed on him.
	2. Intent to mislead is not required and neither is privity of contract.
Breach of warranty	1. Product liability may arise from breach of an express warranty or the implied warranties of merchantability and fitness for a particular purpose.
	2. Lack of privity of contract is no defense.

STRICT LIABILITY

Theory	1. In strict liability cases, the focus of attention is on the product.
	2. A manufacturer selling a defective product in a defective condition that is unreasonably dangerous to the user or his property is liable for physical injuries caused by the defect.
	3. A plaintiff need not prove negligence of the manufacturer or seller. Disclaimers and notice of breach are not problems, and lack of privity of contract is immaterial.
	4. The theory may apply to leases as well as sales.
Product defects	1. A manufacturer, distributor, or seller of a product is liable to compensate a person injured by a defective product.
	2. Products include tangible personal property, items such as electricity, and containers for goods such as pop bottles.
	3. The consumer expectations test is used to determine if a product is defective. A product is defective if it does not meet the standards of safety consumers expect.
	4. A product is defective when it is in a condition not contemplated by the ultimate consumer, which will be unreasonably dangerous to him. A product is unreasonably dangerous when it is dangerous to the extent beyond that

which would be contemplated by the ordinary consumer.

5. Product defects may be design defects, production defects, and marketing defects.

6. The typical marketing defect is a failure to warn.

Defenses

1. Contributory negligence is not a defense to a suit based on the theory of strict tort liability.

2. Misuse and abnormal use of a product are defenses.

3. Assumption of the risk is a defense.

4. Comparative negligence is often used to reduce verdicts in strict products liability cases.

CASES

Donnelly Const. Co. v. Oberg/Hunt/ Gilleland
677 P.2d 1292 (Ariz. 1984)

GORDON, J. . . . In June of 1976, the Board of Supervisors of Coconino County solicited bids on behalf of Page School District Number Eight for improvements to the Page School complex. The site improvements included the construction of retaining walls and sidewalks, grading and filling, and the installation of a sprinkler system. Among the documents available to the bidders was a site plan, including engineering site specifications, prepared by Oberg/Hunt/Gilleland [hereinafter "O/H/G"], a firm of architects. Plaintiff, Donnelly Construction Company, relied on the plans, specifications, and information contained in the site plan to prepare its bid on the improvements. Donnelly's bid was accepted and a contract with the county board of supervisors was entered on July 6, 1976. Upon beginning work, Donnelly found the plans and specifications prepared by O/H/G to be in substantial error. The errors resulted in increased costs of construction to Donnelly.

After substantially completing work, Donnelly sued O/H/G for its increased costs. Donnelly

asserted three claims against O/H/G: negligence, negligent misrepresentation, and breach of the implied warranty that O/H/G's plans and specifications were accurate. . . . (The trial court dismissed the complaint.)

O/H/G's . . . basis for the motion to dismiss was that, absent privity of contract, they owed no duty and could not be liable to a contractor such as Donnelly.

. . . There is no requirement of privity in this state to maintain an action in tort. . . . Rather, an action in negligence may be maintained upon the plaintiff's showing that the defendant owed a duty to him, that the duty was breached, and that the breach proximately caused an injury which resulted in actual damages. Duty and liability are only imposed where both the plaintiff and the risk are foreseeable to a reasonable person. This Court has held that a broad view will be taken of the class of risks and the class of victims that are foreseeable.

Design professionals have a duty to use ordinary skill, care, and diligence in rendering their professional services. When they are called upon to provide plans and specifications for a particular job, they must use their skill and care to provide plans and specifications which are sufficient and adequate. This duty extends to those with whom the design professional is in privity, . . . and to those with whom he or she is not. . . .

We find it foreseeable . . . that Donnelly, hired to follow the plans and specifications prepared by O/H/G, would incur increased costs if those plans and specifications were in error. . . . The complaint did state a cause of action in negligence and its dismissal was error. . . .

Donnelly's second cause of action against O/H/G was for negligent misrepresentation. Such an action . . . is governed by §552 of the Restatement (Second) of Torts. Section 552 provides:

> INFORMATION NEGLIGENTLY SUPPLIED FOR THE GUIDANCE OF OTHERS (1) One who, in the course of his business, profession or employment, or in any other transaction in which he has a pecuniary interest, supplies false information for the guidance of others in their business transactions, is subject to liability for pecuniary loss caused to them by their justifiable reliance upon the information, if he fails to exercise reasonable care or competence in obtaining or communicating the information. . . .

By its terms, this section does not require privity to maintain a cause of action. . . . Illustration 9 of the comments to §552 is particularly enlightening and is pertinent to the case before us:

> The City of A is about to ask for bids for work on

a sewer tunnel. It hires B Company, a firm of engineers, to make boring tests and provide a report showing the rock and soil conditions to be encountered. It notifies B Company that the report will be made available to bidders as a basis for their bids and that it is expected to be used by the successful bidder in doing the work. Without knowing the identity of any of the contractors bidding on the work, B Company negligently prepares and delivers to the City an inaccurate report, containing false and misleading information. On the basis of the report C makes a successful bid, and also on the basis of the report D, a subcontractor, contracts with C to do a part of the work. By reason of the inaccuracy of the report, C and D suffer pecuniary loss in performing their contracts. B company is subject to liability to B [sic] and to D.

Donnelly's complaint stated a cause of action in negligent misrepresentation and its dismissal was error.

Donnelly's third cause of action was for breach of the implied warranty that O/H/G's plans and specifications were accurate. Design professionals, in the absence of an express guarantee, do not "warrant" that their work will be "accurate." Rather, . . . they "warrant" merely that they have exercised their skills with care and diligence and in a reasonable, non-negligent manner. A claim for breach of a common law warranty does not require privity, and thus, the dismissal of it was error. . . .

Reversed and remanded.

Greenman v. Yuba Power Products, Inc. 377 P.2d 897 (Cal. 1963)

TRAYNOR, J. . . . Plaintiff brought this action for damages against the retailer and the manufacturer of a Shopsmith, a combination power tool that could be used as a saw, drill, and wood lathe. He saw a Shopsmith demonstrated by the retailer and studied a brochure prepared by the manufacturer. He decided he wanted a Shopsmith for his home workshop, and his wife bought and gave him one for Christmas in 1955. In 1957 he bought the necessary attachments to use the Shopsmith as a lathe for turning a large piece of wood he wished to make into a chalice. After he had worked on the piece of wood several times without diffi-

culty, it suddenly flew out of the machine and struck him on the forehead, inflicting serious injuries. About ten and a half months later, he gave the retailer and the manufacturer written notice of claimed breaches of warranties and filed a complaint against them alleging such breaches and negligence.

After a trial before a jury, the court ruled that there was no evidence that the retailer was negligent or had breached any express warranty and that the manufacturer was not liable for the breach of any implied warranty. Accordingly, it submitted to the jury only the cause of action alleging breach of implied warranties against the retailer and the causes of action alleging negligence and breach of express warranties against the manufacturer. The jury returned a verdict for the retailer against plaintiff and for plaintiff against the manufacturer in the amount of $65,000. The manufacturer and plaintiff appeal. Plaintiff seeks a reversal of the part of the judgment in favor of the retailer, however, only in the event that the part of the judgment against the manufacturer is reversed.

Plaintiff introduced substantial evidence that his injuries were caused by defective design and construction of the Shopsmith. His expert witnesses testified that inadequate set screws were used to hold parts of the machine together so that normal vibration caused the tailstock to the lathe to move away from the piece of wood being turned permitting it to fly out of the lathe. They also testified that there were other more positive ways of fastening the parts of the machine together, the use of which would have prevented the accident. The jury could therefore reasonably have concluded that the manufacturer negligently constructed the Shopsmith. The jury could also reasonably have concluded that statements in the manufacturer's brochure were untrue, that they constituted express warranties, and that the plaintiff's injuries were caused by their breach.

The manufacturer contends, however, that plaintiff did not give it notice of breach of warranty within a reasonable time and that therefore his cause of action for breach of warranty is barred by section 1769 of the Civil Code. Since it cannot be determined whether the verdict against it was based on the negligence or warranty cause of action or both, the manufacturer concludes that the error in presenting the warranty cause of action to the jury was prejudicial.

Section 1769 of the Civil Code provides: "In the absence of express or implied agreement of the parties, acceptance of the goods by the buyer shall not discharge the seller from liability in damages or other legal remedy for breach of any promise or warranty in the contract to sell or the sale. But, if, after acceptance of the goods, the buyer fails to give notice to the seller of the breach of any promise or warranty within a reasonable time after the buyer knows, or ought to know of such breach, the seller shall not be liable therefor."

Like other provisions of the uniform sales act, section 1769 deals with the rights of the parties to a contract of sale or a sale. It does not provide that

notice must be given of the breach of a warranty that arises independently of a contract of sale between the parties. Such warranties are not imposed by the sales act, but are the product of common-law decisions that have recognized them in a variety of situations.

The notice requirement of section 1769, however, is not an appropriate one for the court to adopt in actions by injured consumers against manufacturers with whom they have not dealt. "As between the immediate parties to the sale [the notice requirement] is a sound commercial rule, designed to protect the seller against unduly delayed claims for damages. As applied to personal injuries, and notice to a remote seller, it becomes a boobytrap for the unwary. The injured consumer is seldom 'steeped in the business practice which justifies the rule,' and at least until he has had legal advice it will not occur to him to give notice to one with whom he has had no dealings." We conclude, therefore, that even if plaintiff did not give timely notice of breach of warranty to the manufacturer, his cause of action based on the representations contained in the brochure was not barred.

Moreover, to impose strict liability on the manufacturer under the circumstances of this case, it was not necessary for plaintiff to establish an express warranty as defined in Section 1732 of the Civil Code. A manufacturer is strictly liable in tort when an article he places on the market knowing that it is to be used without inspection for defects, proves to have a defect that causes injury to a human being. Recognized first in the case of unwholesome food products, such liability has now been extended to a variety of other products that create as great or greater hazards if defective.

Although in these cases strict liability has usually been based on the theory of an express or implied warranty running from the manufacturer to the plaintiff, the abandonment of the requirement of a contract between them, the recognition that the liability is not assumed by agreement but imposed by law . . . and the refusal to permit the manufacturer to define the scope of its own responsibility for defective products . . . make clear that the liability is not one governed by the law of contract warranties but by the law of strict liability in tort. Accordingly, rules defining and governing warranties that were developed to meet the needs of commercial transactions cannot properly be invoked to govern the manufacturer's liability to those injured by their defective products unless those rules also serve the purposes for which such liability is imposed.

The purpose of strict liability is to insure that the costs of injuries resulting from defective products are borne by the manufacturers that put such products on the market rather than by the injured persons who are powerless to protect themselves. Sales warranties serve this purpose fitfully at best. In the present case, for example, plaintiff was able to plead and prove an express warranty only because he read and relied on the representations of the Shopsmith's ruggedness contained in the manufacturer's brochure. Implicit in the machine's presence on the market, however, was a representation that it would safely do the jobs for which it was built. Under these circumstances, it should not be controlling whether plaintiff selected the machine because of the statement in the brochure, or because of the machine's own appearance of excellence that belied the defect lurking beneath the surface, or because he merely assumed that it would safely do the jobs it was built to do. It should not be controlling whether the details of the sales from manufacturer to retailer and from retailer to plaintiff's wife were such that one or more of the implied warranties of the sales act arose. "The remedies of injured consumers ought not to be made to depend upon the intricacies of the law of sales." To establish the manufacturer's liability it was sufficient that plaintiff proved that he was injured while using the Shopsmith in a way it was intended to be used as a result of a defect in design and manufacture of which plaintiff was not aware that made the Shopsmith unsafe for its intended use.

Judgment affirmed.

Winkler v. Am. Safety Equipment Corp. 604 P.2d 693 (Colo. App. 1980)

SMITH, J. . . . In this personal injury action, one theory of recovery asserted by Plaintiff, Donald Winkler, was misrepresentation by a seller of chattels to a consumer as expressed in the *Restatement (Second) of Torts* §402B (1965). The court refused Winkler's tendered jury instruction based upon this theory. From a defendant's verdict, Winkler appeals. We reverse.

Donald Winkler was an officer in the Denver Police Department. As permitted by department policy, he obtained for his own personal use a helmet which, because of its appearance, had been discarded by the department. The helmet, manufactured by the defendant, American Safety Equipment Corporation, was originally purchased by the Denver Police Department for use in crowd or riot control. It was originally packaged in a carton which depicted a motorcyclist wearing the seller's helmet. Winkler prior to acquiring his helmet had become familiar with the cartons in which they were originally delivered. Believing that the helmet was intended for motorcycle use, Winkler used the helmet for that purpose. While riding his motorcycle, he collided with a pickup truck. Upon impact, the helmet, performing as designed, i.e., for quick release, came off of his head, and as a result he suffered head injuries. Although the helmet performed as designed, Winkler claims that it did not perform as represented on the packaging carton, that is, as a motorcycle helmet. It is this asserted misrepresentation upon which Winkler bases a cause of action under §402B. . . .

The *Restatement (Second) of Torts* §402B . . . imposes strict tort liability upon sellers of products which are *not* defective in design or manufacture, but which are misrepresented to the consuming public.

Section 402B reads as follows:

> One engaged in the business of selling chattels who, by advertising, labels, or otherwise, makes to the public a misrepresentation of a material fact concerning the character or quality of a chattel sold by him is subject to liability for physical harm to a consumer of the chattel caused by justifiable reliance upon the misrepresentation, even though
>
> (a) it is not made fraudulently or negligently, and
>
> (b) the consumer has not bought the chattel from or entered into any contractual relation with the seller.

Under §402B the seller of chattels who misrepresents material facts concerning their character or quality is subject to liability for the physical harm caused to a consumer who relies on the misrepresentation. This rule has evolved because a consumer, out of necessity, must rely upon the representations made by sellers when he makes his purchase decision.

Thus, when a product fails to perform to the level, or in the manner that the consumer has been led, by the seller, to believe it will, and that failure causes physical harm, the seller is liable for that harm. Liability under §402B does not, however, depend upon the factors giving rise to the misrepresentation, nor does it require contractual privity normally associated with warranty. It is a rule of strict liability, which, even in the absence of bad faith or negligence, makes sellers liable if a consumer of their product suffers physical harm as a result of justifiable reliance on the seller's misrepresentation.

In a complex society where sellers offer apparently similar but in reality fundamentally different products, the rationale behind the rule is most persuasive. It is the manufacturing seller who knows the capabilities of his products, for he is the one who has designed and tested them. The consumer, on the other hand, knows only the information he has been able to glean from the seller's marketing material. Logic dictates, then, that the seller should bear the responsibility for his misrepresentation because of his superior knowledge. That this is the logic of the rule is evidenced by the fact that the rule applies only to those engaged in the business of selling, and thus, excludes the casual seller who cannot be expected to know the capabilities of the product to any greater extent than the consumer.

Imposing strict liability upon sellers who misrepresent their products does not create an undue burden upon them. Rather, the rule merely mandates that in order to gain the economic benefits a seller can expect to receive from the representations it makes to the public, the seller must likewise assume the economic consequences for the physical harm resulting from even inadvertent misrepresentations it has made about the products. To permit sellers to benefit from representations made to the public, and at the same time to relieve them of liability for errors in their representations would be to allow them to avoid an integral part of the appropriate costs of manufacturing and marketing their products.

Here, Winkler established a prima facie cause of action based on §402B for misrepresentation by a seller of chattels. The carton from which the helmet or similar helmets came depicted a motorcyclist using the helmet. This illustration constituted a representation, and its materiality, and whether it was relied upon, were questions for the jury.

Section 402B requires that the misrepresentation be made to the public. *Restatement, Comment h,* indicates that if a misrepresentation is intended to reach the public, or indeed does reach the public, the rule will be applied. We hold that a misrepresentation has been made to the public when a seller, as part of his merchandising program, communicates the misrepresentation to potential purchasers or users of his product, even when they constitute only a small or a select portion of the consuming public.

The fact that the merchandising effort is aimed at governmental bodies, such as police departments, is of no import in determining whether the misrepresentation is public. The key factor is that the misrepresentation is made as part of the merchandising of the product. Once a misrepresentation is made to the public, any user who justifiably relies upon the misrepresentation and suffers physical harm as a result thereof may recover. . . .

That Winkler did not purchase the helmet from the defendant is not a defense because §402B applies "even though . . . the consumer has not bought the chattel from or entered into any contractual relation with the seller." It is the reliance upon the seller's misrepresentation that gives rise to the cause of action under this rule and not privity of contract.

For the foregoing reasons, we conclude that the trial court erred in refusing to instruct the jury regarding Winkler's claim for relief based on misrepresentation of a chattel under the *Restatement (Second) of Torts* §402B.

Reversed.

Dewberry v. LaFollette
598 P.2d 241 (Okl. 1979)

DOOLIN, J. . . . This appeal arises out of an attempt by an injured plaintiff to plead a cause of action in manufacturers' products liability against a lessor of personal property.

Plaintiff's son and his wife occupied a mobile home under a lease-purchase agreement with defendants. As part of the agreement, defendants supplied a set of access steps to the home. Plaintiff was seriously injured when the stairs collapsed while she was descending them.

Plaintiff filed the present action against defendants as lessors of the mobile home and steps. The trial court sustained defendants' demurrer to the petition for failure to state a cause of action. Plaintiff appeals.

The policy of strict liability in tort defined as manufacturer's products liability extends its *protection* to any person using the defective product for its intended purpose. This would include the present plaintiff. The decision further extends *liability* to "suppliers" of the defective product as well as manufacturers and sellers. This may be read to impose liability on all those who inject a product into the stream of commerce whether through a sale or other means. One Oklahoma court holds this includes lessors and bailors engaged in the business of leasing chattels to the public where no sale is involved.

The evident trend of other jurisdictions is to expand the concept of strict liability to include commercial lessors on the basis such persons put products into the stream of commerce in a fashion not unlike a manufacturer or retailer. However, the property must have been placed in the stream of commerce; a casual or isolated transaction does not bring the doctrine into play.

[The decisions in other states have] premised their holdings on these pertinent factors: (1) In some instances the lessor, like the seller, may be the only member of the marketing chain available to the injured plaintiff for redress; (2) As in the case of the seller, imposition of strict liability upon the lessor serves as an incentive to safety; (3) The lessor will be in a better position than the consumer to prevent the circulation of defective products; and (4) The lessor can distribute the cost of compensating for injuries resulting from defects by charging for it in his business, i.e., by adjustment of the rental terms. We find the reasoning of these opinions to be highly persuasive and hold that all suppliers of products engaged in the business of supplying products for use or consumption by the public are subject to strict liability for injuries caused by "a defective condition unreasonably dangerous to the user or consumer or his property."

We adopt this reasoning. . . . We perceive no substantial difference between sellers of personal property and non-sellers of personal property such as lessors. In each instance the seller or lessor places an article in the stream of commerce; it makes no difference that lessor has retained title.

Here plaintiff did not plead liability of defendant based on a landlord-tenant relationship. She alleged defendants were in the business of leasing mobile home accessories, which are personal property. She alleged the steps were defective and unreaasonably dangerous when they left the defendants' possession and control. She further pleaded they were the cause of her injuries. These are the necessary elements of a cause of action in manufacturers' products liability, which we hereby make applicable to lessor-lessee relationships. . . .

Reversed and remanded.

Belle Bonfils Memorial Blood Bank
v. Hansen
379 P.2d 1158 (Colo. 1978)

Muriel Hansen, while a patient at Mercy Hospital, received a blood transfusion consisting of several units of blood supplied by the defendant blood bank. She filed suit against the blood bank, claiming she had contracted serum hepatitis as a result of the transfusion, and that the blood bank was liable by reason of strict liability and breach of implied warranties. The trial judge granted the blood bank's motion for summary judgment, basing its ruling upon *St. Luke's Hospital* v. *Schmaltz,* 188 Colo. 353 (1975). The court of appeals reversed holding that the opinion in *Schmaltz* did not apply here.

GROVES, J. . . . In *Schmaltz* the plaintiff claimed that she contracted serum hepatitis from blood used in a transfusion, which blood was furnished by the defendant hospital.

There a majority of this court adopted the rationale of *Perlmutter v. Beth David Hospital,* 308 N.Y. 100 (1954). *Perlmutter* established the sales/service distinction for blood transfusion cases. In *Schmaltz* the majority followed *Perlmutter,* and held that a hospital was not *selling* blood but rather was *providing services.* It was stated:

> We are persuaded by the rationale expressed in the leading case on the question, *Perlmutter v. Beth David Hospital,* wherein the supplying by a hospital of blood for transfusion to a patient was viewed as only incidental to the basic function of the hospital, that of providing medical services through trained personnel and specialized facilities, for the care and treatment of the patient in an effort to restore his health.

> Although respondent's complaint alleges that petitioner "sold" blood for the purposes of transfusion, such being essential to raise the issue of warranty, the totality of the allegations does not change the true character of the transaction from that of furnishing medical services to that of a simple sale. We simply do not view it as realistic to hold the transfusion of blood, in these circumstances, is a sale of a product.

In the instant case the blood bank was selling blood, and was not *supplying medical services* as was held as to the hospital in *Schmaltz.* While supplying blood may be "only incidental to the basic function of the hospital," it is not an incidental function for a blood bank. Rather than incidental, supplying blood for transfusions is the basic function of a blood bank. It is not a small part of an overall range of services provided, as in the case of a hospital.

This is a *sales* and not a *services* situation. As a "sale" is involved, we reach the question as to whether blood is a "product" such that §402A of the Restatement (Second) of Torts may be applied. . . .

This court expressly approved §402A in the case of *Hiigel* v. *General Motors Corp.,* Colo., 544 P.2d 983 (1975). We now . . . hold that blood is a "product" for purposes of §402A.

While whole blood may well be viable, human tissue, and thus not a manufactured article of commerce, we believe that it must in this instance be considered a product in much the same way as other articles wholly unchanged from their natural state which are distributed for human consumption.

The plaintiff's claims on strict liability and breach of implied warranties should not have been dismissed on the basis of *Schmaltz.*

Judgment affirmed.

Spencer v. Nelson Sales Co., Inc.
620 P.2d 477 (Okla. 1980)

Melvin Spencer, the 52-year-old plaintiff, was doing some arc welding in his garage on a cold day in January, 1973. He had on a suit of long, quilted, insulated underwear that ignited when a hot spark penetrated his coveralls. The fire spread rapidly, severely burning his right leg. He sued the distributor of the insulated underwear. From a judgment for the defendant, Spencer appealed, claiming it was error not to instruct the jury on the word "defective."

BRIGHTMIRE, J. . . . The first and most obvious instructional shortcoming is the absence of a relevant definition of the vital term "defective."

[We apply] the rule stated in Restatement (Second) of Torts §402A (1964). The basic rule stated in this section is "One who sells any product in a defective condition unreasonably dangerous to the user or consumer or to his property is subject to liability" for the harm it causes.

Comments accompanying the principal statement of §402A reveal that the authors considered a product to be defective if the supplier fails to give directions or a warning as to its use or characteristics, if such is required to prevent the product from being unreasonably dangerous to the user.

But how could the jury go about making such a finding without knowing the legal meaning of the critical word "defective" in terms of the presented factual situation? Obviously they could not. This failure of the trial court to adaptively define "defective"—that is, in a way compatible with the pleadings and evidence—operated to deprive plaintiff of having his theory of recovery presented to the jury. As a consequence the trial judge breached his nondelegable duty to properly instruct the jury on a fundamental matter—a default that constituted prejudicial error necessitating a new trial.

Perhaps it would be helpful to discuss what definition should have been given. Courts have tended to avoid a stiff or inflexible definition of "defective" and have considered the term pliable and amenable to situational molding in an almost endless variety of product design, function and performance contexts. For example, it has been held that a product, though properly manufactured, is defective if its design is unreasonably dangerous, if it is not fit for the ordinary purposes for which such articles are sold and used, if it fails to perform its intended function safely, if it does not meet reasonable expectations of an ordinary consumer as to its safety, if it is rendered dangerous by failing to perform in a manner which can be reasonably expected in light of its nature and intended use, if the manufacturer uses material which results in an unreasonably dangerous design and a product unsafe for an intended use, if known risks inherent in the product that would lead a reasonable and humane seller to withhold it from the market, if the risks are greater than a reasonable buyer would expect, or if the product does not fulfill a policy assumption that it will serve in normal use without causing injury.

With regard to polio vaccine, the Oklahoma Supreme Court has held that a manufacturer's failure to warn prospective injectees of known risks renders the product defective. A product lacking safety devices necessary for a reasonably safe use of it is defective. In fact, the terms "dangerous" and "defective" have been treated as nearly synonymous in the text of a long-arm statute, and the words "defective condition" and "unreasonably dangerous" were considered to be "essentially synonymous" in a strict liability food case.

Here the evidence is that the particular undergarment worn by plaintiff—not some other similar one—possessed extraordinary ignition and flame characteristics. The user could not be expected to know this. Thus the jury should have been informed that a garment is defective (1) if its ignitability or flammability is extraordinary—that is, it ignites more readily and burns more rapidly and intensely than cotton or other conventional clothing materials—rendering it unreasonably dangerous; or (2) if it bears no label either instructing the user of the undergarment's high ignition and intense flame capability, or warning that because of its quilted design it is more combustible than conventional clothing and that it should not be permitted to come in contact with fire or anything hot.

Once the term defect is defined the explanation of the term unreasonably dangerous becomes both meaningful and useful. The jury should have been instructed that if they found the underwear caught fire and burned in the manner plaintiff testified it did, then it was defective and unreasonably dangerous.

The cause is reversed and remanded for a new trial.

Ilosky v. Michelin Tire Corp.
307 S.E.2d 603 (W.Va. 1983)

In June 1974, Edward Ilosky purchased a 1966 Ford Mustang from a neighbor for his daughter Karen to drive to work. At this time, Karen was 22 years old. At the time of purchase, the automobile was equipped with Michelin radial tires on the rear axle and either radial or conventional tires on the front axle.

At his daughter's request, Mr. Ilosky took the automobile to Ferguson's Tire. Co. on October 22, 1974, to purchase snow tires and to have them mounted on the rear axle. Mr. Ilosky purchased two recapped conventional snow tires and a Ferguson employee mounted them on the rear axle. At Mr. Ilosky's direction, the employee moved the radial tires on the rear axle to the front axle because the rear tires carried more tread than the front tires. As a result, the automobile was then equipped with radial tires on the front axle and conventional tires on the rear axle. Ferguson's employee did not advise Mr. Ilosky that mixing tire types in this manner was not recommended or that it could create a driving condition which could result in injury.

Michelin tires did not carry a warning about mixing tire types, even though the company had been aware for decades of the dangers. Michelin had undertaken a campaign against mixing radial and conventional tires and its literature recommended against such use. This literature, however, only went to direct purchasers and not to persons who purchased a used car equipped with Michelin radials.

Later that day Karen was traveling at between 20 and 30 miles per hour when she was unable to control her automobile, and it left the highway, crashing into a utility pole and splitting in two parts. She was seriously injured and sued Michelin, using the theory of strict liability. She alleged that the failure to provide an adequate warning of the dangers of mixing constituted a defect which made the radial tires unreasonably dangerous.

The trial court awarded $500,000 as damages and Michelin appeals.

McGRAW, J. . . . The starting point of our inquiry must be to determine whether Michelin is subject to the appellee's strict liability cause of action. . . .

In this jurisdiction the general test for establishing strict liability in tort is whether the involved product is defective in the sense that it is not reasonably safe for its intended use. The standard of reasonable safeness is determined not by the particular manufacturer, but by what a reasonably prudent manufacturer's standards should have been at the time the product was made. . . .

A defective product may fall into three broad, and not mutually exclusive, categories: design defectiveness; structural defectiveness; *and use defectiveness arising out of the lack of, or the adequacy of, warnings, instructions, and labels.* In use defectiveness, the focus is not so much on a flawed physical condition of the product, as on its unsafeness arising out of the failure to adequately label, instruct, or warn. Use defectiveness covers situations when a product may be safe as designed and manufactured, but which becomes defective because of the failure to warn of dangers which may be present when the product is used in a particular manner.

This case fits the use defectiveness category. The appellee does not claim that the Michelin radials were manufactured or designed in a defective manner. Rather, the appellee claims that when radials are used in combination with conventional tires in certain instances, they become dangerous, and that the manufacturer or other responsible party has a duty to warn of the danger and its potential consequences.

For the duty to warn to exist, the use of the product must be foreseeable to the manufacturer or seller. The question of what is an intended use of a product carries with it the concept of *all those uses* a reasonably prudent person might make of the product, having in mind its characteristics, warnings and labels. The Oklahoma Supreme Court has succinctly explained the concept of foreseeable use in strict liability cases.

> Foreseeability as applied to manufacturer's products liability is a narrow issue. A manufacturer must anticipate all foreseeable uses of his product. In order to escape being *unreasonably* dangerous, a *potentially* dangerous product must contain or reflect warnings covering all foreseeable uses. These warnings must be readily understandable and make the product safe.

The jury concluded that the appellee's use of the radial tires was a foreseeable use. We agree. The evidence at trial showed that Michelin had been aware of the hazards created by mixing radial and conventional tires in the manner utilized by the appellee. The company had taken steps to warn against such use. The tire industry itself recommended against such practice. Mixing radial and conventional tires has been outlawed in Great Britain, and radials are sold in only in sets of four in France. Both these actions presumably have been taken to prevent mixing tire types. Therefore, the appellee's use of the tires was foreseeable, and the appellant was under a duty to warn of the hazards associated with such use.

Having established that a strict liability cause of action could be maintained against Michelin, we must decide whether the appellee proved her case. . . .

Product unsafeness arising from failure to warn is to be tested by what the reasonably prudent manufacturer would accomplish in regard to the safety of the product, having in mind the general state of the art of the manufacturing process, including design, labels and warnings, as it relates to the economic costs, at the time the product was made. The determination of whether a defendant's efforts to warn of a product's dangers are adequate is a jury question.

The jury . . . concluded that Michelin's efforts to warn did not meet the legal standard. . . . To demonstrate ways Michelin could have attempted to warn, the plaintiff presented evidence that a warning could have been incorporated into the tire design itself for a few cents per tire. . . . Given this, we cannot say that the jury's conclusion that Michelin failed to adequately warn was not supported by the evidence. We do wish to make clear, however, that we are not saying that the jury found that the only method to ensure an adequate warning was to incorporate it into the tire. Whether that would be an adequate warning was not the issue; the legal question was whether Michelin's actual attempts at warning were legally sufficient. . . .

Additionally, the evidence supported the appellee's theory of causation, and the jury was entitled to find that the defect proximately resulted in the appellee's injuries. Therefore, we must affirm the jury's finding of liability against the appellant Michelin premised on a strict liability in tort cause of action.

Affirmed.

Coney v. J. L. G. Industries, Inc.
454 N.E.2d 197 (Ill. 1983)

Jasper died as a result of injuries sustained while operating a hydraulic aerial work platform manufactured by defendant, J. L. G. Industries, Inc. Plaintiff, administrator of Jasper's estate, filed suit based on a strict products liability theory. Defendant asserted that Jasper was guilty of comparative negligence or fault in his operation of the platform. It also contended that Jasper's employer was also guilty of comparative negligence in failing to instruct and train Jasper on the operation of the platform and by failing to provide a groundman. In these defenses, defendant requested that its fault, if any, be compared to the total fault of all parties and any judgment against defendant reflect only its percentage of the overall liability—i.e. that defendant not be held jointly and severally liable.

The trial court certified the following question for appeal: "Whether the doctrine of comparative negligence or fault is applicable to actions or claims seeking recovery under products liability or strict liability in tort theories?"

MORAN, J. . . . Imposition of strict liability was not meant to make the manufacturer an absolute insurer. The plaintiff must prove that the injury or damage resulted from the condition of the product, that the condition was an unreasonably dangerous one, and that the condition existed at the time the product left the manufacturer's control. Moreover, the court has heretofore followed the reasoning of the Restatement concerning the available defenses to a strict liability action. It has been held that a manufacturer can assert a user's negligence as a complete bar to recovery when it rises to the level of misuse of the product, or assumption of the risk; but contributory negligence is not a defense.

Traditionally in negligence actions, however, any contributory negligence by the plaintiff was an absolute defense which barred recovery. In response to the harshness of this doctrine, the court adopted comparative negligence and indicated that this concept produced "a more just and socially desirable distribution of loss" and was "demanded by today's society." Defendant maintains "total justice" can only be achieved where the relative fault of all the parties is considered in apportioning damages. To illustrate its argument, defendant points to the anomalous situation where, in a single case with alternate counts of negligence and strict liability, the identical conduct by the plaintiff which amounts to an assumption of the risk will completely bar recovery in the strict liability count, yet, . . . will only reduce his award under the negligence count. Moreover, if the plaintiff is only contributorily negligent, he recovers all his damages under strict liability, but his recovery is diminished under the negligence count. Defendant argues that common sense mandates an approach which is consistent in its treatment of all the parties to an action, whether founded on common law negligence or strict liability.

We are not the first to consider the impact of comparative negligence upon strict liability. Some jurisdictions have declined to apply comparative negligence or fault principles in strict liability actions. The vast majority, though, have found comparative negligence theory applicable in strict liability cases. . . .

We believe that application of comparative fault principles in strict products liability actions would not frustrate this court's fundamental reasons for adopting strict products liability. . . . The plaintiff will still be relieved of the proof problems associated with negligence and warranty actions. Privity and a manufacturer's negligence continue to be irrelevant. Nor would comparative fault lessen the manufacturer's duty to produce reasonably safe products. The manufacturer's liability remains strict; only its responsibility for damages is lessened by the extent the trier of facts finds the consumer's conduct contributed to the injuries.

Further, the risk associated with the product defect is still spread among all consumers. Only that portion due to plaintiff's own conduct or fault is borne by the plaintiff. Where the allocation of losses properly can be apportioned, we see no reason to spread the cost of the loss resulting from plaintiff's own fault on to the consuming public. We believe that equitable principles require that the total damages for plaintiff's injuries be apportioned on the basis of the relative degree to which the defective product and plaintiff's conduct proximately caused them. Accordingly, we hold that the defense of comparative fault is applicable to strict liability cases.

Amicus curiae argues that, if comparative fault is to be applied in strict products liability cases, we should not reduce a plaintiff's award if he merely fails to "inspect," "discover," or "guard against" a defective product.

Following the Restatement, this court adopted misuse and assumption of the risk as complete defenses to a strict products liability action. But, at the same time, it was said there that "[c]ontributory negligence of the plaintiff is not a defense when such negligence consists merely in a failure to discover the defect in the product, or to guard against the possibility of its existence." We adhere to this statement. We believe that a consumer's unobservant, inattentive, ignorant, or awkward failure to discover or guard against a defect should not be compared as a damage-reducing factor. . . .

However, the defenses of misuse and assumption of the risk will no longer bar recovery. Instead, such misconduct will be compared in the apportionment of damages. Specifically, we hold: Once defendant's liability is established, and where both the defective product and plaintiff's misconduct contribute to cause the damages, the comparative fault principle will operate to reduce plaintiff's recovery by that amount which the trier of fact finds him at fault.

Thus, the defendant remains strictly liable for the harm caused by its defective product, except for that part caused by the consumer's own misconduct.

Therefore, in response to the question posed, we conclude that comparative fault is applicable to strict products liability actions.

REVIEW QUESTIONS

1. Automobile driver and passenger brought products liability action, alleging defective design, against automobile manufacturer for injuries sustained when the automobile was rear-ended, causing the gas tank to rupture and burn. What theories would support such a lawsuit? Explain each.

2. Pat sued the seller of a reconditioned clothes dryer. The dryer overheated, and a blanket being dried caught fire. The fire spread to the rest of the house, causing $25,000 in damages. What theory will support the plaintiff's cause of action? Explain.

3. Smith sued Ariens for injuries sustained while operating a snowmobile in a field. The snowmobile hit a rock that was partially covered by snow. On impact, the right side of Smith's face came down and hit a brake bracket on the left side of the snowmobile. The brake bracket had two sharp metal protrusions on the inside which were toward the plaintiff's face. What theory of recovery best supports plaintiff's case? Explain. With what result? Why?

4. Davis claims damages for breach of the implied warranty of merchantability resulting from the use of 1-inch floor decking in the construction of a 48-unit apartment complex. The product was manufactured by the defendant, Homasote Company, and was sold to Davis by Homasote's distributor, North Pacific Lumber Company. The flooring was not sound-deadening and not weatherproof. Defendants moved to dismiss for lack of privity of contract. With what result? Why?

5. The plaintiff bought a rotary power mower from the defendant. He had used similar mowers before and was thoroughly familiar with them. The rear of the housing of plaintiff's mower is embossed with the warning: "Keep Hands & Feet From Under Mower." The instruction booklet twice advises the operator to mow slopes lengthwise, not up and down. While mowing up and down, plaintiff fell and lifted the mower onto his feet. Plaintiff sues, using strict liability as his theory. With what result? Why?

6. Claude, a ski instructor, was injured while riding a chair lift at a ski area when the chair in front of him slipped back along the cable, striking his chair and knocking him 30 feet to the ground. The cause of the mishap was the failure of a cable clamp unit to secure the chain to the cable. What must Claude prove in order to recover? Explain.

7. Plaintiff was injured while seeking to avoid a collision with a truck. He overturned his convertible as it left the road. As the car rolled over, the roof was deformed, and plaintiff broke his back. He sued the manufacturer, using the theory of strict liability. With what result? Why?

8. Plaintiff was injured when a propane gas heater leaked gas and exploded. The propane did not contain ethyl mercaptan, which provides the smell of gas. Plaintiff sues on a theory of negligence. With what result? Why?

9. Hammond, an asbestos worker, contracted asbestosis. He sued the manufacturer of the raw material, using strict liability as a theory. The plant at which he worked bought the raw material from the defendant and used it to make various insulating products. The defendant contended that raw asbestos is not a product for purpose of strict liability. With what result? Why?

10. Plaintiffs, owners of a house which was destroyed by fire as a result of electricity overload, brought a products liability action against the electric power company. The company contended that electricity was not a product. With what result? Why?

11. A forklift truck operator was injured when the equipment failed to function properly. The truck had been leased by his employer from State Trucking Lines, the manufacturer. The operator sued State, claiming that it be charged with strict liability. Did the operator win? Why or why not?

12. Maude bought a plastic waste container, and when she got it home she found the lid did not fit properly on the top of the container. In an attempt to make it fit, she hit the corner of the lid with her hand and suffered a deep gash in her hand. Will Maude successfully recover on a theory of strict liability against the manufacturer of the plastic waste container? Explain.

13. Plaintiff is a 15-year-old girl employed at a fast food restaurant. She was injured when in the midst of filling a customer's order, she made a split-second decision to remove a paper towel covering a roast without turning off the power. The meat was on a moving tray approaching a stationary blade and her hand hit the blade. Is the manufacturer strictly liable? Why?

14. An electrician sued the manufacturer of an aluminum five-way combination ladder. The ladder collapsed and the plaintiff fell. A rail of the ladder had buckled near the bottom rail. There was no evidence of abnormal use of the ladder. Is the defendant liable? Why?

27 INTRODUCTION TO COMMERCIAL PAPER

The term *commercial paper* describes two basic types of negotiable instruments: the *note* (a promise to pay, other than a certificate of deposit) and the *draft* (an order to some other entity to pay). A *check* is a typical draft, an order from the drawer, directing the drawee (bank) to pay money to the payee of the check.

Negotiable means that the written instrument can move freely as a substitute for money. That is one of the functions of commercial paper. The other is its use as a credit device. If an appliance dealer buys an air conditioner from a manufacturer and pays by check, the check substitutes for money. If the dealer pays with a 60-day note, the note is a credit device. The manufacturer may sell the note and receive money for it.

1. The Concept of Negotiability

Negotiable instruments developed because of the commercial need for something that would be readily acceptable in lieu of money and would accordingly be readily transferable in trade or commerce. Substantial protection and assurance of payment must be given to any person to whom the paper might be transferred. To accomplish this protection, it is necessary to insulate the transferee from most of the defenses that a primary party, such as the maker of a note, might have against the payee. The purpose of the negotiability trait is to prevent the primary party from asserting defenses to the instrument against the person to whom the paper was transferred.

To accomplish the foregoing, Article 3 of the Code provides that a person to whom commercial paper is negotiated takes it free of personal defenses of the maker or drawer. This basic theory of negotiability can be further explained by noting the difference between the *assignment* of a contract and the negotiation of a negotiable instrument. Assume that the dealer owes the manufacturer $100, but he has a counterclaim because the product was defective. If a third party such as a bank purchased the right from the manufacturer, it would be subject to the dealer's defense of failure of consideration. The bank, as assignee, would secure no better right against the dealer than the original right held by the manufacturer, the assignor. The bank therefore could not collect $100 from the dealer.

In this example, if the evidence of the debt is not a simple contract for money but a negotiable promissory note given by the dealer to the manufacturer, and if it is properly negotiated, the bank is in a position superior to that which it occupied when it was an assignee. Assuming that it is a "holder in due course," the bank has a better title because it is free of the personal defenses that are available against the manufacturer, the original party to the paper. The dealer, therefore, cannot use the defense of failure of consideration, and the bank can collect the $100.

Transfer of the instrument free of personal defenses is the very essence of negotiability. Three requirements must be met before a holder is free from personal defenses. First, the instrument must be negotiable; that is, it must comply with the statutory formalities and language requirements. An instrument that does not qualify is nonnegotiable, and any transfer is an assignment subject to defenses. Second, the instrument must be properly *negotiated* to the transferee. Third, the party to whom negotiable commercial paper is negotiated must be a *holder in due course* or have the rights of a holder in due course. Each of these concepts is discussed in the next chapters.

The defenses that cannot be asserted against a holder in due course are called *personal defenses. Real defenses,* on the other hand, may be asserted against anyone, including a holder in due course. Real defenses are matters that go to the very existence of the instruments. Personal defenses such as failure of consideration involve less serious matters and usually relate to the transaction out of which they arose, or events such as payment of the note.[1]

2. Kinds of Commercial Paper

Article 3 of the Code, Commercial Paper, is restricted in its coverage to the note, certificate of deposit, draft, and check. A note is two-party paper, as is a certificate of deposit. The draft and the check are three-party instruments. A draft presupposes a debtor-creditor relationship between the *drawer* and the *drawee* or some other obligation on the part of the drawee in favor of the drawer. The drawee is the debtor; the drawer is the creditor. The drawer-creditor orders the drawee-debtor to pay money to a third party, who is the *payee.* The mere execution of the draft does not obligate the drawee on the paper. The drawee's liability on the paper arises when it formally *accepts* the obligation to pay in writing upon the draft itself. By accepting, the drawee becomes primarily liable on the paper [3-410(1)]. Thereafter, the drawee is called an *acceptor,* and its liability is similar to the liability of the maker of a promissory note.

---

[1] Bank of Miami v. Florida City Express, Inc., p. 608.

$5,000   July 1, 1985

For value received, I, the undersigned, promise
to pay to the order of Paul Payee on demand
the principal sum of $5,000 (five thousand dollars).

/s/ _____ (seal)

FIGURE 27–1

Form of a simple note.

Note.   A *note* initially is a two-party instrument in which the issuer (the *maker*) promises to pay to the order of a *payee* or to bearer. A note is used to evidence an obligation to pay in the future and is typically employed in loan and secured sales transactions (Fig. 27–1 above).

Certificate of Deposit.   A *certificate of deposit* (commonly called a *CD*) is a two-party, usually short-term, instrument in which a bank is the maker [3-104(2)(c)]. A CD is a bank's written acknowledgment of money on deposit which the bank promises to pay to the depositor or to his order or to some third person. The promise to repay distinguishes the CD from a deposit slip. A CD basically is a promissory note issued by a bank as a means of investment. People buy CDs to earn the interest they bear. The bank may pay higher rates of interest than on a savings account, since a CD may not be redeemed until the date specified without significant penalties. A CD may be negotiable or nonnegotiable; Figure 27–2 shows a negotiable one.

CERTIFICATE OF DEPOSIT
First Athens Bank
Athens, GA

Has received on deposit and on May 1, 1992 will pay to the
order of Darlene Depositor $20,000.00 (twenty thousand dollars)
with interest at a rate of fifteen percent (15%) payable upon return
of this certificate properly indorsed. No payment before maturity. No
interest after maturity.

                                   First Athens Bank

_____   _____
   May 1, 1985   /s/
   (date of issue)   (authorized signature)

FIGURE 27–2

Form of negotiable CD.

Draft. A *draft* (sometimes called a bill of exchange) is a simple order to pay money [3-104(2)(a)]. It is addressed by one person (the *drawer*) to another person (the *payor* or *drawee*), requiring that person to pay on demand or at a fixed future time a definite amount to the order of a named person (the *payee* or *holder*) or to bearer. A seller of goods or services may draw a draft on the buyer for purchase price of the goods, making the instrument payable to himself. In this case, the seller is both the drawer and the payee, while the buyer is the drawee of the draft. In drawing this draft, the seller implicitly promises to pay its amount to any holder if it is not paid by the drawee [3-413(2)]. By putting his demand for payment in the stylized form of a draft, the seller thereby facilitates the transfer to a financer of the seller's right to receive payment from the buyer.

Drafts may be payable on demand or at a fixed or determinable time. Usually demand drafts are presented to the drawee for payment and are said to be payable *on sight.*

Checks. The check is the most common form of commercial paper. It is a demand draft drawn on a bank. A check drawn by a bank upon itself is a *cashier's check. Traveler's checks* are like cashier's checks in that the financial institution issuing them is both the drawer and the drawee. Traveler's checks are negotiable when they have been completed by the identifying signature. A *bank draft* is a banker's check; that is, it is a check drawn by one bank on another bank, payable on demand.

A *certified check* is one that has been accepted by the drawee bank. Either the drawer or the holder of a check may present it to the drawee bank for certification. The bank will stamp "certified" on the check, and an official of the bank will sign it and date it. By certifying, the bank assumes responsibility for payment and sets aside funds from its customer's account to cover the check.

Certification may or may not change the legal liability of the parties upon the instrument. When the *drawer* has a check certified, such a certification merely acts as additional security and does not relieve the drawer of any liability. On the other hand, when the *holder* of a check secures certification by the drawee bank, he thereby accepts the bank as the only party liable. Such an act discharges the drawer and all prior indorsers from liability [3-411(1)]. The effect of such certification is similar to a payment by the bank and redeposit by the holder.

The refusal of a bank to certify a check at the request of a holder is not a dishonor of the instrument. The bank owes the depositor a duty to pay, but not necessarily the duty to certify checks that are drawn on it, unless there is a previous agreement to certify [3-411(2)]. A drawer cannot stop payment on a check after the bank has certified it.

Checks are sometimes postdated. A postdated check creates different legal relationships than does a "regular" check. It does not represent that funds are currently available to cover the check. A postdated check is in effect a credit transaction.[2]

---

[2] Wilson v. Lewis, p. 609.

3. Terminology

Article 4 of the Code, Bank Deposits and Collections, provides uniform rules to govern the collection of checks and other instruments for the payment of money. These rules govern the relationship of banks with one another and with depositors in the collection and payment of *items.*

Timing is important in the check collection process. Many of the technical rules of law refer to a *banking day,* which is defined as "that part of any day on which a bank is open to the public for carrying on substantially all of its banking functions" [4-104(1)(c)]. A bank is permitted to establish a cutoff hour of 2 P.M. or later, so that the bank may have an opportunity to process items, prove balances, and make the necessary entries to determine its position for the day. If an item is received after the cutoff hour or after the close of the banking day, it may be treated as having been received at the opening of the next banking day [4-107]. The term *midnight deadline* with respect to a bank means midnight on its banking day following the banking day on which it receives a check or a notice regarding the check [4-104(1)(h)].

4. The Debtor-Creditor Relationship

The legal relationship between a bank and its depositors is that of debtor and creditor. If the depositor is a borrower of the bank, the reverse relationship (creditor-debtor) also exists between the bank and its customers. The dual relationship provides the bank with a prompt and easy method of protecting itself in the event of a depositor's default or pending insolvency. A bank can "seize" bank deposits under its right of setoff (an independent right to deduct debts from customers' accounts) if such action becomes necessary to protect its account receivable.

A bank is under a duty to honor checks drawn by its customer when there are sufficient funds in his account to cover the checks. If there are insufficient funds, the bank may honor the checks, even though this action creates an overdraft. The customer is indebted to the bank for the overdraft and implicitly promises to reimburse the bank [4-401(1)].[3]

5. Stop Payments

A customer has the right to stop payment on checks drawn on his account. Only the drawer has this right; it does not extend to holders—payees or indorsees. To be effective, a stop-payment order must be received at a time and in a manner that will afford the bank a reasonable opportunity to stop payment before it has taken other action on the item [4-403]. A bank must act reasonably in complying with the stop-payment order. It cannot avoid liability by asserting immaterial differences between the check and the stop-payment order.[4]

---

[3] Continental Bank v. Fitting, p. 610.

[4] FJS Electronics, Inc. v. Fidelity Bank, p. 610.

If a check has been certified, the depositor cannot stop payment, whether he or the payee procured the certification. An oral stop order is binding on the bank for only 14 days unless confirmed in writing within that period. Unless renewed in writing, a written stop order is effective for only 6 months [4-404].

A bank that honors a check upon which payment has been stopped is liable to the drawer of the check for any loss he has suffered because of the failure to obey the stop order. The burden is on the customer to establish the amount of his loss. It may be that the customer cannot establish any loss. Thus, if the drawer did not have a valid reason to stop payment, he cannot collect from a bank that fails to obey the stop-payment order [4-403(3)]. The bank cannot by agreement disclaim its responsibility for its failure to obey stop-payment orders [4-103(1)]. Thus, a form signed by a customer agreeing not to hold the bank responsible for failure to pay could not be enforced.

Because of the concept of negotiability previously noted, a stop order on a check gives the drawer only limited protection. If the check is negotiated by the payee to a holder in due course, that holder can require payment of the amount by the drawer of the check, notwithstanding the stop order.

6. Wrongful Dishonor

If a bank wrongfully dishonors a check, it is liable to its customer for damages proximately caused by the wrongful dishonor. When the dishonor occurs by mistake, as distinguished from a malicious or willful dishonor, liability is limited to the *actual* damages *proved* [4-402]. These damages may include *consequential damages* proximately caused by the wrongful dishonor, damages such as for arrest or prosecution of the customer. If the wrongful dishonor is willful, punitive damages in addition to actual damages may be awarded.[5] The Code rejects early common-law decisions holding that, if the dishonored item were drawn by a merchant, he was defamed in his business because of the reflection on his credit. Consequently, a merchant cannot recover damages on the basis of defamation because of wrongful dishonor of a check.

7. Banks' Rights and Duties

If a bank in good faith pays an altered check, it can charge the account of its customer only according to the original tenor of the check. Thus, if a check is raised, the bank can charge its customer's account only with the original amount of the check [4-401(2)(a)]. If a person signs his name to an incomplete check and it is thereafter completed and presented to the drawee bank that pays it, the bank can charge the customer's account for the full amount if it pays in good faith and does not know that the completion was improper [4-401(2)(b)]. The improperly completed check is not an altered check.

A bank is entitled, but not *obligated,* to pay a check that is over 6 months old, and it may charge the check to the customer's account [4-404]. Certified checks do not fall within the 6-month rule; they are the primary obligation of the certifying bank, and the obligation runs directly to the holder of the check.

---

[5] Yacht Club Sales v. First Nat. Bank of North Idaho, p. 611.

In paying stale checks, the bank must act in good faith and exercise ordinary care.[6] It must ask questions and if a reasonable person would be put on notice that something is wrong, it should contact the drawer for authority to pay the stale item.

As a general proposition, the death or incompetence of a person terminates the authority of others to act on his behalf. If this principle were applied to banks, a tremendous burden would be imposed upon them to verify the continued life and competence of drawers. A bank's authority to pay checks therefore continues until it knows that a customer has died or has been judged incompetent and the bank has had a reasonable opportunity to act [4-405].

8. Depositors' Rights and Duties

Banks make available to their customers a statement of account and canceled checks. Within a reasonable time after they are received, the customer must examine them for forgeries and for alterations. The bank does not have the right to charge an account with forged checks, but the customer's failure to examine and to notify will prevent him from asserting the forgery (or alteration) against the bank if the bank can establish that it suffered a loss because of this failure. The bank may be able to prove that prompt notification would have enabled it to recover from the forger [4-406(2)].

The Code does not specify the period of time within which the customer must report forgeries or alterations. It does specify that if the same wrongdoer commits successive forgeries or alterations, the customer must examine and notify the bank within 14 days after the first item and statement were available to him. Otherwise, he cannot assert the same person's forgeries or alterations paid in good faith by the bank [4-406(2)(b)]. This rule is intended to prevent the wrongdoer from having the opportunity to repeat his misdeeds. If the customer can establish that the bank itself was negligent in paying a forged or altered item, the bank cannot avail itself of a defense based on the customer's tardiness in examining and reporting [4-406(3)].[7] The same result occurs when a bank processes an item that has been materially altered or contains an unauthorized indorsement. If a person's negligence contributes to the alteration or unauthorized signature, the bank is not liable for the item paid unless the bank failed to observe reasonable commercial standards. Thus, if both parties are "at fault," the bank is liable, because its fault prevents it from asserting the fault of the other party.

A customer is precluded from asserting a forgery of the drawer's signature or alteration on a check after 1 year from the time the check and statement were made available even though the bank was negligent. Forged indorsements must be reported within 3 years [4-406(4)]. If a payor bank, as a matter of policy or public relations, waives its defense of tardy notification by its customer, it cannot thereafter hold the collecting bank or any prior party for the forgery [4-406(5)].

---

[6] Charles Ragusa & Son v. Community State Bank, p. 613.

[7] K & K Mfg., Inc. v. Union Bank, p. 614

SUMMARY

CONCEPT OF NEGOTIABILITY

Contrasted with assignments

1. An assignee of a contract takes it subject to any defense the obligor may have against the assignor.
2. The goal of negotiability is to insulate a transferee from personal defenses that a primary party, such as a maker of a note, might have against the transferor.

Freedom from personal defenses

1. For a holder to take an instrument free of personal defenses, the instrument must be negotiable, must be properly negotiated, and the holder must be a holder in due course.

KINDS OF COMMERCIAL PAPER

Note

1. A promissory note is a two-party instrument in which the maker promises to pay a stated amount to the payee.

Certificate of deposit

1. A certificate of deposit is a two-party instrument in which a financial institution such as a bank promises to repay a stated sum with interest on a certain date.

Draft

1. A draft is a bill of exchange in which a drawer orders a drawee to pay a stated amount to a payee.

Checks

1. A check is a draft drawn on a bank. A check drawn by a bank on itself is a cashier's check. Travelers' checks are cashier's checks in which the financial institution is both the drawer and the drawee.
2. A certified check is one that has been accepted by the drawee bank, and by the acceptance it assumes the obligation of the drawer. Certification at the request of a holder releases the drawer from any further liability. A bank has no duty to certify a check.

BANKS AND THEIR CUSTOMERS

Terminology

1. A banking day is that part of the day in which a bank is open, and which usually ends at 2:00 P.M. so that the bank may process items before it closes. Items received after 2:00 P.M. are generally posted the following day.

2. A midnight deadline is midnight on the banking day following the day the item or notice is received by the bank.

Debtor-creditor relationship

1. The relationship between a bank and its depositors is that of debtor and creditor: If the depositor borrows money from the bank, the opposite relationship also exists.

2. A bank can seize deposits and set them off against debts owed to the bank.

3. A bank has a duty to honor checks when there are sufficient funds on deposit. It may also pay other checks and collect the amounts from its depositors.

Stop payments

1. A customer has the right to stop payment on checks drawn on his account.

2. The stop order must be received in a time and manner that will allow the bank a reasonable opportunity to stop payment.

3. Oral stop orders expire in 14 days unless confirmed in writing.

4. Written stop orders are effective for only 6 months, but may be renewed in writing.

5. A bank that fails to stop payment upon proper notice is liable to the drawer of the check for any proven losses.

6. A bank may not contractually disclaim liability for failure to obey a stop order.

Bank's rights and duties

1. A bank can charge a customer's account for an altered check only with the original amount of the check.

2. If an incomplete check is signed by a depositor and it is completed improperly, a bank can in good faith charge the account with the completed amount.

Depositor's rights and duties	3. Banks must act in good faith and exercise ordinary care in processing checks. If they are put on notice, then they have a duty to inquire of the drawer about the item. 4. A bank may pay a check more than 6 months old but need not do so. 1. Upon receipt of the statement of account and canceled checks, the depositor has a duty to examine them within a reasonable time for forged, unauthorized, or altered checks. 2. Although the bank does not initially have the right to charge the customer's account for forged, unauthorized, or altered checks, the customer's failure to examine and notify may prevent him from asserting the improper charge to his account. 3. If both the customer and the bank are at fault in allowing the forged, altered, or unauthorized check to be paid, the bank is liable. 4. The customer cannot assert a forged, altered, or unauthorized check after 1 year from the time the canceled check or the statement of account was available for examination. 5. Forged indorsements must be reported within 3 years.

CASES

Bank of Miami v. Florida City Express, Inc.
367 So.2d 683 (Fla.App. 1979)

SCHWARTZ, J. . . . Florida City Express, Inc., the maker of negotiable promissory notes, must pay twice because the Bank of Miami, a holder in due course, was not paid once. That is the impact of the law of negotiable instruments, as now embodied in the Uniform Commercial Code, upon the undisputed facts of this case.

On November 1, 1974, Florida City Express, Inc., in return for merchandise, executed an ordinary "short form" promissory note for $3,292.12 payable to Latin American Tire Co.; the maturity date was February 3, 1975. On January 17, 1975, it gave Latin American a similar note for $3,500.00 due on March 3, 1975. On November 18, 1974 and January 30, 1975, respectively, Latin American endorsed and discounted the notes with the Bank of Miami. The bank took the notes before maturity for value, and without notice of the existence of any defenses to them; hence, it was indisputably a holder in due course of both instruments. At each maturity date, the bank, after making unsuccessful demands on Latin American, called upon Florida City Express, as the maker of the notes, to pay them. Therein lies the unhappy tale told by this case.

For Florida City had already paid all the amounts due to Latin American by virtue of payments made by several checks given both before and after the negotiation of the notes by Latin American to the bank. However, the maker had not required, as to the payments made before the transfer, that any notation of those payments be made on the notes themselves. Furthermore, it had not demanded that they be displayed or surrendered by Latin American when payments were made after the payee *had* negotiated them and when they were therefore no longer in Latin American's possession. When, however, the bank sued Florida City on the notes in this action, it raised the defense of payment. After a non-jury trial, the court below upheld that defense and entered judgment for the defendant. We disagree and reverse.

Our holding is based on the long familiar, universal rule, . . . that a holder in due course takes and holds a negotiable instrument free of all defenses of which he is not on notice. And it is very

clear that this rule includes the defense of discharge or payment. . . .

When an instrument is paid in whole or in part before maturity, it is the duty of the party making payment to have the payment indorsed or to require surrender of the instrument, and if he omits these precautions and the instrument is transferred before maturity to a holder in due course without notice of the payments, he may not avail himself of the defense of prior payment against such a holder. Since the maker neither required an endorsement of its payments on the notes, nor demanded their surrender, it must therefore take the unpleasant consequences of that failure by making a second payment to the present holder.

Florida City argues that the bank should have given it notice of its acquisition of the notes. No authority is cited, because none exists, to support this proposition. The maker's claim that a double payment of over $6,000.00 could have been avoided had the bank used a 15-cent stamp has some obvious surface attraction. But we agree with the appellant that the imposition of a notice requirement would be contrary not only to every decided case on the subject but also to the important policy that negotiable instruments must flow freely and without such impediments in the stream of commerce.

Reversed and remanded.

Wilson v. Lewis
165 Cal.Rptr. 396 (1980)

A real estate broker, Anny, sued the owner of real estate, Lewis, to collect a real estate commission. The defendant had signed a sale contract with Wilson which recited that a $500 good faith deposit check had been posted by purchasers. In fact the purchasers had given him only a postdated check because they did not have sufficient funds in drawee bank. Lewis contended that this concealment justified rescission of the agreement.

ELKINGTON, J. . . . Anny orally represented to defendant Lewis that a good faith deposit *check* for $500 had been posted. "A 'check' . . . is a draft drawn on a bank and payable on demand. . . . Its unqualified tender is a representation that there are

sufficient funds to cover it on deposit with the drawee bank which will pay it instantly on demand. The presentation of a postdated check is not subject to the civil or penal sanctions normally attending the knowing tender of a check without sufficient funds for a valuable consideration.

A *postdated check* is not such a check as was represented by Anny and the Wilsons' offer. Ordinarily as here its purpose is to obtain an extension of credit. Where the instrument offered by the buyer is not a payment but a credit instrument such as a note or a check *post dated by even one day*, the seller's acceptance of the instrument insofar as third parties are concerned, amounts to a delivery on credit. In accepting a postdated check the payee is looking to the promise of payment in the future; it is no more than a mere promise to discharge a present obligation at a future date. And it has been held that a postdated check being irregular and not in due course of business, he who takes it holds it subject to that objection. . . .

Where there is a duty to disclose, the disclosure must be full and complete, and any material concealment or misrepresentation will amount to fraud. And a real estate agent undeniably owes a "fiduciary obligation" to his principal "to disclose all material facts which might affect her decision with regard to the transaction. . . ."

There was accordingly . . . a material misrepresentation to or concealment from (defendant) . . . by Anny.

Under the circumstances defendant Lewis was entitled to rescind the agreement. . . .

Reversed.

Continental Bank v. Fitting
559 P.2d 218 (Ariz. 1977)

SCHROEDER, J. . . . The appellant, Continental Bank, brought this action to recover the amount of an overdraft which it paid on a check drawn on appellee's account. The appellee, Fitting, resisted the bank's action on the ground that the bank should not have paid the overdraft. . . . The judgment was entered in favor of Fitting . . . and the bank appeals.

The check leading to the overdraft claim was written by Fitting in the amount of $800. After writing the check, she had second thoughts and contacted the bank about the possibility of stopping payment. A bank employee advised that a stop payment order could not be submitted until the bank opened the following morning. Fitting then discussed with the bank employee the possibility of deliberately creating an overdraft situation by withdrawing enough money so that there would remain insufficient funds to cover the check in question. The bank employee indicated that in those circumstances the bank would not pay the check.

Early the next morning, Fitting proceeded to withdraw money from the account, leaving enough money to cover other checks she had written. The bank nevertheless paid the $800 check in question, and sought recovery of the amount of the overdraft from Fitting in this action.

In defense of her judgment below, Fitting's sole reliance is upon evidence . . . showing that under the bank's usual internal procedures and policies, the bank would have known the check represented an overdraft and would not have paid it. . . . Fitting does not contend that her conversations with the bank employees concerning overdraft policies constituted a contractual agreement that the check would be dishonored. . . .

In those circumstances, the sole issue with respect to the overdraft is whether the bank was lawfully entitled to pay it and to seek recourse from Fitting. The matter is governed by A.R.S. §44-2627 [U.C.C. §4-401] which clearly gives the bank the option to pay an overdraft and to charge the customer's account for that overdraft when the check is otherwise properly payable.

The bank, therefore, by paying the overdraft and charging the customer's account, was acting in accordance with procedures specifically authorized by law, and violated no claimed contractual agreement with its customer. Fitting offers no support for her theory that the bank's own internal policies may in and of themselves give rise to a duty to follow such policies in every case, despite provisions of the statute authorizing contrary conduct. We perceive no basis for such a holding as a matter of sound policy. As the comment to section 4-401 of the Uniform Commercial Code states:

> It is fundamental that upon proper payment of a draft the drawee may charge the account of the drawer. This is true even though the draft is an overdraft since the draft itself authorizes the payment for the drawer's account and carries an implied promise to reimburse the drawee. . . .

Reversed.

FJS Electronics, Inc. v. Fidelity Bank
431 A.2d 326 (Pa. Super. 1981)

Electro Corp. drew check number 896 in the amount of $1,844.98 on the Fidelity Bank. The next day an official of Electro Corp. telephoned Fidelity Bank and ordered a stop payment on the check. The official correctly stated the check number as 896 but incorrectly stated the amount as $1,844.48. Fidelity Bank sent written confirmation of the stop-payment order to Electro Corp. with a notice that contained the following request, "PLEASE ENSURE AMOUNT IS CORRECT." (The entire notice was in block letters.) The confirmation stated the check number as 896 and the amount as $1,844.48. Fidelity Bank's computer is programmed to stop payment only if the amount of the check is correct. The Bank's computer was not programmed to pull checks where there was a discrepancy in a digit of the amount of the stop payment request and the computer digits of the amount on the bottom of the check nor was it designed for stop payment purposes to read the number of the check. Upon presentation, the computer overlooked the check and the check was paid. Electro Corp sued Fidelity Bank for the amount of the check. The trial court found for the plaintiff.

BROSKY, J. . . . We must decide whether the court below was correct in holding that a customer's error in the amount of a check in a stop payment request does not relieve the bank of liability.

Section 4-403(1) of the Uniform Commercial Code addresses the problem of stop payment orders:

A customer may by order to his bank stop payment of any item payable for his account but the order must be received at such time and in such manner as to afford the bank a reasonable opportunity to act on it. . . .

It is clear that the order here was timely received. The court below determined that even though it contained an error, the order was given in such manner as to give the bank a reasonable opportunity to act. Fidelity, in essence, asserts that the section should be read to require compliance with the procedures of a particular bank, regardless of what they are and regardless of whether the customer has been made aware of them. Fidelity argues that since its technique for ascertaining whether

payment had been stopped required absolute accuracy as to the amount of a stopped check, this section would require absolute precision in order for the notice to be reasonable. Such a narrow view is not consistent with the intent being §4-403, expressed in Comment 2 following the section:

The position taken by this section is that stopping payment is a service which depositors expect and are entitled to receive from banks notwithstanding its difficulty, inconvenience and expense. The inevitable occasional losses through failure to stop should be borne by the banks as a cost of the business of banking.

Fidelity does not contend that it could not have used a technique which required less precision in the stop payment order. It does not contend that it could not have found the check had it used a more thorough system. It merely asserts that since it chose a system which searched only by amount, notice is not reasonable unless it conforms to the requirements of this system.

Fidelity made a choice when it elected to employ a technique which searched for stopped checks by amount alone. It evidently found benefits to this technique which outweighed the risk that an item might be inaccurately described in a stop order. This is precisely the type of inevitable loss which was contemplated by the code drafters and addressed by the comment quoted above. The focus of §4-403 is the service which may be expected by the *customer,* and a customer may expect a check to be stopped after the bank is given reasonable notice. A bank's decision to reduce operating costs by using a system which increases the risk that checks as to which there is an outstanding stop payment order will be paid invites liability when such items are paid.

An error of fifty cents in the amount of a stop payment order does not deprive the bank of a reasonable opportunity to act on the order. . . .

Affirmed.

Yacht Club Sales v. First Nat. Bank of North Idaho
623 P.2d 464 (Idaho 1980)

Yacht Club Sales and Services, Inc. (Y.C.S.S.) operated its business on land owned by Yacht Club, Inc., a different corporation although similarly

named. On June 18, 1975, when Y.C.S.S. had on deposit over $11,000, a sheriff served the defendant bank with a writ of execution upon which Yacht Club, Inc., was named as judgment debtor. The bank responded:

We are holding funds in the name of Yacht Club Sales & Service, Inc. in the amount of $11,930.72, pending clarification as to whether Yacht Club Sales & Service, Inc. and Yacht Club, Inc. are one and the same.

The same day, the bank placed a "hold" on the [Y.C.S.S.] account, but Y.C.S.S., Inc., was not notified that such action was taken. Respondent continued making deposits into the account in the amount of $39,872 between June 23 and June 25, and these funds were also affected by the "hold."

Eight checks drawn on the account were presented to the bank between June 19 and June 23. These checks were returned with the notation "refer to maker."

The bank removed the "hold" from the account on the afternoon of June 26, after their attorney advised them to release the "hold" because Yacht Club, Inc., and Y.C.S.S., Inc., were two separate entities. However, the funds were not released until June 27. Y.C.S.S. sues the bank for damages for wrongful dishonor. The lower court found for Y.C.S.S. and the bank appeals.

McFADDEN, J. . . . On appeal, the Bank contends that the trial court erred in its instructions to the jury . . . on its liability to respondent. Section 4-402 governs a bank's liability to its customer for the wrongful dishonor of a check. It states:

> Bank's liability to customer for wrongful dishonor.—A payor bank is liable to its customer for damages proximately caused by the wrongful dishonor of an item. When the dishonor occurs through mistake, liability is limited to actual damages proved. If so proximately caused and proved, damages may include damages for an arrest or prosecution of the customer or other consequential damages. Whether any consequential damages are proximately caused by the wrongful dishonor is a question of fact to be determined in each case.

First, appellant claims that the trial court erred in refusing to give the following proposed instruction:

> You are instructed that when a bank dishonors a check by mistake, the bank's liability is limited to actual damages proved.

Although in light of the second sentence of 4-402 the above instruction is a correct statement of the law, we find no error in the trial court's refusal to instruct the jury on dishonor by mistake.

"Mistaken dishonor" means a wrongful dishonor done erroneously or unintentionally. Dishonors resulting from inadvertent bookkeeping errors and other unintentional employee errors would be mistaken dishonors. On the other hand, where a dishonor is caused by a setoff or charge made by a bank under an erroneous belief that it had a legal right to do so, the wrongful dishonor resulting from the improper setoff or charge is not classified as mistaken. In accord is White and Summers' treatise on the Uniform Commercial Code, wherein the authors state:

> We would . . . find the bank guilty of willful dishonor . . . any time it dishonored its Customer's checks because it had previously reduced his account through its own improper setoff, improper garnishment or the like. Moreover we would find such reduction 'improper' even though the bank acted in a good faith but mistaken belief that the garnishment or setoff was valid. Although such dishonors might be the result of a 'mistake' in the sense that the bank official was mistaken about his legal rights, we would classify them as willful for they represent the bank's deliberate judgment to sacrifice the customer's interest to those of some other party.

Ordinarily, whether a dishonor is willful or intentional is a question of fact for the jury. However, when the evidence on an issue of fact is undisputed, and the inferences to be drawn therefrom are plain and not open to doubt by reasonable men, the issue is no longer one of fact to be submitted to the jury, but becomes a question of law. In the instant case it is uncontroverted that appellant Bank intentionally dishonored eight of respondent's checks, although it did so with the belief that it was legally entitled to do so. Under the authorities cited above, the Bank's action cannot be classified as simply a mistaken dishonor. We therefore hold that the trial court was correct when it implicitly ruled that as a matter of law the eight checks had not been dishonored by mistake and we find no error in its refusal to instruct the jury as to the mistake language of the wrongful dishonor sections, 4-402.

Affirmed.

Charles Ragusa & Son v. Community State Bank
360 So.2d 231 (La. App. 1978)

On June 30, 1972, Charles Ragusa & Son, a partnership, issued check #2668, drawn on Community State Bank in the amount of $5,000, to Southern Masonry. Subsequently, Ragusa & Son was advised by the payee that the check had been lost and that a replacement check should be issued. A second check for the same amount was issued and forwarded to the payee as a substitute for check #2668. Contemporaneously, a verbal stop payment order was given to the bank on the lost check. The replacement check was cashed by the payee and paid by the bank in due course.

In July, 1975, check #2668 was deposited by the payee in its account at BNO; presented to and accepted by Community State Bank; and charged to the Ragusa & Son account on July 17, 1975. Ragusa & Son was not aware of this transaction until August 4, 1975, when it received its monthly bank statement. Charles Ragusa returned the check to the bank on August 4, 1975, and demanded that the account be credited for the amount of the check because a stop payment had been issued on the check and the check had a "stale" date. The bank accepted the return of the check and credited the account for the $5,000.

The bank marked the check "returned stale date" and sent the check to the Federal Reserve Bank, seeking a refund. On August 6, 1975, the Federal Reserve Bank returned the check, noting that they would not accept the check since it was not returned timely. The bank held the check until September 10, 1975, when it was again charged to the Ragusa & Son account. Angelo (a bank official) then sent a letter . . . to Ragusa, informing him of the bank's actions.

Ragusa received this letter on September 13, 1975. . . . In the interim, however, the $5,000 debit overdrew the account and caused the dishonor of another check, dated September 11, 1975, in the amount of $3,100.50, issued to a third party.

This suit was filed on September 19, 1975, by Ragusa & Son against the bank, to collect the amount of the check ($5,000) and to recover damages. The trial court held for the plaintiff.

EDWARDS, J. . . . The bank contends that it is not liable to plaintiffs in that it acted properly in accepting check #2668 since there was no valid stop payment order in effect and since it was acting in "good faith" under LSA-R.S. 10:4-404.

We do not view the issue of the stop payment as controlling in view of the undisputed testimony that the stop payment was never renewed. Consequently, the stop payment expired in 1972.

Regarding the bank's good faith in paying a stale check, LSA-R.S. 10:4-404 provides:

> A bank is under no obligation to a customer having a checking account to pay a check, other than a certified check, which is presented more than six months after its date, but it may charge its customer's account for a payment made thereafter in good faith.

Additionally, LSA R.S. 10:1-201 defines "good faith" as meaning "honesty in fact in the conduct or transaction concerned."

We have been unable to find any Louisiana case specifically dealing with the payment of a stale check and the aspect of good faith. However, it seems obvious that although LSA R.S. 10:4-404 protects a bank which pays a stale check so long as it acts in "good faith", it does not eliminate the requirement of ordinary care which a bank must observe in all its dealings.

Considering this burden on a bank seeking the protection of the statute, we do not believe that it is sufficient for a bank merely to utter the conclusionary allegation of good faith. On the contrary, when a bank's actions are put at issue, it is incumbent upon the bank to show that it exercised the requisite care with regard to its customer. This the bank has failed to do in the instant case. In fact, the bank did not introduce any evidence in support of its actions or to prove its alleged good faith.

We believe that the payment of such an obviously stale check, three years old, demonstrates the bank's lack of due care and prevents it from claiming the defense of good faith.

Affirmed.

K&K Mfg., Inc. v. Union Bank
628 P.2d 44 (Ariz. 1981)

HATHAWAY, J. . . . In this case we must apply articles three and four of the Uniform Commercial Code to determine who should bear the risk of loss when a dishonest employee forges her employer's name as drawer on a number of checks on his business and personal checking accounts, then appropriates the proceeds for her personal use.

Appellant Bill J. Knight is the president and majority stockholder of K & K Manufacturing, Inc. K & K Manufacturing employed only two persons when the events which form the basis of this action occurred. These two employees were Knight and a bookkeeper, Eleanor Garza. The bookkeeper's duties at K & K Manufacturing were very broad, including picking up the company mail and Knight's personal mail from a common post office box, preparing checks for Knight's signature to pay both company and personal bills, and making entries in a cash disbursement journal reflecting the expenses for which the checks were written. Most importantly, it was her responsibility to reconcile the monthly statements prepared and sent by appellee Union Bank, where Knight kept both his business and personal checking and savings accounts.

Between March 1977 and January 1978, Miss Garza forged Knight's signature on some 66 separate checks drawn on his personal or business accounts at Union Bank. The majority of these checks were made payable to her. The total amount of the forgeries on the K & K Manufacturing account was $49,859.31. The total on Knight's personal account was $11,350. The bank paid each such check and Miss Garza received or was credited with the proceeds.

Appellant brought this action against appellee for breach of contract, seeking repayment of the funds the bank paid out on checks with unauthorized signatures. After a court trial, judgment was entered in favor of appellant Knight for $5,500, representing the amount paid out of his personal account on forged checks from March 28 to May 20, 1977. This figure included eight forged checks paid by the bank prior to the mailing of its monthly statement containing a record of the payments and the checks themselves to Knight on May 6, plus a 14-day period. Since no forged checks on the K & K Manufacturing account were paid prior to May 20, judgment was entered for appellee against it. Both Knight and K & K Manufacturing have appealed.

We turn to the question of whether appellants met their burden of proof of demonstrating appellee did not exercise ordinary care in paying the bad checks. The issue is whether its method of ascertaining unauthorized signatures on its depositor's checks met the standard of care under the circumstances.

Implied in the debtor/creditor relationship between a bank and its checking account depositor is the contractual undertaking on the part of the bank that it will only discharge its obligations to the depositor upon his authorized signature. The mere fact that the bank has paid a forged check does not mean the bank has breached its duty of ordinary care, however.

At trial, an operations officer for appellee testified as to the methods employed during the period the forgeries occurred to discover unauthorized signatures on depositors' checks. She testified that checks were organized so that a bundle from the same account could be compared with the authorized signature on the bank's signature card. A staff of five filing clerks handled an average of approximately 1,000 checks each per hour in this manner. She testified it was common for a file clerk to become familiar with the drawer's signature in large accounts such as appellants'. An official of a large Arizona bank testified that tellers and file clerks are not trained to be handwriting experts. He testified that in his opinion, because most large banks have completely abandoned physical comparison of checks with the signature card, the system employed by appellee was better than the norm of the banking community in Southern Arizona.

In view of this and other evidence, we conclude that there was sufficient evidence to support . . . the judgment entered below. Similar methods of comparing drawer's signatures have been upheld as constituting ordinary care and being within reasonable commercial standards across the country. Appellant Knight and his controller admitted the forgeries were quite good. Appellants also argue that because the bank tellers recognized Miss Garza was cashing large checks made to herself and her boyfriend and that she was driving an expensive sports car, they had a further duty to check the validity of the drawer's signature. This evidence was balanced by testimony that Miss Garza thoroughly explained the reasons for the large checks as increased salary, bonuses, and payment of Knight's expenses while he was out of town. Knight and Miss Garza were in the bank together on a regular basis and the tellers knew Miss Garza was authorized to handle large amounts of Knight's money.

Finally, there was evidence that some K & K Manufacturing checks were forged with a rubber stamp facsimile of Knight's signature, which was only authorized for use with the Knight Foundry account. Appellants argue appellee fell below the standard of ordinary care in honoring these checks.

The trial court personally examined appellee's expert witness on this subject. There was testimony that if facsimile signatures appear "all of a sudden" on the checks, the depositor may be contacted, but there was sufficient evidence that the piecemeal use of the stamp here, which was at times authorized by appellants, was not such that appellee should be held to bring it to their attention. The finding of fact that appellee's acts, including those regarding the facsimile signature, did not fall below ordinary care or reasonable commercial standards was not clearly erroneous.

Affirmed.

REVIEW QUESTIONS

1. Identify the terms in column A by matching each with the appropriate statement in column B.

A	B
1. Check	**a.** Period after which a forged indorsement may no longer be asserted.
2. Personal defense	**b.** Period after which written stop payment order expires.
3. Midnight deadline	**c.** Period after which a forged check may no longer be asserted by depositor.
4. Six months	**d.** Intended to circulate for shorter periods of time than most other negotiable instruments.
5. Fourteen days	**e.** Part of next banking day.
6. Certification	**f.** Period after which an oral stop payment order expires.
7. Real defense	**g.** Precludes a bank from honoring a stop order.
8. One year	**h.** May not be asserted against a holder in due course.
9. Three years	**i.** May be asserted against a holder in due course.

2. Dolly's bank wrongfully dishonored two small checks that she had drawn. She brought an action against the bank and recovered a judgment of $831.50 for the following: $1.50 for a telephone call to one of the payees; $330 for two weeks' lost wages; and $500 for illness, embarrassment, and inconvenience. Should a court uphold this judgment on appeal? Why or why not?

3. Grain Elevator Company owed State Bank $272,000 on certain promissory notes. Grain, in negotiating a new loan, told State Bank's officers that it lost $22,000 during the last year and that its checking account had been overdrawn by $35,000. The bank turned down the new loan request. It set off Grain's $71,000 checking account balance against the old loans and returned all of Grain's checks when presented for payment. Is State Bank liable for refusing to cash the checks? Why?

4. Newton, a holder in due course, presented a check to the Marshall Bank, the drawee bank named on the face of the instrument. The bank examined the signature of the drawer very carefully, but the signature was such an exact forgery of the drawer's signature that only a handwriting expert could have detected a difference. The bank therefore paid the check. Assume that the check was promptly returned to the drawer-depositor but that he did not discover the forgery until 13 months after the check was returned to him. Can he compel the bank to credit his account for the loss? Why?

5. Franklin, a depositor of the Milltown Bank, orally ordered the cashier of the bank to stop payment on a check he had issued. The check was issued in payment for goods that were not received. Franklin learned that the seller was a notorious confidence man. The cashier in turn notified the tellers that an oral stop order had been given. Ten days later one of the tellers, who was not paying much attention to his business, paid the seller's wife, who had been sent to the bank to cash the check for the seller. Franklin, while examining his canceled checks at the end of the month, discovered the error and promptly demanded that his account be credited for the amount of the check. Is he entitled to the credit? Why?

6. On January 29 Edwards, a wholesale grocer, made a large deposit in cash to his account at Cattlemen's Bank. In error, Edwards' deposit was posted to the account of Edmunds, another depositor. On the following day, Nevins, a local produce jobber, deposited a check to his account at Watermill Bank drawn on Cattlemen's Bank to Nevins' order by Edwards. When the check was presented for payment, Cattlemen's Bank refused to honor it and stamped it "Insufficient Funds." The check was promptly returned to Nevins by Watermill Bank. If Edwards' deposit on January 29 had been properly posted, his bank account balance would have been substantially greater than the amount of his check to Nevins. Edwards sues the Cattlemen's Bank for damages. With what result? Why?

7. The facts are as in problem 6. Assume that Edwards' check had been given to Nevins in payment for a carload of produce that Edwards had arranged to resell at a large profit, that the Bank was aware of this, that on dishonor of the check Nevins stopped the goods in transit, and that Edwards as a result lost his profit on the resale of the goods. May Edwards recover such lost profits from the bank? Explain.

8. Kilpatrick made a check payable to the order of Shaefer, who then had the check certified. Kilpatrick made a stop payment order to the bank before the check was presented for payment. Is the bank obligated to pay the check even if Kilpatrick has a valid defense on the instrument? Explain.

9. Men's Wear drew a check payable to Zino & Co. When Zino did not receive it in the mail, Men's Wear placed a stop payment order in writing with the Drawee Bank. Approximately one year later, Drawee Bank paid on the check to a collecting bank and charged Men's Wear's account. Men's Wear had not renewed its stop payment order. Is Drawee Bank liable to Men's Wear for failing to honor the stop payment order? Why or why not?

10. Lucas was a depositor in the Bank of the Potomac. Certain indorsements on checks drawn by Lucas were forged, but he did not inform the bank of the forgeries for over 3 years. Lucas claims that he was excused from giving earlier notice. Is the bank liable for honoring these checks with forged indorsements? Why or why not?

11. Equipment Company bought equipment from Wells and paid him with a check drawn upon Citizens Bank. When the equipment was not delivered the next day, Equipment Company stopped payment on the check. Wells cashed the check at his own bank, Fargo Bank. When the check was presented to Citizens Bank, it refused to honor the check because of the stop order. Can Fargo Bank successfully collect from Wells? Why or why not?

12. By agreement with its bank, all checks drawn upon plaintiff corporation's account must be signed by two corporate officers. In 1982, a number of checks are issued signed only by the president of the corporation. The bank paid the checks and returned them with a monthly statement. In 1985, the corporation sued the bank for the amount of the checks because they did not contain the two signatures required by the agreement. May the corporation recover the amount of the checks? Why?

28 NEGOTIABLE INSTRUMENTS

Chapter 27 introduced the concept of negotiability. We learned that a holder in due course of a negotiable instrument is not subject to personal defenses asserted by prior parties to the instrument. The negotiability principle is our primary concern in this chapter. We will examine the legal requirements that must be met if an instrument is to qualify for the special treatment afforded negotiable instruments.

The negotiability of an instrument is determined by the terms written on the face of the instrument. In order to be negotiable, it must satisfy four basic requirements: It must (1) be signed by the maker or drawer, (2) contain an unconditional promise or order to pay a sum certain in money, (3) be payable on demand or at a definite time, and (4) be payable to order or to bearer [3-104(1)].

The first requirement is simply that there be a writing signed by the maker or drawer [3-104(1)(a)]. It is not required that any particular type or kind of writing be used, nor is it necessary that the signature be at any particular place upon the instrument. The instrument may be in any form that includes "printing, typewriting, or any other intentional reduction to tangible form" [1-201(46)]. A symbol is a sufficient signature if "executed or adopted by a party with present intention to authenticate a writing" [1-201(39)]. The use of the word *authenticate* in the definition of *signed* makes it clear that a complete signature is not required. The authentication may be printed or written and may be placed on the instrument by stamp.

For purposes of internal control, many businesses and other organizations require that instruments be signed by at least two persons or that they be countersigned. When the agreement requires two signatures, the drawee may not pay on only one signature, even if the one signing is authorized. The authority is limited or divided; both must sign.

1. The Necessity of a Promise or Order

A negotiable note must contain a *promise* to pay. Although the word *promise* is used in almost all notes, a word or words expressing an undertaking to pay may be substituted. The promise must be derived from the language of the instrument, not from the fact that a debt exists. A mere acknowledgment of a debt in writing (an IOU) does not contain a promise. Even though it is a valid enforceable instrument upon which recovery may be had, it is not negotiable.

A draft must contain an *order* to pay. The purpose of the instrument is to order the drawee to pay money to the payee or his order. The drawer must use plain language to show an intention to make an order and to signify more than an authorization or request. It must be a direction to pay. Thus, an instrument in the following form would not be negotiable: "To John Doe. I wish you would pay $1,000 to the order of Richard Roe. [Signed] Robert Lee." This would nevertheless be a valid authorization for John Doe to make payment to Richard Roe. The correct method to create an order to pay would be: "To John Doe. Pay $1,000 to the order of Richard Roe. [Signed] Robert Lee."

2. The Promise or Order Must Be Unconditional

Negotiable instruments serve as a substitute for money and as a basis for short-term credit. If these purposes are to be served, it is essential that the instruments be readily received in lieu of money and be freely transferable. Conditional promises or orders would defeat these purposes, for it would be necessary that every transferee determine whether or not the condition had been performed prior to taking the instrument. The instruments would not freely circulate. In recognition of these facts, the law requires that the promise or order be unconditional.

The question of whether or not the promise or order is conditional arises when the instrument contains language in addition to the promise or order to pay money. The promise or order is conditional if the language of the instrument provides that payment is controlled by, or is subject to, the terms of some other agreement [3-105(2)(a)]. Clearly, a promise or order is conditional if reference to some other agreement is *required* and if payment is *subject to* the terms of another contract.[1]

Negotiability is also destroyed if reference to another writing is necessary to determine the exact nature of the promise or order. Such a reference imposes the terms of the other writing. However, a mere reference to some other contract or document does not condition the promise or order, and does not impair negotiability. Such reference simply gives information about the transaction that gave rise to the instrument. Thus, the words "subject to contract" condition the promise or

---

[1] Mitchell v. Riverside Nat. Bank, p. 627.

order, but the words "as per contract" do not render the promise or order conditional. The latter is informative rather than restrictive.

Statements of the consideration for which the instrument was given and statements of the transaction out of which the instrument arose are simply informative [3-105(1)(b)]. A draft may have been drawn under a letter of credit, and a reference to this fact does not impose a condition [3-105(1)(d)]. Notes frequently contain a statement that some sort of security has been given, such as a mortgage on property, or that title to goods has been retained as security for the payment of the note. In either case, the purpose is to make clear to the holder that the promise to pay is secured by something in addition to the general credit of the maker; and as a consequence, a mere reference to the security does not destroy negotiability [3-105(1)(e)].

Normally implied or constructive conditions in an agreement which underlies the instrument do not make the instrument conditional. For example, a promise that payment will be made when the contract is performed does not make the promise to pay conditional [3-105(1)(a)].[2] However, express conditions stated in the instrument itself can make the promise to pay conditional.

Notes given in payment for property purchased on installment often provide that title to the property shall not pass to the maker of the note until all necessary payments have been made. A statement to this effect in a note does not condition the promise to pay.

3. The Particular Fund Concept

A maker or drawer must engage or pledge his general credit, or his promise or order is conditional. A statement that an instrument is to be paid only out of a particular fund imposes a condition [3-105(2)(b)]. Such an instrument does not carry the general personal credit of the maker or drawer. It is contingent on the sufficiency of the fund on which it is drawn. For example, if a note states: "I promise to pay to the order of John only out of my corn profits," the note is conditioned on having corn profits. The promise is conditional, and the instrument is nonnegotiable. This result is due to the *particular fund doctrine.*

There are three exceptions to this doctrine. First, an instrument is not considered conditional merely because it makes reference to a particular source or fund from which payment is expected but not required. For example, although a check indicates it will be paid out of a particular account, it still may be negotiable. The second exception involves an instrument which is issued by a government or governmental unit and which is limited to payment out of a particular fund [3-105(1)(g)].[3]

Third is where an unincorporated association, such as a partnership, trust, or an estate limits its obligation to pay the instrument only from the assets of the organization and eliminates liability of the individual members, such as partners. The instrument may still be negotiable. For purposes of negotiability, the code

---

[2] Lialios v. Home Ins. Companies, p. 628.

[3] Sanitary & Imp. Dist. v. Continental Western, p. 629.

recognizes partnerships and other unincorporated associations as "commercial entities" which may execute negotiable instruments as an entity [3-105(1)(h)].

4. Sum Certain in Money

To be negotiable, an instrument must be payable in money. Instruments payable in chattels such as wheat or platinum are not payable in money. *Money* means a medium of exchange that is authorized or adopted by a domestic or foreign government as a part of its currency [1-201(24)]. The amount payable may be stated in foreign as well as domestic money [3-107(2)]. If the sum payable is stated in foreign currency, payment may be made in the dollar equivalent unless it is specified in the instrument that the foreign currency is the only medium of payment.

The language used in creating commercial paper must be certain with respect to the amount of money promised or ordered to be paid. Otherwise, its value at any period could not be definitely determined. If the principal sum to be paid is definite, negotiability is not affected by the fact that it is to be paid with interest, in installments, with exchange at a fixed or current rate, or with cost of collection and attorney's fees in case payment is not made at maturity [3-106].

If at any time during the term of the paper its full value can be ascertained, the requirement that the sum must be certain is satisfied. The obligation to pay costs and attorney's fees is part of the security contract, separate and distinct from the primary promise to pay money; therefore, it does not affect the required sum certain. The certainty of amount is not affected if the instrument specifies different rates of interest before and after default; nor is the certainty affected by a provision for a stated discount for early payment or an additional charge if payment is made after the date fixed [3-106(1)(c)]. The principal amount to be paid, however, must be certain in order for the note to be negotiable.[4]

5. Time of Payment Must Be Certain

As a substitute for money, negotiable instruments would be of little value if the holder were unable to determine when he could demand payment. A negotiable instrument, therefore, must be payable on demand or at a "definite time" [3-104(1)(c)].

An instrument is payable on demand when it so states, when payable at sight or on presentation, or *when no time of payment is stated* [3-108]. In general, the words "payable on demand" are used in notes, and the words "at sight" in drafts. If nothing is said about the due date, the instrument is demand paper. A check is a good illustration of such an instrument. The characteristic of demand paper is that its holder can require payment at any time by making a demand upon the person who is obligated on the paper.

Not every instrument that indicates no time of payment is a demand instrument. If the instrument provides for periodic payment of interest or contains

---

[4] Branch Banking & Trust Co. v. Creasy, p. 629.

an acceleration clause without specifying the actual due date, such instruments are nonnegotiable. The interest clauses and acceleration clauses clearly indicate an intent that it not be payable on demand.[5]

The requirement of a definite time is in keeping with the necessity for certainty in instruments. It is important that the value of an instrument can always be determined. This value will be dependent upon the ultimate maturity date of the instrument. If an instrument is payable only upon an act or event, the time of its occurrence being uncertain, the instrument is not payable at a definite time even though the act or event has occurred [3-109(2)]. Thus, an instrument payable "30 days after my father's death" would not be negotiable.

The requirement of certainty as to the time of payment is satisfied if it is payable on or before a specified date [3-109(1)(a)]. Thus, an instrument payable "on or before" June 1, 1986, is negotiable. The obligor on the instrument has the privilege of making payment prior to June 1, 1986, but is not required to pay until the specified date. An instrument payable at a fixed period after a stated date, or at a fixed period after sight, is payable at a definite time [3-109(1)(b)]. The expressions "1 year after date" or "60 days after sight" are definite as to time.

6. Acceleration and Extension Clauses

Two types of provisions appearing on the face of instruments may affect the definite time requirement. The first, an *acceleration clause,* hastens or accelerates the maturity date of an instrument. Accelerating provisions may be of many different kinds. One often provides that in case of default in payment, the entire note shall become due and payable. Another kind gives the holder an option to declare the instrument due and payable when he feels insecure about ultimate payment. An instrument payable at a definite time subject to any acceleration is negotiable [3-109(1)(c)]. If, however, the acceleration provision permits the holder to declare the instrument due when he feels insecure, the holder must act in good faith in the honest belief that the likelihood of payment is impaired. The presumption is that the holder has acted in good faith, placing the burden on the obligor-payor to show that such act was not in good faith [1-208].

The second type of provision affecting time is an *extension clause,* the converse of the acceleration provision. An extension lengthens the time for payment beyond that specified in the instrument. A note payable in 2 years might provide that the maker has the right to extend the time of payment 6 months. An instrument is payable "at a definite time subject to extension at the option of the holder, or to extension to a further definite time at the option of the maker or acceptor or automatically upon or after a specified act or event" [3-109(1)(d)]. If an extension is at the option of the holder, no time limit is required. The holder always has a right to refrain from undertaking collection. An extension at the option of the maker or acceptor, however, or an automatic extension must specify a definite time for ultimate payment, or negotiability is destroyed.

---

[5] P.P. Inc. v. McGuire, p. 630.

THE MAGIC WORDS OF NEGOTIABILITY

7. Introduction

The *words of negotiability* express the intention to create negotiable paper. The usual words of negotiability are *order* and *bearer* [3-110; 3-111]. When these words are used, the maker or drawer has in effect stated that the instrument may be negotiated to another party. When the word *bearer* is used, it means that payment will be made to anyone who *bears* or possesses it. When the word *order* is used, it means that it will be paid to the designated payee or anyone to whom the payee orders it to be paid.

Other words of equivalent meaning may be used, but to ensure negotiability it is preferable to use the conventional words. If the instrument is not payable to "order" or to "bearer," it is not negotiable, and all defenses are available in suits on the instrument.[6]

8. Order Paper

If the terms of an instrument provide that it is payable to the order or assigns of a person who is specified with reasonable certainty, the instrument is payable to order [3-110(1)]. The expressions "Pay to the order of John Doe" or "Pay to John Doe or order" or "Pay to John Doe or assigns" create order paper. (See Fig. 28-1.)

An instrument may be payable to the order of two or more payees together, such as A and B, or in the alternative, A or B. An instrument payable to A and B must be indorsed by both. One payable to the order of A or B may be indorsed and negotiated by either [3-116].

An instrument may be payable to the order of an estate, a trust, or a fund. Such instruments are payable to the order of the representative of the estate, trust, or fund [3-110(1)(e)]. An instrument payable to the order of a partnership or an unincorporated association such as a labor union is payable to such partnership or

---

[6] First Inv. Co. v. Andersen, p. 631.

FIGURE 28-1

Order paper, payable to the order of John Doe [3-110(1)]. It requires John Doe's indorsement if it is to be negotiated.

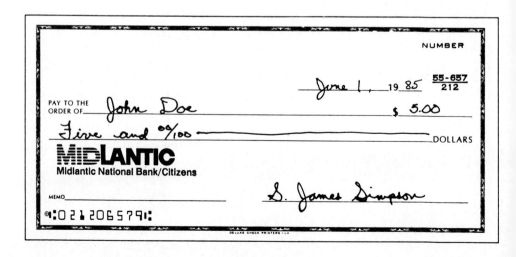

association. It may be indorsed by any person authorized by the partnership or association. [3-110(1)(g)].

9. Bearer Paper

The basic characteristic of bearer paper as distinguished from order paper is that it can be negotiated by delivery without indorsement. (See Fig. 28–2.) An instrument is payable to bearer when created if it is payable (1) to bearer, (2) to the order of bearer (as distinguished from the order of a specified person or bearer), (3) to a specified person or bearer (notice that it is not to *the order of* a specified person or bearer), or (4) to "cash" or "the order of cash," or any other indication that does not purport to designate any specific payee [3-111].

Although bearer paper can be negotiated without indorsement, the person to whom it is transferred will often require an indorsement. The reason for this is that an indorser has a greater liability than one who negotiates without indorsement. Also, if the instrument is dishonored, identification of the person who negotiated the paper becomes easier with an indorsement.

10. Terms and Omissions Not Affecting Negotiability

Some additional terms, usually for the benefit of the payee or other holder, may be included in commercial paper without impairing negotiability. Many instruments contain statements indicating that collateral has been given. These statements, including provisions relating to the rights of the payee or holder in the collateral, do not affect negotiability [3-112(1)(b)(c)].

The drawer of a check or draft may include a provision that the payee, by indorsing or cashing it, acknowledges full satisfaction of an obligation of the drawer. The provision will not affect negotiability [3-112(1)(f)]. Checks or drafts drawn by insurance companies in settlement of claims usually contain such a provision.

OTHER FACTORS AFFECTING NEGOTIABILITY

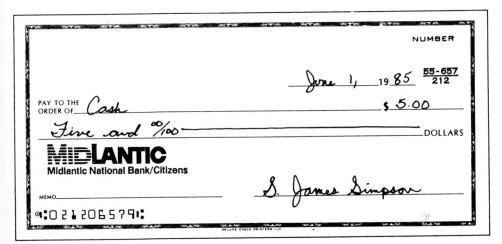

FIGURE 28–2

Bearer paper. Its negotiation is effective without an indorsement [3-111].

Often, the consideration for which an instrument was given is set forth in the instrument, and it is common to include words such as "for value received" or "in payment for services rendered." The omission of words stating the consideration for which an instrument was given will not affect its negotiability. Nor is the negotiable character of an instrument otherwise negotiable impaired by omission of a statement of the place where the instrument is drawn or payable [3-112(1)(a)].

Whether there is no date, a wrong date, an antedate, or a postdate is not important from the standpoint of negotiability [3-114(1)]. Any date that does appear on the instrument is presumed correct until evidence is introduced to establish a contrary date [3-114(3)]. Any fraud or illegality connected with the date of the instrument does not affect its negotiability, but merely gives a defense.

11. Incomplete Instruments

A person may sign an instrument that is incomplete in that it lacks one or more of the necessary elements of a complete instrument. Thus, a paper signed by the maker or drawer in which the payee's name or the amount is omitted is incomplete.

An incomplete instrument cannot be enforced until it is completed [3-115(1)]. If the blanks are subsequently filled in by any person in accordance with the authority or instructions given by the party who signed the incomplete instrument, it is then effective as completed. A person might leave blank signed checks with an employee who must pay for goods to be delivered. When the employee fills in the amounts and names of the payees, the checks are perfectly valid.

A date is not required for an instrument to be negotiable; however, if a date is necessary to ascertain maturity ("payable 60 days from date"), an undated instrument is an incomplete instrument. The date may be inserted by the holder. If an instrument is payable on demand or at a fixed period after date, the date that is put on the instrument controls, even though it is antedated or postdated [3-114(2)].

12. Ambiguous Terms and Rules of Construction

In view of the millions of negotiable instruments that are made and drawn daily, it is to be expected that a certain number of them will be ambiguously worded. Accordingly, the Code provides a number of rules to be applied in interpreting negotiable instruments.

Some instruments are drawn in such a manner that it is doubtful whether the instrument is a draft or a note. It may be directed to a third person but contain a promise to pay, rather than an order to pay. The holder may treat it as either a draft or a note and present it for payment to the person who signed it or the apparent drawee. Where a draft is drawn on the drawer, it is treated as a note [3-118(a)].

An instrument may contain handwritten terms, typewritten terms, or printed terms. Where there are discrepancies in the instrument, handwritten terms control typewritten and printed terms, and typewritten terms control printed terms [3-

118(b)]. Thus, a printed note form may state that it is payable on demand, but there may be typed or written on the note "payable 30 days from date." Such an instrument would be payable in 30 days.

There may also be a conflict between the words and the figures of an instrument. Thus a check may have the words "fifty dollars" and the figures "$500." The words control, and the check would be for 50 dollars. If the words are ambiguous, the figures will control [3-118(c)]. In a check with the words "Five seventy five dollars" and the figures "$5.75," the figures will control. In some cases, the ambiguity may arise from the context of the words.

If an instrument provides for the payment of interest but does not state the rate, the rate will be at the judgment rate at the place of payment. An unsatisfied money judgment bears interest at a rate specified by statute, and whatever this judgment rate is in a particular state will be applicable in this situation. Interest will run from the date of the instrument or, if it is undated, from the date of issue [3-118(d)].

If two or more persons sign an instrument as maker, acceptor, drawer, or indorser as part of the same transaction, they are jointly and severally liable unless the instrument otherwise specifies. This means that the full amount of the obligation could be collected from any one of them or that all of them might be joined in a single action. Joint and several liability is imposed even though the instrument contains such words as "I promise to pay" [3-118(e)].

SUMMARY

GENERAL REQUIREMENTS

The writing	1. The negotiable instrument must be signed by the maker or drawer.
	2. The signature can be anything intended to authenticate the instrument, and it can be applied by mechanical forms.
Promise or order	1. A note must contain a promise, and a draft must contain an order.
	2. The promise or order must be unconditional. A promise is conditional if reference to some other document is required or the instrument is subject to the terms of another document.
	3. A recital of considerations does not destroy negotiability.
	4. A promise that is limited to a particular fund is conditional, and the instrument is not negotiable.

	5. Exceptions to the particular fund concept involve unincorporated associations and governmental units.
Sum certain in money	**1.** The unconditional promise or order must involve a sum certain in money.
	2. Money is any currency adopted by a government.
	3. A sum certain is present if the amount of money involved can be calculated from the information contained on the face of the instrument.
Time of payment	**1.** A negotiable instrument must be payable on demand or at a definite time.
	2. An instrument is payable on demand when no time of payment is stated.
	3. An acceleration clause that changes the maturity date does not destroy negotiability.
	4. An extension clause that extends the time of payment at the option of the maker or acceptor without specifying the time limit of the extension destroys negotiability.
	5. An extension clause exercised at the holder's option does not destroy negotiability even when no time limitations are stated.

WORDS OF NEGOTIABILITY

Order paper	**1.** To be negotiable, a note must be payable to the order of some person or to bearer. A note or check that is simply payable to a specified person is nonnegotiable.
	2. An instrument payable to the order of two people must be indorsed by both.
	3. An instrument payable to an estate, trust, or fund may be indorsed by the appropriate representative.
Bearer paper	**1.** Bearer paper may be negotiated without indorsement by delivery.
	2. An instrument is bearer paper if it specifies that it is payable to bearer or to cash.
	3. Bearer paper may be negotiated by a finder or thief, and anyone in possession of it is entitled to collect.

OTHER FACTORS	
Terms and omissions	1. Many terms do not affect negotiation. For example, a statement acknowledging satisfaction of an obligation on a check does not destroy negotiability.
	2. An undated instrument is nevertheless negotiable, as is a postdated instrument.
Incomplete instruments	1. An incomplete instrument cannot be enforced until it is completed.
	2. Instruments may be completed as authorized or not. Unauthorized completion is a personal defense that cannot be asserted against a holder in due course.
Ambiguous terms	1. Handwritten terms prevail over typewritten terms or printed terms, and typewritten terms control printed terms.
	2. If there is a conflict between words and figures, the words generally control.
	3. If an instrument provides for interest without stating the rate, the rate on judgments will be applied.

CASES

Mitchell v. Riverside Nat. Bank
613 S.W.2d 802 (Tex. 1981)

JUNELL, J. This is an appeal from a judgment ordering that defendant Riverside National Bank ("Riverside") retain its lien against plaintiff Mitchell's property in the amount of $3,548.00 and ordering a default judgment in favor of Mitchell against defendant Naylor in the amount of $3400.00. Mitchell contends the court erred in determining the amount of the lien, Riverside's recovery on the note being subject to any defenses available to Mitchell under the contract.

On June 27, 1973, Mitchell executed a builder's and mechanic's lien contract and a note, both in the amount of $4,435.00 and payable to Naylor, a contractor, for the construction of certain improve-

ments to the property the subject of the lien. Prior to the note's maturity Naylor assigned it to Riverside for $3,548.00 and began, but never completed, the improvements. Mitchell subsequently hired another contractor to complete the improvements at a cost of $3,400.00. When Mitchell refused to pay Riverside the principal and interest due and owing on the assigned note, Riverside filed its lien against Mitchell's property. Mitchell thereafter filed suit against Naylor and Riverside to clear title to the property.

The terms of the note include that it is payable on or before ninety days from its date or upon completion of the improvements provided for in the lien contract, whichever occurred first, and that payment of the note is secured by the lien created in the lien contract and "is subject to and governed by said contract, which is hereby expressly referred to, incorporated herein and made a part hereof. . . ." The lien contract provides that in the event the improvements for any reason are not completed, the owner and holder of the note shall have a lien against the property for the contract price less the cost to complete the improvements according to the contract.

Mitchell contends that the quoted language making reference to the contract burdens the note with the conditions of the contract, thereby making the note non-negotiable and subject recovery on the note to any defenses available under the contract. We agree. Use of the terms "subject to and gov-erned by" in referring to an extrinsic contract in an otherwise negotiable instrument destroys the negotiability of the instrument and renders the instrument burdened by the terms within the extrinsic contract.

The face amount of the note being $4,435.00 and the cost of completion being stipulated by the parties to be $3,400.00, we hold that Riverside has lien against Mitchell's property for $1,035.00, plus interest at the rate of ten percent per annum from September 25, 1973, the date the note was due, until paid. . . .

Judgment reformed.

Lialios v. Home Ins. Companies
410 N.E.2d 193 (Ill. App. 1980)

O'CONNOR, J. . . . Plaintiff, Gregory Lialios, brought suit against defendant, The Home Insurance Companies, the drawer of a draft, alleging that he was a holder in due course and seeking $1,275, the face amount of the draft.

On December 21, 1978, defendant settled a Workman's Compensation claim with Costas Moulopoulos for $1,275. On that date, defendant through its duly authorized agent, issued draft No. 19668648, drawn upon defendant, payable through Citibank, New York, New York, and made payable to Moulopoulos. The draft states on its face "upon acceptance pay to the order of Costas Moulopoulos."

On December 28, 1978, Moulopoulos returned to defendant and stated that he lost draft No. 19668648 and requested another draft. Defendant issued a stop payment order on draft No. 19668648 and issued Moulopoulos another draft.

Moulopoulos had not lost draft No. 19668648, but instead had negotiated it to plaintiff. When plaintiff's bank presented draft No. 19668648 to Citibank, payment was refused due to defendant drawer's stop payment order.

Plaintiff brought action against defendant drawer, alleging he was a holder in due course. Defendant filed a motion to strike plaintiff's complaint, alleging the draft was conditional and therefore not a negotiable instrument. (The trial court found for the plaintiff.)

The sole issue upon review is whether draft No. 19668648 was a negotiable instrument. Ill.Rev.Stat.1977, ch. 26, par. 3–104(1) sets the requirements for negotiability:

(1) Any writing to be a negotiable instrument within this Article must

(a) be signed by the maker or drawer; and

(b) contain an unconditional promise or order to pay a sum certain in money and no other promise, order, obligation or power given by the maker or drawer except as authorized by this Article; and

(c) be payable on demand or at a definite time; and

(d) be payable to order or to bearer.

Defendant contends that the words "upon acceptance" indicate a conditional promise to pay. . . . The instrument indicates that Citibank is merely the collecting bank and that defendant is both drawer and drawee.

"UPON ACCEPTANCE" does not destroy the negotiability of this instrument because it is only a restatement of an "implied or constructive condition" of any draft or check, which must be accepted to charge the drawee. "A promise or order otherwise unconditional is not made conditional by the fact that the instrument (a) is subject to implied or constructive conditions.". . .

Affirmed.

Sanitary & Imp. Dist. v. Continental Western
343 N.W.2d 314 (Neb. 1983)

To finance construction of a public golf course, the Sanitary District of Sarpy County sold short-term, interest-bearing warrants. The warrants stated they were to be paid from "the construction account of The Sanitary District." When the company hired to build the golf course went out of business, the golf course project was abandoned. Holders of the warrants sued the county. The county defended, claiming that the instruments were nonnegotiable because they were payable out of a particular fund. Since they were nonnegotiable, the holders took the notes subject to the defense of failure of consideration because the golf course was not completed. Plaintiffs contend that the warrants were negotiable and that as holders in due course, they took the notes free of the defense of failure of consideration. The trial court found for plaintiffs.

CAPORALE, J. . . . The question (is) whether (the warrants) are negotiable instruments within the contemplation of article 3 of the Uniform Commercial Code.

Since its enactment in 1963, Neb.U.C.C. §3–104 has provided in part:

(1) Any writing to be a negotiable instrument within this article must (a) be signed by the maker or drawer, and (b) contain an unconditional promise or order to pay a sum certain in money and no other promise, order, obligation or power given by the maker or drawer except as authorized by this article; and (c) be payable on demand or at a definite time; and (d) be payable to order or to bearer.

The warrants are in writing, are signed by the district as the maker, and are payable to order. See Neb.U.C.C. §3–110, which provides that an instrument is payable to order when by its terms it is payable to the order or assigns of any person therein specified with reasonable certainty. Thus, the requirements of §3–104(1)(a) and (d) are clearly met.

The requirement of §3–104(1)(b) is likewise met. Neb.U.C.C. §3–105 has always provided in part: "(1) A promise or order otherwise unconditional is not made conditional by the fact that the instrument . . . (g) is limited to payment out of a particular fund or the proceeds of a particular source, if the instrument is issued by a government or governmental agency or unit." A sanitary and improvement district is such a governmental unit, as is contemplated by §3–105(1)(g), under the provisions of Neb.Rev.Stat. §31–705, which has always stated that such a district shall be "a body corporate and politic."

The requirement of §3–104(1)(c) is met as well. Neb.U.C.C. §3–108 has, at all relevant times, provided: "Instruments payable on demand include those payable at sight or on presentation and those in which no time for payment is stated."

We conclude, therefore, that the subject warrants are negotiable instruments.

Affirmed.

Branch Banking & Trust Co. v. Creasy
269 S.E.2d 117 (N.C. 1980)

Defendant's husband owed plaintiff bank $35,000 on a promissory note which was due October 30, 1975. The husband sought to renew the note in October 1975, and the bank agreed, provided defendant would guarantee payment. On October 20, 1975, defendant signed a "Guaranty Agreement." The paper states that "the undersigned hereby absolutely and unconditionally guarantees to you and your successors and assigns the due and punctual payment of any and all notes, drafts, debts, obligations, and liabilities."

BRITT, J. . . . The Court of Appeals held that the materials which were before the trial court were insufficient to establish as a matter of law that plaintiff was a holder in due course of the agreement and was entitled to take it free of the defense of nondelivery. In order to reach this conclusion, it is essential that there first be a determination that the paper writing upon which the bank relies is a negotiable instrument.

To be a negotiable instrument, a writing must be signed by the maker or drawer, must contain an unconditional promise to pay a sum certain in money and no other promise except as authorized by statute, must be payable on demand or at a definite time, and must be payable to order or bearer. The "continuing guaranty" which was signed by defendant does not meet these requirements.

First, the document which was signed by defendant does not have the attribute of certainty; it provides that: "The aggregate amount of principal of all indebtedness, obligations and liabilities at any one time outstanding for which the undersigned shall be liable shall not exceed the sum of $35,000."

For the requirement of a sum certain to be met, it is necessary that at the time of payment the holder is able to determine the amount which is then payable from the instrument itself, with any necessary computation, without any reference to an outside source. It is necessary for a negotiable instrument to bear a definite sum so that subsequent holders may take and transfer the instrument without having to plumb the intricacies of the instrument's background.

The document in question calls for a ceiling on the amount of defendant's liability. It does not specify the amount of the liability that is to be paid. That data may be obtained only after resorting to sources of information which are external to the agreement itself. Such an absence is enough by itself to foreclose any finding that the paper at issue is negotiable.

The document upon which plaintiff relies is inadequate as a negotiable instrument in one other respect: At no place in the agreement is there any provision that it is "payable to order or bearer." For an instrument to be fully negotiable within the scope of Article Three, it must be "payable to order or bearer."

Reversed.

P.P., Inc. v. McGuire
509 F.Supp. 1079 (N.J. law 1981)

McGuire bought Tursi's clothes boutique, paying $10,000 in cash and executing a promissory note for $65,000. The note had an acceleration clause and stated that "interest payments of $541.66 shall be due and payable at a rate of 10 percent per annum on the fifth day of October, November, and December, 1979." Tursi refused to close the sale to McGuire and sold the note to Parker in another deal. When Parker sued McGuire on the $65,000 note, McGuire defended on the basis of failure of consideration, since Tursi refused to close the sale of his boutique. Parker contended that failure of consideration on a negotiable instrument is not a defense against a holder in due course. McGuire responded that the note was not negotiable because the note was not payable on demand or at a definite time.

DEBEVOISE, J. . . . It is not necessary to decide whether plaintiff meets the requisites of a holder in due course because the note on which he sues is clearly not a negotiable instrument. For an instrument to be negotiable, it must satisfy each of the requirements outlined in U.C.C. §3–104(1). It must:

> (a) be signed by the maker or drawer; and
>
> (b) contain an unconditional promise or order to pay a sum certain in money and no other promise, order, obligation or power given by the maker or drawer except as authorized by this Article; and
>
> (c) be payable on demand or at a definite time; and
>
> (d) be payable to order or bearer.

If any one of elements (a) through (d) is lacking, the instrument is not negotiable and Article 3 of the Uniform Commercial Code does not apply.

The McGuires' note upon which plaintiff seeks to recover fails of negotiability because it is not, on its face, payable either on demand or at a definite time. The note calls for three installments of interest to be paid on "the 5th day of October, November, and December, 1979." It also contains an acceleration clause giving the holder the option of declaring the entire balance of principal, with interest, due and payable prior to maturity upon the makers' default on any installment of "principal or interest." Nowhere on the instrument's face, however, has a time for repayment of principal been specified.

Under U.C.C. §3–109:

An instrument is payable at a definite time if by its terms it is payable

(a) on or before a stated date or at a fixed period after a stated date; or

(b) at a fixed period after sight; or

(c) at a definite time subject to any acceleration; or

(d) at a definite time subject to extension at the option of the holder, or to extension to a further definite time at the option of the maker or acceptor or automatically upon or after a specified act or event.

This promissory note clearly contains none of the provisions necessary to make it payable at a definite time.

An instrument may also be negotiable if it is payable on demand. "Instruments payable on demand include those payable at sight or on presentation and those in which no time for payment is stated." If the note had merely stated that the McGuires promised to pay the Tursis $65,000 at a given rate of interest, there can be no question that the note would have been payable on demand. Here, however, it is apparent from the face of the instrument that the parties did not intend for this note to be payable on demand, nor would any reasonable person so interpret it. Were the note payable on demand, for example, there would be no need for an acceleration clause. Moreover, no note payable on demand would specify a fixed amount of interest payable for the following three months and make no provision for interest thereafter. One can speculate that the parties intended the note to mature at a definite time approximately three months after the date it was signed. Exactly what time was intended, however, is impossible to ascertain from the face of the note. When a note is payable only at an indefinite time in the future, and parol evidence is required to supplement its terms, the note is not a negotiable instrument within the meaning of Article 3 of the Uniform Commercial Code. . . .

Summary judgment denied.

First Inv. Co. v. Andersen
621 P.2d 683 (Utah 1980)

Andersen gave a promissory note to Great Lakes in return for Great Lakes' promise to deliver 65,000 trees for Andersen's nursery business. The note recited:

For value received, Robert Andersen of Nephi, Utah, promises to pay to Great Lakes Nursery Corp. at Waukesha, Wisconsin six thousand four hundred twelve dollars payable as follows: $100 per month beginning Oct. 1, 1965 for 24 months and then $111.30 per month for 36 months including interest computed at 7% per annum added to the principal amount of $4,750.00.

This note may be prepaid with adjustment of interest at any time.

In return for a loan, Great Lakes transferred the note to First Investment. When Great Lakes failed to deliver the trees, Andersen refused to pay First Investment. First Investment sued Andersen, claiming the note was negotiable so it took free of Andersen's defense of failure of consideration. The trial court found for the defendant.

MAUGHAN, J. . . . Defendants prevailed before the trial court on the ground the notes were not negotiable, and failure of consideration was a defense against any person not a holder in due course.

The primary issue is whether the two promissory notes were negotiable. A negotiable promissory note . . . is an unconditional promise in writing made by one person to another, signed by the maker, engaging to pay on demand, or at a fixed or determinable future time, a sum certain in money, *to order or to bearer.*

An instrument to be negotiable . . . must be payable to order or to bearer. An instrument is payable to order where it is drawn payable to the order of a specified person, or to him or his order.

Under . . . the U.C.C. 70A-3-104(1)(d), one of the requirements to qualify a writing as a negotiable instrument is that it contain the time-honored "words of negotiability," such as "pay to the order" or "pay to the bearer." The mere promise to pay, absent the magic words "payable to order or to bearer" renders the note nonnegotiable, and the liability is determined as a matter of simple contract law.

In the instant case, the notes were payable simply to the payee, and were not payable to the order of the payee or to the payee or its order and were thus not negotiable instruments. Since the notes were not negotiable, the transfer by the Nursery to plaintiff must be deemed an assignment, and the assignee (plaintiff) stood in the shoes of the assignor and took subject to existing equities and defense. . . .

Affirmed.

REVIEW QUESTIONS

1. Match each term in column A with the appropriate statement in column B.

A	B
1. I.O.U.	**a.** Varying exchange rates have no impact.
2. Particular fund concept	**b.** A statement of the transaction out of which the instrument arose.
3. Sum certain in money	**c.** Requires good faith in its execution.
4. Demand	**d.** Bearer paper.
5. Negotiability unaffected	**e.** Not a promise.
6. Acceleration clause	**f.** Does not destroy negotiability if a government unit is the maker or drawer.
7. Extension clause	**g.** May or may not destroy negotiability.
8. Cash	**h.** If nothing is stated, the instrument included this term.

2. Comment briefly on the provisions described in these instruments as to their bearing on negotiability; in each instance the other portions of the instrument are in proper form.

    a. A bill of exchange drawn by Y on Z directs Z to pay $1,000 to the order of A and charge this amount to Y's "Book Fund."

    b. The XYZ Co. (a partnership) signed a note promising to pay $1,000 and bearing the notation "limited to payment out of the entire assets of the maker."

    c. X signed a note promising to pay $5,000 or deliver 100 barrels of oil at the option of the holder.

    d. One of the notes is payable "5 days after the death of the maker."

    e. A note containing the following notation: "with interest at bank rates."

    f. A note payable in 10 ounces of gold.

3. Horace Brace has in his possession the following instrument:

> November 1, 1985
>
> I, Walter Forgel, hereby promise to pay Charles Smidlap ONE THOUSAND DOLLARS ($1,000.00) one year after date. This instrument was given for the purchase of FIVE HUNDRED (500) shares of Beefstake Mining Corporation. Interest at 10 percent.
>
> /s/ Walter Forgel

Horace Brace purchased the instrument from Charles Smidlap at a substantial discount. Smidlap specializes in the sale of counterfeit mining stock. Walter Forgel is one of his innocent victims. What are the rights of Brace against Forgel on the instrument? Explain.

4. Albert executed a contract with Blake for the construction of a factory building. Albert gave Blake a signed promissory non-interest-bearing demand note in the amount of $14,000, payable to bearer, as down payment on the contract. On the lower left corner of the note, Albert wrote: "This payment arises out of a construction contract." Blake sold the note to his bank. A few days later, the bank demanded payment and Albert refused because Blake had not started construction. The bank sues Albert on the note. With what result? Why?

5. Mary executed a note and a purchase money mortgage to Al. Al negotiated the note to Tiger Bank. The note contained the following stipulation: "This note with interest is secured by a mortgage on real estate, of even date herewith, made by the maker hereof in favor of the said payee. The terms of said mortgage are by this reference made a part hereof." Is the note negotiable? Explain.

6. Skyblast Freight executed a note which contained the following provisions: "This note is payable only from the proceeds of the sale of the Skyblast Freight Building." Is the note negotiable? Why or why not?

7. Nestrick executed a note with the Bank of Viola to secure an uninterrupted line of credit. The note, in pertinent part, recited that it was "payable in installments of $80.00 per week from the *Jack and Jill* contract." Is this note negotiable? Explain.

8. Employer gave Pension Fund Company a note stating that Employer promised to pay Pension Fund Company "all current contributions as they become due under the collective bargaining agreement in addition to the sum of $15,606.44 with interest." Is this note negotiable? Why or why not?

9. Joanna executed a $5,000 note stating that it was due on request with 30 days notice. Is this note negotiable? Explain.

10. Standard Oil executed a note payable to the order of Texas Oil Industries, which was due "as soon as Texas Oil Industries shall deliver to Standard Oil Company fifty thousand gallons of crude oil." Was this a negotiable instrument? Explain.

11. A note provides: "Payable on January 1, 1986, but payable at any time T&J Partnership dissolves." Is this note negotiable? Why or why not?

12. Locke sued Shields to recover on two notes that stated: "Buyer agrees to pay to Seller. . . ." Is Locke a holder of a negotiable note? Why or why not?

29 THE TRANSFER OF COMMERCIAL PAPER

The general rule governing the transfer of almost all types of property is that a person can transfer no greater interest than he owns. *Assignments* follow that general rule. The general law of assignments was discussed in chapter 13. When one attempts to transfer rights by assignment, it is generally stated that the assignee steps into the shoes of the assignor. Thus, the transfer of an instrument by assignment, whether negotiable or nonnegotiable, vests in the assignee only those rights the assignor had.

By contrast, the key feature of negotiability is that a *negotiation* might confer on a transferee greater rights than were held by the transferor. If the transfer is by negotiation, the transferee becomes a *holder* [3-202(1)]. A holder has, for example, the legal power to transfer the instrument by assignment or negotiation; he can usually enforce it in his own name [3-301]; he can discharge the liability of any party in several ways (as we shall later explain); and he enjoys several procedural advantages. Moreover, the holder has the opportunity to become a holder in due course which, as the next chapter demonstrates, gives him rights not granted by the instrument. Thus, in an *assignment,* only the rights of the transferor are passed to the transferee, but in a *negotiation,* there is the possibility of granting greater rights. Any contract can be assigned; only a negotiable instrument can be negotiated.

1. Transfer by Negotiation

Two methods of negotiating an instrument make the transferee a holder. If the instrument is payable to bearer, it may be negotiated by delivery alone; if it is order paper, indorsement and delivery are required [3-202(1)]. The indorsement must be placed on the instrument itself or on a paper so firmly affixed to it that it becomes a part. thereof. The indorsement paper that is annexed is called an *allonge.* The indorsement must be made by the holder or by someone who has the authority to do so on behalf of the holder [3-202(2)]. If the payee is a corporation, an officer will indorse on its behalf. The indorsement should include the corporate name, but this is not actually required.

The indorsement, to be effective as a negotiation, must convey the entire instrument or any unpaid balance due on the instrument. If it purports to indorse less than the entire instrument, it will be effective only as a partial assignment [3-202(3)]. An indorsement reading "Pay to A one-half of this instrument" would not be a negotiation, and A's position would be that of an assignee.

The indorser may add to his indorsement words of assignment, condition, waiver, guarantee, or limitation or disclaimer of liability, and the like. The indorsement is nevertheless effective to negotiate the instrument [3-202(4)]. Thus if A, the payee of a negotiable instrument, signs his name on the reverse side with the words, "I hereby assign this instrument to B," he has effectively indorsed the instrument, and upon delivery to B, B is a holder.

If the name of the payee is misspelled, the payee may negotiate by indorsing either the name appearing on the instrument or in his true name, or both. A person who pays the instrument or gives value for it may require that both names be indorsed [3-203]. The desirable practice is to indorse in both names when the name of the payee is misspelled.

Instruments payable to multiple parties must be indorsed by all parties in order to negotiate the instrument. If authorized, one party may sign for the other. As will be discussed later, a bank may supply missing indorsements for its depositors. If there is a joint account, it may add the indorsement of either party or both in the event an item is payable to both.[1]

2. Introduction

INDORSEMENTS

The ordinary indorsements used in negotiating paper are either special or blank. If added terms condition the indorsement, it is also a restrictive indorsement, which limits the indorsee's use of the paper. Also, the indorser may *limit* or *qualify* his liability as an indorser by adding words such as "without recourse." This qualified indorsement has the effect of relieving the indorser of his contractual liability as an indorser—that he will pay if the primary obligor refuses to do so. A qualified indorsement will also be a blank or a special indorsement. These indorsements are discussed in the sections that follow.

3. Blank Indorsements

A blank indorsement consists of the indorser's name written on the instrument. If an instrument drawn payable to order is indorsed in blank, (see Fig. 29-1), it becomes payable to bearer [3-204(2)]. After the blank indorsement, if it is indorsed specially, it reverts to its status as order paper, and an indorsement is required for further negotiation [3-204(1)]. If a check, on its face payable to the

---

[1] Beyer v. First Nat. Bank of Dillon, p. 645.

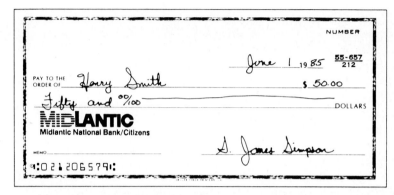
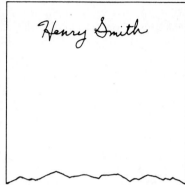

FIGURE 29–1

Order paper, payable to the order of Henry Smith. With his blank indorsement, shown at right, the order paper becomes bearer paper, negotiable by mere delivery.

order of Henry Smith, is indorsed "Henry Smith," it becomes bearer paper and can be negotiated by mere delivery. A thief or finder could pass title to the instrument.

4. Special Indorsements

A special indorsement specifies the person to whom or to whose order it makes the instrument payable. (See Fig. 29–2.) When an instrument is specially indorsed, it becomes payable to the *order of* the special indorsee and requires his indorsement for further negotiation. Thus an indorsement "Pay to John Jones" or "Pay to the order of John Jones" is a special indorsement and requires the further indorsement by John Jones for negotiation. If a bearer instrument is indorsed specially, it requires further indorsement by the indorsee. This is true if the instrument was originally bearer paper or if it became bearer paper as the result of a blank indorsement. In other words, the last indorsement determines whether the instrument is order paper or bearer paper [3-204].

The holder of an instrument may convert a blank indorsement into a special indorsement by writing above the blank indorser's signature any contract consistent with the character of the indorsement [3-204(3)]. Thus, Richard Roe, to whom an instrument has been indorsed in blank by John Doe, could write above Doe's signature, "Pay to Richard Roe." The paper would require Roe's indorsement for further negotiation.

5. Restrictive Indorsements

A person who indorses an instrument may impose certain restrictions upon his indorsement; that is, the indorser may protect or preserve certain rights in the paper and limit the rights of the indorsee. Of the four types of restrictive indorsement, one is conditional (for example, "Pay John Doe if Generator XK-711 arrives by June 1, 1986"). Or the indorsement may purport to prohibit further

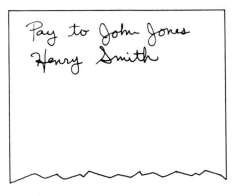

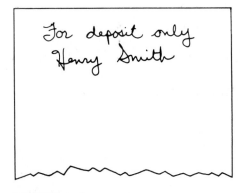

FIGURE 29–2

A special indorsement by Henry Smith. For negotiation, it requires further indorsement by John Jones.

FIGURE 29–3

A restrictive indorsement by Henry Smith. Subsequent holders should be only the banks in the collection process.

transfer of the instrument, such as, "Pay to John Doe only" [3-205(a)(b)]. When a check is deposited in a bank and will be processed through bank collection, the indorsements "For collection," "For deposit only," and "Pay any bank" are restrictive [3-205(c)]. In the fourth type, the indorser stipulates that it is for the benefit or use of the indorser or some other person, such as, "Pay John Doe in trust for Richard Roe" [3-205(d)].

A restrictive indorsement does not prevent further transfer or negotiation of the instrument [3-206(1)]. Thus, an instrument indorsed "Pay to John Doe only" could be negotiated by John Doe in the same manner as if it had been indorsed "Pay to John Doe."

The most common restrictive indorsement is "For deposit only." It is a common practice for payees of checks to use such an indorsement in order to safeguard checks. Once a check is stamped "For deposit only," a thief or finder of the check cannot cash it. The only action the bank can take is to deposit it into the indorser's account. If it fails to do so, it has liability to the indorser. (See Fig. 29–3).[2]

The effect of restrictive indorsements is substantially limited when applied to banks. An intermediary bank or a payor bank that is not a depositary bank can disregard any restrictive indorsement except that of the bank's immediate transferor. This limitation does not affect whatever rights the restrictive indorser may have against the bank of deposit or his right against parties outside the bank's collection process [3-206(2)]. Under a conditional indorsement or an indorsement for collection or deposit, a transferee (other than an intermediary bank) becomes a holder for value if it pays consistent with the indorsement [3-206(3)].

When the indorsement is for the benefit of the indorser or another person, such as "Pay to John Doe in trust for Richard Roe," only the first taker is required to act consistently with the restrictive indorsement [3-206(4)]. John Doe has the

---

[2] Rutherford v. Darwin, p. 646.

obligation to use the instrument or the proceeds from it for the benefit of Richard Roe. John Doe could negotiate the instrument to John Smith, who could qualify as a holder and ignore the restriction.

TRANSFER OF CHECKS

6. Terminology

The following terminology of section 4-105 of the Code is significant with regard to the designation of the various banks in the collection process for checks.

1. "Depositary bank" means the first bank to which an item is transferred for collection even though it is also the payor bank.
2. "Payor bank" means a bank by which an item is payable as drawn or accepted.
3. "Intermediary bank" means any bank to which an item is transferred in course of collection except the depositary or payor bank.
4. "Collecting bank" means any bank handling the item for collection except the payor bank.
5. "Presenting bank" means any bank presenting an item to a payor bank.
6. "Remitting bank" means any payor or intermediary bank remitting for an item.

It should be kept in mind that a bank may occupy more than one status in the collecting process. For example, a bank that receives a customer's deposit drawn on another bank is both a depositary and a collecting bank. A bank accepting a deposit of a check drawn by another customer is both a depositary and a payor bank.

7. The Bank Collection Process

If a check is deposited in a bank other than the bank on which it is drawn, it must be sent to the payor bank for payment. This collection process may involve routing the item through a number of banks that typically credit or debit accounts they maintain with one another. In particular, the regional Federal Reserve Banks, with which most banks have accounts, play a major role in this process. An example may help you understand the collection process.

Suppose that Carson in Athens, Georgia, mails his check drawn on the First Athens Bank to Exxon in Houston, Texas, in payment of an obligation. Exxon deposits the check in the First National Bank of Houston, which forwards it to the Federal Reserve Bank of Houston, which sends it to the Federal Reserve Bank of Atlanta, which presents it to the First Athens Bank for payment. The relationship of these parties is depicted in Fig. 29-4.

As Figure 29-4 indicates, the collection process begins when the customer (Exxon) deposits a check to its account. The account is provisionally credited by the bank. The check then passes through the collecting banks, each of which provisionally credits the account of the prior bank. When the check finally reaches

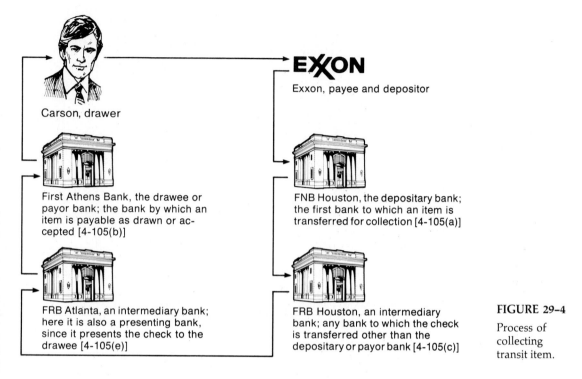

Carson, drawer

Exxon, payee and depositor

First Athens Bank, the drawee or payor bank; the bank by which an item is payable as drawn or accepted [4-105(b)]

FNB Houston, the depositary bank; the first bank to which an item is transferred for collection [4-105(a)]

FRB Atlanta, an intermediary bank; here it is also a presenting bank, since it presents the check to the drawee [4-105(e)]

FRB Houston, an intermediary bank; any bank to which the check is transferred other than the depositary or payor bank [4-105(c)]

FIGURE 29–4

Process of collecting transit item.

the payor-drawee bank (First Athens Bank), that bank debits the drawer's (Carson's) account.

The payor bank then credits the account of the presenting bank, remits to it or, if both belong to the same clearinghouse, includes the check in its balance there. If the payor bank honors the check, the settlement is final. Transactions prior to this final settlement by the payor bank are called "provisional settlements," because it is not known until final settlement whether the check is "good." If the payor bank dishonors the check, as in the case of an "N.S.F." (not sufficient funds) check, the presenting bank will revoke its provisional settlement and charge the item back to the account of the next prior collecting bank. Likewise, other banks in the chain of collection will charge back. The final step is a chargeback to the customer's account by the depositary bank and the return of the check to the customer. Each of the collecting banks must return the item or send notification of the facts by its midnight deadline. The right to charge back by the depositary bank is not affected by the fact that the depositor may have drawn against the provisional credit.

A depositor does not have the right to draw against uncollected funds. Accordingly, he is not entitled to draw against an item payable by another bank until the provisional settlement his depositary bank has received becomes final [4-213(4)(a)]. Many banks allow their customers this privilege, even though they have no legal duty to do so.

A customer who deposits an item for collection should indorse it, but quite frequently a customer forgets that signature. The depositary bank may supply the missing indorsement. If the bank states on the item that it was deposited by a customer or credited to his account, such a statement is as effective as the customer's indorsement. This is a practical rule intended to speed up the collection process by making it unnecessary to return to the depositor any items he may have failed to indorse [4-205]. The term *customer* is broadly construed and may include parties other than depositors.[3]

8. Collecting Banks

When a bank has received a check for collection, it has the duty to use ordinary care in performing its collection operations. These operations include presenting the check to the drawee or forwarding it for presentment, sending notice of nonpayment if it occurs and returning the check after learning that it has not been paid, and settling for the check when it receives final payment. Failure of the collecting bank to use ordinary care in handling a check subjects the bank to liability to the depositor for any loss or damage sustained.

To act seasonably, a bank is generally required to take proper action before the midnight deadline following the receipt of a check, a notice, or a payment. Thus, if a collecting bank receives a check on Monday and presents it or forwards it to the next collecting bank any time prior to midnight Tuesday, it has acted seasonably. If it fails to do so, it has liability unless it is excused by matters beyond its control. In this case the bank must use due diligence, and excuses are difficult to establish.[4]

9. Payor Banks

An item is finally paid by a payor bank when the bank (1) pays the item in cash, (2) settles for the item without reserving the right to revoke the settlement, (3) completes the process of posting the item, or (4) makes a provisional settlement and fails to revoke it within the time prescribed [4-213(1)]. Upon final payment, the payor bank is accountable for the item, and it has substituted its own obligation for that of the drawer. Final payment usually occurs whenever the payor bank makes a provisional settlement for the item (a credit) and then fails to revoke its credit within its midnight deadline after receipt of the item. If the payor bank makes a provisional settlement for an item on the banking day it is received, that bank has until final payment of the check—but not later than the midnight deadline on the following day—to decide whether or not the item is good. Within this time the bank may revoke the settlement and return the item or, if this is not possible, send written notice of nonpayment. This enables the bank to defer posting until the next day. When a check drawn by one customer of a bank is *deposited by another customer of the same bank* for credit on its books, the bank

[3] Marine Midland Bank, N.A. v. Price, Etc., p. 647.
[4] First Wyo. Bank v. Cabinet Craft Distrib., p. 648.

may return the item and revoke any credit given at any time on the following day. The deposit of an item on which the depository bank is itself the payor ("on us" items) becomes final on the opening of the second banking day following receipt of the item [4-213(4)(b)].

Failure of the payor-drawee bank to take action within the prescribed time limits may make it accountable to the person who deposited the check if the check is not paid. This liability is imposed if the bank (1) retains a check presented to it by another bank without settling for it by midnight of the banking day of receipt or (2) does not pay or return the check or send notice of dishonor within the period of its midnight deadline [4-302(a)].

Another problem relates to the *order of payment of checks.* There is no priority among checks drawn on a particular account and presented to a bank on any particular day. The checks and other items may be accepted, paid, certified, or charged to the indicated account of its customer in any order convenient to the bank [4-303(2)].

An item does not always proceed through the clearinghouse. It may be presented directly to the payor bank for payment over the counter. If the payor bank pays the item in cash, it may not later collect back the payments if its customer has insufficient funds on deposit [4-213(1)(a)].

10. Forgeries

Banks have a special problem in connection with forgeries. Checks presented to payor banks for payment may bear forged signatures of drawers or forged indorsements. If the drawer's signature was forged, the bank that honors the check has not followed the order of the drawer and cannot charge the account [3-418]. If charged, it must be recredited. Likewise, the bank will have to make restitution to the party whose name was forged on the check as an indorsement [3-419(1)(c)]. In either case, the loss initially is that of the bank that pays the instrument bearing the forgery.

In the case of a forged drawer's signature, the payor bank as a general rule cannot collect payment from the party who received it. The bank has the signature of the drawer on file and is charged with knowledge of the forgery. This general rule is subject to the exception that if the party receiving payment is the forger or dealt with the forger and was negligent in doing so, the payor may recover the payment. Thus, if a collecting bank was negligent, the payor bank that paid on a forged drawer's signature could recover from the collecting bank.

A payor-bank who pays on a forged indorsement has greater rights in seeking to recover the payment than does the payor who pays on a forged drawer's signature. In the case of a forged indorsement, the payor has no way of knowing about the forgery, and thus it can collect from the person to whom payment was made, who in turn can collect from all prior parties back to the forger.

A bank sometimes cashes a check indorsed by an agent who lacks authority. When it does, the bank is held liable to the payee if the bank is charged with knowledge of the lack of authority. Just as in the case of forgery by a stranger, the drawer can insist that the drawee recredit his account with the amount of any unauthorized payment. An unauthorized signature is a forgery and a real defense.

11. Impostors: Fictitious Payees

A situation similar to forgery arises when an instrument is made payable to a fictitious person or to an impostor. The drawer's signature is genuine, but the instrument is indorsed in the fictitious name or the name of the person who is being impersonated. In the impostor situation, one person poses as someone else and induces the drawer to issue a check payable to the order of the person being impersonated. In the fictitious payee case, the person who induces the issuance of the instrument simply makes up the name of the payee. In both cases the instrument is then indorsed in the name of the person being impersonated or the name made up. The indorsement in the name of the payee is effective because it was made by the person that the drawer intended to indorse, and the named payee was not intended to have an interest in the check. The loss falls on the drawer rather than on the person who took the check or the bank that honored it [3-405(1)(a)]. *Note*: If the check is intended for the party named but is diverted and forged by an employee, the indorsement is not effective because the instrument is not indorsed by the party intended by the drawer.

A typical fictitious payee case involves a dishonest employee authorized to sign his employer's name to checks, or one who draws checks that he presents to his employer for the latter's signature. Thus the employee may draw payroll checks or checks payable to persons with whom the employer would be expected to do business. He either signs the checks or obtains his employer's signature and then cashes the checks, indorsing the name of the payee. If he is in charge of the company's books, he is able to manipulate the books when the canceled checks are returned and may thus avoid detection. The Code imposes this loss on the employer; the dishonest employee can effectively indorse in the payee's name [3-405(1)(c)].[5]

---

[5] Brighton, Inc. v. Colonial First Nat'l. Bank. p. 649.

SUMMARY

TRANSFER OF COMMERCIAL PAPER

Negotiation	
	1. The term *negotiation* is used to describe the method of transferring a negotiable instrument in a manner that makes the transferee a holder.
	2. A transfer that is not a proper negotiation is an assignment, and the assignee has the same rights as the assignor.

3. Bearer paper is negotiated by delivery. Order paper requires indorsement and delivery.

4. For proper negotiation, the whole instrument must be negotiated.

INDORSEMENTS

Blank

1. A blank indorsement consists of the indorser's name, usually written on the back of the instrument.

2. A blank indorsement converts order paper to bearer paper.

Special

1. Special indorsements indicate the person to whom the instrument is payable. Special indorsements require the indorsement of such person for further negotiation.

Restrictive

1. Restrictive indorsements allow the indorser to preserve rights and limit the options of the indorsee.

2. The most common restrictive indorsement is "For deposit only." This means that the bank may not cash the check, but must deposit the proceeds into the account of the indorser.

3. A restrictive indorsement when applied to banks does not prevent further negotiation and is applicable only to the immediate indorsee.

THE TRANSFER OF CHECKS

Terminology

1. Depositary bank—the first bank to which an item is transferred for collection.

2. Payor bank—the bank by which an item is payable as drawn or accepted.

3. Intermediary bank—any bank to which an item is transferred in the course of collection except the depositary or payor bank.

4. Collecting bank—any bank handling the item for collection except the payor bank.

5. Presenting bank—any bank presenting an item to a payor bank.

	6. Remitting bank—any payor or intermediary bank remitting an item.
The collection process	**1.** A check deposited in the account is a provisional settlement until the check is honored by the payor bank.
	2. If the payor bank dishonors a check, provisional settlements are revoked. This must occur for each bank by its midnight deadline.
	3. Depositors do not have the right to draw against provisional settlements, although many banks allow them to do so.
Missing indorsements	**1.** Items deposited for collection without indorsement may be indorsed by the depositary bank on behalf of its customer. The indorsement indicates that it was deposited to the account of the customer.
	2. Depositary banks may not supply indorsements of persons who are not customers.
Collecting banks	**1.** Banks have a duty to use ordinary care in the collection process. Failure to do so creates liability for losses sustained.
	2. Banks must take action before the midnight deadline on checks, notices from other banks, and making payments.
Payor banks	**1.** An item is paid by a payor bank when it actually pays the item, settles for it without reserving the right to revoke the settlement, completes the posting of the item, or makes a provisional settlement and does not revoke it within the time allowed.
	2. A provisional settlement may be revoked until the midnight deadline.
	3. If a check is drawn on the payor bank by a customer of the same bank, the bank may revoke the credit any time until the close of business the next day.
	4. There is no priority in the order of paying checks presented on the same day.
Forgeries	**1.** A bank that pays on a forged signature of the drawer cannot charge the drawer's account.
	2. A bank paying on the forged signature of an indorser must return the instrument to the party whose name was forged.

3. In the event of the forged signature of a drawer, the bank cannot collect from the party receiving payment unless that party is the forger or the party dealt with the forger negligently.

4. A payor-bank who pays on a forged indorsement can collect from the person to whom payment was made.

Impostors or fictitious payees

1. If a check is payable to an impostor or fictitious payee and indorsed by the impostor or by the person supplying the name of the fictitious person, the indorsement is effective as a negotiation. In such a case the loss falls on the drawer and not the bank.

2. These situations usually are a part of an embezzlement scheme, and the loss is placed on the employer who was in a position to prevent it from occurring.

CASES

Beyer v. First Nat. Bank of Dillon
612 P.2d 1285 (Mont. 1980)

Fred Beyer and his wife Peggy Beyer opened a joint account at the defendant bank. Both deposited checks to the account and wrote checks on it. As a part of a settlement with an insurance company, they received a check payable to "Fred Beyer and Peggy Beyer." It was deposited to the joint account without indorsement. The bank negotiated the check after a bank employee stamped the check with the following indorsement:

Deposited to the account of the within named payee in accordance with payee's instruction. Absence of the indorsement guaranteed by the First National Bank of Dillon, Montana.

The Beyers had marital difficulties and Peggy took all of the money out of the account. Fred sued the bank for the funds, alleging that it was liable to him for the check because he had not indorsed it.

The trial court held for the bank.

DALY, J. . . . This check is governed by section 30-3-116, MCA which provides:

Instruments payable to two or more persons: An instrument payable to the order of two or more persons:

(a) if in the alternative is payable to any one of them and may be negotiated, discharged or enforced by any of them who has possession of it;

(b) *if not in the alternative is payable to all of them and may be negotiated, discharged, or enforced only by all of them.*

Since the check is payable only to "Fred Beyer and Peggy Beyer" together, subsection (b) applies and "both must endorse in order to negotiate the instrument, although one, of course, may be authorized to sign for the other." The mere fact that the copayees are husband and wife does not authorize one to sign for the other:

Normally, when a check is made payable to husband and wife, it is considered to be payable to them jointly and the check must be endorsed by both of them. . . .

It is undisputed that neither Peggy Beyer nor Fred Beyer endorsed the $5,899 check, and that it was deposited to Account No. 2-227-7 by Peggy Beyer and stamped with the Bank's guaranteed endorsement. As a general proposition, Courts in a number of cases have held or recognized that a cashing or collecting bank which pays a check drawn to joint payees, other than partners, without obtaining the authentic endorsement of all such payees, is liable to a nonsigning payee for the value of his interest in the check, unless the nonsigning payee has authorized or ratified such payment. . . .

Section 30-3-419(3), MCA, however, gives the depository or collecting bank a defense to a suit for conversion and limits the bank's liability where the bank acts in good faith and in accordance with reasonable commercial standards:

> . . . a representative, including a depositary or collecting bank, who has in good faith and in accordance with the reasonable commercial standards applicable to the business of such representative dealt with an instrument or its proceeds on behalf of one who was not the true owner is not liable in conversion or otherwise to the true owner beyond the amount of any proceeds remaining in his hands.

Therefore, if the defendant-respondent, First National Bank of Dillon, acted in good faith and in accordance with reasonable commercial standards when it permitted Peggy Beyer to deposit the $5,899 check payable to "Fred Beyer and Peggy Beyer" in Checking Account No. 2-227-7 without the endorsement of either payee, the Bank would not be liable to Fred Beyer beyond the amount of any proceeds remaining in the Bank. Since the record indicates that neither the instrument itself nor any proceeds of it remained in the Bank at the time of suit, the Bank would not be liable at all if it acted in good faith and in accordance with reasonable commercial standards.

The Bank's good faith has not been challenged, and since the account to which the check was deposited was in fact the joint account of Fred and Peggy Beyer, as the trial court found, the Bank has complied with reasonable commercial standards.

Affirmed.

Rutherford v. Darwin
622 P.2d 245 (N.M.App. 1980)

ANDREWS, J. . . . Tom Darwin was a general partner of both Rancho Village Partners and The Settlement, Ltd., which are New Mexico limited partnerships. He had full authority to manage the funds of both entities with his signature alone.

On May 17, 1977, Darwin made a $300,000 draw against a construction loan made by Albuquerque National Bank (ANB) to Rancho Village Partners. He received the money in the form of a money order payable to "Rancho Village Partnership, Ltd." He endorsed the money order with "Deposit to the account of Rancho Village Partners, Ltd.", and took it to the First National Bank in Albuquerque (FNBIA), where both Rancho Village Partners and The Settlement had accounts. Darwin gave the money order to the teller with a pre-printed deposit slip for the account of The Settlement, and the teller wrote out the account number of The Settlement on the reverse side of the money order, below the endorsement. The teller then deposited the money order to the account of The Settlement, notwithstanding the endorsement, which directed otherwise.

Darwin intended that the deposit be made into The Settlement account. He then withdrew the bulk of the $300,000 within two weeks of the deposit of the money order, and the account was almost entirely depleted before any of the other members of the Rancho Village partnership learned of the draw seven months later. . . . Rancho Village Partners acted promptly to notify FNBIA and to protect its interest after the other members of the partnership learned of Darwin's action.

Rancho Village Partners brought suit against FNBIA to recover the $300,000 and the trial court entered summary judgment against the bank. FNBIA appeals from this summary judgment.

The words "Deposit to the account of Rancho Village Partnership, Ltd." clearly constitute a restrictive endorsement under §55-3-205. Section 55-3-206 imposes upon FNBIA the duty to pay consistently with the restrictive endorsement, and this duty gives rise to liability for the bank if it fails to do so.

FNBIA contends that Darwin "waived" the restrictive endorsement, and thus released it from its duty to pay as directed by the endorsement. We conclude, however, that New Mexico does not recognize any doctrine of the waiver of restrictive endorsements, and thus we cannot accept FNBIA's theory.

We hold, as a matter of law, that the bank had a duty to refuse to deposit the money to the account of The Settlement. The money order was restrictively endorsed to the account of an entity entirely different from that named, on the accompanying deposit slip. The trial court observed that, particularly in light of the sum involved, the bank had an obligation to be sure that the money went into the proper account. . . .

The presence of a restriction imposes upon the depositary bank an obligation not to accept that item other than in accord with the restriction. By disregarding the restriction, it not only subjects itself to liability for any losses resulting from its actions, but it also passes up what may well be the best opportunity to prevent the fraud. The presentation of a check in violation of a restrictive endorsement is an obvious warning sign, and the depositary bank is required to investigate the situation rather than blindly accept the check. Based on such a failure to follow the mandates of due care and commercially reasonable behavior, it is appropriate to shift ultimate responsibility from the drawer to the depositary bank.

Affirmed.

Marine Midland Bank, N.A. v. Price, Etc. 446 N.Y.S.2d 797 (App.Div. 1981)

MEMORANDUM: The issue is whether plaintiff bank became a holder in due course of checks drawn by defendant law firm when, upon receiving the checks from the payee, it stamped them "Credited to the account of the payee herein named/Marine Midland Chautauqua National Bank," despite the fact that the payee had no account with plaintiff and plaintiff was actually cashing the checks for the payee by wiring funds to Oklahoma. We hold that because plaintiff was a bank it was entitled to supply the payee's endorsement under U.C.C. section 4-205[1] and so become a holder in due course entitled to payment from defendant drawer of the checks.

The parties have stipulated the following facts: On January 3, 1979, defendant drew two checks totalling $36,906.54 on an account at the First National Bank of Jamestown payable to Leo Proctor Construction Company, Inc. and delivered the checks to Proctor. On January 4, 1979 an employee of Proctor presented the checks, unindorsed, to plaintiff and requested that $36,906.54 be wire-transferred to Proctor's account at a bank in Oklahoma. Plaintiff took the unindorsed checks and stamped each on the reverse side, "Credited to the account of the Payee herein named/Marine Midland Chautauqua National Bank" although Proctor has never maintained an account with plaintiff, and plaintiff wire-transferred the funds to the Oklahoma bank account as requested.

. . . The two checks at issue in the instant case, . . . were returned to plaintiff by the Oklahoma bank, having been stamped "payment stopped" by the First National Bank of Jamestown. Defendant had stopped payment on the checks immediately upon learning that Proctor was in default on the construction contracts for which the checks were drawn. Plaintiff's timely demands for payment by Proctor and/or by defendant were refused, the Oklahoma bank advising plaintiff that Proctor had filed a petition in bankruptcy. . . .

The parties agree that defendant has a valid defense on the checks as against Proctor. By our holding we find that defendant should not be permitted to transfer to plaintiff the loss resulting from Proctor's default on the construction contract with defendant when plaintiff was in no way involved with that contract, had no notice of Proctor's default and paid out funds to Proctor in good faith.

Plaintiff's right to recover depends upon whether it was a holder in due course. To establish that it must first establish that it was a "holder" of the check, i.e., a person to whom an instrument has been indorsed. If it was a holder in due course then it is entitled as a matter of law to judgment for the amount of the funds it has paid out to the payee before collecting on the check against the drawer who stopped payment.

Prior to the passage of the Uniform Commercial Code, the Court of Appeals held that a transferor's inadvertent failure to indorse a check prevented the transferee from being a bona fide holder for value, reasoning that that was a special status which required compliance with the technical requisites of the law of negotiable instruments. Article 3 of the

Uniform Commercial Code has not changed that result. Uniform Commercial Code, §3-302(1) requires a "holder in due course" first to be a "holder," and "holder" is defined to be a person to whom an instrument has been negotiated by indorsement.

Plaintiff, as a bank, enjoys a special status, however, under article 4 of the Code. Section 4-102(1) provides that the provisions of article 4 prevail over conflicting provisions of article 3 and section 4-205(1) provides that a "depositary bank which has taken an item for collection may supply any indorsement of the customer which is necessary to title." Thus, the bank was not required to prove that Proctor endorsed the checks to it because it is authorized by the Code to supply his indorsement.

Furthermore, we do not believe the bank was required to extend provisional credit to the payee, Proctor, pending collection or else forfeit its rights or that Proctor's non-depositor status is material to its right to recover in this proceeding. A customer, within the intendment of the Code, includes "any person . . . for whom a bank has agreed to collect items." The bank agreed to collect the checks here for Proctor and the stipulated facts establish that doing so was part of a course of conduct between the parties.

Judgment is granted to plaintiff against defendant Price, Miller, Evans & Flowers for $36,906.54 with interest and with costs.

First Wyo. Bank v. Cabinet Craft Distrib. 624 P.2d 227 (Wyo. 1981)

The plaintiff presented a check payable to itself to the defendant bank. The payor had insufficient funds on deposit with the bank to cover the check. The bank dishonored the check but failed to do so within its midnight deadline. It charged back the deposit. The bank's normal procedure was to collect all checks and send them for processing to a computer center in Billings.

The untimely dishonor of the check was due to delay in delivering checks from the computer center in Billings, Montana, to the bank in Sheridan. Normally, the same courier delivering the checks to the Montana computer center from Sheridan would have driven them back to Sheridan after the center had processed them. However, after the check in issue had been taken to Billings, the main road between Billings and Sheridan became flooded. Although the courier could have taken an alternate route back to Sheridan, the check was instead given to Western Airlines by the computer center to be placed on the next morning's flight to Sheridan. For unknown reasons Western Airlines failed to deliver the check to Sheridan although it made its usual flight. Western Airline's failure to deliver the check to Sheridan as planned caused the bank to miss its Uniform Commercial Code deadline for dishonoring the check.

ROSE, J. . . . The trial court found for plaintiff. The bank has appealed and argues that its "excuse" for failing to timely dishonor the check is sufficient under the Code to enable it to escape liability.

Section 34-21-408(b) (U.C.C. §4-108(2)), provides:

> (b) Delay by a collecting bank or payor bank beyond time limits prescribed or permitted by this act or by instructions is excused if caused by interruption of communication facilities, suspension of payments by another bank, war, emergency conditions *or other circumstances beyond the control of the bank provided it exercises such diligence as the circumstances required.*

Courts generally interpret U.C.C. §4-302 as imposing strict liability upon a bank which fails to dishonor a check in time unless the bank meets its burden of proving a valid defense. . . . If it is shown that a check has not been dishonored within the Code time limit, a prima facie case is established for imposing liability on the bank and the bank has the obligation of proving an excuse for untimely dishonor. . . .

It is obvious that the flooded road between Billings and Sheridan which disrupted the normal procedure for delivery of the check was a "circumstance beyond the control of the bank" as contemplated by §34-21-408(b) (U.C.C. §4-108(2)). Our inquiry is whether the bank used "such diligence as the circumstances required," in allowing the Montana computer center to give the check to Western Airlines for delivery and in not following up the failure of the airline to deliver the packet on schedule. In answering this question we must consider that the stipulated facts show that the bank had an alternative to using Western Airlines: its courier could have taken a different route.

. . . [O]ur appellee urges that we note that there is no evidence in the record that the appellant bank made any efforts to trace the checks when they did not arrive in Sheridan aboard the Western Airlines flight as scheduled. Perhaps a trace started on the missing checks that morning would have enabled the bank to obtain the checks that day and meet the midnight deadline for dishonoring the insufficient funds check which is the focus of this appeal.

The appellant bank has failed to prove an excuse sufficient under U.C.C. §4–103(2), to enable it to escape liability under U.C.C. §4–302 for its failure to dishonor the check in question by the midnight deadline imposed by the U.C.C.

Affirmed.

Brighton, Inc. v. Colonial First Nat'l. Bank
422 A.2d 433 (N.J. 1980)

MORGAN, J. . . . This appeal presents issues, . . . which deal with bank collection problems and the liabilities of depositary and drawee banks with respect to checks drawn by a so-called "faithless employee." The matter was adjudicated summarily in favor of the banks. Plaintiffs appeal.

The facts are, in the main, uncontroverted. They focus on the activities of Norman Hirschfield, the faithless employee of the plaintiffs, a group of real estate management firms, who between 1973 and 1978 embezzled well over $300,000 from plaintiffs' accounts with several of the defendant payor drawee banks. The fraudulent scheme used was not complex. His employment carried with it the authority to draw checks on his employers' bank accounts. He used this authority to draw such checks, payable to actual companies and individuals who were in fact creditors of his principals but to whom no money was then owing. He would then indorse the checks in the names of those payees and obtain payment from several of the defendant banks. The depositary banks would present the checks for payment at the payor-drawee banks and the appropriate account would then be debited. . . .

We start with the general proposition that a drawee bank may not properly debit the account of a customer whose check bears the forged indorsement of a payee. Where it does so and where the drawee is so notified within three years from the date the statement, and the challenged item is made available to the customer that such is the case, it will be required to recredit the customer's account by the amount of the check bearing the forged indorsement. A forged indorsement is normally ineffective to pass title to the instrument on which it appears.

With respect to checks bearing forged indorsements the amounts of which were debited to a plaintiff's account more than three years prior to return of the forged item, no claim against a drawee may be pressed for reasons given in the first point. With respect to the many items not so barred as untimely, summary judgment was entered in the drawees' favor on the basis of the so-called fictitious payee rule.

§3–405(1)(b) provides: "[a]n indorsement by any person in the name of a named payee is effective if . . . a person signing as or on behalf of a maker or drawer intends the payee to have no interest in the instrument. . . ."

This statute was designed to place the loss from the activities of a typical "faithless employee" upon the employer rather than upon the bank. As stated in Official Comment 4:

> . . . The principle followed is that the loss should fall upon the employer as a risk of his business enterprise rather than upon the subsequent holder or drawee. The reasons are that the employer is normally in a better position to prevent such forgeries by reasonable care in the selection or supervision of his employees, or, if he is not, is at least in a better position to cover the loss by fidelity insurance; and that the cost of such insurance is properly an expense of his business rather than of the business of the holder or drawee.

The loss is shifted by making the indorsement effective rather than by explicitly imposing it upon the drawer. By declaring a forged indorsement "effective," a collecting bank's liability on a warranty and a drawee bank's liability to its customer are precluded, with the result that loss is borne by the drawer. A typical situation to which §3–405 applies is given as an example in Official Comment 3 to §3-405:

> c. The drawer makes the check payable to P, an existing person whom he knows, intending to receive the money himself and that P shall have no interest in the check.

Plaintiffs' complaint pleads facts directly congruent to the given example. Hirschfield drew checks to the order of payees he intended to have no interest therein. In such circumstances . . . anyone's indorsement for the payee, even Hirschfield's, is "effective," thus passing title and making the item properly payable. . . . A drawee receiving that item, as did the three drawee banks in this matter, is authorized to debit the customer's account in the amount of such a check. Any loss thereon is borne by the customer as the Code clearly intended. . . .

Accordingly, we hold that a drawee bank bears no liability to its customer with respect to forged indorsements validated under an applicable fictitious payee rule. Such items are regarded as properly payable under §401(a) in furtherance of the Code design to cast the loss for such items on the customer rather than on his bank.

Affirmed.

REVIEW QUESTIONS.

1. Identify the terms in column A by matching each with the appropriate statement in column B.

A	B
1. Allonge	**a.** Without recourse.
2. Blank indorsement	**b.** May be revoked if payor bank dishonors check.
3. Qualified indorsement	**c.** The first bank to which an item is transferred for collection.
4. Special indorsement	**d.** May be supplied by depositary bank.
5. Provisional credit	**e.** A paper added to an instrument.
6. Presenting bank	**f.** Pay to John Jones. /s/ Paul Pringle.
7. Restrictive indorsement	**g.** Item deposited by one customer of a bank drawn on the same bank.
8. Depositary bank	**h.** A signature.
9. Missing indorsement	**i.** Any bank presenting an item except a payor bank.
10. On us	**j.** For deposit only.

2. Forger signs drawer's name to a $5,000 check and issues it to payee. Payee indorses and delivers it to Jane, who takes for value, in good faith and without notice of the forgery. Jane presents the check to drawee for payment, and drawee pays.

   a. Drawer discovers the forgery and requests drawee to recredit his account for $5,000. Will drawer win? Why?

   b. May drawee now recover from Jane? Why?

   c. May drawee now recover from forger? Why?

3. Drawer issues a check "to the order of Payee" for $5,000. Forger steals the check from payee, forges payee's name on the check and sells the check to Jane, who deposits it in her account with Depositary Bank. The check proceeds through the bank collection process, where it is ultimately paid by drawee. Because the check was stolen, payee was not paid.

a. May payee require drawer to issue another check? Why?

b. Can drawer now require drawee to recredit his account for the first check that was stolen and forged? Why?

c. Assume that payee seeks recovery from drawee, rather than requiring drawer to issue a new check. Will payee win? Why?

d. If drawee has either recredited drawer's account or paid payee for conversion of the check, may drawee now recover from Depositary Bank? Why?

e. Will Depositary Bank now be able to recover from Jane? Why?

f. Can Jane now recover from forger? Why?

4. One of plaintiff's employees, who was authorized to draw checks on plaintiff's account, drew several checks to the firm's creditors. He indorsed the checks in the name of the payees himself and cashed them. The depositary bank presented the checks to the payor bank, which paid them and debited plaintiff's accounts. When the embezzlement was discovered, plaintiff sued its bank. Is the bank liable for the amount of the checks? Why?

5. A check payable to a limited partnership was stamped "Deposit to the account of Rancho Village Partnership, Ltd." The check was deposited by a partner in his personal account and the proceeds were later withdrawn. The partnership sues the bank to collect the proceeds of the check. With what result? Why?

6. A check is issued payable jointly to Sam and Chuck. Sam indorses the check and deposits it in his account with National Bank. Chuck does not indorse the check, nor has Chuck ever been a customer of National Bank. National Bank supplies Chuck's missing indorsement and forwards the check to the drawee bank. Chuck sues National Bank for cashing the check without his indorsement. With what result? Why?

7. Roberts was a holder in due course of a properly drawn check payable to "Bearer." He indorsed the check as follows:

"Pay to the order of Wilson Hall without recourse.

"(s) Peter Roberts"

What type of indorsement did Roberts make? If Hall wishes to negotiate the instrument, what is required? Explain.

8. Casey held a negotiable instrument payable to his order. He transferred the instrument to Dale for value. At the time of transfer, Casey failed to indorse his name on the back of the instrument and Dale accepted the instrument as given to him. What rights does Dale have on the instrument? Explain.

9. Pearl is the holder of a check drawn by Sharpe on Washington State Bank. Pearl also maintains an account at Washington State Bank. The check is deposited at the bank on Monday. On that same day, Sharpe's account is overdrawn, but she promises to make a substantial deposit, so the bank holds the check until Thursday. Sharpe does not make the deposit, and the bank, on Friday, returns the check to Pearl marked "Insufficient Funds." Can Pearl require the bank to make good on the check? Why or why not?

10. A caterer, holder of a check, wishes to protect herself against its loss or theft. It has been indorsed to her in blank. Describe two methods by which she may gain this protection. Explain.

11. Quincey signed a promissory note payable to the order of Unger, who indorsed the note in blank over to Pritchard. Pritchard then transferred the note to Truax by delivery. Is Truax a holder of the instrument? Explain.

12. Bob issued a check payable to the order of Gary, who lost it without indorsing it. Can a finder of the check negotiate it? Why or why not?

30 HOLDERS IN DUE COURSE AND DEFENSES

If a person in possession of an instrument is the original party to whom the instrument was issued or drawn, he has the right to transfer the instrument to a third person. But a third party in possession may be a thief or finder whose rights and powers will be determined by whether the paper is order or bearer paper. A thief or finder may negotiate bearer paper, but neither has the right or power to negotiate order paper.

When an instrument is rightfully in possession of a third party, the third party transferee may be an *assignee,* a *holder,* or a *holder in due course.* An assignee has a simple contract, in contrast to a negotiable instrument. A transferee has the status of an assignee if a negotiable instrument has not been properly negotiated. A holder is in possession of a negotiable instrument that has been properly negotiated. After certain special requirements are met, the holder may qualify as a holder in due course.

A *holder* is a person in possession of a negotiable instrument payable to him or which has been properly negotiated to him [1-201(20)]. Thus, either the original payee or a third party may qualify as a holder of an instrument and may transfer or negotiate it. A holder may legally discharge it or enforce payment in his own name [3-301]. A thief or finder may qualify as a holder of a bearer instrument. A holder who does not qualify as a holder in due course is in a position equivalent to that of an assignee of a simple contract in that he cannot enforce payment in the event that a defense to the instrument legally exists.

A *holder in due course* is a holder who, because he meets certain require-ments, is given a special status and a preferred position in the event that there is a claim or a defense to the instrument [3-302]. If there is no claim or defense to the instrument, it is immaterial whether the party seeking to enforce it is a holder or a holder in due course. The Code makes all holders the functional equivalent of holders in due course until a defense is claimed. The burden of proving a defense is on the party asserting it. When the defense is proved, the holder has the burden of proving that he is a holder in due course [3-307(3)]. If he can prove that, he can enforce payment, notwithstanding the presence of a personal defense to the instrument. (Later in the chapter we discuss both types of defenses: personal and real.) A holder in due course will not be able to enforce the instrument in the event that a real defense is asserted. The preferred status of a holder in due course exists only where the defense to the instrument is a personal defense.

Issues as to whether or not a party is a holder in due course usually arise when the party seeks to collect on the instrument. But occasionally a party is sued on a negligence theory for losses incurred in transactions involving an instrument. To avoid liability, the defendant must establish that he is or was a holder in due course. Thus, a holder in due course is free of claims and is not subject to personal defenses.

1. Requirements

In order to qualify as a holder in due course, a holder must meet three basic requirements. He must take the instrument (1) for value, (2) in good faith, and (3) without notice that it is overdue, that it has been dishonored, or that any other person has a claim to it or defense against it [3-302(1)].

A payee may be a holder in due course if all the requirements are met. Ordinarily, a holder in due course is free of only personal defenses to parties with whom he had not dealt. Most payees deal with the maker or drawer. However, a payee may be a holder in due course when the instrument is not delivered to the payee by the maker, but is delivered by an intermediary or agent of the maker. A payee that participates in the transaction out of which the instrument arises cannot be a holder in due course.

When an instrument is acquired in a manner other than through the usual channels of negotiation or transfer, the holder will not be a holder in due course. Thus, if an instrument is obtained by an executor in taking over an estate, is purchased at a judicial sale, is obtained through legal process by an attaching creditor, or is acquired as a transaction not in the regular course of business, the party acquiring it is not a holder in due course [3-302(3)].

2. Value

A holder must have given value for an instrument in order to qualify as a holder in due course. A person to whom an instrument was transferred as a gift would not qualify as a holder in due course. *Value* does not have the same meaning as *consideration* in the law of contracts. A mere promise is consideration, but it is not value. As long as a promise is executory, the value requirement to be a holder in due course has not been met [3-303].

HOLDERS IN DUE COURSE

While a mere promise is not value, if the promise to pay is negotiable in form, it does constitute value [3-303(c)]. A drawer who issues his check in payment for a negotiable note that he is purchasing from the holder becomes a holder for value even before his check is cashed. A bank which cashes a check has given value.[1]

A holder who takes an instrument in payment of an existing debt is a holder for value [3-303(b)]. Thus, if Ada owed Brenda $500 on a past-due account and transferred a negotiable instrument to Brenda in payment of such account, Brenda would qualify as a holder for value. The same holds true if the instrument is received as collateral for an existing debt, whether the debt is due or not.[2]

A purchaser of a limited interest in paper can be a holder in due course only to the extent of the interest purchased [3-302(4)]. If a negotiable instrument is transferred as collateral for a loan, the transferee may be a holder in due course, but only to the extent of the debt that is secured by the pledge of the instrument. For example, George loans Gerry $2,500. To secure the loan, Gerry negotiates Ron's note in the amount of $4,000 to George. George is a holder in due course only to the extent of $2,500.

A person who purchases an instrument for less than its *face value* can be a holder in due course to the full amount of the instrument. Cora is the payee of a note for $1,000. She may discount the note and indorse it to Wick for $800. Wick has nevertheless paid value and is entitled to collect the full $1,000.

3. Good Faith

A holder must take the instrument in good faith in order to qualify as a holder in due course [3-304]. *Good faith* is defined as "honesty in fact in the conduct or transaction concerned" [1-201(19)]. If a person takes an instrument under circumstances that clearly establish the fact that there is a defense to the instrument, he does not take it in good faith. Failure to follow accepted business practices or to act reasonably by commercial standards, however, does not establish lack of good faith.

Taking a note on large discount does not in and of itself establish lack of good faith.[3] A large discount may result from factors other than the existence of a defense to the instrument. The burden is on the party seeking to deny the holder in due course status to prove lack of good faith. Good faith is presumed in the absence of facts to show bad faith.

Under a doctrine known as *close connectedness*, a transferee does not take an instrument in good faith when the transferee is so closely connected with the transferor that the transferee may be charged with knowledge of an infirmity in the underlying transaction. The rationale for the close connectedness doctrine is the basic philosophy of the holder in due course concept: to encourage free negotiability of commercial paper by removing certain anxieties from one who takes the paper as an innocent purchaser, knowing no reason why the paper is not

---

[1] Suit & Wells Equip. Co. v. Citizens Nat. Bank of So. Md., p. 662.

[2] Barclays Discount Bank Ltd. v. Bogharian Brothers, p. 663.

[3] Johnson v. Citizens and Southern Bank, p. 664.

sound as its face would indicate. Therefore, the more the holder knows about the underlying transaction, and particularly the more he controls or participates or becomes involved in it, the less he fits the role of a good-faith purchaser for value. The closer his relationship to the underlying agreement which is the source of the note, the less need there is for giving him the tension-free rights.

Among the factors that tend to establish the close connection are (1) drafting by the transferee of forms for the transferor; (2) approval of the transferor's procedures by the transferee (e.g., setting the interest rate); (3) an independent check by the transferee on the credit of the debtor; (4) heavy reliance by the transferor upon the transferee (e.g., transfer by the transferor of all or substantial part of his paper to the transferee); and (5) common or connected ownership or management of the transferor and transferee.

As a result of the close connectedness doctrine, many courts have held that a transferee of a negotiable note does not take in "good faith" and is not a holder in due course of a note given in the sale of consumer goods where the transferee is a finance company involved with the seller of the goods, and which has a pervasive knowledge of factors relating to the terms of the sale.

The good-faith requirement has often been challenged by consumers using the close connection doctrine when consumer paper was immediately transferred by a seller to a bank. If the bank qualified as a holder in due course, the consumer would have to pay, even though the goods were defective. This issue has been significantly eliminated today by a 1976 Federal Trade Commission ruling allowing consumers to use all defenses when sued on consumer paper. This FTC rule will be discussed in detail later in this chapter.

4. Without Notice

Closely related to "good faith" is the requirement that the transferee must not have notice of any claim or defense to the instrument, that it is overdue or has been dishonored [3-304]. A person has notice of a fact if he has actual knowledge of it, has received notification of it, or (from the facts and circumstances known to him) has "reason to know" that it exists [1-201(25)].[4] The law generally provides that a person has reason to know a fact if his information would indicate its existence to a person of ordinary intelligence (or of the intelligence of the person involved, if that is above the ordinary). He also has reason to know the facts if they are so highly probable that a person exercising reasonable care will assume their existence.

If there is visible evidence of forgery or alteration, a purchaser is put on notice of a claim or defense [3-304(1)(a)]. Certain irregularities on the face of an instrument also put a purchaser on notice that there may be a claim or defense to the instrument.[5]

If an instrument is incomplete in some important respect at the time it is purchased, notice is imparted [3-304(1)(a)]. Blanks in an instrument that do not relate to material terms do not give notice of a claim or defense; but if the

---

[4] Money Mart Check Cashing Center v. Epicycle, p. 664.

[5] Arcanum National Bank v. Hessler, p. 666.

purchaser has notice that the completion was improper, he is not a holder in due course [3-304(4)(d)].

Knowledge that a defense exists or that the instrument has been dishonored prohibits the status of a holder in due course. In some situations, knowledge of certain facts does *not,* of itself, give the purchaser notice of a defense or claim. Awareness that an instrument is antedated or postdated does not prevent a holder from taking in due course [3-304(4)(a)]. Knowledge of a separate contract is not notice. Although a defense will arise if the contract is not performed, such knowledge does not prevent one from becoming a holder in due course. Of course, if the purchaser is aware that the contract has been breached or repudiated, he will not qualify as a holder in due course.

Actual notice to prevent a party from being holder in due course must be received at a time and in a way that will give a reasonable opportunity to act on it [3-304(6)]. A notice received by the president of a bank one minute before the bank's teller cashes a check is not effective in preventing the bank from becoming a holder in due course.

5. Before Overdue

To be a holder in due course, a purchaser of an instrument must take it without notice that it is overdue [3-304(1)(c)]. A purchaser of overdue paper is charged with knowledge that some defense may exist.[6] A purchaser has notice that an instrument is overdue if he has reason to know that any part of the principal amount is overdue [3-304(3)(a)]. Past-due interest does not impart notice to the holder [3-304(4)(f)].

Demand paper poses a special problem, since it does not have a fixed date of maturity. A purchaser of demand paper cannot be a holder in due course if he has reason to know that he is taking it after a demand has been made, or if he takes it more than a reasonable length of time after its issue [3-304(3)(c)]. What is a reasonable or an unreasonable time is determined on the basis of a number of factors—the kind of instrument, the customs and usages of the trade or business, and the particular facts and circumstances involved. In the case of a check, a reasonable time is presumed to be 30 days [3-304(3)(c)]. The 30-day period is a presumption rather than an absolute rule.

6. Holder from a Holder in Due Course

A transferee may have the rights of a holder in due course, even though he personally does not meet all the requirements. Because a transferee obtains all the rights that the transferor had, a person who derives title through a holder in due course also has those rights. Code section 3-201(1) states this principle, the shelter provision, which advances the marketability of commercial paper.

The main significance of the shelter provision is that it permits one who is not a holder in due course to share the shelter from claims and defenses enjoyed by the holder in due course from whom he got the instrument. For example (see

---

[6] Richardson v. Girner, p. 667.

Fig. 30–1): Paul fraudulently induces Mary to execute and deliver a note to him. Paul then negotiates the note to Tom, and Tom qualifies as a holder in due course. Tom makes a gift of the note to Al, who sells it to Bob, a friend of Paul's who knew of Paul's fraud. Bob sells it to Carl after maturity. Is Carl a holder in due course? No. Were Bob and Al holders in due course when they owned the instrument? No. Is Carl subject to Mary's defense? No. While Al, Bob, and Carl are not and were not holders in due course, they have the rights of a holder in due course. They have Tom's rights and are free of the personal defense. Mary's defense was cut off by Tom's status as a holder in due course.

FIGURE 30–1

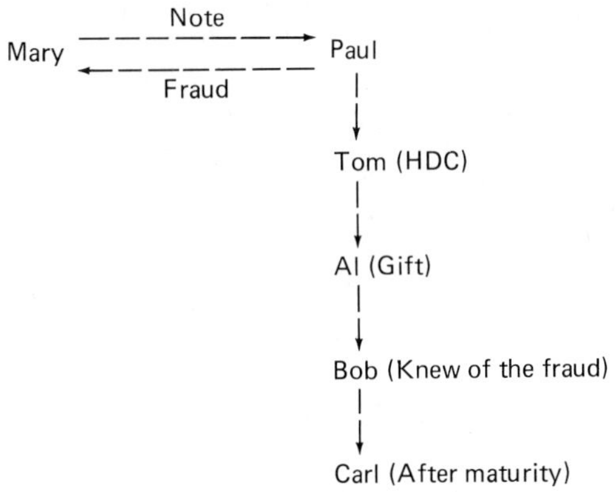

The shelter provision is subject to a limitation. A person who formerly held the paper cannot improve his position by later reacquiring it from a holder in due course. If a former holder was himself a party to any fraud or illegality affecting the instrument, or if he had notice of a defense or claim against it as a prior holder, he cannot claim the rights of a holder in due course by taking from a later holder in due course.

7. Classifications

DEFENSES

A holder in due course takes commercial paper free from the *personal* defenses of the parties to the paper [3-305]. One who is not a holder in due course or who does not have the rights of one under the shelter provision is subject to such defenses. All transferees, including holders in due course, are subject to what are referred to as *real* defenses.

In general, real defenses relate to the existence of any obligation on the part of the person who asserts them. The most obvious real defense is forgery of the signature of a maker of a note or the drawer of a check. The person whose signature was forged has not entered into any contract, and he has an absolute defense even against a holder in due course.

The Code generally specifies which defenses are real and which are personal. A few defenses—infancy being one—are real in some states and personal in others, but Table 30–1 groups them according to their usual status. Note that the

TABLE 30–1

Commercial
paper: typical
defenses

PERSONAL DEFENSES	REAL DEFENSES
Lack of failure of consideration	Unauthorized signature
Nonperformance of a condition precedent	Material alteration
Nondelivery, conditional delivery, or delivery for a special purpose	Infancy, if it is a defense to a simple contract
Payment	Lack of capacity
Slight duress	Extreme duress
Fraud in the inducement	Fraud in the execution
Theft by the holder or one through whom he holds	Illegality
Violation of a restrictive indorsement	Discharge in bankruptcy
Unauthorized completion	Discharge of which the holder has notice
Other defenses to a simple contract	
Any real defense where the party was negligent	

basic aspects of most personal defenses were discussed in the materials on contracts.

8. Personal Defenses

A distinction exists between fraud in the *inducement* and fraud in the *execution.* Inducement pertains to the consideration for which an instrument is given. The primary party intended to create an instrument, but was fraudulently induced to do so. Such a defense is personal and is not available against a holder in due course. Fraud in the execution exists where a negotiable instrument is procured from a party when circumstances are such that the party does not know that he is giving a negotiable instrument. Fraud in the execution is a real defense [3-305(2)(c)]. The theory is that since the party primarily to be bound has no intention of creating an instrument, none is created. Such fraud is rare because persons are usually charged with knowledge of what they sign.

Another personal defense, acquisition of title by or through a thief, is easily preventable. Conversion of bearer paper to order paper precludes its negotiation by a thief or finder.

A holder in due course is not subject to the defense of unauthorized completion of an instrument [3-407(3)]. The defense is personal. The person who left the blank space must bear the risk of wrongful completion.

Negligence of a party, frequently present in situations of fraud and material alteration, will reduce a real defense to a personal defense [3-406]. A check written with a wide, blank space preceding the amount offers a wrongdoer an easy place to raise that amount. The negligent check writer has reduced the defense to a personal one. The defense may be asserted, however, if the bank fails to follow reasonable commercial standards.[7]

---

[7] Owensboro National Bank v. Crisp, p. 667.

9. Real Defenses

The real defense of unauthorized signature includes signatures by agents without authority and forgeries [3-404(1)]. It applies to indorsements as well as to the signature creating the instrument.

The most common example of a material alteration is the "raising" of a check. A check drawn in the amount of $50 might be raised by alteration to $500. This creates a real defense to the extent of $450. A subsequent holder in due course could enforce the check only in the amount of its original $50. In the next chapter, we shall see that a material alteration of an instrument operates to discharge it. A basic change in the contract without the permission of its creator will cancel it.

The defense of lack of capacity is a real defense if the state law so provides. If it is a defense to a simple contract, it is a real defense [3-305(2)(a)]. The same is true for all forms of illegality. If a contract is merely voidable, the defense is personal; if the contract is void or unenforceable, the defense is a real one. If state law provides that usurious contracts are null and void, usury is a real defense.

10. FTC Rule Protecting Consumers from a Holder in Due Course

The holder in due course concept was predicated on the need for commercial paper to move quickly, freely, and as "a courier without luggage" in the financial community. Negotiable instruments were intended to be the equivalent of money. Use of commercial paper was encouraged by freeing it of personal defenses if its holder is a holder in due course. Today, consumer advocates argue that protection of the consumer is more important than the reasons for the holder in due course concept, and that all defenses should always be available to the consumer-debtor. They feel that the best protection for a consumer is the right to withhold payment if goods are defective or not delivered.

A number of states have enacted statutes prohibiting the use of enforcement of clauses that cut off defenses. Courts in many states have held that a holder was not a holder in due course when the finance company was closely connected with the seller. Courts have also strictly construed the application of the holder in due course rule. Doubts about the negotiability of instruments have been resolved against negotiability. Several states have achieved this result by the enactment of the Uniform Consumer Credit Code, whose provisions are applicable to instruments other than checks. This code offers two alternative approaches to the problem. A state legislature can select the one it considers best suited to the needs of the state.

One alternative simply gives maximum protection to the consumer by allowing him to assert all claims and defenses against the assignee of any paper that he signed. The other alternative provides that the assignee can give written notice of the assignment to the debtor. The consumer is then given the right to assert defenses for 3 months. After the 3-month period, the assignee is free of any defense, and the debtor's only remedy is against the seller.

Since these state efforts were not universal, in 1976 the Federal Trade Commission, acting under its authority to prohibit unfair or deceptive methods of competition, adopted a rule that prohibits the use of the holder in due course concept against consumers. It also provides that a clause purporting to cut off defenses is an unfair method of competition and illegal.

The FTC rule is designed to eliminate substantial abuses often inflicted upon the purchaser of consumer goods. Under the holder in due course concept, consumers were often required to pay for defective merchandise and even for merchandise not received. Since consumer paper was usually sold to a bank or other financial institution, the purchaser of the paper would qualify as a holder in due course. As such, it would be able to collect, and the consumer was left to fight it out with the seller when a problem arose.

The FTC rule is applicable to any sale or lease of goods or services to consumers in commerce. In such a transaction, it is an unfair or deceptive act or practice for a seller to receive a credit contract that does not contain the following provision in at least 10-point bold type:

NOTICE

**ANY HOLDER OF THIS CONSUMER CREDIT CONTRACT
IS SUBJECT TO ALL CLAIMS AND DEFENSES
WHICH THE DEBTOR COULD ASSERT AGAINST THE SELLER
OF GOODS OR SERVICES OBTAINED PURSUANT HERETO
OR WITH THE PROCEEDS HEREOF.**

Thus the holder could not be a holder in due course, because the holder agrees to be subject to all defenses.

To prevent sellers from sending buyers directly to the lender and thus circumventing the law, the rule has a special provision relating to lending institutions. It declares that it is an unfair or deceptive practice for a seller to accept in payment the proceeds of a purchase-money loan unless a similar notice is included in the loan agreement in 10-point bold type.

For the purpose of the foregoing rule, a purchase-money loan exists if the seller refers the consumer to the creditor or is affiliated with the creditor by common control, contract, or business arrangement. This means that if the lending institution regularly does business with the seller or has an understanding that its customers may obtain financing, the provision must be included in the loan contract. Again, it provides that all defenses are available to the consumer.

As a result of the FTC rule, if a consumer-purchaser or buyer has any defense against the seller, it may assert that defense against the bank or other financial institution that seeks to collect the debt. Thus, banks and other financial institutions must make sure that the seller stands behind the products sold. In addition, they must deal only with responsible parties on a recourse basis if losses are to be avoided.

SUMMARY

STATUS OF THIRD PARTIES

Alternatives

1. A person in possession of commercial paper may be an assignee, a transferee, a holder, or a holder in due course.
2. An assignee has a simple contract.
3. A transferee has a negotiable instrument which has not been properly negotiated and thus has the same rights as an assignee.
4. A holder has a negotiable instrument that has been properly negotiated.
5. A holder that meets certain requirements is a holder in due course and takes instruments free of personal defenses.

HOLDERS IN DUE COURSE

Requirements

1. A holder in due course must take the instrument for value and not as a gift. A mere promise is not value, but a preexisting debt is value.
2. A holder in due course must take in good faith. Good faith is honesty in fact. If the holder knows that there is a defense, he is not a good-faith taker.
3. A holder in due course must take without notice that it is overdue, has been dishonest, or that there is a claim or defense to the instrument. A person has notice if he has actual knowledge or reason to know the fact.
4. An instrument is overdue if it is demand paper and more than a reasonable length of time has passed. In the case of a check, this time period is 30 days.

Shelter provision

1. A transferee from a holder in due course has the rights of a holder in due course and thus is free of personal defenses. Thus, a person may take by gift, with

knowledge of a defense, or after maturity and still be able to collect on an instrument if it has passed through the hands of a holder in due course.

2. The shelter provision is not applicable to a reacquirer.

DEFENSES

Personal defenses

1. A personal defense is one that arises out of the transaction that created the instrument and is generally based on the law of contracts.
2. Payment is a very important personal defense.
3. Negligence reduces a real defense to a personal defense.

Real defenses

1. A real defense may be asserted against any party including a holder in due course.
2. Real defenses go to the essence of the instrument. The most important real defense is forgery.
3. Material alteration is a real defense only to the extent of the alteration.

The FTC rule

1. The FTC rule prevents the use of the holder in due course concept against a consumer.
2. In a transaction involving consumers, the contract must contain a notice in 10-point bold type informing all holders that any defense available against the seller of goods can be asserted against the holder.
3. The same notice must be contained in purchase-money loan documents.

CASES

Suit & Wells Equip. Co. v. Citizens Nat. Bank of So. Md.
282 A.2d 109 (Md. 1971)

SINGLEY, J. . . . This case poses the question whether, under certain circumstances, the holder of a check on which payment has been stopped can require payment by the maker.

. . . On 3 September 1966, Suit and Wells Equipment Co., Inc. (Suit and Wells) issued a check on its account at First National Bank of Southern Maryland (First National), payable to the order of

Joseph F. Tayman in the amount of $4,200. The check had been given to Tayman in payment for some equipment which he had promised to deliver the following day. When the equipment was not delivered, Suit and Wells stopped payment on the check early on the morning of 6 September, the next banking day. Later that day Tayman attempted to cash the check at First National, and when payment was refused, took the check to his own bank, Citizens National Bank of Southern Maryland (Citizens National), and cashed it. Citizens National seasonably presented the check for payment, which was refused and later brought suit. From a judgment for $4,200 with interest and costs in favor of Citizens National against Suit and Wells, Suit and Wells has appealed.

The principal thrust of Suit and Wells' argument is that Citizens National was Tayman's agent for purposes of collecting the check, and therefore could not be a holder in due course. We conclude that Suit and Wells' [argument is wrong].

It is clear that there are circumstances in which a collecting bank may acquire the rights of a holder. UCC §4-208 provides, in part:

> (1) A bank has a security interest in an item and any accompanying documents or the proceeds of either . . .
>
> (c) If it makes an advance on or against the item.

UCC §4-209 continues:

> For purposes of determining its status as a holder

in due course, the bank has given value to the extent that it has a security interest in an item provided that the bank otherwise complies with the requirements of §3-302 on what constitutes a holder in due course.

A bank which cashes a check drawn on another bank has a security interest and is a holder for value. Whether it is a holder in due course is determined by UCC §3-302, which provides, in part:

> (1) A holder in due course is a holder who takes the instrument
>
> (a) For value; and
>
> (b) In good faith; and
>
> (c) Without notice that it is overdue or has been dishonored or of any defense against or claim to it on the part of any person.

In the instant case, Tayman placed an unrestricted endorsement on the check, took it to Citizens National and cashed it, without disclosing that payment had been refused by First National. The check was not credited to Tayman's account but was purchased by Citizens National. Once Citizens National had advanced funds against the check, whether it was a purchaser or Tayman's agent, it acquired a security interest and became a holder in due course, if it acted in good faith and without notice of any informity in the instrument. . . .

Affirmed.

Barclays Discount Bank Ltd. v. Bogharian Bros.
568 F. Supp. 1116 (Cal. law 1983)

TASHIMA, J. . . . Plaintiffs seek summary judgment in these five actions for collection of promissory notes. Plaintiffs are banks operating out of the Diamond Exchange in Ramat Gan, Israel. Defendants, three American diamond merchants, issued a total of seven notes to Leo Siegman, a leading Israeli diamond dealer, as security for diamonds purchased by the defendants. Siegman endorsed three notes to plaintiff Barclays Discount Bank Ltd. ("Barclays") and four notes to plaintiff Israel Discount Bank Ltd. ("IDB") as collateral for his pre-existing obligations to the banks and as

collateral for the diamonds shipped to defendants. Plaintiffs presented the notes for payment as they came due; they were returned unpaid. Plaintiffs then commenced these actions for collection of the dishonored notes.

Plaintiffs contend that they are holders in due course; therefore, that they are entitled to recover on the notes. . . .

A holder in due course of a note is a holder who takes a note for value, in good faith, and without notice of any defense to the payment of the note.

A holder takes a note for value, . . . [w]hen he takes the instrument in payment of or as security for an antecedent claim against any person whether or not the claim is due. Plaintiffs took the notes as partial security for Siegman's loans and as additional collateral for Siegman's entire outstanding debt to plaintiffs. This outstanding debt was an antecedent claim of plaintiffs against Siegman. Therefore, plaintiffs took the notes for value when they accepted them as additional collateral for Siegman's debts.

Summary judgment is proper if there does not exist any genuine issue of material fact and, on those uncontroverted facts, the movant is clearly entitled to judgment as a matter of law. In the absence of any evidence controverting their showing, plaintiffs have satisfied the requirements of Cal. Comm. Code §3302(1) in that they took the notes for value, in good faith, and without notice of any claims or defenses. Plaintiffs are holders in due course of the notes at issue in these actions. Therefore, they are entitled to summary judgment.

So ordered.

Johnson v. Citizens and Southern Bank
241 S.E.2d 625 (Ga. 1978)

C & S Bank sued Johnson to collect a $50,000 note. Johnson had signed the note payable to Peek. Peek had transferred the note to the bank as security for a $20,000 loan. Johnson seeks to assert a defense of fraud and lack of consideration. The bank contends that it is a holder in due course and not subject to such defenses. The trial court entered summary judgment for the plaintiff.

BIRDSONG, J. . . . In substance, Johnson asserts that the gross lack of consideration paid by C & S to Peek for the . . . note raises a question for jury as to whether C & S was aware of the deficiencies in that note. In opposition to that position, C & S offered evidence that it took the note for value, in good faith, and without notice of any defects or defenses. Other than the inferences arising from the evidence of value paid by C & S to Peek, Johnson presented no other substantial factual evidence showing that C & S was not a holder in due course.

The mere fact that there might have been an inadequacy of consideration does not give rise to the conclusion proffered by Johnson. Johnson has presented no specific facts to show that C & S was aware that the . . . note was defective or that C & S was not a holder in due course other than bare assertions and conclusions in his defensive pleadings.

. . . When a motion for summary judgment is made and supported . . . an adverse party may not rest upon the mere allegations or denials of his pleadings, but his response, by affidavits or as otherwise provided . . . must set forth specific showing that there is a genuine issue for trial. If he does not so respond, summary judgment, if appropriate, shall be entered against him.

The evidence is uncontroverted that C&S Bank has held the note in question without interruption, obtained it in good faith and paid value therefor. Johnson has presented no credible evidence to show that the bank is not a holder in due course. Johnson admitted executing the note and does not deny that he is jointly and severally liable if the bank is indeed a holder in due course. Under such a state of facts, the trial court did not err in granting the motion for summary judgment.

Judgment affirmed.

Money Mart Check Cashing Center v.
Epicycle
667 P.2d 1372 (Colo. 1983)

Money Mart cashes payroll and government checks for a fee. Epicycle Corporation pays its employees by check. On February 16, 1980, Epicycle issued a payroll check, payable to John Cronin, in the amount of $278.59. During the term of his employment, Cronin had borrowed money from Epicycle to be offset by subsequent wages.

Cronin's employment was terminated, and an Epicycle employee who was unaware of Cronin's indebtedness gave Cronin his final payroll check. Epicycle ordered payment on the check stopped. Cronin cashed the check at one of Money Mart's locations on February 22, 1980. Money Mart deposited the check, sending it through normal banking channels. The check was returned to Money Mart marked "Payment Stopped."

Money Mart sued the employer for the amount of the check, claiming to be a holder in due course. The defendant contended that Money Mart who is in the business of cashing checks was negligent in not verifying that the check was good prior to cashing it and was therefore not entitled to holder-in-due-course status. The lower court found for the defendant.

ROVIRA, J. . . . The question before us is whether Money Mart is a holder in due course. If it is, it takes the check free of any of Epicycle's claims to the check or defenses against Cronin. Section 4-3-302(1), C.R.S.1973, provides:

(1) A holder in due course is a holder who takes the instrument:

(a) For value; and

(b) In good faith; and

(c) Without notice that it is overdue or has been dishonored or of any defense against or claim to it on the part of any person.

That Money Mart took the check for value is undisputed, leaving the questions of "good faith" and "notice."

"Good faith" is defined as "honesty in fact in the conduct or transaction concerned." The drafters of the Uniform Commercial Code intended that this standard be a subjective one. Thus, the question is "[W]as this alleged holder in due course acting in good faith, however stupid and negligent his behavior might have been?"

The only testimony on the question of good faith is that Money Mart cashed the check without knowing that a stop payment order had been issued on it. The Superior Court concluded that Money Mart was not a holder in due course because it "did not inquire as to the check itself and had no knowledge as to whether the check was stolen, incomplete, or secured by fraud." Under a subjective standard, an absence of knowledge is not equivalent to a lack of good faith. Consequently, if the Superior Court's reversal was based upon a lack of good faith on the part of Money Mart, it was in error.

We now consider whether Money Mart had "notice" of the fact that payment had been stopped on the check or that Cronin had obtained the check improperly. A person has "notice" of a fact when:

(a) He has actual knowledge of it; or

(b) He has received a notice or notification of it;

or

(c) From all the facts and circumstances known to him at the time in question he has reason to know that it exists.

As can be seen, tests other than "actual knowledge" may be used in determining whether a person is a holder in due course. There is no allegation that Money Mart had received notification of the defenses, so we must now determine whether Money Mart had "reason to know" of them.

The County Court referee found that Money Mart had no reason to know of the defenses because there was nothing inherently suspicious in the transaction and Money Mart had no duty to inquire about any possible defenses or ensure that the check was good. The Superior Court held that Money Mart's failure to inquire about the validity of the check constituted negligence. However, there is nothing in the Uniform Commercial Code and nothing in the record to support such a conclusion.

A determination of whether a holder has "reason to know" is based upon "all the facts and circumstances known to him." A person "knows" of a fact when he has "actual knowledge" of it. The question therefore is whether Money Mart had actual knowledge of facts giving it reason to know that a defense existed. There is nothing to distinguish the facts of this case from any other of the thousands of checks that Money Mart and others cash each year: A man came to Money Mart to cash his paycheck; Money Mart is in the business of cashing paychecks; the face of the check disclosed nothing to raise even a suspicion that there was something wrong with it.

It has often been held that where an instrument is regular on its face there is no duty to inquire as to possible defenses unless the circumstances of which the holder has knowledge are of such a nature that failure to inquire reveals a deliberate desire to evade knowledge because of a fear that investigation would disclose the existence of a defense. There is nothing in using a check-cashing service instead of a bank that would lead to a rule imposing different standards on the two kinds of institutions.

Accordingly, we hold that Money Mart is a holder in due course and, as such, is not subject to the defenses Epicycle may have against Cronin. . . .
Reversed.

Arcanum Nat. Bank v. Hessler
433 N.E.2d 204 (Ohio 1982)

Ken Hessler was in the business of raising hogs for J and J Farms, Inc. JJ Farms would deliver the hogs to Hessler and require him to sign a promissory note payable to JJ Farms to cover the cost of the hogs and feed. After raising the hogs, JJ Farms would take them to be sold at auction. The proceeds were applied to satisfy Hessler's notes and his fees for raising the hogs. Business went well until January 4, 1977, when JJ Farms' representative asked Hessler to sign his wife's name to the promissory note for the hogs delivered that week. Hessler signed his wife's name, then placed his initials "K.H." after the signature. JJ Farms then immediately sold the note to Arcanum National Bank. Unfortunately for Hessler, the hogs delivered to him on January 4 had been previously sold by JJ Farms to another buyer who repossessed the hogs from Hessler. The note became due and Arcanum demanded payment from Hessler. Arcanum claimed to be a holder in due course. Hessler contended Arcanum was subject to the defense of lack of consideration since the note on its face gave notice of a defense.

KRUPANSKY, J. . . . The sole issue in this case is whether appellee is a holder in due course who takes the note free from appellant's defense of want of consideration.

In a suit by the holder of a note against the maker, the holder obtains a great advantage if granted the status of holder in due course. R.C. Chapter 1303 (Article 3, U.C.C.) provides that a holder in due course takes the instrument free from most defenses and claims. One such defense which is of no avail when raised against a holder in due course is want of consideration, the defense raised by appellant.

Whether one is a holder in due course is an issue which does not arise unless it is shown a defense exists. Once it is established a defense exists, the holder has the full burden of proving holder in due course status in all respects.

There are five requirements which one must meet in order to establish holder in due course status: viz, (1) one must be a "holder"; (2) one must be in possession of an "instrument"; (3) "value" must have been given for the instrument; (4) the instrument must have been taken in "good faith"; and (5) the purchaser must take the instrument without notice that it is overdue or has been dishonored or of any defense against or claim to it on the part of any person. All five of these requirements must be met to qualify as a holder in due course. A transferee who otherwise qualifies as a holder in due course, but who takes an instrument with notice of a defense to it on the part of any person is therefore not a holder in due course. Likewise, one who does not take an instrument in good faith is not a holder in due course.

Appellant contends appellee has not established holder in due course status because appellee took the instrument with notice of a defense against it. We agree.

The requirement that the purchaser take the instrument without notice of a claim or defense in order to qualify as a holder in due course is explained, under the heading of "Notice to Purchaser," at R.C. 1303.33 (UCC 3-304), which provides in relevant part:

(A) The purchaser has notice of a claim or defense if:

(1) The instrument is so incomplete, bears such visible evidence of forgery or alteration, or is otherwise so irregular as to call into question its validity, terms, or ownership or to create an ambiguity as to the party to pay.

Whether a transferee has taken an instrument with notice of a defense depends upon all the facts and circumstances of a particular situation and is generally a question of fact to be determined by the trier of fact. . . .

The trial court, sitting as fact finder, weighed the evidence of the relationship between appellee and appellants and reasoned: "The defect on the promissory note is that the signature of Carla Hessler was added by Kenneth Hessler and, since the Arcanum National Bank handled the Hesslers' personal finances, it should have noticed that there was a defect on the face of the instrument. . . . The note also bears the initials 'K.H.' indicating that Kenneth Hessler had signed Carla Hessler's name." Accordingly, the trial court specifically found "this 'irregularity' does call into question the validity of the note, the terms of the note, the ownership of the note or create an ambiguity as to the party who is to pay the note." Thus, the trial court, while specifically finding appellee took the note with notice of a defense, nonetheless erroneously held appellee bank qualified as a holder in due course.

We hold, therefore, when the trier of fact finds a transferee took a note with notice of a defense, the legal conclusion which follows from such finding is the transferee cannot benefit from holder in due course status and the maker may assert all valid defenses. Since the fact finder in this case specifically found appellee bank took the note with notice of a defense, appellee cannot qualify as a holder in due course.

Reversed.

Richardson v. Girner
668 S.W.2d 523 (Ark. 1984)

Girner executed a $5,000 promissory note to First Realty Corporation on September 25, 1980. Monthly payments on the note were to commence on January 15, 1981. A schedule was printed on the back of the note. The note was assigned by First Realty to Imran Bohra in exchange for property. On July 27, 1981, Bohra transferred the note to his attorney, F. Eugene Richardson, in payment for legal services rendered by Richardson. At that time there was no entry of any payment on the back of the note. At that time Girner had claims against Bohra far in excess of the amount of the note. The trial court found for the defendant and plaintiff appeals.

PURTLE, J. . . . The trial court held that the appellant was not a holder in due course and took the note by assignment subject to the defense of set-off by the makers against an intervening assignee. . . .

The primary issue before us is whether appellant took the note without notice that it was overdue or was otherwise subject to defense on the part of any holder prior to appellant. Arkansas Stat.Ann. §85–3–302 defines a holder in due course to be one who in good faith takes an instrument for value and without notice that it is overdue or has been dishonored or is subject to any defense against or claim to it on the part of any person. The facts in this case clearly reveal that at the time appellant acquired the note no payments had been entered in the schedule on the back of the note. Six payments should have been made at the time of the transfer to appellant. Appellant found out during the meeting with Bohra, at the time of the assignment, that the note was past due. Appellant argues that the note was not declared to be in default until after he contacted the maker. It is not necessary to have the holder of the note declare that it is in default when this fact is obvious in other ways. Unless a person is a holder in due course the note is subject to all valid claims to it on the part of any person, and all defenses, counterclaims and set-offs.

According to Ark.Stat.Ann. §85–3–201(1) (Add.1961), transfer of an instrument vests in the transferee such rights as a transferor possesses. In the present case Bohra knew that the Girners had claims against him far in excess of the amount of the note here in question. From the record there is an indication that Bohra had been told by the Girners, prior to assignment of the note to Richardson, that he should consider the note paid. He was given credit in the amount of the note by the Girners on their claim against him.

In view of the fact that appellant had notice that payments on the note were overdue at the time he took the note, he was not a holder in due course. Therefore, the note was subject to the defense by the Girners against Bohra. . . . It was proper for the court to . . . dismiss appellant's claim.

Affirmed.

Owensboro Nat. Bank v. Crisp
608 S.W.2d 51 (Ky. 1980)

Sam Crisp was approached by Bill Carter to do some repair work on Crisp's lightning rod. Carter said he would do the work for $12.50. Crisp made out the check for $12.50 but left the name of payee blank and an open space preceding the amount for which the check was issued. Carter took the check and altered the amount to where it read

$6,212.50. Owensboro National Bank paid the check and Crisp sued the bank to recover his losses. The bank claimed Crisp's negligence precluded him from asserting the alteration and that they paid the check in good faith.

At the trial the judge submitted the issues to the jury in an interrogatory which required the jury to decide whether the employees of the bank failed to follow reasonable commercial standards in paying the check. Ten of the twelve jurors found in the affirmative. Accordingly, a judgment was entered in Crisp's favor in the sum of $6,200.

STERNBERG, J. . . . We must . . . determine whether the bank was required to exercise reasonable commercial standards in cashing the check. . . . KRS 355.3-406 is designed for the benefit of the bank and provides as follows:

> Negligence contributing to alteration or unauthorized signature.
>
> Any person who by his negligence substantially contributes to a material alteration of the instrument or to the making of an unauthorized signature is precluded from asserting the alteration or lack of authority against a holder in due course or against a drawee or other payor who pays the instrument in good faith and in accordance with the reasonable commercial standards of the drawee's or payor's business.

Crisp was negligent as the word is used therein and would, as a matter of law, be compelled to stand the loss except for the requirement contained therein that the check must be paid in "good faith and in accordance with the reasonable commercial standards of the drawee's or payor's business." In other words, even though the drawer of the check (Crisp) may have been negligent in substantially contributing to a material alteration or to the making of an unauthorized signature, the bank may still be responsible if it does not act in good faith and in accordance with the reasonable commercial standards of the banking industry. Although Crisp was negligent, his negligence may be overcome by the negligence of the bank in cashing the check. This was a question of fact which properly was submitted to the jury. The jury found that the cashier of the bank failed to follow reasonable commercial standards in paying Crisp's check and that such failure was a substantial factor in causing Crisp's loss.

Movant argues that the evidence conclusively shows that the bank exercised reasonable commercial standards in cashing the check and that the trial court should have directed a verdict for the bank. The evidence is conflicting as to whether the cashier of the bank exercised reasonable commercial standards in cashing the check. . . . Not only does it appear to be clearly reasonable from the evidence for the jury to find in favor of Crisp, but, as a matter of fact, the jury did find in his favor. The trial court did not err in refusing to direct a verdict for the bank. . . .

Affirmed.

REVIEW QUESTIONS

1. Identify the terms in column A by matching each with the appropriate statement in column B.

A	B
1. Shelter provision	**a.** May be a real defense or a personal one depending on state law.
2. Value	**b.** Prohibits consumers from holder in due course status.
3. Good faith	**c.** Always a real defense.
4. Holder	**d.** Eliminates real defenses.
5. FTC Rule	**e.** Allows a transferee to have the rights of a holder in due course.

6. Fraud in the execution

7. Infancy

8. Negligence

f. A promise does not qualify as this.

g. Has possession of a negotiable instrument that has been properly negotiated.

h. Honesty in fact.

2. Andrews owed Martin, his accountant, a fee for services rendered. Andrews drew a check on his bank payable to "Cash" and signed it. He left the amount blank because he was not sure of the exact amount owed. On his way to Martin's office Andrews lost the check. Oliver found the check, filled it in for $500, and handed it to Ernest to satisfy a $500 debt which Oliver owed to Ernest. Ernest accepted the check in good faith as payment for the debt and immediately presented it to the drawee bank. The drawee bank refused to cash it because of a stop payment order. Is Andrews liable to Ernest for the $500? Why?

3. Arthur purchased securities from William, giving William his check payable to William's order and drawn on Produce Bank in payment. William immediately indorsed the check to the order of Robert, "without recourse," and it was accepted by Robert in payment of a debt owed him by William. Robert indorsed the check in blank and delivered it to his son, Charles, as a birthday gift. Arthur has discovered that the securities sold him by William are worthless and has directed Produce Bank to stop payment. When Produce Bank refuses to pay Charles on the check and Charles sues Arthur, may Arthur assert the defense of failure of consideration against Charles? Explain.

4. Pat fraudulently misrepresented certain goods he was attempting to sell Mike. Mike relied on these misstatements and purchased the goods, giving Pat in exchange a negotiable promissory note for $100, made by Mike, payable to Pat's order, and maturing on November 14, 1984. Pat indorsed and delivered the note to Art, a holder in due course. On November 15, 1984, Art indorsed and delivered the note to Harry, in exchange for Harry's promise to pay Art $95. Harry did not know of Pat's fraud until he attempted to collect from Mike and Mike refused payment. Is Harry a holder in due course? Why? Is Harry free of the defense? Why?

5. Hadley drew a check to the order of Larsen, who indorsed it to Richards in payment of an existing indebtedness. Hadley stopped payment on the check before Richards cashed it. Hadley seeks to assert a personal defense against Richards. Should Hadley succeed? Why or why not?

6. On September 28, 1985, Margaret bought a series of art lessons. As payment, she transferred two checks payable to the order of Margaret Kearney, one dated December 29, 1985, and the other dated January 14, 1986. On October 3, 1985, Sussex Enterprises acquired the checks and a week later transferred them for a discount (deduction from the gross sum of the checks) to Rennie's Retreat. On November 1, 1985, Margaret returned the lessons and stopped payment on the checks. She claims that Rennie's Retreat cannot sue since it is not a holder in due course. Is she correct? Explain.

7. A bank received a check to deposit in Seve's account. Seve subsequently wrote checks withdrawing most of the proceeds of the deposited check. The bank paid these checks before receiving notice that the deposited check was bad. Does the bank qualify as a holder in due course? Explain.

8. Dolan owed Luboff $3,046. Fiske gave Dolan her signed blank check with instructions to cash it for $800 and give the cash to Luboff as a partial payment. Instead, Dolan wrote out the check for $3,046 and delivered it to Luboff, who then negotiated the check to Weil. Fiske stopped payment on the check. Is Weil a holder in due course? Why?

9. Nevers executed a note payable to the order of Young due on January 1, 1985. On March 1, 1985, Young negotiated the note to Glassen. Will Glassen be subject to the personal defenses of Nevers? Why?

10. Pellato acquired a negotiable instrument as a gift from her friend, Gaines. Gaines was given the note for laundering services and was a holder in due course. Is Pellato a holder in due course? Explain.

11. Pam bought equipment from a dealer who was to supply additional equipment weekly. These additional items would permit Pam to make tapes that the dealer was to purchase. Pam gave the dealer a note for the equipment; but the additional equipment was never delivered and the dealer went out of business. Before closing, the dealer discounted the note at a bank that had purchased other notes from the dealer. The bank had a very close relationship with the dealer and apparently knew of the dealer's shady business practices. The bank now sues Pam to collect the proceeds of the note. Is it a holder in due course? Why?

12. Merck gave a merchant a check in the amount of $500 in payment for some linoleum installed in Merck's home. When the check was dishonored, the merchant sued to recover on the check. Merck contends that the linoleum was not satisfactory. Is this a valid defense? Why?

13. In the previous question, assume that Merck signed a consumer note instead of the $500 check. Would the FTC rule change the result if the note had been duly negotiated by the merchant to ABC Company, which became a holder in due course? Explain.

14. Smith delivered to Janett his check drawn on National Bank payable to Janett. Janett had the check certified and delivered it to Cook as payment on account. The certification was stamped on the face of the check. It said "certified payable as originally drawn." The original check was for $1,000. Janett had raised the amount to $4,000 prior to the certification. No one but an expert would have realized that the check had been raised. How much can Cook collect on the check? How much can the bank charge to Smith's account? Explain.

31 LIABILITY OF PARTIES TO COMMERCIAL PAPER

In our discussions of the rights of holders and holders in due course, we usually assumed that the party being sued had liability unless a valid defense could be asserted against the plaintiff. In this chapter, we go to the basic issue of the liability of a defendant in the absence of a defense.

In a transaction involving commercial paper, liability may be predicated on either the instrument itself or on the underlying contract. No person is liable on the instrument itself unless his signature appears thereon, but the signature may be affixed by a duly authorized agent [3-401(1)]. Persons whose signatures appear on instruments may have different types of liability, depending on their status. This chapter will discuss the liability of various parties to commercial paper transactions. Unless indicated otherwise, liability is predicated on the instrument itself and on the rules of the Code relating to commercial paper.

1. Liability Based on Signatures

A person's liability on commercial paper results from his signature on the instrument. The signature may be affixed as a maker, drawer, or acceptor on the face of the instrument, or it may be an indorsement on the back. In either case, the person signing may be an accommodation party or surety.

The general principles of the law of agency are applicable to commercial paper. A principal is bound by the duly authorized acts of his agent.[1] If the agent

---

[1] First Sec. Bank v. Fastwich, Inc., p. 683.

is not authorized to sign, the principal is not bound unless it (1) ratifies the signature or (2) is estopped from asserting lack of authority. An agent who fails to bind his principal because of lack of authority will usually be personally liable to third parties. To be bound on the instrument, the principal's name must be on it.

An agent is also personally liable if he fails to show his representative capacity [3-403(2)(a)]. This may occur when the principal is not named on the instrument.[2] Even if the principal's name appears on the instrument, the agent may fail to indicate that he is signing in a representative capacity. In such cases, the agent is also personally liable [3-403(2)(a)].[3]

An agent can relieve himself of liability to the person to whom he issued the paper by proving that such party knew he was acting only as an agent for his principal [3-403(2)(b)]. Between the parties, parol evidence is admissible to show the intent of the parties where the principal's name appears on the instrument and the status of the agent's signature is ambiguous.

2. Capacity of the Signature

Another issue concerning signatures relates to the capacity in which the signature is affixed. The liability of primary parties such as makers of notes is different from the liability of secondary parties such as indorsers. A person signing as a primary or secondary party may sign to accommodate someone else and have a special status insofar as liability is concerned. The capacity of a signature may be ambiguous because of its physical location or because of the language used.

The capacity in which a person signs is usually obvious because of the location of the signature. Makers and drawers usually sign in the lower right-hand corner of an instrument, and indorsers sign on the back of an instrument. A drawee normally places his signature of acceptance on the face of the instrument, but his signature on the back would clearly indicate that he was signing as an acceptor unless he could establish otherwise. When the signature does not reveal the obligation of the party who signs, the signature is an indorsement [3-402].

If a person signs as co-maker of an instrument, he or she is primarily liable for the total instrument. The holder may collect all that is due from either maker. However, the party that pays the total due is entitled to collect from his or her co-maker.[4]

3. Classification of Parties

LIABILITY BASED ON STATUS

For the purposes of liability, the Code divides the parties to commercial paper into two groups—primary parties and secondary parties. The *primary parties* are the makers of notes and acceptors of drafts. These parties have incurred a definite obligation to pay and are the parties who, in the normal course of events, will *actually* pay the instrument.

---

[2] Farmers & Merch. Nat. Bank of Hatton v. Lee, p. 684.

[3] Bank v. Cannon, p. 684.

[4] Grimes v. Grimes, p. 685.

The *secondary parties* are drawers of drafts, drawers of checks, and indorsers of any instrument. These parties do not expect to pay the instrument but assume, rather, that the primary parties will fulfill their obligations. The drawer and indorsers expect that the acceptor will pay the draft. The indorsers of a note expect that the maker will pay when the note matures. Drawers and indorsers have a responsibility to pay if the primary parties do not, *provided* that certain conditions precedent are satisfied. The drawer and the indorser are, in effect, saying that they will pay if the primary party (acceptor or maker) does not, but only if the party entitled to payment has made proper demand upon the primary party and due notice of the primary party's dishonor of the instrument has then been given to the secondary parties [3-413(2)]; [3-414(1)].

4. Liability of Primary Parties

A primary party engages that he will pay the instrument according to its terms. The maker thus assumes an obligation to pay the note as it was worded at the time he executed it. The acceptor assumes responsibility for the draft as it was worded when he gave his acceptance [3-413(1)].

If a maker signs an incomplete note, when the note is completed—even though the completion is unauthorized—it can be enforced against him by a holder in due course. On the other hand, if an instrument is materially altered after it is made, the maker has a real defense in the absence of negligence. The maker confirms to all subsequent parties the existence of the payee and his capacity to indorse [3-413(3)].

The drawee of a check or draft is not liable on the instrument until acceptance. Upon acceptance, the acceptor is primarily liable. An acceptance must be in writing on the draft and signed by the drawee-acceptor [3-410(1)]. Acceptance is usually made by the drawee's writing or stamping the word *Accepted,* with the name and the date, across the face of the instrument. The usual means for accepting a check is to have it certified.

A party presenting a draft for acceptance is entitled to an *unqualified acceptance* by the drawee. Thus, when the drawee offers an acceptance that in any manner varies or changes the direct order to pay or accept, the holder may refuse the acceptance [3-412(1)]. The paper is dishonored; and upon notice of dishonor or protest, the holder may hold responsible all prior parties on the paper—back to, and including, the drawer.

5. Drawers

The drawer engages that upon *dishonor* of the draft and any necessary notice of dishonor or protest, he will pay the amount of the draft to the holder or to any indorser who has paid it [3-413(2)]. In effect, the drawer assumes a conditional liability on the instrument. The party who draws a draft or check, like one who makes a note or accepts a draft, affirms to all subsequent parties the existence of the payee and the payee's capacity to indorse [3-413(3)]. In addition, most drawers have liability on the underlying contract or transaction in which they deliver the

THE LIABILITY OF SECONDARY PARTIES

instrument as drawer. In other words, if the drawer delivered a check for goods and the check is dishonored, the drawer has liability for the goods which were not paid for, in addition to any liability on the check itself.

6. Indorsers

Indorsers of checks, drafts, or notes have two kinds of liability. First, they are liable on their *contract of indorsement* [3-414(1)]. The indorsement contract can either be unqualified or qualified. The majority of transferors indorse without qualification. The unqualified indorser does not say "I will pay," but rather says "I will pay if the instrument is dishonored and any necessary notice of dishonor is given and any necessary protest is made." The unqualified indorser's liability, which runs to subsequent parties [3-414(1)] is discussed later in this chapter. A *qualified* indorser indorses with the words "without recourse." By indorsing "without recourse," the qualified indorser disclaims conditional liability.

Second, an indorser has *unconditional* liability. This unconditional liability is based on breach of warranty. An indorser makes warranties with reference to the instrument that is transferred [3-417(2)]. He warrants that he has good title to the instrument, that all signatures are genuine or authorized, that the instrument has not been materially altered, and that no defense of any party is good against him. He also warrants that he does not know of any insolvency proceedings with respect to any of the parties involved [3-417(2)(*e*)].

The warranties are made whether the transfer is by delivery only, by qualified indorsement (without recourse), or by unqualified indorsement. A qualified indorsement eliminates only conditional liability; it does not eliminate unconditional liability or prevent a breach of warranty. It is also important to note that liability is automatic if any of the warranties are breached. The indorser and transferor by delivery must make good without regard to the performance of any conditions precedent, such as presentment or notice of dishonor.

7. Transferors without Indorsement

All secondary parties have unconditional liability because this liability is based on a theory of breach of warranty. Technically speaking, the party who presents an instrument for payment and signs it is not an indorser. The signature is a receipt for the payment; but in presenting the instrument, the person warrants that no indorsements are forged, that so far as he knows the signature of the maker or drawer is genuine, and that it has not been materially altered [3-417(1)]. The person who pays or accepts will thus have recourse against the presenting party if the warranties are breached. There is no warranty that the drawer has sufficient funds on deposit to cover a check. If a drawee pays a check when the drawer has insufficient funds on deposit, the party presenting the check is not liable for breach of warranty. The warranty with regard to the drawer's signature is not absolute; it assures only that the warrantor has no knowledge that such signature is forged or unauthorized.

A transferor without an indorsement (bearer paper) also makes warranties to the transferee. They are the same warranties an unqualified indorser makes, except the warranties run only to the immediate transferee, whereas the indorser's warranties extend to subsequent holders [3-417(2)]. The qualified indorser's warranty about defenses is simply that he has no *knowledge* of any defense [3-417(3)].

8. Accommodation Parties and Guarantors

One who signs an instrument for the purpose of lending his name and credit to another party to an instrument is an *accommodation party* [3-415(1)]. He may sign as an indorser, maker, or acceptor or as a co-maker or co-acceptor. The accommodation party is liable in the capacity in which he signed [3-415(2)]. As an indorser, he does not indorse for the purpose of transferring the paper, but rather to lend security to it.

Since any party, including a co-maker, may be an accommodation party, and accommodation parties are treated somewhat differently from other parties, issues as to the status of a party frequently arise. The intention of parties is the significant element in determining whether one who signs a note is an accommodation party or a principal maker. The primary factors to be considered in determining the intent of the parties are: (1) whether or not the proceeds of the instrument are received by the party, and (2) whether the signature was required as a condition of the loan. If the party did not receive the proceeds but the creditor demanded the signature as a condition for the loan, the party signing is an accommodation party. Whether the signature is as a co-maker or indorser, it should be recognized that the liability of an accommodation party is supported by the consideration which flows from the creditor to the principal debtor, and the fact that no consideration flowed directly to the accommodation party is no defense. Lack of benefit to a party does tend to show the status of the party, however.

The significance of being an accommodation party is found in the law of *suretyship*. An accommodation party is a *surety*. In some situations a surety is entitled to a discharge from liability where other parties are not. The right to discharge may be asserted against one who is not a holder in due course [3-415(3)]. Sureties have a right of contribution from co-sureties.[5] Sureties are not liable to the party accommodated. If a surety is required to pay, he can obtain reimbursement from the accommodated party. [3-415(5)].

The liability of an accommodation party arises without express words. A guarantor's liability is based on words of guaranty. If the words "Payment guaranteed" or their equivalent are added to a signature, the signer engages that if the instrument is not paid when due, he will pay it without previous resort by the holder to other parties on the paper [3-416(1)]. If the words "Collection guaranteed" are added to a signature, the signer becomes liable only after the holder has reduced his claim against the maker or acceptor to judgment, and execution has been returned unsatisfied, or after the maker or acceptor has become insolvent or it is otherwise apparent that it is useless to proceed against him [3-416(2)].

[5] King v. Finnell, p. 686.

A guarantor waives the conditions precedent of presentment, notice of dishonor, and protest. The words of guarantee do not affect the indorsement as a means of transferring the instrument but impose upon such indorser the liability of a co-maker [3-416(5)]. Such a person in effect becomes a primary party.

9. Conditional Liability

The term *conditional liability* is used to describe the secondary liability that results from the status of parties as drawers or unqualified indorsers. The adjective *conditional* refers to the fact that certain conditions precedent must be fulfilled to establish liability [3-501]. The conditions precedent are *presentment, dishonor, notice of dishonor,* and in some instances *protest.* The importance of exact compliance with the conditions precedent cannot be overemphasized. Failure to comply may result in the discharge of the secondary parties.

10. Presentment—Generally

Presentment is a demand made upon a maker or drawee [3-504(1)]. In relation to a note, it is a demand for payment made by the holder on the maker. In the case of a draft, it may be either a demand for acceptance or a demand for payment.

The drawee of a draft is not bound on the instrument as a primary party until acceptance. The holder will usually wait until maturity and present his draft to the drawee for payment, but he may present it to the drawee for acceptance before maturity in order to give credit to the instrument during the period of its term. The drawee is under no legal duty to the holder to accept; but if he refuses, the draft is dishonored by nonacceptance. A right of recourse arises immediately against the drawer and the indorsers, and no presentment for payment is necessary. The refusal to accept is similar to an anticipatory breach of contract. The holder need not wait until the due date to see if it will be paid. He may assume that it will not and proceed against the other parties with liability.

In most instances, it is not necessary to present an instrument for acceptance. Presentment for payment alone is usually sufficient, but presentment for acceptance must be made in order to charge the drawer and indorsers of some drafts. For example, if the date of payment depends on presentment, as in the case of a draft payable after sight, presentment for acceptance is required in order to fix the maturity date of the instrument [3-501(1)(a)]. Failure to make a proper presentment for payment results in the complete discharge of an indorser [3-501(1)(b)].

11. Presentment—How and Where

Presentment may be made by personally contacting the primary party and making a demand for acceptance or payment. Presentment may be made by mail or through a clearinghouse [3-504(2)(a)(b)]. Presentment by mail is effective when received. If the instrument specifies the place of acceptance or payment, presentment is made there. If no place is specified, presentment may be made at the place of business of the party to accept or to pay. Presentment is excused if neither the party to accept or pay nor anyone authorized to act for him is present or accessible at such place [3-504(2)(c)]. A draft accepted or a note made payable at a bank in the United States must be presented at that bank [3-504(4)]. Presentment of a check to the data processing center of the payor bank is effective if the records are maintained at the center. This is important when a bank has several branches.[6]

To balance the liberal attitude regarding what will suffice as a presentment, Section 3-505(1) empowers the party on whom presentment is made to require

1. Exhibition of the instrument
2. Reasonable identification of the person making presentment
3. Evidence of authority if presentment is made for another
4. Production of the instrument at a place specified in it or (if none is specified) at any reasonable place
5. A signed receipt on the instrument for any partial or full payment and its surrender upon full payment

If the primary party does not avail himself of these rights, the presentment is perfectly valid, no matter how or where the presentment is made. If he does require proper presentment, a failure to comply invalidates the presentment, but the instrument is not dishonored. The requirement of identification of the presenting party applies to bearer paper as well as order paper [3-505].

12. Presentment—When

In general, an instrument must be presented for payment on the day of maturity. The presentment must be made at a reasonable hour and if at a bank, during banking hours.

When an instrument is payable on demand, it must be presented or negotiated within a reasonable time after such secondary party became liable, for example, after his indorsement [3-503(1)(e)]. Thus, in the case of a demand note, an indorser would be discharged if presentment were not made within a reasonable time after he indorsed the note.

Note that presentment within a "reasonable time" is required when a definite maturity date is not included in the instrument; that is, sight and demand instruments. A reasonable time for presentment is determined by the nature of the instrument, any usage of banking or trade, and the facts of the particular case [3-503(2)].

The drawer of a check is liable for it for a reasonable time, presumed to be 30 days after date or issue, whichever is later. In that time, a check should be presented for payment or to initiate bank collection [3-504(2)(a)]. The presumed reasonable time for presentment in order to hold the indorser liable is 7 days after the indorsement [3-503(2)(b)].

---

[6] Chrysler Credit Corp. v. First Nat. Bank & Trust, p. 687.

13. Dishonor

The party who presents an instrument is entitled to have the instrument paid or accepted. If the party to whom the instrument is presented refuses to pay or accept, the instrument is dishonored [3-507(1)]. The presenting party then has recourse against indorsers or other secondary parties, provided he gives proper notice of such dishonor.

When a draft is presented to the drawee for *acceptance,* the drawee may wish to ascertain some facts from the drawer before he assumes the obligation of an acceptor. As a result, the law allows the drawee to defer acceptance until the close of the next business day following presentment [3-506(1)]. If the drawee needs more time within which to obtain information, the holder can give him one additional business day within which to accept. The secondary parties are not discharged by the one-day postponement. The holder who presents the draft for *acceptance* is seeking the drawee's obligation on the paper and will not receive payment until a later date. For this reason, the Code permits a longer period of time within which to accept a draft than is allowed when the draft is presented for payment. When an instrument is presented for *payment,* the party to whom presentment is made is allowed a reasonable time to examine the instrument, to determine whether the instrument is properly payable, but payment must be made in any event on the same day that it is presented and before the close of business on that day [3-506(2)].

14. Notice of Dishonor

When an instrument has been dishonored on proper presentment, the holder must give prompt notice of the dishonor in order to have a right of recourse against unqualified indorsers [3-507(2)]. Failure to give prompt and proper notice of dishonor results in the discharge of indorsers.

Notice of dishonor should also be given to the drawer, even though failure to do so discharges the drawer only to the extent of a loss caused by the improper notice. Such a loss could arise if the bank failed after dishonor and before notice to the drawer [3-502(1)]. Although this is a rare occurrence, the notice will expedite settlement for the item.

Generally, notice is given to secondary parties by the holder or by an indorser who has received notice. Any party who may be compelled to pay the instrument may notify any party who may be liable on it [3-508(1)].

Except for banks, notice must be given before midnight of the third business day after dishonor [3-508(2)]. A person who has received notice of dishonor and wishes to notify other parties must do so before midnight of the third business day after receipt of the notice.

Banks must give any necessary notice before the bank's "midnight deadline"—before midnight of the next banking day following the day on which a bank receives the item or notice of dishonor [3-508(2)].

Notice may be given in any reasonable manner, including oral notice, notice by telephone, and notice by mail. The notice must identify the dishonored instrument and state that it has been dishonored. Written notice is effective when sent, even though it is not received, if it bears proper address and postage [3-508(4)].

Proper notice preceded by any necessary presentment and dishonor imposes liability upon secondary parties to whom such notice of dishonor is given. Proper notice operates for the benefit of all parties who have rights on the instrument against the party notified [3-508(8)]. Thus it is necessary to notify a party only once for his liability to be fixed. Assume that A, B, C, and D are indorsers in that order.

- Holder gives notice to A and C only.
- C will not be required to give additional notice to A.
- If C is compelled to pay, he would have recourse against A.
- B and D are discharged if they are not notified by the holder or one of the indorsers.

This occurs because indorsers are in general liable in the order of their indorsement. An indorser who is required to pay can recover from an indorser prior to him. But each indorser is entitled to notice of dishonor, so that he can take appropriate steps to pass the responsibility on to those prior to him on the paper.

15. Protest

Protest is a certificate stating the following: an instrument was presented for payment or acceptance, it was dishonored, and the reasons, if any, given for refusal to accept or pay [3-509]. It is a formal method for satisfying the conditions precedent and is required only for drafts that are drawn or payable outside the United States. The protest requirement is in conformity with foreign law in this respect. In other cases, protest is optional with the holder. Protest serves as evidence both that presentment was made and that notice of dishonor was given. It creates a presumption that the conditions precedent were satisfied.

16. Excuses for Failure to Perform Conditions Precedent

An unexcused delay in making any *necessary* presentment or in giving notice of dishonor discharges parties who are entitled to performance of the conditions precedent. Indorsers are completely discharged by such delay; and drawers, makers of notes payable at a bank, and acceptors of drafts payable at a bank are discharged to the extent of any loss caused by the delay [3-502]. Delay in making presentment, in giving notice of dishonor, or in making protest is excused when the holder has acted with reasonable diligence and the delay is not due to any fault of the holder. He must, however, comply with these conditions or attempt to do so as soon as the cause of the delay ceases to exist [3-511(1)].

The performance of the conditions precedent is entirely excused if the party to be charged has *waived* the condition. When such waiver is stated on the face of the instrument, it is binding on all parties; when it is written above the signature of the indorser, it binds him only [5-511(6)]. Most promissory notes contain such a waiver.

The performance of the conditions precedent is also excused if the party to be charged has himself dishonored the instrument or has countermanded payment or otherwise has no reason to expect or right to require that the instrument be accepted or paid [3-511(2)(b)]. If a drawer of a check has stopped payment on the check, the drawer is not in a position to complain about slow presentment or any lack of notice of dishonor.

17. Discharge

The liability of various parties may be discharged in a variety of ways, many of them previously noted [3-601]. Certification of a check at the request of a holder discharges all prior parties [3-411]. Any ground for discharging a simple contract also discharges commercial paper [3-601(2)].

Payment usually discharges a party's liability. This is true even if the payor has knowledge of the claim of another person. Payment does not operate to discharge liability if the payor acts in bad faith and pays one who acquired the instrument by theft. Payment is also no defense if paid in violation of a restrictive indorsement [3-603].

A holder may discharge any party by intentionally canceling the instrument or by striking out or otherwise eliminating a party's signature. The surrender of the instrument to a party will also discharge that party [3-605].

If a holder agrees not to sue one party or agrees to release collateral, then all parties with rights against such party or against the collateral are discharged from liability. This assumes that there is no express reservation of rights by the holder and that the party claiming discharge did not consent to the holder's actions [3-606].

When an instrument is reacquired by a prior party, he may cancel all intervening indorsements. In this event, all parties whose indorsements are canceled are discharged [3-208].

Fraudulent and material alteration of an instrument discharges any party whose liability is affected by the alteration. Of course, this is not true if the alteration is agreed to or if the party seeking to impose liability is a holder in due course [3-407]. In fact, no discharge is effective against a holder in due course unless he has notice of the discharge when he takes the instrument [3-602].

SUMMARY

LIABILITY BASED ON SIGNATURE

Agency	**1.** No person is liable on an instrument unless his signature is on the instrument, but it may be affixed by an agent.

2. A principal is bound by acts of his agent. If the agent is not authorized to sign, the principal is not bound unless he ratifies the signature or is estopped from asserting lack of authority.

3. An agent is personally liable if he fails to show his representative capacity or fails to bind the principal.

Other aspects

1. When the instrument requires two signatures, the drawee may not pay the instrument on only one signature, even if the one signing is authorized.

2. Makers and drawers usually sign in the lower right-hand corner of the face and indorsers usually sign on the back.

3. Acceptance is usually shown on the face.

LIABILITY BASED ON STATUS

Primary parties

1. Makers of notes and acceptors of drafts agree they will pay the instrument according to its terms.

2. The usual means for acceptance of a check is to certify it.

Secondary parties

1. Drawers of drafts and checks and unqualified indorsers agree to pay if the primary party does not.

2. A drawer admits the existence of the payee and its capacity to indorse.

3. Indorsers are liable on their contract of indorsement. If an unqualified indorsement, there is both conditional and unconditional liability.

4. A qualified indorser has only unconditional liability.

5. Transferors who do not indorse have unconditional liability to their immediate transferee.

6. Unconditional liability is based on breach of warranty. Secondary parties not receiving payment warrant that they have good title to the instrument, no defense of any party is good against him, all signatures are genuine, and the instrument has not been materially altered.

Accommodation parties and guarantors	1. An accommodation party is a surety. Such a party may sign as a maker, acceptor, or indorser.
	2. Such an indorser does not indorse to negotiate but to lend credit to the instrument.
	3. These parties are in the same position as other parties insofar as the conditions precedent to conditional liability are concerned.
	4. An accommodation party may collect from the co-maker and is not liable to the party accommodated.

CONDITIONAL LIABILITY

Presentment	1. Presentment is a demand on a maker or drawee for payment or acceptance. Failure to make a proper presentment results in complete discharge of indorsers.
	2. Presentment by mail or through a clearinghouse is effective. It may also be made at the place of business of the party to accept or pay. The party on whom presentment is made has the power to require exhibition of the instrument.
	3. Presentment must be made on the day of maturity, or if payable on demand, it must be presented or negotiated within a reasonable time after such secondary party became liable.
	4. Drawer of a check is liable for 30 days after date or issue, whichever is later. An indorser is liable for 7 days after his indorsement. Presentment beyond these time periods releases indorsers, but the drawer may remain liable.
Dishonor	1. If an instrument is presented and not paid or accepted, it is dishonored.
	2. If presentment for acceptance, the drawee must act prior to the close of the next business day following presentment. If needed, the holder can give the drawee one additional day to act.
	3. If presentment for payment, drawee has a reasonable time to act but must do so on the same day or it is an honor.

Notice of dishonor	**1.** When an instrument is dishonored, the presenting party has recourse against indorsers or other secondary parties, provided that he gives notice of dishonor.
	2. Notice of dishonor requires the holder to be prompt in order to have a right of recourse against unqualified indorsers. Except for a bank, the notice must be given before midnight of the third business day.
	3. Banks must give notice of dishonor before the bank's midnight deadline.
	4. Notice may be by any reasonable manner. It may be written, oral, or by phone.
Other aspects	**1.** Protest is a certificate stating the instrument was presented for payment, it was dishonored, and the reasons for refusal to accept or pay. It is used primarily in foreign transactions.
	2. Conditions precedent of notice of dishonor, presentment, or protest may be waived by the party to be charged. Such waivers are contained in most notes.
	3. Discharge of a party's liability may be accomplished by: a. Payment. b. Canceling the instrument. c. Surrender of the instrument. d. Fraudulent and material alteration of an instrument.

CASES

First Sec. Bank v. Fastwich, Inc.
612 S.W.2d 799 (Mo. 1981)

The First Security Bank of Brookfield sued a corporate borrower, Fastwich, Inc., and certain guarantors of the note. The note was signed as follows:

[typed] FASTWICH, INC.
[/s/] John J. Smith II [/s/] Carolyn Smith
[/s/] Gary D. Smith [/s/] Cheryl J. Smith

The trial court held that the corporation was bound as having signed the note, and Fastwich appealed.

SOMMERVILLE, J. . . . Fastwich resolutely contends that it was not liable on the promissory note as the note failed to "clearly" show on its face that Fastwich's signature was "made on . . . [its] behalf". According to them, Fastwich was not liable on the promissory note even though (1) its officers were authorized to borrow money on its behalf and execute such "evidence of indebtedness as . . . [might] be required" and (2) it was named on the promissory note. . . . Comment 1 of the Uniform Commercial Code Comment appended to Section 3-401 reads, in part as follows:

1. No one is liable on an instrument unless and until he has signed it. The chief application of the rule has been in cases holding that a principal whose name does not appear on an instrument signed by his agent is not liable on the instrument even though the payee knew when it was issued that it was intended to be the obligation of one who did not sign. . . .

Fastwich's name, appearing in the lower right hand corner of the promissory note, albeit typed, constituted its signature within the prescription of Section 3-401. In *O. P. Ganjo, Inc. v. Tri-Urban Realty Co.,* 108 N.J. Super. 517,261 A.2d 722 (1969), a corporate principal was held liable as a maker on a promissory note which was signed in the following manner:

> Tri-Urban Realty Co., Inc.
> George Moskowitz

The authority relied upon by the court for holding that the corporate principal's signature was affixed to the note as a maker being that Section 3-401(2) provides that "a signature is made by use of any name, including any trade or assumed name, upon an instrument, or by any word or mark used in lieu of a written signature" . . . [and] [t]he comment to this section points out that "a signature may be handwritten, typed, printed or made in any other manner." . . .

Affirmed.

Farmers & Merch. Nat. Bank of Hatton v. Lee
333 N.W.2d 792 (N.D. 1983)

In June 1981 Lee executed and delivered a promissory note due November 1, 1981, to the plaintiff bank. The note was a consolidation of previous loans made to Village Homes, Inc., which were in default. The note was signed by Lee personally. "Village Homes, Inc." does not appear anywhere on the note.

The bank began an action to recover the moneys owing on the promissory note after it became due. The trial court granted the bank's motion for summary judgment and Lee appeals.

PAULSON, J. . . . On an appeal from a summary judgment, we view the evidence in the light most favorable to the party against whom the motion was granted.

In the instant case, Lee contends . . . that he is not personally liable for the note and that the issue of his liability involves a question of material fact.

Although Lee contends that he is not personally liable on the note because the note is actually an obligation of his corporation, Village Homes, Inc., Lee's signature alone is on the note. Generally, the maker contracts to pay the instrument according to its terms. [U.C.C. 3-403(2)] provides, in relevant part, that

> 2. An authorized representative who signs his own name to an instrument "a. is personally obligated if the instrument neither names the person represented nor shows that the representative signed in a representative capacity;

In *Ristvedt v. Nettum*, 311 N.W.2d 574, 578 (N.D.1981), we stated: " . . . courts have long held that the signature of a representative without any indication that he was signing in a representative capacity leaves him personally liable."

There is no indication on the note in issue that Lee signed the note in a representative capacity. Therefore, under North Dakota law Lee is liable for the note. The trial court correctly found that there was no genuine issue of material fact regarding Lee's liability that would preclude summary judgment.

Affirmed.

Bank v. Cannon
414 So.2d 926 (Ala. 1982)

Plaintiff Bank sues M. O. Cannon to collect a promissory note for $60,000. Mr. Cannon was an officer of Slocumb & Cannon, a corporation in serious financial difficulty. The note was signed as follows:

> Slocumb & Cannon
> By: M. O. Cannon
> (Debtor)
> M. O. Cannon
> (Debtor)

The note did not identify the debtor in any other place on the note.

Mr. Cannon testified that he did not intend to be liable on the note and that the bank's employees did not discuss the issue of personal liability with him. They simply told him where to sign. The trial court found for the defendant.

FAULKNER, J. . . . This Court is again faced with the issue of whether an agent signed in a representative capacity or whether the agent is to be held liable on an instrument. Section 7-3-403(2) provides that a representative who signs his own name to an instrument is personally liable if the instrument "names the person represented, but does not show that the representative signed in a representative capacity.". . .

Parol evidence is not admissible in the present case to vary the terms of the note dated August 28, 1978. The signature included the name of the corporation, Slocumb & Cannon, and Mr. Cannon signed "By: M. O. Cannon." Then Mr. Cannon signed again. This second signature neither names the person representated nor shows that Mr. Cannon signed in a representative capacity.

Parol evidence is not admissible under § 7-3-403(2)(a) if the instrument neither "names the person represented nor shows that the representative signed in a representative capacity."

In order to avoid personal liability on an instrument, the agent should (1) name the organization represented; (2) sign his or her name and office; and (3) make the name of the agent and principal refer to each other so that a reasonable person could understand from the face of the instrument that the agent signed as a representative.

The Official Comments to § 7-3-403 clearly provide an example of an unambiguous way to make an agent's representation clear. "Assuming that Peter Pringle is a principal and Arthur Adams is his agent," Adams should sign an instrument "Peter Pringle by Arthur Adams, Agent." An agent may easily indicate his representative capacity by signing in the manner prescribed above. . . .

Reversed and remanded.

Grimes v. Grimes
267 S.E.2d 372 (N.C.App.,1980)

Plaintiff seeks to recover from his former wife $13,800, one-half of the amount he paid to retire a debt owed Lexington State Bank of Lexington, North Carolina, in the amount of $27,600. The note was executed by both plaintiff and defendant while they were separated though still married. At a nonjury trial, defendant moved for and was granted an involuntary dismissal. Plaintiff appeals.

MORRIS, J. . . . At common law, a note evidencing a debt executed jointly by husband and wife rendered the husband liable on the note, but not the wife. However, this rule no longer obtains. Now where the wife executes a promissory note as a co-maker, she is primarily liable thereunder. This result follows from the rule that nothing else appearing, a person signing his or her name at the bottom of the face of a promissory note is a maker thereof, and is primarily liable thereon.

With respect to the applicability of the Uniform Commercial Code, . . . on the negotiable note in question, it is clear that the liability of a person signing a negotiable instrument is determined by the capacity in which one executes the instrument. Under G.S. 25-3-413(1), the maker "engages that he will pay the instrument according to its tenor at the time of his engagement. . . ." A maker's liability is unconditional and absolute. When two or more persons execute a note as makers, they are jointly and severally liable, unless the language of the note clearly indicates the contrary. Because of the joint and several nature of a maker's obligation under a note, when one co-maker pays the instrument he is entitled to contribution from other co-makers.

We are of the opinion that a co-maker's right to contribution is unaffected by the marital relationship of the parties to a note. This case is different from those situations to which a presumption of gift attaches, because in those cases the wife had been given merely a transfer of value from the husband. Here, . . . the wife has personally obligated herself under the note. Defendant, as a co-maker, has an absolute and unconditional obligation under the note. The fact that the proceeds from the loan were used during the marriage is of no moment. At any rate, plaintiff and defendant were divorced at the time plaintiff paid the balance due under the note. No presumption of gift arises, therefore, from plaintiff's retiring the debt. Accordingly, we overrule the trial court's conclusions in this regard.

Reversed and remanded.

King v. Finnell
603 P.2d 754 (Okl. 1979)

Dixie Neeley executed a note to the City Bank and Trust Company. King executed a separate guarantee agreement for the debt. Ms. Neeley had financial difficulty and was not making payments on the note. She arranged for her former husband, Finnell, to lend his name to the note by adding his signature to the back of the note. After Finnell signed, King paid off the note and it was assigned to him. King then sued Finnell to collect the note. The trial court entered summary judgment for the plaintiff.

BARNES, J. . . . The first question to be answered is, in what capacity Mr. Finnell lent his name to the note. Mr. King argues that Mr. Finnell is an accommodation maker, and therefore not a mere guarantor. We cannot agree with that analysis.

Mr. Finnell's signature on the instrument does not contain any written indication of the capacity in which he signed the instrument. He merely signed the back of the instrument in blank.

As Mr. Finnell's signature did not indicate the capacity in which he signed the instrument, the provisions of 12A O.S.1971, §3–402, apply. That Section provides that:

> Unless the instrument clearly indicates that a signature is made in some other capacity it is an indorsement.

Thus, Mr. Finnell was an indorser and not a maker of the instrument.

We next determine in what capacity Mr. Finnell indorsed the note. Under the provisions of §3–415(4), an indorsement *not in the chain of title* is an *accommodation* indorsement. That Section provides:

> An indorsement which shows that it is not in the chain of title is notice of its accommodation character.

In the case before us, Mr. Finnell's indorsement was clearly *not* in the chain of title. The note was given to the Bank by Ms. Neely, and then the Bank negotiated the instrument by transferring it to Mr. King. At the time Mr. King took the instrument, it contained Mr. Finnell's indorsement. Thus, as the note was clearly one given to the Bank, and

being transferred by the Bank and not by the indorser of the instrument, the indorsement was not in the chain of title. Under the provisions of Section 3–415(4), quoted above, the indorsement thus had the effect of making Mr. Finnell an *accommodation indorser.*

For the above stated reasons, we hold, first, that Mr. Finnell was an indorser, and not a maker, and, secondly, that he was an accommodation indorser.

Having held that Mr. Finnell was an accommodation indorser, we next determine what rights and obligations flow from that status. Section 3–415(2) of the Uniform Commercial Code provides:

> When the instrument has been taken for value before it is due the *accommodation party is liable in the capacity in which he has signed even though the taker knows of the accommodation.*

. . . Under both the Uniform Commercial Code and pre-code Oklahoma law, an accommodation party is a surety.

Uniform Commercial Code Comment 1 to Section 3–415 provides in part:

> 1. *Subsection (1) recognizes that an accommodation party is always a surety.* . . . His obligation is . . . determined by the capacity in which he signs. An accommodation maker or acceptor is bound on the instrument without any resort to his principal, *while an accommodation indorser may be liable only after presentment, notice of dishonor and protest.* The subsection recognizes the defenses of a surety in accordance with the provisions subjecting one not a holder in due course to all simple contract defenses, as well as his rights against his principal after payment. . . .

In the case before us, Mr. King and Mr. Finnell were both sureties and may possibly be co-sureties, as they were both bound for the same debt of a principal.

If the parties are co-sureties, the right of contribution which exists between them would only entitle a co-surety to collect his pro rata share of a debt paid, and not the entire amount.

Whether or not Mr. King and Mr. Finnell are in fact co-sureties, or sub-sureties, is not clear, as the so-called guarantee agreement signed by Mr. King was not introduced. This being the case, we can hardly say that the granting of summary judgment was appropriate, as there is no definite proof that Mr. King was a guarantor. If the document signed by Mr. King does not in fact obligate him to pay upon Ms. Neely's default, he may be nothing more than a volunteer, in which case he would be entitled to no reimbursement contribution at all. . . .

For these reasons, we must reverse the summary judgment granted by the trial court and remand the case for a trial on the merits.

So ordered.

Chrysler Credit Corp. v. First Nat. Bank & Trust
582 F.Supp. 1436 (Pa. Law 1984)

Plaintiff, Chrysler Credit Corporation, sues to recover the sum of $53,337.75 from First National Bank and Trust of Washington County, Pennsylvania (First National). Plaintiff and Al Barry, Inc., executed financing agreements whereby plaintiff agreed to finance the purchase of new and used vehicles for sale by the dealer. Al Barry drew 10 checks on January 18 and 19, 1979, payable to Chrysler Credit Corporation in the total sum of $53,337.75. The checks were drawn on the Barry account at the Charleroi branch office of First National. Chrysler deposited the checks in its account at the Monroeville branch of Mellon Bank on January 19, 1979. The checks were routed through the Federal Reserve and received at the main branch and data processing center of First National at Washington, Pennsylvania, on January 22, 1979.

The checks were processed by employees at the processing center, placed in a reader-sorter memory machine, and posted in a reject journal because they were drawn on uncollected funds. The checks were then withdrawn or pulled by employees of central operations.

On January 23, 1979, at approximately 10:30 a.m., the Charleroi branch received a copy of the posting reject journal by courier from the main branch. The branch manager made a decision to pay the checks the same day. However, on January 24, the branch manager reversed the decision, dishonored the checks and notified the processing center. The central operations department returned the checks to plaintiff.

Chrysler Credit contends that the checks were "presented on and received by" the Charleroi branch within the meaning of the Uniform Commercial Code on January 22, 1979. Thus the bank is liable for the amount of each check because it failed to dishonor within 24 hours of presentment.

ZIEGLER, J. . . . This case presents the question whether presentment of a check at the data processing center of a payor bank requires the bank to give notice of dishonor or return the check prior to midnight of the next banking day. . . . We conclude that when a check is received at the data processing center of the payor bank, where the bookkeeping services for the branch offices are conducted, the bank's failure to send notice of dishonor or return the check before midnight of the next business day renders the bank liable for the amount of a worthless check pursuant to 13 Pa.C.S.A. §4302. . . .

The Uniform Commercial Code provides that a payor bank must pay, return or dishonor a check within the midnight deadline following presentment to or receipt by the bank. The Code defines midnight deadline as "midnight on its next banking day following the banking day on which it receives the relevant item." These limitations require that payor banks make decisions on demand items to insure prompt payment to a chain of individuals and institutions in a fluid commercial transaction. Otherwise, a situation is created where a series of banks are extending credit to each other. And as one commentator has noted:

> If payor banks delay too long the rights of others may be compromised. Often the depositor may be a seller whose rights will be impaired if he must wait too long to discover if the check has been paid.

The foregoing policy determinations make clear that First National was required to pay, return or dishonor the 10 checks before midnight on the day following presentment. Failure to act renders the bank accountable. First National contends that the checks were "presented on and received by" the payor bank when the Charleroi branch received the posting reject journal on the morning of January 23, because the branch is treated as a separate bank for the purpose of computing the time within which action must be taken under the Commercial Code.

Thus, according to defendant, the bank had until midnight on January 24 to meet its deadline. We disagree. . . . Presentment at a processing center operated by a bank, rather than the banking office where the check is drawn, is effective to trigger the time limits of the midnight deadline.

The official comments to the Commercial Code support our conclusion. Comments 4 and 5 to §4-106 provide:

> 4. Assuming that it is not desirable to make each branch a separate branch for all purposes, this Section provides that a branch or separate office is a separate bank for certain purposes. . . .
>
> 5. Whether a branch functions as a separate bank may vary depending upon the type of activity taking place and upon practices in the different states. If the activity is that of a payor bank paying items, a branch will usually function as a separate bank if it maintains its own deposit ledgers. Similarly whether a branch functions as a separate bank in the collection of items usually depends also on whether it maintains its own deposit ledgers. Conversely, if a particular bank having branches does all of its bookkeeping at its head office, the branches of that bank do not usually function as separate banks either in the payment or collection of items.

Given these comments, we conclude that the drafters would consider a computer center as part of a branch bank where: (1) the computer center is the designated place of presentment for checks drawn on the branch's accounts; (2) the computer center performs services specifically for that branch; (3) these services are not customarily performed by the branch itself; (4) these services are an integral part of the branch's processing of checks, and (5) the checks are never physically delivered to the branch but only computerized information is forwarded to the branch. . . .

In summary, the language of §4106 is ambiguous and this court must consider the official comments and other authorities to determine the definition of a "branch bank." As rehearsed, the comments recommend that a branch be judged by the functions it performs, without regard to where those functions are physically performed. . . . Because we interpret the intent of §4302 to favor the expeditious processing of commercial paper and because we find that the banking industry as a whole will benefit if all banks are held to a standard of prompt processing of checks, we hold that the midnight deadline of §4302 is to be measured from the time checks are presented to a payor bank's computer processing center, where the center is a designated place of presentment and where the center performs an integral and necessary check processing function. . . . We find that First National is accountable for the face value of the 10 checks in question, plus 6 percent interest calculated from January 23, 1979, when the bank failed to meet its statutory midnight deadline.

So ordered.

REVIEW QUESTIONS

1. Match each term in column A with the appropriate statement in column B.

A	B
1. Presentment	**a.** On who signs an instrument for the purpose of lending his name and credit to another party.
2. Dishonor	**b.** The secondary liability that results from the status of parties as drawers or unqualified indorsers.
3. Notice of dishonor	**c.** A person who agrees to pay an instrument according to its terms.
4. Accommodation party	**d.** A person who is primarily liable on a draft.

5. Protest

6. Primary party

7. Acceptor

8. Unconditional liability

9. Conditional liability

e. The liability of one who negotiates by use of a qualified indorsement.

f. A refusal to pay or to accept.

g. A requirement for conditional liability.

h. A formal method of satisfying conditions precedent.

i. A demand made upon a maker or drawee.

2. A note recited that the makers were jointly and severally liable. It was signed on behalf of a corporation and by the officers individually on the face of the note. One of the officers claimed to be an accommodation party and a surety. Is he liable as a maker? Why?

3. A corporation executed a promissory note to its bank. The corporation's president signed the note on the back with his name and without any other identifying or limiting designation. When the note was not paid, the bank sought to hold both the corporation and its president liable. Is the president personally liable on the note? In what capacity? Explain.

4. Motz indorsed a promissory note of an organization. When the maker defaulted, Motz was sued. He defended on the ground of lack of consideration. With what result? Why?

5. Anne loaned Donna's son David money to start a business, which later failed. David offered to sign a promissory note for the debt to prevent Anne from instituting legal proceedings against the remaining assets of the failed business. Anne agreed, but would only accept a note co-signed or indorsed by Donna. Donna signed the back of her son's note. Anne sued Donna to collect the note when David could not be located. With what result? Why?

6. Mark delivers a negotiable promissory note to Peter. Peter specially indorses it and delivers it to Art. Art adds his signature and delivers it to Bill. Bill, without signing it, delivers it to Carl. Carl indorses without recourse and delivers it to Dick. Dick presents the instrument to Mark, who replies: "I'm sorry, but I have no money." From whom can Dick collect the note? What must he do to collect? Explain.

7. The facts are as in problem 6, except Mark informs Dick that the signature on the note is a forgery. From whom can Dick collect the note? Explain.

8. Hopkins, the holder of a note, transferred the note by a blank indorsement to Beggs. Beggs did not present the note to the maker for payment nor did he notify Hopkins of any dishonor. Can Beggs maintain an action against Hopkins as an indorser? Why or why not?

9. The defendant received a check drawn on plaintiff's bank. The defendant indorsed the check and received payment from his bank. That bank sent the check for collection to the plaintiff bank, and the check was honored. Several days later, the bank discovered that the drawer of the check did not have an account and that it had mistakenly charged the check to another of its customers. Plaintiff then sought to recover from defendant as an indorser. He contended that the check had not been dishonored within the time allowed by law. Is he liable as an indorser? Why or why not?

10. A check was indorsed on the back by three persons, Johns, Baker, and Charles. When Johns was sued, he sought to prove that he signed after Baker and Charles. Is he entitled to offer such proof? Explain the significance of the evidence.

11. Chrysler Credit Corp. was the payee on a check for $53,000 drawn on First National Bank and Trust. Chrysler Credit Corp. deposited the check in its own bank on January 19. The check reached First National Bank through normal banking channels on January 22. First National did not pay or return the check or send notice of dishonor until after midnight of January 23. Is the bank entitled to collect back from Chrysler Credit? Why?

12. On Thursday, May 15, Fox, the payee on a check drawn by Owens on Riverside Bank, indorsed the check to the order of Granger who, on the same date, indorsed the check to the order of Hines, a mutual friend of Granger and Owens. On Friday, May 16, Hines presented the check for payment at the Bank and payment was refused because of insufficient funds in Owens's account. Not wishing to embarrass Owens, Hines telephoned and advised Owens of the bank's refusal to pay and the reason. Owens promised to make a deposit to his bank account on the following Monday and told Hines to present the check again at the bank on that day and it would be paid. Hines agreed but unexpectedly had to go out of town on business and could not again present the check for payment until the following Thursday, May 22. When Hines then presented the check at the bank, payment was again refused for the same reason. Hines thereupon promptly and properly notified Granger, Fox, and Owens of the dishonor of the check. It was later determined that Owens was insolvent. Does Hines have a cause of action against Granger and Fox? Explain. Assuming Hines may recover from Granger and Fox and recovers from Fox only, may Fox recover from Granger? Explain.

13. Winston Corporation purchased five $1,000 thirty-day notes of the Fubor Corporation. The notes were clever forgeries. The forger, William Claude, drew the notes to his own order and signed the name of Oscar Fubor to the notes as the maker. He then indorsed them to Bernard Oldfield, signing his own name in blank. Oldfield negotiated them to Winston Corporation using a "without recourse" indorsement. What are the rights, if any, of Winston against Fubor, Claude, and Oldfield? Explain.

32 Introduction to Article 9 Transactions

With this chapter we begin an in-depth examination of the creditor-debtor relationship. The creation of this relationship is one of the most common examples of contracts in our society today. Literally billions of dollars in debt are incurred each month. The extension of credit occurs at every level of business as well as in our personal lives. For example, manufacturers finance raw materials and equipment; wholesalers and retailers finance inventory; and consumers finance their purchases. The common denominator of all these financial transactions is that the creditor wants to be repaid.

Since most debtors repay their obligations, the safeguard for lenders and sellers of goods on credit is the willingness of the debtor to repay voluntarily. Because the vast majority of borrowers do repay, creditors sometimes agree to depend only on the debtor's personal promise to pay. This creditor is said to be *unsecured.* In other words, an unsecured creditor does not have any collateral from which the debt can be collected. A credit sales transaction wherein the seller is unsecured is often called a sale on *open account* or *open credit.* The danger of lacking collateral is illustrated by the steps an unsecured creditor must take if the debtor fails to repay voluntarily.

The unsecured creditor must first sue the debtor and obtain a judgment. Then, as a *judgment creditor,* it may pursue the enforcement procedures available to a judgment creditor. These postjudgment procedures include obtaining a writ of execution, having a law enforcement official levy the execution on the debtor's property, and having the property sold at a public auction. The process of litigation and enforcement of the judgment are costly in terms of both time and money.

In order to avoid the difficulty of collecting unpaid debts, most creditors insist on being secured. In other words, creditors often want at least a second source of repayment in addition to the debtor's personal promise to repay. This security may take several forms. Very often, if the debtor owns any real estate, it is used as collateral. The use of real estate as security is discussed in chapter 34. Another source of repayment is a second person's commitment to pay the debt. This source creates a suretyship, which is discussed in chapter 35. A third source is the use of the debtor's personal property as collateral. It is this use of personal property which this chapter and the next one consider.

1. Secured Creditors

Article 9 of the Uniform Commercial Code is an attempt to make all state laws uniform with respect to creditors' use of personal property as collateral. Article 9 provides for the creation of a secured transaction. This transaction involves a security interest which is granted by a debtor to a creditor. The *security interest,* as defined by Article 9, is that interest in the debtor's personal property or fixtures which the creditor can use to obtain satisfaction of the debt in the event of nonpayment [9-102(1)(a)]. A *fixture* is an item of personal property that has become attached to real estate. Items of personal property and fixtures used as security are called *collateral* [9-105(1)(c)]. A creditor who is protected by a valid Article 9 security interest is known as a *secured creditor.* A creditor obtains a security interest by entering into a *security agreement* with the debtor. In order to be secured, the creditor must *perfect* the security interest [9-301].

In general, perfected secured creditors are in a much more favorable position than unsecured creditors. For example, the secured creditor, upon the debtor's default, can seize the collateral. If the secured creditor cannot seize the collateral peacefully, it can institute formal foreclosure proceedings and have the collateral applied to the payment of the debt. The right of foreclosure is cheaper and less time-consuming than the procedure an unsecured creditor must follow. These rights of a secured creditor upon the debtor's default are explained further in chapter 33.

Secured creditors enjoy an advantage when a debtor becomes insolvent or files bankruptcy. The secured creditor has personal property from which repayment may be obtained. By having a security interest in the debtor's personal property, a secured creditor, in effect, is given priority over unsecured creditors.

2. Article 9 of the Code

The study of Article 9 is made more difficult because there are two versions. Originally, Article 9 on secured transactions was proposed for adoption by the states in 1962. This 1962 version was adopted by every state except Louisiana, but two problems quickly arose with the version. First, the states enacted numerous alterations of the recommended Article 9. These nonuniformities meant that the purpose of having a uniform law was not satisfied. Second, there were some inherent flaws with the recommended version itself. Article 9 was the most novel article of the entire Uniform Commercial Code. In other words, the 1962 version of Article 9 attempted to substitute a simple, unified body of law for the confusing and haphazard nineteenth-century developments concerning the use of personal property as collateral.

In an attempt to establish greater uniformity, Article 9 was redrafted. In 1972, the revised Article 9 was proposed to the states for adoption. To date, over 40 of the states have adopted the revision. Since it now is the law in almost every state, our concentration will be on the 1972 revision. This revision is included in the reprint of the Code at the end of this text, and the text refers to it. When it is necessary to discuss the 1962 version, it will be described as the 62 Code or 62 version. Otherwise, all references to Article 9 are to the 1972 revision.

Even though there are two versions of Article 9 and many nonuniformities have been passed by various states, some concepts of the secured transaction apply in all situations. In order to gain an appreciation for how an Article 9 secured transaction protects creditors, our study is divided into 5 parts:

1. The scope of Article 9
2. The creation of a security interest
3. The perfection of a security interest
4. The priorities to the collateral
5. The creditors' rights and duties when a debtor defaults

Helping you understand these objectives is the goal of this chapter and the next. The first three objectives are discussed in this chapter. Priority issues and the creditors' rights and duties on the debtor's default are discussed in chapter 33.

3. In General

SCOPE OF ARTICLE 9

Although Article 9 deals primarily with secured transactions, it also covers outright sales of certain types of property, such as accounts receivable [9-102(1)(b)]. Thus, a sale of the accounts receivable of a business must comply with the Code requirements as if the accounts were security for a loan.

Except for sales such as those of accounts receivable, the main test to be applied in determining whether a given transaction falls within the purview of Article 9 is whether it was intended to have effect as security. Every transaction with such intent is covered [9-102(1)(a)]. A lease with option to buy may be considered a security transaction rather than a lease if the necessary intent is present.

Certain credit transactions are expressly excluded from Article 9 coverage [9-104]. In general, these exclusions involve transactions that are not of a commercial nature. Examples of common exclusions include a landlord's liens, an assignment of wages, and a transfer of an insurance policy. Another important exclusion is the lien created by state law in favor of those who service or repair personal property, such as automobiles. This lien, known as an *artisan's lien,* is discussed in more detail in chapter 35.

Despite the excluded transactions, Article 9's coverage is very broad indeed. This broad application can be seen best by examining the various types of collateral covered by Article 9. As the following sections indicate, there is not an item of personal property that cannot be used as collateral in a secured transaction. The only limitation to what is acceptable as collateral is the creditor's willingness to accept an interest in a particular item of personal property.

4. Classifications of Collateral

Collateral may be classified according to its physical makeup into (1) tangible, physical property or goods, (2) documentary property that has physical existence, such as a negotiable instrument, but is simply representative of a contractual obligation, and (3) purely intangible property, such as an account receivable. Each type of collateral presents its own peculiar problems, and the framework of Article 9 is structured on the peculiarities of each type. Table 32–1 summarizes the various classifications of personal property that may be the collateral which is the subject of a security interest. The following three sections also discuss each of these three classifications.

TABLE 32–1

Collateral Subject to a Security Interest

TANGIBLE PROPERTY ("GOODS")	DOCUMENTARY COLLATERAL	INTANGIBLE PROPERTY
Any personal property that is movable at the time the security interest attaches or that is a fixture [9-105 (1)(h)]. A fixture is a special type of Article 9 collateral [9-313].	Involves some indispensable piece of paper and has both tangible and intangible aspects.	Not evidenced by an indispensable writing, which distinguishes it from documentary collateral.
Goods are classified as one of the following:	Documentary collateral is classified into one of the following:	Intangible property consists of one of the following:
Consumer goods [9-109 (1)]	Chattel paper [9-105 (1) (b)]	Account [9-106]
Equipment [9-109 (2)]	Documents of title [9-105 (1) (f)]	Contract right [9-106 62 Code]; deleted by 72 Code and definition of account, above, reworded to cover it
Farm products [9-109 (3)]	Instruments [9-105 (1) (i)]	
Inventory [9-109 (4)]		General intangibles [9-106]

5. Tangible Goods

In secured transactions under either version of Article 9, four categories of tangible goods are established. These categories include the following:

1. Consumer goods   **3.** Farm Products

2. Equipment   **4.** Inventory

In determining the classification of any particular item of goods, it is necessary to take into account not only the physical attributes of the collateral, but also the status of the debtor who is buying the property or using it as security for a loan and the use the debtor will make of the goods. Keep in mind that the classification will determine the place of filing to perfect the security interest against third parties. It may also affect the rights of the debtor on default.

Consumer Goods. Goods fall into this classification if they are used or bought primarily for personal, family, or household purposes [9-109(1)].

Equipment. Goods that are used or bought for use primarily in a business, in farming, in a profession, or by a nonprofit organization or government agency fall within this category [9-109(2)]. The category is something of a catchall, embracing goods that otherwise defy classification. Since equipment often is attached to realty and becomes a "fixture," the discussion of fixtures later is especially significant for the equipment classification.

Farm Products. This category includes crops and livestock, supplies used or produced in farming operations, and the products of crops or livestock in their unmanufactured state (ginned cotton, wool, milk, and eggs), provided that the items are in the possession of a debtor who is engaged in farming operations [9-109(3)]. Farm products are *not* equipment or inventory. Note that goods cease to be farm products and must therefore be reclassified when (1) they are no longer in the farmer's possession, or (2) they have been subjected to a manufacturing process. Thus, when the farmer delivers his farm products to a marketing agency for sale or to a frozen-food processor as raw materials, the products in the hands of the other party are inventory. Likewise, if the farmer maintained a canning operation, the canned product would be inventory, even though it remained in his possession.

Inventory. Inventory consists of goods that are held by a person for sale or lease or are to be furnished under a contract of service. They may be raw materials, work in process, completed goods, or material used or consumed in a business [9-109(4)]. The basic test to be applied in determining whether goods are inventory is whether they are held for immediate or ultimate sale or lease. The reason for the inclusion of materials used or consumed in a business (e.g., supplies of fuel, boxes, and other containers for packaging the goods) is that they will soon be used in making an end product for sale.

The proper classification of goods is determined on the basis of its nature and intended use by the debtor. A television set in a dealer's warehouse is inventory to the dealer. When the set is sold and delivered to a consumer customer, it becomes a consumer good. If an identical set were sold on the same terms to the owner of a tavern, to be used for entertaining customers, the set would be equipment in the hands of the tavern owner. The secured party generally cannot rely on the classification furnished by the debtor. The secured party must analyze all facts to ensure proper classification of the collateral and proper perfection of the security interest.[1]

6. Documentary Collateral

In secured transactions, three types of paper are considered to represent such valuable property interests that they are included as potential collateral. These items of paper property include documents of title, chattel paper, and instruments. These items comprise various categories of paper frequently used in commerce. These papers may be negotiable or nonnegotiable. Each of these items of potential collateral is evidenced by a writing, and each represents rights and duties of the parties who signed the writing.

Documents of Title. Included under this heading are bills of lading, warehouse receipts, and any other document that in the regular course of business or financing is treated as sufficient evidence that the person in possession of it is entitled to receive, hold, and dispose of the document and the goods it covers [1-201(15)].

Chattel paper. Chattel paper refers to a writing or writings that evidence both (1) an obligation to pay money, and (2) a security interest in, or a lease of, specific goods [9-105(1)(b)]. The chattel paper is *itself* a security agreement. A security agreement in the form of a conditional sales contract, for example, is often executed in connection with a negotiable note or a series of notes. The group of writings (the contract plus the note) taken together as a composite constitutes *chattel paper.* A typical situation involving chattel paper as collateral is one in which a secured party who has obtained it in a transaction with his customer may wish to borrow against it in his own financing. To illustrate: A dealer sells an electric generator to a customer in a conditional sales contract, and the customer signs a negotiable installment note. At this point, the contract is the security agreement; the dealer is the secured party; the customer is the debtor; and the generator is the collateral (equipment). The dealer, needing funds for working capital, transfers the contract and the note to a finance company as security for a loan. In the transaction between dealer and finance company, the contract and note are the collateral (chattel paper), the finance company is the secured party, the dealer is the debtor, and the customer is now designated as the *account debtor.*

Instruments. As distinguished from chattel paper, an *instrument* means (1) negotiable instrument, (2) an investment security such as stocks and bonds, or (3) any other writing that evidences a right to the payment of money and is not itself a security agreement or lease [9-105(1)(i)]. To qualify as an instrument, the other writing must also be one that is in the ordinary course of business transferred by indorsement or assignment. Thus, the classification includes, in addition to negotiable instruments, those that are recognized as having some

---

[1] First State Bank v. Producers Livestock Marketing Association Non-Stock Cooperative, p. 709.

negotiable attributes. Instruments are frequently used as collateral, and they present certain problems in this connection because of their negotiable character. These problems are discussed further in the part of this chapter concerning perfection. Due to the readily transferable nature of negotiable instruments, priority issues also are complicated when this type of collateral is used in a secured transaction. These complications are explained in the next chapter.

7. Intangible Collateral

In the law of secured transactions there is a third basic classification of collateral called *intangibles*. This classification includes the following three categories: (1) accounts, (2) contract rights, and (3) general intangibles. These categories are distinguished from documentary collateral by virtue of the fact that they are not represented by a writing. In other words, these three categories of potential collateral are truly lacking any physical characteristics.

Accounts.   An account is any right to payment arising out of a sale of goods or services if that right is not evidenced by a writing, such as with an instrument or chattel paper [9-106]. An account receivable, which arose from a sale on open credit, is a typical example of an account.

Contract Rights.   A contract right is the right to payment under a contract that has not yet been performed [9-106]. In other words, a contract right exists only until the party performs his obligations under the contract. After contractual performance occurs, the contract right becomes an account receivable. Due to the slight distinction between this and the previous category of collateral, the concept of contract rights was deleted in the 1972 revision of Article 9. In that revision, the word "account" is redefined to include contract rights.

General Intangibles.   This heading includes miscellaneous intangible personal property that may be used as commercial security, but does not fall within any of the preceding classifications of collateral. Examples of general intangibles include goodwill, literary rights, patents, and copyrights [9-106].

8. Introduction

The ultimate goal of the secured party is to have an enforceable, attached, and perfected security interest. The remainder of this chapter is devoted to these three concepts: *enforceability, attachment,* and *perfection.* Completing the steps as outlined in section 9-203, causes a security interest to spring into existence. This moment of creation is called "attachment." At the time of attachment, the security interest is also enforceable against the debtor and third parties [9-203(1), 9-201]. However, third parties may defeat the security interest if it is not perfected. Perfection will be discussed later in this chapter.

The following four simple steps are required to create a security interest:

1. Make a security agreement with the debtor.
2. Make sure the debtor has "rights in the collateral."

**CREATION OF
A SECURITY
INTEREST**

3. Give value.

4. Make the security interest enforceable either by putting the security agreement in writing, which the debtor signs, or take possession of the collateral pursuant to the agreement.

The four steps can occur in any order. A security agreement may be executed and the secured party may give value (such as a loan) before the debtor acquires rights in the collateral. Assume that Sewall, a small manufacturing company, is seeking a loan of $5,000 from a bank. Sewall intends to buy a Model 711 Reaper sewing machine, which will be the collateral. Assume that the following progressive steps occur:

1. *A security agreement is signed by Sewall, but not by the bank. Sewall has yet to deal with Reaper.* Only the debtor is required to sign this document.

2. *Now Sewall contracts with Reaper to buy the Model 711 machine.* According to Article 2, a buyer does not have any rights in the goods until the goods are identified to the contract [2-501(1)(b)].

3. *Reaper removes a Model 711 machine from its inventory and marks it for delivery to Sewall.* Now the goods are identified to the contract. Therefore, the debtor, Sewall, has rights in the collateral [2-501].

4. *The bank, for the first time, makes a binding commitment to lend Sewall the $5,000.* The requirement that the secured party give value is met. Agreeing to lend money, as well as actually making a loan, is the giving of value [1-201(44)].

Not until step 4 is completed does an Article 9 security interest exist. Only after these four steps are completed has a security interest attached to the collateral (sewing machine). After step 4, we find a written security agreement signed by the debtor; the debtor has rights in the collateral; and the secured party has given value. Thus, an attached and enforceable security interest comes into existence. The following three sections describe a few more rules about the elements of creating a valid security interest.

9. The Security Agreement

The basic instrument in a secured transaction is the security agreement [9-105(1)(l)]. It must be in writing, unless the security arrangement is a possessory one and the secured party is in possession of the collateral [9-203(1)].[2] Allowing the creditor to possess the collateral is not always feasible. Indeed, most circumstances require that the debtor have possession of the collateral. In these situations, the security agreement must be in writing, and it must be signed by the debtor. Regardless of whether the security agreement is in oral or written form, this agreement must describe the collateral in a manner sufficient so that it can be reasonably identified [9-110].

---

[2] Gibbs v. King, p. 710.

When it is in a written form, the security agreement usually will contain many other provisions. The forms in general use include a statement of the amount of the obligation and the terms of repayment, the debtor's duties in respect to the collateral, such as insuring it, and the rights of the secured party on default. In general, the parties can include such terms and provisions as they may deem appropriate to their particular transactions.

10. Debtor's Rights in Collateral and Creditor's Value

Another requirement for attachment (or creation of a valid security interest) is that the debtor must have rights in the collateral. It is clear that the debtor-buyer gets rights in the collateral against his seller upon delivery of the goods. A number of recent cases have held that the buyer can acquire rights prior to shipment, the earliest time being when the seller identifies the goods to the contract. The rights acquired by the buyer are subject to the seller's right of reclamation if the buyer fails to pay or if the buyer's check bounces.[3] If a security interest created by the buyer attaches to the goods prior to the seller exercising a right to reclaim, the secured party generally prevails over the unpaid seller holding the bounced check.

For purposes of attachment, value is defined somewhat differently than it is in commercial paper (Article 3). Basically, *value* means that a secured party has furnished to the debtor any consideration sufficient to support a simple contract [1-201(44)]. When a bank loans money or makes a binding executory promise to extend credit to a merchant and takes a security interest in the merchant's inventory, value is given. Value is also given when the secured party takes his security interest to secure a preexisting claim against the debtor.

11. Introduction

Between the debtor and secured party, the security agreement protects the secured party's security interest. But the secured party also wants protection against third parties, who may later make claims against the secured collateral. *Perfection* of the security interest will give this desired protection to the secured party. Perfection is designed to give notice to third parties that financing is occurring on the basis of collateral described. In general, an unperfected secured party's claim is subordinate to the claims of others who acquire an interest in the collateral without knowledge of the unperfected security interest.

Article 9 provides numerous ways in which a security interest can be perfected. The methods of perfection include (1) filing a financing statement, (2) taking possession of the collateral, or (3) simply creating a security interest (automatic perfection). Several factors must be taken into account in determining which of the three methods is appropriate in any given transaction: (1) the kind of collateral in which security interest was created, (2) the use the debtor intends to make of the collateral, and (3) the status of the debtor in relation to the secured party.

PERFECTION OF A SECURITY INTEREST

---

[3] Chapman Parts Warehouse, Inc. v. Guderian, p. 711.

12. Perfection by Filing

The most common method of perfecting a security interest occurs when the creditor files a *financing statement* in the appropriate public office. This financing statement, which is to be distinguished from the security agreement, is signed by the debtor only, but includes the addresses of both parties. This statement must contain a description of the collateral. It also must indicate that the debtor and secured party have entered into a security agreement. Simple forms are available with spaces for additional provisions as agreed upon by the parties, but this basic information is all that is required. If crops or fixtures constitute the collateral, then the financing statement must include a description of the real estate concerned [9-402].[4]

A financing statement is not a substitute for a security agreement. A security agreement may be filed as a financing statement if it contains the required information and is signed by the debtor. However, a financing statement usually will not qualify as a security agreement. Most businesspeople use a separate financing statement, because filing a security agreement would make public some information the parties might prefer to keep confidential.

The purpose of filing is to give notice that the secured party has a security interest in the described collateral.[5] Potential creditors are charged with the task of going to a public office to check to see if the proposed collateral is already encumbered. A person searching the records finds only minimal information and may obtain more from the parties listed in the financing statement.

A secured party can file a financing statement before the security interest attaches to the collateral. In fact, since the filing serves as notice to third parties, it is wise for the secured party to file at the earliest possible moment. Nevertheless, the filing of a financing statement does not perfect a security interest until it is in existence by attachment [9-303(1)].

The financing statement may provide a maturity or expiration date, but more often it is silent on this point. In the absence of such data, the filing is effective for a period of 5 years, subject to being renewed by the filing of a continuation statement signed by the secured party [9-403(2)]. In order to be effective, a continuation statement must be filed within 6 months of the financing statement's termination. If it is properly renewed, the original financing statement continues to be valid for another 5 years [9-403(3)].

The presence in the records of a financing statement constitutes a burden upon the debtor, since it reveals to all persons with whom he may be dealing that his property is or may be subject to the claims of others. The Code therefore provides for the filing of a *termination statement* to clear the record when the secured party is no longer entitled to a security interest. Failure of the secured party to send a termination statement within 10 days after written demand by the debtor subjects the secured party to a $100 penalty and makes him liable for any loss suffered by the debtor [9-404(1)].

---

[4] First National Bank in Creston v. Francis, p. 712.

[5] Matter of Glasco, Inc., p. 714.

Filing a financing statement is *required* in order to perfect a nonpossessory security interest in most secured transactions. As a general rule, filing is required in the case of an assignment of accounts receivable or contract rights. An exception exists for certain isolated transactions. If the assignment does not encompass a significant portion of the outstanding accounts or contract rights of the assignor, filing is not required [9-302(1)(e)].

The Code allows the states to require that the financing statement be filed in a central filing system, a local filing system, or a combination [9-401]. A central filing system means that all filing is in the state capital except for fixtures, which are filed locally. Local filing means that filing is at the county level. Most states have enacted dual filing systems. The usual system requires local filing for fixtures, local filing for farm-related collateral and consumer goods, and central filing for other business-related collateral, such as inventory and equipment. If the appropriate office for filing is unclear, the secured party should file the financing statement in every office that might be considered proper.

The Code makes special provisions for goods such as motor vehicles that have a certificate of title. The filing requirements of the Code do not apply, and the usual method of indicating a security interest is to have it noted on the certificate of title [9-302(3)].[6] If the security interest is properly perfected on the certificate of title, the security interest is valid even though a substitute certificate of title fails to disclose the interest of the secured party.

13. Perfection by Possession

The simplest way to give notice of a security interest is for the secured party to take possession of the collateral [9-305]. This transfer of the collateral's possession from the debtor to the secured party is called a *pledge.* Since a secured party's possession of the collateral gives notice of his security interest, no public filing is required. As noted previously, the possessory security interest is very easy to accomplish because a written security agreement is not required. However, the use of possession as perfection is quite limited because most debtors either need or want possession of the collateral.

Possession is the required method of perfection of a security interest in instruments. Filing a financing statement is deemed inappropriate since instruments are created to be freely transferable in commercial transactions. Because a third party accepting an instrument as security or as payment would not think to check for the existence of a financing statement, the Code limits the method of perfection in instruments to possession.

Possession is an optional method of perfection if the collateral consists of goods, negotiable documents of title, and chattel paper [9-305]. Since intangible collateral lacks a physical existence, it cannot be possessed. Therefore, the filing of a financing statement is essential for perfection if the collateral is an account, a contract right, or a general intangible.

Although it usually is considered an alternative to filing, possession of the

---

[6] Noble v. Bonnett, p. 715.

collateral is the only method whereby complete protection in documents and chattel paper can be obtained. The reason possession of documents is necessary for absolute perfection is because the rights of good faith holders to whom a document has been negotiated by the debtor will prevail over the secured party, even though there has been a filing. Possession of chattel paper is necessary in order to prevent buyers who purchase chattel paper in the ordinary course of their business from obtaining a superior claim to the paper [9-308]. These situations involving issues of priority to the collateral are discussed in more detail in the next chapter.

For a variety of commercial reasons, it may be necessary or desirable that the secured party with a possessory security interest temporarily release possession of the collateral, to the debtor. Since the release is of short duration, it would be cumbersome to require a filing. The Code therefore provides that a security interest *remains perfected* for a period of 21 days without filing when a secured party having a perfected security interest releases the collateral to the debtor. This grace period applies only to (1) instruments, (2) negotiable documents, and (3) goods in the hands of a bailee not covered by a negotiable document of title.

If an *instrument* is temporarily released to the debtor, the purpose must be to enable the debtor to make a presentation of it, collect it, renew it, obtain registration of a transfer, or make an ultimate sale or exchange. The risks associated with such a release involve the debtor's improper or unauthorized negotiation of the instrument, or the debtor's sale of the instrument to a bona fide purchaser. If the debtor has possession of the instruments, these risks always are present.

The purposes for which *goods* or *documents* may be released to the debtor are limited. The release to the debtor of these items of collateral must be for the purpose of (1) ultimate sale or exchange; or (2) loading, unloading, storing, shipping, transshipping, manufacturing, processing, or otherwise dealing with them in a manner preliminary to their sale or exchange [9-302(5)].

14. Perfection by Attachment

Another method of perfection simply involves the attachment of the security interest to the collateral. In other words, in some situations, the creation of the security interest is perfection. In these situations, the secured party is automatically perfected by attachment. One example of this type of perfection is the 21-day time period mentioned in the preceding section. A much more common application of perfection by attachment occurs in transactions involving a purchase-money security interest.

There are two types of purchase-money security interests (often referred to as PMSI). The first one is called the seller's PMSI. This occurs when a seller of goods finances the purchase price and retains a security interest in the goods sold as collateral [9-107(1)(a)]. The second example of a PMSI involves the lender's PMSI. This situation arises when a lender advances money to enable a debtor to acquire the collateral, and the money is, in fact, used to buy the collateral [9-107(1)(b)].

Perfection by attachment is possible when a PMSI is created in any item of consumer goods [9-302]. Creditors are allowed to be automatically perfected when they have taken a PMSI in consumer goods because it would be very burdensome to have to file a financing statement after every consumer credit sales transaction. Furthermore, this perfection by attachment prevents the official recordkeepers from being overworked with a multitude of filings.

A secured party perfected by attachment enjoys only limited protection from third-party claims. In the next chapter we will examine some situations in which the secured party who relies on perfection by attachment loses rights in the collateral to good-faith buyers.

15. In General

Often a creditor may create a security interest in collateral that is likely to be sold by the debtor. This event is very common when the collateral is inventory. In order to remain secured, the creditor will want to create a floating lien. A *floating lien* is created when the security agreement describes the collateral as including property acquired in the future by the debtor [9-204(1)]. The security agreement may also provide that future advances made to the debtor will be covered [9-204(3)]. The secured party can also have a security interest in the proceeds of the sale of collateral in the debtor's ordinary course of business.

The secured party's floating lien is protected against the claims of third parties by virtue of the public notice that such a financing arrangement has been made. The amount of the debt and the actual collateral can be constantly changing if the security agreement is worded to include after-acquired property, future advances of money, and the proceeds of any sale. This sort of arrangement allows the secured party to tie up most of the assets of a debtor, a possibility considered acceptable in business financing but restricted toward consumers, as the next section indicates.

FLOATING LIENS

16. After-Acquired Property

The security agreement may provide that property acquired by the debtor at any later time shall also secure some or all of the debtor's obligation under the security agreement. Many security agreements contain a clause called an *after-acquired property clause* such as the following:

> The security interest of the secured party under this security agreement extends to all collateral of the type that is the subject of this agreement and is acquired by the debtor at any time during the continuation of this agreement.

Under this clause, as soon as the debtor acquires rights in new property, a security interest in the new property vests in favor of the secured party [9-204(1)].

This clause obviously binds a debtor severely. The Code limits the effect of after-acquired property clauses in relation to consumer goods, since the clauses seem best suited to commercial transactions and might work undue hardship on a consumer. Unless a consumer obtains goods within 10 days after the secured party gives value, a security interest usually cannot attach under an after-acquired property clause in consumer goods contracts [9-204(2)].

17. Future Advances

A creditor may include in a security agreement that the collateral protects him with respect to future advances in addition to the original loan. A *future advance* occurs when the secured party makes a second loan to the debtor. This additional loan is a future advance covered by a properly worded security agreement even if the secured party was not obligated to make the second loan. A problem that arises with future advances occurs in this context: SP-1 lends money, files a financing statement, and has perfected his security interest. SP-2 later lends money, files, and perfects his interest in the same collateral. SP-1 generally would have priority since he was the first to file. But what happens when SP-1 lends additional money after SP-2 has filed and perfected? SP-1 still has priority.

If the future advance is made while a security interest is perfected, the secured party with priority to the original collateral has the same priority with respect to the future advance. Likewise, if a perfected secured party makes a commitment to lend money later, that party has the same priority regarding the future advance as he has with respect to the original collateral. These rules are justified by the necessity of protecting the filing system. In other words, a secured party that is perfected by filing remains perfected when future advances are made without having to check for filings made later than his financing statement.

18. Proceeds

The passing of the security interest from goods to the proceeds of the sale is an important part of the floating lien concept. A debtor may sell or otherwise dispose of the collateral, but the secured party may have an interest in the identifiable proceeds. These proceeds may take the form of cash or noncash proceeds. Examples of noncash proceeds include receivable, instruments, chattel paper, documents of title, or any form of goods [9-306(1)]. In those states that have adopted the 1972 revision, insurance payments also clearly are proceeds.

Two different factual situations concerning proceeds may arise. A debtor may have the authority to dispose of the collateral, as in a sale of inventory. Or he may dispose of the collateral without authority to do so. In either situation, the secured party has an interest in the proceeds. In the former, he loses his security interest in the collateral that is sold in the ordinary course of business, but retains an interest in the proceeds. If the debtor sells the collateral without authority, the secured party retains a security interest in the original collateral, and he gains an interest in the proceeds [9-306(2)].

An interest in the proceeds from the sale of collateral may remain perfected even if the original financing statement does not specifically mention proceeds. This continuous perfection occurs if the original financing statement's description of collateral includes the type of collateral which covers the proceeds. For example, suppose that the original financing statement described the collateral as inventory and accounts. If an item of inventory is sold on account, the proceed is an account receivable. The secured party is perfected with respect to this account by the original financing statement. However, suppose that the item of inventory is sold and the buyer signs a promissory note. This note, as an instrument, is not covered by the original financing statement. Indeed, in order to be perfected the secured party must take possession of this note. In this situation, the 1972 revision provides that the secured party is automatically perfected for 10 days with regard to the proceeds not covered by the original financing statement. In order to remain perfected, the secured party must perfect the interest in these proceeds by some acceptable method during this 10-day period [9-306(3)].

Special provisions relate to the secured party's interest in proceeds if the debtor becomes involved in bankruptcy or other insolvency proceedings [9-306(4)]. In general, the secured party is entitled to reclaim from the trustee in bankruptcy proceeds that can be identified as relating to the original collateral. If the proceeds are no longer identifiable because they have been commingled or deposited in an account, the secured party nonetheless has a perfected security interest in an amount up to the proceeds received by the debtor within 10 days prior to the commencement of the bankruptcy proceedings. Other priority issues are discussed in the next chapter.

SUMMARY

INTRODUCTION

Unsecured creditors	1. An unsecured creditor has only the debtor to look to for payment of a debt or performance of a contractual promise.
	2. If the debtor fails to perform, the unsecured creditor must file suit and try to collect.
	3. An unsecured creditor who has obtained a judgment is a judgment creditor. This creditor must obtain a writ of execution, have the writ levied on the debtor's property, and have the property sold at public auction.
Secured creditors	1. In order to avoid the time and expenses of seeking a judgment and having the debtor's property sold, creditors often seek an interest in collateral.
	2. Collateral may take many forms. However, Article 9 is limited to the debtor's personal property and fixtures.

	3. Secured creditors have many advantages in collecting unpaid debts over unsecured creditors.
Scope of Article 9	1. Article 9 includes any commercial transaction wherein the purpose is to use the debtor's personal property or fixtures as collateral.
	2. Article 9 also covers transactions involving the outright sale of accounts receivable.
	3. Article 9 does not govern transactions involving security interests that are not commercial in nature.
	4. Such excluded transactions are the creation of a landlord's lien, an assignment of wages, and a transfer of an insurance policy.
Classifications of collateral	1. Collateral is classified on the basis of its physical characteristics and on the basis of the debtor's use of the collateral.
	2. Article 9 collateral can be classified as tangible goods, documentary collateral, or intangible collateral.
	3. Tangible goods can be categorized as consumer goods, equipment, farm products, and inventory.
	4. Documentary collateral can be subdivided into documents of title, chattel paper, and instruments.
	5. Intangible collateral consists of accounts, contract rights, and general intangibles. Contract rights, as a category of collateral, was eliminated by the 1972 revision of Article 9.

CREATION OF A SECURITY INTEREST

Attachment	1. To create a valid Article 9 security interest, the interest must attach to the collateral and become enforceable.
	2. This process is achieved by (a) the existence of a security agreement, (b) the debtor having rights in the collateral, (c) the creditor granting value, and (d) the debtor signing the agreement or the creditor taking possession of the collateral.

	3. These steps of attachment may occur in any order as long as all have occurred.
Security agreement	1. The agreement is the grant of a security interest by the debtor to the creditor.
	2. The agreement must name the parties and describe the collateral involved.
	3. The agreement may be oral if the creditor takes possession of the collateral. If possession remains with the debtor, this agreement must be in writing and signed by the debtor.
Debtor's rights in collateral	1. In general a debtor has rights in the collateral when it is identified to a sales contract.
	2. Clearly, the debtor has rights in the collateral when the debtor has possession.
Creditor's value	1. Value is defined as consideration sufficient to support a contract.
	2. Therefore, a creditor's executory promise to lend money is value.

PERFECTION OF A SECURITY INTEREST

Purpose	1. Perfection is that step which notifies the public that a creditor has an interest in the described collateral.
	2. Perfection generally gives a secured creditor priority to collateral over the claims of third parties.
Perfection by filing	1. The most common method of perfection is filing a financing statement.
	2. The financing statement is a separate document from a security agreement. The debtor must sign a written financing statement.
	3. A financing statement is effective for 5 years unless a shorter time period is clearly stated or unless a continuation statement is filed to extend the statement's duration.
	4. To be valid, a financing statement must be filed in the appropriate office, as required by state law.
Perfection by possession	1. Notice of the creditor's interest in collateral clearly is given if the creditor has possession of the collateral.

	2. Possession is an optional method of perfection if the collateral is tangible goods, negotiable documents, or chattel paper.
	3. Possession is mandatory if the collateral is instruments.
	4. An interest in intangible collateral cannot be perfected by possession. A financing statement must be filed when the collateral is intangible in form.
Perfection by attachment	**1.** In some situations, the creation (or attachment) of a security interest automatically perfects the secured creditor.
	2. The 21-day exceptions to the creditor's having possession of instruments is one example of perfection by attachment.
	3. The more common example of perfection by attachment involves the secured party's PMSI in consumer goods.

FLOATING LIENS

Definition	**1.** A floating lien is created when a creditor's security interest covers after-acquired collateral, future advances, and proceeds.
	2. This concept avoids the necessity of the secured party having to create a new security interest and file a new financing statement every time the debtor acquires additional property or borrows additional money.
After-acquired property	**1.** A clause granting the creditor an interest in new property acquired by the debtor may be included in the security agreement.
	2. This clause's application is limited to a 10-day period if the property is consumer goods.
Future advances	**1.** A security agreement may state that the security interest covers future loans made by the creditor.
	2. In general, priority with respect to future advances made is determined by the date of original perfection.

Proceeds	**1.** A secured party's floating lien also gives that party's interest in the proceeds of a sale of collateral.
	2. These proceeds may be in the form of cash or noncash collateral.
	3. Under the 1972 Code, an interest in proceeds continues as perfected if the original financing statement included a description of the type of collateral that covers the proceeds. Otherwise, the secured party is perfected by attachment for a 10-day period.

CASES

First State Bank v. Producers Livestock Marketing Association Non-Stock Cooperative
261 N.W.2d 854 (Neb. 1978)

BOSLAUGH, J. This case involves a controversy concerning a security interest in cattle owned by James W. Faden. Faden, who died on January 12, 1971, was a farmer and rancher who lived in southern Banner County, Nebraska. On November 8, 1965, he executed and delivered a financing statement and security agreement to the plaintiff, First State Bank at Kimball, Nebraska. On that date he borrowed $12,200 from the bank. His total indebtedness to the bank was then $38,360. The financing statement and security agreement was filed in Banner County on November 9, 1965, and a continuation agreement was filed on August 14, 1970. At the time of his death Faden owed the bank nearly $150,000.

The security agreement secured future advances and granted a security interest in "livestock" including any "increase, additions, accessions and substitutions thereto.". . .

The defendant, Producers Livestock Marketing Association Non-Stock Cooperative, hereinafter referred to as Producers, operates a livestock auction business in Gering, Nebraska. In a series of six transactions between February 1, 1969, and March 28, 1970, Faden sold 112 head of cattle at the auction in Gering and deposited the proceeds in the Scottsbluff National Bank at Scottsbluff, Nebraska. The plaintiff claims these cattle were covered by the security agreement and that Producers is liable to the plaintiff for the proceeds from the sale of the cattle. . . .

The trial court found generally for the plaintiff on its petition. . . . The trial court found specifically that the plaintiff had a security interest in all the livestock owned by Faden and involved in this action. The defendant has appealed.

The first transaction which is in dispute took place on February 1, 1969. On that date Faden sold 2 head of cattle at Gering, through Producers for net proceeds of $719.35.

On May 17, 1969, Faden sold 5 head of cattle at Gering, through Producers for net proceeds of $1,199.55. The evidence does not show where the cattle sold on these two dates originated.

On December 19, 1969, Faden purchased 47 head of cattle at the Torrington Livestock Commission Company at Torrington, Wyoming, for $9,464.19 and paid for them with a check on the plaintiff bank. The cattle were shipped to Gering, Nebraska, and sold through Producers on December 20, 1969, for net proceeds of $8,326.88. Two days later Faden borrowed $9,500 from the plaintiff to cover his December 19, 1969, check.

On January 16, 1970, Faden purchased 37 head of cattle at Torrington for $8,079.77. The cattle were shipped to Gering and sold through

Producers on the following day, January 17, 1970, for net proceeds of $7,496.72. Three days later, Faden borrowed $8,000 from the plaintiff bank to cover his check of January 16, 1970.

On February 20, 1970, Faden purchased 9 head of cattle at Torrington for $2,054. The cattle were shipped to Gering and sold the following day, February 21, 1970, through Producers for net proceeds of $1,883.48. On February 26, 1970, Faden borrowed $2,100 from the plaintiff bank to cover his check of February 20, 1970.

On March 26, 1970, Faden purchased 21 head of cattle at Torrington for $5,697. Twelve of these cattle were shipped to Gering and sold through Producers on March 28, 1970, for net proceeds of $2,850.65. On March 31, 1970, Faden borrowed $5,700 from the plaintiff bank to cover his check of March 26, 1970.

The defendant contends that the security agreement did not cover the cattle sold through Producers in the transactions described above because they were not "farm products." The defendant claims that Faden was actually engaged in two occupations and that in addition to being a farmer and rancher he was a cattle trader or speculator.

Under the Uniform Commercial Code, goods are classified as consumer goods, equipment, farm products, or inventory. Livestock used or produced in farming operations and in the possession of a debtor engaged in raising, fattening, grazing, or other farming operations are farm products. If goods are farm products they are neither equipment nor inventory.

Goods which are held for sale or lease are classified as inventory. The Comment to Section 9-109, U.C.C., states that the classifications are mutually exclusive and that the principal test to deter-mine whether goods are inventory is whether they are held for immediate or ultimate sale. In borderline cases the principal use to which the property is put should be considered determinative.

As to the cattle which were sold on February 1, 1969, and May 17, 1969, there is no evidence as to their origin. In the absence of any evidence to show affirmatively that these cattle were not a part of the farming and ranching operation of Faden the trial court could have concluded that they were farm products.

As to the cattle which were sold on December 20, 1969, January 17, 1970, February 21, 1970, and March 28, 1970, the evidence shows affirmatively and without dispute that they were purchased in Torrington, Wyoming, 1 or 2 days before they were shipped to Gering, Nebraska, for sale. These cattle were goods held for immediate sale and there is nothing to indicate they had any connection whatsoever with Faden's farming and ranching operation in Banner County. Under the facts in this case these cattle were inventory as a matter of law.

It is clear from the terms of the security agreement that the plaintiff and Faden intended to create a security interest in livestock used or bought primarily for farming operations and not business operations. The bank may not have been aware of Faden's activities as a cattle trader but the record establishes that the transactions involved in this case were not isolated instances. . . .

The evidence in this case does not support the finding of the trial court that the plaintiff had a security interest in all the livestock owned by Faden and involved in this action. The judgment must, therefore, be

Reversed and remanded.

Gibbs v. King
564 S.W.2d 515 (Ark. 1978)

HOWARD, J. We are to decide whether the holding of the trial court, sitting without a jury, that the possession of a Caterpillar D8 tractor, hereinafter referred to as tractor, by appellee is held pursuant to a pledge, as claimed by appellee, rather than pursuant to a sale, as asserted by appellant, is supported by substantial evidence.

Sometime during the early part of 1973, appellant, Jim Gibbs, acquired a truck from Interna-tional Harvester Company . . . hereinafter referred to as International, where appellee, Vernie King, is employed as a salesman. Appellant immediately discovered that the truck needed necessary repairs—the replacement of a defective clutch and the repair of the truck's brakes—in order to make the truck operative upon the highways. Consequently, the truck was returned to International by appellant.

Approximately one month after the truck had been returned to International, appellant was advised that the truck had been repaired and appellant was presented "a pretty big bill." Appellant decided that he did not want the truck, but appellee persuaded appellant to accept the truck and, as a further inducement to get appellant to keep the truck, appellee loaned appellant $1,250.00 to be applied to the repair bill.

Appellee prepared a financing statement, which was signed by appellant, that identifies appellant as debtor, appellee as the secured party and identifies the property covered as the tractor in question, serial number 8D81776 with the figure "$1,248.05" written on the face of the document. This document was filed with the Circuit Clerk of Jefferson County on March 12, 1973. However, the record does not reflect that a security agreement was ever executed nor was possession of the tractor delivered to appellee at the time the financing statement was executed and filed.

On September 12, 1974, appellee went to appellant's home . . . and took possession of the tractor. However, before taking possession, a written instrument which is a printed retail order containing blank spaces and used by International in connection with the sale of used vehicles, was executed by both appellant and appellee after certain blank spaces had been filled in by appellee. This written document designates appellant as seller and appellee as purchaser of "1 D8 Cat., serial No. 8D81776" and "1 Set of Rails and Rollers" for a "cash price of $5,000.00" and a down payment of "$1,248.05" with an "unpaid cash price of $4,752.05." The written document further provides that the unpaid balance shall be paid in "12 installments of $396.00 each." The document further specifies that "This vehicle is sold 'As Is' with no warranty as to mechanical condition unless otherwise endorsed by seller on the reverse side.". . .

On September 7, 1977, appellant instituted action in the Circuit Court of Jefferson County seeking judgment against appellee for the unpaid balance due on the tractor. . . . [The trial court held]

that the subject of this lawsuit, this Caterpillar D8 Tractor, was never anything more than a pledge for the indebtedness of Mr. Gibbs to Mr. King in the amount of One Thousand Two Hundred and Forty-eight and 05/100 ($1,248.05) Dollars.

As a consequence of this holding, appellant-plaintiff's complaint was dismissed. . . .

Inasmuch as this record is void of any security agreement executed by appellant granting a security interest in the tractor to appellee and the evidence further reflects that appellee did not take possession of the tractor when the financing statement was executed, appellee had no valid security interest in the tractor even though the financing statement was filed for record in the office of the Circuit Clerk of Jefferson County, Arkansas.

Appellee argues that when he took possession of the tractor on September 12, 1974, some twenty months after the execution and filing of the financing statement, he received the tractor as a pledge to secure the indebtedness owed by appellant to appellee. This argument is neither persuasive nor convincing inasmuch as if we accepted this argument, we would be required to close our eyes completely to the existence of a written agreement prepared by appellee which clearly and conclusively shows that the tractor was delivered to appellee on September 12, 1974, in connection with a sale and purchase agreement made between appellant and appellee. The document sets forth in detail the contract price, designates appellant's indebtedness owed to appellee as a down payment and the unpaid balance is to be paid out in 12 monthly installments of $396.00 each. These facts do not support a pledge.

After carefully reviewing all of the evidence in this case and giving every reasonable inference derived therefrom in the light most favorable to appellee, we conclude that the trial court's holding is not supported by substantial evidence, and consequently, we reverse and remand this case.

So ordered.

Chapman Parts Warehouse, Inc. v. Guderian
609 S.W.2d 317 (Tex. 1980)

SHANNON, J. . . . On December 7, 1977, Bill Senter and Chapman Parts signed a franchise agreement whereby Chapman Parts was to provide Senter, among other things, an initial inventory of

automobile parts and assistance in opening a "Mr. C Auto Parts Store" in Austin, at 6325 Cameron Road. Pursuant to the agreement, Chapman Parts delivered the initial inventory to Bill Senter, Inc., on June 8, 1978. Bill Senter, Inc., paid for the inventory by check drawn by Senter, dated June 8, 1978, in the sum of $38,317.00. That check was dishonored and returned to Chapman Parts.

Upon return of the check, and within ten days from date of the delivery of the inventory, Chapman Parts gave notice to Bill Senter, Inc., by letter dated June 15, 1978, that the franchise agreement was revoked. The next day, Chapman Parts also gave Senter notice of foreclosure and repossession of the inventory located at the store on Cameron Road. In an effort to effect repossession, Chapman Parts caused the locks on the Cameron Road store to be changed on June 16, 1978. Chapman Parts did not file a financing statement with the Secretary of State concerning the inventory.

On June 22, 1978, Senter and Bill Senter, Inc., entered into a financing arrangement with Travis Bank and Trust whereby a note and security agreement were executed and the bank lent Bill Senter, Inc., $4,500.00. By the security agreement, the bank took as security "all inventory located [at the Cameron Road store] or wherever located in the future," and "all inventory now owned or hereafter acquired." The bank filed a financing statement (Form UCC-1) with the Secretary of State on June 28, 1978.

The bank sold the note to appellee Guderian for $4,500.00 on July 24, 1978. Contemporaneous with the purchase of the note, the bank assigned the security agreement and security interest in the inventory to appellee. On the following day, appellee filed suit.

After a bench trial, the district court entered judgment favorable to appellee.

Chapman Parts' pivotal point of error is that the district court erred in holding that the security interest of appellee had priority over appellant's claim to the inventory. Appellee defends the judgment of the district court upon the basis that she, as a secured party, had a perfected prior interest in the inventory.

Appellee's security interest was not enforceable against Chapman Parts with respect to the collateral unless the security interest had "attached" to the collateral. A security interest "attaches" when it becomes enforceable against the debtor with respect to the collateral. Section 9.203(b) provides that attachment occurs as soon as all of the following events have transpired.

(1) the collateral is in the possession of the secured party pursuant to agreement or the debtor has signed a security agreement which contains a description of the collateral; and

(2) value has been given; and

(3) the debtor has rights in the collateral.

Chapman Parts claims that the debtor Bill Senter, Inc., had no rights in the inventory of parts because the debtor's rights were terminated by Chapman Parts' prior reclamation of the inventory. The argument is that since the debtor had no rights in the collateral, appellee's security interest had not "attached" to the collateral, and cannot be given priority over Chapman Parts interest obtained through reclamation. . . .

Those courts recognizing reclamation under §2.507 have adhered to the express requirement in §2.507 Comment 3 that demand for return be made within ten days after receipt of the goods by the buyer, or else the right is lost.

This Court has concluded that Chapman Parts, by timely exercise of its right of reclamation, terminated the debtor's rights in the inventory of parts. Appellee's security interest, therefore, was not enforceable against Chapman Parts since her security interest had not "attached."

Chapman Parts followed the procedure for reclamation. As previously noticed, Chapman Parts gave timely notice of reclamation, foreclosure, and repossession to Bill Senter, Inc. Further, Chapman Parts caused the locks to be changed on the Cameron Road store. By changing the locks, and thereby excluding Bill Senter, Inc., from the store, Chapman Parts, in effect, repossessed the parts inventory prior to the execution of the security agreement under which appellee claims a prior right.

Any right Bill Senter, Inc., may have had in the inventory of parts was extinguished by Chapman Parts' reclamation. Accordingly, neither Bill Senter nor Bill Senter, Inc., could thereafter transfer or sell any interest in the inventory.

Reversed and remanded.

First National Bank in Creston v. Francis 342 N.W.2d 468 (Ia. 1984)

WOLLE, J. Plaintiff First National Bank in Creston, Iowa, appeals from the district court's order granting defendant Farmers Cooperative Company's motion for summary judgment. The sole issue presented is whether the bank's incorrect description of real estate on which encumbered crops would be found nevertheless imparted constructive notice to the cooperative of the claimed security interest. . . .

The bank loaned money to David Francis for his farming operations. To secure the loan the bank prepared and had Francis execute a security agreement and financing statement in favor of the bank. Both documents secured, among other items, growing crops (and proceeds) on land described as the southeast one-quarter of section 24, township 71 north, range 32 in Grant Township, Adams County, Iowa. That description was in error, the bank had intended to refer not to section 24 but to section 25 (where Francis lived on a farm his father owned). The financing statement was duly filed with the secretary of state.

The bank brought this action against Francis when his financial situation worsened; the cooperative was joined as a defendant because it had purchased grain from Francis after the bank's financing statement had been filed. Neither Francis nor the cooperative had paid the bank the proceeds from the sale of grain which Francis had produced on section 25 and on land he was farming in three other counties. . . . [T]he district court granted the cooperative's motion for summary judgment, finding the bank's description seriously misleading because it erroneously referred to crops located on a specific quarter of section 24 when the bank intended to encumber other crops. We must answer the question of law arising from these undisputed facts by applying Iowa statutes which require that a secured party sufficiently describe its secured property.

Two provisions of the Iowa Commercial Code specifically provide that when a financing statement covers crops growing or to be grown, the filed documents must include a description of the real estate concerned. Iowa Code Section 9-203 provides in pertinent part that:

> a security interest is not enforceable against . . . third parties with respect to the collateral and does not attach unless . . . a security agreement . . . contains a description of the collateral and in addition, when the security interest covers crops growing or to be grown . . . a description of the land concerned;

Similarly, Iowa Code section 9-402(1) provides:

> When the financing statement covers crops growing or to be grown, the statement must also contain a description of the real estate concerned.

Two other code provisions relax somewhat these and other description requirements. Iowa Code section 9-402(8) provides:

> A financing statement substantially complying with the requirements of this section is effective even though it contains minor errors which are not seriously misleading.

Additionally, Iowa Code section 9-110 provides:

> For the purpose of this Article any description of personal property or real estate is sufficient whether or not it is specific if it reasonably identifies what is described.

Thus, a person securing crops, as distinguished from other personal property, must include a description of the real estate where the crops are produced or located. That description, however need not be specific "if it reasonably identifies what is described," and the description may even contain "minor errors which are not seriously misleading.". . .

Our decision must turn not on whether the description was sufficient to secure crops but whether it was so specific that it could only reasonably be read to secure the crops on the described land. We agree with the trial court's conclusion that the bank's erroneous specific description was "seriously misleading" and did not encumber the crops which the cooperative purchased.

The description was misleading because a person checking the filed documents would reasonably conclude that the only crops the bank intended to secure were those in the southeast one-quarter of section 24. Nothing in the bank's description would have caused the cooperative or some other person checking the record to suspect the section number was wrong or that the bank intended to encumber crops on other land. Consequently, this case is not controlled by the rule that a description is sufficient if the property "is described in such a manner as to enable third persons, aided by inquiries which the instrument itself indicates and directs, to identify the property. . . ." The purpose of the Code's description requirements for financing statements is to give notice to purchasers and third-party creditors and allow them to identify what property is secured. For crops, our legislature has required a description of the land to assist the third person in making that identification. When, as here, nothing in the instrument itself indicates or directs that further inquiry should be made concerning the location of the secured crops, the third person need not make further inquiry. The bank can point to nothing within the financing statement or security agreement which would have alerted third persons that the bank had made a mistake, and in fact intended to cover crops other than those at the specified location.

We do not imply by our decision that the party securing crops must give an exact legal description of the real estate where crops may be found. The description need only reasonably identify the land. . . .

The trial court correctly applied the Iowa Commercial Code to the undisputed facts in this case. The cooperative did not have constructive notice of the bank's claimed security interest in crops on land other than that specifically described in the instruments it filed with the Secretary of State.

Affirmed.

Matter of Glasco, Inc.
642 F.2d 793 (Fla. law 1981)

RONEY, J. The sole issue on appeal is whether a financing statement, filed with the Florida Secretary of State by a creditor, perfected a security interest in certain property of the bankrupt debtor. The bankruptcy court held the financing statement to be inadequate because it listed the debtor by the name in which it did business rather than its legal corporate name. The district court affirmed. . . .

To perfect a security interest in collateral, a creditor must file a financing statement which complies with the filing requirements of the Uniform Commercial Code, as adopted in Florida. The purpose of the filing system is to give notice to creditors and other interested parties that a security interest exists in property of the debtor. Perfect accuracy, however, is not required as long as the financing statement contains sufficient information to "put any searcher on inquiry." The emphasis of the Uniform Commercial Code is thus on commercial realities rather than on corporate technicalities. Section 9-402(5) reflects this emphasis by providing: "A financing statement substantially complying with the requirements of this section is effective even though it contains minor errors which are not seriously misleading."

The effect of errors in the listing of the debtor's name has been the subject of extensive litigation. The decisions appear generally to turn on the particular factual circumstances involved. The case here, then, must be judged on its own facts, with the focus on whether potential creditors would have been misled as a result of the name the debtor was listed by in the bank's financing statement.

It is undisputed the debtor held itself out to the community and to creditors as "Elite Boats, Division of Glasco, Inc." Its checks, stationery, and bank account all bore the latter name. Apparently the same name was used in its bills, contracts and telephone listing, because there is no indication in the record the debtor ever used the name of just "Glasco, Inc.," or any other name. Thus, listing the debtor by the sole name in which it did business was not misleading, because any reasonably prudent creditor would have requested the Secretary of State to search under "Elite Boats" in addition to "Glasco, Inc." Of course, the trustee in bankruptcy is considered to be in the position of a hypothetical but prudent creditor.

The trustee relies on several cases each involving an individual who is engaged in business under an assumed trade name. These cases generally hold that a financing statement listing only the trade name as the debtor will be insufficient to perfect a security interest effective against the individual. There is a crucial distinction, however, between these cases and the case here. In the former, a single debtor is necessarily held out to the credit community under two names, that of the individual and of the business. The individual's credit for personal needs is unrelated to the business. A personal creditor would not necessarily be aware of the business or trade name, and thus may not discover security interests filed solely under the business name. In the present case, where the company does business only under one name, the opportunity for creditors to be misled is substantially reduced, even though that name is not the company's "true name."

We hold the listing of the debtor as "Elite Boats, Division of Glasco, Inc." rather than as

"Glasco, Inc." was not seriously misleading. The financing statement was therefore in substantial compliance with the filing requirements under Florida law and was sufficient to perfect the bank's security interest. . . .

Reversed.

Noble v. Bonnett
577 P.2d 248 (Ariz. 1978)

GORDON, J. Contemporaneously with a loan of money and credit by Lila Bonnett, to her son, Louis, Louis transferred the title to his 1971 Dodge to Lila, the appellee herein. It was understood between the parties that Louis was to remain the owner of the car and that Lila was to hold the title in her name solely as a security device until Louis satisfied his obligations under the loans. Soon thereafter William and Virginia Noble, judgment creditors of Louis and appellants herein, levied upon the Dodge which Louis had retained in his possession. . . .

After the trial of appellee's claim, the trial judge determined that, although Louis was the owner of the Dodge, and hence had a property interest theoretically subject to execution by his judgment creditors, appellee had a security interest in the vehicle in an amount equal to its value that was superior to the claim of appellants. The Court of Appeals agreed that Louis had interests in the Dodge that were subject to execution. However, in a memorandum decision, it reversed holding that appellee did not have a valid security interest as a matter of law because she failed to properly perfect her interest. . . . We accepted review to resolve questions as to the proper method of perfecting a security interest in an automobile.

As a preliminary matter, it should be noted that the Uniform Commercial Code on Secured Transactions defers to any state statute that requires indication of a security interest on a certificate of title as the exclusive source of law under which a security interest can be perfected in property subject to that statute. For automobiles the special statute in Arizona states:

> No conditional sale contract, conditional lease, chattel mortgage or other lien or encumbrance, title retention instrument or other instrument affecting or evidencing title to, ownership of, or reservation of title to any registered vehicle, other than a lien dependent upon possession, is valid as against the creditors of an owner acquiring a lien by levy or attachment, or subsequent purchasers or encumbrancers without notice, until the requirements of this section have been complied with.

. . . [Other sections of the Arizona law] proceed to dictate a detailed process by which a security interest in an automobile is perfected. First, the secured party must deposit a copy of the instrument creating the security interest with the motor vehicle division along with the certificate of title last issued for the vehicle. If the vehicle has not yet been registered, the copy of the instrument creating the lien must be accompanied by the owner's application for an original registration and certificate of title.

When satisfied as to the genuineness of the application, the motor vehicle division issues a new certificate of title, listing the name of the owner and a statement of all encumbrances that have been certified to the division as existing against the vehicle. The issuance of a new certificate of title constitutes constructive notice to creditors or subsequent purchasers of all liens against the vehicle except those authorized by law that are dependent upon possession. . . .

It is clear that the appellant's unorthodox method of taking a security interest did not meet the requirements of . . . [the Arizona law]. Hence, the issue on appeal is reduced to whether her failure to do so automatically rendered her security interest invalid vis-a-vis the appellants.

It is appellee's contention . . . that the sole problem envisaged by the Legislature when drafting this provision was the situation where title to the vehicle is in the name of the owner and a secured creditor of the owner who has not recorded his interest in any manner attempts to assert that interest against a bona fide purchaser or subsequent creditor of the owner. By contrast, appellee contends that where the secured party takes title in her own name, there is no hidden interest and, hence, no potential for fraud because subsequent creditors are on notice of the interest of the secured party. . . .

Regardless of whether the Legislature considered the specific problem presented in this case, it is our view that the goal of preventing fraud in automobile transactions will be well served by our refusal to sanction the taking of title in the name of the secured party as a valid security device. If we were to approve of this method, there would always be the danger that the secured party, having the indicia of ownership, would defraud the true owner of the vehicle by transferring it to a bona fide purchaser. . . .

This case is remanded for proceedings not inconsistent with this opinion.

So ordered.

REVIEW QUESTIONS

1. Match each term in column A with the appropriate statement in Column B.

A	B
1. Unsecured creditor	**a.** The essential element in the creation and enforceability of a security agreement.
2. Tangible goods	**b.** Exists when either a seller or lender, as a secured party, lends the money that enables the debtor to buy the collateral.
3. Inventory	**c.** A general classification of collateral that has a physical nature.
4. Chattel paper	**d.** The document that must be filed to perfect a security interest.
5. General intangible	**e.** A category of collateral held by a business debtor for resale.
6. Attachment	**f.** A party whose only collateral is the debtor's promise to repay.
7. Security agreement	**g.** A catchall category of collateral.
8. Financing statement	**h.** Another name for perfection by attachment.
9. Automatic perfection	**i.** A writing that evidences both an obligation to pay money and a security interest or lease.
10. Purchase money security interest	**j.** An essential document that must be signed by the debtor if he retains possession of the collateral if a security interest is to be created.
11. Floating lien	**k.** Arises from the sale of collateral.
12. Proceed	**l.** Created when a creditor's security interest covers after-acquired collateral or future advances or both.

2. Donald Laughlin signed a contract to lease an airplane from U C Leasing, Inc., as lessor. The fair market value of the plane involved was $55,000. The lease agreement required Laughlin, as lessee, to make rental payments of $1,144 per month for 5 years. At the end of the lease, Laughlin could retain possession of the plane by paying an additional $5,500. Under the terms of the contract, Laughlin was to bear the risk of loss, pay all taxes and fees, and pay insurance premiums. The lessor disclaimed all implied and expressed warranties. The contract also provided that if the lease was terminated prematurely, Laughlin would become liable to pay a dollar amount equal to the percentage of lessor's original purchase price as revealed in the contract. After only nine monthly payments, Laughlin did default. The lessor reacquired the plane, sold it, and sued for the deficiency owed by the lessee. Laughlin argued that this lease was really an instrument of security and that the lessor had not complied with Article 9 provisions governing rights and duties on default. The lessor contended this contract was a lease governed by its own terms. Which party has the more correct argument? Why?

3. Classification of collateral may not be as easy as the text indicates. Try to classify the following collateral correctly:

   a. Burns Rentals leases and sells TV sets and cars. Burns obtains financing from City Bank, enabling him to buy 25 new cars and 100 new TV sets. Classify the cars and TV sets.

   b. Burns has 50 cars on his lot for lease. Classify the cars.

   c. Burns sells a truck to Boyce and retains a security interest in the truck. Boyce uses the truck exclusively for weekend camping and fishing trips. Classify the truck.

   d. Burns assigns Boyce's promissory note and security agreement to City Bank as collateral for a loan. Classify the collateral.

   e. Burns Rentals buys 300 new Philco TV sets for his annual summer sale. Classify the TV sets in the hands of Philco; in Burns's possession. Virgil, owner of Virgil's Truck City and Bar, buys a TV set during the sale. The set is delivered to Virgil in its original carton and put in the back of his sixteen-wheeler. What type of goods did Virgil buy?

   f. When Philco sells TV sets to Burns, it packages them in special shipping cartons, using packaging materials such as styrofoam and excelsior. Philco maintains a large supply of these materials. Classify them.

   g. Burns has a large supply of diesel fuel and oil for his fleet of trucks. Classify the diesel fuel, oil, and trucks.

4. The categories of instruments and chattel paper, as potential collateral, frequently are confused. What is the basic difference between an instrument and chattel paper?

5. The 1972 revision of Article 9 requires *attachment* for the creation of a security interest. Describe the required steps necessary for attachment to occur.

6. Walker purchased Terminal Moving & Storage Company by making a small down payment and signing a promissory note for the remainder of the purchase price. On the same day, Walker, as sole owner, granted a security interest in all the corporation's assets to the seller. The seller later assigned the security interest and the note to a third party, who assigned them to Putnam. When the corporation went bankrupt a few years later, the bankruptcy trustee contended that Putnam did not have a valid security interest. The trustee argued that the security interest was given without any consideration being given to the corporation itself. Therefore, the security interest did not attach because no value had been given. Did Putnam have a valid security interest? Explain.

7. Tom and Marie Shafer purchased a household washing machine and dishwasher on credit from the Georgia Power Company (GPC). GPC took purchase money security interests in each of these appliances that were perfected by attachment. Later, the Shafers granted security interests in these same appliances to Personal Thrift as collateral for a loan. Personal Thrift perfected its interests by filing a proper financing statement. The Shafers defaulted on all these loans, and Personal Thrift took possession of the appliances. GPC sued Personal Thrift, seeking to recover the two appliances. Personal Thrift argued that GPC's automatic perfection was unconstitutional as a violation of equal protection and due process. Is perfection by attachment constitutional? Explain.

8. Paula, an accountant, lent money to a company already indebted to her for services rendered. As security for the loan and to secure payment for the services, the company assigned to Paula a portion of its expected recovery of a pending lawsuit. Paula did not file a financing statement with regard to the assignment. Subsequently, Debra was awarded a judgment against the company in another lawsuit. Debra, without knowledge of the assignment to Paula, had the sheriff levy against the company's property. At the sheriff's execution sale, all the company's rights in the pending lawsuit were sold to

Debra. When that lawsuit was settled, Paula claimed rights to the proceeds. Is Paula entitled to the proceeds of the lawsuit under her security interest? Explain.

9. Cable Services of Florida, Inc., purchased a backhoe and financed the purchase with ITT Industrial Credit Company. ITT prepared a security agreement that required Cable to insure the backhoe. Cable did acquire insurance through the Insurance Management Corporation (IMC), which agreed to lend Cable the money for the insurance premium. This insurance actually was issued by U.S.F.&G. Company. The backhoe was stolen, and the parties claimed the benefits under this insurance policy. IMC received a check from U.S.F.&G. as payment under the policy. ITT, as a secured party, claimed this insurance money as a proceed from the backhoe. IMC claimed a portion of these insurance benefits as payment of its loan to Cable for the insurance premiums. Is money paid under an insurance policy a proceed to which the secured party is entitled? Why?

10. By answering the following, check your knowledge of the business decisions involved in secured transactions:

   a. Assume you are a retailer with a large amount of outstanding accounts receivable and you are in need of cash to pay expenses. How might you raise the necessary cash? Explain.

   b. Assume you are considering lending to Fred Tauber of Tauber & Sons and taking a security interest in certain property of Tauber & Sons. What should you do prior to lending the money? Explain.

   c. Assume you are arranging to finance another's business. It will be a secured financing plan that works on a continuing basis. What provisions should you require for inclusion in the security agreement and in the financing statement? Explain.

   d. Assume you are a secured party and are in doubt about whether you have to file and, if so, where. What do you do? Explain.

33 ISSUES IN ARTICLE 9 TRANSACTIONS

The previous chapter covers how a security interest is created and how it is perfected. For the most part, in this chapter we assume that these essential steps have been accomplished. The dominant theme of this chapter is whether a perfected secured party has priority over others claiming an interest in the personal property being used as collateral. By "priority," we mean the party first in line to have its claim paid from the proceeds made from the sale of the collateral.

This chapter examines two issues: First, when does a perfected secured party not have priority to the collateral? Second, what is the logic for allowing a third party to defeat a secured party's claim of priority? The answers to these questions make up the majority of this chapter. In particular, sections 1 through 15 address the issues of priority. The last portion of this chapter (sections 16 through 22) is concerned with the parties' rights and duties when the debtor defaults.

1. Priority Issues in General

Collateral is frequently the subject of conflicting claims. Two or more persons may claim a security interest in the same collateral, or a person may claim that he has a better right to the collateral than does the secured party. Interests that may compete with the secured party's claim of priority fall into the following two basic categories: (1) those who purchase the collateral from the debtor, and (2) those who are creditors of the debtor. These creditors may be further subdivided into those that have a conflicting security interest in the same collateral and those that have some other lien on the collateral. Among the many ways in which conflicting claims to collateral may arise, the following are some of the more important situations:

1. A debtor sells the collateral to a good-faith purchaser who may or may not know of the security interest.

2. A debtor gives more than one security interest in the same collateral.

3. Collateral becomes attached to real property, so that it is a fixture.

4. Collateral becomes attached to personal property that belongs to another or in which another has security interest.

5. Collateral has been processed (such as raw material, in which there is a security interest, being converted into a finished product).

6. The government or some other creditor claims a lien on the property.

7. Collateral has been repaired or improved by the services or materials of another.

8. A trustee in bankruptcy claims the collateral in connection with a bankruptcy case involving the debtor.

In all these situations, as well as in many others, it is necessary to sort out the conflicting interests and determine the priority among them. Keep in mind that the priority of a secured party's claim often is determined by whether or not the secured party has perfected his security interest. The general rule of Article 9 regarding priority is that after perfection, the secured party is protected against (1) those who purchase the collateral from the debtor, (2) those who are creditors of the debtors, and (3) those who represent creditors in insolvency proceedings instituted by, or against, the debtor. The bulk of the following material involves exceptions to this general rule. In addition to these exceptions, a secured party that has priority to collateral may agree, explicitly or implicitly, to subordinate its claim in preference to the rights of a third party.

SECURED PARTY VERSUS BUYERS OF COLLATERAL

2. Introduction

We now turn our attention to the secured party's priority when the collateral is sold or transferred to a third party. In general, the secured party's security interest continues in any collateral sold or transferred unless the security agreement authorizes such a sale or transfer. This general rule makes sense, since the secured party and the debtor are free to make any legal agreement they wish. The more difficult issue arises when the debtor sells the collateral without the secured party's approval. Under Section 9-306(2), if the debtor makes an unauthorized sale or transfer, the security interest usually continues in the collateral in the hands of the buyer.[1] However, there are three situations when buyers take priority over the secured party, even though the sale was unauthorized. These situations are considered in the next three sections.

---

[1] Matteson v. Harper, p. 743.

3. Buyers in the Ordinary Course of Business

A buyer in the ordinary course of business "takes free of a security interest created by his seller even though the security interest is perfected and even though the buyer knows of its existence" [9-307(1)]. A buyer in the ordinary course of business is a buyer who buys goods from a seller who is in the business of selling goods of that kind [1-201(9)].[2] When you buy goods at the grocery store, department store, and gas station, you are a buyer in the ordinary course of business. In general, a transaction in the ordinary course of business involves the sale of a seller's inventory.

The reason for giving priority to a buyer in the ordinary course of business is obvious. When you buy goods from a professional seller, you expect to get clear title to the goods and would never think that they might be subject to a security interest. This rule, then, simply codifies the customary expectations of buyers in our society. It has been applied to buyers of new cars from a dealership and to a dealer buyer who buys from another dealer. Generally this rule would not apply if you bought a used car from a car repair garage, since the garage is not in the business of selling cars on a daily basis. In other words, the garage does not sell cars in the ordinary course of its business.

The buyer-in-ordinary-course-of-business rule does not apply to a person buying farm products from a person engaged in farming operations [9-307(1)]. Typically, farmers or ranchers get loans and grant security interests in their crops or cattle. This rule allows the secured party to follow its security interest into the hands of a cattle buyer or a grain elevator or food processor. To understand the reason for this exception, you need only ask who makes most of the loans to farmers and ranchers—the federal government. If state law did not grant priority to the government's security interest over buyers of farm products, then the government might refuse to lend money to farmers. Due to this exception to the buyer-in-ordinary-course-of-business rule, it becomes very important to determine what type of collateral is involved in the creation of a security interest.

4. Buyers of Consumer Goods

The rules stated in the preceding section do not apply when a buyer purchases consumer goods from a consumer debtor. The consumer debtor, by definition, cannot sell his property in the ordinary course of business. This is because, as a consumer, the seller is not engaged in a business activity. In chapter 32, we learned that a secured party with a purchase-money security interest (PMSI) in consumer goods is automatically perfected when the security interest is created. In other words, a PMSI in consumer goods is perfected by attachment. Nevertheless, a secured party who relies on this automatic perfection may lose his priority. As the next paragraph explains, a secured party with a PMSI in consumer goods has to file a financing statement to be assured of priority over a consumer buyer of the collateral.

Section 9-307(2) allows a consumer buyer of consumer goods from a

---

[2] Antigo Co-op Credit Union v. Miller, p. 743.

consumer debtor to take free of the PMSI "unless prior to the purchase the secured party has filed a financing statement covering such goods." Suppose that Smith buys a sofa from Furniture Company and gives it a PMSI in the sofa for the unpaid purchase price. Furniture Company does not file a financing statement. A few months later, Smith sells the sofa to her next-door neighbor, Jones, who uses the sofa in his home. Although Furniture Company has an automatically perfected security interest in the sofa, the sale is free of that PMSI if Jones paid value, did not know of the PMSI, and uses the sofa for consumer purposes [9-307(2)]. This example shows that Section 9-307(2) applies when a consumer debtor (Smith) sells consumer goods (sofa) to another consumer (Jones). If Furniture Company had filed a financing statement, Jones's purchase would be subject to the PMSI. In the alternative, if Jones had purchased this sofa from Smith for a resale in his used furniture store, Jones's purchase would be subject to the Furniture Company's security interest even if the Furniture Company had not filed a financing statement. This result is logical because, in this latter example, Jones is not a consumer buyer and the sofa no longer is a consumer good. This sofa has become inventory in Jones's used furniture store.

5. Buyers of Chattel Paper and Instruments

In the preceding section we saw that the secured party's reliance on automatic perfection by attachment does not assure priority to the collateral. There are situations other than the PMSI in consumer goods when a secured party may be automatically perfected by attachment. First, remember the 21-day time periods with respect to perfection of an interest in instruments. (Review section 14 of chapter 32.) Second, recall the possibility of a secured party's being perfected by attachment for 10 days with respect to proceeds. (See section 18 of the preceding chapter.) In order to be consistent with the rules regarding a PMSI in consumer goods, Article 9 also provides rules governing priority between a buyer of chattel paper or instruments or both and a secured party who has an interest in these items of collateral and who is relying on automatic perfection by attachment [9-308].

There are three typical situations in which a secured party may rely on perfection by attachment when the collateral is chattel paper or instruments or both. These three situations are as follows:

1. The chattel paper or instruments or both are proceeds from the sale of inventory collateral.
2. The chattel paper or instruments or both are proceeds from the sale of noninventory collateral.
3. The instruments are the original collateral. (If chattel paper is the original collateral, the secured party must file a financing statement or take possession in order to perfect the interest in chattel paper. Perfection by attachment is not possible if the original collateral is chattel paper.)

To illustrate the first situation, suppose that a retail merchant has financed its inventory with the First State Bank. This bank has a security interest in the merchant's inventory, and it has perfected this interest by filing a financing statement describing the inventory. As a part of its daily business activity, the merchant will sell some of its inventory. Assume that one buyer signs an installment sales contract which grants the merchant a security interest in the items sold. This installment sales contract, as a proceed from the sale of inventory, is chattel paper. Further assume that another buyer simply signs a promissory note when buying some of the merchant's inventory. This transaction creates an instrument as a proceed. Now assume that these two transactions are repeated numerous times. Since the merchant probably is in need of money, he may wish to sell these "paper" proceeds. Assume that the merchant does sell these items of chattel paper and instruments to the Second State Bank within 5 days of selling the inventory from which these items are proceeds. Which bank has priority to the proceeds? The First State Bank claims to have priority with respect to these proceeds as a secured party perfected under the 10-day rule of automatic perfection. The Second State Bank claims priority as a buyer who has possession of and who has paid value for these proceeds. The Second State Bank has priority. A purchaser of chattel paper or an instrument who pays value and who takes possession of it in the ordinary course of business takes priority over a security interest in the chattel paper or instrument which is claimed merely as proceeds from the sale of inventory [9-308(b)]. This rule applies even if the purchaser had knowledge of the secured party's security interest in these proceeds.

The rule that governs the other two situations described above is a little different. If the chattel paper or instruments were proceeds from the sale of noninventory collateral or if the instruments were the original collateral, a buyer of these items in the ordinary course of business has priority only if he does not have any knowledge of the secured party's security interest in the chattel paper or instruments [9-308(a)]. For example, suppose that the merchant granted to the First State Bank a security interest in equipment as well as inventory. Assume that this bank files a financing statement describing the collateral as inventory, equipment, and chattel paper. Now suppose that the merchant sells a piece of equipment in return for chattel paper and then sells the chattel paper to the Second State Bank. That bank is subject to the First State Bank's interest in the chattel paper, since Second State Bank had constructive knowledge of First State Bank's interest in chattel paper via the financing statement's being properly filed.

Of course, a financing statement describing the collateral as instruments does not protect a secured party. Remember, perfection in instruments can be achieved only through possession. Indeed, the real lesson of Section 9-308 and of this discussion is that a secured party has not *absolutely* perfected its interest in chattel paper as proceeds or in instruments as proceeds or original collateral until it has taken possession of these items of collateral.

6. Introduction

Two or more creditors may obtain security interests covering the same collateral. If the value of the collateral is less than the total of the claims it secures, upon the debtor's default it will be necessary to determine the priority of competing security interests.

Section 9-312 governs most secured party versus secured party priority

SECURED PARTY VERSUS SECURED PARTY

contests. It contains special rules to be applied when the conflicting security interests are regular or when at least one of the interests is a purchase-money security interest. The general rule governing priority between regular perfected security interests in the same collateral is found in Section 9-312(5)(a) of the Code.

This section basically provides a first-in-time rule. In other words, the first creditor to file or to perfect, *whichever occurs first,* will have priority. This rule emphasizes the special status of filing a financing statement. Remember, filing can occur at any time, even prior to attachment. The Code adopts a pure "race type" statute; the first to file or perfect wins. Knowledge is unimportant. The benefit of a race statute is that it provides for certainty and predictability. Whichever party wins the race has priority.

This first-in-time rule also makes it advantageous to be perfected by attachment. Suppose a retail merchant sold a refrigerator to Smith to be used in Smith's home. Assume the merchant sold this refrigerator to Smith on credit, and the merchant had Smith sign a security agreement. This merchant is automatically perfected by attachment, since he has a PMSI in consumer goods. If Smith then granted a security interest in this refrigerator to a bank in return for a loan, the bank must file a financing statement to be perfected. If Smith defaults on his payments to both the merchant and the bank, which party has priority to the refrigerator? The merchant has priority, since he was perfected before the bank filed. Section 9-312(5)(a) states that the creditor who files *or* perfects first has priority.

There are a number of exceptions to this general rule, and each is designed to meet the needs of a specific commercial situation. The next five sections examine some of these exceptions. For example, a secured party with a PMSI enjoys a preferred status in some situations.

7. PMSI in Inventory Collateral

In order to be really protected, a secured party with a security interest in inventory usually will insist upon having the security agreement contain an after-acquired inventory clause. If that security interest is perfected by filing, the general rule is that this secured party will have priority over a later secured party, since he was first in time. However, what happens if the debtor wants to finance a new line of inventory? This general rule effectively stops the debtor unless the secured party is willing to make a future advance. For the purpose of allowing the debtor more control over his inventory, Section 9-312(3) creates an exception to this general rule.

For example, a bank lends a store money secured by all the store's inventory now owned or hereafter acquired. The bank properly files a financing statement. A year later, a loan company advances money to allow the store to acquire a new line of appliances. Before the new appliances arrive, the loan company properly files a financing statement covering the appliances. An officer of the loan company then writes to the loan officer of the bank and explains that the loan company intends to finance the new appliances for the store on a PMSI. The loan company now has priority over the bank, but only in relation to the new appliances.

The requirements of Section 9-312(3) are rather simple. First, the PMSI secured party must perfect its PMSI and give the other secured party *written* notice that it has (or expects to have) a PMSI in certain described inventory. Perfection and notice must occur prior to the debtor's receiving the inventory. The purpose of the notice is to protect the first secured party so that he will not make new loans based on the after-acquired inventory or otherwise rely on the new inventory as his collateral.

It is not important whether the perfection of the PMSI or the notification to the preexisting secured party occurs first. What is important is that these steps must occur before the debtor takes possession of the new inventory.[3]

8. PMSI in Noninventory Collateral

For collateral other than inventory, a purchase-money security interest is superior to conflicting security interests in the same collateral, provided the purchase-money security interest is perfected at the time the debtor receives the collateral or within ten days thereafter [9-312(4)]. Thus, prior notice to other secured parties is not required in cases of equipment if the security interest is perfected within 10 days after the debtor receives the equipment. The prior notice requirement is limited to a PMSI in new inventory under Section 9-312(3).

Why is prior notice required for inventory, but not other classifications of collateral? The answer is that secured parties are likely to rely on the debtor's inventory more than on other types of collateral as a primary source of repayment. In other words, the sale of inventory is much more likely to produce regular income from which debts can be paid. Therefore, the secured parties need to be informed more readily about the fact that they cannot rely on new inventory. The lack of prior notice about new equipment being purchased on credit, for example, does not create a problem for the preexisting secured parties, since their reliance on that equipment should be minimal.

A secured party with a purchase-money security interest in noninventory collateral is given a special status for 10 days after the debtor receives the property. The protection during this period is limited. It gives priority over the rights of only (1) transferees in bulk (buyers of all or a substantial portion of a business) from the debtor, and (2) lien creditors, to the extent that such rights arise between the time the purchase-money security interest attaches and the time of filing [9-301(2)]. The purchase-money secured party is not protected against (1) a sale by the debtor to another party, or (2) a secured transaction in which the collateral is given as security for a loan during the period prior to filing. Of course, to remain continuously perfected, the secured party must file a financing statement or otherwise perfect during this 10-day period.

9. Fixtures

Personal property that is collateral for a secured party may be annexed to real estate. This annexation transforms the personal property into a fixture. Examples of fixtures would include an installed heating/air conditioning unit, a

---

[3] King's Appliance v. Citizens & Southern Bank, p. 745.

built-in kitchen appliance, and lighting and plumbing fixtures. The use of fixtures or potential fixtures as collateral raises a question of priority between the Article 9 secured party and one who has an interest in the real estate. These third parties with possible conflicting interests could include the owner of the real estate or a party who has a security interest in that real estate. (Chapter 34 discusses in detail the use of real property as security.)

The party that has priority is entitled, upon default, to remove the fixtures. This party is required to reimburse an encumbrancer or owner other than the debtor for the cost of repair of any physical damages caused by the removal [9-313(5)].

Building materials are clearly not classified as fixtures [9-313(2)]. The revised Code recognizes three categories of goods: (1) those that retain their chattel character and are not part of the real estate, (2) building materials that lose their chattel character entirely and are a part of the real estate, and (3) an intermediate class that becomes a part of the real estate for some purposes but may be a part of a secured transaction. The third category is *fixtures.*

The term *fixture filing* is used to require filing where a mortgage on real estate would be filed. The financing statement for fixture filing must (1) show that it covers fixtures, (2) recite that it is to be filed in the real estate records, (3) describe the real estate, and (4) show the name of the record owner if the debtor does not own the real estate.[4]

A mortgage may describe fixtures and thus be used as a financing statement. In such cases, the mortgage is exempt from the 5 year limitation on financing statements.

Two basic priority rules are based on fixture filing. First, there is the general rule that governs the potential conflict between a nonpurchase-money security interest in fixtures and a real estate interest. This rule is another one based on the first-in-time principle. For example, if the Article 9 security interest is fixture-filed before a mortgage is recorded, the fixture filer has priority. Of course, if the mortgage is recorded first, it has priority [9-313(4)(b)]. The second rule concerns purchase-money security interest in fixtures. If the fixture filing for a PMSI occurs before the goods become fixtures or within 10 days thereafter, the security interest is superior to any *earlier* realty interest, such as a prior recorded mortgage [9-313(4)(a)].

A special filing rule applies to soft fixtures (readily removable factory or office machines or readily removable replacements of domestic appliances). These fixtures can be perfected by any method allowed under Article 9, such as filing, taking possession, fixture filing, or automatic perfection. If you replace a stove (a fixture) in your house and give a PMSI to the seller, the PMSI in consumer goods (stove) would thus automatically be perfected [9-313(4)(c)].

A special priority provision for a construction loan gives it total priority [9-313(6)]. Thus, a security interest in fixtures added as part of new construction is always subordinate to the construction mortgage or to a mortgage given to refinance a construction mortgage.

---

[4] The Corning Bank v. The Bank of Rector, p. 746.

10. Accessions

In addition to being affixed to real estate, goods may be installed in or affixed to other goods. In general, this occurs when parts are added to personal property in order to repair that object. These parts are called *accessions*. When accessions are present, there is a possibility for conflict between a party with an interest in the repaired object and a party with an interest in the accessions. The confusing thing in determining which of these parties has priority is that the attachment (creation) of a security interest is as important as the perfection of that interest.

Two basic rules govern priority to accessions. First, a security interest that attaches to goods *before* they become accessions generally has priority over all persons' claims to the whole object. This rule applies regardless of whether the claims to the whole object arose before or after the accessions were installed [9-314(1)]. The second rule is applied when a security interest in goods attaches *after* they become accessions. In general, this security interest is superior to all subsequent claims to the whole object. However, preexisting claims to the whole object have priority over the security interest in the accessions [9-314(2)].

To help in your understanding of Section 9-314, consider this example. The Houston Oil Company owns a large air compressor which it uses in its oil and gas drilling operations. This compressor is part of the equipment in which the Bank of the Southwest has perfected a security interest. The basis of the bank's perfection is a financing statement filed on June 1, 1985. Last month, the company had the compressor repaired by the Hughes Tool Company. These repairs cost $30,000, and the company signed a security agreement granting to Hughes an interest in the parts installed in the compressor. If the company defaults on its payments to both the bank and Hughes, the rules stated above determine which party has priority to the accessions. If the Hughes Tool Company created its security interest before the repairs were made, it has priority. If the repairs were made and then the security interest was created (attached), the bank has priority. Upon the debtor's default, the secured party with priority can remove its collateral from the whole. However, this party must make payment for the cost of repair of any physical damage caused by removal [9-314(4)].

These general rules on priority to accessions are subject to two exceptions. First, any party with an interest in the whole object who has priority can consent to subordinate his interest in favor of the party with an interest in the accessions. To be binding, this consent must be in writing. The second exception is a bit more confusing, since it reintroduces the concept of perfection as the basis for priority. Notice that in the example above we never mentioned that Hughes had to perfect its interest in the parts in order to have priority over the bank. If Hughes does not perfect its interest by filing a financing statement, it can lose whatever priority it has to (1) a subsequent purchaser of the whole object, (2) a subsequent judgment creditor who levies on the whole object, and (3) a creditor with a prior perfected security interest to the extent that this creditor makes subsequent advances [9-314(3)]. Therefore, to be assured of priority to the parts installed, the repairer who extends credit must create and perfect its security interest in the parts (accessions) prior to installing them.

11. Commingled and Processed Goods

In a manufacturing process, several items—including raw materials and components, each of which may be subject to different security interests—may combine to make a finished product. The collateral to which the financing party is entitled will ultimately be the product that results from the combination of the materials in which he has a security interest. If a security interest in the raw materials was perfected, the security interest continues in the product if the identity of the goods is lost *or* the original financing statement provided for a security interest that covered the "product" [9-315(1)]. In a situation in which component parts are assembled into a machine, the secured party would generally have a choice of claiming either (1) a security interest in the machine or (2) an interest in a component part as provided for security interests in accessions [9-314(1)]. If he stipulates "product," he cannot claim an accession. When more than one security interest exists in the product, the secured parties share in the product in proportion to the costs of their materials used [9-315(2)].

SECURED PARTY VERSUS LIEN CREDITORS

12. Introduction

In addition to other secured parties and buyers of the collateral, a secured party's security interest can conflict with parties holding liens arising from operation of law. Four types of liens created by law may come into conflict with an Article 9 security interest: (1) federal tax lien; (2) laborer's, artisan's, or materialman's lien; (3) judgment creditor's lien; and (4) the bankruptcy trustee's lien. In general, the rule determining priority between a secured party and a lienholder is the first-in-time rule. In other words, the party that is first to indicate its interest on the public record has priority.

For example, failure to pay federal taxes allows the Internal Revenue Service to file a notice of a tax lien on any property of the delinquent taxpayer. The property described in a federal tax lien may also be subject to an Article 9 security interest. The secured party has a priority claim to this property if the notice of the tax lien is filed *after* the security interest is perfected. If the notice of the tax lien is filed *before* the security interest is perfected, the Internal Revenue Service has priority.

Although the federal tax lien follows the first-in-time priority rule, other liens do create some exceptions to this general rule. The following sections discuss some of these exceptions.

13. Laborer's, Artisan's, and Materialman's Lien

These liens are discussed in detail in chapter 35. For now, it is sufficient to know that these liens may be created by judges under common law or by statute. The *common-law lien* on goods—allowed for repair, improvement, storage, or transportation—is superior to a perfected security interest as long as the lien claimant retains possession of the property. *Statutory liens* also may have such priority. Even though a lien is second in point of time, it will be granted priority over a perfected security interest in the goods unless the statute creating the lien provides that it is subordinate [9-310]. The reason for giving superiority to a second-in-time lien is the presumption that the service rendered by the lienholder has added to or protected the value of the collateral.

14. Judgment Creditor's Lien

Article 9 defines a lien creditor as a creditor who acquired a lien on the debtor's property by a sheriff's levy based on the creditor's judgment, or a trustee in bankruptcy [9-301(3)]. The lien creditor is more generally called a judgment creditor and was discussed in the introduction to chapter 32. This creditor, having obtained a judgment in a lawsuit, seeks to collect that judgment by levy, attachment, execution, or the like on the debtor's property. Article 9 has some awkward language in Section 9-301(1)(b) that covers conflicts between a lien creditor and an Article 9 security interest. It states in the negative that an unperfected security interest is subordinate to the rights of a person who becomes a lien creditor before the security interest is perfected. Stated positively, the Code provides a first-in-time rule. A secured party who perfects before the judicial lien creditor levies will prevail. To apply the rule, look to the time that the levy is made (October 3). If the secured party has perfected at any time prior to that levy on October 3, the secured party's security interest has priority over the judicial lien creditor. Stated in another affirmative way, priority goes to the lien creditor if the lien is levied before the security interest is perfected.

There is one important exception to this general first-in-time rule. Under Section 9-301(2), the Code has a 10-day grace period for filing a PMSI, regardless of the type of collateral. Assume that a secured party makes a PMSI loan to a debtor on May 1 and that the secured party files to perfect on May 8. Since filing was within the 10-day period, the security interest relates back to May 1 under Section 9-301(2). Therefore, if a lien is levied on May 3, the security interest is perfected and is superior to a lien creditor under Section 9-301(1)(b).

15. Bankruptcy Trustee's Lien

The subject of bankruptcy is thoroughly explained in chapter 37. Bankruptcy is a remedy for financial difficulties granted by the federal Bankruptcy Reform Act of 1978. When a debtor (voluntarily or involuntarily) is put into bankruptcy, his nonexempt assets are required to be turned over to a trustee to be sold to satisfy the claims of unsecured creditors. If a secured party has a security interest in some of those assets, then the security interest is threatened. The bankruptcy trustee is another third party who may attempt to defeat certain Article 9 secured parties. It is the trustee's job to gather and liquidate the debtor's estate, reduce it to cash, and make a pro rata payment to the bankrupt's *unsecured* creditors.

The trustee will attempt to show that the Article 9 security interest is ineffective. If the attempt is successful, it will increase the available assets and, in turn, increase the pro rata distribution to the unsecured creditors. The acid test for an Article 9 security interest is said to be its ability to survive the trustee's attack. Several sections of the 1978 Bankruptcy Act give the trustee powers to avoid an Article 9 security interest; many of them—such as the power to avoid the security interest as a *preference* under Section 547—will be considered in chapter 37. For now, we analyze one important right of the bankruptcy trustee in his quest to set aside a security interest.

The most frequent clash between the secured party and the trustee occurs when the security interest is not perfected. The trustee will prevail over an unperfected security interest by using the bankruptcy law and the Code. The trustee generally has the rights of a hypothetical lien creditor. This allows the trustee to pretend he is a lien creditor on the date the bankruptcy petition is filed. In essence, on this *date,* the trustee can assert the same rights that a lien creditor would have on that same date under Article 9. (See the preceding section for the rights of a lien creditor.) The following example illustrates that this rule is easy to apply.

Assume that the bankruptcy petition was filed on October 10, and the secured party filed a financing statement on October 11. As we already know, the lien creditor's levy has priority over an unperfected security interest but is inferior to a previously perfected security interest. Now, apply that reasoning to the time the bankruptcy petition is filed. If before that date (October 10 in our example) the security interest is perfected, the trustee loses. But in our example, perfection occurred on October 11. Since the security interest was unperfected on October 10, the trustee will have priority.

RIGHTS AND DUTIES ON DEBTOR'S DEFAULT

16. Introduction

A debtor's default is the event that illustrates the real benefits of being an Article 9 secured party. Unsecured creditors are required to sue and get a judgment against a defaulting debtor. But secured creditors may invoke Part 5 of Article 9. This part defines the rights and duties of both secured parties and debtors in default situations. The provisions of Part 5 permit the secured party to take possession of the collateral and dispose of it to satisfy his claim. He may obtain the collateral by self-help (if this procedure does not breach the peace) or by court action [9-503]. Once the collateral is in hand, the secured party has two alternatives. The first one is to conduct a *foreclosure sale* with the proceeds to be applied to the unpaid debt. The second option is *strict foreclosure*, which occurs when the secured creditor retains the collateral in satisfaction of the debt. At any time before either alternative regarding disposition of the collateral becomes final, the debtor has the right to *redeem* his interest in the collateral by paying off the debt.

The following sections discuss the parties' rights and duties on the debtor's default from a chronological perspective. First, the secured party must take possession of the collateral. This act often is called *repossession* since the secured party may have sold the collateral to the debtor. Next, the secured party must decide whether to sell the collateral or to keep it. Finally, the secured party must give the debtor the opportunity to exercise his rights.

Prior to discussing the secured party's ability to repossess the collateral, a special rule concerning some types of collateral should be noted. If the collateral is accounts, chattel paper, instruments, or general intangibles, repossession is not necessary. The secured party can simply proceed to collect whatever may become due on the collateral. He may give reasonable notice to the person who owes the account receivable or instrument to make payment directly to the secured party [9-502(1)]. A failure to give reasonable notice prevents the secured party from collecting these debts from any party other than the original debtor.

17. Repossession of Collateral

By Self-Help.   Generally, a secured party will attempt "peaceable" self-help repossession, since it is swift and inexpensive. The main drawback is that self-help techniques must not result in a breach of the peace. Countless judicial opinions have considered whether self-help repossession is peaceable or not under particular situations.

The following three sets of circumstances usually are deemed peaceable in connection with a repossession. First, the secured party removes the collateral (a car) from the street or parking lot without the knowledge or objection of the debtor. More than likely, starting the car without the use of the ignition key will be considered peaceful. If the removal is from the debtor's open premises such as a driveway, it is not objectionable. Second, removal without the debtor's consent (or even if debtor knows but does not make an express objection) is not a breach of the peace. Finally, removal of the collateral from the premises of a third party (such as a garage, parking lot, neighbor's yard) is lawful so long as neither the debtor nor third person expressly objects.

In four other situations, however, repossession will usually involve a "breach of the peace." First, it is a breach to threaten or to appear to threaten violence to the debtor or other person who is present, whether or not any violence occurs. Second, removal of the collateral over the express objection of the debtor (even if there is no violence) is a breach. Most courts also find a breach of the peace when the removal is over the express objection of a third party. Third, the use of trickery is a breach of the peace. Posing as a police officer or obtaining the aid of a police officer or other law enforcement officer who acts beyond his official authority is improper. Fourth and finally, unauthorized entry into the debtor's home, garage, or other building for the purpose of repossession is unlawful.[5]

By Judicial Action.   If a secured party cannot obtain possession of the collateral by the peaceful self-help method, a judicial action becomes necessary. Repossession by judicial action may be accomplished by several means. The secured party may bring a *replevin* action, which is a judicial action for the actual recovery of the possession of an item of personal property. Or the action may be for a personal judgment against the debtor, with that judgment being levied on the collateral. In some states, the judicial action may be brought to obtain a foreclosure sale of specific personal property.

Obviously, repossession by judicial action is more expensive than self-help; however, the Code does make the debtor liable for most court costs, including attorney's fees. The secured party is well advised to use the courts when the debtor

---

[5] Quest v. Barnett Bank of Pensacola, p. 747.

will not part with the goods without a fight. Under the typical judicial action, the plaintiff files a complaint, makes an affidavit, and posts a required bond. Then, the sheriff seizes the property. Unless the debtor objects within a specified time, the property is delivered to the secured party.

Alternatives to Repossession. By including specific provisions in the security agreement, a secured party can tailor his rights on the debtor's default to suit his particular needs. In other words, secured parties may provide for alternative remedies to the self-help repossession or the judicial action allowed by Article 9. The security agreement can, for instance, put the debtor to work. It can provide that the debtor assemble the collateral and make it available to the secured party at a place reasonably convenient to both parties [9-503]. If the debtor refuses, the secured party may use judicial help in requiring a debtor in possession of collateral that is spread out over a number of places to gather the collateral at one place.

In the case of collateral such as heavy equipment, the physical removal from the debtor's plant and storage elsewhere pending resale may be excessively expensive and, in some cases, impractical. Thus, the Code allows the secured party, without removal, to render equipment unusable and to dispose of the collateral on the debtor's premises [9-503]. Any such action must, of course, be "commerciably reasonable."

18. Rights and Duties of Secured Party in Possession

The secured party has certain rights against the debtor who has defaulted. First, any reasonable expenses incurred in connection with the collateral are chargeable to the debtor and are secured by the collateral [9-207(2)(a)]. Second, the risk of accidental loss or damage to the collateral is on the debtor to the extent that the loss is not covered by insurance [9-207(2)(b)]. Finally, the secured party is entitled to hold as additional security any increase or profits received from the collateral, unless the increase or profit is money [9-207(2)(c)].

Once the secured party has obtained possession of the collateral, that party must decide what to do with the collateral. The secured party may sell the collateral and apply the sale proceeds to satisfy the debt. Sections 19 and 20 discuss the legal issues associated with a foreclosure sale. Or the secured party may decide to keep the collateral in satisfaction of the debt. Because of the potential harshness of strict foreclosure, the secured party's right to keep the collateral may be limited under certain circumstances. In other words, there are situations when a debtor or other interested party can force the secured party to sell the collateral. Section 21 examines the rules associated with strict foreclosures.

The Code imposes certain duties on a secured party in possession of the collateral [9-207]. The most important is to exercise reasonable care in the custody and preservation of the collateral. If the collateral is chattel paper or instruments, reasonable care includes taking steps to preserve rights against prior parties unless otherwise agreed. Example: Debtor pledged its stock in ABC Corporation to creditor to secure a loan. While creditor was in possession, ABC issued rights to current stockholders to buy additional shares, which rights would expire if not exercised by a stated date. Knowing of this right, creditor failed to notify debtor about it before the expiration date. Creditor thus failed to exercise due care and would be liable to debtor for any loss caused by the failure to notify.

19. Foreclosure Sale

After default, a secured party may sell, lease, or otherwise dispose of the collateral [9-504]. The usual disposition is by public or private foreclosure sale. These sales often are called *resales* since the collateral often was sold originally to the debtor. Code provisions governing foreclosure sales are extremely liberal. They are based on the rationale that the primary concern is to get the best possible price on the resale, since that benefits both the debtor and the secured party. For example, the higher the foreclosure sale price, the greater is the likelihood of a surplus for the debtor. Also, the likelihood of a deficiency is diminished.

The foreclosure sale can be public or private, and it can be by one or more contracts [9-504(3)]. A *public sale* is a sale by auction open to the general public. A public sale often occurs on the courthouse steps. A *private sale* is a sale through commercial channels to a buyer arranged by the secured party. Such a buyer could be a dealer who regularly buys and sells goods like the collateral.

Although the Code provides flexible rules for the foreclosure sale, it does not leave the debtor unprotected and at the secured party's mercy. Indeed, the Code imposes definite restrictions on the secured party, who must adhere to these restrictions or risk losing the remedies provided by the Code. Of these restrictions, three are the most important. They are (1) *reasonable notification* of the foreclosure sale given to the debtor by the secured party, (2) *reasonable timing* of the foreclosure sale, and (3) every aspect of the foreclosure sale being *commercially reasonable*.

Notice Required.   A secured party is not free to assume that repossession of the collateral serves as *notice* of a possible public or private foreclosure sale. The Code requires the secured party to give reasonable notice of either the time and place of any public sale or of the time after which a private sale may occur [9-504(3)]. This notice gives the debtor a deadline within which to protect himself in whatever manner he sees fit.

When notification is required by the Code, it must be reasonable in all situations. Upon the failure to give reasonable notice of a foreclosure sale, the secured party usually is denied the right to sue the debtor for a deficiency judgment. It should be emphasized that this notice must be given, not necessarily received.[6]

The notice must be sent to the debtor and (to be reasonable) must be sent in time for the debtor to take appropriate steps to protect his interests if he so desires. The notice of resale need not be given if the debtor has signed *after default* a statement renouncing or modifying his right to notification of sale.

In the case of consumer goods, notice must be given only to the debtor. With the exception of consumer goods, the Code requires that notice be sent to any

---

[6] First National Bank & Trust Company of Lincoln v. Hermann, p. 749.

other secured party from whom the secured party has received written notice of an interest.

Notification of an impending disposition is not required if the collateral is (1) perishable, or (2) threatens to decline speedily in value, or (3) is of a type customarily sold on a recognized market [9-504(3)]. Examples of goods sold on a recognized market include commodities or corporate stock sold on a public exchange. Used cars and similar items are not considered customarily sold in a recognized market, since there is no established price for these items.

Time of Sale. In general, the Code does not establish any stated *time* limitation within which the foreclosure sale or disposition of collateral must occur. This absence of a stated time period for resale conforms to the Code philosophy of encouraging disposition by private sale through regular commercial channels. For example, it may not be wise to dispose of goods if the market collapses. Likewise, the sale of large amounts of inventory in parcels over time may be more reasonable than a forced sale of the entire amount in bulk. The foreclosure sale must be commercially reasonable. The secured party is not allowed to delay when no reason exists for not making a prompt sale.

An exception to this general rule of no time restriction does apply if the collateral is consumer goods and if the debtor has paid over 60 percent of the purchase price or loan amount. Under these circumstances, the consumer goods must be sold within 90 days after the secured party has taken possession of the collateral. This exception is necessary to protect the debtor since, in most cases, a sale of the consumer goods will produce proceeds in excess of the debt.

Commercial Reasonableness. Every aspect of the resale, including the *method, manner, time, place, and terms* must be commercially reasonable.[7] The term *commercially reasonable* is not defined in the Code, but case law has developed some rules to assist in making the determination in future cases. First, the fact that a better price could have been obtained at another time or by another method is not of itself sufficient to establish that the resale was unreasonable. However, recent case law indicates that a resale at a price substantially under what might well have been received is not commercially reasonable. In particular, if the sale is followed by a second sale at a substantially greater price, it is not reasonable. If the secured party has not exerted much effort (as in failing to contact a number of prospective buyers), the sale may be held not commercially reasonable.

The Code allows the secured party to buy the collateral at any public sale, but the right to buy in at a private sale is restricted. Only if the collateral is of a type normally sold in a recognized market or is subject to universal price quotations can the secured party buy in at a private sale [9-504(3)]. This prohibition against the creditor's buying at a private sale acknowledges that creditors can overreach the debtor's rights by conducting a sham sale. A *sham sale* occurs if the collateral is purchased by the creditor at an unreasonably low price

---

[7] Mack Financial Corporation v. Scott, p. 750.

which allows the creditor to make the debtor liable for a substantial deficiency. Obviously, this type of resale is commercially unreasonable.

A resale is recognized as commercially reasonable if the secured party either (1) sells the collateral in the customary manner in a recognized market or (2) sells at a price current in such market at the time of resale or (3) sells in conformity with reasonable commercial practices among dealers in the type of property sold.

20. Rights of Parties after Foreclosure

The buyer of the collateral at a foreclosure sale receives it free of the security interest under which the sale was held. This buyer also is free of any inferior security interest [9-504(4)]. Thus, the good-faith purchaser at a disposition sale receives substantial assurance that he will be protected in his purchase. After the sale has been made, the proceeds of the sale will be distributed and applied as follows. First, the expenses the secured party incurred in taking repossession and conducting the foreclosure sale will be paid. After these expenses are paid, the sale's proceeds are used to satisfy the debt owed to the secured party. Third, any indebtedness owed to persons who have inferior security interests in the collateral will be paid. Fourth and finally, any surplus remaining after all these debts are satisfied will be returned to the debtor [9-504(1)]. If the foreclosure sale is commercially reasonable in all respects, but does not produce enough to satisfy all these charges, the debtor is liable for any deficiency [9-504(2)].

21. Strict Foreclosure

Notice Required.   The secured party who intends to keep the collateral in satisfaction of the debt rather than conduct a foreclosure sale must send written notice to the debtor indicating this intent [9-505(2)]. This notice is not required if the debtor has signed after default a statement modifying or renouncing his right to this notice. If the collateral is consumer goods, only the debtor needs to be given notice of the proposed strict foreclosure. Notice to other interested parties is not necessary when consumer goods are involved, since most of the secured parties claiming a conflicting interest will have PMSI and will be relying on perfection by attachment. Thus, the secured party proposing a strict foreclosure will not even know of conflicting interests.

When collateral other than consumer goods is involved, written notice proposing strict foreclosure must be sent to all persons who have filed a financing statement covering the collateral or who are known to have a security interest in it. Within the time period discussed in the next section, the debtor or any interested party may object in writing to the proposed strict foreclosure. If no objections are received, the secured party can retain the collateral in satisfaction of the debt [9-505(2)].

Prevention of Strict Foreclosure.   Strict foreclosure is disallowed in two situations. First, special provisions relate to consumer transactions. Disposition of consumer goods is *compulsory,* and a sale must be made within 90 days after possession is taken by the secured party. This resale of the collateral is mandatory when there exists either (1) a purchase-money security interest in consumer goods and 60 percent of the purchase price has been paid, or (2) an interest in consumer goods to secure a nonpurchase-money loan and 60 percent of the loan has been repaid [9-505(1)]. As stated previously, these rules exist because there is a presumption that the resale will result in surplus proceeds. The resale within 90 days ensures that the consumer debtor will not be deprived of this surplus. Of course, it is possible that even though a large percentage of the purchase price or loan amount has been paid, the resale of the collateral clearly will not produce a surplus. Thus, the consumer debtor is allowed to waive the right of mandatory resale. This waiver must be in writing and must be signed by the debtor after default [9-505(1)].

The second situation when strict foreclosure may be prevented involves an objection to the secured party keeping the collateral. As noted in the preceding section, the debtor and all other interested parties must be sent written notice that a strict foreclosure is proposed. Any of these parties may object to this proposal. This objection must be made in writing, and it must be received by the secured party's proposing the strict foreclosure within 21 days of the original notice's being sent. If these requirements for objecting to a strict foreclosure are met, the collateral must be sold [9-505(2)].

22. Debtor's General Remedies

Except for the 90-day period for consumer goods, the secured party is not required to make disposition of the repossessed goods within any time limit. The debtor has the right to *redeem* or reinstate his interest in the collateral until (1) that property has been sold or contracted to be sold, or (2) the obligation has been satisfied by the retention of the property. The debtor must, as a condition to redemption, tender the full amount of the obligation secured by the collateral plus expenses incurred by the secured party in connection with the collateral and (if so provided in the security agreement) attorney's fees and legal expenses [9-506].

If the secured party fails to comply with the provisions of the Code relating to default, a court may order disposition or restrain disposition, as the situation requires. If the sale has already taken place, the secured party is liable for any loss resulting from his noncompliance, and he may lose his right to recover any deficiency. If the collateral is consumer goods, the consumer debtor is entitled to recover from the secured party (1) the credit service charge plus 10 percent of the principal amount of the debt, or (2) the time-price differential plus 10 percent of the cash price, whichever is greater [9-507(1)]. The secured party who forecloses a security interest in consumer goods must be very careful to comply with the law as it relates to their sale.

Note that if the creditor fails to follow the compulsory sale of consumer goods under the 60 percent–90 day rule of Section 9-505(1), the debtor may recover in conversion or under the liability provisions of Section 9-507(1). Under the latter provision, the debtor may recover any loss caused by the secured party's failure to comply with Code provisions. In addition to recovering damages caused by the secured party, if consumer goods are involved the debtor also can recover the Code penalty discussed in the preceding paragraph.

SUMMARY

SECURED PARTY VERSUS BUYERS OF COLLATERAL

General rule	1. Secured parties who are perfected generally have priority over buyers of collateral. However, there are at least three exceptions.
Buyers in the ordinary course of business	1. Such a buyer takes free from a perfected secured party's interest.
	2. A buyer in the ordinary course of business is a buyer who buys goods from a seller who is in the business of selling goods of that kind.
	3. A buyer in the ordinary course of business usually will purchase a debtor's inventory.
	4. This rule of priority does not apply when the collateral is farm products.
Buyers of consumer goods	1. A buyer of consumer goods cannot make this purchase in the ordinary course of business. A consumer seller does not ordinarily sell such goods.
	2. A buyer of consumer goods has priority over a secured party who has relied on perfection by attachment of a purchase money security interest if the buyer has no knowledge of the security interest and if the buyer uses the goods as consumer goods.
	3. A secured party can be assured of priority with respect to consumer goods if a financing statement is properly filed.
Buyers of chattel paper and instruments	1. A buyer of chattel paper or instruments which are proceeds from the sale of inventory collateral has priority over a secured party even if that buyer has knowledge of the security interest. This buyer must make the purchase in the ordinary course of business for value and must take possession of the chattel paper or instruments.

2. A buyer of chattel paper or instruments which are proceeds from the sale of noninventory collateral takes priority over a secured party only if that secured party relies on the 10-day automatic perfection rule and if the buyer lacks knowledge of the security interest.

3. A buyer of instruments that were original collateral takes priority over a secured party only if that secured party relies on the 21-day automatic perfection rules and if the buyer lacks knowledge of the security interest.

SECURED PARTY VERSUS SECURED PARTY

General rule

1. The secured party who is first to file or perfect has priority to the described collateral. When PMSI's are involved, exceptions do exist.

PMSI in inventory collateral

1. A second-in-time secured party who has a PMSI in inventory may have priority over a preexisting secured party.

2. This purchase-money secured party must notify the preexisting secured party in writing and must file a financing statement before the debtor gets possession of the collateral.

PMSI in noninventory collateral

1. A second-in-time secured party who has a PMSI in noninventory collateral may have priority over a preexisting secured party.

2. This purchase-money secured party does not have to give notice of its PMSI. However, this party must file a financing statement before or within 10 days after the debtor takes possession of the collateral.

Fixtures

1. The financing of fixtures or potential fixtures creates the possible conflict between an Article 9 secured party and a party with an interest in the real estate.

2. The Code requires a fixture filing. It specifically provides rules concerning priority in certain situations when a fixture-secured party and a real estate secured party have conflicting interests.

	3. These situations include the financing of building materials, the financing of soft fixtures, the creation of PMSI and non-PMSI in fixtures, and the rights of construction mortgages.
Accessions	**1.** An *accession* is a good or part which is added to or installed in a larger good. Accessions typically arise in repairs of personal property.
	2. A secured party who creates a security interest in accessions before they are affixed to the whole object has priority to the accessions.
	3. If the security interest in accessions is created after the parts are added to the whole object, the party secured by the accessions has priority over anyone who subsequently takes an interest in the whole. However, this secured party's interest is inferior to parties who have a preexisting interest in the whole object.
	4. To be assured of priority, the party who is secured by accessions should perfect as well as create the security interest *prior* to the parts being added to the whole object.
Commingled and processed goods	**1.** A creditor with a perfected security interest in raw materials or component parts generally has a security interest in the finished product as well.
	2. Secured parties with conflicting interests in the finished products must share in proportion to the costs of their materials which were used in manufacturing the finished product.

SECURED PARTY VERSUS LIEN CREDITORS

General rule	**1.** Whichever party, the secured party or the lien creditor, who is on record first in time has priority.
	2. Federal tax liens follow this general rule. A tax lien is considered to be on record when the notice of the lien is filed.
Laborer's, artisan's, and materialman's liens	**1.** These liens may be of common law or statutory origin.
	2. Article 9 provides an exception to the general priority rule stated above.

	3. These lienholders have priority since value has been added to the collateral.
Judgment creditor's liens	1. These lienholders usually are subject to the general rule stated above. A judicial lien is on record when it is levied on the debtor's property.
	2. A PMSI-secured party may defeat a preexisting judgment creditor's lien if the secured party perfects within 10 days after debtor receives possession of collateral and if the judicial lien is levied between the time the security interest attaches and the time it is perfected.
Bankruptcy trustee's liens	1. The bankruptcy trustee is considered a hypothetical lien creditor. Therefore, the trustee is in the same priority position as the judgment creditor.
	2. The bankruptcy trustee's lien arises on the date the bankruptcy petition is filed.

RIGHTS AND DUTIES ON DEBTOR'S DEFAULT

Repossession of collateral	1. The secured party's basic right on the debtor's default is to obtain possession of the collateral.
	2. The collateral may be possessed through peaceful self-help or through judicial action.
	3. Upon the debtor's default, a secured party may take possession of the collateral as long as there is not a breach of the peace.
	4. If the repossession of the collateral cannot be done peacefully, the secured party must seek the court's assistance.
	5. This judicial action may take the form of a replevin action, a suit for judgment and levy, or a suit for an order of foreclosure.
	6. In general, repossession by judicial action is more expensive than the self-help method. However, most of these expenses will be passed on to the debtor.
	7. The secured party can include any legal provision in the security agreement providing an alternative remedy to repossession.

	8. These provisions can require the debtor to assemble all collateral in one location or the secured party may be allowed to make heavy equipment unusable and sell it from the debtor's place of business.
Rights and duties of secured party in possession	**1.** The secured party can recover the cost of repossession from the debtor.
	2. Any increase in the collateral is additional security protecting the secured party.
	3. Once the secured party has possession of the collateral, that party must decide to conduct a foreclosure sale or to keep the collateral in satisfaction of the debt, which is called strict foreclosure.
	4. In general, the secured party must handle the collateral with reasonable care.
Foreclosure sale	**1.** A foreclosure sale may be public or private. A public sale is open to the general public and usually is an auction.
	2. A private sale is arranged by the secured party who locates one or more buyers of the collateral.
	3. The secured party always must give the debtor notice of the foreclosure sale. This notice must include the time and place of a public sale. The notice need only inform the debtor of the time after which a private sale may occur.
	4. If the collateral is consumer goods, notice of resale needs to be given only to the debtor. If other types of collateral are involved, notice also must be given to the other secured parties who have notified the secured party arranging the sale of their interest.
	5. This type of notice is not required if the collateral is perishable, threatens to decline in value rapidly, or is sold on a recognized market.
	6. In general, there is no time limit within which a foreclosure sale must occur.
	7. The applicable standard is that the sale must occur within a reasonable time.
	8. All aspects of a foreclosure sale must be handled in a commercially reasonable manner.

	9. This standard has been and continues to be developed by case law, since the Code does not provide a definition.
Rights of parties after foreclosure	1. A buyer at a commercially reasonable foreclosure sale takes the property free from the security interest of the seller and all inferior security interests.
	2. The proceeds of a resale of collateral will be distributed to the secured party to pay for the expenses of repossession and resale and for the debt. Any remaining proceeds will be paid to other parties secured by the same collateral. Any surplus is paid to the debtor. Any deficiency is owed by the debtor.
Strict foreclosure	1. A secured party who proposes to keep the collateral in satisfaction of the debt must send the debtor written notice of this proposal unless the debtor has waived after default the right to such notice.
	2. If the collateral is not consumer goods, written notice of strict foreclosure also must be sent to all other known interested parties.
	3. If the collateral is consumer goods and 60 percent of the purchase price or loan amount has been paid, the consumer goods must be sold within 90 days of the secured party's possession of them.
	4. Any debtor or interested party may object to the strict foreclosure and force a foreclosure sale. This objection must be given in writing within 21 days of the secured party's notice of strict foreclosure being sent.
General debtor's remedies	1. The debtor has a right to redeem his interest in the collateral any time prior to final action being taken by the secured party.
	2. To redeem interests in default, the debtor must pay all amounts owed to the secured party.
	3. If the secured party fails to comply with any Code provision, the debtor can sue for actual damages plus any applicable Code remedy.

CASES

Matteson v. Harper
682 P.2d 766 (Ore. 1984)

JONES, J. Plaintiff sued defendant for conversion of collateral in which plaintiff had a perfected security interest. The trial court granted summary judgment for plaintiff in the amount of $17,000, representing the fair market value of the equipment on the date of the conversion. The Court of Appeals reversed. . . .

Matteson, plaintiff, owned a bulldozer, which he purchased as an investment. He sold the bulldozer to the Thorson group and retained and perfected a security interest by filing a financing statement on October 6, 1980. The security agreement prohibited sale of the bulldozer without Matteson's written consent.

The Thorson group defaulted on payments and delivered, for sale, the bulldozer to Walker, an auctioneer who dealt in earth-moving equipment. In March, 1981, upon discovering that the Thorson group had made the delivery, Matteson wrote Walker:

> . . . Mr. Bob Thorson . . . has indicated that the John Deer [sic] 4500 he is purchasing from me is to be at an auction in Seattle on March 26, 1981.
>
> A minimum sales price must be $22,400.00, plus auctioneer's fee, any transportation costs, storage and handling fees, etc., or I cannot consent to the sale. . . .

Walker did not respond to the letter.

On April 18, 1981, defendant, Harper, purchased the bulldozer from Walker in Tigard, Oregon, for $20,500. Walker kept the proceeds of the sale and thereafter went bankrupt. Matteson demanded that Harper return the bulldozer to him. Harper refused and Matteson brought this action for conversion of property. . . .

Harper contends that Matteson's letter to Walker "authorized" the sale of the bulldozer . . . and, therefore, Matteson's security interest did not continue. . . .

Here, Matteson expressly conditioned the sale of the bulldozer requiring a sales price of at least $22,400 plus fees and costs. The sale of the bulldozer to Harper for $20,500 violated the condition imposed by Matteson and does not constitute an authorized sale. . . .

Defendant, Harper, contends that as a policy matter the secured party is in a better position to protect his interest in the collateral than is the buyer. Defendant suggests Matteson could have affixed a notice on the bulldozer at the place of sale, informing would-be buyers of Matteson's security interest. The purpose behind filing a financing statement to perfect a security interest is to inform potential buyers of the existing interest. . . .

Requiring the secured party to follow the collateral to every sale and post a notice to unwary buyers would undermine the simplicity, uniformity and reliability of the filing system.

The purpose of the Uniform Commercial Code generally and the secured transaction provisions specifically is . . .

> to provide a simple and unified structure within which the immense variety of present-day secured financing transactions can go forward with less cost and with greater certainty.

This purpose is best served by providing a comprehensive system by which parties may perfect a security interest and on which they may rely.

The Court of Appeals is reversed and the trial court is affirmed.

So ordered.

Antigo Co-op Credit Union v. Miller
271 N.W.2d 642 (Wis. 1978)

HEFFERNAN, J. The principal issue presented on this appeal is whether a buyer in the ordinary course of business takes free of a security interest when the secured party did not know that the seller was in the business of selling goods of the kind which constituted the collateral. We conclude that a buyer under those circumstances takes free of the security interest even though that security interest is perfected by proper execution and filing of a financing statement.

An important question to be resolved under the facts of this case is whether the buyer, James L. Miller, purchased the horse trailer from Peggy Sparks in the ordinary course of business. . . .

Peggy Sparks purchased a horse trailer from Walter Hoffmeister. Her purchase from Hoffmeister was financed by the Antigo Co-op Credit Union. She picked up the trailer from Hoffmeister on May 7, 1974, and on that date she made application to the Antigo Co-op Credit Union for amendment of a security agreement entered into in November of 1973. The purpose of her application was to substitute as collateral the trailer received from Hoffmeister in May of 1974 for the trailer financed in the previous November and which she had sold.

On May 18, 1974, Peggy Sparks displayed the trailer at a horse show. James L. Miller saw the "for sale" sign on the trailer, looked it over, and eventually bought the trailer from Sparks on July 2, 1974. The sum of $2,700 was paid by Miller to Sparks for the trailer.

Sparks failed to pay Antigo Co-op Credit Union. Because of Sparks' default, Antigo brought an action against Miller, claiming that the trailer was subject to Antigo's perfected security interest. Miller answered, denying any knowledge of the prior security interest and asked for the dismissal of the plaintiff's complaint.

At trial, the defendant urged . . . that purchase of the trailer was in the ordinary course of business; and, hence, even were the security interest perfected by proper filing, Miller took free of the security interest.

The trial court in its memorandum decision accepted the . . . defense and ordered the dismissal of the complaint.

Sections 9.307(1) and 1.209(9) are controlling. Sec. 9.307(1) provides:

> (1) A buyer in ordinary course of business other than a person buying farm products from a person engaged in farming operations takes free of a security interest created by his seller even though the security interest is perfected and even though the buyer knows of its existence.

A buyer in the ordinary course of business is defined in sec. 1.201(9) as follows:

> (9) 'Buyer in ordinary course of business' means a person who in good faith and without knowledge that the sale to him is in violation of the ownership rights or security interest of a 3rd party in the goods buys in ordinary course from a person in the business of selling goods of that kind but does not include a pawnbroker. . . .

Under these statutes, Miller, if a buyer in the ordinary course of business, takes free of Antigo's prior security interest. . . .

The only contested factual issue was whether Peggy Sparks, at the time Miller bought the horse trailer, was "in the business of selling goods of that kind." In the trial court's memorandum decision, the court made the finding that, prior to Miller's purchase, Sparks showed the trailer at a horse show and advertised it for sale. The court also found that there was another new trailer on Peggy Sparks' farm on the date of the sale. It found that Sparks bought trailers from Hoffmeister with the intent of reselling them. It found that she carried trailer parts for resale and color charts, which were provided by Hoffmeister. When she conveyed the trailer to Miller, she did so by the means of a "Sales and Production Order," which had been furnished her by Hoffmeister. She signed the sales instrument on the line provided for the dealer's signature. In addition to having a new trailer on the premises on the date she sold the trailer to Miller, the court found that she had sold another trailer immediately before she purchased the trailer eventually sold to Miller.

Whether she was a "dealer" in the sense that she had a manufacturer's franchise to sell is irrelevant. She was in the business of selling trailers. It is thus apparent, under the facts, that the application of sec. 9.307(1) requires the conclusion that Miller, a buyer in the ordinary course of business, took the horse trailer free of any security interest of Antigo Co-op Credit Union.

Antigo asserts, however, that, even though Miller was a buyer in good faith in the ordinary course of business, Antigo was ignorant of the fact that Sparks was in the business of selling trailers. It contends, therefore, that its security interest would be subordinate to the rights of Miller only if it knew, or should have known, that Peggy Sparks was in the business of selling trailers.

We conclude that the knowledge or lack of knowledge, whether actual or constructive, of a security holder is immaterial to the rights of a buyer in the ordinary course of business. . . .

The status of a buyer in the ordinary course of business does not depend on what the secured party knew. . . .

Article 9 of the Uniform Commercial Code is not designed to reward a secured party for its ignorance of the business of its debtor. The philosophy of the Uniform Commercial Code is that it is more reasonable to expect a secured party to investigate its debtor's business than to impose such a duty on a good-faith consumer. The purpose of sec. 307(1) of Article 9 is to protect consumers. . . .

The fact that in this case Antigo Co-op Credit Union financed Peggy Sparks without knowing her ordinary course of business was selling horse trailers, does not change the law's basic policy to protect the consumer. Antigo properly must bear the burden of failing to investigate its debtor. . . .

We accordingly conclude that the trial court's finding that Peggy Sparks was selling in the ordinary course of business when she sold the horse trailer to Miller, a buyer in good faith, is not contrary to the great weight and clear preponderance of the evidence. As a buyer in the ordinary course of business, Miller takes free and clear of Antigo Co-op Credit Union's security interest, whether or not that interest was perfected. The complaint was properly dismissed.

Order affirmed.

King's Appliance v. Citizens & Southern Bank
278 S.E.2d 733 (Ga. 1981)

CARLEY, J. The instant appeal involves priority between conflicting security interests in the same collateral and interpretation of Code Ann. §109A-9-312. The relevant facts are as follows: On August 3, 1978, The Citizens and Southern Bank (C&S) filed a financing statement listing itself as the secured party and Randall B. Helton, d/b/a United TV (Helton) as the debtor. The financing statement covered the following types of property:

> All equipment of the Debtor of every description used or useful in the conduct of the Debtor's business, now or hereafter existing or acquired, and all accessories, parts and equipment now or hereafter affixed thereto or used in connection therewith. All inventory, accounts receivable and contract rights of borrower whether now or hereafter existing or acquired; all chattel paper and instruments, whether now or hereafter existing or acquired, evidencing any obligation to borrow for payment for goods sold or leased or services rendered; and all products and proceeds of any of the foregoing.

On November 27, 1978, Helton entered into an "Inventory Financing Agreement" with Appliance Buyers Credit Corporation (ABCC) "to finance the acquisition by [Helton] of certain merchandise of inventory from time to time from" King's Appliance & Electronics, Inc. (King's Appliance). On November 29, 1978, ABCC filed a financ-

ing statement listing itself as the secured party and Helton as the debtor. The financing statement covered the following property:

> Television sets, phonographs, stereos, radios and combinations, tape recorders, organs, pianos and other musical instruments, refrigerators, freezers, ice makers, dish and clothes washers and dryers, ranges, food waste disposers, trash conpactors, dehumidifiers, humidifiers, room air conditioners, heating and air conditioning equipment, vacuum cleaners, and other types of mechanical or electrical, commercial, household or industrial equipment and accessories or replacement parts for any of such merchandise.

On December 1, 1978, pursuant to Code Ann. §109A-9-312(3)(d), ABCC sent notification to C&S that it "has or expects to acquire a purchase money security interest in the inventory of [Helton]" and described the inventory by item or type.

Thereafter, King's Appliance apparently began to ship to Helton merchandise which had been financed by ABCC as well as certain merchandise on consignment. The security interest held by ABCC in that part of Helton's inventory financed under the agreement with ABCC was eventually assigned to King's Appliance. When Helton subsequently defaulted on his obligations to both C&S and King's Appliance, C&S took possession of all of Helton's inventory and gave notice of its intent to sell the inventory and apply the amount realized to Helton's indebtedness to it. King's Appliance, contending that as ABCC's assignee it held a perfected security interest in part of the inventory under Code Ann. §109A-9- 302(2), filed a complaint seeking, in effect, a determination that its security interest in the inventory had priority over that of C&S under Code Ann. §109A-9-312(3). C&S answered and, after discovery, both parties moved for summary judgment. The trial court entered its order granting summary judgment to C&S and denying summary judgment to King's Appliance. The order was based upon the trial court's following interpretation of Code Ann. §109A-9-312:

> Subpart (3)(b)(i) absolutely requires the purchase money secured party to give notification in writing to the holder of the conflicting security interest *before* the date of the filing [of the financing statement] by the purchase money secured party. . . . The notice given C&S [dated December 1, 1978] was *after* the filing of the security interest of [ABCC on November 29, 1978] . . . Failure to give a timely notice prevents priority from being accorded the purchase money security interest. . . .

King's Appliance appeals, urging that the trial court misconstrued Code Ann. §109A-9-312(3)(b) and that summary judgment was erroneously granted to C&S and denied to it. . . .

Code Ann. §109A-9-312(3) provides that a perfected purchase money security interest in inventory has priority over a conflicting prior security interest in the same property if:

(a) The purchase money security is perfected at the time the debtor receives possession of the inventory; and:

(b) The purchase money secured party gives written notice to those holders of conflicting prior security interests who have perfected their interest in the same types of inventory before the purchase money secured party perfects his; and

(c) The holder of the previously perfected security interest receives the notification no more than five years before the date the debtor receives possession of the inventory secured by the purchase money interest; and

(d) The notification states that a purchase money security interest in the debtor's inventory, described by item or type, has been or is expected to be acquired.

Insofar as the trial court in the instant case misconstrued Code Ann. §109A-9-312(3) and granted summary judgment to C&S on the basis of this misconstruction, the judgment must be reversed.

We conclude, however, that summary judgment for King's Appliance was not authorized under the evidence. Under the proper construction of Code Ann. §109A-9-312(3), even if C&S has been given proper notification in compliance with subsections (b) and (d), the record before us shows neither the date upon which Helton, the debtor, received possession of the inventory in which King's Appliance holds the assigned purchase money security interest nor the date that C&S received notification of that security interest. Under subsections (a) and (c) of the current Code Ann. §109A-9-312(3) the security interest of King's Appliance is entitled to priority only to that part of the inventory received by and in the possession of Helton (1) after the purchase money security interest therein was first perfected *and* (2) after C&S received notification. If Helton received possession of any items of inventory before a purchase money security interest therein was perfected *or* before C&S received notification of the conflicting purchase money security interest in Helton's inventory the purchase money security interest of King's Appliance in those items is not entitled to priority over the prior security interest of C&S in Helton's inventory. We conclude, therefore, that there remain genuine issues of material fact for jury resolution and it was not error to deny the motion of King's Appliance for summary judgment.

Reversed.

The Corning Bank v. The Bank of Rector
576 S.W.2d 949 (Ark. 1979)

A dispute arose between two banks as to which one had the better rights to grain bins located on the debtor's real estate. The Bank of Rector,

appellee, had financed the debtor's purchase of the real estate involved and had recorded its mortgage on May 17, 1976. The Corning Bank, appellant, had previously financed the grain bins and had filed a financing statement on March 19, 1976. This financing statement did not describe the real estate where the bins were located nor was it referenced into the real estate records. When the debtor became insolvent, these banks sought a judicial determination establishing which one had priority to the grain bins. The trial court held that the Bank of Rector had priority. The Corning Bank appealed this decision.

FOGELMAN, J. . . . The critical issues in this case, according to appellant, are whether the property involved is a fixture and whether a "fixture filing" was required to preserve the priority of appellant's security interest. The chancellor held that each of the grain bins consisted of a floor, roof and sides and that they constituted buildings, were "permanent property" and a part of the real estate. He also held that there was nothing on file to put appellee on notice of appellant's security interest. We cannot say that the chancellor erred.

Under the Uniform Commercial Code, goods are fixtures when they become so related to the real estate that an interest in them arises under real estate law. Unless the facts are undisputed and reasonable minds could only reach one conclusion, the question whether particular property constitutes a fixture is sometimes one of fact only, but usually is a mixed question of law and fact.

In reviewing the evidence on this question . . . we simply are unable to say that the finding that the property involved here constituted a fixture is clearly against the preponderance of the evidence.

. . . [T]he decision in this case turns upon the effect of the filing by appellate as notice to appellee. In this connection, . . . the only description relied upon by the appellant as a land description was the statement that the property would be located at the Greenway Elevator Company at Greenway, Arkansas, which . . . was identified only by a post-office box number. We do not consider this as a sufficient key to identification of real estate to meet Uniform Commercial Code requirements. . . .

In a financing statement filed as a fixture filing, the description of the real estate must be sufficient to have given constructive notice of a real estate mortgage under the law of this state if it had been included in a mortgage of the real estate described. This description did not meet this test. It is true that a real estate mortgage will not be held void for uncertainty, even as to third persons, where the description used in the mortgage furnishes a key whereby one, aided by extrinsic evidence, can ascertain what property is covered. The name and address of the mortgagor would hardly furnish that key, particularly when the address is a post-office box number. To be sufficient, the description must make reference to something *tangible* by which the property can be located. This requirement was not met.

On the basis of the evidence before him, the chancellor was justified in holding that appellant's collateral was goods which were, or were to become, fixtures, so that, in order to establish the priority of its security agreement, a "fixture filing" must have been made in the office where a mortgage on real estate would be filed or recorded, before the interest of a subsequent encumbrancer is placed of record. There is no indication that appellant complied or attempted to comply with the requirements for a "fixture filing." There was no recitation in the instrument that it was to be filed for record in the real estate records and it did not contain a description of the real estate sufficient to give constructive notice of a mortgage of the real estate. Thus, the circuit clerk was not called upon to index the instrument as he would have if it had been a real estate mortgage. . . .

Appellant has failed to demonstrate error in the decree, so it is

Affirmed.

Quest v. Barnett Bank of Pensacola
397 So.2d 1020 (Fla. 1981)

ERVIN, J. Quest and Sea-Sky Travel Agency, Inc., appeal an order granting a directed verdict at the close of their case-in-chief in an action which had sought damages against the bank based upon alternative theories of trespass, conversion, negligence, and a count filed pursuant to Section 9.507, Florida Statutes (1975), authorizing a statutory right of action against a secured party who does not proceed against a debtor in accordance with the procedure required by Part V of Chapter 679. Appellants contend that the court erred in directing a verdict because the bank's self-help measures constituted a breach of the peace and were therefore unlawful. . . .

On January 27, 1977, the bank seized possession of appellants' assets without judicial process. On that date, a bank agent phoned Mrs. Quest, who was at home ill, and requested her to come immediately to her place of business, because he intended to close it down. Mrs. Quest informed the agent that she could solve the cash flow problem in 48 hours, but he declined any further extensions. During a later telephone conversation, she advised the agent that there were very important papers in her office and that she needed more time to place her business affairs in order. He responded that she could come to the office and that the bank would not do anything until then. When she arrived at the scene, the bank's agents had already taken action; many of the business's contents had been removed, and the records were scattered on the floor. An employee of Sea-Sky testified that when one of the agents first arrived at the premises, she told him that she was not authorized to take any action, and that he would have to talk first with Mrs. Quest. The bank's agent testified as an adverse witness, and did not refute the essence of Mrs. Quest's or the employee's testimony.

The bank defends its self-help remedy by asserting that its actions were sanctioned by its security agreement giving it "immediately and without demand any and all rights and remedies granted to a secured party upon default under the Uniform Commercial Code." More specifically, the bank contends that its actions were authorized by Section 9.503, permitting a secured creditor to take possession of collateral "if this can be done without breach of the peace. . . ."

This statute has been construed as providing a creditor a very limited right of possession. A two-pronged test has been established to determine whether a " 'breach of the peace has occurred' " within the meaning of the statute: " '(1) whether there was entry by the creditor upon the debtor's premises, and (2) whether the debtor or one acting in his behalf consented to the entry and repossession.' " There is no dispute in the record that there was entry by the bank upon Mrs. Quest's business premises.

A thorough analysis of the question whether consent was given the creditor to enter the debtor's premises requires consideration of the following factors. First, a debtor's consent to a creditor to enter into an enclosed area, even if expressed, must be freely and voluntarily given. There are ample facts in the record from which the jury could have inferred that Mrs. Quest's consent was not voluntarily given. Although it is true that Mrs. Quest never ejected the bank's agents from the premises, she did request that they delay their action. It could also be inferred from the record that resistance to the bank's actions would have been fruitless, since at the time Mrs. Quest first arrived at the business after being notified by the bank's agent, the process of closing the business down had already begun.

Second, permission to come upon one's premises may be implied from custom, usage, or conduct; but such implied consent is limited to those acts that are within a fair and reasonable interpretation of the terms of the grant.

In the instant case, it is arguable whether the facts reveal that implied consent was given the bank, either by appellants' custom or conduct, to enter and repossess. Yet, even if that issue were conclusively established against appellants by the facts, it would be a jury question whether the bank overreached the consent given. There was evidence that Mrs. Quest's acquiescence was obtained by promises from the bank's agents which were not kept. She was told over the phone by the bank's agent to come down to the business premises because it was his intention to close the business. Yet, this action had already been taken before she arrived. The evidence is even stronger that the bank's agent also violated his promise to Mrs. Quest that the bank would give her until the following morning to put her business papers in order.

A creditor has been held liable for trespass when the self-help remedy has been accomplished through the use of fraud and deceit. The evidence in this case is such that a jury could infer that the bank willfully misinformed its debtor as to the time its self-help remedy would be exercised.

Moreover, even if the bank's entry of the premises could be said to have been accomplished without a breach of the peace, there is evidence in the record that the manner in which it carried out its self-help remedy was improper. A breach of peace can occur if the secured party damages property of the debtor while affecting repossession. Also, a creditor is liable for any negligence resulting in damage to the debtor's collateral. We conclude that as to the second point raised, the facts taken as a whole establish a prima facie case for a jury's consideration.

Reversed and remanded.

First National Bank & Trust Company of Lincoln v. Hermann
286 N.W.2d 750 (Neb. 1980)

Carol Hermann had borrowed money from and granted a security interest in a mobile home to the First National Bank. When Carol defaulted on her payments, the Bank sent a certified letter to her at her last known address. This letter contained notice of the time when and the place where the bank would be selling Carol's mobile home. Since Carol had moved, the letter was forwarded to her new address. Twice the post office attempted to deliver this certified letter, but no one would come to the door. Indeed, two notices that a certified letter was at the post office were left in Carol's mailbox. Finally, after a week of no response, the letter was marked "unclaimed" and returned to the bank. The mobile home was sold, and the bank sued Carol to recover a deficiency judgment. Carol argued that the deficiency judgment should be disallowed since she never received notice of the foreclosure sale. The lower courts held in favor of the bank. Thereafter, Carol appealed.

BOSLAUGH, J. . . . The rule in this state is that compliance with the requirements of the Uniform Commercial Code for notification as to the disposition of collateral is a condition precedent to a secured creditor's right to recover a deficiency.

The code requirement for a private sale is that "reasonable notification of the time after which any private sale or other intended disposition is to be made shall be sent by the secured party to the debtor." We have interpreted this to mean that a written notice is required and that it should be sent in such time that the debtors will have a minimum of 3 business days to arrange to protect their interests.

The issue in this case is whether the defendant was given "reasonable notification" of the sale of the collateral as required by the Uniform Commercial Code. Subsection (26) of section 1–201 of the code provides that, "A person 'notifies' or 'gives' a notice or notification to another by taking such steps as may be reasonably required to inform the other in ordinary course *whether or not such other actually comes to know of it.*" (Emphasis supplied.) In other words, notification under the code does not depend upon whether the notification actually reached the person to whom it was sent. The statute is satisfied if the steps taken were such as would be reasonably required to inform the person to be notified in ordinary course.

Subsection (38) of section 1–201 of the code provides that, " 'Send' in connection with any writing or notice means to deposit in the mail or deliver for transmission by any other usual means of communication with postage or cost of transmission provided for and properly addressed. . . ." Under this provision a notice sent by ordinary mail will comply with the statute.

The rule concerning notification under section 9–504(3) of the code is stated in White and Summers, Uniform Commercial Code, §26–10, p. 983, at pp. 984 and 985, as follows: "The secured creditor can satisfy the notice requirement merely by sending notification; it is not necessary that the debtor receive it. If the mailman loses the notice or the debtor's wife throws it in the wastebasket, that is the debtor's tough luck; he bears such risks under the Code. . . ."

Although there is authority to the contrary, we believe the notification requirement of the code was satisfied in this case even though the notice was not received by the defendant. The notification sent by the bank would have been delivered to the Knox street address if it had been sent by ordinary mail. This would have been sufficient. The fact that the notice was returned to the bank "unclaimed" by the defendant because the bank had taken the additional precaution of sending the notice by certified mail should not destroy its efficacy.

The judgment of the District Court is affirmed.

So ordered.

Mack Financial Corporation v. Scott
606 P.2d 993 (Id. 1980)

Scott Trucking purchased several Mack trucks and financed the transaction through Mack Financial Corporation (Mack). Shortly thereafter, Scott became delinquent and returned the trucks to Mack in February 1970. These trucks remained in Mack's possession until they were sold at a public auction on January 25, 1972. In February, 1970, Scott owed Mack $127,600. In January 1972, the trucks were sold for $44,700. Therefore, Scott still owed over $85,000 in principal and interest after the resale. When Mack sued to recover this deficiency, Scott argued the foreclosure sale was not a reasonable one due to the long time delay. Scott, therefore, claimed it was not liable for the deficiency. The trial court agreed with Scott, and Mack appealed.

BAKES, J. . . . Plaintiff appellant Mack Financial Corporation urges on appeal that the district court erred in its analysis and application of the law governing a secured creditor's right to a deficiency judgment following repossession and sale of the collateral securing the conditional sales agreement. Mack argues that the effect of the court's rulings was to grant the debtor, Scott Trucking, a setoff on Mack's claim for a deficiency without requiring Scott Trucking to prove its entitlement to the setoff.

Under the provisions of Article IX of the Uniform Commercial Code a repossessing creditor must give notice to the debtor of the time and place of a public sale of the collateral or the time after which a private sale will be effective. Further, "every aspect" of the creditor's disposition of the collateral repossessed after a debtor's default in a secured transaction "including the method, manner, time, place and terms must be commercially reasonable." However, nowhere does the code specify the consequences of a creditor's failure to meet the two requirements of proper notice and commercially reasonable disposition. Courts have reached varying results in cases where a creditor has failed to comply with the code's provisions governing disposition of the collateral.

One line of authority holds that the creditor's failure to comply with the requirements governing disposition of repossessed collateral serves as an absolute bar to the creditor's right to a deficiency judgment. These courts view the code's requirements of proper notice to the debtor of the proposed disposition and commercially reasonable disposition of the collateral as conditions precedent to the creditor's right to recover a deficiency judgment.

A second line of authority, adopted by but a few courts, permits the secured party to recover a deficiency judgment despite his non-compliance with the requirements of notice and commercially reasonably disposition, subject to the debtor's rights under U.C.C. §9–507(1) to recover from the secured party any loss occasioned by the creditor's failure to comply with the code. Under this approach the debtor's claim for damages is generally asserted as a counterclaim in the creditor's action for a deficiency judgment.

A third line of authority embodies the analysis utilized by the district court below and is that which we adopt. Under this approach, failure of the secured party to dispose of the repossessed collateral in a commercially reasonable manner or to give proper notice of the proposed disposition to the debtor does not constitute an absolute bar to the secured party's recovery of a deficiency judgment. However, where the requirements in §9–504(3) are not met by a secured party, it will be presumed that the fair market value of the collateral at the time of repossession was equal to the outstanding debt and that the debtor owes no deficiency. The secured party will then have the burden of proving the actual fair market value of the collateral at the time of repossession in order to establish its right to a deficiency judgment. . . .

The court below found that Mack's unexcused delay of nearly two years between its repossession of the collateral and its sale of the collateral at public auction resulted in a reduced price as a consequence of depreciation and constituted a commercially unreasonable disposition of the collateral in violation of the requirements of §9–504(3). The trial record establishes that the collateral did depreciate between the time of repossession in February of 1970 and Mack's sale of the trucks at public auction in January, 1972, and readily supports the court's finding that the disposition was commercially unreasonable. The record also supports the trial court's finding that Mack failed to prove the actual fair market value of the collateral at the time of its repossession in February, 1970. Consequently, it is to be presumed that the collateral at the time of its repossession was equal in value to the debt, and the trial court's denial of a deficiency judgment against Scott Trucking is therefore affirmed.

So ordered.

REVIEW QUESTIONS

1. Match each term in column A with the appropriate statement in column B.

A	B
1. Buyer in the ordinary course of business	**a.** May be of common law or statutory origin.
2. Accession	**b.** A judicial action seeking possession of personal property.
3. Laborer's lien	**c.** The reinstatement of a defaulting debtor's interest in collateral.
4. Judicial lien	**d.** A foreclosure sale involving an unreasonably low price.
5. Self-help	**e.** A party who purchases an item from a seller in the business of selling such items.
6. Replevin	**f.** A foreclosure when anyone may be the buyer.
7. Public sale	**g.** A public exchange involving specific prices for items sold.
8. Recognized market	**h.** The rights of a judgment creditor who levies on the debtor's property.
9. Sham sale	**i.** A secured party's retention of collateral in satisfaction of the debt.
10. Strict foreclosure	**j.** Personal property affixed to personal property.
11. Redemption	**k.** A method of repossession that is available as long as it is peaceful.

The following factual situation is to be used to answer review problems 2 to 10. Assume that the following events occur. Answer each question based on these and any additional facts given.

The First National Bank agrees to lend $500,000 to Custom Sound Stereo and Television Company. To secure its position, the bank takes a security interest in Custom Sound's inventory; equipment; accounts; chattel paper; and after-acquired inventory, equipment, accounts and chattel paper. A security agreement and financing statement is filed in the proper location to give the bank a perfected security interest.

2. Corliss purchases a TV set for her personal use. If Custom Sound defaults on its loan payments, who has priority between the bank and Corliss?

3. Deborah, a doctor, purchases a stereo for her office waiting room. If Custom Sound defaults on its loan payments, who has priority to the stereo between the bank and Deborah?

4. Suppose Deborah purchased her stereo on credit. She signed a promissory note, but not a security agreement. Does the bank have any interest in this note? If so, how is this interest perfected?

5. If Custom Sound sells this note to the Second Financial Institution three days after Deborah signed it, who has priority to the note between the bank and the Institution?

6. Suppose Corliss purchased her TV set on credit. She signed a promissory note and a security agreement. What are all the ways that Custom Sound can perfect its interest in Corliss's TV set?

7. Assume Corliss, while still owing Custom Sound, sells the TV set to Freddie. Who has priority to the TV set between Custom Sound and Freddie if Corliss defaults on her payments to Custom Sound? What assumption do you have to make?

8. What interest does the bank have at this point with respect to the Corliss transaction? How can this interest be perfected?

9. Suppose Custom Sound is in need of new computerized stereo testing equipment. It agrees to buy on credit new equipment worth $50,000 from Hi-Fi Diagnostic Corporation. This corporation wants to keep a security interest in the equipment sold to Custom Sound. What must Hi-Fi Diagnostic Corporation do to be sure of having priority to the equipment in case Custom Sound defaults?

10. How would your previous answer change if Custom Sound were planning to stock these items as inventory for resale?

11. Acme Glass Company sells Welch four mirrors on credit and installs the mirrors in Welch's house. The glass company retains a security interest in the mirrors and immediately fixture files. Will the company's security interest be superior under the revised Code to that of (a) First Bank, which has a mortgage on the house? (b) A new owner who buys the house from Welch? Explain both answers.

12. SP-1 takes a security interest in Don's inventory on February 1. Don files a bankruptcy petition on February 5. SP-1 files a financing statement on February 9 to perfect its security interest in Don's inventory. May the trustee prevail over SP-1's security interest? Would your answer change if SP-1's security interest were a PMSI? Explain.

13. To answer parts "a" through "g" of this question, rely on the following situation: A debtor was in arrears in his auto payments. When he failed to respond to requests for payment from the secured party, the secured party sent an agent to repossess the car. Is the agent's repossession of the car peaceful in the following instances?
    a. When the agent repossesses, the car is parked in front of the debtor's house.
    b. The agent at 11:00 P.M. tows away the car from the parking lot at the apartment house complex where the debtor had an assigned space.
    c. The car is parked in the debtor's unlocked garage.
    d. The car is parked in the debtor's locked garage. The agent unlocks the garage door, removes the car, and locks the garage.
    e. The car is parked at a service station after a tuneup. The station owner permits the agent to remove the car.
    f. The car is parked on the road in front of the debtor's house. As the agent starts to enter the car, the debtor bursts from the door of his house, shouting epithets and demanding that his car not be moved. But the agent is able to start the car and drive away before the debtor can get to the car.
    g. The agent comes to the debtor's house and states that he is from the city water department and needs to check the debtor's pipe system. The agent then sneaks into the garage and drives the car away.

14. A furniture manufacturer, secured by a security agreement, sold furniture to Daniel on credit. When Daniel did not pay as agreed, the creditor repossessed the furniture. This creditor approached one possible buyer for the items but failed to sell them. The creditor then bought the collateral at a private sale and sued Daniel for a deficiency of $7,000. Daniel contends that he is entitled to credit for the full value of the repossessed goods because the private sale was improper. Is Daniel correct? Why?

34 REAL PROPERTY AS SECURITY

The chapters on contracts and the Uniform Commercial Code dealt with many aspects of the law that are of substantial consequence to creditors. We saw basic legal procedures available to creditors—their right to sue for breach of contract and to use certain collection methods to enforce judgments obtained in such suits. The secured transaction, discussed in the previous chapters, involves the use of personal property as a significant method used by creditors to ensure the collection of debts.

In this chapter and the next one, we are concerned with additional aspects of the law that protect creditors. The use of real estate as security is the topic of this chapter: we discuss real estate mortgages and mechanic's liens. The next chapter includes material on other laws assisting creditors, especially the use of a third party's commitment as assurance to the creditor that a debt will be repaid.

1. Terminology

MORTGAGE TRANSACTIONS

A real estate *mortgage* is an interest in real property, an interest created for the purpose of securing the performance of an obligation, usually the payment of a debt. A mortgage is not a debt—only security for a debt. The owner of the estate in land that is being used as security for the debt is called the *mortgagor,* since that owner is granting a mortgage interest to the creditor. This party to whom the security interest in the real estate is conveyed is called the *mortgagee.*

2. Theories of Mortgages

Three distinct legal theories relate to mortgages. The first of these, the *title theory*, was developed under common law. Originally, a mortgage on land was an absolute conveyance of the title to the land by the owner to the mortgagee. However, title reverted to the mortgagor when the obligation was performed or the money was repaid. If the mortgagor failed to repay the debt, the property remained the property of the mortgagee. Under the title theory, the mortgagee could not be forced to sell the land to satisfy the debt. The process of not having a forced sale is known as strict foreclosure. Furthermore, anytime after default, the mortgagor lost all rights to redeem the interest in the real property. Due to the harshness of its application, the title theory has very little support today.

The second theory of mortgages is usually known as the *lien theory*, although it is sometimes called the *equitable theory*. Under this theory, a mortgage is not a conveyance of title, but only a method of creating a lien on the real estate. The lien or equitable theory avoids the harshness that results under the title theory. Under the lien theory, a mortgagee does not have title when the mortgagor defaults; he simply has a lien that can be foreclosed. Upon foreclosure of the lien, any proceeds of the sale are used to pay the debt and the costs of the sale. Any excess from the proceeds remains the property of the mortgagor. In addition, the lien theory grants to the mortgagor a right to redeem his property after the default and foreclosure. These rights to redeem are discussed in section 13, later in this chapter.

Many states do not follow the title or the lien theory; they have reached a compromise between the two, an *intermediate theory*. Under it, a mortgage is a conveyance of title, but the equitable theories are applied to it. Mortgages must be foreclosed; and the mortgagor has the right to redeem the interest prior to the foreclosed sale. This right of redemption exists even though the mortgagee has "title." The great majority of states are either lien- or intermediate-theory states.

3. Documents Involved

Remember that a mortgage is evidence of the security interest a lender is receiving; it is not evidence of the loan being made. Therefore, typically there are two documents involved in the mortgage financing transaction. The *promissory note* is the piece of paper that evidences the borrower's agreement to repay the amount of the loan. This note should include the principal borrowed, the interest rate charged, the term or the life of the loan, and the amount of the periodic payments.

In addition to the note, the mortgage document must be prepared. Since a mortgage is a contract, it must meet all the requirements of an enforceable agreement. A mortgage must be in writing and contain (1) the names of the mortgagor and mortgagee, (2) an accurate description of the mortgaged property, (3) the terms of the debt (incorporated from the note), and (4) the mortgagor's signature. This document must be executed with all the formalities of a deed. (For a review of these formalities, see chapter 19, section 9.)

In order that the mortgagee may give notice to the third parties that he has an interest in the real estate, it is necessary that the mortgage be recorded in the recording office of the county where the real estate is situated. Recording serves to notify subsequent parties of the lien or encumbrance of the mortgage.

4. Mortgage Clauses

In addition to the essential requirements just mentioned, mortgage documents are often several pages long because they contain many optional clauses. Some of the more typical mortgage provisions include (1) an acceleration clause, (2) a prepayment penalty clause, and (3) a dragnet clause. These clauses are discussed below. A mortgage also usually contains provisions on the rights and duties of the mortgagor and mortgagee. These rights and duties are discussed in the next section.

Acceleration Clauses. An acceleration clause enables the mortgagee to declare the entire outstanding balance of the loan immediately due and payable if stated conditions occur. For example, a due-on-default clause allows the mortgagee at his option to demand full payment if the mortgagor has failed to make a payment or a series of payments within a stated time period. A default may also occur whenever the mortgagor fails to comply with any other provision of the mortgage.

A *due-on-encumbrance clause* allows the mortgagee to accelerate the debt owed any time the mortgagor encumbers the real property without the mortgagee's consent. Examples of encumbering the property might include creating an easement in favor of a third party, agreeing to the application of restrictive covenants on the use of the land, failing to pay for work done to improve the property, or failing to pay taxes as they become due. The occurrence of any of these events entitles the mortgagee to demand full payment in order to protect the security interest the mortgagee already has.

The most controversial acceleration clause has been the *due-on-sale clause.* This type of clause permits the mortgagee to call the loan due whenever the mortgagor sells the collateral. The purpose of this clause originally was to protect the mortgage from purchasers with a questionable ability to repay the loan. In other words, with the due-on-sale acceleration clause, the mortgagee could prevent the assumption of the mortgage-secured loan by a buyer who was not creditworthy.

During periods of rapidly increasing interest rates, the due-on-sale clause has been utilized by mortgagees to adjust their below-market interest rates to a higher level. This clause has been used to prevent assumptions without an upward adjustment of the interest rate being charged. During the late 1970s and early 1980s, many states passed laws limiting the use of due-on-sale clauses as a means of adjusting the mortgagee's portfolio regarding interest rates. In 1982, the United States Supreme Court ruled that federally chartered financial institutions are exempt from state laws and regulations limiting the enforceability of due-on-sale clauses, regardless of the mortgagee's purpose. Since this decision, many states have decided that state-chartered financial institutions should be allowed to enforce due-on-sale clauses regardless of the circumstances. This trend has been necessary to keep state and federally created institutions on an equal competitive level.[1] Despite these rules and regulations, the enforcement of due-on-sale clauses becomes less important during times of relatively stable or declining interest rates.

Prepayment Penalty Clause. A mortgagor has the right without penalty to pay the loan off earlier than the agreed time unless the mortgage or note includes a prepayment penalty clause. This clause is used to protect the mortgagee when interest rates are falling. The prepayment penalty clause usually is limited to the situation where the mortgagor borrows funds at a lower rate in order to pay off the original loan. This clause is not applicable when the mortgagor prepays the loan due to the sale of the mortgaged property. This use would likely be prohibited as a restraint on the transferability of property.

If a mortgage contains both a due-on-sale and a prepayment penalty clause, the mortgagee probably is taking unfair advantage of the mortgagor—especially if the mortgagor is a consumer borrower. Most courts probably would refuse to allow the combined effect of these clauses. These clauses could be declared unenforceable as being unconscionable or contrary to public policy.

Dragnet Clause. A mortgage may be created prior to the time when money is advanced to the mortgagor. Such a mortgage is called a *mortgage to secure future advances.* The clause in a mortgage that makes the security interest cover future advances is referred to as a *dragnet clause.* This clause gives the mortgagee a valid interest in the real property described in the mortgage as of the date the mortgage is recorded to the extent of the amount stated in the mortgage.

For example, assume Rick E. Olsen, an owner of real estate, signs a mortgage containing a dragnet clause naming First Federal Savings and Loan as the mortgagee. This mortgage secures a loan First Federal makes to Rick in the amount of $50,000 and is recorded on September 2, 1980. Suppose Second National Bank then lends Rick $20,000 and receives a mortgage describing the same land as that described in the mortgage protecting First Federal. Second National's mortgage is recorded on April 10, 1983. Further assume that as of today's date, Rick has paid off half of the loan he owes First Federal ($25,000 of the $50,000), and it lends him another $15,000 without taking any new security. If Rick defaults the next day and if his land is sold for $45,000, who gets what of the proceeds? *Answer*: First Federal would get the full $40,000 Rick owes it, and Second National would get the remaining $5,000 of the proceeds. Second National would then be unsecured with respect to the remainder of what Rick owed it. The lesson of this example is to beware of dragnet clauses unless they are protecting you.

5. Rights and Duties of the Parties

Payment of the mortgage debt terminates the mortgage. Upon payment, the mortgagor is entitled to a release or satisfaction of the mortgage. This release should be recorded in order to clear the title to the land; otherwise, the unreleased

---

[1] Schulte v. Benton Savings and Loan Association, p. 770.

mortgage will remain a cloud on the title. If the mortgagee refuses to give a release, he can be compelled to do so in a court of equity.

The mortgagor is entitled to retain possession of the real estate during the period of the mortgage unless a different arrangement is provided for in the mortgage. The mortgagor may not use the property in a manner that will reduce materially its value. Mining ore, pumping oil, or cutting timber are operations that cannot be conducted by the mortgagor during the period of the mortgage unless the right to do so is reserved in the mortgage agreement. The rights will be implied when they are being conducted at the time the mortgage is created.

Any parcel of real estate may be subject to more than one mortgage. In addition, mortgaged land may be subject to a lien for property taxes. A mortgagee has a right to pay off any superior mortgage in order to protect his security, and he can charge the amount so paid to the mortgagor. Likewise, he may pay taxes or special assessments that are a lien on the land and recover the sum expended. The mortgagor is under a duty to protect the security; but should he fail to do so, the mortgagee has the right to make any reasonable expenditures necessary to protect the security for a debt.

The rights and duties of the parties may change when the mortgaged property is transferred. This situation, involving the transfer of the mortgage itself, is discussed in the next section.

6. Transfer of Mortgaged Property

The mortgagor may sell, will, or give away the mortgaged property, subject, however, to the rights of the mortgagee. A transferee from a mortgagor has no greater rights than the mortgagor. For example, a grantee of the mortgagor's interest may redeem the land by paying off the debt. A grantee of mortgaged property is not personally liable for the mortgage debt, unless he impliedly or expressly assumes and agrees to pay the mortgage. An assumption of a debt secured by a mortgage must be established by clear and convincing evidence. A purchase "subject to" a mortgage is usually considered not to be a legally enforceable assumption. If the grantee assumes the mortgage, he becomes personally liable for the debt, even when the land is worth less than the mortgage.

To illustrate, assume that Berg purchases real estate worth $88,000, which is subject to a mortgage of $60,000. Berg pays the former owner $28,000 cash. If she assumes and agrees to pay the mortgage, she is personally liable for the $60,000 debt. If the property is sold at a foreclosure sale, Berg is liable for any deficiency. However, if she merely purchased the property "subject to" the mortgage when she paid the $28,000, Berg would have no liability for any deficiency on foreclosure.

If the grantee of the mortgaged property assumes and agrees to pay the indebtedness, he thereby becomes the person primarily liable for the debt. Between the grantee and the mortgagor, by virtue of his promise to the mortgagor to pay the debt, he is the principal debtor, and the mortgagor is a surety. This assumption by the grantee, however, does not relieve the mortgagor of his obligation to the mortgagee, and the mortgagor continues to be liable unless he is released from his indebtedness by the mortgagee. Such a release must comply with all the requirements for a novation.

7. Alternatives to the Mortgage

Now that some of the basic principles of a mortgage have been discussed, at least three alternatives to the mortgage should be considered. First, a document known as a *deed of trust* or *trust deed* may be used as a substitute for a mortgage for the purpose of securing debts. Through this document, title to the real property is conveyed to a third party, who is the trustee, to be held for the benefit of the creditor. Whereas a mortgage involves two parties—the mortgagor (debtor) and the mortgagee (creditor)—the deed of trust involves three parties—the trustor (debtor), the trustee, and the beneficiary (creditor).

The trustee's title does not affect the debtor's use of the land as long as the loan is being repaid. If the debt is paid fully at the time required by the contract, the trustee reconveys the title to the debtor and releases the lien thereon. If there is a default, the trustee sells the property and applies the proceeds to the payment of the secured loan. Under this power of sale, the trustee transfers to the new purchaser all right, title, and interest that the debtor had at the time the deed trust was executed.

Deeds of trust are used instead of mortgages when the note is likely to be negotiated and when numerous notes are secured by the same property. The nature of the deed of trust is that the note secured by it can be freely transferred, separate and apart from the deed of trust. When the debtor pays the note, he surrenders it to the trustee under the trust deed, and the latter makes it a matter of record that the obligation has been satisfied.

A second alternative concerns a deed absolute on its face (one which purports to be only a deed with no qualifications) that may be shown by parol evidence to be a mortgage. If such evidence indicates that the intention of the parties was to make the transfer as security for a loan, the deed will be construed as a mortgage. The grantor of the deed must prove by clear, precise, and positive evidence that it was the intention of the parties to use the deed for the purpose of securing a loan.[2]

The third alternative to a mortgage occurs when the seller of real estate finances the transaction through a contract for a deed rather than with the use of a formal mortgage. Recall from chapter 20 that when a contract for a deed governs the transaction, there is no legal title being transferred. Therefore, in general, if the buyer/borrower defaults, no foreclosure sale is necessary since the seller/lender still owns the property.

MORTGAGE FORECLOSURE

8. Introduction

The issue of how the mortgage really protects the mortgagee is based on the assumption that the mortgagor has defaulted or will default prior to the loan being paid fully. If no default occurs, the mortgagee will recover that which it wants—

---

[2] White v. Ford, p. 771.

repayment of the loan. However, upon a default, the real property described in the mortgage can be used as leverage to encourage the mortgagor to pay what is owed. If payment still is not forthcoming, foreclosure becomes the valuable, albeit last, means of collection. In the following sections, you will read about the methods of foreclosure, the priority of claims to the proceeds, the mortgagor's rights to redeem his interest in the real property, and the mortgagee's rights to seek a deficiency.

9. Types of Foreclosures

The statutes of the various states specify the procedure by which mortgages are foreclosed. The common types of foreclosure proceedings are (1) strict foreclosure, (2) foreclosure by judicial action, and (3) foreclosure by exercise of the power of sale.

Strict Foreclosure. Strict foreclosure gives the mortgagee clear title to the land. A decree of strict foreclosure provides that if the debt is not paid by a certain date, the mortgagor loses the described real estate and the mortgagee takes it free from the rights of junior mortgagees and lienholders. It is used only where it is clear that the mortgaged property is not worth the mortgage indebtedness, the mortgagor is insolvent, and the mortgagee accepts the property in full satisfaction of the indebtedness. The substitution of the property for the debt has a historical basis in this country in those states that followed the absolute title theory. Since the title theory has very little impact today, strict foreclosure seldom arises by operation of law.

Today the mortgagor may agree to transfer title to the mortgagee in satisfaction of a debt by use of a deed in lieu of foreclosure. Obtaining title by this deed is not synonymous with the strict foreclosure process. Unlike foreclosure, a deed in lieu of foreclosure does not extinguish all the junior liens that may be on the property. Therefore, the mortgagee who accepts a deed in lieu of foreclosure may become involved in legal disputes with other creditors. These disputes usually involve the issue of whether the mortgagee took advantage of a defaulting mortgagor and thereby received property of more value than the debt satisfied.

Foreclosure by Judicial Action. The usual method of foreclosing a mortgage is a proceeding in a court of equity. If the mortgagor is in default, the court will authorize the sale of all the land at public auction. Following the sale, the purchaser receives a deed to the land. The funds received from the sale are used to pay court costs, the mortgage indebtedness, and inferior liens in the order of their priority. If any surplus remains, it is paid to the former owner of the property.

Statutes in many states provide a period of time after the sale within which the mortgagor or other persons having an interest are entitled to redeem the property. Where such statutes are in force, the purchaser is not entitled to a deed until after the expiration of the period within which redemption may be made. If the mortgagor remains in possession of the property sold, the purchaser may request that the court appoint a receiver and order the mortgagor to pay rent during the redemption period. The purchaser is entitled to the net rent during this period.

Foreclosure by Power of Sale. Particularly in states following the intermediate theory of mortgages, the mortgage often provides that upon default by the mortgagor, the mortgagee may sell the real property without resorting to judicial action. This method of foreclosure can be made only in strict conformity with the mortgage's provisions. Such provisions usually require the mortgagee to advertise several times in the local newspaper the time and location of the public auction.

This type of power of sale makes the mortgagee the agent of the mortgagor for the purposes of selling the property. The power of sale creates in the mortgagee's favor an agency coupled with an interest, which means that the mortgagee's appointment as the mortgagor's agent is irrevocable. Therefore, the mortgagor's death, insanity, bankruptcy, or withdrawal of consent does not destroy the validity of the power of sale. This type of agency and its termination are discussed in more detail in chapter 17.

As the mortgagor's agent, the mortgagee cannot purchase the property at the sale unless there is an explicit grant of such authority. Whoever the purchaser is at a foreclosure pursuant to a power of sale receives only the title the mortgagor had when he made the mortgage. In some states, a power of sale is expressly forbidden from appearing in a mortgage. In these jurisdictions, foreclosures can occur only after a judicial hearing.

10. Priority to Proceeds

A mortgage that holds senior priority on a property and that will be paid first in the event of default and foreclosure is known as a first mortgage. The amount of money that can be raised through a first mortgage is often less than the borrower needs to complete a purchase. In such cases junior mortgages—that is, second, third, and fourth mortgages, which are subordinate to the first mortgage—are sometimes used. Such mortgages carry more risk than first mortgages and usually are issued for shorter periods of time and at higher interest rates.

The priority given to various mortgages on the same real estate normally is determined by which mortgagee is the first to record the mortgage document with the public records. However, order of recording does not always determine priority. One mortgagee whose mortgage is already on record may agree to subordinate its priority to another mortgagee. For example, a mortgagee that holds a security interest on a vacant land probably would agree to let a second mortgagee who has lent funds for a construction project have priority if the construction of an improvement will increase the land's value by more than the amount of the additional mortgage.

Junior mortgages also are commonly used to help in the financing of the sale of an existing home or income properties. For example, a homeowner may be able to get a higher price for his house if the purchaser can assume an existing mortgage at an interest rate lower than those currently charged by banks. The required down payment may be larger than the buyer can pay, however, and the seller may be willing to take a second mortgage for part of the purchase price. Furthermore, second mortgages commonly are used for home-improvement loans. A family that wants to add a room or make extensive repairs to its home can usually get the money to do so at a lower rate through a junior mortgage than by taking out a personal installment loan.

Foreclosure of an inferior mortgage is made subject to all superior liens. In other words, the foreclosure of a second mortgage does not affect a first mortgage. The buyer at the foreclosure sale takes title, and the first mortgage remains a lien on the property. A foreclosure does cut off the enforceability of all inferior liens. For instance, the foreclosure of a first mortgage eliminates the rights of the second and subsequent mortgages.

11. Mortgagor's Rights of Redemption

A mortgagor who is in default on a note secured by a mortgage can terminate the foreclosure process prior to its completion by exercising a right called the *equity of redemption.* Upon the mortgagor's payment of an amount equal to the debt then owing plus interest and any expenses incurred by the mortgagee, the mortgagor's interest in the property is restored. In other words, the debt and the mortgage will be reinstated if the mortgagor redeems his or her interest by making payment prior to the foreclosure sale.

Any person who acquires the mortgagor's interest while a default situation exists also acquires the right to redeem the property interest equitably prior to foreclosure. Because the mortgagee may have the right to accelerate the amount owed upon default, the entire debt may have to be paid in order to redeem the interest. Normally the mere payment of the amount in default is not sufficient if the debt has been accelerated properly.

In many states (including Alabama, Arizona, California, Colorado, Connecticut, Hawaii, Idaho, Illinois, Indiana, Iowa, Kansas, Kentucky, Maine, Michigan, Minnesota, Missouri, Montana, Nevada, New Jersey, North Dakota, Oregon, South Dakota, Utah, and Washington), the mortgagor is allowed to redeem his property even after foreclosure. This right to redeem property after a foreclosure sale is called the *statutory right of redemption.* The statutory redemption period varies from state to state, being as short as 6 months and as long as 2 years. The most common statutory period is 1 year. In states that have this statutory right of redemption, the purchaser at a foreclosure sale does not obtain full and clear title until the statutory period of redemption has passed.

12. Mortgagee's Rights to Deficiency Judgments

A person who executes the note or bond secured by the mortgage is personally liable for the debt. If the property that is the security for the debt does not sell for a sum sufficient to pay the indebtedness, the mortgagor remains liable for the deficiency, and a judgment may be entered for this unpaid balance. This judgment may be collected from the mortgagor's other property or income. In other words, additional assets of the mortgagor may be seized and sold by an officer of the court to satisfy the mortgagee's claim of deficiency.

Property that is sold at a foreclosure sale seldom brings a price that reflects the market value of the property under normal circumstances. During the Great

Depression of the 1930s, prices at foreclosure sales fell to extremely low levels, often leaving debtors with large deficiency judgments against them even after they had lost their mortgaged property. As might be expected, a great deal of antideficiency legislation was passed during that period. To recover the full amount of a deficiency, the mortgagee must be able to prove the foreclosure sale was conducted according to commercially reasonable standards.[3] Indeed, the mortgagee should have the foreclosure price approved by the appropriate court prior to or concurrent with the filing of a motion for a deficiency judgment. In the alternative, the mortgagee may waive the right to collect the amount of a deficiency.

In order not to impose too great a hardship on mortgagors, different schemes have been devised to limit the amount of these parties' liability for deficiencies. Some states, including Nebraska, New Jersey, and Oregon, have simply outlawed all deficiency judgments. Many other states have antideficiency statutes that are applicable only to purchase-money mortgages. When a mortgage is given to secure payment of the balance of the purchase price of real property, the mortgagee is not entitled to a deficiency judgment. In these states, if the mortgage proceeds are not used to finance the purchase of the real property, deficiency judgments are allowed. The elimination of liability for deficiencies rests on several theories: that the mortgagee lent his money on the security of the real estate and not the personal credit of the purchaser; that a mortgagee should share with the mortgagor the risk of declining real estate values; and that if the real estate is the limit of the security, sounder loans and fewer inflationary ones will be made.

MECHANIC'S LIENS

13. Introduction

Mechanic's lien laws provide for the filing of liens upon real estate that has been improved. An improvement is any addition to the land. While the term *improvement* does not always mean that the land's value has been increased, most improvements usually do increase the real estate's value. The purpose of a mechanic's lien is to protect contractors, laborers, and materialmen in the event of nonpayment of their accounts. Because state laws vary slightly in the protection accorded and the procedure required to obtain it, the laws of the state in which the property is located should be consulted.

To gain an understanding of how mechanic's liens generally are used to secure payment for one who contributed to an improvement, the following sections discuss: (1) potential lienholders, (2) the perfection and enforcement of liens; (3) priority issues; and (4) protection against liens.

14. Potential Lienholders

The persons usually entitled to a lien include those who (1) deliver material, fixtures, apparatus, machinery, forms, or form work to be used in repairing, altering, or constructing a building upon the premises; (2) fill, sod, or do landscape work in connection with the premises; (3) act as architect, engineer, or superin-

---

[3] Danvers Savings Bank v. Hammer, p. 772.

tendent during the construction of a building; or (4) furnish labor for repairing, altering, or constructing a building.

Persons who contract with the owner, whether they furnish labor or material or agree to construct the building, are known as *contractors*. Thus, virtually any contract between the owner and another that has for its purpose the improvement of real estate gives rise to a lien on the premises in favor of those responsible for the improvement. Improvements include fixtures.

In addition to contractors, anyone who furnishes labor, materials, or apparatus to contractors, or anyone to whom a distinct part of the contract has been sublet, has a right to a lien. These latter parties are customarily referred to as *subcontractors*. Their rights differ slightly from those of contractors, and some of these differences will be considered in later sections.

Prior to studying the nature of a mechanic's lien, you must understand that not every act related to real estate is an improvement and leads to a lien.[4] The statutes creating mechanic's liens are crucial in determining who is protected by these liens.

14. Perfection and Enforcement

In some states, a contractor has a lien as soon as the contract to repair or to improve the real estate is entered into. In others, the lien attaches as soon as the work is commenced. A supplier of materials usually has a lien as soon as the materials are furnished. A laborer has a lien when the work is performed. The statutes relating to mechanic's liens provide for the method of perfecting these mechanic's liens and for the time period during which they may be perfected. The time period begins when the work is substantially completed. Minor corrections to the work or trivial work done after substantial completion does not extend the period.

The usual procedure is that the party seeking to perfect a mechanic's lien files or records a notice of lien in the office of the county in which deeds to real estate are recorded. Some statutes provide for filing in the county of residence of the owner. A copy of the notice is sent to the owner of record and to the party contracting for the repair or improvement. This notice must be filed within the prescribed statutory period. The law then requires a suit to foreclose the lien and specifies that it be commenced within an additionally prescribed period such as one year. Anything less than strict observance of the filing requirements eliminates the mechanic's lien, but not the debt.[5]

Most mechanic's lien laws provide a relatively long period, such as 1 year, during which a contractor may file a mechanic's lien and proceed to enforce it against the property interest of the party with whom he contracted. This time period is relatively long because the obligation is known to the owner, and he is in no way prejudiced if the lien is not promptly filed.

A much shorter time period is set for subcontractors, laborers, and materialmen to file their mechanic's liens. The owner of the premises may not know the

---

[4] Johnson v. Barnhill, p. 773.

[5] Smith Pipe & Steel Company v. Mead, p. 774.

source of materials and may not know the names of all persons performing services on the premises. To this extent, the liens of subcontractors, materialmen, and workers may be secret, and the owner may pay the wrong person. Therefore, the time period in which the statutory procedures must be followed is relatively short, such as 60 to 90 days.

If the property is sold or mortgaged, the existence of any mechanic's lien often would be unknown to the purchaser or mortgagee. For this reason the statutes on mechanic's liens usually specify the same short period of time for the perfection of the mechanic's lien—whether by a contractor, subcontractor, materialman, or laborer, if it is to be effective against good-faith purchasers of the property or subsequent mortgagees. Under these statutory provisions, a mechanic's lien that could be enforced against the property interest of the original contracting owner cannot be enforced against the property interest of the new owner or mortgagee after the expiration of the prescribed statutory period. Thus, during the relatively short statutory period, a mechanic's lien is good against innocent third parties even though it has not been properly perfected. Consequently, a purchaser of real estate should always ascertain if any repairs or improvements have been made to the premises within the time period for filing mechanic's liens. If it is determined that repairs or improvements have been made, the procedures outlined in the next section should be followed.

If a contractor, subcontractor, supplier of material, or laborer fails to file his notice of lien within the appropriate prescribed time period or fails to commence suit within the additional period, the lien is lost.

Since a person entitled to a mechanic's lien has a prescribed period within which to file his lien, the date on which this time period starts to run is frequently quite important. Most statutes provide that in the case of a supplier, the time period starts to run from the date the materials are delivered; and in the case of a contractor or subcontractor performing services, the time for filing starts to run from the completion of the work. This latter concept requires further clarification, however.

Should a contractor or subcontractor be able to postpone the time for filing by performing additional services at a later date? Assume that a contractor has allowed the time for filing his lien to elapse. Should the time period start all over if he makes a minor repair, such as adjusting a doorknob or touching up a paint job? Common sense would say no, and most statutes provide that a contractor or subcontractor cannot extend the statutory period of time by performing minor, trifling repairs after the work has been substantially completed. In other words, trivial work done or materials furnished after the contract has been substantially completed will not extend the time in which a lien claim can be filed.[6]

15. Priorities

Two basic situations create issues of priorities concerning mechanic's liens. The first concerns priority among similar mechanic's liens. The second situation involves the priority of a mechanic's lienholder compared with the rights of a mortgagee to the proceeds from the forced sale of the real estate.

---

[6] Mitchell v. Flandro, p. 775.

If there are several mechanic's liens filed as the result of the same improvement project, the liens are entitled to priority on the basis of when the lienholder began work on the project. If several liens are considered equal in priority and there are insufficient funds to satisfy all these claims, the lienholders must share the proceeds on a pro-rata basis. Each lienholder is entitled to that portion of the proceeds which his work represented of the entire improvement.

When determining the priority of a mechanic's lien and a mortgage on the same property, the date of attachment is crucial. Nearly all states provide that a mortgage attaches when it is properly recorded. If the state where the land is located is one of the few providing that a mechanic's lien attaches when a notice of lien is filed, then priority is given to the creditor who is first to file.

The majority of states' laws on mechanic's liens say that these liens attach when work first begins or when supplies are first delivered. In these states a mortgage may be filed before a notice of lien is filed, and yet the lien has priority. A mortgagee must therefore make sure there are no potential mechanic's liens or obtain an agreement from contractors, laborers, and suppliers that their liens are subordinated to the mortgage. Without these actions, a mortgagee may lose all or at least part of the foreclosure proceeds to a mechanic's lienholder.

Still other states give priority to mechanic's liens over a previously recorded mortgage because the lienholder has increased the value of the real property. This added value should be evident in the greater proceeds obtained at the foreclosure sale. After the lienholder is paid, the mortgagee still has the remaining proceeds, which should be the same as if no improvement had been made. This priority given to the mechanic's lien may not apply if the items added to the real estate become inseparable from the entire improvement.[7]

16. Protection against Liens

Mechanic's lien statutes usually provide that an owner is not liable for more than the contract price if he follows the procedures outlined in the law. These usually require that the owner, prior to payment, obtain from the contractor a sworn statement setting forth all the creditors and the amounts due, or to become due, to each of them. It is then the duty of the owner to retain sufficient funds at all times to pay the amounts indicated by the sworn statements. In addition, if any liens have been filed by the subcontractors, it is the owner's duty to retain sufficient money to pay them. He is at liberty to pay any balance to the contractor.

An owner has a right to rely upon the truthfulness of the sworn statement of the contractor. If the contractor misstates the facts and obtains a sum greater than that to which he is entitled, the loss falls upon the subcontractors who dealt with him, rather than upon the owner. Under such circumstances, the subcontractors may look only to the contractor for payment. Payments made by the owner, without his first obtaining a sworn statement, may not be used to defeat the claims of subcontractors, materialmen, and laborers. Before making any payment, the owner has the duty to require the sworn statement and to withhold the amount necessary to pay the claims indicated.

The owner may also protect himself by obtaining waivers of the contractor's

---

[7] Exchange Savings & Loan Association v. Monocrete Pty. Ltd., p. 776.

lien and of the liens of subcontractors, suppliers, and laborers. A *waiver* is the voluntary relinquishment of the right to a lien before a notice of lien is filed. In a few states, a waiver of the lien by the contractor is also a waiver of the lien of the subcontractors, as they derive their rights through those of the contractor. However, in most states, lien waivers are effective only against those who agree not to claim a mechanic's lien.

Even after a notice of lien is filed, lienholders may extinguish their right to enforce the lien. This post-filing process is known as a *release* of the lien. Very often, the concept of waivers and that of releases is confused. A waiver occurs before a notice of lien is filed, whereas a release is used after there is a public filing. A mechanic's lien commonly is released when the landowner pays the lienholder after a notice of lien has been filed.

SUMMARY

MORTGAGE TRANSACTION

Terms	1. A mortgage is the document wherein a borrower grants to a lender a security interest in the borrower's real estate.
	2. A mortgagor is the borrower who grants the security interest in real estate to the lender.
	3. A mortgagee is the lender who receives a security interest in real estate.
Theories	1. Originally, a mortgage conveyed legal title or ownership to the mortgagee.
	2. Today, the law of a state usually views a mortgage as creating only a lien on the real estate or, in the alternative, a mortgagee has title which is created as a lien for security purposes.
	3. These modern theories are known as the lien (or equity) theory and the intermediate theory, respectively.
Documents involved	1. The borrower in a mortgage transaction usually signs a promissory note, which is evidence of the borrower's personal obligation to repay.
	2. The borrower also signs a mortgage, which is the document that grants the lender a security interest in described real estate.
Mortgage clauses	1. Mortgages often include acceleration clauses which allow the mortgagee to

make the entire debt due and payable upon the occurrence of certain events. These clauses may be classified as due on default, due on encumbrance, and due on sale.

2. A prepayment penalty clause is often included in a mortgage. It allows the mortgagee to collect a penalty if the debt is paid off early without permission.

3. A dragnet clause allows one mortgage to serve as security for any future loan the mortgagee grants to the mortgagor.

Transfer of mortgaged property

1. When real estate and the mortgage describing such real estate are transferred, the question arises about whether the original mortgagor or the transferee or both are liable.

2. The transferee who takes the property "subject to" the mortgage does not become personally liable for any deficiency should there be a foreclosure sale.

3. The transferee who takes the property and who "assumes" the mortgage does become personally liable for any deficiency.

4. In either of the two situations above, the original mortgagor remains personally liable for the debt unless there has been a novation.

Alternatives to mortgages

1. In many states, a three-party document, known as a deed of trust, is often used instead of a mortgage.

2. A deed, which is absolute on its face, may be treated as a mortgage if the parties' intent was for the deed to serve as security and not as an outright conveyance.

3. A contract for a deed can be used instead of a mortgage when the seller agrees to finance a purchase of real estate.

MORTGAGE FORECLOSURE

Types of foreclosure

1. Strict foreclosure occurs when a mortgagee simply keeps title to the real estate rather than conducting a foreclosure sale. This process was most

closely associated with the title theory. Due to the rejection of the title theory, strict foreclosure seldom is allowed today.

2. Foreclosure by judicial action requires court approval to conduct a sale of the mortgaged real estate. In states that follow a lien theory of mortgages, this type of foreclosure is most common.

3. Foreclosure by the power of sale usually is allowed in states that have adopted an intermediate theory of mortgages if the mortgage contains a power-of-sale clause.

Priorities

1. Mortgagees have priority to the proceeds of a sale in the same order in which their mortgages were recorded.

2. An exception to this order occurs if a mortgagee with a superior priority subordinates its claim to an inferior mortgagee.

3. Upon the foreclosure of a superior mortgage, all inferior mortgages are extinguished. However, the buyer at a foreclosure sale of an inferior mortgage takes subject to all superior mortgages.

Rights of redemption

1. A mortgagor in default has the right to redeem or reinstate his interest in the real estate by paying the debt plus necessary expenses.

2. All mortgagors may exercise the equitable right of redemption prior to the foreclosure sale.

3. Even after the foreclosure sale, some states allow the mortgagor to exercise a statutory right of redemption. This statutory right is more likely to exist in states recognizing the lien theory of mortgages.

Deficiency judgment

1. After a foreclosure sale that has not produced proceeds equal to the debt, the mortgagee may sue the mortgagor for the deficiency.

2. In order to recover a deficiency judgment, the mortgagee must prove that the foreclosure sale was commercially reasonable.

3. A few states have abolished this right to collect a deficiency judgment, particularly

when a purchase money mortgage is
involved.

MECHANIC'S LIENS

Purpose

1. A mechanic's lien gives leverage to any
   party who has contributed to an
   improvement of real estate.
2. An improvement does not necessarily
   increase the value of the real estate.

Potential lienholders

1. Those parties who contract directly or
   indirectly with an owner for an
   improvement are potential lienholders.
   Typically, these parties include general
   contractors and subcontractors.
2. Suppliers of materials and laborers who
   provide work also are potential
   lienholders.

Perfection and enforcement

1. Since mechanic's liens are created by state
   law, each state's requirements for a valid
   lien vary to some degree.
2. In general, a lienholder must file a notice
   of a lien within a statutory time period
   after work is completed.
3. In addition to the notice of lien, a lawsuit
   must be filed within the time provided.
4. As a result of the lawsuit, a court may
   order that the improved real estate be
   sold in order to satisfy the lienholder's
   claim for payment.

Priorities

1. Among mechanic's lienholders, priority
   usually is determined by the beginning of
   that lienholder's work or delivery of
   materials.
2. If lienholders are equal in priority, they
   share the proceeds on a pro-rata basis.
   Each should receive the same percentage
   of the proceeds that their work
   contributed to the whole improvement.
3. The priority between mechanic's liens and
   mortgages depends on the state's law and
   the time each claim attached to the real
   estate.

Protection against liens

1. A real estate owner who is improving his
   land should obtain a sworn statement
   from the contractor prior to making any

payment. This statement should explain who are potential lienholders. The owner then can take steps to satisfy these parties' claims.

2. An owner generally can prevent claims by making payment to the lienholders or by having these lienholders waive or release their rights to a mechanic's lien.

CASES

Schulte v. Benton Savings and Loan Association
651 S.W.2d 71 (Ark. 1983)

HOLT, J. The issue in this case involves the enforceability of a "due on sale" clause in a mortgage where the mortgagee is a state chartered savings and loan association. . . .

In 1977, the appellant, Ballard Construction Company, executed a promissory note payable to the appellee and secured by a mortgage on commercial real property. Included in the mortgage contract was the following due on sale clause:

> (j) Acceleration. The maturity of the principal indebtedness secured hereby may be accelerated in any of the following events: . . .

> (7) If the mortgagor or assignee sells or conveys (or contracts to sell or convey) all or any part of the mortgaged property without the written consent of the holder of said note.

In 1981, appellant Ballard Construction Company sold the mortgaged real estate to the appellant Schulte without the written consent of the appellee. The appellee elected to accelerate the maturity of the indebtedness. The appellant Schulte refused the appellee's demand that she pay the full indebtedness within 30 days. However, she tendered into the registry of the court the regular monthly installments, which appellee refused to accept, pursuant to the terms of the promissory note. The appellee declared the note to be in default and brought this action to collect the full balance of the note plus attorney's fees. The trial court granted summary judgment in favor of the appellee, holding that the appellants were liable to the appellee for the $82,285.58 balance. . . . Hence this appeal.

Appellants argue that the default is based upon a technical provision in the mortgage absent any showing that the security is impaired by the prohibited sale. They cite *Tucker v. Pulaski Federal Savings & Loan*, 481 S.W.2d 725 (1972). There, we held that a due on sale clause, such as the one presented here, could not be enforced unless the mortgagee reasonably believed its security was impaired by the sale. However in 1976 the Federal Home Loan Bank Board issued a regulation, 12 C.F.R. §545.8 3(f) (1982), permitting federally chartered savings and loans to enforce due on sale clauses without a showing that the security is impaired by the sale. . . . Here the appellee is a state chartered savings and loan association, not a federal savings and loan. . . .

[This Court discussed the Arkansas legislation that granted state chartered financial institutions the same rights and powers as federally chartered financial institutions. The purpose of this legislation is to ensure against federal institutions having an unfair competitive advantage over state institutions.]

The recited statute and rules clearly place state savings and loan associations on the same footing as federally chartered associations doing business in this state. Since we held that federally chartered associations may enforce due on sale clauses in cases without the requirement of showing the security is impaired, it follows that state associations are duly empowered to do the same. . . .

Since we affirm the trial court on the legal issue that the rule that governs federally chartered associations in Arkansas has been made applicable to state chartered associations and the Arkansas Savings and Loan Association Board, we must affirm the summary judgment. There is no genuine issue as to any material fact and the appellee is entitled to judgment as a matter of law.

Affirmed.

White v. Ford
471 A.2d 1176 (N.H. 1984)

PER CURIAM. . . . The plaintiff, Robert R. White, is executor under the will of John E. Ford, who died February 6, 1978. Fred H. Ford, Jr., the defendant, is a nephew of the deceased. By deed dated March 30, 1962, the deceased purported to convey to the defendant by specific description, . . . approximately ten acres of land in the town of Hudson. At that time, title to the land was held by the town under a tax collector's deed.

At the time of the conveyance to the defendant, there was an outstanding mortgage on the property running to a third party, which was assigned to the defendant as part of the same transaction. There is evidence which indicates that, shortly before the deed was executed, the defendant had lent the deceased $1,000 to pay back taxes. There is further evidence indicating that the defendant had lent the decedent money over a period of years. There is a notation on the mortgage instrument that the mortgage note was paid in full by the deceased on January 9, 1963.

On May 3, 1963, the deceased purchased the property from the town. Until his death, the deceased lived there and personally paid whatever taxes were paid on the property, with an undetermined amount of the money being furnished by the defendant.

[The issue before this Court is whether the deed of conveyance involved in this case actually was given to secure a debt.]

. . . [T]he master ruled that the decedent's deed was given to the defendant as security for a debt. A deed absolute on its face may be proven by parol evidence to have been intended by the parties to operate as security for a debt. The intentions of the parties at the time of the conveyance is determinative, but those intentions may be inferred from the situation of the parties and their actions after the contract was executed. Where, as here, the trial court must look to extrinsic evidence to deduce the intentions of the parties, we will adopt the trial court's interpretation of the contract if supported by sufficient evidence.

Our review of the record compels us to conclude that the evidence does support the finding that the deed was given to the defendant as security for a debt. Factors pointing to this conclusion include the impecunious state of the decedent at the time of the transfer, his close relationship to the defendant and the inadequacy of the consideration, as well as the fact that the decedent was permitted to remain in possession of the real estate without accounting for rent.

The true intention of the parties to the transfer having been found by the master, the deed should be deemed a mortgage running from the decedent to the defendant, with the decedent having an equitable right of redemption. The master also found that the debt for which the deed originally acted as security was extinguished when the mortgage assigned to the defendant was paid and discharged as noted on the mortgage by notation dated January 9, 1963. Again, the evidence supports this finding, and therefore, the granting of the petition to quiet title is affirmed.

The master, however, indicated that the defendant viewed the deed as being security for money lent to the decedent over the course of several years. The master went on to state: "No ruling is made nor intended on the defendant's rights to enforce a claim for any amount owed to him by the estate on the security interest established."

It was by virtue of the superior court's equitable powers that the petition to quiet title was granted. For the plaintiff to invoke the court's equitable power to quiet title, he must also act equitably. . . . Consequently, as a condition precedent to the superior court's granting the petition to quiet title, the court may require the plaintiff to satisfy any claims made by the defendant against the estate that are properly proven by him to the satisfaction of the court.

Affirmed.

Danvers Savings Bank v. Hammer
440 A.2d 435 (N.H. 1982)

DOUGLAS, J. On February 9, 1970, Richard Hammer borrowed $7,000 from the Danvers Savings Bank and executed a promissory note in favor of the bank. The note was secured by land in Boxford, Massachusetts. After the defendant defaulted, the bank foreclosed on his property. No potential buyers attended the foreclosure sale except bank representatives. They purchased the defendant's real estate for $100, and later resold it for $2,025. The bank sought a $10,040.02 deficiency judgment against Hammer, consisting of the sum of the $7,000 principal due under the note, $1,523.55 in accrued interest, $1,237.88 in taxes, $709.50 for legal notices of the foreclosure sale, $150 for an auctioneer, and $1,444.09 for legal fees and expenses, less a credit of $2,025, the resale price. The Superior Court granted the bank's motion for a directed verdict on July 9, 1980, awarding the bank a $10,040.02 deficiency judgment. The defendant appealed to this court. . . .

Richard Hammer's mortgage included a statutory power of sale that allowed the bank to sell his property if he defaulted. In conducting the foreclosure sale, the bank complied with the proper statutory procedures, but Richard Hammer argues that the price paid for his land was so inadequate that we should infer bad faith and invalidate the sale or award him damages.

When a mortgagee seeks to uphold a foreclosure sale in order to bring a deficiency action against the mortgagor, courts scrutinize the sale price very closely to assure that the mortgagee acted with strict impartiality. We will review this sale with particular caution because the bank purchased the mortgaged property at its own foreclosure sale.

The validity, method and effect of a mortgage foreclosure are determined by the law of the place where the land is located, and therefore we will apply Massachusetts law. Under Massachusetts law, the bank had the right to purchase at its own foreclosure sale. The price paid, however, was so grossly disproportionate to Hammer's debt and the value of the property, "as to indicate bad faith or lack of reasonable diligence." Generally, an inadequate price will not invalidate a sale or entitle the debtor to damages. A grossly disproportionate price, however, indicates that the sale was improperly conducted, entitling the debtor to relief.

The debtor in this case is entitled to relief. At trial, a bank official testified that the bank had "no particular reason" for bidding only $100 for property securing a $7,000 debt and which the bank later resold for $2,025 over twenty times the bid price. The bank did not have the land appraised, and had no opinion at trial as to what the land was worth when sold. The bank was not reasonably diligent, in submitting such an arbitrary bid. In addition, in its advertisements of the foreclosure sale, the bank stated that a minimum of $1,000 of the purchase price had to be paid at the time and place of sale. Nothing in the Massachusetts statutes or cases indicates that this advertisement chilled bidding or established a mandatory minimum bid, but it does illustrate the inadequacy of the bank's $100 bid. Thus, the trial court erred in ruling that the defendant did not sustain his "burden of showing misconduct on the part of the plaintiff."

Because title to the property has passed to bona fide purchasers, we will not set aside the foreclosure sale. We therefore remand for a reassessment of damages. The trial court must first determine the fair market value of the real estate at the time of foreclosure. The damages should consist of the difference between that market value and the defendant's outstanding debt plus costs.

If the proven market value exceeds the outstanding debt plus costs, the excess should be awarded to the defendant.

The defendant argues that the bank should not have been allowed to recover a deficiency judgment. We disagree. When a mortgagee notifies the debtor of its intention to foreclose, and of the debtor's possible liability for a deficiency judgment, a deficiency may be recovered.

Richard Hammer next contends that the trial court should not have allowed the bank to recover the various costs it incurred in conducting the foreclosure sale. The defendant's mortgage allows the bank only to "retain" costs, charges, and expenses from the proceeds of a foreclosure sale. The defendant argues that there was no fund from which these expenses could be retained, therefore the bank has no right to recover them. In *Security Co-operative Bank v. Corcoran*, 10 N.E.2d 57, 58 (1937), the court held that reasonable foreclosure expenses may be charged to the debtor. In that case, "[t]he bank made no mistake in adding to the balance of principal due on the note . . . the expenses of foreclosure and then crediting on account the full price for which the premises were sold. This was a proper method of ascertaining the deficiency. . . ." Foreclosure expenses, therefore, were properly included in the bank's deficiency judgment.

Remanded for reassessment of damages.

Johnson v. Barnhill
306 S.E.2d 216 (S.C. 1983)

LEWIS, J. While other issues are presented in this appeal, the dispositive one is whether, under the South Carolina Mechanic's Lien statutes respondent Johnson, a surveyor, is entitled to a Mechanic's Lien upon the real property of appellant Barnhill for surveying work done in connection with the property.

Appellant employed respondent to survey, plat, and lay out approximately 194 acres of land known as Cassina Plantation in the Mount Pleasant area of Charleston County. The work consisted solely of subdividing the land into smaller tracts and laying out roads, bridle paths, and drainage ditches.

Disagreement arose between the parties over payment for the work, which resulted in the institution of this action to foreclose a mechanic's lien previously filed by respondent to secure payment for the work allegedly done. Among other defenses, appellant moved to dismiss the action on the ground that work done by respondent did not entitle it to a lien under the terms of the foregoing statutes. The lower court denied the motion, holding that surveyors were entitled to a mechanic's lien for their services. The present issue arises on appeal from that ruling. . . .

Respondent seeks to bring itself within the terms of both Sections 29–5–10 and 29–5–20. Section 29–5–10 grants a lien to any person for labor performed or furnished in the erection, alteration or repair of any building or structure upon any real estate, which includes "the work of making such real estate suitable as a site for such building or structure." Section 29–5–20 gives a lien to every laborer or person "furnishing material for the improvement of real estate."

. . . [R]espondent contends that the work of surveying and laying out lots was essential to the beginning of construction, hence it was "work of making such real estate suitable as a site." Respondent further argues that the work of surveying and laying out of lots constituted it a laborer and the services an "improvement." . . .

The statute, in granting a lien for labor performed or furnished in making the real estate upon which a building is to be placed "suitable as a site for such building," has reference, and is limited, to labor performed in the preparation of the location on which the building is to be placed. The survey and laying out of the subdivision was not labor in the preparation of the actual site for any building or other improvement to be located thereon. The laying out of the lot was nothing more than the designation of the site or place where the improvement might be placed by a subsequent purchaser.

Neither did the work of the surveyor constitute an improvement to the real estate. . . . In order to establish a mechanic's lien, it is generally necessary that the labor performed go into something which has attached to and become a part of the real estate, adding to the value thereof. The survey and marking of the lots simply designated an area to be sold; and the surveyor's service did not go into anything which attached to or become a part of the realty.

. . . [T]his Court approved the settled principle that statutory liens may not be extended by courts to claims not specified in the statute and that a claimant must bring himself within the expressed intention of the lawmakers.

There was no language in Sections 29–5–10 or 29–5–20 which expressly or by implication indicated a legislative intent that the services of a surveyor were covered by these statutes.

The lower court was therefore in error in holding that respondent was entitled to a lien for its services. Judgment is accordingly reversed and the cause remanded for entry of judgment in favor of appellant.

Reversed and remanded.

[We note that under a 1978 amendment (Code

Section 29-5-21, Code Supplement) the provisions of Code Section 29-5-20 were extended to grant a mechanic's lien to surveyors. However, since the

agreement and work performed in this case predated the 1978 amendment, it has no effect on this decision.]

Smith Pipe & Steel Company v. Mead
634 P.2d 962 (Ariz. 1981)

HAYS, J. This is an action by Smith Pipe & Steel Co. (hereinafter "Smith") to foreclose a materialman's lien on certain property held in trust by William A. Mead. The Superior Court granted Mead's motion for summary judgment and Smith appeals. . . .

The facts pertinent to this appeal are brief and undisputed. Mead was a trustee for a trust which owned adjacent parcels of real property in Maricopa County. Smith sold and furnished construction materials to Flood Plumbing Company, a licensed plumbing subcontractor, for use in the construction of structures and improvements on the *south* parcel of the adjacent lots. Flood completed the work but subsequently went bankrupt and failed to pay Smith for the materials. Smith then recorded a Notice and Claim of Lien. . . . The Notice and Claim of Lien, however, gave the legal description of the *north* parcel, instead of the south parcel upon which the improvements were made. After Smith filed a complaint to foreclose the lien, Mead moved for summary judgment arguing that the erroneous description rendered the lien invalid. The trial court agreed and granted Mead's motion.

The sole issue presented is whether a lien claimant may perfect a materialman's lien where the Notice and Claim of Lien contains an erroneous legal description.

Smith contends that the erroneous description was sufficient to give notice to Mead which parcel was intended to be impressed with the lien. In making this argument, reliance is placed upon the familiar rule that the Arizona Mechanics' and Materialmen's Lien Statutes are to be liberally construed in favor of laborers and materialmen. Because the record is devoid of any indication that Mead was prejudiced by the erroneous legal description and no third party rights were involved,

Smith concludes that a liberal construction of the statute requires a finding that the lien was valid.

With regard to the content of the lien, . . . in 1973, . . . the legislature amended §33-993 to provide that the notice and claim of lien contain "[t]he *legal description* of the lands and improvements to be charged with a lien." (Emphasis added.) In light of this change, Mead submits that Smith has not achieved even substantial compliance with the statute's "legal description" requirement in that the legal description contained in its Notice and Claim of Lien is "unambiguously erroneous" and fails to describe the correct parcel of property. . . .

The 1973 amendment to §33-993(1) clarifies the manner in which the property to be charged with the lien is to be described. The inexact provision under former §33-993(1), "[a] description . . . sufficient for identification" did not give any indication whether a legal description, street address, or physical description of the land or improvements would suffice. The amended version, however, removed this obvious ambiguity by requiring a legal description to be used when describing the property to be charged with the lien. Significantly, the legislature not only added the legal description requirement, but at the same time omitted the "sufficient for identification" language from the old statute. We believe this reflects a legislative intent that substantial compliance with the legal description requirement is necessary in order to perfect a lien. As was aptly stated by the Supreme Court of Idaho in a case with virtually identical facts, "[a]lthough the rule may be different with regard to a description which is merely loose, vague, or ambiguous, where the real property description in a mechanic's lien claim notice is 'unambiguously erroneous' and describes with exactitude the wrong parcel of real property, substantial compliance is not achieved, and the claim of lien is invalid."

Affirmed.

Mitchell v. Flandro
506 P.2d 455 (Idaho 1973)

A contractor instituted a suit to foreclose a mechanic's lien. On November 10, 1964, the architect signed a certificate acknowledging the substantial completion of the construction. Thereafter, the contractor continued to do finishing work until January 2, 1965. The lien was filed March 11, 1965. The lower court denied recovery on the ground that the lien was not timely filed, and the contractor appealed.

BAKES, J. . . . Of primary importance in this appeal is the district court's conclusion that respondent's lien was not timely filed as required in I.C. 45-507. At the time that respondent filed his lien, the section provided:

> Every original contractor claiming the benefit of this chapter must, within ninety (90) days. . . . after the completion of any building, improvement or structure, or after the completion of the alteration or repair thereof, or in case he cease to labor thereon before the completion thereof, then after he so ceases to labor or after he has ceased to labor thereon for any cause, or after he has ceased to furnish materials therefor . . . file for record with the county recorder for the county in which such property or some part thereof is situated, a claim containing a statement of his demand, after deducting all just credits and offsets, with the name of the owner, or reputed owner, if known, and also the name of the person by whom he was employed or to whom he furnished the materials. . . .

It is respondent's position that due to the fact that he allegedly performed work on the structure up until January 2, 1965, that the lien application filed March 11, 1965, was in fact filed within ninety days of the cessation of work under the contract and hence was timely filed. In finding that the lien was not timely filed, the trial court stated:

> . . . as a matter of fact, that from the November [1964] date through the March [1965] date that plaintiff did not prove services of such a nature as to expand the time for filing his lien and the court

concludes, therefore, as a matter of law, that the lien was not timely filed. . . .

Since there is competent evidence in the record supporting the trial court's factual determination that no substantial work was proven done after November, 1964, we do not disturb it on appeal.

It is undisputed in the record that the certificate of "substantial completion" was submitted by respondent and approved by appellants' architect on November 10, 1964. According to the architect, the certificate issued when the construction was completed to the extent that appellants could assume occupancy. On issuance of the certificate, the respondent-builders were entitled to submit their final estimate for payment. From respondent Mitchell's own testimony it appears that the issuance of the certificate also marked the effective completion of construction under the contract.

It is established that "trivial" work done or materials furnished after the contract has been substantially completed will not extend the time in which a lien claim can be filed under I.C. 45-507. As well articulated in *Gem State Lumber Co.* v. *Whitty,* 37 Idaho 489, 217 P. 1027:

> While the time fixed in the contract for the completion of a building is not controlling against laborers or materialmen, it has a direct bearing upon the time when the building was to be completed under the contract, so that the time for filing liens for material and labor would begin to run. The statute provides that this time shall be computed from the date of the last item of material furnished, or from the last work performed. *The rule very generally prevails that such time begins to run from a substantial completion of the contract, and that new items thereafter added to the account will not extend the time in which to claim a lien or revive a lien already expired.* The more difficult question is to determine when under this doctrine the contract has been completed. By the weight of authority, this is to be ascertained by the conditions of the contract, the conduct of the parties with reference thereto, and the surrounding facts and circumstances. *Ordinarily, furnishing an article or performing a service trivial in character is not sufficient to extend the time for claiming a lien or to revive an expired lien, where the article is*

furnished or the service rendered after a substantial completion of the contract, and the article is not expressly required by the terms thereof.

Since it is undisputed that the contract was substantially completed on November 10, 1964, and since the trial court found inadequate proof that any material or substantial work was performed or supplies furnished after that date which would extend the time for filing a lien, we conclude that the trial court was correct in ruling that the lien was not timely filed. . . .

Affirmed.

Exchange Savings & Loan Association v. Monocrete Pty. Ltd.
629 S.W.2d 34 (Tex. 1982)

CAMPBELL, J. This case concerns the priority of a deed of trust lien and a later perfected statutory mechanic's and materialman's lien. Monocrete Pty. Ltd., d/b/a Monier Company (Monier), a roofing company, furnished and installed concrete roofing tiles on condominium homes. The roofing company perfected a mechanic's and materialman's lien . . . Exchange Savings & Loan Association (Exchange Savings), the first lien deed of trust holder, foreclosed its lien upon the lots and bought the condominiums at the trustee's sale. The roofing company, unpaid for the materials and labor, sued Exchange Savings to foreclose its materialman's lien and to remove the concrete roofing tile.

The trial court held the concrete roofing tile could not be removed without material injury to the land, the remaining structure, existing improvements and the tiles themselves; and denied foreclosure of the materialman's lien. That court also held the deed of trust lien of Exchange Savings was superior and its foreclosure extinguished the materialman's lien. The court of civil appeals held the trial court's finding of material injury is against the great weight and preponderance of the evidence. The court of civil appeals reversed the trial court's judgment and remanded the part of the judgment denying foreclosure of the materialman's lien on lots H–28, L–98 and H–18. . . .

While this Court does not have jurisdiction to review the question of factual sufficiency of the evidence, we do possess jurisdiction to determine whether the court of civil appeals applied the proper rules of law in reaching its conclusion.

. . . [A] perfected materialman's lien upon improvements is superior to a prior recorded deed of trust lien if the materials furnished can be removed without material injury to (1) the land, (2) the existing improvements, or (3) the materials themselves. . . . The question is whether removal of the roofing tiles constitutes material injury to the existing structure or the roofing tiles.

Monier contends the existing structure would not be materially injured in the process of removing the tiles. The evidence is that nail holes may be left in the plywood decking; paint on the lead flashing may crack; and the felt paper may be torn in places. Exchange Savings suggests the evidence also shows possible damage to the fascia board around the perimeter of the roof.

Whether the removal of a specific improvement will cause material injury is generally a question for the fact finder. The materialman may have his materials sold separately, provided the prior lien ". . . shall not be affected thereby. . . ." The purpose of the statutory proviso is to protect the security of the prior lien holder. Accordingly, evidence of the effect of removal of improvements upon the security of the prior lien holder is pertinent. In weighing the evidence, the court of civil appeals incorrectly refused to consider evidence of the nature of the improvements sought to be removed and the probabilities of post-removal damage to the existing structure. Some factors that may be considered are: the manner and extent of attachment to the land or existing improvements; the extent to which removal would necessitate repairs, modification and/or protection of the land or existing improvements; the stage of completion of improvements under construction at the time removal is sought; and the function of the improvements sought to be removed.

. . . Improvements found removable, even though connected to the realty, are separable from the basic structure. . . .

Cement roofing tiles necessary to prevent penetration of the elements through the roof of a completed structure become an integral part of its construction and necessary to its completion as a livable dwelling. The roofing tiles became an integral part of the basic structure of the townhomes. At the time the roofing tiles were furnished and affixed to the roof, the townhomes were of such a nature as to give notice to Monier that the roofing tiles could not be separated from the basic structure without material injury and had necessarily become a part thereof. We hold, as a matter of law, removal of the roofing tiles would cause material injury to the existing improvements on the land. Thus, Mo-

nier's statutory lien is not superior to Exchange Savings' prior deed of trust lien. . . .

The deed of trust liens are superior to the materialman's liens upon lots H–28, L–98 and H–18. Exchange Savings, as purchaser at the trustee's sale, acquired title to the lots free of Monier's inferior lien. We reverse the judgment of the court of civil appeals and affirm the judgment of the trial court.

Reversed.

REVIEW QUESTIONS

1. Identify the terms in column A by matching each with the appropriate statement in column B.

A		B	
1. Mortgagee		**a.**	A clause which allows one mortgage to secure future advances.
2. Mortgagor		**b.**	Allows the mortgagor to reinstate his interest after a foreclosure sale has occurred.
3. Lien theory		**c.**	A clause found in a mortgage which permits the mortgagee to conduct a foreclosure sale without court approval.
4. Due on default		**d.**	The party who lends money and is secured by an interest in real estate.
5. Dragnet		**e.**	The voluntary relinquishment of the right to a mechanic's lien prior to a notice of lien being filed.
6. Strict foreclosure		**f.**	A view of mortgages that does not involve the conveyance of title.
7. Power of sale		**g.**	A seldom-used process whereby the mortgagee gets to keep mortgaged property regardless of the property's value and the amount of the debt.
8. Equitable right of redemption		**h.**	The voluntary relinquishment of a mechanic's lien after the notice of lien has been filed.
9. Statutory right of redemption		**i**	The filing of this is a required step in the perfection and enforcement of a mechanic's lien.
10. Notice of a lien		**j.**	A type of acceleration clause often included in a mortgage.
11. Waiver		**k.**	A borrower of money who grants the creditor a security interest in real estate.

12. Release

l. Allows the mortgagor to reinstate his interest after default but before a foreclosure sale occurs.

2. The First National Bank agreed to lend Mike and Michelle $50,000 if they would grant their personal residence as security for repayment of the loan. In this transaction, name the mortgagor and the mortgagee.

3. List the three theories of mortgage law the various states have adopted. What distinguishes these theories?

4. New Mexico Bank & Trust sued Lucas Bros. and Liberty National Bank to foreclose on a mortgage. Liberty National Bank held a mortgage on Lucas Bros. property recorded subsequent to a New Mexico Bank & Trust mortgage in the amount of $20,000. The New Mexico Bank & Trust mortgage contained a dragnet clause which provided that the mortgaged real estate would secure all future loans made to Lucas Bros. Does the dragnet clause in the mortgage allow all subsequent loans made by New Mexico Bank & Trust to enjoy the same priority as the original mortgage? Why?

5. Mort owned real estate that he had mortgaged. Mort sold this property to Pat, who agreed to take it subject to the mortgage. Pat ascertained the balance of the debt Mort owed at the date of purchase of the land. When Pat failed to make payments, the mortgage was foreclosed. What does the term "taking subject to a mortgage" mean? Explain.

6. In the previous question, is Mort still liable for the payments made by Pat? Why?

7. What is the distinction between an equitable right of redemption and a statutory right of redemption?

8. Garland paid $72,000 down and signed a purchase-money mortgage note for the $287,000 balance due on realty. When Garland defaulted, over $300,000 in principal and interest was still owing. At a public auction, Hill, the mortgagee, bid $25,000 for the property and agreed to forgive the balance of principal and interest due. Garland filed suit to enjoin the sale on the equitable ground that the price was "shockingly inadequate." May an inadequate purchase price be made adequate by the mortgagee's waiver of his right to claim a deficiency against the mortgagor? Explain.

9. Describe the nature and purpose of mechanic's liens.

10. Bowen Hardware Company claimed that materials it had furnished were used in the construction of Collins's building. Collins argued that Bowen could not prove that the materials it had furnished were used in Collins's building. Do materials which are furnished to construct a building actually have to be used in the building to give rise to a materialman's lien? Why?

11. At the time Bill bought a new home, his attorney examined the recorded documents affecting interests in the property. No mechanic's liens were revealed. A short time after Bill had bought this home, Ralph, a roofer, demanded payment for a roof installed prior to Bill's purchase. Is it possible that Ralph has any rights against Bill's property? Why?

12. Carver Lumber filed a suit to foreclose a mechanic's lien. Commercial Bank, which held a purchase-money mortgage on the same property, claimed priority over Carver Lumber's lien. Commercial Bank's mortgage was recorded after Carver Lumber began work on the property. Is the bank correct? What assumptions have you made in reaching your answer? Explain.

35 ADDITIONAL LAWS ASSISTING CREDITORS

Chapter 34 deals with the use of mortgages or similar documents as one way a creditor has security. Chapters 32 through 33 discuss the taking of a security interest in personal property as another way a creditor can be secured when extending credit. These discussions on the methods of how creditors become secured are incomplete. In this chapter we examine three more legal areas designed to assist creditors in the collection of debts: (1) artisan's liens, (2) Article 6 on bulk transfers, and (3) suretyship. In essence, this chapter discusses additional laws designed to give creditors leverage, or a source in addition to the debtor, from which the debt can be collected.

1. Artisan's Liens

An *artisan's lien* is a security interest in personal property in favor of one who has performed services on the personal property. Such services often take the form of a repair. From a very early date, the common law permitted one who expended labor or materials on the personal property of another to retain possession of the property as security for his compensation. This right to possession creates a lien against the owner's personal property when the task is completed. By court decisions, such a lien typically has been interpreted to exist in favor of public warehousemen and common carriers of goods entrusted to their care. Today, in almost every state, the artisan's lien has been extended by statute to cover all cases of storage or repair.

Because the artisan's lien is perfected by possession, voluntary surrender of the property generally terminates the lien. If the artisan parts with possession, reacquisition of the goods involved will not re-create the lien.[1] The artisan's lien is personal to the party who performs the services. In other words, this lien is not assignable.

Despite the general rules just stated, a lienholder may temporarily surrender possession, with an agreement that the lien will continue. However, if rights of a third party arise while the lienholder is not in possession of the property, the lien is lost. Surrender of part of the goods will not affect the lien on the remaining goods. Perhaps most important, the release of possession will not terminate the lien if a notice of lien is recorded in accordance with state lien and recording statutes prior to surrender. This notice of an artisan's lien in the public records serves as an adequate substitute for possession as a way of informing the public of the artisan's claim in specific personal property.

Under common law, the lienholder had to retain the property until a judgment was obtained; then he levied execution on the property. Modern statutes permit the lienholder to have the property sold to satisfy the claim. These statutes usually require notice to the owner prior to the sale. With respect to the proceeds of a forced sale, the artisan generally has a superior claim when compared with a preexisting Article 9 secured party. The lienholder has priority because the law presumes that the work or improvement done on the personal property has increased that property's value at least in an amount equal to the lienholder's claim. Therefore, the secured creditor has not been damaged by having inferior status. Any surplus proceeds left after all claims against the property are satisfied are paid to the owner of the property.

BULK TRANSFERS

2. In General

Chapter 33 explained that a buyer in the ordinary course of business takes free of a security interest previously created in the property purchased. We said that the property typically purchased in the ordinary course of business will be items of inventory. (A review of section 3 of chapter 33 may be helpful.) However, Article 9 did not address the situation of a purchase of inventory that is not in the ordinary course of business. For example, what happens when an entire business is purchased? What are the rights of the creditors of the purchased business? What are the rights of the purchaser to whom property has been transferred? Is the purchaser liable for the debts of the purchased business, or is the purchaser free from all claims?

Article 6 of the Uniform Commercial Code is concerned with these bulk transfer situations, and it provides answers to the questions just asked. Prior to reading the following material, an understanding of the terminology used in Article 6 is essential. A *bulk transfer* covers sales of inventory if (1) the sale is in bulk and not in the ordinary course of business; (2) it is of the major part of the materials, supplies, merchandise, or other inventory; and (3) the seller's principal business is the sale of merchandise from stock. Ordinarily, a sale of a manufactur-

---

[1] Rocky Mountain Turbines v. 660 Syndicate, p. 800.

ing concern is not subject to the law; however, this sale would be subject to Article 6 if the firm included a retail outlet that also was being sold. Enterprises that manufacture what they sell—certain bakeries, for example—would be included. Enterprises whose principal business is the sale of services rather than merchandise are not covered. Article 6 is applicable to transfers of a substantial part of the equipment of an enterprise only if the equipment is sold in connection with bulk transfers of inventory. A sale of just the equipment of a business is not subject to the law.

The parties involved in a bulk transfer are usually referred to as the transferor, the transferee, and the creditors of the transferor. The *transferor* is the business selling the bulk of its inventory. The *transferee* is the party who is the buyer in the bulk transfer.

In a bulk transfer, the transferor's creditors have presumably extended credit on the strength of the assets transferred. The sale of these assets could jeopardize the ability of the creditor to collect the debt, since the transferor might fail to pay the debt after receiving the proceeds of the sale. Article 6 has attempted to remedy this situation by imposing certain requirements on the transferee who purchases inventory in bulk, if the sale is to pass title to the property free of the claims of creditors.

Article 6 does not govern the relationship between a transferor and transferee. A contract of sale is valid without compliance. However, if the statutory requirements are not met, the property in the hands of the transferee is subject to the claim of the transferor's creditors. The following sections describe the duties of the transferee and the rights of the transferor's creditors.

3. Duties of the Transferee

An optional provision of Article 6 requires the transferee to make mandatory payment to the transferor's creditors to satisfy their claims. The states are free to adopt or not adopt this provision, which gives additional protection to these creditors. If this provision is not adopted, the proceeds of the bulk transfer do not have to be paid directly to the creditors.

Regardless of whether this optional provision is enacted, Article 6 imposes two other requirements on the transferee. This party must first obtain from the transferor a schedule of the property transferred and a sworn list of the transferor's creditors. This list must include the creditors' addresses and the amount owed to each. The transferee can rely on the accuracy of this list. This schedule of property and list of creditors must be kept for at least 6 months, and be always available to creditors. Or the transferee can file these documents in the designated public office.

The second requirement concerns the notification process. The transferee must give notice personally or by registered mail to all persons on the list of creditors and to all other persons who are known to the transferee to have claims against the transferor. Notice must be given at least 10 days before the transferee takes possession of the goods or pays for them (whichever happens first). This notice must contain the following information: (1) that a bulk transfer is about to be made; (2) names and business addresses of both the transferor and transferee;

and (3) whether the debts of the creditors are to be paid in full as a result of the transaction. If the debts are to be paid, the address to which the creditors should send their bills must be included. If no provision is made for payment in full of the creditors, the notice must contain the following additional information: (1) estimated total of transferor's debts; (2) location and description of property to be transferred; (3) the address where the creditor list and property schedule may be inspected; (4) whether the transfer is in payment of, or security for, a debt owing to transferee and, if so, the amount of the debt; and (5) whether the transfer is a sale for new consideration and, if so, the amount of the consideration and the time and place of payment.

In states that have adopted the optional provision of Article 6, the transferee is obligated, in effect, to see that creditors are paid in full or pro rata from the "new consideration" paid by the transferee. Failure to do so creates personal liability for the value of the property.

Article 6 is applicable to bulk sales by auction. The auctioneer is required to obtain a list of creditors and of the property to be sold. All persons who direct, control, or are responsible for the auction are collectively called the *auctioneer.*The auctioneer is also required to give 10 days' notice of sale to all persons on the list of creditors.

4. Rights of the Creditors

If the required procedures have been followed, the transferor's creditors will have had ample opportunity to take any necessary steps to protect their interests. Their action might include the levying of execution against the property or obtaining a writ of attachment or a temporary injunction to stop the sale. If Code procedures have not been followed, the transfer is ineffective as to the creditors, and they may collect the debt from the transferee to the extent of the value of the transferred property.[2]

The creditors must take action within 6 months after the transferee takes possession if the Article 6 provisions have not been followed. If the transferee and the bulk transfer are concealed, the creditors must act within 6 months after they learn of the transfer. A purchaser who buys for value and in good faith from the transferee obtains the property free of objection based on noncompliance with the Code. However, the transferee who sells the property becomes personally liable to the transferor's creditors to the extent of the value received.

The failure to comply with Article 6 by those in charge of an auction sale of the bulk of a business' inventory creates personal liability to the extent of the auction's proceeds.

SURETYSHIP IN GENERAL

5. Introduction

Suretyship provides security for a creditor without involving an interest in property. In suretyship, the security for the creditor is provided by a third person's promise to be responsible for the debtor's obligation.

---

[2] Anderson & Clayton Co. v. Earnest, p. 801.

Suretyship may have commenced with the beginning of civilization. Although there is evidence of surety contracts as far back as 2750 B.C., and in the Code of Hammurabi, about 2250 B.C., the earliest written contract of suretyship that has been found dates to 670 B.C. By A.D. 150, the Romans had developed a highly technical law of suretyship. The concept of a corporate surety did not evolve until the Industrial Revolution. Today, suretyship plays a major role in many business transactions, especially construction contracts. Suretyship also is involved in a substantial percentage of loan transactions.

6. Terminology

A *principal,* or *principal debtor,* or *obligor* is the party who borrows money or assumes direct responsibility to perform a contractual obligation. The party entitled to receive payment or performance is called the *creditor* or *obligee.* Any party who promises the creditor to be liable for a principal's payment or performance is either a *surety* or *guarantor.* The word *party* includes individuals as well as all types of business organizations. What is the difference between a surety and a guarantor? Historically, this distinction has involved the difference between a third party being primarily and secondarily liable. Also involved is the distinction between assuring a creditor that the principal will perform a noncredit contractual promise and that the principal will repay money borrowed.

Surety.   A surety's promise to be liable for a principal's obligation is created as a part of and dependent on the principal's agreement to perform. In a narrow sense, a surety is considered primarily liable for the principal's performance. In other words, a creditor could demand performance from the surety rather than the principal. From this concept came the general rule that no notice of the principal's default had to be given in order for the creditor to hold the surety liable. This notice requirement and its ramifications are discussed in section 11.

Since a surety's promise is part of the creditor-debtor relationship, a creditor may sue the surety simultaneously when action is taken against the principal. Finally, a surety's obligation can be summarized as being a promise to do what the principal agreed to do.

Guarantor.   On the other hand, a guarantor's promise to be liable for a principal's obligation is created separate from and independent of the principal's agreement to perform. In other words, a guarantor's promise is only related to, but not an essential part of, the principal's obligation. A guarantor will become liable to the creditor only when the principal has defaulted. Therefore, the principal is primarily liable and the guarantor is secondarily liable. Historically, this concept has required the creditor to give the guarantor notice of the debtor's default before action could be commenced against the guarantor. Furthermore, a creditor, if necessary, must bring two legal actions—first against the principal, and second and separately against the guarantor. To summarize—a guarantor promises that the principal will do what the principal promised to do.

There are two types of guaranty agreements: general and special. A *general* guarantor is a party whose promise is not limited to a single transaction or to a single creditor. For example, a principal may have an open line of credit and may borrow from the creditor many times within the overall credit limitation. A guarantor who promises to be liable for the principal's default regardless of the number of transactions within the credit line is called a general guarantor.[3] Furthermore, a creditor secured by a general guarantor's obligation may assign the rights to expect the principal's performance to a second creditor.

A *special* guarantor is a party who limits the promise made to a single transaction or to a single creditor or both. A special guarantor's obligation would not protect a creditor to the full extent of an open line of credit if the initial loan transaction was for a lesser amount. In addition, a creditor cannot assign the special guarantor's promise to a new creditor.

Guaranty agreements also are classified as absolute or conditional. Under an *absolute* guaranty, a creditor can go directly to the guarantor to collect. In a *conditional* guaranty, the creditor must have made reasonable but unsuccessful attempts to collect from the principal before the guarantor can be held liable.

Legal Significance between Surety and Guarantor. Fortunately, today the distinction between a surety and a guaranty has very little significance. This result is due in large part to the *Restatement of Security,* which is a legal treatise on the subject of suretyship. Although the *Restatement* is not the law, its influence on the law is quite substantial. Those scholars who prepared the *Restatement of Security* considered surety to be interchangeable with guarantor. Therefore, unless it is stated otherwise, the general principles presented below are applicable to sureties as well as guarantors.

7. Suretyship versus Indemnity

A contract of suretyship should be distinguished from a contract of indemnity. Both contracts ultimately provide protection that what has been promised will be performed. However, the approach to accomplishing this purpose is vitally different. A surety makes a promise to a person (creditor) who is *to receive* the performance of an act or payment of a debt by another (principal). In a contract of indemnity, the assurance of performance is made to the party (principal) who is promising *to do* an act or *to pay* a debt. Whereas suretyship provides security to creditors, indemnity provides security to principal debtors. In other words, indemnity is a promise to the debtor, or obligor, to hold him harmless from any loss he may incur as a result of nonpayment of a debt or nonperformance of a promise. Most insurance contracts are examples of indemnification agreements between the insurer and the insured.

8. Creation of Suretyship Contracts

Two basic situations exist when a surety's promise would benefit the creditor: (1) when the creditor is concerned about the principal's ability to repay a loan; and (2) when the creditor is concerned about the principal's completion of a

---

[3] Chemical Bank v. Sepler, p. 802.

contractual promise other than repayment. Each of these situations is discussed briefly below, followed by a subsection on methods of creating suretyship agreements.

Payment of a Debt.   Typically, the creation of this relationship involves a relative, a friend, or a business associate of the principal debtor serving as a surety for the creditor's benefit. This surety's promise to the creditor is made gratuitously. The consideration (or money) given to the principal is sufficient consideration to make the surety's promise enforceable. In other words, sureties who promise to pay a principal's debt if the principal fails to are generally known as *uncompensated sureties.*

Uncompensated sureties are viewed as being protected by the law. Although they are bound to perform as promised, uncompensated sureties' liabilities are often limited. Many of the legal principles discussed in the following sections have a restricted application with respect to uncompensated sureties. Therefore, it is vital that the surety's compensation or lack thereof always be known.

Performance of Other Contractual Promises.   Suretyship agreements also are useful whenever a creditor (obligee) is worried about a principal's performance of a contractual promise other than the repayment of a loan. Performance bonds and fidelity bonds are examples of suretyship. A *performance bond* provides protection against losses that may result from the failure of a contracting party to perform the contract as agreed. The surety (bonding company) promises the party entitled to performance to pay losses caused by nonperformance by the principal in an amount not to exceed the face of the bond. *Fidelity bonds* give protection against the dishonest acts of a person. In other words, such a bonding company promises to repay the employer any loss, not to exceed a stated amount, caused by the covered employees' embezzlement. Bonding companies are sureties in the sense that the term *surety* includes security either for the payment of money or for the faithful performance of some other duty.

Whenever bonding companies serve as a surety, they receive some consideration separate and distinct from the consideration promised to the debtor. This additional consideration paid to them makes these parties *compensated sureties.* Whereas uncompensated sureties are favorites of the law, compensated sureties are perceived as being able to take care of themselves. This difference is illustrated in the interpretation of the contract. Ambiguous provisions of surety agreements are construed in favor of the unpaid surety and against the creditor. Ambiguous provisions of surety agreements involving compensated sureties are resolved against the surety. This distinction results from the fact that ambiguous language is generally construed against the party writing it. In the case of unpaid sureties, the language is usually framed by the creditor and signed by the surety. In the case of compensated sureties, the contract is usually prepared by the surety.

Methods of Creation.   Suretyship agreements most often result from an express written contract between the surety and the creditor, whereby the surety assumes responsibility for the principal's performance for the creditor. The surety agrees that he may be called upon to pay or to perform in case the principal defaults. The contract of suretyship requires consideration. In most instances, the consideration that supports the surety's promise is the same consideration received by the principal.

Contracts of suretyship also may result by operation of law. Assume that Jones sells his retail lumber business to Smith, who assumes and agrees to pay, as part of the purchase price, all of Jones's outstanding liabilities. Between Smith and Jones, Smith has now become the primary debtor. Jones is a surety and secondarily liable. As soon as the creditors are notified of the sale, they are obligated to respect the new relationship by attempting to recover from Smith before looking to Jones for payment.

9. Liability of the Parties—In General

Now we turn our attention to a discussion of the legal principles concerning the surety's liability or freedom from liability. The surety's liability is dependent on the many factors that exist in at least a three-party relationship. In other words, the various interrelationships all have an impact on the issue of the surety's liability. Therefore, the following discussion is divided into three parts, each based on the following relationships:

1. Creditor-surety (sections 10 through 12)
2. Creditor-principal (sections 13 through 17)
3. Principal-surety (sections 18 through 20).

CREDITOR–SURETY RELATIONSHIP

10. Fiduciary Nature

The suretyship relation is, within limits, fiduciary in character, involving special trust and confidence between the creditor and the surety. It requires good faith and fair dealing. For this reason, a creditor possessing information affecting the risk must communicate such information to the surety before the contract is made. This duty applies only to information that is *significant* to the risk. It does not cover *all* matters that might affect the risk. If some facts make the risk a materially greater one than the surety intends to assume, and if the creditor knows this, he has a duty to disclose those facts. The duty to disclose exists only if the creditor has reason to believe that the surety does not know the facts and the creditor has a reasonable opportunity to communicate them to the surety.

When we concentrate on a typical loan transaction, the surety generally will have as much, if not more, knowledge about the principal than will the creditor. Therefore, the fiduciary duty of disclosure will seldom arise as long as the surety is a relative of or otherwise related in a business sense to the principal. However, in keeping with conservative lending practices—when in doubt about its appropriateness—the creditor should disclose what it knows about the principal when the surety inquires.[4]

Since the contract is between the surety and the creditor, any misconduct of the principal that induces a party to become a surety does not allow that surety to avoid the contract. At the time of the contract, however, a creditor who is aware of

---

[4] First National Bank and Trust Company of Racine v. Notte, p. 803.

the principal's misrepresentation is obligated to inform the surety of the misrepresentation. This duty to inform probably occurs most frequently when a creditor learns that a principal has misrepresented its financial condition to a prospective surety. Particularly when the surety does not have access to the principal's records and books, the creditor is obligated to warn the surety of the increased risk. In this situation, a creditor's failure to warn the surety will release that surety from liability.

Perhaps the most common application of these fiduciary duties occurs when a financial institution is bonding its employees. An employer who knows of an employee's past financial transgressions (such as embezzlement) must inform the bonding company of this fact at the time a bond is sought. Furthermore, an employer who discovers that a bonded employee has been guilty of misappropriation of funds should immediately discharge the employee unless the surety assents to his continued employment. To allow the employee to continue subjects the surety to a risk not contemplated. Rehabilitation of the employee by giving him a second chance can be undertaken only with the consent of the surety. If the surety does not consent, and if the employee is guilty of misappropriation a second time, the surety is not liable on the surety bond.

11. Principal's Default

By the nature of the agreement, a surety has no obligation to the creditor unless the principal fails to perform. Although no performance is owed prior to that time, a surety is liable to the creditor *as soon as* the principal defaults. This simple-sounding rule means that the creditor usually does not have to exhaust his remedies against the principal before seeking to recover from the surety. Additionally, a creditor may take action against the surety without having to give notice to the surety that the principal has defaulted. The principal that no notice need be given the surety is subject to the following three important exceptions:

1. A surety may require that notice of the principal's default be given prior to the creditor's holding the surety liable.

2. A surety who is a drawer or indorser of commercial paper is entitled to notice.

3. A surety who only guarantees collection is entitled to notice.

Surety–Creditor Agreement.   Since a suretyship generally is created by agreement, the relationship is of a contractual nature. Like most contracts, the contract of a suretyship will be enforceable as long as its terms have a legal purpose. A surety may insist on including a clause in the contract with the creditor requiring that notice of the principal's default be given within a specified time. Whenever such a clause is included, courts will enforce it. If such a clause is binding on the parties, the creditor's failure to notify the surety of the principal's default discharges the surety from liability. However, the notice requirement must be reasonably, and not strictly, interpreted.[5]

---

[5] Local No. 1179 v. Merchants Mutual Bonding Co., p. 805.

Surety as Drawer or Indorser of Commercial Paper. Any drawer of a draft (check) and any indorser of a note, draft, or certificate of deposit becomes liable on the instrument signed if (1) presentment for payment or acceptance was made within a reasonable time, (2) dishonor occurred, and (3) notice of dishonor was given within the time allowed. Since this notice of dishonor must be given, parties who become a surety through their status as an accommodating drawer or indorser or both are entitled to be notified of the principal's (primary party's) default (dishonor). Chapter 31 on the liability of parties to commercial paper gives further details of the logic behind the notice requirement in this exception.

Surety as Collection Guarantor. Again, chapter 31 also explains that a collection guarantor under the terms of the Uniform Commercial Code assures the creditor that collection can be obtained from the guarantor if all efforts to collect from the principal prove unsuccessful. Due to the nature of this assurance, equity requires that the guarantor's potential liability not be unresolved indefinitely while the creditor pursues its claim against the principal. Technically, this guarantor is not entitled to immediate notice that the principal has defaulted. However, the creditor should keep the collection guarantor informed of what actions are being taken to collect from the principal.

To the extent a collection guarantor does suffer from a lack of notice, that guarantor is discharged. For example, assume that a creditor attempts to collect a debt owed by the principal for 2 years without notifying the collection guarantor of any such actions. Then the creditor seeks to collect from the guarantor. Also assume that the guarantor can prove that 2 years before, the guarantor could have recovered 75 percent of the obligation owed from the principal, but now the guarantor can recover nothing. The creditor's lack of notice relieves the guarantor of 75 percent of the original obligation.

The collection guarantor is not damaged by a lack of notice if that guarantor is aware of what actions the creditor is taking to collect from the principal. In the example above, if the guarantor knew of the creditor's efforts despite no notice being received, that guarantor has not been prejudiced in any way. In other words, the guarantor could have satisfied its potential obligation at any time and pursued its rights against the principal. Therefore, in this situation, the collection guarantor remains liable for 100 percent of the obligation.

12. Surety's Performance and Subrogation Rights

In general, when a principal defaults, the surety immediately becomes liable to the creditor. The surety can satisfy its obligation to the creditor by performing as promised or by showing that it has a valid excuse for not performing. The following sections present several situations in which the surety is relieved of liability. However, for the time being, assume that upon the principal's default, the surety does perform as promised. When performance has been completed, the surety's most important right involves the concept of subrogation.

The term *subrogation* literally means the substitution of one person in the place of another. The surety who fully performs the obligation of the principal is subrogated to the creditor's rights against the principal. The surety who pays the principal's debt becomes entitled to any security interest the principal has granted to the creditor regarding the debt paid. Furthermore, whenever the creditor obtains a judgment against the principal, the surety receives the benefit of this judgment when the surety satisfies the principal's debts.

Because of the right of subrogation, a creditor in possession of collateral given to him by the principal is not at liberty to return it without the consent of the surety. Any surrender of security releases the surety to the extent of its value, his loss of subrogation damaging him to that extent. Failure of the creditor to make use of the security, however, does not release the surety, since the latter is free to pay the indebtedness and to obtain the security for his own protection. If the creditor loses the benefit of collateral by inactivity—failure to record a mortgage or notify an indorser—the surety is released to the extent that he is injured. In general, if the person who is entitled to protection under the contract of suretyship does anything that will materially prejudice the rights of the surety, the surety will, to that extent at least, be discharged.

The right of subrogation protects the creditor as well as the surety. In other words, a creditor has the right to step into the shoes of the surety and to enforce the surety's rights against the principal. Assume that the principal delivered corporate stock to the surety in order to protect the surety in the event of the principal's default. The creditor, to the extent of his claim, may substitute his position for that of the surety with reference to the stock. In the event of the return of the stock by the surety to the principal, the creditor is entitled to follow the stock into the hands of the debtor and subject it to a lien. The creditor may also secure an injunction against return of the stock to the principal, thus having it impounded by the court until the principal debt falls due, at which time the stock may be sold for the benefit of the creditor.

13. Introduction

As has been stated previously, a surety generally becomes liable only when the principal defaults. Therefore, if the principal does not default, the surety never becomes liable to the creditor; no default occurs if the principal performs as promised. However, there may be other situations in which the principal has not defaulted because he has a valid excuse for nonperformance. These situations may involve (1) a defense the principal can assert against the creditor, (2) a release of the principal by the creditor, or (3) a modification of the creditor-principal relationship. Any of these possible situations may have an impact on the surety's liability.

14. Principal's Defenses

In general, any defense the principal can use to reduce liability to the creditor may also be used by a surety to reduce his liability. This idea of making the principal's defenses available to the surety is not conditioned on the principal's utilizing the defense first. The surety is protected by the defense regardless of whether or not the principal is relieved of liability.

One important defense is that of lack of a primary obligation. In other words, the surety is not bound if the principal is not bound. This may occur when

**CREDITOR–
PRINCIPAL
RELATIONSHIP**

the principal fails to sign a contract, although expected to do so. Other common examples of defenses that may be available to the principal and surety include mutual mistake, fraud, duress, undue influence, illegality, impossibility, and lack or failure of consideration.

There are three important exceptions to the general rule that defenses available to the principal may be used by the surety to avoid liability to the surety: (1) the principal's lack of capacity, (2) the principal's discharge in bankruptcy, and (3) the principal's performance excused due to the statute of limitations having run.

Lack of capacity and discharge in bankruptcy are not available to the surety as defenses because the surety promised in the first instance to protect the creditor against the principal's inability to perform. Most creditors, particularly those in loan transactions, anticipate the principal's lack of capacity or discharge in bankruptcy. A creditor is likely to protect against the consequences of these possible events by insisting that a surety becomes involved.

When a principal who lacks capacity avoids a contract and fails to return the consideration that was received from the creditor, the surety is required to make up any deficiency between the value of whatever the principal has performed and the complete performance. If, on the other hand, the principal returns all or some of the consideration received from the creditor, the surety's liability is reduced by the value of the consideration returned.

The principal's defense that the statute of limitations prevents a proper claim by the creditor may not be used by the surety. The principal and the surety have separate time periods for which they remain liable to the creditor, and that period may be longer for the surety. For example, the principal may be liable only on the basis of an oral promise (2-year statute of limitations, for instance). The surety's obligation may be based on a written agreement subject to a 6-year statute of limitations. Obviously, the creditor who waits for 3 years after the principal's default cannot recover from the principal. Nevertheless, in this situation, the surety remains liable.

Setoffs and counterclaims of both the principal and the surety may be used as a defense by the surety under certain circumstances. The surety can set off any claim it has against the creditor and use the setoff to reduce or eliminate the liability. If the debtor is insolvent, if the principal and surety are sued jointly, or if the surety has taken an assignment of the claim of the debtor, the surety is entitled to use as a defense any setoff that could be used by the principal debtor in a suit by the creditor.

15. Releases

In general, a creditor who voluntarily releases the principal from liability also releases the surety. The logic of this general rule is based on the fact that the surety becomes liable only upon the principal's default. If the principal never defaults since the creditor relinquishes its claim against the principal, the surety never becomes liable either. Any conclusion to the contrary would mean the creditor could indirectly require the principal's performance even after a release. If a creditor could hold the surety liable, the surety could seek reimbursement from the principal. Therefore, the creditor would be requiring indirectly the principal's performance.

As always, we must consider some exceptions to this general rule. The following three are discussed here: (1) A surety that consents to a principal's release is not released; (2) a creditor that reserves rights against a surety does not release that surety; and (3) a release obtained by that principal's fraud does not release the surety if the creditor rescinds the release prior to the surety's reliance.

The Surety's Consent. It is hard to imagine why any commercial surety would voluntarily consent to remain liable when a principal is released from liability. Indeed, most situations involving a surety's consent to remain personally liable probably will involve a friendship or kinship between the surety and the principal. For example, a surety may wish to help a friend or relative by improving that principal's financial record. In order to achieve this result, the surety may actually seek the principal's release by consenting to remain liable.

Furthermore, a surety may be secured by the principal in return for acting as a security. We could assume that a business, as principal, granted its president, as surety, a security interest in all its accounts and general intangibles. A creditor may be willing to take the surety's security interest in full satisfaction of the performance owed. The creditor might agree to release the principal from further personal liability if the surety consents to the creditor's having the right to pursue its claim against the accounts and general intangibles. The basis for this conclusion is the creditor's right of subrogation, discussed in section 12 previously.

Reservation of Rights. Even a nonconsenting surety is not released when a principal is released if the creditor reserves rights against the surety. In essence, the creditor's reservation of rights is interpreted to be a promise by the creditor that the principal will not be sued. The creditor can still hold the surety liable, and the surety can seek reimbursement from the principal upon the surety's performance. Therefore, in essence the principal ultimately remains liable despite the prior release. The creditor really has promised only that the creditor will not sue the principal. In order to protect the surety's potential claim against the principal, the surety may perform for the creditor any time after that creditor has released the principal and has reserved rights against the surety. Due to its vital importance and its impact on the surety's liability, notice of the reservation of rights against a surety should be given in writing to both the surety and the principal.

Principal's Fraud. With the use of false financial statements, the principal may induce a creditor to accept less than full performance from the principal or no performance at all in return for the creditor's release. Once that creditor learns of this fraudulent scheme by the principal, the creditor may rescind its release agreement. What impact these events have on a surety's liability depends on the factual situation. Normally a surety (that has not consented and has not had rights reserved against it) is released when the principal is released. However, if the release is obtained by fraud by the principal, the creditor would be greatly disadvantaged if the surety is released altogether. Therefore, if the surety had no knowledge of the fraud, that surety is released only to the extent it has relied on the release and the changed legal position as a result of the release. If the surety had knowledge of the principal's wrongful acts, the surety is not justified in relying on the release. In this latter situation, the creditor still may hold the surety liable for the principal's uncompleted performance.

16. Extensions of Time for Payment

Before discussing the rules regarding the surety's liability, we need to have a clear understanding of what is meant by an extension of time for performance. To affect the surety's liability, the extension agreement must be a binding, enforceable contract. As such, it must be for a definite time and supported by consideration. In other words, the principal must induce the creditor to extend the time originally involved by promising something in addition to what the principal is already obligated to do. A principal's consideration for an extension may take the form of a refinancing agreement or an advance payment of interest. Merely promising to pay the original debt at a future date will not supply the consideration, because performance of a preexisting obligation is not consideration.

The creditor's gratuitous indulgence or passive permission to the principal to take more time than the contract provides has no impact on the surety's liability. Such conduct by the creditor does not injure the surety in any way. Upon the principal's default, the surety is free to perform at any time and pursue all available remedies.

If there is a formalized agreement between creditor and principal whereby the time for performance is extended to a definite time, a nonconsenting, uncompensated surety is discharged from liability. This rule is necessary since the extension of time delays any potential default by the principal. Such a delay could adversely affect the surety's ability to recover from the principal if the surety has to perform. During the extension, the principal's financial condition could worsen, which could increase the surety's ultimate risk of loss.

As with releases, this general rule does not apply if the surety consents to the extension. Furthermore, a surety is not discharged by a formal extension of time if the creditor expressly reserves rights against the surety. This reservation of rights must be a part of the extension agreement. The creditor's stipulation that rights are reserved against the surety does not bind the surety to the extension agreement. Thus, this surety may proceed to satisfy the creditor's claim and sue the principal for reimbursement at any time. The principal, therefore, is not really protected by an extension agreement that includes the creditor's reservation of rights against the surety. This type of extension agreement simply is a limited promise by the creditor not to sue the principal during the extension period.

Finally, a formalized extension of the time for performance discharges a compensated surety only to the extent that surety is injured by the extension. Of course, this rule assumes that the surety does not consent to the extension agreement. A compensated surety is perceived as being capable of protecting itself by anticipating possible extension agreements and charging a premium in accordance with expectations.

17. Other Modifications

In addition to an extension of the time for payment, any other modification of the creditor-principal agreement generally discharges the surety. The logic behind this general rule is that a surety should not be liable for the performance of some agreement made after the surety's commitment to the creditor. A modification agreed to by creditor and principal is a novation that relieves the surety from its obligation. In general, evidence of a renewed obligation is not considered to be a modification that relieves the surety of liability.[6] However, if the renewal note increases the principal's obligation, the surety is relieved of further liability unless the surety consents to the renewal agreement.

An examination of the exceptions or qualifications to this general rule, may make the philosophy behind it clearer. These exceptions include the following: (1) A surety that consents to the modification is not discharged. (2) An uncompensated but nonconsenting surety is not discharged to the extent the modification benefits the surety. (3) A compensated surety is not discharged if the modification does not materially increase the surety's risk.

Surety's Consent.   As in other areas of suretyship, the parties can override the application of the general rule on modification by their agreement. A surety who consents to remain liable is not discharged by a modification to the creditor-principal agreement. This exception is applicable regardless of when the surety consents. Whether consent to modifications occurs before, at the time of, or after the modification, the consenting surety remains liable to the creditor.

If the surety's consent is not a part of the original agreement signed by the surety, the creditor has the responsibility to notify the surety of the modification and to obtain the surety's consent. Failure to obtain this consent upon full notice of the modification automatically discharges the surety.

Uncompensated Sureties.   The surety who is not paid is a favorite of the law. In fact, the uncompensated surety is so protected in some states that any modification to the principal's obligation results in an absolute discharge of this surety, assuming no consent.[7]

Courts in some states have disliked the harshness of the rule which discharges an uncompensated surety whenever any modification is made without that surety's consent. Therefore, there are decisions which hold that an uncompensated (and nonconsenting) surety should not be discharged if the creditor-principal modification benefits the surety. This benefit must be so obvious that there is no way to doubt its beneficial nature. Typically, such a modification occurs only when the creditor agrees to reduce the amount due or the rate of interest. In some states, a change in interest rates (up or down) does not discharge a continuing surety. Since interest rates are expected to change in today's economy, that change should not discharge the continuing surety.

---

[6] Commerce Union Bank v. Burger-in-a-Pouch, Inc., p. 806.

[7] Inter-Sport, Inc. v. Wilson, p. 807.

Compensated Sureties. Sureties that receive consideration (separate from that received by the principal) in return for their promises are *not* protected by the law to the same extent as uncompensated sureties. Thus, with respect to the impact of creditor-principal modifications, a compensated surety is discharged altogether only if that surety's risk has materially increased. If the increased risk to the surety cannot be readily determined, it is immaterial. To the extent that a compensated surety's risk is increased only slightly by the modification, that surety is discharged only to the extent of the increased risk. And if the compensated surety's risk is not affected by the modification, the surety remains liable as promised.

Why is an extension of time for payment treated differently from other modifications? This distinction in treatment basically is due to the creditor's ability to reserve rights against the surety upon an extension of the time of performance. In this section on modification, there has been no mention of reservation of rights. A creditor cannot reserve rights against a surety when a general modification of the principal's agreement is made.

PRINCIPAL–SURETY RELATIONSHIP

18. Introduction

Not only does the principal owe a duty to perform to the creditor, but the principal also owes that same duty to the surety. This duty arises by express agreement or by implication. Whenever a surety is present, the principal owes the duty to protect that surety from liability regardless of whether the surety has a contract with that principal or with the creditor. The only exception to this general rule is when the principal is relieved of liability due to a defense assertable against the creditor's claim. It is this general duty the principal owes the surety that justifies the surety's right to be reimbursed by the principal after the surety has satisfied the creditor's claim.

The surety owes a duty to account to the principal for any profits obtained after the surety performs. For example, suppose a principal gave a creditor a security interest in some equipment. And assume that a surety personally paid $100,000 in order to satisfy the principal's delinquent obligation. As noted previously, the surety has the right to the security interest via subrogation. If the surety sold the equipment for $175,000, that surety would have to return $75,000 to the principal. This surety's duty to account emphasizes the fact that the surety is liable for the principal's performance of an obligation. In essence, the surety should be liable for no more than, and should not benefit from, the commitment made.

19. Right to Reimbursement

Generally, after the surety has performed, the surety is entitled to be reimbursed by the principal. As you have come to expect, this general rule on the surety's right to be reimbursed is subject to at least two exceptions. First, a principal may inform a surety of a valid defense that a principal can assert to deny the creditor's claim. If the surety fails to use this defense as a means of reducing liability, that surety is not entitled to be reimbursed by the principal. Basically, the law requires the principal to bear the burden of informing the surety of available defenses. However, this requirement to inform does not apply when the principal's defense cannot be asserted by the surety. For example, the principal's defenses of (1) lack of capacity, (2) discharge in bankruptcy, and (3) expiration of the statute of limitations cannot be asserted by the surety. Regardless of whether a surety knows of these defenses, that surety cannot force the principal to reimburse expenses after the surety has satisfied the creditor's claim. In other words, these defenses extinguish the principal's liability altogether.

A second exception to the principal's duty to reimburse occurs when a surety has performed for a creditor after a principal already has performed or been released. By performance, the principal is *discharged* from liability. On the other hand, the principal may be *released* from performing by agreement of the creditor. Although a discharge and a release may be asserted by the principal as a defense against the creditor's claim, these concepts are treated separately from the more typical defenses justifying nonperformance. This separate treatment is necessary since the law generally puts the burden of discovering the existence of a discharge or a release on the surety, not the principal. In the preceding paragraph, the general rule was that a principal must inform the surety of defenses.

A surety that performs is not entitled to be reimbursed by the principal if the principal has been discharged by performance or released by the creditor's agreement. This rule makes logical sense, since it would be fraudulent for a creditor of a discharged or released principal to seek performance from a surety. If a surety does perform under these circumstances, the surety has a right to have the value of performance returned from the creditor.

This rule relieving the principal of the duty to reimburse the surety is subject to a further exception when the creditor releasing the principal reserves rights against the surety. As discussed in sections 15 and 16 above, a surety remains liable to perform the principal's obligations if the creditor reserves rights against the surety. If the surety must perform for the creditor, it is only fair that the surety is reimbursed by the principal. The use of the concept of reservation of rights is allowed when a principal is released by a creditor or when time for payment is extended formally.

20. Liability of Co-Sureties

Throughout this chapter to this point, there has been an implicit assumption that only one surety was involved in protecting the creditor. This assumption is too simplistic to reflect the actual situation in the marketplace. In any contract, a creditor may insist upon or otherwise be benefited by the existence of two or more sureties. Generally, these sureties may exist as co-sureties or as sub-sureties. *Co-sureties* are jointly and severally liable to the creditor. This term *joint and several* means the creditor may sue the co-sureties jointly for the performance promised or may sue each surety separately for the entire performance due. A *sub-surety* promises to be liable only in the event that the surety refuses to perform and thereby defaults. A sub-surety is a surety's surety. Unless the sureties involved in a transaction agree otherwise, they are considered co-sureties. A sub-suretyship normally must be created by the agreement of the parties, whereas a co-suretyship may be created by implication.

Numerous legal principles govern the rights of all the parties involved in a transaction with two or more sureties. In general, all the basic rules and exceptions discussed in this chapter remain applicable. For example, a release of the principal is a release of the surety if the surety does not consent to the release and if the creditor does not reserve rights against the surety. When a creditor releases one surety but not the other sureties, the general rule is that the remaining sureties are released to the extent that they cannot seek contribution against the released surety. Once again, this rule is not applicable if the remaining sureties consent or if the creditor reserves rights against the remaining sureties.

In addition to the applicability of the legal principles discussed above, there are rules that govern the liability of co-sureties one to another. Similar to the surety's right to be reimbursed by the principal, the fundamental rule among co-sureties is their right of contribution. This right is how co-sureties work out among themselves their fair share of the performance completed for the creditor. Whereas a creditor can hold one surety liable for all of the principal's obligation, that surety is liable for only a pro-rata share (among the co-sureties) of the performance rendered. The right of contribution works to allocate the liability 50–50 among two co-sureties, $33\frac{1}{3}$–$33\frac{1}{3}$–$33\frac{1}{3}$ among three co-sureties, and so forth. Before one co-surety can collect from another, proof of payment of the obligation is required. In general, any recovery does not include attorney's fees, although interest calculated at the statutory rate may be recovered.[8]

[8] Collins v. Throckmorton, p. 808.

SUMMARY

ARTISAN'S LIENS

Definition	1. The right to possess, for leverage in the collection process, personal property that one has serviced or repaired.
Perfection	1. The "improved" personal property must be possessed at all times.
	2. If possession is surrendered voluntarily, the lien is lost unless a claim of lien is filed in the public records.
	3. Artisan's liens are personal and cannot generally be assigned.
Enforcement	1. The property is sold and the proceeds are used to satisfy the lienholder's claim.
	2. In general, artisan's lienholders have priority to the sale proceeds.

BULK TRANSFERS

Terms	1. A bulk transfer is the sale of such a large amount of inventory that the sale is not in the ordinary course of business.
	2. The parties involved in a bulk transfer are called the transferor, the transferee, and the transferor's creditor.
Duties of transferees	1. The transferee must obtain and then maintain for 6 months a schedule of property being transfered and a list of the transferor's creditors.
	2. The transferee also must give notice to all the transferor's creditors that a bulk transfer is occurring.
Rights of creditors	1. The creditors' action upon receiving notice of a bulk transfer is to levy against the property transferred or enjoin that transfer.
	2. This action must be taken within 6 months of the transfer if Article 6 is not followed.

SURETYSHIP IN GENERAL

Terminology	1. A principal is a debtor or one who is obligated to perform a contractual promise.
	2. A creditor is the party to whom money is owed or who is entitled to some other contractual performance.
	3. A surety is a party who assures the creditor that the principal will perform as promised.
	4. The term *surety* should be compared and contrasted with *guarantor* and *indemnitor*.
Creation of suretyship contracts	1. These contracts usually arise in relationship to the principal's obligation to repay a debt or to complete some other promised performance.
	2. These contracts may be created as expressed written agreements or by operation of law.

CREDITOR–SURETY RELATIONSHIP

Fiduciary nature	1. A suretyship is based on trust and confidence.
	2. Both creditor and surety must share any information that may adversely affect that party's potential liability.
Principal's default	1. A surety becomes liable to the creditor when the principal defaults.
	2. In general, the creditor does not have to give notice of default in order to hold the surety liable.
	3. However, notice of default is required if the creditor-surety agreement requires it, if the surety is a drawer or indorser of commercial paper, of if the surety is a collection guarantor.
Surety's performance and subrogation rights	1. A surety satisfies its obligation upon performance.
	2. Having performed, the surety is entitled to any rights of the creditor.
	3. Likewise, the creditor is entitled to be protected by any rights held by the surety.

CREDITOR–PRINCIPAL RELATIONSHIP

Principal's defenses	1. Sureties generally can utilize any defense a principal has against the creditor to reduce liability.
	2. The principal's defenses of lack of capacity, discharge in bankruptcy, and expiration of the statute of limitation cannot be asserted by the surety.
Releases	1. In general, a creditor who releases a principal from liability also releases any surety.
	2. The principal's release does not relieve the surety of liability if the surety consents to the release, if the creditor reserves rights against the surety, or if the release is obtained by the principal's fraud.

Extensions of time for payment	1. An extension must be a valid agreement supported by consideration if it is to have an impact on the surety's liability.
	2. A formal extension does discharge the surety's liability unless the surety consents, unless the creditor reserves rights against the surety, or unless the surety is compensated and not injured by the extension.
Other modifications	1. In general, any modification of the creditor-principal relationship discharges the surety.
	2. Exceptions to this general rule include the surety's consent to the modification, the uncompensated surety to the extent of any benefit, and the compensated surety as long as the modification does not materially increase that surety's risk.

PRINCIPAL–SURETY RELATIONSHIP

Surety's duty to account	1. The surety must account to the principal for any benefits the surety receives from performance.
Surety's right to reimbursement	1. In general, after performance a surety is entitled to be reimbursed by the principal. This right of the surety is based on the principal's obligation not to default.
	2. The surety's right to reimbursement does not apply if the principal has informed the surety of a valid defense that would defeat the creditor's claim of performance.
	3. The right to reimbursement is also lacking if the surety performs after the principal has been discharged or released by the creditor, unless the creditor reserves rights against the surety.
Liability of co-sureties	1. In general, the liability of co-sureties is based on the same principles as the liability of one surety.
	2. Co-sureties are jointly and severally liable. Generally, the right of contribution assures that co-sureties share liability on a pro-rata basis.

CASES

Rocky Mountain Turbines v. 660 Syndicate
623 P.2d 758 (Wyo. 1981)

Plaintiff (660 Syndicate) sued the defendant (Rocky Mountain) to obtain possession of an airplane. The defendant had repaired the airplane at the request of Wyoming Airlines, which had leased it from the plaintiff. The defendant had returned possession of the airplane to Wyoming after the repairs had been completed and had later reacquired possession of the plane. It sought to enforce a lien on the plane and to foreclose it as a defense to the suit by the plaintiff. The trial court held that the defendant had no lien, and it appealed.

ROONEY, J. . . . Wyoming Airlines took the aircraft from Rocky Mountain and flew it after the repairs on which Rocky Mountain claims a lien were made. Rocky Mountain did not file a lien statement. Rocky Mountain contends that its lien was valid by virtue of subsequent acquisition by it of possession of the aircraft.

Following are pertinent portions of the statutes which are dispositive of this issue.

Section 29-7-10 (a), W.S.1977:

(a) Any person, firm or corporation who makes, alters, repairs, bestows labor upon, transports, stores or keeps any goods or chattels, or who feeds, herds, pastures or cares for any domestic or wild animal, at the request of the owner or any person in possession thereof, has a lien on such goods, chattels or animal for his or its reasonable charges for the labor, services, materials and feed performed or provided.

Section 29-7-102, W.S.1977:

A lienor may retain possession of the property to which the lien pertains until paid for the labor, services, materials and feed which entitle the lienor to assert the lien; provided the right of possession shall terminate six (6) months after the date upon which the charges for the labor, services, materials and feed become due and payable unless the lienor has commenced proceedings to foreclose the lien . . . within such six (6) months.

Section 29-7-103(a) and (b), W.S.1977:

(a) A lienor desiring to continue a lien without retaining possession may, with the written consent of the owner, before releasing possession, file a lien statement in the office of the county clerk of the county where the property is located.

(b) A lien statement shall set forth the name and address of the lienor, the name and address of the owner of the property, a description of the property, the amount of the lien and the nature of the labor, services, feed and materials giving rise to the lien, and shall contain a statement that the lienor was in possession of the property at the time the lien statement was filed. A lien statement shall be verified under oath by the lienor or his agent or attorney.

Section 29-7-104, W.S.1977:

(a) A lien under this act [§§29-7-101 to 29-7-106] shall terminate:

(i) Upon a lienor's voluntary surrender of possession of the property, unless a lien statement has previously been filed as provided in section [§29-7-103];

(ii) Six (6) months after the date upon which the charges for labor, services-materials and feed giving rise to the lien become due and payable, unless a lien statement has previously been filed as provided in section 3 or unless action to enforce and foreclose the lien has been commenced; and

(iii) Six (6) months after a lien statement has been filed as provided in section 3, unless action to enforce and foreclose the lien has been commenced.

(b) Upon termination of a lien, the lienor shall have no further right to possession of the property and no further interest therein.

The foregoing language is plain in that the lien established thereby is a possessory lien which terminates upon the "voluntary surrender of possession" unless "a lien statement has previously been filed." The common-law lien was similar:

The right to a common-law lien is based directly on the idea of possession, and it is indispensable that one claiming it have an independent and exclusive possession of the property. Such a lien arises only when possession is obtained, and exists only so long as it is retained. . . .

As a general rule a common-law or other lien dependent on possession is waived or lost by the lienholder voluntarily and unconditionally parting with possession or control of the property to which it attaches; and such lien cannot be restored thereafter by resumption of possession. . . .

The statutes are too plain and unambiguous to require further discussion. Rocky Mountain's lien terminated when it relinquished possession of the aircraft without having previously filed a lien statement. A subsequent obtaining of possession of the aircraft does not restore the terminated lien. . . .

Affirmed.

Anderson & Clayton Co. v. Earnest
610 S.W.2d 846 (Tex. App. 1980)

Earnest purchased an operating livestock feed and supply store. However, Earnest did not satisfy the requirements of the Bulk Transfers Act (Article 6). Anderson & Clayton Company (ACCO) was a creditor of Earnest's transferor. ACCO filed a lawsuit seeking to hold Earnest personally liable for the debts owed to ACCO. ACCO argued that Earnest should be personally liable for the transferor's debts since Earnest did not comply with the Bulk Transfers Act.

COUNTISS, J. . . . After a nonjury trial, a take-nothing judgment was rendered and the trial court filed findings of fact and conclusions of law. . . .

[I]t is necessary to review the purpose and nature of the Act that is the basis of the litigation before us. The debt in question was not contracted by Earnest and is not his direct personal obligation. Thus, if he has any liability, it is of a derivative nature. The Bulk Transfers Act and related predecessors were enacted for the protection of creditors who sell goods and merchandise to others on credit for inventory and resale. When a bulk sale of, or by, the debtor entity, of the kind described in section 6.102 of the Act, and not subject to the exceptions specified in section 6.103, occurs, the remaining provisions of the Act are applicable. The subsequent provisions establish, among other things, procedures for assembling a property schedule and a list of creditors and notifying the creditors of the proposed bulk transfer.

The Act does not, however, spell out the remedies available to a creditor if the notice provisions are not followed. It simply states that the bulk transfer is "ineffective against any creditor of the transferor" unless the requirements of the Act are

followed. Apparently the creditor is relegated to whatever remedial relief is afforded by state law outside the code. Thus, if the creditor already has a judgment against the transferor and the bulk sale of the assets is ineffective as to the creditor, the creditor would have the same right to levy execution on the assets as would have existed prior to the bulk sale. If the creditor does not have a judgment against the transferor, an alternate remedy would be to seek one and also seek to have the bulk sale set aside, further transfers enjoined, and a receiver or trustee appointed or designated to gather the assets and preserve them for distribution pro rata among the creditors.

Regardless of the remedy pursued by the creditor, it is apparent that relief is obtained primarily from and against the assets transferred in bulk. . . .

The purchaser becomes personally liable to the creditors only under the narrow circumstances described as follows in *South-western Drug,* 172 S.W.2d at 487:

> However, if a purchaser or receiver disposes of or converts to his own use property acquired in violation of the Bulk Sales Law, placing it beyond the reach of creditors, he will be held personally liable for the value thereof. . . .

When the foregoing principles are applied to this case, it is apparent that the judgment must be affirmed for two reasons. First, ACCO brought this proceeding seeking a personal judgment against Earnest. There is no evidence in the record, however, that would support a personal judgment against him. At the trial, Earnest testified that he had sold some of the property and still had some of it. There is no evidence of the value of the property sold, no evidence of the value of the property still on hand at the time of trial and no evidence that the property sold has been disposed of or converted in such a manner as to place it beyond the reach of creditors.

Even if we were to construe ACCO's pleadings as seeking to enforce its claim only against the assets transferred to Earnest in violation of the Act, the proof is still deficient. . . . ACCO established a transfer in violation of the Act and established the amount of its debt. It did not present any evidence, however, of the assets on hand and available for satisfaction of the debt. As noted above, Earnest had sold part of the assets and still had some, but we have no evidence of the nature or value of either.

Since the assets at the time of transfer did not exceed the debts owed to creditors, and since there was an unknown but apparently lesser quantity of assets on hand at the time of trial, it would have been impossible for the trial court to make an award to ACCO, had it been desirous of doing so. It simply could not determine, from the evidence, what to award ACCO.

For all of the reasons discussed above, the trial court's conclusions were proper.

Affirmed.

Chemical Bank v. Sepler
457 N.E.2d 714 (N.Y. 1983)

KAYE, J. Personal guarantees issued in connection with loans to a corporation may survive repayment of the corporate indebtedness where the guarantees provide that they are continuing until terminated by written notice. . . .

Appellants Sandy Sepler, David Sepler and Lawrence Roth were officers of Damsel Manufacturing Company (Damsel), a closely held corporation in the apparel business. In June, 1972, in order for Damsel to obtain financing from respondent, each appellant signed a guarantee of Damsel's obligations to respondent. Those identical instruments provided that they were continuing guarantees of all present and future liabilities of the corporation to respondent, whether created directly or acquired by respondent through assignment; they were to remain in effect irrespective of any interruptions in the business relations of Damsel with respondent, subject to appellants' right at any time to terminate the guarantees by written notice; and their terms could be modified or waived only in writing. Respondent thereafter extended loans to the corporation.

In March, 1974 Damsel, seeking alternate financing arrangements, entered into an agreement with another lender, United Virginia Factors Corporation. By November, 1975, Damsel had paid off all loans received from respondent, and did not borrow directly from respondent thereafter. Respondent continued, however to factor accounts receivable for several suppliers of Damsel, and as a consequence the corporation continued to issue checks payable to respondent on those accounts.

Between 1975 and 1980, Damsel issued approximately 350 such checks to respondent.

Damsel filed for reorganization under chapter 11 of the Bankruptcy Act in August, 1980. At the time, the corporation was obligated to respondent for merchandise purchased on credit between April and July, 1980 from three suppliers who had in turn factored their accounts receivable to respondent. In March, 1981, respondent brought suit against appellants to enforce their personal guarantees. Special Term granted respondent's motion for summary judgment, finding that no written notice of termination had ever been sent by appellants to respondent, and concluding that neither the repayment of the initial loans nor the length of time between that repayment and the transactions eventually giving rise to appellants' liability served to terminate the guarantees. The Appellate Division affirmed. . . .

Any analysis of appellants' liability under the guarantees must of course begin with the words of the instruments themselves. Each guarantee provides, in relevant part, as follows:

NOW THEREFORE, in consideration of the premises and of other good and valuable consideration and in order to induce the Bank from time to time, in its discretion, to extend or continue credit to the Borrower, the undersigned hereby guarantees, absolutely and unconditionally, to the Bank the payment of all liabilities of the Borrower to the Bank of whatever nature, whether now existing or hereafter incurred, whether created directly or acquired by the Bank by assignment or otherwise, whether matured or unmatured and whether absolute or contingent. . . .

This guaranty is a continuing guaranty and shall remain in full force and effect irrespective of any interruptions in the business relations of the Borrower with the Bank; provided, however, that the undersigned may by notice in writing, delivered personally to or received by registered mail by, an officer of the Bank at the Bank's office at 349 Fifth Ave., New York, New York, terminate this guaranty with respect to all Liabilities of the Borrower incurred or contracted by the Borrower or acquired by the Bank after the date on which such notice is so delivered or received. . . .

While appellants gave no written notice of termination, they nonetheless contend that they should not be liable under the guarantees because no "business relationship" existed after the loans were satisfied, and the guarantees accordingly terminated due to the conduct of the parties, the passage of time, and the fact that there was no continuing consideration to support the continuing guarantees. This contention is at odds with both the terms of the guarantees and the applicable law.

Where, as here, a guarantee is continuing, applicable to after-acquired obligations and termi-

nable only by writing, it may not be said to have terminated due to lack of further consideration, or cessation of what one party may have regarded as the "business relationship." A single, unlimited, continuing guarantee, supported by consideration given once and for all time, is not automatically terminated by a change in the parties' relationship. Unless the parties to a continuing guarantee provide otherwise in the writing, such a guarantee is not limited to the life of loans executed contemporaneously therewith and generally cannot expire by mere conduct, change of circumstances, or lapse of time. Here, the parties expressly provided that the guarantee would apply to obligations acquired in the future by assignment, and would be continuing "irrespective of any interruptions in the business relations of the Borrower with the Bank". No clearer showing of intent is required.

Accordingly, the order of the Appellate Division should be affirmed.

Affirmed.

First National Bank and Trust Company of Racine v. Notte
293 N.W.2d 530 (Wis. 1980)

DAY, J. The First National Bank and Trust Company of Racine (First National) brought this action against Robert Notte to recover the balance owing on a "Consumer Installment Note and Chattel Security Agreement" in the amount of $16,372.85 plus interest and costs. Mr. Notte acted as a gratuitous co-signer for the principal debtor, Pauline McCloud, who defaulted on the obligation and later filed a petition in bankruptcy.

The question presented for review is under what circumstances will a contractual surety obligation be rendered voidable based on the material misrepresentation or non-disclosure of a creditor. We conclude that the creditor has a duty to make disclosure to a proposed surety if the creditor knows of facts that materially increase the risk beyond that which the creditor has reason to believe the surety intends to assume, and the creditor has reason to believe that the surety does not know these facts and the creditor has a reasonable opportunity to communicate them to the surety. Failure

to disclose under these circumstances will be a defense to the surety obligation. . . .

Pauline McCloud, the principal debtor on the note, owned and operated a beauty salon business. Prior to the loan in controversy here, she had taken out seventeen loans with First National since 1958. All of these loans were paid within the end term of the contract. . . .

The developments leading up to the issuance of the defaulted loan in controversy here began in 1974. In February of that year, Ms. McCloud applied for a loan of $41,000 from First National to remodel and equip the "Tartan Room," one of her hair-styling establishments. In March that loan application was denied. Then in November, 1974 and again in April, 1975, loans were made by First National in the amount of $2,500 and $3,000 respectively for the purpose of remodeling and buying fixtures for the Tartan Room. Both of these loans were secured by the cash surrender value of life insurance owned by Ms. McCloud.

In May, 1975, Pauline McCloud spoke with the vice-president in charge of lending at First National, Till A. Bruett. . . . [S]he requested another $13,000 from First National so that she could purchase fixtures. First National agreed to make the loan on the condition that she provide the bank with a third mortgage on real estate that she owned on Douglas Avenue, a lien on the fixtures, and a suitable co-signer. . . .[Later], it was "decided that based on Bob Notte's credit record and reputation" they would go ahead with the loan without the third mortgage.

Sometime later, Mr. Notte called Mr. Bruett to inquire about Pauline McCloud's credit record with the bank. Mr. Bruett stated that Ms. McCloud's credit record with the bank was good and that she had always paid her loans. After talking with Mr. Bruett, Mr. Notte signed the note and the explanation of the co-signer obligation.

Problems arose immediately. Ms. McCloud was late with the first payment. She then made a couple of more payments and then all payments ceased. Mr. Notte made payments for a number of months and then he too ceased making them after consulting with his attorney.

The loan agreement which Mr. Notte signed stated. . . . that there would be a lien on real estate and a security interest taken in all furniture, fixtures, and equipment in the Tartan Room. . . .

The trial court . . . entered [a verdict] in favor of First National in the amount of $10,305.82. . . . A notice of appeal and cross-appeal were duly filed by the parties. The court of appeals . . . reversed the trial court, holding that strict liability would be imposed for First National's misrepresentations and that Mr. Notte was therefore entitled to rescission of the transaction. . . .

We first address the duty of a creditor to disclose information to a surety. Although the creditor owes a surety a duty of continuous good faith and fair dealing, there is no general obligation imposed upon the creditor to disclose to the surety all matters which the creditor knows might affect the surety's risk. There are, however, circumstances under which the creditor may be required to make disclosure and the failure to do so will discharge the surety. In such circumstances it is not necessary that the concealment or the failure to disclose facts material to the surety be wilfully done by the creditor, or that the creditor have the intent to deceive. The motive behind the concealment or misrepresentation is immaterial. . . .

After careful consideration, we conclude that the rule as stated in the Restatement of *Security,*

§124(1) (1941) is a correct reflection of the current state of the law. We hereby adopt the disclosure rule provided in that section which states:

> Where before the surety has undertaken his obligation the creditor knows facts unknown to the surety that materially increase the risk beyond that which the creditor has reason to believe the surety intends to assume, and the creditor also has reason to believe that these facts are unknown to the surety and has a reasonable opportunity to communicate them to the surety, failure of the creditor to notify the surety of such facts is a defense to the surety.

To be noted is the fact that there is no duty imposed on the creditor to conduct an investigation for the surety regarding the risk to be undertaken. Therefore, if the creditor is nothing more than negligent in not discovering facts which affect the risk the surety will not be discharged of his obligation. As the comments to this section indicate, there may be some difficulty in ascertaining the precise degree of knowledge possessed by the surety and in determining the materiality of facts which were not disclosed. But these ordinarily will be questions for the trier of fact. . . .

We next address under what circumstances a surety will be entitled to avoid his contractual obligation because the creditor made assertions which the surety later discovers are false. . . .

The most innocent misrepresentation may result in unforeseen liability to a likewise innocent surety. In circumstances such as these, where both parties, the misrepresenter and the surety, are innocent of any wrongdoing there is a dilemma as to the proper treatment to be accorded each. But between two innocent parties, the party making the misrepresentation will bear the loss. There is a basic inequity of allowing one party to benefit from his own misstatements or misrepresentations, however honestly he believed them to be at the time made. . . .

There has been considerable discussion in the parties' briefs concerning the justifiable reliance of Mr. Notte and his alleged negligence in failing to discover the facts behind the misrepresentations made. The recipient's fault in failing to discover the facts before entering the contract does not make his reliance unjustified unless his fault amounts to a failure to act in good faith or to conform his conduct to reasonable standards of fair dealing.

Application of the foregoing principles to the facts of this case requires that the case be remanded for a new trial. . . .

Reversed and remanded.

Local No. 1179 v. Merchants Mutual Bonding Co.
613 P.2d 944 (Kan. 1980)

The Floor Covering Association agreed with Local Union No. 1179 to fund certain health, welfare, pension, and other fringe benefits payments. As a part of their collective bargaining agreement, the Association was required to furnish a surety bond covering the agreed-upon payments. Merchants Mutual Bonding Company signed a bond covering up to $10,000 of the Association's fringe benefits payment. This bond contained a requirement that Merchants Mutual be notified within thirty days of the Association's failure to perform. In March, 1975, Driscoll, a member of the Association, defaulted on making its fringe benefit payments. In March or April, an agent of the union orally told Merchants Mutual that there may be a claim filed on the bond. Formal written notice of a claim was not sent until September, 1975. The union, as a creditor, filed suit against Merchants Mutual. This defendant argued it was not liable since the bond's notice requirement had not been satisfied. Furthermore, there had been no action taken against the defaulting Association.

HERD, J. . . . The controlling issues are these: . . . whether notice of default was timely, and, if not, whether the surety is absolved of liability; and whether evidence supports the trial court's findings and judgment. We turn to these issues in order.

The Association was formed, according to its articles of incorporation, for the primary purpose of negotiating, entering into, and administering collective bargaining agreements with the employees of the member firms. This is borne out by the testimony of the officers of the Association. The Association itself had no employees; it simply presented a united front, a single entity for the purpose of negotiating and entering into a collective bargaining agreement with the Union. The Union represented its members, the employees; the Association represented management, its member floor covering contractors.

The Association itself paid no wages and no fringe benefits. Each member firm paid to its workmen the union scale provided by the April 1, 1973, collective bargaining agreement or the later amendments thereto, and each remitted monthly to the Union and the trustees the amounts required for vacation pay, health and welfare, pension, and other fringe benefits. The Association had no financial dealings with plaintiffs; it was a nonprofit corporation, was not authorized to issue capital stock, and there is no evidence that it had any assets. The Association was acting as an agent for its member contractors when it negotiated and signed the collective bargaining agreement and when it applied for and secured the surety bond required by that agreement. The bond makes reference to and incorporates the terms of the collective bargaining agreement insofar as it requires payment of dues, vacation and holiday pay, health, welfare, and pension contributions and other fringe benefits.

The union proceeded against Driscoll, the actual employer who was obligated to make the fringe benefit payments, and it secured a judgment against him. Looking through form to substance, as we are required to do, it is obvious that the bond was intended to protect the plaintiffs from default by Driscoll or the other member contractors in the payment of fringe benefits. A surety bond is to be construed in the light of the circumstances in which it is given, so as to effectuate its purpose. . . . The bond provides that in the event of default, the obligees (plaintiffs) shall notify the surety within 30 days after the obligees shall have had knowledge of such default. No penalty is provided in the bond for failure to give prompt notice.

The evidence, outlined above, is that Driscoll was obligated to pay fringe benefits for his employees by early March, 1975, and that he did not do so. The plaintiffs then knew that Driscoll was in default. In either March or April, the Union notified the resident agent of the surety by telephone, of the default and the possibility that a claim would be made on the bond. A formal written claim was made in September. There was no evidence that the surety was disadvantaged or that its position was adversely affected because of delay in the giving of notice. We agree with the trial court that "there was substantial compliance with the notice requirement. . . . " . . .

In *School District v. McCurley,* 92 Kan. 53, 142 P. 1077 (1914) we held that bonding companies engaged in the business of insuring the performance of contracts of others for pay are not "favorites of the law" in the sense the term is applied to accommodation sureties; that such companies are in fact insurers; and that the failure of the obligee to give notice of the principal's default in strict compliance with the terms of the bond does not relieve the surety of liability when the failure to notify resulted in no actual loss or prejudice to the surety. We said:

> The breach of a condition precedent in a bond given by an insurer for pay will not relieve the

insurer from liability for any loss for which he would otherwise be liable unless such breach contributed to the loss."

We conclude that under no construction of the evidence is the surety entitled to discharge in this case.

Finally, we turn to the claim that the record does not support the trial court's findings and judgment. It would unduly prolong this opinion to detail the various documents in the record, as well as the testimony of the Union officials, the agent who wrote the bond, officers of the Association, and former employees of Driscoll. We have carefully examined the evidence and find full and adequate support for the trial court's findings and conclusions. . . .

Affirmed.

Commerce Union Bank v. Burger-in-a-Pouch, Inc.
657 S.W.2d 88 (Tenn. 1983)

HUMPHREYS, J. This case is before this Court on appeal from the Court of Appeals. It arises under the uniform negotiable instrument law, a part of the Uniform Commercial Code. It involves a $24,900 promissory note of a corporation first named Burger-in-a-Pouch, a name later changed to Best of Both, and a surety contract signed by appellee Heatherly and others, guaranteeing absolutely and unconditionally the payment to appellant bank of that note. . . .

On September 27, 1976, appellee Heatherly, at that time a stockholder in, and president of, the debtor corporation, together with the other stockholders and officers, Kenneth H. Mitchell, and Jimmy L. Darnell, and Mitchell's wife, Linda S. Mitchell, signed a contract guaranteeing payment of $25,000 to appellant bank in consideration of money loaned, and to be loaned, to the debtor corporation. At that time the debtor corporation owed appellant $25,000, $13,000 of which had been borrowed after appellee Heatherly joined the corporation.

Heatherly, Mitchell and Darnell disagreed about the management of the corporation and Heatherly resigned and supposedly disposed of his

stock. . . . This happened in February 1977. In April of 1978 the corporate charter of the debtor corporation was forfeited for non-payment of state franchise taxes. Subsequent to appellee's resignation and the charter forfeiture, Mitchell and Darnell signed notes in their name and in the name of the defunct corporation renewing the original $25,000 note. Appellee Heatherly did not sign any renewal notes expressly refusing appellant bank's request that he do so, advising the bank at that time that he had no further connection with the corporate enterprise.

In July 1980 this suit was brought to recover $24,900, the balance owing on the debt, and interest and attorney's fees. All of the parties who had signed the notes and surety contracts were made defendants. None of these parties except appellee Heatherly defended the suit, and judgment was taken against them. The other parties not having appealed, have no interest in these proceedings.

The trial court held appellee liable on his surety contract and awarded the bank judgment for the principal, $24,900, and interest and attorney's fees in the amount of $8,408.76. Appellee Heatherly appealed and the Court of Appeals reversed. . . .

As it is the law that a renewal note does not discharge the original note unless this is intended, and it is against reason to presume that a creditor would act against his own interest by accepting a renewal note with intent to discharge an original note, and so release a solvent surety; and as it is the common practice of which the Court will take notice for lenders to extend payment of original notes by renewal notes, we are compelled to the conclusion that there is no presumption that the renewal note extinguishes the old. . . .

Absent presumptions on either side, where do the facts lead? The appellee offered no proof at all as to the intention of the parties. Although he could have called Darnell or Mitchell, the makers of the original and renewal notes, to testify about intent, he didn't. So there is not only no evidence on his side, there is at least a warranted inference that these parties may not have testified in his favor. This inference is weakened by the fact that relations between appellee and these two were strained, but there is still the presumption they would have told the truth and the burden being on appellee to prove the intent was to discharge the original note and release the surety he should have called them, or, at least, explained why he did not.

On the other hand, appellant bank retained possession of the security contract, producing it at the trial. The last renewal note included a reference to the security contract, indicating that in the minds of the appellant and the maker the original note and contract were not to be affected by the renewal. Finally, the appellant bank evinced an intention not to discharge the original note by asking appellee from time-to-time to sign renewal notes.

All of this, together with the proposition that it would have been absurd for appellant to take a renewal note from two doubtful debtors with intent to release a solvent debtor, proves to this Court that it was not the intention of the parties to discharge the original note by the making and acceptance of the renewal note. The appellant bank has borne the burden of proof on this issue. . . .

A question bitterly contested by the parties in their briefs is whether or not the agreement sued on is one of suretyship or guaranty. The distinction between these two at the common law is that a surety is primarily liable while a guarantor is secondarily liable. This distinction has been virtually abolished by new provisions of the Uniform Commercial Code. . . . It will be observed that, to the extent applicable, this new provision abolishes the distinction between suretyship and guarantyship, making a guarantor as primarily liable as a surety. . . .

Here, the appellee assumed primary liability to pay the note both as surety and guarantor, merging the nature of the two into the greater, that of surety, and since neither the note nor the instrument have been discharged, appellee remains primarily liable according to his clear and express undertaking in the suretyship agreement. . . .

The judgment of the Court of Appeals is reversed and set aside. The judgment of the Chancery Court of Davidson County is reinstated. The case is remanded.

Reversed and remanded.

Inter-Sport, Inc. v. Wilson
661 S.W.2d 367 (Ark. 1983)

ADKISSON, J. . . . On June 18, 1976, 3–W Enterprises, Inc. (hereinafter 3–W) entered into a franchise agreement with appellant, Inter-Sport, Inc. As a part of that franchise agreement, appellees, Steve Wilson and Vicki Wilson, his wife, executed a guaranty regarding payment of royalties arising from the agreement.

On May 10, 1981, 3–W and Inter-Sport, Inc. entered into a compromise agreement, evidenced by a promissory note, reducing to a sum certain the amount due under the franchise agreement. The issue on appeal is whether the execution of the promissory note discharged appellee's personal liability on the guaranty agreement.

Arkansas has adopted the well-settled principle of the law of guaranty that a material alteration in the obligation assumed, made without the assent of the guarantor, discharges him from liability as guarantor. A guarantor is not liable where the underlying agreement was changed in form or in substance. Guarantors are entitled to a strict construction of their undertaking and cannot be held liable beyond the strict terms of their contract. According to the better rule of law, a material alteration in or departure from the contract of guaranty, without the guarantor's consent, will discharge him, whether or not he is prejudiced thereby.

Here, the underlying agreement between appellees and Inter-Sport, Inc. was a guaranty of the franchise agreement. The subsequent execution of the promissory note from 3–W to Inter-Sport, Inc. in satisfaction of sums owed on the franchise agreement constituted a material change in both the form and substance of the original understanding and, therefore, extinguishes any liability the appellees may have had as guarantors of the franchise agreement.

Affirmed.

Collins v. Throckmorton
425 A.2d 146 (Del. 1980)

McNEILLY, J. Plaintiff Philip Throckmorton and defendant Robert Collins were the sole stockholders (as well as the officers and directors) in Central Ceilings, Inc. (hereinafter referred to as "Central"). On March 26, 1973, Central borrowed $10,000 from the Wilmington Trust Company ("the bank"); a demand note therefore was executed by the corporate officers. On the back of the note, the plaintiff, his wife and the defendants (then husband and wife) signed a provision unconditionally guaranteeing payment of the note on behalf of Central. Subsequent to this transaction, relations between Mr. Throckmorton and Mr. Collins deteriorated to the point where, in August, 1973, Mr. Collins left the employ of Central and ceased to be actively involved in the management of the company. . . .

After Mr. Collins' departure from Central, the plaintiff continued to operate the business. However, by mid-1975, Central had become insolvent and simply ceased to do business. . . .

On May 30, 1975, pursuant to negotiations between the Throckmortons and the bank, the plaintiff and his wife took out a loan in the amount of $15,402. All of these proceeds were used to satisfy Central's debts to the bank. Of the total, $9,668.73 was paid to satisfy the 1973 note, i.e., $8,800 in unpaid principal plus $868.73 in interest at eight and three-quarters percent per year as specified in the note. In return, the bank assigned its rights under the 1973 note to the plaintiff, individually.

On June 4, 1975, the plaintiff demanded that the defendants reimburse him in full for the amounts he paid in satisfaction of the 1973 note; the defendants refused. The plaintiff subsequently, in his complaints and at trial, reduced his claims against each defendant to one-quarter of the amounts thus paid by him. The Superior Court entered judgment against each defendant in the amount of $3,492.86 allocated as follows: $2,417.18 representing the proportionate one-quarter share of each defendant on the demand note as paid by the plaintiff on May 30, 1975; $909.35 representing interest on such proportionate shares at the rate of eight and three-quarters percent per year from June 15, 1975 to November 1, 1979 and $166.33 representing awards of attorney fees at the rate of five percent of the amounts otherwise assessed against each defendant.

In order to understand the defendants' argument, it is necessary to state the general rule governing contribution rights among co-guarantors. The Restatement of the Law of Security, *supra*, §154 provides in pertinent part:

> (1) A surety who has discharged more than his proportionate share of the principal's duty is entitled to contribution from a co-surety.
> (a) who has consented to the surety's becoming bound, in the proportionate amount of the net outlay property expended. . . .

The undisputed facts show that the 1973 note was guaranteed by four persons.

Consequently, each was potentially liable for one-quarter of Central's default on the note. Although the complaint alleged the plaintiff personally satisfied Central's default by paying the entirety of the principal and interest owed on the note in May, 1975, the defendants argue that the trial proofs show that the plaintiff's wife, the fourth co-guarantor, contributed equally with the plaintiff to this satisfaction. Thus, of the $9,688.73 paid to satisfy the 1973 note, the defendants claim the plaintiff contributed only half ($4,834.36). Of that amount the plaintiff was personally liable for half, which constituted one-quarter of Central's total default ($2,417.18). Thus argue the defendants, the maximum amount of contribution which the plaintiff could recover from the two defendants was $2,417.18, i.e., the amount in excess of his share of Central's default which the plaintiff personally paid to satisfy the 1973 note. Therefore, the defendants argue that the Trial Court's decision, which was premised on the assumption that the plaintiff satisfied the entire default by Central (or at least three-quarters thereof), erroneously awarded judgment against each defendant in the amount of $2,417.18, double the excess amount which the plaintiff allegedly paid in satisfaction of the note and, thus, double the total amount of contribution which he was entitled to recover from the defendants collectively. . . .

Considering the evidentiary aspect of the argument on the merits, we are not persuaded that the defendants are entitled to appellate relief. Although there was no direct testimony concerning the respective amounts which the plaintiff and his wife contributed to satisfaction of the 1973 note, the bank's assignment of the note to the plaintiff, individually, gives rise to a reasonable inference that, as between the plaintiff and his wife, the plaintiff alone was entitled to seek contribution from the defendants. Therefore, we will not disturb that portion of the Trial Court's judgment which requires each defendant to pay the plaintiff $2,417.18 for their contributive shares on the demand note as satisfied.

The defendants' final argument is that the Trial Court erred in its awards of pre-judgment interest and attorney fees. The language of the Trial Court's order clearly shows that these amounts were determined pursuant to the terms of the demand note assigned to the plaintiff. We conclude that this was erroneous.

The plaintiff's rights to recover from the defendants are based on the equitable principles governing contribution between co-guarantors, not the terms of the instrument on which the co-guarantors have become liable. Allowing the plaintiff to expand his rights as co-guarantor against the defendants simply because he obtained an assignment of the note upon satisfaction thereof would serve to undermine the basic tenets of guaranty law. We believe that the more equitable and proper rule is that:

> The judgment against defendant guarantors should carry interest at the legal rate and should not impose an attorney's fee in the absence of any express contract [between co-guarantors] or statute providing for such fee.

Therefore, the plaintiff was not entitled to the award of attorney fees.

As for the award of pre-judgment interest, we reach the same conclusion but for a different reason. The general rule cited above gave the plaintiff a theoretical entitlement to pre-judgment interest, but at the legal rate of six percent not the note rate of eight and three-quarters percent as ordered by the Trial Court. However, this right is not self-executing; in order to get such interest in his judgment, the plaintiff had to request it, (and he failed to do so). . . .

In conclusion, we modify the judgment below to eliminate the awards of interest and attorney fees, and we affirm the judgment as so modified. *Affirmed, as modified.*

REVIEW QUESTIONS

1. Identify the terms in column A by matching each with the appropriate statement in column B.

A	B
1. Artisan's lien	**a.** In modern law, another term for a guarantor.
2. Bulk transfer	**b.** The right that exists between co-sureties.
3. Schedule of property	**c.** Literally means to stand in the place of another.
4. Surety	**d.** A sale of a large quantity of inventory outside the ordinary course of business.
5. Indemnity	**e.** Usually associated along with a list of creditors.

6. Subrogation

f. Not created when a repairman agrees to do work on credit.

7. Reimbursement

g. A promise to hold someone harmless.

8. Contribution

h. A surety's right against a principal.

2. Mary took her car to the local Chevrolet dealer for service and necessary repairs. After the dealer performed the desired work, Mary paid the bill in full. However, the dealer refused to relinquish possession of her car, since Mary had not paid for repairs previously made on the same car. Does the dealer have a lien on her car so that Mary cannot regain possession of it? Why?

3. Jack, Dick, and Bob opened an office for their accounting practice. They purchased office furniture on credit. Before they had paid fully for this furniture, they decided to sell it and buy new furniture. Does the sale of this furniture fall within the scope of Article 6? Explain.

4. National Bank failed to file the financing statement necessary to perfect its security interest in Frye's inventory. Therefore, the bank was a general, unsecured creditor. Before Frye filed a petition in bankruptcy, he sold all his inventory in bulk to Unclaimed Freight. Frye and Unclaimed Freight did not comply with Article 6 of the U.C.C. Specifically, Unclaimed Freight did not demand that Frye provide it with a list of all existing creditors and the amounts owed to each. The bank filed suit to recover Frye's inventory from Unclaimed Freight. Does a general, unsecured creditor have priority over a transferee in bulk who failed to comply with Article 6 requirements? Why?

5. Peterson Company, an appliance store, purchased appliances from Cooper's Appliance Wholesale, Ltd. Often Cooper's financed the purchases made by Peterson. However, Cooper's required Stuart Peterson, president of his company, to guarantee personally the debts incurred by Peterson Company. The language of this surety contract established that Stuart's guaranty was a special one in favor of Cooper's only. Cooper's assigned the right to collect the Peterson Company's debts to Financeamerica, which sued Stuart on the basis of his guaranty. Stuart defended on the ground that a special guaranty cannot be assigned. Is Stuart correct? Explain.

6. Sam wrote a letter of guaranty to Carl on behalf of Rex, a retailer. The letter stated that Sam "does guarantee payment of any credit granted by you not to exceed ten thousand dollars ($10,000)." Rex was involved in a series of individual transactions with Carl, of which none exceeded $10,000, and the total amount did not exceed $10,000. Rex failed to pay, but Sam contends that his total liability is limited to one transaction. Is Sam correct? Why?

7. Give an example of a creditor-surety relationship that arises by operation of law.

8. Lee signed as guarantor of a promissory note signed by Akins and payable to Vaughn. Lee expressly inserted a provision into the note that if the principal debtor defaulted, Lee must be notified promptly if he was to be liable. After the maker defaulted, no notice was given of that fact by Vaughn to Lee. When Vaughn sued Lee for payment, Lee contended that the lack of notice discharged his liability. When a surety contract expressly requires notice of the default, is the surety liable on the note if the payee does not promptly notify the surety? Why?

9. Owens hired Terry, a general contractor, to build a house. Terry, in turn, hired Paint-It-All, a subcontractor, to paint the house. Being concerned about Paint-It-All's reputation, Terry required that a performance bond be obtained. Paint-It-All paid the Aetna Insurance Company to assure its performance. Paint-It-All failed to do the job, and Terry brought an action against Aetna alone. May he do so? Explain.

10. Donald Dunwoody borrowed money from the First National Bank and in return granted a security interest in his office equipment. In addition to this security, the bank required that Donald's sister, Sarah, sign as surety of her brother's performance. Donald did default on his payment. Sarah paid the loan in full and now claims to have rights in her brother's office equipment. Is she correct? Explain.

11. Name three exceptions to the general rule that defenses available to the principal are available to the surety.

12. With regard to surety contracts, what does the term *reservation of rights* mean? How is this term typically applied?

13. Davis was indebted to Carter in the amount of $2,000. Davis agreed to pay monthly installments of $100. Smith agreed that if Davis defaulted in a monthly payment, he would make up the payment. Davis made one payment of $100, two payments of $37.50, then disappeared. Smith claims that Carter's acceptance of partial payment without Smith's consent constituted an extension of time, which released him from liability. Is Smith correct? Why?

14. Lamar and Carolyn Upshaw guaranteed payment up to $4,000 on a loan from First State Bank to James Chaney. The Upshaws gave the bank a loan deed to a parcel of property they owned as security for payment. Subsequently, Chaney signed a new note with the bank renewing his obligations and canceling all prior notes. Chaney defaulted, and the bank seeks to foreclose on the Upshaw realty. Could the bank foreclose on the Upshaw property based on their surety agreement in the original note? Explain.

36 LAWS ASSISTING DEBTORS

The four previous chapters are dedicated to the discussion of laws designed to assist creditors in the collection of debts. Numerous laws also attempt to protect consumers from financial and physical harm. These laws seek to protect consumers in their contracts, especially those that involve credit, and from injury caused by products.

Debtor and consumer protection is a goal of all branches of government. Many principles discussed in this chapter are based on statutes enacted by federal and state governments. Courts have also been active in extending protection to consumers. The demise of privity of contract in the breach-of-warranty cases is an example of judicial consumer protection. Finally, administrative agencies such as the Federal Trade Commission and Federal Reserve Board are active in the protection of consumer debtors.

The law has been aiding debtors and consumers for several reasons. Debtors and consumers frequently have less bargaining power than creditors and sellers. Many are financially unsophisticated, easily deceived, and lack information needed to make intelligent decisions. Therefore, much of the consumer movement has been directed at providing all the relevant information, so that borrowers and purchasers will be able to make reasonably intelligent decisions in the marketplace. Other laws are aimed at equalizing the bargaining power between buyer and seller. This equalization is often accomplished by declaring a provision illegal if it is one that would not be agreed to by a party with equal bargaining power.

This chapter covers the laws regulating both debtor and consumer protections. The concerns for debtors and consumers are so interrelated that many laws were enacted specifically to protect consumer debtors. Sections 1 through 17 concentrate on the laws that assist such debtors. The last portion of this chapter deals with laws that protect consumers who are not necessarily debtors.

1. Debtor Protection in General

Since 1968, federal legislation has had a substantial impact in the area of consumer credit. In addition to this federal legislation, state laws governing consumer credit also remain important. This chapter will introduce, analyze, and discuss compliance with the laws and regulations affecting consumer credit transactions. Unless stated otherwise, the laws discussed here are applicable to any consumer credit transaction regardless of whether the lender is a secured or unsecured creditor, or whether the loan is secured by personal property, by an individual's promise, or by real property.

The term *consumer* means those individuals involved in transactions concerning personal, family, or household needs as opposed to commercial or business purposes. The term *credit* involves any situation in which money is lent with repayment to be made in the future. This chapter concentrates on what a loan officer of a financial institution must keep in mind while making loans for the customer's personal benefit.

The following materials discuss the lender's requirements (1) to refrain from discriminatory lending practices, (2) to use and report the consumer's credit history validly, (3) to disclose pertinent information about the loan, and (4) to collect the debt properly.

2. Equal Credit Opportunity Act

The Equal Credit Opportunity Act (ECOA), as it was passed in 1974, originally prohibited discrimination in credit transactions on the basis of sex or marital status. The ECOA was enacted in response to findings of studies which indicated that women had a much more difficult time borrowing money than did their male counterparts. Lenders' fears that a woman may drop out of the work force can no longer be used when extending credit. In 1976, the ECOA was amended to add age, race, color, religion, national origin, receipt of public assistance benefits, and the good-faith exercise of any right under the Consumer Credit Protection Act as categories of prohibited discrimination in credit transactions.

A *creditor* subject to the ECOA is an individual or a business organization, in the ordinary course of business, participating in a decision whether or not to extend credit. Creditors include financial institutions, retail stores, and credit card issuers. *Discrimination* occurs when an applicant is treated less favorably than other applicants. An *applicant* is any individual or business organization requesting or receiving an extension of credit from a creditor. An *application* is defined as an oral or written request for an extension of credit made in accordance with procedures established by a creditor for the type of credit requested. These terms and the provisions of the ECOA are applicable to lease transactions as well as sales transactions if credit decisions are involved.[1]

CREDIT
APPLICATIONS

---

[1] Brothers v. First Leasing, p. 835.

The ECOA allows suits for dollar damages by victims of credit discrimination. Individual victims are entitled to recover actual damages, which can include a recovery for embarrassment and mental distress. In addition to actual damages, victims can sue for attorney's fees, other legal costs, and punitive damages up to $10,000. Punitive damages may be awarded even in the absence of actual damages being proved. In addition to these private remedies, governmental entities may bring suit to enjoin violations of the ECOA and to assess civil penalties. Punitive damages may not be recovered by the government.

Generally any action to enforce the ECOA must be begun within 2 years from the date the violation occurred. An exception to this statute of limitations arises if an administrative agency or the attorney general begins an enforcement action within 2 years of the violation's occurrence. Any applicant who has been a victim of wrongful discrimination then has 1 year after the governmental enforcement action is commenced to bring a civil action to enforce the ECOA.

3. Discrimination Prohibited

A creditor must not advertise the availability of credit in any way that implicitly discriminates. For example, a picture of potential applicants must not include only males or females, whites or blacks, young or old, and so on. Such a picture must be representative of all potential applicants. Furthermore, an ad campaign must not be directed to a target audience that could result in possible discrimination due to the makeup of the target audience. Advertising must be directed to the entire community in a nondiscriminatory manner. A creditor found guilty of discriminatory advertising may be ordered to conduct an affirmative advertising campaign specifically aimed at the group suffering from past discrimination.

In addition to concerns about advertising, creditors must be aware of what information can be properly requested on an application. Recall that the purpose of the ECOA is to prohibit discrimination when extending credit on the basis of the applicant's race, color, religion, national origin, sex, marital status, age, receipt of income from a public assistance program, or exercise of a right under the law. A creditor is smart to remember that the best way to avoid discrimination is not to have any information request on which discrimination can be based. With respect to the application form, the following are six general rules regarding information that should *not* be requested from the applicant:

1. A creditor should not inquire about an applicant's spouse or former spouse.
2. A creditor should not inquire about the applicant's marital status when the applicant will be individually liable.
3. A creditor should not inquire whether an applicant's income is derived from alimony, child support, or separate maintenance payments.
4. A creditor should not inquire about the sex of an applicant.
5. A creditor should not inquire about the applicant's birth control practices, capacity to bear children, or intention to have children.

6. A creditor should not inquire about an applicant's race, color, religion, or national origin.

4. Fair Credit Reporting Act

Shortly after an applicant has applied for a loan, the creditor normally will check on the applicant's credit history. This check may be conducted simply by examining the applicant's past record with this creditor. Or the creditor may contact a third party for a credit report. When this latter step occurs, the Fair Credit Reporting Act (FCRA) must be followed. The basic reason for the FCRA's enactment was to prevent abuses in credit reporting systems. Furthermore, with this law, Congress provided a means to protect all individuals' privacy and to ensure accuracy with respect to the information in the reports covered.

The FCRA covers the compilation, distribution, and utilization of credit reports on consumers. Reports on businesses are not within the scope of this law. Typically the FCRA governs the activities of both the consumer reporting agencies and the users of information provided by such agencies. The term *consumer reporting agency* includes any person who or entity that regularly collects information on consumers and furnishes it to third parties. In essence, these agencies are in the business of selling consumer reports for a fee. A *consumer report* is a written or oral communication relating to a consumer's creditworthiness, credit standing, credit capacity, character, general reputation, personal characteristics, or mode of living. This report must be furnished by a consumer reporting agency.

By these definitions, it should be clear that a report containing information solely about transactions or experiences between the consumer and the party making the report is not covered by the FCRA. For example, a financial institution may be asked about its credit experience with one of its customers. If that institution reports only its experience with the customer, a consumer report, as defined in the FCRA, is not involved. In other words, with respect to collecting and furnishing information on consumers to third parties, the FCRA covers only consumer reporting agencies.

Despite this limitation of the FCRA's coverage, this law does regulate some activities of the parties that *use* the information in a consumer report. The user's requirements are discussed in section 6.

5. Consumer Reporting Agencies

A consumer report furnished to any party (other than a court or the consumer himself) must be for use in connection with at least one of the following:

1. Extending credit
2. Hiring, transferring, promoting, or firing an employee
3. Selling insurance
4. Issuing a license, particularly one of a professional nature
5. Determining eligibility for governmental financial assistance

The consumer reporting agency must ensure that the reports given are furnished for a proper purpose. For example, the agency must obtain a certification from the user with respect to (1) that user's identity, (2) the purpose for which the report is to be used, and (3) the fact the report will not be used for any other purpose. Furthermore, the agency must take additional steps to verify that the user's identity and the user's stated purpose are accurate. It would be a violation of the FCRA if an agency furnished a consumer report when that agency knew, or had reasonable grounds to know, that the report was to be used for an unjustified purpose.

In addition to making sure the report is used properly, the reporting agency must take steps not to include obsolete information. In general, adverse information over 7 years old is obsolete and should not be included in a consumer report. Information on bankruptcy cases over 10 years old also is considered obsolete. Furthermore, all consumer reporting agencies must establish procedures which, when implemented, will prevent improper or inaccurate information from being included in a consumer report.[2]

6. Users of Information

Those parties that decide whether a consumer will be extended credit, sold insurance, employed, or licensed may use information from two sources other than themselves. These two outside sources of information are (1) consumer reporting agencies or (2) someone else. Users of this information have an obligation to disclose the source of such information to the consumer. However, the duty to disclose and the extent of such disclosure depends on the source of information.

First, assume that adverse action was taken regarding a consumer's credit, insurance, or employment application. [*Note:* Adverse action includes the application being denied or the cost of credit or insurance being increased.] Further, suppose that this adverse action was taken because of some information contained in a consumer report. When the user of this information notifies the consumer of the adverse action, the user automatically must disclose the name and address of the consumer reporting agency that furnished the report. Without this requirement, the consumer would find it difficult to determine whether the information in the report was accurate.

Second, again assume that adverse action is taken with respect to a consumer's application for credit, insurance, or employment. Also assume that this action was taken because of some information furnished to the user by a party other than a consumer reporting agency. Before the FCRA requires the user to disclose the information relied on, that user and the consumer must follow several steps. (1) At the time notice of adverse action is given to the consumer, the user also must notify the consumer that he or she has the right to request in writing the reasons for the adverse action being taken. (2) Within 60 days after receiving the user's notice, the consumer must make a written request for an explanation of why this adverse action was taken. (3) After receiving the consumer's request for an explanation, the user must disclose the information on which the adverse decision was based.

---

[2] Bryant v. TRW, Inc., p. 837.

7. Rights of Consumer Debtors

Any consumer debtor has the right to learn about and the consumer reporting agency has the duty to disclose the following items contained in that consumer's file:

1. The nature and substance of all information except medical records
2. The sources of that information
3. The parties receiving a consumer report for employment purposes within the prior 2 years and the parties receiving a consumer report for any other purposes within the prior 6 months

Before disclosing the information contained in the consumer's file, the consumer reporting agency must ask the consumer to provide proper identification. This information must not be disclosed to anyone other than the consumer unless the information is in a consumer report furnished for a proper purpose. One exception to this rule of nondisclosure arises when the consumer is accompanied by one other person chosen by the consumer. This person must provide reasonable identification, and the consumer may be required to furnish a written statement authorizing the agency to reveal information in the presence of this additional person. Furthermore, when information from the consumer's file is made available to the consumer, he or she has the right to have the information explained by a competently trained employee of the consumer reporting agency.

The consumer has a right to the information in his or her file without any charge if the request is made within 30 days after that consumer receives either (1) notice of adverse action on an application for credit, insurance, or employment; or (2) notice from a debt collection agency that his or her credit rating may be adversely affected. In other situations, consumers may be charged a reasonable fee when examining the contents of their files. This fee is collected by the consumer reporting agency.

Another important protection of consumers is their right to challenge the accuracy of information contained in the file. For instance, suppose that a consumer examines his or her file and has a justifiable reason to dispute the correctness or relevance of some information. The consumer must communicate this dispute's existence to the consumer reporting agency. Upon receiving this notice of dispute, the agency must reinvestigate the appropriateness of this information being in the consumer's file. As the result of such a reinvestigation, one of two steps must be followed.

First, if the consumer reporting agency determines that the information is inaccurate or cannot be verified, such information must be deleted from the file. Second, the reinvestigation may result in a finding that the disputed information is accurate and relevant. This second finding by the consumer reporting agency means that the dispute is not resolved. In this event, the consumer must be allowed to write a brief statement describing his or her position, to be included in that consumer's file. This statement may be limited to 100 words if the consumer reporting agency provides assistance to the consumer regarding the writing of the statement.

The consumer has the right to insist that this or some similar statement be included in any future consumer report furnished by the agency. Furthermore, upon the consumer's request, the agency must give notice that information has been deleted or give notice of a statement of the consumer's position to any user of a consumer report if that user received (1) a report related to an employment purpose within a 2-year period, or (2) a report related to any other purpose within a 6-month period prior to the consumer's request.

To encourage enforcement of its provisions, the FCRA provides for both civil and criminal sanctions. Regarding civil liability, any consumer reporting agency or user of credit reports that *negligently* fails to comply with FCRA is liable to the consumer for that person's actual damages plus costs of the action and reasonable attorney's fees. Additionally, if the consumer reporting agency or user is shown to have *willfully* violated the FCRA's provisions, that party is liable for any punitive damages the court might award. Willful noncompliance will be proved with evidence of an agency's or user's intent to not comply. Furthermore, unreasonable reliance on what may be perceived as a legal right could result in a finding of willfulness. For example, if an agency repeatedly refused to reinvestigate information disputed by a consumer because it wrongfully relied on the belief the dispute was frivolous, that agency could be found to have willfully violated the FCRA. Civil actions must be filed within 2 years of the date the violation occurred. If the violation involves misrepresentation of information, the statute of limitations begins running when the misrepresentation is discovered.

In the cases in which someone obtains information about a consumer from a consumer reporting agency under false pretenses, criminal sanctions may be imposed. When false pretenses are knowingly and willfully utilized, the perpetrator may be fined up to $5,000 or confined for up to 1 year or both.

CREDIT TRANSACTIONS

8. Introduction

Once a creditor has examined an applicant's credit application and credit history, a decision on whether or not to extend credit must be made. If the decision is to deny the requested credit, the ECOA and the FCRA require that the applicant be informed of the reasons for this decision. A decision to extend the applicant credit also creates a number of legal requirements that must be satisfied. These requirements are found in the federal Truth-in-Lending Act and in the Uniform Consumer Credit Code if your state has adopted this code.

9. Truth-in-Lending Act

Although this law was originally passed in 1968, the Truth-in-Lending Simplification and Reform Act was adopted by Congress in 1980. As important as the law itself, Regulation Z has been issued by the Board of Governors of the Federal Reserve System to implement the actual law. Following the 1980 amendment, Regulation Z was substantially revised in 1981.

The Truth-in-Lending Act (T in L Act) and Regulation Z apply to any individual or business organization offering or extending credit whenever the following four conditions are met:

1. The applicant for credit is a consumer with respect to the credit requested. In other words, the proceeds of the loan are used for a personal as opposed to a business purpose.

2. Credit is offered or extended on a regular basis, which means the creditor extended consumer credit more than 25 times during the previous calendar year. If the creditor extended consumer credit secured by a dwelling at least 5 times, the regularity requirement is met.

3. The repayment of the credit extended is subject to a finance charge or is evidenced by a written agreement that allows for more than four installments.

4. Finally, the credit is for family, household, or personal uses. This fourth element of the T in L Act's coverage once again emphasizes the consumer versus business nature of the loan covered by the act.

Consumer credit transactions are exempt from the act if the amount of credit extended exceeds $25,000. The reason for this exemption seems to be that consumer debtors who borrow over $25,000 have the sophistication to protect themselves. However, even untrained and inexperienced consumers borrow substantially more than $25,000 when they purchase a personal residence and use that residence as security. Therefore, mortgage transactions involving personal residences are not exempted from the act's requirements regardless of the dollar amount involved.

10. Disclosures Required

The basic purpose of the T in L Act has been and continues to be to encourage potential consumer debtors to shop for credit. In order to facilitate this comparison shopping, the act requires the creditor to disclose certain items of information. Although there are numerous and technical disclosure requirements, the most important items to be revealed include the following:

1. The identity of the creditor[3]
2. The amount financed
3. An itemization of the amount financed
4. The finance charge
5. The annual percentage rate
6. The payment schedule
7. The total amount of all payments

Of these, items 2, 4, 5 and 7 frequently are the most important.

Amount financed. The amount financed by the creditor is calculated by taking the amount of the loan's principal, adding other amounts financed by the creditor which are not a part of the finance charge, and then subtracting the amount of any prepaid finance charge. This amount must be stated as a dollar figure and must be clearly marked as the "Amount Financed."

---

[3] Ford Motor Credit Company v. Cenance, p. 838.

Finance charge. This item is considered one of the most important, and it is one of the most complex to calculate. Once again, this disclosure is in the form of a dollar figure. This finance charge figure quickly shows the consumer applicant what this credit transaction is costing over its term. In essence, this figure includes all charges paid by the consumer applicant when securing the extension of credit. This dollar figure is more than the total amount of all interest payments. The finance charge also includes fees charged by the creditor as a cost of extending credit. Especially in long-term mortgage-secured loans, it is not unusual for the finance charge to be several times higher than the amount financed.

Annual percentage rate. Along with the finance charge, the annual percentage rate (APR) is the second part of the all-important disclosure requirements of the T in L Act. The APR can be used by consumer applicants to compare the cost of obtaining credit. This cost is expressed in terms of a percentage rate rather than in dollars, as with the finance charge. The APR is the cost of the credit expressed as a yearly rate. This rate is a measure that relates the amount and timing of the credit received by the consumer applicant to the amount and timing of the payments to be made by the applicant. The complex method of calculating the APR is beyond our purpose in this chapter. However, since the finance charge includes items in addition to interest payments, the APR should be higher than the quoted interest rate.

Total amount of all payments. Under the heading "Total Amount of All Payments," the creditor must disclose in a dollar figure the total amount the consumer debtor will have paid after all the payments have been made. A simple way to check the accuracy of this figure is to add the amount financed and the finance charge. This addition should equal the total amount of all payments. If the consumer applicant desires to do so, this figure can be a helpful source in comparing credit opportunities.

The T in L Act also protects borrowers by prohibiting misleading advertising, such as representing lower down payments and lower installment payments than are actually available. If an advertisement contains any details of a credit plan, it must also include as disclosures substantial information on finance charges, rates, cash price, down payment, and other information included in the specific regulations used to enforce the law.

11. Sanctions for Truth-in-Lending Violations

The T in L Act provides for both civil and criminal sanctions against creditors that fail to comply with the applicable provisions. For example, in a civil suit based on the creditor's failure to make all necessary disclosures, an individual plaintiff may recover two times the finance charge subject to a minimum of $100 and a maximum of $1,000. In a class action for improper disclosures, there is no limit on an individual's claim, but the class can recover only the lesser of $500,000 or 1 percent of the creditor's net worth.

Not all improper disclosures result in civil liability. Creditors that make bona fide errors in their disclosures are not necessarily liable. A bona fide error may include an inaccurate disclosure due to clerical, printing, or computer malfunctions. Also, the recent amendments to the T in L Act limit the creditor's liability for failures to disclose material information. Therefore, technical but immaterial violations do not create a ground to hold creditors liable for dollar damages.

Although it is rare, the Justice Department can bring criminal charges against a creditor for violating the T in L Act. To be a crime, failure to make adequate and accurate disclosures must be done knowingly and willfully. The criminal violation is punishable by up to a $5,000 fine or up to 1 year in confinement or some combination of the two.

12. Uniform Consumer Credit Code

All the federal laws discussed in this chapter do not preempt state consumer credit protection laws so long as these state laws do not narrow the protection provided by Congress. Because of the diversity among the states concerning protection of consumers in credit transactions, the commissioners on Uniform State Laws have prepared a proposed uniform law similar to many of the federal laws. The Uniform Consumer Credit Code (UCCC) attempts to protect consumers by utilizing the technique of full disclosure of all pertinent facts about the credit transaction to buyers. The UCCC is applicable to virtually every transaction involving credit: retail installment sales, consumer credit, small loans, and usury.

The UCCC does not fix rates of interest, but rather sets maximums that may be charged. When the amount financed is $300 or less, the maximum is 36 percent per year; and when the amount is more than $300 but less than $1,000, it is 21 percent per year. The credit code has detailed provisions covering matters such as delinquency charges, deferral charges, service charges on refinancing or loan consolidation, and revolving charge accounts. It also prohibits most deficiency judgments when goods sold as a part of a consumer credit sale are repossessed.

The UCCC requires a written disclosure that conspicuously sets forth the required facts prior to a sale or loan. Just as in the Truth-in-Lending Act, the annual percentage rate is the key fact that must be disclosed. The difference between the cash price and the credit price is also essential as a part of the disclosure. The provisions on advertising generally require that the ad include the rate of the credit service charge as well as the amount of the charge.

In addition to regulating the cost of credit, the UCCC prohibits certain types of agreements. It prohibits the use of the holder-in-due course concept and outlaws agreements cutting off defenses. It prohibits the use of multiple agreements to obtain higher interest. It also prohibits *balloon payments.* If any scheduled payment is more than twice as large as the average payment, the buyer has the right to refinance the balloon payment, without penalty, on terms no less favorable than the original terms. The balloon-payment provision is not applicable to a sale for agricultural purposes or one pursuant to a revolving charge account.

The UCCC prohibits debtors from assigning their earnings as part of a credit sale. In addition, lenders are not allowed to take an assignment of earnings for payment of a debt arising out of a consumer loan. The UCCC also prohibits referral sales schemes in which the buyer is given credit on a purchase for furnishing the names of other possible purchasers.

Violations of the UCCC may be punished criminally. In addition, debtors are relieved of their obligation to pay the finance charge, and they are entitled to recover, from creditors who violate the law, up to three times the finance charge actually paid. Of course, debtors are not obligated to pay charges in excess of those allowable by the act. If a debtor entitled to a refund is refused a refund, the debtor is entitled to recover the total amount of the credit service charge or 10 times the excess charge, whichever is greater. If the excess charge was in deliberate violation of the act, the penalty may be recovered even if the excess has been repaid.

This UCCC proposal has received only modest approval. The UCCC has been adopted by only nine states: Colorado, Idaho, Indiana, Iowa, Kansas, Maine, Oklahoma, Utah, and Wyoming. The states of South Carolina and Wisconsin have legislation substantially similar to the UCCC.

PAYMENTS AND COLLECTIONS

13. Introduction

From the creditor's perspective, after credit has been extended the next stage of the transaction is collection from the debtor. The collection may be as simple as billing the debtor and waiting for payment. If payment is not made voluntarily, the creditor may have to seek the assistance of a third party to collect the debt. Of concern to the debtor is property that is exempt from the creditor's attempt to collect past-due debts. The following sections discuss the laws that protect debtors in this billing, payment, and collection process.

14. Fair Credit Billing Act

Prior to being able to collect an amount owed, the creditor must inform the consumer debtor what is owed. This information is conveyed through a billing. Due to the problem a mistake in a billing could cause, the Fair Credit Billing Act (FCBA) was originally passed in Congress in 1974 and amended in 1980. The FCBA is applicable only to open-ended consumer credit transactions. A billing error associated with any business loan or with a consumer closed-end transaction is *not* covered by the FCBA.[4]

Definitions. The term *billing error,* as used in the FCBA, can consist of a periodic statement containing any of the following: (1) a reflection of credit not actually extended, (2) a reflection of credit extended of which the debtor seeks clarification, (3) a reflection of the cost of goods and services not received by the debtor or by an authorized agent, (4) a reflection of a computational error made by the creditor, (5) a failure to reflect a payment made by the debtor, and (6) a failure to reflect the type of transaction involved. A billing error also occurs when the creditor fails to send the periodic statement to the borrower's last known address

---

[4] American Express Co. v. Koerner, p. 839.

if that address has been given to the creditor at least 20 days before the end of a billing cycle.

A *billing error notice* is a written notice received by a creditor from a consumer debtor. This notice must contain the consumer debtor's statement that a billing error exists, and there must be a statement as to why the consumer believes such error exists. Furthermore, this notice must enable the creditor to identify the following items: (1) the consumer debtor's name; (2) his or her account number; and (3) the type, date, and amount of the billing error. Finally, this notice must be received by the creditor within 60 days after the first periodic statement containing the error was sent by the creditor.

Creditor's general duties.   If a creditor receives a billing error notice, that creditor must first of all acknowledge in writing to the consumer debtor the receipt of the notice within 30 days of its actual receipt. Second, the creditor, within two billing cycles but not more than 90 days after the notice is received, must either (1) correct the error, credit the account for the correct amount, and send a notice of the correction made; or (2) send a written statement of clarification to the consumer debtor as to why the creditor believes no error has been made.

Until a billing error has been corrected or until an explanation of the billing's accuracy has been sent and received, the creditor cannot (1) restrict the credit available to the consumer debtor, (2) close that account, and (3) report or even threaten to report the consumer debtor's nonpayment to a credit rating organization. A report to a credit reporting agency may be made after the creditor has sent an explanation of why there is no billing error and after the time for payment has passed if the consumer debtor has not reasserted the billing error's existence. If a dispute continues to exist, the creditor may make a credit report if the following steps are satisfied: (1) The report must indicate that the amount or account is in dispute; (2) the creditor must mail or otherwise deliver to the consumer debtor a written notice of the name and address of all persons receiving the credit report; and (3) the creditor promptly must make a report of any subsequent resolution of the dispute to all those who received the original report.

The FCBA also regulates some of the accounting practices of creditors. For example, prompt posting of all payments is required in order to prevent additional finance charges being billed to the consumer debtor's account. Furthermore, creditors of revolving charge accounts cannot impose finance charges on a new purchase made by the consumer debtor unless a statement including the amount upon which the finance charge for that period is based is mailed at least 14 days before the date the finance charge will be imposed if full payment is not made.

15. Credit Card Protection

Lost or stolen credit cards are often used for unauthorized purchases, resulting in a loss to (1) the business that dealt with the wrong person, (2) the credit card company [which may be the same as (1), as in the case of an oil company's gasoline credit card], or (3) the actual cardholder. The T in L Act seeks to limit the cardholder's loss and to impose most of the losses on the issuer of the card. For example, the law prohibits the issuance of credit cards except upon application or upon the renewal of an existing card. Thus, the person to whom a card is issued has no liability for unauthorized purchases if that card was issued without being requested.

The T in L Act further provides that a cardholder is liable only up to the lesser of the amount charged or $50 for the unauthorized use of a credit card, and then only if all the following conditions are met:

1. The credit card is an accepted card, one that the cardholder had requested.
2. The charge is made prior to the cardholder's giving notice to the issuer that the card was lost or stolen.
3. Within 2 years before the unauthorized use, the issuer warned the cardholder of his potential liability for unauthorized use.
4. The issuer had provided the cardholder with a preaddressed notice form that may be mailed to the issuer in the event the card is lost or stolen.

The warning to the cardholder mentioned in condition 3 may be given by printing it on the card. This notice must state that the liability in the case of loss or theft shall not exceed $50. The cardholder also must be informed in a clear manner that the notice of loss or theft may be given orally as well as in writing.

Finally, no cardholder is liable unless the issuer has provided a method whereby the user of the card can be identified as the person authorized to use it. This identification traditionally has been by the cardholder's signature, photograph, or fingerprint on the card. In order to reduce the problem of counterfeiting credit cards, the means of identifying the cardholder has shifted to mechanical and electronic devices.

16. Fair Debt Collection Practices Act

In 1977, Congress passed the Fair Debt Collection Practices Act (FDCPA), and it has been in effect since 1978. The underlying reason for the passage of this act was the congressional finding of "abundant evidence of the use of abusive, deceptive, and unfair debt collection practices by many debt collectors." In order to prevent the adverse impact of improper debt collection procedures on bankruptcies, marriages, employment, and personal privacy, the FDCPA was passed. This law is also intended to ensure the competitiveness of those debt collectors that are not utilizing abusive tactics.

Coverage of the FDCPA. The FDCPA is directed toward regulating those individuals and business entities that are in the business of collecting debts owed to someone else. For example, creditors are not subject to the FDCPA's provisions unless they attempt to collect a debt by using a name that does not reveal that creditor's identity. Creditors are exempt from this law because it is believed that creditors will not engage in unfair debt collection practices. This belief is based on the fact that creditors will not jeopardize their goodwill with their debtors by using questionable practices.

The FDCPA is applicable only to the collection of consumers' debts. As has been the case throughout this entire chapter, a *consumer debt* consists of any obligation of a human being (as opposed to a business organization) to repay money used for a personal, family, or household purpose (as opposed to a business purpose). The law presumes that business debtors are able to protect themselves from unfair debt collection practices.

Collection practices.   The law permits a bill collector to communicate with third parties, such as neighbors or employers of the debtor, but it limits the contact. Third parties may not be informed that the consumer owes a debt. When an attorney represents the debtor, and the bill collector knows it, the collector may not get in touch with anyone else except the attorney, unless the attorney fails to respond to the collector's communication.

The act also restricts the methods that may be used in the collection process. The collector may not (1) physically threaten the debtor, (2) use obscene language, (3) pretend to be an attorney unless he is, (4) threaten the debtor with arrest or garnishment unless the collector or creditor is legally entitled to such action and intends to take it, or (5) telephone the debtor repeatedly with intent to annoy. In telephoning the debtor, the collector must make a meaningful disclosure of his identity and may not telephone collect or call before 8:00 A.M. or after 9:00 P.M. In addition to these specific prohibitions, the act forbids the collector from using any "unfair or unconscionable" means to collect the debt.

If a debtor desires to stop repeated contacts, he need only notify the collector in writing of this wish. Any further contact by the collector following such notification violates the act. The collector's sole remedy in such cases is to sue the debtor. Violations of the law entitle the debtor to sue the collector for actual damages, including damages for invasion of privacy and infliction of mental distress, court costs, and attorney's fees. In the absence of actual damages, the court may still order the collector to pay the debtor up to $1,000 for violations.

Many states have enacted laws similar to the FDCPA. In general, these laws are interpreted very liberally in order to provide the greatest protection reasonably possible.[5]

17. Limitations on Garnishments

A logical source from which a debt can be collected from a consumer borrower is that person's earnings. Particularly when the creditor has an inadequate security interest in some property, legal action may be taken to ensure that the debtor's earnings are withheld and used to pay the debt. This legal process is known as *garnishment.* Due to the findings that excessive garnishments (in the amount of earnings withheld or in the actual number of actions filed) may adversely affect the consumer's employment and the ultimate production and consumption of goods in interstate commerce, Congress has statutorily limited the amount of earnings that can be subject to garnishment.

Disposable earnings are that part of a consumer's earnings left after all withholdings required by law are deducted from the earnings. In general, the federal maximum amount of the total disposable earnings subject to garnishment

---

[5] Campbell v. Beneficial Finance Company of Dallas, p. 841.

in any week may not exceed the *lesser* of the following: (1) 25 percent of the disposable earnings for the week, or (2) the amount by which the disposable earnings for that week exceed 30 times the federal minimum hourly wage prescribed by the Fair Labor Standards Act. *Example:* Suppose that a consumer debtor has disposable earnings of $200 per week and these earnings are subject to garnishment. What is the federal limit on the amount garnished? The answer is $50. The calculation of 25 percent of disposable earnings is $50, whereas this amount of disposable earnings exceeding 30 times the minimum wage ($3.35 per hour) is $99.50. Since $50 is the lesser of the amounts calculated, it is the garnishment limit.

In the past some employers have discharged employees when their earnings were garnished. The federal law now prohibits this discharge on the basis that the employee's earnings have been subject to garnishment for only one indebtedness. (By implication, the law seems to permit the dismissal of an employee from employment if there are garnishments involving two or more indebtednesses owed by that employee.) If an employer violates this provision limiting the discharge of employees, the employer may be fined up to $1,000 or imprisoned up to 1 year, or any combination of these two sentences.

The federal law does not preempt the field of garnishment or affect any state law. Many state laws exempt larger amounts than does the federal law, and the net effect of the federal law is to exempt the larger amount that either provides. Both the state and the federal law illustrate a public policy against using a wage earner's income to pay judgment debts. In some states, the amount exempt is left to the courts, in order to avoid undue hardship on the debtor.

OTHER CONSUMER PROTECTIONS

18. Magnuson-Moss Warranty Act

In the past, warranties have been written in language so technical and misleading that many so-called warranties on products were actually disclaimers of warranties. Prior to the adoption of the federal law on warranties and the Federal Trade Commission (FTC) rules designed to accomplish its goals, a wide gap separated what the consumer was led to believe and what the manufacturer and seller would do under a warranty. To alleviate this problem, to provide consumers with adequate information about express warranties, and to prevent deceptive warranties, Congress enacted the Magnuson-Moss Warranty Act. This law and the FTC rules adopted under it are applicable to all products costing over $5.

This law does not require that a warranty has to be given. However, if a warranty is made by the seller, that warranty must satisfy the requirements stated in the following paragraphs. Specifically, the Magnuson-Moss Act provides guidance concerning express warranties, implied warranties, and mechanisms for resolving disputes.

Express warranties.   The first requirement of the law is that a warrantor of a consumer product must, by means of a written warranty, fully and conspicuously disclose in simple and readily understood language the terms and conditions of the warranty. The law and the rules then specify what must be included in the written warranty. Such a warranty must include, among other things, a statement of what the warrantor will do in the event of a defect or breach of warranty, at whose expense, and for what period of time. Furthermore, the warranty must set forth the step-by-step procedure the consumer is to follow in order to obtain performance of the warranty.

Any exceptions or limitations of the warranty must be indicated. A warrantor may not exclude or limit consequential damages for breach of any warranty unless the exclusion or limitation appears conspicuously on the face of the warranty.

The law also requires that each warranty be labeled "full" or "limited" if the product sells for over $15. A *full warranty* must indicate its duration. Products covered by a full warranty must be repaired or replaced by the seller without charge and within a reasonable time in the event there is a defect, malfunction, or failure to conform to the written warranty. A purchaser of a *limited warranty* is put on notice to find out its limits.

To assist the consumer in making an intelligent purchase decision, sellers are required to make available all information about the warranties. Prior to the sale, this information must be clearly and conspicuously displayed in close connection with the warranted product.

Implied warranties.   Under the federal law, a warrantor may not impose any limitation on the duration of any implied warranty. No supplier may disclaim or modify any implied warranty if there is a written warranty or if, at the time of sale or within 90 days, the supplier enters into a service contract with the buyer. The latter restriction does not prevent a seller from limiting the time period of a written warranty. The time period of the warranty must also be set forth in clear and unmistakable language on the face of the warranty.

Mechanisms to resolve disputes.   A significant aspect of the federal law deals with informal mechanisms for the resolution of consumer disputes. The law does not require such mechanisms, but it strongly encourages sellers to use them. If a seller establishes a procedure for an independent or government entity to resolve disputes with its buyers, the consumer must resort to the procedure before filing suit against the seller. Consumers are given access to these informal dispute procedures free of charge.

Violations of the warranty law subject the business to a suit for damages. The law also authorizes class action suits for damages for breach of warranty if at least 100 persons are affected. The law also allows consumers to collect attorney's fees if legal counsel is required to enforce a warranty. This makes litigation a reasonable alternative even though the cost of the product is not substantial. Without the provision authorizing attorney's fees, consumer suits in breach-of-warranty cases would rarely be the subject of litigation.

19. Consumer Product Safety Act

In 1972 Congress enacted the Consumer Product Safety Act, creating the Consumer Product Safety Commission and a Product Safety Advisory Council. This law imposes safety standards on manufacturing and commercial operations relating to consumer products and, with a few exceptions, identifies and regulates almost all aspects of safety in products sold to the public. Since there is no requirement that the goods be sold, the law covers free samples and products sold to others but used by consumers. The breadth of the law is apparent from its definition of a *consumer product.* The term includes any article produced or distributed for sale to, or use by, a consumer in or around a permanent or temporary household or residence, a school, in recreation or otherwise.

Manufacturers of consumer products are required to furnish information about their products to the commission. This information may include technical data; it must include all information on new products. The law also requires manufacturers to notify the commission whenever they learn that a product is defective or fails to meet applicable standards. Notice also must be given to the general public and to known purchasers whenever it is found that a product is defective or in violation of a safety rule.

Once a product safety rule has been adopted, a variety of private and public enforcement procedures are available. Courts are authorized to issue injunctions, which may result in the removal of a product from the market. The law provides a penalty of $2,000 for each violation, up to a maximum of $500,000 for each product involved in a violation. A consumer is authorized to sue in federal courts for injuries caused by a product if the manufacturer is knowingly in violation of a product safety rule, provided the claim meets the jurisdictional amount ($10,000) of the federal courts.

20. Unfair Business Practices

By federal statute, the Federal Trade Commission (FTC) is responsible for preventing unfair or deceptive acts or practices in commerce. As a result of this law, the FTC has a Bureau of Consumer Protection actively engaged in regulating advertising and the sale of goods. Advertising is unfair or deceptive if it has a tendency or capacity to mislead consumers.

The FTC has found numerous unfair and deceptive promotional devices and advertisements. One ad violated the law by comparing the seller's price to a higher "regular" price or a manufacturer's list price. It is deceptive to refer to a "regular price" unless the seller usually and recently sold the items at that price in the regular course of business. Also it has been held deceptive to refer to the "manufacturer's list price" when that list price is not the ordinary and customary retail sales price of the item in the locality. Bait and switch promotions are another violation of the FTC act. In a *bait and switch* sales technique, a product is advertised at a low price that will bring in customers whom the advertiser then tries to switch to other products he prefers to sell.

Ads that are false or misleading about the quality of a product or its source are also unfair and deceptive. Disparaging the product of a competitor may be stopped by the FTC on the ground that such ads are unfair. Words that are technically not false may be held to be deceptive if they give the wrong impression to consumers. The words "guaranteed for life" were held to be deceptive when the seller intended the life to be the life of the product, and consumers thought that the guarantee was for the life of the purchaser of the product.

Many states have laws designed to aid and protect consumers in a multitude of transactions. These laws, which are enacted pursuant to the police power, are usually enforced by the state attorney general, but they may be enforced by consumers and class action suits.[6]

21. Home Solicitation

Under its authority to prevent unfair and deceptive business practices, the Federal Trade Commission has regulated door-to-door selling. The FTC rule covers any sale, lease, or rental of consumer goods with a purchase price of $25 or more, at places of business other than the normal place of business of the seller. It does not cover mail-order or telephone sales or sales in which the buyer has requested the seller to visit his home.

The law requires the seller to furnish the buyer with a copy of the contract in the same language—e.g., Spanish—used in the oral presentation. The contract must, in 10-point type, notify the buyer that the transaction may be canceled at any time prior to midnight of the third business day after the date of the transaction. The seller is required to furnish the buyer with a form to be used to cancel, so that all the buyer is required to do is to sign the form and send it to the seller. The seller also must orally inform the buyer of the right to cancel.

The law requires the seller to honor the notice of cancellation within 10 days, refund all payments made and all property traded in, and return any instruments assigned by the buyer. If the purchase is canceled, all security arrangements are null and void. If the goods have been delivered to the buyer prior to cancellation, the seller must, within 10 days, notify the buyer whether the seller intends to repossess or to abandon the goods.

22. Real Estate Settlement Procedures Act

Since the purchase of a home is the most significant transaction ever entered into by most people, the law contains provisions aimed at assisting buyers with this transaction. At one time, the amount of settlement costs or closing costs in real estate transactions often came as a surprise, if not a shock, to many purchasers. To aid home buyers and borrowers, Congress in 1974 enacted a law requiring the disclosure of all costs to buyers and borrowers prior to the consummation of a real estate transaction. The law assumes that the disclosure of the total cost will allow buyers and borrowers to shop for credit and thus reduce the settlement costs in many cases. The disclosure statement also gives advance notice of the cash required at settlement.

The law requires the use of a standard form for advance disclosure of closing costs and for recording the actual charges incurred at settlement in all covered transactions. Some settlement costs are typically paid by sellers; others are the obligation of buyers. The form covers both categories of expenses. Among the common items disclosed are loan origination fees, loan discount points, appraisal fees, attorney's fees, inspection fees, title charges, and the cost of surveys.

---

[6] Bondanza v. Peninsula Hospital and Med. Ctr., p. 842.

The law also outlaws certain practices that are contrary to the interest of the home-buying public. Among these are giving kickbacks for referring a borrower to a lender, charging or accepting a fee for something other than services actually performed, and requiring that a home seller purchase title insurance from any particular title company. For the title insurance violation, there is a liability equal to three times the cost of the title insurance.

In addition to the foregoing, this law prevents a lender from requiring that an unreasonable amount be paid in advance for the purposes of paying real property taxes and insurance when they are due. These payments generally are known as *escrow* payments. A lender can require the borrower to pay at closing, as escrow, the amount equal to the number of months between the closing date and the last time the bill was paid. In addition, the lender can collect at closing a cushion of 2 months of the total estimated bill for taxes and insurance.

An example should help illustrate this confusing-sounding formula. Assume that a buyer is closing the purchase of a house on April 1, 1986. Also assume that the 1985 taxes were paid on December 1, 1985, and they amounted to $720. At closing the lender could require that this buyer pay $360 into a tax escrow account. This figure is determined by counting the number of months from the time the taxes were last paid to closing. This involves 4 months. The additional cushion is 2 months. Each month's tax escrow payment equals $60. Six months times $60 amounts to a total advance escrow payment for taxes of $360. These calculations should provide the lender with a sufficient fund from which to pay even the increased property taxes on December 1, 1986.

SUMMARY

Debtor protection in general	1. Since 1968, the federal government has enacted into law numerous acts designed to protect the consumer debtor in credit transactions.
	2. A consumer debtor is an individual involved in a credit transaction for the purpose of satisfying personal, family, or household needs.
	3. Credit is applicable to any transaction in which money is lent with repayment to be made in the future.

APPLICATIONS FOR CREDIT

Equal Credit Opportunity Act	1. This law prevents discrimination in granting credit on the basis of sex, race, color, age, religion, national origin, the

receipt of welfare, or the exercise of any right under the law.

2. Victims of illegal discrimination may collect actual damages, attorney's fees, other legal expenses, and punitive damages.

3. The ECOA prohibits discriminatory advertising concerning the availability of credit.

4. The creditor must take care not to request on a credit application any information that may lead to discrimination in the extension of credit.

Fair Credit Reporting Act

1. This law was designed to prevent abuses in the credit reporting industry and to ensure a person's right to privacy.

2. The FCRA's protection is limited to reports on consumers. Businesses are presumed to be able to protect themselves.

3. The FCRA regulates those who distribute reports on consumers and the users of such reports.

Consumer reporting agencies

1. Such an agency exists when it regularly collects information on consumers and furnishes it to third parties.

2. These agencies must make certain that consumer reports are used for a justifiable purpose.

3. These agencies also must take precautions to ensure the accuracy of the information distributed. Such information must not be obsolete.

Users of information

1. Whenever a user of a consumer report takes adverse action on a consumer's credit, insurance, employment, or license application, that user must disclose from which reporting agency the information was obtained.

Rights of consumer debtors

1. A consumer debtor has the right to inspect the report an agency has compiled on him or her.

2. This debtor may challenge the accuracy of any information.

3. If the information is retained by the consumer reporting agency, the consumer

debtor may prepare and require the agency to include in any report a written statement about the dispute.

CREDIT TRANSACTIONS

Truth in Lending Act

1. The T in L Act is applicable only if the credit transaction involves a consumer debtor who will repay a debt that is payable in more than four installments or is subject to a finance charge.
2. The T in L Act attempts to encourage consumer debtors to shop for the best credit opportunities. This purpose is accomplished through disclosure requirements which provide the information to make comparison possible.
3. The T in L Act's most important required disclosures are the amount financed, the finance charge, the annual percentage rate, and the total amount of all payments.
4. Failure to make these disclosures accurately exposes the creditor to liability for twice the finance charge within the range of $100 to $1,000.

Uniform Consumer Credit Code

1. This law, which has been adopted by a few states, has many of the same purposes as the federal T in L Act.
2. It does not fix interest rates, but does set maximum rates of interest.
3. This law prohibits certain types of transactions such as those requiring balloon payments after the end of a relatively short period of time. The law prohibits a seller from taking a wage assignment from a consumer.

PAYMENTS AND COLLECTIONS

Fair Credit Billing Act

1. This law specifies the rights of consumer debtors and the duties of creditors if there is a billing error in an open-ended credit transaction.

2. After a consumer debtor has submitted a billing error notice, the creditor must respond by correcting the error or explaining why the bill is accurate.

3. The FCBA establishes criteria for how the creditor is to treat the consumer debtor during the resolution of a dispute.

4. This law also provides creditors with accounting principles that must be followed when a payment is credited to the consumer debtor's bill.

Credit card protection

1. A cardholder is liable only up to $50 for the unauthorized use of a credit card.

2. There is no liability for unauthorized purchases by credit card which were not requested by the cardholder.

3. There is no liability unless the card has a method for identification of the user.

Fair Debt Collection Practices Act

1. The FDCPA was passed to prevent the abuses that may occur in the debt collection process.

2. This law regulates only third parties who act as debt collectors. Creditors who collect from their own debtors are exempt.

3. The FDCPA covers only the collection of consumer debts. Again, businesses are presumed to be able to protect themselves.

4. A number of collection practices are allowed and a number are considered illegal under the FDCPA.

5. Any person abused during a third party's efforts to collect a consumer debt may recover actual damages, attorney's fees, and other legal expenses.

Limitations on garnishments

1. Both federal and state governments limit the amount of wages that can be used to pay debts.

2. The federal law limits garnishment to 25 percent of take-home pay or the amount that disposable earnings exceed 30 times the federal minimum wage, whichever is less.

3. Employers may not discharge an employee because one garnishment proceeding has been instituted against that employee.

OTHER CONSUMER PROTECTIONS

Magnuson-Moss Warranty Act

1. Warranties of consumer products must be in writing and must fully and conspicuously disclose in simple, readily understood language the terms of the warranty.
2. The warranty must include a statement of what the warrantor will do in the event of a breach of warranty, at whose expense, and for what time period.
3. The warranty must inform the consumer of the steps to be followed to obtain performance.
4. Warranties must be labeled full or limited, and information about warranties must be readily available.
5. A warrantor may exclude or limit consequential damages only in conspicuous writing on the face of the warranty.
6. Informal procedures established by the warrantor in order to resolve disputes concerning warranties must be followed by the customers.

Consumer Product Safety Act

1. The Consumer Product Safety Commission imposes safety standards on manufacturers of consumer products. Manufacturers are required to furnish information to the commission.
2. There are sanctions in addition to common law liability, and the statute allows suits in the federal courts in the event that product safety rules are violated.

Unfair business practices

1. The Federal Trade Commission may prohibit deceptive business practices by issuing cease and desist orders.
2. State statutes also attempt to prohibit deception of consumers. They generally create liability not only to consumers, but

	also to competitors for false and deceptive advertising.
Home solicitation	**1.** The Federal Trade Commission has rules regulating door-to-door selling. These cover goods costing $25 or more.
	2. The rules require written contracts in at least 10-point type, and the contract must allow cancellation anytime prior to midnight of the third business day after the transaction.
	3. The buyer must be orally informed of the right to cancel and obtain a refund.
Real Estate Settlement Procedures Act	**1.** This law applies to the purchase of homes. It requires the disclosure of all costs to buyers and borrowers in advance of the closing of the transaction.
	2. The buyer is furnished a completed standard form informing him as to the amount of such costs and which party is expected to pay them.

CASES

Brothers v. First Leasing
724 F.2d 789 (9th Cir. 1984)

REINHARDT, J. The district court dismissed plaintiff's claim that her application for an automobile lease had been denied on the basis of sex or marital status in violation of the Equal Credit Opportunity Act (ECOA). The sole issue on appeal is whether the ECOA applies to consumer leases. We hold that it does.

In January 1982, plaintiff-appellant, Patricia Ann Brothers, attempted to lease an automobile for her personal use from defendant-appellee, First Leasing. First Leasing required Brothers to submit a completed "Application for Lease Credit," which was to provide First Leasing with information with which to evaluate her financial condition.

Brothers informed First Leasing that she intended to lease the automobile in her own name rather than jointly with her husband, James A. Garske. Nonetheless, First Leasing insisted that

Brothers include on the "Application for Lease Credit" information concerning Mr. Garske's financial history. In addition, First Leasing required Mr. Garske, as well as Brothers, to sign the application. Brothers submitted the application, signed by her husband, with the requested information about his finances. First Leasing then obtained TRW Credit Reports on Brothers and her husband. Mr. Garske's credit report indicated that he previously had filed for bankruptcy.

In a form entitled "Statement of Credit Denial, Termination, or Change," which complies with the requirements of the ECOA, and is almost identical to the form suggested in the ECOA regulations, First Leasing rejected Brothers' application. The "principal reason" given for the denial of Brothers' lease credit application was her husband's previous bankruptcy. The form used by First Leasing also contained a statement that the ECOA bars "creditors from discriminating against credit applicants on the basis of sex [or] marital status."

Brothers filed a claim against First Leasing that alleged that (1) the requirement that Mr. Garske sign her lease credit application, and (2) the denial of *her* application because of *his* credit record, constitute unlawful discrimination on the basis of sex or marital status under the ECOA. Contending that the ECOA does not apply to leases, First Leasing moved to dismiss the action for failure to state a claim upon which relief can be granted. The district court held that the lease was not covered by the ECOA and granted the motion. . . .

The use of the broad term "credit transactions" in the ECOA does not, by itself, answer the question whether consumer leases are covered by the Act, although a literal reading of the language supports the view that they are. On the one hand, the lease obligation that Brothers would have incurred under the automobile lease falls within the ECOA's definition of "credit." So would the obligations incurred under most consumer leases. Moreover, the credit investigation engaged in by First Leasing is specifically included within the Federal Reserve Board's definition of "credit transaction."

Although "credit transactions" might in some contexts lend itself to a narrow interpretation, we cannot give it such a construction in the ECOA in view of the overriding national policy against discrimination that underlies the Act and in view of the current structure of the Consumer Credit Protection Act, the umbrella statute. We must construe the literal language of the ECOA in light of the clear, strong purpose evidenced by the Act and adopt an interpretation that will serve to effectuate that purpose. . . .

The purpose of the ECOA is to eradicate credit discrimination waged against women, especially married women whom creditors traditionally refused to consider for individual credit. Congress reaffirmed the goal of antidiscrimination in credit in the 1976 amendments to the ECOA by adding race, color, religion, national origin, and age to sex and marital status as characteristics that may not be considered in deciding whether to extend credit.

In enacting and amending the ECOA, Congress recognized that a prohibition against discrimination in credit provides a much-needed addition to the previously existing strict prohibitions against discrimination in employment, housing, voting, education, and numerous other areas. The ECOA is simply one more tool to be used in our vigorous national effort to eradicate invidious discrimination "root and branch" from our society.

In view of the strong national commitment to the eradication of discrimination in our society, we see no reason why Congress would have wanted to subject the leasing of durable consumer goods to regulation under the disclosure provisions of the Consumer Credit Protection Act, but to exclude those transactions from the scope of the antidiscrimination provisions of that Act. Certainly, abolishing discrimination in the affording of credit is at least as important as compelling the disclosure of information regarding finance charges. To conclude that discrimination in consumer leasing transactions is exempt from the ECOA simply because Congress did not add express language covering consumer leases when it amended the ECOA for entirely unrelated reasons would be inconsistent with the broad purpose of the statute and the liberal construction we must give it. It is far more reasonable to conclude that Congress thought that an express amendment was unnecessary because the ECOA on its face applies to all credit transactions and, therefore, the language already in the Act was broad enough to cover consumer leases.

In enacting the Consumer Leasing Act, Congress explicitly recognized the "recent trend toward leasing automobiles and other durable goods for consumer use as an alternative to installment credit sales." Prospective lessors run extensive credit checks on consumer lease applicants just as they do in the case of credit sales applicants. . . . Therefore, interpreting "credit transactions" so that the ECOA applies to lease transactions, as well as to credit sales and loans, is essential to the accomplishment of the Act's antidiscriminatory goal. . . .

Finally, to interpret the term "credit transactions" narrowly, so as to exclude consumer leases, would nullify Congress' use of flexible language necessary "to insure the effective application of legislative policy to changing circumstances."

Because the language of the ECOA is broad and its antidiscriminatory purpose is overriding, . . . we conclude that the ECOA applies to consumer leases.

The district court's order dismissing appellant's claim is reversed and the case is remanded. *So ordered.*

Byrant v. TRW, Inc.
689 F.2d 72 (6th Cir. 1982)

EDWARDS, J. Defendant, a credit reporting agency, appeals from an adverse judgment based on a jury verdict of $8,000 in actual damages and an attorney's fee award of $13,705, which resulted from a suit prosecuted by plaintiff, an individual who was seeking credit for the purchase of a house. The verdict represented a finding that defendant had supplied inaccurate information to a mortgage company and had thereby caused the denial of plaintiff's home loan application. . . .

The credit reporting agency was TRW Inc., an Ohio corporation; the prospective mortgagor was an individual named Bennie E. Bryant; and the mortgage company was the Hammond Mortgage Corporation of Southfield, Michigan.

The central issue in this case is whether or not defendant violated section 607(b) of the Fair Credit Reporting Act (FCRA), 15 U.S.C. §1681e(b), which reads:

> Whenever a consumer reporting agency prepares a consumer report it shall follow reasonable procedures to assure maximum possible accuracy of the information concerning the individual about whom the report relates.

Negligent noncompliance with any requirement of the FCRA gives rise to liability for "any actual damages" and "reasonable attorney's fees;" . . . willful noncompliance, in addition, gives rise to liability for punitive damages.

[The consumer report that TRW gave Hammond Mortgage Corporation contained inaccurate information. These inaccuracies were information TRW obtained from Hudson and Grinnell, who were creditors of Bryant.]

Defendent does not contest . . . the inaccuracies.

Its basic defense is that the inaccuracies were those of plaintiff's creditors and that, under section 607(b), all it had to do was report accurately whatever information the creditors furnished.

Thus, it appears to this court that the critical legal issue in this case is whether or not section 607(b) requires a consumer reporting agency to do more than correctly report the information supplied to it by creditors. Reviewing the language and legislative history of the statute, we answer this question affirmatively. . . .

Acceptance in full of the position urged on this court by defendant . . . would, we believe, serve essentially to repeal by judicial decree a statute that Congress adopted after much consideration in lengthy hearings. Congress chose to require consumer reporting agencies to "follow reasonable procedures to assure *maximum possible accuracy of the information* about whom the report relates."

Although the legislative history of section 607(b) is sketchy and compels neither acceptance nor rejection of defendant's position, two aspects of that history dealing with amendments to the original Senate bill insisted on by the House conferees support a broad reading of the duties imposed by the statute:

(1) Procedures to Insure Accuracy

The Senate bill required reporting agencies who prepared investigative reports to follow reasonable procedures to assure the maximum possible accuracy of such report. The House conferees felt that this requirement should be extended to all reporting agencies, whether they prepared investigative reports or conventional credit reports. The Senate conferees felt that this was a reasonable requirement and accepted the House amendment.

Investigative consumer reports contain "information on a consumer's character, general reputation, personal characteristics, or mode of living," which is gathered through personal interviews. These reports are generally used by employers in their hiring practices and by insurance companies and are put together with greater care than conventional credit reports because of the sensitive and subjective nature of the information involved and the manner in which the information is obtained. We are persuaded that by extending to conventional credit reports the requirement of "reasonable procedures to assure maximum possible accuracy," Congress evinced its desire that agencies that assemble conventional credit reports be more than conduits of information and its belief that accurate credit information is as important as accurate personal information.

(2) Civil Liability for Negligent Noncompliance

The House amendment . . . which was agreed to by the conferees, would establish liability for actual damages sustained as a result of ordinary negligence, instead of only as a result of gross negligence as provided in the Senate bill.

This tends to show, we believe, that Congress rejected the imposition of only a nominal standard of care on the credit reporting industry.

In sum, we hold that a consumer reporting agency does not *necessarily* comply with section 607(b) by simply reporting in an accurate manner the information it receives from creditors.

Each case under this statute will vary on the facts, and each must be judged on its own merits. It is clear, as defendant contends, that liability does not flow automatically from the fact that a credit reporting agency, such as defendant, reports inaccurate information. Instead, liability flows from failure to follow "[(1)] *reasonable procedures [(2)] to assure maximum possible accuracy of the information [(3)] concerning the individual about whom the information relates.*"

Defendant's effort to "assure maximum possible accuracy of the information" in the mortgage report comprised two phone calls, the record indicates. The calls, one to Hudson's, the other to Grinnell's, simply reconfirmed the information— inaccurate information it turns out—furnished earlier to defendant by the creditors concerned.

On the record of this case, we believe that defendant was required to do more under section 607(b). It would have taken little added effort immediately to advise the creditors of plaintiff's complaints and to request investigation and re-evaluation based on the most recent data. . . . Although the inaccuracies were eventually corrected, the corrections were made after the rejection of plaintiff's home loan application, his consequent frustration, and the denigration of his name and creditworthiness. . . .

We have no doubt from this record that plaintiff offered proofs from which the jury could properly have found that defendant's failure in timely fashion to use "reasonable procedures to assure maximum possible accuracy" occasioned damage to plaintiff's name and consequent anguish and humiliation.

Furthermore, we do not find any reason to set aside the District Judge's award of attorney's fees. . . . We have no doubt that Congress intended in authorizing attorney's fees in lawsuits under the FCRA, to make use of the private attorney general concept.

The fact that the attorney's fees in this case, $13,705, exceeded plaintiff's actual damages, $8,000, does not argue for a reduction of the former. The fees were calculated on the basis of an hourly rate, but defendant contends that the purpose of the FCRA's allowance for attorney's fees could be as efficaciously achieved by calculating fees on the basis of a contingent fee.

We reject this contention because we believe that . . . a fee calculated in terms of hours of service provided is the fairest and most manageable approach. . . .

Affirmed.

Ford Motor Credit Company v. Cenance
101 S.Ct. 2239 (1981)

PER CURIAM. These cases were consolidated in the Court of Appeals. In each, a prospective purchaser of an automobile entered into an installment sales transaction with an automobile dealer. Prior to completion of the transaction the dealer submitted the buyer's credit application to petitioner Ford Motor Credit Company (FMCC). Once the dealer was notified that the buyer met FMCC's credit standards, the buyer and the dealer executed a retail installment contract. On each contract the following legend appeared: "The foregoing contract hereby is accepted by the Seller and assigned to Ford Motor Credit Company in accordance with the terms of the Assignment set forth on the reverse side hereof." Pursuant to the arrangement between the dealer and FMCC, FMCC purchased each contract without recourse against the dealer. Although FMCC did not assist in the actual negotiations, it provided the dealer with credit forms, including blank retail installment contracts.

Subsequently, each buyer brought suit in

federal district court, alleging violations of . . . the Truth-in-Lending Act.

The allegations common to all suits were that FMCC was a creditor within the meaning of the Act and that the statement concerning assignment to FMCC did not adequately disclose that status. The respective district courts agreed and the Court of Appeals for the Fifth Circuit affirmed. . . .

Having concluded that FMCC was a creditor within the meaning of the Act, the Court of Appeals went on to hold that the statement in the retail sales agreement notifying the buyer of the assignment to FMCC was an insufficient disclosure of creditor status. . . .

FMCC's petition for certiorari challenges these holdings. We grant the petition in major part, affirm the holding that FMCC is a creditor within the meaning of the Act, but reverse the holding that the statement revealing the assignment to FMCC was not a sufficient disclosure of creditor status. . . .

The Truth-in-Lending Act, as it stood prior to recent amendments, defined creditors in pertinent part as those "who regularly extend, or arrange for the extension of, credit. . . ." Regulation Z, promulgated pursuant to the Act, defines the term consistently with the above: " 'Creditor' means a person who in the ordinary course of business regularly extends or arranges for the extension of consumer credit. . . ." On the facts of this case, the above definition easily encompasses both the dealers and FMCC. Each dealer *arranged* for the extension of credit but FMCC actually *extended* the credit. The facts negate any suggestion that the dealers anticipated financing any of these transactions. The sales were contingent upon FMCC's approval of the credit worthiness of the buyer. The acceptance of the contract and the assignment became operational simultaneously and the assignment divested the dealer of any risk in the transaction. In short, we agree with the Court of Appeals that it would be elevating form over substance to conclude that FMCC is not a creditor within the meaning of the Act.

Equally formalistic, however, is the conclusion below that the statement notifying the buyer of the assignment to FMCC was an insufficient disclosure of FMCC's creditor status. As the Court of Appeals recognized, other Circuit Courts of Appeals that have addressed this precise point have held that such a statement adequately disclosed FMCC's role in the transactions. Those courts have reasoned that the statement notifying the buyer that the contract was, upon acceptance, assigned to FMCC served the purpose of the Act by disclosing the nature of the relationship of the finance company to the transaction. It was unneccessary precisely to characterize FMCC as a "creditor." Contrary to the court below, we agree with those Courts of Appeals that have found the notification of assignment to be a sufficient disclosure of creditor status. . . .

> The concept of "meaningful disclosure" that animates TILA . . . cannot be applied in the abstract. *Meaningful* disclosure does not mean *more* disclosure. Rather, it describes a balance between "competing considerations of complete disclosure . . . and the need to avoid . . . [informational overload]."

Here, requiring more disclosure would not meaningfully benefit the consumer and consequently would not serve the purposes of the Act.

The decision of the Court of Appeals is accordingly affirmed in part and reversed in part.

So ordered.

American Express Co. v. Koerner
101 S.Ct. 2281 (1981)

Plaintiff, a former credit card holder, sued the credit card issuer for damages, alleging a violation of the Fair Credit Billing Act. The credit card was issued to a corporation for a company account with the plaintiff, as president, authorized to use it. The plaintiff agreed to be liable jointly and severally for the account. Later a dispute arose over the account; and when plaintiff attempted to use the account to purchase plane tickets, the card was cancelled. This suit followed for damages, alleging retaliatory cancellation. The plaintiff sought damages for "inconvenience, mental anguish, grief, aggravation and humiliation." The district court dismissed the complaint but the court of appeals reversed.

BLACKMAN, J. . . . The question presented is whether a creditor must follow the requirements specified in 1974 by the Fair Credit Billing Act, for the correction of billing errors, when both a corporation and an individual officer are liable for a debt.

The Fair Credit Billing Act . . . applies whenever a creditor transmits to an obligor "a statement of the obligor's account in connection with an extension of consumer credit." If the obligor believes that the statement contains a billing error, he may send the creditor a written notice setting forth that belief, indicating the amount of the error and the reasons supporting his belief that it is an error. If the creditor receives this notice within 60 days of transmitting the statement of account, §161(a) imposes two separate obligations upon the creditor. Within 30 days, it must send a written acknowledgment that it has received the notice. And, within 90 days or two complete billing cycles, whichever is shorter, the creditor must investigate the matter and either make appropriate corrections in the obligor's account or send a written explanation of its belief that the original statement sent to the obligor was correct. The creditor must send its explanation before making any attempt to collect the disputed amount.

A creditor that fails to comply with §161(a) forfeits its right to collect the first $50 of the disputed amount including finance charges. In addition, §161(d) provides that, pursuant to regulations of the Federal Reserve Board, a creditor operating an "open end consumer credit plan" may not restrict or close an account due to an obligator's failure to pay a disputed amount until the creditor has sent the written explanation required by §161(a).

Every creditor under an "open end consumer credit plan" must disclose the protections available under §161 to the obligor. This disclosure must occur at the time the account is open and at semiannual intervals thereafter.

This case presents a dispute over the applicability of §161. . . .

The threshold inquiry under §161(a) is whether the creditor has transmitted to an obligor "a statement of the obligor's account in connection with an extension of consumer credit." If there has been no extension of "consumer credit," the section imposes no obligation upon a creditor, and the creditor is free to adopt its own procedures for responding to a customer's complaint about a billing error. We conclude that, on the undisputed facts of this case, respondent has failed to show that American Express has extended him "consumer credit" in any relevant transaction. Section 161(a), therefore, is not applicable to the dispute between these parties. . . .

An extension of credit is an extension of "consumer credit" if the conditions specified in the statute's definition of "consumer" are also satisfied. Section 103(h) of the TILA, 15 U.S.C. §1602(h), defines "consumer" as follows:

> The adjective "consumer," used with reference to a credit transaction, characterizes the transaction as one in which the party to whom credit is offered or extended is a natural person, and the money, property, or services which are the subject of the transaction are primarily for personal, family, household, or agricultural purposes.

Two elements thus must be present in every "consumer credit" transaction: the party to whom the credit is extended must be a natural person, *and* the money, property, or services received by that person must be "primarily for personal, family, household, or agricultural purposes."

The only permissible conclusion [is] that the undisputed facts of this case establish that the threshold requirement of §161(a)—an "extension of consumer credit"—has not been satisfied because none of the credit transactions relevant to the billing dispute was entered into "primarily" for consumer purpose. . . .

The undisputed facts of this case reveal that the Koerner Company obtained the right "to incur debt and defer its payment" from American Express primarily for business, not consumer, purposes. In addition, the specific transactions that were the subject of the dispute between the company and American Express also were business transactions. The facts of this case, therefore are not encompassed within any possible interpretation of the phrase "extension of consumer credit" in §161(a). . . .

We do not suggest that it always will be easy to determine whether the opening of a credit account involves an extension of consumer credit. The Court of Appeals noted that often it is difficult to characterize the overall purpose of a credit card account that allows for a large number of individual transactions. It is clear, however, that the Fair

Credit Billing Act requires creditors and the courts to undertake this task. On this record, there can be no dispute that the Koerner Company's account was not covered by §103(h)'s definition of "consumer," because it was not opened "primarily for personal, family, household, or agricultural purposes." . . .

Inasmuch as the record establishes that there was no dispute between petitioner and respondent concerning "a statement of [respondent's] account in connection with an extension of consumer credit," petitioner was not required to follow the procedures mandated by §161(a).

Because Congress has restricted the operation of §161(a) to disputes concerning extensions of consumer credit, and because the dispute between American Express and respondent did not concern an extension of consumer credit, the judgment of the Court of Appeals must be, and is, reversed.

It is so ordered.

Campbell v. Beneficial Finance Company of Dallas
616 S.W.2d 375 (Tex. App. 1981)

CORNELIUS, J. This is an appeal from the grant of a summary judgment. Clara Campbell brought suit against Beneficial Finance Company and its employee, Raymond Bernard Johnson, alleging a cause of action for harassment and abusive debt collection practices.

Campbell's daughter and son-in-law, Sue and Bobby Rice, were indebted to Beneficial and became delinquent in their payments. The loan was apparently taken for the purpose of purchasing household goods and furnishings. Campbell alleged in her suit that Beneficial and its employees, specifically Mr. Johnson threatened and harassed her because she apparently would not or could not disclose the whereabouts of Mr. and Mrs. Rice. She alleged a number of specific acts of harassment, and alleged that those acts caused her embarrassment, humiliation, loss of sleep and extreme mental suffering.

The appellees filed a motion for summary judgment on the basis that Mrs. Campbell had no standing to sue for the injuries under the Debt Collection Act because she was not the debtor. . . .

It is appellees' position that Campbell has no cause of action under the Debt Collection Act for two reasons: (1) a bystander, i.e., one not a debtor under the Act, has no standing to assert a cause of action, and (2) allegation and proof of physical injury are necessary elements of such a cause of action, and no such allegation was made in this case.

Appellees assert that a bystander is not a person within the class of persons intended by the legislature to be protected by the Debt Collection Act. We first note that Mrs. Campbell was not a bystander in the usual meaning of that term. The alleged abuses were committed directly against her. In addition, the language of the Act clearly authorizes a cause of action such as that alleged here. By the express terms of the Act, if a debt collector in connection with the collection or the attempted collection of a debt owed by a consumer oppresses, harasses or abuses *any person* by one of the four enumerated practices, a cause of action may be maintained. Likewise, certain threats and coercive activities against *any* person are prohibited. Further, *any person* may maintain an action for actual damages sustained as a result of the violation of the Act. It is thus clear that while the threat, coercion, harassment or abuse must occur in connection with the collection or attempted collection of a debt allegedly owed by a consumer, persons other than the debtor may maintain an action for violations of the Act. To hold otherwise would be to find a legislative intent to protect debtors from the abuses the Act is designed to prevent, but to leave their families, friends and employers subject to those same abuses. The commission of such threatening and harassing acts against the debtor's family or friends is no less obnoxious or despicable, and surely no less worthy of prevention, than the commission of those same acts against the debtor himself. Indeed, just the opposite is true. . . . [I]t is more unreasonable to harass someone who does not owe a debt than it is to harass someone who does owe a debt. . . .

The Act requires that the wrong complained of must arise out of a debtor/creditor relationship, but it does not limit the cause of action to the debtor. Any person against whom the prohibited acts are committed may maintain an action for actual damages sustained as a result of those violations. . . .

Appellees also assert that allegations and proof of physical injury are necessary to maintain a cause of action under the Act. This Court has expressly ruled that an action for unreasonable debt collection efforts may be maintained absent a plea of physical illness or injury.

Appellees failed to establish as a matter of law the grounds of defense set out in their motion for summary judgment. The judgment is therefore reversed and the cause is remanded for trial.

So ordered.

Bondanza v. Peninsula Hospital & Med. Ctr.
590 P.2d 22 (Cal. 1979)

Plaintiffs were patients at the defendant hospital. At the time of admission, each of them signed an agreement that obligated them to pay the hospital charges due on the date of discharge. The agreement also provided that if the account was referred to a collection agency or an attorney for collection, the debtor would pay "reasonable attorney's fees and collection expense." Plaintiffs were each assessed collection costs equal to one-third of the amount due on their bills. This one-third was the amount the hospital had agreed to pay a collection agency for collecting the accounts. Plaintiffs contend that this practice is an unlawful business practice in violation of state statutes because the collection costs assessed against plaintiffs amounted to a penalty, the charge was greatly in excess of the actual expense of collection, and it was fixed before any costs had been incurred by the agency. Plaintiffs sought to enjoin the practice. The trial court dismissed the complaint, and the plaintiffs appealed.

MOSK, J. . . . The Code authorizes any person to bring an action on behalf of the general public to enjoin an "unlawful, unfair or fraudulent business practice." Plaintiffs do not complain solely of the requirement of the admission agreement that they pay a "reasonable" collection charge, but also of defendants' practice of implementing that condition by assessing the debtor a charge of one-third of the balance due on the debt at the time of assignment without regard to the actual collection costs incurred. Thus, in discussing the validity of the collection charge, we consider not only the promise made by plaintiffs but the manner in which defendants enforced that promise. We have no doubt that defendants' conduct constitutes a business practice within the meaning of the statutory language.

The Code . . . prohibits contracts in which the amount of damages is determined in advance unless "it would be impracticable or extremely difficult to fix the actual damage."

. . . Here, there was no agreement between plaintiffs and the hospital as to the amount of collection costs to be paid in the event of default and no effort made between them to estimate a fair compensation for the breach. Instead, plaintiffs agreed to pay a "reasonable" expense; only the hospital and a third party, the collection agency, determined that expense would amount to one-third of the balance due at the time of assignment. Moreover, although defendants have the burden of demonstrating that it would have been impracticable or extremely difficult to fix actual collection costs, the record does not disclose they attempted to make any such showing below. In these circumstances, defendants' practice of assessing a debtor a "collection" charge of one-third of the amount due is plainly unlawful.

The underlying unfairness of the practice is also clear, as the admission agreement—including the promise to pay collection costs—is an adhesion contract which a patient must sign as a condition of admission to the hospital in all except limited emergency situations. Medical bills often add up to many thousands of dollars; one-third of the balance due could amount to a substantial sum. Furthermore, as in the present case, a patient who cannot personally pay the charges but who relies on his medical insurance to do so may be penalized for the delays or errors of his insurer—circumstances usually well beyond his control.

Finally, there may be no relationship whatever between the charge assessed against the patient and the actual expense required to collect an amount. The charge is calculated on the amount due at the time of assignment, yet it may be that the patient or his insurer has paid all or most of the obligation shortly *after* assignment and before the collection agency has expended any significant effort to collect the debt.

Since we have concluded that defendants' conduct constitutes an unlawful and unfair business practice, plaintiffs are entitled to an injunction prohibiting defendants from assessing patients who sign the admission agreement a collection expense of one-third of the amount owed at the time of assignment, or any other sum which does not represent the actual costs of collection.

Reversed.

REVIEW QUESTIONS

1. Identify the terms in column A by matching each with the appropriate statement in column B.

A		B
1. Consumer debtor	a.	A third party who collects information on consumers and furnishes it to creditors, insurers, employers, and similar parties.
2. Equal Credit Opportunity Act	b.	Designed to inform buyers of closing costs.
3. Fair Credit Reporting Act	c.	Enacted to encourage consumer applicants to shop for the best credit opportunity.
4. Consumer reporting agency	d.	Exists to provide funds to ensure that debtors have housing.
5. Truth-in-Lending Act	e.	An individual involved in a credit transaction for the purposes of satisfying personal, family, or household needs.
6. Billing error	f.	Passed to prevent abuses that may occur in the debt collection process.
7. Fair Debt Collection Practices Act	g.	This law regulates those parties that either distribute or use information on consumers.
8. Homestead exemption	h.	Regulated by the Federal Trade Commission and state laws.
9. Magnuson-Moss Act	i.	Law enacted to prevent discrimination based on several factors in the granting of credit.
10. Consumer Product Safety Act	j.	The federal law that establishes requirements concerning manufacturers' warranties.
11. Unfair business practices	k.	A mistake in an open-ended credit statement.
12. Real Estate Settlement Procedures Act	l.	Enacted to impose safety standards on manufacturers of consumer products.

2. The Equal Credit Opportunity Act was passed to prevent discrimination in the credit extension transaction. What are the criteria on which the credit decision cannot be legally based?

3. Alice was rejected for life insurance on the basis of a report from an independent consumer reporting agency. What are her rights concerning the report?

4. Lamb's automobile insurance policy was canceled due to information in a report furnished by Equifax Services, Inc. (Equifax) to the insurance company. Lamb contacted Equifax to discover the contents of the report. He was verbally told the contents but was not given a copy. Lamb disputed the following two items contained in the report: (1) the reason for his first divorce, and (2) information concerning an arrest. Because of the dispute, Equifax reinvestigated Lamb's background and issued a new report. It deleted the first disputed item but retained the second based on a verification by police records. Lamb was given a copy of this second report, and he took no exception to it. The second report was furnished to another source, but Lamb was not told this fact. When he learned that Equifax had reported the information about his arrest, Lamb instituted this suit alleging defamation and violation of the FCRA. Did Equifax violate the disclosure requirements of the FCRA? Explain.

5. What are the four principal disclosure requirements that a creditor must satisfy under the Truth in Lending Act?

6. Ferguson Finance held a mortgage on Dandy's six-unit apartment building. Dandy fell behind on his payments and, to avoid foreclosure, agreed to execute a mortgage on his home in favor of Ferguson. This second mortgage secured a note for the amount that Dandy was in arrears on his payments. When the second mortgage was entered, Ferguson did not comply with the Truth-in-Lending law. Dandy now sues Ferguson for his actual damages, plus twice the amount of the finance charge. Should Dandy succeed? Why?

7. A salesman for Plumbing Company sold a water-softening unit to Baker. The sales agreement included a "referral sale" credit. For every sale to a buyer Baker had referred to Plumbing, Baker would get a $40 credit toward payment for Baker's unit. Is this a valid sales agreement? Explain.

8. The Charge-It Company issued a credit card to Albert at his request. Albert's card was stolen, and he immediately notified Charge-It. The thief used Albert's card for motel and gasoline purchases. Who bears the loss in this situation? Why?

9. Boudreaux owed the Allstate Company $185, payable in 24 monthly installments. When Boudreaux became unemployed, he fell behind in his payments. Allstate hired the Debtor's Collection Agency to collect the amount owed by Boudreaux. This agency began calling his neighbors repeatedly, since the Boudreaux phone was disconnected. It used insulting language in speaking to these neighbors about Boudreaux. Mrs. Boudreaux was also insulted when an agent attempted to collect the amount owed. Does Mr. Boudreaux have any recourse against the agency for these debt collection actions? Explain.

10. Harry, a wage earner, earns $200 per week. His employer withholds 20 percent for income and FICA taxes. A garnishment proceeding is commenced against Harry and his employer to collect a judgment owed by Harry. Under the applicable federal law, how much of Harry's wages may be garnished each week? Explain your calculations.

11. The Ideal Sound and Stereo Company advertised a radio for $39.95 in the local campus paper. When students attempted to purchase this radio, they were told it was of poor quality. The store clerks suggested a special on a better-quality radio for $64.95. Several students wished to complain. What sales tactic is involved, and to whom should the students protest?

12. The Real Estate Settlement Procedures Act was enacted to control the amount of closing costs associated with real estate secured loans. What four requirements does this act impose in an attempt to achieve its purpose?

37 BANKRUPTCY

The law of bankruptcy provides possible solutions to problems that arise when a person, partnership, corporation, or municipality is unable, or finds it difficult, to satisfy obligations to creditors. Bankruptcy has its roots in the law of the Roman Empire and has been a part of English jurisprudence since 1542. The bankruptcy laws in the United States have been amended periodically. The last major revision occurred in 1978, when Congress and the president approved the Bankruptcy Reform Act, which became effective on October 1, 1979.

This revision really was a total rewriting of the bankruptcy laws in this country. In short, the 1978 act made bankruptcy a much more acceptable alternative for debtors in financial difficulty. Under this act, filing for bankruptcy no longer was socially unacceptable or an admission of failure. More than ever before, bankruptcy became an acceptable solution to the financial distress individuals or businesses could not otherwise overcome. In fact, the 1978 act was criticized as actually encouraging debtors to avoid obligations that could be paid. Creditors argued that this revision was too pro-debtor to become an effective bankruptcy law. Other problems concerning the structure of the bankruptcy courts and the appointment of bankruptcy judges also arose. Finally, a Supreme Court decision allowing collective bargaining agreements to be avoided in bankruptcy created enough pressure that the 1978 act was amended by Congress. On July 10, 1984, President Reagan signed the Bankruptcy Amendments and Federal Judgeship Act of 1984.

This chapter's coverage of bankruptcy laws involves an examination of the 1978 act as it has been amended through 1984. The following materials describe the types of bankruptcy proceedings, the basic purpose of the bankruptcy law, some procedural aspects of a bankruptcy case, and rights and duties of the parties involved in a bankruptcy case.

Prior to studying these materials, you should be aware of some terminology used in the bankruptcy law. For example, the *debtor* is an individual, a business organization, or a municipality that the bankruptcy case concerns. A *claim* is a right to payment from the debtor. Claims are held and asserted by creditors. An *order of relief* is entered by the bankruptcy judge when he or she finds that the debtor is entitled to the protection of the bankruptcy law. A *trustee* is the person responsible for managing the debtor's assets.

TYPES OF PROCEEDINGS

1. In General

The federal bankruptcy laws have two distinct approaches to the problems of debtors. One approach is to liquidate debts. The liquidation approach recognizes that misfortune and poor judgment often create a situation in which a debtor will never be able to pay his debts by his own efforts, or at least it will be very difficult to do so.

The second approach is to postpone the time of payment of debts or to reduce some of them to levels that make repayment possible. This approach is found in the reorganization sections for businesses and in the adjustment of debts provisions for municipalities and individuals with regular incomes. The reorganization and adjustment provisions are aimed at rehabiliation of debtors. These procedures, if utilized, prevent harassment of debtors and spare them undue hardship, while enabling most creditors eventually to obtain some repayment.

There are four types of bankruptcy proceedings, each identified by a chapter of the statute: Chapter 7, Liquidation; Chapter 9, Adjustment of Debts of a Municipality; Chapter 11, Reorganization; Chapter 13, Adjustment of Debts of an Individual with Regular Income. Chapter 9 adjustment proceedings recognize the financial plight of many governmental units such as New York City and Cleveland, Ohio. A municipal governmental entity may be a debtor under Chapter 9 if state law or a public official authorized by state law permits it. The municipality must be unable to meet its debts as they mature, and it must desire to effect a plan to adjust its debts. Because of the special and limited use of these proceedings, they will not be discussed further in this text.

2. Liquidation Proceedings

Liquidation proceedings are used to eliminate most of the debts of a debtor. In exchange for having the debts declared uncollectible, the debtor must allow many, if not most, of his assets to be used to satisfy creditors' claims. Cases under Chapter 7 may involve individuals, partnerships, or corporations, but only individuals may receive a discharge from the court. A discharge voids any judgment against the debtor to the extent that it creates a personal liability. A discharge covers all scheduled debts that arose before the date of the order for relief. It is irrelevant whether or not a claim was filed or allowed. A discharge also operates as an injunction against all attempts to collect the debt—by judicial proceedings, telephone calls, letters, personal contacts, or other efforts. Under all types of proceedings, once they are commenced, creditors are prohibited from attempting to collect their debts.

The debts of partnerships and corporations that go through liquidation proceedings are not discharged. These businesses are still technically liable for their debts; however, the lack of discharge is immaterial unless the partnership or corporation acquires assets later. This lack of discharge stops people from using "shell" businesses after bankruptcy for other purposes.

Certain businesses are denied the right to liquidation proceedings. Railroads, insurance companies, banks, savings and loan associations, homestead associations, and credit unions may not be debtors under Chapter 7. These organizations are subject to the jurisdiction of administrative agencies that handle all aspects of such organizations, including problems related to insolvency. Under this arrangement, there are alternative legal provisions for their liquidation.

Chapter 7 has special provisions relating to liquidation proceedings involving stockbrokers and commodity brokers. These special provisions are necessary to protect their customers, because bankruptcies of this kind usually involve large indebtedness and substantial assets. Stockbrokers and commodity brokers are subject only to Chapter 7. Chapter 11 and Chapter 13 proceedings are not available to them.

3. Reorganization Proceedings

Reorganization proceedings are utilized when debtors wish to restructure their finances and attempt to pay creditors over an extended time period, as required by a court-approved plan. Chapter 11 of the Bankruptcy Act contains detailed provisions on all aspects of the plan of reorganization and its execution. As soon as practicable after the order for relief, the court appoints a committee of creditors holding unsecured claims. The committee ordinarily consists of persons with the seven largest claims, and it may employ attorneys, accountants, or other agents to assist it. Working with the trustee and the debtor concerning the administration of the case, it represents the interests of the creditors. It may investigate the financial condition of the debtor and will assist in the formulation of the reorganization plan.

The court in reorganization cases will usually appoint a trustee before approval of the plan of reorganization. If the court does not appoint a trustee, it will appoint an examiner who conducts an investigation into the affairs of the debtor, including any mismanagement or irregularities.

After the trustee or the examiner conducts the investigation of the acts, conduct, assets, liabilities, financial conditions, and other relevant aspects of the debtor, a written report of this investigation is filed with the court. The trustee may file a plan of reorganization if the debtor does not, or it may recommend conversion of the case to liquidation proceedings. The trustee will also file tax returns for the debtor, file reports with the court, and may even operate the debtor's business unless the court orders otherwise. The debtor may file a plan of reorganization with the voluntary petition or later, in an attempt to extricate the business from its financial difficulties and help it to survive. The plan will classify claims, and all claims within a class will be treated the same. All unsecured claims for less than a specified amount may be classified together. The plan will designate those classes of claims that are unimpaired under the plan and will specify the treatment to be given claims that are impaired.

The plan must provide a means for its execution. It may provide that the debtor will retain all or part of the property of the estate. It may also propose that property be sold or transferred to creditors or other entities. Mergers and consolidations may be proposed. In short, the plan will deal with all aspects of the organization of the debtor, its property, and its debts. Some debts will be paid in full, some will be partially paid over an extended period of time, and others may not be paid at all. The only limitation is that all claimants must receive as much as they would receive in liquidation proceedings.

Holders of claims or interests in the debtor's property are allowed to vote and to accept or reject the proposed plan of reorganization. A class of claims has accepted a plan if at least two-thirds in amount and more than half in number of claims vote yes. Acceptance by a class of interests such as equity holders requires a two-thirds yes vote.

A hearing is held on the confirmation of a plan, to determine if it is fair and equitable. The statute specifies several conditions, such as good faith, which must be met before the plan is approved. Also before approval, it must be established that each holder of a claim or interest has either accepted the plan or will receive as much under the reorganization plan as would be received in liquidation proceedings. For secured creditors, this means that they will receive the value of their security either by payment or by delivery of the property. Confirmation of the plan makes it binding on the debtor, equity security holders, and creditors. Confirmation vests the property of the estate in the debtor and releases the debtor from any payment not specified in the reorganization plan.

As a general rule, any debtor subject to liquidation (Chapter 7) is also subject to reorganization (Chapter 11). An exception exists for railroads. The public interest in railroads prevents their liquidation, but the law recognizes that financial reorganization of railroads is not only possible but often desirable.

4. Adjustment of Individuals' Debts

Chapter 13 proceedings are used to adjust the debts of individuals with regular income whose debts are small enough and whose income is significant enough that substantial repayment is feasible. Such persons often seek to avoid the stigma of bankruptcy. Unsecured debts of individuals utilizing Chapter 13 proceedings cannot exceed $100,000, and the secured debts cannot exceed $350,000. Persons utilizing Chapter 13 are usually employees earning a salary, but persons engaged in business also qualify. Self-employed persons who incur trade debts are considered to be engaged in business.

The debtor files a plan that provides for the use of all or a portion of his future earnings or income for the payment of debts. The income is under the supervision and control of the trustee. Except as provided in the plan, the debtor keeps possession of his property. If the debtor is engaged in business, the debtor continues to operate the business. The plan must provide for the full payment of all claims entitled to priority unless the creditors with priority agree to a different treatment. If a plan divides unsecured claims into classes, all claims within a class must be given the same treatment.

Unsecured claims not entitled to priority may be repaid in full or reduced to a level not lower than the amount that would be paid upon liquidation. Since this amount is usually zero, any payment to unsecured creditors will satisfy the law. The secured creditors may be protected by allowing them to retain their lien, by payment of the secured claim in full, or by the surrender of the property to the secured claimant. The usual plan will provide for payments over 3 years, but the court may extend the payment period up to a total of 5 years. A typical plan allocates one-fourth of a person's take-home pay to repay debts.

The plan may modify the rights of holders of secured and unsecured claims, except that the rights of holders of real estate mortgages may not be modified. Claims arising after the filing of the petition may be included in the plan. This is a realistic approach, because all the debts of the debtor must be taken into account if the plan is to accomplish its objectives.

When the court conducts a hearing on the confirmation of the plan, if it is satisfied that the debtor will be able to make all payments to comply with it, the plan will be approved. Of course, the plan must be proposed in good faith, be in compliance with the law, and be in the best interest of the creditors.

As soon as the debtor completes all payments under the plan, the court grants the debtor a discharge of all debts, unless the debtor waives the discharge or the debts are not legally dischargeable. (See sections 8 and 9.)

Courts, after a hearing, may also grant a discharge, even though all payments have not been made, if the debtor's failure to complete the payments is due to circumstances for which the debtor should not justly be held accountable. In such cases, the payments under the plan must be not less than those which would have been paid on liquidation, and modification must not be practicable.[1]

5. Fresh Financial Start

PURPOSE OF
BANKRUPTCY

The basic concept underlying all bankruptcy laws has been to allow a debtor who is in a difficult financial situation a fresh financial start. In other words, the bankruptcy laws permit a deserving debtor the opportunity to come out from under overwhelming financial burdens and to begin anew the job of building financial security. However, this "fresh start" is not granted without the debtor's paying something for the opportunity. In essence, the bankruptcy laws always have attempted to balance the rights of the debtor with the rights of the creditors. In order to protect the creditors, the debtor must turn over his assets to the court. These assets become the property of the bankruptcy estate from which creditors' claims will be paid. However, to take every asset the debtor has would deprive that debtor the opportunity for a fresh financial start. Therefore, the debtor may

---

[1] Public Finance Corp. v. Freeman, p. 870.

exempt certain items from the bankruptcy estate and retain them as the basis for a new beginning.

As it was originally enacted, the 1978 act was criticized as being too pro-debtor. These criticisms were based mostly on the expansive federal exemptions given to the debtor. The 1984 amendments have narrowed these exemptions somewhat. The points discussed in section 7 below reflect the amended exemptions.

In addition to retaining exempt assets, the debtor also is benefited by having the creditors' unsatisfied claims discharged. However, once again, the law provides for a balance between the debtor and creditors. (Sections 8 and 9 describe circumstances under which debts will not be discharged.)

6. Property of the Estate

The *bankruptcy estate* consists of all legal or equitable interests of the debtor in property, wherever located. The property may be tangible or intangible and includes causes of action. All property is included in the estate to begin with, but the debtor may exempt portions entitled to exemption, as discussed in the next section.

The estate includes property that the trustee recovers by using his power to avoid prior transactions. It also includes property inherited by the debtor or received as a beneficiary of life insurance within 180 days of the petition. Proceeds, products, offspring, rents, and profits generated by or coming from property in the estate are also part of the estate.

In general, property acquired by the debtor after commencement of the case—including earnings from employment—belongs to the debtor. Property held in trust for the benefit of the debtor under a *spendthrift trust* does not become a part of the estate. In essence, the trustee in bankruptcy acquires the same interest with the same restrictions as the debtor had at the time the bankruptcy petition is filed. However, this trustee can require creditors to turn over possession of assets which are held by the creditors at the time the petition is filed.[2] In return, the *trustee* must provide adequate protection for these creditors' claims.

7. Exemptions

Technically, all property of the debtor becomes property of the bankruptcy estate, but an individual debtor is then permitted to claim some of it as exempt from the proceedings. That property is then returned to the debtor. Exemptions are granted by federal, state, and local laws. The 1978 Bankruptcy Act, as it has been amended, allows the following exemptions in the debtor's property:

1. Real property used as a residence, up to $7,500.
2. The debtor's interest, not to exceed $1,200, in one motor vehicle.
3. The debtor's interest, not to exceed $200 in any particular item or $4,000 in aggregate value, in household furnishings, wearing apparel,

---

[2] United States v. Whiting Pools, Inc., p. 871.

appliances, books, animals, crops, or musical instruments that are held primarily for the personal family or household use of the debtor and his dependents.

4. The debtor's interest in jewelry, not to exceed $500.

5. The debtor's interest in other property, not to exceed $400, plus up to $3,750 of any unused real property exemption.

6. The debtor's interest, not to exceed $750, in any implements, professional books, or tools of the trade of the debtor, or the trade of his dependents.

7. Unmatured life insurance contracts.

8. The cash value of life insurance, not to exceed $4,000.

9. Professionally prescribed health aids.

10. The debtor's rights to receive benefits such as social security, unemployment compensation, public assistance, disability benefits, alimony, child support and separate maintenance reasonably necessary, and payments of pension, profit-sharing, annuity, or similar plans.

11. The debtor's right to receive payment traceable to the wrongful death of an individual on whom the debtor was dependent or to life insurance on the life of such a person or to payments for personal injury not to exceed $7,500.

The 1984 amendments placed a cap of $4,000 on the total amount of household items that can be exempt. These amendments also restrict tenants to an additional amount of $3,750 when exempting personal property under exemption 5 above. Prior to this change, debtors who did not own a residence could use the entire real estate exemption of $7,500 (see exemption 1) to exempt additional personal property not exempted by another provision of the federal exemptions. Creditors have praised these amendments as a more equitable balance of debtors' and creditors' rights.

Every state has enacted statutes granting exemptions to debtors domiciled there, but these exemptions vary greatly from state to state. For example, some state exemptions exceed those provided by the federal bankruptcy laws. Other state exemptions are too small to give a debtor a real chance at a fresh financial start. Debtors may claim the larger exemptions offered by their state if it is to their advantage to do so. In order to encourage some states to raise their exemptions, the 1978 act provides that the federal exemptions will be available to debtors unless the state specifically passes a law denying its residents the federal exemptions. Over half of the states have adopted laws denying debtors the use of the federal exemptions; however, these states have substantially increased their own exemptions.

As a general rule, exempt property is not subject to any debts that arise before the commencement of the case. Exceptions to the general rule apply to tax claims, alimony, child support, and separate maintenance. Exempt property can be used to collect such debts after the proceeding. The discharge in bankruptcy does not prevent enforcement of valid liens against exempt property; however, judicial liens and nonpossessory, nonpurchase money security interests in household goods, wearing apparel, professional books, tools, and professionally prescribed health aids may be avoided. A debtor may redeem such tangible personal property from a lien securing a dischargeable consumer debt by paying the lien holder the amount of the secured claim. Exempt property is free of such liens after the proceedings. Waivers of exemptions are unenforceable, to prevent creditors from attempting to deny debtors the necessary property to gain a fresh start.

While exemptions are necessary to aid debtors in their financial fresh start, these exemptions generally must be narrowly applied so that the creditors' rights to payment can be balanced properly against the needs of the debtors.[3]

8. Debts That Are Not Discharged

Although the purpose of bankruptcy proceedings and especially those under Chapter 7 is to eliminate the debts of the debtor, not all debts are discharged. A discharge in bankruptcy does not discharge an individual debtor from the following debts:

1. Certain taxes and customs duties.
2. Debts for obtaining money, property, services, or credit by false pretenses, false representations, or actual fraud.
3. Consumer debts over $500 for luxury goods and services incurred within 40 days of the order of relief.
4. Cash advances over $1,000 that are extensions of consumer credit under an open end credit plan within 20 days of the order of relief.
5. Unscheduled debts.
6. Debts for fraud or defalcation while acting in a fiduciary capacity and debts created by embezzlement or larceny.
7. Alimony, child support, and separate maintenance.
8. Liability for willful and malicious torts.
9. Tax penalties if the tax is not dischargeable.
10. Student loans less than 5 years old.
11. Debts incurred as a result of an accident caused by driving while intoxicated.
12. Debts owed before a previous bankruptcy to which discharge was denied for grounds other than the 6-year rule.

The taxes that are not discharged are the same ones that receive priority under the second, third, and seventh categories discussed in Section 23 on priorities. If the debtor failed to file a return, filed it beyond its last due date, or filed a fraudulent return, those taxes are not discharged. One of the most common tax liabilities that is not discharged in bankruptcy is the one for unpaid withholding and social security taxes.

Items 3 and 4, which were added by the 1984 amendments, now prevent the debtor from going on a spending spree at creditors' expense just before filing a

---

[3] In re Clark, p. 873.

bankruptcy petition. The phrase "luxury goods and services" is defined as not including goods or services acquired for the support or maintenance of the debtor or his dependents.

For a debt to be denied discharge because of fraud, the creditor must have placed reasonable reliance on a false statement in writing. The denial of unscheduled debts means that the claim of any creditor who is not listed or who does not learn of the proceedings in time to file a claim is not discharged. The debtor, under such circumstances, remains liable for it unless he can prove that the creditor did have knowledge of the proceedings in time to file a claim. Proof of actual knowledge is required; and although such knowledge often exists, care should be taken to list all creditors, so that all claims will unquestionably be discharged.

Tort liability claims based on negligence are discharged. Tort liability claims arising from willful and malicious acts are not discharged. A judgment arising out of an assault and battery is not discharged. Reason 11 was added by the 1984 amendments. The logic behind making this tort liability nondischargeable indicates support in the battle to discourage drunk driving.

The provision generally denying discharge to student loans was added in the 1978 revision. It seeks to give creditors and the government 5 years to collect student loans. There is an exception if the debtor is able to convince the court that undue hardship on him and his dependents will result if the student loan debt is not discharged. If the debtor fails to prove the undue hardship caused by the student loan, a general discharge will not relieve the debtor of the obligation to pay that student loan.[4]

9. Grounds for Denying Discharge

A discharge in bankruptcy is a privilege, not a right. Therefore, in addition to providing that certain debts are not discharged, the Bankruptcy Act specifies the following grounds for denying an individual debtor a discharge:

1. Fraudulent transfers.
2. Inadequate records.
3. Commission of a bankruptcy crime.
4. Failure to explain a loss of assets or deficiency of assets.
5. Refusing to testify in the proceedings or to obey a court order.
6. Any of the above within 1 year in connection with another bankruptcy case of an insider.
7. Another discharge within 6 years.
8. Approval by the court of a waiver of discharge.

The first three grounds for denying discharge are predicated on wrongful conduct by the debtor in connection with the case. Fraudulent transfers involve acts such as removing, destroying, or concealing property with the intent to hinder, delay, or defraud creditors or the trustee. The conduct must occur within 1 year preceding the case, or it may occur after the case is commenced.

---

[4] Massachusetts Higher Education Assistance Corporation v. Taylor, p. 873.

A debtor is also denied a discharge if he has concealed, destroyed, mutilated, falsified, or failed to keep or preserve any books and records relating to his financial condition. A debtor is required to keep records from which his financial condition may be ascertained, unless the act or failure is justified.

Bankruptcy crimes are generally related to the proceedings. They include a false oath, the use or presentation of a false claim, or bribery in connection with the proceedings and with the withholding of records.

The 6-year rule, which allows a discharge only if another discharge has not been ordered within 6 years, extends to Chapter 11 and Chapter 13 proceedings, as well as to those under Chapter 7. Confirmation of a plan under Chapters 11 or 13 does not have the effect of denying a discharge within 6 years if all the unsecured claims were paid in full, or if 70 percent of them were paid and the debtor has used his best efforts to pay the debts.

Either a creditor or the trustee may object to the discharge. The court may order the trustee to examine the facts to see if grounds for the denial of the discharge exist. Courts are also granted the authority to revoke a discharge within 1 year if it was obtained by fraud on the court.

PROCEDURAL STEPS

10. Introduction

Chapter 3 of the 1978 Bankruptcy Reform Act is concerned with procedural aspects and administration of all types of bankruptcy cases, regardless under which chapter the case is filed. The provisions of Chapter 3 give guidance in how to and who can file a case, in how the automatic stay prohibits any action against the debtor, and in how creditors are informed of the debtor's status. These provisions are discussed in the next five sections. The most technical portion of Chapter 3 is entitled "administrative powers." These provisions grant the bankruptcy court and the trustee a wide range of powers to accomplish the purposes of the bankruptcy law. Sections 16 through 20 present a more detailed examination of these powers and duties.

11. Voluntary Commencement

A debtor may voluntarily instigate a bankruptcy case under any appropriate chapter by filing a petition with the bankruptcy court. In recognition of the fact that husbands and wives often owe the same debts, a joint case may be filed. A *joint case* is a voluntary one concerning a husband and wife, and it requires only one petition. The petition must be signed by both spouses, since one spouse cannot take the other into bankruptcy without the other's consent. Insolvency is not a condition precedent to any form of voluntary bankruptcy action.

All petitioners must pay a filing fee of $60, in installments if they prefer. Only one filing fee is required in a joint case. A petition filed by a partnership as a firm is not a petition on behalf of the partners as individuals. If they intend to obtain individual discharges, separate petitions are required.

The petition contains lists of secured and unsecured creditors, all property owned by the debtor, property claimed by the debtor to be exempt, and a statement of affairs of the debtor. The statement of affairs of a debtor engaged in business is much more detailed than the one filed by a debtor not in business. In general, the filing of a voluntary petition constitutes an order of relief indicating that the debtor is entitled to the bankruptcy court's protection. This concept of an automatic order of relief upon the debtor's filing caused creditors to argue that some debtors were filing voluntary petitions when the debtor did not need the court's protection. In 1984, Congress amended Chapter 7 to allow the bankruptcy judge, on his own initiative, to dismiss a case filed voluntarily if the debtor's obligations are primarily consumer debts and if the order of relief would be an abuse of the bankruptcy law. However, there is a presumption in favor of granting the relief requested by the debtor.

If the bankruptcy judge decides the petition was properly filed and an order of relief is effective, an interim trustee will be appointed. The roles of this trustee and the permanent one are discussed in sections 16 through 20.

12. Involuntary Commencement

Involuntary cases are commenced by one or more creditors filing a petition. If there are 12 or more creditors, the petition must be signed by at least 3 creditors whose unsecured claims are not contingent and aggregate at least $5,000. If there are fewer than 12 creditors, only one need sign the petition, but the $5,000 amount must still be met. Employees, insiders, and transferees of voidable transfers are not counted in determining the number of creditors. Insiders are persons such as relatives, partners of the debtor, directors and officers of the corporation involved. The subject of voidable transfers is discussed later in this chapter.

Creditors may commence involuntary proceedings in order to harass the debtor. To protect the debtor, the court may require the petitioning creditors to file a bond to indemnify the debtor. This bond will cover the amounts for which the petitioning creditors may have liability to the debtor. The liability may include court costs, attorney's fees, and damages caused by taking the debtor's property.

Until the court enters an order for relief in an involuntary case, the debtor may continue to operate his business and to use, acquire, and dispose of his property. However, the court may order an interim trustee appointed to take possession of the property and to operate the business. If the case is a liquidation proceeding, the appointment of the interim trustee is mandatory unless the debtor posts a bond guaranteeing the value of the property in his estate.

Since some debtors against whom involuntary proceedings are commenced are, in fact, not bankrupt, the debtor has a right to file an answer to the petition of the creditors and to deny the allegations of the petition. If the debtor does not file an answer, the court orders relief against the debtor. If an answer is filed, the court conducts a trial on the issues raised by the petition and the answer. A court will order relief in an involuntary proceeding against the debtor only if it finds that the debtor is generally not paying his debts as they become due. Insolvency in the balance sheet sense (liabilities exceeding assets) is not required. Relief may also be ordered if, within 120 days before the filing of the petition, a custodian, receiver, or agent has taken possession of property of the debtor for the purpose of enforcing a lien against the debtor.

The statute specifies which debtors under each chapter are subject to involuntary proceedings. Farmers and not-for-profit corporations are not subject to involuntary proceedings, under either Chapter 7 or Chapter 11. A *farmer* is defined as a person who receives more than 80 percent of gross income for the taxable year preceding the bankruptcy case from a farming operation he owns and operates. The term *farming operation* includes tillage of the soil; dairy farming; ranching; production or raising of crops, poultry, or livestock; and production of poultry or livestock products in an unmanufactured state.

Creditors also are prohibited from forcing any debtor into a Chapter 13 proceeding. The reason for this rule is that a Chapter 13 debtor is required to pay off his debts pursuant to an approved plan. To force an individual debtor to work to pay his debts is equivalent to involuntary servitude, which violates the Thirteenth Amendment of the Constitution.

13. Conversion of Cases

Because a case may be filed voluntarily or involuntarily under the various chapters, the issue arises as to whether the debtor or the creditors can convert a filing to another type of proceeding. If the original filing is under Chapter 7, the debtor can request a conversion to a Chapter 11 or 13 proceeding. Creditors can have a Chapter 7 case converted to Chapter 11, but not to Chapter 13. If the case was filed voluntarily as a Chapter 11 reorganization proceeding, the debtor may request that the case be converted to a Chapter 7 or 13 proceeding. However, if the Chapter 11 proceeding was begun involuntarily, the creditors must consent to a conversion to Chapter 7. Creditors may seek to convert a Chapter 11 proceeding to Chapter 7 as long as the debtor is neither a farmer nor a nonprofit corporation. Creditors cannot convert a case from Chapter 11 to Chapter 13 without the debtor's consent.

In general, a debtor may convert a Chapter 13 proceeding to Chapter 7 or 11, whichever is more appropriate. Creditors also may ask the court to convert a case filed under Chapter 13 to Chapter 7 or 11 unless that debtor is a farmer. If the debtor is a farmer, any conversion must be agreed to by that farmer before that conversion will occur.

14. Automatic Stay

Bankruptcy cases operate to *stay* other judicial or administrative proceedings against the debtor. These stays of proceedings may operate to the detriment of a creditor or third party. For example, a stay would prevent a utility company from shutting off service. Despite this potential harm to creditors, the stay automatically becomes applicable immediately upon the bankruptcy petition being filed.[5]

When the trustee continues to operate the debtor's business, it is frequently necessary to use, sell, or lease property of the debtor. In order to prevent irreparable harm to creditors and other third parties as a result of stays, a trustee may be required to provide "adequate protection" to third parties. In some cases,

---

[5] United Northwest Federal Credit Union v. Arens, p. 875.

adequate protection requires that the trustee make periodic cash payments to creditors. In others, the trustee may be required to provide a lien to the creditor. When the sale, lease, or rental of the debtor's property may decrease the value of an entity's interest in property held by the trustee, a creditor may be entitled to a lien on the proceeds of any sale, lease, or rental. The court is empowered to determine if the trustee has furnished adequate protection; and when the issue is raised, the burden of proof is on the trustee.

The automatic stay is designed to protect both debtor and creditor. The stay provides the debtor time and freedom from financial pressures to attempt repayment or to develop a plan of reorganization. Creditors are protected by the stay, since it forces them to comply with the orderly administration of the debtor's estate. In other words, the stay prevents some creditors from grabbing all the debtor's assets while other creditors receive nothing.

Despite these advantages of staying all proceedings against the debtor who files a bankruptcy petition, there are exceptions to the application of the automatic stay. These exceptions apply to proceedings that are not directly related to the debtor's financial situation. Proceedings that are not automatically stayed when a bankruptcy petition is filed include (1) criminal actions against the debtor; (2) the collection of alimony, maintenance, or support from property that is not part of the estate; and (3) the commencement or continuation of an action by a governmental unit to enforce that governmental unit's police power. Although these actions are not stayed automatically by the filing of a bankruptcy petition, the trust may seek to enjoin these actions if they harm the debtor's estate.

15. Meeting of Creditors

In a voluntary case, the debtor has filed the required schedules with the petition. In an involuntary case, if the court orders relief, the debtor will be required to complete the same schedules as the debtor in a voluntary proceeding. From this point, the proceedings are identical. All parties are given notice of the order for relief. If the debtor owns real property, notice is usually filed in the public records of the county where the land is situated. The notice to creditors will include the date by which all claims are to be filed, and the date of a meeting of the creditors with the debtor. This meeting of creditors must be within a reasonable time after the order for relief. The debtor appears at the meeting with the creditors, and the creditors are allowed to question the debtor under oath. The court may also order a meeting of any equity security holders of the debtor.

At the meeting of creditors, the debtor may be examined by the creditors to ascertain if property has been omitted from the list of assets, if property has been conveyed in defraud of creditors, and other matters that may affect the right of the debtor to have his obligations discharged.

In liquidation cases, the first meeting of creditors includes the important step of electing a *permanent trustee.* This trustee will replace the interim trustee appointed by the court at the time the order for relief was entered. The unsecured creditors who are not insiders elect this permanent trustee. To have a valid election, creditors representing at least 20 percent of the amount of unsecured claims held against the debtor must vote. The election is then determined by a majority of the unsecured creditors voting.

16. Trustee and the Estate

The trustee may be an individual or a corporation that has the capacity to perform the duties of a trustee. In a case under Chapter 7 or 13, an individual trustee must reside or have an office and the corporate trustee must have an office in the judicial district in which the case is pending or in an adjacent district. Prior to becoming a trustee in a particular case, the trustee must file with the court a bond in favor of the United States. This bond may be used as a source of collection if the trustee should fail to faithfully perform his duties.

The trustee is the representative of the estate and has the capacity to sue and to be sued. Trustees are authorized to employ professional persons such as attorneys, accountants, appraisers, and auctioneers and to deposit or invest the money of the estate during the proceedings. In making deposits or investments, the trustee must seek the maximum reasonable net return, taking into account the safety of the deposit or investment.

The statute has detailed provisions on the responsibilities of the trustee under the tax laws. As a general rule, the trustee has responsibility for filing tax returns for the estate. After the order for relief, income received by the estate is taxable to it and not to an individual debtor. The estate of a partnership or a corporation debtor is not a separate entity for tax purposes. While the technical requirements of the tax laws are beyond the scope of this text, it should be remembered that the bankruptcy laws contain detailed rules complementary to the Internal Revenue Code in bankruptcy cases, and both must be followed by the trustee.

17. Duties and Powers—In General

The statutory duties of the trustee in liquidation proceedings are to: (1) collect and reduce to money the property of the estate; (2) account for all property received; (3) investigate the financial affairs of the debtor; (4) examine proofs of claims and object to the allowance of any claim that is improper; (5) oppose the discharge of the debtor if advisable; (6) furnish information required by a party in interest; (7) file appropriate reports with the court and the taxing authorities, if a business is operated; and (8) make a final report and account and file it with the court.

A trustee that is authorized to operate the business of the debtor is authorized to obtain unsecured credit and to incur debts in the ordinary course of business. These debts are paid as administrative expenses.

A trustee in bankruptcy has several rights and powers with respect to the property of the debtor. First of all, the trustee has a judicial lien on the property, just as if the trustee were a creditor. Second, the trustee has the rights and powers of a judgment creditor who obtained a judgment against the debtor on the date of the adjudication of bankruptcy and who had an execution issued that was returned unsatisfied.

Third, the trustee has the rights of a bona fide purchaser of the real property of the debtor as of the date of the petition. Finally, the trustee has the rights of an actual unsecured creditor to avoid any transfer of the debtor's property and to avoid any obligation incurred by the debtor that is voidable under any federal or state law. As a result of these rights, the trustee is able to set aside transfers of property and to eliminate the interests of other parties where creditors or the debtor could do so.

The trustee also has the power to avoid certain liens of others on the property of the debtor. Liens that first become effective on the bankruptcy or insolvency of the debtor are voidable. As a general rule, liens that are not perfected or enforceable against a bona fide purchaser of the property are also voidable. Assume that a seller or creditor has an unperfected lien on goods in the hands of the debtor on the date the petition is filed. The lien is perfected later. That lien is voidable if it could not be asserted against a good-faith purchaser of the goods. Liens for rent and for distress for rent are also voidable.

The law imposes certain limitations on all these rights and powers of the trustee. A purchase-money security interest under Article 9 of the Code may be perfected after the petition is filed if it is perfected within 10 days of delivery of the property. Such a security interest cannot be avoided by the trustee if properly perfected.

The rights and powers of the trustee are subject to those of a seller of goods in the ordinary course of business who has the right to reclaim goods if the debtor was insolvent when the debtor received them. The seller must demand the goods back within 10 days, and the right to reclaim is subject to any superior rights of secured creditors. Courts may deny reclamation and protect the seller by giving his claim priority as an administrative expense.

18. Executory Contracts and Unexpired Leases

Debtors are frequently parties to contracts that have not been performed. Also, there are often lessees of real property, and the leases usually cover long periods of time. As a general rule, the trustee is authorized, subject to court approval, to assume or to reject an executory contract or unexpired lease. If the contract or lease is rejected, the other party has a claim subject to some statutory limitations. A rejection by the trustee creates a prepetition claim for the rejected contract or lease debt subject to these limitations.

If the contract or lease is assumed, the trustee will perform the contract or assign it to someone else, and the estate will presumably receive the benefits. If the trustee assumes a contract or lease, he must cure any default by the debtor and provide adequate assurance of future performance. In shopping-center leases, adequate assurance includes protection against declines in percentage rents and preservation of the tenant mix, among other things.

A trustee may not assume an executory contract that requires the other party to make a loan, deliver equipment, or issue a security to the debtor. A party to a contract based on the financial strength of the debtor is not required to extend new credit to a debtor in bankruptcy.

Contracts and leases often have clauses prohibiting assignment. The law also prohibits the assignment of certain contract rights, such as those which are personal in nature. The trustee in bankruptcy is allowed to assume contracts, notwithstanding a clause prohibiting the assumption or assignment of the contract or lease. The trustee is not allowed to assume a contract if applicable nonbankruptcy law excuses the other party from performance to someone other than the debtor, unless the other party consents to the assumption.

The statute invalidates contract clauses that automatically terminate contracts or leases upon filing of a petition in bankruptcy or upon the assignment of the lease or contract. The law also invalidates contract clauses that give a party other than the debtor the right to terminate the contract upon assumption by the trustee or assignment by the debtor. Such clauses hamper rehabilitation efforts and are against public policy. They are not needed, because the court can require the trustee to provide adequate protection and can insure that the other party receives the benefit of its bargain.

Debtors are sometimes lessors instead of lessees. If the trustee rejects an unexpired lease of a debtor lessor, the tenant may treat the lease as terminated or may remain in possession for the balance of the lease. There is a similar provision for contract purchasers of real estate. They may treat the rejection as a termination, or they may remain in possession and make the payments due under the contract. A purchaser that treats a contract as terminated has a lien on the property to the extent of the purchase price paid.

If the trustee assigns a contract to a third party and the third party later breaches the contract, the trustee has no liability. This is a change of the common law in which an assignor is not relieved of his liability by an assignment. An assignment by a trustee in bankruptcy is, in effect, a novation if the assignment is valid.

In 1984, the United States Supreme Court held that the trustee's power gave the trustee the right to terminate employees who were working under a collective bargaining contract. Unions were so upset by this ruling that they convinced Congress the court's decision had to be changed by legislation. Indeed, the union's efforts were a major reason that the 1984 amendments were passed by Congress and signed by President Reagan. When an employer files a petition under Chapter 11, the amended law requires the trustee to apply to the court to reject the collective bargaining contract. After the application is filed, the trustee and the employees' representative must negotiate about how the collective bargaining contract can be changed to allow the debtor-employer to reorganize successfully. If these negotiations are unsuccessful in reaching a mutual agreement, the trustee may seek the bankruptcy court's approval to reject the collective bargaining contract. The court must conduct a hearing within 14 days after the trustee filed an application to reject the contract. The court's ruling on this application must be announced within 30 days of the hearing.

19. Voidable Preferences

One of the goals of bankruptcy proceedings is to provide an equitable distribution of a debtor's property among his creditors. To achieve this goal, the trustee in bankruptcy is allowed to recover transfers that constitute a preference of one creditor over another. As one judge said, "A creditor who dips his hand in a pot which he knows will not go round must return what he receives, so that all may share." To constitute a recoverable preference the transfer must (1) have been made by an insolvent debtor; (2) have been made to a creditor for, or on account of, an antecedent debt owed by the debtor before the transfer; (3) have been made within 90 days of the filing of the bankruptcy petition; and (4) enable the creditor to receive a greater percentage of his claim than he would receive under a distribution from the bankruptcy estate in a liquidation proceeding.

Insofar as the time period is concerned, there is an exception when the transfer is to an insider. Then, the trustee may avoid the transfer if it occurred within one year of the date of filing the petition, provided the insider had reasonable cause to believe the debtor was insolvent at the time of the transfer.

A debtor is presumed to be insolvent during the 90-day period prior to the filing of the petition. Any person contending that the debtor was solvent has the burden of coming forward with evidence to prove solvency. Once credible evidence is introduced, the party with the benefit of the presumption of insolvency has the burden of persuasion on the issue.

Recoverable preferences include not only payments of money but also the transfer of property as payment of, or as security for, a prior indebtedness. Since the law is limited to debts, payments by the debtor of tax liabilities are exempt from the preference provision and are not recoverable. A mortgage or pledge may be set aside as readily as direct payments. A pledge or mortgage can be avoided if received within the immediate 90-day period prior to the filing of the petition in bankruptcy, provided it was obtained as security for a previous debt. The effective date of a transfer or a mortgage of real property may be questioned if the date the legal documents are signed is different from the date these documents are recorded. A logical solution to this potential problem seems to be to rely on the date the document is recorded in the public records.[6]

Payment of a fully secured claim does not constitute a preference and therefore may not be recovered. Transfers of property for a contemporaneous consideration may not be set aside, because there is a corresponding asset for the new liability. A mortgage given to secure a contemporaneous loan is valid even when the mortgagee took the security with knowledge of the debtor's insolvency. An insolvent debtor has a right to attempt to extricate himself, as far as possible, from his financial difficulty. If the new security is personal property, it must be perfected within ten days after the security interest attaches. The trustee's power to avoid a preference does not apply in a case filed by an individual debtor whose debts are primarily consumer debts if the aggregate value of the property subject to the preferential transfer is less than $600.

The law also creates an exception for transfers in the ordinary course of business or in the ordinary financial affairs of persons not in business. The payment of such debts within 45 days after they are incurred is not recoverable if the payment is made in the ordinary course of business. This exception covers ordinary debt payments such as utility bills. The law on preferences is directed at unusual transfers and payments, not those occurring promptly in the ordinary course of the debtor's affairs.

---

[6] In re Brown Iron & Metal, Inc., p. 876.

20. Fraudulent Transfers

A transfer of property by a debtor may be fraudulent under federal or state law. The trustee may proceed under either to set aside a fraudulent conveyance. Under federal law, a fraudulent conveyance is a transfer within one year of the filing of the petition, with the intent to hinder, delay, or defraud creditors. Under state law, the period may be longer and is usually within the range of 2 to 5 years.

Fraudulent intent may be inferred from the fact that the consideration is unfair, inadequate, or nonexistent. Solvency or insolvency at the time of the transfer is significant, but it is not controlling. Fraudulent intent exists when the transfer makes it impossible for the creditors to be paid in full or for the creditors to use legal remedies that would otherwise be available.

The intent to hinder, delay, or defraud creditors may also be implied. Such is the case when the debtor is insolvent and makes a transfer for less than a full and adequate value. Fraudulent intent is present if the debtor was insolvent on the date of the transfer or if the debtor becomes insolvent as a result of the transfer.

If the debtor is engaged in business or is about to become so, the fraudulent intent will be implied when the transfer leaves the businessperson with an unreasonably small amount of capital. The businessperson may be solvent; nevertheless, he has made a fraudulent transfer if the net result of the transfer leaves him with an unreasonably small amount of capital, provided the transfer was without fair consideration. Whether or not the remaining capital is unreasonably small is a question of fact.

The trustee may also avoid a transfer made in contemplation of incurring obligations beyond the debtor's ability to repay as they mature. Assume that a woman is about to enter business and that she plans to incur debts in the business. Because of her concern that she may be unable to meet these potential obligations, she transfers all her property to her husband, without consideration. Such a transfer may be set aside as fraudulent. The requisite intent is supplied by the factual situation at the time of the transfer and the state of mind of the transferor. The actual financial condition of the debtor in such a case is not controlling but does shed some light on the intent factor and state of mind of the debtor.

The trustee of a partnership debtor may avoid transfers of partnership property to partners if the debtor was or thereby became insolvent. This rule was made to prevent a partnership's preferring partners who are also creditors over other partners. Such transfers may be avoided if they occurred within 1 year of the date of filing the petition.

If a transferee is liable to the trustee only because the transfer was to defraud creditors, the law limits the transferee's liability. To the extent that the transferee does give value in good faith, the transferee has a lien on the property. For the purpose of defining value in the fraudulent transfer situation, the term includes property or the satisfaction or securing of a present or existing debt. It does not include an unperformed promise to support the debtor or a relative of a debtor.

CREDITORS

21. Creditors and Claims

Creditors are required to file proof of their claims if they are to share in the debtor's estate. Filed claims are allowed unless a party in interest objects. If an objection is filed, the court conducts a hearing to determine the validity of the claim. A claim may be disallowed if it is: (1) unenforceable because of usury, unconscionability, or failure of consideration, (2) for unmatured interest, (3) an insider's or attorney's and exceeds the reasonable value of the services rendered, (4) for unmatured alimony or child support, (5) for rent, and (6) for breach of an employment contract. These latter two claims may be disallowed to the extent that they exceed the statutory limitations for such claims.

Illegality can be raised, because any defense available to the debtor is available to the trustee. Postpetition interest is not collectible, because interest stops accruing at the date of filing the petition. Bankruptcy operates as an acceleration of the principal due. From the date of filing, the amount of the claim is the total principal plus interest to that date.

Unreasonable attorney's fees and claims of insiders are disallowed because they encourage concealing assets or returning them to the debtor. Since alimony claims are not dischargeable in bankruptcy, there is no reason to allow a claim for postpetition alimony and child support.

The amount of rent that may be included in a claim is limited. The law is designed to compensate the landlord for his loss, but not to allow the claim to be so large that other creditors will not share in the estate. A landlord's damages are limited to the rent for the greater of 1 year or 15 percent of the remaining lease term, not to exceed 3 years. In liquidation cases, the time is measured from the earlier of the date of filing the petition and the date of surrender of possession. In cases filed under Chapters 9, 11, and 13, the claim is limited to 3 years' rent. Of course, these limitations are not applicable to rent owed by the trustee, an administrative expense for which the estate is liable.

Landlords often have a security deposit for rent. To the extent that the security deposit exceeds the rent allowed as a claim, it must be paid over to the trustee to be a part of the bankruptcy estate. If the security deposit is less than the claim, the landlord keeps the security deposit, and it will be applied in satisfaction of the claim. The limitations on claims for rent are applicable to bona fide leases, not to leases of real property, which are financing or security leases.

The limitation for damages resulting from termination of employment contracts is similar to the one for rent. Damages are limited to compensation for the year following the earlier of the date of the petition and that of the termination of employment.

Claims are sometimes contingent or otherwise unliquidated and uncertain. The law authorizes the court to estimate and to fix the amount of such claims, if necessary, to avoid undue delay in closing the estate. The same is true for equitable remedies such as specific performance. Courts will convert such remedies to dollar amounts and proceed to close the estate.

If a secured claim is undersecured—that is, if the debt exceeds the value of the collateral—the claim is divided into two parts. The claim is secured to the extent of the value of the collateral. It is an unsecured claim for the balance.

22. Right of Setoffs

Any person owing money to the debtor may set off against the amount owed any sum that the debtor owes him, provided such amount would be allowable as a claim. To the extent of this setoff, he becomes a preferred creditor, but he is legally entitled to this preference. This, however, does not apply when the claim against the debtor has been purchased or created for the purpose of preferring the creditor. Assume that a bank has lent a debtor $2,000 and that the debtor has $1,500 on deposit at the time of bankruptcy. The bank is a preferred creditor to the extent of the deposit. This setoff will be allowed unless the evidence discloses that the deposit was made for the purpose of preferring the bank. In that case, the deposit becomes a part of the debtor's estate because of the collusion.

Since the filing of the petition in bankruptcy operates as a stay of all proceedings, the right of setoff operates at the time of final distribution of the estate. Since the law allows the trustee to use the funds of the debtor with court approval, parties who wish to exercise the right of setoff should seek "adequate protection."

The right of setoff will usually be exercised by a creditor against a deposit that has been made within 90 days of the filing of a petition in bankruptcy. Quite frequently, there are several such deposits, and there also may have been several payments on the debt during the 90-day period. As a result of these variables, the application of offset principles is sometimes difficult.

The law seeks to prohibit a creditor from improving his position during the 90-day period. It does so by allowing the trustee to recover that portion of the setoff which would be considered a preference. This amount recoverable by the trustee is the insufficiency between the amount owed and the amount on deposit on the first day of the 90-day period preceding the filing of a bankruptcy petition that a deficiency occurred to the extent that this insufficiency is greater than the insufficiency existing on the day the petition is filed. If the deposit on first day of the preceding 90-day period exceeds the creditor's claim, look for the first insufficiency during the 90-day period and calculate the setoff based on the first insufficiency.

Assume that a bankruptcy petition was filed on September 2. Throughout the 90 days prior to this filing, the debtor owes $2,000 to the creditor. On June 4, the debtor has on deposit with the creditor $1,500. On July 15, the amount on deposit is reduced to $700. On September 1, the debtor's balance is increased to $1,800. At the time of the filing, the creditor seeks to use the entire $1,800 on deposit to set off its claim against the debtor. The trustee would be able to recover $300 of this attempted setoff, since there was a greater insufficiency of that amount on the first day of the 90-day period prior to the petition's being filed. In other words, the creditor's setoff would be limited to $1,500.

23. Priorities

The bankruptcy law establishes certain priorities in the payment of claims. After secured creditors have had the opportunity to benefit from a security interest in collateral, the general order of priority is as follows:

1. Claims as administrative expenses.
2. Claims of involuntary GAP creditors.
3. Claims as wages, salaries, and commissions.
4. Claims as contributions to employee benefit plans.

5. Claims against debtors who operate either a grain storage facility or a fish produce storage or processing facility.

6. Claims as consumer deposits.

7. Claims by governmental units for certain taxes.

Administrative expenses include all costs of administering the debtor's estate, including taxes incurred by the estate. Typical costs include attorney's fees, appraiser's fees, and wages paid to persons employed to help preserve the estate.

The term *involuntary GAP creditor* describes a person who extends credit to the estate after the filing of an involuntary petition under Chapter 11 and before a trustee is appointed or before the order for relief is entered. Such claims include taxes incurred as the result of the conduct of business in this period.

The third class of priority is limited to amounts earned by an individual within 90 days of the filing of the petition or the cessation of the debtor's business, whichever occurred first. The priority is limited to $2,000 for each individual, but it includes vacation, severance, and sick leave pay as well as regular earnings. The employee's share of employment taxes is included in the third priority category, provided the wages and the employee's share of taxes have been paid in full. The category does not include fees paid to independent contractors.

The fourth priority recognizes that fringe benefits are an important part of many labor-management contracts. The priority is limited to claims for contributions to employee benefit plans, arising from services rendered within 120 days before commencement of the case or cessation of the debtor's business, whichever occurs first. The priority is limited to $2,000 multiplied by the number of employees less the amount paid under priority 3. The net effect is to limit the total priority for wages and employee benefits to $2,000 per employee.

The fifth priority was included in the 1984 amendments. It is designed to protect the farmer who raises grain and the fisherman if their grain or fish are held by the owner of a production or storage facility. If the farmers or fishermen have not been paid for the grain or fish transferred, they have a priority claim to the extent of $2,000 per creditor.

The sixth priority was added in 1978 as an additional method of consumer protection. It protects consumers who have deposited money in connection with the purchase, lease, or rental of property or the purchase of services for personal, family, or household use that were not delivered or provided. The priority is limited to $900 per consumer.

The seventh priority is for certain taxes. Priority is given to income taxes for a taxable year that ended on or before the date of filing the petition. The last due date of the return must have occurred not more than three years before the filing. Employment taxes and transfer taxes such as gift, estate, sale, and excise taxes are also given sixth-class priority. Again the transaction or event that gave rise to the tax must precede the petition date, and the return must have been due within 3 years. The bankruptcy law has several very technical aspects relating to taxation, and they must be reviewed carefully for tax returns filed by the trustee and claims for taxes.

In liquidation cases, the property available is first distributed among the priority claimants in the order just discussed. Then the property is distributed to general unsecured creditors who file their claims on time. Next, payment is made to unsecured creditors who tardily file their claims. Thereafter distribution is made to holders of penalty, forfeiture, or punitive damage claims. Punitive penalties, including tax penalties, are subordinated to the first three classes of claims, as a matter of policy. Regular creditors should be paid before windfalls to persons and entities collecting penalties. Finally, postpetition interest on prepetition claims is paid if any property is available to do so. After the interest is paid, any surplus goes to the debtor. Claims within a particular class are paid pro rata if the trustee is unable to pay them in full.

SUMMARY

Introduction	1. Of major importance today is the Bankruptcy Reform Act of 1978 as it has been amended through 1984.
	2. Terms to remember include debtor, claim, order of relief, and trustee.

TYPES OF PROCEEDINGS

In general	1. The bankruptcy law has two basic approaches to resolving a debtor's financial problems—one is liquidation and the other is reorganization.
Liquidation	1. This proceeding is governed by Chapter 7.
	2. In general, a debtor surrenders all assets from which creditors are paid as much as possible.
	3. Individual debtors generally have all unpaid debts discharged or forgiven. Technically, a business organization's debts are not discharged.
Reorganization	1. This proceeding is governed by Chapter 11.
	2. In essence, the debtor attempts to restructure the financial situation so that creditors can be substantially paid over time.
	3. The key to a successful reorganization is the court's approval of a reasonable confirmation plan.
Adjustment of individual's debts	1. This proceeding is governed by Chapter 13.

2. The debtor must be an individual who has regular income and who has unsecured debts not exceeding $100,000 and secured debts not exceeding $350,000.

3. Again, a plan of repayment must be approved. The unsecured creditors must receive at least as much as they would under a Chapter 7 liquidation proceeding.

PURPOSE OF BANKRUPTCY

In general	1. The basic purpose of the bankruptcy law is to give a debtor in financial difficulty an opportunity to overcome these difficulties.
	2. Balanced against the debtor's need for a fresh start is the creditors' right to payment.
	3. In essence, the bankruptcy law attempts to strike a balance between the rights and duties of the debtor and creditors.
Property of the estate	1. All the property interests of a debtor are used to create an estate.
	2. The trustee, in essence, has whatever interests a debtor had at the time a bankruptcy petition was filed.
Exemptions	1. To enhance the debtor's fresh start, the debtor may exempt certain property from the estate.
	2. These exemptions are governed by either federal or state law, whichever the state provides.
Dischargeability of debts	1. Certain debts are not discharged; therefore, they survive the bankruptcy case and remain payable to the creditor.
	2. There also are grounds for denying a discharge.
	3. Basically, in its balancing process, the drafters of the law decided that debts created in certain situations should not be forgiven.

PROCEDURAL STEPS

Beginning the case	1. Any proceeding may be started by a debtor filing a petition in bankruptcy.

	2. The voluntary filing acts as an order of relief unless the bankruptcy judge decides that a consumer debtor is not entitled to Chapter 7 protection.
	3. In general, cases may also be started by creditors with at least $5,000 in claims filing a petition. This creditor-commenced action is known as an involuntary case.
	4. In an involuntary case, the bankruptcy judge must decide whether an order of relief is appropriate.
	5. An involuntary case cannot be filed under Chapter 13 regardless of who the debtor is. And an involuntary case under Chapters 7 and 11 cannot be filed when the debtor is a farmer or a nonprofit corporation.
Automatic stay	**1.** The filing of a bankruptcy petition protects the debtor against any action taken by creditors.
	2. This stay is automatic even before the creditors learn of the petition's being filed.
	3. The stay remains in effect until the bankruptcy judge permits actions by creditors.
Meeting of creditors	**1.** After the order of relief is entered, a meeting of the creditors will be scheduled. At this meeting, creditors can question the debtor and examine documents.
	2. Also at this meeting, unsecured creditors will elect a permanent trustee.

TRUSTEE AND CASE ADMINISTRATION

Trustee and the estate	**1.** The trustee must satisfy statutory prerequisites before he, she, or it is qualified.
	2. The trustee has the responsibility to preserve the estate for the benefit of all creditors.
	3. The trustee must fulfill the administrative duties with regard to taxes and similar matters.
	4. In general, the trustee is a fiduciary of the estate.

General duties and powers	1. The trustee may employ professionals in representing the estate. The trustee also may sue and be sued in a representative capacity.
	2. The trustee has several statutory duties designed to ensure the proper workings of the bankruptcy law.
	3. The trustee may operate the business of the debtor and may incur expenses associated with such an operation.
	4. The trustee may assume the position of a lienholder or a good-faith purchaser if such positions enhance the estate.
	5. The trustee also may avoid certain liens on the debtor's property.
Power to avoid agreements	1. The trustee has the general power to perform or avoid executory contracts and unexpired leases, regardless of what the agreement may state about the debtor's right to assign.
	2. The trustee's power to avoid or modify a collective bargaining contract has been limited, but not removed, by the 1984 amendments.
Power to avoid preferences	1. In order to keep all creditors on an equal basis, the trustee can avoid any transfer or payment to a creditor if such was made within 90 days of the petition being filed, if such was made to satisfy all or part of antecedent debts, if such was made while the debtor was insolvent, and if such was indeed a preference.
	2. The debtor is presumed to be insolvent during the 90 days prior to the petition's being filed.
	3. If the preferred creditor is an insider, the time period of concern is 1 year, not 90 days, before the petition was filed.
Power to avoid fraudulent transfers	1. A transfer of property may be fraudulent under either federal or state law.
	2. In general, any transfer within a statutory time period prior to the filing of a bankruptcy petition is fraudulent if the debtor intended to hinder, delay, or defraud creditors.
	3. The trustee has the power to declare these transfers invalid in order to protect the estate for the creditors' benefit.

CREDITORS

Claims	1. Creditors must be able to prove their claims in order to be paid from the debtor's estate.
	2. There are numerous reasons why a claim may be disallowed altogether or otherwise limited.
Right of setoffs	1. Because the debtor may have a claim against the creditor, that creditor can set off the amount owed to the debtor against the claims the creditor makes on the debtor's estate.
	2. This setoff must not give an unreasonable preference to the creditor. The trustee will examine all events during the 90 days prior to the filing of the bankruptcy in order to determine the proper amount of the setoff.
Priorities	1. The creditors' claims are subject to payment according to the priority established by the bankruptcy law.
	2. Seven categories of priority claims must be paid before the first general unsecured creditor's claim is paid.

CASES

Public Finance Corp. v. Freeman
712 F.2d 219 (5th Cir. 1983)

POLITZ, J. Public Finance Corporation, an unsecured creditor, objected to the debtors' plan proposed by Eddie and Angela Freeman pursuant to Chapter 13 of the Bankruptcy Code. The bankruptcy court's approval of the plan was affirmed by the district court. Public Finance appeals.

The Freemans' petition reflects a combined monthly income of $1,304, and monthly expenses of the debtors and their eight-year-old daughter of $988. The secured creditors are to be paid in full. The debtors propose to make monthly payments of $147.51 into the Chapter 13 plan, scheduling pay-

ment in full to First National Bank and Merchants and Planters Bank, creditors on co-signed promissory notes. No payment is proposed for the other unsecured creditors, including Public Finance which filed a proof of claim for $2,176.80.

Public Finance objected on the grounds that the plan failed to meet the good faith requirement . . . and discriminated against creditors of the same class. . . . The bankruptcy judge concluded that the plan was filed in good faith and that the unsecured creditors would receive nothing if the debtors' estate were liquidated under Chapter 7.

The bankruptcy judge also found that the requisites for confirmation of a plan . . . had been met and that the plan was consistent with the provisions . . . which require "the same treatment for each claim within a particular class." The bankruptcy court's findings of fact are not clearly erroneous. . . .

Good Faith

Section 1325(a)(3) requires that the plan be "proposed in good faith." . . . Public Finance suggests that good faith exists only when the debtor proposes payment to all unsecured creditors. It argues that a good faith proposal would also avoid differentiation in the treatment accorded unsecured creditors. This argument poses the inherent inquiry whether any plan may be considered in good faith if it does not provide for payment to all creditors, and if so, how much?

We agree with our colleagues of the Ninth Circuit that good faith does not necessarily require substantial repayment of the unsecured claims. Congress addressed only the minimum payment permitted, doing so explicitly in §1325(a)(4) by directing that the amount to be paid on each unsecured claim cannot be "less than the amount that would be paid on such claim if the estate of the debtor were liquidated under Chapter 7." . . . [W]e consider the existence of this explicit statutory standard sufficient grounds to reject the suggestion that by prescribing the good faith requirement Congress implicitly intended a more rigorous standard.

We underscore that we do not examine a plan which proposes no repayment at all. The Freemans propose to pay the secured creditors and the unsecured creditors holding co-signed promissory notes. . . .

We are persuaded that the phrase "proposed in good faith" must be viewed in light of the totality of the circumstances surrounding confection of a given Chapter 13 plan. This analysis must be accomplished mindful of the purpose of the Bankruptcy Code and its legislative predecessors. Debtors are to be given a reasonable opportunity to make a fresh start. Debtors proposing some payment under Chapter 13 are not to be treated more harshly than those opting for a Chapter 7 liquidation.

In the instant case the bankruptcy judge found that the unsecured creditors would receive nothing in a liquidation under Chapter 7. . . . It is not clearly erroneous. The judges also found that the plan proposed by the Freemans was reasonable and that the Freemans could be expected to maintain the payment schedule outlined. These findings are not clearly erroneous on the record before us.

The bankruptcy judge was in a position to determine whether the Freemans were making a reasonable proposal consistent with the realities of the distressful economic situation in which they found themselves. He could best assess whether their proposal constituted a reasonable repayment effort or was an attempt to abuse the spirit of the Bankruptcy Code. He concluded that the Freeman proposal met the requirements of §1325. We agree.

Discriminatory Treatment

Public Finance complains that the proposed plan is not consistent with §1322, which requires that all claims in a particular class be accorded the same treatment. The Freemans propose to pay First National Bank and Merchants and Planters Bank in full while providing no payment to other unsecured creditors. These named creditors hold co-signed notes. Their position differs from the other unsecured creditors, with the concomitant effect that difference has on the debtors. Under §1322(b)(1), these creditors may be designated as members of a separate class. Thereafter, §1322(a)(3) requires only that all claims in each class be accorded identical treatment. Different classes may be treated differently. The proposed plan conforms to this requirement.

Affirmed.

United States v. Whiting Pools, Inc.
103 S.Ct. 2309 (1983)

Whiting Pools, Inc., sold, installed and serviced swimming pools. When the corporation became obligated for $92,000 in FICA taxes, the IRS seized all of the corporation's tangible personal property. The estimated liquidation value of the property seized was $35,000 at most, but its estimated going concern value in Whiting's hands was $162,876. One day after the seizure, Whiting filed a Chapter 11 bankruptcy petition. The Bankruptcy

Court ruled that the seized assets were property of the debtor's estate. It ordered the IRS to turn the property over to the bankruptcy trustee on the condition that the trustee provide the IRS with protection for its interests. The District Court reversed, but the Court of Appeals in turn reversed the District Court. The Supreme Court granted certiorari in order to review what becomes the property of the debtor estate.

BLACKMUN, J. . . . By virtue of its tax lien, the Service holds a secured interest in Whiting's property. We first examine whether §542(a) of the Bankruptcy Code generally authorizes the turnover of a debtor's property seized by a secured creditor prior to the commencement of reorganization proceedings. Section 542(a) requires an entity in possession of "property that the trustee may use, sell, or lease . . ." to deliver that property to the trustee. . . .

In proceedings under the reorganization provisions of the Bankruptcy Code, a troubled enterprise may be restructured to enable it to operate successfully in the future. Until the business can be reorganized pursuant to a plan, . . . the trustee or debtor-in-possession is authorized to manage the property of the estate and to continue the operation of the business. By permitting reorganization, Congress anticipated that the business would continue to provide jobs, to satisfy creditors' claims, and to produce a return for its owners. Congress presumed that the assets of the debtor would be more valuable if used in a rehabilitated business than if "sold for scrap." The reorganization effort would have small chance of success, however, if property essential to running the business were excluded from the estate. Thus, to facilitate the rehabilitation of the debtor's business, all the debtor's property must be included in the reorganization estate.

This authorization extends even to property of the estate in which a creditor has a secured interest. Although Congress might have safeguarded the interests of secured creditors outright by excluding from the estate any property subject to a secured interest, it chose instead to include such property in the estate and to provide secured creditors with "adequate protection" for their interests. At the secured creditor's insistence, the bankruptcy court must place such limits or conditions on the trustee's power to sell, use, or lease property as are necessary to protect the creditor. The creditor with a secured interest in property included in the estate must look to this provision for protection, rather than to the nonbankruptcy remedy of possession.

Both the congressional goal of encouraging reorganizations and Congress' choice of methods to protect secured creditors suggest that Congress intended a broad range of property to be included in the estate.

The statutory language reflects this view of the scope of the estate. . . . [Section] 541(a) provides that the "estate is comprised of all the following property, wherever located: . . . all legal or equitable interests of the debtor in property as of the commencement of the case." . . . Most important, in the context of this case, §541(a)(1) is intended to include in the estate any property made available to the estate by other provisions of the Bankruptcy Code. Several of these provisions bring into the estate property in which the debtor did not have a possessory interest at the time the bankruptcy proceedings commenced.

Section 542(a) is such a provision. It requires an entity (other than a custodian) holding any property of the debtor that the trustee can use to turn that property over to the trustee. Given the broad scope of the reorganization estate, property of the debtor repossessed by a secured creditor falls within this rule, and therefore may be drawn into the estate. . . .

As does all bankruptcy law, §542(a) modifies the procedural rights available to creditors to protect and satisfy their liens. In effect, §542(a) grants to the estate a possessory interest in certain property of the debtor that was not held by the debtor at the commencement of reorganization proceedings. The Bankruptcy Code provides secured creditors various rights, including the right to adequate protection, and these rights replace the protection afforded by possession.

This interpretation of §542(a) is supported by the section's legislative history. Although the legislative reports are silent on the precise issue before us, the House and Senate hearings from which §542(a) emerged provide guidance. Several witnesses at those hearings noted, without contradiction, the need for a provision authorizing the turnover of property of the debtor in the possession of secured creditors. Section 542(a) first appeared in the proposed legislation shortly after these hearings.

The section remained unchanged through subsequent versions of the legislation.

We conclude that the reorganization estate includes property of the debtor that has been seized by a creditor prior to the filing of a petition for reorganization.

We see no reason why a different result should obtain when the IRS is the creditor. The Service is bound by §542(a) to the same extent as any other secured creditor. The Bankruptcy Code expressly states that the term "entity," used in §542(a), includes a governmental unit. Moreover, Congress carefully considered the effect of the new Bankruptcy Code on tax collection and decided to provide protection to tax collectors, such as the IRS, through grants of enhanced priorities for unsecured tax claims and by the nondischarge of tax liabilities. . . . Nothing in the Bankruptcy Code or its legislative history indicates that Congress intended a special exception for the tax collector in the form of an exclusion from the estate of property seized to satisfy a tax lien.

The judgment of the Court of Appeals is affirmed.

So ordered.

In re Clark
711 F.2d 21 (3d Cir. 1983)

GIBBONS, J. Robert H. Clark, a discharged debtor, appeals from a final order of the Bankruptcy Court for the District of New Jersey denying his claim for exemption of $17,466 in his Keogh retirement plan. The appeal is to this court by agreement of the parties. . . .

On September 18, 1981, Clark, a 43-year old licensed family therapist, filed a Chapter 7 petition in bankruptcy and claimed an exemption for his Keogh retirement plan. Contributions to such a plan are tax-deductible, and income tax on the fund and its earnings is deferred until withdrawn. Funds may be withdrawn when a participant becomes 59½, dies, or is disabled. If funds are withdrawn before these events, the participant must pay a penalty tax of 10% in addition to regular income taxes, and is barred from making contributions to the plan for five years.

Thomas J. O'Neill, the interim trustee, filed an objection to the claimed exemption, and Clark filed a complaint against the trustee seeking a denial of the objection. The bankruptcy court noted that the case involved only the issue of exemption; not whether the fund was property of the bankruptcy estate. The court agreed with the trustee that because Clark had no present right to receive payments from the plan, his exemption claim did not fall within the literal terms of section 522(d)(10)(E).

The general purpose of the exemption provisions of the Bankruptcy Code is to give debtors a fresh start. . . . The exemption of present Keogh payments, to the extent they are necessary for the support of the debtor, is consistent with this goal. The exemption of *future* payments, however, demonstrates a concern for the debtor's long-term security which is absent from the statute.

The result of denying the exemption with respect to future payments is in accord with the caselaw. . . . The court in *Matter of Kochell,* 26 B.R. 86 (Bkrtcy. W.D. Wis. 1982), squarely faced the issue of whether section 522(d)(10)(E) exempts pension plans themselves rather than present payments. The *Kochell* court agreed that the underlying purpose of the section was to alleviate present rather than long-term need, a condition which the 44-year old debtor, a doctor in apparent good health, could not demonstrate. . . .

The judgment appealed from will be affirmed.

So ordered.

Massachusetts Higher Education Assistance Corporation v. Taylor
459 N.E.2d 807 (Mass. 1984)

LYNCH, J. This is an action of contract in which the plaintiff, Massachusetts Higher Education Assistance Corporation, seeks to recover the sum of $8,697 loaned to the defendant, Marshall A. Taylor, plus interest and costs.

The plaintiff's motion for summary judgment was granted by a judge of the Municipal Court of the City of Boston. The Appellate Division of the

Boston Municipal Court vacated that judgment and directed instead that summary judgment be entered for the defendant. . . .

The facts in this case are not disputed. Between September 19, 1974, and April 27, 1977, Taylor executed four promissory notes to Baybank, Middlesex (Baybank) in conjunction with loans granted pursuant to the Guaranteed Student Loan Program. In Massachusetts this program is administered by the plaintiff. Should the student borrower default on a loan, the lender may assign its rights to the Federal guarantor and be reimbursed. In this case, Baybank assigned all its rights under the promissory notes to the plaintiff.

In October of 1977, Taylor filed a petition for voluntary bankruptcy in the United States Bankruptcy Court. Numerous creditors were listed on his schedule of debts, including Baybank. Baybank was notified of the petition through the procedures required by the Bankruptcy Court, but apparently did not enter an appearance at any time. On December 8, 1977, the Bankruptcy Court allowed Taylor's petition, and an order for payment of dividends was issued. Baybank was not listed as one of the creditors to receive a dividend.

When the plaintiff filed suit in the Boston Municipal Court in 1981 to collect the amount of the loans, Taylor asserted that the judgment of the Bankruptcy Court precluded the plaintiff's recovery. The Appellate Division of the Boston Municipal Court agreed with Taylor. It found that Baybank did not dispute the fact that the loans had been discharged in the bankruptcy proceeding, despite the restrictions which would make loans of this type nondischargeable during the first five years of the repayment period unless a judge specifically found that payment would impose undue hardship on the debtor. The court further found that the bankruptcy court has exclusive jurisdiction to revoke a discharge, therefore summary judgment was granted in Taylor's favor. On appeal, the plaintiff argues that, since the Bankruptcy Court did not have the authority to discharge the educational debts, the general discharge should not be understood to include them. . . .

Nonchalance toward the repayment of student loans has become a nationwide scandal. Of an estimated $28.2 billion provided under the Guaranteed Student Loan Program, loans totaling approximately $1.7 billion are in default. More than 800,000 recipients have not repaid their loans.

Congress has sought to thwart this trend by, among other things, excluding student loans from the category of debts that may be discharged in a bankruptcy proceeding. The statutes relevant to discharge of educational loans in effect at the time Taylor filed for bankruptcy specifically provided that educational loans were not dischargeable in the absence of a finding by the Bankruptcy Court of undue hardship. The defendant does not contend that the finding of undue hardship was made. . . .

When Taylor was adjudged bankrupt in 1977, he received a discharge from his debts. He contends that, since there is no indication to the contrary from the bankruptcy judge, this general discharge covers all the debts he listed on his schedule of debts. Under the current Bankruptcy Act, it is clear that the debts for Taylor's educational loans would not have been discharged by a general discharge. . . . A discharge does not operate to release an individual debtor from certain debts which are specifically excepted. . . . Nondischargeable debts owed to creditors are not released even though the individual debtor receives a general discharge. . . . When a debtor receives a general discharge from the Bankruptcy Court, the official form states: "The above-named debtor is released from all *dischargeable* debts."

Educational loans are not the only debts to which this principle applies. Other debts, such as taxes, alimony, support and maintenance, and non-scheduled debts are not affected by a general discharge even though there is no express order to that effect. . . .

It is clear, therefore, that under existing law in the absence of special circumstances a student loan is assumed to be nondischarged. The Bankruptcy Court does not have the power to discharge a student loan unless [the payment of that loan would impose an undue hardship on the debtor]. . . . There is no reason to expect the Bankruptcy Court to mention student loans in an order of discharge unless special circumstances apply.

Because student loans are not discharged automatically, the creditor need not appear at the bankruptcy proceedings and file a complaint for nondischargeability. "The Code is self-executing and Congress has declared such debts not discharged." . . .

Given the expressions of Congressional intent, we conclude that the general discharge in bankruptcy granted Taylor did not discharge him from his debt to the plaintiff. Faced with his failure to show undue hardship in the Bankruptcy Court, we assume that that court meant its judgment to comply with the law. There is no reason to assume otherwise.

The order of the Appellate Division is reversed and the judgment entered for the defendant is vacated. Judgment is to be entered for the plaintiff.

So ordered.

United Northwest Federal Credit Union v. Arens
664 P.2d 811 (Kan. 1983)

HERD, J. This is an action on a note and to foreclose a security interest in a mobile home. The trial court granted the United Northwest Federal Credit Union default judgment. The Arens appeal.

On September 8, 1980, appellants, William H. Arens and Katherine Arens, filed a voluntary petition in bankruptcy seeking relief pursuant to Chapter 7, Title 11, of the U.S.Code. On September 9, 1980, appellee filed a petition for recovery of money advanced to William H. Arens and Katherine Arens pursuant to its open-ended loan agreement to purchase a 1972 Kingwood mobile home. Appellee sought recovery of money and foreclosure of its security interest in the purchase money collateral. The omnibus order and notice of the bankruptcy court was issued on September 10, 1980. A summons was issued in Norton County on September 10, 1980, and served on the appellants on September 16, 1980.

No further action was taken in Norton County until after the bankruptcy petition was dismissed on May 4, 1981, for failure of the debtors to appear. A default judgment against appellants on May 11, 1981, was set aside on September 15, 1981, but reentered on January 4, 1982. Appellants challenge the entry of default judgment in favor of the Credit Union.

Chapter 7 of the Bankruptcy Code authorizes establishment of priorities of claims and the liquidation of the assets of an insolvent debtor for pro rata payment to creditors. When a petition is filed under a Chapter 7 case, a trustee is appointed by the court and the debtor submits schedules to the trustee listing his debts and assets. The trustee then takes possession of the bankrupt estate, liquidates the assets subject to prior liens, and discharges the debts.

11 U.S.C. §362(a) provides for an automatic stay of all proceedings against the debtor once the bankruptcy petition is filed. . . . The House Report on section 362 offers insight into the purpose behind the stay:

> The automatic stay is one of the fundamental debtor protections provided by the bankruptcy laws. It gives the debtor a breathing spell from his creditors. It stops all collection efforts, all harassment, and all foreclosure actions. It permits the debtor to attempt a repayment or reorganization plan, or simply to be relieved of the financial pressures that drove him into bankruptcy.

> "The automatic stay also provides creditor protection. Without it, certain creditors would be able to pursue their own remedies against the debtor's property. Those who acted first would obtain payment of the claims in preference to and to the detriment of other creditors.

The automatic stay of section 362(a) is in force from the moment the bankruptcy petition is filed. The fact a creditor has not received notice of the filing is irrelevant. Further, formal service is not required to effectuate the stay. The stay terminates automatically when the bankruptcy proceeding is closed or dismissed.

Appellants argue the district court was without jurisdiction to enter judgment against them because appellee's lawsuit was filed after the bankruptcy petition and thus in violation of the automatic stay. We agree. The import of section 362(a)(1) is that all legal actions pending or to be taken against the debtor are halted. As such, no new lawsuit can be commenced. The filing of appellee's foreclosure action on September 9, 1980, was thus in violation of the automatic stay. It is settled that acts done in violation of the stay are "void and without effect."

Since the filing of the foreclosure action against appellants was "void and without effect," there was no action on file when the appellants' bankruptcy petition was eventually dismissed. We note parenthetically this would not be the case had the action been filed before the petition in bankruptcy. In that situation the action would have remained on file because it was not filed in violation of the stay. Only further proceedings pursuant to the action would have been stayed. The instant case, however, arises under different circumstances.

Here the trial court was without jurisdiction to enter its order.

The judgment of the trial court is reversed. *Reversed.*

In re Brown Iron & Metal, Inc.
28 B.R. 426 (E.D. Tenn. 1983)

BARE, B.J. The trustee in bankruptcy seeks to avoid a transfer of real property by the debtor to the Jerrolds on the basis the transfer was preferential. A warranty deed effecting the transfer was executed more than ninety days before the date of the filing of the debtor's petition in bankruptcy but was filed for registration within the ninety-day period. . . .

. . . [T]he trustee contends the deed was not effective until it was filed for registration. Averring the transfer as between the debtor and themselves was effective upon delivery of the deed, the Jerrolds deny that the trustee is entitled to avoid the transfer. . . .

Jerrolds obtained a warranty deed to the property from the debtor in favor of himself and his wife, defendant Linda R. Jerrolds. Although this deed is dated May 25, 1982, it was not recorded until August 17, 1982, less than thirty days previous to the filing of the debtor's petition. Jerrolds testified he had no explanation for his delay in recording the deed from the debtor. . . . [Jerrolds obtained this deed by assuming to pay the obligation the debtor owed on the property transferred.]

The trustee in bankruptcy asserts the transfer of the property from the debtor to Jerrolds and his wife is clearly preferential. This assertion is disputed by the Jerrolds. . . .

The only value, if any, received by the debtor in connection with the transfer was the assumption by the Jerrolds of the unpaid balance on the debtor's note . . . secured by the first deed of trust. The court assumes *arguendo* this assumption constituted value. The amount of this unpaid balance was $16,000.00, according to the provisions of the May 25, 1982, deed from the debtor to the Jerrolds. Since there is no evidence of any increase in the fair market value of the property between May 25, 1982, and December 9, 1982, when the appraisal value of the property was reportedly $27,100.00, the debtor clearly received less than a reasonably equivalent value in exchange for the property. Furthermore, since a bona fide purchaser without notice from the debtor could have acquired an interest superior to any interest of Jerrolds prior to the filing of his deed for registration, the transfer in question was not "made" until the deed was filed for registration on August 17, 1982. Thus, the transfer from the debtor to the Jerrolds was made only twenty-four days prior to the filing of debtor's bankruptcy petition. This transfer was made in furtherance of the agreement that the debtor's obligation to J.R.C., Inc. would be satisfied by transfer of the property. Since the debtor's bankruptcy schedules reflect assets of $136,354.81 and liabilities of $302,641.29, the court has no difficulty in finding the debtor was insolvent when the transfer was made on August 17, 1982. . . .

[Having found all the elements of voidable preference, the transfer to Jerrolds is voided as requested by the bankruptcy trustee.]

So ordered.

REVIEW QUESTIONS

1. Match the term in column A with the appropriate statement in column B.

A	B
1. Liquidation	a. A creditor's right to payment.
2. Reorganization	b. Entered by bankruptcy judge whenever debtor is entitled to the court's protection.
3. Claim	c. The creditor's right to reduce the amount of its claim by the amount it owes the debtor.
4. Discharge	d. The proceeding pursued under Chapter 7.

5. Order of relief

6. Meeting of creditors
7. Voidable preference
8. Right of setoff

e. A transfer that gives a creditor an unfair advantage over other creditors.
f. The legal forgiveness of a debt.
g. The proceeding pursued under Chapter 11.
h. The event when, among other things, a permanent trustee is elected.

2. What is the basic purpose of the federal bankruptcy law?

3. The bankruptcy law has two distinct approaches to resolving the financial burdens of debtors. It has four types of proceedings. Describe these approaches and list the four types of proceedings.

4. Fred Murray owns 350 acres of farmland on which he raises cattle, pigs, and other livestock. He also grows hay and has a large garden. In addition to these responsibilities related to his farming operations, Fred works for the state cooperative extension service. In fact, 50 percent of his income comes from his salary paid by the state. Through mismanagement, Fred became involved in financial difficulties and was not paying his debts as they became due. His creditors commenced an involuntary bankruptcy proceeding against him. Is the creditors' action proper? Explain.

5. What is the amount of unsecured debts an individual debtor may owe and still be entitled to begin a Chapter 13 proceeding? What amount of secured debts? What is the minimum amount a debtor must owe before an involuntary proceeding may be begun?

6. The Chocolate Cookie Company entered into a 20-year lease at an annual rental of $4,000 a year. This lease contained a clause that the lease was not assignable without the lessor's consent. Eighteen months after the lease was signed, the Chocolate Cookie Company commenced voluntary liquidation proceedings. The trustee sought to enforce the lease, despite the nonassignability clause. May the trustee enforce the lease as written? Why?

7. With the facts as in problem 6, how much could the lessor claim in the bankruptcy proceeding if the trustee terminated the lease 6 months after the petition was filed (after 2 years of the lease term had passed)? Explain.

8. Pauline lives in a state that exempts $800 for an automobile owned by a debtor in a bankruptcy proceeding. Pauline's car was worth more than $800, so she sought to recover $800 of the sales price when the court sold the car to satisfy her debts. Her creditors contend that she is not entitled to any exemption for a car worth more than $800. Who is correct? Explain.

9. Despite financial difficulties, Barney bought one gray and one blue suit for a total of $500. When he received a bill for the suits 2 weeks later, he was insolvent, but he paid this bill fully in cash. One month later, he filed a petition in bankruptcy. The appointed trustee sued to recover the $500 paid, contending that the payment was a preferential transfer. Was the trustee correct? Why?

10. Tracy filed a bankruptcy petition on November 2. The State Bank seeks to establish its right of setoff, based upon the following facts. For the 6 months prior to the petition's being filed, Tracy owed the bank $8,000 at all times. Tracy had a savings account that had the following balances:

July 1–August 30	$10,000.00
August 31–September 15	5,000.00
September 16–October 2	500.00
October 3–November 2	7,000.00

What is the maximum amount of setoff to which the bank is entitled? Why? Would your answer change if the balance on November 2 were only $500? Explain.

11. White is an attorney who performed professional services for Smith & Smyth Insurance Company. This company did not pay White before it filed a voluntary liquidation proceeding. White seeks to have his claim given priority in the distribution of the debtor's estate, since his fees should qualify as a wage claim. Is White's contention correct? Why?

38 CHOOSING THE FORM OF BUSINESS ORGANIZATION

Business organizations may operate under a variety of legal forms. The common ones are sole proprietorships, partnerships, limited partnerships, and corporations. There are also some specialized organizations, such as professional service corporations, authorized by statute so that doctors, lawyers, dentists, and other professional persons are able to obtain the tax advantages of corporations.

This chapter will examine the various forms of organization and the factors that influence the actual selection of a particular form. The factors involved in this selection are applicable to all businesses, from the smallest to the largest, but the relative influence of the various factors varies greatly, depending on the size of the business. As a practical matter, the very large business must be incorporated, because that is the only method that can bring a large number of owners and investors together for an extended period of time.

The difficulty of deciding which is the best form of organization to select is most often encountered in the closely held business. Taxation is usually the most significant factor. Although a detailed discussion of the tax laws is beyond the scope of this text, some of the general principles of taxation will be presented in order to illustrate the influence of taxation in choosing among organizational forms.

1. General Partnerships

Partnerships developed logically in the law merchant, and the common law of partnerships has been codified in the Uniform Partnership Act. A *partnership* is an association of two or more persons to carry on, as co-owners, a business for profit. It is the result of an agreement.

A partnership form of organization has many advantages.

1. Since it is a matter of contract between individuals, to which the state is not a party, it is easily formed.

2. Costs of formation are minimal.

3. It is not a taxable entity.

4. Each owner, as a general rule, has an equal voice in management.

5. It may operate in more than one state without being required to comply with many legal formalities.

6. Partnerships are generally subject to less regulation and less governmental supervision than corporations.

The fact that a partnership is not a taxable entity does not mean that partnership income is tax-free. A partnership files an information return allocating its income among the partners, and each partner pays income tax on the portion allocated to him.

Several aspects of partnerships may be considered disadvantageous. First, as a personal matter, only a limited number of people may own such a business. Second, a partnership is dissolved any time a member ceases to be a partner either by withdrawal or by death. Although dissolution is the subject matter of chapter 41, it should be observed here that the perpetual existence of a corporation is often a distinct advantage, compared to easily dissolved partnerships. Third, the liability of a partner is unlimited, contrasted with the limited liability of a shareholder. The unlimited liability of a partner is applicable both to contract and tort claims. Fourth, since a partner is taxed on his share of the profits of a partnership, whether distributed to him or not, a partner may be required to pay income tax on money that is not received. This burden is an important consideration in a new business that is reinvesting its profits for expansion. A partner in such a business would have to have an independent means of paying the taxes on such income.

2. Joint Ventures

A *joint venture,* or *joint adventure,* occurs when two or more persons combine their efforts in a particular business enterprise and agree to share the profits or losses jointly or in proportion to their contributions. It is distinguished from a partnership in that the joint venture is a less formal association and contemplates a single transaction or a limited activity, whereas a partnership contemplates the operation of a general business. A joint venture is a specific venture without the formation of a partnership or corporation.

A partnership in most states is a legal entity, apart from the partners; a joint venture is not. A joint venture cannot sue or be sued. A suit must be by, on behalf of, or against the joint venturers individually.

Joint ventures file a partnership tax return and have many of the other legal aspects of partnerships. The parties stand in a fiduciary relationship with each other and are agents for purposes of tort liability.

LIMITED PARTNERSHIPS

3. Characteristics

A *limited* partnership, like other partnerships, comes into existence by virtue of an agreement. Like a corporation, it is authorized by statute, and the liability of one or more, but not all, of the partners is limited to the amount of capital contributed at the time of the creation of the partnership. For liability purposes, a limited partnership is, in effect, a hybrid between the partnership and the corporation.

One or more *general partners* manage the business and are personally liable for its debts. One or more *limited partners* also contribute capital and share in profits and losses, but take no part in running the business and incur no liability with respect to partnership obligations beyond their contribution to capital. It is from the limited liability of the limited partners that the organization gets its name.

Limited partnerships are governed in most states by the Uniform Limited Partnership Act provisions. The purpose of this statute is to encourage trade by permitting persons to invest in a business and reap their share of the profits without becoming liable for debts or risking more than the capital contributed. This reduced risk is based on the investor's not being a general partner or participating actively in the conduct of the business. The risk cannot be further reduced by taking a security interest in the property of the limited partnership.[1]

4. Creation

To create a limited partnership under the Uniform Limited Partnership Act, the parties must sign and swear to a certificate containing, among other matters, the following information: the name of the partnership, the character of the business, its location, the name and place of residence of each member, those who are to be the general and those who are to be the limited partners, the term for which the partnership is to exist, the amount of cash or the agreed value of property to be contributed by each partner, and the share of profit or compensation each limited partner shall receive. Strict compliance with the statutory requirement is necessary if the limited partners are to achieve the goal of limited liability.[2] Some states by statute require only substantial compliance, however, especially between the partners.

The certificate must be recorded in the county where the partnership has its principal place of business, and a copy must be filed in every community where it conducts business or has a representative office. Most states require notice by newspaper publication. In the event of any change in the facts contained in the certificate as filed—such as a change in the name of the partnership, the capital, or other matters—a new certificate must be filed. If such a certificate is not filed and the partnership continues, the limited partners immediately become liable as general partners.

The statutes of most states require the partnership to conduct its business in

---

[1] Kramer v. McDonald's System, Inc., p. 890.

[2] Wisniewski v. Johnson, p. 890.

a firm name that does not include the name of any of the limited partners or the word *company*. Some states specify that the word *limited* shall be added.

5. Operation and Dissolution

Unless a limited partner participates in management and control of the business, his liability to creditors does not extend beyond his contribution to the business. Participation in management makes the limited partner a general partner with unlimited liability.

In many states, but not all, this unlimited liability cannot be avoided by making the general partner a corporation if the limited partners would be in control of the corporate general partner. Thus, in some states, the officers and directors of a corporate general partner who are also individually limited partners have liability as general partners, and in other states they do not.[3]

While a limited partner has no right to participate in management, a limited partner does have the right (1) to have the partnership books kept at the principal place of business of the partnership, and at all times to inspect and copy any of them, (2) to have on demand true and full information of all things affecting the partnership and a formal account of partnership affairs whenever circumstances render it just and reasonable, (3) to have dissolution and winding up by decree of court, and (4) to have the right to receive a share of the profits or other compensation by way of income, and to return of his contribution upon dissolution. He is a quasi-shareholder. In addition, the limited partner does not become a general partner by engaging in activities that are of an advisory nature and do not amount to control of the business.[4]

To dissolve a limited partnership voluntarily before the time for termination stated in the certificate, notice of the dissolution must be filed and published. Upon dissolution, the distribution of the assets of the firm is prescribed by statute. As a general rule, the law gives priority to limited partners over general partners after all creditors are paid.

A limited partnership is dissolved only when there is a change in the general partners. Because limited partners have no active voice in the daily management of the organization, the limited partners' interests are treated like corporate shareholders' stock. Therefore, unless there is an agreement to the contrary, limited partners are free to transfer their interests without causing a dissolution of the limited partnership.

The limited partnership as a tax shelter is of special value in many new businesses, especially real estate ventures such as shopping centers and apartment complexes. It gives the investor limited liability and the operators control of the venture. It allows maximum use of the tax advantages of accelerated depreciation and the investment credit. Accelerated depreciation usually results in a tax loss in early years, which can be immediately deducted by the limited partner. Offsetting this tax loss, usually, is a cash flow that gives a limited partner an income at the

---

[3] DeLaney v. Fidelity Lease Limited, p. 891.
[4] Trans-Am Builders, Inc. v. Woods Mill Ltd., p. 892.

same time he has a loss for tax purposes. When such ventures start to show a taxable gain, the limited partnership is often dissolved and a corporation is formed, or the venture is sold.

6. Revised Uniform Limited Partnership Act

In 1976, the Commissioners on Uniform State Laws issued a revised Uniform Limited Partnership Act. Although this act has not yet been adopted by very many states, it will in all probability become the law in most states in the future. The revised act tends to make a limited partnership even more like a corporation than does the original act.

Under the revised act, the name of the limited partnership must contain the words *limited partnership*. The name may not contain the name of a limited partner unless his name is also the name of a general partner or one that had been used prior to the admission of that limited partner.

A limited partnership under the new law is required to maintain a registered office within the state and an agent to receive notices for it. The law requires that certain records, such as a list of all partners and a copy of the certificate of the limited partnership, be maintained at this office. Copies of the partnership tax returns and copies of all financial statements must be kept for three years.

Under the revised act, the certificate creating the partnership is filed with the state's secretary of state. If it is later amended or canceled, the certificates of amendment and cancellation are also filed in that office.

The revised act makes a substantial change in the liability of a limited partner who participates in control of the business. The liability of a general partner is imposed on a limited partner who participates in the control of the business only if the third party had knowledge of the participation. In addition, the act provides that a limited partner does not participate in the control of the business by (1) being an agent or employee of the business, (2) consulting with or advising a partner with respect to the partnership, (3) acting as surety for the limited partnership, (4) approving or disapproving of an amendment to the certificate, and (5) voting on matters such as dissolution, sale of assets, or a change of name.

THE BUSINESS CORPORATION

7. Advantages and Disadvantages

The corporation comes into existence when the state issues the corporate charter. A *corporation* is a legal entity that usually has perpetual existence. The liability of the owners is limited to their investment, unless there is a successful "piercing of the corporate veil." (See chapter 42 for a further discussion of "piercing the corporate veil.")

A corporation, as a general rule, is a taxable entity paying a tax on its net profits. Dividends paid to stockholders are also taxable, giving rise to the frequently made observation that corporate income is subject to double taxation. The accuracy of this observation will be discussed later.

The advantages of the corporate form of organization may be briefly summarized as follows:

1. It is the only method that will raise substantial capital from a large number of investors.
2. Tax laws have several provisions that are favorable to corporations.
3. Control can be vested in those with a minority of the investment by using techniques such as nonvoting or preferred stock.
4. Ownership may be divided into many separate and unequal shares.
5. Investors have limited liability.
6. The organization can have perpetual existence.
7. Certain laws, such as those relating to usury, are not applicable to corporations.
8. Investors, notwithstanding their status as owners, may also be employees entitled to benefits such as worker's compensation.

Among the frequently cited disadvantages of the corporate form of organization are these:

1. Cost of forming and maintaining the corporate form with its rather formal procedures.
2. Expenditures such as license fees and franchise taxes that are assessed against corporations but not against partnerships.
3. Double taxation of corporate income and the frequently higher rates.
4. The requirement that it must be qualified to do business in all states where it is conducting intrastate commerce.
5. Subject to more regulation by government at all levels than are other forms.
6. Being required to use an attorney in litigation, whereas an ordinary citizen can proceed on his or her own behalf.[5]

The fact that corporations are required to use an attorney in litigation is listed as a disadvantage of the corporate form of organization. As a practical matter, all forms of organization must use an attorney in any litigation of much significance, so to that extent the requirement is not a significant disadvantage. It does emphasize, however, the fact that corporations do require the services of lawyers on an ongoing basis. The role of the lawyer and his relationship to a business corporation is colorfully stated by Roy A. Redfield in *Factors of Growth in a Law Practice 30* (1962):

> When the business corporation is born, the lawyer is the midwife who brings it into existence; while it functions he is its philosopher, guide and friend; in trouble he is its champion, and when the end comes and the last

---

[5] Land Management v. Department of Envir. Protec., p. 892.

sad rites must be performed, the lawyer becomes the undertaker who disincorporates it and makes final report to the Director of Internal Revenue.

8. Taxation of Corporate Income

The fact that taxation was listed as both an advantage and a disadvantage of the corporate form illustrates the importance of the tax factor in choosing this particular form of organization. Corporate tax law provisions change from time to time, depending on the economy and the effect of tax policy on employment, economic growth, and so on. The current rates (1985) are:

INCOME ($)	TAX RATE
0–25,000	15%
25–50,000	18
50–75,000	30
75–100,000	40
Over 100,000	46

Prior to 1984, the tax laws that relate to pension and profit-sharing plans favored corporate plans over those of partnerships and the self-employed. Congress generally eliminated this favorable treatment, and the law on retirement benefits is no longer dictating that many closely held businesses and professional practices be incorporated.

Among the tax laws that favor corporations over partnerships are the following: (1) Health insurance payments are fully deductible and are not subject to the limitations applicable to individuals. (2) Deferred compensation plans may be adopted. (3) Retained earnings below $100,000 per year are taxed at graduated rates that are frequently lower than the individual tax rates of the shareholders. (4) Income that is needed in the business is not taxed against a person who does not receive it. (5) Accumulated income can be taken out as a capital gain on dissolution. The net effect of the capital gain treatment is that 60 percent of the gain is not taxable. (6) The corporation may provide life insurance for its employees as a deductible expense. (7) Medical expenses in excess of health insurance coverage may be paid on behalf of employees as a deductible expense.

The corporate form is frequently at a disadvantage from a tax standpoint because of the double taxation aspect and because the 46 percent rate often exceeds the individual rate of the owners of the business. Some states impose a higher tax on corporate income than on individual income. There are also many taxes that are imposed on corporations, but not on individuals or partnerships.

9. Avoidance of Double Taxation

Certain techniques may be used to avoid, in part, the double taxation of corporate income. First of all, reasonable salaries paid to corporate employees may be deducted in computing the taxable income of the business. Thus, in a closely held corporation in which all or most shareholders are officers or employees, this technique can be used to avoid double taxation of much of the corporate income. The Internal Revenue Code disallows a deduction for excessive or unreasonable compensation, and unreasonable payments to shareholder employees are taxable as dividends. Therefore, the determination of the reasonableness of corporate salaries is an ever-present tax problem in the closely held corporation that employs shareholders.

Second, the capital structure of a corporation may include both common stock and interest-bearing loans from shareholders. Envision a company that needs $200,000 to begin business. If $200,000 of stock is purchased, there will be no expense to be deducted. But suppose that $100,000 worth of stock is purchased and $100,000 is loaned to the company at 10 percent interest. In this case, $10,000 of interest each year is deductible as an expense of the company, and thus subject to only one tax as interest income to the owners. Just as in the case of salaries, the Internal Revenue Code contains a counteracting rule relating to corporations that are undercapitalized. If the corporation is undercapitalized, interest payments will be treated as dividends and disallowed as deductible expenses.

The third technique for avoiding double taxation, at least in part, is simply not to pay dividends and to accumulate the earnings. After the earnings have been accumulated, the shareholders can sell their stock or dissolve the corporation. In both situations the difference between the original investment and the amount received is given capital gains treatment. Here again we have tax laws designed to counteract the technique. There is a special income tax imposed on "excessive accumulated earnings" in addition to the normal tax and rules relating to collapsible corporations.

Finally, a special provision in the Internal Revenue Code treats small, closely held business corporations and partnerships similarly for income tax purposes. These corporations are known as Sub-Chapter S corporations.

10. The Sub-Chapter S Corporation

The limited partnership is a hybrid between a corporation and a partnership in the area of liability. A similar hybrid known as a *tax-option* or *Sub-Chapter S* corporation exists in the tax area of the law. Such corporations have the advantages of the corporate form without the double taxation of income.

The tax-option corporation is one that elects to be taxed in a manner similar to that of partnerships; that is, to file an information return allocating income and losses among the shareholders for immediate reporting, regardless of dividend distributions, thus avoiding any tax on the corporation.

Sub-Chapter S corporations cannot have more than 35 shareholders, each of whom must sign the election to be taxed in the manner similar to a partnership. There are many technical rules of tax law involved in Sub-Chapter S corporations. But as a rule of thumb, this method of taxation has distinct advantages for a business operating at a loss, because the loss is shared and immediately deductible on the returns of the shareholders. It is also advantageous for businesses capable of paying out net profits as earned, thereby avoiding the corporate tax. If net profits must be retained in the business, Sub-Chapter S tax treatment is disadvantageous, because income tax is paid by the shareholders on earnings not received.

11. The Professional Service Association

Traditionally, professional services, such as those of a doctor, lawyer, or dentist, could be performed only by an individual and could not be performed by a corporation, because the relationship of doctor and patient or attorney and client was considered a highly personal one. The impersonal corporate entity could not render the personal services involved.

For many years there were significant tax advantages in corporate profit-sharing and pension plans that were not available to private persons and to partnerships to the same extent. An individual proprietor or partner was limited to a deduction of 15 percent of income or $15,000 under a *Keogh* pension plan provision. Professional persons therefore often incorporated or created professional associations in order to obtain the greater tax advantages of corporate pension and profit-sharing plans. To make this possible, every state enacted statutes authorizing *professional associations.* As legal entities similar to corporations, their payments to qualified pension and profit-sharing plans qualify for deductions equal to those of business corporations.

As previously noted, the tax laws were changed in 1984 in an attempt to equalize the tax treatment of Keogh plans and corporate pension and profit-sharing plans. While this has been generally achieved, there remain a few advantages to corporate plans. Most professional corporations that were created earlier remain in existence, and new ones are still being formed.

The law authorizing professional corporations does not authorize business corporations to practice a profession such as law or medicine.[6] Professional corporations are special forms of business organization that must meet strict statutory requirements. In addition, professional persons practicing a profession as a professional corporation do not obtain any limitation on their liability to third persons.

Today, there are thousands of professional corporations in all states. They can be identified by the letters *S.C.* (Service Corporation), *P.C.* (Professional Corporation), or *Inc.* (Incorporated), or by the word *company* in the name of the professional firm.

12. Making the Decision

A few pages back, we listed advantages of incorporating a business with substantial capital. If the business is to be owned and operated by relatively few people, their choice of form of organization will be made with those factors in mind—especially taxation, control, liability, perpetual existence, and legal capacity. *Legal capacity* is the power of the business, in its own name, to sue or be sued, own and dispose of property, and enter into contracts.

---

[6] Carter v. Berberian, p. 894.

In evaluating the impact of taxation, an accountant or attorney will look at the projected profits or losses of the business, the ability to distribute earnings, and the tax brackets of the owners. An estimate of the tax burden under the various forms of organization will be made. The results will be considered along with other factors in making the decision on the form of business organization.

The generalization that partners have unlimited liability and stockholders limited liability must be qualified in the case of a closely held business. A small, closely held corporation with limited assets and capital will find it difficult to obtain credit on the strength of its own credit standing alone; and as a practical matter, the shareholders will usually be required to add their individual liability as security for the debts. If Tom, Dick, and Jane seek a loan for their corporation, they usually will be required to guarantee repayment of the loan. This is not to say that closely held corporations do not have some degree of limited liability. The investors in those types of businesses are protected with limited liability for contractlike obligations imposed as a matter of law (such as taxes) and for debts resulting from torts committed by company employees while engaged in company business. If the tax aspects dictate that a partnership and limited liability are desired by some investors, the limited partnership will be considered.

Issues of liability are not restricted to the investors in the business or to financial liability. Corporation law has developed several instances in which the directors and officers of the corporation will have liability to shareholders or the corporation for acts or omissions by those directors or officers in their official capacity. These matters will be discussed more fully in chapter 43.

The significance of the law relating to control will be apparent in the discussions on formation and operation of partnerships and corporations in the chapters that follow. The desire of one or more individuals to control the business is a major factor in selecting the form, and the control issues are second only to taxation in importance.

SUMMARY

PARTNERSHIPS

Advantages

1. The partnership is easily formed, and the costs of formation are minimal.
2. The partnership is not a taxable entity, and losses are immediately deductible.
3. Each partner as a general rule has an equal voice in management.
4. It can operate in any state and is subject to less government regulation.

Disadvantages	1. A partnership may involve only a limited number of people and is easily dissolved.
	2. Partners have unlimited liability.
	3. Income is taxed to a partner whether received or not.

LIMITED PARTNERSHIPS

Characteristics	1. A limited partnership has at least one general partner with unlimited liability.
	2. It is not a taxable entity, and any losses are immediately deductible.
	3. The general partners manage the business.
Characteristics of a corporation	1. A certificate containing vital information is filed in a public office.
	2. Limited partners do not participate in management and are thus similar to shareholders.
	3. The name used gives notice of the limited liability of some owners.
Creation	1. The steps necessary to establish a limited partnership are governed by statute and must be followed closely.
Operation and dissolution	1. Usually, the limited partners forego their right to participate in management in exchange for having their liability limited to their investment.
	2. Limited partners do have the right to inspect the books, to have an accounting, to dissolve the organization by court decree, and to share in the distribution of profits.
	3. In general, the transfer of a limited partner's interest does not dissolve the limited partnership.
The Revised Uniform Limited Partnership Act	1. Limited partnerships have additional requirements concerning their offices and records.
	2. Limited partners who participate in management assume unlimited liability only to persons who know of the participation.

THE BUSINESS CORPORATION

Advantages	1. Investors have limited liability, and the business may have perpetual existence.
	2. It is a method by which even hundreds of thousands of persons can own a business together and in varying percentages of ownership.
	3. Several provisions in the tax law favor corporations.
	4. As a separate entity, there are many laws covering only corporations.
Disadvantages	1. There are significant costs in forming and maintaining a corporation.
	2. Corporate income is taxed to the corporation, and dividends are taxed to the shareholders.
	3. It must qualify in every state where it conducts intrastate business and is subject to greater government regulation.
	4. It must have an attorney represent it in litigation.
Taxation of corporate income	1. Several provisions of the Internal Revenue Code, such as those relating to health insurance, have special advantages for corporations.
	2. There are several techniques for avoiding double taxation of corporate income, such as the payment of salaries and expenses on behalf of the owners of the corporation.
	3. The Sub-Chapter S corporation, which is a corporation taxed in the same manner as a partnership, is of special importance in avoiding the double taxation of corporate income.

CASES

Kramer v. McDonald's System, Inc.
396 N.E.2d 504 (Ill. 1979)

Kramer, a limited partner in a McDonald's franchise, invested $90,000 in the limited partnership. To secure his investment, he took a security agreement from the franchisee covering all equipment, inventory, and receivables. When the business failed, another creditor caused a public sale of the assets, which McDonald's bought. Kramer sued McDonald's, the franchisor, for conversion of his property. The lower reviewing court held for the franchisor, and Kramer appealed.

CLARK, J. . . . The issue herein is not whether a limited partner may secure a loan but whether a limited partner may secure his capital contribution. . . .

A limited partner is prohibited from taking collateral to secure repayment of his capital contribution. To do so would give him an unfair priority over the creditors of the partnership contrary to the express provisions of section 16(1) of the ULPA:

> (1) A limited partner shall not receive from a general partner or out of partnership property any part of his contribution until (a) All liabilities of the partnership, except liabilities to general partners and to limited partners on account of their contributions, have been paid or there remains property of the partnership sufficient to pay them.

> (b) The consent of all members is had, unless the return of the contribution may be rightfully demanded under the provision of paragraph (2), and

> (c) The certificate is cancelled or so amended as to set forth the withdrawal or reduction.

A limited partnership interest is in the nature of an investment. Through his contribution, the limited partner becomes entitled to share in the profits and losses of the partnership, though his share of the losses will not exceed the amount of capital initially contributed to the enterprise. However, when the limited partner makes the contribution, he is placing that amount at risk. He is not permitted to insure that risk or to guarantee a return to himself by taking some form of security. He may not vie with creditors for the assets available to pay the partnership's obligations. [The ULPA] was designed to prevent illegal competition between the limited partner and creditors of the partnership for the assets of the partnership. It would therefore defeat the purpose of the ULPA to permit Kramer to enforce a security interest against the property purchased by the partnership to operate the restaurant.

We therefore hold that Kramer is prohibited by the express provisions of section 16 of the ULPA from accepting collateral as security for his capital contribution. . . .

Affirmed.

Wisniewski v. Johnson
286 S.E.2d 223 (Va. 1982)

STEPHENSON, J. . . . The dispositive question in this appeal is whether a certificate of limited partnership satisfies the requirements of . . . Code §50-45 when the partners have their signatures acknowledged by a notary but do not swear to the truth of the document.

Michael Wisniewski, Walter M. Luchaka, and Olga G. Luchaka (the appellants) and Harold R. Gearhart executed and recorded a certificate in an effort to establish the River Bend Limited Partnership. Gearhart was listed as general partner and the appellants as limited partners. This certificate was signed and acknowledged by all the partners before a notary.

Thomas and Suzanne Johnson purchased a house from the partnership in 1975. Subsequently, they brought suit against the partners, alleging breach of warranty in the construction of the dwelling. The trial court found for the Johnsons and held the appellants liable as general partners, ruling that since they had not sworn to the statements in the certificate, a limited partnership had not been formed.

The appellants argue that an acknowledgment is constructively the same as swearing to a document. . . . We cannot agree.

There is a marked difference between acknowledging a signature and signing a document under oath. An acknowledgment merely verifies that the person named executed the document in question. . . . We hold, therefore, that the appellants' failure to "swear to" the certificate was such a noncompliance with the requirements of Code §50-45 as to render the certificate ineffective for the creation of a limited partnership.

Accordingly, the judgment of the trial court will be affirmed.

Affirmed.

DeLaney v. Fidelity Lease Limited
526 S.W.2d 543 (Tex. 1975)

Fidelity Lease Limited is a limited partnership consisting of 22 limited partners and a corporate general partner. Three of the limited partners were the officers and directors of the corporate general partner. When the limited partnership breached a contract with the plaintiff, suit was brought against three of the limited partners individually. It was contended that they had become general partners by participating in the management of the limited partnership. The lower courts held that the individuals were not liable, and the plaintiff appealed.

DANIEL. J. . . . The question here is whether limited partners in a limited partnership become liable as general partners if they "take part in the control of the business" while acting as officers of a corporation which is the sole general partner of the limited partnership. . . .

Pertinent portions of the Texas Uniform Limited Partnership Act, Article 6132a, provide:

> Sec. 8. A limited partner shall not become liable as a general partner unless, in addition to the exercise of his rights and powers as a limited partner, he takes part in the control of the business. . . .

It was alleged by plaintiffs, and there is summary judgment evidence, that the three limited partners controlled the business of the limited partnership, albeit through the corporate entity. The defendant limited partners argue that they acted only through the corporation and that the corporation actually controlled the business of the limited partnership. In response to this contention, we adopt the following statements in the dissenting opinion of Chief Justice Preslar in the court of civil appeals:

> I find it difficult to separate their acts for they were at all times in the dual capacity of limited partners and officers of the corporation. Apparently the corporation had no function except to operate the limited partnership and Appellees were obligated to their other partners to so operate the corporation as to benefit the partnership. Each act was done then, not for the corporation, but for the partnership. Indirectly, if not directly, they were exercising control over the partnership. Truly "the corporation fiction" was in this instance a fiction.

Thus, we hold that the personal liability, which attaches to a limited partner when "he takes part in the control and management of the business," cannot be evaded merely by acting through a corporation.

Crombie, Kahn, and Sanders argue that, since their only control of Fidelity's business was as officers of the alleged corporate general partner, they are insulated from personal liability arising from their activities or those of the corporation. This is a general rule of corporate law, but one of several exceptions in which the courts will disregard the corporate fiction is where it is used to circumvent a statute. That is precisely the result here, for it is undisputed that the corporation was organized to manage and control the limited partnership. Strict compliance with the statute is required if a limited partner is to avoid liability as a general partner. It is quite clear that there can be more than one general partner. Assuming that Interlease Corporation was a legal general partner . . . this would not prevent Crombie, Kahn, and Sanders from taking part in the control of the business in their individual capacities as well as their corporate capacities. In no event should they be permitted to escape the statutory liability which would have devolved upon them if there had been no attempted interposition of the corporate shield against personal liability. Otherwise, the statutory requirement of at least one general partner with general liability in a limited partnership can be circumvented or vitiated by limited partners operating the partnership through a corporation with minimum capitalization and therefore minimum liability. We hold that . . . if . . .

either of these three limited partners took part in the control of the business, whether or not in his capacity as an officer of Interlease Corporation, he should be adjudged personally liable as a general partner.

Reversed.

Trans-Am Builders, Inc.
v. Woods Mill, Ltd.
210 S.E.2d 866 (Ga. 1974)

STOLZ, J. . . . The litigation before us arose out of the construction of an apartment complex involving Trans-Am Builders, Inc., as general contractor (appellant) and Woods Mill, Ltd., a limited partnership (appellee) with a number of individuals as limited partners and The Baier Corporation as the general partner. . . .

During the construction of the project, financial difficulties arose, resulting in appellant's either abandoning or being removed from the project. Suits and countersuits were filed. However, there is but one issue before us, that is, have the limited partners conducted themselves in such a manner as to "take part in the control of the business" and thus become liable as a general partner? . . .

Code Ann. §75-411 provides as follows: (1) A limited partner shall have the same rights as a general partner to (a) Have the partnership books kept at the principal place of business of the partnership, and at all times to inspect and copy any of them. (b) Have on demand true and full information of all things affecting the partnership, and a formal account of partnership affairs whenever circumstances render it just and reasonable. (c) Have dissolution and winding up by decree of court. (2) A limited partner shall have the right to receive a share of the profits or other compensation by way of income, and to the return of his contribution. . . .

The evidence before us reveals that the limited partners (with one exception) held at least two meetings after it became apparent that the project was in financial difficulty. At these meetings the situation was presented by a representative of the general partner, discussions were participated in, and additional money was raised to meet financial obligations. At least one of the limited partners went to the project and went over it with the appellant's superintendent, and "obnoxiously" complained and objected to the way the work was being conducted, but there is nothing to indicate that he gave any directions which may have been followed by the plaintiff's superintendent. . . . The appellant contends that these actions violated Code Ann. §75-411, *supra,* and that the limited partners thus became general partners. The trial judge held otherwise and sustained the limited partners' motion for summary judgment, from which judgment the plaintiff appeals. . . .

It is well established that just because a man is a limited partner in an enterprise he is not by reason of that status precluded from continuing to have an interest in the affairs of the partnership, from giving advice and suggestions to the general partner or his nominees, and from interesting himself in specific aspects of the business. Such casual advice as limited partners may have given to [the employees] can hardly be said to be interference in day-to-day management. Certainly common sense dictates that in times of severe financial crisis all partners in such an enterprise, limited or general will become actively interested in any effort to keep the enterprise afloat and many abnormal problems will arise that are not under any stretch of the imagination mere day-to-day matters of managing the partnership business. This is all that occurred in this instance. . . .

It would be unreasonable to hold that a limited partner may not advise with the general partner and visit the partnership business, particularly when the project is confronted with a severe financial crisis.

Judgment affirmed.

Land Management v. Department
of Envir. Protec.
368 A.2d 602 (ME) 1977

ARCHIBALD, J. . . . The sole issue raised by this appeal is whether the presiding Justice acted properly in dismissing the plaintiff's complaint on the ground that the plaintiff was a corporation not represented by a duly admitted attorney. We conclude that the Justice below correctly dismissed the complaint, and we therefore deny the plaintiff's appeal.

The plaintiff, Land Management, Inc., is a corporation doing business in the State of Maine. On April 9, 1976, it commenced an action in the Superior Court seeking declaratory and injunctive relief against the defendants. Throughout the proceedings in the Superior Court the plaintiff was represented by its president who, admittedly, is not an attorney admitted to practice law in Maine.

All of the defendants filed motions to dismiss the plaintiff's complaint. . . . [These were granted] solely on the basis that the Plaintiff Land Management, Inc. is not entitled to proceed in this action *pro se* by and through a person who is not an attorney licensed to practice law.

In support of its position that a corporation may represent itself in Maine courts through a corporate officer who is not a duly admitted attorney, the plaintiff relies upon language found in 4 M.R.S.A. §§807 and 811.

4 M.R.S.A. §807 provides:

> Unless duly admitted to the bar of this State, no person shall practice law or any branch thereof, or hold himself out to practice law or any branch thereof, within the State or before any court therein, or demand or receive any remuneration for such services rendered in this State. Whoever, not being duly admitted to the bar of this State, shall practice law or any branch thereof, or hold himself out to practice law or any branch thereof, within the State or before any court therein, or demand or receive any remuneration for such services rendered in this State, shall be punished by a fine of not more than $500 or by imprisonment for not more than three months, or by both. This section shall not be construed to apply to practice before any Federal Court by any person duly admitted to practice therein nor to a person pleading or managing his own cause in court. . . .

4 M.R.S.A. §811 defines a "person" as "any individual, corporation, partnership or association."

On the basis of these statutory provisions, the plaintiff contends that since a corporation can only act through its agents, it may authorize a non-attorney to represent it in court. We do not agree with the plaintiff's assertion that the Legislature, in enacting §§807 and 811, intended to permit a corporation to be represented before the courts of this State by a person who is not authorized to practice law. To accept plaintiff's argument would require us to hold that a corporation may authorize a non-attorney to represent it in court, while an individual may not. We do not believe that the Legislature intended such an illogical result. The purpose of §811 for including a corporation within the definition of the word "person" was to make it clear that a corporation, as well as anyone else, is prohibited from engaging in the unauthorized practice of law. This section modified the §807 prohibition against unauthorized practice rather than expanding the right of individuals to represent themselves in either the Federal or State courts.

The rule that a corporation may appear in court only through a licensed attorney was stated succinctly in *Paradise* v. *Nowlin,* 86 Cal. App.2d 897, 195 P.2d 867 (1948):

> A natural person may represent himself and present his own case to the court although he is not a licensed attorney. A corporation is not a natural person. It is an artificial entity created by law and as such it can neither practice law nor appear or act in person. Out of court it must act in its affairs through its agents and representatives and in matters in court it can act only through licensed attorneys. A corporation cannot appear in court by an officer who is not an attorney and it cannot appear in *propria persona.*

Sound public policy reasons also require such a rule. As stated by the Ohio Supreme Court:

> To allow a corporation to maintain litigation and appear in court represented by corporate officers or agents only would lay open the gates to the practice of law for entry to those corporate officers or agents who have not been qualified to practice law and who are not amenable to the general discipline of the court.

There is abundant authority, both state and federal, rejecting the argument, as advanced by the plaintiff, that a corporation has the right to appear in court without the aid of a licensed attorney.

Since the plaintiff was not represented by counsel licensed to practice law, its complaint was a nullity and was properly dismissed by the presiding Justice.

Appeal denied.

Carter v. Berberian
434 A.2d 255 (R.I. 1981)

Berberian, an attorney at law, was one of the incorporators of Plantations Legal Defense Services, Inc. (PLDS), a Rhode Island nonbusiness corporation. PLDS was incorporated for the express purpose of rendering legal defense aid and assistance to persons in Rhode Island. Berberian was the executive director of PLDS since its incorporation. It handled both civil and criminal cases and collected fees from clients. Berberian was the chief lawyer and handled all litigation and legal research for cases handled by PLDS.

The State Bar Disciplinary Board brought charges against Berberian for violation of DR 3-101 A of the Code of Professional Responsibility in that he aided a nonlawyer (PLDS) in the unauthorized practice of law. The Board recommended that he be disciplined. Berberian appeals.

PER CURIAM. . . . By way of defense . . . respondent . . . contends that DR 3 101(A) relates only to unauthorized practice by "human beings." This position is untenable. . . . [T]he professional-service-corporation law does not permit ordinary business corporations to practice law and only corporations organized under the act [chapter 5.1 of title 7] are permitted to do so. . . . Clearly, a corporation, as well as an association or an individual, may engage in the unauthorized practice of law, and an attorney who aids in such unauthorized practice of law violates DR 3-101(A).

As his second issue, respondent contends that PLDS is a legal-aid or public-defender office operated by a bona fide nonprofit community organization and that therefore his "dignified cooperation" is protected by DR 2-103(D)(1)(b). He argues that PLDS should not be treated differently from the Legal Aid Society or from Rhode Island Legal Services, Inc., both of which have been specifically authorized by the General Assembly to represent indigent persons. The Board found that PLDS was not a bona fide community organization but was "virtually a one-man show, that man being the respondent." The Board further found that in general PLDS charged or sought to charge its clients for its services instead of serving indigents without charge as do the Legal Aid Society and Rhode Island Legal Services, Inc. Therefore the Board recommended to this court that it censure respondent and order him to cease and desist from aiding PLDS in its unauthorized practice of law.

* * *

. . . In essence, the respondent was carrying on in association with this corporation a general practice of law, both civil and criminal. Most of the clients were being charged for services rendered; retainer agreements were signed, and every effort was made to obtain fees for services. . . .

Consequently, it is clear from the evidence and the findings that the respondent, instead of forming a professional-service corporation . . . , which corporation would be subject to regulation by this court and subject to the obligations set forth by the General Assembly in chapter 5.1 of title 7 (including the providing of malpractice insurance), chose to follow a course not authorized by law. In aiding PLDS in the unauthorized practice of law, the respondent violated DR 3-101(A).

We therefore adopt the recommendation of the Board and hereby order the respondent to cease and desist forthwith from aiding Plantations Legal Defense Services, Inc. in its unauthorized practice of law, and further, we hereby publicly censure the respondent for violation of DR 3-101(A).

So ordered.

REVIEW QUESTIONS

1. Identify the terms in column A by matching each with the appropriate statement in column B.

A	B
1. Partnership	**a.** A business owned by one person who is personally liable for all losses.
2. Proprietorship	**b.** An artificial being created by a state.
3. Limited partnership	**c.** Two or more persons combine their efforts for a single transaction.
4. Corporation	**d.** Created when shareholders elect to be treated as partners for tax purposes.
5. Professional corporation	**e.** Created by an agreement between two or more persons who agree to share profits and losses.
6. Capital gain	**f.** 60 percent is not taxed.
7. Sub-Chapter S corporation	**g.** Shareholders do not have limited tort liability.
8. Joint venture	**h.** Exists when some partners are treated like shareholders for liability purposes.

2. Gerald and Lionel purchased a tavern. They orally agreed that Lionel would manage the business at a stated salary and receive 50 percent of all profits for his interest as a *limited* partner. Subsequently, the Internal Revenue Service assessed a deficiency in cabaret taxes in the amount of $46,000. Lionel contended that since he was a limited partner, he was not personally liable for the taxes. Is Lionel correct? Why or why not?

3. Garrett and Lewis signed an agreement creating a limited partnership. Garrett was the general partner, and Lewis was a limited partner. Neither the agreement nor the certificate required by statute were filed with the secretary of state. This limited partnership purchased merchandise on credit from Products, Ltd., which assumed that the business was a general partnership. Should the failure to file pertinent documents related to the limited partnership make Lewis liable to Products, Ltd., as if he were a general partner? Explain.

4. Describe at least four advantages and four disadvantages of the general partnership as a form of business organization.

5. Linda and Gladys formed a limited partnership, with Gladys as general partner. The partnership purchased land from Sandy, giving a promissory note on behalf of the partnership to Sandy. The partnership subsequently defaulted on its payments. Sandy brought suit to hold Gladys personally liable. With what result? Why?

6. A corporation was a defendant in a mortgage foreclosure suit. It failed to appear in the trial court, and a decree of foreclosure was entered. Defendant filed a notice of appeal signed by the corporate secretary. Plaintiff moved to strike the appeal because the notice was not signed by an attorney. What was the ruling? Why?

7. John Thompson and Richard Allenby wish to enter the camping equipment manufacturing business. If the following facts exist, which type of business organization would be most advantageous?
  a. Thompson is an expert in the field of camping gear production and sale but has no funds. Allenby knows nothing about such production but is willing to contribute all necessary capital.
  b. Camping gear production requires large amounts of capital, much more than Thompson and Allenby can raise personally or together, yet they wish to control the business.
  c. Some phases of production and sale are rather dangerous, and a relatively large number of tort judgments may be anticipated.
  d. Sales will be nationwide.

    e. Thompson and Allenby are both 65 years old. No profits are expected for at least 5 years, and interruption of the business before that time would make it a total loss.

    f. Several other persons wish to put funds into the business but are unwilling to assume personal liability.

    g. The anticipated earnings over cost, at least for the first few years, will be approximately $70,000. Thompson and Allenby wish to draw salaries of $25,000 each; they also want a hospitalization and retirement plan, all to be paid from these earnings.

    h. A loss is expected for the first three years, owing to the initial capital outlay and the difficulty in entering the market.

8. Describe four techniques for avoiding double taxation of corporate income.

9. List the characteristics of a limited partnership that are similar to those of a (a) general partnership and (b) corporation.

10. Vaughan is a limited partner in the Grand Limited Partnership, a real estate syndication. He purchased his interest for $5,000 when the partnership was created. The partnership has prospered, and Vogel has offered to buy Vaughan's interest for $6,500. The general partners are opposed to the sale because they dislike Vogel. Is Vaughan entitled to sell the interest without the consent of the general partners? Why?

39 FORMATION OF PARTNERSHIPS

A *partnership* is defined as an association of two or more persons to carry on as co-owners of a business for profit. It is the result of an agreement between competent parties to place their money, property, or labor in a business and to divide the profits and losses. Each partner is personally liable for the debts of the partnership, since the partnership is in effect a mutual agency relationship.

Express partnership agreements may be either oral or written, but a carefully prepared written agreement is highly preferable to an oral one. The provisions usually contained in articles of partnership will be discussed later in this chapter.

Issues concerning the existence of a partnership may arise between the parties or between the alleged partnership and third parties. The legal issues in these two situations are substantially different. When the issue is between the alleged partners, it is essentially a question of intention. Between the alleged partners, a partnership arises only from an express or implied agreement between them. It is never established by implication or operation of law. When the issue concerns liability to a third person, the question involves not only intention to create the partnership, but issues of estoppel as well.

A partnership must be formed to carry on a business for profit. As such, it is subject to all laws regulating businesses. In addition, the concept of a partnership cannot be used to circumvent laws such as those regulating the sale of alcoholic beverages.[1]

---

[1] Roby v. Day, p. 904.

1. Implied Partnerships

Between the parties, the intention to create a partnership may be expressed or implied from their conduct. The basic question is whether the parties intend a relationship that includes the essential elements of a partnership, not whether they intend to be partners. In fact, under certain circumstances, a corporation may be held to be a partnership at least between the owners of the business.

If the essential elements of a partnership are present, the mere fact that the parties do not think they are becoming partners is immaterial. If the parties agree upon an arrangement that is a partnership in fact, it is immaterial whether they call it something else or declare that they are not partners. On the other hand, the mere fact that the parties themselves call the relation a partnership will not make it so if they have not, by their conduct, agreed upon an arrangement that by the law is a partnership in fact.

The essential attributes of a partnership are a common interest in the business and management and a share in the profits and losses.[2] This common interest may be established by a holding of property and a sharing of the profits and losses related to the property. If there is a sharing of profits, a partnership may be found to exist even though there is no sharing of losses.

The presence of a common interest in property and management is not enough to establish a partnership by implication. Nor, of itself, does an agreement to share the gross returns of a business, sometimes called gross profits, prove an intention to form a partnership. If a person receives a share of real or net profits in a business, that is *prima facie* but not conclusive evidence of partnership. It may be overcome by evidence that the share in the profits is received for some other purpose, such as payment of a debt by installments, wages, rent, annuity to a widow of a deceased partner, interest on a loan, or payment of goodwill by installments. Bonuses are frequently paid as a percent of profit, but they do not make the employee a partner. Likewise, many leases provide for rent based on profits.

Whether a partnership exists is an inference of law based on established facts. The existence of a partnership is often implied from the conduct of the parties.[3]

2. Partnership by Estoppel

Insofar as third persons are concerned, partnership liability, like the apparent authority of an agent, may be predicated upon the legal theory of estoppel. If a person by words spoken or written or by conduct represents himself, or consents to another's representing him, as a partner in an existing partnership, that person is not a partner but is liable to any party to whom such representation has been made.[4] If the representation is made in a public manner either personally or with consent of the apparent partner, the apparent partner is liable if credit is

---

[2] Beck v. Indiana Surveying Co., p. 905.

[3] Lupien v. Malsbenden, p. 906.

[4] Montana Farm Service Co. v. Marquart, p. 907.

extended to the partnership, even if the creditor did not actually know of the representation. This is an exception to the usual estoppel requirement of actual reliance.

The courts are not in accord as to whether a person must affirmatively disclaim a reputed partnership that he did not consent to or claim. Some court cases hold that if a person is held out as a partner and he knows it, he should be chargeable as a partner unless he takes reasonable steps to give notice that he is not, in fact, a partner. These courts impose a duty on a person to deny that he is a partner, once he knows that third persons are relying on representations that he is a partner. Other cases indicate that there is no duty to deny false representations of partnership if the ostensible partner did not participate in making the misrepresentation. Also there is no duty to seek out all those who may represent that he is a partner, so that he may deny it.

3. Introduction

THE PARTNERSHIP AGREEMENT

The partnership agreement, usually called the *articles of partnership*, will vary from business to business. Among the subjects usually contained in such agreements are the following: the names of the partners and of the partnership, its purpose and duration, the capital contributions of each partner, the method of sharing profits and losses, the effect of advances, the salaries (if any) to be paid the partners, the method of accounting and the fiscal year, the rights and liabilities of the parties upon the death or withdrawal of a partner, and the procedures to be followed upon dissolution.

The Uniform Partnership Act or other partnership statute is a part of the agreement as if it had actually been written into the contract or had been made part of its stipulations. The sections that follow discuss some of the more important provisions of the partnership agreement and indicate the effect of the Uniform Partnership Act on the agreement.

4. Profit-and-Loss Provision

Unless the agreement is to the contrary, each partner has a right to share equally in the profits of the enterprise, and each partner is under a duty to contribute equally to the losses. Capital contributed to the firm is a liability owing by the firm to the contributing partners. If, on dissolution, there are not sufficient assets to repay each partner his capital, the amount is considered as a loss; and like any other loss of the partnership, it must be met. For example, a partnership is composed of A, B, and C. A contributed $20,000, B contributed $10,000, and C contributed $4,000. The firm is dissolved, and upon the payment of debts only $10,000 of firm assets remain. Because the total contribution to capital was $34,000, the operating loss is $24,000. This loss must be borne equally by A, B, and C, so that the loss for each is $8,000. This means that A is entitled to be reimbursed to the extent of her $20,000 contribution less $8,000, her share of the loss, or net of $12,000. B is entitled to $10,000, less $8,000, or $2,000. Because C has contributed only $4,000, he must now contribute to the firm an additional $4,000, in order that his loss will equal $8,000. The additional $4,000 contributed by C, plus the $10,000 remaining, will now be distributed so that A will receive $12,000 and B $2,000.

Occasionally, articles of copartnership specify the manner in which profits are to be divided, but they neglect to mention possible losses. In such cases the losses are borne in the same proportion that profits are to be shared. In the event that losses occur when one of the partners is insolvent and his share of the loss exceeds the amount owed him for advances and capital, the excess must be shared by the other partners. They share this unusual loss in the same ratio that they share profits. Thus, in the above example, if C were insolvent, A and B would each bear an additional $2,000 loss.

In addition to the right to be repaid his contributions, whether by way of capital or advances to the partnership property, the partnership must indemnify every partner for payments made and personal liabilities reasonably incurred by him in the ordinary and proper conduct of its business or for the preservation of its business or property.

5. Partnership Capital Provision

Partnership capital consists of the total credits to the capital accounts of the various partners, provided the credits are for permanent investments in the business. Such capital represents the amount that the partnership is obligated to return to the partners at the time of dissolution, and it can be varied only with the consent of all the partners. Undivided profits that are permitted by some of the partners to accumulate in the business do not become part of the capital. They, like temporary advances by firm members, are subject to withdrawal at any time unless the agreement provides to the contrary.

The amount that each partner is to contribute to the firm, as well as the credit he is to receive for assets contributed, is entirely dependent upon the partnership agreement. A person may become a partner without a capital contribution. For example, he may contribute services to balance the capital investment of the other partners. Such a partner, however, has no capital to be returned at the time of liquidation.[5] Only those who receive credit for capital investments—which may include goodwill, patent rights, and so forth, if agreed upon—are entitled to the return of capital when dissolution occurs.

If the investment is in a form other than money, the property no longer belongs to the contributing partner. He has vested the firm with title, and he has no greater equity in the property than has any other party. At dissolution, he recovers only the amount allowed to him for the property invested.

6. Provisions Relating to Partnership Property

In conducting its business, a partnership may use its own property, the property of the individual partners, or the property of some third person. It frequently becomes important, especially on dissolution and where claims of firm

---

[5] Badran v. Bertrand, p. 908.

creditors are involved, to ascertain exactly what property constitutes partnership property, in order to ascertain the rights of partners and firm creditors to specific property.

As a general rule, the agreement of the parties will determine what property is properly classified as partnership property. In the absence of an express agreement, what constitutes partnership property is ascertained from the conduct of the parties and from the purpose for, and the way in which, property is used in the pursuit of the business.

The Uniform Partnership Act provides that all property specifically brought into partnership or acquired by it is partnership property. Therefore, unless a contrary intention appears, property acquired with partnership funds is partnership property. In other words, there is a presumption that property acquired with partnership funds is partnership property, but this presumption is rebuttable.

Property acquired by a partner individually is often transferred to the partnership as a part of a partner's contribution to capital. If this property is purchased on credit, the creditor has no claim against the partnership, even though the property can be traced to it. A personal loan made to a partner does not become a partnership debt unless it is expressly assumed by the partnership.[6]

Because a partnership has the right to acquire, own, and dispose of personal property in the firm name, legal documents affecting the title to partnership personal property may be executed in the firm name by any partner. The Uniform Partnership Act also treats a partnership as a legal entity for the purposes of title to real estate that may be held in the firm name. Title so acquired can be conveyed in the partnership name. Many of the legal principles relating to partnership property will be discussed in the next chapter.

7. The Firm Name

Because a partnership is created by the agreement of the parties, they select the name to be used. This right of selection is subject to two limitations by statute in many states. First, a partnership may not use the word *company* or other language that would imply the existence of a corporation. Second, if the name is other than that of the partners, they must comply with assumed name statutes that require the giving of public notice as to the actual identity of the partners. Failure to comply with this assumed name statute may result in the partnership's being denied access to the courts to sue its debtors, or it may result in criminal actions being brought against those operating under the assumed name.

The firm name is an asset of the firm, and as such it may also be sold, assigned, or disposed of in any manner upon which the parties agree. At common law, a partnership was not a legal entity that could sue and be sued in the firm name. All actions had to be brought on behalf of, or against, all the partners as individuals. Today, statutes in most states have changed the common law and allow partnerships to sue or be sued in the firm name. Partnerships may also

---

[6] Waldrop v. Holland, p. 909.

declare bankruptcy as a firm. To this extent, and to the extent that it can own and dispose of property in the firm name, a partnership is a legal entity. It is not a legal entity to the extent that a corporation is, however.

8. Provisions Relating to Goodwill

Goodwill, which is usually transferred with the name, is based upon the justifiable expectation that a firm's good reputation, satisfied customers, established location, and past advertising will result in continued patronage of old customers and the probable patronage of new customers. Goodwill is usually considered in an evaluation of the assets of the business, and it is capable of being sold and transferred. Upon dissolution caused by the death of one of the partners, the surviving partner must account for it to the legal representative of the deceased partner, unless otherwise agreed upon in the *buy and sell agreement.*

When goodwill and the firm name are sold, an agreement not to compete is usually part of the sales agreement. Such an agreement may be implied, but it should be a part of the buy and sell provisions.

9. Buy and Sell Provisions

Either as part of the partnership agreement or by separate contract, the partners should provide for the contingency of death or withdrawal of a partner. This contingency is covered by a *buy and sell agreement,* and it is imperative that the terms of the buy and sell provisions be agreed upon before either party knows whether he is a buyer or a seller. After the status of the parties becomes known, agreement may be very difficult. If such agreement is lacking, many additional problems will arise upon the death or withdrawal of a partner, and there are many possibilities of litigation and economic loss to all concerned.

A buy and sell agreement avoids these types of problems by providing a method whereby the surviving partner or partners can purchase the interest of the deceased partner, or the remaining partner or partners can purchase the interest of the withdrawing partner. A method of determining the price to be paid for such interest is provided. The time and method of payment are usually stipulated. The buy and sell agreement should specify whether a partner has an option to purchase the interest of a dying or withdrawing partner or whether he has a duty to do so.

It is common for partners to provide for life insurance on each other's lives as a means of funding the buy and sell provisions. In the event of a partner's death, proceeds of the insurance are used to purchase the deceased partner's interest. Premiums on such life insurance are not deductible for tax purposes, but are usually treated as an expense for accounting purposes. There are a variety of methods for holding title to the insurance. It may be individually owned or business owned. The provisions of the policy should be carefully integrated into the partnership agreement; each partner's estate plan should also properly consider the ramifications of this insurance and of the buy and sell agreement.

SUMMARY

THE EXISTENCE OF A PARTNERSHIP

Issues between the partners

1. A partnership may be created by express agreement or may be implied from conduct. In either case, it is a question of the intent of the parties.
2. The essential elements of a partnership are a common interest in the business and a share in the profits and losses.
3. The receipt of a share of the profits is *prima facie* evidence of a partnership, but this presumption may be overcome by evidence that the share of profits is for some other purpose.

Issues between the partnership and third parties

1. While parties may not be partners as between themselves, a partnership may exist insofar as third parties are concerned.
2. A partnership by estoppel is created if a person by words or conduct represents himself or consents to another's representing him as a partner.

THE PARTNERSHIP AGREEMENT

Profit and loss provision

1. Unless there is an agreement to the contrary, profits and losses are shared equally.
2. If the agreement does not cover losses, they are shared in the same manner as profits.

The capital provision

1. Partnership capital is the amount contributed by a partner and the amount that is to be returned on dissolution.
2. Undivided profits are not a part of capital.
3. A party may become a partner without a capital contribution.

Partnership property provisions

1. All property brought into the partnership or acquired by it is partnership property.

	2. Property contributed as part of a capital contribution is partnership property.
	3. Partnership property may be acquired and disposed of in the partnership name.
The partnership name	**1.** The partnership may not use words indicating that it is a corporation.
	2. The partnership name is other than the names of the partners and must comply with the assumed name statute.
	3. The firm name is an asset and may be treated as such.
	4. Partnerships can sue and be sued in the firm name.
Goodwill	**1.** Goodwill is an asset that may be transferred to others and that must be accounted for upon the death of a partner.
The buy and sell provision	**1.** The partnership agreement must provide for the contingency of the death, withdrawal, or expulsion of a partner.
	2. Such agreements are usually funded with life insurance as an expense of the partnership.

CASES

Roby v. Day
635 P.2d 611 (Okl. 1981)

The Oklahoma Constitution prohibits the sale of alcoholic beverages in an "open saloon." Retail sales of alcoholic beverages are limited to sales in the original sealed package. The plaintiff in an attempt to circumvent this prohibition formed a limited partnership whose capital would be used to purchase liquor. The limited partners would be individual consumers of alcoholic beverages. The partnership would enter into storage and service agreements with various private clubs to store the liquor and serve it to the partners upon proof of identification.

The plaintiff filed a registration statement with the state as required for a public sale of interests in a limited partnership. The Oklahoma Attorney General advised that the plaintiff's pro-

posed business purpose was illegal, and the Department of Securities issued an order denying the effectiveness of the registration statement.

LAVENDER, J. . . . In essence the partnership represents a scheme for distribution of alcoholic beverages which is outside of the framework of the statute and the Constitution of Oklahoma that govern licensing, distribution, and regulation of alcoholic beverages.

However, we perceive . . . [a] hurdle.

Section 144 of The Oklahoma Uniform Limited Partnership Act provides:

A limited partnership may carry on any business which a partnership without limited partners may carry on, except banking and insurance.

Section 206 of The Uniform Partnership Act insofar as pertinent, states:

(1) A partnership is an association of two or more persons to carry on as co-owners a business for profit.

(2) . . . this Act shall apply to limited partnerships except insofar as the statutes relating to such partnerships are inconsistent herewith.

The limited partnership contemplated by plaintiff is neither a "business" nor is it "for profit" within the meaning of § 144, supra. Without the presence of both, plaintiff's whole scheme crumbles.

This court has held that associations and clubs, the objects of which are political rather than for purposes of trade and profit are not partnerships. . . .

. . . The general rule is: [T]hose persons are partners who contribute either property or services to carry on a joint business for their common benefit, and who own and share the profits thereof in certain proportions. If they do this, the incidents or consequences follow that the acts of one in conducting the partnership business are the acts of all; that each is agent of the firm and for the other partners; that each receives part of the profit as profits, and takes part of the fund to which the creditors of the partnership have a right to look for the payment of their debts; that all are liable as partners upon contracts made by any of them with third persons within the scope of the partnership business; and that even an express stipulation between them that one shall not be so liable, though good between themselves, is ineffectual as against third persons. And participating in profits is presumptive, but not conclusive, evidence of partnership. . . .

The only enterprise which plaintiff's scheme contemplates "carrying on" is the replenishment of alcoholic consumables as the common supply diminishes, a project which falls short of a program which the contemplated partners will "carry on as co-owners a business for profit." . . .

Affirmed.

Beck v. Indiana Surveying Co.
429 N.E.2d 264 (Ind. App. 1981)

Beck and Kirk entered into a "land development agreement" which provided that Beck would contribute land and Kirk would furnish her expertise to create a residential housing development to be called "Beckhaven Estates." Beck and Kirk agreed to divide any profits. Kirk employed the plaintiff, Indiana Surveying, to plot the development. When Kirk failed to pay for the survey, suit was instituted against Beck and Kirk as partners to collect. The trial court found for the plaintiff and Beck appeals.

ROBERTSON, J. . . . Beck argues that there was insufficient evidence to support the trial court's finding that the business activities of Beck and Kirk constituted a partnership. A partnership has been defined as an association of two or more persons to carry on as co-owners a business for a profit. . . .

The receipt by a person of a share of the profits of a business is prima facie evidence that he is a partner in the business, but no such inference shall be drawn if such profits were received in payment:

(a) As a debt by installments or otherwise,

(b) As wages of an employee or rent to a landlord,

(c) As an annuity to a widow or representative of a deceased partner,

(d) As interest on a loan, though the amount of payments vary with the profits of the business,

(e) As the consideration for the sale of a good will of a business or other property by installments or otherwise.

Beck and Kirk agreed to split the profits from their activities. The receipt of a share of the profits is prima facie evidence of the existence of a partnership. . . . Beck argues that his receipt of the profits is not evidence of a partnership, but merely the consideration for the sale of property by installments. . . . We believe that the scope of this exception is limited to transactions between the immediate buyer and seller, such that the receipt of a share of the buyer's profits by the seller is not evidence that the seller is a partner of the buyer. We believe that [the installment sale exception] is inapplicable to future sales to third parties.

Beck also argues that there was insufficient evidence that he was a "co-owner of a business". . . .

There was further evidence demonstrating that Beck and Kirk's activities constituted a partnership. The agreement clearly intended the creation of a housing development, which must be construed to be the intent to create a business enterprise, and not just an investment in real estate. The development was to be named Beckhaven Estate after Beck. The use of a firm name is evidence of the existence of a partnership. . . . The partnership agreement provided that sales under a minimum amount needed Beck's approval. The trustee was directed to convey the land in question at the direction of either Beck or Kirk. This established that Beck could participate in the management. The lack of involvement in the daily management of the enterprise is not per se indicative of the absence of a partnership. . . .

Affirmed.

Lupien v. Malsbenden
477 A.2d 746 (Me. 1984)

Plaintiff, Lupien, entered into a contract with Cragin doing business as York Motor Mart for the construction of a Bradley automobile from a kit. The price was $8,020, and plaintiff paid $4,450 down. He visited York Motor Mart each week to check on the progress being made on his car. During those visits plaintiff generally dealt with the defendant Malsbenden because Cragin was seldom present. On one such visit Malsbenden told plaintiff to sign over ownership of his pickup truck so that the proceeds from the sale of the truck could be used to complete construction of the Bradley. When plaintiff complied, Malsbenden provided plaintiff with a rental car and later with a "demo" model of the Bradley. Plaintiff never received the Bradley he had contracted to purchase, and he sued Malsbenden for a refund of the purchase price.

Malsbenden asserts that his interest in the Bradley operation of York Motor Mart was only that of a banker. He stated that he had lent $85,000 to Cragin, without interest, to finance the Bradley portion of York Motor Mart's business. The loan was to be repaid from the proceeds of each car sold. Malsbenden acknowledged that Bradley kits were purchased with his personal checks and that he had also purchased equipment for York Motor Mart. He also stated that after Cragin disappeared, he had physical control of the premises of York Motor Mart and that he continued to dispose of assets there even to the time of trial in 1983.

McKUSICK, J. . . . The Uniform Partnership Act defines a partnership as "an association of 2 or more persons . . . to carry on as co-owners a business for profit." . . . Whether a partnership exists is an inference of law based on established facts. . . . A finding that the relationship between two persons constitutes a partnership may be based upon evidence of an agreement, either express or implied,

> to place their money, effects, labor, and skill, or some or all of them, in lawful commerce or business with the understanding that a community of profits will be shared. . . . No one factor is alone determinative of the existence of a partnership. . . .

. . . If the arrangement between the parties otherwise qualifies as a partnership, it is of no matter that the parties did not expressly agree to form a partnership or did not even intend to form one:

> It is possible for parties to intend no partnership and yet to form one. If they agree upon an arrangement which is a partnership in fact, it is of no importance that they call it something else, or that they even expressly declare that they are not to be partners. The law must declare what is the legal import of their agreements, and names go for nothing when the substance of the arrangement shows them to be inapplicable. . . .

Here the trial justice concluded that, notwithstanding Malsbenden's assertion that he was only a "banker," his "total involvement" in the Bradley operation was that of a partner. The testimony at trial, both respecting Malsbenden's financial interest in the enterprise and his involvement in day-to-day business operations, amply supported the Superior Court's conclusion. Malsbenden had a financial interest of $85,000 in the Bradley portion of York Motor Mart's operations. Although Malsbenden termed the investment a loan, significantly he conceded that the "loan" carried no interest. His "loan" was not made in the form of a fixed payment or payments, but was made to the business, at least in substantial part, in the form of day-to-day purchases of Bradley kits, other parts and equipment, and in the payment of wages. Furthermore, the "loan" was not to be repaid in fixed amounts or at fixed times, but rather only upon the sale of Bradley automobiles.

The evidence also showed that, unlike a banker, Malsbenden had the right to participate in control of the business and in fact did so on a day-to-day basis. According to Urbin Savaria, who worked at York Motor Mart from late April through June 1980, Malsbenden during that time opened the business establishment each morning, remained present through part of every day, had final say on the ordering of parts, paid for parts and equipment, and paid Savaria's salary. On plaintiff's frequent visits to York Motor Mart, he generally dealt with Malsbenden because Cragin was not present. It was Malsbenden who insisted that plaintiff trade in his truck prior to the completion of the Bradley because the proceeds from the sale of the truck were needed to complete the Bradley. When it was discovered that the "demo" Bradley given to plaintiff while he awaited completion of his car actually belonged to a third party, it was Malsben-

den who bought the car for plaintiff's use. As of three years after the making of the contract now in litigation, Malsbenden was still doing business at York Motor Mart, "just disposing of property."

Malsbenden and Cragin may well have viewed their relationship to be that of creditor-borrower, rather than a partnership. At trial Malsbenden so asserts, and Cragin's departure from the scene in the spring of 1980 deprives us of the benefit of his view of his business arrangement with Malsbenden. In any event, whatever the intent of these two men as to their respective involvements in the business of making and selling Bradley cars, there is no clear error in the Superior Court's finding that the Bradley car operation represented a pooling of Malsbenden's capital and Cragin's automotive skills, with joint control over the business and intent to share the fruits of the enterprise. As a matter of law, that arrangement amounted to a partnership. . . .

The entry is:

Judgment affirmed.

Montana Farm Service Co. v. Marquart
578 P.2d 315 (Mont. 1978)

HASWELL, J. Defendant Leo Marquart, appeals from a judgment . . . granting plaintiff . . . the sum of $5,301.27 plus attorney fees of $1,500 and costs.

On or about September 1, 1973, defendants entered into a written agreement with plaintiff, whereby defendants were designated as the service agent for plaintiff in Missoula, Montana. Under the agreement, defendants were authorized to merchandise tires, batteries, and accessories delivered to them by plaintiff.

At trial, the testimony concerning the execution of this agreement was conflicting. Plaintiff's agent, Stewart Burwell, testified that defendants signed the agreements together and he personally witnessed such signing. He testified (1) that when the agreements were signed they were not blank agreements, (2) that defendant Marquart introduced him to defendant Roth, and (3) that defendant Marquart informed him that he and defendant Roth were going into a joint venture together to merchandise plaintiff's goods. This joint venture,

according to Burwell, was Southside Tire and Clinic. . . . (Defendants testified to a wholly different set of facts.)

Between September 1, 1973 and January 7, 1974, plaintiff delivered merchandise to defendants for resale, in accordance with their agreement. Defendants made no attempt to pay for any of the merchandise delivered to them. . . .

The sole issue on appeal is whether the evidence is sufficient to sustain the . . . judgments . . . requiring defendant Marquart to pay for the merchandise received by Southside Tire and Clinic.

The evidence in this case is conflicting. Plaintiff's witness gave one version of the facts and defendants gave another version. . . .

Where there is a conflict in the evidence, . . . the findings of the trial court, in a nonjury trial, will not be reversed on appeal, unless there is a clear preponderance of evidence against the findings. Applying those rules to this case, we find there is substantial credible evidence to support the findings of the trial court and there is no clear preponderance of evidence against such findings.

We recount the evidence supporting the findings: the testimony of Burwell concerning the execution of the agreements; his testimony that defendant Marquart stated that he and defendant Roth were going into a joint venture as the service agent for plaintiff; the agreements themselves which both defendants signed on the same signature line and next to each other's signature; and defendant Marquart's testimony that he had taken over the property owned by defendant Roth, which indicates some business dealing between the two men. The only evidence presented by defendants against the court's findings was their own testimony and a calendar which was introduced into evidence. The calendar read that defendant Roth was the owner and manager of Southside Tire and Clinic.

In our view the evidence indicates that a partnership existed between the defendants as far as their relationship with the plaintiff is concerned. One may become a partner of a firm, as to third persons, without intending to, by words spoken or written or by conduct, and thereby become liable to those who have, on the faith thereof, given credit to the actual or apparent partnership. We hold then that defendant Marquart, by signing the service agency agreement and never having his name removed from it, is liable to plaintiff for the merchandise delivered to Southside Tire and Clinic.

Affirmed.

Badran v. Bertrand
334 N.W.2d 184 (Neb. 1983)

The parties first met in July, 1975, at Grand Island, Nebraska, where Sam was selling bedspreads and linens from his car. Shortly thereafter, the parties orally agreed to a partnership type venture, financed by Virginia and promoted by Sam, to sell Indian jewelry and other gift items. On February 12, 1976, they opened the Holdrege Gift Shop, Holdrege, Nebraska. All funds for the purchase of merchandise and early business operations were paid from Virginia's personal funds, except money generated from sales. On June 23, 1976, the parties executed a partnership agreement, terminating in two years. The partnership never made a profit, and the shop was closed in January, 1979, when the merchandise was moved to Omaha, Nebraska, where the parties were operating Nasr's Restaurant. Some of the Indian jewelry was displayed at Nasr's and the rest was stored in the trunk of a car owned by Virginia and possessed by Sam. There are no records of any purchases or sales in 1979. On January 7, 1980, Virginia forcibly obtained possession of all the merchandise, which she still has. This suit by Sam for an accounting followed. The trial court awarded all assets to Virginia. Sam appeals, claiming his personal business expertise was a contribution of partnership capital.

COLWELL, J. . . . Plaintiff's . . . assignment of error is that the trial court failed to find that his business expertise was a contribution of capital to the partnership. His expertise is described as a vast

amount of time, experience, and knowledge as a self-employed salesman.

The partnership agreement provides in part, "(5) The initial capital of the Partnership shall be One Hundred Thousand Dollars . . . and each partner agrees to contribute *cash or property* as follows:

	Amount	Percent
Virginia Bertrand	$50,000.00	50%
Sam Badran	50,000.00	50%

*   *   *

The record is clear that plaintiff contributed no money and that defendant knew that he could not do so; she expected him to contribute his money from future profits. Plaintiff contends that he contributed his business skills and expertise, which was "property." This claim being contrary to the agreement, and there being no competent evidence varying its terms, we look to the conduct of the parties. . . .

Sam had 35 years of experience as an itinerant, self-employed salesman dealing in bedspreads, rugs, and linens. He had no prior experience in Indian jewelry merchandising. His first purchases of jewelry were made through the assistance of his two brothers, who were dealers. An example of his claimed expertise was his ability to buy jewelry at one-third to one-fourth of its retail value, which Virginia could not do. Virginia does not deny his skill as a merchant; rather, she denies that it was more than that. During the 1976–78 period, when the shop failed to make a profit, plaintiff requested of defendant and obtained money, a car, living quarters, and other family gratuities amounting to more than $80,000, a part being deemed salary by the trial court. His conduct is inconsistent with his claim.

As we view the record, plaintiff performed the services that the parties intended; those services were not unusual considering plaintiff's sales experience, skills, the attending circumstances, and bearing in mind the failure of the venture. We conclude that plaintiff made no contribution to his capital account as required and intended by the partnership agreement.

This leaves the question of the distribution of the remaining partnership assets and the settlement of its debts. . . .

It is a general rule that capital furnished by any partner, in the absence of agreement to the contrary, is a debt owing by the firm to the contributing partner, and necessarily is to be repaid him, if the firm assets are sufficient after paying the firm liabilities to outsiders.

. . . [U]pon dissolution, where one has contributed capital and another services, the one contributing the capital is entitled to withdraw its value. . . .

Affirmed.

Waldrop v. Holland
588 P.2d 1237 (Wash.App.) 1979

GREEN, J. . . . As a matter of law, does a partnership assume an antecedent loan obtained by one of the partners to purchase equipment later transferred to the partnership? . . .

The defendants loaned money to Dalton Waldrop in 1974. In mid-1975, Dalton Waldrop and Thomas Waldrop, his brother, formed a partnership for the drilling of wells. In January 1976, this partnership was incorporated as Waldrop Drilling & Pipe Co., Inc. In May 1976, Dalton Waldrop left the corporation and his interest was taken over by Thomas Waldrop. Neither the partnership nor the corporation assumed the obligation of Dalton Waldrop to the defendants for the loan to Dalton Waldrop by the defendants in 1974. In August 1976, defendants employed Waldrop Drilling & Pipe Co., Inc., to repair one of their pumps. This repair work was completed on August 24, 1976, at a reasonable cost of $2,873.75. On November 4, 1976, at the request of defendants, the corporation performed additional repair services in the reasonable amount of $710.54. Neither of these bills was paid.

The corporation brought this action to collect the amount due. Defendants sought to offset these amounts against the balance owed to them by Dalton Waldrop. The trial court rejected the offset and entered judgment in favor of the corporation for these amounts plus interest and costs.

It is defendants' position that because Dalton Waldrop, the original debtor, used the loan proceeds to purchase well-drilling equipment which later became an asset of the partnership between Dalton and Thomas Waldrop, and later a corporate asset, the partnership and the corporation are liable for the original loan. Consequently, defendants contend that the repair cost should have been offset against the balance owed to them by Dalton Waldrop. We disagree.

Thomas Waldrop testified he was unaware of this obligation until the business entity performed some work for defendants, and the defendants thereafter sought to offset the cost of the work against the amount of their loan to Dalton Waldrop. The court found that at the time the repairs in question were performed, Thomas Waldrop, president of the corporation, told the defendants that they would be responsible for payment for the services. The court further found that neither the partnership nor the corporation in fact assumed Dalton Waldrop's personal obligation to the defendants. In these circumstances, the trial court was correct in concluding that neither entity became obligated for Dalton Waldrop's personal obligation to the defendants. A loan made to a partner in his individual capacity before formation of the partnership is not a partnership debt unless it is expressly assumed by the partnership. Therefore, defendants are obliged to look to Dalton Waldrop for collection of their loan.

Affirmed.

REVIEW QUESTIONS

1. Identify the terms in column A by matching each with the appropriate statement in column B.

A	B
1. Partnership by estoppel	**a.** An agreement that covers the rights of parties on dissolution.
2. Implied partnership	**b.** The contribution of partners to the partnership.
3. Ostensible partner	**c.** A partnership created by conduct.
4. Articles of partnership	**d.** Failure to comply may be a crime.
5. Partnership capital	**e.** Partnership liability that is imposed on one who has held himself out to be a partner when in fact he is not a partner.
6. Advance	**f.** Synonymous with a partner by estoppel.
7. Assumed name statute	**g.** The agreement creating a partnership.
8. Buy and sell agreement	**h.** A loan to the partnership by a partner.

2. Holler owned grazing land and was looking for someone to pasture cattle on his land. Plaintiff, a cattle rancher, entered into a grazing contract with Holler, which provided in part that "net money" from the sale of cattle was to be split evenly between the parties. For many years the operation was a success. However, in 1984 plaintiff suffered an $89,000 loss. Plaintiff sued Holler, contending that the agreement made the parties "partners" and that Holler was liable for half of the loss. Holler contended that he was not a partner, but only a landlord receiving profits as rent. Were the parties partners? Why?

3. Plaintiff, a newspaper, sued Elliott to recover an account for advertising. Filip had ordered the advertising, and in order to obtain credit, Peoples, an employee of Filip, had represented that Elliott was a co-owner of the business. Plaintiff relied upon this representation, but made no effort to verify the fact. Elliott was not a co-owner and had not held himself out to be one. Is the defendant liable? Explain.

4. Jenkins obtained an option to purchase 10 acres of land for $60,000. He approached Petty with a proposal of combining for development the 10-acre parcel with the adjacent 26-acre parcel owned by Petty. After negotiations Jenkins and Petty entered into a written agreement which provided for the transfer of Jenkins's option to Petty for $20,000 and the purchase of the optioned property by Petty. There also was a provision requiring both parties to promote the development as soon as rezoning was obtained, and a provision on payback of investments and profit sharing. Were Jenkins and Petty partners? Explain.

5. Les and Turner entered into a written agreement whereby Turner was to farm Les's land in exchange for one-third of the crop as rental. The contract also provided that Les was to advance financing and Turner was to furnish the equipment. It was also agreed that after delivery of one-third of the crops, all net proceeds and losses were to be shared equally. The contract specifically stated that Les and Turner were not partners, but landlord and tenant. Are Les and Turner partners? Why?

6. Charlotte and Gia, both attorneys, agreed to share office space and other overhead expenses, but they did not agree to form a partnership. The sign outside their offices and their common letterhead read "Charlotte Gifford and Gia Hammond, Attorneys at Law." Using this stationery, Charlotte purchased some office equipment from Descor. Gia did not join in the contract in any way. Charlotte did not pay for the equipment. Is Gia liable to Descor? Discuss.

7. Pursuant to an oral agreement, Andy and Jeff formed a partnership to do kitchen remodeling. It was agreed that Andy was to invest $10,000 and manage the business affairs. Jeff who would invest $1,000, was to work as job superintendent and manage the work. Profits were to be split fifty-fifty, but possible losses were not discussed. The business proved unprofitable, and Andy brought action against Jeff for one-half of the losses. To what extent is Jeff liable? Explain.

8. Describe four situations in which a person may receive a percentage of business income without its being presumed that this person is a partner.

9. A partnership is to be liquidated. Smith has contributed $6,000 to capital, Charles $3,000 to capital, and Black has made no contribution to capital, but has merely contributed his services. Liabilities of the partnership exceed assets by $9,000. How much must each partner contribute to pay off the liabilities? Explain.

10. A partnership known as Stein Properties used its firm name when it sued a defendant for breach of contract. The partnership had not complied with the state's assumed-name statute. The defendant moved to dismiss the suit, contending that the partnership could not sue because of its failure to comply with the state statute. Should the suit be dismissed? Why?

11. Pat and Doris were equal partners in a real estate business. Doris purchased a piece of real estate in her own name; however, she reimbursed herself for the down payment from the partnership's checking account. This property was shown on the partnership's books, and all expenses connected with it were paid by the partnership. Is this real estate partnership property, each partner being entitled to one-half of the profits from its sale? Why?

12. An agent for a general partnership entered into a contract in the name of the partnership to purchase certain real estate. The seller refused to close the transaction, and a suit for specific performance of the sales agreement was brought in the partnership's name without naming the partners. The defendant moved to dismiss the complaint on the ground that the plaintiff does not have legal capacity to sue. With what result? Why?

13. Why should a buy and sell provision be included in a partnership agreement? How can the partnership be sure of having sufficient funds to comply with a buy and sell provision?

40 Operation of Partnerships

The operation of a partnership is governed by the provisions of the partnership agreement and the applicable statutory law, which in most states is the Uniform Partnership Act. Thus the rights, duties, and powers of partners are both expressed (those in the agreement) and implied (those created by law). Many of the expressed rights, duties, and powers were discussed in chapter 39. Those that are implied will be discussed in this chapter, along with additional observations about the partnership agreement as it affects operations. Throughout this discussion, remember that a partner is essentially an agent for the other partners, and that the general principles of the law of agency are applicable.

Before examining the rights, duties, and powers of partners, certain terminology must be understood. A *silent partner* in a general partnership is one who does not participate in management. If the silent partner is to have limited liability, the provisions of the Uniform Limited Partnership Act must be followed. A *secret partner* is unknown to third parties. He may advise management and participate in decisions, but his interest is not known to third parties. A *dormant partner* is both secret and silent.

THE RIGHTS OF PARTNERS

1. Right to Participate in Management

All partners have equal rights in the management and conduct of the firm's business. These rights are not determined by the share that each partner has invested in the business. The partners may, however, agree to place the management within the control of one or more partners.

The majority of the partners decide ordinary matters arising in the conduct of the partnership business. If the firm consists of only two persons who are unable to agree, and the articles of partnership make no provision for the settlement of disputes, dissolution is the only remedy. The partnership agreement usually provides for some form of arbitration of deadlocks between partners in order to avoid dissolution.

The majority cannot, however, without the consent of the minority, change the essential nature of the business by altering the partnership agreement or by reducing or increasing the capital of the partners. It cannot embark upon a new business or admit new members to the firm. In a limited partnership, the agreement cannot be modified without the unanimous consent of all partners.

Certain acts other than those enumerated previously require the unanimous consent of the partners in order to bind the firm, namely: (1) assigning the firm property to a trustee for the benefit of creditors; (2) confessing a judgment: (3) disposing of the goodwill of the business; (4) submitting a partnership agreement to arbitration; and (5) doing any act that would make impossible the conduct of the partnership business.

2. Right to Be Compensated for Services

It is the duty of each partner, in the absence of an agreement to the contrary, to give his entire time, skill, and energy to the pursuit of the partnership affairs. No partner is entitled to payment for services rendered in the conduct of the partnership business, unless an agreement to that effect has been expressed or may be implied from the conduct of the partners.[1] An agreement to compensate may be implied from the practice of actually paying a salary. If an agreement or practice contemplates a salary to one or more partners but no amount is specified, it may be presumed that the payment of reasonable compensation is intended. This often occurs when one partner is actually engaged in the business and others are not. Often, one of the partners does not desire to participate in the management of the business. The partnership agreement in such case usually provides that the active partners receive a salary for their services in addition to their share in the profits. A surviving partner is entitled to reasonable compensation for his services in winding up the partnership affairs, unless he is guilty of misconduct in winding up the affairs.

3. Right to Interest

Contributions to capital are not entitled to draw interest unless they are not repaid when the repayment should be made. The partner's share in the profits constitutes the earnings on his capital investment. In the absence of an expressed provision for the payment of interest, it is presumed that interest will be paid only on advances above the amount originally contributed as capital. Advances in excess of the prescribed capital, even though credited to the capital account of the contributing partners, are entitled to draw interest from the date of the advance.

---

[1] Sharp v. Laubersheimer, p. 921.

Unwithdrawn profits remaining in the firm are not entitled to draw interest. They are not considered advances or loans merely because they are left with the firm, although custom, usage, and circumstances may show an intention to treat them as loans.

4. Right to Information and to Inspection of Books

Every partner is entitled to full and complete information concerning the conduct of the business and to inspect the books to secure that information. The partnership agreement usually contains provisions relative to the records that the business will maintain. Each partner is under a duty to give the person responsible for keeping the records whatever information is necessary to carry on the business efficiently and effectively. It is the duty of the person keeping the records to allow each partner access to them, but no partner has a right to remove the records from the agreed-upon location without the consent of the other partners. Each partner is entitled to make copies of the records, provided he does not make his inspection for fraudulent purposes.

Each partner has implied authority to receive notices and information for all other partners concerning matters within the pursuit of the partnership business. Knowledge held by any partner in his mind but not revealed to the other partners is nevertheless notice to the partnership. Knowledge of one partner is legally knowledge of all partners, provided that the facts became known or were knowledge obtained within the scope of the partnership business. A partner has a duty to communicate known facts to the other partners and to add them to the records of the partnership. Failure to do so is fraud on the partnership by the partner possessing the knowledge. This failure to inform is also a breach of the duty to assist in the maintenance of accurate records.

5. Right to an Accounting

The partners' proportionate share of the partnership assets or profits, when not determined by a voluntary settlement of the parties, may be ascertained in a suit for an accounting. Such suits are equitable in nature; and in states that still distinguish between suits at law and suits in equity, these actions must be filed in the court of equity.

As a general rule, a partner cannot maintain an *action at law* against other members of the firm on the partnership agreement because until there is an accounting and all partnership affairs are settled, the indebtedness among the firm members is undetermined. This general rule is subject to a few commonsense exceptions.[2] For example, if the partnership is formed for the carrying out of a single venture or transaction, or the action involves a segregated or single unadjusted item of account, or a personal covenant or transaction entirely independent of the partnership affairs, a suit at law may be filed. Since the affairs of a partnership usually involve multiple and complicated transactions, the requirement of an accounting before a suit for damages is usually applied.

---

[2] Mitchell Resort Enterprises, Inc. v. C & S Builders, Inc., p. 922.

Because partners ordinarily have equal access to the partnership records, there is usually no need for formal accountings to determine partnership interests. A suit for an accounting is not permitted for settling incidental matters or disputes between the partners. If a dispute is of such grievous nature that the continued existence of the partnership is impossible, a suit for an accounting in equity is allowed.

In all cases, a partner is entitled to an accounting upon the dissolution of the firm. Without a dissolution of the firm, he has a right to a formal accounting in the following situations:

1. There is an agreement for an accounting at a definite date.
2. One partner has withheld profits arising from secret transactions.
3. There has been an execution levied against the interest of one of the partners.
4. One partner does not have access to the books.
5. The partnership is approaching insolvency, and all parties are not available.

Upon an agreement between themselves, the partners may make a complete accounting and settle their claims without resort to a court of equity.

6. Property Rights

A partner is a co-owner with the other partners of partnership property. Subject to any agreement among partners, a partner has an equal right to possess partnership property for partnership purposes. A partner has no right to possess partnership property for other purposes without the consent of the partners.

A partner has a right that the property will be used in the pursuit of the partnership business and to pay firm creditors. Since a partner does not own any specific item of the partnership property, he has no right in specific partnership property that is transferable by him. A partner has no right to use the firm property in satisfaction of personal debts; conversely, his personal creditors cannot make a levy upon specific partnership property.

When a partner dies, his interest in specific partnership property passes to the surviving partner or partners, who have the duty of winding up the affairs of the partnership in accordance with the partnership agreement and the applicable laws. When the winding-up process is complete, the estate of the deceased partner will be paid whatever sum the estate is entitled to, according to law and the partnership agreement. The surviving partner may sell the property, real and personal, of the partnership in connection with winding up the business, in order to obtain the cash to pay the estate of the deceased partner.

A partner's interest *in the firm* consists of his rights to share in the profits that are earned and, after dissolution and liquidation, to the return of his capital and undistributed profits. This assumes, of course, that his capital has not been absorbed or impaired by losses.

A partner may assign his interest, or his right to share in the profits of the partnership. Such an assignment will not of itself cause the dissolution of the firm.

The assignee is not entitled to participate in the management of the business. The only right of the assignee is to receive the profits to which the assignor would otherwise have been entitled and, in the event of dissolution, to receive his assignor's interest.

A partner's interest in the partnership cannot be levied upon by his separate creditors and sold at public sale. A judgment creditor of a partner must proceed by obtaining a "charging order" from the court. This order charges the interest of the debtor partner with the unsatisfied amount of the judgment debt. The court will ordinarily appoint a receiver, who will receive the partner's share of the profits and any other money due or to fall due to him in respect of the partnership and apply that money upon the judgment. Likewise, the court may order that the interest charged be sold. Such a sale is not a sale of the partnership assets or property.[3] Neither the charging order nor the sale of the interest will cause a dissolution of the firm unless the partnership is one that is terminable at will.

If there is more than one judgment creditor seeking a charging order, the first one to seek it is usually paid in full before others are paid anything. There is no pro rata distribution unless the partnership is dissolved.

DUTIES AND POWERS OF PARTNERS

7. Duties

A partnership is a fiduciary relationship. Each partner owes the duty of undivided loyalty to the other. Therefore, every partner must account to the partnership for any benefit and hold as a trustee for it any profits gained by him without consent of the other partners. This duty also rests upon representatives of deceased partners engaged in the liquidation of the affairs of the partnership.

The partnership relation is a personal one, obligating each partner to exercise good faith and to consider mutual welfare of all the partners in his conduct of the business. If one partner attempts to secure an advantage over the others, he thereby breaches the partnership relation, and he must account for all benefits that he obtains. This includes transactions with partners and with others. It also includes transactions connected with winding up the business. The duty continues, even though the partnership is dissolved, if the partnership opportunity arose prior to dissolution.[4]

8. The Power to Contract

A partner is an agent of the partnership for the purpose of its business, and the general rules of agency are applicable to all partnerships. Each partner has authority to bind the partnership with contractual liability whenever he is apparently carrying on the business of the partnership in the usual way. If it is apparent that he is not carrying on business of the partnership in the usual way, his act does not bind the partnership unless it is authorized by the other partners.[5]

---

[3] Bohonus v. Amerco, p. 923.

[4] Leff v. Gunter, p. 924.

[5] Hodge v. Garrett, p. 925.

The rules of agency relating to authority, ratification, and secret limitations on the authority of a partner are applicable to partnerships, but the extent of implied authority is generally greater for partners than for ordinary agents. Each partner has implied power to do all acts necessary for carrying on the business of the partnership. Admissions or representations pertaining to the conduct of the partnership business and made by a partner may be used as evidence against the partnership.

The nature and scope of the business and what is usual in the particular business determine the extent of the implied powers. Among the common implied powers are the following: to compromise, adjust, and settle claims or debts owed by or to the partnership; to sell goods in the regular course of business and to make warranties; to buy property within the scope of the business for cash or upon credit; to buy insurance; to hire employees; to make admissions against interest; to enter into contracts within the scope of the firm; and to receive notices. In a trading partnership, a partner has the implied authority to borrow funds and to pledge the assets of the firm. Some of these implied duties are discussed more fully in the sections that follow.

9. The Power to Impose Tort Liability

A partner has the power to impose tort liability through the doctrine of *respondeat superior*. The law imposes tort liability upon a partnership for all wrongful acts or omissions of any partner acting in the ordinary course of the partnership and for its benefit.[6]

If a partnership has liability because of a tort of a partner, the firm has the right to collect its losses from the partner at fault. In effect, a partnership that is liable in tort to a third person has a right of indemnity against the partner at fault. Likewise, if the injured third party collects directly from the partner at fault, the partner cannot seek contribution from his co-partners.

10. Powers over Property

Each partner has implied authority to sell to good-faith purchasers personal property that is held for the purpose of resale and to execute any documents necessary to effect a transfer of title. Of course, if his authority in this connection has been limited and that is known to the purchaser, the transfer of title will be ineffective or voidable. A partner has no power to sell the fixtures and equipment used in the business unless he has been duly authorized. His acts are not a regular feature of the business, and a prospective purchaser should make certain that the particular partner has been given authority to sell. The power to sell, where it is present, also gives the power to make warranties that normally accompany similar sales.

The right to sell a firm's real property is to be inferred only if the firm is engaged in the real estate business. In other cases there is no right to sell and convey realty unless it has been authorized by a partnership agreement. In most

---

[6] Martin v. Barbour, p. 926.

states, a deed by one partner without authority is not binding on the firm, but it does convey the individual interest of the parties executing and delivering the deed. This conveyance, however, is subject to the rights of creditors of the partnership.

Under the Uniform Partnership Act, title to real property may be taken in the firm name as a "tenancy in partnership," and any member of the firm has power to execute a deed thereto by signing the firm name. If that happens, what is the effect of a wrongful transfer of real estate that has been acquired for use in the business and not for resale? The conveyance may be set aside by the other partners, because the purchaser should have known that one partner has no power to sell real estate without the approval of the others. However, if the first purchaser has resold and conveyed the property to an innocent third party, the latter takes good title.

If the title to real estate is held in the firm name, a conveyance by the partners as individuals is not effective to convey title to the real estate. The conveyance must be in the firm name.[7] This is true even if the conveyance is to a partner as part of a settlement agreement between the partners.

If the title to firm property is not held in the firm name but is held in the names of one or more of the partners, a conveyance by those in whose names the title is held passes good title, unless the purchaser knows or should know that title was held for the firm. There is nothing in the record title in such a situation to call the buyer's attention to the fact that the firm has an interest in the property.

The power to mortgage or pledge a firm's property is primarily dependent upon the power to borrow money and bind the firm. A partner with authority to borrow may, as an incident to that power, give the security normally demanded for similar loans. Because no one partner without the consent of the others has the power to commit an act that will destroy or terminate the business, the power to give a security interest on the entire stock of merchandise and fixtures of a business is usually denied. Such a security interest would make it possible, upon default, to liquidate the firm's assets and thus destroy its business. Subject to this limitation, the power to borrow carries the power to provide security.

11. Financial Powers

To determine the limit of a partner's financial powers, partnerships are divided into two general classes—trading and nontrading partnerships. A *trading partnership* is one that has for its primary purpose the buying and selling of merchandise. In such a trading firm, each partner has an implied power to borrow money and to extend the credit of the firm, in the usual course of business, by signing negotiable paper.

A *nontrading partnership* is one that does not buy and sell commodities, but has for its primary purpose the production of commodities or is organized for the purpose of selling services; for example, professional partnerships in law, medicine, or accounting. In such partnerships, a partner's powers are more

---

[7] Simmons v. Quick Stop Food Mart, Inc., p. 926.

limited, and a partner does not have implied power to borrow money or to bind the firm on negotiable paper. However, if the partner's act is within the scope of partnership business, a member of a nontrading partnership may bind the firm by the exercise of implied authority, just as a partner in a trading partnership may.

SUMMARY

THE RIGHTS OF PARTNERS

Management	1. Unless the agreement provides to the contrary, each partner has an equal right to manage and to conduct the firm's business.
	2. The majority of partners can make final decisions concerning normal operations.
	3. Certain actions require unanimous consent to bind the firm.
Compensation	1. Partners are not generally compensated, other than with a share of the profits, unless the agreement provides otherwise.
	2. A partner engaged in winding up the partnership is entitled to compensation for doing so.
	3. Unless the agreement is to the contrary, partners have a duty to devote all of their time, skill, and energy to partnership affairs.
Interest	1. Capital contributions do not earn interest.
	2. Interest is paid on advances above capital contributions.
	3. Interest is not paid on unwithdrawn profits.
Information and inspection of books	1. Each partner is entitled to all information concerning the business and to inspect the books and records of the partnership.
	2. Partners have a duty to furnish information necessary to operate the business.
	3. Partners have a right to make copies of partnership records.
Accounting	1. In the event of a dispute as to the rights of the parties to assets or income, the

	equity action of an accounting is available to determine the rights of the partners.
	2. As a general rule, partners are not allowed to sue each other in courts of law for dollar damages.
	3. The suit for an accounting cannot be brought for minor disputes.
	4. The suit for an accounting is usually a part of the dissolution process.
Property	1. Each partner has an equal right to possess partnership property for partnership purposes.
	2. A partner has no right in specific partnership property and no right to use partnership property for personal purposes.
	3. Upon the death of a partner, the property belongs to the surviving partners, who have a duty to wind up the affairs. These surviving partners must pay the deceased partner's estate the sum to which the deceased partner was entitled.
	4. A partner's interest cannot be levied upon by his separate creditors. Creditors are entitled to obtain a charging order and to collect the partner's share of profits to satisfy the judgment.

DUTIES OF PARTNERS

The duty of loyalty and good faith	1. A partnership is a fiduciary relationship, and each partner must act only on behalf of the partnership.
	2. A partner cannot take for himself an opportunity of the partnership, and any gains which should have belonged to the partnership must be paid to it.
	3. All acts of partners are subject to the good-faith standard.
Notice	1. Since knowledge of any partner is charged to all partners, there is a duty on one partner to inform all other partners of all facts affecting the partnership business.

POWERS OF PARTNERS

Contracts

1. A partner is an agent of the partnership business, and the general rules of agency are applicable.
2. The implied authority of a partnership is greater than that of an ordinary agent. A partner has the implied power to do all acts necessary to carry on the business.

Torts

1. The doctrine of *respondeat superior* is applicable to the partnership relationship.
2. If the partnership incurs liability because of the tort of a partner, it has the right to collect the loss from the partner.

Property

1. Partners have authority to sell personal property held by the partnership for resale in the ordinary course of business.
2. A partner has no right to sell firm real estate unless it is engaged in the business of selling real estate.
3. Real property held in the partnership name can be conveyed only with the agreement of all partners.

Financial transactions

1. In a trading partnership, each partner has the implied power to borrow money to extend the credit of the firm in the usual course of business.
2. In a nontrading partnership, a partner does not have the implied power to borrow money.

CASES

Sharp v. Laubersheimer
347 N.W.2d 268 (Minn. 1984)

In July, 1976, Sharp, Zelinsky, and Laubersheimer entered into a written agreement to form the general partnership of Maple Investments. Shortly thereafter, Salo joined as a fourth partner with the consent of the three original partners. Sharp contributed land valued at $50,000; Zelinsky, Salo, and Laubersheimer made cash contributions of $10,000, $10,000, and $5,000, respectively. The partnership agreement did not provide for compensation to the partners for services rendered to Maple.

Maple Investments began construction of commercial warehouses on the partnership property. These warehouses were sold. Laubersheimer handled the closing for the partnership. Instead of depositing the proceeds of the sale ($104,000) into the partnership's account, he placed the money in a new account that only Laubersheimer and Salo had access to. When these partners refused to release the $104,000 of partnership assets, Sharp and Zelinsky sued to recover the assets, to dissolve the partnership, and to recover compensation owed Sharp for services rendered. The trial court ruled for the plaintiffs, including the payment of $60,000 as compensation to Sharp.

PETERSON, J. . . . We reverse the trial court's award of $60,000 compensation to Sharp for services rendered. We hold as a matter of law that the trial court erred when it awarded Sharp, a partner under an express partnership agreement, reimbursement for services rendered on a theory of quasi-contract when the partnership and joint venture agreements did not expressly provide for such compensation.

The partnership and joint venture agreements in this case did not provide for compensation to the partners of Maple. . . . According to the partnership agreement, each partner was required to contribute reasonable time and attention to the business and affairs of the partnership. Apart from the partners' sharing Maple's profits in accordance with their

ratio of partnership units, no other form of remuneration is mentioned. Since the partnership agreement is silent regarding compensation, the Minnesota Uniform Partnership Act does not allow plaintiffs to be reimbursed for services rendered on behalf of the partnership. Minn.Stat. §323-17 (1982) provides in pertinent part:

> The rights and duties of the partners in relation to the partnership shall be determined, subject to any agreement between them, by the following rules: . . .
> (6) No partner is entitled to remuneration for acting in the partnership business, except that a surviving partner is entitled to reasonable compensation for his services in winding up the partnership affairs. . . .

Moreover, . . . [i]t is fundamental that proof of an express contract precludes recovery in *quantum meruit.*

Because there was an express contract in this case, the trial court's award of compensation under a quasi-contract or an unjust enrichment theory, which in essence amounted to an award in *quantum meruit,* was contrary to well-established Minnesota case law. . . .

We therefore reverse the trial court's award of $60,000 to Sharp for services rendered and remand with direction to order judgment consistent with this opinion.

So ordered.

Mitchell Resort Enterprises Inc. v. C & S Builders, Inc.
570 S.W.2d 465 (Tex. 1978)

C & S Builders, Inc., sued Mitchell Resort Enterprises, Inc., for the reasonable profit of joint ventures between them. The joint ventures involved the construction and sale of townhouses. The lower court awarded the plaintiff $75,000 for lost profits, and the defendant appealed.

BROWN, J. . . . Mitchell entities contend the court erred in rendering judgment for damages because C & S failed to plead, prove or request jury findings that the partnership between the parties had been dissolved and terminated which is an

essential element of a cause of action for damages between partners. We agree. . . .

The law is well settled that one partner may not sue another partner on a claim arising out of partnership business until an accounting and settlement of partnership affairs is made. . . . Subject to certain exceptions, the general rule is that an accounting between partners is a condition precedent to an action on partnership claims and transactions. . . .

. . . [T]his broad general rule is subject to many exceptions—such, for instance, as where the partnership was formed for the carrying out of a single venture or transaction, or the action involves a segregated or single unadjusted item of account, or a personal covenant or transaction entirely independent of the partnership affairs. These exceptions, of course, are based upon the theory that such cases do not necessarily involve an accounting, and, therefore, that resort need not be had to an equity forum. Broadly speaking, it might be said that one partner may maintain an action at law against a copartner if the relief sought does not involve the taking of an accounting of complicated or numerous partnership transactions, but not if such accounts are involved.

C & S argues the applicability in the instant case of one of the exceptions to the general rule. We disagree.

This is not a case where the cause of action is not connected with partnership accounts and is distinct and separate from partnership dealings. Nor is the case one in which the partnership involves a single venture which is completed. Neither is the instant case one for breach of a contract to form a partnership where the partnership has never existed. This partnership was formed to build and sell townhouses. C & S seeks lost profits to that partnership.

C & S contends that it is not suing for assumpsit or breach of contract, but on breach of a fiduciary duty and negligence. Its claim, however, either in contract or tort, involves partnership affairs and the ultimate purpose of the partnership. C & S's pleadings disclose a partnership relationship existing between it and Mitchell Enterprises; a partnership that has not been terminated; the claim sued upon is not one separate and distinct from partnership affairs, nor does the partnership involve a single completed venture bringing the claim within an exception to the general rule, but to the contrary the claim involves loss of profits to the partnership. . . .

> An accounting and settlement between partners is generally a condition precedent to an action by one against another based on partnership claims and transactions. For this reason a suit for a share of property or profits or an action for contribution to losses or debts may not be maintained by a partner.

C & S having failed to plead or prove an accounting and settlement of partnership affairs, the court erred in rendering judgment for damages against Mitchell Enterprises. . . .

Reversed and remanded.

Bohonus v. Amerco
602 P.2d 469 (Ariz.) 1979

HAYS, J. . . . The first issue before us is: May the trial court order the sale of partnership property to satisfy the individual debt of a partner?

The appellee, Amerco, after it secured a judgment against the appellant, Bohonus, sought a charging order from the court pursuant to . . . the Uniform Partnership Act. The court granted the request for a charging order and as a part of that order mandated the sale of appellant's interest in the assets and property of the partnership business, including a spiritous liquor license. The sheriff proceeded with the sale and filed his return.

We now look at the partnership statute. A.R.S. §29-225(b)(3) says: "A partner's right in specific partnership property is not subject to attachment or execution, except on a claim against the partnership. . . ."

A.R.S. §29-224 sets forth the extent of the property rights of the partner:

The property rights of a partner are:

1. His rights in specific partnership property.

2. His interest in the partnership.

3. His right to participate in the management.

A.R.S. §29-226 defines "a partner's interest": "A partner's interest in the partnership is his share of the profits and surplus, and the same is personal property."

A.R.S. §29-228 reads, in pertinent part, as follows:

> A. On due application to a competent court by any judgment creditor of a partner, the court which entered the judgment, order, or decree, or any other court, may charge the interest of the debtor partner with payment of the unsatisfied amount of such judgment debt with interest thereon; and may then or later appoint a receiver of his share of the profits, and of any other money due or to fall due to him in respect of the partnership, and make all other orders, directions, accounts and inquiries which the debtor partner might have made, or which the circumstances of the case may require.

With the foregoing statutes in mind, we note that it is only a partner's interest in the partnership which may be charged and, in some jurisdictions, sold. It cannot be overemphasized that "interest in the partnership" has a special limited meaning in the context of the Uniform Partnership Act and hence in the Arizona statutes.

The appellee urges that somehow A.R.S. §29-228(a), supra, authorizes the sale of partnership assets and property. We note that the record reflects that pursuant to the provisions of the same statute a receiver was appointed in this case. The conclusion is that only the "interest in the partnership" may be charged and we find no provision therein for sale of assets of property of the partnership. . . .

We concur with appellee's position that the charged interest of a debtor-partner can be sold, but further enforcement of the creditor's rights must be pursuant to statute. However, this in nowise makes the sale of the partnership assets valid. . . . The Uniform Partnership Act prohibits the sale of partnership property in order to satisfy the nonpartnership debts of individual partners. . . .

Reversed.

Leff v. Gunter
189 Cal. Rptr. 377 (1983)

Leff, plaintiff, and Sender agreed to enter a joint bid for the construction of an Internal Revenue Service (IRS) Center in Fresno, California. Sender had already submitted a joint bid with others on a similar project in Memphis, Tennessee, and he suggested to the plaintiff that it would be advantageous to have this same group join them in bidding on the Fresno project. It was agreed that plaintiff and Sender would place a joint bid with that group, which included the defendant, Gunter. Thereafter, the plaintiff kept Sender informed on all aspects of the Fresno project, and the two worked to establish the group's bid. In similar fashion, Sender forwarded all relevant information about the Fresno project to Gunter, including construction estimates.

Sometime after the proposed final bid had been forwarded to him, Gunter advised Sender that he and his associates wished to withdraw from the Fresno joint venture. Later, the government informed the plaintiff that his proposed annual rent was too high and that his bid was rejected. Unknown to the plaintiff, Gunter and his associates had submitted their own bid, and they were awarded the contract. Plaintiff thereafter initiated this suit, alleging a breach of fiduciary duties by the defendants. The trial court held for the plaintiff in the amount of $416,666, and the defendants appealed.

RICHARDSON, J. . . . Defendants challenge jury instructions Nos. 44 and 45. No. 44 stated: "You are instructed that where one partner secretly enters into a contract sought to be contracted by the partnership which another partner is negotiating on behalf of the partnership such partner is in violation of his fiduciary duty to the excluded partner." No. 45 directed: "You are further instructed that such fiduciary duty continues for so long as the other party is negotiating on behalf of the original partnership."

Defendants assert that these instructions misstate the law by acknowledging a previously unrecognized cause of action for breach of fiduciary duty through fair competition by a former partner after termination of the partnership. Although conceding that it would be improper for one partner to engage in "secret preemptive activities" while the partnership is still in existence, defendants claim that any such taint of impropriety was removed by their withdrawal from the joint venture before Russell & Associates made its independent bid on the Fresno project. . . .

Defendants further contend that to the extent that these instructions may be construed as asserting only defendants' illegality in competing with a partnership while still members thereof, the instructions were erroneous because there was no evidence of such activity.

We do not agree with these contentions. The instructions advise the jury that a partner's duty not to compete with his partnership with respect to a partnership opportunity which is actively being pursued by the partnership survives his withdrawal therefrom. . . . There is an obvious and essential unfairness in one partner's attempted exploitation of a partnership opportunity for his own personal benefit and to the resulting detriment of his copartners. It may be assumed, although perhaps not always easily proven, that such competition with one's own partnership is greatly facilitated by access to relevant information available only to partners. Moreover, it is equally obvious that a formal disassociation of oneself from a partnership does not change this situation unless the interested parties specifically agree otherwise. It is no less a violation of the trust imposed between partners to permit the personal exploitation of that partnership information and opportunity to the prejudice of one's former associates by the simple expedient of withdrawal from the partnership. . . .

The foregoing reasoning has been well established, and the underlying ethical principles firmly and consistently supported by precedent. We have often stated that "Partners are trustees for each other, and in all proceedings connected with the conduct of the partnership every partner is bound to act in the highest good faith to his copartner and may not obtain any advantage over him in the partnership affairs by the slightest misrepresentation, concealment, threat or adverse pressure of any kind." . . .

Affirmed.

Hodge v. Garrett
614 P.2d 420 (ID. 1980)

Plaintiff Hodge sued for specific performance of a contract for the sale of a small parcel of land belonging to a partnership. The contract was signed by Rex E. Voeller, the managing partner of the partnership, which operated a drive-in theater. The parcel, adjacent to the theater, was part of the theater's driveway. The other partners contended that Voeller did not have authority to sell the parcel of land. They appealed from a trial court decision granting specific performance.

BISTLINE, J. . . . At common law one partner could not, "without the concurrence of his copartners, convey away the real estate of the partnership, bind his partners by a deed, or transfer the title and interest of his copartners in the firm real estate." This rule was changed by the adoption of the Uniform Partnership Act. The relevant provisions are . . . as follows:

> I.C. §53-310(1); Where title to real property is in the partnership name, any partner may convey title to such property by a conveyance executed in the partnership name; but the partnership may recover such property unless the partner's act binds the partnership under the provisions of paragraph 1 of section 53-309, unless such property has been conveyed by the grantee or a person claiming through such grantee to a holder for value without knowledge that the partner, is making the conveyance, has exceeded his authority.
>
> I.C. §53-309(1): Every partner is an agent of the partnership for the purpose of its business, and

the act of every partner, including the execution in the partnership name of any instrument, for apparently carrying on in the usual way the business of the partnership of which he is a member binds the partnership, unless the partner so acting has in fact no authority to act for the partnership in the particular matter, and the person with whom he is dealing has knowledge of the fact that he has no such authority.

The meaning of these provisions was stated in one text as follows:

> If record title is in the partnership and a partner conveys in the partnership name, legal title passes. But the partnership may recover the property (except from a bona fide purchaser from the grantee) if it can show (a) that the conveying partner was not apparently carrying on business in the usual way or (b) that he had in fact no authority and the grantee had knowledge of that fact. The burden of proof with respect to authority is thus on the partnership.

Thus this contract is enforceable if Voeller had the actual authority to sell the property, or, even if Voeller did not have such authority, the contract is still enforceable if the sale was in the usual way of carrying on the business and Hodge did not know that Voeller did not have this authority.

As to the question of actual authority, such authority must affirmatively appear, "for the authority of one partner to make and acknowledge a deed for the firm will not be presumed. . . ." Although such authority may be implied from the nature of the business, or from similar past transactions, nothing in the record in this case indicates that Voeller had express or implied authority to sell real property belonging to the partnership. There is no evidence that Voeller had sold property belonging to the partnership in the past, and obviously the partnership was not engaged in the business of buying and selling real estate.

The next question, since actual authority has not been shown, is whether Voeller was conducting the partnership business in the usual way in selling this parcel of land.

The (trial) court made no finding that it was customary for Voeller to sell real property, or even personal property, belonging to the partnership. Nor was there any evidence to this effect. Nor did the court discuss whether it was in the usual course of business for the managing partner of a theater to sell real property. . . . For a theater, "carrying on in the usual way the business of the partnership," means running the operations of the theater; it does not mean selling a parcel of property adjacent to the theater. Here the contract of sale stated that the land belonged to the partnership, and, even if Hodge believed that Voeller as exclusive manager had authority to transact all business for the firm, Voeller still could not bind the partnership through a unilateral act which was not in the usual business of the partnership. We therefore hold that the trial court erred in holding that this contract was binding on the partnership.

Judgment reversed.

Martin v. Barbour
558 S.W.2d 200 (Mo. 1977)

A jury returned a verdict for the plaintiff, Martin, in the amount of $125,000 against Drs. Barbour and Egle. The case was based on allegations of negligence by Dr. Barbour in performing an operation for a rectal condition that resulted in permanent incontinence.

The defendant, Dr. Egle, did not assist or participate in the surgery and did not treat the plaintiff. He was a partner in the practice of medicine with Dr. Barbour at the time of the surgery.

The trial court entered a judgment, notwithstanding the verdict in favor of Dr. Egle. The plaintiff appealed.

HOUSER, J. . . . Pursuant to general rules, partners in the practice of medicine are all liable for an injury to a patient resulting from the lack of skill or the negligence, either in omission or commission, of any one of the partners within the scope of their partnership business. And where several physicians are in partnership, they may be held liable in damages for the professional negligence of one of the firm. It is plain, too, that when physicians and surgeons are in partnership, all are liable in damages for the professional negligence of one of the firm, for the act of one, within the scope of the partnership business, is the act of each and all, as fully as if each is present, participating in all that is done. On this record Dr. Egle is liable for Dr. Barbour's professional negligence on the basis of their partnership. . . .

Reversed.

Simmons v. Quick Stop Food Mart, Inc.
286 S.E.2d 807 (N.C. 1982)

On May 21, 1970, Johnny L. Wood and Oscar H. Simmons executed a partnership agreement creating Wood and Simmons Investments. On the same day, Wood conveyed to the partnership two tracts of land on which was situated a store building. On May 28, the partnership leased the building to the defendant.

On June 30, 1976, Wood and Simmons dissolved the partnership. Wood and his wife conveyed all their interest in the above-mentioned property to Simmons and his wife. In 1979, Simmons and his wife separated, and he conveyed the property and building to her as part of their settlement. Subsequently, the former Mrs. Simmons, who is the plaintiff in this action, notified the defendant to vacate the store building. Defendant refused; and when suit was filed, the defendant contended that the title to the land remained with the partnership and that the partnership still is the landlord since it did not convey "out" its interest in the property.

HILL, J. . . . [T]he question is whether the 21 May 1970 conveyance "in" to "Johnny L. Wood and Oscar Harold Simmons d/b/a Wood and Simmons Investments, a partnership" vested title in the partnership or in the partners as individuals.

"All property originally brought into the partnership stock or subsequently acquired by purchase or otherwise, on account of the partnership, is partnership property."

Partners' interests in partnership property has been described as a "tenancy in partnership." When title to the property is *in the partnership name,* it may be conveyed "out" by any partner *in the partnership name.* In such cases, however, when the partner conveys partnership property "out" *in his own name,* he merely "passes the equitable interest of the partnership. . . ."

In deciding whether the 21 May 1970 deed is *in the partnership name,* we must look to the "four corners" of the document. Thus, the grantor's intended grantee may be ascertained by reviewing the granting clause, which provided,

> [t]hat said parties of the first part, in consideration of other good and valuable consideration and the sum of Ten—Dollars to them paid by *party* of the second part the receipt of which is hereby acknowledged have bargained and sold, and by these presents do grant, bargain, sell and convey to said party of the second part, its successors, heirs and assigns, a certain tract or parcel of land. . . .

Further, the habendum clause provided, "TO HAVE AND TO HOLD the aforesaid tract or parcel of land, and all privileges and appurtenances thereto belonging, to the said *party* of the second part, *its* successors, heirs and assigns, to *its* only use and behoof forever."

The . . . language of the deed quoted above indicates that the grantor intended the partnership entity to be the grantee rather than the partners as individuals. Under G.S. 59–40(a), then, the conveyance "out" must be *in the partnership name.* However, the deed recorded on 16 July 1976 was executed by "Johnny L. Wood and wife, Zula Wood," *individually,* rather than in the partnership name. At most, this deed conveyed "out" the "equitable interest of the partnership." The deed of 5 November 1979 has the same effect . . . since the named grantor is "Oscar Harold Simmons." Legal title therefore remains in the partnership despite the deeds through which plaintiff claims title. . . .

[W]e conclude that plaintiff has no legal title to the property and no standing to pursue summary ejectment proceedings as owner of the property and defendant's landlord.

Affirmed.

REVIEW QUESTIONS

1. Identify the terms in column A by matching each with the appropriate statement in column B.

A		B
1. Silent partner	**a.**	A partnership that is engaged in the buying and selling of goods.
2. Secret partner	**b.**	Describes the title to property held in the partnership name.
3. Dormant partner	**c.**	A partner that does not participate in management.
4. Tenancy in partnership	**d.**	A partnership engaged in providing services.
5. Charging orders	**e.**	A loan to a partnership by a partner.
6. Trading partnership	**f.**	A partner that is unknown to third parties.
7. Nontrading partnership	**g.**	A court procedure for collecting an undivided debt of a partner from the partnership.
8. Advance	**h.**	A partner that is both secret and silent.

2. The partners in a partnership composed of seven members have differing views on several partnership issues. If the partnership agreement makes no provision for the number of partners required to decide particular issues, how many votes does it take:

a. To discharge a clerk accused of stealing
b. To cause the dissolution of the partnership
c. To require the change of the partnership business from a wholesale to a retail operation
d. To require the submission of a partnership claim to arbitration
e. To submit to a confession of judgment on behalf of the partnership

3. Agatha, Alicia, and Hilary operated the AAH Family Health Spa. Agatha and Hilary paid themselves salaries of $18,000 a year, but paid Alicia only $5,000 annually. Agatha and Hilary sold spa memberships to their families at below the normal rate. They also refused to discuss partnership affairs with Alicia. Does Alicia have cause of action against Agatha and Hilary? Explain.

4. Defendants Smith and Brook were partners in the automobile business under the name of Greenwood Sales and Service. Defendant Brook borrowed $6,000 from plaintiff and gave a partnership note in return. Is Smith liable on the note? Why?

5. Huffington was the managing partner of an oil and gas investment firm. He learned of an "Indonesian" oil deal and acquired 10 percent of it for himself. Is the partnership entitled to the investment? Explain.

6. Waite was a limited partner in Ozark Skyrise, Ltd., a limited partnership whose purpose was to build and manage a resort complex. The general partners were Salestrom and Gardner. Salestrom agreed to refund Waite his partnership contribution if the building was not completed. When the project failed, Waite sued to recover his partnership contribution from both general partners. Is Gardner liable? Why?

7. Two people have been partners for a number of years. Upon the death of one, the other spent considerable time in winding up the partnership affairs. Is the surviving partner legally entitled to compensation for services? Why?

8. Albert and Maria were partners in a grocery business. The firm was in need of additional working capital, and Albert advanced $20,000. Is Albert entitled to interest on the advance? Why?

9. Bedford and Eckhart formed a partnership and built a shopping center. Three years later, Bedford, the managing partner, informed Eckhart that the business was in deep financial trouble and that he had tried to sell the complex but had failed. Bedford said that the best thing to do would be for one to buy the other out, and that their equity in the business was not worth more than $3 million. Eckhart sold his half interest in the partnership to Bedford for $1.5 million. Later he discovered that their equity in the business amounted to over $10 million and that Bedford had received several offers to purchase the business. Eckhart brought suit to rescind the sale, to have the partnership dissolved, and for an accounting. Should Eckhart succeed? Why?

10. Martin, Lewis, and Davis are partners in a CPA firm. Martin negligently causes an automobile accident while on his way to perform an audit. Are the firm and the other partners liable? Explain.

11. The Viking Partnership consisted of seven equal partners. Wells, one of the partners, purchased six shares of the Azuma Dairy Farm Corporation stock. He used partnership funds to purchase the stock. Subsequently another share was purchased, and each partner's capital account was debited for an amount equal to one-seventh of the total purchase price. Is the stock partnership property? Why?

12. A partner in an accountancy firm borrowed $10,000 in the firm name and used the proceeds to pay an individual debt. Is the firm liable for this debt? Why?

13. Preston obtained a judgment against Daniel. He sought a charging order against Daniel's interest in a general partnership in order to collect the judgment. Jeff also obtained a judgment against Daniel. Jeff seeks to intervene in Preston's suit for a charging order, so that he (Jeff) may share in it. Preston claims that he has a right to full payment before Jeff is entitled to anything. Should the charging order against Daniel's partnership interest pro rate the payment between Preston and Jeff? Explain.

41 DISSOLUTION OF PARTNERSHIPS

Three steps are necessary to end a partnership: dissolution, winding up, and termination. *Dissolution,* the legal destruction of the partnership relation, occurs whenever any partner ceases to be a member of the firm or whenever a new partner is admitted. It is the change in the relation of the partners caused by any partner's ceasing to be associated in carrying on—as distinguished from winding up—the business. Dissolution alone does not terminate the partnership, but designates the time when partners cease to carry on business together. *Winding up* involves the process of reducing the assets to cash, paying off the creditors, and distributing the balance to the partners. *Termination* occurs only when the winding-up process is completed.[1]

Dissolutions will occur without violation of the partnership agreement: (1) at the end of the stipulated term or particular undertaking specified in the agreement; (2) by the express will of any partner when no definite term or particular undertaking is specified; (3) by the agreement of all the partners; or (4) by the expulsion, in good faith, of any partner from the business, in accordance with power conferred by the partnership agreement. Dissolutions also may occur by operation of law or by an order of a court of equity.

1. Dissolution by Act of the Partners

When a definite term of a particular undertaking is not specified, it is a *partnership at will.* In such a partnership, any partner may, without liability, legally

---

[1] Howe v. Horton, Davis & McCaleb, p. 939.

dissolve it at any time. Dissolution may be accomplished by giving notice to the other parties.

No particular form of notice is required; it will be implied from circumstances inconsistent with the continuation of the partnership. When a partner whose services are essential leaves the community, his departure is an act and notice of dissolution.

Expulsion of a partner is a breach of the partnership agreement unless the agreement confers the power of expulsion upon a majority of the partners. Assume that A, B, and C are partners. A and B cannot expel C unless that power is specifically granted in the agreement. Without power to expel, partners may seek judicial dissolution if one partner is guilty of violating the partnership agreement (see the next section). If C in the above case was not devoting his time to the business, as he was required to do in the partnership agreement, A and B could seek a dissolution on these grounds, although they could not expel C.

Dissolution may also occur in violation of the partnership agreement. Although the agreement stipulates the length of time the partnership is to last, dissolution is always possible because the relationship is essentially a mutual agency not capable of specific performance. Each partner therefore has the *power,* but not the *right,* to revoke the relationship. In the event of wrongful dissolution, the wrongdoer is liable for damages.

2. Dissolution by Operation of Law

If during the period of the partnership, events make it impossible or illegal for the partnership to continue, it will be dissolved by operation of law. Such events or conditions are the death or bankruptcy of one of the partners or a change in the law that makes the continuance of the business illegal. Of course, a partnership may also be illegal at its inception. In such a case, the courts will leave the partners where it finds them and will not grant relief to a partner in a suit against the other partner or partners.

Since a partnership is a personal relationship existing by reason of contract, when one of the partners dies, the partnership is dissolved. It is not terminated on dissolution, but it continues for the purpose of winding up the partnership's affairs. The process of winding up is, in most states, the exclusive obligation and right of the surviving partner or partners. The executor or administrator of the deceased partner has no right to participate in, or interfere with, the winding-up processes, unless, of course, the deceased was the last surviving partner. The only right of the personal representative of a deceased partner is to demand an accounting upon completion of the winding up of the partnership's affairs. As a general rule, the estate of the deceased partner is not bound on contracts entered into by the surviving partners if the contracts are unconnected with the winding up of the affairs of the partnership. This is discussed more fully later in the chapter.

The bankruptcy of a partner will dissolve the partnership because the control of his property passes to the trustee in bankruptcy for the benefit of the creditors. The mere insolvency of a partner will not be sufficient to justify a dissolution. The bankruptcy of the firm itself is a cause for dissolution, as is a valid assignment of all the firm's assets for the benefit of creditors.

3. Dissolution by Court Decree

When a partnership by its agreement is to be continued for a term of years, circumstances sometimes make continued existence of the firm impossible and unprofitable. Upon application of one of the partners to a court of equity, the partnership may be dissolved. Under the following circumstances and situations, a court of equity may order dissolution:

1. Total incapacity of a partner to conduct business and to perform the duties required under the contract of partnership.

2. A declaration by judicial process that a partner is insane.

3. Willful and persistent commitment of a breach of the partnership agreement, misappropriation of funds, or commitment of fraudulent acts.

4. An innocent party's application for dissolution because the partnership was entered into as a result of fraud.

5. Gross misconduct and neglect or breach of duty by a partner to such an extent that it is impossible to carry out the purposes of the partnership agreement.

6. In some states, any grounds that make dissolution equitable or in the best interests of the partners.

Courts will not interfere and grant a decree of dissolution for mere discourtesy, temporary inconvenience, minor differences of opinion, or errors in judgment. The misconduct mentioned above must be of such gross nature that the continued operation of the business would be unprofitable. In those states that have incorporated item 6 into their law, courts of equity will order dissolution if there is serious disharmony among the partners.[2]

4. Effect of Dissolution on Powers of Partners

The process of winding up, except when the agreement provides for continuation by purchase of former parties' shares, involves liquidation of the partnership assets, so that cash may be available to pay creditors and to make a distribution to the partners. When the agreement provides for continuation and purchase of a deceased partner's interest, the technical dissolution is followed by valuation and payment, and the new firm immediately commences business.

As a general rule, dissolution terminates the actual authority of any partner to act for the partnership except as far as necessary to wind up partnership affairs, to liquidate the assets of the firm in an orderly manner, or to complete transactions begun but not finished. Insofar as third persons who had dealings with the firm are concerned, apparent authority still exists until notice of termination is given.

This apparent authority means that one partner of a dissolved partnership binds the firm on contracts unconnected with winding up the firm's affairs. When he does so, issues arise as to whether or not the new obligations may be met with

---

[2] First Western Mortgage Co. v. Hotel Gearhart, Inc., p. 940.

partnership funds or whether the contracting partner is entitled to contribution toward payment of the debt or obligation from the other partners.

The resolution of these issues depends upon the cause of the dissolution. If the dissolution is caused by (1) the act of a partner, (2) bankruptcy of the partnership, or (3) the death of a partner, each partner is liable for his share of any liability incurred on behalf of the firm after dissolution, just as if there had been no dissolution, unless the partner incurring the liability had knowledge of the dissolution. In these situations, if knowledge of the dissolution is present, the partner incurring the liability is solely responsible, and cannot require the other partners to share the burden of an unauthorized act. If the dissolution is not caused by the act, bankruptcy, or death of a partner but by some event such as a court decree, no partner has authority to act and therefore has no right to contribution from other partners for liabilities incurred after dissolution.

When dissolution results from the death of a partner, title to partnership property remains in the surviving partner or partners for purposes of winding up and liquidation. Both real and personal property is, through the survivors, thus made available to a firm's creditors. All realty is treated as though it were personal property. It is sold, and the surviving partners finally account, usually in cash, to the personal representative of the deceased partner for the latter's share in the proceeds of liquidation.

5. Rights of Partners after Dissolution

Upon dissolution, a withdrawing partner who has not breached the partnership agreement has certain options with regard to his interest in the dissolved partnership. He may require the partnership to be wound up and terminated. The partnership will be liquidated and the assets distributed among the partners. The alternative is to allow the business to continue, or accept the fact that it has continued.

If the withdrawing partner allows the business to continue, the value of his interest in the partnership as of the date of dissolution is ascertained. He then has the right to receive, at his option after an accounting, either the value of this interest in the partnership with interest or, in lieu of interest, the profits attributable to the use of his rights in the property of the dissolved partnership. The portion of profits to which a withdrawing partner is entitled because of the use of property will almost always be less than his portion prior to dissolution. This is true because a portion of the profit is usually attributable to services of the continuing partners.

When dissolution is caused in any way other than breach of the partnership agreement, each partner has a right to insist that all the partnership assets be used first to pay firm debts. After firm obligations are paid, remaining assets are used to return capital contributions and then to provide for a distribution of profits. All the partners except those who have caused a wrongful dissolution of the firm have the right to participate in the winding up of the business. The majority selects the method and procedures to be followed in the liquidation. The assets are turned into cash unless all agree to distribute them in kind.

If a partnership that is to continue for a fixed period is dissolved by the wrongful withdrawal of one partner, the remaining members may continue as partners under the same firm name for the balance of the agreed term of the partnership. They are required to settle with the withdrawing partner for his interest in the partnership and to compensate him, but they are allowed to subtract from the amount due in cash the damages caused by his wrongful withdrawal. In the calculation of his share, the goodwill of the business is not taken into consideration. The fact that a partner breached the agreement does not take away the right to an accounting and to receive his share of the partnership after deducting any damages caused by the breach of the agreement.[3]

Upon dissolution, it is the duty of the remaining partner or partners to wind up the affairs. If they fail to do so and instead continue the business, they have liability to the withdrawing partner, his assignee, or personal representative for use of partnership assets. The liability may include interest if the value of the former partner's portion of the partnership can be ascertained. It may also include liability for a share of postdissolution profits. This liability arises because the business is continuing to use the assets of all of the former partners.

Just as a partner whose property is used to earn postdissolution profits is entitled to share in those profits, one who continues the partnership business after dissolution and contributes substantial labor and management services is entitled to compensation for that share of the profits attributable to such services. A partner who withdraws from a partnership has no interest in profits that are attributable to labor and management services of continuing partners and which are earned after dissolution and before final accounting. Therefore, in determining profits attributable to use of a withdrawing partner's right in the property of dissolved partnership, a court is entitled to make an equitable allowance for services of partners who continue the partnership business.

It is often difficult to value accurately the interest of a withdrawing or deceased partner when the business continues. The buy and sell provisions will control the method for establishing the value of the interest as of the date of dissolution. If there are no buy and sell provisions and the parties cannot agree, a judicial decision on the value may be required. This decision may sometimes involve which of the parties is to continue the business, as well as the amount to be paid the withdrawing partner, but it cannot be made with mathematical certainty.

6. Dissolution and Third Parties

Dissolution of a partnership terminates the authority of the partners to create liability, but it does not discharge any existing liability of any partner. An agreement between the partners themselves that one or more of the partners will assume the partnership liabilities and that a withdrawing partner will not have any liability does not bind the firm's creditors. However, a partner may be discharged from any existing liability by an agreement to that effect with the creditors. Such an agreement may be express or even implied from the conduct of the parties.[4]

When a firm's assets are insufficient to pay its debts, the individual property

---

[3] Hoppen v. Powell, p. 940.
[4] Munn v. Scalera, p. 941.

of partners, including the estate of a deceased partner, is subject to claims of third parties for all debts created while the partnership existed. This liability is subject to the payment of individual debts, however.

After dissolution, two categories of parties are entitled to notice of the dissolution. First of all, the firm's creditors, including all former creditors, are entitled to actual notice of the dissolution. Transactions entered into after dissolution without such notice continue to bind withdrawing partners and the estate of deceased partners. If proper notice is given, former partners are not liable for contracts unconnected with winding up the partnership's affairs. Notice eliminates the apparent authority to bind the former firm and its partners.

Notice of dissolution is required, whether the dissolution is caused by an act of the parties or by operation of law, unless a partner becomes bankrupt or the continuation of the business becomes illegal. Therefore, upon death of a partner, the personal representative should give immediate notice of the death and dissolution in order to avoid further liability.

The second category of parties entitled to notice of dissolution consists of persons who knew about the partnership but who were not creditors. When the dissolution is caused by an act of the parties, the partners will continue to be liable to all such parties unless public notice of dissolution is given. Notice by publication in a newspaper in the community where the business has been transacted is sufficient public notice.

If a partner has not actively engaged in the conduct of the partnership business, if creditors have not learned that he was a partner and have not extended credit to the firm because of their faith in him, there is no duty to give notice to either of the groups mentioned above on his withdrawal.

7. New Partners and New Firms

A person admitted as a partner into an existing partnership is liable to the extent of his capital contribution for all obligations incurred before his admission, as though he had previously been a partner. The new partner is not personally liable for such obligations, and the creditors of the old firm can look only to the firm's assets and to members of the old firm.

If a business is continued without liquidation of the partnership affairs, creditors of the first, or dissolved, partnership are also creditors of the partnership continuing the business. Likewise, if the partners assign all their interest to a former partner or a third person who continues the business without liquidation of the partnership affairs, creditors of the dissolved partnership are also creditors of the person continuing the business.

DISTRIBUTIONS ON DISSOLUTION

8. Solvent Partnerships

Upon the dissolution of a solvent partnership and winding up of its business, an accounting is made to determine its assets and liabilities. Before the partners are entitled to participate in any of the assets, whether or not the firm owes them money, all firm creditors other than partners are entitled to be paid. After firm creditors are paid, the assets of the partnership are distributed among the partners as follows:

1. Each partner who has made advances to the firm or has incurred liability for, or on behalf of, the firm is entitled to be reimbursed.[5]
2. Each partner is then entitled to the return of the capital that he has contributed to the firm.
3. Any balance is distributed as profits in accordance with the partnership agreement.

In many partnerships, one partner contributes capital, the other contributes labor, so the partner contributing labor has nothing to be returned in step 2. Of course, the original agreement could place a value on such labor; but unless it does, only the partner who contributes cash or other property will be repaid in step 2.

In the absence of agreement to the contrary, goodwill is a partnership asset that should be accounted for on termination of a partnership.[6] If one partner appropriates the goodwill or retains it for his own use, he must account for it to the other partner.

9. Insolvent Partnerships

When the firm is insolvent and a court of equity is responsible for making the distribution of the assets of the partnership, the assets are distributed in accordance with a rule known as *marshaling of assets.* Persons entering into a partnership agreement impliedly agree that the partnership assets will be used for the payment of the firm debts before the payment of any individual debts of the partners. Consequently, a court of equity, in distributing the assets, will give them to the firm's creditors before awarding them to separate creditors or individual partners. The court will give separate assets of the partners to their private creditors before awarding these assets to the firm's creditors. Neither class of creditors is permitted to use the funds belonging to the other until the claims of the other have been satisfied. The firm's creditors have available two funds out of which to seek payment: assets of the firm and the individual assets of the partners. Individual creditors of the partners have only one fund: the personal assets of the partners. Because of this difference, equity compels the firm's creditors to exhaust the firm's assets before having recourse to the partners' individual assets.

The doctrine of marshaling of assets does not apply if a partner conceals his existence and permits the other member of the firm to deal with the public as the sole owner of the business. Under these circumstances, the secret partner's conduct has led the creditors of the active partner to rely upon the firm's assets as the separate property of the active partner; and by reason of his conduct, the secret partner is estopped from demanding an application of the equity rule that the firm's assets shall be used to pay the firm's creditors first and individual assets used to pay individual creditors. Thus the firm's assets must be shared equally with its creditors and the individual creditors of the active partner. In such a case, because the firm's assets may not be sufficient to pay all its debts when depleted by

[5] Park Cities Corporation v. Byrd, p. 943.
[6] Swann v. Mitchell, p. 943.

payments to individual creditors, there may be unpaid firm creditors, and secret partners will be personally liable.

Just as the individual creditors are limited to individual assets, firm creditors are limited to firm assets. Therefore, firm creditors are not entitled to payment out of the individual assets of the partners until the individual creditors have been paid. This rule applies even though the firm creditors may at the same time be individual creditors of a member of the firm. There are two main exceptions to this general rule: (1) The rule for the limit of firm creditors to firm assets applies only where there are firm assets. If no firm assets or no living solvent partner exists, the firm creditors may share equally with the individual creditors in the distribution of the individual estates of the partners. (2) If a partner has fraudulently converted the firm assets to his own use, the firm's creditors will be entitled to share equally with individual creditors in the guilty partner's individual assets.

The doctrine of marshaling of assets is not applicable to tort claims under the Uniform Partnership Act. Partners are individually liable in tort for the acts of the firm, its agent and servants. The liability is joint and several. Thus, the injured party may sue the partners individually or as a partnership. The firm assets need not be first used to collect a judgment, and direct action may be taken against individual assets.

SUMMARY

INTRODUCTION

Terminology	1. Dissolution occurs whenever there is a change (deletion or addition) in the partners as members of a partnership.
	2. Winding up is the process of reducing the assets to cash, paying creditors, and distributing the balance to the partners.
	3. Termination of a partnership occurs when the winding-up process is completed.

METHODS OF DISSOLUTION

| Acts of the partners | 1. In a partnership at will, any partner may dissolve the partnership at any time without liability. |
| | 2. Expulsion of a partner is a breach of the partnership agreement unless it provides for such expulsion. |

	3. Dissolution may occur in violation of the partnership agreement, in which case there is liability for wrongful dissolution.
Dissolution by court decree	1. A court of equity may order dissolution if a partner is incapacitated or is in willful and persistent breach of the partnership agreement.
	2. Other grounds such as gross misconduct also may justify a court in ordering dissolution.
Dissolution by operation of law	1. Any event that makes it impossible or illegal to continue the partnership operates as a dissolution.
	2. Death or bankruptcy of a partner or the partnership operates as a dissolution.
	3. Insolvency of a partner is not a basis for dissolution.

THE EFFECT OF DISSOLUTION

Powers of partners	1. Dissolution terminates the authority of a partner to act except to wind up partnership affairs.
	2. The winding-up process includes liquidating the assets, completing transactions, paying debts, and distributing the balance.
	3. Partners possess apparent authority to bind the dissolved partnership unless persons dealing with the partners have actual or constructive notice of the dissolution.
	4. On the death of a partner, title to partnership property remains with the surviving partners for the purpose of winding up the partnership.
Rights of partners	1. A withdrawing partner has the right to be paid the value of his interest in the partnership as of the date of dissolution.
	2. A partner has the right to have partnership property used to pay firm debts.
	3. If a partnership is wrongfully dissolved, the remaining partners may continue for the agreed term of the partnership. They must settle with the withdrawing partner,

	but may deduct damages caused by the wrongful dissolution.
	4. A partner who withdraws is entitled to the earnings resulting from property remaining in the partnership, but is not entitled to earnings attributable to the efforts of the remaining partners.
Third parties	1. An agreement between partners that a withdrawing partner will have no liability is not binding on firm creditors.
	2. A withdrawing partner or the estate of a deceased partner has liability for firm debts in the event firm assets are insufficient to discharge them.
Notice to third parties	1. Notice of dissolution must be given to third parties in order to abolish the partners' apparent authority to act on behalf of the firm.
	2. This notice may be actual (personal) or constructive (public).
	3. All creditors (past and present) must receive actual notice of dissolution if the dissolution is caused by the acts of partners or by a partner's death or incompetency.
	4. All other third parties can be informed by constructive notice.
	5. No notice needs to be given any third party if the dissolution was caused by bankruptcy or illegality.
New partners and firms	1. A new partner in an existing partnership is liable for firm debts incurred prior to admission only to the extent of his capital contribution.
	2. The partnership is continued without liquidation. Creditors of the dissolved partnership are creditors of the new partnership.

DISTRIBUTIONS ON DISSOLUTION

Solvent partnerships	1. After firm creditors are paid, the assets are distributed in the following order: (1) partnership advances, (2) partnership capital, and (3) undistributed profits.

Insolvent partnerships

2. Goodwill is a partnership asset which must be accounted for if either partner retains it.

1. If the partnership is unable to pay all of its debts, the doctrine of marshaling of assets will be followed.

2. Firm assets are paid to firm creditors. Individual assets are used to pay individual creditors. Each class must be paid in full before assets can be used to pay the other class.

3. If a firm has no assets, the firm creditors may share in the individual assets. The same is true if a partner has fraudulently converted firm assets to his own use.

4. The doctrine of marshaling assets is not applicable to tort claims.

CASES

Howe v. Horton, Davis & McCaleb
407 N.E.2d 766 (Ill.App. 1980)

McNAMARA, J. A claim was brought in the probate division of the circuit court of Cook County against the estate of Earl E. Howe, deceased. The claim was filed on behalf of and in the name of a law partnership, Horton, Davis & McCaleb, and was signed by a surviving member of the firm. The claim was for the balance due on an outstanding bill for legal services rendered to decedent by the claimant law firm. During a hearing on the claim, the trial court learned that claimant was not in existence and, . . . dismissed the claim. Claimant appeals.

At the hearing, the trial court was informed that at least two partners of claimant had died and that the firm was not engaged in the practice of law. The court also learned that there were two successors to the claimant law firm. Counsel for the claimant informed the court:

I am suing on behalf of the law firm that provided those services. The law firm does not any longer exist. My law firm is a successor to that law firm.

We are paying the heirs of the deceased members of the claimant's law firm as accounts are received. . . .

Claimant contends that the trial court erred in dismissing the partnership's claim based upon an asserted lack of legal existence. Claimant maintains that in dismissing the claim the court failed to perceive the distinction between dissolution and termination of a partnership.

Section 29 of the Uniform Partnership Act provides as follows:

The dissolution of a partnership is the change in the relation of the partners caused by any partner ceasing to be associated in the carrying on as distinguished from the winding up of the business.

Section 30 of the Act sets forth the effect of dissolution:

On dissolution the partnership is not terminated, but continues until the winding up of the partnership affairs is completed. . . . The terms "dissolution" and "termination" as employed in the Partnership Act are not synonyms and, as used, have different meanings. Dissolution does not terminate the partnership and does not end completely the authority of the partners. The order of events is: (1) dissolution; (2) winding up; and (3) termination. Termination extinguishes their authority. It is the ultimate result of the winding up and occurs at the conclusion of the wind up.

Thus a dissolved partnership has legal existence. It is apparent that the claimant partnership had not terminated its existence but had dissolved and was in the process of winding up its affairs. Part of the winding up includes collection of debts owed the partnership. The filing of this claim itself and the aforementioned remarks of claimant's counsel to the trial court indicate that the claimant was in the process of winding up its affairs by attempting to collect an amount due for legal services rendered to decedent. The trial court erred in dismissing the claim. . . .

Reversed.

First Western Mortgage Co. v. Hotel Gearhart, Inc.,
488 P.2d 450 (Or. 1971)

Plaintiff and defendant were partners in a motel, restaurant, and condominium development. Plaintiff was responsible for building and selling the condominiums; defendant ran the motel and restaurant. After the condominiums were built and sold, a dispute arose between the parties. Plaintiff charged defendant with failure to pay taxes and with commingling partnership funds with his own money. Defendant accused plaintiff of improper accounting methods on the condominiums and charging excessive interest. In addition, both partners were entering into contracts involving partnership property without the knowledge or consent of the other. The lower court refused to enter a decree of dissolution, and the plaintiff appealed.

HOWELL, J. . . . The plaintiff was entitled to a decree of dissolution. Although the parties were engaged in a joint venture, the law applicable to partnerships applies to joint ventures. Under ORS 68.540, on application of a partner the court shall decree a dissolution for various reasons, including circumstances which render a dissolution equitable.

In the instant case the parties had the right to dissolve the partnership by the express will of either party as the partnership had no definite term. However, this does not preclude a partner from bringing a suit for dissolution by judicial decree. In such event, a court of equity may decree a dissolution because of any circumstances which render such dissolution just and equitable or where the interests of the partners will be best served by a dissolution. While a court of equity will not decree dissolution because of trifling disputes among the partners, dissolution will be granted where the dissensions are so serious and persistent as to make continuance impracticable, or where all confidence and cooperation between the parties have been destroyed.

In the instant case the trial court refused dissolution on the ground that the disputes were trifling. We disagree. The evidence definitely establishes that serious disharmony exists between the parties. This fact is not disputed, and both parties want a termination of their joint venture. The cause is reversed and remanded with directions to enter a decree granting a dissolution of the May 1, 1968, agreement, a winding up of the joint venture, and directing an accounting.

So ordered.

Hoppen v. Powell
600 S.W.2d 736 (Tenn. 1980)

In July 1977, the plaintiff, Hoppen, and the defendant, Powell, entered into a verbal partnership agreement. The defendant was to work full-time at the partnership business at a salary of $2,000 per month, and the plaintiff was to work part-time at a salary of $300 per month. Net profits were to be divided equally. In October 1977, Hoppen insisted that he be paid $2,000 per month, like Powell, even though he continued to work only part-time. Powell would not agree unless Hoppen quit his other job and came to work for the partnership full-time. Hoppen notified Powell on October 19, 1977, that he wanted the partnership terminated. On October 31, 1977, Hoppen filed suit to dissolve the partnership on the ground that a dispute between the partners rendered a dissolution equitable and desirable. He also asked the court to wind up the business and distribute the net proceeds.

On February 2, 1979, the trial judge ruled that the partnership had terminated on October 31, 1977, when the complaint was filed. He found that prior to the dissolution, the defendant Powell had breached his fiduciary duties to the partnership by engaging in a similar business in competition with the partnership after October 1977. For that reason, the judge awarded *all* partnership property to the plaintiff without an accounting.

MATHERNE, J. . . . The chancellor did not render an accounting, but merely held that Powell came into court with unclean hands and divested him of all interest in the partnership. . . . The chancellor . . . decreed all assets to Hoppen. The chancellor stated that he was acting under the doctrine of equity. We disagree with this method of partnership accounting upon a dissolution of a partnership by court decree.

The parties seem to agree that dissolution occurred on October 31, 1977, when Hoppen filed this lawsuit. Even though Hoppen gave notice of dissolution in the month of October 1977, and withdrew from the business on or about October 15, 1977, neither party treated this action as amounting to a dissolution. The request for dissolution was not based upon a contravention of the partnership agreement; rather, this lawsuit was brought under T.C.A. §61-131(f) on the ground that under the circumstances dissolution was equitable and desirable.

The filing of a lawsuit seeking dissolution does not necessarily effect a dissolution upon the filing of the cause—the court could refuse dissolution. Where, as here, the court determines that dissolution is proper, an order of dissolution should be entered. Such an order is not absolutely necessary, however, where as here, all partners agree that dissolution be effected.

Under the facts of this case, considering the admissions of the two partners and the findings of the chancellor, we hold that dissolution was effected on October 31, 1977, the date this lawsuit was filed.

There were no provisions in the partnership agreement relative to dissolution, distribution of assets or accounting upon dissolution. Absent such agreement, the provisions of the Uniform Partnership Act apply as between the two partners. In a suit for dissolution the partners are entitled to an accounting, whether it be simple or complicated.

If dissolution results because of the wrongful acts of a partner, that partner is not summarily thrown out of the partnership and all assets turned over to the partner who did no wrong. The correct procedure is covered by the Uniform Act. T.C.A. §61-137(2). The chancellor erred in the application of the clean hands doctrine—equity follows the law.

The decree of the chancellor is affirmed insofar as finding a dissolution of the partnership as of October 31, 1977. The chancellor's decree is in all other aspects overruled and this cause is remanded to the chancery court for a complete accounting as between the partners and the partnership and as between each other. After the accounting is approved by the chancellor a final decree will be entered adjudging the rights and liabilities of the partners, all receiver fees, expenses and costs. . . .

So ordered.

Munn v. Scalera
436 A.2d 18 (Conn. 1980)

The defendants Peter Scalera and Robert Scalera were doing business as a partnership known as Constructors I when they agreed, in 1972, to build a house for the plaintiffs. The project fell into default almost immediately. During the first half of 1973, having run into financial and other difficulties, the partners discussed dissolution of their partnership and phasing out of partnership business. Peter Scalera and Robert Scalera individually met with the plaintiffs to inform them that the brothers were no longer doing business as partners. Each of them offered to complete the construction contract individually, and the plaintiffs elected to have Robert do so.

Robert Scalera resumed construction of the plaintiffs' house in the late summer of 1973. A year later the work was substantially completed, but there were sizable outstanding payments owed to a materialman, the Washington Supply Company. Eventually those obligations had to be met by the plaintiffs, and they incurred some other expenses as well in having the construction totally completed. These elements of damages to the plaintiffs led to the court's rendering of a judgment against Robert Scalera in the amount of $10,127, but the court found Peter Scalera to have no liability, and the plaintiffs appeal that decision.

PETERS, J. . . . Dissolution of partnerships is governed by a number of provisions in the Uniform Partnership Act. Section 34–74, entitled Discharge From Partnership Liability, provides in subsection (1) that "dissolution of a partnership does not of itself discharge the existing liability of any partner." However, subsection (3) goes on to state: "Where a person agrees to assume the existing obligations of a dissolved partnership, the partners whose obligations have been assumed shall be discharged from any liability to any creditor of the partnership who, knowing of the agreement, consents to a material alteration in the nature or time of payment of such obligations." We have not previously had the opportunity to interpret this section. Other courts, in their analysis of this language in the Uniform Partnership Act, have described the relationship of the assuming partner to the withdrawing partner as the relationship of principal to surety, and have bound creditors to knowledge of the legal consequences of such a relationship if they knew of the assumption agreement.

The defendant raises three issues with regard to the applicability of §34–74(3). Did the trial court err in concluding that: (1) the partnership between Peter Scalera and Robert Scalera had been dissolved? (2) Robert Scalera had assumed the partnership obligation to complete the plaintiffs' construction project? and (3) there had been a material alteration in the nature or payment of the obligation owed to the plaintiffs?

The first two of these issues are easily resolved for they are essentially questions of fact. . . . The evidence in the record amply supports the trial court's conclusions . . . that the two brothers had determined to go separate ways, and that thereafter Robert Scalera alone intended to undertake the responsibility to complete the plaintiffs' construction project.

The third claim, concerning the applicability of §34–74(3) as a matter of law, raises a more serious issue. The language of §34–74(3) fits most aptly the situation in which (1) all of the obligations of the partnership are assumed by the remaining partner and (2) all of the assumed obligations are in the form of obligations to pay. In such circumstances, the statute discharges the withdrawing partner, as surety, whenever the creditor and the remaining partner, as principal, agree to a material variation in the assumed debts by an alteration in the nature or manner of payment of those debts. For example, extension in the time of payment by the issuance and acceptance of renewal notes in substitution for the original partnership obligations has been held to discharge the withdrawing partner.

In our case, it is undisputed that the defendant Robert Scalera assumed only one of the various partnership obligations that were outstanding when Constructors I was dissolved, the obligation to construct the plaintiffs' house. That deviation from the normal pattern is of no significance. There is no discernible reason of policy to distinguish between the unitary assumption of all partnership obligations and the singular assumption of one partnership contract, so long as all the parties are fully and accurately informed of what has transpired.

The second aspect of the coverage of §34–74(3) is potentially more troublesome. The statute is not clear about the range of suretyship defenses which it incorporates, about the extent to which material alterations in the assumed obligation may be a basis for discharge if the material alteration relates to some aspect of the assumed obligation other than its payment terms. In the case before us, the plaintiffs agreed to changes in the nature and time of payment *to* the defendant Robert Scalera, the remaining partner, rather than to changes in the nature and time of payment *by* these defendants. The plaintiffs agreed to underwrite the procurement of materials, by adding their own credit to that of Robert Scalera, when the partnership contract assigned this responsibility solely to the defendants. In effect, the plaintiffs overpaid and prepaid Robert Scalera by not insisting that he discharge the claims of these materialmen before he himself was paid in full. There can be no doubt that the plaintiffs materially altered the partnership contract, and altered it in respect to its payment terms. We hold that this alteration fell within both the literal terms and the understood policy of §34–74(3), so as to afford a firm basis for the discharge of the defendant Peter Scalera.

There is no error.

Park Cities Corporation v. Byrd
522 S.W.2d 572 (Tex. 1975)

Mrs. Byrd was the general partner in a limited partnership. She made numerous loans to the partnership during her lifetime. These loans were evidenced by promissory notes bearing interest. When Mrs. Byrd died, the executors of her estate filed this suit for instruction as to the proper method for winding up the partnership. The limited partners contended that the loans were capital contributions and should be repaid as such.

KEITH, J. . . . The partnership agreement provided that the general partner "shall have the sole and exclusive control of the management of the business of the partnership and shall devote part of her time, attention, talent, capital, credit and business capacity to the business of the partnership as is necessary for its successful operation." The agreement did *not* require Mrs. Byrd to contribute a fixed or stated dollar amount of capital contribution; and, although granting her sole and exclusive control of the management, did not contain any provision prohibiting the borrowing of funds.

Upon a complete record, the trial court found as a fact that the loans so made by Mrs. Byrd were actual "bona fide loans made to the Limited Partnership by the General Partner, and are not capital contributions." Whether an advance by a partner is a loan or an added contribution to the capital of the firm is a question of fact. . . .

It is neither illegal nor improper for a partner to make a loan to a partnership of which he is a member. As stated in 60 Am. Jur. 2d, *Partnership* §309 at 204 (1972):

> Under the Uniform Partnership Act, the second rank in order of payment is for those liabilities owing to partners other than for capital and profits. This provision is in accord with the general rule that in the absence of an agreement which will determine rights as to advances, each partner is a creditor of the firm as to money loaned it and has a right to repayment after the debts to other creditors have been met. The payment of interest on advances apparently also falls within the second rank in order of payment if there is an express or implied agreement to pay interest. . . .

In *Moore* v. *Steele,* 67 Tex. 435, 3 S.W. 448, 450 (1887), Judge Gaines held that a partner "who has advanced money to the firm beyond his share of the capital is entitled to retain the amount due him before the other partners are entitled to recover any of the assets."

In Crane & Bromberg, *supra* (§65 at 369), the authors state:

> Before profits are shared on dissolution, payments must be made to creditors, and partners must be *repaid their advances* and their capital contributions. Presumably the partner making advances is entitled to interest thereon until paid.

. . . We hold that . . . the partner is entitled to be repaid the advances, with interest, before payments are made for those owing to partners in respect of capital or in respect of profits. . . .

Affirmed.

Swann v. Mitchell
435 So.2d 797 (Fla. 1983)

The defendants, Mitchells, own and operate an automobile dealership called Mitchell Motors. The dealership operated as a corporation from 1940 until 1954, and as a partnership thereafter. Swann served as business manager of Mitchell Motors from 1940 until 1967. In 1966, he entered into the partnership with an agreement that provided Swann would receive 5 percent of the profits and losses of the partnership. The agreement also provided that upon Swann's death, the partnership would pay his estate any undistributed profits of the partnership. In 1967, Swann retired. On June 30, 1979, the Mitchells dissolved the partnership without notifying Swann. They transferred all the partnership's assets to a corporation and issued stock to themselves. Swann discovered the conversion to corporate form in 1980 when he received a final payment from the Mitchells intended to represent his percentage of the profits of the business to the date of dissolution. Swann sues for wrongful dissolution of the partnership and to recover a portion of the capital surplus, including the value of the goodwill of the business. The lower court held that he had no interest in the goodwill of the business.

ADKINS, J. . . . The goodwill of a business may be defined as the advantage or benefit the business has beyond the mere value of its property and capital. Goodwill is usually evidenced by general public patronage and is reflected in the increase in profits beyond those that may be expected from the mere use of capital. Accordingly, goodwill should be recognized as an asset of a business, in the absence of a contract to the contrary, and taken into consideration in any sale or valuation of assets.

Courts have frequently recognized goodwill as an asset subject to consideration on an accounting between partners where its disposition is not controlled by the partnership articles and the dissolution was not caused by the wrongful act of one of the partners. . . .

Where some or all of the partners retain possession of any of the assets after dissolution of the partnership, whether their purpose is to use those assets to continue the business in another form or otherwise, they should be required to account to the partnership for the value of those assets at the time of dissolution. . . . The partnership laws of this state also forbid any number less than *all* of the partners in a partnership to dispose of the goodwill of the business. . . .

Upon dissolution of a partnership, the general rule is that it is the right of each partner to have the partnership property converted into money by sale. But, where a sale would be prejudicial to an innocent partner or where circumstances exist which would render distribution in kind, or another method of disposition, to be more favorable to the interests of the parties, such a distribution is per-missible and desired. . . . [W]here an actual sale of partnership property does not occur, there are methods available to use to determine the value of the goodwill. Two methods have often been used to calculate the value of goodwill; the capitalization of earnings method and the method of subtracting the value of tangible assets of a business from the sale price of that business. Under the capitalization of earnings methods, the goodwill is evaluated by determining the average annual net earnings of the business, determining the value of the business and tangible assets, deducting from the total net earnings those earnings attributable to the tangible property and then capitalizing the balance. Not all aspects of goodwill as a whole are reflected by the use of these formulas. These formulas would not necesarily be reflective of the goodwill which is personal to some particular individual. Elements of goodwill attributable to the personality, skill, or business acumen of the person disposing of a business, for instance, may be evaluated by comparing the profit margin of similar businesses where no such unusual personal elements of goodwill exist to obtain a value for the portion of the goodwill attributable to such personal factors.

We do not attempt to value the goodwill of Mitchell Motors in this case. That determination is properly left to the trial court after receiving the evidence. We merely give a brief discussion of these methods to demonstrate that it is possible to value goodwill in the absence of an actual sale. . . . Accordingly, the decision of the district court is . . . for further proceedings consistent with this opinion.

It is so ordered.

REVIEW QUESTIONS

1. Identify the terms in column A by matching each with the appropriate statement in column B.

A	B
1. Dissolution	a. Notice in a newspaper of general circulation.
2. Winding up	b. A partnership that may be dissolved at any time for any reason.

3. Termination

 c. The process of reducing assets to cash, paying creditors, returning capital contributions, and distributing the balance to the partners.

4. Partnership at will

 d. The advantage or benefit a business has beyond its tangible assets.

5. Marshaling of assets

 e. The legal destruction of the partnership relationship which occurs whenever any partner ceases to be a member of the firm or whenever a new partner joins the firm.

6. Accounting

 f. A method for allocating property among the firm creditors and the individual creditors of the partner.

7. Notice of publication

 g. A formal determination of the partnership's financial condition.

8. Goodwill

 h. The completion of the winding-up process.

2. Williams brought action against Burrus for dissolution of partnership and for accounting and distribution to plaintiff of his claimed share of partnership assets. The partnership operated a cocktail lounge under a Class H liquor license. The business was purchased in defendant's name alone, since plaintiff was unacceptable to State Liquor Control Board as a licensee. Is plaintiff entitled to dissolution? Why?

3. Alex, Ben, and Carl formed the ABC Company, a partnership, with Alex contributing $12,000 of capital, Ben contributing $8,000, and Carl contributing $6,000. The partnership agreement provided that the partnership was to exist for 20 years, but the partners made no provision as to the proportions in which profits and losses were to be shared. During the course of operating the partnership, Alex made a loan of $1,000 to the partnership that has not been repaid, and the partnership also owes outside creditors additional amounts that exceed the value of partnership assets by $3,000. How much will each be required to pay, and how much will each receive upon dissolution? Explain.

4. A partnership was dissolved. Subsequently suit was filed against the partnership and a summons was served on a former partner. Is the service valid to support a judgment against the partnership? Why?

5. Carson, Crocket, and Kitt were partners in the importing business. They needed additional capital to expand. They located an investor named White, who agreed to purchase a one-fourth interest in the partnership by contributing $50,000 in capital. At the time he became a partner, there were several large creditors who had previously lent money to the partnership. The partnership subsequently failed, and the creditors are attempting to assert personal liability against White. Is he liable for these debts? Explain.

6. Ashley, Raines, and Jackson operated a large canning company as a partnership. Jackson died suddenly and unexpectedly. Dempsey, an attorney, has been appointed as executor of Jackson's estate. Does Dempsey have a right to participate in the winding up of this partnership? Why?

7. Metals Suppliers was a partnership that bought and sold precious gems and metals. Cooper, one of the partners, flew to New York City to negotiate a major contract. While Cooper was away, Golden died in an automobile accident. Before he received the news of Golden's death, Cooper signed a contract committing the partnership to buy $500,000 worth of diamonds. Is the partnership bound to this contract? Why?

8. Bush and Baker formed a partnership, but a year later mutually agreed to dissolution. The only notice of dissolution was by publication in a newspaper in the community where their business had been transacted. By agreement, Bush continued to operate the business. O'Neill Company, a previous creditor of the partnership, continued to extend credit to the business. When O'Neill Company was not paid, it brought suit against both Baker and Bush. Should Baker be held liable for the credit extended after dissolution? Why?

9. IBM sold machinery to a limited partnership on credit. Before this debt was paid in full, the partnership was dissolved, and the capital contributions were returned to the limited partners. Thereafter, the partnership could not pay its debts. Can IBM collect from the limited partners? To what extent? Explain.

10. A partnership consists of three partners, Perkins, Adams, and Halloway, who share profits equally. The partnership agreement is silent on the sharing of losses. Perkins lent the partnership $10,000 and made a capital contribution of $20,000; Adams made a $10,000 capital contribution; Halloway made no capital contribution. The partnership now has assets of $80,000 and owes outside creditors $55,000. The partners have decided to dissolve the firm. How much is each partner entitled to receive on dissolution? Explain.

11. Patrick and Douglas operated a sawmill business as partners. The First Bank made a loan to the partnership, which was secured by a deed of trust on Patrick's home. When the partnership defaulted on this loan, the bank commenced foreclosure proceedings on the house. Patrick seeks to enjoin this foreclosure until a partnership accounting is completed. He contends that partnership assets will discharge this and all other debts. Should an injunction be issued? Why?

12. Bradley and Smith are the only partners in an insolvent partnership. The firm has assets of $10,000 and liabilities of $100,000. The creditors are Donaldson ($50,000), Charles ($40,000), and Williams ($10,000). The three creditors rank equally in order of priority. Bradley does not have any personal assets or liabilities. Smith has personal assets of $80,000, but he owes the Security Bank $50,000. Smith has no other personal debts. How much are Donaldson, Charles, Williams, and Security Bank each entitled to receive? Explain.

13. Rose, Morgan, and Carlton were partners under an agreement whereby the firm was to continue in business for 10 years. Rose caused a wrongful dissolution of the partnership and demanded his interest therein. May he demand that firm's assets be liquidated? Is he entitled to the return of all his capital contribution? Explain.

42 THE FORMATION OF CORPORATIONS

Corporations may be classified in a variety of ways: public or private, for profit (business corporations) or not-for-profit. Each state classifies corporations doing business within the state as foreign or domestic, to denote the state where incorporation took place. Moreover, each state has a variety of statutes relating to specialized corporations such as cooperatives, church and religious corporations, and fraternal organizations. In this chapter and those that follow, we are primarily concerned with the private business corporations.

Statutes relating to business corporations vary from state to state, yet they are quite similar. For our discussion, the principles of the Model Business Corporation Act will be used as the basic statute. This model act, prepared by the Commissioners on Uniform State Laws, has been wholly adopted by a few states, and largely adopted by others. A major influence on the law of corporations throughout the country, its application to any particular issue must nevertheless be checked in each state.

A corporation is an artificial, intangible person or being, created by the law. Incorporating is a method by which individual persons are united into a new legal entity. For this new legal entity, they select a common name and the purposes that it is to accomplish. As a legal entity separate and apart from the persons who had it created, the corporate existence is not affected by the death, incapacity, or bankruptcy of any of the persons involved in its creation or in its operation. Its owners do not have personal liability on its contracts,[1] and it has no liability for

---

[1] Morgan v. O'Neil, p. 962.

the obligations of its shareholders. As a legal entity, a corporation is able to own property and to sue or be sued in its own name in the same manner as a natural person. It has rights and duties separate and apart from its shareholders, and the law recognizes this separation in a variety of situations.

A corporation is also a person for purposes of both tort and criminal law. As an impersonal entity, it can act only through agents and servants, but the corporation is subject to the doctrine of *respondeat superior* and may be punished for certain criminal acts of its agents or servants.

Although a corporation is considered a person under most statutes, there are a few, such as those allowing the appointment of "suitable persons" as parole officers, in which it is not a "person." A corporation is a person for the purposes of the due process clause of the Fifth and Fourteenth Amendments to the United States Constitution. For purposes of the privilege against compulsory self-incrimination, it is not a person.

1. Procedure for Incorporation

The law prescribes the steps for the creation of the corporation. Most corporate laws provide that a specified number of adult persons, usually not less than three, may file an application for a charter. The application contains the names and addresses of the incorporators, the name of the proposed corporation, the object for which it is to be formed, its proposed duration, the location of its registered office, the name of its registered agent, and information about the stock of the corporation.

The *registered agent* is the person designated to receive notices for the corporation. The *registered office* is the location where notices may be delivered. A registered agent of a corporation need not simultaneously serve as an officer or director of such corporation, but an officer usually serves as registered agent.

The information that is supplied about the corporate stock usually includes (1) whether there will be preferred stock or only common stock; (2) the stated or par value of the stock (if the stock has no stated value, then it is called no-par stock); (3) the number of shares of stock that will be authorized; and (4) the number of shares of stock that will actually be issued.

Some states also require the names and addresses of the subscribers to the stock and the amount subscribed and paid in by each. Most applications usually indicate whether the stock is to be paid for in cash or in property.

The application, signed by all the incorporators, is forwarded to a state official, usually the secretary of state. If the application is in order, the official then issues a charter. If the application is not in proper form or if the corporation is being formed for an illegal purpose, the secretary of state will refuse to create the corporation and deny it a charter.[2]

Upon return of the charter properly signed by the secretary of state, it is filed by the incorporators in the proper recording office. The receipt of the charter and its filing are the operative facts that bring the corporation into existence and give it authority and power to do business. It is not necessary that stock be issued or bylaws be adopted for the corporation to exist as a legal entity.

---

[2] Smith v. Director, Corp. & Securities Bureau, p. 962.

After the charter has been received and filed, the incorporators and all others who have agreed to purchase stock meet and elect a board of directors. They may also approve the bylaws of the corporation if the applicable law so provides. In most instances, the bylaws are approved by the board, not by the shareholders. The board of directors that has been elected then meets, approves the bylaws, elects the officers, calls for the payment of the subscription price for the stock, and makes whatever decisions are necessary to start business.

2. Corporate Names

One of the provisions in the application for a corporate charter is the proposed name of the corporation. In order that persons dealing with a business will know that it is a corporation and that the investors therefore have limited liability, the law requires that the corporate name include one of the following words or end with an abbreviation of them: *corporation, company, incorporated,* or *limited.* A corporate name must not be the same as, or deceptively similar to, the name of any domestic corporation or a foreign corporation authorized to do business in the state to which the application is made.[3]

Most states have procedures for reserving a corporate name for a limited period. Inquiry is usually made concerning the availability of a name; if it is available, it is reserved while the articles are being prepared. The name may be changed by charter amendment at any time without affecting corporate contracts or title to corporate property in any way.

3. Powers of Corporations

The application for a charter includes a statement of the powers desired by the corporation. These are usually stated in quite broad language. A corporation has only such powers as are conferred upon it by the state that creates it. The charter, together with the statute under which it is issued, sets forth the express powers of the corporation. All powers reasonably necessary to carry out the expressed powers are implied.

The following general powers are ordinarily granted to the corporation by statute: (1) to have perpetual existence; (2) to sue and be sued; (3) to have a corporate name and corporate seal; (4) to own, use, convey, and deal in both real and personal property; (5) to borrow and lend money other than to officers and directors; (6) to purchase, own, and dispose of securities; (7) to enter into contracts of every kind; (8) to make charitable contributions; (9) to pay pensions and establish pension plans; and (10) all powers necessary or convenient to effect any of the other purposes.

Any acts of a corporation that are beyond the authority, express or implied, given to it by the state in the charter are said to be *ultra vires* acts—"beyond the authority." If a corporation performs acts or enters into contracts to perform acts that are *ultra vires,* the state creating such a corporation may forfeit its charter for misuse of its corporate authority. The extent of the misuse is controlling in determining whether the state will take away its franchise or merely enjoin the corporation from further *ultra vires* conduct.

---

[3] First Nat. Bank of Lander v. First Wyoming S & L, p. 963.

Although third parties have no right to object to the *ultra vires* acts of a corporation, a stockholder may bring court action to enjoin a corporation from performing an *ultra vires* contract. If the corporation sustains losses or damages because of the *ultra vires* venture, the corporation may recover from the directors who approved the contracts. When the directors exceed corporate powers, they may become personally liable for resulting losses.

At common law, a corporation had no liability on contracts beyond its corporate powers because the corporation had capacity to do only those things expressly authorized within its charter or incidental thereto. Most modern statutes, including the Model Business Corporation Act, provide that all *ultra vires* contracts are enforceable. Neither party to such a contract may use *ultra vires* as a defense. *Ultra vires* conduct on the part of the corporation may be enjoined by the state or any shareholder; otherwise, contracts previously made are binding, whether they be wholly executory, partially executed, or fully performed.

4. Bylaws

A *bylaw* is a rule for governing and managing the affairs of the corporation. It is binding upon all shareholders but not third parties, unless the third parties have knowledge of it. The bylaws contain provisions establishing the corporate seal and the form of the stock certificate, the number of officers and directors, the method of electing them and removing them from office, as well as the enumeration of their duties. Bylaws specify the time and place of the meetings of the directors and the shareholders. Together with the articles of incorporation and the applicable statute, the bylaws provide rules for operating the corporation. The bylaws are subservient to the articles of incorporation and the statute but are of greater authority than, for instance, a single resolution of the board. Failure to follow the bylaws constitutes a breach of the fiduciary duties of a director or officer.

Bylaws are valid if they are reasonable and are consistent with the corporate charter and the applicable statutes. Bylaws may be illegal and void. For example, a bylaw of a corporation gave the president the power to manage the corporation's affairs. Such a bylaw is void because the law provides that the affairs of corporations shall be managed by a board of directors.

The power to alter, amend, or revoke the bylaws is vested in the board of directors unless reserved to the shareholders by statute or by the articles of incorporation. The board cannot, however, repeal, amend, or add to the bylaws if the change will affect the vested rights of a shareholder.

5. Domestic and Foreign Corporations

To a state or country, corporations organized under its laws are *domestic* corporations; those organized under the laws of another state or country are *foreign* corporations.

Domestic corporations become qualified to do business upon receipt and recording of their charter. Foreign corporations with significant intrastate activities must also "qualify" to do business by obtaining a certificate of authority and by paying the license fees and taxes levied on local businesses. A foreign corporation engaged wholly in *interstate* commerce through a state need not qualify in that state.

Most state statutes require foreign corporations to qualify to do business by filing a copy of their articles of incorporation with the secretary of state. They are also required to appoint an agent upon whom service of process may be served, and to maintain an office in the state. Failure to comply results in a denial of the right of access to the courts as a plaintiff. Of course, such a corporation could be sued in a state if it had sufficient minimum contacts to satisfy due process. Generally, subjecting a foreign corporation to a state's qualification statutes requires more activity within a state than for service of process or for taxation of its income and property.[4] Qualification is essential if these are local activities that constitute transacting business.

In a real sense, this denial of access to the courts as a plaintiff prevents a corporation from conducting business, because its contracts are not enforceable by suit, and debtors would thus be able to avoid payment to the corporation. Transacting business within the state without complying with the statute also subjects the corporation and its officers to statutory penalties, such as fines.

The term *doing business* is not reducible to an exact and certain definition. The Model Business Corporation Act defines the term by saying that a foreign corporation is *doing business* when "some part of its business substantial and continuous in character and not merely casual or occasional" is transacted within a state. A corporation is not *doing business* in a state merely because it is involved in litigation or maintains a bank account or an office within a state for the transfer of its stock. It also states that a foreign corporation is not required to obtain a license to do business by reason of the fact that (1) it is in the mail-order business and receives orders from a state that are accepted and filled by shipment from without the state, and (2) it uses salespeople within a state to obtain orders that are accepted outside the state. If the orders are accepted or filled within the state, or if any sale, repair, or replacement is made from stock physically present within the state in which the order is obtained, a foreign corporation is required to obtain a license.

6. Promoters

A *promoter,* as the name implies, promotes the corporation and assists in bringing it into existence. One or more promoters will be involved in making application for the charter, holding the first meeting of shareholders, entering into preincorporation subscription agreements, and engaging in other activities necessary to bring the corporation into existence. Promoters are responsible for compliance with the applicable blue-sky laws (statutes relating to the sale of securities), including the preparation of a prospectus if required.

Many of these activities involve the incurring of contractual obligations or debts. Preparation of the application for a charter usually requires the assistance

---

[4] Johnson v. MPL Leasing Corp., p. 964.

of a lawyer, and it must be accompanied by the required filing fee. Legal questions about who has liability for these obligations and debts frequently arise. Is the promoter liable? Is the corporation after formation liable? Are both liable?

Certain general principles of contract and agency law prevent simple answers to these questions. First of all, a promoter is not an agent prior to incorporation, because there is no principal. A party who purports to act as an agent for a nonexistent principal is generally liable as a principal. Thus, a promoter is liable on preincorporation contracts unless the other party is aware that the corporation has not been formed and agrees that the promoter is not to be bound by the contract personally. Second, the corporation technically cannot ratify the contracts of promoters because ratification requires capacity to contract both at the time of the contract and at the time of the ratification.

To avoid the difficulties caused by these legal theories, the law has used certain fictions to create an obligation on the part of the corporation and to provide a means to eliminate liability on the part of the promoters. One fiction is that a novation occurs. This theory proceeds on the premise that when the corporation assents to the contract, the third party agrees to discharge the promoter and to look only to the corporation. Establishing a novation often fails because of a lack of proof of any agreement to release the promoter.

Another theory that is used to determine liability on preincorporation obligations may be described as the *offer and acceptance theory*. Under this theory, a contract made by a promoter for the benefit of the corporation is an offer that may be accepted by the corporation after it comes into existence. Acceptance of the benefits of the contract constitutes a formal ratification of it. If the corporation does not accept the offer, it is not liable. The promoter may or may not be liable, depending on the degree of disclosure.

Corporations have also been held liable on promoters' contracts on theories that may be called the *consideration theory* and the *quasi-contract theory*. After incorporation, directors may promise to pay for expenses and services of promoters. Under the consideration theory, their promise will be binding and supported by sufficient consideration, on the theory of services previously rendered. The quasi-contract theory holds that corporations are liable by implication for the necessary expenses and services incurred by the promoters in bringing them into existence, because such expenses and services accrue or inure to the benefit of the corporation. Finally, it should be noted that some states have abandoned trying to justify corporate liability with a legal theory and have simply provided by statute that corporations are liable for the reasonable expenses incurred by promoters.

The parties frequently do not intend the promoter to be liable on a preincorporation contract. A promoter may avoid personal liability by informing the other party that he does not intend to be liable and that he is acting in the name of, and solely on, the credit of a corporation to be formed. But if the promoter represents that there is an existing corporation when there is none, the promoter is liable. A promoter should make sure that contracts entered into on behalf of the proposed corporation are worded to relieve him of personal liability, if that is the intent.

Promoters occupy a fiduciary relationship toward the prospective corporation. Their position does not give them the right to secure any benefit or advantage over the corporation itself or over other shareholders. A promoter cannot purchase property and then sell it to the corporation at a profit, nor has he a right to receive a commission from a third party for the sale of property to the corporation. In general, however, he may sell property acquired by him prior to the time he started promoting the corporation, provided he sells it to an unbiased board of directors after full disclosure of all pertinent facts.

7. Disregarding the Corporate Entity

One of the basic advantages of the corporate form of business organization is the limitation of shareholder liability. Corporations are formed for the express purpose of limiting one's risk to the amount of his investment in the stock. Sometimes suits are brought to hold the shareholders personally liable for an obligation of a corporation or to hold a parent corporation liable for debts of a subsidiary.

Such suits attempt to "pierce the corporate veil." They ask the court to look behind the corporate entity and take action as though no entity separate from the members existed. They may not ask that the corporate entity be disregarded simply because all the stock is owned by the members of a family or by one person or by another corporation.

The lending of money to a corporation one controls or guaranteeing its debts is not enough to justify piercing the corporate veil. It would frustrate the purposes of corporate law to expose directors, officers, and shareholders to personal liability for the debts of the corporation when they contribute funds to, or on behalf of, a corporation for the purpose of assisting the corporation to meet its financial obligations. The loan or guarantee may assist the corporate efforts to survive thus benefiting the creditors. If such acts were grounds to eliminate the separate corporate entity, such loans and guarantees usually would not be forthcoming.

In certain situations, the corporate entity may be disregarded. First, if the use of the corporation is to defraud or to avoid an otherwise valid obligation, the court may handle the problem as though no corporation existed. Let us assume that A and B sold a business and agreed not to compete with the buyer for a given number of years. In violation of the contract, A and B organized a corporation in which they became the principal stockholders and managers; the buyer may enjoin the corporation from competing with him, and he may do so effectively as he could have enjoined A and B from establishing a competing business. Second, if the corporate device is used to evade a statute, the corporate entity may be disregarded. If a state law provides that a person may not hold more than one liquor license at a time, this law cannot be circumvented by forming multiple corporations. The attempt to evade the statute would justify "piercing the corporate veil."

The fiction of the corporate entity also may be disregarded when one corporation is organized, controlled, and conducted to make it a mere instrumentality of another corporation. In such circumstances one corporation is said to be the *alter ego* of another. The *alter ego theory,* by which the corporate veil is pierced, may also be used to impose personal liability upon corporate officers and stockholders. If the corporate entity is disregarded by the principals themselves, so that there is such a unity of ownership and interest that separateness of the corporation has ceased to exist, the alter ego doctrine will be followed.

Some of the factors considered significant in justifying a disregard of the corporate entity are: (1) undercapitalization of a corporation,[5] (2) failure to observe corporate formalities such as annual meetings, (3) nonpayment of dividends, (4) siphoning of corporate funds by the dominant stockholders, (5) nonfunctioning of other officers or directors, (6) absence of corporate records, (7) use of the corporation as a facade for operations of the dominant stockholders, and (8) use of the corporate entity in promoting injustice or fraud. In other words, the corporate veil will be pierced if the ends of justice require it. Justice will require the disregarding of the corporate entity if the liability-causing activity did not occur only for the benefit of the corporation or because the liable corporation has been gutted and left without funds by those controlling it in order to avoid actual or potential liability.

Sometimes the shareholders seek to disregard the separate corporate entity. This usually arises when multiple corporations are subjected to multiple taxation. Such taxes may be income, property, or sales taxes.

CORPORATE STOCK

8. Kinds of Stock

A *stock certificate* is written evidence of the ownership of a certain number of shares of stock of a corporation. The certificate recognizes a certain person as being a shareholder with rights in the corporation, primarily the right to share in profits, to participate indirectly in the control of the corporation, and to receive a portion of the assets at the time of dissolution. A share of stock gives the holder no right to share in the active management of the business.

Stock must be distinguished from a bond. A *bond* is an obligation of the corporation to pay a certain sum of money in the future at a specified rate of interest. It is comparable to a corporation's promissory note. A bondholder is a creditor of the corporation, whereas a shareholder is an owner of the corporation. A shareholder has a right to receive dividends if they are declared by the board of directors and to participate in the assets of the corporation after all creditors have been paid. A bondholder has no right to vote or to participate in the management and control of a corporation. A shareholder has a right to participate in management to the extent of electing the directors and voting on matters such as dissolution.

Common stock is the simplest type of corporate stock. It entitles the owner to share in the control, profits, and assets of the corporation in proportion to the amount of common stock held. Such a shareholder has no advantage, priority, or preference over any other class of shareholders unless otherwise specified.

Preferred stock has priority over other classes of stock in claiming dividends or assets on dissolution. The most important right given to a preferred shareholder

---

[5] Pierson v. Jones, p. 964.

is the right to receive a certain specified dividend, even though the earnings are not sufficient to pay like dividends to common shareholders.

Preferred stock may be *cumulative or noncumulative.* If cumulative, any dividends that are not paid because of lack of earnings accrue and are paid when earnings are available. If noncumulative, only the current year's preferred dividend is paid out of current earnings. If nothing is stated about the payment of the dividends, the preferred stock is cumulative.

The statutes of most states provide that a corporation may issue stock with *no par value.* The value of no-par stock is determined by its sale price in the open market or by the price set by the directors as a "stated value." Shareholders, creditors of the corporation, and the public are not misled or prejudiced by this type of stock, because there is no holding out that the stock has any particular face value. All persons dealing in no-par stock are put on notice that they should investigate the corporation's assets and its financial condition. Stock with no par value represents its proportionate part of the total assets of the corporation.

A *stock warrant* is a certificate that gives its holder the right to subscribe for and purchase a given number of shares of stock in a corporation at a stated price. It is usually issued in connection with the sale of other shares of stock or of bonds, although the law of some states permits the issuance of stock warrants entirely separate and apart from the sale of other securities. Warrants are transferable. The option to purchase contained in the warrant may or may not be limited as to time or otherwise conditioned. Warrants have value and can readily be sold on the market in the same fashion as other securities.

Watered stock is stock that has been issued as fully paid, when in fact its full par value has not been paid in money, property, or services. The original owner of watered stock has liability for the unpaid portion of its stated value. If Catherine exchanges property worth $200 for 1,000 shares of $1 par value stock, she owes the corporation $800. If the corporation becomes insolvent, a creditor may require that the balance due be paid.

The liability for watered stock arises because the capital stock of a corporation represents the total par value of all the shares of the corporation (plus the stated value of no-par stock). The public, including corporate creditors, has a right to assume that the capital stock issued has been paid for in full. The corporation in effect represents that assets have been received in payment equal in amount to its issued capital stock. If stock is issued in excess of the actual assets in money value received for it by the corporation, there is watered stock.

Treasury stock is that which has been issued by the corporation for value and returned to the corporation by gift or purchase. It may be sold at any price, including below par, and the proceeds returned to the treasury of the corporation for working capital. It differs from stock originally issued below par in that the purchaser is not liable for the difference between par and the sale price. It may be sold at any price the company sees fit to charge.

A corporation is restricted in its power to purchase treasury stock because the purchase might effect a reduction of its capital, to the detriment of creditors. In most states a corporation is permitted to purchase treasury stock only out of accumulated profits or surplus. This restriction retains the stockholders' investment, equivalent to the original capital, as a protective cushion for creditors in case subsequent losses develop.

A corporation may redeem its preferred stock if there is no injury to, or objection by, creditors. Here again, many of the states require the preferred stock to be redeemed out of surplus, or they demand that authority to reduce the capital stock be obtained from the state.

9. Stock Subscriptions

A *preincorporation stock subscription* is an agreement to purchase stock in a corporation. It is a binding agreement (a subscriber cannot revoke his subscription) created among the subscribers for stock in a corporation to be formed. The subscription is usually drafted in a manner that creates a contract. Some states by statute have provided that a preincorporation subscription constitutes a binding, irrevocable offer to the corporation, by reason of the mutual promises of the parties. The offer is usually limited to a specified period of time, such as 6 months.

Certain conditions are inherent in the preincorporation subscription contract. The subscriber will not be liable unless: the corporation is completely organized; the full amount of the capital stock is subscribed; and the purpose, articles, and bylaws of the corporation are as originally stated and relied upon by the subscriber. Conditions, expressed or implied, are often waived by the subscriber if, with knowledge of the nonperformance, he participates in stockholders' meetings, pays part or all of his subscription, or acts as an officer or director of the corporation.

A subscription to stock of a corporation already in existence is a contract between the subscriber and the corporation. Such a contract may come into existence by reason of an offer made by the corporation and accepted by the subscriber or made by the subscriber and accepted by the corporation. If the corporation opens subscription books and advertises its stock, it is seeking an offer to be made by the subscriber. The corporation may, however, make a general offer to the public, which may be accepted by the subscriber in accordance with the terms of the general offer.

10. Right to Transfer of Stock

A share of stock is personal property, and the owner has the right to transfer it just as he may transfer any other personal property. The right to transfer freely one's share in the corporation is one of the features of the corporation that distinguishes it from a partnership. A share of stock is generally transferred by an indorsement and the delivery of the certificate of stock and by surrender of the certificate to the stock transfer agent for reissue.

Shareholders of close corporations usually attempt to restrict the transfer of stock. Such attempts may be part of a contract, or they may be included in the bylaws. These restrictions may be a simple right of first refusal to the corporation, the other shareholders, or both, or there may be a binding buy and sell agreement among the shareholders. In the latter case, there is a sale of the stock upon the happening of a specified event even if the owner or the estate of the owner does not desire to sell.[6]

A corporate bylaw that makes shares of stock transferable only to the corporation or to those approved by the board of directors is unenforceable. It places too severe a restraint upon the alienation of property. Society is best protected when property may be transferred freely, but an agreement or bylaw approved by all shareholders to the effect that no transfer of stock shall be made until it has first been offered to the other shareholders or to the corporation is generally enforced. Notice of the bylaw or agreement should be set forth in the stock certificate because an innocent purchaser without notice of the restriction on alienation receives ownership free from the restriction.

In a close corporation, sometimes the buy and sell agreements between shareholders provide for matters such as salary continuation in the event of death or disability and the amount of dividends to be paid in the future. Some agreements even commit the shareholders to vote for certain persons in the election of directors. Such agreements are valid in closely held corporations, providing the duration of the agreement is not so long that it becomes contrary to public policy and providing the agreement does not adversely affect minority interests in the corporation. These agreements are used by the majority owners to ensure the election of the desired board of directors. Corporations are governed by the republican principle that the whole are bound by lawful acts of the majority. It is not against public policy, nor is it dishonest, for shareholders to contract for the purpose of control.

The importance of shareholder buy and sell provisions must not be overlooked. It is just as important to have a means of getting a shareholder out of a closely held corporation as it is to have a means of getting a partner out of a partnership.

Shareholder buy and sell provisions should be worked out before any shareholder knows whether he is a buyer or a seller. Although withdrawal from active participation will not effect a dissolution, it can have the serious effect of precipitating a lawsuit, or a shareholder may continue to participate in management when he does not desire to do so. Frequently, a withdrawing shareholder will be forced to sell his stock for less than it is worth because a buy and sell agreement was not worked out in advance.

11. Mechanics of Transfer

A share of stock is generally transferred by an endorsement and the delivery of the certificate of stock and by surrender of the certificate to the stock transfer agent for reissue. A share may be transferred or assigned by a bill of sale or by any other method that will pass title to a *chose in action* (a right to recover money or property from another through judicial procedure) or other intangible property. Whenever a share of stock is sold and a new stock certificate issued, the name of

---

[6] Renberg v. Zarrow, p. 965.

the new owner is entered on the stock records of the corporation. In a small corporation, the secretary of the corporation usually handles all transfers of stock and also the canceling of old certificates and issuing of new. Large corporations, in which there are hundreds and even thousands of transactions, employ transfer agents. The transfer agents transfer stock, cancel old certificates, issue new ones, keep an up-to-date list of the names of shareholders of the corporation, distribute dividends, mail out shareholders' notices, and perform many functions to assist the corporation secretary. Stock exchange rules provide that corporations listing stock for sale must maintain a transfer agency and registry, operated and maintained under exchange regulations. The registrar of stock is an agent of the corporation whose duty is to see that no stock certificates are issued in excess of the authorized capitalization of the corporation.

Article 8 of the Uniform Commercial Code deals with investment securities. The general approach of Article 8 is that securities are negotiable instruments and that bona fide purchasers have greater rights than they would have "if the things bought were chattels or simple contracts." The particular rules of Article 3 that relate to the establishment of preferred status for commercial paper are applied to securities. Defenses of the issuer are generally not effective against a purchaser for value who has received the securities without being given notice of the particular defense raised.

A bona fide purchaser is one who purchases in good faith and without notice of any adverse claim. He is the equivalent of a holder in due course. A bona fide purchaser takes free of "adverse claims," which include a claim that a transfer was wrongful or that some other person is the owner of, or has an interest in, the security.

SUMMARY

PROCEDURE

The charter	1. The incorporators prepare an application for a charter which includes basic information such as the purpose of the corporation, the location of its office and registered agent, and information about its stock.
	2. The application will indicate the amount of authorized stock and the amount to be issued.
	3. When the application is approved, it is returned as a charter which is filed in the proper recording office.

The name	1. The name of a corporation must include words such as *corporation, company, incorporated,* or *limited,* which provide notice of the limited liability of the shareholders.
	2. A corporate name must not be deceptively similar to names of other corporations.
Powers	1. A corporation has all the powers granted in its charter and those set forth in the statutes of the state of incorporation.
	2. The usual powers, include the power to sue and be sued; to own, convey, and deal in property; to enter into contracts; and to purchase and dispose of securities.
	3. An *ultra vires* act is one beyond the authority of the corporation.
	4. Neither the corporation nor parties dealing with it may avoid liability on the ground of *ultra vires.*
	5. *Ultra vires* conduct on the part of the corporation may be enjoined at the request of the shareholders or may be the basis of a revocation of the charter by the state.
Bylaws	1. After filing the charter, the incorporators meet with all stock subscribers and elect a board of directors. The board in turn meets and adopts bylaws.
	2. The bylaws provide the rules for managing the corporation. They cover such activities as the corporate seal, stock certificates, the number and manner of election of officers, and the time and place of meetings of shareholders as well as the board of directors.
Foreign corporations	1. A corporation incorporated in one state is a foreign corporation in all other states.
	2. Foreign corporations transacting local business in a state must qualify to do business in that state. If they fail to do so, they are denied access to the courts and are subject to other sanctions.
	3. If a business is engaged only in interstate commerce and is not conducting intrastate activities, it is not required to obtain a license to do business.

Promoters	1. A promoter is usually an incorporator and is active in obtaining preincorporation agreements. Promoters are responsible for compliance with all applicable laws.
	2. A promoter may be personally liable for contracts prior to incorporation, but this liability may be avoided.
	3. A corporation after it is formed may have liability on preincorporation agreements under a variety of theories.
	4. Promoters stand in a fiduciary relationship to the corporation and cannot secure benefits at the expense of other shareholders or the corporation.

DISREGARDING THE CORPORATE ENTITY

Piercing the corporate veil	1. Creditors may seek to look through the corporation to the shareholders and seek to impose liability as if the corporate entity did not exist.
	2. The corporate entity is not disregarded simply because all the stock is owned by one person.
	3. Courts will pierce the corporate veil to avoid fraud and to prevent the evasion of statutes.
The alter ego theory	1. This theory is used to pierce the corporate veil where a corporation is actually nothing more than the alter ego of another corporation or of an individual.
	2. This theory is used where the business is actually operated as if the separate corporate entity did not exist.

CORPORATE STOCK

Kinds of stock	1. Some stock is preferred over others in either dividends, distributions on dissolution, or both.
	2. Stock may be issued without par value, in which case the directors provide a stated value for balance sheet purposes.

3. A stock warrant gives a person a right to subscribe and to purchase corporate stock at a stated price. Such warrants are transferable.

4. Watered stock is stock that is issued as fully paid when in fact an equivalent value has not been paid to the corporation.

5. Treasury stock is stock of the corporation that has been purchased by or returned to the corporation.

6. Treasury stock may be purchased only out of accumulated earnings. Otherwise, the purchase could constitute a reduction of capital.

Stock subscriptions

1. A preincorporation stock subscription is binding and irrevocable for a stated period of time after its execution.

2. Preincorporation subscriptions are usually conditioned on such things as final organization of the corporation and subscription to all the stock.

3. Stock may also be subscribed after incorporation, and such contracts are subject to the same rules as other contracts.

The right to transfer stock

1. In a close corporation, the bylaws may grant a right of first refusal to the corporation or to other shareholders.

2. A buy and sell agreement may require the purchase of stock on death or withdrawal of a shareholder.

3. Stock is transferred on the records of the corporation by surrender of the stock certificate and issuing a new one. Large corporations retain stock transfer agents to perform this task.

4. Article 8 of the Uniform Commercial Code deals with investment securities. If its provisions are complied with, a party purchasing stock has greater rights than the seller.

CASES

Morgan v. O'Neil
652 S.W.2d 83 (Ky. 1983)

Plaintiffs obtained a judgment against a corporation in Indiana. They then sued the sole stockholder in Kentucky to collect the judgment. The corporation had been dissolved in the meantime.

ENGLISH, J. . . . The amended complaint seeks to hold O'Neil, a stockholder, liable for payment of the Indiana judgment against the corporation, which is a corporate debt.

In general, a shareholder may be liable for a corporate debt either by "piercing the corporate veil" or by statutory authorization.

It is fundamental corporate law that a shareholder is not liable for a debt of the corporation unless extraordinary circumstances exist to impose liability. Such extraordinary liability may be imposed either by "piercing the corporate veil" or by violation of a particular statute imposing liability.

No allegations appear in the complaint to state a claim on "piercing the corporate veil." Likewise, the complaint made no allegation of any statutory basis to impose personal liability upon O'Neil, the sole shareholder in the corporation. . . .

No allegation was made that O'Neil was an officer of the corporation. The bland allegation in the pleadings that O'Neil, the sole shareholder in the corporation, allowed the corporation to proceed through dissolution procedures while having knowledge of the claim of the Plaintiffs is not sufficient to state a cause of action so as to impose personal liability on the shareholders for the payment of the Indiana judgment.

Holding a shareholder in a corporation individually liable for a corporate debt is an extraordinary procedure and should be done only when the strict requirements for imposing individual liability are met. . . .

Case dismissed.

Smith v. Director, Corp. & Securities Bureau
261 N.W.2d 228 (Mich. 1978)

Plaintiff Smith (P) attempted to file proposed articles of incorporation on behalf of a mortgage company. The proposed articles contained a statement of purpose, which expressed the rates of interest the mortgage company would charge its borrowers. These rates of interest were usurious under state law.

Defendant (D), the secretary of state, rejected the articles of incorporation because they contained an illegal purpose. P filed suit to force D to issue the charter. The lower court held for the defendant, and the plaintiff appealed.

KEYES, J. . . . Plaintiff asserts that the Business Corporation Act, does not give defendant legal authority to reject newly filed articles of incorporation and that, therefore, defendant is required by law to issue a certificate of incorporation to plaintiff. M.C.L.A. §450.1131; M.S.A. §21.200(131) reads:

(1) A document required or permitted to be filed under this act shall be filed by delivering the document to the administrator together with the fees and accompanying documents required by law. If the document substantially conforms to the requirements of this act, the administrator shall indorse upon it the word 'filed' with his official title and the dates of receipt and of filing thereof, and shall file and index the document or a microfilm or other reproduced copy thereof in his office. . . .

The defendant argues that the proposed articles failed to substantially conform to the requirements of the BCA because sections M.C.L.A. §450.1130; M.S.A. §21.200(103) and M.C.L.A. §450.1251; M.S.A. §21.200(251) require a lawful purpose which these articles do not contain. We agree that proposed articles of incorporation which state an unlawful corporate purpose do not substantially conform to the requirements of the B.C.A. We also agree that the defendant has no duty to accept and file such articles. . . . The interest rates set out in the proposed articles are not authorized by Michigan statute. Such rates of interest on loans secured by second mortgages on single family residential property are usurious; they would be in violation of the statute and therefore unlawful. The stated corporate purpose contained in the proposed articles, contracting for unlawful interest rates, is unlawful. Therefore, the proffered articles do not conform to the provisions of the BCA and were properly rejected by defendant. We hold that the Business Corporation Act contains an implicit grant of authority to the defendant to reject such articles of incorporation. . . .

Affirmed.

First Nat. Bank of Lander v. First Wyoming S & L
592 P.2d 697 (Wyo. 1979)

ROSE, J. We are concerned here with the name change sought by the Wyoming Bancorporation's subsidiary in Lander, Wyoming—The First National Bank of Lander. First National, like the other subsidiary banks, planned to change its name to First Wyoming Bank, N.A.—Lander. On December 9, 1976, the appellee-plaintiff, First Wyoming Savings and Loan Association, filed a complaint seeking permanently to enjoin the defendant from making the name change in Lander or elsewhere in Wyoming. The basis of the complaint against First National Bank was that First Wyoming Savings had established a trade name in the words "First Wyoming" and that the use of the name "First Wyoming Bank—Lander" would result in confusion and deception to the general public in Fremont County. . . . The complaint was, in part, premised on the alleged protection provided by the First Wyoming Savings' registration of its service mark pursuant to the Wyoming statutes. The district court granted permanent injunctive relief, enjoining the use by the First National Bank of the name "First Wyoming Bank—Lander" in Fremont County. . . .

The defendant contends that the trial court's finding—that the words "First Wyoming" had taken on a secondary meaning and had been appropriated by plaintiff as a common-law trade name in Fremont County—is not supported by the law and the evidence. . . .

Questions regarding trade-name infringement are largely factual determinations to be made by the trier-of-fact and, therefore, we will not disturb a trial court's findings thereon unless they are clearly erroneous or contrary to the great weight of the evidence. We also set forth the applicable standard of law as follows:

> . . . Unless a trade name is confusing and deceptive on its face, those seeking such protection must take the burden of proving that they have given to their trade names a secondary meaning through years of usage and if in this case defendant was to be allowed to use its new name, the public would be confused by its similarity to the trade names of plaintiffs. This confusion, in turn, must be such as to warrant issuance of an injunction. That is, potential customers must be confused or deceived into patronizing one bank in the mistaken belief that they are dealing with another bank. . . .

A secondary meaning is supplier to geographic or generic words—like those at issue here—when by the process of association the words become distinctive and distinguish the producer of a particular service and the name of that producer. With regard to the likelihood of confusion, the consumer bears some responsibility for using reasonable care.

A review of the record discloses that, in Fremont County, questions of fact were present with respect to the likelihood of confusion and the acquisition of a secondary meaning by plaintiff in the words "First Wyoming." The plaintiff presented evidence of one of its signs located in Lander on which the words "First Wyoming" were predominant. It presented various radio announcements—covering the period from March 1975 to August 1976—in which the words "First Wyoming" were emphasized. Five witnesses testified that they commonly referred to plaintiff as "First Wyoming." Finally, a portion of a study entitled "The Effect of a Proposed Name Change in Lander, Wyoming," prepared for the plaintiff, was admitted into evidence. The study concludes that "the proposed name change would likely create an awkward and confusing situation in Lander." The study contains data which, if believed by the trial court, would support the trial court's findings.

We hold that the trial court did not clearly err

in finding that the defendants' proposed name-change would infringe upon the secondary meaning acquired by plaintiff in the words "First Wyoming"

and that injunctive relief in Fremont County was necessary to avoid confusion and deception.

Affirmed.

Johnson v. MPL Leasing Corp.
441 So.2d 904 (Ala. 1983)

MPL Leasing Corporation (MPL), the plaintiff, is a California corporation organized for the purpose of financing people who desire to sell Saxon Business Products. Johnson and MPL signed an agreement which provided for Johnson to lease copiers with the option to buy them. MPL shipped the copiers to Alabama, Johnson's home state, and filed the appropriate financing papers.

After several months, Johnson became delinquent with his payments to MPL. MPL sued in the Alabama courts, alleging a breach of contract. Johnson moved to dismiss on the ground that MPL was a foreign corporation not qualified to do business in Alabama and that the state's constitution prevented unqualified corporations from enforcing their contracts in Alabama's courts. The trial court denied the defendant's motion, and he appealed.

TORBERT, J. . . . The question to be considered by this Court is whether a foreign corporation, not qualified to do business in this state, may nevertheless utilize Alabama courts to enforce a contract which concerns the lease or sale, or both, of products within Alabama to Alabama citizens. . . .

Section 232 of the Alabama Constitution and 10-2A-247, Code 1975, bar foreign corporations not qualified to do business in this state from enforcing

their contracts through our courts. These laws only come into play when the business conducted in the state by non-qualified corporations is considered "intrastate" in nature. MPL's activities within Alabama are limited to (1) delivering copying machines by common carrier and (2) filing this action. This Court has never held previously that contacts as minimal as those of MPL constitute "intrastate business." . . .

The appellant cites several cases for the proposition that solicitation of sales constitutes "doing business." In *Marcus v. J.R. Watkins Co.,* 279 Ala. 584 (1966), the Court confused the test for minimum contacts for service of process with the test for determining whether a foreign corporation must qualify to do business in order to sue in state court. The minimum contacts test for service of process protects *defendants* against the burden of litigating in a distant forum. The doing business test for qualifying foreign corporations is governed by the limits on state regulation inherent in the Commerce Clause of the United States Constitution. . . . It is far easier to find that a foreign corporation is "doing business" for service of process than it is to find that the corporation is conducting intrastate business subject to state regulation in view of the Commerce Clause.

Therefore, we hold that MPL is welcome to use Alabama courts to enforce rights arising from the agreement with Johnson. The judgment is.

Affirmed.

Pierson v. Jones
625 P.2d 1085 (Id. 1981)

Pierson sues Jones to hold him personally liable for a corporate debt. Jones operated a sheet metal business as a sole proprietorship until it was incorporated in September of 1975. At that time, Jones transferred the assets of that business to a corporation in exchange for an equal amount of stock. Jones and his wife were the only directors at the outset of the corporation, although the bylaws required three directors.

After Jones and his wife were divorced, Jones held a corporate meeting at which the corporation was authorized to borrow $90,000 from Pierson. At that time Jones represented that he was the sole director and shareholder of the corporation. It was not until August of 1976 that the corporate bylaws were amended to permit fewer than three directors.

Pierson was an employee of the corporation from July 1976 to December 1976, and in such capacity he had occasion to work with and check the business records of the corporation on a daily basis. During that period of time Pierson lent the corporation $80,571.42. Prior to making those loans, Pierson was aware that he was dealing with a corporation and had reviewed a corporate financial statement of May 31, 1976.

The business began sustaining financial losses and on February 9, Pierson's attorney threatened suit against the corporation and Jones if a security interest for the Pierson debt was not obtained. On February 10, 1977, Jones assigned corporate accounts receivable of $34,000 to Pierson. The corporation filed bankruptcy on June 24, 1977, at which time it owed Pierson $33,187.64.

SHEPARD, J. . . . On appeal, Pierson contends. . . the trial court erred in not piercing the corporate veil. . . . It is held that to justify piercing the corporate veil, it must . . . be shown that there is such a unity of interest and ownership that the individuality of such corporation and such person has ceased; and it must further appear from the facts that the observance of the fiction of separate existence would, under the circumstances, sanction a fraud or promote injustice. Here the trial court

held that the facts disclosed by the evidence did not, as a matter of law, justify piercing the corporate veil. We find ample, substantial and competent evidence to support those findings upon which the trial court based its conclusion.

Pierson . . . asserts that the corporation was undercapitalized at the time he lent it money and that this is a justification for piercing the corporate veil. We disagree. It is held that undercapitalization is one factor to be considered in determining whether or not to pierce the corporate veil. However, financial inadequacy is measured by the nature and magnitude of the corporate undertaking or the reasonableness of the cushion for creditors at the time of the *inception* of the corporation. Here the corporate accountant testified that at the time of its inception the corporation was not undercapitalized. Clearly, a corporation adequately capitalized at its inception can become undercapitalized at a later time for any of a variety of legitimate reasons. . . .

Affirmed.

Renberg v. Zarrow
667 P.2d 465 (Okla. 1983)

In 1963, the shareholders of a closely held corporation executed an agreement which provided that upon the death of any shareholder, the survivors had an option for one year from the date of death to buy a deceased shareholder's shares at a price set by the majority shareholders each year. If no price was established for a given year, the most recently set price prevailed.

Dorothy Renberg died April 22, 1978. During April of 1979, the surviving shareholders notified Dorothy's husband that they wished to purchase her shares pursuant to the buy-sell agreement. The husband refused to sell and initiated this suit to prevent the transfer of stock. The trial court enforced the agreement and the plaintiff appealed.

HODGES, J. . . . Absolute restrictions forbidding the alienation of corporate stock are invalid, but reasonable restrictions are not. The usual purpose of shareholders' agreements which restrict the sale of corporate stock is to prevent transfers to outsiders without first providing an opportunity for

the shareholders to acquire the stock. The agreement evolved as a device to assure the succession in interest of persons most likely to act in harmony with the other stockholders. Stock in a corporation creates a personal relationship analogous to a partnership, and shareholders in a close corporation should have the same right to choose one's associates in a corporation as in a firm. Restrictive agreements designed to prevent sale of stock to outsiders must be strictly construed and cannot be applied to transactions which are not expressly mentioned in the agreement; nor can they be enlarged by implication.

A basic reason for buy-sell agreements is to provide methodology to determine the value of the stock. The difficulty of determining the price to be paid arises because shares of a close corporation are not traded on the open market and, therefore, the value cannot be readily ascertained. To induce shareholders to purchase decedents' shares and to provide a market for the stock, the price must be attractive. A great deal of leeway is permitted because the shares represent more than a mere interest in property.

The Sooner shareholders considered several

factors other than income tax implications in the periodic revaluation of the option price. These included: the ability of the surviving shareholders to pay the purchase price; maintenance of the option price at a level which would be attractive enough to the survivors to exercise their options; and provision of a market for the shares.

Buy-sell agreements are construed to comply with the manifest intent of the parties. After parties in a close corporation agree on a price formula, the validity of the restriction on transfer does not rest on any abstract notion of intrinsic fairness of price. Before the restriction can be declared invalid, it must be shown that there is more than a mere disparity between option price and current market value. In the absence of fraud, overreaching, or bad faith, an agreement between the stockholders that upon the death of any of them, the stock may be acquired by the corporation is binding. Even a great disparity between the price specified in a buy-sell agreement and the actual value of the stock is not sufficient to invalidate the agreement. Although this agreement inured to the benefit of the Zarrows, it might very well have resulted in benefit to Dorothy had she survived. Under the actuarial tables in effect at the time of the 1963 Agreement, Dorothy stood to gain most by the agreement; she was consistently advised of the value of the stock; she and her attorney had access to Sooner's financial records; and could have called a shareholders' meeting to reassess the stock had she so desired. . . . The language of a written contract governs the rights and obligations of the contracting parties. The courts may not rewrite a shareholders' agreement under the guise of relieving one of the parties from the apparent hardship of an improvident bargain; nor may the courts rewrite an agreement which is clear and unambiguous on its face. We agree with the trial court's finding that the stipulated price provision wherein no one knows for certain at the time the price is set whether he is to be a buyer or a seller is inherently fair and provides mutuality of risk. . . .

A court of equity will not enforce stock trans-fer restrictions adopted under circumstances which indicate bad faith and inequitable treatment of stock purchasers. Because close corporations are usually family affairs, a special relationship may exist between the majority shareholder of a close corporation and a minority shareholder. If a fiduciary relationship exists, and circumstances result in the enhancement of the value of the stock which are known to the officers, directors or the majority shareholders because of their position in the corporation, but which are unknown to the minority, the officers, directors, or the majority shareholders are required to make a full disclosure to the minority. Failure to do so may amount to fraud or deceit sufficient to vitiate a sale, and entitle the minority to relief for unjust enrichment.

The relationship of brother and sister does not of itself create a fiduciary relationship between the parties. However, a majority shareholder has a fiduciary duty not to misuse his power by promoting his personal interests at the expense of the corporation, and the majority shareholder has the duty to protect the interests of the minority. Unless minority shareholders have been systematically excluded from directors and shareholders' meetings, minority stockholders in a close corporation usually have access, apart from the corporate records, to inside information which may affect the value of the stock. It has been held that absent circumstances from which fraud or unfair dealing may be inferred, an officer or director of a close corporation has no duty to volunteer information to a stockholder from whom he purchases stock.

There is no evidence that there was fraud or overreaching in connection with the buy-sell agreement. It operated equally concerning all shareholders. The fact that surviving shareholders were allowed to purchase Dorothy's shares on stated terms and conditions which resulted in purchase for less than actual value of the stock does not subject the agreement to attack as a breach of the relation of trust and confidence. . . .

Affirmed.

REVIEW QUESTIONS

1. Identify the terms in column A by matching each with the appropriate statement in column B.

A	B
1. Incorporator	**a.** A theory used to pierce the corporate veil.
2. Bylaw	**b.** Stock repurchased by the issuing corporation.
3. Foreign corporation	**c.** Right to subscribe for stock.
4. Promoter	**d.** One who signs an application for a corporate charter.
5. Ultra vires	**e.** One who assists in organizing a corporation.
6. Alter ego	**f.** A corporation operating in a state other than the state which issued its charter.
7. Treasury stock	**g.** Stock not fully paid for.
8. Stock warrant	**h.** A rule for governing a corporation.
9. Watered stock	**i.** A contract defense unavailable to the parties to a contract today.
10. Stock dividend	**j.** A transfer of earned surplus to capital stock and the issue of stock to current shareholders in the proportion to their current holdings.

2. The plaintiffs entered into a series of contracts involving coal excavations with Doral Coal Company and Dean Coal Company. Robert W. William, defendant, was president of both coal companies. When royalty payments owed were not made by the corporations as agreed, plaintiffs canceled the agreements and filed suit against the defendant individually. They contended that the defendant was personally liable because he was the sole shareholder of each corporation. Is the defendant liable? Why or why not?

3. Alorna Coat Corporation is in the business of selling women's clothing. The officers bought merchandise on credit when the corporation was in serious financial condition, a fact which they fraudulently concealed. The seller sought to hold the officers personally liable. With what result? Why?

4. Lyon, a legal secretary, fell and sustained injuries while employed by a professional law corporation. The defendant, Barrett, was the sole owner of the corporate stock. The injury occurred in a building owned by Barrett individually and rented by him to the corporation and other tenants. Lyon received workers' compensation benefits that prevented a tort suit for the injuries against the corporation. Thereafter, she instituted suit against Barrett individually as landlord of the building, claiming he negligently maintained the building. Barrett defended, arguing that he also was immune from suit. With what result? Why?

5. A contract on behalf of a corporation was entered into 2 weeks prior to its incorporation. The corporation benefited from the contract. Is it bound by its terms? Explain.

6. Vodopich entered into a contract with the promoters for a corporation to be formed. The contract called for commissions to be paid Vodopich on sales of real estate. He later sued the promoters of the corporation to collect the commissions. Is the promoter liable? Why?

7. Plaintiff does virtually all its business in Mississippi and less than 1 percent of its business in Arkansas. It is not registered to do business in the State of Arkansas as required by law. Its agents went to Arkansas and entered into a contract in Arkansas to do some work on a residence near Lake Village.

It was not paid for its work and filed an action to impose a lien against the Arkansas residence. May the lien be judicially enforced? Why?

8. Dearmin was president and the sole shareholder of Dearmin Brothers Excavating, Inc. The corporation experienced severe cash flow problems in 1975. To help alleviate this problem, Dearmin lent $30,000 to the corporation and personally guaranteed several loans that were made to the corporation. Hill sold oil products to the corporation. When his bill for $6,268.46 was not paid, he instituted this suit against Dearmin personally, using the alter ego doctrine. With what result? Why?

9. The XYZ Corporation was to be formed by Peter, a promoter. In order to operate the corporation after incorporation, it was necessary for Peter to lease certain facilities. Peter executed a lease in the corporate name for office space without revealing to the lessor that the corporation had not yet been organized. The corporation subsequently came into existence, and the board declined to accept the lease of office space that Peter had executed in the corporate name.
   a. Can the corporation validly decline the lease of office space? Explain.
   b. Does Peter have any liability on any of the leases he made? Explain.

10. The Endo Corporation was duly incorporated in state Y in 1980. During all years prior to the current year, its operations and activities were all of an intrastate nature, taking place in state Y. In 1984, however, a sales office was established in state Z, and two resident salesmen authorized to contact prospective customers in that state, to solicit orders, and to make sales. The corporation has taken no action in respect to state Z. What is the danger that this set of facts raises in respect to the Endo Corporation? Discuss.

11. Through its president, a religious corporation leased liquor-dispensing equipment from the Drink-n-Crown Beverage Company. When the lessor defaulted, Drink-n-Crown filed suit for the unpaid rent. The religious corporation's board of directors asserted *ultra vires* as a defense. Is the defense justified? Explain.

12. A corporation decided to repurchase stock of a shareholder that recently died. The corporation was in existence for 3 years and had lost $50,000 during this period. The original shareholders had invested $25,000 in the business, of which the deceased had invested $5,000. How much may the corporation pay for the stock of the deceased? Explain.

13. LST Company was the parent company and BAG Company was a subsidiary. LST Company extended credit to BAG Company. The latter became insolvent, and the other creditors objected to LST's sharing equally in the assets. Is LST entitled to its pro rata share of BAG's assets? Why?

14. Albert sold Betty some stock representing ownership of the Cobra Corporation. Albert delivered the stock certificate to Betty, but he failed to indorse it. Albert died, and the executor of his estate claims that the stock certificate should be returned, since it was not indorsed. Betty contends she is entitled to have the certificate indorsed by Albert's representative. Who is correct? Explain.

43 Operating the Corporation

The preceding chapter was concerned with the legal aspects of forming a corporation. Many of the legal principles that were discussed there also apply to the operation of a corporate entity. Many bylaw provisions, for example, are directly concerned with operations. Because some of the subjects dealt with in this chapter, such as the rights of shareholders, have a bearing on formation problems, the preceding chapter and this one should be considered complementary.

Three distinct groups participate in the management of a corporation. *Shareholders* or *stockholders* (the words are synonymous) comprise the basic governing body. Shareholders exercise their control by electing the *board of directors,* sometimes by approving the bylaws, and by voting on matters such as merger, consolidation, or dissolution. The board of directors is the policy-making group, with responsibility for electing *officers,* who carry out the policies. The duties and powers of the shareholders, the board of directors, and the various officers are regulated by statute, by the bylaws of the corporation, and by corporate resolutions passed by the board of directors.

1. Rights

SHARE-
HOLDERS

A shareholder has the following rights, usually created by statute and reiterated in the bylaws: (1) the right to inspect the books and papers of the corporation,[1] (2) the right to attend shareholders' meetings and to vote for

---

[1] Bank of Heflin v. Miles, p. 983.

directors and on certain other matters such as dissolution or merger, (3) the right to share in the profits when a dividend is declared, (4) the preemptive right, and (5) the right to bring a shareholder's derivative suit. In some states, a shareholder has the additional right of cumulative voting.

The right to inspect the books and papers is limited to good-faith inspections for proper and honest purposes at the proper time and the proper place. A *proper purpose* is one that seeks to protect the interest of the corporation as well as the interest of the shareholder seeking the information. A shareholder is legitimately entitled to know anything and everything which the records, books, and papers of the company would show to protect his interests. A shareholder must have an honest motive and not proceed for vexatious or speculative reasons. He must seek something more than satisfaction of his curiosity and must not be conducting a general fishing expedition. A shareholder's desire to learn the reasons for lack of dividends or low dividends, and suspicion of mismanagement arising from such dividend policy, will constitute a proper purpose. The burden of proving good faith and proper purpose for a shareholder's examination of corporate records rests with him, but proof of actual mismanagement or wrongdoing is not necessary, and good-faith fears of mismanagement are sufficient.

The business hours of the corporation are the reasonable and proper hours in which stockholders are entitled to inspect the books. They also have the right to the assistance of accountants and attorneys in that inspection. The assistance of qualified professionals is often required to understand the books and records and to know what to ask for.

In some states, a shareholder who is refused access to the books and records is entitled to damages as provided by statute. A typical statute provides that a shareholder who is denied the right to inspect books and records is entitled to damages equal to 10 percent of the value of the stock owned. This right to inspect includes contracts and correspondence as well as books and records. The right extends even to confidential records.

2. Meetings

Action by the shareholders normally binds the corporation only when taken in a regular or properly called special meeting after notice required by the bylaws or statute has been given. It is generally conceded, however—and most states so provide by statute—that action approved informally by *all* shareholders will bind the corporation. If there is less than unanimous approval, informal action is not possible.

Notice. Notice of a special meeting must include a statement concerning matters to be acted upon at the meeting; any action taken on other matters will be ineffective. If unusual action, such as a sale of corporate assets, is to be taken at the regular annual meeting, notice of the meeting must call specific attention to that fact; but otherwise, any business may be transacted at the annual meeting.

Failure to give proper notice of a meeting generally invalidates the action taken at the meeting. A stockholder who has not received notice but attends and participates in a meeting is said to waive the notice by his presence.

Quorum.   A quorum of shareholders must be present in person or by proxy (a *proxy* is the authority to vote another's stock) in order to transact business. If shareholders leave the meeting, they can no longer be counted as present. A *quorum* is usually a majority of the voting shares outstanding, unless some statute or the bylaws provide for a larger or smaller percentage. Affirmative action is approved by majority vote of the shares represented at a meeting, provided a quorum exists. Under common law, certain unusual matters such as a merger or sale of all corporate assets required a unanimous vote. Today, statutes usually provide that such actions can be taken by vote of two-thirds or three-fourths of the shareholders. Many of these statutes also provide that the dissenting shareholders have the right to surrender their shares and receive their fair value if they disapprove of the action taken.

Purposes.   In large, publicly held corporations, the annual meeting of shareholders serves a variety of purposes. Management has usually solicited enough proxies in advance to control any vote that is taken, so the outcome is usually a certainty. Nevertheless, many shareholders attend meetings in order to question management on a variety of issues and to lobby for certain policies. Management uses the annual meeting of shareholders of large corporations as a public relations opportunity, to educate the shareholders on company accomplishments as well as its problems.

3. Voting

Statutes of the states and the charters issued under their authority prescribe the matters on which shareholders are entitled to vote. Usually, they vote on the election of directors; on major policy issues such as mergers and consolidations and on dissolution; and, in some instances, on a change in the bylaws.

Some state laws allow a corporation to deny some shareholders the vote on certain issues, such as the election of directors. This denial allows a minority of shareholders to obtain control. But since public policy supports the right of an investor to vote, the status of stock as nonvoting must be communicated to the investor, or the stock purchase may be rescinded.

As a general rule, every shareholder is entitled to as many votes as he owns shares of stock. The shareholder whose name appears in the corporate records is usually designated by the bylaws as the person entitled to vote. Owners of preferred stock, depending on their contract with the corporation, may or may not be entitled to vote.

The statutes of some states provide for cumulative voting in the election of directors. In *cumulative voting,* a shareholder may cast as many votes for one board candidate as there are board members to be filled, multiplied by the number of his shares of stock, or he may distribute this same number of votes among the candidates as he sees fit. A shareholder owning 100 shares of stock has 300 votes if three directors are to be elected. He may cast all 300 for one candidate, or they may be spread among the candidates.

A shareholder is entitled to vote only by virtue of his ownership of the stock, but he may specifically authorize another to vote his stock. Authorization is made by power of attorney and must specifically state that the agent of the shareholder has power to vote his principal's stock. This *voting by proxy* is a personal relationship that the shareholder may revoke before the authority is exercised. Laws pertaining to principal and agent control this relationship.

A shareholder, unlike a director, is permitted to vote on a matter in which he has a personal interest. Although in certain respects he represents the corporate welfare in his voting, in most respects he votes to serve his interest. But a majority of shareholders is not permitted to take action that is clearly detrimental to the corporate and minority interest.

4. Preemptive Right

The original application for a charter specifies the amount of stock the corporation will be authorized to issue and the amount that will be issued without further notice to the state. The amount of authorized stock and the amount of issued stock are used to compute the license fees and franchise taxes due to the state of incorporation. These amounts cannot be increased or exceeded without the authority of the state.

Shareholders may authorize an increase in the authorized capital stock, but such action may not be taken by the directors. An increase in the authorized capital stock is an amendment to the corporate charter, which requires state approval.

The board of directors may authorize the sale of unissued capital stock when the amount previously issued is less than that authorized. This authorization does not require an amendment to the charter. All that is required is that the state be informed of the additional issue of the stock, so that the correct taxes may be collected.

When an increase in the capital stock has been properly authorized, the existing shareholders have a prior right over third parties to subscribe to the increased capital stock. This right is called the shareholder's *preemptive right.* It is based upon the shareholder's right to protect and maintain his proportionate control and interest in the corporation. The preemptive right may be limited or waived by contract and by provisions in the charter or bylaws of the corporation in most states. In many states it is not applicable to treasury stock. Many publicly held corporations, such as IBM, have eliminated it.

The preemptive right is applicable to new authorizations of stock. It is generally not applicable to new issues of stock previously authorized. If the new issue of an original authorization takes place a long time after the original issue, many states provide that the preemptive right exists. Most states approve the issuance of stock to employees under stock option plans without regard to the preemptive right.

5. Derivative Suits

A shareholder cannot maintain an *action at law* for injuries to the corporation, because the corporation is a legal entity and by law has a right to bring a suit in its own name. Any cause of action based on conduct injurious to the corporation accrues in the first instance to the corporation. Nor can a shareholder bring a suit against the directors or other officers of the corporation for negligence, waste, and mismanagement in the conduct of the corporate business. The right to sue for injuries to the corporation rests strictly with the corporation itself, unless modified by statute.

A shareholder may, however, bring a *suit in equity* known as a shareholder's *derivative suit* to enjoin the officers of a corporation from entering into *ultra vires* contracts or from doing anything that would impair the corporate assets. Likewise, the shareholder has a right to bring suit for dollar damages on behalf of the corporation if the officers are acting outside the scope of their authority, are guilty of negligent conduct, or are engaging in fraudulent transactions that are injurious to the corporation itself. The shareholder bringing the derivative suit must have been a shareholder at the time of the action complained of and at the time the suit is filed.[2] Individuals are not allowed to acquire stock for the purpose of filing a derivative action.

Before a shareholder may bring a derivative suit, he must show that he has done everything possible to secure action by the managing officers and directors and that they have refused to act. Shareholders upset at a corporate failure to bring a lawsuit may not initiate a derivative suit without first demanding of the directors to bring the action. If the directors refuse and the derivative action challenges that refusal, courts normally accept the business judgment of the directors. The directors' decision will hold unless bad faith is proved. The corporate decision not to file a lawsuit against directors or others will not be challenged by a court if it is made on the basis of a recommendation by outside directors or disinterested investigators. This deference to objective board decisions is known as the *business judgment rule.*

When, however, there is a conflict of interest in the directors' decision not to sue because the directors themselves have profited from the transaction underlying the litigation, no demand need be made and shareholders can proceed directly with the derivative suit. In such cases, the business judgment rule does not come into play. Any judgment received in such an action is paid to the corporation. The shareholder who initiates the action is permitted to recover the expenses involved in the suit.

Mere dissatisfaction with the management of the corporation will not justify a derivative suit. In the law of corporations, it is fundamental that the majority shareholders control the policies and decisions of the corporation. Every shareholder impliedly agrees that he will be bound by the acts and decisions of a majority of the shareholders or by the agents of the corporation they choose. Courts will not undertake to control the business of a corporation, although it may be seen that better decisions might be made and the business might be more successful if other methods were pursued.

The majority of shares of stock are permitted to control the business of a corporation. They may not act in violation of its charter or some public law or corruptly, oppressively, and fraudulently subversive of the rights and interests of the corporation or of a shareholder. If a majority of disinterested directors acting

---

[2] Vista Fund v. Garis, p. 984.

in good faith and with reasonable business judgment adopt a course of action, it will not be overturned by a derivative suit.

6. Dividends

Although a shareholder has a right to share in dividends when declared, whether or not a dividend is declared is within the discretion of the board of directors. Shareholders are not entitled to the payment of a dividend simply because earned surplus exists. The board of directors may see fit to continue the profits in the business for the purpose of expansion, but it must act reasonably and in good faith. Where fraud or a gross abuse of discretion is shown, and there are profits out of which dividends may be declared, the shareholders may compel the board of directors to declare dividends. Before there is a right to interfere by asking a court to order the payment of dividends, however, it must be clear that the board of directors has illegally, wantonly, and without justification refused to declare a dividend.

When a cash dividend is declared, it becomes a debt of the corporation. It will be paid to the person whose name appears on the corporate stock records as the owner of the share on the record date the dividend is payable. This is known as the *ex-dividend date*. The fact that it is paid to this person does not necessarily mean that the payee is entitled to keep it. If the stock has been sold prior to the dividend date but not transferred on the books of the corporation, the buyer is entitled to the dividend. If there is only a contract to sell the stock, the seller is entitled to any dividend paid prior to the delivery of the stock.[3]

A *cash dividend,* once its declaration has been made public, may not be rescinded. A declaration of dividends is proper so long as it does not impair the capital stock. Any declaration that reduces the net assets of the corporation below the outstanding capital stock is illegal.

Dividends are permissible only after provision has been made for all expenses, including depreciation. In industries with wasting or depleting assets, such as mines and oil wells, it is not necessary to allow for the depletion before declaring dividends.

Directors are personally liable to creditors for dividends improperly declared. In most states, shareholders who receive such dividends may be compelled to return them.

A *stock dividend* is a transfer of retained earnings to capital and is used when the earnings are required for growth of the business. Stock dividends of the issuing company are not taxable income to shareholders. A *stock split* differs from a *stock dividend* in that in the former there is no transfer of surplus to capital, but only a reduction in par value and an increase in the number of shares.

7. Fiduciary Aspects

The law as it relates to close corporations is somewhat different from the law as it relates to publicly held corporations. Publicly held corporations have many shareholders, none of whom owns a majority of the stock. As a general rule, there

---

[3] Deering Milliken v. Clark Estates, Inc., p. 985.

is no fiduciary relationship between shareholders in publicly held corporations. One owner of stock listed on the New York Stock Exchange owes no duty to other owners of the same stock unless, of course, the shareholder is also an insider subject to regulation by the Securities and Exchange Commission.

A *close corporation* is one in which management and ownership are substantially identical, to the extent that it is unrealistic to believe that the judgment of the directors will be independent of that of the shareholders. The shareholders in a close corporation owe one another substantially the same fiduciary duty that partners owe one another. They must discharge their management and shareholder responsibilities in conformity with the strict good-faith standard, and they may not act out of avarice, expediency, or self-interest in derogation of their loyalty to other shareholders and to the corporation. A shareholder in a close corporation may not permit his private interests to clash with those of the corporation and other shareholders.

Some courts have called close corporations "incorporated partnerships." They are corporations for liability, perpetual existence, and taxation, but the shareholders expect to act and to be treated as partners in their dealings among themselves. The practical realities dictate that the relationship be considered a fiduciary one, demanding fairness, honesty, and full disclosure of all functions. Close corporations are held to a higher moral standard than that of the marketplace.

Suits alleging a breach of fiduciary duty often involve the purchase of stock by a majority shareholder or director from a minority shareholder. Such purchases usually involve the use of inside information. A seller under these circumstances should be aware that the buyer has superior knowledge. In deciding such cases, there are three different views among the various states. The majority view is that a director does not stand in a fiduciary relationship to a shareholder in the acquisition of stock and therefore has no duty to disclose inside information. The minority view is that a director has a duty to disclose all material information. The third view is that although a director ordinarily owes no fiduciary duty to shareholders when acquiring stock, under special circumstances a fiduciary relationship arises. The special facts creating the fiduciary relationship may include the familial relationship of the parties, the forthcoming sale of corporate assets,[4] the director's initiation of the sale, and the relative ages and experience in financial affairs of the directors and the selling shareholder.

---

8. Powers   DIRECTORS

Directors of a corporation are elected by the shareholders. They ordinarily attend meetings, exercise judgment on propositions brought before the board, vote, and direct management, although they need not be involved actively in the day-to-day operation of the business. A director has no power to issue orders to any officer or employee, nor can he institute policies by himself or command or veto any other action by the board.

It is not essential that directors hold stock in the corporation. Because they

---
[4] Sampson v. Hunt, p. 986.

are to supervise business activities, select key employees, and plan for the future development of the enterprise, they are presumably selected for their business ability.

At one time, most directors of major publicly held corporations were insiders—officials of the corporation. Today, insider-dominated corporate boards seem to be on the way out. Outside directors now constitute the majority on almost nine out of ten boards of directors. These outside directors provide greater independence, more minority representation, and greater diversification in the backgrounds of the directors. Moreover, many people feel that such boards accept more corporate social responsibility and greater accountability for their actions. They also demand higher standards of performance by corporate officers.

Directors have power to take action necessary or proper to conduct the ordinary business activities of the company. They may not amend the charter, approve a merger, or bring about a consolidation with another corporation without the approval of the shareholders.

9. Meetings

The bylaws usually provide for the number of directors. Historically, not less than three directors were required; but in recent years, many corporate statutes have authorized two directors—and in some cases, one director. This development is especially prevalent in professional associations or corporations, which frequently have only one shareholder and thus only one director.

Since the board of directors must act as a unit, it is traditional that it assemble at board meetings. The bylaws provide for the method of calling directors' meetings and for the time and the place of the meeting. A record is usually kept of the activities of the board of directors, and the evidence of the exercise of its powers is stated in resolutions kept in the corporate minute book. A majority of the members of the board of directors is necessary to constitute a quorum unless a bylaw provides to the contrary. Special meetings are proper only when all directors are notified or are present at the meetings. Directors may not vote by proxy, having been selected as agents because of their personal qualifications.

Modern statutes make it possible for a board to take informal action (usually by telephone), provided the action is subsequently expressed in writing and signed by all the directors. This gives a board the flexibility and capability to make decisions without delay. Failure to have unanimous approval of such informal actions or to give proper notice is fatal to informal actions attempted by the board of directors.

Traditionally, a director was forbidden to vote on any matter in which he had a personal interest. Even though his vote was not necessary to carry the proposition considered, many courts would regard any action to be voidable if it was taken as a result of that vote. Some courts went so far as to hold that if he was present at the meeting, favorable action was not binding. Most courts held that if his presence was required to make a quorum, no transaction in which he was interested could be acted upon. These rather severe rules were developed so that directors would not be tempted to use their position to profit at the expense of the corporation.

Today, many states have relaxed some of the traditional rules on directors' voting and participation. The trend of the law is to allow interested directors to be present and to be counted as a part of the quorum. Actions taken with interested directors are valid if the participating director's interest is fully and completely disclosed, provided the action is approved by a majority of disinterested directors. Even in states that have changed the earlier common-law view, a director with a personal interest in a subject is not allowed to vote on the matter. The problem of acting in good faith is discussed later in this chapter.

10. Compensation

The charter, bylaws, or a resolution by the shareholders usually stipulates payment of directors' fees. If not, service as a director is uncompensated. Directors who are appointed as officers of the corporation should have their salaries fixed at a meeting of the shareholders or in the bylaws. Because directors are not supposed to vote on any matter in which they have a personal interest, director officers of small corporations usually vote on salaries for each other but not their own. The action to set salaries should be ratified by the shareholders in order to ensure the validity of the employment contracts.

11. In General

The officers and directors of a corporation may have personal liability both in tort and in contract. The principles of the law of agency are applicable; liability is usually to the corporation, although it may extend to shareholders and third parties as well.

The liability of corporate officers and directors for tortious conduct is predicated on basic common-law principles. A director who participates in a tort has personal liability to the third party on the usual common-law tort theories, as does any other agent or servant. This liability is based on the participation theory.[5]

Several statutes impose liability on directors and officers. Officers and directors who have responsibility for federal withholding and social security taxes may be liable to the federal government for failure to collect and transfer these taxes for their employees. Likewise, a director or officer is subject to third-party liability for aiding a corporation in such acts as patent, copyright, or trademark infringements, unfair competition, antitrust violations, violation of the laws relating to discrimination, or violations of the securities laws. They are also personally liable when they issue stock as fully paid when it is not paid in full or when dividends are declared or treasury stock is purchased without the requisite retained earnings.[6]

The relationship between the officers and directors and a corporation is a fiduciary one. Liability is often imposed for violation of the fiduciary duties owed

LIABILITY OF OFFICERS AND DIRECTORS

---

[5] Wicks v. Milzoco Builders, Inc., p. 987.

[6] Sec. Nat. Bank v. Peters, Writer, & Christensen, p. 988.

to the corporation. This fiduciary relationship requires that directors act in good faith and with due care. It prohibits conflicts of interest and imposes a duty of undivided loyalty on officers and directors.

12. Loyalty and Good Faith

A director occupies a position of trust and confidence with respect to the corporation and cannot, by reason of his position, directly or indirectly derive any personal benefits that are not enjoyed by the corporation or the shareholders. This duty of loyalty or the duty to act in good faith prohibits directors from acting with a conflict of interest. The most common violation of this duty occurs when a director enters into a contract with, or personally deals with, the corporation. A conflict of interest also arises in transactions between the director's corporation and another entity in which he may be a director, employee, investor, or one who is otherwise interested. In all circumstances, the director or officer must fully disclose his conflict of interest to the corporation. If he fails to do so, the contract may be rescinded.

Under common law, a contract between a corporation and one of its directors was voidable unless it was shown to be approved by a disinterested board *and* "fair" to the corporation, in that its terms were as favorable as those available from any other person. Under some modern statutes, the transaction is valid if it is approved, with knowledge of the material facts, by a vote of disinterested directors or shareholders *or* if the director can show it to be "fair."

Issues of good faith frequently arise when a corporation is in financial difficulty. For example, the good faith of a director or officer is an issue when such a person is attempting to collect a personal loan to the corporation. Directors and officers may make loans to their corporations, and they may use the same methods as other creditors to collect bona fide corporation debts owed to them, but only as long as the corporation is solvent. When a corporation is insolvent or on the verge of insolvency, its directors and officers become fiduciaries of corporate assets for the benefit of creditors. As fiduciaries, directors and officers cannot by reason of their special position give themselves preference over other creditors in collecting bona fide business debts.

Many cases involve the *corporate opportunity doctrine.* This doctrine precludes corporate fiduciaries from diverting to themselves business opportunities in which the corporation has an expectancy, property interest, or right, or which in fairness should otherwise belong to the corporation. The doctrine follows from a corporate fiduciary's duty of undivided loyalty to the corporation. The good-faith requirement is lacking when a director or officer takes for himself an opportunity that the corporation should have had.

A director must present all possible corporate opportunities to the corporation first. Only after disinterested, informed directors have determined that the corporation should not pursue such opportunities can a director pursue them for his own benefit. If a corporate director acquires property for himself, knowing the corporation desires it, he breaches his fiduciary relation to the corporation, and it may obtain the property.

Persons charged with violating the corporate opportunity doctrine sometimes seek to avoid liability by claiming that the corporation was not in a financial position to take advantage of the opportunity. In most states, if the corporation is solvent, financial inability to undertake an opportunity does not absolve a corporate fiduciary from liability for diverting what is otherwise a corporate opportunity. Financial insolvency will, however, excuse corporate fiduciaries from liability in most states. The fiduciary has the burden of proving insolvency; mere financial difficulty is not enough.

To allow a corporate fiduciary to take advantage of a business opportunity when the fiduciary determines the corporation to be unable to avail itself of it would create the worst sort of temptation for the fiduciary to rationalize an inaccurate and self-serving assessment of the corporation's financial ability and thereby compromise the duty of loyalty to the corporation. If a corporate fiduciary's duty of loyalty conflicts with his personal interest, the latter must give way.

The appropriate method to determine whether or not a corporate opportunity exists is to let the corporation decide at the time the opportunity is presented. If a fiduciary is uncertain whether a given opportunity is corporate or not, or whether the corporation has the financial ability to pursue it, he needs merely to disclose the existence of the opportunity to the directors and let them decide. Disclosure is a fundamental fiduciary duty. It cannot be burdensome, and it resolves the issue for all parties concerned and eliminates the necessity for a judicial determination after the fact.

A corporate officer or director does not become free to appropriate a business opportunity of the corporation by resigning his office. The duty continues after the resignation.

13. Due Care

In addition to good faith, directors must exercise due care. In its simplest terms, the duty to exercise *due care* is synonymous with a duty not to be negligent. As a general rule, directors owe that degree of care that a businessman of ordinary prudence would exercise in the management of his own affairs. The nature and extent of reasonable care depends upon the type of corporation, its size, and its financial resources. A bank director is held to stricter accountability than the director of an ordinary business. In large corporations many duties must be delegated, so intimate knowledge of details by the directors is not possible. In corporations invested with a public interest—such as insurance companies, banks, building and loan associations, and public utilities—rigid supervision and specific obligations are imposed upon directors. If a director fails to exercise the requisite degree of care and skill, the corporation will have a right of action against him for any resulting losses.

As a general rule, a director should acquire at least a rudimentary understanding of the business of the corporation and should be familiar with the fundamentals of that business. Since directors are bound to exercise ordinary care, they cannot set up as a defense to a suit against them lack of knowledge needed to exercise the requisite degree of care. If one has not had sufficient business experience to perform the duties of a director, he should either acquire the knowledge by inquiry, or refuse to serve.

Directors must keep informed about the activities of the corporation. Otherwise, they may not be able to participate in the overall management of corporate affairs. Directors may not shut their eyes to corporate misconduct and then claim that because they did not see the misconduct, they did not have a duty to look. They have a duty to protect the corporation. This does not require a detailed inspection of day-to-day activities, but a general monitoring of corporate affairs and policies. Accordingly, a director should attend board meetings regularly. Indeed, a director who is absent from a board meeting is presumed to concur in action taken on a corporate matter, unless a dissent is filed with the secretary of the corporation within a reasonable time after learning of such action.

Although directors are not required to audit corporate books, they should be familiar with the financial affairs of the corporation through a regular review of its financial statements. In some circumstances, directors may be charged with ensuring that bookkeeping methods conform to industry custom and usage. The extent of review, as well as the nature and frequency of financial statements, depends not only on the customs of the industry, but also on the nature of the corporation and the business in which it is engaged. Financial statements of some small corporations may be prepared internally and only on an annual basis; in a large, publicly held corporation, the statements may be produced monthly or at some other regular interval. Adequate financial review normally would be more informal in a private corporation than in a publicly held corporation.

Generally directors are immune from liability if, in good faith, they rely upon the opinion of counsel for the corporation or upon written reports prepared by a certified public accountant or upon financial statements, books of account, or reports of the corporation represented to them to be correct by the president, the officer of the corporation having charge of its books of account, or the person presiding at a meeting of the board. The review of financial statements, however, may give rise to a duty to inquire further into matters revealed by those statements. Upon discovery of an illegal course of action, a director has a duty to object and, if the corporation does not correct the conduct, to resign.

In certain circumstances, the fulfillment of the duty of a director may call for more than mere objection and resignation; sometimes a director may be required to seek the advice of legal counsel. A director may require legal advice concerning the propriety of his or her own conduct, the conduct of other officers and directors, or the conduct of the corporation. A director should consult with corporate counsel or his own legal adviser whenever there is doubt regarding a proposed action. Sometimes the duty of a director may require more than consulting with outside counsel. A director may have a duty to take reasonable means to prevent illegal conduct by co-directors, including the threat of suit.

A director is not an ornament, but an essential component of corporate governance. Consequently, a director cannot protect himself behind a paper shield bearing the motto "dummy director." A director may incur liability by failing to do more than passively rubber-stamp the decisions of the active managers.

Directors must use their best business judgment. They have no liability for honest mistakes. Directors are liable to the corporation for negligence in management. As a general rule, since no duty extends to third-party creditors,[7] there is no liability to them or to the shareholders individually. Of course, a shareholder may enforce this liability through a derivative suit.

14. Indemnification and Insurance

In recent years, dissenting shareholders, public interest groups, and government regulators have caused a dramatic increase in the number of lawsuits filed against directors and officers of publicly held corporations. Many of the lawsuits result from the failure of directors to prevent activities such as bribery of foreign officials and illegal political contributions. Most large corporations carry liability insurance for directors, and costs for this insurance are soaring because of the increased number of suits.

In order to reimburse directors and officers for the expenses of defending lawsuits if the insurance is nonexistent or inadequate, most states provide by statute for indemnification by the corporation. The Model Business Corporation Act provides that the standard for indemnification is that the director must have "acted in good faith and in a manner he reasonably believed to be in or not opposed to the best interests of the corporation" and if a criminal action, "had no reasonable cause to believe his conduct was unlawful." The indemnification is automatic if the director has been successful in the defense of any action.

---

[7] Equitable Life & Cas. Ins. Co. v. Inland Printing Co., p. 989.

SUMMARY

SHAREHOLDERS

Meetings	**1.** Shareholders are entitled to notice of the annual meeting and of special meetings as well. The notice must include the matters to be acted upon at special meetings and all unusual matters that are on the agenda of the annual meeting.
	2. Informal action by all shareholders may be taken without an actual meeting.
	3. A quorum is usually a majority of the voting stock.
Voting	**1.** Shareholders usually vote to elect directors and on issues such as dissolution.

	2. Election of directors by cumulative voting is possible in some states.
	3. Shareholders may vote by proxy.
	4. Shareholders may vote on matters in which they have a personal interest.
Other rights of shareholders	1. Shareholders have rights created by statute. These usually include the right to inspect the books and papers of the corporation, the right to attend meetings and to vote, and the right to dividends.
	2. A shareholder also has a preemptive right, which is the right to buy a proportionate share of new stock issues.
	3. A shareholder has the right to bring a suit on behalf of the corporation when the directors fail to do so. Shareholders usually must demand that the directors take action before filing such a suit.
	4. The minority shareholders of a corporation agree tacitly to be bound by the acts of the majority. The majority controls the business unless acting illegally, oppressively, or fraudulently.
Dividends	1. A shareholder has a right to dividends declared, but has no right to have dividends declared.
	2. It is generally up to the board of directors to declare a dividend.
	3. A stock dividend is a transfer of retained earnings to capital and in effect gives the shareholder nothing of additional value.
Fiduciary aspects	1. In a publicly held corporation, the shareholders do not stand in a fiduciary relationship with each other.
	2. In a closely held corporation, the shareholders do stand in a fiduciary relationship to the enterprise and to each other.
	3. Shareholders in a close corporation must act in good faith. In many states, this includes the duty to disclose relevant information.

DIRECTORS

Powers	1. The directors determine policy in the ordinary course of business and elect the officers.

Meetings	**2.** Directors need not be shareholders.
	1. The bylaws provide the procedures for calling and conducting directors' meetings, and minutes of them are maintained.
	2. The majority of the directors constitute a quorum, and action is usually by a majority.
	3. Directors may not vote by proxy, but informal action that is unanimous is allowed in most states.
	4. Directors may not vote on matters in which they have a personal interest, although their presence may be used to constitute a quorum.
Compensation	**1.** Directors are compensated as provided in the bylaws.
	2. Directors fix the salary of officers, but they cannot vote on their own salary.
Liabilities of directors	**1.** Directors and officers may have personal liability both in tort and in contract. This liability may be to the corporation or to third parties.
	2. Directors are liable to the corporation for breach of their fiduciary duties or of duties imposed by statute.
	3. Directors must act in good faith and with due care. The duty of good faith creates liability if there is a conflict of interest.
	4. Directors may rely on experts such as accountants or attorneys in exercising their responsibilities.
	5. Directors are not liable to third parties for negligence in management.
	6. Corporations usually carry liability insurance to protect directors.

CASES

Bank of Heflin v. Miles
318 So.2d 697 (Ala. 1975)

FAULKNER, J. . . . M. M. Miles wrote two letters, dated 12 and 19 August 1974, to the Bank of Heflin, requesting an unlimited inspection of the books and records of the bank. The second letter alleged one or more proper purposes for an inspection: to ascertain whether any action had been taken contrary to the best interests of the stockholders, such as misuse of corporate funds; abuse of corporate office; diversion of corporate assets to the personal benefit of any officer, director, employee, or stockholder; misapplication of corporate assets, or favoring of certain customers of the bank because of personal connections with officers or directors of the bank; and to determine whether the directors have lived up to their fiduciary obligation to the stockholders.

Uncertain of the propriety of disclosing all of its records, the bank filed a complaint for declaratory judgment, asking the circuit court to determine what records the defendant, Miles, was entitled to. . . .

Mileses assert that they have, since they have made a proper demand alleging a proper purpose, a right of access to any and all records and writings of any kind of nature relating to the Bank of Heflin.

The position of the bank . . . is that it has a duty to its customers not to disclose certain confidential memoranda, individual files, and materials from which the books and records of the account are prepared. This duty exists because of the bank's fiduciary relationship with its customers and because of the strictures imposed on it by the banking laws and regulations. Stockholders can examine certain records if they have a "proper purpose"; certain others can never be viewed by the stockholders. The bank is unsure which records should be disclosed; for this reason it argues that the trial court properly used its powers in appointing a master to ascertain which records the stockholders have a right to examine. . . .

In addition to common law inspection rights, stockholders now have rights under statutes. Alabama's statute is based largely on the Modern Business Corporation Act, §52, which enlarged and extended the common law right. Numerous cases in Alabama have upheld the shareholders' inspection rights based on the common law and statutes. . . . At common law the inspection right covered all the books and records of the corporation, including corporate documents, contracts and papers, but not including secret researches and the results of skilled and technical investigations.

The only express limitation of our statutory right of inspection is that it must be exercised at reasonable and proper times; an implied limitation is that it must not be exercised from idle curiosity, or for improper or unlawful purposes. In all other respects the statutory right is absolute. The purpose of the statute, like that of the common law right, is to protect small and minority shareholders against the mismanagement and faithlessness of their agents and officers, by furnishing the mode and opportunity to ascertain, establish, and maintain their rights.

What inspection can be made by a stockholder of a bank? One that is for a proper purpose and does not interfere with the bank's conduct of its business. The inspection rights of stockholders of a bank are the same as stockholders of a corporation generally. . . .

It is obvious that certain activities of the bank are not reflected in the ledger of official action. The principles of equity, fair dealing, and good faith give the stockholders the right to know how the affairs of the bank are conducted, and whether the capital, a part of which they contributed, is being prudently and profitably employed. The petitioners do not want to ramble through the books and records; they want merely an inspection by their accountants.

The right to inspect was a broad right at common law; Alabama has codified the common law, with slight exceptions. Banks are to be regarded as corporations under the Alabama statute. The applicable statute is not limited to "relevant" books and records; it is to be liberally construed. The shareholders advanced a proper purpose for inspection; their request was not overly broad, as it tracked the language of the statute. Hostility on the shareholders' part toward the officers of the bank will not defeat their request; neither will the fact of mere confidentiality of the books and records sought. The inspection by the petitioners will not unnecessarily interfere with the bank's conduct of business.

Inspection ordered.

Vista Fund v. Garis
277 N.W.2d 19 (Minn. 1979)

Plaintiffs (Vista) brought a stockholder's derivative action alleging fraud, negligence, and breach of fiduciary duties against a corporation, its officers and directors. Plaintiff was a stockholder at the time of the transactions complained of, but later sold its stock. Just prior to filing the suit, plaintiff repurchased 100 shares of stock in the defendant corporation. Plaintiff had made a proper demand on the corporation to take action itself. The lower court found for the defendants, and the plaintiff appeals.

SCOTT, J. . . . Rule 23.06, Rules of Civil Procedure, requires that a plaintiff meet certain stock ownership requirements before he may invoke the equitable remedy of a shareholder's derivative suit. The rule states, in pertinent part, as follows:

> In a derivative action brought by one or more shareholders or members to enforce a right of a corporation or of an unincorporated association, the corporation or association having failed to enforce a right which may properly be asserted by it, the complaint shall allege that the plaintiff was a shareholder or member at the time of the transaction of which he complains or that his share or membership thereafter devolved on him by operation of law.

Vista argues that a plaintiff need not be a shareholder at the time stockholder's derivative suit is commenced because Rule 23.06 requires only that "the complaint shall allege that the plaintiff was a shareholder at the time of the transaction of which he complains." This contention is without merit. The rule states that a derivative action is one "brought by one or more shareholders." The use of the term "shareholders" requires that the plaintiff own stock in the corporation at the time he brings suit. Indeed, the Federal counterpart to Rule 23.06 has been so interpreted. . . .

The trial court interpreted Rule 23.06 as requiring a plaintiff, in order to have standing to maintain a derivative action, to continuously and uninterruptedly own stock in the corporation from the time of the alleged wrongs through the time suit is commenced. Since Vista sold its stock before it commenced suit (although it purchased 100 shares of stock shortly before bringing this action), the district court ruled that it lacked standing to maintain the instant derivative action. Vista argues . . . uninterrupted ownership of the stock from the time of the alleged wrongs until commencement of suit is not required. Again, this contention is without merit.

It is consistent with the policy underlying Rule 23.06 to require continuous stock ownership. The purpose of the stockholding requirements of the rule is to prevent persons from purchasing stock solely for purposes of maintaining shareholders' derivative actions. In other words, the share ownership requirement is intended to prevent the litigating of purchased grievances or speculating in wrongs done to corporations. Once a shareholder has sold his stock he is in the same position as any other non-shareholder. Accordingly, when he reacquires stock and brings suit based on a corporate wrong occurring during his prior ownership he is in effect purchasing a grievance or speculating in corporate wrongs. Indeed, this is what occurred here. Based on the above reasoning, we conclude that continuous ownership must be required to effectuate the policy behind Rule 23.06. . . .

We find that the trial court was correct in concluding that insofar as the complaint asserts any derivative claims on behalf of Vista summary judgment was proper dismissing such claims. We agree to the extent that Rule 23.06, Rules of Civil Procedure, requires that in a derivative action the plaintiffs must be shareholders in the corporation in whose benefit it sues from the time the alleged improper acts occurred, continuously and uninterruptedly, until the time such action is commenced. . . .

Affirmed.

Deering Milliken v. Clark Estates, Inc. 373 N.E.2d 1212 (N.Y. 1979)

JONES. J. When a contract is made for the future transfer of beneficial interest in stock and no provision is made therein by the buyer and seller as to which shall be entitled to receive regular dividends declared before the purchase price is paid and delivery of the stock certificates made, such dividends remain the property of the seller.

On March 31 and April 5, 1967 Deering Milliken, Inc., executed agreements for the purchase from defendants, executors under the will of Susan Vanderpoel Clark and the Clark Estates, Inc., of some 480,000 shares of stock of Albany Felt Company. Under the first agreement, with the executors, a minimal payment was to be made at the time the contract was signed, a partial payment on May 1, 1967 and the substantial balance on August 1, 1967. Under the April agreement, with

Clark Estates, payment was to be made on such date between May 1 and August 1, 1967 as might be specified by the seller. Under each contract delivery of the stock certificates was to take place when the total purchase price was paid. . . . Absent from both contracts was any provision as to which party would be entitled to dividends declared by Albany Felt between the dates of the agreements and the dates of transfer of the shares.

On May 24, 1967 the corporation declared a regular quarterly dividend payable on July 1 to stockholders of record on June 16. Payment of the purchase price and delivery of the stock certificates held by Clark Estates took place on June 19, 1967; final payment and delivery of the stock certificates held by the executors was made on August 1. The sellers' rejection of the buyer's demand under both contracts for delivery to it of the dividends distributed July 1 gave rise to the present litigation.

In the circumstances of this case, we agree with the Appellate Division that the dividend declared on May 24 belonged to the sellers.

As in most contract questions, the intention of the parties, if manifested, would have controlled. In the March and April agreements between the parties, however, there were no express provisions with respect to entitlement to interim dividends, and no extrinsic evidentiary proof of the intention of the parties as to that subject has been tendered. . . .

Critical to the determination whether buyer or sellers were entitled to the May dividend is the question whether present sales—current transfers of substantial beneficial interest—or only agreements to make future sales were manifested by the execution of the contracts of March 31 and April 5, 1967. A purchaser of stock acquires by a contract of present sale a right to the benefits which may accrue upon the stock bought, and that right is, for convenience, called the 'beneficial ownership' of the stock. A different result attends the execution of a contract to make a sale in the future. In the absence of an agreement to the contrary, the buyer under an executory contract to sell stock is not entitled to dividends until the legal title to the stock has passed to him, which is not until delivery is made to him or is due to him and is offered to be made, unless there is something in the contract specifying or implying a contrary intention. Where there is a sale of stock in praesenti, but the date of delivery and payment is postponed, the vendee is entitled to all dividends declared between the date of the agreement and the date of closing to the purchaser.

Looking to the terminology used by these parties in their agreements, in addition to provisions for future dates for payments of the purchase price and deliveries of the stock certificates, we find: "Seller will sell to Buyer;" "Buyer will purchase such shares from Seller"; the seller "agrees to cause to be sold to" the purchaser; the purchaser "agrees to buy such shares"; reference to "shares to be sold"—all terminology looking to future occurrences and inconsistent with a present transfer of beneficial ownership of the stock. . . . We conclude that, while at the time of execution of the March and April agreements Deering Milliken acquired certain enforceable rights with respect to a sale of the Albany Felt stock, there was then no present sale and no transfer of such beneficial interest as to carry with it the right to the regular quarterly dividend declared May 24, 1967. Defendants, as the actual and beneficial owners of the shares when the dividend was declared, were entitled to the distribution. . . .

Affirmed.

Sampson v. Hunt
564 P.2d 489 (Kan. 1977)

There were two shareholders of Bonanza, Inc., and each owned 50 percent of the stock. The defendant, Hunt, was president, and he managed the business. The plaintiff was secretary but inactive. The business operated a shopping center.

The defendant purchased the plaintiff's stock for $75,000. At the time of the sale, the defendant did not inform the plaintiff of (1) additional leases that had been obtained, (2) a commitment for financing of a third phase of the development, and (3) sale of part of the stock to three doctors. When the plaintiff learned these facts, he sued to recover the difference between the selling price and the fair market value of the stock at the time of the sale, alleging a breach of fiduciary duties. The lower court awarded the plaintiff $93,000, and the defendant appealed.

PRAGER, J. . . . Hunt's appeal raises a

question of law involving the duty of a director or managing officer of a corporation to disclose to another stockholder material information as to the status of the corporation's affairs prior to a sale and purchase of corporate stock. It is the established rule in this state that a director of a corporation owes a high fiduciary duty to the other stockholders of the corporation. The Kansas rule is exemplified by *Stewart v. Harris,* 69 Kan. 498 (1904), where we held:

> The managing officers of a corporation are not only trustees of the corporate entity and the corporate property, but they are to some extent, and in many respects, trustees for the corporate shareholders.
>
> When two parties occupy to each other a confidential or fiduciary relation, and a sale is made by one to the other, equity raises a presumption against the validity of the transaction. To sustain it the buyer must show affirmatively that the transaction was conducted in good faith, without pressure or influence on his part, and with express knowledge of the circumstances and entire freedom of action on the part of the seller.
>
> A director or managing officer of a corporation having knowledge of the condition of its affairs, because of the trust relation and the superior opportunities afforded for acquiring information, must inform a stockholder not actively engaged in the management of the true condition of the corporation before he can rightfully purchase his stock.

The defendant Hunt on this appeal concedes that such a fiduciary relationship exists where a director or managing officer of a corporation seeks to purchase the corporate shares of a stockholder not actively engaged in the management of a corporation. He maintains, however, that such a fiduciary relationship does not exist where the stockholder who sold his shares is another director or officer of the corporation as is true in the present case where the plaintiff was both a director and secretary of Bonanza, Inc. Although the majority of the earlier cases held to the contrary, the more recent cases hold that in a closely held corporation where one director or officer has a superior knowledge of corporate affairs because he is intimately involved in the daily operations of the corporation while the other director or officer has only a limited role in corporate management, the fiduciary duty is the same as if the latter were a stockholder not actively engaged in corporate affairs.

We hold that the rule of law to be followed in Kansas is that where knowledge of facts affecting the value or price of stock comes to an officer or director of a corporation by virtue of his office or position, he is under a fiduciary duty to disclose such facts to other stockholders before dealing in company stock with them, even if they too are directors or officers, and regardless of whether these facts pertain to intracompany matters, such as the value of assets, or relate to events "outside" the corporation, such as the existence of favorable contracts, the availability of additional financing, or any other matters which would tend to increase the value of the corporation's stock. Applying this rule to the facts and circumstances of the present case we must conclude that the defendant Hunt, as president and director of Bonanza, Inc., breached his fiduciary duty to the plaintiff Sampson, a director and secretary of the corporation, by Hunt's failure to disclose material information affecting the value of the stock of Bonanza, Inc. before contracting to purchase Sampson's shares.

The judgment of the district court is affirmed.

Wicks v. Milzoco Builders, Inc.
470 A.2d 86 (Pa. 1983)

Plaintiffs are residents of Monroe Acres, a housing development built by two corporations. The defendants include the president, vice-president, and secretary of the corporations.

The plaintiffs allege that due to faulty planning, their home was built in an area that is often flooded by the drainage of the other areas of the development. This suit is for the resulting damage for their homes and yards.

The trial court dismissed the suit holding that the officers could not be held personally liable for the alleged torts of their corporation. Plaintiffs appeal.

HUTCHINSON, J. . . . In the instant case, . . . appellants have not . . . alleged that appellees have used the corporate form merely as a vehicle by which they seek to engage in illegal or improper acts with impunity. Instead, appellants seek to hold Miller, Cook and Zollers liable on the theory that they personally participated in the alleged tortious acts committed on behalf of the corporations. There is a distinction between liability for individual participation in a wrongful act and an individual's responsibility for any liability-creating act performed behind the veil of a sham corporation. Where the court pierces the corporate veil, the owner is liable because the corporation is not a bona fide independent entity; therefore, its acts are truly his. Under the participation theory, the court imposes liability on the individual as an actor rather than as an owner. Such liability is not predicated on a finding that the corporation is a sham and a mere alter ego of the individual corporate officer. Instead, liability attaches where the record establishes the individual's participation in the tortious activity.

Pennsylvania law recognizes the participation theory as a basis of liability.

> The general, if not universal, rule is that an officer of a corporation who takes part in the commission of a tort by the corporation is personally liable therefor; but that an officer of a corporation who takes no part in the commission of the tort committed by the corporation is not personally liable

to third persons for such a tort, nor for the acts of other agents, officers or employees of the corporation in committing it, unless he specifically directed the particular act to be done or participated, or cooperated therein.

Liability under this theory attaches only where the corporate officer is an actor who participates in the wrongful acts. Therefore, corporate officers may be held liable for misfeasance. . . .

. . . Nevertheless, corporate officers and directors may not be held liable for mere nonfeasance.

. . . [T]he pertinent averments in these complaints can be read as setting forth, generally, that the individual appellees actually knew that the location of the proposed Monroe Acres Development created, at least, an unreasonable risk of the drainage problems which occurred and that, having the power to do so, they deliberately ordered the work to proceed. This complaint . . . when read as a whole, does state ultimate facts on which the appellants depend to show Miller, Cook and Zollers' liability, in the most general terms.

Accordingly, we vacate the order of the Superior Court and remand . . . for further proceedings consistent with this opinion.

So ordered.

Sec. Nat. Bank v. Peters, Writer & Christensen
569 P.2d 875 (Colo.App. 1977)

Plaintiffs, preferred shareholders of a corporation (PWC), sued the directors for violating the Corporate Code. At a meeting of directors and common shareholders, the directors had voted to liquidate the corporate assets and to dissolve the company. Plaintiffs were not given notice of the meeting or an opportunity to vote.

The company was in arrears on five of its preferred dividends but paid the sixth dividend anyway, because the stock subscription agreement provided that if six dividends were omitted, the preferred shareholders were entitled to assume control of the company. The dividends were paid while the capital was impaired. In addition, the corporation had purchased preferred stock from three shareholders.

The trial court dismissed plaintiff's case as

being an action based on fraud, which must be filed within one year. Plaintiffs appealed.

BERMAN, J. . . . Plaintiffs' complaint sets forth specific sections of the Colorado Corporation Code which were allegedly violated, and specific sections of the Code granting relief therefrom. Moreover, the evidence at trial was, in part, clearly directed to whether the capital of the company was impaired at the time dividends were paid or the treasury stock purchased, which evidence related solely to whether statutory violations occurred.

And a showing of fraud is not required to impose liability under the statutes allegedly violated. The statutes in question expressly make directors personally liable to the corporation for assenting to or voting for the payment of illegal dividends, for the wrongful purchase of treasury shares, or, in certain cases, for making a loan to an officer or director. . . . Accordingly, the court erred in dismissing plaintiffs' two claims for relief premised on the purchase of treasury shares and on the payment of dividends out of capital and a new trial is required as to those claims.

However, defendants argue that dismissal of plaintiffs' . . . claims was proper because both claims were barred by the applicable statute of limitations. It is asserted that the liability imposed upon directors for the payment of improper dividends and the purchase of treasury shares is in the nature of a penalty, and that the one year limitation contained in C.R.S. 1963, 87-1-4 applies as to those claims. Accordingly, they assert that plaintiffs' claims for relief were not timely. We disagree.

Liability for improper payment of dividends and improper purchase of treasury shares is imposed upon directors pursuant to C.R.S.1963, 31-5-14(1). Based upon the wording of these sections and the amount of liability imposed upon directors thereunder, it is apparent that the statutes are remedial in nature as to the corporation, merely requiring directors to indemnify the corporation for amounts actually lost. As such, there is no burdensome liability as was imposed under prior statutes. Under the present statutes, damages are based directly upon injuries suffered by the corporation, as opposed to a liquidated measure without regard to injury. Accordingly, we hold that these statutes in question are not penal in nature, and that the one-year statute of limitations does not apply thereto.

Directors are fiduciaries to the corporation and its shareholders and thus, we hold that the five-year limitation period . . . governs the instant case. That statute provides that actions falling thereunder "shall be filed within five years after the cause thereof shall accrue, and not thereafter." Accordingly, we must determine when a cause of action accrues under the applicable statutes.

Under C.R.S.1963, 31-2-2(4), "No purchase of or payment for its own shares shall be made at a time when the corporation is insolvent or when the purchase or payment would make it insolvent." Hence, a cause of action accrues at the time an improper purchase of treasury shares is made, and any liability imposed on directors for violating this section would therefore attach at the time of the purchase. Thus, under the explicit terms of C.R.S.1963, 87-1-15 a claim . . . must be commenced within five years of the improper purchase. Similarly, any claim against directors based upon an improper dividend payment would have to be commenced within five years of such payment.

Thus, on the retrial of these claims, if the court determines that improper payments of dividends of improper purchases of treasury shares were made, and that the purchases or payments occurred within five years of the filing of this suit, the defendants must be held liable. . . .

Reversed.

Equitable Life & Cas. Ins. Co. v. Inland Printing Co.
484 P.2d 102 (Utah 1971)

ELLETT, J. The appellant herein held a note signed by the defendant corporation and secured by a chattel mortgage and also a mortgage on realty. The present action is to foreclose the mortgages and to recover the amount of the deficiency, if any there be, from the officers and directors of the corporation because of alleged negligent mismanagement of the corporate business.

The question to be determined on this appeal is what rights, if any, does a creditor of a corporation have against officers and directors for negligent mismanagement of its affairs. The appellant does not claim that there was any fraudulent or deceitful acts committed by any of the respondents. . . .

The law relative to mismanagement by, and negligence on the part of, officers and directors of a corporation is set out in 19 Am.Jur.2d, Corporations §1350, as follows:

> Directors or officers may be liable to the corporation or stockholders for mismanagement of the business of the corporation or waste of its assets; but according to a number of cases, they are not liable to its creditors for mere mismanagement or waste of assets constituting a wrong or breach of duty as to the corporation. The rule generally followed by the authorities is that a creditor of a corporation may not maintain a personal action at law against the officers or directors of a corporation who have, by their mismanagement or negli-

gence, committed a wrong against the corporation to the consequent damage of the creditor. The reason given for the rule is the entire lack of privity between the parties. There is certainly no contractual relation between them, nor any other legal relation which would raise a duty, on the part of directors or officers, to the creditor to exercise care in the management of the affairs of the corporation. The duty to exercise diligence and care is one owed to the corporation, and it is elementary law that one person cannot maintain an action against another for a wrong to a third person which injures him only incidentally. How-

ever, there are other cases which seem to hold an opinion contrary to the general proposition as expressed above. These actions seem to be maintained upon the theory that directors are trustees for creditors, but generally these cases have some element of fraud and deceit involved therein.

We think the trial court correctly held that the complaint did not state a cause of action against the individual defendants, the judgment is affirmed with costs to the respondents.

Affirmed.

REVIEW QUESTIONS

1. Identify the terms in column A by matching each with the appropriate statement in column B.

	A		B
1.	Cumulative voting	**a.**	A lawsuit filed on behalf of a corporation by a shareholder as the result of the failure of the officers and directors to file the suit.
2.	Preemptive right	**b.**	A majority of the shares of a corporation.
3.	Derivative suit	**c.**	The record date on which a dividend is payable.
4.	Quorum	**d.**	A reduction in par value and an increase in the number of shares outstanding.
5.	Proxy	**e.**	Prevents some derivative suits.
6.	Ex dividend date	**f.**	A shareholder is entitled to the number of votes in electing directors that is the product of number of shares times number of directors to be elected. All the shareholder's votes may be cast for one director.
7.	Stock split	**g.**	The right to vote someone else's stock.
8.	Business judgment rule	**h.**	The right of a shareholder to purchase additional stock of subsequent stock issues so that he may maintain his overall percentage of total stock outstanding.

2. A well-organized minority group of common shareholders have asserted that the Endo Corporation's directors and officers have been guilty of mismanagement and negligence and have allowed corporate assets to be shamefully wasted. They demand to see the books and records of the Endo Corporation in order to obtain all the relevant facts. Furthermore, they demand to be permitted to make copies of the lists of shareholders. They also demand that they be permitted to bring in their attorney and their accountant. Do the shareholders have the right (1) to examine the books, (2) make copies of the lists of stockholders, and (3) bring along their attorney and their accountant? Explain.

3. Jackson, Baker, and Cronin were directors of the ABC Corporation. During the early years, the corporation met with moderate success and showed a small annual profit each year. There was nothing in the corporate charter or bylaws about compensation for directors, and during this initial period the directors did not seek or receive any compensation. In 1980 the corporation had a banner year: several new contracts were obtained, and a new product line that the directors decided the corporation should make and sell proved highly profitable. The directors performed the usual services and duties of their office in a highly competent and skillful manner, and their efforts were to a large extent responsible for the large profits obtained in 1980. After the 1980 income statement was received and examined by the directors, they met on March 15, 1981, and voted themselves a retroactive bonus of $10,000 each as the reasonable value for the services of the past years. Sherman, a stockholder of record, objected to this action and now brings a derivative stockholder's action against the directors and seeks to obtain a judgment against each of them to the extent of the bonus he received. With what result? Why?

4. Andrews, a director of Omega Corporation, learned of a very valuable mineral discovery on certain land that could be acquired at a bargain price. Without revealing this information to Omega, Andrews, acting through his brother-in-law, acquired the mineral rights for the property and resold them to Omega at a large profit. Did Andrews incur any liability to Omega as a result of these transactions? Explain.

5. Abner owned a majority of the stock of Sarin Company, and he ran the corporation by himself. The balance of the stock was owned by Abner's brother and sister, who agreed to sell all their stock to him. At the time of the purchase Abner was negotiating a sale of the company, but he did not reveal this fact to his brother and sister. The sale of the company resulted in a great profit to Abner. The brother and sister brought suit to recover the difference. Should the brother and sister succeed? Why?

6. On March 1, a company declared a cash dividend of $1 per share, payable on June 1 to all stockholders of record on May 1. On April 10, Ann sold 10 shares of her stock to Bob, but the transfer was not recorded on the corporation's books until May 15. To whom will the company pay the dividend? Who is entitled to the dividend? Explain.

7. George brought a shareholder's derivative suit against the Danver Corporation, alleging financial improprieties by officials of Danver. The events upon which this derivative action was based had occurred prior to George's becoming a shareholder. Is a shareholder entitled to maintain a derivative action complaining of transactions that occurred prior to his becoming a shareholder? Why?

8. A Michigan statute requires all corporations to provide funds to meet any worker's compensation claim presented by an employee. Failure to so provide, by insurance or otherwise, renders the officers and directors jointly and severally liable. Plaintiff was injured during the course of his employment with the corporate defendant and was awarded 215 weeks of compensation. Shortly thereafter, the corporation went bankrupt without paying the claim. Plaintiff seeks to hold the directors and officers personally liable. With what result? Why?

9. Wilkes and three other individuals formed a corporation to operate a nursing home many years ago. The four corporate shareholders were also elected directors, and they served as employees of the close corporation. Plaintiff had a quarrel with one of the other directors after years of successful operation. As a result, the other board members canceled plaintiff's salary, refused to reelect him as director, and stopped paying dividends in an attempt to freeze him out. He sued for damages on the ground that the majority had breached the fiduciary duty owed to him. With what result? Why?

10. A corporation board authorized a director, Wilson, to negotiate the purchase of some land. Instead, Wilson secretly bought the land himself and sold it to the corporation at a profit. After learning of the deceit, the corporation failed to act. Do the minority shareholders have any remedy? Explain.

11. Alan is chairman of the board of directors of Shipping Corporation. The bylaws of the corporation provide for a seven-person board of directors, one of whom has just died. The bylaws have no provision for filling a vacancy, and Alan would like to appoint his brother. Alan attempted to telephone the other directors and inform them of what he would like to do. Two directors agreed by

telephone. A third director could not be reached. The fourth director agreed to Alan's plan on behalf of himself and the fifth director, who had given his proxy to the fourth director. The substance of the telephone calls was not then expressed in writing. Can Alan legally appoint his brother as a director? Explain.

12. A corporation has only two stockholders: Andrew who owns 70 shares, and Bob who owns 30 shares. Three directors are to be elected by cumulative voting. How many directors will Andrew be able to elect? Explain.

44 CORPORATE DISSOLUTIONS, MERGERS, AND CONSOLIDATIONS

Corporate existence terminates upon the expiration of the period set forth in the charter or upon the voluntary or involuntary dissolution of the corporation. Voluntary dissolutions may occur when corporations consolidate or merge. In a *consolidation,* corporate existence technically ceases for both corporations when the new corporation is formed. In a *merger,* it ceases for the corporation that is merged into the continuing one. This chapter will discuss various methods for terminating the corporate existence. Since a corporation is a creation of a statute, it can be dissolved only according to statute. Thus the statute of the state of incorporation is very important.

Most corporate charters provide for perpetual existence. If the charter stipulates that the corporation shall exist for a definite period, it automatically terminates at the expiration of the period, unless application to continue the corporation is made and approved by the authority granting the charter. Since almost every corporation has perpetual existence, formal action is almost always required to end the life of a corporation.

1. Voluntary Dissolution

A corporation that has obtained its charter but has not begun business may be dissolved by its incorporators. The incorporators file articles of dissolution with the state, and a certificate of dissolution is issued if all fees are paid and the articles are in order.

A corporation that has begun business may be voluntarily dissolved either by the written consent of *all* its shareholders or by corporate action instituted by its board of directors and approved by the requisite percentage (usually two-thirds) of the shareholders. The board action, usually in the form of a recommendation, directs that the issue be submitted to the shareholders. A meeting of shareholders is called to consider the dissolution issue, and if the vote is in favor of it to the degree required by statute, the officers follow the procedures for dissolution.

These procedures require the corporate officers to file a statement of *intent to dissolve.* The statement is filed with the state of incorporation, and it includes either the consent of all shareholders or the resolutions instituted by the board of directors. Upon filing the statement of intent to dissolve, the corporation must cease to carry on its business, except for winding up its affairs, even though corporate existence continues until a certificate of dissolution is issued by the state.

The filing of a statement of intent to dissolve is not irrevocable. If the shareholders change their minds before the articles of dissolution are issued, the decision may be revoked by filing a statement of revocation of voluntary dissolution proceedings. When such a statement is filed, the corporation may resume its business.

In winding up its affairs, the corporation must give notice to all known creditors of the corporation. Directors become personally liable for any debt of which notice is not given.[1]

In dissolution proceedings, corporate assets are first used to pay debts. After all debts are paid, the remainder is distributed proportionately among the shareholders. If there are insufficient assets to pay all debts, a receiver will be appointed by a court, and the proceedings will be similar to those of involuntary dissolutions, discussed later.

When all funds are distributed, the corporation will prepare duplicate "articles of dissolution" and forward them to the state for approval. When signed by the appropriate state official, usually the secretary of state, one copy is filed with state records, and one copy is returned to the corporation to be kept with the corporate records.

INVOLUNTARY DISSOLUTION

2. Proceedings Commenced by the State

The state, having created the corporation, has the right to institute proceedings to cancel the charter. Suits by a state to cancel or forfeit a charter are known as *quo warranto* proceedings. They are filed by the attorney general, usually at the request of the secretary of state. Statutes often allow charters to be canceled by executive action also.

Charters may be canceled by suit or executive action if a corporation (1) did not file its annual report, (2) neglected to pay its franchise tax and license fees, (3) procured its charter by fraud, (4) abused and misused its authority, (5) failed to appoint and maintain a registered agent for the service of notices and process or has not informed the state of the name and address of its registered agent, or (6) ceased to perform its corporate functions for a long period of time. By proper

[1] Bonsall v. Piggly Wiggly Helms, Inc., p. 1002.

proceedings and without charter forfeiture, the attorney general may also enjoin a corporation from engaging in a business not authorized by its charter. If a corporation is dissolved for any of these reasons, it may not continue its business. Its officers and directors may wind up the business, but any other contract is null and void.

By statute in most states, the officers and directors do not have personal liability for debts incurred on behalf of the corporation when its charter is suspended for failure to comply with state laws. Such statutes only suspend the right of a corporation to transact business while the corporation is delinquent for failure to file its annual report or pay its annual fees to the state. They do not expose the corporation's officers or directors to personal liability for debts incurred during the period of delinquency.

3. Proceedings Commenced by Shareholders

Involuntary dissolution may be ordered by a court of equity at the request of a shareholder when the directors are deadlocked in the management of corporate affairs or the shareholders are deadlocked and unable to elect a board of directors. Deadlocks require proof that irreparable injury is likely and that the deadlock cannot be broken. A mere deadlock in voting to elect directors is not sufficient in most states to cause a court to order dissolution.[2]

The general rule throughout the country is that a minority shareholder or group of shareholders of a going and solvent corporation cannot, without statutory authority, maintain a suit to have it dissolved. Most states have statutes that authorize courts of equity to liquidate a corporation at the request of a shareholder when it is proved that those in control of the corporation are acting illegally, fraudulently, or oppressively. It is so difficult to define oppressive conduct that each case must be decided on its own facts.

Actions intended to squeeze out or freeze out minority shareholders may provide grounds for dissolution or other equitable relief. Minority shareholders have been granted relief when the majority have refused to declare dividends, but have paid out all profits to themselves in the form of salaries and bonuses. Relief was also granted in a recent case where the majority shareholders of a corporation that was *not* in need of funds sold additional stock in order to dilute the percentage of control of the minority, who the majority knew were unable financially to exercise their preemptive right. Such conduct is a breach of the fiduciary relationship.

Today, conduct that is not illegal or fraudulent may be held to be oppressive. Although controlling shareholders in a closely held corporation are not fiduciaries in the strict sense of the word, the general concepts of fiduciary duties are useful in deciding if conduct is oppressive. The law imposes equitable limitations on dominant shareholders. They are under a duty to refrain from using their control to profit for themselves at the expense of the minority. Repeated violations of these duties will serve as a ground for dissolution. Even though it takes substan-

---

[2] Henry George & Sons, Inc. v. Cooper-George, Inc., p. 1003.

tially less evidence to justify dissolution of a partnership than of a close corporation, the trend is to treat the issues as similar. *Oppressive conduct* may be summarized as conduct that is burdensome, harsh, and wrongful. It is a substantial deviation from fair dealing and a violation of fair play. It is a violation of the fiduciary duty of good faith in those states that recognize such a duty.

All states allow minority shareholders to obtain dissolution when it is established that corporate assets are being wasted or looted or the corporation is unable to carry out its purposes. Some states have by statute broadened the grounds for court-ordered dissolution. These states allow courts to order dissolution when it is reasonably necessary for the protection of the rights or interests of minority shareholders.[3] Even in these states, a corporation will not be dissolved by a court for errors of judgment or because the court confronted with a question of policy would decide it differently than would the directors. Dissolutions by decree at the request of a shareholder are rare; but as previously noted, the trend is to give greater protection to the minority shareholders.

4. Proceedings Commenced by Creditors

A corporation is in the same position as a natural person insofar as its creditors are concerned. A suit may be brought against it; and when a judgment is obtained, an execution may be levied against its property, which may then be sold. Corporate assets may be attached; and if the corporation has no property subject to execution, its assets may be traced by a bill in a court of equity.

The creditors have no right, because they are creditors, to interfere with the management of the business. A creditor who has an unsatisfied judgment against a corporation may bring a bill in equity to set aside conveyances and transfers of corporate property that have been fraudulently transferred for the purpose of delaying and hindering creditors. Creditors may also, in these circumstances, ask for a receiver to take over the assets of the corporation and to apply them to the payment of debts.

When there is an unsatisfied execution and it is established that the corporation is insolvent, a court may order a dissolution. The same is true if the corporation admits its insolvency. Dissolution in such cases proceeds in the same manner as if instituted by the state or by voluntary proceedings when insolvent.

5. Procedure in Involuntary Dissolution

In liquidating a corporation, courts have the full range of judicial powers at their disposal. They may issue injunctions, appoint receivers, and take whatever steps are necessary to preserve the corporate assets for the protection of creditors and shareholders. The receiver will usually collect the assets, including any amount owed to the corporation for shares. The receiver will then sell the assets, pay the debts and expenses of liquidation, and if any funds are left, divide them proportionately among the shareholders. Courts usually require creditors to prove their claims in court in a manner similar to that in bankruptcy proceedings. When

[3] Stumpf v. C. S. Stumpf & Sons, Inc., p. 1004.

all funds in the hands of a receiver are paid out, the court issues a decree of dissolution that is filed with the secretary of state. Funds due persons who cannot be located are deposited with the state treasurer and held for a specified number of years. If not claimed by the creditor or shareholder within the declared period, the funds belong to the state.

6. Liability of Shareholders

As a general rule, shareholders are not personally liable for the debts of the firm, but a shareholder who has not paid the corporation for his original issue of stock in full is liable to the receiver or to a creditor for the unpaid balance. In addition, statutes in most states allow creditors to reach assets of the former corporation that are in the hands of shareholders. The assets of a corporation are a trust fund for the payment of creditors, and the directors must manage this fund for their benefit. The liability of shareholders to creditors of the corporation is predicated on the theory that the transfer of corporate assets on dissolution is in fraud of creditors, and a shareholder knowingly receiving such assets ought to have liability.

Claims that existed before dissolution may be enforced afterward by statute in most states. For a specified period after dissolution, remedies survive against a corporation, its directors, officers, and shareholders. Suits against the corporation may be prosecuted or defended in the corporate name even though the corporate existence has technically ended. A judgment on such a claim may be collected from the corporation if it has property or from any former insurance carrier of the corporation. A claim may also be collected from property distributed to shareholders on dissolution, or the creditor may proceed directly against the shareholder receiving property. As previously noted, failure to give notice to creditors of intent to dissolve stops the time period from running.

The time period to sue after dissolution was created to protect creditors from losses that could easily result from the "death" of the corporate debtor. However, this protection is limited to whatever period is specified by the law of the state of incorporation; liability does not continue indefinitely.[4] In addition, there is no liability for postdissolution causes of action unless a statute imposes it. If liability existed for postdissolution causes of action, corporate existence might never end.

7. Definitions

A business may acquire other businesses in a variety of ways. It may singly purchase the assets of the other firm. Such purchases include the plant, equipment, and even the goodwill of the other business. In such cases, the selling business retains its liabilities and its corporate structure.

Businesses may also consolidate or merge. *Consolidation* is the uniting of two or more corporations. A new corporation is created and the old entities are dissolved. The new corporation takes title to all the property, rights, powers, and privileges of the old corporations, subject to the liabilities and obligations of the

ACQUISITIONS, CONSOLIDATIONS, AND MERGERS

---

[4] Hunter v. Fort Worth Capital Corp., p. 1005.

old corporations. In a *merger,* one of the corporations continues its existence but absorbs the other corporation, which ceases to have an independent existence. The continuing corporation may expressly or impliedly assume and agree to pay the debts and liabilities of the absorbed corporation, whose creditors become third-party creditor beneficiaries. By statute in most states, the surviving corporation is deemed to have assumed all the liabilities and obligations of the absorbed corporation.

Mergers and acquisitions comprise a major part of the antitrust laws, and this aspect is discussed more fully in chapter 47. They also are subject to the securities laws and to regulation by the SEC; these topics are discussed in chapter 49.

8. Procedures

The procedures for consolidations and mergers are statutory. Usually, the board of directors gives its approval by resolution that sets forth in detail all facts of the planned merger or consolidation. The plan is submitted to the shareholders for approval. Notice of the meeting typically includes the resolution passed by the directors. If proxies are submitted for the vote, proxy material must disclose all material facts required for an intelligent decision by the shareholders. In most states the shareholders must approve the plan by a two-thirds vote of all shares and two-thirds of each class if more than one class of stock is voting. If the consolidation or merger is approved by the shareholders of both corporations, articles of consolidation or articles of merger will be prepared and filed with the state. If the papers are in order and all fees are paid, a certificate of consolidation or a certificate of merger will be issued.

9. Rights of Dissenting Shareholders

Statutes of the appropriate state may be strictly complied with, yet the courts may block a merger or acquisition. A merger may not be effected for the purpose of freezing out or squeezing out minority shareholders. If a merger has no valid business purpose other than the elimination of minority shareholders, courts will enjoin the merger or consolidation. Even if the minority shareholders receive the investment value of their interest in the merged corporation, the policy favoring corporate flexibility is not furthered by permitting the elimination of minority interests for the benefit of the majority, when no benefit accrues to the corporation. Moreover, the majority shareholders owe the minority shareholders a fiduciary obligation in dealing with corporate assets. This duty includes the protection of corporate interests and restraint from doing anything that would injure the corporation or deprive it of profits or the ability to exercise its powers. Since dissolution may cause these effects, the majority may not dissolve when the only purpose is to get rid of the minority.

A shareholder who dissents from a consolidation or merger, and who makes his dissent a matter of record by serving a written demand that the corporation purchase his stock, is entitled to be paid the fair value of his stock on the day preceding the vote on the corporate action. Procedures are established for ascertaining the fair value and for a judicial decision of that issue if necessary. Among the relevant factors to be considered in evaluating a dissenting shareholder's stock are the nature of the corporation; the market demand for the stock; the business of the corporation; its earnings, dividends, and net assets; general economic conditions; the market prices of comparable companies; the market price and earnings ratio; management and policies; revenues for various contingencies; tax liabilities; future earnings; and the permanence of the business. One method for determining this fair price is known as the *weighted average method.* This method assigns a particular weight to the elements of value—assets, market price, and earnings. The results are added to determine the value per share.[5]

There is no rule of thumb for the weight to be given any factor. Moreover, the weighted average method is not exclusive, and many courts today believe it is outmoded. Other techniques that are acceptable in the financial community, such as discounted cash flow analysis and comparisons with other tender offers, may be used. All relevant factors are considered in determining a fair price; fair value cannot be computed according to any precise mathematical formula. If the stock is regularly traded in an exchange, market value may be the dominant factor.

The laws relating to dissenting shareholders petitioning for appraisal and the right to be paid the fair values for their stock apply to a cash-for-stock merger as well as a stock-for-stock merger. Also, a shareholder who dissents from a sale or exchange of all or substantially all the assets or property of the corporation, other than in the usual course of business, has the same right to be paid for his stock. When the statutory procedures are followed, the dissenting shareholder ceases to be a shareholder when notice is given; he then becomes a creditor.

Tender offers create problems in valuing the stock of dissenting shareholders. Such offers usually include a premium, in order to overcome objections of many shareholders; but dissenting shareholders who refuse a tender offer and insist on a judicial determination of the fair value of shares are not entitled to receive the tender offer premium. A premerger tender offer price does not establish a floor on the amount that the court may fix as the value of shares in an appraisal proceeding, but it does have some evidentiary significance.

10. Liability of Successors

In the case of a merger or a consolidation of corporations, the changed entity ordinarily remains liable for prior debts; a business cannot shrug off personal liability to its creditors simply by merging, consolidating, switching from the partnership to the corporate form or vice versa, or changing its name. By statute in most states, the surviving corporation is deemed to have assumed all the liabilities and obligations of the absorbed corporation or of the former corporations.

In order to avoid assuming the debts and liabilities of corporations that are being acquired, the acquiring businesses often purchase the assets of a corporation without assuming the liabilities and without any change of organization. The buyer does not become involved with the seller, and there is no merger or

---

[5] Brown v. Hedahl's–Q B & R, Inc., p. 1006.

consolidation. As a general rule, if one corporation acquires only the assets of another corporation, the acquiring corporation is not liable for the debts and liabilities of the transfer. An exception exists if the transfer is an attempt to defraud creditors.

This general rule is subject to attack today. Under what circumstances should an acquiring corporation have liability for the debts and the obligations of the business whose assets it acquired? This becomes a difficult question when the assets acquired include the firm name and its product line. The contract of acquisition usually provides for no assumption of liabilities, but should such a provision bind third parties when the selling corporation dissolves as soon as the sale is complete? This issue arises quite frequently in product liability cases.[6] It is not surprising that the courts of different states have answered the liability issue differently in product liability cases. The majority view is to find no liability, but many states take the opposite view.

---

[6] Bernard v. Kee Mfg. Co., Inc., p. 1009.

SUMMARY

VOLUNTARY DISSOLUTION

Procedures	1. A chartered corporation that has not begun business may be dissolved by its incorporators' filing articles of dissolution with the state.
	2. A corporation that has begun business may be dissolved by all its shareholders.
	3. A corporation that has begun business may be dissolved by its board of directors with the approval of two-thirds of the shareholders.
	4. A corporation must give notice to all creditors of its intent to dissolve. The directors are personally liable to creditors to whom notice is not given.
Distributions	1. Corporate assets are first used to pay debts. Any remaining assets are distributed proportionately among the shareholders.
	2. If there are not enough assets to pay debts, a receiver will be appointed, and

the dissolution will proceed as if it were involuntary.

INVOLUNTARY DISSOLUTION

Proceedings commenced by the state	1. The state may file a *quo warranto* proceeding to cancel a corporate charter.
	2. Such proceedings are brought for failure of the corporation to comply with the law in such areas as annual reports, franchise taxes, and registered agents.
Proceedings commenced by shareholders	1. Shareholders may petition a court of equity to dissolve a corporation if there is a deadlock in management and irreparable injury is likely.
	2. Shareholders may obtain dissolution if the directors are acting illegally, fraudulently, or oppressively.
	3. Modern statutes do not allow the majority to freeze out minority shareholders, and dissolution is an appropriate remedy in such cases.
	4. Shareholders in closely held corporations have duties similar to partners in a partnership.
Proceedings commenced by creditors	1. Creditors have no right to interfere with the management of a corporation.
	2. Creditors may ask for a receiver to be appointed when they have an unsatisfied judgment. If insolvency is established, dissolution is possible.
Procedures	1. Courts of equity have the full range of procedures to protect corporate assets, the creditors, and shareholders.
	2. Creditors are required to prove their claims before they share in assets.
Liability of shareholders in dissolution	1. Shareholders have no personal liability to creditors unless the stock is not paid for in full or assets have been transferred to them to defraud creditors.
	2. Claims against the corporation exist for a specified time after dissolution and may be enforced against shareholders receiving corporate assets.

CONSOLIDATIONS AND MERGERS

Procedures

1. Certain statutory procedures must be followed. These usually require submission to the shareholders for approval.
2. Each class of shareholders must approve the plan, and usually by a two-thirds vote.
3. Minority shareholders who dissent to a merger or consolidation are entitled to be paid the fair value of their stock immediately prior to the change in the corporation. Various methods are in use for determining fair market value.
4. A tender offer does not establish fair market value, but it is evidence of the value.

Liability of successors

1. In a merger or consolidation, the new corporation is liable for the debts of the old corporation.
2. When one corporation acquires the assets of another, there may be liability in some states if the facts warrant it.

CASES

Bonsall v. Piggly Wiggly Helms, Inc.
274 S.E.2d 298 (S.C. 1981)

Bonsall was injured in a "slip and fall" accident while shopping at the defendant's grocery store. She telephoned the store and notified them of her injury. Defendant notified its insurance company, and an adjuster contacted the plaintiff and her attorney.

Thereafter, the defendant corporation was dissolved. It failed to give actual notice of intent to dissolve to the plaintiff, although it published notice of dissolution in the newspaper. The South Carolina law on corporate dissolution provides:

After the filing by the Secretary of State of a statement of intent to dissolve, . . . (b) The

corporation shall immediately cause notice of the filing of the statement of intent to dissolve to be mailed to each *known creditor* of the corporation. . . .

LEWIS, J. . . . The sole question in this appeal is whether or not respondent was a "known creditor" . . . so as to require notice to her of appellant's dissolution in order to bar her claim under the two year limitation provisions of Code Section 33–21–220. We affirm the holding of the lower court that respondent was a "known creditor" to whom notice was required to be given in order to bar her tort claim.

The preponderance of the evidence supports this finding. The call by respondent to a woman at

Piggly Wiggly, notifying it of her fall, resulted in an adjuster of the store contacting the respondent. This gives rise to the reasonable inference, . . . that Piggly Wiggly had notice of the respondent's fall and her resulting claim for damages.

We next consider the question of a tort claimant as a creditor. *Stewart, Admr. v. Walterboro and Western Ry. Co.,* 64 S.C. 92, considered the magnitude of the term creditor in the context of a corporate merger. The Court held that the defendant, which had since pursued a merger into a new corporation, was not dissolved as a corporation insofar as the rights of the plaintiff. Although the statute involved concerned merger and not dissolution, as pointed out by the appellant, this distinction is not of significance. Both address the viability of actions against corporate entities seeking to end their corporate existence as it existed at the time of the claim.

The respondent's tort claim made her a creditor within the meaning of Section 33–21–60, entitling her to notice of dissolution. Since notice was not given to respondent, who was a known creditor, the corporation was not dissolved insofar as the rights of the respondent. . . .

Judgment affirmed.

Henry George & Sons, Inc. v. Cooper-George, Inc.
632 P.2d 512 (Wash. 1981)

Shareholders of Cooper-George, Inc., failed to elect new directors at two successive annual meetings due to a deadlock in voting power. The corporation has continued, however, to transact business, and the former board remained in office.

In April 1979 a shareholder initiated this suit, seeking dissolution under a Washington statute granting courts jurisdiction to liquidate the assets and business of a corporation when it is established that the shareholders are deadlocked in voting power and have failed for a period of at least two years to elect successor directors. The trial court interpreted the code section to be mandatory and the grounds sufficient for dissolution of a corporation.

DIMMICK, J. . . . This appeal raises the question of whether the failure of shareholders of a Washington corporation to elect new directors at two successive annual meetings is, by itself, sufficient grounds for dissolution of a corporation under RCW 23A.28.170(1)(c). . . .

We conclude that this provision is not mandatory, but gives the court jurisdiction to exercise its discretion in the best interests of all the shareholders. Therefore, we reverse.

At common law, many courts refused to intervene in shareholder disputes since the State licensed the corporation, and as such the State and not the courts had the authority to dissolve the corporation.

In a few jurisdictions, courts of equity began to carve out areas in which they would use the powers of the chancellors to liquidate the assets and business of the corporation. A few courts asserted the power to liquidate on a showing of irreparable injury to the shareholders and the corporation due to gross or fraudulent mismanagement.

More recently, many states have adopted statutory provisions granting courts of equity power to dissolve corporations in suits brought by shareholders where irreparable injury to the shareholders or the corporation occurred or was threatened. Some states adopted legislation permitting liquidation and dissolution because of deadlocks among the owners or the directors of the corporation. In determining whether to grant dissolution under either the common law or statute, the principal inquiry appears to be whether dissolution would be beneficial to the shareholders and not injurious to the public.

Under the predecessor statutes to RCW 23A.28.170, the Washington courts permitted dissolution based on shareholder dissension or deadlock only under the most egregious circumstances.

It is within this background that our legislature saw fit to pass the Model Business Corporation Act. Section 97 of the act, as adopted as RCW 23A.28.170(1), permits involuntary dissolutions by shareholders in four different situations. Although RCW 23A.28.170(1) clearly provides that it is within the power of the court to order dissolution upon finding one of the four situations, we hold that the power is discretionary. Thus, under subsection .170(1)(c), the court need not order a dissolution merely because a party proved, at trial, that the shareholders were deadlocked in voting power and unable to elect a slate of directors at two consecutive meetings. . . .

A . . . reason for adopting such an interpretation is that to construe the statute otherwise (that is, to construe the statute as merely requiring a showing of the requisite deadlock requirements), would be manifestly unjust for it would dictate that the courts grant the harsh sanctions of dissolution regardless of the consequences to shareholders or to the public at large.

The question is essentially one for resolution through the familiar balancing process and flexible remedial resources of courts of equity. We agree with the conclusion of the text writer of corporations:

> Involuntary dissolution proceedings, although generally statutory in most jurisdictions, are fundamentally equitable in nature, and the statutes should be construed and applied consistent with equitable principles. While the general effect of the statutes is to prescribe the procedures and particularize the grounds for dissolution, the inherent power of equity is not thereby impaired but, to the contrary, such power gives meaning to the statutory provisions.

Therefore, we conclude . . . that our present statute contemplates that once the requisite showing of the jurisdictional requirements are met, the trial court, in its discretion, shall determine whether there exist equitable grounds for ordering dissolution of the corporation. In so ruling, the trial court should consider the seriousness of the deadlock and whether the corporation is able to conduct business profitably despite the deadlock. Moreover, the trial court should consider whether such a dissolution will be beneficial or detrimental to all the shareholders, or injurious to the public. For example, the court may consider such factors as the length of time the company has been in business, the stated purpose of the business, the original incorporators, whether one shareholder has shown a clear design to take over the business and is in a financial posture to do so to the detriment of other shareholders who may be injured financially by tax consequences, what the market for sale and purchase is at the instant time, whether the shareholders are in a relatively equal bargaining position, and whether it is in the best interests of all the shareholders to leave them to find their own solutions by one party buying out the others in a fair market value situation rather than by a forced sale.

Reversed and remanded.

Stumpf v. C.S. Stumpf & Sons, Inc. 120 Cal.Rptr. 671 (1975)

A father and his two sons formed a corporation to conduct a general contracting business. The business had previously been conducted as a partnership, and each shareholder had an equal number of shares in the new corporation. Three years later, plaintiff, one of the sons, ceased to be employed by the corporation. There had been a dispute, and the plaintiff had been removed as an officer and director of the corporation. The corporation pays no dividends but invests its profits in real estate. There was no evidence of abuse of authority or persistent unfairness by the defendants. Plaintiff filed suit to dissolve the corporation. California law allows courts to order dissolution where "liquidation is reasonably necessary" for the protection of the rights or interests of the complaining shareholders. The lower court ordered dissolution, and the defendants appealed.

CHRISTIAN, J. . . . . Appellant contends that respondent's rights and interests are not jeopardized and that dissolution was not justified. Implied in this contention is the argument that [the statute] is not applicable in the absence of some finding of deadlock, mismanagement of the corporation, or display of unfairness toward respondent. The court specifically found that there had been no mismanagement or unfairness; there was no evidence of corporate deadlock. . . .

It is true that courts of some states have narrowly construed provisions similar to subdivision (f), requiring a showing of some kind of management misconduct or deadlock before relief will be granted. In California, a narrow construction of the involuntary dissolution statute has been urged by Ballantine, who suggested that a broad construction of the statute "make[s] it too easy for an obstreperous minority to interfere with the legitimate control and management of the majority by creating a cash nuisance value."

But the danger of minority abuse was evidently recognized and dealt with by the Legislature. The procedure created by the statute does not authorize dissolution at will. The minority must persuade the court that fairness requires drastic relief under section 4651, subdivision (f); involuntary dissolution is not an automatic remedy but, rather, a matter for the court's discretion.

> [A] minority stockholder suing under a statute, just as if he were suing in the absence of statute, must still convince the court that his application is meritorious. If the objection were that, because of the possibility of abuse, minority stockholders should not be permitted to ask a court to wind up a corporation, however meritorious the case, the solution would seem to lie in total abolition of the remedy. The reluctance to authorize winding-up a corporation even where such action would be just and equitable contrasts strangely with the arbitrary manner in which a ministerial state official terminates, at a stroke, the existence of great numbers of corporations for failure to comply

with comparatively unimportant formalities, such as filing reports or paying a nominal annual tax. . . .

The court's exercise of discretion to order dissolution under section 4651, subdivision (f), was consistent with the intent of the Legislature in adopting that provision.

Appellant next contends that the court's conclusion that the case called for relief under section 4651, subdivision (f), was not supported by the evidence. . . . There was, however, substantial evidence supporting the findings and judgment. The hostility between the two brothers had grown so extreme that respondent severed contact with his family and was allowed no say in the operation of the business. After respondent's withdrawal from the business, he received no salary, dividends, or other revenue from his investment in the corporation. . . .

The decree is affirmed.

Hunter v. Fort Worth Capital Corp.
620 S.W.2d 547 (Tex. 1981)

Theodore Moeller was injured in 1975 by an elevator installed by the Hunter-Hayes Elevator Company in 1960. The company was dissolved in 1964. The injured worker brought an action against the former shareholders. He alleged the shareholders were personally liable to him, to the extent of the assets they received on dissolution, under the trust fund theory.

The shareholders moved for summary judgment on the ground that a state statute (Article 7.12) required actions against dissolved corporations and their shareholders be brought within 3 years after the company is dissolved. The trial court granted the motion, and the appellate court reversed.

McGEE, J. . . . Article 7.12 provides statutory remedies for pre-dissolution claims only and thus is in the nature of a survival statute. Moeller's cause of action did not accrue until he was injured more than eleven years after the company dissolved. Consequently, Moeller cannot recover against the shareholders for his post-dissolution claim against

the corporation, unless his suit is authorized by some other statute or legal theory.

The shareholders contend the court of civil appeals erred in holding that Moeller could maintain suit against them under the "trust fund theory." More specifically, they argue Article 7.12 supplants the trust fund theory and Moeller must look solely to that statute in order to determine if the legislature provided him with a remedy.

This contention calls for a construction of Article 7.12. In doing so, our primary objective will be to ascertain the legislative intent. . . .

At common law, dissolution terminated the legal existence of a corporation. Once dissolved, the corporation could neither sue nor be sued, and all legal proceedings in which it was a party abated.

To alleviate the harsh effects of the common law on creditors, an equitable doctrine evolved. This doctrine provided that when the assets of a dissolved corporation are distributed among its shareholders, a creditor of the dissolved corporation may pursue the assets on the theory that in equity they are burdened with a lien in his favor. This doctrine is often referred to as the "trust fund theory." Actually, the equitable doctrine has a much broader application. The trust fund theory applies whenever the assets of a dissolved corporation are held by any third party, including corporate officers and directors, so long as the assets are traceable and have not been acquired by a bona fide purchaser.

Prior to the enactment of Article 7.12, Texas courts had long applied the trust fund theory to dissolved corporations, but only as it was embodied within the general framework of certain remedial statutes. Under these remedial statutes, the legislature had given creditors of a dissolved corporation "the same broad measure of relief which equity would have afforded in the absence of legislation." . . . The effect of these statutes was to supplant the equitable trust fund theory by declaring a statutory equivalent. In Texas, recognition of the trust fund theory, as applied to dissolved corporations, did not exist apart from these statutes.

We find no indication that the legislature intended for Article 7.12 to be interpreted any differently. Because the statute applies to officers, directors, and shareholders of a dissolved corporation, it embodies the trust fund doctrine but only to the extent that the doctrine allows recovery for pre-dissolution claims. Therefore, Article 7.12 expresses a legislative policy to restrict the use of the trust fund theory to pre-dissolution claims, and to protect shareholders, officers and directors of a dissolved corporation from prolonged and uncertain liability.

. . . Accordingly, we hold Article 7.12 bars resort to the trust fund theory as it exists apart from the statute. . . .

We agree with defendant that extension of the trust fund theory to cover plaintiff's claim would mean that the corporation could never completely dissolve but would live on indefinitely through its shareholders. We do not believe that this result would be in accordance with the spirit of the laws governing the dissolution of corporations.

If the legislature had intended for shareholders of a dissolved corporation to be liable for causes of action which accrue after dissolution, it could have easily provided so within the statutory language of Article 7.12. Only when it is necessary to give effect to the clear legislative intent can we insert additional words into a statutory provision. A provision was included to provide creditors with a statutory remedy for pre-dissolution claims. A similar provision could have been included to encompass post-dissolution claims as well. We believe the exclusion of such a provision to be significant. In the absence of such a provision in Article 7.12 or some other statute, we hold Moeller cannot recover from the shareholders for his post-dissolution negligence claim against Hunter-Hayes.

We reverse the judgment of the court of civil appeals and affirm the judgment of the trial court.

Brown v. Hedahl's–Q B & R, Inc.
185 N.W.2nd 249 (N.Dak. 1971)

The owner of shares of stock in a closely held corporation dissented to a proposed merger that was approved by the remaining shareholders. By state statute, the dissenting shareholder who filed written objections to the merger was entitled to be paid the "fair value" of his shares as of the day preceding the approval of the merger by the other shareholders. The shareholder contended that the stock was worth $322 per share, and the corporation contended that it was worth $100 per share. The lower court found the "fair value" to be $230 per share, and the corporation which had to purchase the stock appealed.

TEIGEN, J. . . . It appears, as a matter of general law, that there are three primary methods used by courts in determining the fair value of shares of dissenting shareholders. These three methods are the market value method, the asset value method, and the investment or earnings value method. The market value method establishes the value of the share on the basis of the price for which a share is selling or could be sold to a willing buyer. This method is most reliable where there is an established market for the stock. The asset value method looks to the net assets of the corporation valued as a "going concern," each share having a pro rata value of the net assets. The net assets value depends on the real worth of the assets as determined by physical appraisals, accurate inventories, and realistic allowances for depreciation and obsolescence. The investment value method relates to the earning capacity of the corporation and involves an attempt to predict its future income based primarily on its previous earnings record. Dividends paid by the corporation are considered in its investment value. Generally, all the elements involved in these methods are considered in determining the value of the dissenter's stock. . . .

In redetermining the "fair value" of a share of Q B & R stock as of March 8, 1968, we have used all three methods of valuation and have established a value under each method which we have assigned a certain percentage weight in determining the fair value of the Q B & R stock. In determining the asset value as of March 8, 1968, we have used the consolidated statement of February 29, 1968, as that is the closest statement to the date in question. We have made certain adjustments to this statement to reflect more properly the true value of the assets of Q B & R as a "going concern." . . . [After explaining the adjustments.] The book value and the adjusted value of the Q B & R assets as of February 29, 1968, are shown in the statement.

Q B & R Consolidated Statement February 29, 1968

	BOOK VALUE	ADJUSTED VALUE
Current assets:		
Cash on hand and in banks	10,583.75	10,583.75
Notes receivable	6,641.27	3,000.00
Accounts receivable	184,800.00	166,320.00
Inventories	469,932.77	469,932.77
Stocks and bonds	5,423.98	4,000.00
Cash value life insurance	10,860.00	10,860.00
Fixed assets:		
Real estate—lots	34,916.73	207,300.00
Real estate—buildings	56,150.59	(Bldgs. included above)
Furniture & fixtures	4,792.50	9,000.00
Shop equipment	13,450.98	20,250.00
Autos & trucks	14,223.92	11,385.00
Total assets:	811,776.89	912,631.52
Total liabilities:	203,228.93	203,228.93
Net asset value:	608,547.96	709,402.59

Total shares outstanding: 2,922
Asset value per share based on the adjusted
statement value of Q B & R:

$$2,922 \overline{\smash{\big)}\ 709{,}402.59}^{\textstyle 242.81}$$

The asset value per share, then, based on the adjusted value of the Q B & R assets as of February 29, 1968, is $242.81 per share.

Under the investment value (or earnings value) method of valuation, the value per share of Q B & R stock as of March 8, 1968, is zero. Q B & R had sustained a series of losses for several years prior to its merger with Hedahl's, Inc. Plaintiffs' exhibit showing the comparative net profits between Q B & R and Hedahl's, Inc., from 1962 through 1967 shows that Q B & R's five-year average net earnings per share, disregarding 1967, the year prior to the merger, was a loss of 14¢ per share. Based on a six-year average, which includes 1967, the earnings per share was a loss of $4.62 per share. Based on its earnings record, Q B & R was not a good investment and its earnings value is properly fixed at zero. . . . It appears that there is no established market for the Q B & R shares and thus there is no apparent market value that can be assigned to a share of Q B & R stock. However, a reconstructed market value can be established based on the limited transactions that have occurred. . . .

Averaging all Q B & R stock transactions from June of 1963 up to December 6, 1967, the result is a reconstructed market price of $69 per share. This figure appears to be a reasonable reconstructed market price and, accordingly, will be established as the market value for a share of Q B & R stock. . . .

We hold that all three methods of valuation must be used in determining the "fair value" of a share of Q B & R stock as of March 8, 1968. We have determined the value of a share of Q B & R stock by each method. The asset value of a share of Q B & R stock is $242.81 per share; the investment or earnings value of a share of Q B & R stock is zero; and the market value of a share of Q B & R stock is $69 per share. Having determined the value of a share of Q B & R stock by each method, the problem becomes one of weighing the various factors to reach a final result that properly takes into consideration all of the elements and factors involved in determining the "fair value" of a share of Q B & R stock as of March 8, 1968. . . .

In weighing the various values involved we have considered all aspects of Q B & R as a "going concern" prior to its merger with Hedahl's, Inc. Although we have assigned weights to the several values involved, we have not used any set formula; rather, we have relied on an analysis of the particular facts of this case as being determinative of the weight given each value. We have assigned a weight of 25% to the market value of Q B & R. Normally, where there is an established market for the stock of a corporation the market price is given great weight. In other cases where there is no reliable market and none can be reconstructed, market price is not considered at all. However, as to the Q B & R stock, there has been a limited market such that we can properly reconstruct a realistic market price for a share of Q B & R stock. We have assigned a weight of 50% to the asset value of Q B & R. Normally, a higher value is assigned only in cases where the primary purpose of the corporation is to hold

assets, such as real estate, for the purpose of allowing them to appreciate in value. In other words, assets are weighed more heavily when they are held for appreciation purposes rather than for commercial retail or wholesale purposes designed to generate earnings. Here the assets of Q B & R primarily consisted of inventories for sale and the necessary buildings and equipment to carry out this business purpose. The inventories held by Q B & R would depreciate in value rather than appreciate but the value of the lots and buildings is substantial in relation to the inventories and will likely appreciate in value. We have assigned a weight of 25% to the investment or earnings value of Q B & R. Normally, in a commercial business, earnings are given great weight as the primary purpose of the business is to generate earnings and not to hold assets that will appreciate in value. Q B & R was such a business, whose primary purpose was to generate earnings for its shareholders. The fact that Q B & R has failed in the past several years to generate such earnings does not mean that earnings are not an important part of the value of Q B & R stock. . . . Although earnings should ordinarily weigh heavily in determining the true value of the stock in a commercial corporation, we believe, under the circumstances, it is proper to give less weight in this case. Accordingly, we have determined that the "fair value" of a share of Q B & R stock as of March 8, 1968, is $138.65 per share.

	VALUE	× WEIGHT	= RESULT
Asset	$242.81 ×	50%	= $121.40
Market	69.00 ×	25%	= 17.25
Earnings	0.00 ×	25%	= 0.00
	Total value per share		$138.65

We therefore direct that the judgment be modified to conform to this opinion and as modified, it is affirmed.

Affirmed.

Bernard v. Kee Mfg. Co., Inc.
409 So.2d 1047 (Fla. 1982)

. . . [T]he Bernards, brought a products liability claim against respondent Kee Manufacturing Company, Inc. (Kee, Inc.). They claimed that a lawn mower manufactured and sold in 1967 by Kee Manufacturing Company (Kee), the predecessor business to Kee, Inc., caused an injury in 1976 to plaintiffs. Kee, Inc., had incorporated in 1972 when it had acquired for cash the assets of Kee from the owner, Flechas J. Kee, who did business as Kee Manufacturing Company. These assets included the manufacturing plant, inventory, goodwill, and the right to use the name "Kee Manufacturing Company." Kee, Inc., by the terms of this acquisition, had not assumed liabilities or obligations of its predecessor, Kee. The former owner of the business had no interest in the new company. Kee, Inc., used these assets to continue the manufacture of lawn mowers, maintaining the same factory personnel and using the trade name of Kee Mowers. The entire manufacturing process was effectively continued, but under a new owner and management. The brochure of Kee, Inc., states that it has been manufacturing lawn mowers since 1948.

SUNDBERG, J. . . . The issue we confront in this case is whether the purchaser of the assets of a manufacturing firm which continues under the same trade name the general product line of the seller can be liable for a defective product manufactured by the seller.

The vast majority of jurisdictions follow the traditional corporate law rule which does not impose the liabilities of the selling predecessor upon the buying successor company unless (1) the successor expressly or impliedly assumes obligations of the predecessor, (2) the transaction is a de facto merger, (3) the successor is a mere continuation of the predecessor, or (4) the transaction is a fraudulent effort to avoid liabilities of the predecessor.

Courts in a few jurisdictions have begun to extend products liability to the successor corporation in an effort to effectuate an acknowledged purpose of strict liability for defective products,

that the costs of a defective product should be included in that product. A first series of cases has expanded the continuity exception to the traditional rule by deleting a historical requirement of substantial identity of ownership. . . . A second line of cases . . . developed a new exception to the general rule of a corporate successor's non-liability, the product-line exception:

> [A] party which acquires a manufacturing business and continues the output of its line of products . . . assumes strict tort liability for defects in units of the same product line previously manufactured and distributed by the entity from which the business was acquired.

This rule has been adopted by only two . . . jurisdictions (New Jersey and Pennsylvania). The courts in these cases based justification of the product-line exception on (1) the lack of remedy for the plaintiff, (2) the successor's ability to spread the risk through insurance by estimating risks in the previously manufactured product, and (3) the fairness of requiring the successor to assume the burdens as well as the benefits of the original manufacturer's good will. Though these justifications have undeniable appeal, we find countervailing considerations more convincing.

We choose not to join this vanguard of courts, due in part to the threat of economic annihilation that small businesses would face under such a rule of expanded liability. Because of their limited assets, small corporations would face financial destruction from imposition of liability for their predecessor's products.

The economy as a whole suffers when small successor corporations lose such cases since corporate acquisitions are discouraged due to business planners' fears of being held so liable. Furthermore, the marketability of on-going corporations is diminished, perhaps forcing the sellers into the undesirable process of liquidation proceedings. Currently, small manufacturing corporations comprise ninety percent of the nation's manufacturing enterprises. If small manufacturing corporations liquidate rather than transfer ownership, the chances that the corporations will be replaced by other successful small corporations are decreased. As a result, there will be fewer small manufacturers and the larger more centralized manufacturers will increase their production to meet the demands of the marketplace. Greater centralization of business is adverse to the long held American notion that the small business represents independence, freedom and perseverance. . . .

. . . [We] . . . perceive other legitimate policy considerations for refusing to expand such liability. Extending liability to the corporate successor is not consistent with at least one major premise of strict liability, which is to place responsibility for a defective product on the manufacturer who placed that product into commerce. The corporate successor has not created the risk, and only remotely benefits from the product. The successor has not invited usage of the product or implied its safety. Since the successor was never in a position to eliminate the risk, a major purpose of strict liability in modifying a manufacturer's behavior is also lost.

Case dismissed.

REVIEW QUESTIONS

1. Identify the terms in column A by matching each with the appropriate statement in column B.

A		B	
1. Consolidation		a.	A merger in which the acquired corporation previously competed with its acquirer.
2. Merger		b.	By what authority.
3. Horizontal merger		c.	A merger between two firms that have nothing in common.
4. Vertical merger		d.	One corporation absorbs another.
5. Conglomerate merger		e.	A technique for valuing the stock of a dissenting shareholder.
6. Quo warranto		f.	Uniting two corporations into a new third one.
7. Weighted average method		g.	A merger between a supplier and one of its customers.

2. Mondati owned 50 percent of the stock of a corporation. He seized a corporate opportunity for himself. As president, he failed to hold annual meetings and refused to allow the other shareholders to take part in the corporation. They petitioned the court to dissolve the corporation. With what result? Why?

3. A corporation filed its notice of intent to dissolve with the secretary of state of the state of incorporation. It failed to give notice of dissolution to the local tax collector. Suit was filed 6 years later against the directors to collect the unpaid corporate property taxes. The law provided that suits against corporations survive for 2 years after dissolution. With what result? Why?

4. In 1975, plaintiff Jones was injured while operating a punch press manufactured by Johnson Machine & Press Company (Johnson) in 1955. In 1956, Johnson transferred all its liabilities and assets to the defendant Amsted, who continued manufacturing the Johnson Press line of products. Amsted expressly disclaimed the assumption of liability for claims arising out of defects in products manufactured by its predecessor. Is the defendant liable? Why?

5. Morejon was injured in a laundromat owned and operated by Washwell, Inc., which was later dissolved. At the time of the injury, Rebozo was an officer, director, and sole stockholder of Washwell. Morejon filed suit against Washwell prior to its dissolution and recovered a judgment in the amount of $150,000, of which $50,000 remained unpaid by insurance. Morejon then brought suit against Rebozo individually. With what result? Why?

6. Bob and David, father and son, entered into an agreement whereby each was 50 percent stockholder of a close corporation operating a luncheonette. The agreement provided that the death of either party would constitute an automatic option to the survivor to purchase, at book value, the shares of stock of the deceased. Upon Bob's death, his daughter Ann (David's sister and administratrix of Bob's estate) refused to sell for the value shown on the books. Having created a deadlock in management, Ann then petitioned for dissolution. Should it be granted? Why?

7. The Paper Corporation breached a contract with Yates. A short while later, Paper merged with the Towel Corporation to form the Paper Towel Corporation. Can Yates collect damages from Paper Towel? Why?

8. Adams, the owner of all capital stock of the Gazette Corporation, a newspaper business, sold all his shares to Burr and promised to serve as adviser to the newspaper for a period of 5 years in return for an annual salary of $20,000. After 3 years, Burr petitioned for dissolution, which was obtained. Does Adams have a right to collect the balance of the salary from the corporation? Explain.

9. Pauline, the past president of a dissolved corporation, brought suit against two shareholders of the corporation to recover the amount of her unpaid salary. The state statute provided that the shareholders are personally liable for unpaid salaries and wages of employees and laborers in an amount equal to the value of the stock owned by them. The stockholders contend that the statute is not applicable to the chief executive officer, who had complete control of the corporation. Should Pauline succeed? Why?

10. David was president of Music, Inc. He owned 53 percent of the common stock. David received a salary of $10,000 per year and bonuses of $7,000 per year. The corporation had a net worth of $100,000 and sales of $245,000. The net profit of the company had been under $2,000 each year, and dividends were either small or nonexistent. Minority shareholders brought suit to compel dissolution of the corporation on the ground of waste, alleging that the waste occurred in the payment of bonuses to David. Should the company be dissolved? Why?

11. The initial incorporation agreement provided that George would manage the corporation. The majority shareholders discharged him, and he brought suit to dissolve the corporation on the ground of oppression. With what result? Why?

12. Dissenting shareholders to a merger filed a suit for damages against the merging corporations and their directors. They alleged breach of fiduciary duties, fraud, and conspiracy to violate the securities laws. The defendants moved to dismiss, contending that the only remedy available to the plaintiffs was to be paid the fair value of their shares. With what result? Why?

13. A corporation brought suit to fix the value of the shares of stock belonging to dissenting shareholders. The shareholders asked the court to declare the merger illegal as an attempt to freeze out the dissenters. May the court block the merger? Why?

14. The plaintiff obtained a judgment against a corporation. Williams was the sole shareholder of the corporation. After the judgment was obtained, Williams caused the corporation to be dissolved. He paid off all the debts of the corporation except the plaintiff's judgment and kept all the corporate assets. The plaintiff seeks to collect the judgment from Williams personally. With what result? Why?

45 THE CONSTITUTION AND BUSINESS

The Constitution of the United States not only provides the foundation for our form of government, but also contains numerous provisions that have a direct impact upon the legal environment in which business operates. Article I establishes the legislative branch of government, and Section 8 of Article I grants Congress numerous powers, including the power to tax and the power to regulate commerce. Article IV covers the relationship between the states and, in effect, prevents a state from becoming an area of economic isolation. Article VI contains the supremacy clause, which makes federal laws supreme over state laws when the two are in conflict. The supremacy clause frequently comes into play when states attempt to regulate a business activity that is also regulated by the federal government. Finally, the protections of the Bill of Rights generally apply to business as well as to private individuals. This chapter will discuss some of the more important constitutional concepts as they relate to business.

1. The Supremacy Clause

Article VI states in part: "This Constitution, and the Laws of the United States which shall be made in pursuance thereof . . . shall be the supreme Law of the Land. . . ." This guarantees federal supremacy, even though the states created the federal government. The effect of this clause is to make the federal law enforceable and the state law unenforceable if the two are in irreconcilable conflict. It also prevents state governments from defeating a national policy by enacting state laws intended to thwart such policies.[1] Federal laws often preempt state laws, in which case the state laws are unconstitutional under the supremacy clause.

2. The Contract Clause

Section 10 of Article I of the United States Constitution provides in part that no state shall pass any law impairing the obligation of contracts. This provision has no application to the federal government, which, in fact, frequently enacts laws and adopts regulations that affect existing contracts. The Department of Agriculture from time to time embargoes grain sales to foreign countries, usually as a result of problems in foreign affairs.

The limitation on state action impairing contracts has not been given a literal application. As a result of judicial interpretation, some state laws that affect existing contracts have been approved, especially when the law is passed to deal with a specific emergency situation. On the other hand, this constitutional provision does limit the alternatives available to state government and prevents the enactment of legislation that changes vested contract rights.

3. The Taxing Power

The taxing power is used by government to raise revenue to defray its expenses. It apportions the cost of government among those who receive its benefits. The taxing power in the broad sense includes all charges and burdens imposed by government upon persons or property for the use and support of government.

Taxes are paid by those able to do so, in order that all persons may share in the general benefits of government. Property can be taxed without an obvious personal benefit to the property owner. The theory supporting taxation is that since governmental functions are a necessity, the government has the right to compel persons and property within its jurisdiction to defray the costs of these functions. The payment of taxes gives no right to a taxpayer. The privilege of enjoying the protection and services of government is not based on taxes paid. As a matter of fact, many examples illustrate that those who receive the most from the government pay the least taxes.

The power of taxation is exercised by the legislative branch of the government. The only limitations on its exercise are found in federal and state constitutions. The fact that a tax may destroy a business or the value of property is no basis for a judicial determination that the tax is unconstitutional. The court must find that the tax violates some specific provision of the Constitution before the tax can be held invalid. The decision as to the wisdom or propriety of the tax is left to the legislature.

The taxing power is used to accomplish many goals other than raising revenue. Taxation is a very important form of regulation. Tax policy is a major

---

[1] Southland Corp. v. Keating, p. 1025.

ingredient in the efforts of government to regulate the economy. Depreciation allowances have been accelerated from time to time to bolster the economy by making additional cash available for business investment. The gasoline tax has been substantially increased in order to raise the price of gasoline and reduce consumption.

Tax laws are also used by the federal government to equalize competition among different businesses. The gasoline tax is an important part of the equalization of costs between truckers and other forms of transportation. The taxing power has been used to encourage uniform legislation among the states. States were encouraged to adopt unemployment compensation taxes by a federal law that gave a 90 percent credit on the federal tax for taxes paid to states.

The federal taxing power is also used to implement social policies. The federal government pays money to the states to encourage certain activities such as education, road building, and slum clearance. Persons in one part of the country may pay for social improvements in another as a direct result of the exercise of the taxing and spending powers of the federal government. An examination of the implementation policies of the federal government will reveal that many of them are tied directly to taxation.

Few questions are raised today concerning the *validity* of a federally imposed tax. The Sixteenth Amendment to the Constitution and the broad scope of the federal taxing power, which has been approved by the courts, eliminates most such issues. Of course, there is a considerable amount of litigation involving the *interpretation* and *application* of the federal tax laws and regulations. Great deference is given to the position taken by the commissioner of Internal Revenue in such cases. Courts tend to hold that federal taxing laws are valid unless there is some clear constitutional infirmity.

4. The Privileges and Immunities Clause

Section 2 of Article IV of the U.S. Constitution contains the so-called privileges and immunities clause, providing that "the Citizens of each State shall be entitled to all Privileges and Immunities of Citizens in the several States." Because of similar language in the Fourteenth Amendment, this clause has not often been involved in litigation; nevertheless, it has played a role in assuring equality of treatment for all citizens.

The clause places the citizens of each state on the same footing as citizens of other states so far as the advantages of citizenship are concerned. It relieves them from the disabilities of alienage in other states: states cannot discriminate against nonresidents. In Maryland, out-of-state practitioners were required to take the full bar examination unless they had actively practiced for 5 of the preceding 7 years in the jurisdiction of their admission. That rule was held to violate Article IV's privileges and immunities clause. It gives all persons the right of free entry into, and exit from, other states. It ensures everyone of the same freedom in the acquisition and enjoyment of property and in the pursuit of happiness. No provision in the Constitution has tended more strongly to constitute the citizens of the United States one people, because it prevents a state from discriminating against citizens of other states in favor of its own.

The privileges and immunities clause does not prevent state citizenship from being used to distinguish among persons. A state may require citizenship for voting, holding office, and paying resident tuition to a state university. Only those privileges and immunities bearing upon the vitality of the nation as a single entity must be granted equally to all citizens—resident and nonresident.

5. In General

THE
COMMERCE
CLAUSE

The power of the federal government to regulate business activity is found in the so-called commerce clause of the Constitution, which states: "Congress shall have power . . . to regulate Commerce with foreign Nations, and among the several States, and with the Indian Tribes. . . ." This grant of three-pronged power has been broadly interpreted to give the federal government considerable power to regulate business, to prescribe the rules by which commerce is conducted. Among the three regulatory powers—foreign, interstate, and Indian—commerce with the Indian tribes is relatively unimportant, although Congress is responsible for the laws applicable to Indian reservations.

6. Foreign Commerce

The power to regulate foreign commerce is vested exclusively in the federal government and extends to all aspects of foreign trade. State and local governments may not regulate foreign commerce, although they do sometimes attempt directly or indirectly to regulate imports and exports to some degree. Such attempts are unconstitutional. State or local laws regulating or interfering with federal regulation of commerce with foreign nations are invalid as violations of the commerce and supremacy clauses.

The right to import includes the right to sell the goods imported. States may not prohibit the sale of imported goods any more than they can prohibit their import. The exclusive federal power over imported goods continues until the goods are mingled with, and become a part of, the general property of the country; so that for all purposes, the imported product is given similar treatment with other property. In most cases, imported goods become a part of internal commerce when the importer or wholesaler disposes of them to retail dealers in local communities. If a state or local law tends to continue to distinguish the goods by their point of origin, the foreign commerce aspect continues, and the law is invalid. One city required that all retail goods originating behind the Iron Curtain be so labeled. The law was unconstitutional.

7. Interstate Commerce

The key language of the commerce clause is the phrase "among the several States." This language has been construed to give Congress power to enact laws covering any business activity in interstate commerce and any intrastate business activity that has a substantial effect—negative or positive—on interstate commerce.[2] The effect of any individual business on interstate commerce need not be substantial if the cumulative effect of all similar businesses is substantial. In recent years this power has been used in a variety of ways. One of the more important pieces of legislation was the public accommodation provisions of the Civil Rights Act of 1964. Activities such as gambling, discrimination in the sale or rental of housing, and loan sharking have been regulated under the commerce clause.

While the power of Congress to regulate an infinite variety of business activities by use of the commerce clause is quite broad, it is subject to some limitations. These limitations are found in other provisions of the Constitution, such as the Sixth Amendment's guarantee of a right to a trial by jury and the Fifth Amendment's Due Process Clause.

8. The Commerce Clause and the States' Police Power

In granting Congress power over commerce, the Constitution did not expressly exclude the states from exercising authority over commerce. The Supreme Court held that the nature of the commerce power did not by *implication* prohibit state action and that some state power over commerce is compatible with the federal power. Because of the commerce clause, nevertheless, state powers over commerce are definitely limited.

State and local governments use their police power to enact laws to promote the public health, safety, morals, and general welfare. Of necessity, such laws frequently result in the regulation of business activity. The commerce clause and the supremacy clause impose several restrictions on the states' use of police power as it affects business.

The first restriction is that state and local governments cannot enact laws on subjects that are considered to be exclusively federal. A state could not pass a law establishing the width of a railroad track or a law concerning air traffic, because those regulations require national uniformity. For this reason, any state law concerning a subject that is exclusively under the federal government's jurisdiction is unconstitutional under the commerce clause and supremacy clause. This is true even if there is no federal law on the subject.

The second limitation concerns subject matters over which the federal government has taken exclusive jurisdiction by enacting legislation. Federal laws that assert exclusive jurisdiction over a subject are said to preempt the field. Preemption may result from express language or by comprehensive regulation showing an intent by Congress to exercise exclusive dominion over the subject matter. When a federal statute has preempted the field, *any* state or local law pertaining to the same subject matter is unconstitutional, and the state regulation is void.

Not every federal regulatory statute preempts the field. When a federal law does not preempt the field and the subject matter is not exclusively federal, state regulation under the police power is permitted. When a state law is inconsistent or

---

[2] Perez v. United States, p. 1026.

irreconcilably in conflict with a federal statute, it is unconstitutional and void because of the supremacy clause that makes federal laws supreme over state laws. Moreover, state laws are unconstitutional under the commerce clause if they discriminate against interstate commerce or impose an undue burden on it.

The commerce clause does not prohibit the imposition of burdens on interstate commerce—only the imposition of undue burdens.[3] A state law that required train locomotives to have spark arrestors did not impose an undue burden on interstate commerce when the trains traveled frequently through heavy forests. Every regulatory measure is a burden to some degree. If a local law furthers a legitimate public interest, it is valid unless the burden on interstate activities is undue. A state law limiting the lengths of trucks imposed an undue burden on interstate commerce.

We have pointed out that the commerce clause prohibits discrimination against interstate commerce in favor of intrastate commerce. On the other hand, state and local governments frequently attempt by legislation to aid local business in its competition with interstate business. The commerce clause requires that all taxes and regulations be the same for local businesses as for businesses engaged in interstate commerce. While interstate commerce is required to pay its fair share of all taxes, it must be placed on a plane of equality with local trade or commerce. A state may not place itself in a position of economic isolation from other states.

Every tax is to some extent regulatory. The commerce clause also imposes limitations on the taxing power of state and local governments. Although the issues involved are varied and complex, it may be said as a general rule that a state may impose a tax such as an income tax or a property tax on a business engaged in interstate commerce, provided that the tax is *apportioned* by some reasonable formula to local activities within the state and does not discriminate against interstate commerce in favor of intrastate commerce. There must be a connection between the tax and the local enterprise being taxed *(nexus),* or the tax will violate the commerce clause. The concepts of nexus and apportionment are used to ensure that interstate commerce pays its fair share for benefits received from the state.

9. General Principles

The first 10 amendments to the Constitution of the United States, often referred to as the Bill of Rights, have numerous provisions that directly affect business and economic activity, as well as on all other aspects of our daily lives.

Before examining some of the business implications of the Bill of Rights, we should keep in mind 3 of their important characteristics. First of all, constitutional rights are not absolutes. They are limited. Mr. Justice Black, dissenting in *Tinker* v. *Des Moines Independent Community School Dist.,* 89 S.Ct. 733 (1969), noted this fact.

> The truth is that a teacher of kindergarten, grammar school, or high school pupils no more carries into a school with him a complete right to freedom of speech and expression than an anti-Catholic or anti-Semitic carries with

---

[3] Kassel v. Consolidated Freightways Corp., etc., p. 1028.

him a complete freedom of speech and religion into a Catholic church or Jewish synagogue. Nor does a person carry with him into the United States Senate or House, or to the Supreme Court, or any other court, a complete constitutional right to go into those places contrary to their rules and speak his mind on any subject he pleases. It is a myth to say that any person has a constitutional right to say what he pleases, where he pleases, and when he pleases.

The same sense of limitation is applicable to all basic constitutional protections.

Second, the limit of any basic constitutional guarantee depends upon the nature of the competing public policy. In constitutional cases, courts are required to weigh and strike a balance between some goal or policy of society and the constitutional protection involved. They may weigh an ethical standard of a profession and balance it against freedom of speech. That is what they did when they were required to decide if professional persons such as lawyers should be allowed to advertise, notwithstanding codes of professional ethics prohibiting advertising. Similarly, the free exercise of religious beliefs is often in conflict with public policy or law enacted to achieve some goal of society.

Finally, constitutional rights vary from time to time. A doctrine known as constitutional relativity means that the Constitution is interpreted in light of current facts and problems. This doctrine is especially applicable to the Bill of Rights, which changes to meet current conditions and emergencies such as war or civil strife.

10. The First Amendment

The First Amendment gives us five basic freedoms: (1) freedom of religion, (2) freedom of speech, (3) freedom of the press, (4) freedom of assembly, and (5) the right to petition the government for a redress of grievances.

Freedom of religion becomes a business issue when Sunday closing laws are enacted for religious purposes. If the laws are based on economic considerations they may be valid, providing there are reasonable exceptions for necessary public services. Another example of freedom of religion restricts unions. It has been held that the laws relating to unionization are not applicable to, nor do they protect, parochial school teachers. If the NLRB were to conduct a union certification election for parochial teachers, it would constitute a violation of the doctrine of separation between church and state.

The publishing business is the only organized private business that is given explicit constitutional protection. Freedom of the press as guaranteed by the First Amendment authorizes a private business to make an organized scrutiny of government. Yet, freedom of the press is not absolute. The press is not free to print anything it chooses, without liability. Rather, freedom of the press is usually construed to prohibit prior restraints on publication. If the press publishes that which is improper, mischievous, illegal, or libelous, it has liability for doing so. This liability may be either criminal or civil for damages. Moreover, freedom of the press is not violated when a government agency (FCC) censors obscene words on TV.

Freedom of speech or expression covers verbal and written communications and conduct or actions that are considered symbolic speech. Clearly, it does not extend to obscenity and pornography; the only issue is whether or not the matters are, in fact, obscene or pornographic. The First Amendment not only prohibits prior restraint, it also guards against fear of punishment for the exercise of the right to free speech. Its protection benefits corporations[4] as well as individuals and unions. The right to picket peacefully for lawful reasons is well recognized.

Historically, *commercial speech* was considered unprotected, but that view is no longer accepted, and those conducting businesses frequently assert their rights of free speech. The protection extends to all businesses, including the professions. Doctors and lawyers are permitted to advertise, but limitations may be imposed. But commercial speech is not protected to the same extent as noncommercial speech. The major requirement is that ads must be truthful and not misleading.

The First Amendment freedoms include the right to assemble and associate and the right to petition the government for a redress of grievances. The purpose of the guarantee of freedom of assembly and association is to prevent guilt by association. It is also designed to ensure privacy in one's association. It has been held that state law may not compel the disclosure of membership lists of a constitutionally valid association. Such a disclosure entails the likelihood of a substantial restraint upon the exercise of the members' rights to freedom of association. The protection extends to the social, legal, and economic benefits of membership in groups; it prevents a state from denying a Communist a license to practice law.

In addition to these enumerated protections, the First Amendment has been interpreted to include the right of privacy and the right to knowledge. Freedom of expression includes freedom of inquiry, freedom of thought, and the freedom to teach. Moreover, the right of association surpasses the right to attend a meeting. It includes the right to express an attitude or philosophy by group membership. Thus, the specifics of the Bill of Rights have penumbras or additional implied rights, such as the right of privacy.

11. The Fourth Amendment

The Fourth Amendment protects individuals and corporations from unreasonable searches and seizures. Its primary object is to protect persons from unwarranted intrusions into their individual privacy. While Fourth Amendment issues usually arise in criminal cases, the protection of the Fourth Amendment extends to civil matters as well. Courts have held that building inspectors do not have the right to inspect for building code violations without a warrant if the owner of the premises objects. Likewise, OSHA inspections cannot be conducted without a search warrant if the business objects. The Occupational Safety and Health Administration (OSHA) has the responsibility to enforce laws requiring that all employees have a safe and healthy place to work. Reports written for one purpose cannot be used for another without running afoul of the Fourth

---

[4] Consolidated Edison Co. v. Public Service Com'n., p. 1029.

Amendment. The Securities and Exchange Commission, having obtained confidential reports in the course of its function, could not use those reports to establish a violation of other federal laws.

12. The Fifth Amendment

The Fifth Amendment, best known for its protection against compulsory self-incrimination, goes further and includes other protections. Specifically, it (1) requires indictment by a grand jury for a capital offense or infamous crime, (2) prohibits double jeopardy, (3) requires just compensation in eminent domain proceedings, and (4) contains a due process clause. Most of these protections are for criminal cases, which are beyond the scope of this text; however, some aspects have special impact for business.

The requirement of just compensation in eminent domain proceedings is very important to many businesses, especially utilities. Public utilities have the power to acquire private property by condemnation and may be required to pay just compensation. Or the property owned by a business may be taken for public purpose by government bodies. The Fifth Amendment requires just compensation in such cases. This is a question of fact for a jury if the property owner and the condemning governmental unit cannot agree on a fair market value of the property taken.

The Fifth Amendment protects life, liberty, and property from deprivation by the federal government without due process of law. The Fourteenth Amendment contains an identical provision that is applicable to the states. While due process is difficult to define, it basically amounts to "fundamental fairness." Since the interpretations of the due process clauses of the Fifth and Fourteenth Amendments are, for all practical purposes, identical, the discussion of due process under the Fourteenth Amendment (next section) will also illustrate due process under the Fifth Amendment.

The protection against compulsory self-incrimination does not apply to corporations. Corporations are citizens for most purposes except this one. Corporate officials do retain their personal privilege against compulsory self-incrimination and cannot be required to testify; but they may be required to deliver all corporate records subpoenaed for evidentiary purposes, since corporations are not protected by the privilege.

13. The Fourteenth Amendment

The Fourteenth Amendment contains three clauses commonly referred to as (1) the privileges and immunities clause, (2) the due process clause, and (3) the equal protection clause. The exact language is as follows:

> No State shall make or enforce any law which shall abridge the privileges or immunities of citizens of the United States; nor shall any State deprive any person of life, liberty or property, without due process of law, nor deny to any person within its jurisdiction the equal protection of the laws.

The language of the original 10 amendments makes them applicable to the federal government, but the Fourteenth Amendment's most significant role has been to make most of the provisions of the Bill of Rights applicable to the states. The courts, by judicial interpretation, have held that the due process clause of the Fourteenth Amendment "incorporates" or "carries over" the Bill of Rights and makes its provisions applicable to the states.

The term *due process of law* is used to describe fundamental principles of liberty and justice. Simply stated, due process means that *government* may not act in a manner that is arbitrary, capricious, or unreasonable. The clause does not prevent private individuals or corporations, including public utilities, from acting in an arbitrary or unreasonable manner.

The issues in due process cases are usually divided into questions of *procedural due process* and *substantive due process.* Substantive due process issues arise when property or other rights are directly affected by governmental action. Procedural due process cases often are concerned with whether proper notice has been given and a proper hearing has been conducted. Such cases frequently involve procedures established by state statute.

Early in this century, many attempts at economic regulation were held to be violations of substantive due process. The judicial attitude toward economic regulation changed in midcentury, and now due process challenges to economic regulation fall on deaf ears. Substantive due process is important in cases involving individual liberties. Today there is a presumption of constitutionality of economic legislation, but legislation that tends to restrict fundamental rights is suspect and subject to more exacting judicial scrutiny under the Fourteenth Amendment. This double standard is often justified because of the crucial importance of these basic freedoms, which must be protected by the judiciary from the "vicissitudes" of political action.

The purpose of the equal protection clause is to prevent "invidious" discrimination.[5] In determining whether or not a statutory classification is "invidious," the courts use two different tests depending on the factual situation. First, the strict judicial scrutiny test is used when a legislative classification interferes with the exercise of a fundamental right or operates to the peculiar disadvantage of a suspect class. A suspect class is one burdened with disabilities or subjected to a history of unequal treatment. Blacks and Chicanos have been held to be members of a suspect class. When a suspect class is involved, the state must prove that its statutory classifications are based upon a compelling state interest, or the classifications will be held to constitute a denial of equal protection. Classifications subject to this test are in effect presumed to be unconstitutional, and the state must convince the court that the classification is fair, reasonable, and necessary to accomplish the objective of the legislation.

The second test in equal protection cases is known as the rational basis standard. Classifications to which the rational basis standard are applied are presumed to be valid. It is only when there is no rational basis for the classification

---

[5] Vil. of Arlington Hts. v. Metro. Housing Dev., p. 1031.

that it is unconstitutional under the equal protection clause. A classification judged by this standard must be rationally related to the state's legitimate objectives. The classification may be imperfect and may not be the best to accomplish the purpose. Yet it is still constitutional if there is a rational basis for the classification. A state statute that allowed females to purchase alcoholic beverages at 18 while requiring males to be 21 was held to be unconstitutional because the age classification was not substantially related to the achievement of state objectives.

SUMMARY

CONSTITUTIONAL CLAUSES

Supremacy clause	1. This clause guarantees that the Constitution will prevail over all laws, if there is a conflict in interpretation and application. Federal statutes prevail over state statutes if there is a conflict.
	2. This clause is the reason for federal law preempting an area of business regulation.
Contract clause	1. This clause prohibits states from passing laws that impair existing contractual relationships.
	2. This clause does not apply to the federal government.
	3. This clause is not absolute. Through judicial interpretation, state laws that impair existing contract rights in a reasonable manner are not invalid under the contract clause.
Taxing power	1. This power is exercised by the legislative branch.
	2. A tax is valid as long as it does not violate a constitutional provision.
	3. This power can be used to accomplish many purposes. For example, the tax laws may be used to increase the government's revenue. Tax laws also may be a form of regulation of the economy. Tax laws are used to increase competition among different businesses and to implement other social policies.

Privileges and immunities clause	1. This clause prohibits states from discriminating against out-of-state residents.
	2. This clause has helped establish citizens of the United States as one people.
	3. In matters of importance to states, this clause does not prohibit distinctions between in-state and out-of-state residents. Such matters include requirements to vote, to hold office, and to be entitled to lower college tuitions.

THE COMMERCE CLAUSE

In general	1. The power of the federal government to regulate business activities is based on this clause.
	2. The federal government has the power to regulate "commerce with foreign nations, and among the several states, and with the Indian Tribes."
Foreign commerce	1. Regulation of commerce with foreign nations is reserved exclusively for the federal government.
	2. State laws that attempt to regulate foreign commerce are invalid as being in violation of the commerce clause and supremacy clause.
Interstate commerce	1. The commerce clause has been interpreted to give almost unlimited power to the federal government in its regulation of businesses.
	2. The federal government can regulate any business which is engaged in or which substantially affects interstate commerce.
Commerce clause and the states' police power	1. The authority of state and local governments to regulate businesses is based on the police power.
	2. The police power allows regulations directed to promote the public health, safety, morals, and general welfare.
	3. The commerce clause in conjunction with the supremacy clause has been interpreted to restrict the exercise of the states' police power.

4. Some areas of regulation are reserved exclusively for the federal government. Other regulatory areas have been preempted by federal statutes. In either of these areas, exercise of the states' police power is unconstitutional.

5. When a federal law does not preempt the area of regulation or when there is no federal law at all, states may have laws that regulate business activities. These state laws must not create an undue burden or discriminate against business activities in interstate commerce.

THE BILL OF RIGHTS AND BUSINESS

General principles

1. The Bill of Rights consists of the first 10 amendments to the United States Constitution.

2. These constitutional rights are not absolute; they are subject to interpretation based on competing social policies, and they vary in meaning from time to time.

The First Amendment

1. This amendment affects business by creating five guarantees or freedoms.

2. These freedoms include: (a) the freedom of religion; (b) the freedom of speech; (c) the freedom of the press; (d) the freedom of assembly; and (e) the freedom to petition the government for a redress of grievances.

The Fourth Amendment

1. This amendment protects individuals and business organizations from unreasonable searches and seizures.

2. In essence, this constitutional right protects against unwarranted interference into one's privacy.

3. The warrant requirement applies to civil inspections as well as criminal investigations.

The Fifth Amendment

1. This amendment includes five more vital constitutional protections.

2. These protections include: (a) the right to a grand jury indictment; (b) the protection against double jeopardy; (c)

the protection against self-incrimination; (d) the right to be compensated for property taken by the government; and (e) the right to due process.

The Fourteenth Amendment

1. Whereas the Bill of Rights protects individuals and business organizations from actions by the federal government, this amendment is directed toward regulating state governments.

2. Because of this amendment, state and local governments must ensure individuals' and business organizations' right to (a) due process and (b) equal protection.

3. Through the due process clause in this amendment, the courts have made state and local governments subject to the constitutional rights contained in the Bill of Rights.

4. Due process has been subdivided into procedural and substantive due process.

5. Courts apply either the strict judicial scrutiny test or the rational basis test to cases brought under the equal protection clause. The test used depends on the type of case.

CASES

Southland Corp. v. Keating
104 S.Ct. 852 (1984)

BURGER, C.J. . . . We noted probable jurisdiction to consider whether the California Franchise Investment Law, which invalidates certain arbitration agreements covered by the Federal Arbitration Act, violates the Supremacy Clause. . . .

Appellant The Southland Corporation is the owner and franchisor of 7-Eleven convenience stores. Southland's standard franchise agreement provides each franchisee with a license to use certain registered trademarks, a lease or sublease of a convenience store owned or leased by Southland, inventory financing, and assistance in advertising and merchandising. The franchisees operate the

stores, supply bookkeeping data, and pay Southland a fixed percentage of gross profits. The franchise agreement also contains the following provision requiring arbitration:

> Any controversy or claim arising out of or relating to this Agreement or the breach thereof shall be settled by arbitration in accordance with the Rules of the American Arbitration Association . . . and judgment upon any award rendered by the arbitrator may be entered in any court having jurisdiction thereof.

Appellees are 7-Eleven franchisees. Between September 1975 and January 1977, several appellees filed individual actions against Southland in California Superior Court alleging, among other things, fraud, oral misrepresentation, breach of contract, breach of fiduciary duty, and violation of the disclosure requirements of the California Franchise Investment Law. Southland's answer . . . included the affirmative defense of failure to arbitrate, . . .

The California Court of Appeal . . . interpreted the arbitration clause to require arbitration of all claims asserted under the Franchise Investment Law, and construed the Franchise Investment Law not to invalidate such agreements to arbitrate. Alternatively, the court concluded that if the Franchise Investment Law rendered arbitration agreements involving commerce unenforceable, it would conflict with §2 of the Federal Arbitration Act and therefore be invalid under the Supremacy Clause. . . . The California Supreme Court interpreted the Franchise Investment Law to require judicial consideration of claims brought under that statute and concluded that the California statute did not contravene the federal Act. . . .

The California Franchise Investment Law provides: "Any condition, stipulation or provision purporting to bind any person acquiring any franchise to waive compliance with any provision of this law or any rule or order hereunder is void." The California Supreme Court interpreted this statute to require judicial consideration of claims brought under the State statute and accordingly refused to enforce the parties contract to arbitrate such claims. So interpreted, the California Franchise Investment Law directly conflicts with §2 of the Federal Arbitration Act and violates the Supremacy Clause.

In enacting §2 of the federal Act, Congress declared a national policy favoring arbitration and withdrew the power of the states to require a judicial forum for the resolution of claims which the contracting parties agreed to resolve by arbitration. . . .

The Federal Arbitration Act rests on the authority of Congress to enact substantive rules under the Commerce Clause. . . . The Arbitration Act creates a body of federal substantive law (which is) . . . applicable in state and federal courts. . . . The problems Congress faced were . . . twofold: the old common law hostility toward arbitration, and the failure of state arbitration statutes to mandate enforcement of arbitration agreements. To confine the scope of the Act to arbitrations sought to be enforced in federal courts would frustrate what we believe Congress intended to be a broad enactment appropriate in scope to meet the large problems Congress was addressing. . . .

We are unwilling to attribute to Congress the intent, in drawing on the comprehensive powers of the Commerce Clause, to create a right to enforce an arbitration contract and yet make the right dependent for its enforcement on the particular forum in which it is asserted. And since the overwhelming proportion of all civil litigation in this country is in the state courts, we cannot believe Congress intended to limit the Arbitration Act to disputes subject only to *federal* court jurisdiction. Such an interpretation would frustrate Congressional intent to place an arbitration agreement upon the same footing as other contracts, where it belongs.

In creating a substantive rule applicable in state as well as federal courts, Congress intended to foreclose state legislative attempts to undercut the enforceability of arbitration agreements. We hold that §31512 of the California Franchise Investment Law violates the Supremacy Clause. . . .

Reversed.

Perez v. United States
91 S.Ct. 1357 (1971)

The defendant was convicted of violating the "loan sharking" provisions of the Federal Consumer Credit Protection Act. It was proved beyond any doubt that the defendant, as a part of organized crime, had used extortion in collecting illegal rates of interest. He challenged the constitutionality of the statute on the ground that Congress has no power to control the local activity of loan sharking.

DOUGLAS, J. . . . The Commerce Clause reaches in the main three categories of problems. First, the use of channels of interstate or foreign commerce which Congress deems are being misused, as for example, the shipment of stolen goods or of persons who have been kidnapped. Second, protection of the instrumentalities of interstate commerce, as for example, the destruction of an aircraft, or persons or things in commerce, as for example, thefts from interstate shipments. Third, those activities affecting commerce. It is with this last category that we are here concerned. . . .

Chief Justice Stone wrote for a unanimous Court in 1942 that Congress could provide for the regulation of the price of intrastate milk, the sale of which, in competition with interstate milk, affects the price structure and federal regulation of the latter. The commerce power, he said, "extends to those activities intrastate which so affect interstate commerce, or the exertion of the power of Congress over it, as to make regulation of them an appropriate means to the attainment of a legitimate end, the effective execution of the granted power to regulate interstate commerce."

Wickard v. Filburn, 317 U.S. 111, soon followed in which a unanimous Court held that wheat grown wholly for home consumption was constitutionally within the scope of federal regulation of wheat production because, though never marketed interstate, it supplied the need of the grower which otherwise would be satisfied by his purchases in the open market. We said:

> . . . even if appellee's activity be local and though it may not be regarded as commerce, it may still, whatever its nature, be reached by Congress if it exerts a substantial economic effect on interstate commerce, and this irrespective of whether such effect is what might at some earlier time have been defined as 'direct' or 'indirect.'

As pointed out in *United States v. Darby,* 312 U.S. 100, the decision sustaining an Act of Congress which prohibited the employment of workers in the production of goods "for interstate commerce" at other than prescribed wages and hours—*a class of activities*—was held properly regulated by Congress without proof that the particular intrastate activity against which a sanction was laid had an effect on commerce. . . .

That case is particularly relevant here because it involved a criminal prosecution, a unanimous Court

holding that the Act was "sufficiently definite to meet constitutional demands." Petitioner is clearly a *member of the class* which engages in "extortionate credit transactions" as defined by Congress and the description of that class has the required definiteness.

It was the "class of activities" test which we employed in *Heart of Atlanta Motel, Inc. v. United States,* 379 U.S. 241, to sustain an Act of Congress requiring hotel or motel accommodations for Negro guests. The Act declared that "any inn, hotel, motel, or other establishment which provides lodging to transient guests affects commerce *per se.*" That exercise of power under the Commerce Clause was sustained. . . . In a companion case, *Katzenbach v. McClung,* 379 U.S. 294, we ruled on the constitutionality of the restaurant provision of the same Civil Rights Act which regulated the restaurant "if . . . it serves or offers to serve interstate travelers or a substantial portion of the food which it serves . . . has moved in commerce." Apart from the effect on the flow of food in commerce to restaurants, we spoke of the restrictive effect of the exclusion of Negroes from restaurants on interstate travel by Negroes. In emphasis of our position that it was the *class of activities* regulated that was the measure, we acknowledged that Congress appropriately considered the "total incidence" of the practice on commerce.

Where the *class of activities* is regulated and that *class* is within the reach of federal power, the courts have no power "to excise, as trivial, individual instances" of the class.

Extortionate credit transactions, though purely intrastate, may in the judgment of Congress affect interstate commerce. In an analogous situation, Mr. Justice Holmes, speaking for a unanimous Court, said ". . . when it is necessary in order to prevent an evil to make the law embrace more than the precise thing to be prevented it may do so." . . .

In the setting of the present case there is a tie-in between local loan sharks and interstate crime. The findings by Congress are quite adequate on that ground. . . .

"Even where extortionate credit transactions are purely intrastate in character, they nevertheless directly affect interstate and foreign commerce." . . .

It appears . . . that loan sharking in its national setting is one way organized interstate crime holds its guns to the heads of the poor and the rich alike and syphons funds from numerous localities to finance its national operations.

Affirmed.

Kassel v. Consolidated Freightways Corp., etc.
101 S.Ct. 1309 (1981)

POWELL, J. The question is whether an Iowa statute that prohibits the use of certain large trucks within the State unconstitutionally burdens interstate commerce.

Respondent, Consolidated Freightways Corporation of Delaware (Consolidated), is one of the largest common carriers in the country. It offers service in 48 states. Among other routes, Consolidated carries commodities through Iowa on Interstate 80, the principal east-west route linking New York, Chicago, and the West Coast, and on Interstate 35, a major north-south route.

Consolidated mainly uses two kinds of trucks. One consists of a three-axle tractor pulling a 40-foot two-axle trailer. This unit, commonly called a single, or "semi" is 55 feet in length overall. Consolidated also uses a two-axle tractor pulling a single-axle trailer which, in turn, pulls a single-axle dolly and a second single-axle trailer. This combination, known as a double, or twin, is 65 feet long overall. Many trucking companies, including Consolidated, increasingly prefer to use doubles to ship certain kinds of commodities. Doubles have larger capacities, and the trailers can be detached and routed separately if necessary. Consolidated would like to use 65-foot doubles on many of its trips through Iowa.

The state of Iowa, however, by statute restricts the length of vehicles that may use its highways. Unlike all other states in the West and Midwest, Iowa generally prohibits the use of 65-foot doubles within its borders. Instead, most truck combinations are restricted to 55 feet in length. Doubles, mobile homes, trucks carrying vehicles such as tractors and other farm equipment, and singles hauling livestock, are permitted to be as long as 60 feet. . . .

Because of Iowa's statutory scheme, Consolidated cannot use its 65-foot doubles to move commodities through the state. Instead, the company must do one of four things: (i) use 55-foot singles; (ii) use 60-foot doubles; (iii) detach the trailers of a 65-foot and shuttle each through the State separately; or (iv) divert 65-foot doubles around Iowa.

Dissatisfied with these options, Consolidated filed this suit in the District court averring that Iowa's statutory scheme unconstitutionally burdens interstate commerce. Iowa defended the law as a reasonable safety measure enacted pursuant to its police power. The State asserted that 65-foot doubles are more dangerous than 55-foot singles and, in any event, that the law promotes safety and reduces road wear within the state by diverting much truck traffic to other states.

In a 14-day trial, both sides adduced evidence on safety, and on the burden on interstate commerce imposed by Iowa's law. On the question of safety, the District Court found that the "evidence clearly establishes that the twin is as safe as the semi." . . .

The District Court . . . concluded that the state law impermissibly burdened interstate commerce. . . . The Court of Appeals for the Eighth Circuit affirmed.

It is unnecessary to review in detail the evolution of the principles of Commerce Clause adjudication. The Clause is both a "Prolific source of national power and an equally prolific source of conflict with legislation of the state(s)." The Clause permits Congress to legislate when it perceives that the national welfare is not furthered by the independent actions of the States. It is now well established, also, that the Clause itself is a limitation upon state power even without congressional implementation. The Clause requires that some aspects of trade generally must remain free from interference by the States. When a state ventures excessively into the regulation of these aspects of commerce, it "trespasses upon national interests," and the courts will hold the state regulation invalid under the Clause alone.

The Commerce Clause does not, of course, invalidate all state restrictions on commerce. It has long been recognized that, "in the absence of conflicting legislation by Congress, there is a residuum of power in the state to make laws governing matters of local concern which nevertheless in some measure affect interstate commerce or even, to some extent regulate it." The extent of permissible state regulation is not always easy to measure. It may be said with confidence, however, that a state's power to regulate commerce is never greater than in matters traditionally of local concern. For example, regulations that touch upon safety—especially highway safety—are those that "the Court has been most reluctant to invalidate." Indeed, "if safety justifications are not illusory, the court will not second guess legislative judgment about their importance in comparison with related burdens on interstate commerce." Those who would challenge such bona fide safety regulations must overcome a "strong presumption of validity."

But the incantation of a purpose to promote the public health or safety does not insulate a state law from Commerce Clause attack. Regulations designed for that salutary purpose nevertheless may further the purpose so marginally, and interfere with commerce so substantially, as to be invalid under the Commerce Clause. . . .

Applying these general principles, we conclude that the Iowa truck-length limitations unconstitutionally burden interstate commerce. . . .

The state failed to present any persuasive evidence that 65-foot doubles are less safe than 55-foot singles. Moreover, Iowa's law is now out of step with the laws of all other midwestern and western states. Iowa thus substantially burdens the interstate flow of goods by truck. In the absence of congressional action to set uniform standards, some burdens associated with state safety regulations must be tolerated. But where, as here, the State's safety interest has been found to be illusory, and its regulations impair significantly the federal interest in efficient and safe interstate transportation, the state law cannot be harmonized with the Commerce Clause. . . .

Consolidated, meanwhile, demonstrated that Iowa's law substantially burdens interstate commerce. Trucking companies that wish to continue to use 65-foot doubles must route them around Iowa or detach the trailers of the doubles and ship them through separately. Alternatively, trucking companies must use the smaller 55-foot singles or 60-foot doubles permitted under Iowa law. Each of these options engenders inefficiency and added expense. The record shows that Iowa's law added about $12.6 million each year to the costs of trucking companies. Consolidated alone incurred about $2 million per year in increased costs. . . .

Because Iowa has imposed this burden without any significant countervailing safety interest, its statute violates the Commerce Clause. The judgment of the Court of Appeals is affirmed.

Affirmed.

Consol. Edison Co. v. Public Service Com'n
100 S.Ct. 2326 (1980)

POWELL, J. . . . The question in this case is whether the First Amendment, as incorporated by the Fourteenth Amendment, is violated by an order of the Public Service Commission of the State of New York that prohibits the inclusion in monthly electric bills of inserts discussing controversial issues of public policy.

The Consolidated Edison Company of New York, . . . placed written material entitled "Independence Is Still a Goal, and Nuclear Power Is Needed To Win The Battle" in its January 1976 billing envelope. The bill insert stated Consolidated Edison's views on "the benefits of nuclear power," saying that they "far outweigh any potential risk" and that nuclear power plants are safe, economical, and clean. The utility also contended that increased use of nuclear energy would further this country's independence from foreign energy sources.

[In 1977 the Public Service Commission of the State of New York issued an order which] . . . prohibited "utilities from using bill inserts to discuss political matters, including the desirability of future development of nuclear power." . . . The Commission concluded that Consolidated Edison customers who receive bills containing inserts are a captive audience of diverse views who should not be subjected to the utility's beliefs. Accordingly, the Commission barred utility companies from including bill inserts that express "their opinions or viewpoints on controversial issues of public policy."

The Commission did not, however, bar utilities from sending bill inserts discussing topics that are not "controversial issues of public policy." . . .

Consolidated Edison sought review of the Commission's order in the New York state courts. . . . The Court of Appeals held that the order did not violate the Constitution because it was a valid time, place, and manner regulation designed to protect the privacy of Consolidated Edison's customers. . . .

The First and Fourteenth Amendments guarantee that no State shall abridge the freedom of speech. Freedom of speech is indispensable to the discovery and spread of political truth and the best test of truth is the power of the thought to get itself accepted in the competition of the market. The First and Fourteenth Amendments remove governmental restraints from the arena of public discussion, putting the decision as to what views shall be voiced largely into the hands of each of us, in the hope that use of such freedom will ultimately produce a more capable citizenry and more perfect polity.

This Court has emphasized that the First Amendment embraces at the least the liberty to discuss publicly and truthfully all matters of public concern. In the mailing that triggered the regulation at issue, Consolidated Edison advocated the use of nuclear power. The Commission has limited the means by which Consolidated Edison may participate in the public debate on this question and other controversial issues of national interest and importance. Thus, the Commission's prohibition of discussion of controversial issues strikes at the heart of the freedom to speak.

The Commission's ban on bill inserts is not, of course, invalid merely because it imposes a limitation upon speech. We must consider whether the State can demonstrate that its regulation is constitutionally permissible. . . . (as) a reasonable time, place, or manner restriction . . . or a narrowly tailored means of serving a compelling state interest.

This Court has recognized the validity of reasonable time, place, or manner regulations that serve a significant governmental interest and leave ample alternative channels for communication. . . . Various methods of speech, regardless of their content, may frustrate legitimate governmental

goals. No matter what its message, a roving soundtrack that blares at 2 a.m. disturbs neighborhood tranquility.

A restriction that regulates only the time, place or manner of speech may be imposed so long as it's reasonable. But when regulation is based on the content of speech, governmental action must be scrutinized more carefully to ensure that communication has not been prohibited merely because public officials disapprove the speaker's views.

As a consequence, we have emphasized that time, place, and manner regulations must be applicable to all speech irrespective of content. Governmental action that regulates speech on the basis of its subject matter "slips from the neutrality of time, place, and circumstance into a concern about content." Therefore, a constitutionally permissible time, place, or manner restriction may not be based upon either the content or subject matter of speech.

The Commission does not pretend that its action is unrelated to the content or subject matter of bill inserts. Indeed, it has undertaken to suppress certain bill inserts precisely because they address controversial issues of public policy. The Commission allows inserts that present information to consumers on certain subjects, such as energy conservation measures, but it forbids the use of inserts that discuss public controversies. The Commission, with commendable candor, justifies its ban on the ground that consumers will benefit from receiving "useful" information, but not from the prohibited information. The Commission's own rationale demonstrates that its action cannot be upheld as a content-neutral time, place, or manner regulation.

Where a government restricts the speech of a private person, the state action may be sustained only if the government can show that the regulation is a precisely drawn means of serving a compelling state interest.

. . . The Commission argues that its prohibition is necessary (i) to avoid forcing Consolidated Edison's views on a captive audience, (ii) to allocate limited resources in the public interest, and (iii) to ensure that ratepayers do not subsidize the cost of the bill inserts.

Even if a short exposure to Consolidated Edison's views may offend the sensibilities of some consumers, the ability of government to shut off discourse solely to protect others from hearing it is dependent upon a showing that substantial privacy interests are being invaded in an essentially intolerable manner. A less stringent analysis would permit a government to slight the First Amendment's role in affording the public access to discussion, debate and the dissemination of information and ideas. Where a single speaker communicates to many listeners, the First Amendment does not permit the government to prohibit speech as intrusive unless the captive audience cannot avoid objectional speech.

Passengers on public transportation or residents of a neighborhood disturbed by the raucous broadcasts from a passing soundtruck, may well be unable to escape an unwanted message. But customers who encounter an objectionable billing

insert may effectively avoid further bombardment of their sensibilities simply by averting their eyes. The customer of Consolidated Edison may escape exposure to objectionable material simply by transferring the bill insert from envelope to wastebasket. . . .

The Commission's suppression of bill inserts that discuss controversial issues of public policy directly infringes the freedom of speech protected by the First and Fourteenth Amendments. The state action is neither a valid time, place, or manner restriction, . . . nor a narrowly drawn prohibition justified by a compelling state interest. Accordingly, the regulation is invalid.

Reversed.

Vil. of Arlington Hts. v. Metro. Housing Dev.
97 S.Ct. 555 (1977).

The Metropolitan Housing Development Corporation (MHDC) contracted to purchase a tract of land within the boundaries of petitioner village in order to build racially integrated, low and moderate income housing. The contract was contingent upon securing rezoning as well as federal housing assistance. MHDC applied to the village for the necessary rezoning from a single-family to a multiple family (R-5) classification. At a series of Village Plan Commission public meetings, both supporters and opponents touched upon the fact that the project would probably be racially integrated. Opponents also stressed that the location had always been zoned single-family, and that the village's apartment policy called for limited use of R-5 zoning, primarily as a buffer between single-family development and commercial or manufacturing districts, none of which adjoined the project's proposed location. After the village denied the rezoning, MHDC and individual minority respondents filed this suit for injunctive and declaratory relief, alleging that the denial was racially discriminatory and violated the Equal Protection Clause of the Fourteenth Amendment. The district court upheld the zoning board, but the court of appeals reversed holding that the ultimate effect of the rezoning

denial was racially discriminatory because of a disproportionate impact on blacks.

POWELL, J. . . . (O)fficial action will not be held unconstitutional solely because it results in a racially disproportionate impact. Disproportionate impact is not irrelevant, but it is not the sole touchstone of an invidious racial discrimination. Proof of racially discriminatory intent or purpose is required to show a violation of the Equal Protection Clause.

[The Law] does not require a plaintiff to prove that the challenged action rested solely on racially discriminatory purposes. Rarely can it be said that a legislature or administrative body operating under a broad mandate made a decision motivated solely by a single concern, or even that a particular purpose was the "dominant" or "primary" one. In fact, it is because legislators and administrators are properly concerned with balancing numerous competing considerations that courts refrain from reviewing the merits of their decisions, absent a showing of arbitrariness or irrationality. But racial discrimination is not just another competing consideration. When there is a proof that a discriminatory purpose has been a motivating factor in the decision, this judicial deference is no longer justified.

Determining whether invidious discriminatory purpose was a motivating factor demands a sensitive inquiry into such circumstantial and direct evidence of intent as may be available. The impact of the official action—whether it "bears more heavily on one race than another"—may provide an important starting point. Sometimes a clear pattern, unexplainable on grounds other than race, emerges from the effect of the state action even when the governing legislation appears neutral on its face. The evidentiary inquiry is then relatively easy. But such cases are rare. Absent a pattern, impact alone is not determinative, and the Court must look to other evidence.

This historical background of the decision is one evidentiary source, particularly if it reveals a series of official actions taken for invidious purposes. The specific sequence of events leading up to the challenged decision also may shed some light on the decision-makers' purposes. For example, if the property involved here always had been zoned R-5 but suddenly was changed to R-3 when the town learned of MHDC's plans to erect integrated housing, we would have a far different case. Departures from the normal procedural sequence also might afford evidence that improper purposes are playing a role. Substantive departures too may be relevant, particularly if the factors usually considered important by the decision maker strongly favor a decision contrary to the one reached.

The legislative or administrative history may be highly relevant, especially where there are contemporary statements by members of the decision making body, minutes of its meetings, or reports. In some extraordinary instances the members might be called to the stand at trial to testify concerning the purposes of the official action, although even then such testimony frequently will be barred by privilege.

The foregoing summary identifies, without purporting to be exhaustive, subjects of proper inquiry in determining whether racially discriminatory intent existed. With these in mind, we now address the case before us.

[The court reviewed the findings of the lower courts which were the zoning policies were not administered in a discriminatory manner.]

We also have reviewed the evidence. The impact of the Village's decision does arguably bear more heavily on racial minorities. Minorities comprise 18% of the Chicago area population, and 40% of the income groups said to be eligible for Lincoln Green. But there is little about the sequence of events leading up to the decision that would spark suspicion. The area around the property has been zoned R-3 since 1959, the year when Arlington Heights first adopted a zoning map. Single-family homes surround the 80-acre site, and the Village is undeniably committed to single-family homes as its dominant residential land use. The rezoning request progressed according to the usual procedures. The Plan Commission even scheduled two additional hearings, at least in part to accommodate MHDC and permit it to supplement its presentation with answers to questions generated at the first hearing.

The statements by the Plan Commission and Village Board members, as reflected in the official minutes, focused almost exclusively on the zoning aspects of the MHDC petition, and the zoning factors on which they relied are not novel criteria in the Village's rezoning decisions. There is no reason to doubt that there has been reliance by some neighboring property owners on the maintenance of single-family zoning in the vicinity. The village originally adopted its buffer policy long before MHDC entered the picture and has applied the policy too consistently for us to infer discriminatory purpose from its application in this case. Finally, MHDC called one member of the Village Board to the stand at trial. Nothing in her testimony supports an inference of invidious purpose.

In sum, the evidence does not warrant overturning the concurrent findings of both courts below. Respondents simply failed to carry their burden of proving that discriminatory purpose was a motivating factor in the Village's decision. This conclusion ends the constitutional inquiry. The Court of Appeals' further finding that the Village's decision carried a discriminatory "ultimate effect" is without independent constitutional significance. . . .

Reversed and remanded.

REVIEW QUESTIONS

1. Match each term in column A with the appropriate statement in column B.

A		B
1. Supremacy clause	**a.**	Provision that prohibits states from discriminating against out-of-state residents.
2. Contract clause	**b.**	Protects against unreasonable searches and seizures.
3. Privileges and immunities clause	**c.**	Consists of the Constitution's first 10 amendments.
4. Commerce clause	**d.**	Includes the equal protection clause.
5. States' police power	**e.**	Guarantees that any law which contradicts the Constitution is invalid.
6. Bill of Rights	**f.**	A right found in the First Amendment.
7. Freedom of speech	**g.**	A clause found in both the fifth and fourteenth amendments.
8. Fourth Amendment	**h.**	Is a grant of authority to the federal government as well as a limitation on state and local governments' authority to regulate business activities.
9. Due process	**i.**	A constitutional provision that does not apply to the federal government.
10. Fourteenth Amendment	**j.**	Used to promote the public health, safety, morals, and general welfare.

2. An Arizona statute authorized the registrar of contracts to revoke the license of any contractor who filed a petition in voluntary bankruptcy. Hull, a licensee, filed a petition in voluntary bankruptcy on January 22. His contractor's license was revoked on May 16. He appealed to the courts, contending that the Arizona statute was unconstitutional. Is Hull correct? Why?

3. In addition to raising revenue, what can be four other goals of the taxation process?

4. The Alaska legislature passed the so-called Alaska Hire Act. It required that all Alaska oil and gas leases, easements, and right-of-way permits for oil and gas pipelines contain a requirement that Alaska residents of more than 1 year be hired in preference to others. Five nonresidents challenged the constitutionality of this statute when they were denied jobs on the Alaska pipeline. What is the basis of their challenge? What should be the result?

5. A New York State statute entitled "An act prohibiting supersonic transport (SST) planes from landing or taking off in the state" provides: "Notwithstanding the provisions of any law, unless there is an emergency, no commercial supersonic transport plane which is not capable of limiting its noise level to one hundred and eight decibels or less while landing, on the ground, or taking off will be permitted to land or to take off in this state." SSTs are engaged in flights from London and Paris to New York City and Washington, D.C. Perkins files suit to have the state law declared unconstitutional. What will be the result? Why?

6. The state of Maryland required nonresident merchants to obtain licenses in order to pursue their trade in the state. No license was required of Maryland residents. A New Jersey resident challenged the constitutionality of the law. Is the law constitutional? Why? NO

priv. + immunities Clause

7. Consumers of prescription drugs challenged a Virginia State Board of Pharmacy regulation on prescription drugs. These consumers sued and argued that the regulation violated the freedom of speech clause. Is commercial speech protected by the First Amendment? Explain.

8. Building inspectors of Metropolis decided on a yearly inspection of all buildings more than 10 years old. When the inspectors arrived at property owned by Simpson, he refused them admission because they did not have a search warrant. Were the building inspectors entitled to search without the warrants? Why?

9. What is the incorporation doctrine of the Fourteenth Amendment?

10. Which constitutional amendments contain the following guaranteed protections?
    a. Freedom of religion.
    b. Eminent domain.
    c. Right to grand jury indictment.
    d. Freedom of assembly.
    e. Right to remain silent.
    f. Freedom of speech.
    g. Protection against unreasonable searches and seizures.
    h. Freedom of the press.
    i. Equal protection clause.

46 ADMINISTRATIVE LAW

In our complex industrial society, social and economic problems are so numerous that courts and legislative bodies cannot possibly deal with all of them. Legislation must be so general in character that it cannot possibly cover everything the law seeks to control or correct. There must be a method of filling in the gaps in legislation and of adding meat to the bones of legislative policy. There must also be special expertise to solve problems created by advancing technology. To handle these and other situations, our society has turned to the administrative process in government. In doing so, it has created a fourth branch of government: the independent regulatory agencies, bureaus, and commissions that the administrative process relies upon to develop laws and enforce them. This fourth branch of government possesses the powers and functions of the other three branches.

1. Reasons for the Administrative Process

Administrative agencies are necessary in order to lighten the burdens that otherwise must be borne by the executive branch, legislative bodies, and courts. The multitude of administrative agencies performing governmental functions today encompasses almost every aspect of business operation and, indeed, almost every aspect of our daily lives. These agencies provide flexibility in the law and adaptability to changing conditions.

The many local, state, and federal administrative agencies have a far greater, direct, day-to-day, legal impact on business than the impact of the courts and legislative bodies. Administrative agencies create and enforce the greater bulk of the laws that make up the legal environment of business.

The fourth branch of government exists in part because laws cannot be particular enough to cover all aspects of a problem. It is impossible for the legislature to write laws in sufficient detail to cover all aspects of many problems. As a consequence, Congress uses general language in stating its regulatory aims and purposes. For example, it is probably not possible for Congress to enact an environmental law that would cover every possible issue that might arise. Therefore, Congress delegates to the Environmental Protection Agency (EPA) the power to make rules and regulations to fill in the gaps and create the necessary details to make the laws relating to the environment workable.

It is also difficult for the courts to handle all the disputes and controversies that arise. Each year, tens of thousands of industrial accidents cause injury or death. If each accident were to result in traditional litigation, the courts simply would not have the time or personnel to handle the multitude of cases. Therefore, we use the administrative process to handle them. Similarly, most cases involving alleged discrimination in employment are decided by the administrative process.

Many agencies exist because of the desire for experts to handle difficult problems. The Federal Reserve Board, Nuclear Regulatory Commission, and Pure Food and Drug Administration are examples of agencies with expertise above that of the Congress or the executive branch. Administrative agencies also provide continuity and consistency in the formulation, application, and enforcement of rules and regulations governing business.

Many governmental agencies exist to protect the public and the public interest from some members of the business community. The protection of the investing public was a major force behind the creation of the Securities and Exchange Commission. The manufacture and sale of dangerous products led to the creation of the Consumer Product Safety Commission. It is our practice to turn to a governmental agency for assistance whenever a business or business practice may injure significant numbers of the general public. There is a belief that a legitimate function of many government agencies is to protect the public from harm.

Agencies are often created to replace competition with regulation. When a firm is given monopoly power, it loses its freedom of contract, and a governmental body is given the power to determine the provisions of its contracts. For example, electric utility companies are usually given a monopoly in the geographic area they serve. A state agency such as a public service commission is then empowered to set the rate structure for the utility. Similar agencies have regulated transportation and banking because of the difference in bargaining power between the business and the public.

Many agencies such as the Post Office Department were created out of necessity. Welfare programs require government personnel to administer them. The social security system cannot function without a federal agency to determine eligibility and to pay the benefits. The mere existence of most government programs automatically causes the creation of a new agency or an expansion of the functions of an existing one.

Today, the legislative and executive branches of government are content to identify problems and to develop policies to solve them. These policies are enacted into law; the responsibility for carrying out the policies and enforcing the law is delegated to the administrative process. The goals of society are determined by the traditional branches of government, and their achievement is the responsibility of the fourth branch.

2. Functions of Administrative Agencies

Administrative agencies both at federal and state levels of government tend to perform the six functions of the other three branches of government: (1) legislative or rule making, (2) adjudicating, (3) prosecuting, (4) advising, (5) supervising, and (6) investigating. These functions are not fulfilled to the same degree by all administrative agencies, but all are of concern to each agency. Some agencies are primarily adjudicating bodies, such as the industrial commissions that rule on worker's compensation claims. Others are primarily supervisory, such as the Securities and Exchange Commission (SEC), which oversees the issue and sale of investment securities.

In the legislative function, rules and regulations are issued to accomplish the goals of the agency. The rule-making function is based on the authority delegated to the agency by the legislature. This delegation of authority is usually stated in broad, general language. A delegation "to make such rules, regulations, and decisions as the public interest, convenience, and necessity may require" is a typical statement of the authority of an agency.

It is the usual practice for administrative agencies in performing their quasi-legislative functions to hold hearings on proposed rules and regulations. The agency receives testimony on the need for, or desirability of, proposed rules and regulations. Notice of such hearings is usually given to the public, and all interested parties are allowed to present evidence for consideration by the agency. Keep in mind that these rules and regulations have the same force and effect as laws passed by a legislative body.

Numerous activities in the administrative process are basically executive functions. For example, agencies investigate activities and practices that may be illegal. This investigative power allows agencies to gather and compile information concerning the organization and business practices of any corporation or industry to determine if there has been a violation of any law. In performing this function, agencies may utilize the subpoena power and require reports, examine witnesses under oath, and examine and copy documents, or they may obtain information from other governmental offices. There is a federal law which makes it a crime to make any false or fraudulent statement in any matter within the jurisdiction of a federal agency. A person may be guilty of a violation without proof that he or she had knowledge that the matter was within the jurisdiction of a federal agency.[1] This power of investigation complements the exercise of the other powers, such as giving advice, prosecuting violations, issuing rules, and deciding cases.

The adjudicating function means that administrative agencies also decide cases or disputes between private parties after they have conducted hearings. This

---

[1] United States v. Yermian, p. 1048.

involves both fact-finding and applying the law to the facts. The purpose of the hearing may be to find if a rule of the agency or an applicable statute has been violated. The National Labor Relations Board conducts hearings to determine if an unfair labor practice has been committed. Other quasi-judicial hearings may be held for the purpose of fixing liability, as in a case of worker's compensation, which provides employer liability for employee deaths, sicknesses, and injury arising out of, and in the course of, employment. The quasi-judicial hearings receive detailed evidence and determine the rights and duties of the parties subject to the jurisdiction of the agency. The rules of procedure used in these quasi-judicial hearings are usually more informal than those of court trials, but on the whole they follow the general pattern set by courts.

An agency usually appoints a person to conduct the hearing—an administrative law judge, sometimes called a *hearing examiner* or *trial examiner.* This person receives the evidence, submits findings of facts, and makes recommendations to the board or commission regarding the disposition to be made in the case. The agency studies the report and issues whatever orders the law in the case appears to demand. The agency may hear objections to the hearing officer's finding, and sometimes it will hear arguments on the issues.

Many cases are settled by agreement before a final agency decision in the same way most lawsuits are settled. Settlement results in the issuance of a *consent order.* Such orders waive all rights to seek a judicial review. A respondent does not have to admit it has been guilty of a violation of the law; but it does agree that it will not engage in the business activities that were the subject of the complaint. A consent order has the same legal force and effect as a final decision after a full hearing. Consent orders save considerable expense. The business involved is not found guilty, but only agrees that it will not do the act complained of in the future.

The quasi-judicial function of administrative agencies is the subject of substantial controversy. A frequent complaint is that administrative agencies make a law and investigate to see if it has been violated; they serve as prosecutor, judge, and jury; then they act in the manner of an appellate court in reviewing the decision. Another frequent objection is that the administrative process denies business and others the right to a trial by jury. Such objections are not constitutionally valid.[2]

CHALLENGING AGENCY DECISIONS

3. Introduction

Each branch of government has some degree of control over the administrative process. The executive branch nominates the top officials of an agency with the advice and consent of the legislative branch. The executive branch also makes budget recommendations to the legislature. The legislature can control administrative activity by abolishing the agency or changing its authority. It can enact legislation changing the rules and regulations adopted by the agency. Of course, it can also limit the appropriation of funds to the agency and curtail its activities.

The courts serve as a check on administrative bodies by exercising the power of judicial review. Rules and regulations adopted by administrative agencies must

---

[2] *Atlas Roofing Co., Inc. v. Occupational Safety, etc.,* p. 1049.

be within the confines of their grant of power from the legislature, or a court will set them aside. However, once having determined that an act of the legislature is constitutional or a rule of an agency is authorized, the courts will not inquire into its wisdom or effectiveness. Unwise rules or regulations adopted by an agency may be corrected by the legislature that gave the agency power to make the rule in the first place, but not by the courts.

Agencies may decide to reverse or change their own rules and regulations. They may also decide to change rules and procedures. The rules created by agencies are not intended to last forever; agencies are given ample latitude to adapt their rules and policies to changing circumstances. However, an agency changing its course by rescinding a rule is obligated to supply a reason for the change beyond that which may be required when an agency does an act in the first place. The agency must explain why it has exercised its discretion to change a rule or eliminate it. The forces of change do not always or necessarily point in the direction of elimination of a rule. There is no more reason to presume that changing circumstances require the rescission of prior action, instead of a revision, or even the extension of, a current regulation. Thus the reasons given are important when the decision is reviewed by courts. While the removal of a regulation may not entail the monetary expenditures and other costs of enacting a new standard, so it may be easier for an agency to justify a deregulatory action, the direction in which an agency chooses to move does not alter the standard of judicial review.

Although a court is not to substitute its judgment for that of the agency, the agency nevertheless must examine the relevant data and articulate a satisfactory explanation for its action; and in reviewing that explanation, a court must consider whether the decision was based on a consideration of the relevant factors and whether there was a clear error of judgment.

How much deference is given to the quasi-legislative and quasi-judicial decisions of administrative agencies? Under what circumstances will a court reverse the decision of an agency? What alternatives are available to a party who is unhappy with either a rule or a decision? What are the powers of courts in reviewing the decision of an administrative agency? The answers to these questions must be clearly understood if one is to appreciate the role of administrative agencies in our system. The principles and issues are somewhat different, depending upon whether the court is reviewing a rule or regulation, or a quasi-judicial decision.

4. Judicial Review in General

Regardless of whether a court is asked to review an agency's quasi-legislative or quasi-judicial actions, there are two issues the court must initially resolve: (1) do the complaining parties have standing to sue? (2) have these parties exhausted their administrative remedies?

Standing to sue. Standing to sue involves two important issues. First, is the action or decision of the agency subject to judicial review? Not all administrative decisions are reviewable. The Federal Administrative Procedure Act provides for judicial review except where "(1) statutes preclude judicial review or (2) agency action is committed to agency discretion by law." Few statutes actually preclude judicial review, and preclusion by inference is rare.

The second issue is whether or not the plaintiff in any particular case is able to obtain judicial review. It is generally required that the plaintiff be "an aggrieved party" before he or she has standing to sue or to obtain judicial review. Persons who may suffer economic loss due to agency action have standing to sue. Persons who have noneconomic interests, such as First Amendment rights, now also have standing to sue.

Exhaustion of remedies.   The doctrine of exhaustion of remedies is based on the proposition that courts should not decide in advance of a hearing that an agency will not conduct it fairly. In general (although there are exceptions), courts refuse to review administrative actions until a complaining party has exhausted all the administrative review procedures available. Otherwise, the administrative system would be denied important opportunities to make a factual record, to exercise its discretion, or to apply its expertise in decision making. Exhaustion gives an agency the opportunity to discover and correct its own errors and thus help to dispense with judicial review.

Exhaustion is most clearly required in cases involving the agency's expertise or specialization, so that exhaustion would not incur unusual expense, or when the administrative remedy is just as likely as the judicial one to provide appropriate relief. If nothing is to be gained from the exhaustion of administrative remedies, and the harm from the continued existence of the administrative ruling is great, the courts have not been reluctant to discard this doctrine. This is especially true when fundamental constitutional guarantees such as freedom of speech or press are involved or the administrative remedy is likely to be inadequate. When the agency is clearly acting beyond its jurisdiction (because its action is not authorized by statute, or the statute authorizing it is unconstitutional), or when the agency's action would result in irreparable injury (such as great expense) to the petitioner, a court probably would not insist upon exhaustion.

5. Judicial Review of Quasi-Legislative Decisions

The rule-making function is essentially legislative in character. Agencies are created, and their powers are derived, from statutes that delegate certain responsibilities or quasi-legislative power to the agency. These statutes usually authorize an administrative agency to "fill in the details" of legislation by making rules and regulations to carry out its goals and purposes.

Two basic issues in litigation challenge the validity of a rule or regulation adopted by an administrative agency. First of all, is the delegation valid; second, has the agency exceeded its authority? Delegation of quasi-legislative authority to an administrative agency must be definite, or it will violate due process. *Definiteness* means that the delegation must be clear enough for reviewing courts to ascertain the extent of the agency's authority, but broad language has been held sufficiently definite to meet the requirements of due process.

The power of administrative agencies to make rules must also be limited. The limited-power concept means that delegation must contain standards by which a court can determine whether the limitations have been exceeded. Just as broad language has been approved as being sufficiently definite for a delegation to be valid under the due process clause, so have broad standards been approved to meet the limited power test since the 1930s. When an agency is given authority to make rules required for the "public interest, convenience and necessity," there is a valid standard for those rules. The law, recognizing that practical considerations often make definite standards impossible, will hold valid a delegation that includes a criterion as concrete as possible within its field and with the factors involved.

While it is highly unlikely that a court would hold a delegation invalid because of indefiniteness or lack of standards, courts sometimes do find that agencies have exceeded their authority. Delegation of quasi-legislative power usually involves grants of substantial discretion to the board or agency involved. It must be kept in mind that the delegation of discretion is to the agency, not to the courts. Courts cannot interfere with the discretion given to the agency and cannot substitute their judgment for that of the agency simply because they disagree with a rule or regulation. Courts will hold that an agency has exceeded its authority if an analysis of legislative intent confirms the view that the agency has gone beyond that intent.

6. Judicial or Quasi-Judicial Decisions

The exercise of quasi-judicial powers of administrative agencies is often criticized because personnel of the agency act as prosecutor, finder of facts, and judge. The law therefore requires that this quasi-judicial power be restricted by procedural safeguards to prevent abuse.

Judicial review of agency adjudications, by its very nature, is quite limited. Since legislatures have delegated authority to agencies because of their expertise and other capabilities, courts usually exercise restraint and give great deference to agency decisions. Courts reviewing administrative interpretations of law do not always decide questions of law for themselves. It is not unusual for a court to accept an administrative interpretation of law as final if it has a rational basis. Administrative agencies are frequently called upon to interpret the statute governing the agency, and the agency's construction is persuasive to courts.

Agencies develop their own rules of procedure or follow those set forth in administrative procedure acts of the legislature—either way being far less formal than judicial procedure. Administrative agencies usually do not follow the strict rules of evidence used by courts, although they do not ignore all rules of evidence. They cannot deny cross-examination of witnesses, and they must meet judicial standards of fairness, such as giving a fair hearing to all parties. In reviewing the procedures of administrative agencies, courts are not empowered to substitute their judgment or their own procedures for those of the agency. Judicial responsibility is limited to ensuring consistency with statutes and compliance with the demands of the Constitution for a fair hearing.

Agencies are frequently called upon to determine questions of fact. Such decisions are similar to those of a jury in traditional litigation. All that is usually required for a decision is a finding that the evidence is preponderant one way or the other. The preponderance of the evidence burden of proof has been carried over to most quasi-judicial hearings.[3]

Federal administrative agencies are free to fashion their own rules of procedure because it is presumed that administrative agencies and administrators will be familiar with the industries they regulate. Thus they will be in a better position than courts or legislative bodies to design procedural rules adapted to the peculiarities of the industry and the tasks of the agency involved.

7. Judicial Review of Factual Decisions

When a court reviews the findings of fact made by an administrative body, it considers them to be prima facie correct. A court of review examines the evidence by analyzing the record of the agency's proceedings and upholds the agency's findings and conclusions on questions of fact if they are supported by substantial evidence in the record as a whole.[4] In other words, the record must contain material evidence from which a reasonable person might reach the same conclusion as did the agency. If substantial evidence in support of the decision is present, the court will not disturb the agency's findings, even though the court itself might have reached a different conclusion on the basis of the evidence. The determination of credibility of the witnesses who testify in quasi-judicial proceedings is for the agency to determine, not the courts.

On review, courts do not (1) reweigh the evidence, (2) make independent determinations of fact, or (3) substitute their view of the evidence for that of the agency. Courts do determine if there is substantial evidence to support the action taken; but in their examination of the evidence, all that is required is evidence sufficient to convince a reasonable mind to a fair degree of certainty. Thus, substantial evidence is evidence that a reasonable mind might accept as adequate to support the conclusion.

For the courts to exercise their function of limited review, it is necessary for the agency to provide a record of the reasons and basis for its decision. If this record shows that the agency did not examine all relevant data and that it ignored issues before it, a court may set aside the decision because it is arbitrary and capricious. Agencies cannot make assumptions in their decisions; the decisions must be based on evidence, and the record must support the decision.

8. Legal Costs

In 1982, Congress passed the Equal Access to Justice Act. It authorizes suits against the government to collect attorney's fees and court costs on behalf of persons unjustly treated. A treatment or action is *unjust* if it is taken without substantial justification. The law applies to small businesses, nonprofit groups, and individuals. Eligibility is limited to persons whose net worth is less than $1 million and businesses with no more than $5 million net worth and 500 employees.

---

[3] Steadman v. Securities and Exchange Commission, p. 1051.

[4] Green v. Carder, p. 1052.

Charitable and religious tax-exempt organizations qualify if they have 500 or fewer employees. The law grants legal fees only to parties that overcome the government position in court, administrative proceedings, or in a settlement. Even then, the government agency is not required to pay if it can show that its original decision was substantially justified.

This remedy is not being used very extensively. During the first nineteen months under the law, the government lost 12,000 lawsuits, but there were only 30 applications for legal fees.

9. Common Criticisms

The regulatory process is subject to a great deal of criticism. Critics charge agencies with being inefficient and ineffective. Many complaints relate directly to the vastness of the size of the fourth branch of government. This vastness exists at all levels of government—federal, state, and local. In a real sense, the bureaucracy actually runs the country.

The administrative process is so extensive it is almost impossible for any business to be aware of all the rules applicable to it. Moreover, the rules and regulations of one agency often conflict with the rules and regulations of other agencies.

The major problems of the fourth branch of government may be grouped under the headings (1) personnel, (2) cost, and (3) procedures. The validity of the criticisms change from time to time and from agency to agency. Keep in mind that they are directed at the total system only to illustrate the types of complaints that are made against some agencies. Many bureaucrats and commissioners are dedicated and competent public servants who work long and hard in the public interest.

Personnel problems.   Personnel problems often include inefficiency and unqualified personnel. Appointments to some positions on boards and commissions often appear to be made as rewards to political friends, rather than on the basis of ability. The Peter Principle that many persons are promoted to their level of incompetence is often applicable. On the other hand, some people's skills are underemployed, and this also causes job dissatisfaction and reduced efficiency.

Bias and lack of political accountability are two of the more often heard complaints. Bias is almost always present to some degree, since an agency tends to attract people who believe in its goals. Lack of political accountability means that voters cannot directly express their dissatisfaction with an agency, its rules, or its decisions. About the best they can do is to get the legislature to take steps to affect agency policy.

It is often alleged that agencies favor the industries they regulate, rather than the public, as a result of the cozy relationship between the regulator and the regulated. One reason for this rapport is that the regulators are often selected from persons in high executive positions in the industries they regulate. This choice is justified by the argument that they possess the expertise required to understand the technical problems. For the same reason, key staff members are often recruited from the regulated industry. Also, it is not unusual for the reverse to occur. Upon completion of their terms in office, commissioners and staff members frequently obtain high-paying jobs in the industries they have been regulating. Sweetheart regulation is sometimes a problem.

Cost problems. Regulation is a form of taxation because it directly increases the cost of government. But these direct costs of regulation are only a small fraction of the total cost. Regulation adds significantly to the cost of doing business, and these costs are passed on to the tax-paying public. Businesses, forced to develop bureaucracies within their own organizations to deal with the regulating agencies, create internal groups that are mirror images of the agencies. The existence of the Equal Employment Opportunity Commission has caused most large corporations to designate affirmative action employees to assist the company in complying with the laws, rules, and regulations enforced by EEOC. Whenever a bureaucracy exists, firms dealing with it must spend time and money in dealing with the agency. As a result, consumers for whose protection many regulations are adopted pay the direct cost of regulation in taxes and the indirect cost in the price of products and services.

Historically, there was little or no cost-benefit analysis of administrative rules and regulations. Government tended to assess only the benefits accruing from a cleaner environment, safer products, healthier working conditions, and so on, in deciding to embark upon vast new regulatory programs. Today, government is trying to balance the costs of the programs against potential benefits. But it is not required to do so.[5]

Procedural problems. One of the most often voiced criticisms of many agencies is that there is unnecessary delay in rendering decisions. Many agencies are unable to resolve controversies quickly, despite the fact that the agencies were created to act faster than courts. Much of this delay is caused by the excessive paperwork typical of all bureaucracies.

Some agencies have been accused of devoting the major part of their time to trivia, while ignoring the more important aspects of their mission. Agencies also have been accused of lack of enforcement and follow-up to ensure compliance with rules and orders after they have been issued. Many agencies operate without clearly defined goals and priorities.

11. Regulatory Reform

There have been numerous recommendations and attempts to deregulate this or that activity or industry, to decrease the number of government programs by reorganizing agencies, and to pare down their functions. Proponents of deregulation argue that we should replace rigid, unnecessary regulation with the free play of competitive market forces. They believe that competition and the market can allocate resources and achieve efficiency better than government rules and regulations. Among the industries where there has been significant deregulation are the airlines, banking, and telephone communications.

Shortly after taking office, President Reagan issued an executive order

---

[5] American Textile Manufacturers Institute, Inc. v. Donovan, p. 1053.

requiring executive agencies to apply cost-benefit analysis before creating "significant" new regulations. The order does not apply to independent regulatory agencies, since they are not under the president's direct control. Many regulations escaped the analysis because a "significant" regulation had to have an "annual effect on the economy of $100 million or more." Finally, as *American Textile* illustrates, some enabling legislation for executive agencies does not require and may not allow the use of cost-benefit analysis.

The constant demand for the use of cost-benefit analysis to evaluate government regulations requires analysis. How do you apply cost-benefit analysis to a rule dealing with human life? How much dollar benefit is to be assigned to a life in measuring it against the cost? Assume that the Department of Transportation rule requiring air bags in all new automobiles adds a cost of $800 to each car. Assume also that it saves 50,000 lives per year. Is the cost worth the benefit? It depends on whether or not you are one of the 50,000. Cost-benefit analysis is not possible for many government rules and regulations. This is not to say that the cost of many agencies cannot be compared with tangible benefits. Cost-benefit analysis applied to some agencies and to some rules and regulations will clearly point toward deregulation, but its use is obviously limited.

President Reagan's most effective technique for reducing the impact of government regulation has been to cut budgets and to appoint critics of various agencies to head them. He has sought reform through ideology. If a commissioner or board member does not believe in certain regulatory activities, chances are that they will not be carried out even if the law would allow the agency to do so. But what is needed is not the elimination of regulation, but the elimination of bad and excessive regulation. Most agencies exist for valid reasons, and they have proper goals and important roles to play in aiding the legitimate needs of society. They exist because of perceived needs of society. The legitimate goal is a balanced approach—free enterprise with effective regulation to protect the public interest.

SUMMARY

Reasons for administrative process	1. Administrative agencies are necessary to lighten the burden on the other branches of government.
	2. Through their rule-making authority, agencies fill in the specifics needed to carry out the legislature's general policies.
	3. Agencies may be created to provide expertise to resolve difficult problems, to protect the public, or to regulate a noncompetitive market.
Functions of administrative agencies	1. Agencies may exercise a quasi-legislative function by issuing rules and regulations that have the authority of statutes enacted by an elected legislative body.

2. Agencies also may have quasi-judicial authority that allows them to resolve a variety of controversies.

3. Other functions performed by agencies include (a) prosecuting, (b) advising, (c) supervising, and (d) investigating.

4. Through the issuance of consent orders, agencies resolve many of their cases in a manner similar to a settlement.

CHALLENGING AGENCY DECISIONS

Introduction

1. All three branches of government have some control over agency decisions.

2. The executive branch can replace administrators through the appointment process.

3. The legislative branch can control the agencies' budgets and the extent of their authority.

4. The courts are often called on to review the various functions of agencies.

Judicial review in general

1. Two issues must be decided by any court at the outset when reviewing agencies' decisions.

2. The first issue is: Do those seeking review have standing to sue? In other words, reviewing courts must decide the agency's decision is subject to review. Courts also must find the review is requested by "aggrieved parties."

3. The second issue is: Have the administrative remedies been exhausted? The agency involved must be given all opportunities to correct any errors that may have occurred.

Judicial review of quasi-legislative decisions

1. Courts generally consider two issues when reviewing agencies' rule-making authority.

2. The first issue is: Is the delegation of authority valid? If the answer is no, the rule is invalid. If the answer is yes, the second issue must be considered.

3. The second issue is: Did the agency exceed the authority granted? If the answer is yes, the rule is invalid. Otherwise, the rule is valid.

Judicial review of quasi-judicial decisions	**1.** Courts hesitate to overrule an agency's decision if there is a rational basis to support that decision.
Judicial review of factual decisions	**1.** A great deal of deference is given to the factual determinations of agencies.
	2. Courts generally do not (a) reweigh the evidence, (b) make independent findings of fact, or (c) substitute their views for that of the agency.
	3. Agencies' factual decisions are not reversed unless they are arbitrary or unreasonable.
Legal costs	**1.** In addition to having courts review an agency's decision, the aggrieved party may collect attorney's fees and court costs from the administrators and the government for money damages.

COMPLAINTS AND REFORM

Common criticisms	**1.** The complaints heard most frequently about agencies involve (a) personnel, (b) cost, and (c) procedural problems.
	2. Personnel problems relate to the appointment process being influenced by politics, to the lack of accountability, and to the close ties administrators have with the regulated businesses.
	3. Cost problems include the expenses businesses incur in keeping up with agencies' decisions. There has seldom been cost-benefit analysis of agencies' decisions.
	4. The basic procedural problem involves the time-consuming delays that often occur in administrative hearings.
Regulatory reform	**1.** President Reagan has attempted to require cost-benefit analysis prior to the development of new regulations.
	2. More effective has been the reduction of the agencies' budgets.

CASES

United States v. Yermian
104 S.Ct. 2936 (1984)

POWELL, J. . . . It is a federal crime under 18 U.S.C. §1001 to make any false or fraudulent statement in any matter within the jurisdiction of a federal agency. To establish a violation of §1001, the Government must prove beyond a reasonable doubt that the statement was made with knowledge of its falsity. This case presents the question whether the Government also must prove that the false statement was made with actual knowledge of federal agency jurisdiction.

Respondent Esmail Yermian was convicted . . . on three counts of making false statements in a matter within the jurisdiction of a federal agency, in violation of §1001. The convictions were based on false statements respondent supplied his employer in connection with a Department of Defense security questionnaire. Respondent was hired in 1979 by Gulton Industries, a defense contractor. Because respondent was to have access to classified material in the course of his employment, he was required to obtain a Department of Defense Security Clearance. To this end, Gulton's security officer asked respondent to fill out a "Worksheet For Preparation of Personnel Security Questionnaire."

In response to a question on the worksheet asking whether he had ever been charged with any violation of law, respondent failed to disclose that in 1978 he had been convicted of mail fraud, in violation of 18 U.S.C. §1341. In describing his employment history, respondent falsely stated that he had been employed by two companies that had in fact never employed him. The Gulton security officer typed these false representations onto a form entitled "Department of Defense Personnel Security Questionnaire." Respondent reviewed the typed document for errors and signed a certification stating that his answers were "true, complete, and correct to the best of [his] knowledge" and that he understood "that any misrepresentation or false statement . . . may subject [him] to prosecution under section 1001 of the United States Criminal Code."

After witnessing respondent's signature, Gulton's security officer mailed the typed form to the Defense Industrial Security Clearance Office for processing. Government investigators subsequently discovered that respondent had submitted false statements on the security questionnaire. Confronted with this discovery, respondent acknowledged that he had responded falsely to questions regarding his criminal record and employment history. On the basis of these false statements, respondent was charged with three counts in violation of §1001.

At trial, respondent admitted to having actual knowledge of the falsity of the statements he had submitted in response to the Department of Defense Security Questionnaire. He explained that he had made the false statements so that information on the security questionnaire would be consistent with similar fabrications he had submitted to Gulton in his employment application. Respondent's sole defense at trial was that he had no actual knowledge that his false statements would be transmitted to a federal agency. . . .

The only issue presented in this case is whether Congress intended the terms "knowingly and willfully" in §1001 to modify the statute's jurisdictional language, thereby requiring the Government to prove that false statements were made with actual knowledge of federal agency jurisdiction. The issue thus presented is one of statutory interpretation. . . .

The statutory language requiring that knowingly false statements be made "in any matter within the jurisdiction of any department or agency of the United States" is a jurisdictional requirement. Its primary purpose is to identify the factor that makes the false statement an appropriate subject for federal concern. Jurisdictional language need not contain the same culpability requirement as other elements of the offense. Indeed, we have held that "the existence of the fact that confers federal jurisdiction need not be one in the mind of the actor at the time he perpetrates the act made criminal by the federal statute." Certainly in this case, the statutory language makes clear that Congress did not intend the terms "knowingly and willfully" to establish the standard of culpability for the jurisdictional element of §1001. The jurisdictional language appears in a phrase separate from the prohibited conduct modified by the terms "knowingly and willfully." Any natural reading of §1001, therefore, establishes that the terms "knowingly and willfully" modify only the making of "false, fictitious or fraudulent statements," and not the predicate circumstance that those statements be made in a matter within the jurisdiction of a federal agency. Once this is clear, there is no basis for requiring proof that the defendant had actual knowledge of federal agency jurisdiction. The statute contains no language suggesting any additional element of intent, such as a requirement that false statements be "knowingly made in a matter within

federal agency jurisdiction," or "with the intent to deceive the federal government." On its face, therefore, §1001 requires that the Government prove that false statements were made knowingly and willfully, and it unambiguously dispenses with any requirement that the Government also prove that those statements were made with actual knowledge of federal agency jurisdiction. Respondent's argument that the legislative history of the statute supports a contrary interpretation is unpersuasive. . . .

There is no support in the legislative history for respondent's argument that the terms "knowingly and willfully" modify the phrase "in any matter within the jurisdiction of a [federal agency]."

Both the plain language and the legislative history establish that proof of actual knowledge of federal agency jurisdiction is not required under §1001. Accordingly, we reverse the decision of the Court of Appeals to the contrary.

It is so ordered.

Atlas Roofing Company Inc. v. Occupational Safety, etc.
97 S.Ct. 1261 (1977)

In 1970 Congress passed the Occupational Safety and Health Act (OSHA) to protect employees from death and injury due to unsafe working conditions. The law allows the Department of Labor (1) to obtain abatement orders requiring employers to correct unsafe working conditions and (2) to impose civil penalties on any employer maintaining unsafe working conditions. An employer may contest a penalty or abatement order in an evidentiary hearing before an administrative law judge of the Occupational Safety and Health Review Commission (Commission). The judge's decision is subject to review by the full Commission. A decision by the Commission may be appealed to the Court of Appeals. On appeal, the Commission's findings of fact, if supported by substantial evidence, are conclusive. If the employer fails to pay the assessed penalty, the Secretary of Labor may commence a collection action in a federal district court in which neither the fact of the violation nor the propriety of the penalty assessed may be retried.

In this case, abatement orders were issued and

penalties proposed against petitioners for violations of safety standards. The case proceeded through the various review procedures, with the Commission affirming the violations and penalties. Petitioners sought judicial review challenging the constitutionality of OSHA's enforcement procedures, contending that the procedures violated the Seventh Amendment. The Court of Appeals affirmed, and the Supreme Court granted certiorari.

WHITE, J. . . . The issue in this case is whether consistent with the Seventh Amendment, Congress may create a new cause of action in the Government for civil penalties enforceable in an administrative agency where there is no jury trial. . . .

The Seventh Amendment provides that "in Suits at common law, where the value in controversy shall exceed twenty dollars, the right of trial by jury shall be preserved. . . ." The phrase "suits at common law" has been construed to refer to cases tried prior to the adoption of the Seventh Amendment in courts of law in which jury trial was customary as distinguished from courts of equity or admiralty in which jury trial was not. Petitioners claim that a suit in a federal court by the Government for civil penalties for violation of statute is a suit for a money judgment which is classically a suit at common law and that the defendant therefore has a Seventh Amendment right to a jury determination of all issues of fact in such a case. Petitioners then claim that to permit Congress to assign the function of adjudicating the Government's rights to civil penalties for violation of the statute to a different forum—an administrative agency in which no jury is available—would be to permit Congress to deprive a defendant of his Seventh Amendment jury right. We disagree. At least in cases in which "public rights" are being litigated—e.g., cases in which the Government sues in its sovereign capacity to enforce public rights created by statutes within the power of Congress to enact—the Seventh Amendment does not prohibit Congress from assigning the factfinding function and initial adjudication to an administrative forum with which the jury would be incompatible.

Congress has often created new statutory obligations, provided for civil penalties for their violation, and committed exclusively to an administrative agency the function of deciding whether a violation has in fact occurred. These statutory schemes have been sustained by this Court, albeit often without express reference to the Seventh Amendment. . . . When Congress creates new statutory "public rights," it may assign their adjudication to an administrative agency with which a jury trial would be incompatible, without violating the Seventh Amendment's injunction that jury trial is to be "preserved" in "suits at common law." Congress is not required by the Seventh Amendment to choke the already crowded federal courts with new types of litigation nor prevented from committing some new types of litigation to administrative agencies with special competence in the relevant field. This is the case even if the Seventh Amendment would have required a jury where the adjudication of those rights is assigned instead to a federal court of law instead of an administrative agency. . . .

It is apparent from the history of the jury trial in civil matters that factfinding, which is the essential function of the jury in civil cases, was never the exclusive province of the jury under either the English or American legal system at the time of the adoption of the Seventh Amendment; and the question whether a fact would be found by a jury turned to a considerable degree on the nature of the forum in which a litigant found himself. Critical factfinding was performed without juries in suits in equity, and there were no juries in admiralty, neither were there in the military justice system. . . .

The Seventh Amendment was declaratory of the existing law, for it required only that jury trial in suits at common law was to be "preserved." It thus did not purport to require a jury trial where none was required before. . . .

The point is that the Seventh Amendment was never intended to establish the jury as the exclusive mechanism for factfinding in civil cases. It took the existing legal order as it found it, and there is little or no basis for concluding that the Amendment should now be interpreted to provide an impenetrable barrier to administrative factfinding under otherwise valid federal regulatory statutes. We cannot conclude that the Amendment rendered Congress powerless—when it concluded that remedies available in courts of law were inadequate to cope with a problem within Congress' power to regulate—to create new public rights and remedies by statute and commit their enforcement, if it chose, to a tribunal other than a court of law—such as an administrative agency—in which facts are not found by juries. Indeed, the "settled judicial construction" was to the contrary "from the beginning."

Thus, history and our cases support the proposition that the right to a jury trial turns not solely on the nature of the issue to be resolved, but also on the forum in which it is to be resolved. Congress found the common law and other existing remedies for work injuries resulting from unsafe working conditions to be inadequate to protect the Nation's working men and women. It created a new cause of action, and remedies therefore, unknown to the common law, and placed their enforcement in a tribunal supplying speedy and expert resolutions for the issues involved. The Seventh Amendment is no bar to the creation of new rights or to their enforcement outside the regular courts of law.

Affirmed.

Steadman v. Securities and Exchange Commission
101 S. Ct. 999 (1981)

BRENNAN, J. . . . In administrative proceedings, the Securities and Exchange Commission applies a preponderance of the evidence standard of proof in determining whether the antifraud provisions of the federal securities laws have been violated. The question presented is whether such violations must be proved by clear and convincing evidence rather than by a preponderance of the evidence.

In June 1971, the Commission initiated a disciplinary proceeding against petitioner and certain of his wholly-owned companies. . . . The Commission alleged that petitioner had violated numerous provisions of the federal securities laws in his management of several mutual funds registered under the Investment Company Act.

After a lengthy evidentiary hearing before an administrative law judge and review by the Commission in which the preponderance of the evidence standard was employed, the Commission held that between December of 1965 and June of 1972, petitioner had violated antifraud, reporting, conflict of interest, and proxy provisions of the federal securities laws. Accordingly, it entered an order permanently barring petitioner from associating with any investment adviser or affiliating with any registered investment company, and suspending him for 1 year from associating with any broker or dealer in securities. . . .

(On Appeal) Petitioner challenged the Commission's use of the preponderance of the evidence standard of proof in determining whether he had violated antifraud provisions of the securities laws. He contended that, because of the potentially severe sanctions that the Commission was empowered to impose and because of the circumstantial and inferential nature of the evidence that might be used to prove intent to defraud, the Commission was required to weigh the evidence against a clear and convincing standard of proof. The Court of Appeals rejected petitioner's argument, holding that in a disciplinary proceeding before the Commission violations of the antifraud provisions of the securities laws may be established by a preponderance of the evidence.

Where Congress has not prescribed the degree of proof which must be adduced by the proponent of a rule or order to carry its burden of persuasion in an administrative proceeding, this Court has felt at liberty to prescribe the standard, for "[i]t is the kind of question which has traditionally been left to the judiciary to resolve." However, where Congress has spoken, we have deferred to "the traditional powers of Congress to prescribe rules of evidence and standards of proof in the federal courts" absent countervailing constitutional constraints. For Commission disciplinary proceedings we conclude that Congress has spoken, and has said that the preponderance of the evidence standard should be applied. . . .

The legislative history, . . ., clearly reveals the Congress' intent. The original Senate version of §7(c) provided that "no sanction shall be imposed . . . except as supported by relevant, reliable, and probative evidence." After the Senate passed this version, the House passed the language of the statute as it reads today, and the Senate accepted the amendment. Any doubt as to the intent of Congress is removed by the House Report, which expressly adopted a preponderance of the evidence standard:

> [W]here a party having the burden of proceeding has come forward with a prima facie and substantial case, he will prevail unless his evidence is discredited or rebutted. In any case the agency must decide "in accordance with the evidence." Where there is evidence pro and con, the agency must weigh it and decide *in accordance with the preponderance*. In short, these provisions require a conscientious and rational judgment on the whole record in accordance with the proofs adduced.

Nor is there any suggestion in the legislative history that a standard of proof higher than a preponderance of the evidence was ever contemplated, much less intended. Congress was primarily concerned with the elimination of agency decisionmaking premised on evidence which was of poor quality—irrelevant, immaterial, unreliable and nonprobative—and of insufficient quantity—less than a preponderance.

The language and legislative history of §7(c) lead us to conclude, therefore, that §7(c) was intended to establish a standard of proof and that the standard adopted is the traditional preponderance of the evidence standard.

Affirmed.

Green v. Carder
667 S.W.2d 660 (Ark. 1984)

HOLLINGSWORTH, J. . . . The Alcoholic Beverage Control Board granted the application of Dr. Edward Stewert Allen for retail liquor and off premise beer permits. On appeal, the circuit court upheld the board's decision. We are being asked to reverse the circuit court and the board and find that there was not substantial evidence to support the granting of the permit. We affirm. . . .

The record made before the ABC Board contains the arguments presented by Allen in favor of granting the permit and by the fourteen people in opposition who attended the hearing. Since these are the facts upon which a finding of substantial evidence must be based, we will set them out in pertinent part. The appellee, Dr. Allen, appeared, representing himself and testified as follows:

> I had planning consultants come out over a year ago to advise me on the best development of this piece of vacant property. I considered a fast food operation and I considered a retail sporting goods store but because of the area that it is in and the traffic and parking it was his advice, his professional advice, that the lowest traffic production and the lowest parking requirements would be a retail liquor outlet. That's my reason for, it's a pure development situation. . . . I would like to comment also on the petitions there in the file. . . . Some of those petitions were gathered at the cash register of two opposing retail liquor outlets. . . . I have outlined the trade area here. This . . . area . . . contains approximately 15,000 to 20,000 people. . . . In this area . . . there are presently two outlets. Two retail liquor outlets. . . . So there is an outlet in the neighborhood already. . . . I am going to oversee [the operation of the outlet] to a major degree. This proposed location is three blocks from my house. . . . I hire competent, experienced managers and I am in direct contact. On some of my other businesses on almost a daily basis. . . .
>
> [A]s far as the parking is concerned. In the file is a proposed plot plan showing the location of the proposed door to the parking lot. Now the parking lot primarily at this point does not serve parking for the businesses there. It serves as a primary parking for the employees that work in the surrounding businesses. . . . There are present on that thirty-one parking spaces. With the proposed development of this lot there will be twenty-nine parking spaces. So I am proposing to eliminate two parking places. . . . All the retail outlets in that area . . . close at 10:00 and that is our intention also.

Sandra Cherry, spokesperson for the opposition, testified as follows:

> The opposition is not based on any opposition to alcohol in particular. The opposition is based primarily on the fact that the neighborhood itself and the shopping center itself are inter-related. . . . [T]hese are some of the considerations. . . . The first one is that we feel that its particular location would lower the property value of the area directly behind the proposed location. . . . Secondly, we are most concerned with the fact that Dr. Allen is a practicing physician and he will not be there, there is no way that he could adequately supervise and be present sufficiently himself to have control over it. There are other considerations . . . mainly with the parking that is available now. . . . [T]he store that Dr. Allen is proposing will take up part of only the remaining parking space. . . . The exit from where the store would be located comes in awkwardly into an intersection which is already a difficult area. . . . [F]or the property located behind the proposed store, the proposed permit, the noise level has been high, will be higher with the store and the stores that are there at the present time close early, . . . around six or seven and at this time pose no problem. It will introduce to this particular block another kind of element, a later night element. . . .

At the original hearing before the Director of the ABC Division when the application was rejected, 103 letters were submitted and 229 signatures on petitions were presented. In the hearing before the ABC Board, where the application was approved, eighty-eight signed copies of a short form protest letter; four signed copies of a long form protest letter; forty-four signatures on a long form petition; and 264 signatures on a short form petition were submitted along with the testimony. . . .

The Alcoholic Beverage Control Board is empowered to determine whether public convenience and advantage will be promoted by issuing liquor permits. . . . Courts may reverse or modify a decision of an administrative board if the decision is not supported by substantial evidence. We do not, however, substitute our judgment for that of an administrative agency, absent an abuse of discretion by that agency. When reviewing administrative decisions, we review the entire record to determine whether there is any substantial evidence to support the agency's decision, or was there arbitrary and capricious action, or was it characterized by abuse of discretion.

It is well settled that administrative agencies are better equipped than courts, by specialization, insight through experience and more flexible procedures to determine and analyze underlying legal issues; and this may be especially true where such issues may be wrought up in a contest between opposing forces in a highly charged atmosphere. This recognition has been asserted, as perhaps, the principal basis for the limited scope of judicial review of administrative action and the refusal of the court to substitute its judgment and discretion for that of the administrative agency.

In examining similar cases, we have held that "[t]he number or official position of persons who object or support the issuance of retail liquor permits is of no significance under the statute. The reasons those persons oppose or support specific permit applications may be very significant." . . .

The burden was upon the appellant to demonstrate that the proof before the administrative tribunal was so nearly undisputed that fair-minded men could not reach its conclusion. The question is not whether the testimony would have supported a contrary finding but whether it supports the finding that was made. Whenever the record contains affirmative proof supporting the view of each side, we must defer to the Board's expertise and experience.

Here, the primary concerns of the parties opposed to the permit were lack of necessity for another liquor store; traffic congestion; general opposition to liquor stores; safety considerations from increased crime and increased traffic; and parking problems. The area where the proposed store would be located is already heavily congested with parking problems and a liquor store already exists a block away. Therefore, it is difficult to see how the addition of this liquor store will suddenly introduce a dangerous element into the neighborhood. We hold that there was substantial evidence to support the Board's action.

Affirmed.

American Textile Manufacturers Institute, Inc. v. Donovan
101 S.Ct. 2478 (1981)

The Occupational Safety and Health Administration issued a health standard in an attempt to limit exposure to cotton dust, which is an airborne particle produced during the manufacture of cotton products. Exposure to cotton dust induces a serious and potentially disabling disease, byssinosis, also known as brown lung disease. The cotton industry challenged the validity of the Cotton Dust Standard. It contended that the Occupational Safety and Health Act requires OSHA to demonstrate that its standard reflects a reasonable relationship between the costs and benefits associated with the standard. The Court of Appeals upheld the standard and ruled that the Act does not require OSHA to compare costs and benefits.

BRENNAN, J. . . . The principal question presented in this case is whether the Occupational Safety and Health Act requires the Secretary, in promulgating a standard pursuant to Section 6(b)(5) of the Act to determine that the costs of the standard bear a reasonable relationship to its benefits. Relying on Sections 6(b)(5) and 3(8) of the Act, petitioners urge not only that OSHA must show that a standard addresses a significant risk of material health impairment, but also that OSHA must demonstrate that the reduction in risk of material health impairment is significant in light of the costs of attaining that reduction. Respondents on the other hand contend that the Act requires OSHA to promulgate standards that eliminate or reduce such risks "to the extent such protection is technologically and economically feasible." To resolve this debate, we must turn to the language, structure, and legislative history of the Occupational Safety and Health Act.

The starting point of our analysis is the language of the statute itself. Section 6(b)(5) of the Act provides:

> The Secretary, in promulgating standards dealing with toxic materials or harmful physical agents under this subsection, shall set the standard which most adequately assures, *to the extent feasible,* on the basis of the best available evidence, that no employee will suffer material impairment of health or functional capacity even if such employee has regular exposure to the hazard dealt with by such standard for the period of his working life.

Although their interpretations differ, all parties agree that the phrase "to the extent feasible" contains the critical language in Section 6(b)(5) for purposes of this case.

The plain meaning of the word "feasible" supports respondents' interpretation of the statute. According to Webster's Third New International Dictionary of the English Language, "feasible" means "capable of being done, executed, or effected." Thus, Section 6(b)(5) directs the Secretary to issue the standard that "most adequately assures . . . that no employee will suffer material impairment of health," limited only by the extent to which this is "capable of being done." In effect then, as the Court of Appeals held, Congress itself defined the basic relationship between costs and benefits, by placing the "benefit" of worker health above all other considerations save those making attainment of this "benefit" unachievable. Any standard based on a balancing of costs and benefits by the Secretary that strikes a different balance than that struck by Congress would be inconsistent with the command set forth in Section 6(b)(5). Thus, cost-benefit analysis by OSHA is not required by the statute because feasibility analysis is. . . .

The legislative history of the Act, . . . demonstrates conclusively, that Congress was fully aware that the Act would impose real and substantial costs of compliance on industry, and believed that such costs were part of the cost of doing business. . . .

Not only does the legislative history confirm that Congress meant "feasible" rather than "cost-benefit" when it used the former term, but it also shows that Congress understood that the Act would create substantial costs for employers, yet intended to impose such costs when necessary to create a safe and healthful working environment. Congress viewed the costs of health and safety as a cost of doing business. Senator Yarborough, a cosponsor of the Williams bill, stated: "We know the costs would be put into consumer goods but that is the price we should pay for the 80 million workers in America." . . .

When Congress passed the Occupational Safety and Health Act in 1970, it chose to place preeminent value on assuring employees a safe and healthful working environment, limited only by the feasibility of achieving such an environment. We must measure the validity of the Secretary's actions against the requirements of that Act. For "[t]he judicial function does not extend to substantive revision of regulatory policy. That function lies elsewhere—in Congressional and Executive oversight or amendatory legislation." Accordingly, the judgment of the Court of Appeals is
Affirmed.

REVIEW QUESTIONS

1. Identify the terms in column A by matching each with the appropriate statement in column B.

A	B
1. Quasi-legislative	a. Doctrine which requires that an agency is given full opportunity to correct its errors.
2. Consent order	b. Needed to make the administrative agencies more efficient.
3. Standing to sue	c. A principle that must be considered when a court is reviewing an agency's rule-making authority.

4. Exhaustion of remedies

5. Delegation of authority

6. Immunity

7. Cost-benefit analysis

8. Regulatory reform

d. A mechanism used to settle disputes.

e. An important defense used by administrators when sued for damages.

f. The initial issue a court must consider when reviewing an agency decision.

g. Another name for an agency's authority to make rules and regulations.

h. A proposed remedy to some of the problems inherent with the administrative process.

2. What are three reasons why it has become necessary to create administrative agencies to assist in the operation of the federal government?

3. List six of the common functions of these administrative agencies.

4. The Environmental Protection Agency (EPA) discovered that a chemical company was dumping toxic waste into a local river. The agency conducted a hearing with proper notice to the chemical company and found the company to be in violation of EPA's regulations. A heavy fine was imposed and the corporation appealed to the court, contending that the hearing had denied it its right to a trial by jury. Is the corporation entitled to a trial by jury? Explain.

5. The initial issue that any court must consider when reviewing an administrative agency's decision is whether the complaining party has standing to sue. What is meant by *standing to sue?*

6. Leonard's, Inc., was charged with violating a rule of an administrative agency. A hearing was conducted by an administrative law judge. The judge found the company guilty. The rules of the agency provided for a review by the full commission, but rather than seek such a review, Leonard's filed a case in the courts to enjoin further agency action. Is Leonard's entitled to an injunction? Why?

7. By what standards do courts determine whether Congress has validly delegated authority to a federal agency?

8. Define the term *consent order* and explain how effective it is as an enforcement device.

9. The Federal Trade Commission (FTC) issued an administrative complaint against several major oil companies alleging unfair methods of competition. After failing to get the FTC to dismiss the complaint, the oil companies brought a separate action against the FTC in federal court asserting that the FTC had issued the complaint without having reason to believe that the companies were violating the law. They sought an order to require the FTC to withdraw the complaint. The gist was that political pressure for a public explanation of the gasoline shortages of 1973 forced the FTC to issue the complaint despite insufficient investigation. Should the case be dismissed? Why?

10. Henry, a person of limited means, had a dispute with a federal administrative agency. When the matter was not resolved before the agency, Henry appealed to a federal court. The court found all of the issues for Henry and observed that the government officials had been arbitrary and capricious in their dealings with Henry. Henry paid his attorney $10,000 to handle his appeal. Is he entitled to recoup this loss from the government? Explain.

11. Discuss the standard by which courts are governed when they review decisions of administrative agencies.

12. What three major problems arise when a government relies heavily on administrative agencies?

47 THE ANTITRUST LAW

A series of laws commonly referred to as the *antitrust laws* serve to protect our economic system from monopolies, attempts to monopolize, and activities in restraint of trade. These laws seek to provide a system of workable competition that will achieve lower prices, product innovation, and equitable distribution of real income among consumers and the factors of production. Antitrust laws are enforced by the Justice Department and the Federal Trade Commission, but competitors and consumers aid enforcement by instituting private damage suits.

In 1890, under its power to regulate interstate commerce, Congress passed the Sherman Antitrust Act, directed at two areas: (1) contracts, combinations, or conspiracies in restraint of trade; and (2) monopoly and attempts to monopolize. The law supplies a means to break up existing monopolies and to prevent others from developing. It is directed at single firms and does not purport to cover shared monopolies and oligopolies.

In 1914 Congress passed two laws, the Clayton Act and the Federal Trade Commission Act. The Clayton Act was designed to make the Sherman Act more specific. The Federal Trade Commission Act created the Federal Trade Commission as an administrative agency staffed with experts to enforce the Clayton Act. Table 47-1 summarizes these laws.

1. Sanctions

The antitrust laws seek to preserve competition by utilization of three basic sanctions. First of all, violation of the Sherman Act is a federal crime punishable by fine or imprisonment or both. Second, the Sherman Act authorizes injunctions

STATUTE	SUBJECT MATTER
I. Sherman Act (1890)	
Section 1	Contracts, combinations and conspiracies in restraint of trade
Section 2	Monopoly and attempts to monopolize
II. Clayton Act (1914)	
Section 2, as amended by the Robinson-Patman Act (1936)	Price discrimination
Section 3	Tying and exclusive contracts
Section 4	Treble damage suits
Section 7, as amended by the Celler-Kefauver Amendment (1950)	Mergers and acquisitions
Section 8	Interlocking directorates
III. Federal Trade Commission Act (1914)	
Section 5	Unfair methods of competition and unfair or deceptive acts or practices

TABLE 47–1

Antitrust laws

to prevent and restrain violations or continued violations of its provisions. Failure to obey may be punished by contempt proceedings. Third, the Clayton Act creates a remedy for those who have been injured by violations. In a civil action, they may collect treble damages plus court costs and reasonable fees for an attorney. Normally, the objective of money damages is to place the injured party in the position he or she would have enjoyed, as nearly as this can be done with money, had rights not been invaded. The treble-damage provision serves not only as a means of punishing the defendant for wrongful acts, but also as a means of compensating the plaintiff for injuries sustained.

Today, criminal violations of the Sherman Act are felonies. An individual found guilty may be fined up to $100,000 and imprisoned for up to 3 years. A corporation found guilty may be fined up to $1 million for each offense.

The treble-damage sanction is probably the most important today. Suit to collect triple damages may be brought by the attorneys general of the various states on behalf of the consumers of their state or by class-action suits. Suits are also brought by competitors, customers of violators, and other members of the general public that suffer economic injury as the result of antitrust law violations. The treble-damage remedy allows the general public to enforce the law if government fails to do so. (For example, H. J. Heinz Company has sued Campbell Soup, alleging predatory market practices designed to eliminate Heinz.)

As previously noted, even consumers may collect triple damages from retailers guilty of violating the law. Consumers and others cannot sue a party that he or she did not deal with directly, however. Treble-damage claims are not passed through the channels of distribution because of the uncertainty of determining the damages at each level. If a manufacturer is guilty of violating the law, only the person who dealt directly with the manufacturer can recover triple damages. However, the theory that prevents indirect purchasers from collecting triple damages does not limit suits by parties indirectly affected if the damages are easily determined.

Parties who conspire to commit torts together are generally said to have "joint and several liability." This means that each party is liable for the total damages caused by the tort of all. The concept of joint and several liability is applied to antitrust suits for triple damages in order to discourage antitrust violations such as price-fixing.

The fact that a company has liability for all of the tort damages caused by co-conspirators is further complicated by the legal principle that a wrongdoer has no right to compel contribution from the other wrongdoers. As a result, one company may end up owing triple damages to customers of other companies when all are guilty of price-fixing or other Sherman Act violations. To illustrate, assume that five companies are charged with price-fixing. Four of them settle out of court for $1 million each, and the fifth proceeds to trial, continuing the contention of all that they were innocent of price-fixing. The jury finds the fifth company guilty, and the plaintiff's total damages are $5 million. The court triples this amount to $15 million and deducts only the $4 million paid by the other defendants, leaving a liability of $11 million. Each company had an equal share of the market, so the company that went to trial has a liability of $8 million more than its share. Such a result has the potential to destroy a company.

THE SHERMAN ACT

2. Monopoly and Attempts to Monopolize

It is a violation of Section 2 of the Sherman Act for a firm to (1) monopolize, (2) attempt to monopolize or (3) conspire to monopolize any part of interstate or foreign commerce. In a case alleging an attempt to monopolize, there must be proof of intent to destroy competition or to achieve monopoly power. Showing that a conspiracy to monopolize existed requires proof of specific intent to monopolize and at least one overt act to accomplish it.

A firm has violated Section 2 if it followed a course of conduct through which it has obtained the power to control price or exclude competition. The mere possession of monopoly power is not a violation. There must be proof that the power has resulted from a deliberate course of conduct or proof of intent to maintain the power by conduct.

Cases involving Section 2 require proof of the power to affect the price of the firm's products in the market. Whether such power exists is determined by an analysis of the reaction of buyers to price changes by the alleged monopolist seller. Related products and geographic markets must be identified, and a study must be made of the degree of concentration within the markets.

Some monopoly cases involve homogenous products; others involve products for which there are numerous substitutes. Aluminum may be considered a product for which it is difficult to find substitutes. If a firm has 90 percent of the virgin aluminum market, a violation would be established. If a firm has 90 percent of the Danish coffee cake market, the decision is less clear, because numerous products compete with Danish coffee cakes. The relevant product is often difficult to define because of differences in products, substitute products, product diversification, and even product clusters.

Courts in monopoly cases examine a variety of factors: the degree of market concentration, barriers to entering the market, structural features such as the market shares of other firms, profit levels, the extent to which prices respond to changes in supply and demand, whether or not a firm discriminates in price among its customers, and the absolute size of the firm. Courts also examine the conduct of the firm. How did it achieve its market share? Was it by internal growth or by acquisition? Does the firm's current conduct tend to injure competition? These and other issues are important aspects in any finding of the existence of monopoly power.

Monopolistic conduct is predatory in that a firm seeks to advance its market share by injuring its actual or potential competitors, not by improved performance. Monopoly power may be used for the purpose of driving out competitors, for keeping them out, or for making them less effective.

3. Restraints of Trade

Section 1 of the Sherman Act prohibits contracts (express or implied), combinations, and conspiracies in restraint of trade. For example, discussion of price with one's competitors taken together with conscious parallel pricing establishes a violation.

Activities that may constitute a contract, combination, or conspiracy in restraint of trade are limitless. An agreement by several competitors to buy exclusively from a single supplier may be a violation. A group boycott may be a violation, even though the victim is just one small merchant. Of course, all forms of price-fixing or other concentrated action among competitors constitute violations. A multiple listing service required that member real estate brokers have favorable credit reports and business reputations, that they keep their offices open for stated hours, and that they purchase stock at a price not related to the operating cost of the service. These practices were held to be a prima facie case of unreasonable restraint of trade.

Analysis.   Under the Sherman Act, agreements and practices are illegal only if they are unreasonable. In deciding if an agreement or practice is unreasonable, courts divide them into two types or categories. Some are said to be illegal per se.[1] This means that they are conclusively presumed to be unreasonable and thus illegal, so plainly anticompetitive and lacking in any redeeming virtue that it is unnecessary to examine the effects of the activity. If an activity is illegal per se, proof of the activity is proof of a violation and proof that it is in restraint of trade.

The second type or category includes activities that are illegal only if the facts establish that they are unreasonable. An act is unreasonable if it suppresses or destroys competition. An act is reasonable if it promotes competition. In cases under this second category, courts analyze the facts to determine the significance of the activity or restraint on competition.

Price-fixing.   The most common type of Sherman Act violation is horizontal price-fixing, which is illegal per se. It is no defense that the prices fixed are fair or reasonable. It also is no defense that price-fixing is engaged in by small competi-

[1] Catalano, Inc. v. Target Sales, Inc., p. 1071.

tors to allow them to compete with larger competitors. It is just as illegal to fix a low price as it is to fix a high price. Today it is as illegal to fix the price of services as it is to fix the price of goods. Price-fixing in the service sector has been engaged in by professional persons as well as by service occupations such as automobile and TV repair workers, barbers, and refuse collectors. For many years it was contended that persons performing services were not engaged in trade or commerce, but the courts today reject such arguments.

Some professional groups have attempted to avoid the foregoing result through the use of ethical standards.[2] Others have attempted to determine the price of services indirectly by the use of formulas and relative value scales. Some medical organizations have determined that a given medical procedure would be allocated a relative value on a scale of 1 to 10. Brain surgery might be labeled a 9 and a face lift a 4. All members of the profession would then use these values in determining professional fees. Such attempts have been uniformly held to be illegal.

Horizontal price-fixing exists when competitors combine together to fix the price of their products. *Vertical* price-fixing occurs when a manufacturer or producer enters into an agreement with its customers on the price to be charged when the product is resold. Vertical price-fixing is sometimes called *resale price maintenance.*

As a general rule, vertical price-fixing is also illegal per se. While a manufacturer may announce its prices and may refuse to deal with retailers that do not follow such prices, a manufacturer cannot coerce dealers to follow such prices and cannot enter into agreements to fix such prices. This makes it difficult for a manufacturer of a brand or trade name product to maintain its retail price and the image of high quality which many consumers often relate to high price.

Whether or not vertical price-fixing should be illegal per se is a matter of debate. The Reagan administration has indicated that it believes some vertical price-fixing is not anticompetitive, but may in fact aid competition. Congress in 1984 adopted a resolution condemning vertical price-fixing and indicating that vertical price-fixing is just as bad as horizontal price-fixing and therefore should be illegal per se.

4. Other Violations

Many violations of the Sherman Act involve concerted activities among competitors. An exchange of price information has been held to be one of the numerous violations.[3] Typical of the cases involving concerted activities was the 1984 Supreme Court decision relating to the televising of college football games. The National Collegiate Athletic Association (NCAA) had adopted a television plan intended to reduce the adverse effect of live television on football games and the number of games that any one college could televise. No member of the NCAA could sell television rights except in accordance with the plan. The NCAA had agreements with ABC and CBS granting each network the right to telecast

---

[2] National Society of Professional Engineers v. United States, p. 1072.

[3] United States v. Container Corporation of America, p. 1073.

games for a specified "minimum aggregate compensation" to the participating NCAA members. When the University of Georgia and the University of Oklahoma challenged the plan under the Sherman Act, the court held the plan to be a violation. Competition in "live" college football television was restrained in three ways: (a) The NCAA fixed the price for particular telecasts; (b) its exclusive network contracts amounted to a group boycott of all other potential broadcasters, and its threat of sanctions against its members constituted a threatened boycott of potential competitors; and (c) its plan placed an artificial limit on the production of televised college football. The activity was not illegal per se even though it involved horizontal price-fixing. It was subject to the rule of reason because some horizontal restraint is essential if the product is to be available at all. The NCAA television plan raised prices and reduced output without regard to consumer preference.

Manufacturers frequently license distributors for their products, assigning them an exclusive territory, getting them to agree not to sell in other areas, and sometimes limiting their customers. Manufacturers who seek to control their products after parting with dominion over them through a sale may or may not be in violation of the Sherman Act. Vertical territorial restrictions imposed by a manufacturer on its dealers are not per se violations, but may be illegal if they have an unreasonable effect on competition. Horizontal territorial restrictions (agreements among competitors) are illegal per se.

5. Introduction

THE CLAYTON ACT

From its adoption, the Sherman Act proved unable to accomplish all its goals. Its language was too broad, and the courts favored big business early in the century. Various amendments designed to make the act more specific have been enacted through the years.

In 1914 Congress enacted the first such amendment, known as the Clayton Act, designed to make the Sherman Act more specific. The Clayton Act declared illegal certain practices that might have an adverse effect on competition but were something less than violations of the Sherman Act. The practices it enumerated were outlawed if they *might* substantially lessen competition or tend to create a monopoly. This effect is sometimes referred to as the *prohibited effect* of the Clayton Act.

The Clayton Act contained four major provisions. Section 2, later amended by the Robinson-Patman Act, made it unlawful for a seller to discriminate in price among purchasers of commodities when the prohibited effect or tendency might result. Section 3 makes it unlawful for a person engaged in commerce to lease or sell commodities or fix a price with the condition that the lessee or purchaser shall not use or deal in the commodities of a competitor of the lessor or seller when the prohibited effect might result.

Section 7 prohibited the acquisition of all or part of the stock of other corporations if the effect *might* be to lessen competition substantially or to *tend* to create a monopoly. This section has been substantially amended also.

Section 8 of the Clayton Act was aimed at interlocking directorates. It prohibits a person from being a member of the board of directors of two or more corporations at the same time when one of them has capital, surplus, and undivided profits totaling more than $1 million and where elimination of competition by agreement between such corporations would amount to a violation of any of the antitrust laws.

6. Price Discrimination—In General

Historical background. Section 2, as originally adopted, outlawed price discrimination that might substantially lessen competition or tend to create a monopoly in any line of commerce. It was not illegal to discriminate in price because of differences in the grade, quality, or quantity of the commodity sold or to make due allowance for difference in the cost of selling or transportation. This latter provision, which allowed quantity discounts among other things, so weakened Section 2 that it was very difficult to prevent price discrimination.

In the 1920s and very early 1930s, large-volume retailers and especially chain stores were able to obtain more favorable prices than those available to smaller competitors. Preferential treatment included quantity discounts, brokerage allowances paid to subsidiaries of customers, and promotional allowances. These practices, which were not prohibited by the Clayton Act, led to the enactment in 1936 of the Robinson-Patman amendment, which attempted to eliminate the advantages of large buyers over a small buyer.

To ensure equality of price to all customers of a seller of commodities for resale, where the result of unequal treatment may be substantially to lessen competition or tend to create a monopoly in any line of commerce, the Robinson-Patman Act forbids any person engaged "in commerce" to discriminate in price if the goods involved in such discrimination are "in commerce" and are for resale. The act does not apply to a sale by retailers to consumers. The term *commerce* refers to transactions in interstate commerce, not to intrastate transactions that only *affect* interstate commerce. A victim of a violation is entitled to collect triple damages from parties in violation. A plaintiff seeking damages must prove actual injury attributable to the violation, not merely a price differential, because there are no automatic damages.

Basic provisions. First of all, the Robinson-Patman amendment made it a crime for a seller to sell at lower prices in one geographical area than elsewhere in the United States in order to eliminate competition or a competitor, or to sell at unreasonably low prices to drive out a competitor. As a result, it is illegal to sell goods below cost for the illegitimate purpose of driving out competition. Not every sale below cost constitutes a violation. Sales for legitimate purposes such as liquidation of excess, obsolete, or perishable merchandise may be legal. It is illegal to charge the low price only where the intention is to drive out a competitor.

Second, it is unlawful for any person to discriminate in price among different purchasers of commodities of like grade and quality if discrimination would substantially lessen competition or tend to create a monopoly in any line of commerce or injure competition with any person. Price discrimination is not illegal per se. An injury to competition may be established by showing injury to a competitor victimized by the discrimination. It is a violation knowingly to receive a benefit of such discrimination or to give such a benefit. The law applies both to buyers and sellers. It also applies to state and local government.[4]

The statute recognizes certain exceptions. (1) Price differentials based on differences in the cost of manufacture, sale, or delivery of commodities are permitted (cost justification defense). (2) Sellers may select their own customers in bona fide transactions and not in restraint of trade. (3) Price changes may be made in response to changing conditions, such as actual or imminent deterioration of perishable goods, obsolescence of seasonal goods, distress sales under court process, or sales in good faith in discontinuance of business in the goods concerned (changing conditions defense). (4) A seller in good faith may meet the equally low price of a competitor (good-faith meeting of competition defense).

The Robinson-Patman amendment also gave the Federal Trade Commission jurisdiction and authority to eliminate quantity discounts. It outlaws certain hidden or indirect discriminations by sellers in favor of certain buyers. Section 2(c) prohibits an unearned brokerage or commission related to a sale of goods. It is unlawful to pay or receive a commission or discount on sales or purchases except for actual services rendered. Section 2(d) outlaws granting promotional allowances or payments on goods bought for resale unless they are available to all competing customers. A manufacturer who gives a retailer a right to purchase three items for the price of two, as a part of a special promotion, must give the same right to all competitors in the market. Section 2(e) prohibits giving promotional facilities or services on goods bought for resale unless they are available to all competing customers.

7. Price Discrimination—Defenses

Two of the several defenses to a charge of price discrimination require further comment.

Cost justification defense.   If a plaintiff proves differential pricing and injury to competition, a prima facie case of price discrimination is established. Theoretically, a defendant may rebut this prima facie case by proof of cost justification. Practically, the cost defense has proved largely illusory. The complexities of determining what is "cost" results in rare use of the defense. As a practical matter, proof of cost involves direct costs and indirect costs. Indirect costs are based on assumptions, and accountants may make different ones. Disputes occur over the technique to determine actual cost, and proof of it is difficult. The status of the defense is such that only the most prosperous and patient business firms can afford pursuit of it.

Good-faith meeting of competition.   On the other hand, the good-faith meeting of competition defense is quite important. The act permits a defendant to demonstrate that price discrimination was not unlawful because the lower price, services, or facility was offered in good faith to meet an equally low price, service, or facility of a competitor. "Good faith" is not easily defined. It is a flexible and

---

[4] Jefferson City Pharmaceutical Ass'n. v. Abbott Labs, p. 1074.

pragmatic, not a technical or doctrinaire concept. The standard of good faith is simply the standard of the prudent businessperson responding fairly to what he reasonably believes is a situation of competitive necessity. The facts and circumstances in each case govern its interpretation and application.

Good faith cannot be established if the purpose of a seller's price discrimination is to eliminate competition. The seller may offer discriminatory prices to customers, whether or not he has done business with them in the past. The timing of the price offers must make it apparent that they are intended to meet an individual competitive situation and are not a part of a general system of competition.

The good-faith meeting of competition defense is available to buyers as well as to sellers. A buyer's liability is based on the seller's liability; therefore, if the seller has a defense, so does the buyer.[5]

8. Tying Arrangements and Exclusive Dealings

Section 3 of the Clayton Act prohibits arrangements and exclusive dealings that may substantially lessen competition or tend to create a monopoly in any line of commerce. If that should be the effect, anyone engaged in commerce may not lease or sell commodities (patented or unpatented) or fix a price on the condition that the lessee or purchaser should not use or deal in the commodities of a competitor or competitors of the lessor or seller. Section 3 covers tying contracts, reciprocal dealings, and exclusive arrangements.

In a *tying contract,* a commodity is sold or leased for use only on condition that the buyer or lessee purchase a different product or service from the seller or lessor. Tying arrangements may be violations of Section 1 of the Sherman Act and Section 3 of the Clayton Act. Tying arrangements are illegal without proof of anticompetitive effects. They are treated as unreasonable in and of themselves whenever economic power over the tying product can appreciably restrain free competition for the tied product and affect a "not insubstantial" amount of interstate commerce. The monopolistic power of a patent might be used to tie in a promise to buy an unpatented item. That would be a typical tying contract in violation of Section 3.

In *full-line forcing,* a common form of tying arrangement, the buyer or lessee is compelled to take a complete product line from the seller. If a major oil company requires its service station dealers to purchase a stated amount of regular gasoline and premium priced gasoline in order to obtain no-lead gasoline, Section 3 is violated.

A *reciprocal dealing* arrangement exists when two parties face each other as both buyer and seller. One party offers to buy the other party's goods, but only if the second party buys other goods from the first party. If one party is both a food wholesaler and a provider of goods used in processing foods, food processors may be faced by a reciprocal requirement. The first party might agree to buy the processors' products only if the processors buy the processing goods from it. One

---

[5] Great Atlantic & Pacific Tea Co., Inc. v. FTC, p. 1076.

side of the transaction uses its power to force those with whom it deals to make concessions in another market. The law declares such conduct to be illegal because of the extension of market power in one market to another market.

Exclusive dealings do not necessarily involve more than one product and the terms of its sale. An exclusive dealing may be a requirements contract, whereby the buyer agrees to purchase all its business needs of a product supplied by the seller during a certain period of time. The buyer may be a manufacturer who has a reasonably ascertainable need for the raw materials or parts agreed to be supplied, or he may be a retailer who needs goods for resale. An exclusive dealing is present also in a contract in which a buyer agrees not to purchase an item or items of merchandise from competitors of the seller. Such a contract might take the form of a franchise, in which a dealer agrees to sell only the product manufactured or distributed by the seller—a particular make of automobile, for instance. Such contracts are not illegal per se. They are illegal only if they tend substantially to lessen competition or tend to create a monopoly. Proof that competition is foreclosed in a substantial line of commerce establishes a violation.

9. Mergers and Acquisitions

Mergers and acquisitions are usually classified as horizontal, market extension, vertical, or conglomerate. A *horizontal* merger combines two businesses in the same field or industry, reducing the number of competitors. A *market extension* merger is an acquisition in which the acquiring company extends its markets. This market extension may be either in new products (product extension) or in new areas (geographical extension).

A *vertical* merger brings together two companies, one being the customer of the other. Such a combination usually removes the customer from the market as far as other suppliers are concerned. It may remove a source of supply also if the acquiring company is a customer of the acquired one. A *conglomerate* merger is one in which the businesses involved are neither competitors nor related as customer and supplier in any given line of commerce.

The law of mergers is based primarily upon three statutes—the Sherman Act, the Bank Merger Act, and the Clayton Act. A horizontal merger violates the Sherman Act if it is a combination in unreasonable restraint of trade or if it results in monopolization of a line of commerce or if it is an attempt to monopolize.

A great deal of merger litigation involves banks. Their mergers are subject to the provisions of the Bank Merger Acts of 1960 and 1966 as well as the usual antitrust laws. Bank mergers are illegal unless approved by one of the agencies that regulate banks. If the merger involves a national bank, the approval of the Comptroller of the Currency is required. If the banks are state banks that are members of the Federal Reserve System, the approval of the Federal Reserve Board is necessary. Other mergers of banks insured by the Federal Deposit Insurance Corporation require approval of that agency.

Section 7 of the Clayton Act is the major statute in the merger and acquisition area. It was originally adopted in 1914 and later amended by the Celler-Kefauver amendment in 1950. Section 7, as amended, provides essentially that no business engaged in commerce shall acquire any of the stock or assets of another such business if the effect may be substantially to lessen competition or to tend to create a monopoly in any line of commerce in any section of the country. Violations require only a finding and conclusion that a given acquisition has a reasonable probability of lessening competition or tendency toward monopoly. Section 7 does not deal with certainties, only with probabilities. The goal of the law is to arrest incipient anticompetitive effects and trends toward undue concentration of economic power. In determining whether or not a merger or acquisition is illegal, courts examine both the product market and the geographic market affected.

The law has neither adopted nor rejected any particular tests for measuring relevant markets. Both the product market and geographical market of the businesses involved are factual issues to be considered by the courts. The more narrowly the product line or geographic area is defined, the greater the impact of a merger or acquisition on competition. Thus, the relevant market frequently determines the probable anticompetitive effects of the merger. A decision that enlarges the line of commerce may be important in establishing that a merger is not anticompetitive.

For a violation of Section 7, courts must also find that within the market the effect of the merger "may be substantially to lessen competition or to tend to create a monopoly." The degree of market concentration prior to the merger and the relative position of the merged parties are important factors to be considered. If there has been a history of tendency toward concentration in an industry, slight increases in further concentration are prohibited because of the policy of the law to curb such tendencies in their incipiency.

Today those responsible for enforcing this law are primarily concerned with horizontal acquisitions. Vertical acquisitions and conglomerate mergers are likely to be challenged only if they involve a highly concentrated industry or monopoly is likely. Many large mergers and acquisitions have been consummated without legal challenge.

10. Interlocking Directorates

Section 8 of the Clayton Act prohibits a person from being a member of the board of directors of two or more competing corporations. The law is applicable when one of the corporations has capital, surplus, and undivided profits totaling more than $1 million and the elimination of competition by agreement between the corporation would amount to a violation of any of the antitrust laws. Such corporations are said to have *interlocking boards of directors.*

There have been numerous Section 8 challenges of directors on the boards of many large companies. These challenges were the result of outside directors—directors who are high-ranking officers of other corporations and who are asked to serve as a director because of their experience and expertise rather than as officials of the corporation. As corporations have tended to diversity, it is not difficult to find some form of competition between two companies that on the surface would seem to be involved in quite different fields. For example, a director on the board of an aluminum manufacturer who also served on the board of a steel company was held to be in violation because aluminum and steel compete under certain circumstances. The number of outside directors seems to have been reduced substantially in highly diversified corporations as the direct result of this law.

Congress enacted a second antitrust law in 1914 creating the Federal Trade Commission as one of the expert, independent regulatory agencies. The Federal Trade Commission was given jurisdiction over cases arising under Section 2, 3, 7, and 8 of the Clayton Act. Originally, the commission was directed to prevent unfair methods of competition in commerce. A later amendment directed it to make "unfair methods of competition in commerce and unfair or deceptive acts or practices in commerce" unlawful. The commission has to determine what methods, acts, or practices are "unfair" or "deceptive" and thus illegal, because Congress did not define these terms. The term "unfair methods of competition" is a flexible concept, the exact meaning of which evolves on a case-by-case basis. It is capable of application to a variety of unrelated activities, including business conduct in violation of any provision of the antitrust laws. Further, anticompetitive acts or practices that *fall short* of transgressing the Sherman or Clayton Acts may be restrained by the FTC as being "unfair methods of competition."

ENFORCEMENT

The antitrust laws are enforced by (1) the Department of Justice, (2) the Federal Trade Commission, and (3) private parties. The Department of Justice alone has the power to bring criminal proceedings; the department shares power with the Federal Trade Commission and private parties in civil proceedings. The civil proceedings may use the injunctive remedy or the treble-damage remedy.

The extent to which the laws are enforced by the Justice Department and by the Federal Trade Commission vary from time to time and from administration to administration. The attitude and philosophy of the president and his appointees play a significant role in antitrust enforcement. For example, President Reagan's desire for less government involvement in economic decisions and for greater reliance on competition to regulate the economy resulted in a shift in antitrust enforcement and especially in the enforcement of Section 7 of the Clayton Act. Mergers that prior administrations would probably have challenged were routinely approved by the Reagan administration and by Reagan's appointees to the Federal Trade Commission. Mergers that could have been challenged successfully were not challenged.

On the other hand, the Reagan administration has stepped up enforcement of the laws relating to horizontal price-fixing. The Justice Department has a "hotline" to encourage people to report price-fixing and other antitrust violations. Criminal price-fixing cases usually result in plea-bargained penalties that include incarceration.

Antitrust enforcement by state government is also very important. State attorneys general may bring triple-damage suits under the Sherman Act on behalf of the citizens of their states. In addition, state legislators have enacted antitrust laws covering both products and services that apply to intrastate activities. For example, one case involved agreements by local golf course operators to fix the price of green fees and golf cart rentals. Another case involved a real estate subdivider whose contracts of sale required that his real estate firm be used as the broker on a subsequent sale. The impact of state antitrust laws is likely to be much greater in the future.

SUMMARY

Introduction	1. The three most important federal antitrust laws are the Sherman Act, the Clayton Act, and the Federal Trade Commission Act.
	2. The relevant sections and subject matters of each of these acts are summarized in Table 47–1.
Sanctions	1. A violation of the Sherman Act is a felony, which is punishable by a fine or imprisonment or both.
	2. The government may also seek to enjoin the alleged violation.
	3. As a third sanction, individuals and business organizations that have been damaged by an antitrust violation may sue for triple damages.

THE SHERMAN ACT

Monopoly and attempts to monopolize	1. Section 2 of the Sherman Act prohibits monopolies or the attempts to monopolize any part of interstate or foreign commerce.
	2. A violation of Section 2 would consist of conduct whereby an organization exhibits the power to control a product's price or to exclude competition.
	3. Many factors are considered by courts in Section 2 cases. The ultimate issue is whether an organization is forcing competitors out of business, keeping them out, or making them less effective.
Restraints of trade	1. Section 1 of the Sherman Act prohibits contracts, combinations, and conspiracies in restraint of trade.
	2. Only those restraints of trade that are unreasonable are illegal under Section 1.

3. Courts have developed two types of analyses for determining unreasonableness. One is the per se rule, and the other is the rule of reason.

4. Price-fixing is the classic case when courts apply the per se rule. All cases of price-fixing are unreasonable regardless of the price which is fixed.

Other violations

1. Concerted activities other than price-fixing among competitors are illegal only if they are unreasonably anticompetitive.

2. Vertical territorial restrictions by a supplier on a customer are subject to the rule of reason. Horizontal territorial restrictions among competitors are illegal per se.

THE CLAYTON ACT

Price discrimination—in general

1. Section 2 of the Clayton Act outlawed price discrimination that might substantially lessen competition or tends to create a monopoly.

2. As originally enacted, the loopholes in Section 2 made enforcement of price discrimination difficult.

3. The Robinson-Patman amendment (1936) succeeded in closing most of the loopholes.

4. Only the price discrimination in commerce is potentially illegal. Price discrimination in intrastate transactions is not covered by Section 2 even when such discrimination affects interstate commerce.

Price discrimination—defenses

1. The cost justification defense to Section 2 has been illusory. The difficulties in establishing the cost of a product make reliance on this defense impractical.

2. A more usable defense is to prove that a price was lowered to one customer in a good-faith attempt to meet the price of a competitor.

3. The lowering of a price to meet an illegal price of a competitor is not in good faith.

Tying arrangements and exclusive dealing	1. Section 3 of the Clayton Act prohibits contracts involving tying arrangements and exclusive dealing that might substantially lessen competition or tend to create a monopoly.
	2. A tying arrangement occurs when a product is sold only if the buyer also purchases an undesired product.
	3. Full-line forcing and reciprocal deals are examples of tying arrangements that may be illegal.
	4. Exclusive dealings may occur through a buyer agreeing not to buy from the seller's competitor or through a seller agreeing not to sell to any other outlet within a stated territory.
Mergers and acquisitions	1. A merger may be classified as horizontal, market extension, vertical, or conglomerate.
	2. Although the Sherman Act and the Bank Merger Act are important laws governing mergers, Section 7 of the Clayton Act, as amended, is the most important law.
	3. Answers to three questions are essential in analyzing a Section 7 case. These questions concern the market involved, the geography involved, and the adverse impact of the merger on competition.
Interlocking directorates	1. Section 8 of the Clayton Act prohibits one person from being a director of two competing companies under certain circumstances.
	2. Section 8 applies if one of the competing companies has capital, surplus, and undivided profits greater than $1 million and the elimination of the competition would be an antitrust violation.
Enforcement	1. The Federal Trade Commission Act created the FTC, whose purpose is to protect the public from unfair or deceptive trade practices and unfair methods of competition.
	2. An individual or business organization may be found to have violated the FTC Act even though a Sherman Act or Clayton Act violation cannot be proven.

3. Antitrust laws may be enforced by the Justice Department, the FTC, or private entities. Only the Justice Department can bring criminal charges.

4. During the Reagan administration enforcement of Section 7 of the Clayton Act has been relaxed, while enforcement against horizontal price-fixing has increased.

5. Despite the federal government's power of enforcement of antitrust laws, the role of states in this area is increasing in importance.

CASES

Catalano, Inc. v. Target Sales, Inc.
100 S.Ct. 1925 (1980)

Plaintiffs (beer retailers) brought suit claiming that various wholesalers had engaged in a conspiracy to restrain trade. The wholesalers had agreed to refuse to sell to retailers unless the retailer paid cash in advance or at the time of delivery. There was an agreement that no wholesaler would grant short-term credit, although such credit had been extended prior to the agreement. Plaintiffs asked the trial court to declare the case one of "per se" illegality. The trial court refused, and the plaintiffs appealed.

PER CURIAM. . . . In construing and applying the Sherman Act's ban against contracts, conspiracies, and combinations in restraint of trade, the Court has held that certain agreements or practices are so "plainly anticompetitive," and so often lack . . . any redeeming virtue, that they are conclusively presumed illegal without further examination under the rule of reason generally applied in Sherman Act cases.

A horizontal agreement to fix prices is the archetypal example of such a practice. It has long been settled that an agreement to fix prices is unlawful per se. It is no excuse that the prices fixed are themselves reasonable. In United States v. Socony-Vacuum Oil Co., 310 U.S. 150, 60 (1940),

we held that an agreement among competitors to engage in a program of buying surplus gasoline on the spot market in order to prevent prices from falling sharply to be unlawful without any inquiry into the reasonableness of the program, even though there was no direct agreement on the actual prices to be maintained. In the course of the opinion, the Court made clear that "the machinery employed by a combination for price-fixing is immaterial."

"Under the Sherman Act a combination formed for the purpose and with the effect of raising, depressing, fixing, pegging, or stabilizing the price of a commodity in interstate or foreign commerce is illegal per se." . . .

It is virtually self-evident that extending interest-free credit for a period of time is equivalent to giving a discount equal to the value of the use of the purchase price for that period of time. Thus, credit terms must be characterized as an inseparable part of the price. An agreement to terminate the practice of giving credit is thus tantamount to an agreement to eliminate discounts, and thus falls squarely within the traditional per se rule against price fixing. While it may be that the elimination of a practice of giving variable discounts will ultimately lead in a competitive market to corresponding decreases in the invoice price, that is surely not necessarily to be anticipated. It is more realistic to view an agreement to eliminate credit sales as extinguishing one form of competition among the sellers. In any event, when a particular concerted activity entails an obvious risk of anticompetitive impact with no apparent potentially redeeming value, the fact that a practice may turn out to be harmless in a particular set of circumstances will not prevent its being declared unlawful per se. . . .

Thus, under the reasoning of our cases, an agreement among competing wholesalers to refuse to sell unless the retailer makes payment in cash

either in advance or upon delivery is "plainly anticompetitive." Since it is merely one form of price fixing, and since price-fixing agreements have been adjudged to lack any "redeeming virtue," it is conclusively presumed illegal without further examination under the rule of reason.

Accordingly, the judgment of the Court of Appeals is reversed, and the case is remanded for further proceedings consistent with this opinion.

It is so ordered.

National Society of Professional Engineers v. United States
98 S.Ct. 1355 (1978)

STEVENS, J. This is a civil antitrust case brought by the United States to nullify an association's canon of ethics prohibiting competitive bidding by its members. The question is whether the canon may be justified under the Sherman Act, 15 U.S.C. Section 1 et. seq., because it was adopted by members of a learned profession for the purpose of minimizing the risk that competition would produce inferior engineering work endangering the public safety. The District Court rejected this justification without making any findings on the likelihood that competition would produce the dire consequences foreseen by the association. The Court of Appeals affirmed. We granted certiorari to decide whether the District Court should have considered the factual basis for the proffered justification before rejecting it. Because we are satisfied that the asserted defense rests on a fundamental misunderstanding of the Rule of Reason frequently applied in antitrust litigation, we affirm. . . .

The charges of a consulting engineer may be computed in different ways. He may charge the client a percentage of the cost of the project, may set his fee at his actual cost plus overhead plus a reasonable profit, may charge fixed rates per hour for different types of work, may perform an assignment for a specific sum, or he may combine one or more of these approaches. Suggested fee schedules for particular types of services in certain areas have been promulgated from time to time by various local societies. This case does not, however, involve any claim that the National Society has tried to fix specific fees, or even a specific method of calculating fees. It involves a charge that the members of the Society have unlawfully agreed to refuse to

negotiate or even to discuss the question of fees until after a prospective client has selected the engineer for a particular project. Evidence of this agreement is found in Section 11(c) of the Society's Code of Ethics, adopted in July 1964.

The District Court found that the Society's Board of Ethical Review has uniformly interpreted the "ethical rules against competitive bidding for engineering services as prohibiting the submission of any form of price information to a prospective customer which would enable that customer to make a price comparison on engineering services." If the client requires that such information be provided, then Section 11(c) imposes an obligation upon the engineering firm to withdraw from consideration for that job. The Society's Code of Ethics thus "prohibits engineers from both soliciting and submitting such price information," and seeks to preserve the profession's "traditional" method of selecting professional engineers. Under the traditional method, the client initially selects an engineer on the basis of background and reputation, not price.

In 1972 the Government filed its complaint against the Society alleging that members had agreed to abide by canons of ethics prohibiting the submission of competitive bids for engineering services and that, in consequence, price competition among the members had been suppressed and customers had been deprived of the benefits of free and open competition. The complaint prayed for an injunction terminating the unlawful agreement.

In its answer the Society admitted the essential facts alleged by the Government and . . . in defense . . . averred that the standard set out in the Code of Ethics was reasonable because competition among professional engineers was contrary to the public interest. It was averred that it would be cheaper and easier for an engineer "to design and specify inefficient and unnecessarily expensive structures and methods of construction." Accordingly, competitive pressure to offer engineering services at the lowest possible price would adversely affect the quality of engineering. Moreover, the practice of awarding engineering contracts to the lowest bidder, regardless of quality, would be dangerous to the public health, safety and welfare. For these reasons, the Society claimed that its Code of Ethics was not an "unreasonable restraint of interstate trade or commerce." (The lower courts held that the canon was a per se violation of Section 1 and illegal without regard to claimed or possible benefits.) . . .

Price is the "central nervous system of the economy," and an agreement that "interferes with the setting of price by free market forces" is illegal on its face. In this case we are presented with an agreement among competitors to refuse to discuss prices with potential customers until after negotiations have resulted in the initial selection of an engineer. While this is not price fixing as such, no elaborate industry analysis is required to demonstrate the anticompetitive character of such an agreement. It operates as an absolute ban on competitive bidding, applying with equal force to both complicated and simple projects and to both inexperienced and sophisticated customers. As the District Court found, the ban "impedes the ordinary give and take of the market place" and substantially deprives the customer of "the ability to utilize and compare prices in selecting engineering services." On its face, this agreement restrains trade within the meaning of Section 1 of the Sherman Act. . . .

The Sherman Act does not require competitive bidding; it prohibits unreasonable restraints on competition. Petitioner's ban on competitive bidding prevents all customers from making price comparisons in the initial selection of an engineer, and imposes the Society's views of the costs and benefits of competition on the entire market place. It is this restraint that must be justified under the Rule of Reason, and petitioner's attempt to do so on the basis of the potential threat that competition poses to the public safety and the ethics of its profession is nothing less than a frontal assault on the basic policy of the Sherman Act.

The Sherman Act reflects a legislative judgment that ultimately competition will not only produce lower prices, but also better goods and services. "The heart of our national economic policy long has been faith in the value of competition." The assumption that competition is the best method of allocating resources in a free market recognizes that all elements of a bargain—quality, service, safety, and durability—and not just the immediate cost, are favorably affected by the free opportunity to select among alternative offers. Even assuming occasional exceptions to the presumed consequences of competition, the statutory policy precludes inquiry into the question whether competition is good or bad.

The fact that engineers are often involved in large-scale projects significantly affecting the public safety does not alter our analysis. Exceptions to the Sherman Act for potentially dangerous goods and services would be tantamount to a repeal of the statute. In our complex economy the number of items that may cause serious harm is almost endless—automobiles, drugs, foods, aircraft components, heavy equipment, and countless others, cause serious harm to individuals or to the public at large if defectively made. The judiciary cannot indirectly protect the public against this harm by conferring monopoly privileges on the manufacturers. . . .

In sum, the Rule of Reason does not support a defense based on the assumption that competition itself is unreasonable. . . .

Affirmed.

United States v. Container Corporation of America
89 S.Ct. 510 (1969)

DOUGLAS, J. This is a civil antitrust action charging a price-fixing agreement in violation of §1 of the Sherman Act. . . .

The case as proved is unlike any other price decisions we have rendered. There was here an exchange of price information but no agreement to adhere to a price schedule. . . . There was here an exchange of information concerning specific sales to identified customers, not a statistical report on the average cost to all members, without identifying the parties to specific transactions. . . .

Here all that was done was a request by each defendant from its competitor for information as to the most recent price charged or quoted, whenever it needed such information and whenever it was not available from another source. Each defendant on receiving that request furnished the data with the expectation that he would be furnished reciprocal information when he wanted it. That concerted action is of course sufficient to establish the combination or conspiracy, the initial ingredient of a violation of §1 of the Sherman Act.

There was of course freedom to withdraw from the agreement. But the fact remains that when a defendant requested and received price information, it was affirming its willingness to furnish such information in return.

There was to be sure an infrequency and irregularity of price exchanges between the defendants; and often the data was available from the records of the defendants or from the customers themselves. Yet the essence of the agreement was to furnish price information whenever requested.

Moreover, although the most recent price charged or quoted was sometimes fragmentary, each defendant had the manuals with which it could compute the price charged by a competitor on a specific order to a specific customer.

Further, the price quoted was the current price which a customer would need pay in order to obtain products from the defendant furnishing the data.

The defendants account for about 90% of the shipment of corrugated containers from plants in the southeastern United States. While containers vary as to dimensions, weight, color, and so on, they are substantially identical, no matter who produces them, when made to particular specifications. The prices paid depend on price alternatives. Suppliers when seeking new or additional business or keeping old customers, do not exceed a competitor's price. It is common for purchasers to buy from two or more suppliers concurrently. A defendant supplying a customer with containers would usually quote the same price on additional orders, unless costs had changed. Yet where a competitor was charging a particular price, a defendant would normally quote the same price or even a lower price.

The exchange of price information seemed to have the effect of keeping prices within a fairly narrow ambit. Capacity has exceeded the demand from 1955 to 1963, the period covered by the complaint, and the trend of corrugated container prices has been downward. Yet despite this excess capacity and the downward trend of prices, the industry has expanded in the Southeast from 30 manufacturers with 49 plants to 51 manufacturers with 98 plants. An abundance of raw materials and machinery makes entry into the industry easy with an investment of $50,000 to $75,000.

The result of this reciprocal exchange of prices was to stabilize prices though at a downward level. Knowledge of a competitor's price usually meant matching that price. The continuation of some price competition is not fatal to the Government's case. The limitation or reduction of price competition brings the case within the ban, for . . . interference with the setting of price by free market forces is unlawful *per se*. Price information exchanged in some markets may have no effect on a truly competitive price. But the corrugated container industry is dominated by relatively few sellers. The product is fungible and the competition for sales is price. The demand is inelastic, as buyers place orders only for immediate, short-run needs. The exchange of price data tends toward price uniformity. For a lower price does not mean a larger share of the available business but a sharing of the existing business at a lower return. Stabilizing prices as well as raising them is within the ban of §1 of the Sherman Act. As we said in *United States v. Socony Vacuum Oil Co.,* "in terms of market operations, stabilization is but one form of manipulation." The inferences are irresistible that the exchange of price information has had an anticompetitive effect in the industry, chilling the vigor of price competition. . . .

Price is too critical, too sensitive a control to allow it to be used even in an informal manner to restrain competition.

Reversed.

Jefferson Cty. Pharmaceutical Ass'n v. Abbott Labs.
103 S.Ct. 1011 (1983)

POWELL, J. . . . The issue presented is whether the sale of pharmaceutical products to state and local government hospitals for resale in competition with private retail pharmacies is exempt from the proscriptions of the Robinson-Patman Act.

Petitioner, a trade association of retail pharmacists and pharmacies doing business in Jefferson County, Alabama, commenced this action in 1978

. . . as the assignee of its members' claims. Respondents are 15 pharmaceutical manufacturers, the Board of Trustees of the University of Alabama, and the Cooper Green Hospital Pharmacy. The University operates a medical center, including hospitals, and a medical school. Located in the University's medical center are two pharmacies. Cooper Green Hospital is a county hospital, existing as a public corporation under Alabama law.

The complaint seeks treble damages and injunctive relief . . . for alleged violations of §2(a) and (f) of the Clayton Act, as amended by the Robinson-Patman Act (the Act). Petitioner contends that the respondent manufacturers violated §2(a) by selling their products to the University's two pharmacies and to Cooper Green Hospital Pharmacy at prices lower than those charged petitioner's members for like products. Petitioner alleges that the respondent hospital pharmacies knowingly induced such lower prices in violation of §2(f) and sold the drugs to the general public in direct competition with privately owned pharmacies. . . .

The District Court held that "government purchases are, . . . beyond the intended reach of the Robinson-Patman Price Discrimination Act, at least with respect to purchases for hospitals and other traditional governmental purposes." The Court of Appeals affirmed. . . .

The issue here is narrow. We are not concerned with sales to the federal government, nor with state purchases for use in traditional governmental functions. Rather, the issue before us is limited to state purchases for the purpose of competing against private enterprise—with the advantage of discriminatory prices—in the retail market.

The courts below held, and respondents contend, that the Act exempts all state purchases. Assuming, without deciding, that Congress did not intend the Act to apply to state purchases for consumption in traditional governmental functions, and that such purchases are therefore exempt, we conclude that the exemption does not apply where a State has chosen to compete in the private retail market.

The Robinson-Patman Act by its terms does not exempt state purchases. . . . Moreover, as the courts below conceded, [t]he statutory language— "persons" and "purchasers"—is sufficiently broad to cover governmental bodies. . . .

We do not perceive any reason to construe the word "person" in that Act any differently than we have in the Clayton Act, which it amends, and it is undisputed that the Clayton Act applies to states. In sum, the plain language of the Act strongly suggests that there is no exemption for state purchases to compete with private enterprise. . . .

Our cases have been explicit in stating the purposes of the antitrust laws, including the Robinson-Patman Act. On numerous occasions, this Court has affirmed the comprehensive coverage of the antitrust laws and has recognized that these laws represent "a carefully studied attempt to bring within [them] every person engaged in business whose activities might restrain or monopolize commercial intercourse among the states."

It has been said, of course, that the antitrust laws, and Robinson-Patman in particular, are to be construed liberally, and that the exceptions from their application are to be construed strictly. The Court has recognized, also, that Robinson-Patman "was enacted in 1936 to curb and prohibit all devices by which large buyers gained discriminatory preferences over smaller ones by virtue of their greater purchasing power." Because the Act is remedial, it is to be construed broadly to effectuate its purposes. . . .

"A general application of the [Robinson-Patman] Act to all combinations of business and capital organized to suppress commercial competition is in harmony with the spirit and impulses of the times which gave it birth." The legislative history is replete with references to the economic evil of large organizations purchasing from other large organizations for resale in competition with the small, local retailers. There is no reason, in the absence of an explicit exemption, to think that congressman who feared these evils intended to deny small businesses, such as the pharmacies of Jefferson County, Alabama, protection from the competition of the strongest competitor of them all. To create an exemption here clearly would be contrary to the intent of Congress.

We hold that the sale of pharmaceutical products to state and local government hospitals for resale in competition with private pharmacies is not exempt from the proscriptions of the Robinson-Patman Act.

Reversed.

Great Atlantic & Pacific Tea Co., Inc. v. FTC
99 S.Ct. 925 (1979)

STEWART, J. . . . The question presented in this case is whether the petitioner, the Great Atlantic and Pacific Tea Company (A&P), violated Section 2(f) of the Robinson-Patman Act by knowingly inducing or receiving illegal price discriminations from the Borden Company (Borden).

The alleged violation was reflected in a 1965 agreement between A&P and Borden, under which Borden undertook to supply "private label" milk to more than 200 A&P stores in a Chicago area that included portions of Illinois and Indiana. This agreement resulted from an effort by A&P to achieve cost savings by switching from the sale of "brand label" milk (milk sold under the brand name of the supplying dairy) to the sale of "private label" milk (milk sold under the A&P label).

To implement this plan, A&P asked Borden, its longtime supplier, to submit an offer to supply under private label certain of A&P's milk and other dairy product requirements. After prolonged negotiations, Borden offered to grant A&P a discount for switching to private label milk, provided A&P would accept limited delivery service. Borden claimed that this offer would save A&P $410,000 a year compared to what it had been paying for its dairy products. A&P, however, was not satisfied with this offer and solicited offers from other dairies. A competitor of Borden, Bowman Dairy, then submitted an offer which was lower than Borden's.

At this point, A&P's Chicago buyer contacted Borden's chain store sales manager and stated, "I have a bid in my pocket. You [Borden] people are so far out of line it is not even funny. You are not even in the ballpark." When the Borden representative asked for more details, he was told nothing except that a $50,000 improvement in Borden's bid "would not be a drop in the bucket."

Borden was thus faced with the problem of deciding whether to rebid. A&P, at the time, was one of Borden's largest customers in the Chicago area. Moreover, Borden had just invested more than five million dollars in a new dairy facility in Illinois. The loss of the A&P account would result in under-utilization of this new plant. Under these circum-stances, Borden decided to submit a new bid which doubled the estimated annual savings to A&P, from $410,000 to $820,000. In presenting its offer, Borden emphasized to A&P that it needed to keep A&P's business and was making the new offer in order to meet Bowman's bid. A&P then accepted Borden's bid after concluding that it was substantially better than Bowman's.

[The FTC filed a complaint against A&P charging that it had violated Section 2(f) of the Robinson-Patman Act by knowingly inducing or receiving price discrimination from Borden. The Commission found that Borden had discriminated in price between A&P and its competitors, that the discrimination had been injurious to competition, and that A&P had known or should have known that it was the beneficiary of unlawful price discrimination. The Commission rejected A&P's defenses that the Borden bid had been made to meet competition and was cost justified. The Court of Appeals affirmed holding that as a matter of law A&P could not successfully assert a meeting competition defense because it, unlike Borden, had known that Borden's offer was better than Bowman's.]

The Robinson-Patman Act was passed in response to the problem perceived in the increased market power and coercive practices of chain stores and other big buyers that threatened the existence of small independent retailers. Notwithstanding this concern with buyers, however, the emphasis of the Act is in Section 2(a), which prohibits price discriminations by sellers. Indeed, the original Patman Bill as reported by Committees of both Houses prohibited only seller activity, with no mention of buyer liability. Section 2(f) of the Act, making buyers liable for inducing or receiving price discriminations by sellers, was the product of a belated floor amendment near the conclusion of the Senate debates.

As finally enacted, Section 2(f) provides: "That it shall be unlawful for any person engaged in commerce, in the course of such commerce, knowingly to induce or receive a discrimination in price which is prohibited by this section."

Liability under Section 2(f) thus is limited to situations where the price discrimination is one "which is prohibited by this section." While the phrase "this section" refers to the entire Section 2 of the Act, only subsections (a) and (b) dealing with seller liability involved discriminations in price. Under the plain meaning of Section 2(f), therefore, a buyer cannot be liable if a prima facie case could not be established against a seller or if the seller has an affirmative defense. In either situation, there is no price discrimination "prohibited by this section." The legislative history of Section 2(f) fully confirms the conclusion that buyer liability under Section 2(f) is dependent on seller liability under Section 2(a). . . .

Thus, a buyer cannot be held liable under Section 2(f) if the lower prices received are justified by reason of one of the seller's affirmative defenses.

The petitioner, relying on this plain meaning of Section 2(f), argues that it cannot be liable under Section 2(f) if Borden had a valid meeting competition defense. The respondent, on the other hand, argues that the petitioner may be liable even assuming that Borden had such a defense. The meeting competition defense, the respondent contends, must in these circumstances be judged from the point of view of the buyer. Since A&P knew for a fact that the final Borden bid beat the Bowman bid, it was not entitled to assert the meeting competition defense even though Borden may have honestly believed that it was simply meeting competition. Recognition of a meeting competition defense for the buyer in this situation, the respondent argues, would be contrary to the basic purpose of the Robinson-Patman Act to curtail abuses by large buyers.

The short answer to these contentions of the respondent is that Congress did not provide in Section 2(f) that a buyer can be liable even if the seller has a valid defense. The clear language of Section 2(f) states that a buyer can be liable only if he receives a price discrimination "prohibited by this section." If a seller has a valid meeting competition defense, there is simply no prohibited price discrimination. . . .

Because both the Commission and the Court of Appeals proceeded on the assumption that a buyer who accepts the lower of two competitive bids can be liable under Section 2(f) even if the seller has a meeting competition defense, there was not a specific finding that Borden did in fact have such a defense. But it quite clearly did.

The test for determining when a seller has a valid meeting competition defense is whether a seller can "show the existence of facts which would lead a reasonable and prudent person to believe that the granting of a lower price would in fact meet the equally low price of a competitor." "A good faith belief, rather than absolute certainty, that a price concession is being offered to meet an equally low price offered by a competitor is sufficient to satisfy the Robinson-Patman's Section 2(b) defense." Since good faith, rather than absolute certainty, is the touchstone of the meeting competition defense, a seller can assert the defense even if it has unknowingly made a bid that in fact not only met but beat his competition.

Under the circumstances of this case, Borden did act reasonably and in good faith when it made its second bid. . . .

Since Borden had a meeting competition defense and thus could not be liable under Section 2(b), the petitioner who did no more than accept the offer cannot be liable under Section 2(f).

Accordingly, the judgment is reversed.

REVIEW QUESTIONS

1. Match each term in column A with the appropriate statement in column B.

A	B
1. Price discrimination	**a.** An agreement or combination by which the conspirators set the market price of a product or service either being sold or purchased, whether high or low.

2. Predatory pricing

    b. The controlling by a manufacturer of a brand or trade name product of the minimum retail price at which it is sold.

3. Exclusive dealing contract

    c. A rule that contracts or conspiracies are illegal only if they constitute undue or unreasonable restraints of trade, or unreasonable attempts to monopolize.

4. Reciprocal dealing

    d. Certain acts are unreasonable and therefore illegal under the Sherman Act in themselves.

5. Tying contract

    e. A merger in which the businesses combined neither compete nor are related as customer and supplier in any given line of commerce.

6. Per se illegality

    f. A merger that combines two businesses which formerly competed in a particular line of commerce.

7. Price-fixing

    g. A merger that brings together a customer in a line of commerce and a supplier.

8. The rule of reason

    h. A commodity is sold or leased for use only on condition that the buyer or lessee purchase certain additional products or services from the seller or lessor.

9. Resale price maintenance

    i. A contract in which a buyer agrees not to purchase an item or items of merchandise from competitors of the seller.

10. Vertical merger

    j. A seller charges different purchasers different amounts for the same commodity.

11. Horizontal merger

    k. This arrangement exists when two parties face each other as both buyer and seller.

12. Conglomerate merger

    l. Selling at prices below average variable cost to close out competition.

2. The four largest real estate brokers in Houston, Texas, agreed upon the real estate commissions to be charged sellers of homes. They were indicted by a federal grand jury and ultimately entered a plea of *nolo contendere*. The usual commission rate prior to the conspiracy was 5 percent. The agreed-upon rate was 7 percent.
    a. What punishment may be imposed on the individuals involved?
    b. If the brokers are incorporated, what punishment may be imposed?
    c. If a suit for triple damages is filed, what proof is required? Explain.
    d. Assume that you had sold your house for $150,000 during the period the conspiracy was in effect. How much could you collect from a broker that was involved?

3. A former employee alleged that his employer and its competitors agreed to fix prices, allocate customers, and boycott anyone who interfered with their plans. He was fired from his job for refusing to participate in the scheme. He alleged that he was unable to find another job in the same industry. He sued for triple damages under Section 4 of the Clayton Act. His employer contended that the plaintiff lacked standing to sue. With what result? Why?

4. The American Medical Association adopted a code of ethics that prohibited all advertising by physicians. Included in the prohibition were ads indicating that physicians would make house calls. Is the code of ethics legal? Explain.

5. Copp Paving Company was sued by Gulford for triple damages, alleging a violation of the Robinson-Patman Act. Copp operates an asphalt concrete "hot plant" in California. The plant manufactures asphalt for surfacing highways, including interstate highways in California. Its whole operation is in intrastate commerce. Does the complaint allege a valid claim? Why?

6. Mary, who recently received a degree in business, has been named general sales manager for a manufacturer. She called a meeting of the salesforce and, among other matters, made the following statement: "We will cut prices so low our competitors will be cut off at the knees." If this policy is carried out, will any law be violated? Explain.

7. Same facts as in problem 6. Mary later called on the corporation's most important customer. While informing this customer of its special importance, Mary said: "To your company, Larry, and to it alone, the price we charge will always be below cost." If this policy is carried out, will it be in violation of any law? Explain.

8. A department store solicited and received contributions from vendors toward the cost of the store's 100th anniversary celebration. The store gave the vendors no direct promotional services for vendors' products. Is the store in violation of Section 2 of the Clayton Act as amended? Why?

9. Magi-Comp Computer Corporation requires its customers who buy or lease Magi-Comp computers to also buy Magi-Comp accessories, such as discs, tapes, and punch cards. The Justice Department sued Magi-Comp to force it to cease employing these contracts. With what result? Why?

10. The national association of repossessors established fee schedules to be used in charging for the services of its members. Repossessors are hired by creditors such as automobile dealers to take possession of items that were bought with loans that are in default. The Justice Department filed suit to enjoin the use of the fee schedules. What was the result? Why?

11. The American Society of Anesthesiologists has an ethical standard that prevents its member doctors from working for salaries at hospitals. It insists on fee-for-service arrangements. Is such a standard a violation of the Sherman Act? Explain.

12. In 1984, Standard Oil of California acquired the Gulf Oil Corporation for $13.4 billion, and it also acquired the Getty Oil Company for $10.1 billion. The Justice Department and the Federal Trade Commission decided not to challenge the acquisition. Could these mergers still be challenged? Explain.

13. The LTV Corporation owns Jones & Laughlin Steel. The Lykes Corporation owns Youngstown Sheet and Tube Company. It is proposed that these two corporations merge, forming a steel company that would rank third in size behind U.S. Steel and Bethlehem Steel. Both companies are major producers of flat-rolled steel. Together they account for 11 percent of that market. They also hold 19 percent of the tube market and 22 percent of the tin-plate business. The steel industry in the United States has difficulty in competing with cheaper foreign imports. Both LTV and Lykes are operating at significant losses. Is it likely that this merger will be challenged? Explain.

14. Illinois Brick Company manufactures concrete blocks and sells them to many different wholesalers. These wholesalers then sell the blocks to general contractors, who use them in the construction of buildings. The State of Illinois purchased a building in which the products of Illinois Brick had been incorporated. Seeking treble damages, the state sued Illinois Brick, alleging it was part of a conspiracy to fix the price of concrete blocks. Should the State of Illinois be able to recover treble damages? Explain.

15. Jack, who had an independent home delivery business, was hired by *The Post* Company to deliver its evening newspaper. The contract provided that carriers with exclusive territories were subject to termination if their prices exceeded $6.50 a month. Jack charged his customers $7.25 a month, and *Post* objected. *Post* hired other carriers to solicit customers away from Jack. Jack sued *Post*, claiming that it was in violation of the Sherman Act. Is Jack correct? Why?

48 LABOR LAWS

The goal of this chapter is to understand the major provisions of laws related to labor-management relations. Labor law is concerned with all aspects of collective bargaining, as well as with the internal operation of labor unions. *Collective bargaining* is concerned with issues such as worker's wages, hours of work, and other terms and conditions of employment. Labor law developed not only by statutes and judicial decisions, but also by the rules, regulations, and decisions of the National Labor Relations Board (NLRB).

To understand labor law, we must recognize and understand its goals. The primary goal of laws relating to collective bargaining may be simply stated: to create equality of bargaining power between management and labor, so that they will be able to settle their differences on mutually satisfactory terms consistent with the public interest. Some statutory provisions are designed to equalize the bargaining power of management with labor, or vice versa. Other statutory provisions are designed to protect the public interest in the collective bargaining process. The law encourages unionization and collective bargaining. This is a result of the inequality of bargaining power between any single employee and a business. The sections that follow will briefly review the various laws that have been enacted to accomplish the goal of equalizing the bargaining power of labor and management.

OVERVIEW OF FEDERAL LABOR LAWS

1. Clayton Act

The Clayton Act of 1914 contained two provisions relating to labor relations. The first attempted to prohibit federal courts from issuing injunctions to prevent strikes and picketing in disputes over terms or conditions of employment. The second provided that the antitrust laws were not applicable to labor unions or their members in carrying out union activities. Prior to the existence of the Clayton Act, the Sherman Antitrust Act was sometimes applied by courts to the activities of those in the labor movement. The Clayton Act provision exempting labor activities followed.

The exemption covers only legitimate union activity such as picketing and striking to advance the interest of workers. The exemption does not cover agreements that are beyond the usual subjects of collective bargaining. Most union activity is thus exempt from the antitrust laws.

2. Railway Labor Act

In 1926 Congress enacted the Railway Labor Act to encourage collective bargaining in the railroad industry, so that labor disputes would not interrupt the transportation of goods in interstate commerce. The act was later extended to airlines, and it is now applicable to both forms of transportation. The Railway Labor Act created a National Mediation Board whose duty it is to designate the bargaining representative for any group of employees in the railway or air transport industries. The selection is made by conducting representation elections. The act also outlaws certain unfair labor practices, such as refusing to bargain collectively.

In 1951, Congress amended the Railway Labor Act to permit the union shop. A *union shop* permits a union and an employer to require all employees in the bargaining unit to join the union as a condition of continued employment. The act does not permit a union to spend an objecting employee's dues to support political causes or other activities unconnected with the negotiation of contracts or the settlement of grievances.

When the parties under the jurisdiction of the National Mediation Board cannot reach a collective bargaining agreement, it is the function of the board to attempt mediation of their differences. If mediation fails, the board encourages voluntary arbitration. If the parties refuse to arbitrate and the dispute is likely to be a substantial interruption of interstate commerce, the board informs the president, who may then appoint a special emergency board. This emergency board investigates the dispute and publishes its findings of fact and recommendations for its resolution. During the investigation, which lasts 30 days, and for an additional 30 days after the report is issued, business is conducted without interruption. The parties, however, have no duty to comply with the special board's proposals. Thus, if no new collective bargaining agreement is reached after the 60-day period, lockouts by management and strikes by workers become legal.

The procedures of the Railway Labor Act sometimes fail to resolve major disputes in transportation, and special action is taken by the president or Congress. The transportation industry's labor problems have such potential for irreparable damage to the public that legislative solutions may be required.

The procedures discussed above apply to assisting employers and unions to arrive at a collective bargaining agreement; they do not apply to issues concerning the interpretation of existing contracts. Such issues in transportation must be submitted to compulsory arbitration. This requirement is peculiar to the transportation industry.

3. Norris-LaGuardia Act

In 1932 Congress enacted the Norris-LaGuardia Act. Prior to that enactment, management could rather effectively prevent union activity by going to court and obtaining an injunction against a strike or against picketing. The Norris-LaGuardia Act encouraged collective bargaining by limiting the jurisdiction of federal courts in enjoining union activity. Federal courts may not issue an injunction to stop an employee or a union from engaging in lawful union activities such as: (a) striking or quitting work, (b) belonging to a labor organization, (c) paying strike or unemployment benefits to participants in a labor dispute, (d) publicizing the existence of a labor dispute or the facts related to it (including picketing), (e) peaceably assembling to promote their interests in a labor dispute, and (f) agreeing with others or advising or causing them to do any of the above acts without fraud or violence.

Although the Norris-LaGuardia Act greatly restricts the use of injunctions in labor disputes, it does not prohibit them altogether. An injunction may be issued to enjoin illegal strikes such as those by public employees. When unlawful acts are threatened, they may be enjoined. Although the Norris-LaGuardia Act restricts the use of federal court injunctions in labor disputes, it does not limit the jurisdiction of state courts in issuing them. The Supreme Court has upheld the jurisdiction of a state court to enjoin a union's work stoppage and picketing in violation of a no-strike clause in its collective bargaining agreement.

The second major provision of the Norris-LaGuardia Act was to make *yellow dog contracts* (those forbidding union membership) unenforceable. Because of this provision, it is illegal for an employer to have employees agree that they will not join or form a union. Norris-LaGuardia attempted to establish a climate in which employees would be free to organize and bargain collectively through a union, without interference or coercion on the part of employers. It did nothing to impose any duty on management to deal with or even recognize unions. As a result, it did little to encourage the growth of collective bargaining.

4. Wagner Act

In 1935 Congress passed the National Labor Relations Act, commonly called the Wagner Act. Noting that employees individually did not possess bargaining power equal to that of their employers, the Wagner Act stated that its policy was to protect by law the right of employees to organize and bargain collectively in order to encourage the "friendly adjustment of industrial disputes." This policy was to be accomplished by creating for employees equality in bargaining position with that of employers. In summary, the Wagner Act:

1. Created an administrative agency, the National Labor Relations Board (NLRB), to administer the act. The NLRB was given broad powers.
2. Authorized the NLRB to conduct union certification elections and to certify the union that was to represent a group of workers.
3. Outlawed certain conduct by employers that generally prevented or at least discouraged union activity. These prohibited acts are known as

unfair labor practices. The NLRB was authorized to enter corrective orders when unfair labor practices had been committed. [Unfair labor practices by management will be discussed later in this chapter.]

Note that the Wagner Act does not cover all workers. Among those exempt from its coverage are employees of the federal and state governments, political subdivisions of the states, nonprofit hospitals, and persons subject to the Railway Labor Act. Also excluded are independent contractors, agricultural laborers, domestic servants, and those employed by their spouse or a parent. Finally, supervisors are not employees. This supervisor exception covers employees properly classified as managerial. For example, university professors who control admissions, faculty hiring and firing, and who participate in budget preparation are supervisors and not covered by the act. Professors who have no power to act in these areas are covered.

The NLRB has a special rule regarding the discharge of supervisors. Under it, the discharge of a supervisor is illegal only if it interferes with the rights of other employees. An employer is entitled to insist on the loyalty of supervisors. Supervisors are not free to engage in activities which if engaged in by other employees would be protected by labor laws. The only exceptions to the rule make it an unfair labor practice (a) to discharge a supervisor for testifying before the NLRB or during a grievance proceeding, (b) to discipline a supervisor for refusing to commit an unfair labor practice, or (c) to discharge a supervisor who has hired a pro-union crew in order to terminate other employees.

6. Taft-Hartley Act

The Wagner Act provided a climate for rapid union growth. By the end of World War II many people believed that the power and influence of unions was greater than that of management. Although employers had superior bargaining power prior to the Wagner Act, by 1946 many persons felt the pendulum had shifted, and the unions—with their power of nationwide, crippling strikes—had greater bargaining power. It was clear that no one company had equal bargaining power with a union that represented all employees in an industry. Moreover, nationwide strikes were having a substantial adverse effect on an important third party—the public.

In 1947 Congress, attempting once again to equalize the bargaining power of management and labor, passed the Taft-Hartley amendment to the Wagner Act. The amendment contains the following important provisions:

1. Equalizes bargaining power by declaring that certain activities by unions are improper. The Wagner Act had been one-sided, recognizing management's unfair treatment of labor but neglecting the other side of the coin.

2. Establishes an 80-day cooling-off period. The president, acting with an emergency board and through the federal courts, may obtain an injunction to stop a strike or lockout that may imperil national safety or health. The injunction is good for 80 days.

3. Creates the Federal Mediation and Conciliation Service to assist in settlement of labor disputes. This federal agency is of special importance in strikes that threaten the national economy.

4. Outlaws the *closed* shop, one in which a person must be a union member as a condition of employment. Taft-Hartley did allow a *union* shop, one in which a worker must join the union within 30 days after being employed. Section 14(b) authorizes states to enact state right-to-work laws, however, and they may prohibit union shops. Thus Taft-Hartley gives employees some freedom of choice in union membership.

5. Allows employers to express their opinions. To meet employers' complaints that the Wagner Act violated their right of free speech, Congress added Section 8(c), which provided that expressing any views, arguments, or opinions is not evidence of an unfair labor practice if such expression contains no threat of reprisal or force or promise of benefit.

6. Allows suits for breach of a contract between an employer and a labor organization to be filed in the federal district courts, without regard to the amount in question. A labor organization is responsible for the acts of its agents and may sue or be sued. Any money judgment against it is enforceable only against its assets, and not against any individual member.

The 80-day cooling-off provisions of Taft-Hartley are extremely important. They may be used in any strike under the jurisdiction of the Wagner Act—almost every industry except transportation. The provisions come into play whenever the president is of the opinion that a strike or lockout will, if permitted to occur or to continue, imperil the national health or safety. The president then appoints a board of inquiry to obtain facts about the strike. The board makes a study of the strike and reports back to the president. If the board finds that the national health or safety is indeed affected by the strike, then the president, through the attorney general, goes to the federal district court for an injunction ordering the union to suspend the strike (or company to suspend the lockout) for 80 days.

During the 80-day period, the Federal Mediation Service works with the two parties to try to achieve an agreement. If no agreement is reached, the presidential board holds new hearings and receives the company's final offer. The members of the union are then allowed to vote on this final proposal. If they vote for the new proposal, the dispute is over. If they vote against the proposal, they may again be called out on strike. At this point the strike may continue indefinitely until the disagreement causing it is resolved by collective bargaining—unless Congress passes additional legislation to solve the problem. Experience has shown that most disputes are settled during the 80-day period. The injunction provided for in the Taft-Hartley Act may not be used for all strikes, but is limited to "national emergency" strikes. These must involve national defense or key industries or have a substantial effect on the economy.

6. Landrum-Griffin Act

After the enactment of Taft-Hartley, Congress turned its attention to the internal operations of labor unions. Hearings before congressional committees in the 1950s revealed widespread corruption, lack of democratic procedures, and domination of labor unions by elements thought to be undesirable. As a result, Congress in 1959 enacted the Landrum-Griffin amendment to the Wagner Act.

In order to eliminate internal corruption and to guarantee that the rank and file union members had control of their union, Landrum-Griffin contained a Bill of Rights protecting the rights of union members:

1. To nominate candidates, to vote in elections, to attend membership meetings, and to have a voice in business transactions, subject to reasonable union rules and regulations.
2. To have free expression in union meetings, business discussions, and conventions subject to reasonable rules and regulations.
3. To vote on an increase of dues or fees.
4. To sue and testify against the union.
5. To receive written, specific charges; to be given a reasonable time for defense; and to be accorded a full and fair hearing before any disciplinary action is taken by the union against them.
6. To be given a copy of the collective bargaining agreement that they work under, upon request.

Landrum-Griffin contains provisions relating to reports that must be filed with the secretary of labor. The purpose of these reports is to reveal practices detrimental to union members. For example, each union must adopt a constitution and bylaws and file them with the secretary of labor. In addition, unions must keep the Department of Labor informed of facts about union operations and their financial affairs.

A major focus of Landrum-Griffin is on union elections. The law requires that elections be held at minimum regular intervals to promote democracy. National unions must hold elections at least every 5 years; locals, every 3 years; intermediate bodies, every 4 years. Elections must be by secret ballot of members or of delegates who were chosen by secret ballot of members. Unions may impose reasonable qualifications for union office.[1] The goal of the law is to ensure democratic procedures that will allow the rank-and-file members to use the ballot box to correct abuses by union officers.

7. In General   NLRB

The National Labor Relations Board conducts union certification elections and hearings on unfair labor practice charges. In addition to the five board members, there is a general counsel who supervises board investigations and serves as prosecutor in cases before the board. The general counsel supervises operations of the NLRB so that the board itself may perform its quasi-judicial function of deciding unfair labor practice cases free of bias.

Congress gave the NLRB jurisdiction over any business "affecting commerce," with the few exceptions previously noted. It has not been able to exercise its powers over all business because of budget and time considerations. It has limited its own jurisdiction to businesses of a certain size. (Table 48–1 lists these businesses). Other businesses are subject to state law.

---

[1] Local 3489 United Steelworkers of America v. Usery, p. 1097.

TABLE 48–1

NLRB jurisdiction

1. *Nonretail operations* with an annual outflow or inflow across state lines of at least $50,000
2. *Retail enterprises* with a gross volume of $500,000 or more a year
3. *Enterprises operating office buildings* if the gross revenues are at least $100,000 per year
4. *Transportation enterprises* furnishing interstate services
5. *Local transit systems* with an annual gross volume of at least $250,000
6. *Newspapers* that subscribe to interstate news services, publish nationally syndicated features, or advertise nationally sold products with a minimum annual gross volume of $250,000
7. *Communication enterprises* that operate radio or television stations or telephone or telegraph services with a gross volume of $100,000 or more per year
8. *Local public utilities* with an annual gross volume of $250,000 per year, or an outflow or inflow of goods or services across state lines of $50,000 or more per year
9. *Hotel and motel enterprises* serving transient guests that gross at least $500,000 in revenues per year
10. All enterprises whose operations have a substantial impact on *national defense*
11. *Nonprofit hospitals*
12. *Private universities and colleges*

The Wagner Act authorizes the NLRB, upon finding that an unfair labor practice has occurred, to issue an order requiring the wrongdoer to cease and desist such practices. The board may also order corrective action if necessary to overcome any injury caused by the unfair labor practice. The board's corrective action will not be disturbed by the courts unless it can be shown that it is an obvious attempt to achieve ends contrary to the policies of the law.

The NLRB may order the reinstatement of an employee who has been discharged wrongfully, with back pay and restoration of full seniority rights. In fact, even a purchaser of a business who acquires and operates it knowing that the seller discharged an employee in violation of the Wagner Act may be ordered by the NLRB to reinstate the employee with back pay. The NLRB may require an employer to bargain collectively with the appropriate union, or vice versa. It may order an employer to post notices at the plant assuring employees that it will no longer commit a particular unfair labor practice of which it has been found guilty. If an unfair labor practice has influenced the outcome of a representation election, the NLRB may set aside the election and hold another one free of such improper conduct.

8. Elections and Certifications

An employer may recognize that its workers want representation by a certain union and it may voluntarily agree to bargain with that union. In other cases, the selection of a union as collective bargaining representative is made by the election process. NLRB-supervised elections are by secret ballot. The board determines the appropriate unit of employees entitled to vote. It may select the total employer unit, craft unit, plant unit, or any subdivision of the plant. The board's decision on the voting unit is often crucial to the outcome of an election.

In order to obtain an election, a petition must be filed with the board by an employee, a labor organization, or an employer. If the petition if filed by either an employee or a labor organization, it must allege either (a) that a substantial number of employees want a collective bargaining representative but their employer refuses to recognize their representative, or (b) that a substantial number of employees assert that the union which has been certified by the board or which the employer currently recognizes as their bargaining representative is no longer such. "Substantial" means that at least 30 percent of the employees support the petition. An employer may petition for an election without making and proving any allegations of fact. However, an employer who files a petition to invalidate certification of an incumbent union must show that it doubts, in good faith, the continued support of the union by a majority of the employees.

The NLRB investigates the allegations of a petition. If it finds an issue to be voted upon, it directs that a representation election be held. After the results are tallied, the board certifies that no union has been selected by majority of the employees, or that a given one has. After any valid election has been conducted by the NLRB, another is not permitted for 1 year. If an election has resulted in board certification of a union, no new election may take place within 1 year of the certification. Also, an election is not allowed within the term of a collective bargaining agreement, or 3 years after it was signed, whichever period is shorter.

A union seeking to represent employees may solicit cards from them indicating their willingness that the union represent them. A bargaining order may be based on such cards if the cards unequivocally and clearly indicate that the employee signing the card is authorizing the union to represent him or her. If a card states on its face that it authorizes collective bargaining, it will be counted for that purpose unless there is clear proof that the employee was told that it would not be used for that purpose. Employers may rely upon the cards and agree to bargain with the union. Most cards simply request an election because of the belief that peer pressure may cause workers who do not actually favor the union to sign the cards. The secret ballot of the election process ensures freedom of choice for the workers.

9. Introduction

The Wagner Act uses the term *unfair labor practice* to describe conduct by management that is unfair to workers and their unions. It lists five general categories of such violations. The Landrum-Griffin amendment added a sixth. These are summarized in Table 48–2.

Conduct may be, and often is, a violation of more than one of the listed unfair labor practices. Most violations constitute interference with the right to engage in concerted activity. For example, retaliation against a union leader for filing charges would constitute a violation of both the first and fourth categories.

If management is guilty of an unfair labor practice, the National Labor

UNFAIR
LABOR
PRACTICES
BY
EMPLOYERS

TABLE 48–2

Unfair labor practices by employers

1. Interference with efforts of employees to form, join, or assist labor organizations, or to engage in concerted activities for mutual aid or protection
2. Domination of a labor organization or contribution of financial or other support to it
3. Discrimination in hiring or tenure of employees for reason of union affiliation
4. Discrimination against employees for filing charges or giving testimony under the act
5. Refusal to bargain collectively in good faith with a duly designated representative of the employees
6. Agreeing with a labor organization to engage in a secondary boycott

Relations Board has a broad range of remedies to use in eliminating the impact of the violation. The NLRB has the capability of righting any wrongs that may have occurred.

10. Interference with Unionization and Concerted Activities

In order to guarantee the worker's right to organize and bargain collectively, any practice that might discourage union activity is considered unfair. Employers may not threaten to fire employees who attempt to organize, nor may they cut back on benefits if unionization takes place. The act also prohibits conferral of benefits on workers if management is using the benefits to discourage union activity. Any attempt by management to prevent or discourage employees' activities for the purpose of collective bargaining or other mutual aid or protection may constitute an unfair labor practice. An employer cannot engage in conduct calculated to erode employee support for the union. This applies to conduct that is otherwise lawful and in some cases proper from the standpoint of other public policy considerations.[2]

Work rules may negatively affect workers' attempts to organize and join a union. For example, a work rule may prohibit the wearing of buttons or insignia. Unless the employer can establish a valid reason for such a rule, it cannot be used to stop the wearing of union buttons or insignia. Similarly, a "no solicitation on the premises" rule that goes beyond the actual needs of the employer based on health, safety, or the like is not enforceable.

Difficult issues are presented in those cases in which an employer is accused of an unfair labor practice as a result of something said or written. Although both parties are entitled to freedom of speech during a campaign to organize workers, management especially must be very careful in what it says. It must make sure that its statements do not contain threats of reprisal if a union is voted in, or promises of benefits if the union is rejected. Coercive statements are an unfair labor practice that may result in the election being set aside. For example, a union organizer told the workers that the union would obtain higher wages for the workers. The company responded, "If the union comes in, the wages may go up, but they may also go down." This was a coercive statement because it contained an implied threat and therefore was an unfair labor practice.

[2] Sure-Tan, Inc. v. N.L.R.B., p. 1098.

The first unfair labor practice covers interference with efforts to form, join, or assist labor organizations, and with concerted activities for mutual aid or protection. The second part of this provision protects any group of employees acting for mutual aid and protection.[3] *Concerted activity* may directly involve the union, or it may involve issues of importance only to workers. For example, some employees refused to work after a heated grievance meeting. They followed their supervisors onto the workroom floor and continued to argue loudly until they were ordered a second time to resume work. The employer issued letters of reprimand alleging insubordination. The employer's action was an unfair labor practice because the employees were engaged in concerted activity.

The concerted activity concept is quite broad. In one case, an employer was investigating a theft. An employee asked that a union representative be present during her interview. She was refused. The Supreme Court held that the employee had a right to have the representative present because there was a perceived threat to her employment security. The presence of a representative assures other employees that they too can obtain aid and protection if needed. Refusing the assistance at the interview was an unfair labor practice. This right to assistance was later expanded to cover nonunion members as well. The right to engage in concerted activity has also been expanded to cover the actions of a sole employee under certain circumstances. If an employee has a grievance that may affect other workers, that employee has rights protected by the concerted activity language of the first unfair labor practice.

11. Domination of a Union

The second unfair labor practice is for an employer to dominate a labor organization or contribute financial or other support to it. The law views the relationship of employer and employee in the collective bargaining process to be adversary in character. The union must be independent of the employer. If two unions are seeking to organize workers, the law requires the employer to be neutral. An employer who takes sides is guilty of an unfair labor practice. Such a practice is committed if the employer supports the union by giving it a meeting place; provides refreshments for union meetings; permits the union to use the employer's telephone, secretary, or copying machine; or allows the union to keep cafeteria or vending machine profits.

12. Discrimination against Union Activity

The third unfair labor practice listed in the Wagner Act prohibits discrimination in the hiring or tenure of employees for reason of union affiliation. Under this section, an employer may neither discharge nor refuse to hire an employee either to *encourage* or to *discourage* membership in any labor organization. Nor may it discriminate in regard to any term or condition of employment for such purposes. Thus, discrimination on account of union affiliation concerning wages, hours, work assignments, promotions, vacations, and the like is forbidden.

---

[3] Eastex, Inc. v. NLRB, p. 1099.

13. Retaliation

A fourth unfair labor practice by management is retaliation against employees for filing charges or giving testimony in proceedings brought under the Wagner Act. This unfair labor practice protects employees from being discharged or from other reprisals by their employers because the workers have sought to enforce their rights under the law. It protects the NLRB's channels of information by preventing employer intimidation of complainants and witnesses.

In cases alleging retaliation for filing charges or giving testimony, the employer will frequently contend that action was taken against the employee for some reason other than filing charges or giving testimony. Thus, most often these cases boil down to a question of proof of what motivated the employer in pursuing his course of action. If discharge is because of misconduct, low production, personnel cutbacks necessitated by economic conditions, or other legitimate consideration, it is not an unfair labor practice.

14. Other Unfair Practices

The fifth unfair labor practice contained in the Wagner Act as originally passed is for management to refuse to bargain collectively with a duly certified union. This requirement to bargain in good faith will be discussed in section 17, below.

The sixth unfair labor practice was added by the Landrum-Griffin amendment. It outlaws hot cargo contracts. A *hot cargo* contract is one in which an employer voluntarily agrees with a union not to handle, use, or deal in the nonunion-produced goods of another person. Such contracts are unfair labor practices for both parties.

UNFAIR LABOR PRACTICES BY UNIONS

15. Introduction

The Taft-Hartley amendment to the Wagner Act declared that certain conduct or activities by labor unions were unfair labor practices and thus illegal. The Landrum-Griffin amendment added two more, and now the list includes the acts and omissions listed in Table 48–3.

TABLE 48–3

Unfair labor practices by unions

1. Restraining or coercing an employee to join a union or an employer in selecting representatives to bargain with the union
2. Causing or attempting to cause the employer to discriminate against an employee who is not a union member, unless there is a legal union shop agreement in effect
3. Refusing to bargain with the employer if it is the NLRB-designated representative of the employees
4. Striking, picketing, and engaging in secondary boycotts for illegal purposes
5. Charging new members excessive or discriminatory initiation fees where there is a union shop agreement
6. Causing an employer to pay for work not performed (featherbedding)
7. Picketing to require an employer to recognize or bargain with a union that is not currently certified as representing its employees in certain cases
8. Agreeing with an employer to engage in a secondary boycott

16. Coercion

The first unfair labor practice above includes misconduct by unions directed toward both employees and employers. Most allegations of unfair labor practices filed against unions are brought under this provision.

It is illegal for a union to restrain or coerce employees in the exercise of their right to bargain collectively, just as it is an unfair labor practice by employers to interfere with the same rights. Employees also are guaranteed the right to refrain from union activities unless required by a legal union shop agreement in force between their employer and a labor organization.

Mass picketing, threats of physical violence aimed at employees or their families, and blocking of entrances to plants physically to bar employees from going in have all been held to be union unfair labor practices.

The words *restrain* and *coerce* have the same meanings in reference to union activity and activities by employers. The test is whether the words or conduct by the union are reasonably likely to have deprived the employees of a free choice. The intent is to ensure that the decision of the employees as to whether or not to be represented by a union in bargaining and also the choice of that representative is arrived at freely, without coercion.

17. Refusal to Bargain

As previously noted, it is an unfair labor practice for either employer or union to refuse to bargain collectively with each other. The term "to bargain collectively" means to bargain in good faith. Although the parties need not agree with each other's demands, conduct such as the failure to make counterproposals may be evidence of bad faith. Employers and unions must approach the bargaining table with a fair and open mind and sincere purpose to find a basis of agreement. Refusing to meet at reasonable times with representatives of the other party, refusing to reduce agreements to writing, and designating persons with no authority to negotiate as representatives at meetings are examples of conduct that constitute this unfair labor practice.

Another issue is also present in the requirement that the parties bargain collectively. This issue, simply stated, is: about what? Must the employer bargain with the union on all management decisions in which the union or the employees are interested? Are there subjects and issues upon which management is allowed to act unilaterally? The law requires or compels bargaining on issues concerned with wages, hours, and other terms and conditions of employment.[4]

Thus, management decisions affecting labor fall into two categories: those that concern *mandatory* or *compulsory* bargaining issues, and those that involve *voluntary* or *permissive* bargaining issues. Classifications must be made on a case-by-case basis.

As the Ford case illustrates, courts tend to defer to the special expertise of the NLRB in classifying collective bargaining subjects, especially in the area of "terms or conditions of employment." Among the issues that have been held to be compulsory bargaining issues are merit-pay increases, incentive-pay plans,

---

[4] Ford Motor Co. v. N.L.R.B., p. 1101.

bonuses, paid vacations and holidays, proposals for effective arbitration and grievance procedures, and no-strike and no-lockout clauses.

Typical of issues that do not involve compulsory bargaining matters are the price of the employer's product, loading and unloading procedures, and other matters that generally qualify as managerial decisions essential to entrepreneurial control.

Neither the employer nor the union is required to make concessions to the other concerning a mandatory subject of bargaining. The law demands only that each negotiate such matters in good faith with the other before making a decision and taking unilateral action. If the parties fail to reach an agreement after discussing these problems, each may take steps that are against the wishes and best interests of the other party. The employer may refuse to grant a wage increase requested by the union, and the union is free to strike.

18. Other Unfair Practices

One of the unfair labor practices listed above concerns the union's applying what are called secondary pressures against an employer. *Secondary pressures* are those whose purpose it is to force an employer to cease using, or dealing in, the products of another. A secondary pressure may take the form of a strike or a boycott or an attempt to encourage a strike or a boycott. It is illegal to strike against an employer for the purpose of forcing it to cease doing business with another employer. Similarly, it is unlawful for a union to boycott an employer because that company uses or deals in the goods of another. As mentioned in section 14, hot cargo contracts involve unfair labor practices by a labor union as well as by an employer.

Featherbedding, another unfair labor practice by unions, occurs when an employer is required to pay for work not performed. It should be understood that "make work" provisions of union contracts are not illegal featherbedding. This provision of Taft-Hartley is not violated as long as some services are performed, even if they are of little or no actual value to the employer.

It also is an unfair labor practice for labor unions to charge excessive and unreasonable initiation fees when the employees are required to join the union due to a valid union shop arrangement. Since employees have no choice but to join the union in this situation, this unfair labor practice is designed to prevent unions from taking unfair advantage of their members.

Organizational picketing to force the recognition of an uncertified union is illegal when:

1. The employer has lawfully recognized another union as the collective bargaining representative of employees.
2. A valid representation election has been conducted by the NLRB within the past 12 months.
3. Picketing has been conducted for a reasonable time, not in excess of 30 days, without a petition for a representation election being filed with the NLRB.

Such organizational picketing is an unfair labor practice because of the policy of the law to encourage NLRB-conducted elections. The NLRB election procedures are reinforced, and unions that represent only a minority of employees are prevented from continuing a jurisdictional dispute with the union representing the majority of workers.

A difficult question in labor-management relations today is whether government employees should have the right to form unions and to bargain collectively. If collective bargaining fails, should government employees have the right to strike? The trend is to answer the first question affirmatively and the second negatively. Unions or employee organizations exist at all levels of government. A union without the right to strike is to a significant degree a "paper tiger," and has much less power than other unions. The right to strike is denied government workers because such strikes directly affect the public interest. Strikes by police, firefighters, teachers, sanitation workers, transportation workers, and other public employees affect vital services directly and immediately. They are detrimental to the health, safety, and welfare of society.

GOVERNMENT EMPLOYEES

Collective bargaining for public employees varies through the country. States vary from having no laws granting bargaining rights to public employees to having statutes with broad guarantees. A few states even give some public employees the right to strike. Unions of public workers are pressing for legislation that would give them the choice of striking or turning to binding arbitration. Some advocate the expansion of the present Wagner and Taft-Hartley acts to cover state and local government employees.

SUMMARY

OVERVIEW OF FEDERAL LABOR LAWS

Clayton Act	**1.** This act attempted to prohibit federal courts from enjoining strikes and pickets.
	2. This act also exempted labor unions from the antitrust provisions of the Sherman Act.
Railway Labor Act	**1.** This act is designed to prevent labor disputes from interrupting the services provided by the railway and airline industries.
	2. The National Mediation Board was created to function as a mediator if a labor dispute exists in the covered industries.
	3. If mediation is not successful, arbitration is encouraged. However, the National Mediation Board has no judicial authority to bind the disputing parties.

4. Despite the board's lack of quasi-judicial authority, this act allows the president to order work not be disrupted if there is a likely and substantial interference with interstate commerce.

Norris-LaGuardia Act

1. This act, which was passed in 1932, restricts federal courts from issuing injunctions to prevent legal union activities. State courts are not restricted in a similar manner.

2. This act also outlaws yellow-dog contracts.

3. Although this law attempts to assist union activities, it does not require management to recognize or bargain with union representatives.

Wagner Act

1. Passed in 1935, this law is formally known as the National Labor Relations Act.

2. This act formally recognized the employee's right to organize and participate in union activities.

3. The Wagner Act created the National Labor Relations Board and established five unfair labor practices by management.

Taft-Hartley Act

1. This amendment to the Wagner Act was adopted in 1947. It was designed to adjust the bargaining process, which Congress perceived as favoring the unions.

2. Among its important provisions, the Taft-Hartley Act provided an 80-day cooling-off period, outlawed the closed shop contract, allowed employers to have free speech, and created the Federal Mediation and Conciliation Service.

3. As a step to balancing the bargaining process, this act also included unfair labor practices by unions.

Landrum-Griffin Act

1. This act also is, in essence, an amendment to the Wagner Act. It was passed in 1959.

2. The major purpose of this act is to remove corruption from the internal government of unions and to ensure each union's members a specific bill of rights.

3. This act requires unions to file reports with the secretary of labor. It also has

provisions intended to ensure union democratic elections.

NATIONAL LABOR RELATIONS BOARD

In general

1. The NLRB is an administrative agency designed to conduct investigations and hold hearings involving allegations of unfair labor practices.
2. The NLRB's other primary function is to conduct union representation elections.

Elections and certifications

1. These elections may involve the certification or decertification of a union as a bargaining representative of a group of employees.
2. Such an election may be requested by the union, the employees, or the employer.
3. All NLRB elections are conducted by secret ballot.
4. A valid NLRB election may not be repeated for at least a 12-month period.
5. As an alternative to the election process, a union may ask employees to sign cards authorizing the union as their bargaining agent. If a sufficient number of these cards are signed by employees, the NLRB can certify the union as a bargaining representative without holding an election.
6. Most cards signed by employees simply request the NLRB to conduct an election. Employees often are hesitant to sign a card authorizing the union as a bargaining agent.

UNFAIR LABOR PRACTICES BY EMPLOYERS

Interference with unionization

1. Management cannot threaten employees who engage in organizational activities.
2. Furthermore, management cannot take steps designed to erode employees' support for a union.
3. Management cannot make coercive statements during the preelection discussion of a union's merits.

	4. This unfair labor practice protects employees' concerted activities as well as actual union activities.
Domination of a union	1. Management must not express a preference for one union over another.
	2. Management cannot give financial support to a union once it is selected as a bargaining agent.
	3. The law is designed to maintain the adversarial role between an employer and a union.
Discrimination against union activity	1. Management cannot discriminate in hiring or promoting practices due to an employee's union involvement.
	2. Other areas where discrimination is prohibited include wages, hours, work assignments, and vacations.
Retaliation	1. Employees are encouraged to exercise their rights under the labor laws.
	2. Management must refrain from retaliatory acts if an employee exercises his rights by filing charges with the NLRB or by testifying before that board.
Other unfair practices	1. Management must not refuse to bargain in good faith.
	2. Management cannot agree with unions to participate in hot cargo contracts.

UNFAIR LABOR PRACTICES BY UNIONS

Coercion	1. Unions cannot unduly coerce employees in their decision on whether to have a bargaining agent.
	2. Without a legal union shop arrangement, unions cannot force employees to participate in the union's activities.
Refusal to bargain	1. Like employers, unions must not refuse to bargain in good faith.
	2. A major issue under this unfair labor practice is what are the parties to bargain about.
	3. In general, compulsory bargaining issues are those that concern wages, hours, and terms and conditions of employment.
Other unfair practices	1. Unions cannot encourage employees to engage in secondary boycotts. Such a

boycott brings indirect pressure on an employer to deal with a union or to use products made by unionized employees.

2. A secondary boycott is just as much an unfair labor practice when the agreement is between the union and an employer as it is when the agreement is between a union and employees.

3. Unions cannot engage in featherbedding, which is the receipt of payment for work not actually done.

4. Unions cannot charge excessive and unreasonable fees to union members when a union shop exists.

5. Unions cannot engage in picketing of an employer's business if another union has been recognized as the employees' bargaining agent, if a valid NLRB election was held during the past 12 months, or if no request for an NLRB election has been made within a reasonable time.

GOVERNMENT EMPLOYEES

1. In general, government or public employees have the right to join a union, but they do not have the right to strike.

2. The right to strike is denied these employees because the performance of their jobs has direct and important impact on the welfare of the public in general.

CASES

Local 3489 United Steelworkers of America v. Usery
97 S.Ct. 611 (1977)

BRENNAN, J. The Secretary of Labor brought this action under §402(b) of the Labor, Management Reporting and Disclosure Act of 1959 (LMRDA) to *invalidate* the 1970 election of officers of Local 3489, United Steelworkers of America. The Secretary alleged that a provision of the Steelworkers' international constitution, binding on the Local, that limits eligibility for local union office to members who have attended at least one-half of the regular meetings of the Local for three years previous to the election (unless prevented by union activities or working hours), violated §401(e) of the

LMRDA. The District Court dismissed the complaint, finding no violation of the Act. The Court of Appeals for the Seventh Circuit reversed. We granted certiorari. . . .

The LMRDA does not render unions powerless to restrict candidacies for union office. The injunction in §401(e) that "every member in good standing shall be eligible to be a candidate and to hold office" is made expressly "subject to reasonable qualifications uniformly imposed." But "Congress plainly did not intend that the authorization . . . of 'reasonable qualifications . . .' should be given a broad reach. The contrary is implicit in the legislative history of the section and in its wording. . . ." The basic objective of Title IV of the LMRDA is to guarantee "free and democratic union elections modeled on political elections in this country" where "the assumption is that voters will exercise common sense and judgment in casting their ballots." . . .

Whether a particular qualification is "reasonable" within the meaning of §401(e) must therefore "be measured in terms of its consistency with the Act's command to unions to conduct 'free and democratic' union elections." . . .

[W]e conclude that here the antidemocratic effects of the meeting-attendance rule out-weigh the interests urged in its support. [A]n attendance requirement that results in the exclusion of 96.5% of the members from candidacy for union office hardly seems to be a "reasonable qualification" consistent with the goal of free and democratic elections. A requirement having that result obviously severely restricts the free choice of the membership in selecting its leaders.

Petitioners argue that . . . a member can assure himself of eligibility for candidacy by attending some 18 brief meetings over a three-year period. In other words, the union would have its rule treated not as excluding a category of member from

eligibility, but simply as mandating a procedure to be followed by any member who wishes to be a candidate.

Even examined from this perspective, however, the rule has a restrictive effect on union democracy. In the absence of a permanent "opposition party" within the union, opposition to the incumbent leadership is likely to emerge in response to particular issues at different times, and member interest in changing union leadership is therefore likely to be at its highest only shortly before elections. Thus it is probable that to require that a member decide upon a potential candidacy at least 18 months in advance of an election when no issues exist to prompt that decision may not foster but discourage candidacies and to that extent impair the general membership's freedom to oust incumbents in favor of new leadership. . . .

Petitioners next argue that the rule is reasonable within §401(e) because it encourages attendance at union meetings, and assures more qualified officers by limiting election to those who have demonstrated an interest in union affairs, and are familiar with union problems. But the rule has plainly not served these goals. It has obviously done little to encourage attendance at meetings, which continue to attract only a handful of members. Even as to the more limited goal of encouraging the attendance of potential dissident candidates, very few members, as we have said, are likely to see themselves as such sufficiently far in advance of the election to be spurred to attendance by the rule. . . .

We therefore conclude that Congress, in guaranteeing every union member the opportunity to hold office, subject only to "reasonable qualifications," disabled unions from establishing eligibility qualifications as sharply restrictive of the openness of the union political process as is petitioners' attendance rule. . . .

Affirmed.

Sure-Tan, Inc. v. N.L.R.B.
104 S.Ct. 2803 (1984)

After a union was certified, the employer sent a letter to the Immigration and Naturalization Service (INS), asking it to check the immigration status of five named employees. After a short investigation, INS agents discovered that each of the five

employees listed in the letter was a Mexican national working illegally in the United States. They were arrested and later accepted the INS grant of voluntary departure as a substitute for deportation. The administrative law judge (ALJ) and the NLRB found that the employer had in effect discharged the employees for voting for and supporting the union. The Court of Appeals affirmed.

O'CONNOR, J. . . . We . . . determine whether the National Labor Relations Board (NLRB or Board) may properly find that an employer engages in an unfair labor practice by reporting to the Immigration and Naturalization Service (INS) certain employees known to be undocumented aliens in retaliation for their engaging in union activity, thereby causing their immediate departure from the United States. . . .

We consider the predicate question whether the NLRA should apply to unfair labor practices committed against undocumented aliens. The Board has consistently held that undocumented aliens are "employees" within the meaning of §2(3) of the Act. . . .

Accepting the premise that the provisions of the NLRA are applicable to undocumented alien employees, we must now address the more difficult issue whether, under the circumstances of this case, petitioners committed an unfair labor practice by reporting their undocumented alien employees to the INS in retaliation for participating in union activities. Section 8(a)(3) makes it an unfair labor practice for an employer "by discrimination in regard to hire or tenure of employment or any term or condition of employment to encourage or discourage membership in any labor organization." The Board . . . has long held that an employer violates this provision not only when, for the purpose of discouraging union activity, it directly dismisses an employee, but also when it purposefully creates working conditions so intolerable that the employee has no option but to resign—a so-called "constructive discharge."

Petitioners do not dispute that the anti-union animus element of this test was, as expressed by the lower court, "flagrantly met." The record is replete with examples of Sure-Tan's blatantly illegal course of conduct to discourage its employees from supporting the Union. Petitioners contend, however, that their conduct in reporting the undocumented alien workers did not force the workers' departure from the country; instead, they argue, it was the employees' status as illegal aliens that was the actual "proximate cause" of their departure.

This argument is unavailing. According to testimony by an INS agent before the ALJ, petitioners' letter was the sole cause of the investigation during which the employees were taken into custody. This evidence was undisputed by petitioners and amply supports ALJ's conclusion that "but for [petitioners'] letter to Immigration, the discriminatees would have continued to work indefinitely." . . .

We observe that the Board quite properly does not contend that an employer may never report the presence of an illegal alien employee to the INS. . . . The reporting of any violation of the criminal laws is conduct which ordinarily should be encouraged, not penalized. It is only when the evidence establishes that the reporting of the presence of an illegal alien employee is in retaliation for the employee's protected union activity that the Board finds a violation of §8(a)(3). Absent this specific finding of anti-union animus, it would not be an unfair labor practice to report or discharge an undocumented alien employee. . . .

Reversed and Remanded to permit formulation by the Board of an appropriate remedial order.

Eastex, Inc. v. NLRB
98 S.Ct. 2505 (1978)

Employees of petitioner corporation sought to distribute a four-part union newsletter in nonworking areas of petitioner's plant during nonworking time. The second section encouraged employees to write the legislators to oppose incorporation of the state "right-to-work" statute into a revised state constitution. The third section criticized a presidential veto of an increase in the federal minimum wage and urged employees to register to vote to "defeat our enemies and elect our friends." Representatives of petitioner refused to permit the re-

quested distribution of the newsletter because of the content of its second and third sections. The union then filed an unfair labor practice charge with the NLRB. The board ruled that petitioner's refusal interfered with the employees' exercise of their rights under Section 7 of the National Labor Relations Act, and thus violated Section 8(a)(1). The board's cease and desist order was enforced by the Court of Appeals, and the Supreme Court granted certiorari.

POWELL, J. . . . [The question presented here] is whether . . . distribution of the newsletter is the kind of concerted activity that is protected from employer interference by §§7 and 8(a)(1) of the National Labor Relations Act. . . .

Section 7 provides that "[e]mployees shall have the right . . . to engage in . . . concerted activities for the purpose of collective bargaining or other mutual aid or protection. . . ." Petitioner contends that the activity here is not within the "mutual aid or protection" language because it does not relate to a "specific dispute" between employees and their own employer "over an issue which the employer has the right or power to affect." In support of its position, petitioner asserts that the term "employees" in §7 refers only to employees of a particular employer, so that only activity by employees on behalf of themselves or other employees of the same employer is protected. . . . Thus, in petitioner's view, under §7 "the employee is only protected for activity within the scope of the employment relationship." Petitioner rejects the idea that §7 might protect any activity that could be characterized as "political," and suggests that the discharge of an employee who engages in any such activity would not violate the Act.

We believe that petitioner misconceives the reach of the "mutual aid or protection" clause. The "employees" who may engage in concerted activities for "mutual aid or protection" are defined by the Act to "include any employee, and shall not be limited to the employees of a particular employer, unless the Act explicitly states otherwise. . . ."

This definition was intended to protect employees when they engage in otherwise proper concerted activities in support of employees of employers other than their own. In recognition of this intent, the Board and the courts long have held that the "mutual aid or protection" clause encompasses such activity. Petitioner's argument on this point ignores the language of the Act and its settled construction.

We also find no warrant for petitioner's view that employees lose their protection under the "mutual aid or protection" clause when they seek to improve terms and conditions of employment or otherwise improve their lot as employees through channels outside the immediate employee-employer relationship. The 74th Congress knew well enough that labor's cause often is advanced on fronts other than collective bargaining and grievance settlement within the immediate employment context. It recognized this fact by choosing, as the language of §7

makes clear, to protect concerted activities for the somewhat broader purpose of "mutual aid or protection" as well as for the narrower purposes of "self-organization" and "collective bargaining." Thus, it has been held that the "mutual aid or protection" clause protects employees from retaliation by their employers when they seek to improve working conditions through resort to administrative and judicial forums, and that employees' appeals to legislators to protect their interests as employees are within the scope of this clause. To hold that activity of this nature is entirely unprotected—irrespective of location or the means employed—would leave employees open to retaliation for much legitimate activity that could improve their lot as employees. As this could "frustrate the policy of the Act to protect the right of workers to act together to better their working conditions," we do not think that Congress could have intended the protection of §7 to be as narrow as petitioner insists. . . .

The Board determined that distribution of the second section, urging employees to write their legislators to oppose incorporation of the state "right-to-work" statute into a revised state constitution, was protected because union security is "central to the union concept of strength through solidarity" and "a mandatory subject of bargaining in other than right-to-work states." The newsletter warned that incorporation could affect employees adversely "by weakening Unions and improving the edge business has at the bargaining table." The fact that Texas already has a "right-to-work" statute does not render employees' interest in this matter any less strong, for, as the Court of Appeals noted, it is "one thing to face a legislative scheme which is open to legislative modification or repeal" and "quite another thing to face the prospect that such a scheme will be frozen in a concrete constitutional mandate." We cannot say that the Board erred in holding that this section of the newsletter bears such a relation to employees' interest as to come within the guarantee of the "mutual aid or protection" clause.

The Board held that distribution of the third section, criticizing a presidential veto of an increase in the federal minimum wage and urging employees to register to vote to "defeat our enemies and elect our friends," was protected despite the fact that petitioner's employees were paid more than the vetoed minimum wage. It reasoned that the "minimum wage inevitably influences wage levels derived from collective bargaining, even those far above the minimum," and "concern by [petitioner's] employees for the plight of other employees might gain support for them at some future time when they might have a dispute with their employer." We think that the Board acted within the range of its discretion in so holding. Few topics are of such immediate concern to employees as the level of their wages. The Board was entitled to note the widely recognized impact that a rise in the minimum wage may have on the level of negotiated wages generally, a phenomenon that would not have been lost on petitioner's employees. The union's call, in the circumstances of this case, for these employees to back persons who support an increase in the minimum wage, and to oppose those who oppose it, fairly is characterized as concerted activity for the "mutual aid or protection" of petitioner's employees and of employees generally.

In sum, we hold that distribution of both the second and the third sections of the newsletter is protected under the "mutual aid or protection" clause of §7. . . .

The judgment of the Court of Appeals therefore is affirmed.

Ford Motor Company v. NLRB
99 S.Ct. 1842 (1979)

The Ford Motor Company provided its employees with in-plant cafeteria and vending machine services of an independent caterer, ARA. Ford had the right to review and approve the quality, quantity, and prices of the food. When Ford notified the union representing its employees that the food prices were to be increased, the union requested bargaining over them. Ford refused to bargain, and the union filed an unfair labor practice charge. Taking the view that in-plant food prices and services are "other terms and conditions of employment," the NLRB ordered Ford to bargain. The Court of Appeals enforced the order.

WHITE, J. . . . Because of the "classification of bargaining subjects as 'terms or conditions of employment' is a matter concerning which the Board has special expertise," its judgment as to what is a mandatory bargaining subject is entitled to considerable deference. . . .

Of course, the judgment of the Board is subject to judicial review; but if its construction of the statute is reasonably defensible, it should not be rejected merely because the courts might prefer another view of the statute. . . .

Construing and applying the duty to bargain and the language of §8(d), "other terms and conditions of employment," are tasks lying at the heart of the Board's function. With all due respect to the courts of appeals that have held otherwise, we conclude that the Board's consistent view that in-plant food prices and services are mandatory bargaining subjects is not an unreasonable or unprincipled construction of the statute and that it should be accepted and enforced.

It is not suggested by petitioner that an employee should work a full 8-hour shift without stopping to eat. It reasonably follows that the availability of food during working hours and the conditions under which it is to be consumed are matters of deep concern to workers, and one need not strain to consider them to be among those "conditions" of employment that should be subject to the mutual duty to bargain. By the same token, where the employer has chosen, apparently in his own interest, to make available a system of in-plant feeding facilities for his employees, the prices at which food is offered and other aspects of this service may reasonably be considered among those subjects about which management and union must bargain. The terms and conditions under which food is available on the job are plainly germane to the "working environment." Furthermore, the company is not in the business of selling food to its employees, and the establishment of in-plant food prices is not among those "managerial decisions, which lie at the core of entrepreneurial control." The Board is in no sense attempting to permit the Union to usurp managerial decisionmaking; nor is it seeking to regulate an area from which Congress intended to exclude it. . . .

As illustrated by the facts of this case, substantial disputes can arise over the pricing of in-plant supplied food and beverages. National labor policy contemplates that areas of common dispute between employers and employees can be funneled into collective bargaining. The assumption is that this (is) preferable to allowing recurring disputes to fester outside the negotiation process until strikes or other forms of economic warfare occur.

The trend of industrial practice supports this conclusion. In response to increasing employee concern over the issue, many contracts are now being negotiated that contain provisions concerning in-plant food services. . . . Although not conclusive, current industrial practice is highly relevant in construing the phrase "terms and conditions of employment."

Ford . . . argues that the Board's position will result in unnecessary disruption because any small change in price or service will trigger the obligation to bargain. The problem it is said, will be particularly acute in situations where several unions are involved, possibly requiring endless rounds of negotiations over issues as minor as the price of a cup of coffee or a soft drink. . . .

The Board apparently assumes that, as a practical matter, requests to bargain will not be lightly made. Moreover, problems created by constantly shifting food prices can be anticipated and provided for in the collective-bargaining agreement. Furthermore, if it is true that disputes over food prices are likely to be frequent and intense, it

follows that more, not less, collective bargaining is the remedy. This is the assumption of national labor policy, and it is soundly supported by both reason and experience.

Finally, Ford asserts that to require it to engage in bargaining over in-plant food service prices would be futile because those prices are set by a third-party supplier, ARA. It is true that ARA sets vending machine and cafeteria prices, but under Ford's contract with ARA, Ford retains the right to review and control food services and prices. In any event, an employer can always affect prices by initiating or altering a subsidy to the third-party supplier such as that provided by Ford in this case, and will typically have the right to change suppliers at some point in the future. To this extent the employer holds future, if not present, leverage over in-plant food services and prices.

We affirm, therefore, the Court of Appeals' judgment upholding the Board's determination in this case that in-plant food services and prices are "terms and conditions of employment" subject to the mandatory bargaining under §8(a)(5) and 8(d) of the National Labor Relations Act.

Affirmed.

REVIEW QUESTIONS

1. Match each term in column A with the appropriate statement in column B.

A		B
1. Clayton Act	**a.**	Created by the Railway Labor Act.
2. National Mediation Board	**b.**	Provided for by the Taft-Hartley Act.
3. Yellow-dog contracts	**c.**	An unfair labor practice by unions which occurs when they insist on employees being paid for work not performed.
4. Wagner Act	**d.**	Exempted labor unions from the Sherman Antitrust Act.
5. 80-day cooling-off period	**e.**	Established the National Labor Relations Board.
6. Landrum-Griffin Act	**f.**	A law enacted to govern the internal operations of labor unions.
7. Featherbedding	**g.**	Declared illegal by the Norris-LaGuardia Act.

2. Describe the general goals of the labor laws in this country.

3. Despite its pro-labor provisions, the Norris-LaGuardia Act did little to stimulate the organized labor movement. Why?

4. The United Mine Workers called a nationwide strike. Thirty days later, the issues remained unresolved, and several related industries began laying off thousands of workers. If this strike threatens the nation's security, is there any legal method available to stop the strike? Explain.

5. The Coastal Dockworkers Union (CDU) suspected that persons who opposed the labor movement were becoming involved in the union in an attempt to disrupt its operation. As the result of this suspicion, the CDU's membership passed a bylaw requiring all persons who ran for a union office to have been active CDU members for at least 2 years. Hamilton, who had been a CDU member for only 20 months, sought the union's presidency. When Hamilton's application for office was rejected, he filed suit challenging the membership requirement. What is the legal basis of Hamilton's suit? Explain.

6. Before a labor union may petition the NLRB to hold a certification election, the union must be able to prove that a substantial number of employees want a collective bargaining agent. What is meant by the phrase "a substantial number of employees"?

7. A group of employees at Wright & Cole, Inc., seeking to become the exclusive bargaining agent for all employees, decided to organize. While the election was pending, management allowed the group to use the company's photocopy machine and in-house mail system for solicitation purposes. A union also seeking to represent the employees filed an unfair labor practice to stop these practices. What should be the result of the union's action? Why?

8. Union members employed by the Hartley Manufacturing Company were dissatisfied with their salary schedule. Since Jackson was one of Hartley's largest customers, the union picketed in front of Jackson's store. This picket line was in protest of Jackson's relationship with Hartley. Is this activity legal? Why?

9. At the request of Mechanics Union, the NLRB conducted a union certification election for the employees of Savair. Prior to the election, recognition slips were circulated among the employees. An employee who signed the slip before the election automatically would become a member of the union without having to pay an initiation fee if the union was voted in. Employees who did not sign a recognition slip would have to pay the fee. The union won the election, but the company seeks to set aside the results. Is the waiver of the initiation fee proper grounds for invalidating the election? Explain.

10. What types of issues require compulsory bargaining between management and labor?

49 SECURITIES REGULATIONS

During the Reagan administration, perhaps no area of governmental regulation has received as much attention as the federal securities regulations. In recent years, the relaxation and the enforcement of the laws and regulations in this area have been of major importance to all businesses, both large and small. This chapter is designed to highlight the issues that a businessperson must be aware of when creating and while operating a business organization. Of particular importance are the two major federal securities acts—the 1933 Securities Act and the 1934 Securities Exchange Act. These laws are designed to regulate the sale of securities in interstate commerce as well as the operation of our national securities exchanges.

The application of these laws can be one of the most complex legal matters discussed in this book. As has been the theme throughout this entire text, the need for a good working relationship with a lawyer is never more evident than when questions about securities arise. The following pages serve as an introduction to some of the issues businesspeople will encounter concerning the federal securities laws. At the end of this chapter we discuss state securities laws. These often are referred to as "Blue Sky" laws, and they generally regulate the sale of securities in intrastate commerce.

As you study this chapter, keep in mind that the trend toward securities regulation began as part of the program to help the United States overcome the Great Depression of the 1930s. In an attempt to restore the public's faith in the stock market and in order to assist businesses in raising capital, the early securities laws were designed to give potential investors financial information so that they could make more intelligent investments. Although the disclosure of vital information remains important today, the securities laws have been expanded to ensure the honest nature of all securities transactions.

Prior to examining any of the securities laws mentioned, it is essential that you have a clear understanding of what the word *security* means. It is also important that you are aware of the administrative agency which regulates this legal area.

1. Meaning of *Security*

Because the objective of securities laws is to protect uninformed people from investing their money without sufficient data, the term *security* has a very broad definition that includes much more than corporate stock. A *security* exists when one person invests money and looks to others to manage the money for profit. The securities laws apply to every investment contract in which a person receives some evidence of indebtedness or a certificate of interest or participation in a profit-sharing agreement. As a result, sales of oil well interests, interests in racehorses, interests in limited partnerships, margin sales of coins, and even the sale of orange trees in a grove come within the scope of the securities laws. Courts seek answers to the following three questions when determining whether a person has purchased a security. (1) Is the investment in a common venture? (2) Is the investment premised on a reasonable expectation of profits? (3) Will these profits be derived from the entrepreneurial efforts of others? If the answer to these questions is yes, a security is involved.[1]

Although the definition of the term *security* is very broad, the United States Supreme Court has ruled that federal securities laws are not designed to provide a remedy for all fraudulent transactions. In recent years, the Court has held that securities laws do not necessarily apply (1) to a compulsory pension plan into which the employee is not required to make contributions, or (2) to certificates of deposit insured by the federal government. In the first instance, the Court found that the employee was protected by the Employee Retirement Income Security Act, and in the second situation that the customer was insured by the Federal Deposit Insurance Corporation. In areas where "an investor" is protected by other means, protection provided by the securities laws is less essential.

2. Securities and Exchange Commission

The Securities and Exchange Commission (SEC) was created in 1934. It is responsible for enforcing the federal securities laws. As an administrative agency, the SEC is subject to the principles discussed in chapter 46. The SEC is composed of five commissioners appointed by the president for terms of 5 years. In addition to the commissioners, the SEC employs staff personnel, including lawyers, accountants, security analysts, and security examiners.

The SEC has both quasi-legislative and quasi-judicial powers. Using its quasi-legislative power, it has adopted rules and regulations relating to financial

---

[1] Securities and Exchange Commission v. W. J. Howey Co., p. 1126.

and other information that must be furnished to the commission. It also has rules requiring information that must be given to potential investors. The SEC regulates the various stock exchanges, utility holding companies, investment trusts, and investment advisors. Utilizing its quasi-judicial authority, the SEC may file actions against those that have allegedly violated the securities laws or the SEC's regulations.

FEDERAL SECURITIES ACT OF 1933

3. Introduction

Congress enacted the 1933 Securities Act to govern the initial sale of securities. Under this law, it is illegal to use the mails or any other instrument of interstate communication or transportation to sell securities without disclosing to potential investors the required financial information. The following sections discuss several aspects of the Federal Securities Act of 1933 in detail, including who is regulated, what documents are required, which transactions are exempted, when civil and criminal liability exists, and what defenses are available. As you study these sections, keep in mind that this law applies only to initial sale of the security. Subsequest transfers are governed by the Securities Exchange Act of 1934, which is discussed in sections 12 through 18.

In essence, the 1933 Act requires the disclosure of information to the potential investor or other interested party. The information given must not be untrue or even misleading. If this information is not accurate, liability may be imposed upon those responsible. The Securities Act of 1933 recognizes three sanctions for violations. There is the criminal punishment, the equitable remedy of an injunction, and civil liability, which may be imposed in favor of injured parties in certain cases. Proof of an intentional violation usually is required before criminal or civil sanctions are imposed. However, proof of negligence will support an injunction.

4. Parties Involved

Every person who promotes or is otherwise involved with the initial sale of securities is governed by the 1933 Securities Act. These persons typically can be classified as an issuer, an underwriter, a controlling person, or a seller. An *issuer* is the individual or business organization offering a security for sale to the public. An *underwriter* is anyone who participates in the original distribution of securities by selling such securities for the issuer or by guaranteeing their sale. (Often, securities brokerage firms or investment bankers act as underwriters with respect to a particular transaction.) A *controlling person* is one who controls or is controlled by the issuer, such as a major stockholder of a corporation. Finally, a *seller* is anyone who contracts with a purchaser or who exerts a substantial role which causes the purchase transaction to occur. By applying these definitions of the parties involved in a broad manner, courts have protected unwary investors who lose money as a result of having incomplete or inaccurate information.[2]

---

[2] Junker v. Crory, p. 1127.

5. Documents Required

As previously indicated, the 1933 Securities Act essentially is a disclosure law. This act requires that, prior to their sale, securities be registered with the SEC and any potential investor be furnished with a prospectus. Therefore, in order to comply with the 1933 Securities Act, an issuer of securities must prepare both a registration statement and a prospectus.

Registration statement. The 1933 Act contains specific provisions relating to the registration of securities. This law also describes the selling activities permitted at the various stages of the registration process. There are three distinct periods during the registration process: (1) the prefiling period, (2) the waiting period, and (3) the posteffective period. A registration becomes effective 20 days (the waiting period) after it is filed, unless the SEC gives notice that it is not in proper form or unless the SEC accelerates the effective date. Any amendment filed without the commission's consent starts the 20-day period running again.

During the prefiling period, it is legal for the issuer to engage in preliminary negotiations and agreements with underwriters. It is illegal to sell a covered security during this period. Offers to sell and offers to buy securities also are prohibited during this period.

During the waiting period, it is still illegal to sell a security subject to the act. However, it is not illegal to make an offer to buy or an offer to sell. Written offers to sell must conform to the prospectus requirements, but oral offers are permissible. Since contracts to sell are still illegal, offers cannot be accepted during the waiting period. As a result of these interpretations, dealers may make offers to buy from underwriters during the waiting period. Sellers also may solicit offers for later acceptance.

Many offers during the waiting period are made in advertisements called *tombstone ads.* These ads are brief announcements identifying the security and stating its price, by whom orders will be executed, and from whom a prospectus may be obtained. Offers may also be made during the waiting period by use of a statistical summary, a summary prospectus, or a preliminary prospectus. These techniques allow dissemination of the facts that are to be ultimately disclosed in the formal prospectus.

Prospectus. During the posteffective period, securities may be sold. A *prospectus* must be furnished to any interested investor, and it must conform to the statutory requirements. Like the registration statement, the prospectus contains financial information related to the issuer. Indeed, the prospectus contains the same information contained in the registration statement. The purpose of the prospectus is to supply the investor with sufficient facts (including financial information) so that he or she can make an intelligent investment decision. The SEC has adopted rules relating to the detailed requirements of the prospectus. The major requirements are detailed facts about the issuer and financial statements, including a balance sheet and statements of operations of the issuer.

Theoretically, any security may be sold under the act, providing the law and regulations are followed. The law does not prohibit the sale of worthless securities.

An investor may foolishly invest money, and a person may legally sell the blue sky if the statutory requirements are met. In order to emphasize its limited purpose, the prospectus must contain the following statement in capital letters and boldface type:

> **THESE SECURITIES HAVE NOT BEEN APPROVED OR DISAP-PROVED BY THE SECURITIES AND EXCHANGE COMMISSION NOR HAS THE COMMISSION PASSED UPON THE ACCURACY OR ADEQUACY OF THIS PROSPECTUS. ANY REPRESENTATION TO THE CONTRARY IS A CRIMINAL OFFENSE.**

6. Relaxation of Disclosure Requirements

Regarding initial sale of securities to the public, the most significant development in some time has been the SEC's relaxation of disclosure requirements. This trend is not a change in the 1933 law, but a new direction for the rules and regulations issued by the SEC pursuant to the federal securities laws.

Rule 415, which provides for *shelf registration* of securities, allows companies to submit a single, comprehensive disclosure statement describing their long-term financing plans. These disclosure statements permit companies to sell securities whenever rapidly changing market conditions appear most favorable. Through Rule 415, the issuer of securities to the public no longer has to prepare a prospectus for the SEC's review every time it plans to sell securities.

Rule 415 has been controversial since it was first proposed by the SEC. Many traditional securities firms and investment bankers argued against shelf registration because it decreases the role of the underwriters and syndicates which traditionally have distributed new securities to the public. Other concerned parties expressed a fear that investors could be misled by the documents filed in the shelf registration process. This concern involved the issuer's financial condition changing after the time of the Rule 415 filing. This concern especially is applicable to smaller, less financially stable companies.

Because of these criticisms as well as the advantage of flexibility in raising capital, the SEC has modified Rule 415 and allowed it to become permanent. Companies with less than $150 million in stock held by investors unaffiliated with the company can no longer use the shelf registration method of selling securities to the public. This revised Rule 415 is intended to protect investors who may not be able to get adequate financial data about these smaller, little-known companies in the short time between the announcement of a shelf issue and its sale. This modification does not prohibit any companies from using Rule 415 procedures for employee stock ownership plans, dividend reinvestment plans, and similar transactions that do not involve a conventional distribution of securities to the general public.

7. Exempt Securities

Despite the broad definition of the term *security*, the 1933 Securities Act does not require that every security and every transaction involving securities comply with the act's disclosure requirements. Indeed, some statutory provisions exempt certain transactions and others exempt certain securities from the registration requirements of the 1933 Act. Exempt securities are discussed in this section and exempt transactions in the next. The major distinction in these exemptions is that an exempt security never needs to satisfy the act's registration requirements. While a transaction may be exempt, the securities involved in such a transaction may not be resold without the registration requirements being satisfied. In essence, exempt securities are called *unrestricted securities,* while securities involved in exempt transactions continue to be *restricted securities.* Whenever there is doubt about whether a security or a transaction is exempt from registration, the parties involved should assume the 1933 Securities Act applies until an expert's opinion can be obtained.

Exempt securities can be categorized as one of two general types. First, Regulation A issued by the SEC provides for *semi-exempt* securities. This regulation applies to an offering of securities of up to $1.5 million in value during any 12-month period. Although a formal registration statement and prospectus do not have to be prepared by the issuer and approved by the SEC, an *offering circular* must be filed with the appropriate SEC regional office. This circular contains less detailed information than a formal registration statement. For example, the financial statements included in the circular do not have to be audited. Despite calling these Regulation A securities exempt from the 1933 Act, the offering circular must be made available to potential purchasers.

The 1933 Securities Act does provide for complete exemption of certain specialized securities. These exempt securities include those subject to regulation by governmental agencies other than the SEC. Examples are securities issued by banks, savings and loan associations, not-for-profit corporations, and companies reorganizing under the protection of a bankruptcy court. Commercial paper arising out of current transactions with a maturity not exceeding 9 months and insurance policies issued by regulated insurance companies also are exempt. Also falling within the category of exempt securities are those that are sold only intrastate. While these securities are exempt from federal registration requirements, the issuer must not forget to comply with the applicable state Blue Sky laws. The intrastate exemption covers securities that are offered and sold only to persons who reside within the state of incorporation. If the issuer is unincorporated, the purchasers must reside within the state of the issuer's residence and place of business. If the sale is to a resident planning to resell to a nonresident, the intrastate exemption is lost. The same is true if the mails or interstate systems of communication are used to sell the security. In order to protect against an unwanted interstate sale, the certificates representing intrastate securities must contain a legend that clearly states these securities have not been registered and that these securities can be resold only to residents within the state. Failure to include this type of legend on the certificate can result in a violation of the 1933 Act.

8. Exempt Transactions

Provisions that exempt certain transactions have the effect of limiting the application of the law to transactions in which a security is sold in a public offering by the issuer, an underwriter, a controlling person, or a seller. Transactions by a securities dealer (as distinguished from an issuer or an underwriter) are exempt after 40 days have elapsed from the effective date of the first public offer. If the security is offered by a company with no prior registration statements, this period is 90 days. This exemption allows a dealer to enter into transactions in securities after a minimum period has elapsed. In addition, brokers' transactions executed on any exchange or in the over-the-counter market are exempt.

Perhaps the most difficult issue in determining whether a sale is an exempt transaction is the concept of a *public offering*. Private sales are exempt; sales to the general public are not. In determining whether or not a sale is being made to the general public, the SEC will examine (1) the number of offerees, (2) their knowledge about the company in which they are investing, (3) the relationship between the offeror and offeree, (4) whether the security remains in the hands of the offeree or is resold, and (5) the amount of advertising involved. The burden of proof is on the issuer to prove the sale is private and not public.

During 1982, the SEC broadened some exemptions of transactions based on the size of the offering. These exemptions fall into one of three categories, depending on the dollar amount of securities sold and on who the investor-purchasers are. First, any business may raise up to $500,000 in capital per 12-month period without filing any registration statement or prospectus with the SEC. This exemption formerly limited companies to raising $100,000 during any 12-month period.

Second, the SEC also now allows issuers to sell up to $5 million in securities without registration during any 12-month period as long as the issuer reasonably believes there are no more than 35 nonaccredited investors who purchased securities from the issuer in any offering. In this category, subject to the $5 million limitation, the number of accredited investors who purchase securities can be unlimited. An individual is an accredited investor if one of the following qualifications are satisfied: (1) He or she is a director, executive officer, or general partner of the issuer; or (2) a person who purchases at least $150,000 of the securities being offered, where the purchaser's total purchase price does not exceed 20 percent of the purchaser's net worth at the time of the purchase; or (3) any person whose individual net worth at the time of the purchase exceeds $1,000,000; or (4) any person whose income was over $200,000 in each of the two most recent years and who reasonably expects an income over $200,000 in the current year. Formerly, this exemption applied to sales of up to $2 million in a 6-month time period.

Third, the SEC approved an exemption allowing any amount of securities to be sold without registration if the number of nonaccredited investors who purchased securities was no more than 35 and the issuer reasonably believed each purchaser who was not an accredited investor had such knowledge and experience in financial and business matters that he or she would be able to evaluate the merits and risks of the prospective investment.

Despite the exemptions granted from filing a registration statement and prospectus, an issuer is not relieved of all responsibility under the Securities Act of 1933. If sales are made only to accredited persons, the SEC does not require that the issuer furnish specified information to them. If sales are made to accredited and nonaccredited persons, or only to nonaccredited persons, the issuer must furnish all purchasers with basic information prior to the sale. This information must include (1) a description of the business; (2) the remuneration of directors and officers; (3) financial projections; (4) capital structure; (5) options disclosures regarding officers, directors, affiliates, and promoters; and (6) the interests of management and others in certain transactions. If accredited persons receive additional information in writing before any nonaccredited person makes a purchase, the nonaccredited person must be given the same information upon request.

Issuers of any of the exempt transactions discussed in this section must realize that no general advertising or solicitation is permitted in association with these transactions. Furthermore, all parties involved in the initial sales of securities from the issuer remain subject to the federal laws' antifraud and civil liability provisions. States also may require compliance with their securities laws, regardless of any applicable federal disclosure exemptions. Finally, the securities sold in these exempt transactions are restricted. In other words, before these securities can be resold, registration requirements must be satisfied unless the resale is a part of another exempt transaction.

Table 49–1 summarizes the exemptions provided in the 1933 Securities Act and regulations issued by the SEC.

9. Criminal Liability

In order to prove a criminal violation of the 1933 Securities Act, the government must establish that the violation was willful. *Willful* means the accused party acted with intent to defraud. Fraud occurs when any material fact is omitted intentionally or recklessly. This omission must cause the statement made to be untrue or at least misleading. The government can satisfy its burden by proving that a defendant deliberately closed his or her eyes to facts he or she had a responsibility to see. This burden of proof also is satisfied if the government shows the defendant recklessly stated things to be facts when that party was

EXEMPT SECURITIES	EXEMPT TRANSACTIONS	TABLE 49–1
1. Securities up to $1.5 million in value during a 12-month period. (Regulation A)	1. Securities dealers' and brokers' transactions	Exemptions
2. Securities subject to governmental regulation other than SEC (Banks, Savings & Loan, not-for-profit corporations, etc.)	2. Private offering (not available to general public)	
3. Securities sold only intrastate	3. $500,000 per 12-month period for any business	
	4. $5,000,000 per 12-month period if there are 35 or fewer nonaccredited investors	
	5. Unlimited offering if there are 35 or fewer nonaccredited investors who have expertise to evaluate investment opportunity	

ignorant of the truth. Clearly, the plea of ignorance of falsehood is no defense when the defendant could have discovered the truth or simply choose not to search for the truth.

As emphasized in the previous sections, exemptions under the 1933 Securities Act apply only to the registration requirements. Fraud in the sale of an exempt security is a criminal violation of the act if the mail or other means of interstate communications are used in promoting or completing the sale transaction. The criminal violation of the 1933 Securities Act is viewed as a felony. Congress has authorized penalties of up to $10,000 or 5 years confinement or any combination of these sanctions.

10. Civil Liability

This section of the chapter discusses three sections of the 1933 Securities Act that apply directly to the potential civil liability of parties involved in issuing securities. Two of these sections (11 and 12 of the act) involve liability for false or misleading documents. The third section (17 of the act) concerns liability for participating in fraudulent interstate securities transactions.

Improper documentation—Sections 11 and 12. Section 11 of the 1933 Act deals with registration statements, and Section 12 relates to the prospectuses and other communications. The civil liability provisions relating to registration statements impose liability on the following persons in favor of purchasers of securities:

1. Every person who signed the registration statement
2. Every director of the corporation or partner in the partnership issuing the security
3. Every person who, with his consent, is named in the registration statement as about to become a director or partner
4. Every accountant, engineer, or appraiser who assists in the preparation of the registration statement or its certification
5. Every underwriter

The persons listed are liable if the registration statement (1) contains untrue statements of material facts, (2) omits material facts required by statute or regulation, or (3) omits information which if not given makes the stated facts misleading. This latter situation describes the factual situation of a statement containing a half-truth which has the net effect of being misleading. The test of accuracy and materiality is as of the date the registration statement becomes effective.

The separate provision relating to liability in connection with prospectuses and communications imposes liability on sellers who fail to comply with the registration requirements of the act. This liability is imposed regardless of wrongful intent or conduct of those who fail to comply with the law. It also imposes liability on sellers who use a prospectus or make communications (by mail, telephone, or other instrument of interstate commerce) that contain an untrue statement of material facts required to be stated or necessary to make statements not misleading.

As it applies to the registration statements, the prospectuses, and other communications with potential investors, the SEC and the courts have attempted to define materiality. The term *material* limits the information required to those matters which an average prudent investor ought to be informed about before purchasing the security registered. What are "matters which an average prudent investor ought reasonably to be informed about"? They are matters an investor needs to know before he or she can make an intelligent, informed decision whether or not to buy the security. As a result, a material fact is one which if correctly stated or disclosed would have deterred or tended to deter the average prudent investor from purchasing the securities in question. The term *material* does not cover minor inaccuracies or errors in matters of no interest to investors. Facts that tend to deter a person from purchasing a security are those that have an important bearing upon the nature or condition of the issuing corporation or its business.

A plaintiff-purchaser need not prove reliance on the registration statement, prospectus, or other communication in order to recover, but proof of actual knowledge of the falsity by the purchaser is a defense. Knowledge of the falsity by a defendant need not be proved. However, except for an issuer, reliance on an expert such as an accountant is a defense. For example, a director may defend a suit based on a false financial statement by showing reliance on a CPA. Purchasers of securities sold pursuant to false or misleading information may sue for their actual damages, or they may seek to rescind the purchase and obtain a refund of the purchase price.

Fraudulent transactions—Section 17.   This provision concerning fraudulent interstate transactions prohibits the use of any instrument of interstate communication in the offer or sale of any securities when the result is (1) to defraud, (2) to obtain money or property by means of an untrue or misleading statement, or (3) to engage in a business transaction or practice that may operate to defraud or deceive a purchaser.

The requirement that a defendant-seller must act with intent (*scienter*) to deceive or mislead in order to prove a Section 17 violation has caused much controversy over the years. In 1980, the Supreme Court resolved this issue with respect to the SEC seeking injunctive relief.[3] You should realize that this decision is limited to the remedy of an injunction, since Section 17 does not explicitly provide for the private remedy of monetary damages.

11. Defenses

The 1933 Securities Act recognizes several defenses that may be used to avoid liability. Lack of materiality is a common defense. Determining whether or not a particular fact is material depends on the facts and the parties involved.

The statute of limitations is a defense for both civil and criminal liability. The basic period is 1 year. The statute does not start to run until the discovery of

---

[3] Aaron v. Securities and Exchange Commission, p. 1128.

the untrue statement or omission or from the time such discovery would have been made with reasonable diligence. In no event may a suit be brought more than 3 years after the sale.

A defense similar to the statute of limitations is also provided. This statute provides that if the person acquiring the security does so after the issuer has made generally available an earnings statement covering at least 12 months after the effective date of the registration statement, this person must prove actual reliance on the registration statement. However, this defense has little applicability in most cases.

A very important defense to experts such as accountants is the *due diligence* defense. The law provides that no person is liable who shall sustain the burden of proof that "as regards any part of the registration statement purporting to be made upon his authority as an expert that he had, after reasonable investigation, reasonable ground to believe and did believe, at the time such part of the registration statement became effective, that the statements therein were true and that there was no omission to state a material fact required to be stated therein or necessary to make the statements therein not misleading." In determining whether or not an expert such as an accountant has made a reasonable investigation, the law provides that the standard of reasonableness is that required of a prudent person in the management of his or her own property. The burden of proof of this defense is on the expert and the test is as of the time the registration statement became effective. The due diligence defense in effect requires proof that a party was not guilty of fraud or negligence.

Table 49–2 summarizes Sections 11, 12, and 17 of the 1933 Act. It includes what the plaintiff must prove and the available defenses.

FEDERAL SECURITIES ACT OF 1934

12. Introduction

Whereas the 1933 Securities Act deals with original offerings of securities, the Federal Securities Exchange Act of 1934 regulates transfers of securities after the initial sale. The 1934 Act, which created the SEC, also deals with regulation of security exchanges, brokers, and dealers in securities.

It is illegal to sell a security on a national exchange unless a registration is effective for the security. Registration under the 1934 Act differs from registration under the 1933 Act. Registration under the former requires filing prescribed forms with the applicable stock exchange and the SEC. As a general rule, all equity securities held by 500 or more owners must be registered if the issuer has more than $1 million in gross assets. This rule picks up issues traded over-the-counter, and applies to securities that might have qualified under one of the exemptions under the 1933 Act.

Provisions relating to stockbrokers and dealers prohibit the use of the mails or any instrument of interstate commerce to sell securities unless the broker or the dealer is registered. The language is sufficiently broad to cover attempted as well as actual sales. Brokers and dealers must keep detailed records of their activities and file annual reports with the SEC.

The SEC requires that issuers of registered securities file periodic reports as

TABLE 49–2
Civil liability under the 1933 Act

SECTION OF 1933 ACT	PURPOSE OF SECTION	PLAINTIFF'S REQUIRED PROOF OF DEFENDANT'S SCIENTER	DEFENDANT'S DEFENSE
Section 11	Creates liability for false or misleading registration statements	Not required to prove defendant's intent to deceive	1. Proof of no false or misleading information is a defense. 2. Proof that plaintiff knew of false or misleading nature of information is a defense. 3. Except for issuer, proof of reliance on an expert (attorney, accountant, etc.) is a defense. 4. Proof of good faith is not a defense.
Section 12	Creates liability for false or misleading prospectus and other communications	Not required to prove defendant's intent to deceive	Same as above
Section 17	In an interstate transaction it is: 1. unlawful to employ device, scheme, or artifice to defraud 2. unlawful to obtain money or property by untrue statement or omission of material fact 3. unlawful to engage in events which operate or would operate as a fraud or deceit	1. Required to prove defendant's intent to deceive 2. Not required to prove defendant's intent to deceive 3. Not required to prove defendant's intent to deceive	1. Proof of no intent to deceive. Good faith is a defense. 2. Proof of no material misstatement or omission is a defense. Good faith is not a defense. 3. Proof of no involvement in unlawful activities is a defense. Good faith is not a defense.

well as report significant developments which would affect the value of the security. For example, the SEC requires companies to disclose foreign payoffs or bribes to obtain or retain foreign business operations. Businesses must disclose their minority hiring practices and other social data that may be of public concern. Business has been forced by the SEC to submit certain shareholder proposals to all shareholders as a part of proxy solicitation. When a new pension law was enacted, the SEC required that financial reports disclose the law's impact on the reporting business. SEC activity concerning information corporations must furnish to the investing public is almost limitless. As a result, SEC regulations are of paramount significance to all persons concerned with the financial aspects of business. This area of regulation directly affects the accounting profession. Since the SEC regulates financial statements, a major aspect of the commission's work is deciding issues of proper accounting and auditing theory and practices.

How the 1934 Securities Exchange Act affects the businessperson, the accountant, the lawyer, the broker, and the investor is discussed in the following sections. They cover some fundamental concepts of this law, such as civil liability in general and insider transactions in particular, as well as criminal violations and penalties.

13. Fraudulent Transactions—In General

Most of the litigation under the 1934 Securities and Exchange Act is brought under Section 10(b) of the act and Rule 10b-5 promulgated by the SEC pursuant to the act. Section 10(b) and Rule 10b-5 declare that it is unlawful to use the mails or any instrument of interstate commerce or any national securities exchange to defraud *any person* in connection with the *purchase or sale* of any security. They provide a private remedy for defrauded investors. This remedy may be invoked against "any person" who indulges in fraudulent practices in the purchase or sale of securities. In actual practice, defendants in such cases tend to fall into four general categories: (1) insiders; (2) broker-dealers; (3) corporations whose stock is purchased or sold by plaintiffs; and (4) those, such as accountants, who "aid and abet" or conspire with a party who falls into one of the first three categories.

Section 10(b) and Rule 10b-5 are usually referred to as the *antifraud provisions* of the 1934 Act. In order to recover money damages under these provisions, a plaintiff must establish the following:

1. The existence of material misrepresentation or omission made in connection with the purchase or sale of a security
2. The culpable state of mind of the defendant
3. The plaintiff's reliance and due diligence
4. Damage as a result of the reliance

Materiality under the 1934 Act is the same as materiality under the 1933 Act. Liability under Rule 10b-5 requires proof of scienter, and not proof of simple negligence. It also requires proof of a practice that is manipulative or deceptive, and not merely corporate mismanagement.[4]

---

[4] Santa Fe Industries, Inc. v. Green, p. 1129.

The concept of fraud under Section 10(b) encompasses not only untrue statements of material facts, but omissions of material facts necessary to prevent statements actually made from being misleading. In other words, a half-truth that misleads is fraudulent. Finally, failure to correct a misleading impression left by statements already made, or silence where there is a duty to speak, gives rise to a violation of Rule 10b-5 because it is a form of "aiding and abetting." In general, there is no duty on the part of all persons with knowledge of improper activities to report them. However, a duty to disclose may arise from the fact of a special relationship or set of circumstances such as exists when an accountant certifies financial statements.

Liability under Rule 10b-5 may be imposed on accountants even though the accountant performs only an unaudited writeup. An accountant is liable for errors in a financial statement whether it is audited or unaudited if the statement is contained in a prospectus or other filed report. This liability exists if the accountant knew or should have known of the errors. Even when performing an unaudited writeup, an accountant must undertake at least a minimal investigation into the figures supplied to him or her, and cannot disregard suspicious circumstances.

The application of Section 10(b) and Rule 10b-5 also applies to all sales of any security if the requisite fraud exists and the interstate aspect is established. The rule requires that those standing in a fiduciary relationship disclose all material facts before entering into transactions. This means that an officer, a director, or a controlling shareholder has a duty to disclose all material facts. Failure to do so is a violation and, in effect, fraudulent. Privity of contract is not required for a violation, and lack of privity of contract is no defense.

14. Fraudulent Transactions—Remedies

A plaintiff in a suit under Rule 10b-5 must prove damages. The damages of a defrauded purchaser are usually out-of-pocket losses or the excess of what was paid over the value of what was received. Courts in a few cases have used the *benefit of the bargain* measure of damages and awarded the buyer the difference between what he or she paid and what the security was represented to be worth. A buyer's damages are measured at the time of purchase.

Computation of a defrauded seller's damages is more difficult. A defrauding purchaser usually benefits from an increase in the value of the securities, while the plaintiff seller loses this increase. Courts do not allow defrauding buyers to keep these increases in value. Therefore, the measure of the seller's damages is the difference between the fair value of all that the seller received and the fair value of what he or she would have received had there been no fraud, except where the defendant received more than the seller's loss. In this latter case, the seller is entitled to the defendant's profit. As a result, defendants lose all profits flowing from the fraudulent conduct.

Plaintiffs under Rule 10b-5 are also entitled to consequential damages. These include lost dividends, brokerage fees, and taxes. In addition, courts may order payment of interest on the funds. Punitive damages are not permitted, as they are in cases of common law fraud based on state laws. This distinction results from the language of the statute, which limits recoveries to "actual damages."

As a general rule, attorney's fees are not recoverable. This is consistent with the rule in most litigation. However, in class action suits, the attorneys are allowed to collect their fees out of the recovery. These fees in a class action suit will often exceed the usual hourly rate and will be close to or equal to the contingent fee rate (one-third of the recovery).

15. Insider Transactions

Section 16, one of the most important provisions of the 1934 Securities Exchange Act, concerns insider transactions. An *insider* is any person (1) who owns more than 10 percent of any security, or (2) who is a director or an officer of the issuer of the security. Section 16 and SEC regulations require that insiders file, at the time of the registration or within 10 days after becoming an insider, a statement of the amount of such issues of which they are the owners. The regulations also require filing within 10 days after the close of each calendar month if there has been any change in an insider's ownership of securities during that month. There are exemptions to the insider rules for executors or administrators of estates.

The reason for prohibiting insiders from trading for profit is to prevent the use of information that is available to an insider but not to the public in general. Because the SEC cannot determine for certain when nonpublic information is improperly used, Section 16 creates a presumption that any profit made within a 6-month time period is illegal. These profits are referred to as *short-swing profits*. If a director, officer, or principal owner realizes profits on the purchase and sale of a security within a 6-month period, the profits inure to and belong to the company or the investor whose purchase of a security from or whose sale of a security to an insider resulted in the insider's profit and investor's loss. The order of the purchase and sale is immaterial. The profit is calculated on the lowest price in and highest price out during any 6-month period. Unlike the required proof of intent to deceive under Section 10(b), the short-swing profits rule of Section 16 does not depend on any misuse of information. In other words, there is an absolute prohibition against short-swing profits by insiders regardless of the insiders' state of mind.

16. Other Uses of Nonpublic Information

The SEC's concern for trading based on nonpublic information goes beyond the Section 16 ban on short-swing profits. Indeed, a person who is not technically an insider but who trades securities without disclosing nonpublic information may violate Section 10(b) and Rule 10b-5. The SEC takes the position that the profit obtained as the result of a trader's silence concerning information that is not freely available to everyone is a manipulation or deception prohibited by Section 10(b) and Rule 10b-5. In essence, users of nonpublic information are treated like insiders if they can be classified as a tippee or a temporary insider.

A *tippee* is a person who learns of nonpublic information from an insider. A tippee is liable for the use of nonpublic information because an insider should not be allowed to do indirectly what he cannot do directly. In other words, a tippee is liable for trading or passing on information that is nonpublic.

In recent years, the United States Supreme Court ruled that a person who learns of nonpublic information from a source other than an insider is not required to reveal that information prior to trading. In the case of *Chiarella* v. *United States,** a financial printer had been hired by certain corporations to print corporate takeover bids. Chiarella, an employee of the printer, was able to deduce the identities of both the acquiring companies and the companies targeted for takeover. Without disclosing the knowledge about the prospective takeover bids, Chiarella purchased stock in the target companies and then sold his purchased shares for a profit immediately after the takeover attempts were made public. After an investigation by the SEC, Chiarella was indicted and convicted for having violated Section 10(b) and Rule 10b-5. The Supreme Court reversed this conviction. The Justices reasoned that Chiarella had no duty to reveal the nonpublic information, since he was not in a fiduciary position with respect to either the acquiring or the acquired companies.

In 1983, the United States Supreme Court followed the Chiarella decision and narrowed the tippee's liability. The Court ruled that a tippee becomes liable under Section 10(b) only if the tipper breaches a fiduciary duty to the business organization or other shareholders. Therefore, if the tipper communicated nonpublic information for reasons other than personal gain, neither the tipper nor the tippee could be liable for a securities violation.[5]

Despite this apparent loophole in the use of nonpublic information, a person will be considered to be a *temporary insider* if the insider conveyed nonpublic information that was to be kept confidential. This logic results in finding a temporary insider liable under Section 10(b) even though there was no breach of a fiduciary duty.[6]

In addition to the required proof of a breached fiduciary duty, the SEC has had difficulty in curbing insider transactions because of the limited civil sanction. Historically, the insider was liable only to return the profit illegally gained. During 1984, President Reagan signed into law authority for the SEC to seek a civil penalty of three times the illegal profits. It is anticipated that the SEC will use this increased penalty to further its campaign against the use of inside information. Since 1978, the SEC has concentrated most of its investigative powers on controlling transactions involving insider information. For example, between 1978 and 1983, the SEC brought 81 cases to court alleging that a trader had illegally used and benefited from nonpublic information. This total is more than double the combined total of insider transaction cases brought in the SEC's previous 44 years.

*100 S.Ct. 1108 (1980)

[5] Dirks v. Securities and Exchange Commission, p. 1130.

[6] Securities and Exchange Commission v. Lund, p. 1132.

17. Additional Civil Liability

Section 18 of the 1934 Securities Exchange Act imposes liability on any person who shall make or cause to be made any false and misleading statements of material fact in any application, report, or document filed under the act. This liability based on fraud is in favor of both purchasers and sellers. Plaintiffs under this section must prove *scienter,* reliance on the false or misleading statement, and damage. It is a defense that the person sued acted in good faith and without knowledge that the statement was false and misleading. In other words, mere negligence in filing improper documents with the SEC does not result in liability under Section 18. The defendant must be guilty of fraud before liability can be imposed.

18. Criminal Liability

The 1934 Securities Exchange Act provides for criminal sanctions for willful violations of its provisions or the rules adopted under it. Liability is imposed for false material statements in applications, reports, documents, and registration statements. The penalty is a fine not to exceed $100,000 or 5 years in prison or both. Failure to file the required reports and documents makes the issuer subject to a $100 forfeiture per day. A person cannot be convicted if he or she proves that he or she has no knowledge of a rule or regulation, but of course lack of knowledge of a statute is no defense.

Criminal liability is important for officers and directors. It is also important for accountants. Accountants have been found guilty of a crime for failure to disclose important facts to shareholder-investors. Compliance with generally accepted accounting principles is not an absolute defense. The critical issue in such cases is whether the financial statements as a whole fairly present the financial condition of the company and whether they accurately report operations for the covered periods. If they do not, the second issue is whether the accountant acted in good faith. Compliance with generally accepted accounting principles is evidence of good faith, but such evidence is not necessarily conclusive. Lack of criminal intent is the defense usually asserted by accountants charged with a crime. They usually admit mistakes or even negligence, but deny any criminal wrongdoing. Although it often is difficult to prove a defendant's criminal intent, the government is not required to prove a motive for filing inaccurate documents.

STATE
"BLUE SKY"
LAWS

19. Introduction

In addition to understanding the federal securities laws discussed in the previous sections, every person dealing with the issuance of securities should be familiar with state securities regulations. Throughout their history, these laws commonly have been referred to as *blue sky laws*—probably because they were intended to protect the potential investor from buying "a piece of the attractive blue sky" (worthless or risky securities) without financial and other information about what was being purchased. Blue Sky laws can apply to securities subject to federal laws as well as those securities exempt from the federal statutes. It is clearly established that the federal laws do not preempt the existence of state Blue Sky laws. Due to their broad application, any person associated with issuing or thereafter transferring securities should survey the Blue Sky laws passed by the various states.

Although the existence of federal securities laws has influenced state legislatures, enactment of Blue Sky laws has not been uniform. Indeed, states typically have enacted laws that contain provisions similar to either (1) the antifraud provisions, (2) the registration of securities provisions, (3) the registration of securities brokers and dealers provisions, or (4) a combination of these provisions of the federal laws. To bring some similarity to the various laws, a Uniform Securities Act was proposed for adoption by all states beginning in 1956. Since that time, the Uniform Securities Act has been the model for Blue Sky laws. A majority of states have used the uniform proposal as a guideline when enacting or amending their Blue Sky laws.

20. Registration Requirements

Despite the trend toward uniformity, state laws still vary a great deal in their methods of regulating both the distribution of securities and the securities industry within each state. One example of the variety of state regulations concerns the requirements of registering securities. States have chosen one of the following types of regulations: (1) registration by notification, or (2) registration by qualification. *Registration by notification* allows issuers to offer securities for sale automatically after a stated time period expires, unless the administrative agency takes action to prevent the offering. This is very similar to the registration process under the 1933 Securities Act. *Registration by qualification* usually requires a more detailed disclosure by the issuer. Under this type of regulation, a security cannot be offered for sale until the administrative agency grants the issuer a license or certificate to sell securities.

The Uniform Securities Act adopts the registration by notification process for an issuer who has demonstrated stability and performance. Registration by qualification is required of those issuers who do not have a proved record and who are not subject to the 1933 Securities Act. In addition, the Uniform Securities Act created a third procedure called *registration by coordination*. For those issuers of securities who must register with the SEC, duplicate documents are filed with the state administrative agency. Unless the state official objects, the state registration becomes effective automatically when the federal registration statement is deemed effective.

21. Exemptions

To further compound the confusion about Blue Sky laws, various exemptions of the securities or transactions have been adopted by the states. Four basic exemptions have been identified. Every state has enacted at least one and perhaps a combination of these exemptions. Among these common four are the exemption

(1) for an isolated transaction, (2) for an offer or sale to a limited number of offerees or purchasers within a stated time period, (3) for a private offering, and (4) for a sale if the number of holders after the sale does not exceed a specified number.

The second type of exemption probably is the most common exemption, since it is part of the Uniform Securities Act. Nevertheless, states vary on whether the exemption applies to offerees or to purchasers. There is also great variation on the maximum number of such offerees or purchasers involved. That number ranges between 5 and 35, depending on the applicable law. The time period for the offers or purchases, as the case may be, also vary; however, 12 months seems to be the most common period.

Usually the applicable time limitation is worded to read, for example, "*any* twelve-month time period." In essence, this language means that each day starts a new time period. For example, assume a security is exempt from Blue Sky registration requirements if the issuer sells (or offers to sell) securities to no more than 35 investors during any 12-month period. Furthermore, assume the following transactions occur, with each investor being a different person or entity:

- On February 1, 1986, issuer sells to 5 investors
- On June 1, 1986, issuer sells to 10 investors
- On September 1, 1986, issuer sells to 10 investors
- On December 1, 1986, issuer sells to 5 investors
- On March 1, 1987, issuer sells to 5 investors
- On May 1, 1987, issuer sells to 10 investors

Only 30 investors are involved during the 12-month period following February 1, 1986. However, 40 investors are purchasers during the 12 months following June 1, 1986. Therefore, this security and the transaction involved are not exempt from the law. Civil as well as criminal liability may result for failure to comply with the applicable legal regulations.

Although Blue Sky laws may cause confusion due to their variation, ignorance of the state legal requirements is no defense. This confusion is furthered when the businessperson considers the applicability of federal securities laws as well as the variety of Blue Sky laws. To diminish this confusion, any person involved in the issuance or subsequent transfer of securities should consult with lawyers and accountants, as well as other experts who have a working knowledge of securities regulations.

SUMMARY

Meaning of *security*	**1.** The term *security* has a broad meaning.
	2. Three elements usually must be present in order for a security to be found.

	3. These elements include (a) an investment of money, (b) with the expectation of profits, (c) from the performance of others.
Securities and Exchange Commission (SEC)	1. Administrative agency created to enforce the federal securities law and to regulate national securities exchanges.
	2. Consists of five commissioners appointed to 5-year terms by the president.
	3. The SEC has both quasi-legislative and quasi-judicial authority.

FEDERAL SECURITIES ACT OF 1933

Purpose	1. The 1933 Act regulates the initial sale of securities.
	2. It is basically a disclosure law to provide potential investors with information on which to base an investment decision.
Parties involved	1. Those subject to the 1933 Act include issuers, underwriters, controlling persons, and sellers.
	2. An issuer offers a security for sale.
	3. An underwriter guarantees the sale of an initial offering.
	4. A controlling person controls the issuer or is controlled by the issuer.
	5. A seller is anyone who plays a substantial role in causing the purchase to occur.
Documents required	1. The 1933 Act requires that securities be registered with the SEC and that a prospectus be available to potential investors.
	2. The registration statement contains specific financial information about the issuer.
	3. Securities that must be registered are subject to the prefiling period, the waiting period, and the posteffective period.
	4. The prospectus is a document that contains essential financial information to help the prospective investors in their direction-making process.
	5. These documents do not assure the investor of a profit. They are designed simply to supply information to investors.

Relaxation of disclosure requirements	1. Rule 415, which allows shelf registration, applies to companies with assets exceeding $150 million.
	2. Shelf registration permits issuers to submit one disclosure statement covering a large amount of securities.
	3. This shelf registration is in lieu of a separate registration statement for each new issue. Thus Rule 415 allows issuers to react quickly to market conditions whenever capital is being raised.
Exempt securities and exempt transactions	See Table 49–1 for summary.
Criminal liability	1. To be criminal, a violation of the 1933 Act must be willful.
	2. Such a violation is punishable by a fine of up to $10,000 or a jail term of up to 5 years or both.
Civil liability	1. Three sections under the 1933 Act are most important for liability purposes.
	2. Section 11 concerns improper registration statements. Section 12 concerns improper prospectuses. Sections 17 governs fraudulent transactions.
	3. See Table 49–2 for a summary of these sections and possible defenses that can be pleaded by the accused.

FEDERAL SECURITIES ACT OF 1934

In general	1. The 1934 Act governs all securities transaction after the issuer's initial sale.
	2. This Act also is concerned with the operation of national exchanges, brokers, and dealers.
Fraudulent transactions	1. Section 10(b) of the 1934 Act and Rule 10b-5 written by the SEC are the key elements of the 1934 Act.
	2. These provisions make it illegal to use the mail or other interstate communications to defraud any person in connection with securities transactions.
	3. Remedies for fraudulent transactions usually are the recovery by the buyer of out-of-pocket losses. The seller who is

	defrauded may recover the value of lost profits.
	4. Consequential damages may be recovered, but punitive damages and attorney's fees seldom are awarded in fraudulent transaction cases.
Insider transactions	**1.** An insider is defined in Section 16 as (a) an owner of 10 percent of an issued security or (b) a director or officer of the issuer.
	2. Insiders are prohibited from earning any short-swing profits during any 6-month period.
	3. The civil penalty for illegal insider trading is loss of three times the illegal short-swing profit.
Other uses of nonpublic information	**1.** Under Section 10(b) and Rule 10b-5, noninsiders who trade on the use of nonpublic information may be liable as tippees or temporary insiders.
	2. In general, these noninsiders must have breached a fiduciary duty or have been aware that the insider-tippee breached a fiduciary duty or intended the nonpublic information to be kept confidential.
Additional civil liability	**1.** Section 18 of the 1934 Act makes those who file documents with the SEC liable for any false or misleading documents.
	2. A plaintiff who files a Section 18 must prove the plaintiff's reliance on the improper document and the defendant's intent to mislead. Thus, good faith is a valid defense, and the proof of negligence does not state a cause of action.
Criminal liability	**1.** Criminal penalties under the 1934 Act are fines up to $100,000 or prison term up to 5 years or both.

STATE BLUE SKY LAWS

Registration requirements	**1.** Typically a state will require registration by notification or, in the alternative, registration by qualification.
Exemptions	**1.** The blue sky laws also vary widely with respect to exemptions.

> **2.** Typical exemptions may be awarded when (a) the offer is for a limited number of purchasers over a stated time period, (b) the offering is private by nature, or (c) the number of offerees does not exceed a statutory limit.

CASES

Securities and Exchange Commission v. W. J. Howey Co.
66 S.Ct. 1100 (1946)

W. J. Howey Company and Howey-in-the-Hills Service, Inc., are Florida corporations under common control and management. Howey Company offered to sell to the public its orange grove, tree by tree. Howey-in-the-Hills Service, Inc., offered these buyers a contract wherein the appropriate care, harvesting, and marketing of the oranges would be provided. Most of the buyers who signed the service contracts were nonresidents of Florida who had very little knowledge or skill needed to care for and harvest the oranges. These buyers were attracted by the expectation of profits. The SEC sought to enjoin these companies from using the mail and other instruments of interstate communications in offering and selling unregistered and nonexempt securities. The district court refused to issue an injunction, and the court of appeals affirmed.

MURPHY, J. . . . It is admitted that the mails and instrumentalities of interstate commerce are used in the sale of the land and service contracts and that no registration statement or letter of notification has ever been filed with the Commission in accordance with the Securities Act of 1933 and the rules and regulations thereunder. . . .

The legal issue in this case turns upon a determination of whether, under the circumstances, the land sales contract, the warranty deed and the service contract together constitute an "investment contract" within the meaning of §2(1). An affirmative answer brings into operation the registration requirements of §5(a), unless the security is granted an exemption under §3(b). The lower courts, in reaching a negative answer to this problem, treated the contracts and deeds as separate transactions involving no more than an ordinary real estate sale and an agreement by the seller to manage the property for the buyer. . . . [A]n investment contract for purposes of the Securities Act means a contract, transaction or scheme whereby a person invests his money in a common enterprise and is led to expect profits solely from the efforts of the promoter or a third party, it being immaterial whether the shares in the enterprise are evidenced by formal certificates or by nominal interests in the physical assets employed in the enterprise. Such a definition embodies a flexible rather than a static principle, one that is capable of adaptation to meet the countless and variable schemes devised by those who seek the use of the money of others on the promise of profits.

The transactions in this case clearly involve investment contracts as so defined. The respondent companies are offering something more than fee simple interests in land, something different from a farm or orchard coupled with management services. They are offering an opportunity to contribute money and to share in the profits of a large citrus fruit enterprise managed and partly owned by respondents. They are offering this opportunity to persons who reside in distant localities and who lack the equipment and experience requisite to the cultivation, harvesting and marketing of the citrus products. Such persons have no desire to occupy the land or to develop it themselves; they are attracted solely by the prospects of a return on their investment. Indeed, individual development of the plots of land that are offered and sold would seldom be economically feasible due to their small size. Such tracts gain utility as citrus groves only when cultivated and developed as component parts of a larger area. A common enterprise managed by respondents or third parties with adequate personnel and equipment is therefore essential if the investors are to achieve their paramount aim of a return on their investments. Their respective shares in this enterprise are evidenced by land sales contracts and warranty deeds, which serve as a convenient method of determining the investors' allocable shares of the profits. The resulting transfer of rights in land is purely incidental.

Thus all the elements of a profit-seeking business venture are present here. The investors provide the capital and share in the earnings and profits; the promoters manage, control and operate the enterprise. It follows that the arrangements whereby the investors' interests are made manifest involve investment contracts, regardless of the legal terminology in which such contracts are clothed. The investment contracts in this instance take the form of land sales contracts, warranty deeds and service contracts which respondents offer to prospective investors. And respondents' failure to abide by the statutory and administrative rules in making such offerings, even though the failure result from a bona fide mistake as to the law, cannot be sanctioned under the Act.

Reversed.

Junker v. Crory
650 F.2d 1349 (5th Cir. 1981)

James Junker owned 162 shares of stock in Reco Investment Corporation. These shares were equal to 16.2 percent of the 1,000 shares Reco had outstanding. Reco became heavily indebted to another corporation known as Road Equipment Company, Inc. In order to resolve Reco's poor financial condition, Frederick Heisler, a lawyer for Reco, suggested and strongly recommended that Reco be merged into Road. Due to what he believed was an unreasonably low appraised value of Reco's stock, Junker voted against the proposed merger. However, the remaining shareholders of Reco approved the merger plan, and it was accomplished. Later, Junker discovered some negative news about Road's financial condition. This information was not revealed at the shareholders' meeting when the merger vote was taken. Junker sued Frederick Heisler alleging a violation of the 1933 Securities Act. Heisler defended the suit by arguing he had no duty to reveal additional information. The district court ruled in Junker's favor, and Heisler appealed.

RUBIN, J. . . . Heisler . . . was not an officer, director or shareholder in either Reco or Road. According to the trial court's findings, he acted as attorney or agent for both corporations. . . . Finding no state law cause of action on which to ground Heisler's liability to Junker, we turn to the federal securities law claims.

The trial court held Heisler liable for violation of the 1933 Act. . . .

To recover . . . , the plaintiff must establish that the defendant as a seller of a security misrepresented or failed to state material facts to the plaintiff in connection with the sale. . . .

A merger may amount to a purchase or sale of a security for purposes of the federal securities laws. Thus, the exchange of Junker's Reco shares for stock in Road pursuant to the merger qualifies Junker as a purchaser of Road stock.

Because a purchaser may recover . . . only from his immediate seller, our inquiry focuses on whether Heisler's role in the merger transaction constituted him a seller for purposes of that section. Mere participation in the events leading up to the transaction is insufficient to constitute one a seller of a security. Only those in privity with the purchaser or those "whose participation in the buy-sell transaction is a substantial factor in causing the transaction to take place" are classified as sellers. . . .

[W]e held in *Croy v. Campbell,* 624 F.2d 709 (5th Cir. 1980), that an attorney whose connection with the sale was limited to advising the purchaser on its tax consequences was not a seller. The attorney in *Croy* did not attempt to persuade the plaintiffs to make the purchase; he made no representations to them concerning the operational aspects of the project in which the plaintiffs ultimately invested. In determining that his involvement was insufficient to constitute a proximate cause of the sale, we noted, "[t]his conclusion should not be interpreted to mean that a lawyer who participates in the transaction can never be a seller." . . .

Heisler's role in bringing about the merger in this case differed significantly from the relatively inactive part played by the lawyer in *Croy.* According to Heisler's testimony, he initially suggested the possibility of a merger. The minutes of the Reco shareholders' meeting at which the merger was discussed reflect that Heisler attended as . . . proxy and advanced the merger as the solution to Reco's financial problems. He also prepared the merger documents. Thus, unlike the attorney in *Croy,* Heisler did attempt to persuade the Reco shareholders to make the purchase of Road stock pursuant to the merger. He also made representations at the Reco shareholders' meeting regarding his investigation into possible sales of Reco property and the feasibility of a liquidation of Reco as compared with the merger. The evidence of Heisler's involvement in the effort to bring about the merger supports the trial court's finding that he was a key participant in the transaction. His role was not that of a passive advisor as was that of the attorney in *Croy;* rather, he was an active negotiator in the transaction, acting as agent-in-fact as well as attorney-at-law, implementor not counsellor. Therefore, we agree with the trial court's conclusion that Heisler's actions brought him within the scope of the seller definition. . . .

Having determined that Heisler's actions constituted him a seller, . . . we also conclude that his representations made to the Reco shareholders at the shareholders' meeting amounted to an oral communication containing misstatements or omissions of material facts relevant to the merger transaction. . . .

Therefore, we conclude that Heisler did not satisfy the burden of proof required to establish that, exercising reasonable care, he could not have been aware of the material misstatements and omissions in his presentation at the Reco shareholders' meeting. . . .

For these reasons the judgment in Junker's favor is

Affirmed.

Aaron v. Securities and Exchange Commission
100 S. Ct. 1945 (1980)

Peter Aaron was the managing employee of a registered securities firm. Two employees, Schrieber and Jacobson, under Aaron's supervision, gave false information about Lawn-A-Mat Chemical & Equipment Corporation. This information was falsified to induce clients to invest in Lawn-A-Mat common stock. After being told of these wrongful acts, Aaron failed to stop the brokers from continuing to make false and misleading statements. The SEC filed a complaint and sought to enjoin Aaron from aiding and abetting continuous violations of §17(a) of the 1933 Securities Act.

STEWART, J. The issue in this case is whether the Securities and Exchange Commission (Commission) is required to establish scienter as an element of a civil enforcement action to enjoin violations of §17(a) of the Securities Act of 1933 (1933 Act). . . .

Following a bench trial, the District Court found that the petitioner had violated and aided and abetted violations of §17(a) . . . during the Lawn-A-Mat sales campaign and enjoined him from future violations of these provisions. The District Court's finding of past violations was based upon its factual finding that the petitioner had intentionally failed to discharge his supervisory responsibility to stop Schreiber and Jacobson from making statements to prospective investors that the petitioner knew to be false and misleading. Although noting that negligence alone might suffice to establish a violation of the relevant provisions in a Commission enforcement action, the District Court concluded that the fact that the petitioner "intentionally failed to terminate the false and misleading statements made by Schreiber and Jacobson, knowing them to be fraudulent, is sufficient to establish his scienter under the securities laws." As to the remedy . . . , the District Court reasoned that injunctive relief was warranted in light of "the nature and extent of the violations. . . ."

The Court of Appeals for the Second Circuit affirmed the judgment. Declining to reach the question whether the petitioner's conduct would support a finding of scienter, the Court of Appeals held instead that when the Commission is seeking injunctive relief, "proof of negligence alone will suffice" to establish a violation of §17(a). . . .

Section 17(a), which applies only to sellers, provides:

It shall be unlawful for any person in the offer or sale of any securities by the use of any means or instruments of transportation or communication in interstate commerce or by the use of the mails, directly or indirectly—

(1) to employ any device, scheme, or artifice to defraud, or

(2) to obtain money or property by means of any untrue statement of a material fact or any omission to state a material fact necessary in order to make the statements made, in the light of the circumstances under which they were made, not misleading, or

(3) to engage in any transaction, practice, or course of business which operates or would operate as a fraud or deceit upon the purchaser. . . .

In determining whether proof of scienter is a necessary element of a violation of §17(a), . . . the controlling principles are well settled.

The language of §17(a) strongly suggests that Congress contemplated a scienter requirement under §17(a)(1), but not under §17(a)(2) or §17(a)(3). The language of §17(a)(1), which makes it unlawful "to employ any device, scheme, or artifice to defraud," plainly evinces an intent on the part of Congress to proscribe only knowing or intentional misconduct. Even if it be assumed that the term "defraud" is ambiguous, given its varied meanings at law and in equity, the terms "device," "scheme," and "artifice" all connote knowing or intentional practices. . . .

By contrast, the language of §17(a)(2), which prohibits any person from obtaining money or property "by means of any untrue statement of a material fact or any omission to state a material fact," is devoid of any suggestion whatsoever of a scienter requirement. . . .

Finally, the language of §17(a)(3), under which it is unlawful for any person "to engage in any transaction, practice, or course of business which *operates* or *would operate* as a fraud or deceit," (emphasis added) quite plainly focuses upon the *effect* of particular conduct on members of the investing public, rather than upon the culpability of the person responsible. . . .

It is our view, in sum, that the language of §17(a) requires scienter under §17(a)(1), but not under §17(a)(2) or §17(a)(3). Although the parties have urged the Court to adopt a uniform culpability requirement for the three subparagraphs of §17(a), the language of the section is simply not amenable to such an interpretation. . . . Indeed, since Congress drafted §17(a) in such a manner as to compel the conclusion that scienter is required under one subparagraph but not under the other two, it would take a very clear expression in the legislative history of congressional intent to the contrary to justify the conclusion that the statute does not mean what it so plainly seems to say. We find no such expression of congressional intent in the legislative history. . . .

For the reasons stated in this opinion, we hold that the Commission is required to establish scienter as an element of a civil enforcement action to enjoin violations of §17(a)(1) of the 1933 Act. . . . We further hold that the Commission need not establish scienter as an element of an action to enjoin violations of §17(a)(2) and §17(a)(3) of the 1933 Act. The Court of Appeals affirmed the issuance of the injunction in this case in the misapprehension that it was not necessary to find scienter in order to support an injunction under any of the provisions in question. Accordingly, the judgment of the Court of Appeals is vacated, and the case is remanded to that court for further proceedings consistent with this opinion.

It is so ordered.

Santa Fe Industries, Inc. v. Green
97 S.Ct. 1292 (1977)

Santa Fe sought to merge under the Delaware "short-form" merger statute and obtained independent appraisal values of the stock. The company complied with the statute and sent to each minority shareholder an information statement containing the appraisal values of the assets. It offered the minority shareholders $150 per share

(the appraisal value was $125) for their stock. Respondents, minority shareholders, did not pursue their appraisal remedy in the state courts. Instead, they filed suit under Rule 10b-5, claiming that Santa Fe used a device to defraud and that the information statement failed to reveal that the stock was actually worth $772 per share. The district court dismissed the complaint holding that it failed to state a cause of action. The court of appeals reversed.

WHITE, J. . . . We granted the petition for certiorari challenging this holding because of the importance of the issue involved to the administration of the federal securities laws. . . .

Section 10(b) of the 1934 Act makes it "unlawful for any person . . . to use or employ . . . any manipulative or deceptive device or contrivance in contravention of [Securities and Exchange Commission rules]"; Rule 10b-5, promulgated by the SEC under §10(b), prohibits, in addition to nondisclosure and misrepresentation, any "artifice to defraud" or any act "which operates or would operate as a fraud or deceit."

. . . [I]n deciding whether a complaint states a cause of action for "fraud" under Rule 10b-5, "we turn first to the language of §10(b), for '[t]he starting point in every case involving construction of a statute is the language itself.' " . . .

The language of §10(b) gives no indication that Congress meant to prohibit any conduct not involving manipulation or deception. Nor have we been cited to any evidence in the legislative history that would support a departure from the language of the statute. "When a statute speaks so specifically in terms of manipulation and deception, . . . and when its history reflects no more expansive intent, we are quite unwilling to extend the scope of the statute. . . ." Thus the claim of fraud and fiduciary breach in this complaint states a cause of action under any part of Rule 10b-5 only if the conduct alleged can be fairly viewed as "manipulative or deceptive" within the meaning of the statute.

It is our judgment that the transaction, if carried out as alleged in the complaint, was neither deceptive nor manipulative and therefore did not violate either §10(b) of the Act or Rule 10b-5.

As we have indicated, the case comes to us on the premise that the complaint failed to allege a material misrepresentation or material failure to disclose. The finding of the District Court, undisturbed by the Court of Appeals, was that there was no "omission" or "misstatement" in the information statement accompanying the notice of merger. On the basis of the information provided, minority shareholders could either accept the price offered or reject it and seek an appraisal in the Delaware Court of Chancery. Their choice was fairly presented, and they were furnished with all relevant information on which to base their decision. . . .

We thus adhere to the position that "Congress by §10(b) did not seek to regulate transactions which constitute no more than internal corporate mismanagement. There may well be a need for uniform federal fiduciary standards to govern mergers such as that challenged in this complaint. But those standards should not be supplied by judicial extension of §10(b) and Rule 10b-5 to "cover the corporate universe."

The judgment of the Court of Appeals is reversed, and the case is remanded. . . .

So ordered.

Dirks v. Securities and Exchange Commission
103 S.Ct. 3255 (1983)

POWELL, J. Petitioner Raymond Dirks received material nonpublic information from "insiders" of a corporation with which he had no connection. He disclosed this information to investors who relied on it in trading in the shares of the corporation. The question is whether Dirks violated the antifraud provisions of the federal securities laws by this disclosure.

In 1973, Dirks was an officer of a New York broker-dealer firm who specialized in providing investment analysis of insurance company securities to institutional investors. On March 6, Dirks received information from Ronald Secrist, a former officer of Equity Funding of America. Secrist alleged that the assets of Equity Funding, a diversified corporation primarily engaged in selling life insurance and mutual funds, were vastly overstated as the result of fraudulent corporate practices. Secrist also stated that various regulatory agencies had failed to act on similar charges made by Equity Funding employees. He urged Dirks to verify the fraud and disclose it publicly.

Dirks decided to investigate the allegations. He visited Equity Funding's headquarters in Los Angeles and interviewed several officers and employees of the corporation. The senior management denied any wrongdoing, but certain corporation employees corroborated the charges of fraud. Neither Dirks nor his firm owned or traded any Equity Funding stock, but throughout his investigation he openly discussed the information he had obtained with a number of clients and investors. Some of these persons sold their holdings of Equity Funding securities, including five investment advisers who liquidated holdings of more than $16 million. . . .

During the two-week period in which Dirks pursued his investigation and spread word of Secrist's charges, the price of Equity Funding stock fell from $26 per share to less than $15 per share. This led the New York Stock Exchange to halt trading on March 27. Shortly thereafter California insurance authorities impounded Equity Funding's records and uncovered evidence of the fraud. Only then did the Securities and Exchange Commission (SEC) file a complaint against Equity Funding and only then, on April 2, did the *Wall Street Journal* publish a front-page story based largely on information assembled by Dirks. Equity Funding immediately went into receivership.

The SEC began an investigation into Dirks' role in the exposure of the fraud. After a hearing by an administrative law judge, the SEC found that Dirks had aided and abetted violations of §17(a) of the Securities Act of 1933, §10(b) of the Securities Exchange Act of 1934, and SEC Rule 10b-5, by repeating the allegations of fraud to members of the investment community who later sold their Equity Funding stock. The SEC concluded: "Where 'tippees'—regardless of their motivation or occupation—come into possession of material 'information that they know is confidential and know or should know came from a corporate insider,' they must either publicly disclose that information or refrain from trading." Recognizing, however, that Dirks "played an important role in bringing [Equity Funding's] massive fraud to light," the SEC only censured him.

Dirks sought review in the Court of Appeals for the District of Columbia Circuit. The court entered judgment against Dirks. . . .

In view of the importance to the SEC and to the securities industry of the question presented by this case, we granted a writ of certiorari. . . .

We were explicit in *Chiarella* in saying that there can be no duty to disclose where the person who has traded on inside information "was not [the corporation's] agent, . . . was not a fiduciary, [or] was not a person in whom the sellers [of the securities] had placed their trust and confidence." . . . This requirement of a specific relationship between the shareholders and the individual trading on inside information has created analytical difficulties for the SEC and courts in policing tippees who trade on inside information. Unlike insiders who have independent fiduciary duties to both the corporation and its shareholders, the typical tippee has no such relationships. In view of this absence, it has been unclear how a tippee acquires the duty to refrain from trading on inside information.

The SEC's position, as stated in its opinion in this case, is that a tippee "inherits" the obligation to shareholders whenever he receives inside information from an insider. . . .

In effect, the SEC's theory of tippee liability appears rooted in the idea that the antifraud provisions require equal information among all traders. This conflicts with the principle set forth in *Chiarella* that only some persons, under some circumstances, will be barred from trading while in possession of material non-public information. . . . We reaffirm today that "[a] duty [to disclose] arises from the relationship between parties . . . and not merely from one's ability to acquire information because of his position in the market." . . .

The conclusion that recipients of inside information do not invariably acquire a duty to disclose or abstain does not mean that such tippees always are free to trade on the information. The need for a ban on some tippee trading is clear. Not only are insiders forbidden by their fiduciary relationship from personally using undisclosed corporate information to their advantage, but they may not give such information to an outsider for the same improper purpose of exploiting the information for their personal gain. . . . Thus, the tippee's duty to disclose or abstain is derivative from that of the insider's duty. . . .

[A] tippee assumes a fiduciary duty to the shareholders of a corporation not to trade on material nonpublic information only when the insider has breached his fiduciary duty to the shareholders by disclosing the information to the tippee and the tippee knows or should know that there has been a breach. . . .

In determining whether a tippee is under an obligation to disclose or abstain, it thus is necessary to determine whether the insider's "tip" constituted a breach of the insider's fiduciary duty. All disclosures of confidential corporate information are not inconsistent with the duty insiders owe to shareholders. . . . In some situations, the insider will act consistently with his fiduciary duty to shareholders, and yet release of the information may affect the market. . . . This standard was identified by the SEC itself: a purpose of the securities laws was to eliminate "use of inside information for personal advantage." Thus, the test is whether the insider personally will benefit, directly or indirectly, from his disclosure. Absent some personal gain, there has been no breach of duty to stockholders. And absent a breach by the insider, there is no derivative breach.

Determining whether an insider personally benefits from a particular disclosure, a question of fact, will not always be easy for courts. But it is essential, we think, to have a guiding principle for those whose daily activities must be limited and instructed by the SEC's inside-trading rules, and we believe that there must be a breach of the insider's fiduciary duty before the tippee inherits the duty to disclose or abstain. . . .

Under the inside-trading and tipping rules set forth above, we find that there was no actionable violation by Dirks. It is undisputed that Dirks himself was a stranger to Equity Funding, with no pre-existing fiduciary duty to its shareholders. He took no action, directly or indirectly, that induced the shareholders or officers of Equity Funding to repose trust or confidence in him. There was no

expectation by Dirk's sources that he would keep their information in confidence. Nor did Dirks misappropriate or illegally obtain the information about Equity Funding. Unless the insiders breached their duty to shareholders in disclosing the nonpublic information to Dirks, he breached no duty when he passed it on to investors as well as to the *Wall Street Journal.*

It is clear that neither Secrist nor the other Equity Funding employees violated their duty to the corporation's shareholders by providing information to Dirks. The tippers received no monetary or personal benefit for revealing Equity Funding's secrets, nor was their purpose to make a gift of valuable information to Dirks. As the facts of this case clearly indicate, the tippers were motivated by a desire to expose the fraud. In the absence of a breach of duty to shareholders by the insiders, there was no derivative breach by Dirks. Dirks therefore could not have been "a participant after the fact in [an] insider's breach of a fiduciary duty."

We conclude that Dirks, in the circumstances of this case, had no duty to abstain from use of the inside information that he obtained. The judgment of the Court of Appeals therefore is

Reversed.

Securities and Exchange Commission v. Lund
570 F.Supp. 1397 (C.D.Cal. 1983)

Lund was the chief executive officer and chairman of the board of Verit Company. Horowitz was the chief executive officer and chairman of the board of P&F. In order to solicit investment funds, Horowitz told Lund about P&F's opportunity to participate in a Las Vegas gambling casino. Horowitz sought investment capital from Verit. After learning of these unannounced plans, Lund purchased 10,000 shares of P&F's stock. Three days later, P&F's plans to participate in the casino joint venture was announced, and the stock doubled in price. Lund sold his shares at a substantial profit. The SEC sued Lund for violating Section 10(b) of the 1934 Securities Exchange Act.

LUCAS, J. . . . The Court must now address the. . . difficult issue raised by this litigation: Lund's contention that under these facts his failure to

disclose the information he received or to refrain from trading in P&F stock does not constitute a violation of §10(b).

The scope of liability under §10(b) has received much attention in recent years. In particular, the Supreme Court's decisions in *Chiarella v. United States,* 100 S.Ct. 1108 (1980) and *Dirks v. SEC,* 103 S.Ct. 3255 (1983), have significantly clarified the parameters of such liability.

It has long been established that, under certain circumstances, a "tippee" may be held liable under §10 for trading on material, non-public information. However, the precise contours of tippee liability were unclear until *Dirks.* Under *Dirks* tippee liability cannot be imposed unless the "tipper" has breached a fiduciary duty to the shareholders by disclosing the information to the tippee and the tippee knows or should know that there has been a breach.

Following the publication of *Dirks,* plaintiff correctly abandoned its argument that Lund could be held liable under §10(b) on a theory of tippee liability. It is clear in this case that Horowitz did not breach his fiduciary duty to P&F or its shareholders by disclosing information concerning the Jockey Club joint venture to Lund. His disclosure of this information was within the scope of his authority as an officer and director of the corporation. Absent a breach of a fiduciary duty by Horowitz, Lund cannot be liable under §10(b) as a tippee.

This determination does not end the Court's inquiry, however. In addition to "tippee" liability discussed above, courts have long imposed liability under §10(b) in cases of "insider" trading. Although corporate insiders are traditionally defined as officers, directors and controlling shareholders of the corporation, a consistent body of case law makes clear that the scope of the concept "insider" is flexible. In one of the earliest "disclose or abstain" cases, the Commission specifically stated that these three groups "do not exhaust the classes of persons upon whom there is [an obligation to disclose or abstain.]" The commission stated that the scope of the disclose or abstain rule is not "circumscribed by fine distinctions and rigid classifications." Rather, the prohibition against insider trading is directed at "those persons who are in a special relationship with the company and privy to its internal affairs."

This flexible understanding of the scope of the concept "insider" for the purposes of §10(b) has been confirmed by this Circuit. . . .

Similarly, in *Dirks,* the Supreme Court noted that "outsiders" may, under certain circumstances, become fiduciaries of shareholders and, thus become subject to the same duty to disclose or abstain as an insider. . . .

Persons who, although not traditional "insiders", nevertheless become fiduciaries of the corporation and the shareholders could be called "temporary insiders." They assume the duties of an insider temporarily, by virtue of a special relationship with the corporation. A temporary insider is subject to liability under §10(b) for trading on the basis of nonpublic material information received in the context of the special relationship.

The Court has concluded that Lund was a temporary P&F insider when he traded on the basis of the information concerning the Jockey Club project. Lund and Horowitz were long time friends and business associates. They often exchanged information about their corporations. Horowitz sat on the Board of Verit. Horowitz told Verit, through Lund, of the Jockey Club joint venture because of this special relationship. The information was made available to Lund solely for corporate purposes. It was not disclosed in idle conversation or for some other purpose. The relationship between Horowitz and Lund was such as to imply that the information was to be kept confidential. Horowitz clearly did not expect Lund to make the information public or to use the information for his personal gain. Lund knew or should have known that the information he received was confidential and that it had been disclosed to him solely for legitimate corporate purposes.

Under these circumstances, Lund became a temporary P&F insider upon receipt of the information concerning the Jockey Club project and assumed an insider's duty to "disclose or abstain" from trading based on that information. Lund's breach of that duty is actionable under §10(b).

So ordered.

REVIEW QUESTIONS

1. Identify the terms in column A by matching each with the appropriate statement in column B.

A	B
1. Registration statement	**a.** An advertisement made during the waiting period. It announces the security, its price, by whom orders will be executed, and from whom a prospectus may be obtained.

2. Prospectus	**b.** Participant in the distribution of a security who guarantees the sale of an issue.
3. Tombstone ad	**c.** The individual or business organization that offers a security for sale.
4. Insider	**d.** The document that contains financial and other information. It must be filed with the SEC prior to any sale of a security.
5. Issuer	**e.** A party who controls or is controlled by the issuer.
6. Controlling person	**f.** A person who owns more than 10 percent of a security of an issuer or who is a director or an officer of an issuer.
7. Underwriter	**g.** Any person who contracts with a purchaser or who plays a substantial role that causes a purchase transaction to occur.
8. Seller	**h.** A document or pamphlet that includes the essential information contained in the registration statement. It is filed with the SEC and made available to potential investors.

2. What are the three elements of the definition of a *security* as used in the federal security laws?

3. What are the basic distinctions between Blue Sky laws, the 1933 Securities Act, and the 1934 Securities Exchange Act?

4. Under the provisions of the 1933 Securities Act, there are three important time periods concerning when securities may be sold or offered for sale. Name and describe these three time periods.

5. In an attempt to increase issuers' flexibility in raising capital, the SEC has adopted Rule 415 on shelf registration. Explain the meaning and purpose of shelf registration. What is the applicability of Rule 415?

6. Patrick, a promoter for a newly organized corporation, began to solicit purchasers for the corporation's stock. The corporation did not limit the number of potential shareholders, but it did not plan to sell more than $400,000 worth of securities. What is Patrick's responsibility under the provisions of the 1933 Securities Act with respect to registering this offering? Explain.

7. In exempting transactions from the registration requirements of the 1933 Securities Act, the SEC uses the terms *accredited investor* and *nonaccredited investor.* Define each of these terms.

8. Betty, a buyer of unregistered securities from the Thornwood Company, lost all her investment when the company filed for bankruptcy. What civil remedies does Betty have if these securities are subject to the 1933 Securities Act?

9. Section 10(b) of the 1934 Securities Exchange Act and Rule 10b-5 are essential in the regulation of securities. What do this section and this rule basically regulate? Explain.

10. Debra, a corporate director, purchased 200 shares of her corporation's stock on January 15, 1986. The purchase price was $7.25. Six weeks later, the corporation announced a major revision in its production process. This revision will save the corporation 25 percent in production costs. After this announcement, Debra sold her 200 shares for $10.50 a share. Are there any problems with Debra's transactions? Why?

11. In addition to civil liability, a person who violates the federal securities laws also faces criminal sanctions. What are the maximum criminal penalties under the 1933 Securities Act and the 1934 Securities Exchange Act?

UNIFORM COMMERCIAL CODE

UNIFORM COMMERCIAL CODE

AN ACT

To be known as the Uniform Commercial Code, Relating to Certain Commercial Transactions in or regarding Personal Property and Contracts and other Documents concerning them, including Sales, Commercial Paper, Bank Deposits and Collections, Letters of Credit, Bulk Transfers, Warehouse Receipts, Bills of Lading, other Documents of Title, Investment Securities, and Secured Transactions, including certain Sales of Accounts, Chattel Paper, and Contract Rights, Providing for Public Notice to Third Parties in Certain Circumstances; Regulating Procedure, Evidence and Damages in Certain Court Actions Involving such Transactions, Contracts or Documents; to Make Uniform the Law with Respect Thereto; and Repealing Inconsistent Legislation.

ARTICLE 1

GENERAL PROVISIONS

PART 1

SHORT TITLE, CONSTRUCTION, APPLICATION AND SUBJECT MATTER OF THE ACT

Section 1-101. Short Title. This act shall be known and may be cited as Uniform Commercial Code.

Section 1-102. Purposes; Rules of Construction; Variation by Agreement.

(1) This Act shall be liberally construed and applied to promote its underlying purposes and policies.

(2) Underlying purposes and policies of this Act are

   (a) to simplify, clarify and modernize the law governing commercial transactions;

   (b) to permit the continued expansion

of commercial practices through custom, usage and agreement of the parties;

(c) To make uniform the law among the various jurisdictions.

(3) The effect of provisions of this Act may be varied by agreement, except as otherwise provided in this Act and except that the obligations of good faith, diligence, reasonableness and care prescribed by this Act may not be disclaimed by agreement but the parties may by agreement determine the standards by which the performance of such obligations is to be measured if such standards are not manifestly unreasonable.

(4) The presence in certain provisions of this Act of the words "unless otherwise agreed" or words of similar import does not imply that the effect of other provisions may not be varied by agreement under subsection (3).

(5) In this Act unless the context otherwise requires

(a) words in the singular number include the plural, and in the plural include the singular;

(b) words of the masculine gender include the feminine and the neuter, and when the sense so indicates the words of the neuter gender may refer to any gender.

Section 1-103. Supplementary General Principles of Law Applicable. Unless displaced by the particular provisions of this Act, the principles of law and equity, including the law merchant and the law relative to capacity to contract, principal and agent, estoppel, fraud, misrepresentation, duress, coercion, mistake, bankruptcy, or other validating or invalidating cause shall supplement its provisions.

Section 1-104. Construction Against Implicit Repeal. This Act being a general act intended as a unified coverage of its subject matter, no part of it shall be deemed to be impliedly repealed by subsequent legislation if such construction can reasonable be avoided.

Section 1-105. Territorial Application of the Act; Parties' Power to Choose Applicable Law.

(1) Except as provided hereafter in this section, when a transaction bears a reasonable relation to this state and also to another state or nation the parties may agree that the law either of this state or of such other state or nation shall govern their rights and duties. Failing such agreement this Act applies to transactions bearing an appropriate relation to this state.

(2) Where one of the following provisions of this Act specifies the applicable law, that provision governs and a contrary agreement is effective only to the extent permitted by the law (including the conflict of laws rules) so specified:

Rights of creditors against sold goods. Section 2-402.

Applicability of the Article on Bank Deposits and Collections. Section 4-102.

Bulk transfers subject to the Article on Bulk Transfers. Section 6-102.

Applicability of the Article on Investment Securities. Section 8-106.

Policy and scope of the Article on Secured Transactions. Sections 9-102 and 9-103.

Section 1-106. Remedies to be Liberally Administered.

(1) The remedies provided by this Act shall be liberally administered to the end that the aggrieved party may be put in as good a position as if the other party had fully performed but neither consequential or special nor penal damages may be had except as specifically provided in this Act or by other rule of law.

(2) Any right or obligation declared by this Act is enforceable by action unless the provision declaring it specifies a different and limited effect.

Section 1-107. Waiver or Renunciation of Claim or Right After Breach. Any claim or right arising out of an alleged breach can be discharged in whole or in part without consideration by a written waiver or renunciation signed and delivered by the aggrieved party.

Section 1-108. Severability. If any provision or clause of this Act or application thereof to any person or circumstances is held invalid, such invalidity shall not affect other provisions or applications of the Act which can be given effect without the invalid provisions or application, and to this end the provisions of this Act are declared to be severable.

PART 2

GENERAL DEFINITIONS AND PRINCIPLES OF INTERPRETATION

Section 1-201. General Definition. Subject to additional definitions contained in the subsequent Articles of this Act which are applicable to specific Articles or Parts thereof, and unless the context otherwise requires, in this Act:

(1) "Action" in the sense of a judicial proceeding includes recoupment, counterclaim, set-off, suit in equity and any other proceedings in which rights are determined.

(2) "Aggrieved party" means a party entitled to resort to a remedy.

(3) "Agreement" means the bargain of the parties in fact as found in their language or by implication from other circumstances including course of dealing or usage of trade or course of performance as provided in this Act (Sections 1-205 and 2-208). Whether an agreement has legal consequences is determined by the provisions of this Act, if applicable; otherwise by the law of contracts (Section 1-103). (Compare "Contract.")

(4) "Bank" means any person engaged in the business of banking.

(5) "Bearer" means the person in possession of an instrument, document of title, or security payable to bearer or indorsed in blank.

(6) "Bill of lading" means a document evidencing the receipt of goods for shipment issued by a person engaged in the business of transporting or forwarding goods, and includes an airbill. "Airbill" means a document serving for air transportation as a bill of lading does for marine or rail transportation, and includes an air consignment note or air waybill.

(7) "Branch" includes a separately incorporated foreign branch of a bank.

(8) "Burden of establishing" a fact means the burden of persuading the triers of fact that the existence of the fact is more probable than its non-existence.

(9) "Buyer in ordinary course of business" means a person who in good faith and without knowledge that the sale to him is in violation of the ownership rights or security interest of a third party in the goods buys in ordinary course from a person in the business of selling goods of that kind but does not include a pawnbroker. "Buying" may be for cash or by exchange of other property or on secured or unsecured credit and includes receiving goods or documents of title under a pre-existing contract for sale but does not include a transfer in bulk or as security for or in total or partial satisfaction of a money debt.

(10) "Conspicuous": a term or clause is conspicuous when it is so written that a reasonable person against whom it is to operate ought to have noticed it. A printed heading in capitals (as: NON-NEGOTIABLE BILL OF LADING) is conspicuous. Language in the body of a form is "conspicuous" if it is in larger or other contrasting type or color. But in a telegram any stated term is "conspicuous." Whether a term or clause is "conspicuous" or not is for decision by the court.

(11) "Contract" means the total legal obligation which results from the parties' agreement as affected by this Act and any other applicable rules of law. (Compare "Agreement.")

(12) "Creditor" includes a general creditor, a secured creditor, a lien creditor and any representative of creditors, including an assignee for the benefit of creditors, a trustee in bankruptcy, a receiver in equity and an executor or administrator of an insolvent debtor's or assignor's estate.

(13) "Defendant" includes a person in the position of defendant in a cross-action or counterclaim.

(14) "Delivery" with respect to instruments, documents of title, chattel paper or securities means voluntary transfer of possession.

(15) "Document of title" includes bill of lading, dock warrant, dock receipt, warehouse receipt or order for the delivery of goods, and also any other document which

in the regular course of business or financing is treated as adequately evidencing that the person in possession of it is entitled to receive, hold and dispose of the document and the goods it covers. To be a document of title a document must purport to be issued by or addressed to a bailee and purport to cover goods in the bailee's possession which are either identified or are fungible portions of an identified mass.

(16) "Fault" means wrongful act, omission or breach.

(17) "Fungible" with respect to goods or securities means goods or securities of which any unit is, by nature or usage of trade, the equivalent of any other like unit. Goods which are not fungible shall be deemed fungible for the purposes of this Act to the extent that under a particular agreement or document unlike units are treated as equivalents.

(18) "Genuine" means free of forgery or counterfeiting.

(19) "Good faith" means honesty in fact in the conduct or transaction concerned.

(20) "Holder" means a person who is in possession of a document of title or an instrument or an investment security drawn, issued or indorsed to him or to his order or to bearer or in blank.

(21) To "honor" is to pay or to accept and pay, or where a credit so engages to purchase or discount a draft complying with the terms of the credit.

(22) "Insolvency proceedings" includes any assignment for the benefit of creditors or other proceedings intended to liquidate or rehabilitate the estate of the person involved.

(23) A person is "insolvent" who either has ceased to pay his debts in the ordinary course of business or cannot pay his debts as they become due or is insolvent within the meaning of the federal bankruptcy law.

(24) "Money" means a medium of exchange authorized or adopted by a domestic or foreign government as a part of its currency.

(25) A person has "notice" of a fact when

(a) he has actual knowledge of it; or

(b) he has received a notice or notification of it; or

(c) from all the facts and circumstances known to him at the time in question he has reason to know that it exists.

A person "knows" or had "knowledge" of a fact when he has actual knowledge of it. "Discover" or "learn" or a word or phrase of similar import refers to knowledge rather than to reason to know. The time and circumstances under which a notice or notification may cease to be effective are not determined by this Act.

(26) A person "notifies" or "gives" a notice or notification to another by taking such steps as may be reasonably required to inform the other person in ordinary course whether or not such other actually comes to know of it. A person "receives" a notice or notification when

(a) it comes to his attention; or

(b) it is duly delivered at the place of business through which the contract was made or at any other place held out by him as the place for receipt of such communications.

(27) Notice, knowledge or a notice or notification received by an organization is effective for a particular transaction from the time when it is brought to the attention of the individual conducting that transaction, and in any event from the time when it would have been brought to his attention if the organization had exercised due diligence. An organization exercises due diligence if it maintains reasonable routines for communicating significant information to the person conducting the transaction and there is reasonable compliance with the routines. Due diligence does not require an individual acting for the organization to communicate information unless such communication is part of his regular duties or unless he has reason to know of the transaction and that the transaction would be materially affected by the information.

(28) "Organization" includes a corporation, government or governmental subdivision or agency, business trust, estate, trust, partnership or association, two or more persons having a joint or common interest, or any other legal or commercial entity.

(29) "Party," as distinct from "third party," means a person who has engaged in a transaction or made an agreement within this Act.

(30) "Person" includes an individual or an organization (See Section 1-102).

(31) "Presumption" or "presumed" means that the trier of fact must find the existence of the fact presumed unless and until evi-

dence is introduced which would support a finding of its non-existence.

(32) "Purchase" includes taking by sale, discount, negotiation, mortgage, pledge, lien, issue or re-issue, gift or any other voluntary transaction creating an interest in property.

(33) "Purchaser" means a person who takes by purchase.

(34) "Remedy" means any remedial right to which an aggrieved party is entitled with or without resort to a tribunal.

(35) "Representative" includes an agent, an officer of a corporation or association, and a trustee, executor or administrator of an estate, or any other person empowered to act for another.

(36) "Rights" includes remedies.

(37) "Security interest" means an interest in personal property or fixtures which secures payment or performance of an obligation. The retention or reservation of title by a seller of goods notwithstanding shipment or delivery to the buyer (Section 2-401) is limited in effect to a reservation of a "security interest." The term also includes any interest of a buyer of accounts, chattel paper, or contract rights which is subject to Article 9. The special property interest of a buyer of goods on identification or such goods to a contract for sale under Section 2-401 is not a "security interest," but a buyer may also acquire a "security interest" by complying with Article 9. Unless a lease or consignment is intended as security, reservation of title thereunder is not a "security interest" but a consignment is in any event subject to the provisions on consignment sales (Section 2-326). Whether a lease is intended as security is to be determined by the facts of each case; however (a) the inclusion of an option to purchase does not of itself make the lease one intended for security, and (b) an agreement that upon compliance with the terms of the lease the lessee shall become or has the option to become the owner of the property for no additional consideration or for a nominal consideration does make the lease one intended for security.

(38) "Send" in connection with any writing or notice means to deposit in the mail or deliver for transmission by any other usual means of communication with postage or cost of transmission provided for and properly addressed and in the case of an instrument to an address specified thereon or otherwise agreed, or if there be none to any address reasonable under the circumstances. The receipt of any writing or notice within the time at which it would have arrived if properly sent has the effect of a proper sending.

(39) "Signed" includes any symbol executed or adopted by a party with present intention to authenticate a writing.

(40) "Surety" includes guarantor.

(41) "Telegram" includes a message transmitted by radio, teletype, cable, any mechanical method of transmission, or the like.

(42) "Term" means that portion of an agreement which relates to a particular matter.

(43) "Unauthorized" signature or indorsement means one made without actual, implied or apparent authority and includes a forgery.

(44) "Value." Except as otherwise provided with respect to negotiable instruments and bank collections (Sections 3-303, 4-208 and 4-209) a person gives "value" for rights if he acquires them

    (a) in return for a binding commitment to extend credit or for the extension of immediately available credit whether or not drawn upon and whether or not a charge-back is provided for in the event of difficulties in collection; or

    (b) as security for or in total or partial satisfaction of a pre-existing claim; or

    (c) by accepting delivery pursuant to a pre-existing contract for purchase; or

    (d) generally, in return for any consideration sufficient to support a simple contract.

(45) "Warehouse receipt" means a receipt issued by a person engaged in the business of storing goods for hire.

(46) "Written" or "writing" includes printing, typewriting or any other intentional reduction to tangible form.

Section 1-202. Prima Facie Evidence by Third Party Documents. A document in due form purporting to be a bill of lading, policy or certificate of insurance, official weigher's or inspector's certificate, consular invoice, or any other document authorized or required by the contract to be issued by a third party shall be prima facie evidence of its own authenticity and genuineness and of the facts stated in the document by the third party.

Section 1-203. Obligation of Good Faith. Every contract or duty within this Act imposes an obligation of good faith in its performance or enforcement.

Section 1-204. Time; Reasonable Time; "Seasonably."

(1) Whenever this Act requires any action to be taken within a reasonable time, any time which is not manifestly unreasonable may be fixed by agreement.

(2) What is a reasonable time for taking any action depends on the nature, purpose and circumstances of such action.

(3) An action is taken "seasonably" when it is taken at or within the time agreed or if no time is agreed at or within a reasonable time.

Section 1-205. Course of Dealing and Usage of Trade.

(1) A course of dealing in a sequence of previous conduct between the parties to a particular transaction which is fairly to be regarded as establishing a common basis of understanding for interpreting their expressions and other conduct.

(2) A usage of trade is any practice or method of dealing having such regularity of observance in a place, vocation or trade as to justify an expectation that it will be observed with respect to the transaction in question. The existence and scope of such a usage are to be proved as facts. If it is established that such a usage is embodied in a written trade code or similar writing the interpretation of the writing is for the court.

(3) A course of dealing between parties and any usage of trade in the vocation or trade in which they are engaged or of which they are or should be aware give particular meaning to and supplement or qualify terms of an agreement.

(4) The express terms of an agreement and an applicable course of dealing or usage of trade shall be construed wherever reasonable as consistent with each other; but where such construction is unreasonable express terms control both course of dealing and usage of trade and course of dealing controls usage of trade.

(5) An applicable usage of trade in the place where any part of performance is to occur shall be used in interpreting the agreement as to that part of the performance.

(6) Evidence of a relevant usage of trade offered by one party is not admissible unless and until he has given the other party such notice as the court finds sufficient to prevent unfair surprise to the latter.

Section 1-206. Statute of Frauds for Kinds of Personal Property Not Otherwise Covered.

(1) Except in the cases described in subsection (2) of this section a contract for the sale of personal property is not enforceable by way of action or defense beyond five thousand dollars in amount or value of remedy unless there is some writing which indicates that a contract for sale has been made between the parties at a defined or stated price, reasonably identifies the subject matter, and is signed by the party against whom enforcement is sought or by his authorized agent.

(2) Subsection (1) of this section does not apply to contracts for the sale of goods (Section 2-201) nor of securities (Section 8-319) nor to security agreements (Section 9-203).

Section 1-207. Performance or Acceptance under Reservation of Rights. A party who with explicit reservation of rights performs or promises performance or assents to performance in a manner demanded or offered by the other party does not thereby prejudice the rights reserved. Such words as "without prejudice," "under protect" or the like are sufficient.

Section 1-208. Option to Accelerate at Will. A term providing that one party or his successor in interest may accelerate payment of performance or require collateral or additional collateral "at will" or "when he deems himself insecure" or in words of similar import shall be construed to mean that he shall have power to do so only if he in good faith believes that the prospect of payment or performance is impaired. The burden of establishing lack of good faith is on the party against whom the power has been exercised.

ARTICLE 2

SALES

PART 1

SHORT TITLE, GENERAL CONSTRUCTION AND SUBJECT MATTER

Section 2-101. Short Title. This Article shall be known and may be cited as Uniform Commercial Code–Sales.

Section 2-102. Scope; Certain Security and Other Transactions Excluded from this Article. Unless the context otherwise requires, this Article applies to transactions in goods; it does not apply to any transaction which although in the form of an unconditional contract to sell or present sale is intended to operate only as a security transaction nor does this Article impair or repeal any statute regulating sales to consumers, farmers or other specified classes of buyers.

Section 2-103. Definitions and Index of Definitions.

(1) In this Article unless the context otherwise requires

    (a) "Buyer" means a person who buys or contracts to buy goods.

    (b) "Good faith" in the case of a merchant means honesty in fact and the observance of reasonable commercial standards of fair dealing in the trade.

    (c) "Receipt" of goods means taking physical possession of them.

    (d) "Seller" means a person who sells or contracts to sell goods.

(2) Other definitions applying to this Article or to specified parts thereof, and the sections in which they appear are:

"Acceptance." Section 2-606.
"Banker's credit." Section 2-325.
"Between merchants." Section 2-104.
"Cancellation." Section 2-106(4)
"Commercial unit." Section 2-105.
"Confirmed credit." Section 2-325.
"Conforming to contract." Section 2-106.
"Contract for sale." Section 2-106.
"Cover." Section 2-712.

"Entrusting." Section 2-403.
"Financing agency." Section 2-104.
"Future goods." Section 2-105.
"Goods." Section 2-105.
"Identification." Section 2-501.
"Installment contract." Section 2-612.
"Letter of Credit." Section 2-325.
"Lot." Section 2-105.
"Merchant." Section 2-104.
"Overseas." Section 2-323.
"Person on position of seller." Section 2-707.
"Present sale." Section 2-106.
"Sale." Section 2-106.
"Sale on approval." Section 2-326.
"Sale or return." Section 2-326.
"Termination." Section 2-106.

(3) The following definitions in other Articles apply to this Article:

"Check." Section 3-204.
"Consignee." Section 7-102.
"Consignor." Section 7-102.
"Consumer goods." Section 9-109.
"Dishonor." Section 3-507.
"Draft." Section 3-104.

(4) In addition Article 1 contains general definitions and principles of construction and interpretation applicable throughout this Article.

Section 2-104. Definitions: "Merchant"; "Between Merchants"; Financing Agency."

(1) "Merchant" means a person who deals in goods of the kind or otherwise by his occupation holds himself out as having knowledge or skill peculiar to the practices or goods involved in the transaction or to whom such knowledge or skill may be attributed by his employment of an agent or broker or other intermediary who by his occupation holds himself out as having such knowledge or skill.

(2) "Financing agency" means a bank, finance company or other person who in the ordinary course of business makes advances against goods or documents of title or who by arrangement with either the seller or the buyer intervenes in ordinary course to make or collect payment due or claimed under the contract for sale, as by purchasing or paying the seller's draft or making advances against it or by merely taking it for collection whether or not documents of title accompany the draft. "Financing agency" includes also a bank or other person who similarly intervenes between persons who are in the position of seller and buyer in respect to the goods (Section 2-707).

(3) "Between merchants" means in any transaction with respect to which both parties are chargeable with the knowledge or skill of merchants.

Section 2-105. Definitions: Transferability; "Goods"; "Future" Goods; "Lot"; "Commercial Unit."

(1) "Goods" means all things (including specially manufactured goods) which are movable at the time of identification to the contract for sale other than the money in which the price is to be paid, investment securities (Article 8) and things in action. "Goods" also includes the unborn young of animals and growing crops and other identified things attached to realty as described in the section on goods to be severed from realty (Section 2-107).

(2) Goods must be both existing and identified before any interest in them can pass. Goods which are not both existing and identified are "future" goods. A purported present sale of future goods or of any interest therein operates as a contract to sell.

(3) There may be a sale or a part interest in existing identified goods.

(4) An undivided share in an identified bulk of fungible goods is sufficiently identified to be sold although the quantity of the bulk is not determined. Any agreed proportion of such a bulk or any quantity thereof agreed upon by number, weight or other measure may to the extent of the seller's interest in the bulk be sold to the buyer who then becomes an owner in common.

(5) "Lot" means a parcel or a single article which is the subject matter of a separate sale or delivery, whether or not it is sufficient to perform the contract.

(6) "Commercial unit" means such a unit of goods as by commercial usage is a single whole for purposes of sale and division of which materially impairs its character or value on the market or in use. A commercial unit may be a single article (as a machine) or a set of articles (as a suite of furniture or an assortment of sizes) or a quantity (as a bale, gross, or carload) or any other unit treated in use or in the relevant market as a single whole.

Section 2-106. Definitions: "Contract"; "Agreement"; "Contract for Sale"; "Sale"; "Present Sale"; "Conforming" to Contract; "Termination"; "Cancellation."

(1) In this Article unless the context otherwise requires "contract" and "agreement" are limited to those relating to the present or future sale of goods. "Contract for sale" includes both a present sale of goods and a contract to sell goods at a future time. A "sale" consists in the passing of title from the seller to the buyer for a price (Section 2–401). A "present sale" means a sale which is accomplished by the making of the contract.

(2) Goods or conduct including any part of a performance are "conforming" or conform to the contract when they are in accordance with the obligations under the contract.

(3) "Termination" occurs when either party pursuant to a power created by agreement or law puts an end to the contract otherwise than for its breach. On "termination" all obligations which are still executory on both sides are discharged but any right based on prior breach or performance survives.

(4) "Cancellation" occurs when either party puts an end to the contract for breach by the other and its effect is the same as that of "termination" except that the cancelling party also retains any remedy for breach of the whole contract or any unperformed balance.

Section 2-107. Goods to Be Severed From Realty: Recording

(1) A contract for the sale of minerals or the like (including oil and gas) or a structure or its materials to be removed from realty is a contract for the sale of goods within this Article if they are to be severed by the seller but until severance a purported present sale thereof which is not effective as a transfer of

an interest in land is effective only as a contract to sell.

(2) A contract for the sale apart from the land of growing crops or other things attached to realty and capable of severance without material harm thereto but not described in subsection (1) or of timber to be cut is a contract for the sale of goods within this Article whether the subject matter is to be severed by the buyer or by the seller even though it forms part of the realty at the time of contracting, and the parties can by identification effect a present sale before severance.

(3) The provisions of this section are subject to any third party rights provided by the law relating to realty records, and the contract for sale may be executed and recorded as a document transferring an interest in land and shall then constitute notice to third parties of the buyer's rights under the contract for sale.

PART 2

FORM, FORMATION AND READJUSTMENT OF CONTRACT

Section 2-201. Formal Requirements; Statute of Frauds.

(1) Except as otherwise provided in this section a contract for the sale of goods for the price of $500 or more is not enforceable by way of action or defense unless there is some writing sufficient to indicate that a contract for sale has been made between the parties and signed by the party against whom enforcement is sought or by his authorized agent or broker. A writing is not insufficient because it omits or incorrectly states a term agreed upon but the contract is not enforceable under this paragraph beyond the quantity of goods shown in such writing.

(2) Between merchants if within a reasonable time a written confirmation of the contract and sufficient against the sender is received and the party receiving it has reason to know its contents, it satisfies the requirements of subsection (1) against such party unless written notice of objection to its contents is given within ten days after it is received.

(3) A contract which does not satisfy the requirements of subsection (1) but which is valid in other respects is enforceable

(a) if the goods are to be specially manufactured for the buyer and are not suitable for sale to others in the ordinary course of the seller's business and the seller, before notice of repudiation is received and under circumstances which reasonably indicate that the goods are for the buyer, has made either a substantial beginning of their manufacture or commitments for their procurement; or

(b) if the party against whom enforcement is sought admits in his pleading, testimony or otherwise in court that a contract for sale was made, but the contract is not enforceable under this provision beyond the quantity of goods admitted; or

(c) with respect to goods for which payment has been made and accepted or which have been received and accepted (Sec. 2-606).

Section 2-202. Final Written Expression: Parol or Extrinsic Evidence.

Terms with respect to which the confirmatory memoranda of the parties agree or which are otherwise set forth in a writing intended by the parties as a final expression of their agreement with respect to such terms as are included therein may not be contradicted by evidence of any prior agreement or of a contemporaneous oral agreement but may be explained or supplemented.

(a) by course of dealing or usage of trade (Section 1-205) or by course of performance (Section 2-208); and

(b) by evidence of consistent additional terms unless the court finds the writing to have been intended also as a complete and exclusive statement of the terms of the agreement.

Section 2-203. Seals Inoperative.

The affixing of a seal to a writing evidencing a contract for sale or an offer to buy or sell goods does not constitute the writing a sealed instrument and the law with respect to sealed instruments does not apply to such a contract or offer.

Section 2-204. Formation in General.

(1) A contract for sale of goods may be made in any manner sufficient to show agreement, including conduct by both

parties which recognizes the existence of such a contract.

(2) An agreement sufficient to constitute a contract for sale may be found even though the moment of its making is undetermined.

(3) Even though one or more terms are left open a contract for sale does not fail for indefiniteness if the parties have intended to make a contract and there is a reasonably certain basis for giving an appropriate remedy.

Section 2-205. Firm Offers. An offer by a merchant to buy or sell goods in a signed writing which by its terms gives assurance that it will be held open is not revocable, for lack of consideration, during the time stated or if no time is stated for a reasonable time, but in no event may such period of irrevocability exceed three months; but any such term of assurance on a form supplied by the offeree must be separately signed by the offeror.

Section 2-206. Offer and Acceptance in Formation of Contract.

(1) Unless otherwise unambiguously indicated by the language or circumstances

(a) an offer to make a contract shall be construed as inviting acceptance in any manner and by any medium reasonable in the circumstances;

(b) an order or other offer to buy goods for prompt or current shipment shall be construed as inviting acceptance either by a prompt promise to ship or by the prompt or current shipment of conforming or non-conforming goods, but such a shipment of non-conforming goods does not constitute an acceptance if the seller reasonably notifies the buyer that the shipment is offered only as an accommodation to the buyer.

(2) Where the beginning of a requested performance is a reasonable mode of acceptance an offeror who is not notified of acceptance within a reasonable time may treat the offer as having lapsed before acceptance.

Section 2-207. Additional Terms in Acceptance or Confirmation.

(1) A definite and seasonable expression of acceptance or a written confirmation which is sent within a reasonable time operates as an acceptance even though it states terms additional to or different from those offered or agreed upon, unless acceptance is ex-

pressly made conditional on assent to the additional or different terms.

(2) The additional terms are to be construed as proposals for addition to the contract. Between merchants such terms become part of the contract unless:

(a) the offer expressly limits acceptance to the terms of the offer;

(b) they materially alter it; or

(c) notification of objection to them has already been given or is given within a reasonable time after notice of them is received.

(3) Conduct by both parties which recognizes the existence of a contract is sufficient to establish a contract for sale although the writings of the parties do not otherwise establish a contract. In such case the terms of the particular contract consist of those terms on which the writings of the parties agree, together with any supplementary terms incorporated under any other provisions of this Act.

Section 2-208. Course of Performance or Practical Construction.

(1) Where the contract for sale involves repeated occasions for performance by either party with knowledge of the nature of the performance and opportunity for objection to it by the other, any course of performance accepted or acquiesced in without objection shall be relevant to determine the meaning of the agreement.

(2) The express terms of the agreement and any such course of performance, as well as any course of dealing and usage of trade, shall be construed whenever reasonable as consistent with each other; but when such construction is unreasonable, express terms shall control course of performance and course of performance shall control both course of dealing and usage of trade (Section 1-205).

(3) Subject to the provisions of the next section on modification and waiver, such course of performance shall be relevant to show a waiver or modification of any term inconsistent with such course of performance.

Section 2-209. Modification, Rescission and Waiver.

(1) An agreement modifying a contract within this Article needs no consideration to be binding.

(2) A signed agreement which excludes modification or rescission except by a signed writing cannot be otherwise modified or rescinded, but except as between merchants such a requirement on a form supplied by the merchant must be separately signed by the other party.

(3) The requirements of the statute of frauds section of this Article (Section 2-201) must be satisfied if the contract as modified is within its provisions.

(4) Although an attempt at modification or rescission does not satisfy the requirements of subsection (2) or (3) it can operate as a waiver.

(5) A party who has made a waiver affecting an executory portion of the contract may retract the waiver by reasonable notification received by the other party that strict performance will be required of any term waived, unless the retraction would be unjust in view of a material change of position in reliance on the waiver.

Section 2-210. Delegation of Performance; Assignment of Rights.

(1) A party may perform his duty through a delegate unless otherwise agreed or unless the other party has a substantial interest in having his original promisor perform or control the acts required by the contract. No delegation of performance relieves the party delegating of any duty to perform or any liability for breach.

(2) Unless otherwise agreed all rights of either seller or buyer can be assigned except where the assignment would materially change the duty of the other party, or increase materially the burden or risk imposed on him by his contract, or impair materially his chance of obtaining return performance. A right to damages for breach of the whole contract or a right arising out of the assignor's due performance of his entire obligation can be assigned despite agreement otherwise.

(3) Unless the circumstances indicate the contrary a prohibition of assignment of "the contract" is to be construed as barring only the delegation to the assignee of the assignor's performance.

(4) An assignment of "the contract" or of "all my rights under the contract" or an assignment in similar general terms is an assignment of rights and unless the language or the circumstances (as in an assignment for security) indicate the contrary, it is a delegation of performance of the duties of the assignor and its acceptance by the assignee constitutes a promise by him to perform those duties. This promise is enforceable by either the assignor or the other party to the original contract.

(5) The other party may treat any assignment which delegates performance as creating reasonable grounds for insecurity and may without prejudice to his rights against the assignor demand assurances from the assignee (Section 2-609).

PART 3

GENERAL OBLIGATION AND CONSTRUCTION OF CONTRACT

Section 2-301. General Obligations of Parties. The obligation of the seller is to transfer and deliver and that of the buyer is to accept and pay in accordance with the contract.

Section 2-302. Unconscionable Contract or Clause.

(1) If the court as a matter of law finds the contract or any clause of the contract to have been unconscionable at the time it was made the court may refuse to enforce the contract, or it may enforce the remainder of the contract without the unconscionable clause, or it may so limit the application of any unconscionable clause as to avoid any unconscionable result.

(2) When it is claimed or appears to the court that the contract or any clause thereof may be unconscionable the parties shall be afforded a reasonable opportunity to present evidence as to its commercial setting, purpose and effect to aid the court in making the determination.

Section 2-303. Allocation or Division of Risks. Where this Article allocates a risk or a burden as between the parties "unless otherwise agreed," the agreement may not only shift the allocation but may also divide the risk or burden.

Section 2-304. Price Payable in Money, Goods, Realty, or Otherwise.

(1) The price can be made payable in

money or otherwise. If it is payable in whole or in part in goods each party is a seller of the goods which he is to transfer.

(2) Even though all or part of the price is payable in an interest in realty the transfer of the goods and the seller's obligations with reference to them are subject to this Article, but not the transfer of the interest in realty or the transferor's obligations in connection therewith.

Section 2-305. Open Price Term.

(1) The parties if they so intend can conclude a contract for sale even though the price is not settled. In such a case the price is a reasonable price at the time for delivery if

(a) nothing is said as to price; or

(b) the price is left to be agreed by the parties and they fail to agree; or

(c) the price is to be fixed in terms of some agreed market or other standard as set or recorded by a third person or agency and it is not so set or recorded.

(2) A price to be fixed by the seller or by the buyer means a price for him to fix in good faith.

(3) When a price left to be fixed otherwise than by agreement of the parties fails to be fixed through fault of one party the other may at his option treat the contract as cancelled or himself fix a reasonable price.

(4) Where, however, the parties intend not to be bound unless the price be fixed or agreed and it is not fixed or agreed there is no contract. In such a case the buyer must return any goods already received or if unable to do so must pay their reasonable value at the time of delivery and the seller must return any portion of the price paid on account.

Section 2-306. Output, Requirements and Exclusive Dealings.

(1) A term which measures the quantity by the output of the seller or the requirements of the buyer means such actual output or requirements as may occur in good faith, except that no quantity unreasonably disproportionate to any stated estimate or in the absence of a stated estimate to any normal or otherwise comparable prior output or requirements may be tendered or demanded.

(2) A lawful agreement by either the seller or the buyer for exclusive dealing in the kind of goods concerned imposes unless otherwise agreed an obligation by the seller to use best efforts to supply the goods and by the buyer to use best efforts to promote their sale.

Section 2-307. Delivery in Single Lot or Several Lots.
Unless otherwise agreed all goods called for by a contract for sale must be tendered in a single delivery and payment is due only on such tender but where the circumstances give either party the right to make or demand delivery in lots the price if it can be apportioned may be demanded for each lot.

Section 2-308. Absence of Specified Place for Delivery.
Unless otherwise agreed.

(a) the place for delivery of goods is the seller's place of business or if he has none his residence; but

(b) in a contract for sale of identified goods which to the knowledge of the parties at the time of contracting are in some other place, that place is the place for their delivery; and

(c) documents of title may be delivered through customary banking channels.

Section 2-309. Absence of Specific Time Provisions; Notice of Termination.

(1) The time for shipment or delivery or any other action under a contract if not provided in this Article or agreed upon shall be a reasonable time.

(2) Where the contract provides for successive performances but is indefinite in duration it is valid for a reasonable time but unless otherwise agreed may be terminated at any time by either party.

(3) Termination of a contract by one party except on the happening of an agreed event requires that reasonable notification is invalid if its operation would be unconscionable.

Section 2-310. Open Time for Payment or Running of Credit; Authority to Ship under Reservation.
Unless otherwise agreed

(a) payment is due at the time and place at which the buyer is to receive the goods even though the place of shipment is the place of delivery; and

(b) if the seller is authorized to send the goods he may ship them under reservation, and may tender the documents of title, but the buyer may inspect the goods after their arrival before payment is due unless such inspection is inconsistent with the terms of the contract (Section 2-513); and

(c) if delivery is authorized and made by way of documents of title otherwise than by subsection (b) then payment is due at the time and place at which the buyer is to receive the documents regardless of where the goods are to be received; and

(d) where the seller is required or authorized to ship the goods on credit the credit period runs from the time of shipment but post-dating the invoice or delaying its dispatch will correspondingly delay the starting of the credit period.

Section 2-311. Options and Cooperation Respecting Performance.

(1) An agreement for sale which is otherwise sufficiently definite (subsection (3) of Section 2-204) to be a contract is not made invalid by the fact that it leaves particulars of performance to be specified by one of the parties. Any such specification must be made in good faith and within limits set by commercial reasonableness.

(2) Unless otherwise agreed specifications relating to assortment of the goods are at the buyer's option and except as otherwise provided in subsections (1) (c) and (3) of Section 2-319 specifications or arrangements relating to shipment are at the seller's option.

(3) Where such specification would materially affect the other party's performance but is not seasonably made or where one party's cooperation is necessary to the agreed performance of the other but is not seasonably forthcoming, the other party in addition to all other remedies

(a) is excused for any resulting delay in his own performance; and

(b) may also either proceed to perform in any reasonable manner or after the time for a material part of his own performance treat the failure to specify or to cooperate as a breach by failure to deliver or accept the goods.

Section 2-312. Warranty of Title and Against Infringement; Buyer's Obligation Against Infringement.

(1) Subject to subsection (2) there is in a contract for a sale a warranty by the seller that

(a) the title conveyed shall be good, and its transfer rightful; and

(b) the goods shall be delivered free from any security interest or other lien or encumbrance of which the buyer at the time of contracting has no knowledge.

(2) A warranty under subsection (1) will be excluded or modified only by specific language or by circumstances which give the buyer reason to know that the person selling does not claim title in himself or that he is purporting to sell only such right or title as he or a third person may have.

(3) Unless otherwise agreed a seller who is a merchant regularly dealing in goods of the kind warrants that the goods shall be delivered free of the rightful claim of any third person by way of infringement or the like but a buyer who furnishes specifications to the seller must hold the seller harmless against any such claim which arises out of compliance with the specifications.

Section 2-313. Express Warranties by Affirmation, Promise, Description, Sample.

(1) Express warranties by the seller are created as follows:

(a) Any affirmation of fact or promise made by the seller to the buyer which relates to the goods and becomes part of the basis of the bargain creates an express warranty that the goods shall conform to the affirmation or promise.

(b) Any description of the goods which is made part of the basis of the bargain creates an express warranty that the goods shall conform to the description.

(c) Any sample or model which is made part of the basis of the bargain creates an express warranty that the whole of the goods shall conform to the sample or model.

(2) It is not necessary to the creation of an express warranty that the seller use formal words such as "warrant" or "guarantee" or that he have a specific intention to make a warranty, but an affirmation merely of the value of the goods or a statement purporting to be merely the seller's opinion or commendation of the goods does not create a warranty.

Section 2-314. Implied Warranty: Merchantability; Usage of Trade.

(1) Unless excluded or modified (Section

2-316) a warranty that the goods shall be merchantable is implied in a contract for their sale if the seller is a merchant with respect to goods of that kind. Under this section the serving for value of food or drink to be consumed either on the premises or elsewhere is a sale.

(2) Goods to be merchantable must be at least such as

(a) pass without objection in the trade under the contract description; and

(b) in the case of fungible goods, are of fair average quality within the description; and

(c) are fit for the ordinary purposes for which such goods are used; and

(d) run, within the variations permitted by the agreement, of even kind, quality and quantity within each unit and among all units involved; and

(e) are adequately contained, packaged, and labeled as the agreement may require; and

(f) conform to the promises or affirmations of fact made on the container or label if any.

(3) Unless excluded or modified (Section 2-316) other implied warranties may arise from course of dealing or usage of trade.

Section 2-315. Implied Warranty: Fitness for Particular Purpose. Where the seller at the time of contracting has reason to know any particular purpose for which the goods are required and that the buyer is relying on the seller's skill or judgment to select or furnish suitable goods, there is unless excluded or modified under the next section an implied warranty that the goods shall be fit for such purpose.

Section 2-316. Exclusion or Modification of Warranties.

(1) Words or conduct relevant to the creation of an express warranty and words or conduct tending to negate or limit warranty shall be construed wherever reasonable as consistent with each other; but subject to the provisions of this Article on parol or extrinsic evidence (Section 2-202) negation or limitation is inoperative to the extent that such construction is unreasonable.

(2) Subject to subsection (3), to exclude or modify the implied warranty of merchantability or any part of it the language must mention merchantability and in case of a writing must be conspicuous, and to exclude

or modify any implied warranty of fitness the exclusion must be by a writing and conspicuous. Language to exclude all implied warranties of fitness is sufficient if it states, for example, that "There are no warranties which extend beyond the description on the face hereof."

(3) Notwithstanding subsection (2)

(a) unless the circumstances indicate otherwise, all implied warranties are excluded by expressions like "as is," "with all faults" or other language which in common understanding calls the buyer's attention to the exclusion of warranties and makes plain that there is no implied warranty; and

(b) when the buyer before entering into the contract has examined the goods or the sample or model as fully as he desired or has refused to examine the goods there is no implied warranty with regard to defects which an examination ought in the circumstances to have revealed to him; and

(c) an implied warranty can also be excluded or modified by course of dealing or course of performance or usage of trade.

(4) Remedies for breach of warranty can be limited in accordance with the provisions of this Article on liquidation or limitation of damages and on contractual modification of remedy (Sections 2-718 and 2-719).

Section 2-317. Cumulation and Conflict of Warranties Express or Implied. Warranties whether express or implied shall be construed as consistent with each other and as cumulative, but if such construction is unreasonable the intention of the parties shall determine which warranty is dominant. In ascertaining that intention the following rules apply:

(a) Exact or technical specifications displace an inconsistent sample or model or general language of description.

(b) A sample from an existing bulk displaces inconsistent general language of description.

(c) Express warranties displace inconsistent implied warranties other than an implied warranty of fitness for a particular purpose.

Section 2-318. Third Party Beneficiaries of Warranties Express or Implied. Note: *If this Act is introduced in the Congress of the United States* *this section should be omitted. (States to select one alternative.)*

Alternative A

A seller's warranty whether express or implied extends to any natural person who is in the family or household of his buyer or who is a guest in his home if it is reasonable to expect that such person may use, consume or be affected by the goods and who is injured in person by breach of the warranty. A seller may not exclude or limit the operation of this section.

Alternative B

A seller's warranty whether express or implied extends to any natural person who may reasonably be expected to use, consume or be affected by the goods and who is injured in person by breach of the warranty. A seller may not exclude or limit the operation of this section.

Alternative C

A seller's warranty whether express or implied extends to any person who may reasonably be expected to use, consume or be affected by the goods and who is injured by breach of the warranty. A seller may not exclude or limit the operation of this section with respect to injury to the person of an individual to whom the warranty extends.

Section 2-319. F.O.B. and F.A.S. Terms.

(1) Unless otherwise agreed the term F.O.B. (which means "free on board") at a named place, even though used only in connection with the stated price, is a delivery term under which

(a) when the term is F.O.B. the place of shipment, the seller must at that place ship the goods in the manner provided in this article (Section 2-504) and bear the expense and risk of putting them into the possession of the carrier; or

(b) when the term is F.O.B. the place of destination, the seller must at his own expense and risk transport the goods to that place and there tender delivery of them in the manner provided in this Article (Section 2-503);

(c) when under either (a) or (b) the term is also F.O.B. vessel, car or other vehicle, the seller must in addition at his own expense and risk load the goods on board. If the term is F.O.B. vessel the buyer must name the vessel and in an appropriate case the seller must comply with the provisions of this Article on the form of bill of lading (Section 2-323).

(2) Unless otherwise agreed the term F.A.S. vessel (which means "free along-side") at a named port, even though used only in connection with the stated price, is a delivery term under which the seller must

(a) at his own expense and risk deliver the goods alongside the vessel in the manner usual in that port or on a dock designated and provided by the buyer; and

(b) obtain and tender a receipt for the goods in exchange for which the carrier is under a duty to issue a bill of lading.

(3) Unless otherwise agreed in any case falling within subsection (1)(a) or (c) or subsection (2) the buyer must seasonably give any needed instructions for making delivery, including when the term is F.A.S. or F.O.B. the loading berth of the vessel and in an appropriate case its name and sailing date. The seller may treat the failure of needed instructions as a failure of cooperation under this Article (Section 2-311). He may also at his option move the goods in any reasonable manner preparatory to delivery or shipment.

(4) Under the term F.O.B. vessel or F.A.S. unless otherwise agreed the buyer must make payment against tender of the required documents and the seller may not tender nor the buyer demand delivery of the goods in substitution for the documents.

Section 2-320. C.I.F. and C. & F. Terms.

(1) The term C.I.F. means that the price includes in a lump sum the cost of the goods and the insurance and freight to the named destination. The term C. & F. or C.F. means that the price so includes cost and freight to the named destination.

(2) Unless otherwise agreed and even though used only in connection with the stated price and destination, the term C.I.F. destination or its equivalent requires the seller at his own expense and risk to

(a) put the goods into the possession of a carrier at the port for shipment and obtain a negotiable bill or bills of lading covering the entire transportation to the named destination; and

(b) load the goods and obtain a receipt from the carrier (which may be contained in the bill of lading) showing that the freight has been paid or provided for; and

(c) obtain a policy or certificate of insurance, including any war risk insurance, of a kind and on terms then current at the port of shipment in the usual amount, in the currency of the contract, shown to cover the same goods covered by the bill of lading and providing for payment of loss to the order of the buyer or for the account of whom it may concern; but the seller may add to the price the amount of the premium for any such war risk insurance; and

(d) prepare an invoice of the goods and procure any other documents required to effect shipment or to comply with the contract; and

(e) forward and tender with commercial promptness all the documents in due form and with any indorsement necessary to perfect the buyer's rights.

(3) Unless otherwise agreed the term C. & F. or its equivalent has the same effect and imposes upon the seller the same obligations and risks as a C.I.F. term except the obligation as to insurance.

(4) Under the term C.I.F. or C. & F. unless otherwise agreed the buyer must make payment against tender of the required documents and the seller may not tender nor the buyer demand delivery of the goods in substitution for the documents.

Section 2-321. C.I.F. or C. & F.: "Net Landed Weights"; "Payment on Arrival"; Warranty of Condition on Arrival. Under a contract containing a term C.I.F. or C. & F.

(1) Where the price is based on or is to be adjusted according to "net landed weights," "delivered weights," "out turn" quantity or quality or the like, unless otherwise agreed the seller must reasonably estimate the price. The payment due on tender of the documents called for by the contract is the amount so estimated, but after final adjustment of the price a settlement must be made with commercial promptness.

(2) An agreement described in subsection (1) or any warranty of quality or condition of the goods on arrival places upon the seller the risk of ordinary deterioration, shrinkage and the like in transportation but has no effect on the place or time of identification to the contract for sale or delivery or on the passing of the risk of loss.

(3) Unless otherwise agreed where the contract provides for payment on or after arrival of the goods the seller must before payment allow such preliminary inspection as is feasible; but if the goods are lost delivery of the documents and payment are due when the goods should have arrived.

Section 2-322. Delivery "Ex-Ship."

(1) Unless otherwise agreed a term for delivery of goods "ex-ship" (which means from the carrying vessel) or in equivalent language is not restricted to a particular ship and requires delivery from a ship which has reached a place at the named port of destination where goods of the kind are usually discharged.

(2) Under such a term unless otherwise agreed

(a) the seller must discharge all liens arising out of the carriage and furnish the buyer with a direction which puts the carrier under a duty to deliver the goods; and

(b) the risk of loss does not pass to the buyer until the goods leave the ship's tackle or are otherwise properly unloaded.

Section 2-323. Form of Bill of Lading Required in Overseas Shipment; "Overseas."

(1) Where the contract contemplates overseas shipment and contains a term C.I.F. or C. & F. or F. O. B. vessel, the seller unless otherwise agreed must obtain a negotiable bill of lading stating that the goods have been loaded on board or, in the case of a term C.I.F. or C. & F., received for shipment.

(2) Where in a case within subsection (1) a bill of lading has been issued in a set of parts, unless otherwise agreed if the documents are not to be sent from abroad the buyer may demand tender of the full set; otherwise only one part of the bill of lading need be tendered. Even if the agreement expressly requires a full set

(a) due tender of a single part is acceptable within the provisions of this Article on cure of improper delivery (subsection (1) of Section 2-508); and

(b) even though the full set is demanded, if the documents are sent from abroad the person tendering an incomplete set may nevertheless require payment upon furnishing an indemnity which the buyer in good faith deems adequate.

(3) A shipment by water or by air or a contract contemplating such shipment is "overseas" insofar as by usage of trade or agreement it is subject to the commercial, financing or shipping practices characteristic of international deep water commerce.

Section 2-324. "No Arrival, No Sale" Term. Under a term "no arrival, no sale" or terms of like meaning, unless otherwise agreed.

(a) the seller must properly ship conforming goods and if they arrive by any means he must tender them on arrival but he assumes no obligation that the goods will arrive unless he has caused the non-arrival; and

(b) where without fault of the seller the goods are in part lost or have so deteriorated as no longer to conform to the contract or arrive after the contract time, the buyer may proceed as if there had been casualty to identified goods (Section 2-613).

Section 2-325. "Letter of Credit" Term; "Confirmed Credit."

(1) Failure of the buyer seasonably to furnish an agreed letter of credit is a breach of the contract for sale.

(2) The delivery to seller of a proper letter of credit suspends the buyer's obligation to pay. If the letter of credit is dishonored, the seller may on seasonable notification to the buyer require payment directly from him.

(3) Unless otherwise agreed the term "letter of credit" or "banker's credit" in a contract for sale means an irrevocable credit issued by a financing agency of good repute and, where the shipment is overseas, of good international repute. The term "confirmed credit" means that the credit must also carry the direct obligation of such an agency which does business in the seller's financial market.

Section 2-326. Sale on Approval and Sale or Return; Consignment Sales and Rights of Creditors.

(1) Unless otherwise agreed, if delivered goods may be returned to the buyer even though they conform to the contract, the transaction is.

(a) a "sale on approval" if the goods are delivered primarily for use; and

(b) a "sale or return" if the goods are delivered primarily for resale.

(2) Except as provided in subsection (3), goods held on approval are not subject to the claims of the buyer's creditors until acceptance; goods held on sale or return are subject to such claims while in the buyer's possession.

(3) Where goods are delivered to a person for sale and such person maintains a place of business at which he deals in goods of the kind involved, under a name other than the name of the person making delivery, then with respect to claims of creditors of the person conducting the business the goods are deemed to be on sale or return. The provisions of this subsection are applicable even though an agreement purports to reserve title to the person making delivery until payment or resale or uses such words as "on consignment" or "on memorandum." However, this subsection is not applicable if the person making delivery

(a) complies with an applicable law providing for a consignor's interest or the like to be evidenced by a sign, or

(b) establishes that the person conducting the business is generally known by his creditors to be substantially engaged in selling the goods of others, or

(c) complies with the filing provisions of the Article on Secured Transactions (Article 9).

(4) Any "or return" term of a contract for sale is to be treated as a separate contract for sale within the statute of frauds section of this Article (Section 2-201) and as contradicting the sale aspect of the contract within the provisions of this Article on parol or extrinsic evidence (Section 2-202).

Section 2-327. Special Incidents of Sale on Approval and Sale or Return.

(1) Under a sale on approval unless otherwise agreed

(a) although the goods are identified to the contract the risk of loss and the title do not pass to the buyer until acceptance; and

(b) use of the goods consistent with the purpose of trial is not acceptance but failure seasonably to notify the seller of election to return the goods is acceptance, and if the goods conform to the contract acceptance of any part is acceptance of the whole; and

(c) after due notification of election to return, the return is at the seller's risk and expense but a merchant buyer must follow any reasonable instructions.

(2) Under a sale or return unless otherwise agreed

(a) the option to return extends to the whole or any commercial unit of the goods while in substantially their original condition, but must be exercised seasonably; and

(b) the return is at the buyer's risk and expense.

Section 2-328. Sale by Auction.

(1) In a sale by auction if goods are put up in lots each lot is the subject of a separate sale.

(2) A sale by auction is complete when the auctioneer so announces by the fall of the hammer or in other customary manner. Where a bid is made while the hammer is falling in acceptance of a prior bid the auctioneer may in his discretion reopen the bidding or declare the goods sold under the bid on which the hammer was falling.

(3) Such a sale is with reserve unless the goods are in explicit terms put up without reserve. In an auction with reserve the auctioneer may withdraw the goods at any time until he announces completion of the sale. In an auction without reserve, after the auctioneer calls for bids on an article or lot, that article or lot cannot be withdrawn unless no bid is made within a reasonable time. In either case a bidder may retract his bid until the auctioneer's announcement of completion of the sale, but a bidder's retraction does not revive any previous bid.

(4) If the auctioneer knowingly receives a bid on the seller's behalf or the seller makes or procures such a bid, and notice has not been given that liberty for such bidding is reserved, the buyer may at his option avoid the sale or take the goods at the price of the last good faith bid prior to the completion of the sale. This subsection shall not apply to any bid at a forced sale.

PART 4

TITLE, CREDITORS AND GOOD FAITH PURCHASERS

Section 2-401. Passing of Title; Reservation for Security; Limited Application of this Section.

Each provision of this Article with regard to the rights, obligations and remedies of the seller, the buyer, purchasers or other third parties applies irrespective of title to the goods except where the provision refers to such title. Insofar as situations are not covered by the other provisions of this Article and matters concerning title become material the following rules apply:

(1) Title to goods cannot pass under a contract for sale prior to their identification to the contract (Section 2-501), and unless otherwise explicitly agreed the buyer acquires by their identification a special property as limited by this Act. Any retention or reservation by the seller of the title (property) in goods shipped or delivered to the buyer is limited in effect to a reservation of a security interest. Subject to these provisions and to the provisions of the Article on Secured Transactions (Article 9), title to goods passes from the seller to the buyer in any manner and on any conditions explicitly agreed on by the parties.

(2) Unless otherwise explicitly agreed title passes to the buyer at the time and place at which the seller completes his performance with reference to the physical delivery of the goods, despite any reservation of a security interest and even though a document of title is to be delivered at a different time or place; and in particular and despite any reservation of a security interest by the bill of lading

(a) if the contract requires or authorizes the seller to send the goods to the buyer but does not require him to deliver them at destination, title passes to the buyer at the time and place of shipment; but

(b) if the contract requires delivery at destination, title passes on tender there.

(3) Unless otherwise explicitly agreed where delivery is to be made without moving the goods,

(a) if the seller is to deliver a document of title, title passes at the time when and the place where he delivers such documents; or

(b) if the goods are at the time of contracting already identified and no documents are to be delivered, title passes at the time and place of contracting.

(4) A rejection or other refusal by the buyer to receive or retain the goods, whether or not justified, or a justified revocation of acceptance revests title to the goods in the seller. Such revesting occurs by operation of law and is not a "sale."

Section 2-402. Rights of Seller's Creditors Against Sold Goods.

(1) Except as provided in subsections (2) and (3), rights of unsecured creditors of the seller with respect to goods which have been identified to a contract for sale are subject to the buyer's rights to recover the goods under this Article (Sections 2-502 and 2-716).

(2) A creditor of the seller may treat a sale or an identification of goods to a contract

for sale as void if as against him a retention of possession by the seller is fraudulent under any rule of law of the state where the goods are situated, except that retention of possession in good faith and current course of trade by a merchant-seller for a commercially reasonable time after a sale or identification is not fraudulent.

(3) Nothing in this Article shall be deemed to impair the rights of creditors of the seller

(a) under the provisions of the Article on Secured Transactions (Article 9); or

(b) where identification to the contract or delivery is made not in current course of trade but in satisfaction of or as security for a pre-existing claim for money, security or the like and is made under circumstances which under any rule of law of the state where the goods are situated would apart from this Article constitute the transaction a fraudulent transfer or voidable preference.

Section 2-403. Power to Transfer; Good Faith Purchase of Goods; "Entrusting."

(1) A purchaser of goods acquires all title which his transferor had or had power to transfer except that a purchaser of a limited interest acquires rights only to the extent of the interest purchased. A person with voidable title had power to transfer a good title to a good faith purchaser for value. When goods have been delivered under a transaction of purchase the purchaser has such power even though

(a) the transferor was deceived as to the identity of the purchaser, or

(b) the delivery was in exchange for a check which is later dishonored, or

(c) it was agreed that the transaction was to be a "cash sale," or

(d) the delivery was procured through fraud punishable as larcenous under the criminal law.

(2) Any entrusting of possession of goods to a merchant who deals in goods of that kind gives him power to transfer all rights of the entruster to a buyer in ordinary course of business.

(3) "Entrusting" includes any delivery and any acquiescence in retention of possession regardless of any condition expressed between the parties to the delivery or acquiescence and regardless of whether the procurement of the entrusting or the possessor's disposition of the goods have been such as to be larcenous under the criminal law.

(4) The rights of other purchasers of goods and of lien creditors are governed by the Articles on Secured Transactions (Article 9), Bulk Transfers (Article 6) and Documents of Title (Article 7).

PART 5

PERFORMANCE

Section 2-501. Insurable Interest in Goods; Manner of Identification of Goods.

(1) The buyer obtains a special property and an insurable interest in goods by identification of existing goods as goods to which the contract refers even though the goods so identified are non-conforming and he has an opinion to return or reject them. Such identification can be made at any time and in any manner explicitly agreed to by the parties. In the absence of explicit agreement identification occurs

(a) when the contract is made if it is for the sale of goods already existing and identified;

(b) if the contract is for the sale of future goods other than those described in paragraph (c), when goods are shipped, marked or otherwise designated by the seller as goods to which the contract refers;

(c) when the crops are planted or otherwise become growing crops or the young are conceived if the contract is for the sale of unborn young to be born within twelve months after contracting or for the sale of crops to be harvested within twelve months or the next normal harvest season after contracting whichever is longer.

(2) The seller retains an insurable interest in goods so long as title to or any security interest in the goods remains in him and where the identification is by the seller alone he may until default or insolvency or notification to the buyer that the identifica-

tion is final substitute other goods for those identified.

(3) Nothing in this section impairs any insurable interest recognized under any other statute or rule of law.

Section 2-502. Buyer's Right to Goods on Seller's Insolvency.

(1) Subject to subsection (2) and even though the goods have not been shipped a buyer who has paid a part or all of the price of the goods in which he has a special property under the provisions of the immediately preceding section may on making and keeping good a tender of any unpaid portion of their price recover them from the seller if the seller becomes insolvent within ten days after receipt of the first installment on their price.

(2) If the identification creating his special property has been made by the buyer he acquires the right to recover the goods only if they conform to the contract for sale.

Section 2-503. Manner of Seller's Tender of Delivery.

(1) Tender of delivery requires that the seller put and hold conforming goods at the buyer's disposition and give the buyer any notification reasonably necessary to enable him to take delivery. The manner, time and place for tender are determined by the agreement and this Article, and in particular

(a) tender must be at a reasonable hour, and if it is of goods they must be kept available for the period reasonably necessary to enable the buyer to take possession; but

(b) unless otherwise agreed the buyer must furnish facilities reasonably suited to the receipt of the goods.

(2) Where the case is within the next section respecting shipment tender requires that the seller comply with its provisions.

(3) Where the seller is required to deliver at a particular destination tender requires that he comply with subsection (1) and also in any appropriate case tender documents as described in subsections (4) and (5) of this section.

(4) Where goods are in the possession of a bailee and are to be delivered without being moved

(a) tender requires that the seller either tender a negotiable document of title covering such goods or procure acknowl-

edgment by the bailee of the buyer's right to possession of the goods; but

(b) tender to the buyer of a non-negotiable document of title or of a written direction to the bailee to deliver is sufficient tender unless the buyer seasonably objects, and receipt by the bailee of notification of the buyer's rights fixes those rights as against the bailee and all third persons; but risk of loss of the goods and of any failure by the bailee to honor the non-negotiable document of title or to obey the direction remains on the seller until the buyer has had a reasonable time to present the document or direction, and a refusal by the bailee to honor the document or to obey the direction defeats the tender.

(5) Where the contract requires the seller to deliver documents

(a) he must tender all such documents in correct form, except as provided in this Article with respect to bills of lading in a set (subsection (2) of Section 2-323); and

(b) tender through customary banking channels is sufficient and dishonor of a draft accompanying the documents constitutes non-acceptance or rejection.

Section 2-504. Shipment by Seller.
Where the seller is required or authorized to send the goods to the buyer and the contract does not require him to deliver them at a particular destination, then unless otherwise agreed he must

(a) put the goods in the possession of such a carrier and make such a contract for their transportation as may be reasonable having regard to the nature of the goods and other circumstances of the case; and

(b) obtain and promptly deliver or tender in due form any document necessary to enable the buyer to obtain possession of the goods or otherwise required by the agreement or by usage of trade; and

(c) **promptly notify the buyer of the shipment.**

Failure to notify the buyer under paragraph (c) or to make a proper contract under paragraph (a) is a ground for rejection only if material delay or loss ensued.

Section 2-505. Seller's Shipment Under Reservation.

(1) Where the seller has identified goods to the contract by or before shipment:

(a) his procurement of a negotiable bill of lading to his own order or otherwise reserves in him a security interest in the goods. His procurement of the bill to the order of a financing agency or of the buyer indicates in addition only the seller's expectation of transferring that interest to the person named.

(b) a non-negotiable bill of lading to himself or his nominee reserves possession of the goods as security but except in a case of conditional delivery (subsection (2) of Section 2-507) a non-negotiable bill of lading naming the buyer as consignee reserves no security interest even though the seller retains possession of the bill of lading.

(2) When shipment by the seller with reservation of a security interest is in violation of the contract for sale it constitutes an improper contract for transportation within the preceding section but impairs neither the rights given to the buyer by shipment and identification of the goods to the contract nor the seller's powers as a holder of a negotiable document.

Section 2-506. Rights of Financing Agency.

(1) A financing agency by paying or purchasing for value a draft which relates to a shipment of goods acquires to the extent of the payment or purchase and in addition to its own rights under the draft and any document of title securing it any rights of the shipper in the goods including the right to stop delivery and the shipper's right to have the draft honored by the buyer.

(2) The right to reimbursement of a financing agency which has in good faith honored or purchased the draft under commitment to or authority from the buyer is not impaired by subsequent discovery of defects with reference to any relevant document which was apparently regular on its face.

Section 2-507. Effect of Seller's Tender; Delivery on Condition.

(1) Tender of delivery is a condition to the buyer's duty to accept the goods and, unless otherwise agreed, to his duty to pay for them. Tender entitles the seller to acceptance of the goods and to payment according to the contract.

(2) Where payment is due and demanded on the delivery to the buyer of goods or documents of title, his right as against the seller to retain or dispose of them is conditional upon his making the payment due.

Section 2-508. Cure by Seller of Improper Tender or Delivery; Replacement.

(1) Where any tender or delivery by the seller is rejected because non-conforming and the time for performance has not yet expired, the seller may seasonably notify the buyer of his intention to cure and may then within the contract time make a conforming delivery.

(2) Where the buyer rejects a non-conforming tender which the seller had reasonable grounds to believe would be acceptable with or without money allowance the seller may if he seasonably notifies the buyer have a further reasonable time to substitute a conforming tender.

Section 2-509. Risk of Loss in the Absence of Breach.

(1) Where the contract requires or authorizes the seller to ship the goods by carrier

(a) if it does not require him to deliver them at a particular destination, the risk of loss passes to the buyer when the goods are duly delivered to the carrier even though the shipment is under reservation (Section 2-505); but

(b) if it does require him to deliver them at a particular destination and the goods are there duly tendered while in the possession of the carrier, the risk of loss passes to the buyer when the goods are there duly so tendered as to enable the buyer to take delivery.

(2) Where the goods are held by a bailee to be delivered without being moved, the risk of loss passes to the buyer

(a) on his receipt of a negotiable document of title covering the goods; or

(b) on acknowledgement by the bailee of the buyer's right to possession of the goods; or

(c) after his receipt of a non-negotiable document of title or other written direction to deliver, as provided in subsection (4) (b) of Section 2-503.

(3) In any case not within subsection (1) or (2), the risk of loss passes to the buyer on his receipt of the goods if the seller is a merchant; otherwise the risk passes to the buyer on tender of delivery.

(4) The provisions of this section are subject to contrary agreement of the parties and to the provisions of this Article on sale on approval (Section 2-327) and on effect of breach on risk of loss (Section 2-510).

Section 2-510. Effect of Breach on Risk of Loss.

(1) Where a tender or delivery of goods so fails to conform to the contract as to give a right of rejection the risk of their loss remains on the seller until cure or acceptance.

(2) Where the buyer rightfully revokes acceptance he may to the extent of any deficiency in his effective insurance coverage treat the risk of loss as having rested on the seller from the beginning.

(3) Where the buyer as to conforming goods already identified to the contract for sale repudiates or is otherwise in breach before risk of their loss has passed to him the seller may to the extent of any deficiency in his effective insurance coverage treat the risk of loss as resting on the buyer for a commercially reasonable time.

Section 2-511. Tender of Payment by Buyer; Payment by Check.

(1) Unless otherwise agreed tender of payment is a condition to the seller's duty to tender and complete any delivery.

(2) Tender of payment is sufficient when made by any means or in any manner current in the ordinary course of business unless the seller demands payment in legal tender and gives any extension of time reasonably necessary to procure it.

(3) Subject to the provisions of this Act on the effect of an instrument on an obligation (Section 3-802), payment by check is conditional and is defeated as between the parties by dishonor of the check on due presentment.

Section 2-512. Payment by Buyer Before Inspection.

(1) Where the contract requires payment before inspection non-conformity of the goods does not excuse the buyer from so making payment unless

(a) the non-conformity appears without inspection; or

(b) despite tender of the required documents the circumstances would justify injunction against honor under the provisions of this Act (Section 5-114).

(2) Payment pursuant to subsection (1) does not constitute an acceptance of goods or impair the buyer's right to inspect or any of his remedies.

Section 2-513. Buyer's Right to Inspection of Goods.

(1) Unless otherwise agreed and subject to subsection (3), where goods are tendered or delivered or identified to the contract for sale, the buyer has a right before payment or acceptance to inspect them at any reasonable place and time and in any reasonable manner. When the seller is required or authorized to send the goods to the buyer, the inspection may be after their arrival.

(2) Expenses of inspection must be borne by the buyer but may be recovered from the seller if the goods do not conform and are rejected.

(3) Unless otherwise agreed and subject to the provisions of this Article on C.I.F. contracts (subsection (3) of Section 2-321), the buyer is not entitled to inspect the goods before payment of the price when the contract provides

(a) for delivery "C.O.D." or on other like terms; or

(b) for payment against documents of title, except where such payment is due only after the goods are to become available for inspection.

(4) A place or method of inspection fixed by the parties is presumed to be exclusive but unless otherwise expressly agreed it does not postpone identification or shift the place for delivery or for passing the risk of loss. If compliance becomes impossible, inspection shall be as provided in this section unless the place or method fixed was clearly intended as an indispensable condition failure of which avoids the contract.

Section 3-514. When Documents Deliverable on Acceptance; When on Payment. Unless otherwise agreed documents against which a draft is drawn are to be delivered to the drawee on acceptance of the draft if it is payable more than three days after presentment; otherwise, only on payment.

Section 2-515. Preserving Evidence of Goods in Dispute. In furtherance of the adjustment of any claim or dispute

(a) either party on reasonable notification to the other and for the purpose of ascertaining the facts and preserving evidence has the right to inspect, test and sample the goods including such of

them as may be in the possession or control of the other; and

(b) the parties may agree to a third party inspection or survey to determine the conformity or condition of the goods and may agree that the findings shall be binding upon them in any subsequent litigation or adjustment.

PART 6

BREACH, REPUDIATION AND EXCUSE

Section 2-601. Buyer's Rights on Improper Delivery. Subject to the provisions of this Article on breach in installment contracts (Section 2-612) and unless otherwise agreed under the sections on contractual limitations of remedy (Sections 2-718 and 2-719), if the goods or the tender of delivery fail in any respect to conform to the contract, the buyer may

(a) reject the whole; or

(b) accept the whole; or

(c) accept any commercial unit or units and reject the rest.

Section 2-602. Manner and Effect of Rightful Rejection.

(1) Rejection of goods must be within a reasonable time after their delivery or tender. It is ineffective unless the buyer seasonably notifies the seller.

(2) Subject to the provisions of the two following sections on rejected goods (Sections 2-603 and 2-604),

(a) after rejection any exercise of ownership by the buyer with respect to any commercial unit is wrongful as against the seller; and

(b) if the buyer has before rejection taken physical possession of goods in which he does not have a security interest under the provisions of this Article (subsection (3) of Section 2-711), he is under a duty after rejection to hold them with reasonable care at the seller's disposition for a time sufficient to permit the seller to remove them; but

(c) the buyer has no further obligations with regard to goods rightfully rejected.

(3) The seller's rights with respect to goods wrongfully rejected are governed by the provisions of this Article on Seller's remedies in general (Section 2-703).

Section 2-603. Merchant Buyer's Duties as to Rightfully Rejected Goods.

(1) Subject to any security interest in the buyer (subsection (3) of Section 2-711), when the seller has no agent or place of business at the market of rejection a merchant buyer is under a duty after rejection of goods in his possession or control to follow any reasonable instructions received from the seller with respect to the goods and in the absence of such instructions to make reasonable efforts to sell them for the seller's account if they are perishable or threaten to decline in value speedily. Instructions are not reasonable if on demand indemnity for expenses is not forthcoming.

(2) When the buyer sells goods under subsection (1), he is entitled to reimbursement from the seller or out of the proceeds for reasonable expenses of caring for and selling them, and if the expenses include no selling commission then to such commission as is usual in the trade or if there is none to a reasonable sum not exceeding ten per cent on the gross proceeds.

(3) In complying with this section the buyer is held only to good faith and good faith conduct hereunder is neither acceptance nor conversion nor the basis of an action for damages.

Section 2-604. Buyer's Options as to Salvage of Rightfully Rejected Goods. Subject to the provisions of the immediately preceding section on perishables if the seller gives no instructions within a reasonable time after notifcation of rejection the buyer may store the rejected goods for the seller's account or reship them to him or resell them for the seller's account with reimbursement as provided in the preceding section. Such action is not acceptance or conversion.

Section 2-605. Waiver of Buyer's Objections by Failure to Particularize.

(1) The buyer's failure to state in connection with rejection a particular defect which is ascertainable by reasonable inspection precludes him from relying on the unstated defect to justify rejection or to establish breach

(a) where the seller could have cured it if stated seasonally; or

(b) between merchants when the seller has after rejection made a request in writing for a full and final written statement of all defects on which the buyer proposes to rely.

(2) Payment against documents made without reservation of rights precludes recovery of the payment for defects apparent on the fact of the documents.

Section 2-606. What Constitutes Acceptance of Goods.

(1) Acceptance of goods occurs when the buyer

(a) after a reasonable opportunity to inspect the goods signifies to the seller that the goods are conforming or that he will take or retain them in spite of their non-conformity; or

(b) fails to make an effective rejection (subsection (1) of Section 2-602), but such acceptance does not occur until the buyer has had a reasonable opportunity to inspect them; or

(c) does any act inconsistent with the seller's ownership but if such act is wrongful as against the seller it is an acceptance only if ratified by him.

(2) Acceptance of a part of any commercial unit is acceptance of that entire unit.

Section 2-607. Effect of Acceptance; Notice of Breach; Burden of Establishing Breach After Acceptance; Notice of Claim or Litigation to Person Answerable Over.

(1) The buyer must pay at the contract rate for any goods accepted.

(2) Acceptance of goods by the buyer precludes rejection of the goods accepted and if made with knowledge of a non-conformity cannot be revoked because of it unless the acceptance was on the reasonable assumption that the non-conformity would be seasonably cured but acceptance does not of itself impair any other remedy pro-vided by this Article for non-conformity.

(3) Where a tender has been accepted

(a) the buyer must within a reasonable time after he discovers or should have discovered any breach notify the seller of breach or be barred from any remedy; and

(b) if the claim is one for infringement or the like (subsection (3) of Section 2-312) and the buyer is sued as a result of such a breach he must so notify the seller within a reasonable time after he receives notice of the litigation or be barred from any remedy over for liability established by the litigation.

(4) The burden is on the buyer to establish any breach with respect to the goods accepted.

(5) Where the buyer is used for breach of a warranty or other obligation for which his seller is answerable over

(a) he may give his seller written notice of the litigation. If the notice states that the seller may come in and defend and that if the seller does not do so he will be bound in any action against him by his buyer by any determination of fact common to the two litigations, then unless the seller after seasonable receipt of the notice does come in and defend he is so bound.

(b) if the claim is one for infringement or the like (subsection (3) of Section 2-312) the original seller may demand in writing that his buyer turn over to him control of the litigation including settlement or else be barred from any remedy over and if he also agrees to bear all expense and to satisfy any adverse judgment, then unless the buyer after seasonable receipt of the demand does turn over control the buyer is so barred.

(6) The provisions of subsections (3), (4) and (5) apply to any obligation of a buyer to hold the seller harmless against infringement or the like (subsection (3) of Section 2-312).

Section 2-608. Revocation of Acceptance in Whole or in Part.

(1) The buyer may revoke his acceptance of a lot or commercial unit whose non-conformity substantially impairs its value to him if he has accepted it

(a) on the reasonable assumption that

its non-conformity would be cured and it has not been seasonably cured; or

(b) without discovery of such non-conformity if his acceptance was reasonably induced either by the difficulty of discovery before acceptance or by the seller's assurances.

(2) Revocation of acceptance must occur within a reasonable time after the buyer discovers or should have discovered the ground for it and before any substantial change in condition of the goods which is not caused by their own defects. It is not effective until the buyer notifies the seller of it.

(3) A buyer who so revokes has the same rights and duties with regard to the goods involved as if he had rejected them.

Section 2-609. Right to Adequate Assurance of Performance.

(1) A contract for sale imposes an obligation on each party that the other's expectation of receiving due performance will not be impaired. When reasonable grounds for insecurity arise with respect to the performance of either party the other may in writing demand adequate assurance of due performance and until he receives such assurance may if commercially reasonable suspend any performance for which he has not already received the agreed return.

(2) Between merchants the reasonableness of grounds for insecurity and the adequacy of any assurance offered shall be determined according to commercial standards.

(3) Acceptance of any improper delivery or payment does not prejudice the aggrieved party's right to demand adequate assurance of future performance.

(4) After receipt of a justified demand failure to provide within a reasonable time not exceeding thirty days such assurance of due performance as is adequate under the circumstances of the particular case is a repudiation of the contract.

Section 2-610. Anticipatory Repudiation.
When either party repudiates the contract with respect to a performance not yet due the loss of which will substantially impair the value of the contract to the other, the aggrieved party may

(a) for a commercially reasonable time await performance by the repudiating party; or

(b) resort to any remedy for breach (Section 2-703 or Section 2-711), even though he has notified the repudiating party that he would await the latter's performance and has urged retraction; and

(c) in either case suspend his own performance or proceed in accordance with the provisions of this Article on the seller's right to identify goods to the contract notwithstanding breach or to salvage unfinished goods (Section 2-704).

Section 2-611. Retraction of Anticipatory Repudiation.

(1) Until the repudiating party's next performance is due he can retract his repudiation unless the aggrieved party has since the repudiation cancelled or materially changed his position or otherwise indicated that he considers the repudiation final.

(2) Retraction may be by any method which clearly indicates to the aggrieved party that the repudiating party intends to perform, but must include any assurance justifiably demanded under the provisions of this Article (Section 2-609).

(3) Retraction reinstates the repudiating party's rights under the contract with due excuse and allowance to the aggrieved party for any delay occasioned by the repudiation.

Section 2-612. "Installment Contract"; Breach.

(1) An "installment contract" is one which requires or authorizes the delivery of goods in separate lots to be separately accepted, even though the contract contains a clause "each delivery is a separate contract" or its equivalent.

(2) The buyer may reject any installment which is non-conforming if the non-conformity substantially impairs the value of that installment and cannot be cured or if the non-conformity is a defect in the required documents; but if the non-conformity does not fall within subsection (3) and the seller gives adequate assurance of its cure the buyer must accept that installment.

(3) Whenever non-conformity or default with respect to one or more installments substantially impairs the value of the whole contract there is a breach of the whole. But

the aggrieved party reinstates the contract if he accepts a non-conforming installment without seasonably notifying of cancellation or if he brings an action with respect only to past installments or demands performance as to future installments.

Section 2-613. Casualty to Identified Goods. Where the contract requires for its performance goods identified when the contract is made, and the goods suffer casualty without fault of either party before the risk of loss passes to the buyer, or in a proper case under a "no arrival, no sale" term (Section 2-324) then

(a) if the loss is total the contract is avoided; and

(b) if the loss is partial or the goods have so deteriorated as no longer to conform to the contract the buyer may nevertheless demand inspection and at his option either treat the contract as avoided or accept the goods with allowance from the contract price for the deterioration or the deficiency in quantity but without further right against the seller.

Section 2-614. Substituted Performance.

(1) Where without fault of either party the agreed berthing, loading, or unloading facilities fail or an agreed type of carrier becomes unavailable or the agreed manner of delivery otherwise becomes commercially impracticable but a commercially reasonable substitute is available, such substitute performance must be tendered and accepted.

(2) If the agreed means or manner of payment fails because of domestic or foreign governmental regulation, the seller may withhold or stop delivery unless the buyer provides a means or manner of payment which is commercially a substantial equivalent. If delivery has already been taken, payment by the means or in the manner provided by the regulation discharges the buyer's obligation unless the regulation is discriminatory, oppressive or predatory.

Section 2-615. Excuse by Failure of Presupposed Conditions. Except so far as a seller may have assumed a greater obligation and subject to the preceding section on substituted performance:

(a) Delay in delivery or non-delivery in whole or in part by a seller who complies with paragraphs (b) and (c) is not a breach of his duty under a contract for sale if performance as agreed has been made impracticable by the occurrence of a contingency and the non-occurrence of which was a basic assumption on which the contract was made or by compliance in good faith with any applicable foreign or domestic governmental regulation or order whether or not it later proves to be invalid.

(b) Where the causes mentioned in paragraph (a) affect only a part of the seller's capacity to perform, he must allocate production and deliveries among his customers but may at his option include regular customers not then under contract as well as his own requirements for further manufacture. He may so allocate in any manner which is fair and reasonable.

(c) The seller must notify the buyer seasonably that there will be delay or non-delivery and, when allocation is required under paragraph (b), of the estimated quota thus made available for the buyer.

Section 2-616. Procedure on Notice Claiming Excuse.

(1) Where the buyer receives notification of a material or indefinite delay or an allocation justified under the preceding section he may by written notification to the seller as to any delivery concerned, and where the prospective deficiency substantially impairs the value of the whole contract under the provisions of this Article relating to breach of installment contracts (Sections 2-612), then also as to the whole,

(a) terminate and thereby discharge any unexecuted portion of the contract; or

(b) modify the contract by agreeing to take his available quota in substitution.

(2) If after receipt of such notification from the seller the buyer fails so to modify the contract within a reasonable time not exceeding thirty days the contract lapses with respect to any deliveries affected.

(3) The provisions of this section may not be negated by agreement except in so far as the seller has assumed a greater obligation under the preceding section.

PART 7

REMEDIES

Section 2-701. Remedies for Breach of Collateral Contracts Not Impaired. Remedies for breach of any obligation or promise collateral or ancillary to a contract for sale are not impaired by the provisions of this Article.

Section 2-702. Seller's Remedies on Discovery of Buyer's Insolvency.

(1) Where the seller discovers the buyer to be insolvent he may refuse delivery except for cash including payment for all goods theretofore delivered under the contract, and stop delivery under this Article (Section 2-705).

(2) Where the seller discovers that the buyer has received goods on credit while insolvent he may reclaim the goods upon demand made within ten days after receipt, but if misrepresentation of solvency has been made to the particular seller in writing within three months before delivery the ten day limitation does not apply. Except as provided in this subsection the seller may not base a right to reclaim goods on the buyer's fraudulent or innocent misrepresentation of solvency or of intent to pay.

(3) The seller's right to reclaim under subsection (2) is subject to the rights of a buyer in ordinary course or other good faith purchaser or lien creditor under this Article (Section 2-403). Successful reclamation of goods excludes all other remedies with respect to them.

Section 2-703. Seller's Remedies in General. Where the buyer wrongfully rejects or revokes acceptance of goods or fails to make a payment due on or before delivery or repudiates with respect to a part or the whole, then with respect to any goods directly affected and, if the breach is of the whole contract (Section 2-612), then also with respect to the whole undelivered balance, the aggrieved seller may

(a) withhold delivery of such goods;

(b) stop delivery by any bailee as hereafter provided (Section 2-705);

(c) proceed under the next section respecting goods still unidentified to the contract;

(d) resell and recover damages as hereafter provided (Section 2-706);

(e) recover damages for non-acceptance (Section 2-708) or in a proper case the price (Section 2-709);

(f) cancel.

Section 2-704. Seller's Right to Identify Goods to the Contract Notwithstanding Breach or to Salvage Unfinished Goods.

(1) An aggrieved seller under the preceding section may

(a) identify to the contract conforming goods not already identified if at the time he learned of the breach they are in his possession or control;

(b) treat as the subject of resale goods which have demonstrably been intended for the particular contract even though those goods are unfinished.

(2) Where the goods are unfinished an aggrieved seller may in the exercise of reasonable commercial judgment for the purposes of avoiding loss and of effective realization either complete the manufacture and wholly identify the goods to the contract or cease manufacture and resell for scrap or salvage value or proceed in any other reasonable manner.

Section 2-705. Seller's Stoppage of Delivery in Transit or Otherwise.

(1) The seller may stop delivery of goods in the possession of a carrier or other bailee when he discovers the buyer to be insolvent (Section 2-702) and may stop delivery of carload, truckload, planeload or larger shipments of express or freight when the buyer repudiates or fails to make a payment due before delivery or if for any other reason the seller has a right to withhold or reclaim the goods.

(2) As against such buyer the seller may stop delivery until

(a) receipt of the goods by the buyer; or

(b) acknowledgement to the buyer by any bailee of the goods except a carrier that the bailee holds the goods for the buyer; or

(c) such acknowledgement to the buyer by a carrier by reshipment or as ware-houseman; or

(d) negotiation to the buyer of any negotiable document of title covering the goods.

(3) (a) To stop delivery the seller must so notify as to enable the bailee by reasonable diligence to prevent delivery of the goods.

(b) After such notification the bailee must hold and deliver the goods according to the directions of the seller but the seller is liable to the bailee for any ensuing charges or damages.

(c) If a negotiable document of title has been issued for goods the bailee is not obliged to obey a notification to stop until surrender of the document.

(d) A carrier who has issued a non-negotiable bill of lading is not obliged to obey a notification to stop received from a person other than the consignor.

Section 2-706. Seller's Resale Including Contract for Resale.

(1) Under the conditions stated in Section 2-703 on seller's remedies, the seller may resell the goods concerned or the undelivered balance thereof. Where the resale is made in good faith and in a commercially reasonable manner the seller may recover the difference between the resale price and the contract price together with any incidental damages allowed under the provisions of this Article (Section 2-710), but less expenses saved in consequence of the buyer's breach.

(2) Except as otherwise provided in subsection (3) or unless otherwise agreed resale may be at public or private sale including sale by way of one or more contracts to sell or of identification to any existing contract of the seller. Sale may be as a unit or in parcels and at any time and place and on any terms but every aspect of the sale including the method, manner, time, place and terms must be commercially reasonable. The resale must be reasonably identified as referring to the broken contract, but it is not necessary that the goods be in existence or that any or all of them have been identified to the contract before the breach.

(3) Where the resale is at private sale the seller must give the buyer reasonable notification of his intention to resell.

(4) Where the resale is at public sale

(a) only identified goods can be sold except where there is a recognized market for a public sale of futures in goods of the kind; and

(b) it must be made at a usual place or market for public sale if one is reasonably available and except in the case of goods which are perishable or threaten to decline in value speedily the seller must give the buyer reasonable notice of the time and place of the resale; and

(c) if the goods are not to be within the view of those attending the sale the notification of sale must state the place where the goods are located and provide for their reasonable inspection by prospective bidders; and

(d) the seller may buy.

(5) A purchaser who buys in good faith at a resale takes the goods free of any rights of the original buyer even though the seller fails to comply with one or more of the requirements of this section.

(6) The seller is not accountable to the buyer for any profit made on any resale. A person in the position of a seller (Section 2-707) or a buyer who has rightfully rejected or justifiably revoked acceptance must account for any excess over the amount of his security interest, as hereinafter defined (subsection (3) of Section 2-711).

Section 2-707. "Person in the Position of a Seller."

(1) A "person in the position of a seller" includes as against a principal an agent who has paid or become responsible for the price of goods on behalf of his principal or anyone who otherwise holds a security interest or other right in goods similar to that of the seller.

(2) A person in the position of a seller may as provided in this Article withhold or stop delivery (Section 2-705) and resell (Section 2-706) and recover incidental damages (Section 2-710).

Section 2-708. Seller's Damages for Non-Acceptance or Repudiation.

(1) Subject to subsection (2) and to the provisions of this Article with respect to

proof of market price (Section 2-723), the measure of damages for non-acceptance or repudiation by the buyer is the difference between the market price at the time and place for tender and the unpaid contract price together with any incidental damages provided in this Article (Section 2-710), but less expenses saved in consequence of the buyer's breach.

(2) If the measure of damages provided in subsection (1) is inadequate to put the seller in as good a position as performance would have done then the measure of damages is the profit (including reasonable overhead) which the seller would have made from full performance by the buyer, together with any incidental damages provided in this Article (Section 2-710), due allowance for costs reasonably incurred and due credit for payments or proceeds of resale.

Section 2-709. Action for the Price.

(1) When the buyer fails to pay the price as it becomes due the seller may recover, together with any incidental damages under the next section, the price

(a) of goods accepted or of conforming goods lost or damaged within a commercially reasonable time after risk of their loss has passed to the buyer; and

(b) of goods identified to the contract if the seller is unable after reasonable effort to resell them at a reasonable price or the circumstances reasonably indicate that such effort will be unavailing.

(2) Where the seller sued for the price he must hold for the buyer any goods which have been identified to the contract and are still in his control except that if resale becomes possible he may resell them at any time prior to the collection of the judgment. The net proceeds of any such resale must be credited to the buyer and payment of the judgment entitles him to any goods not resold.

(3) After the buyer has wrongfully rejected or revoked acceptance of the goods or has failed to make a payment due or has repudiated (Section 2-610), a seller who is held not entitled to the price under this section shall nevertheless be awarded damages for non-acceptance under the preceding section.

Section 2-710. Seller's Incidental Damages. Incidental damages to an aggrieved seller include

any commercially reasonable charges, expenses or commissions incurred in stopping delivery, in the transportation, care and custody of goods after the buyer's breach, in connection with return or resale of the goods or otherwise resulting from the breach.

Section 2-711. Buyer's Remedies in General; Buyer's Security Interest in Rejected Goods.

(1) Where the seller fails to make delivery then with respect to any goods involved, and with respect to the whole if the breach goes to the whole contract (Section 2-612), the buyer may cancel and whether or not he has done so may in addition to recovering so much of the price as has been paid

(a) "cover" and have damages under the next section as to all the goods affected whether or not they have been identified to the contract; or

(b) recover damages for non-delivery as provided in this Article (Section 2-713).

(2) Where the seller fails to deliver or repudiates the buyer may also

(a) if the goods have been identified recover them as provided in this Article (Section 2-502); or

(b) in a proper case obtain specific performance or replevy the goods as provided in this Article (Section 2-716).

(3) On rightful rejection or justifiable revocation of acceptance a buyer has a security interest in goods in his possession or control for any payments made on their price and any expenses reasonably incurred in their inspection, receipt, transporation, care and custody and may hold such goods and resell them in like manner as an aggrieved seller (Section 2-706)).

Section 2-712. "Cover"; Buyer's Procurement of Substitute Goods.

(1) After a breach within the preceding section the buyer may "cover" by making in good faith and without unreasonable delay any reasonable purchase of or contract to purchase goods in substitution for those due from the seller.

(2) The buyer may recover from the seller as damages the difference between the cost of cover and the contract price together with any incidental or consequential damages as hereinafter defined (Section 2-715), but less expenses saved in consequence of the seller's breach.

(3) Failure of the buyer to effect cover

within this section does not bar him from any other remedy.

Section 2-713. Buyer's Damages for Non-Delivery or Repudiation.

(1) Subject to the provisions of this Article with respect to proof of market price (Section 2-723), the measure of damages for non-delivery or repudiation by the seller is the difference between the market price at the time when the buyer learned of the breach and the contract price together with any incidental and consequential damages provided in this Article (Section 2-715), but less expenses saved in consequence of the seller's breach.

(2) Market price is to be determined as of the place for tender or, in cases of rejection after arrival or revocation of acceptance, as of the place of arrival.

Section 2-714. Buyer's Damages for Breach in Regard to Accepted Goods.

(1) Where the buyer has accepted goods and given notification (subsection (3) of Section 2-607) he may recover as damages for any non-conformity of tender the loss resulting in the ordinary course of events from the seller's breach as determined in any manner which is reasonable.

(2) The measure of damages for breach of warranty is the difference at the time and place of acceptance between the value of the goods accepted and the value they would have had if they had been as warranted, unless special circumstances show proximate damages of a different amount.

(3) In a proper case any incidental and consequential damages under the next section may also be recovered.

Section 2-715. Buyer's Incidental and Consequential Damages.

(1) Incidental damages resulting from the seller's breach include expenses reasonably incurred in inspection, receipt, transportation and care and custody of goods rightfully rejected, any commercially reasonable charges, expenses or commissions in connection with effecting cover and any other reasonable expense incident to the delay or other breach.

(2) Consequential damages resulting from the seller's breach include

    (a) any loss resulting from general or particular requirements and needs of which the seller at the time of contracting had reason to know and which could not reasonably be prevented by cover or otherwise; and

    (b) injury to person or property proximately resulting from any breach of warranty.

Section 2-716. Buyer's Right to Specific Performance or Replevin.

(1) Specific performance may be decreed where the goods are unique or in other proper circumstances.

(2) The decree for specific performance may include such terms and conditions as to payment of the price, damages, or other relief as the court may deem just.

(3) The buyer has a right of replevin for goods identified to the contract if after reasonable effort he is unable to effect cover for such goods or the circumstances reasonably indicate that such effort will be unavailing or if the goods have been shipped under reservation and satisfaction of the security interest in them has been made or tendered.

Section 2-717. Deduction of Damages from the Price.

The buyer on notifying the seller of his intention to do so may deduct all or any part of the damages resulting from any breach of the contract from any part of the price still due under the same contract.

Section 2-718. Liquidation or Limitation of Damages; Deposits.

(1) Damages for breach by either party may be liquidated in the agreement but only at an amount which is reasonable in the light of the anticipated or actual harm caused by the breach, the difficulties of proof of loss, and the inconvenience or non-feasibility of otherwise obtaining an adequate remedy. A term fixing unreasonably large liquidated damages is void as a penalty.

(2) Where the seller justifiably withholds delivery of goods because of the buyer's breach, the buyer is entitled to restitution of any amount by which the sum of his payments exceeds

    (a) the amount to which the seller is entitled by virtue of terms liquidating the seller's damages in accordance with subsection (1), or

    (b) in the absence of such terms, twenty per cent of the value of the total performance for which the buyer is obligated under the contract or $500, whichever is smaller.

(3) The buyer's right to restitution under subsection (2) is subject to offset to the extent that the seller establishes

(a) a right to recover damages under the provisions of this Article other than subsection (1), and

(b) the amount or value of any benefits received by the buyer directly or indirectly by reason of the contract.

(4) Where a seller has received payment in goods their reasonable value or the proceeds of their resale shall be treated as payments for the purposes of subsection (2); but if the seller has notice of the buyer's breach before reselling goods received in part performance, his resale is subject to the conditions laid down in this Article on resale by an aggrieved seller (Section 2-706).

Section 2-719. Contractual Modification or Limitation of Remedy.

(1) Subject to the provisions of subsections (2) and (3) of this section and of the preceding section on liquidation and limitation of damages,

(a) the agreement may provide for remedies in addition to or in substitution for those provided in this Article and may limit or alter the measure of damages recoverable under this Article, as by limiting the buyer's remedies to return of the goods and repayment of the price or to repair and replacement of non-conforming goods or parts; and

(b) resort to a remedy as provided is optional unless the remedy is expressly agreed to be exclusive, in which case it is the sole remedy.

(2) Where circumstances cause an exclusive or limited remedy to fail of its essential purpose, remedy may be had as provided in this Act.

(3) Consequential damages may be limited or excluded unless the limitation or exclusion is unconscionable. Limitation of consequential damages for injury to the person in the case of consumer goods is prima facie unconscionable but limitation of damages where the loss is commercial is not.

Section 2-720. Effect of "Cancellation" or "Rescission" on Claims for Antecedent Breach.

Unless the contrary intention clearly appears, expressions of "cancellation" or "rescission" of the contract or the like shall not be construed as a renunciation or discharge of any claim in damages for an antecedent breach.

Section 2-721. Remedies for Fraud.

Remedies for material misrepresentation or fraud include all remedies available under this Article for non-fraudulent breach. Neither rescission or a claim for rescission of the contract for sale nor rejection or return of the goods shall bar or be deemed inconsistent with a claim for damages or other remedy.

Section 2-722. Who can sue Third Parties for Injury to Goods. Where a third party so deals with goods which have been identified to a contract for sale as to cause actionable injury to a party to that contract

(a) a right of action against the third party is in either party to the contract for sale who has title to or a security interest or a special property or an insurable interest in the goods; and if the goods have been destroyed or converted a right of action is also in the party who either bore the risk of loss under the contract for sale or has since the injury assumed that risk as against the other;

(b) if at the time of the injury the party plaintiff did not bear the risk of loss as against the other party to the contract for sale and there is no arrangement between them for disposition of the recovery, his suit or settlement is, subject to his own interest, as a fiduciary for the other party to the contract;

(c) either party may with the consent of the other sue for the benefit of whom it may concern.

Section 2-723. Proof or Market Price: Time and Place.

(1) If an action based on anticipatory repudiation comes to trial before the time for performance with respect to some or all of the goods, any damages based on market price (Section 2-708 or Section 2-713) shall be determined according to the price of such goods prevailing at the time when the aggrieved party learned of the repudiation.

(2) If evidence of a price prevailing at the times or places described in this Article is not readily available the price prevailing within any reasonable time before or after the time described or at any other place which in commercial judgment or under

usage of trade would serve as a reasonable substitute for the one described may be used, making any proper allowance for the cost of transporting the goods to or from such other place.

(3) Evidence of a relevant price prevailing at a time or place other than the one described in this Article offered by one party is not admissible unless and until he has given the other party such notice as the court finds sufficient to prevent unfair surprise.

Section 2-724. Admissibility of Market Quotations. Whenever the prevailing price or value of any goods regularly bought and sold in any established commodity market is in issue, reports in official publications or trade journals or in newspapers or periodicals of general circulation published as the reports of such market shall be admissible in evidence. The circumstances of the preparation of such a report may be shown to affect its weight but not its admissibility.

Section 2-725. Statute of Limitations in Contracts for Sale.

(1) An action for breach of any contract for sale must be commenced within four years after the cause of action has accrued.

By the original agreement the parties may reduce the period of limitation to not less than one year but may not extend it.

(2) A cause of action accrues when the breach occurs, regardless of the aggrieved party's lack of knowledge of the breach. A breach of warranty occurs when tender of delivery is made, except that where a warranty explicitly extends to future performance of the goods and discovery of the breach must await the time of such performance the cause of action accrues when the breach is or should have been discovered.

(3) Where an action commenced within the time limited by subsection (1) is so terminated as to leave available a remedy by another action from the same breach such other action may be commenced after the expiration of the time limited and within six months after the termination of the first action unless the termination resulted from voluntary discontinuance or from dismissal for failure or neglect to prosecute.

(4) This section does not alter the law on tolling of the statute of limitations nor does it apply to causes of action which have accrued before this Act becomes effective.

ARTICLE 3

COMMERCIAL PAPER

PART 1

SHORT TITLE, FORM AND INTERPRETATION

Section 3-101. Short Title. This article shall be known and may be cited as Uniform Commercial Code–Commercial Paper.

Section 3-102. Definitions and Index of Definitions.

(1) In this Article unless the context otherwise requires

(a) "Issue" means the first delivery of an instrument to a holder or a remitter.

(b) An "order" is a direction to pay and must be more than an authorization or request. It must identify the person to pay with reasonable certainty. It may be addressed to one or more such persons jointly or in the alternative but not in succession.

(c) A "promise" is an undertaking to pay and must be more than an acknowledgment of an obligation.

(d) "Secondary party" means a drawer or endorser.

(e) "Instrument" means a negotiable instrument.

(2) Other definitions applying to this Article and the sections in which they appear are:

"Acceptance." Section 3-410.
"Accommodation party." Section 3-415.
"Alteration." Section 3-407.
"Certificate of deposit." Section 3-104.
"Certification." Section 3-411.
"Check." Section 3-104.
"Definite time." Section 3-109.
"Dishonor." Section 3-507.
"Draft." Section 3-104.
"Holder in due course." Section 3-302.
"Negotiation." Section 3-202.
"Note." Section 3-104.

"Notice of dishonor." Section 3-508.

"On demand." Section 3-108.

"Presentment." Section 3-504.

"Protest." Section 3-509.

"Restrictive Indorsement." Section 3-205.

"Signature." Section 3-401.

(3) The following definitions in other Articles apply to this Article:

"Account." Section 4-104.

"Banking Day." Section 4-104.

"Clearing house." Section 4-104.

"Collecting bank." Section 4-105.

"Customer." Section 4-104.

"Depositary Bank." Section 4-105.

"Documentary Draft." Section 4-104.

"Intermediary Bank." Section 4-105.

"Item." Section 4-104.

"Midnight deadline." Section 4-104.

"Payor bank." Section 4-105.

(4) In addition Article 1 contains general definitions and principles of construction and interpretation applicable throughout this Article.

Section 3-103. Limitations on Scope of Article.

(1) This Article does not apply to money, documents of title or investment securities.

(2) The provisions of this Article are subject to the provisions of the Article on Bank Deposits and Collections (Article 4) and Secured Transactions (Article 9).

Section 3-104. Form of Negotiable Instruments: "Draft"; "Check"; "Certificate of Deposit"; "Note."

(1) Any writing to be a negotiable instrument within this Article must

(a) be signed by the maker or drawer; and

(b) contain an unconditional promise or order to pay a sum certain in money and no other promise, order, obligation or power given by the maker or drawer except as authorized by this Article; and

(c) be payable on demand or at a definite time; and

(d) be payable to order or to bearer.

(2) A writing which complies with the requirements of this section is

(a) a "draft" ("bill of exchange") if it is an order;

(b) a "check" if it is a draft drawn on a bank and payable on demand;

(c) a "certificate of deposit" if it is an acknowledgment by a bank of receipt of money with an engagement to repay it;

(d) a "note" if it is a promise other than a certificate of deposit.

(3) As used in other Articles of this Act, and as the context may require, the terms "draft," "check," "certificate of deposit" and "note" may refer to instruments which are not negotiable within this Article as well as to instruments which are so negotiable.

Section 3-105. When Promise or Order Unconditional.

(1) A promise or order otherwise unconditional is not made conditional by the fact that the instrument

(a) is subject to implied or constructive conditions; or

(b) states its consideration, whether performed or promised, or the transaction which gave rise to the instrument, or that the promise or order is made or the instrument matures in accordance with or "as per" such transaction; or

(c) refers to or states that it arises out of a separate agreement or refers to a separate agreement for rights as to prepayment or acceleration; or

(d) states that it is drawn under a letter of credit; or

(e) states that it is secured, whether by mortgage, reservation of title or otherwise; or

(f) indicates a particular account to be debited or any other fund or source from which reimbursement is expected; or

(g) is limited to payment out of a particular fund or the proceeds of a particular source, if the instrument is issued by a government or governmental agency or unit; or

(h) is limited to payment out of the entire assets of a partnership, unincorporated association, trust or estate by or on behalf of which the instrument is issued.

(2) A promise or order is not unconditional if the instrument

(a) states that it is subject to or governed by any other agreement; or

(b) states that it is to be paid only out of a particular fund or source except as provided in this section.

Section 3-106. Sum Certain.

(1) The sum payable is a sum certain even though it is to be paid

(a) with stated interest or by stated installments; or

(b) with stated different rates of interest before and after default or a specified date; or

(c) with a stated discount or addition if paid before or after the date fixed for payment; or

(d) with exchange or less exchange, whether at a fixed rate or at the current rate; or

(e) with costs of collection or an attorney's fee or both upon default.

(2) Nothing in this section shall validate any term which is otherwise illegal.

Section 3-107. Money.

(1) An instrument is payable in money if the medium of exchange in which it is payable is money at the time the instrument is made. An instrument payable in "currency" or "current funds" is payable in money.

(2) A promise or order to pay a sum stated in a foreign currency is for a sum certain in money and, unless a different medium of payment is specified in the instrument, may be satisfied by payment of that number of dollars which the stated foreign currency will purchase at the buying sight rate for that currency on the day on which the instrument is payable or, if payable on demand, on the day of demand. If such an instrument specifies a foreign currency as the medium of payment the instrument is payable in that currency.

Section 3-108. Payable on Demand.

Instruments payable on demand include those payable at sight or on presentation and those in which no time for payment is stated.

Section 3-109. Definite Time.

(1) An instrument is payable at a definite time if by its terms it is payable

(a) on or before a stated date or at a fixed period after a stated date; or

(b) at a fixed period after sight; or

(c) at a definite time subject to any acceleration; or

(d) at a definite time subject to extension at the option of the holder, or to extension to a further definite time at the option of the maker or acceptor or automatically upon or after a specified act or event.

(2) An instrument which by its terms is otherwise payable only upon an act or event uncertain as to time of occurrence is not payable at a definite time even though the act or event has occurred.

Section 3-110. Payable to Order.

(1) An instrument is payable to order when by its terms it is payable to the order or assigns of any person therein specified with reasonable certainty, or to him or his order, or when it is conspicuously designated on its face as "exchange" or the like and names a payee. It may be payable to the order of

(a) the maker or drawer; or

(b) the drawee; or

(c) a payee who is not maker, drawer or drawee; or

(d) two or more payees together or in the alternative; or

(e) an estate, trust or fund, in which case it is payable to the order of the representative of each estate, trust or fund or his successors; or

(f) an office, or an officer by his title as such in which case it is payable to the principal but the incumbent of the office or his successors may act as if he or they were the holder; or

(g) a partnership or unincorporated association, in which case it is payable to the partnership or association and may be indorsed or transferred by any person thereto authorized.

(2) An instrument not payable to order is not made so payable by such words as "payable upon return of this instrument properly indorsed."

(3) an instrument made payable both to order and to bearer is payable to order unless the bearer words are handwritten or typewritten.

Section 3-111. Payable to Bearer.

An instrument is payable to bearer when by its terms it is payable to

(a) bearer or the order of bearer; or

(b) a specified person or bearer; or

(c) "cash" or the order of "cash," or any other indication which does not purport to designate a specific payee.

Section 3-112. Terms and Omissions Not Affecting Negotiability.

(1) The negotiability of an instrument is not affected by

(a) the omission of a statement of any

consideration or of the place where the instrument is drawn or payable; or

(b) a statement that collateral has been given to secure obligations either on the instrument or otherwise of an obligor on the instrument or that in case of default on those obligations the holder may realize on or dispose of the collateral; or

(c) a promise or power to maintain or protect collateral or to give additional collateral; or

(d) a term authorizing a confession of judgment on the instrument if it is not paid when due; or

(e) a term purporting to waive the benefit of any law intended for the advantage or protection of any obligor; or

(f) a term in a draft providing that the payee by indorsing or cashing it acknowledges full satisfaction of an obligation of the drawer; or

(g) a statement in a draft drawn in a set of parts (Section 3-801) to the effect that the order is effective only if no other part has been honored.

(2) Nothing in this section shall validate any term which is otherwise illegal.

Section 3-113. Seal. An instrument otherwise negotiable is within this Article even though it is under a seal.

Section 3-114. Date, Antedating, Postdating.

(1) The negotiability of an instrument is not affected by the fact that it is undated, antedated or postdated.

(2) Where an instrument is antedated or postdated the time when it is payable is determined by the stated date if the instrument is payable on demand or at a fixed period after date.

(3) Where the instrument or any signature thereon is dated, the date is presumed to be correct.

Section 3-115. Incomplete Instruments.

(1) When a paper whose contents at the time of signing show that it is intended to become an instrument is signed while still incomplete in any necessary respect it cannot be enforced until completed.

(2) If the completion is unauthorized the rules as to material alteration apply (Section 3-407), even though the paper was not delivered by the maker or drawer; but the burden of establishing that any completion is unauthorized is on the party so asserting.

Section 3-116. Instruments Payable to Two or More Persons. An instrument payable to the order of two or more persons

(a) if in the alternative is payable to any one of them and may be negotiated, discharged or enforced by any of them who has possession of it;

(b) if not in the alternative is payable to all of them and may be negotiated, discharged or enforced only by all of them.

Section 3-117. Instruments Payable with Words of Description. An instrument made payable to a named person with the addition of words describing him

(a) as agent or officer of a specified person is payable to his principal but the agent or officer may act as if he were the holder;

(b) as any other fiduciary for a specified person or purpose is payable to the payee and may be negotiated, discharged or enforced by him;

(c) in any other manner is payable to the payee unconditionally and the additional words are without effect on subsequent parties.

Section 3-118. Ambiguous Terms and Rules of Construction. The following rules apply to every instrument:

(a) Where there is doubt whether the instrument is a draft or a note the holder may treat it as either. A draft drawn on the drawer is effective as a note.

(b) Handwritten terms control typewritten and printed terms, and typewritten control printed.

(c) Words control figures except that if the words are ambiguous figures control.

(d) Unless otherwise specified a provision for interest means interest at the judgment rate at the place of payment from the date of the instrument, or if it is undated from the date of issue.

(e) Unless the instrument otherwise specifies two or more persons who sign as maker, acceptor or drawer or indorser and as a part of the same transaction are jointly and severally liable even though the instrument contains such words as "I promise to pay."

(f) Unless otherwise specified consent to extension authorizes a single extension for not longer than the original period. A consent to extension, expressed in the instrument, is binding on secondary parties and accommodation makers. A holder may not exercise his option to extend an instrument over the objection of a maker or acceptor or other party who in accordance with Section 3-604 tenders full payment when the instrument is due.

Section 3-119. Other Writings Affecting Instrument.

(1) As between the obligor and his immediate obligee or any transferee the terms of an instrument may be modified or affected by any other written agreement executed as a part of the same transaction, except that a holder in due course is not affected by any limitation of his rights arising out of the separate written agreement if he had no notice of the limitation when he took the instrument.

(2) A separate agreement does not affect the negotiability of an instrument.

Section 3-120. Instruments "Payable Through" Bank. An instrument which states that it is "payable through" a bank or the like designates that bank as a collecting bank to make presentment but does not of itself authorize the bank to pay the instrument.

Section 3-121. Instruments Payable at Bank.

NOTE: *If this Act is introduced in the Congress of the United States this section should be omitted.*

(States to select either alternative)

Alternative A—

A note or acceptance which states that it is payable at a bank is the equivalent of a draft drawn on the bank payable when it falls due out of any funds of the maker or acceptor in current account or otherwise available for such payment.

Alternative B—

A note or acceptance which states that it is payable at a bank is not of itself an order or authorization to the bank to pay it.

Section 3-122. Accrual of Cause of Action.

(1) A cause of action against a maker or an acceptor accrues

(a) in the case of a time instrument on the day after maturity;

(b) in the case of a demand instrument upon its date or, if no date is stated, on the date of issue.

(2) A cause of action against the obligor of a demand or time certificate of deposit accrues upon demand, but demand on a time certificate may not be made until on or after the date of maturity.

(3) A cause of action against a drawer of a draft or an indorser of any instrument accrues upon demand following dishonor of the instrument. Notice of dishonor is a demand.

(4) Unless an instrument provides otherwise, interest runs at the rate provided by law for a judgment

(a) in the case of a maker, acceptor or other primary obligor of a demand instrument, from the date of demand;

(b) in all other cases from the date of accrual of the cause of action.

PART 2

TRANSFER AND NEGOTIATION

Section 3-201. Transfer: Right to Indorsement.

(1) Transfer of an instrument vests in the transferee such rights as the transferor has therein, except that a transferee who has himself been a party to any fraud or illegality affecting the instrument or who as a prior holder had notice of a defense or claim against it cannot improve his position by taking from a later holder in due course.

(2) A transfer of a security interest in an instrument vests the foregoing rights in the transferee to the extent of the interest transferred.

(3) Unless otherwise agreed any transfer for value of an instrument not then payable to bearer gives the transferee the specifically enforceable right to have the unqualified indorsement of the transferor. Negotiation takes effect only when the indorsement is made and until that time there is no presumption that the transferee is the owner.

Section 3-202. Negotiation.

(1) Negotiation is the transfer of an instrument in such form that the transferee becomes a holder. If the instrument is payable to order it is negotiated by delivery

with any necessary indorsement; if payable to bearer it is negotiated by delivery.

(2) An indorsement must be writted by or on behalf of the holder and on the instrument or on a paper so firmly affixed thereto as to become a part thereof.

(3) An indorsement is effective for negotiation only when it conveys the entire instrument or any unpaid residue. If it purports to be of less it operates only as a partial assignment.

(4) Words of assignment, condition, waiver, guaranty, limitation or disclaimer of liability and the like accompanying an indorsement do not affect its character as an indorsement.

Section 3-203. Wrong or Misspelled Name. Where an instrument is made payable to a person under a misspelled name or one other than his own he may indorse in that name or his own or both; but signature in both names may be required by a person paying or giving value for the instrument.

Section 3-204. Special Indorsement; Blank Indorsement.

(1) A special indorsement specifies the person to whom or to whose order it makes the instrument payable. Any instrument specially indorsed becomes payable to the order of the special indorsee and may be further negotiated only by his indorsement.

(2) An indorsement in blank specifies no particular indorsee and may consist of a mere signature. An instrument payable to order and indorsed in blank becomes payable to bearer and may be negotiated by delivery alone until specially indorsed.

(3) The holder may convert a blank indorsement into a special indorsement by writing over the signature of the indorser in blank any contract consistent with the character of the indorsement.

Section 3-205. Restrictive Indorsements. An indorsement is restrictive which either

(a) is conditional; or

(b) purports to prohibit further transfer of the instrument; or

(c) includes the words "for collection," "for deposit," "pay any bank" or like terms signifying a purpose of deposit or collection; or

(d) otherwise states that it is for the benefit or use of the indorser or of another person.

Section 3-206. Effect of Restrictive Indorsement.

(1) No restrictive indorsement prevents further transfer or negotiation of the instrument.

(2) An intermediary bank, or a payor bank which is not the depositary bank, is neither given notice nor otherwise affected by a restrictive indorsement of any person except the bank's immediate transferor or the person presenting for payment.

(3) Except for an intermediary bank, any transferee under an indorsement which is conditional or includes the words "for collection," "for deposit," "pay any bank," or like terms (subparagraphs (a) and (c) of Section 3-205) must pay or apply any value given by him for or on the security of the instrument consistently with the indorsement and to the extent that he does so he becomes a holder for value. In addition such transferee is a holder in due course if he otherwise complies with the requirements of Section 3-302 on what constitutes a holder in due course.

(4) The first taker under an indorsement for the benefit of the indorser of another person (subparagraph (d) of Section 3-205) must pay or apply any value given by him for or on the security of the instrument consistently with the indorsement and to the extent that he does so he becomes a holder for value. In addition such taker is a holder in due course if he otherwise complies with the requirements of Section 3-302 on what constitutes a holder in due course. A later holder for value is neither given notice nor otherwise affected by such restrictive indorsement unless he has knowledge that a fiduciary or other person has negotiated the instrument in any transaction for his own benefit or otherwise in breach of duty (subsection (2) of Section 3-304).

Section 3-207. Negotiation Effective Although it may be Rescinded.

(1) Negotiation is effective to transfer the instrument although the negotiation is

(a) made by an infant, a corporation exceeding its power, or any other person without capacity; or

(b) obtained by fraud, duress or mistake of any kind; or

(c) part of an illegal transaction; or

(d) made in breach of duty.

(2) Except as against a subsequent holder

in due course such negotiation is in an appropriate case subject to rescission, the declaration of a constructive trust or any other remedy permitted by law.

Section 3-208. Reacquisition. Where an instrument is returned to or reacquired by a prior party he may cancel any indorsement which is not necessary to his title and reissue or further negotiate the instrument, but any intervening party is discharged as against the reacquiring party and subsequent holders not in due course and if his indorsement has been cancelled is discharged as against subsequent holders in due course as well.

PART 3

RIGHTS OF A HOLDER

Section 3-301. Rights of a Holder.
The holder of an instrument whether or not he is the owner may transfer or negotiate it and, except as otherwise provided in Section 3-603 on payment or satisfaction, discharge it or enforce payment in his own name.

Section 3-302. Holder in Due Course.
(1) A holder in due course is a holder who takes the instrument
    (a) for value; and
    (b) in good faith; and
    (c) without notice that it is overdue or has been dishonored or of any defense against or claim to it on the part of any person.
(2) A payee may be a holder in due course.
(3) A holder does not become a holder in due course of an instrument:
    (a) by purchase of it at judicial sale or by taking it under legal process; or
    (b) by acquiring it in taking over an estate; or
    (c) by purchasing it as part of a bulk transaction not in regular course of business of the transferor.
(4) A purchaser of a limited interest can be a holder in due course only to the extent of the interest purchased.

Section 3-303. Taking for Value. A holder takes the instrument for value
    (a) to the extent that the agreed consideration has been performed or that he acquires a security interest in or a lien on the instrument otherwise than by legal process; or
    (b) when he takes the instrument in payment of or as security for an antecedent claim against any person whether or not the claim is due; or

    (c) when he gives a negotiable instrument for it or makes an irrevocable commitment to a third person.

Section 3-304. Notice to Purchaser.
(1) The purchaser has notice of a claim or defense if
    (a) the instrument is so incomplete, bears such visible evidence of forgery or alteration, or is otherwise so irregular as to call into question its validity, terms or ownership or to create an ambiguity as the party to pay; or
    (b) the purchaser has notice that the obligation of any party is voidable in whole or in part, or that all parties have been discharged.
(2) The purchaser has notice of a claim against the instrument when he has knowledge that a fiduciary has negotiated the instrument in payment of or as security for his own debt or in any transaction for his own benefit or otherwise in breach of duty.
(3) The purchaser has notice that an instrument is overdue if he has reason to know
    (a) that any part of the principal amount is overdue or that there is an uncured default in payment of another instrument of the same series; or
    (b) that acceleration of the instrument has been made; or
    (c) that he is taking a demand instrument after demand has been made or more than a reasonable length of time after its issue. A reasonable time for a check drawn and payable within the states and territories of the United States and the District of Columbia is presumed to be thirty days.
(4) Knowledge of the following facts does

not of itself give the purchaser notice of a defense of claim

(a) that the instrument is antedated or postdated;

(b) that it was issued or negotiated in return for an executory promise or accompanied by a separate agreement, unless the purchaser has notice that a defense or claim has arisen from the terms thereof;

(c) that any party has signed for accommodation;

(d) that an incomplete instrument has been completed, unless the purchaser has notice of any improper completion;

(e) that any person negotiating the instrument is or was a fiduciary;

(f) that there has been default in payment of interest on the instrument or in payment of any other instrument, except one of the same series.

(5) The filing or recording of a document does not of itself constitute notice within the provisions of this Article to a person who would otherwise be a holder in due course.

(6) To be effective notice must be received at such time and in such manner as to give a reasonable opportunity to act on it.

Section 3-305. Rights of a Holder in Due Course. To the extent that a holder is a holder in due course he takes the instrument free from

(1) all claims to it on the part of any person; and

(2) all defenses of any party to the instrument with whom the holder has not dealt except

(a) infancy, to the extent that it is a defense to a simple contract; and

(b) such other incapacity, or duress, or illegality of the transaction, as renders the obligation of the party a nullity; and

(c) such misrepresentation as has induced the party to sign the instrument with neither knowledge nor reasonable opportunity to obtain knowledge of its character or its essential terms; and

(d) discharge in insolvency proceedings; and

(e) any other discharge of which the holder has notice when he takes the instrument.

Section 3-306. Rights of One Not Holder in Due Course. Unless he has the rights of a holder in due course any person takes the instrument subject to

(a) all valid claims to it on the part of any person; and

(b) all defenses of any party which would be available in an action on a simple contract; and

(c) the defenses of want or failure of consideration, non-performance of any condition precedent, non-delivery, or delivery for a special purpose (Section 3-408); and

(d) the defense that he or a person through whom he holds the instrument acquired it by theft, or that payment or satisfaction to such holder would be inconsistent with the terms of a restrictive indorsement. The claim of any third person to the instrument is not otherwise available as a defense to any party liable thereon unless the third person himself defends the action for such party.

Section 3-307. Burden of Establishing Signatures, Defenses and Due Course.

(1) Unless specifically denied in the pleadings each signature on an instrument is admitted. When the effectiveness of a signature is put in issue

(a) the burden of establishing it is on the party claiming under the signature; but

(b) the signature is presumed to be genuine or authorized except where the action is to enforce the obligation of a purported signer who has died or become incompetent before proof is required.

(2) When signatures are admitted or established, production of the instrument entitles a holder to recover on it unless the defendant establishes a defense.

(3) After it is shown that a defense exists a person claiming the rights of a holder in due course has the burden of establishing that he or some person under whom he claims is in all respects a holder in due course.

PART 4

LIABILITY OF PARTIES

Section 3-401. Signature.

(1) No person is liable on an instrument unless his signature appears thereon.

(2) A signature is made by use of any name, including any trade or assumed name, upon an instrument, or by any word or mark used in lieu of a written signature.

Section 3-402. Signature in Ambiguous Capacity.

Unless the instrument clearly indicates that a signature is made in some other capacity it is an indorsement.

Section 3-403. Signature of Authorized Representative.

(1) A signature may be made by an agent or other representative, and his authority to make it may be established as in other cases of representation. No particular form of appointment is necessary to establish such authority.

(2) An authorized representative who signs his own name to an instrument

(a) is personally obligated if the instrument neither names the person represented nor shows that the representative signed in a representative capacity;

(b) except as otherwise established between the immediate parties, is personally obligated if the instrument names the person represented but does not show that the representative signed in a representative capacity, or if the instrument does not name the person represented but does show that the representative signed in a representative capacity.

(3) Except as otherwise established the name of an organization preceded or followed by the name and office of an authorized individual is a signature made in a representative capacity.

Section 3-404. Unauthorized Signatures.

(1) Any unauthorized signature is wholly inoperative as that of the person whose name is signed unless he ratifies it or is precluded from denying it; but it operates as the signature of the unauthorized signer in favor of any person who in good faith pays the instrument or takes it for value.

(2) Any unauthorized signature may be ratified for all purposes of this Article. Such ratification does not of itself affect any rights of the person ratifying against the actual signer.

Section 3-405. Impostors; Signature in Name of Payee.

(1) An indorsement by any person in the name of a named payee is effective if

(a) an impostor by use of the mails or otherwise has induced the maker or drawer to issue the instrument to him or his confederate in the name of the payee; or

(b) a person signing as or on behalf of a maker or drawer intends the payee to have no interest in the instrument; or

(c) an agent or employee of the maker or drawer has supplied him with the name of the payee intending the latter to have no such interest.

(2) Nothing in this section shall affect the criminal or civil liability of the person so indorsing.

Section 3-406. Negligence Contributing to Alteration or Unauthorized Signature.

Any person who by his negligence substantially contributes to a material alteration of the instrument or to the making of an unauthorized signature is precluded from asserting the alteration or lack of authority against a holder in due course or against a drawee or other payor who pays the instrument in good faith and in accordance with the reasonable commercial standards of the drawee's or payor's business.

Section 3-407. Alteration.

(1) Any alteration of an instrument is material which changes the contract of any party thereto in any respect, including any such change in

(a) the number or relations of the parties; or

(b) an incomplete instrument, by completing it otherwise than as authorized; or

(c) the writing as signed, by adding to it or by removing any part of it.

(2) As against any person other than a subsequent holder in due course

(a) alteration by the holder which is both fraudulent and material discharges any party whose contract is thereby changed unless that party assents or is precluded from asserting the defense;

(b) no other alteration discharges any party and the instrument may be enforced according to its original tenor, or as to incomplete instruments according to the authority given.

(3) A subsequent holder in due course may in all cases enforce the instrument according to its original tenor, and when an incomplete instrument has been completed, he may enforce it as completed.

Section 3-408. Consideration. Want or failure of consideration is a defense as against any person not having the rights of a holder in due course (Section 3-305), except that no consideration is necessary for an instrument or obligation thereon given in payment of or as security for an antecedent obligation of any kind. Nothing in this section shall be taken to displace any statute outside this Act under which a promise is enforceable notwithstanding lack or failure of consideration. Partial failure of consideration is a defense pro tanto whether or not the failure is in an ascertained or liquidated amount.

Section 3-409. Draft Not an Assignment.

(1) A check or other draft does not of itself operate as an assignment of any funds in the hands of the drawee available for its payment, and the drawee is not liable on the instrument until he accepts it.

(2) Nothing in this section shall affect any liability in contract, tort or otherwise arising from any letter of credit or other obligation or representation which is not an acceptance.

Section 3-410. Definition and Operation of Acceptance.

(1) Acceptance is the drawee's signed engagement to honor the draft as presented. It must be written on the draft, and may consist of his signature alone. It becomes operative when completed by delivery or notification.

(2) A draft may be accepted although it has not been signed by the drawer or is otherwise incomplete or is overdue or has been dishonored.

(3) Where the draft is payable at a fixed period after sight and the acceptor fails to date his acceptance the holder may complete it by supplying a date in good faith.

Section 3-411. Certificate of a Check.

(1) Certification of a check is acceptance.

Where a holder procures certification the drawer and all prior indorsers are discharged.

(2) Unless otherwise agreed a bank has no obligation to certify a check.

(3) A bank may certify a check before returning it for lack of proper indorsement. If it does so the drawer is discharged.

Section 3-412. Acceptance Varying Draft.

(1) Where the drawee's proffered acceptance in any manner varies the draft as presented the holder may refuse the acceptance and treat the draft as dishonored in which case the drawee is entitled to have his acceptance cancelled.

(2) The terms of the draft are not varied by an acceptance to pay at any particular bank or place in the United States, unless the acceptance states that the draft is to be paid only at such bank or place.

(3) Where the holder assents to an acceptance varying the terms of the draft each drawer and indorser who does not affirmatively assent is discharged.

Section 3-413. Contract of Maker, Drawer and Acceptor.

(1) The maker or acceptor engages that he will pay the instrument according to its tenor at the time of his engagement or as completed pursuant to Section 3-115 on incomplete instruments.

(2) The drawer engages that upon dishonor of the draft and any necessary notice of dishonor or protest he will pay the amount of the draft to the holder or to any indorser who takes it up. The drawer may disclaim this liability by drawing without recourse.

(3) By making, drawing or accepting the party admits as against all subsequent parties including the drawee the existence of the payee and his then capacity to indorse.

Section 3-414. Contract of Indorser; Order of Liability.

(1) Unless the indorsement otherwise specifies (as by such words as "without recourse") every indorser engages that upon dishonor and any necessary notice of dishonor and protest he will pay the instrument according to its tenor at the time of his indorsement to the holder or to any subsequent indorser who takes it up, even though the indorser who takes it up was not obligated to do so.

(2) Unless they otherwise agree indorsers

are liable to one another in the order in which they indorse, which is presumed to be the order in which their signatures appear on the instrument.

Section 3-415. Contract of Accommodation Party.

(1) An accommodation party is one who signs the instrument in any capacity for the purpose of lending his name to another party to it.

(2) When the instrument has been taken for value before it is due the accommodation party is liable in the capacity in which he has signed even though the taker knows of the accommodation.

(3) As against a holder in due course and without notice of the accommodation oral proof of the accommodation is not admissible to give the accommodation party the benefit of discharges dependent on his character as such. In other cases the accommodation character may be shown by oral proof.

(4) An indorsement which shows that it is not in the chain of title is notice of its accommodation character.

(5) An accommodation party is not liable to the party accommodated, and if he pays the instrument has a right of recourse on the instrument against such party.

Section 3-416. Contract of Guarantor.

(1) "Payment guaranteed" or equivalent words added to a signature means that the signer engages that if the instrument is not paid when due he will pay it according to its tenor without resort by the holder to any other party.

(2) "Collection guaranteed" or equivalent words added to a signature mean that the signer engages that if the instrument is not paid when due he will pay it according to its tenor, but only after the holder has reduced his claim against the maker or acceptor to judgment and execution has been returned unsatisfied, or after the maker or acceptor has become insolvent or it is otherwise apparent that it is useless to proceed against him.

(3) Words of guaranty which do not otherwise specify guarantee payment.

(4) No words of guaranty added to the signature of a sole maker or acceptor affect his liability on the instrument. Such words added to the signature of one of two or more makers or acceptors create a presumption that the signature is for the accommodation of the others.

(5) When words of guaranty are used presentment, notice of dishonor and protest are not necessary to charge the user.

(6) Any guaranty written on the instrument is enforcible notwithstanding any statute of frauds.

Section 3-417. Warranties on Presentment and Transfer.

(1) Any person who obtains payment or acceptance and any prior transferor warrants to a person who in good faith pays or accepts that

(a) he has a good title to the instrument or is authorized to obtain payment or acceptance on behalf of one who has a good title; and

(b) he has no knowledge that the signature of the maker or drawer is unauthorized, except that this warranty is not given by a holder in due course acting in good faith

(i) to a maker with respect to the maker's own signature; or

(ii) to a drawer with respect to the drawer's own signature, whether or not the drawer is also the drawee; or

(iii) to an acceptor of a draft if the holder in due course took the draft after the acceptance or obtained the acceptance without knowledge that the drawer's signature was unauthorized; and

(c) the instrument has not been materially altered, except that this warranty is not given by a holder in due course acting in good faith

(i) to the maker of a note; or

(ii) to the drawer of a draft whether or not the drawer is also the drawee; or

(iii) to the acceptor of a draft with respect to alteration made prior to the acceptance, even though the acceptance provided "payable as originally drawn" or equivalent terms; or

(iv) to the acceptor of a draft with respect to an alteration made after the acceptance.

(2) Any person who transfers an instrument and receives consideration warrants to

his transferee and if the transfer is by indorsement to any subsequent holder who takes the instrument in good faith that

(a) he has a good title to the instrument or is authorized to obtain payment or acceptance on behalf of one who has a good title and the transfer is otherwise rightful; and

(b) all signatures are genuine or authorized; and

(c) the instrument has not been materially altered; and

(d) no defense of any party is good against him; and

(e) he has no knowledge of any insolvency proceeding instituted with respect to the maker or acceptor or the drawer of an unaccepted instrument.

(3) By transferring "without recourse" the transferor limits the obligation stated in subsection (2) (d) to a warranty that he has no knowledge of such a defense.

(4) A selling agent or broker who does not disclose the fact that he is acting only as such gives the warranties provided in this section, but if he makes such disclosure warrants only his good faith and authority.

Section 3-418. Finality of Payment or Acceptance. Except for recovery of bank payments as provided in the Article on Bank Deposits and Collections (Article 4) and except for liability for breach of warranty on presentment under the preceding section, payment or acceptance of any instrument is final in favor of a holder in due course, or a person who has in good faith changed his position in reliance on the payment.

Section 3-419. Conversion of Instrument; Innocent Representative.

(1) An instrument is converted when

(a) a drawee to whom it is delivered for acceptance refuses to return it on demand; or

(b) any person to whom it is delivered for payment refuses on demand either to pay or to return it; or

(c) it is paid on a forged indorsement.

(2) In an action against a drawee under subsection (1) the measure of the drawee's liability is the face amount of the instrument. In any other action under subsection (1) the measure of liability is presumed to be the face amount of the instrument.

(3) Subject to the provisions of this Act concerning restrictive indorsements a representative, including a depositary or collecting bank, who has in good faith and in accordance with the reasonable commercial standards applicable to the business of such representative dealt with an instrument or its proceeds on behalf of one who was not the true owner is not liable in conversion or otherwise to the true owner beyond the amount of any proceeds remaining in his hands.

(4) An intermediary bank or payor bank which is not a depositary bank is not liable in conversion solely by reason of the fact that proceeds of an item indorsed restrictively (Sections 3-205 and 3-206) are not paid or applied consistently with the restrictive indorsement of an indorser other than its immediate transferor.

PART 5

PRESENTMENT, NOTICE OF DISHONOR AND PROTEST

Section 3-501. When Presentment, Notice of Dishonor, and Protest Necessary or Permissible.

(1) Unless excused (Section 3-511) presentment is necessary to charge secondary parties as follows:

(a) presentment for acceptance is necessary to charge the drawer and indorsers of a draft where the draft so provides, or is payable elsewhere than at the residence or place of business of the drawee, or its date of payment depends upon such presentment. The holder may at his option present for acceptance any other draft payable at a stated date;

(b) presentment for payment is necessary to charge any indorser;

(c) in the case of any drawer, the acceptor of a draft payable at a bank or the maker of a note payable at a bank, presentment for payment is necessary, but failure to make presentment discharges such drawer, acceptor or maker only as stated in Section 3-502(1) (b).

(2) Unless excused (Section 3-511)

(a) notice of any dishonor is necessary to charge any indorser;

(b) in the case of any drawer, the acceptor of a draft payable at a bank or the maker of a note payable at a bank, notice of any dishonor is necessary, but failure to give such notice discharges such drawer, acceptor or maker only as stated in Section 3-502(1) (b).

(3) Unless excused (Section 3-511) protest of any dishonor is necessary to charge the drawer and indorsers of any draft which on its face appears to be drawn or payable outside of the states and territories of the United States and the District of Columbia. The holder may at his option make protest of any dishonor of any other instrument and in the case of a foreign draft may on insolvency of the acceptor before maturity make protest for a better security.

(4) Notwithstanding any provision of this section, neither presentment nor notice of dishonor nor protest is necessary to charge an indorser who has indorsed an instrument after maturity.

Section 3-502. Unexcused Delay; Discharge.

(1) Where without excuse any necessary presentment or notice of dishonor is delayed beyond the time when it is due

(a) any indorser is discharged; and

(b) any drawer or the acceptor of a draft payable at a bank or the maker of a note payable at a bank who because the drawee or payor bank becomes insolvent during the delay is deprived of funds maintained with the drawee or payor bank to cover the instrument may discharge his liability by written assignment to the holder of his rights against the drawee or payor bank in respect of such funds, but such drawer, acceptor or maker is not otherwise discharged.

(2) Where without excuse a necessary protest is delayed beyond the time when it is due any drawer or indorser is discharged.

Section 3-503. Time of Presentment.

(1) Unless a different time is expressed in the instrument the time for any presentment is determined as follows:

(a) where an instrument is payable at or a fixed period after a stated date any presentment for acceptance must be made on or before the date it is payable;

(b) where an instrument is payable after sight it must either be presented for acceptance or negotiated within a reasonable time after date or issue whichever is later;

(c) where an instrument shows the date on which it is payable presentment for payment is due on that date;

(d) where an instrument is accelerated presentment for payment is due within a reasonable time after the acceleration;

(e) with respect to the liability of any secondary party presentment for acceptance or payment of any other instrument is due within a reasonable time after such party becomes liable thereon.

(2) A reasonable time for presentment is determined by the nature of the instrument, any usage of banking or trade and the facts of the particular case. In the case of an uncertified check which is drawn and payable within the United States and which is not a draft drawn by a bank the following are presumed to be reasonable periods within which to present for payment or to initiate bank collection:

(a) with respect to the liability of the drawer, thirty days after date or issue which ever is later and

(b) with respect to the liability of an indorser, seven days after his indorsement.

(3) Where any presentment is due on a day which is not a full business day for either the person making presentment or the party to pay or accept, presentment is due on the next following day which is a full business day for both parties.

(4) Presentment to be sufficient must be made at a reasonable hour, and if at a bank during its banking day.

Section 3-504. How Presentment Made.

(1) Presentment is a demand for acceptance or payment made upon the maker, acceptor, drawee or other payor by or on behalf of the holder.

(2) Presentment may be made

(a) by mail, in which even the time of presentment is determined by the time or receipt of the mail; or

(b) through a clearing house; or

(c) at the place of acceptance or payment specified in the instrument or if there be none at the place of business or residence of the party to accept or pay. If neither the party to accept or pay nor anyone authorized to act for him is present or accessible at such place presentment is excused.

(3) It may be made

(a) to any one of two or more makers, acceptors, drawees or other payors; or

(b) to any person who has authority to make or refuse the acceptance or payment.

(4) A draft accepted or a note made payable at a bank in the United States must be presented at such bank.

(5) In the cases described in Section 4-210 presentment may be made in the manner and with the result stated in that section.

Section 3-505. Rights of Party to Whom Presentment is Made.

(1) The party to whom presentment is made may without dishonor require

(a) exhibition of the instrument; and

(b) reasonable identification of the person making presentment and evidence of his authority to make it if made for another; and

(c) that the instrument be produced for acceptance or payment at a place specified in it, or if there be none at any place reasonable in the circumstances; and

(d) a signed receipt on the instrument for any partial or full payment and its surrender upon full payment.

(2) Failure to comply with any such requirement invalidates the presentment but the person presenting has a reasonable time in which to comply and the time for acceptance or payment runs from the time of compliance.

Section 3-506. Time Allowed for Acceptance or Payment.

(1) Acceptance may be deferred without dishonor until the close of the next business day following presentment. The holder may also in good faith effort to obtain acceptance and without either dishonor of the instrument or discharge of secondary parties allow postponement of acceptance for an additional business day.

(2) Except as a longer time is allowed in the case of documentary drafts drawn under a letter of credit, and unless an earlier time is agreed to by the party to pay, payment of an instrument may be deferred without dishonor pending reasonable examination to determine whether it is properly payable, but payment must be made in any event before the close of business on the day of presentment.

Section 3-507. Dishonor; Holder's Right of Recourse; Term Allowing Representment.

(1) An instrument is dishonored when

(a) a necessary or optional presentment is duly made and due acceptance or payment is refused or cannot be obtained within the prescribed time or in case of bank collections the instrument is seasonably returned by the midnight deadline (Section 4-301); or

(b) presentment is excused and the instrument is not duly accepted or paid.

(2) Subject to any necessary notice of dishonor and protest, the holder has upon dishonor an immediate right of recourse against the drawers and indorsers.

(3) Return of an instrument for lack of proper indorsement is not dishonor.

(4) A term in a draft or an indorsement thereof allowing a stated time for representment in the event of any dishonor of the draft by nonacceptance if a time draft or by nonpayment if a sight draft gives the holder as against any secondary party bound by the term an option to waive the dishonor without affecting the liability of the secondary party and he may present again up to the end of the stated time.

Section 3-508. Notice of Dishonor.

(1) Notice of dishonor may be given to any person who may be liable on the instrument by or on behalf of the holder or any party who has himself received notice, or any other party who can be compelled to pay the instrument. In addition an agent or bank in whose hands the instrument is dishonored may give notice to his principal or customer or to another agent or bank from which the instrument was received.

(2) Any necessary notice must be given by a bank before its midnight deadline and by any other person before midnight of the third business day after dishonor or receipt of notice of dishonor.

(3) Notice may be given in any reasonable manner. It may be oral or written and in

any terms which identify the instrument and state that it has been dishonored. A misdescription which does not mislead the party notified does not vitiate the notice. Sending the instrument bearing a stamp, ticket or writing stating that acceptance or payment has been refused or sending a notice of debit with respect to the instrument is sufficient.

(4) Written notice is given when sent although it is not received.

(5) Notice to one partner is notice to each although the firm has been dissolved.

(6) When any party is in insolvency proceedings instituted after the issue of the instrument notice may be given either to the party or to the representative of his estate.

(7) When any party is dead or incompetent notice may be sent to his last known address or given to his personal representative.

(8) Notice operates for the benefit of all parties who have rights on the instrument against the party notified.

Section 3-509. Protest; Noting for Protest.

(1) A protest is a certificate of dishonor made under the hand and seal of a United States consul or vice consul or a notary public or other person authorized to certify dishonor by the law of the place where dishonor occurs. It may be made upon information satisfactory to such person.

(2) The protest must identify the instrument and certify either that due presentment has been made or the reason why it is excused and that the instrument has been dishonored by a nonacceptance or nonpayment.

(3) The protest may also certify that notice of dishonor has been given to all parties or to specified parties.

(4) Subject to subsection (5) any necessary protest is due by the time that notice of dishonor is due.

(5) If, before protest is due, an instrument has been noted for protest by the officer to make protest, the protest may be made at any time thereafter as of the date of the noting.

Section 3-510. Evidence of Dishonor and Notice of Dishonor.

The following are admissible as evidence and create a presumption of dishonor and of any notice or dishonor therein shown:

(a) a document regular in form as provided in the preceding section which purports to be a protest;

(b) the purported stamp or writing of the drawee, payor bank or presenting bank on the instrument or accompanying it stating that acceptance or payment has been refused for reasons consistent with dishonor;

(c) any book or record of the drawee, payor bank, or any collecting bank kept in the usual course of business which shows dishonor, even though there is no evidence of who made the entry.

Section 3-511. Waived or Excused Presentment, Protest or Notice of Dishonor or Delay Therein.

(1) Delay in presentment, protest or notice of dishonor is excused when the party is without notice that it is due or when the delay is caused by circumstances beyond his control and he exercises reasonable diligence after the cause of the delay ceases to operate.

(2) Presentment or notice or protest as the case may be is entirely excused when

(a) the party to be charged has waived it expressly or by implication either before or after it is due; or

(b) such party has himself dishonored the instrument or has countermanded payment or otherwise has no reason to expect or right to require that the instrument be accepted or paid; or

(c) by reasonable diligence the presentment or protest cannot be made or the notice given.

(3) Presentment is also entirely excused when

(a) the maker, acceptor or drawee of any instrument except a documentary draft is dead or in insolvency proceedings instituted after the issue of the instrument; or

(b) acceptance or payment is refused but not for want of proper presentment.

(4) Where a draft has been dishonored by nonacceptance a later presentment for payment and any notice of dishonor and protest for nonpayment are excused unless in the meantime the instrument has been accepted.

(5) A waiver of protest is also a waiver of presentment and of notice of dishonor even though protest is not required.

(6) Where a waiver of presentment or

notice or protest is embodied in the instrument itself it is binding upon all parties; but where it is written above the signature of an indorser it binds him only.

PART 6

DISCHARGE

Section 3-601. Discharge of Parties.
(1) The extent of the discharge of any party from liability on an instrument is governed by the section on
  (a) payment or satisfaction (Section 3-603; or
  (b) tender of payment (Section 3-604); or
  (c) cancellation or renunciation (Section 3-605); or
  (d) impairment of right of recourse or of collateral (Section 3-606); or
  (e) reacquisition of the instrument by a prior party (Section 3-208); or
  (f) fraudulent and material alteration (Section 3-407); or
  (g) certification of a check (Section 3-411); or
  (h) acceptance varying a draft (Section 3-412); or
  (i) unexcused delay in presentment or notice of dishonor or protest (Section 3-502).
(2) Any party is also discharged from his liability on an instrument to another party by any other act or agreement with such party which would discharge his simple contract for the payment of money.
(3) The liability of all parties is discharged when any party who has himself no right of action or recourse on the instrument
  (a) reacquires the instrument in his own right; or
  (b) is discharged under any provision of this Article, except as otherwise provided with respect to discharge for impairment of recourse or of collateral (Section 3-606).

Section 3-602. Effect of Discharge Against Holder in Due Course. No discharge of any party provided by this Article is effective against a subsequent holder in due course unless he has notice thereof when he takes the instrument.

Section 3-603. Payment or Satisfaction.
(1) The liability of any party is discharged to the extent of his payment or satisfaction to the holder even though it is made with knowledge of a claim of another person to the instrument unless prior to such payment or satisfaction the person making the claim either supplies indemnity deemed adequate by the party seeking the discharge or enjoins payment or satisfaction by order of a court of competent jurisdiction in an action in which the adverse claimant and the holder are parties. This subsection does not, however, result in the discharge of the liability
  (a) of a party who in bad faith pays or satisfies a holder who acquired the instrument, by theft or who (unless having the rights of a holder in due course) holds through one who so acquired it; or
  (b) of a party (other than an intermediary bank or a payor bank which is not a depositary bank) who pays or satisfies the holder of an instrument which has been restrictively indorsed in a manner not consistent with the terms of such restrictive indorsement.
(2) Payment or satisfaction may be made with the consent of the holder by any person including a stranger to the instrument. Surrender of the instrument to such a person gives him the rights of a transferee (Section 3-201).

Section 3-604. Tender of Payment.
(1) Any party making tender of full payment to a holder when or after it is due is discharged to the extent of all subsequent liability for interest, costs and attorney's fees.
(2) The holder's refusal of such tender wholly discharges any party who has a right or recourse against the party making the tender.
(3) Where the maker or acceptor of an instrument payable otherwise than on demand is able and ready to pay at every place of payment specified in the instrument when it is due, it is equivalent to tender.

Section 3-605. Cancellation and Renunciation.
(1) The holder of an instrument may even without consideration discharge any party

(a) in any manner apparent on the face of the instrument or the indorsement, as by intentionally cancelling the instrument or the party's signature by destruction or mutilation, or by striking out the party's signature; or

(b) by renouncing his rights by a writing signed and delivered or by surrender of the instrument to the party to be discharged.

(2) Neither cancellation nor renunciation without surrender of the instrument affects the title thereto.

Section 3-606. Impairment of Recourse or of Collateral.

(1) The holder discharges any party to the instrument to the extent that without such party's consent the holder

(a) without express reservation of rights releases or agrees not to sue any person against whom the party has to the knowledge of the holder a right of recourse or agrees to suspend the right to enforce against such person the instrument or collateral or otherwise discharges such person, except that failure or delay in effecting any required presentment, protest or notice of dishonor with respect to any such person does not discharge any party as to whom presentment, protest or notice of dishonor is effective or unnecessary; or

(b) unjustifiably impairs any collateral for the instrument given by or on behalf of the party or any person against whom he has a right of recourse.

(2) By express reservation of rights against a party with a right of recourse the holder preserves

(a) all his rights against such party as of the time when the instrument was originally due; and

(b) the right of the party to pay the instrument as of that time; and

(c) all rights of such party to recourse against others.

PART 7

ADVICE OF INTERNATIONAL SIGHT DRAFT

Section 3-701. Letter of Advice of International Sight Draft.

(1) A "letter of advice" is a drawer's communication to the drawee that a described draft has been drawn.

(2) Unless otherwise agreed when a bank receives from another bank a letter of advice of an international sight draft the drawee bank may immediately debit the drawer's account and stop the running of interest pro tanto. Such a debit and any resulting credit to any account covering outstanding drafts leaves in the drawer full power to stop payment or otherwise dispose of the amount and creates no trust or interest in favor of the holder.

(3) Unless otherwise agreed and except where a draft is drawn under a credit issued by the drawee, the drawee of an international sight draft owes the drawer no duty to pay an unadvised draft but if it does so and the draft is genuine, may appropriately debit the drawer's account.

PART 8

MISCELLANEOUS

Section 3-801. Drafts in a Set.

(1) Where a draft is drawn in a set of parts, each of which is numbered and expressed to be an order only if no other part has been honored, the whole of the parts constitutes one draft but a taker of any part may become a holder in due course of the draft.

(2) Any person who negotiates, indorses or accepts a single part of a draft drawn in a set thereby becomes liable to any holder in due course of that part as if it were the whole set, but as between different holders in due course to whom different parts have been negotiated the holder whose title first accrues has all rights to the draft and its proceeds.

(3) As against the drawee the first presented part of a draft drawn in a set is the part entitled to payment, or if a time draft to acceptance and payment. Acceptance of any subsequently presented part renders the drawee liable thereon under subsection (2). With respect both to a holder and to the drawer payment of a subsequently presented part of a draft payable at sight has the same effect as payment of a check notwithstanding an effective stop order (Section 4-407).

(4) Except as otherwise provided in this section, where any part of a draft in a set is discharged by payment or otherwise the whole draft is discharged.

Section 3-802. Effect of Instrument on Obligation for Which it is Given.

(1) Unless otherwise agreed where an instrument is taken for an underlying obligation

(a) the obligation is pro tanto discharged if a bank is drawer, maker or acceptor of the instrument and there is no recourse on the instrument against the underlying obligor; and

(b) in any other case the obligation is suspended pro tanto until the instrument is due or if it is payable on demand until its presentment. If the instrument is dishonored action may be maintained on either the instrument or the obligation; discharge of the underlying obligor on the instrument also discharges him on the obligation.

(2) The taking in good faith of a check which is not postdated does not of itself so extend the time on the original obligation as to discharge a surety.

Section 3-803. Notice to Third Party.

Where a defendant is sued for breach of an obligation for which a third person is answerable over under this Article he may give the third person written notice of the litigation, and the person notified may then give similar notice to any other person who is answerable over to him under this Article. If the notice states that the person notified may come in and defend and that if the person notified does not do so he will in any action against him by the person giving the notice be bound by any determination of fact common to the two litigations, then unless after seasonable receipt of the notice the person notified does come in and defend he is so bound.

Section 3-804. Lost, Destroyed or Stolen Instruments. The owner of an instrument which is lost, whether by destruction, theft or otherwise, may maintain an action in his own name and recover from any party liable thereon upon due proof of his ownership, the facts which prevent his production of the instrument and its terms. The court may require security indemnifying the defendant against loss by reason of further claims on the instrument.

Section 3-805. Instruments Not Payable to Order or to Bearer. This Article applies to any instrument whose terms do not preclude transfer and which is otherwise negotiable within this Article but which is not payable to order to bearer, except that there can be no holder in due course of such an instrument.

ARTICLE 4

BANK DEPOSITS AND COLLECTIONS

PART 1

GENERAL PROVISIONS AND DEFINITIONS

Section 4-101. Short Title. This Article shall be known and may be cited as Uniform Commercial Code—Bank Deposits and Collections.

Section 4-102. Applicability.

(1) To the extent that items within this Article are also within the scope of Articles 3 and 8, they are subject to the provisions of those Articles. In the event of conflict the provisions of this Article govern those of Article 3 but the provisions of Article 8 govern those of this Article.

(2) The liability of a bank for action or non-action with respect to any item handled by it for purposes of presentment, payment or collection is governed by the law of the place where the bank is located. In the case of action or non-action by or at a branch or separate office of a bank, its liability is gov-

erned by the law of the place where the branch or separate office is located.

Section 4-103. Variation by Agreement; Measure of Damages; Certain Action Constituting Ordinary Care.

(1) The effect of the provisions of this Article may be varied by agreement except that no agreement can disclaim a bank's responsibility for its own lack of good faith or failure to exercise ordinary care or can limit the measure of damages for such lack or failure; but the parties may by agreement determine the standards by which such responsibility is to be measured if such standards are not manifestly unreasonable.

(2) Federal Reserve regulations and operating letters, clearing house rules, and the like, have the effect of agreements under subsection (1), whether or not specifically assented to by all parties interested in items handled.

(3) Action or non-action approved by this Article or pursuant to Federal Reserve regulations or operating letters constitutes the exercise of ordinary care and, in the absence of special instructions, action or non-action consistent with clearing house rules and the like or with a general banking usage not disapproved by this Article, prima facie constitutes the exercise of ordinary care.

(4) The specification or approval of certain procedures by this Article does not constitute disapproval of other procedures which may be reasonable under the circumstances.

(5) The measure of damages for failure to exercise ordinary care in handling an item is the amount of the item reduced by an amount which could not have been realized by the use of ordinary care, and where there is bad faith it includes other damages, if any, suffered by the party as a proximate consequence.

Section 4-104. Definitions and Index of Definitions.

(1) In this Article unless the context otherwise requires

(a) "Account" means any account with a bank and includes a checking, time, interest or savings account;

(b) "Afternoon" means the period of a day between noon and midnight;

(c) "Banking day" means that part of any day on which a bank is open to the public for carrying on substantially all of its banking functions;

(d) "Clearing house" means any association of banks or other payors regularly clearing items;

(e) "Customer" means any person having an account with a bank or for whom a bank has agreed to collect items and includes a bank carrying an account with another bank;

(f) "Documentary draft" means any negotiable or non-negotiable draft with accompanying documents, securities or other papers to be delivered against honor of the draft;

(g) "Item" means any instrument for the payment of money even though it is not negotiable but does not include money;

(h) "Midnight deadline" with respect to a bank is midnight on its next banking day following the banking day on which it receives the relevant item or notice or from which the time for taking action commences to run, whichever is later;

(i) "Properly payable" includes the availability of funds for payment at the time of decision to pay or dishonor;

(j) "Settle" means to pay in cash, by clearing house settlement, in a charge or credit or by remittance, or otherwise as instructed. A settlement may be either provisional or final;

(k) "Suspends payments" with respect to a bank means that it has been closed by order of the supervisory authorities, that a public officer has been appointed to take it over or that it ceases or refuses to make payments in the ordinary course of business.

(2) Other definitions applying to this Article and the sections in which they appear are:

"Collecting bank." Section 4-105.
"Depositary bank." Section 4-105.
"Intermediary bank." Section 4-105.
"Payor bank." Section 4-105.
"Presenting bank." Section 4-105.
"Remitting bank." Section 4-105.

(3) The following definitions in other Articles apply to this Article:

"Acceptance." Section 3-410.
"Certificate of deposit." Section 3-104.
"Certification." Section 3-411.
"Check." Section 3-104.
"Draft." Section 3-104.
"Holder in due course." Section 3-302.

"Notice of dishonor." Section 3-508.
"Presentment." Section 3-504.
"Protest." Section 3-509.
"Secondary party." Section 3-102.
(4) In addition Article 1 contains general definitions and principles of construction and interpretation applicable throughout this Article.

Section 4-105. "Depositary Bank"; "Intermediary Bank"; "Collecting Bank"; "Payor Bank"; "Presenting Bank"; "Remitting Bank." In this Article unless the context otherwise requires:

(a) "Depositary bank" means the first bank to which an item is transferred for collection even though it is also the payor bank;
(b) "Payor bank" means a bank by which an item is payable as drawn or accepted;
(c) "Intermediary bank" means any bank to which an item is transferred in course of collection except the depositary or payor bank;
(d) "Collecting bank" means any bank handling the item for collection except the payor bank;
(e) "Presenting bank" means any bank presenting an item except a payor bank;
(f) "Remitting bank" means any payor or intermediary bank remitting for an item.

Section 4-106. Separate Office of a Bank. A branch or separate office of a bank [maintaining its own deposit ledgers] is a separate bank for the purpose of computing the time within which and determining the place at or to which action may be taken or notices or orders shall be given under this Article and under Article 3.
NOTE: *The words in Brackets are optional.*

Section 4-107. Time of Receipt of Items.
(1) For the purpose of allowing time to process items, prove balances and make the necessary entries on its books to determine its position for the day, a bank may fix an afternoon hour of two P.M. or later as a cut-off hour for the handling of money and items and the making of entries on its books.
(2) Any item or deposit of money received on any day after a cut-off hour so fixed or after the close of the banking day may be treated as being received at the opening of the next banking day.

Section 4-108. Delays.
(1) Unless otherwise instructed, a collecting bank in a good faith effort to secure payment may, in the case of specific items and with or without the approval of any person involved, waive, modify or extend time limits imposed or permitted by this Act for a period not in excess of an additional banking day without discharge of secondary parties and without liability to its transferor or any prior party.
(2) Delay by a collecting bank or payor bank beyond time limits prescribed or permitted by this Act or by instructions is excused if caused by interruption of communication facilities, suspension of payments by another bank, war, emergency conditions or other circumstances beyond the control of the bank provided it exercises such diligence as the circumstances require.

Section 4-109. Process of Posting. The "process of posting" means the usual procedure followed by a payor bank in determining to pay an item and in recording the payment including one or more of the following or other steps as determined by the bank:
(a) verification of any signature;
(b) ascertaining that sufficient funds are are available;
(c) affixing a "paid" or other stamp;
(d) entering a charge or entry to a customer's account;
(e) correcting or reversing an entry or erroneous action with respect to the item.

PART 2

COLLECTION OF ITEMS: DEPOSITARY AND COLLECTING BANKS

Section 4-201. Presumption and Duration of Agency Status of Collecting Banks and Provisional Status of Credits; Applicability of Article; Item Indorsed "Pay any Bank."

(1) Unless a contrary intent clearly appears and prior to the time that a settlement given by a collecting bank for an item is or becomes final (subsection (3) of Section 4-211 and Sections 4-212 and 4-213) the bank is an agent or sub-agent of the owner of the item and any settlement given for the item is provisional. This provision applies regardless of the form of indorsement or lack of indorsement and even though credit given for the item is subject to immediate withdrawal as of right or is in fact withdrawn; but the continuance of ownership of an item by its owner and any rights of the owner to proceeds of the item are subject to rights of a collecting bank such as those resulting from outstanding advances on the item and valid rights of setoff. When an item is handled by banks for purposes of presentment, payment and collection, the relevant provisions of this Article apply even though action of parties clearly establishes that a particular bank has purchased the item and is the owner of it.

(2) After an item has been indorsed with the words "pay any bank" or the like, only a bank may acquire the rights of a holder

(a) until the item has been returned to the customer initiating collection; or

(b) until the item has been specially indorsed by a bank to a person who is not a bank.

Section 4-202. Responsibility for Collection; when Action Seasonable.

(1) A collecting bank must use ordinary care in

(a) presenting an item or sending it for presentment; and

(b) sending notice of dishonor or non-payment or returning an item other than a documentary draft to the bank's transferor [or directly to the depositary bank under subsection (2) of Section 4-212] (*see note to Section 4-212*) after learning that the item has not been paid or

accepted, as the case may be; and

(c) settling for an item when the bank receives final settlement; and

(d) making or providing for any necessary protest; and

(e) notifying its transferor of any loss or delay in transit within a reasonable time after discovery thereof.

(2) A collecting bank taking proper action before its midnight deadline following receipt of an item, notice or payment acts seasonably; taking proper action within a reasonably longer time may be seasonable but the bank has the burden of so establishing.

(3) Subject to subsection (1) (a), a bank is not liable for the insolvency, neglect, misconduct, mistake or default of another bank or person or for loss or destruction of an item in transit or in the possession of others.

Section 4-203. Effect of Instructions. Subject to the provisions of Article 3 concerning conversion of instruments (Section 3-429) and the provisions of both Article 3 and this Article concerning rectrictive indorsements only a collecting bank's transferor can give instructions which affect the bank or constitute notice to it and a collecting bank is not liable to prior parties for any action taken pursuant to such instructions or in accordance with any agreement with its transferor.

Section 4-204. Methods of Sending and Presenting; Sending Direct to Payor Bank.

(1) A collecting bank must send items by reasonably prompt method taking into consideration any relevant instructions, the nature of the item, the number of such items on hand, and the cost of collection involved and the method generally used by it or others to present such items.

(2) A collecting bank may send

(a) any item direct to the payor bank;

(b) any item to any non-bank payor if authorized by its transferor; and

(c) any item other than documentary drafts to any non-bank payor, if authorized by Federal Reserve regulation or operating letter. clearing house rule or the like.

(3) Presenting may be made by a present-

ing bank at a place where the payor bank has requested that presentment be made.

Section 4-205. Supplying Missing Indorsement; No Notice from Prior Indorsement.

(1) A depositary bank which has taken an item for collection may supply any indorsement of the customer which is necessary to title unless the item contains the words "payee's indorsement required" or the like. In the absence of such a requirement a statement placed on the item by the depositary bank to the effect that the item was deposited by a customer or credited to his account is effective as the customer's indorsement.

(2) An intermediary bank, or payor bank which is not a depositary bank, is neither given notice nor otherwise affected by a restrictive indorsement of any person except the bank's immediate transferor.

Section 4-206. Transfer Between Banks. Any agreed method which identifies the transferor bank is sufficient for the item's further transfer to another bank.

Section 4-207. Warranties or Customer and Collecting Bank on Transfer or Presentment of Items; Time for Claims.

(1) Each customer or collecting bank who obtains payment or acceptance of an item and each prior customer and collecting bank warrants to the payor bank or other payor who in good faith pays or accepts the item that

(a) he has a good title to the item or is authorized to obtain payment of acceptance on behalf of one who has a good title and the transfer is otherwise rightful; and

(b) he has no knowledge that the signature of the maker or drawer is unauthorized, except that this warranty is not given by any customer or collecting bank that is a holder in due course and acts in good faith

(i) to a maker with respect to the maker's own signature; or

(ii) to a drawer with respect to the drawer's own signature, whether or not the drawer is also the drawee; or

(iii) to an acceptor of an item if the holder in due course took the item after the acceptance or obtained the acceptance without knowledge that the drawer's signature was unauthorized; and

(c) the time has not been materially altered, except that this warranty is not given by any customer or collecting bank that is a holder in due course and acts in good faith

(i) to the maker of a note; or

(ii) to the drawer of a draft whether or not the drawer is also the drawee; or

(iii) to the acceptor of an item with respect to an alteration made prior to the acceptance if the holder in due course took the item after the acceptance provided "payable as originally drawn" or equivalent terms; or

(iv) to the acceptor of an item with respect to an alteration made after the acceptance.

(2) Each customer and collecting bank who transfers an item and receives a settlement or other consideration for it warrants to his transferee and to any subsequent collecting bank who takes the item in good faith that

(a) he has a good title to the item or is authorized to obtain payment or acceptance on behalf of one who has a good title and the transfer is otherwise rightful; and

(b) all signatures are genuine or authorized; and

(c) the item has not been materially altered; and

(d) no defense of any party is good against him; and

(e) he has no knowledge of any insolvency proceeding instituted with respect to the maker or acceptor or the drawer of an unaccepted item.

In addition each customer and collecting bank so transferring an item and receiving a settlement or other consideration engages that upon dishonor and any necessary notice of dishonor and protest he will take up the item.

(3) The warranties and the engagement to honor set forth in the two preceding subsections arise notwithstanding the absence of indorsement or words of guaranty or warranty in the transfer or presentment and a collecting bank remains liable for their breach despite remittance to its transferor. Damages for breach of such warranties or engagement to honor shall not exceed the consideration received by the customer or collecting bank responsible plus finance

charges and expenses related to the item, if any.

(4) Unless a claim for breach of warranty under this section is made within a reasonable time after the person claiming learns of the breach, the person liable is discharged to the extent of any loss caused by the delay in making claim.

Section 4-208. Security Interest of Collecting Bank in Items, Accompanying Documents and Proceeds.

(1) A bank has a security interest in an item and any accompanying documents or the proceeds of either

(a) in case of an item deposited in an account to the extent to which credit given for the item has been withdrawn or applied;

(b) in case of an item for which it has given credit available for withdrawal as of right, to the extent of the credit given whether or not the credit is drawn upon and whether or not there is a right of charge-back; or

(c) if it makes an advance on or against the item.

(2) When credit which has been given for several items received at one time or pursuant to a single agreement is withdrawn or applied in part the security interest remains upon all the items, any accompanying documents or the proceeds of either. For the purpose of this section, credits first given are first withdrawn.

(3) Receipt by a collecting bank of a final settlement for an item is a realization on its security interest in the item, accompanying documents and proceeds. To the extent and so long as the bank does not receive final settlement for the item or give up possession of the item or accompanying documents for purposes other than collection, the security interest continues and is subject to the provisions of Article 9 except that

(a) no security agreement is necessary to make the security interest enforceable (subsection (1) (b) of Section 9-203); and

(b) no filing is required to perfect the security interest; and

(c) the security interest has priority over conflicting perfected security interests in the item, accompanying documents or proceeds.

Section 4-209. When Bank Gives Value for Purposes of Holder in Due Course.

For purposes of determining its status as a holder in due course, the bank has given value to the extent that it has a security interest in an item provided that the bank otherwise complies with the requirements of Section 3-302 on what constitutes a holder in due course.

Section 4-210. Presentment by Notice of Item Not Payable by, through or at a Bank; Liability of Secondary Parties.

(1) Unless otherwise instructed, a collecting bank may present an item not payable by, through or at a bank by sending to the party to accept or pay a written notice that the bank holds the item for acceptance or payment. The notice must be sent in time to be received on or before the day when presentment is due and the bank must meet any requirement of the party to accept or pay under Section 3-505 by the close of the bank's next banking day after it knows of the requirement.

(2) Where presentment is made by notice and neither honor nor request for compliance with a requirement under Section 3-505 is received by the close of business on the day after maturity or in the case of demand items by the close of business on the third banking day after notice was sent, the presenting bank may treat the item as dishonored and charge any secondary party by sending him notice of the facts.

Section 4-211. Media or Remittance; Provisional and Final Settlement in Remittance Cases.

(1) A collecting bank may take in settlement of an item

(a) a check of the remitting bank or of another bank on any bank except the remitting bank; or

(b) a cashier's check or similar primary obligation of a remitting bank which is a member of or clears through a member of the same clearing house or group as the collecting bank; or

(c) appropriate authority to charge an account of the remitting bank or of another bank with the collecting bank; or

(d) if the item is drawn upon or payable by a person other than a bank, a cashier's check, certified check or other bank check or obligation.

(2) If before its midnight deadline the collecting bank properly dishonors a remittance check or authorization to charge on itself or presents or forwards for collection a remittance instrument of or on another bank which is of a kind approved by subsection (1) or has not been authorized by it, the collecting bank is not liable to prior parties in the event of the dishonor of such check, instrument or authorization.

(3) A settlement for an item by means of a remittance instrument or authorization to charge is or becomes a final settlement as to both the person making and the person receiving the settlement

(a) if the remittance instrument or authorization to charge is of a kind approved by subsection (1) or has not been authorized by the person receiving the settlement and in either case the person receiving the settlement acts seasonally before its midnight deadline in presenting, forwarding for collection or paying the instrument or authorization is finally paid by the payor by which it is payable;

(b) if the person receiving the settlement has authorized remittance by a non-bank check or obligation or by a cashier's check or similar primary obligation of or a check upon the payor or other remitting bank which is not of a kind approved by subsection (1)(b),—at the time of the receipt of such remittance check or obligation; or

(c) if in case not covered by sub-paragraphs (a) or (b) the person receiving the settlement fails to seasonably present, forward for collection, pay or return a remittance instrument of authorization to it to charge before its midnight deadline,—at such midnight deadline.

Section 4-212. Right of Charge-Back or Refund.

(1) If a collecting bank has made provisional settlement with its customer for an item and itself fails by reason of dishonor, suspension of payments by a bank or otherwise to receive a settlement for the item which is or becomes final, the bank may revoke the settlement given by it, charge back the amount of any credit given for the item to its customer whether or not it is able to return the items if by its midnight deadline or within a longer reasonable time after it learns the facts it returns the item or sends notification of the facts. These rights to revoke, charge-back and obtain refund terminate if and when a settlement for the item received by the bank is or becomes final (subsection (3) of Section 4-211 and subsections (2) and (3) of Section 4-213).

[(2) Within the time and manner prescribed by this section and Section 4-301, an intermediary or payor bank, as the case may be, may return an unpaid item directly to the depositary bank and may send for collection a draft on the depositary bank and obtain reimbursement. In such case, if the depositary bank has received provisional settlement for the item, it must reimburse the bank drawing the draft and any provisional credits for the item between banks shall become and remain final.]

NOTE: *Direct returns is recognized as an innovation that is not yet established bank practice, and therefore, Paragraph 2 has been bracketed. Some lawyers have doubted whether it should be included in legislation or left to development by agreement.*

(3) A depositary bank which is also the payor may charge-back the amount of an item to its customer's account or obtain refund in accordance with the section governing return of an item received by a payor bank for credit on its books (Section 4-301).

(4) The right to charge-back is not affected by

(a) prior use of the credit given for the item; or

(b) failure by any bank to exercise ordinary care with respect to the item but any bank so failing remains liable.

(5) A failure to charge-back or claim refund does not affect other rights of the bank against the customer or any other party.

(6) If credit is given in dollars as the equivalent of the value of an item payable in a foreign currency the dollar amount of any charge-back or refund shall be calculated on the basis of the buying site rate for the foreign currency prevailing on the day when the person entitled to the charge-back or refund learns that it will not receive payment in ordinary course.

Section 4-213. Final Payment of Item by Payor Bank; When Provisional Debits and Credits become Final; When Certain Credits become Available for Withdrawal.

(1) An item is finally paid by a payor bank when the bank has done any of the following whichever happens first:

(a) paid the item in cash; or

(b) settled for the item without reserving a right to revoke the settlement and without having such right under statute, clearing house rule or agreement; or

(c) completed the process of posting the item to the indicated account of the drawer, maker or other person to be charged therewith; or

(d) made a provisional settlement for the item and failed to revoke the settlement in the time and manner permitted by statute, clearing house rule or agreement.

Upon a final payment under subparagraphs (b), (c) or (d) the payor bank shall be accountable for the amount of the item.

(2) If provisional settlement for an item between the presenting and payor banks is made through a clearing house or by debits or credits in an account between them, then to the extent that provisional debits or credits for the item are entered in accounts between the presenting and payor banks or between the presenting and successive prior collecting banks seratim, they become final upon final payment of the item by the payor bank.

(3) If a collecting bank receives a settlement for an item which is or becomes final (subsection (3) of Section 4-211, subsection (2) of Section 4-213) the bank is accountable to its customer for the amount of the item and any provisional credit given for the item in an account with its customer becomes final.

(4) Subject to any right of the bank to apply the credit to an obligation of the customer, credit given by a bank for an item in an account with its customer becomes available for withdrawal as of right

(a) in any case where the bank has received a provisional settlement for the item,—when such settlement becomes final and the bank has had a reasonable time to learn that the settlement is final;

(b) in any case where the bank is both a depositary bank and a payor bank and the item is finally paid,—at the opening of the bank's second banking day following receipt of the item.

(5) A deposit of money in a bank is final when made but, subject to any right of the bank to apply the deposit to an obligation of the customer, the deposit becomes available for withdrawal as of right at the opening of the bank's next banking day following receipt of the deposit.

Section 4-214. Insolvency and Preference.

(1) Any item in or coming into the possession of a payor or collecting bank which suspends payment and which item is not finally paid shall be returned by the receiver, trustee or agent in charge of the closed bank to the presenting bank or the closed bank's customer.

(2) If a payor bank finally pays an item and suspends payments without making a settlement for the item with its customer or the presenting bank which settlement is or becomes final, the owner of the item has a preferred claim against the payor bank.

(3) If a payor bank gives or a collecting bank gives or receives a provisional settlement for an item and thereafter suspends payments, the suspension does not prevent or interfere with the settlement becoming final if such finality occurs automatically upon the lapse of certain time or the happening of certain events (subsection (3) of Section 4-211, subsections (1)(d), (2) and (3) of Section 4-213).

(4) If a collecting bank receives from subsequent parties settlement for an item which settlement is or becomes final and suspends payments without making a settlement for the item with its customer which is or becomes final, the owner of the item has a preferred claim against such collecting bank.

PART 3

COLLECTION OF ITEMS: PAYOR BANKS

Section 4-301. Deferred Posting; Recovery of Payment by Return of Items; Time of Dishonor.

(1) Where an authorized settlement for a demand item (other than a documentary draft) received by a payor bank otherwise than for immediate payment over the counter has been made before midnight of the banking day of receipt the payor bank may revoke the settlement and recover any payment if before it has made final payment (subsection (1) of Section 4-213) and before its midnight deadline it

(a) returns the item; or

(b) sends written notice of dishonor or nonpayment if the item is held for protest or is otherwise unavailable for return.

(2) If a demand item is received by a payor bank for credit on its books it may return such item or send notice of dishonor and may revoke any credit given or recover the amount thereof withdrawn by its customer, if it acts within the time limit and in the manner specified in the preceding subsection.

(3) Unless previous notice of dishonor has been sent an item is dishonored at the time when for purposes of dishonor it is returned or notice sent in accordance with this section.

(4) An item is returned:

(a) as to an item received through a clearing house, when it is delivered to the presenting or last collecting bank or to the clearing house or is sent or delivered in accordance with its rules; or

(b) in all other cases, when it is sent or delivered to the bank's customer or transferor or pursuant to his instructions.

Section 4-302. Payor Bank's Responsibility for Late Return of Item. In the absence of a valid defense such as breach of a presentment warranty (subsection (1) of Section 4-207), settlement effected or the like, if an item is presented on and received by a payor bank the bank is accountable for the amount of

(a) a demand item other than a documentary draft whether properly payable or not if the bank, in any case where it is not also the depositary bank, retains the item beyond midnight of the banking day of receipt without settling for it or, regardless of whether it is also the depositary bank, does not pay or return the item or send notice of dishonor until after its midnight deadline; or

(b) any other properly payable item unless within the time allowed for acceptance or payment of that item the bank either accepts or pays the item or returns it and accompanying documents.

Section 4-303. When Items Subject to Notice, Stop-Order, Legal Process or Setoff; Order in which Items may be Charged or Certified.

(1) Any knowledge, notice or stop-order received by, legal process served upon or setoff exercised by a payor bank, whether or not effective under other rules of law to terminate, suspend or modify the bank's right or duty to pay an item or to charge its customer's account for the item, comes too late to so terminate, suspend or modify such right or duty if the knowledge, notice, stop-order or legal process is received or served and a reasonable time for the bank to act thereon expires or the setoff is exercised after the bank has done any of the following:

(a) accepted or certified the item;

(b) paid the item in cash;

(c) settled for the item without reserving the right to revoke the settlement and without having such right under statute, clearing house rule or agreement;

(d) completed the process of posting the item to the indicated account of the drawer, maker or other person to be charged therewith or otherwise has evidenced by examination of such indicated account and by action its decision to pay the item; or

(e) become accountable for the amount of the item under subsection (1) (d) of Section 4-213 and Section 4-302 dealing with the payor bank's responsibility for late return of items.

(2) Subject to the provisions of subsection (1) items may be accepted, paid, certified or charged to the indicated account of its customer in any order convenient to the bank.

PART 4

RELATIONSHIP BETWEEN PAYOR BANK AND ITS CUSTOMER

Section 4-401. When Bank May Charge Customer's Account.

(1) As against its customer, a bank may charge against his account any item which is otherwise properly payable from that account even though the charge creates an overdraft.

(2) A bank which in good faith makes payment to a holder may charge the indicated account of its customer according to

(a) the original tenor of his altered item; or

(b) the tenor of his completed item, even though the bank knows the item has been completed unless the bank has notice that the completion was improper.

Section 4-402. Bank's Liability to Customer for Wrongful Dishonor. A payor bank is liable to its customer for damages proximately caused by the wrongful dishonor of an item. When the dishonor occurs through mistake liability is limited to actual damages proved. If so proximately caused and proved damages may include damages for an arrest or prosecution of the customer or other consequential damages. Whether any consequential damages are proximately caused by the wrongful dishonor is a question of fact to be determined in each case.

Section 4-403. Customer's Right to Stop Payment; Burden of Proof of Loss.

(1) A customer may by order to his bank stop payment of any item payable for his account but the order must be received at such time and in such manner as to afford the bank a reasonable opportunity to act on it prior to any action by the bank with respect to the item described in Section 4-303.

(2) An oral order is binding upon the bank only for fourteen calendar days unless confirmed in writing within that period. A written order is effective for only six months unless renewed in writing.

(3) The burden of establishing the fact and amount of loss resulting from the payment of an item contrary to a binding stop payment order is on the customer.

Section 4-404. Bank not Obligated to Pay Check more than Six Months old. A bank is under no obligation to a customer having a checking account to pay a check, other than a certified check, which is presented more than six months after its date, but it may charge its customer's account for a payment made thereafter in good faith.

Section 4-405. Death or Incompetence of Customer.

(1) A payor or collecting bank's authority to accept, pay or collect an item or to account for proceeds of its collection if otherwise effective is not rendered ineffective by incompetence of a customer of either bank existing at the time the item is issued or its collection is undertaken if the bank does not know of an adjudication of incompetence. Neither death nor incompetence of a customer revokes such authority to accept, pay, collect or account until the bank knows of the fact of death or of an adjudication of incompetence and has reasonable opportunity to act on it.

(2) Even with knowledge a bank may for ten days after the date of death pay or certify checks drawn on or prior to that date unless ordered to stop payment by a person claiming an interest in the account.

Section 4-406. Customer's Duty to Discover and Report Unauthorized Signature or Alteration.

(1) When a bank sends to its customer a statement of account accompanied by items paid in good faith in support of the debit entries or holds the statement and items

pursuant to a request or instructions of its customer or otherwise in a reasonable manner makes the statement and items available to the customer, the customer must exercise reasonable care and promptness to examine the statement and items to discover his unauthorized signature or any alteration on an item and must notify the bank promptly after discovery thereof.

(2) If the bank establishes that the customer failed with respect to an item to comply with the duties imposed on the customer by subsection (1) the customer is precluded from asserting against the bank

    (a) his unauthorized signature or any alteration on the item if the bank also establishes that it suffered a loss by reason of such failure; and

    (b) an unauthorized signature or alteration by the same wrongdoer on any other item paid in good faith by the bank after the first item and statement was available to the customer for a reasonable period not exceeding fourteen calendar days and before the bank receives notification from the customer of any such unauthorized signature or alteration.

(3) The preclusion under subsection (2) does not apply if the customer establishes lack of ordinary care on the part of the bank in paying the item(s).

(4) Without regard to care or lack of care of either the customer or the bank a customer who does not within one year from the time the statement and items are made available to the customer (subsection (1))

discover and report his unauthorized signature or any alteration on the face or back of the item or does not within three years from that time discover and report any unauthorized indorsement is precluded from asserting against the bank such unauthorized signature or indorsement or such alteration.

(5) If under this section a payor bank has a valid defense against a claim of a customer upon or resulting from payment of an item and waives or fails upon request to assert the defense the bank may not assert against any collecting bank or other prior party presenting or transferring the item a claim based upon the unauthorized signature or alteration giving rise to the customer's claim.

Section 4-407. Payor Bank's Right to Subrogation on Improper Payment. If a payor bank has paid an item over the stop payment order of the drawer or maker, or otherwise under circumstances giving a basis for objection by the drawer or maker, to present unjust enrichment and only to the extent necessary to prevent loss to the bank by reason of its payment of the item, the payor bank shall be subrogated to the rights

    (a) of any holder in due course on the item against the drawer or maker; and

    (b) of the payee or any other holder of the item against the drawer or maker either on the item or under the transaction out of which the item arose; and

    (c) of the drawer or maker against the payee or any other holder of the item with respect to the transaction out of which the item arose.

PART 5

COLLECTION OF DOCUMENTARY DRAFTS

Section 4-501. Handling of Documentary Drafts; Duty to Send for Presentment and to Notify Customer of Dishonor. A bank which takes a documentary draft for collection must present or send the draft and accompanying documents for presentment and upon learning that the draft has not been paid or accepted in due course must seasonably notify its customer of such fact even though it may have discounted or bought the draft or extended credit available for withdrawal as if right.

Section 4-502. Presentment of "On Arrival" Drafts. When a draft or the relevant instructions require presentment "on arrival," "when goods arrive" or the like, the collecting bank need not present until in its judgment a reasonable time for arrival of the goods has expired. Refusal to pay or accept because the goods have not arrived is not dishonor; the bank must notify its transferor of such refusal but need not present the draft again until it is instructed to do so or learns of the arrival of the goods.

Section 4-503. Responsibility of Presenting Bank for Documents and Goods; Report or Reasons for Dishonor; Referee in Case of Need. Unless otherwise instructed and except as provided in Article 5 a bank presenting a documentary draft

> (a) must deliver the documents to the drawee on acceptance of the draft if it is payable more than three days after presentment; otherwise, only on payment; and

> (b) upon dishonor, either in the case of presentment for acceptance or presentment for payment, may seek and follow instructions from any referee in case of need designated in the draft or if the presenting bank does not choose to utilize his services it must use diligence and good faith to ascertain the reason for dishonor, must notify its transferor of the dishonor and of the results of its effort to ascertain the reasons therefor and must request instructions.

But the presenting bank is under no obligation with respect to goods represented by the documents except to follow any reasonable instructions seasonably received; it has a right to reimbursement for any expense incurred in following instructions and to prepayment of or indemnity for such expenses.

Section 4-504. Privilege of Presenting Bank to Deal with Goods, Security Interest for Expenses.

(1) A presenting bank which, following the dishonor of a documentary draft, has seasonably requested instructions but does not receive them within a reasonable time may store, sell, or otherwise deal with the goods in any reasonable manner.

(2) For its reasonable expenses incurred by action under subsection (1) the presenting bank has a lien upon the goods or their proceeds, which may be foreclosed in the same manner as an unpaid seller's lien.

ARTICLE 6

BULK TRANSFERS

Section 6-101. Short Title. This Article shall be known and may be cited as Uniform Commercial Code–Bulk Transfers.

Section 6-102. "Bulk Transfers"; Transfers of Equipment; Enterprises Subject to this Article; Bulk Transfers Subject to this Article.

(1) A "bulk transfer" is any transfer in bulk and not in the ordinary course of the transferor's business of a major part of the materials, supplies, merchandise or other inventory (Section 9-109) of an enterprise subject to this Article.

(2) A transfer of a substantial part of the equipment (Section 9-109) of such an enterprise is a bulk transfer if it is made in connection with a bulk transfer of inventory, but not otherwise.

(3) The enterprises subject to this Article are all those whose principal business is the sale of merchandise from stock, including those who manufacture what they sell.

(4) Except as limited by the following section all bulk transfers of goods located within this state are subject to this Article.

Section 6-103. Transfers Excepted from this Article. The following transfers are not subject to this Article:

(1) Those made to give security for the performance of an obligation;

(2) General assignments for the benefit of all the creditors of the transferor, and subsequent transfers by the assignee thereunder;

(3) Transfers in settlement or realization of a lien or other security interest;

(4) Sales by executors, administrators, receivers, trustees in bankruptcy, or any public officer under judicial process;

(5) Sales made in the course of judicial or administrative proceedings for the dissolution or reorganization of a corporation and of which notice is sent to the creditors of the corporation to order of the court or administrative agency;

(6) Transfers to a person maintaining a known place of business in this State who becomes bound to pay the debts of the transferor in full and gives public notice of that fact, and who is solvent after becoming so bound;

(7)   A transfer to a new business enterprise organized to take over and continue the business, if public notice of the transaction is given and the new enterprise assumes the debts of the transferor and he receives nothing from the transaction except an interest in the new enterprise junior to the claims of creditors;

(8)   Transfers of property which is exempt from execution.

Public notice under subsection (6) or subsection (7) may be given by publishing once a week for two consecutive weeks in a newspaper of general circulation where the transferor had its principal place of business in this state an advertisement including the names and addresses of the transferor and transferee and the effective date of the transfer.

Section 6-104. Schedule of Property, List of Creditors.

(1)   Except as provided with respect to auction sales (Section 6-108), a bulk transfer subject to this Article is ineffective against any creditor of the transferor unless:

(a)   The transferee requires the transferor to furnish a list of his existing creditors prepared as stated in this section; and

(b)   The parties prepare a schedule of the property transferred sufficient to identify it; and

(c)   The transferee preserves the list and schedule for six months next following the transfer and permits inspection of either or both and copying therefrom at all reasonable hours by any creditor of the transferor, or files the list and schedule in (a public office to be here identified).

(2)   The list of creditors must be signed and sworn to or affirmed by the transferot or his agent. It must contain the names and business addresses of all creditors of the transferor, with the amounts when known, and also the names of all persons who are known to the transferor to assert claims against him even though such claims are disputed. If the transferor is the obligor of an outstanding issue of bonds, debentures or the like as to which there is an indenture trustee, the list of creditors need include only the name and address of the indenture trustee and the aggregate outstanding principal amount of the issue.

(3)   Responsibility for the completeness and accuracy of the list of creditors rests on the transferor, and the transfer is not rendered ineffective by errors or omissions therein unless the transferee is shown to have had knowledge.

Section 6-105. Notice to Creditors.

In addition to the requirements of the preceding section, any bulk transfer subject to this Article except one made by auction sale (Section 6-108) is ineffective against any creditor of the transferor unless at least ten days before he takes possession of the goods or pays for them, whichever happens first, the transferee gives notice of the transfer in the manner and to the persons hereafter provided (Section 6-107).

Section 6-106. Application of the Proceeds.

In addition to the requirements of the two preceding sections:

(1)   Upon every bulk transfer subject to this Article for which new consideration becomes payable except those made by sale at auction it is the duty of the transferee to assure that such consideration is applied so far as necessary to pay those debts of the transferor which are either shown on the list furnished by the transferor (Section 6-104) or filed in writing in the place stated in the notice (Section 6-107) within thirty days after the mailing of such notice. This duty of the transferee runs to all the holders of such debts, and may be enforced by any of them for the benefit of all.

(2)   If any of said debts are in dispute the necessary sum may be withheld from distribution until the dispute is settled or adjudicated.

(3)   If the consideration payable is not enough to pay all of the said debts in full distribution shall be made pro rata]

NOTE: *This section is bracketed to indicate division of opinion as to whether or not it is a wise provision, and to suggest that this is a point on which state enactments may differ without serious damage to the principle of uniformity.*

In any State where this section is omitted, the following parts of sections also bracketed in the text, should also be omitted, namely:
Section 6-107(2)(e).
6-108(3)(c).
6-109(2).

In any State where this section is enacted, these other provisions should be also.

Optional Subsection (4) [(4) The transferee may within ten days after he takes possession of the goods pay the consideration into the (specify court) in the county where the transferor had its principal place of business in this state and thereafter may discharge his duty under this section by giving notice by registered or certified mail to all the persons to whom the duty runs that the consideration has been paid into that court and that they should file their claims there. On motion of any interested party, the court may order the distribution of the consideration to the persons entitled to it.]

NOTE: *Optional subsection (4) is recommended for those states which do not have a general statute providing for payment of money into court.*

Section 6-107. The Notice.
(1) The notice to creditors (Section 6-105) shall state:
   (a) that a bulk transfer is about to be made; and
   (b) the names and business addresses of the transferor and transferee, and all other business names and addresses used by the transferor within three years last past so far as known to the transferee; and
   (c) whether or not all the debts of the transferor are to be paid in full as they fall due as a result of the transaction, and if so, the address to which creditors should send their bills.
(2) If the debts of the transferor are not to be paid in full as they fall due or if the transferee is in doubt on that point then the notice shall state further:
   (a) the location and general description of the property to be transferred and the estimated total of the transferor's debts;
   (b) the address where the schedule of property and list of creditors (Section 6-104) may be inspected;
   (c) whether the transfer is to pay existing debts and if so the amount of such debts and to whom owing;
   (d) whether the transfer is for new consideration and if so the amount of

such consideration and the time and place of payment; [and]
   [(e) if for new consideration the time and place where creditors of the transferor are to file their claims.]
(3) The notice in any case shall be delivered personally or sent by registered mail to all the persons shown on the list of creditors furnished by the transferor (Section 6-104) and to all other persons who are known to the transferee to hold or assert claims against the transferor.

NOTE: *The words in brackets are optional.*

Section 6-108. Auction Sales; "Auctioneer."
(1) A bulk transfer is subject to this Article even though it is by sale at auction, but only in the manner and with the results stated in this section.
(2) The transferor shall furnish a list of his creditors and assist in the preparation of a schedule of the property to be sold, both prepared as before stated (Section 6-104).
(3) The person or persons other than the transferor who direct, control or are responsible for the auction are collectively called the "auctioneer." The auctioneer shall:
   (a) receive and retain the list of creditors and prepare and retain the schedule of property for the period stated in this Article (Section 6-104);
   (b) give notice of the auction personally or by registered or certified mail at least ten days before it occurs to all persons shown on the list of creditors and to all other persons who are known to him to hold or assert claims against the transferor; [and]
   [(c) assure that the net proceeds of the auction are applied as provided in this Article (Section 6-106).]
(4) Failure of the auctioneer to perform any of these duties does not affect the validity of the sale or the title of the purchasers, but if the auctioneer knows that the auction constitutes a bulk transfer such failure renders the auctioneer liable to the creditors of the transferor as a class for the sums owing to them from the transferor up to but not exceeding the net proceeds of the auction. If the auctioneer consists of several persons their liability is joint and several.

NOTE: *The words in brackets are optional.*

Section 6-109. What Creditors Protected; Credit for Payment to Particular Creditors.

(1) The creditors of the transferor mentioned in this Article are those holding claims based on transactions or events occurring before the bulk transfer, but creditors who become such after notice to creditors is given (Sections 6-105 and 6-107) are not entitled to notice.

[(2) Against the aggregate obligation imposed by the provisions of this Article concerning the application of the proceeds (Section 6-106 and subsection (3) (c) of 6-108) the transferee or auctioneer is entitled to credit for sums paid to particular creditors of the transferor, not exceeding the sums believed in good faith at the time of the payment to be properly payable to such creditors.]

Section 6-110. Subsequent Transfers. When the title of a transferee to property is subject to a defect by reason of his noncompliance with the requirements of this Article, then:

(1) a purchaser of any of such property from such transferee who pays no value or who takes with notice of such non-compliance takes subject to such defect, but

(2) a purchaser for value in good faith and without such notice takes free of such defect.

Section 6-111. Limitation of Actions and Levies. No action under this Article shall be brought nor levy made more than six months after the date on which the transferee took possession of the goods unless the transfer has been concealed. If the transfer has been concealed, actions may be brought or levies made within six months after its discovery.

NOTE TO ARTICLE 6: *Section 6-106 is bracketed to indicate division of opinion as to whether or not it is a wise provision, and to suggest that this is a point on which State enactments may differ without serious damage to the principle of uniformity.*

In any State where Section 6-106 is not enacted, the following parts of sections, also bracketed in the text, should also be omitted, namely:

Sec. 6-107(2)(e)

6-109(3)(c)

6-109(2).

In any State where Section 6-106 is enacted, these other provisions should be also.

REVISED ARTICLE 9

SECURED TRANSACTIONS; SALES OF ACCOUNTS AND CHATTEL PAPER

PART 1

SHORT TITLE, APPLICABILITY AND DEFINITIONS

Section 9-101. Short Title. This Article shall be known and may be cited as Uniform Commercial Code—Secured Transactions.

Section 9-102. Policy and Subject Matter of Article.

(1) Except as otherwise provided in Section 9-104 on excluded transactions, this Article applies

(a) to any transaction (regardless of its form) which is intended to create a security interest in personal property or fixtures including goods, documents, instruments, general intangibles, chattel paper or accounts; and also

(b) to any sale of accounts or chattel paper.

(2) This Article applies to security interests created by contract including pledge, assignment, chattel mortgage, chattel trust, trust deed, factor's lien, equipment trust, conditional sale, trust receipt, other lien or title retention contract and lease or consignment intended as security. This Article does not apply to statutory liens except as provided in Section 9-310.

(3) The application of this Article to a security interest in a secured obligation is not affected by the fact that the obligation is itself secured by a transaction or interest to which this Article does not apply.

Section 9-103. Perfection of Security Interests in Multiple State Transactions.

(1) Documents, instruments and ordinary goods.

(a) This subsection applies to documents and instruments and to goods other than those covered by a certificate of title described in subsection (2), mobile goods described in subsection (3), and minerals described in subsection (5).

(b) Except as otherwise provided in this subsection, perfection and the effect of perfection or non-perfection of a security interest in collateral are governed by the law of the jurisdiction where the collateral is when the last event occurs on which is based the assertion that the security interest is perfected or unperfected.

(c) If the parties to a transaction creating a purchase money security interest in goods in one jurisdiction understand at the time that the security interest attaches that the goods will be kept in another jurisdiction, then the law of the other jurisdiction governs the perfection and the effect of perfection or non-perfection of the security interest from the time it attaches until thirty days after the debtor receives possession of the goods and thereafter if the goods are taken to the other jurisdiction before the end of the thirty-day period.

(d) When collateral is brought into and kept in this state while subject to a security interest perfected under the law of the jurisdiction from which the collateral was removed, the security interest remains perfected, but if action is required by Part 3 of this Article to perfect the security interest,

(i) if the action is not taken before the expiration of the period of perfection in the other jurisdiction or the end of four months after the collateral is brought into this state, whichever period first expires, the security interest becomes unperfected at the end of that period and is thereafter deemed to have been unperfected as against a person who became a purchaser after removal;

(ii) if the action is taken before the expiration of the period specified in subparagraph (i), the security interest continues perfected thereafter;

(iii) for the purpose of a priority over a buyer of consumer goods (subsection (2) of Section 9-307), the period of the effectiveness of a filing in the jurisdiction from which the collateral is removed is governed by the rules with respect to perfection in subparagraphs (i) and (ii).

(2) Certificate of title.

(a) This subsection applies to goods covered by a certificate of title issued under a statute of this state or of another jurisdiction under the law of which indication of a security interest on the certificate is required as a condition of perfection.

(b) Except as otherwise provided in this subsection, perfection and the effect of perfection or non-perfection of the security interest are governed by the law (including the conflict of laws rules) of the jurisdiction issuing the certificate until four months after the goods are removed from that jurisdiction and thereafter until the goods are registered in another jurisdiction, but in any event not beyond surrender of the certificate. After the expiration of that period, the goods are not covered by the certificate of title within the meaning of this section.

(c) Except with respect to the rights of a buyer described in the next paragraph, a security interest, perfected in another jurisdiction otherwise than by notation on a certificate of title, in goods brought into this state and thereafter covered by a certificate of title issued by this state is subject to the rules stated in paragraph (d) of subsection (1).

(d) If goods are brought into this state while a security interest therein is perfected in any manner under the law of the jurisdiction from which the goods are removed and a certificate of title is issued by this state and the certificate does not show that the goods are subject to the security interest or that they may be subject to security interests not shown on the certificate, the security interest is subordinate to the rights of a buyer of the goods who is not in the business of selling goods of that kind to the extent that he gives value and receives delivery of the goods after issuance of the certificate and without knowledge of the security interest.

(3) Accounts, general intangibles and mobile goods.

(a) This subsection applies to accounts (other than an account described in subsection (5) on minerals) and general intangibles and to goods which are mobile and which are of a type normally used in more than one jurisdiction, such as motor vehicles, trailers, rolling stock, airplanes, shipping containers, road building and construction machinery and commercial harvesting machinery and the like, if the goods are equipment or are inventory leased or held for lease by the debtor to others, and are not covered by a certificate of title described in subsection (2).

(b) The law (including the conflict of laws rules) of the jurisdiction in which the debtor is located governs the perfection or non-perfection of the security interest.

(c) If, however, the debtor is located in a jurisdiction which is not a part of the United States, and which does not provide for perfection of the security interest by filing or recording in that jurisdiction, the law of the jurisdiction in the United States in which the debtor has its major executive office in the United States governs the perfection and the effect of perfection or non-perfection of the security interest through filing. In the alternative, if the debtor is located in a jurisdiction which is not a part of the United States or Canada and the collateral is accounts or general intangibles for money due or to become due, the security interest may be perfected by notification to the account debtor. As used in this paragraph, "United States" includes its territories and possessions and the Commonwealth of Puerto Rico.

(d) A debtor shall be deemed located at his place of business if he has one, at his chief executive office if he has more than one place of business, otherwise at his residence. If, however, the debtor is a foreign air carrier under the Federal Aviation Act of 1958, as amended, it shall be deemed located at the designated office of the agent upon whom service of process may be made on behalf of the foreign air carrier.

(e) A security interest perfected under the law of the jurisdiction of the location of the debtor is perfected until the expiration of four months after a change of the debtor's location to another jurisdiction, or until perfection would have ceased by the law of the first jurisdiction, whichever period first expires. Unless perfected in the new jurisdiction before the end of that period, it becomes unperfected thereafter and is deemed to have been unperfected as against a person who became a purchaser after the change.

(4) Chattel paper.

The rules stated for goods in subsection (1) apply to a possessory security interest in chattel paper. The rules stated for accounts in subsection (3) apply to a non-possessory security interest in chattel paper, but the security interest may not be perfected by notification to the account debtor.

(5) Minerals.

Perfection and the effect of perfection or non-perfection of a security interest which is created by a debtor who has an interest in minerals or the like (including oil and gas) before extraction and which attaches thereto as extracted, or which attaches to an account resulting from the sale thereof at the wellhead or minehead are governed by the law (including the conflict or laws rules) of the jurisdiction wherein the wellhead or minehead is located.

Section 9-104. Transactions Excluded From Article. This Article does not apply

(a) to a security interest subject to any statute of the United States to the extent that such statute governs the rights of parties to and third parties affected by transactions in particular types of property; or

(b) to a landlord's lien; or

(c) to a lien given by statute or other rule of law for services or materials except as provided in Section 9-310 on priority of such liens; or

(d) to a transfer of a claim for wages, salary or other compensation of an employee; or

(e) to a transfer by a government or governmental subdivision or agency; or

(f) to a sale of accounts or chattel paper as part of a sale of the business out of which they arose, or an assignment of accounts or chattel paper which is for the purpose of collection only, or a transfer of a right to payment under a contract to an assignee who is also to do the performance under the contract or a transfer of a single account to an assignee in whole or partial satisfaction of a preexisting indebtedness; or

(g) to a transfer of an interest in or claim in or under any policy of insurance, except as provided with respect to proceeds (Section 9-306) and priorities in proceeds (Section 9-312); or

(h) to a right represented by a judgment (other than a judgment taken on a right to payment which was collateral); or

(i) to any right of set-off; or

(j) except to the extent that provision is made for fixtures in Section 9-313, to the creation or transfer of an interest in or lien on real estate, including a lease or rents thereunder; or

(k) to a transfer in whole or in part of any claim arising out of tort; or

(l) to a transfer of an interest in any deposit account (subsection (1) or Section 9-105), except as provided with respect to proceeds (Section 9-306) and priorities in proceeds (Section 9-312).

Section 9-105. Definitions and Index of Definitions.

(1) In this Article unless the context otherwise requires:

(a) "Account debtor" means the person who is obligated on an account, chattel paper or general intangible,

(b) "Chattel paper" means a writing or writings which evidence both a monetary obligation and a security interest in or a lease of specific goods, but a charter or other contract involving the use or hire of a vessel is not chattel paper. When a transaction is evidenced both by such a security agreement or a lease and by an instrument or a series of instruments, the group of writings taken together constitutes chattel paper;

(c) "Collateral" means the property subject to a security interest, and includes accounts and chattel paper which have been sold;

(d) "Debtor" means the person who owes payment or other performance of the obligation secured, whether or not he owns or has rights in the collateral, and includes the seller of accounts or chattel paper. Where the debtor and the owner of the collateral are not the same person, the term "debtor" means the owner of the collateral in any provision of the Article dealing with the collateral, the obligor in any provision dealing with the obligation, and may include both where the context so requires;

(e) "Deposit account" means a demand, time, savings, passbook or like account maintained with a bank, savings and loan association, credit union or like organization, other than an account evidenced by a certificate of deposit;

(f) "Document" means the document of title as defined in the general definitions of Article 1 (Section 1-201), and a receipt of the kind described in subsection (2) of Section 7-201;

(g) "Encumbrance" includes real estate

mortgages and other liens on real estate and all other rights in real estate that are not ownership interests;

(h) "Goods" includes all things which are movable at the time the security interest attaches or which are fixtures (Section 9-313), but does not include money, documents, instruments, accounts, chattel paper, general intangibles, or minerals or the like (including oil and gas) before extraction. "Goods" also includes standing timber which is to be cut and removed under a conveyance or contract for sale, the unborn young of animals, and growing crops;

(i) "Instrument" means a negotiable instrument (defined in Section 3-104), or a security (defined in Section 8-102) or any other writing which evidences a right to the payment of money and is not itself a security agreement or lease and is of a type which is in ordinary course of business transferred by delivery with any necessary indorsement or assignment;

(j) "Mortgage" means a consensual interest created by a real estate mortgage, a trust deed on real estate, or the like;

(k) An advance is made "pursuant to commitment" if the secured party has bound himself to make it, whether or not a subsequent event of default or other event not within his control has relieved or may relieve him from his obligation;

(l) "Security agreement" means an agreement which creates or provides for a security interest;

(m) "Secured party" means a lender, seller or other person in whose favor there is a security interest, including a person to whom accounts or chattel paper have been sold. When the holders of obligations issued under an indenture of trust, equipment trust agreement or the like are represented by a trustee or other person, the representative is the secured party;

(n) "Transmitting utility" means any person primarily engaged in the railroad, street railway or trolley bus business, the electric or electronics communications transmission business, the transmission of goods by pipeline, or the transmission or the production and transmission of electricity, steam, gas or water, or the provi-

sion of sewer service.

(2) Other definitions applying to this Article and the sections in which they appear are:

"Account". Section 9-106.
"Attach". Section 9-203.
"Construction mortgage". Section 9-313(1).
"Consumer goods". Section 9-109(1).
"Equipment". Section 9-109(2).
"Farm products". Section 9-109(3).
"Fixture". Section 9-313(1).
"Fixture filing". Section 9-313(1).
"General intangibles". Section 9-106.
"Inventory". Section 9-109(4).
"Lien creditor". Section 9-301(3).
"Proceeds". Section 9-306(1).
"Purchase money security interest". Section 9-107.
"United States". Section 9-103.

(3) The following definitions in other Articles apply to this Article:

"Check". Section 3-104.
"Contract for sale". Section 2-106.
"Holder in due course". Section 3-302.
"Note". Section 3-104.
"Sale". Section 2-106.

(4) In addition Article 1 contains general definitions and principles of construction and interpretation applicable throughout this Article.

Section 9-106. Definitions: "Account"; "General Intangibles." "Account" means any right to payment for goods sold or leased or for services rendered which is not evidenced by an instrument or chattel paper, whether or not it has been earned by performance. "General intangibles" means any personal property (including things in action) other than goods, accounts, chattel paper, documents, instruments, and money. All rights to payment earned or unearned under a charter or other contract involving the use or hire of a vessel and all rights incident to the charter or contract are accounts.

Section 9-107. Definitions: "Purchase Money Security Interest." A security interest is a "purchase money security interest" to the extent that it is

(a) taken or retained by the seller of the collateral to secure all or part of its price; or

(b) taken by a person who by making advances or incurring an obligation gives value to enable the debtor to acquire rights in or the use of collateral if such value is in fact so used.

Section 9-108. When After-Acquired Collateral Not Security for Antecedent Debt. Where a secured party makes an advance, incurs an obligation, releases a perfected security interest, or otherwise gives new value which is to be secured in whole or in part by after-acquired property his security interest in the after-acquired collateral shall be deemed to be taken for new value and not as security for an antecedent debt if the debtor acquired his rights in such collateral either in the ordinary course of his business or under a contract of purchase made pursuant to the security agreement within a reasonable time after new value is given.

Section 9-109. Classification of Goods; "Consumer Goods"; "Equipment"; "Farm Products"; "Inventory." Goods are

(1) "consumer goods" if they are used or bought for use primarily for personal, family or household purposes;

(2) "equipment" if they are used or bought for use primarily in business (including farming or a profession) or by a debtor who is a non-profit organization or a governmental subdivision or agency or if the goods are not included in the definitions of inventory, farm products or consumer goods;

(3) "farm products" if they are crops or livestock or supplies used or produced in farming operations or if they are products or crops or livestock in their unmanufactured states (such as ginned cotton, wool-clip, maple syrup, milk and eggs), and if they are in the possession of a debtor engaged in raising, fattening, grazing or other farming operations. If goods are farm products they are neither equipment nor inventory;

(4) "inventory" if they are held by a person who holds them for sale or lease or to be furnished under contracts of service or if he has so furnished them, or if they are raw materials, work in process or materials used or consumed in a business. Inventory of a person is not to be classified as his equipment.

Section 9-110. Sufficiency of Description. For the purposes of this Article any description of personal property or real estate is sufficient whether or not it is specific if it reasonably identifies what is described.

Section 9-111. Applicability of Bulk Transfer Laws. The creation of a security interest is not a bulk transfer under Article 6 (see Section 6-103).

Section 9-112. Where Collateral is Not Owned by Debtor. Unless otherwise agreed, when a secured party knows that collateral is owned by a person who is not the debtor, the owner of the collateral is entitled to receive from the secured party any surplus under Section 9-502(2) or under Section 9-504(1), and is not liable for the debt or for any deficiency after resale, and he has the same right as the debtor

(a) to receive statements under Section 9-208;

(b) to receive notice of and to object to a secured party's proposal to retain the collateral in satisfaction of the indebtedness under Section 9-505;

(c) to redeem the collateral under Section 9-506;

(d) to obtain injunctive or other relief under Section 9-507(1); and

(e) to recover losses caused to him under Section 9-208(2).

Section 9-113. Security Interests Arising Under Article on Sales. A security interest arising solely under the Article on Sales (Article 2) is subject to the provisions of this Article except that to the extent that and so long as the debtor does not have or does not lawfully obtain possession of the goods

(a) no security agreement is necessary to make the security interest enforceable; and

(b) no filing is required to perfect the security interest; and

(c) the rights of the secured party on default by the debtor are governed by the Article on Sales (Article 2).

Section 9-114. Consignment.

(1) A person who delivers goods under a consignment which is not a security interest and who would be required to file under this Article by paragraph (3) (c) of Section 2-326 has priority over a secured party who is or becomes a creditor of the consignee and who would have a perfected security interest in the goods if they were the property of the consignee, and also has priority with respect to identifiable cash proceeds received on or before delivery of the goods to a buyer, if

(a) the consignor complies with the filing provision of the Article on Sales with respect to consignments (paragraph (3) (c) of Section 2-326) before the consignee receives possession of the goods;

and

(b) the consignor gives notification in writing to the holder of the security interest if the holder has filed a financing statement covering the same types of goods before the date of the filing made by the consignor; and

(c) the holder of the security interest receives the notification within five years before the consignee receives possession of the goods; and

(d) the notification states that the con-

signor expects to deliver goods on consignment to the consignee, describing the goods by item or type.

(2) In the case of a consignment which is not a security interest and in which the requirements of the preceding subsection have not been met, a person who delivers goods to another is subordinate to a person who would have a perfected security interest in the goods if they were the property of the debtor.

PART 2

VALIDITY OF SECURITY AGREEMENT AND RIGHTS OF PARTIES THERETO

Section 9-201. General Validity of Security Agreement. Except as otherwise provided by this Act a security agreement is effective according to its terms between the parties, against purchasers of the collateral and against creditors. Nothing in this Article validates any charge or practice illegal under any statute or regulation thereunder governing usury, small loans, retail installment sales, or the like, or extends the application of any such statute or regulation to any transaction not otherwise subject thereto.

Section 9-202. Title to Collateral Immaterial. Each provision of this Article with regard to rights, obligations and remedies applies whether title to collateral is in the secured party or in the debtor.

Section 9-203. Attachment and Enforceability of Security Interest; Proceeds; Formal Requisites.

(1) Subject to the provisions of Section 4-208 on the security interest of a collecting bank and Section 9-113 on a security interest arising under the Article on Sales, a security interest is not enforceable against the debtor or third parties with respect to the collateral and does not attach unless

(a) the collateral is in the possession of the secured party pursuant to agreement, or the debtor has signed a security agreement which contains a description of the collateral and in addition, when the security interest covers crops growing or to be grown or timber to be cut, a description of the land concerned; and

(b) value has been given; and

(c) the debtor has rights in the collateral.

(2) A security interest attaches when it

becomes enforceable against the debtor with respect to the collateral. Attachment occurs as soon as all of the events specified in subsection (1) have taken place unless explicit agreement postpones the time of attaching.

(3) Unless otherwise agreed a security agreement gives the secured party the rights to proceeds provided by Section 9-306.

(4) A transaction, although subject to this Article, is also subject to ....*, and in the case of conflict between the provisions of this Article and any such statute, the provisions of such statute control. Failure to comply with any applicable statute has only the effect which is specified therein.

Section 9-204. After-Acquired Property; Future Advances.

(1) Except as provided in subsection (2), a security agreement may provide that any or all obligations covered by the security agreement are to be secured by after-acquired collateral.

(2) No security interest attaches under an after-acquired property clause to consumer goods other than accessions (Section 9-314) when given as additional security unless the debtor acquires rights in them within ten days after the secured party gives value.

(3) Obligations covered by a security agreement may include future advances or other value whether or not the advances or value are given pursuant to commitment (subsection (1) of Section 9-105).

Section 9-205. Use or Disposition of Collateral Without Accounting Permissible. A security interest is not invalid or fraudulent against creditors by reason of liberty in the debtor to use, commingle or dispose of all or part of the collateral (including returned or repossessed goods) or to collect or compromise accounts or chattel paper, or to accept the return of goods or make repossessions, or to use, commingle or dispose of proceeds, or by reason of the failure of the secured party to require the debtor to account for proceeds or replace collateral. This section does not relax the requirements of possession where perfection of a security interest depends upon possession of the collateral by the secured party or by a bailee.

Section 9-206. Agreement Not to Assert Defenses Against Assignee; Modification of Sales Warranties Where Security Agreement Exists.

(1) Subject to any statute or decision which establishes a different rule for buyers or lessees of consumer goods an agreement by a buyer or lessee that he will not assert against an assignee any claim or defense which he may have against the seller or lessor is enforceable by an assignee who takes his assignment for value, in good faith and without notice of a claim or defense, except as to defenses of a type which may be asserted against a holder in due course of a negotiable instrument under the Article on Commercial Paper (Article 3). A buyer who as part of one transaction signs both a negotiable instrument and a security agreement makes such an agreement.

(2) When a seller retains a purchase money security interest in goods the Article on Sales (Article 2) governs the sale and any disclaimer, limitation or modification of the seller's warranties.

Section 9-207. Rights and Duties When Collateral Is In Secured Party's Possession.

(1) A secured party must use reasonable care in the custody and preservation of collateral in his possession. In the case of an instrument or chattel paper reasonable care includes taking necessary steps to preserve rights against prior parties unless otherwise agreed.

(2) Unless otherwise agreed, when collateral is in the secured party's possession

(a) reasonable expenses (including the cost of any insurance and payment of taxes or other charges) incurred in the custody, preservation, use or operation of the collateral are chargeable to the debtor and are secured by the collateral;

(b) the risk of accidental loss or damage

is on the debtor to the extent of any deficiency in any effective insurance coverage;

(c) the secured party may hold as additional security any increase or profits (except money) received from the collateral, but money so received, unless remitted to the debtor, shall be applied in reduction of the secured obligation;

(d) the secured party must keep the collateral identifiable but fungible collateral may be commingled;

(e) the secured party may repledge the collateral upon terms which do not impair the debtor's right to redeem it.

(3) A secured party is liable for any loss caused by his failure to meet any obligation imposed by the preceding subsections but does not lose his security interest.

(4) A secured party may use or operate the collateral for the purpose of preserving the collateral or its value or pursuant to the order of a court of appropriate jurisdiction or, except in the case of consumer goods, in the manner and to the extent provided in the security agreement.

Section 9-208. Request for Statement of Account or List of Collateral.

(1) A debtor may sign a statement indicating what he believes to be the aggregate amount of unpaid indebtedness as of a specified date and may send it to the secured party with a request that the statement be approved or corrected and returned to the debtor. When the security agreement or any other record kept by the secured party identifies the collateral a debtor may similarly request the secured party to approve or correct a list of the collateral.

(2) The secured party must comply with such a request within two weeks after receipt by sending a written correction or approval. If the secured party claims a security interest in all of a particular type of collateral owned by the debtor he may indicate that fact in his reply and need not approve or correct an itemized list of such collateral. If the secured party without reasonable excuse fails to comply he is liable for any loss caused to the debtor thereby; and if the debtor has properly included in his request a good faith statement of the obligation or a list of the collateral or both the secured party may claim a security in-

terest only as shown in the statement against persons misled by his failure to comply. If he no longer has an interest in the obligation or collateral at the time the request is received he must disclose the name and address of any successor in interest known to him and he is liable for any loss caused to the debtor as a result of failure to disclose.

A successor in interest is not subject to this section until a request is received by him. (3) A debtor is entitled to such a statement once every six months without charge. The secured party may require payment of a charge not exceeding $10 for each additional statement furnished.

PART 3

RIGHTS OF THIRD PARTIES; PERFECTED AND UNPERFECTED SECURITY INTERESTS; RULES OF PRIORITY

Section 9-301. Persons Who Take Priority Over Unperfected Security Interests; Rights of "Lien Creditor."

(1) Except as otherwise provided in subsection (2), an unperfected security interest is subordinate to the rights of

(a) persons entitled to priority under Section 9-312;

(b) a person who becomes a lien creditor before the security interest is perfected;

(c) in the case of goods, instruments, documents, and chattel paper, a person who is not a secured party and who is a transferee in bulk or other buyer not in ordinary course of business or is a buyer of farm products in ordinary course of business, to the extent that he gives value and receives delivery of the collateral without knowledge of the security interest and before it is perfected;

(d) in the case of accounts and general intangibles, a person who is not a secured party and who is a transferee to the extent that he gives value without knowledge of the security interest and before it is perfected.

(2) If the secured party files with respect to a purchase money security interest before or within ten days after the debtor receives possession of the collateral, he takes priority over the rights of a transferee in bulk or of a lien creditor which arise between the time the security interest attaches and the time of filing.

(3) A "lien creditor" means a creditor who has acquired a lien on the property involved by attachment, levy or the like and includes an assignee for benefit of creditors from the time of assignment, and a trustee in bankruptcy from the date of filing of the petition or a receiver in equity from the time of appointment.

(4) A person who becomes a lien creditor while a security interest is perfected takes subject to the security interest only to the extent that it secures advances made before he becomes a lien creditor or within 45 days thereafter or made without knowledge of the lien pursuant to a commitment entered into without knowledge of the lien.

Section 9-302. When Filing is Required to Perfect Security Interest; Security Interests to Which Filing Provisions of This Article Do Not Apply.

(1) A financing statement must be filed to perfect all security interests except the following:

(a) a security interest in collateral in possession of the secured party under Section 9-305;

(b) a security interest temporarily perfected in instruments or documents without delivery under Section 9-304 or in proceeds for a 10 day period under Section 9-306;

(c) a security interest created by an assignment of a beneficial interest in a trust or a decedent's estate;

(d) a purchase money security interest in consumer goods; but filing is required for a motor vehicle required to be registered; and fixture filing is required for priority over conflicting interests in fixtures to the extent provided in Section 9-313;

(e) an assignment of accounts which does not alone or in conjunction with other assignments to the same assignee transfer a significant part of the outstanding accounts of the assignor;

(f) a security interest of a collecting bank

(Section 4-208) or arising under the Article on Sales (see Section 9-113) or covered in subsection (3) of this section;

(g) an assignment for the benefit of all the creditors of the transferor, and subsequent transfers by the assignee thereunder.

(2) If a secured party assigns a perfected security interest, no filing under this Article is required in order to continue the perfected status of the security interest against creditors of and transferees from the original debtor.

(3) The filing of a financing statement otherwise required by this Article is not necessary or effective to perfect a security interest in property subject to

(a) a statute or treaty of the United States which provides for a national or international registration or a national or international certificate of title or which specifies a place of filing different from that specified in this Article for filing of the security interest; or

(b) the following statutes of this state; [list any certificate of title statute covering automobiles, trailers, mobile homes, boats, farm tractors, or the like, and any central filing statute*.]; but during any period in which collateral is inventory held for sale by a person who is in the business of selling goods of that kind, the filing provisions of this Article (Part 4) apply to a security interest in that collateral created by him as debtor; or

(c) a certificate of title statute of another jurisdiction under the law of which indication of a security interest on the certificate is required as a condition of perfection (subsection (2) of Section 9-103).

(4) Compliance with a statute or treaty described in subsection (3) is equivalent to the filing of a financing statement under this Article, and a security interest in property subject to the statute or treaty can be perfected only by compliance therewith except as provided in Section 9-103 on multiple state transactions. Duration and renewal of perfection of a security interest perfected by compliance with the statute or treaty are governed by the provisions of the statute or treaty; in other respects the security interest is subject to this Article.

Section 9-303. When Security Interest Is Perfected; Continuity of Perfection.

(1) A security interest is perfected when it has attached and when all of the applicable steps required for perfection have been taken. Such steps are specified in Sections 9-302, 9-304, 9-305 and 9-306. If such steps are taken before the security interest attaches, it is perfected at the time when it attaches.

(2) If a security interest is originally perfected in any way permitted under this Article and is subsequently perfected in some other way under this Article, without an intermediate period when it was unperfected, the security interest shall be deemed to be perfected continuously for the purposes of this Article.

Section 9-304. Perfection of Security Interest in Instruments, Documents, and Goods Covered by Documents; Perfection by Permissive Filing; Temporary Perfection Without Filing or Transfer of Possession.

(1) A security interest in chattel paper or negotiable documents may be perfected by filing. A security interest in money or instruments (other than instruments which constitute part of chattel paper) can be perfected only by the secured party's taking possession, except as provided in subsections (4) and (5) of this section and subsections (2) and (3) of Section 9-306 on proceeds.

(2) During the period that goods are in the possession of the issuer of a negotiable document therefor, a security interest in the goods is perfected by perfecting a security interest in the document, and any security interest in the goods otherwise perfected during such period is subject thereto.

(3) A security interest in goods in the possession of a bailee other than one who has issued a negotiable document therefor is perfected by issuance of a document in the name of the secured party or by the bailee's receipt of notification of the secured party's interest or by filing as to the goods.

(4) A security interest in instruments or negotiable documents is perfected without filing or the taking of possession for a period of 21 days from the time it attaches to the extent that it arises for new value given under a written security agreement.

(5) A security interest remains perfected for

a period of 21 days without filing where a secured party having a perfected security interest in an instrument, a negotiable document or goods in possession of a bailee other than one who has issued a negotiable document therefor

(a) makes available to the debtor the goods or documents representing the goods for the purpose of ultimate sale or exchange or for the purpose of loading, unloading, storing, shipping, transshipping, manufacturing, processing or otherwise dealing with them in a manner preliminary to their sale or exchange, but priority between conflicting security interests in the goods is subject to subsection (3) of Section 9-312; or

(b) delivers the instrument to the debtor for the purpose of ultimate sale or exchange or of presentation, collection, renewal or registration of transfer.

(6) After the 21 day period in subsections (4) and (5) perfection depends upon compliance with applicable provisions of this Article.

Section 9-305. When Possession by Secured Party Perfects Security Interest Without Filing. A security interest in letters of credit and advices of credit (subsection (2) (a) of Section 5-116), goods, instruments, money, negotiable documents or chattel paper may be perfected by the secured party's taking possession of the collateral. If such collateral other than goods covered by a negotiable document is held by a bailee, the secured party is deemed to have possession from the time the bailee receives notification of the secured party's interest. A security interest is perfected by possession from the time possession is taken without relation back and continues only so long as possession is retained, unless otherwise specified in this Article. The security interest may be otherwise perfected as provided in this Article before or after the period of possession by the secured party.

Section 9-306. "Proceeds"; Secured Party's Rights on Disposition of Collateral.

(1) "Proceeds" includes whatever is received upon the sale, exchange, collection or other disposition of collateral or proceeds. Insurance payable by reason of loss or damage to the collateral is proceeds, except to the extent that it is payable to a person other than a party to the security agreement. Money, checks, deposit accounts, and the like are "cash proceeds." All other proceeds are "non-cash proceeds."

(2) Except where this Article otherwise provides, a security interest continues in collateral notwithstanding sale, exchange or other disposition thereof unless the disposition was authorized by the secured party in the security agreement or otherwise, and also continues in any identifiable proceeds including collections received by the debtor.

(3) The security interest in proceeds is a continuously perfected security interest if the interest in the original collateral was perfected but it ceases to be a perfected security interest and becomes unperfected ten days after receipt of the proceeds by the debtor unless

(a) a filed financing statement covers the original collateral and the proceeds are collateral in which a security interest may be perfected by filing in the office or offices where the financing statement has been filed and, if the proceeds are acquired with cash proceeds, the description of collateral in the financing statement indicates the types of property constituting the proceeds; or

(b) a filed financing statement covers the original collateral and the proceeds are identifiable cash proceeds; or

(c) the security interest in the proceeds is perfected before the expiration of the ten day period.

Except as provided in this section, a security interest in proceeds can be perfected only by the methods or under the circumstances permitted in this Article for original collateral of the same type.

(4) In the event of insolvency proceedings instituted by or against a debtor, a secured party with a perfected security interest in proceeds has a perfected security interest only in the following proceeds:

(a) in identifiable non-cash proceeds and in separate deposit accounts containing only proceeds;

(b) in identifiable cash proceeds in the form of money which is neither commingled with other money nor deposited in a deposit account prior to the insolvency proceedings;

(c) in identifiable cash proceeds in the form of checks and the like which are not deposited in a deposit account prior to the insolvency proceedings; and

(d) in all cash and deposit accounts of the debtor in which proceeds have been commingled with other funds, but the perfected security interest under this paragraph (d) is

(i) subject to any right to set-off; and
(ii) limited to an amount not greater than the amount of any cash proceeds received by the debtor within ten days before the institution of the insolvency proceedings less the sum of (I) the payments to the secured party on account of cash proceeds received by the debtor during such period and (II) the cash proceeds received by the debtor during such period to which the secured party is entitled under paragraphs (a) through (c) of this subsection (4).

(5) If a sale of goods results in an account or chattel paper which is transferred by the seller to a secured party, and if the goods are returned to or are repossessed by the seller or the secured party, the following rules determine priorities:

(a) If the goods were collateral at the time of sale, for an indebtedness of the seller which is still unpaid, the original security interest attaches again to the goods and continues as a perfected security interest if it was perfected at the time when the goods were sold. If the security interest was originally perfected by a filing which is still effective, nothing further is required to continue the perfected status; in any other case, the secured party must take possession of the returned or repossessed goods or must file.

(b) An unpaid transferee of the chattel paper has a security interest in the goods against the transferor. Such security interest is prior to a security interest asserted under paragraph (a) to the extent that the transferee of the chattel paper was entitled to priority under Section 9-308.

(c) An unpaid transferee to the account has a security interest in the goods against the transferor. Such security interest is subordinate to a security interest asserted under paragraph (a).

(d) A security interest of an unpaid transferee asserted under paragraph (b) or (c) must be perfected for protection against creditors of the transferor and purchasers of the returned or repossessed goods.

Section 9-307. Protection of Buyers of Goods.

(1) A buyer in ordinary course of business (subsection (9) of Section 1-201) other than a person buying farm products from a person engaged in farming operations takes free of a security interest created by his seller even though the security interest is perfected and even though the buyer knows of its existence.

(2) In the case of consumer goods, a buyer takes free of a security interest even though perfected if he buys without knowledge of the security interest, for value and for his own personal, family or household purposes unless prior to the purchase the secured party has filed a financing statement covering such goods.

(3) A buyer other than a buyer in ordinary course of business (subsection (1) of this section) takes free of a security interest to the extent that it secures future advances made after the secured party acquires knowledge of the purchase, or more than 45 days after the purchase, whichever first occurs, unless made pursuant to a commitment entered into without knowledge of the purchase and before the expiration of the 45 day period.

Section 9-308. Purchase of Chattel Paper and Instruments.

A purchaser of chattel paper or an instrument who gives new value and takes possession of it in the ordinary course of his business has priority over a security interest in the chattel paper or instrument

(a) which is perfected under Section 9-304 (permissive filing and temporary perfection) or under Section 9-306 (perfection as to proceeds) if he acts without knowledge that the specific paper or instrument is subject to a security interest; or

(b) which is claimed merely as proceeds of inventory subject to a security interest (Section 9-306) even though he knows that the specific paper or instrument is subject to the security interest.

Section 9-309. Protection of Purchasers of Instruments and Documents. Nothing in this Article limits the rights of a holder in due course of a negotiable instrument (Section 3-302) or a holder to whom a negotiable document of title has been duly negotiated (Section 7-501) or a bona fide purchaser of a security (Section 8-301) and such holders or purchasers take priority over an earlier security interest even though perfected. Filing under this Article does not constitute notice of the security interest to such holders or purchasers.

Section 9-310. Priority of Certain Liens Arising by Operation of Law. When a person in the ordinary course of his business furnishes services or materials with respect to goods subject to a security interest, a lien upon goods in the possession of such person given by statute or rule of law for such materials or services takes priority over a perfected security interest unless the lien is statutory and the statute expressly provides otherwise.

Section 9-311. Alienability of Debtor's Rights: Judicial Process. The debtor's rights in collateral may be voluntarily or involuntarily transferred (by way of sale, creation of a security interest, attachment, levy, garnishment or other judicial process) notwithstanding a provision in the security agreement prohibiting any transfer or making the transfer constitute a default.

Section 9-312. Priorities Among Conflicting Security Interests in the Same Collateral.

(1) The rules of priority stated in other sections of this Part and in the following sections shall govern when applicable: Section 4-208 with respect to the security interests of collecting banks in items being collected, accompanying documents and proceeds; Section 9-103 on security interests related to other jurisdictions; Section 9-114 on consignments.

(2) A perfected security interest in crops for new value given to enable the debtor to produce the crops during the production season and given not more than three months before the crops become growing crops by planting or otherwise takes priority over an earlier perfected security interest to the extent that such earlier interest secured obligations due more than six months before the crops become growing crops by planting or otherwise, even though the person giving new value has knowledge of the earlier security interest.

(3) A perfected purchase money security interest in inventory has priority over a conflicting security interest in the same inventory and also has priority in identifiable cash proceeds received on or before the delivery of the inventory to a buyer if

(a) the purchase money security interest is perfected at the time the debtor receives possession of the inventory; and

(b) the purchase money secured party gives notification in writing to the holder of the conflicting security interest if the holder had filed a financing statement covering the same types of inventory (i) before the date of the filing made by the purchase money secured party, or (ii) before the beginning of the 21 day period where the purchase money security interest is temporarily perfected without filing or possession (subsection (5) of Section 9-304); and

(c) the holder of the conflicting security interest receives the notification within five years before the debtor receives possession of the inventory; and

(d) the notification states that the person giving the notice has or expects to acquire a purchase money security interest in inventory of the debtor, describing such inventory by item or type.

(4) A purchase money security interest in collateral other than inventory has priority over a conflicting security interest in the same collateral or its proceeds if the purchase money security interest is perfected at the time the debtor receives possession of the collateral or within ten days thereafter.

(5) In all cases not governed by other rules stated in this section (including cases of purchase money security interests which do not qualify for the special priorities set forth in subsections (3) and (4) of this section), priority between conflicting security interests in the same collateral shall be determined according to the following rules:

(a) Conflicting security interests rank according to priority in time of filing or perfection. Priority dates from the time a filing is first made covering the collateral or the time the security interest is first perfected, whichever is earlier, provided that there is no period thereafter when there is neither filing nor perfection.

(b) So long as conflicting security interests are unperfected, the first to attach has priority.

(6) For the purposes of subsection (5) a date of filing or perfection as to collateral is also a date of filing or perfection as to proceeds.

(7) If future advances are made while a security interest is perfected by filing or the taking of possession, the security interest has the same priority for the purposes of subsection (5) with respect to the future advances as it does with respect to the first advance. If a commitment is made before or while the security interest is so perfected, the security interest has the same priority with respect to advances made pursuant thereto. In other cases a perfected security interest has priority from the date the advance is made.

Section 9-313. Priority of Security Interests in Fixtures.

(1) In this section and in the provisions of Part 4 of this Article referring to fixture filing, unless the context otherwise requires

(a) goods are "fixtures" when they become so related to particular real estate that an interest in them arises under real estate law

(b) a "fixture filing" is the filing in the office where a mortgage on the real estate would be filed or recorded of a financing statement covering goods which are or are to become fixtures and conforming to the requirements of subsection (5) of Section 9-402

(c) a mortgage is a "construction mortgage" to the extent that it secures an obligation incurred for the construction of an improvement on land including the acquisition cost of the land, if the recorded writing so indicates.

(2) A security interest under this Article may be created in goods which are fixtures or may continue in goods which become fixtures, but no security interest exists under this Article in ordinary building materials incorporated into an improvement on land.

(3) This Article does not prevent creation of an encumbrance upon fixtures pursuant to real estate law.

(4) A perfected security interest in fixtures has priority over the conflicting interest of an encumbrancer or owner of the real estate where

(a) the security interest is a purchase money security interest, the interest of the encumbrancer or owner arises before the goods become fixtures, the security interest is perfected by a fixture filing before the goods become fixtures or within ten days thereafter, and the debtor has an interest of record in the real estate or is in possession of the real estate; or

(b) the security interest is perfected by a fixture filing before the interest of the encumbrancer or owner is of record, the security interest has priority over any conflicting interest of a predecessor in title of the encumbrancer or owner, and the debtor has an interest of record in the real estate or is in possession of the real estate; or

(c) the fixtures are readily removable factory or office machines or readily removable replacements of domestic appliances which are consumer goods, and before the goods become fixtures the security interest is perfected by any method permitted by this Article; or

(d) the conflicting interest is a lien on the real estate obtained by legal or equitable proceedings after the security interest was perfected by any method permitted by this Article.

(5) A security interest in fixtures, whether or not perfected, has priority over the conflicting interest of an encumbrancer or owner of the real estate where

(a) the encumbrancer or owner has consented in writing to the security interest or has disclaimed an interest in the goods as fixtures; or

(b) the debtor has a right to remove the goods as against the encumbrancer or owner. If the debtor's right terminates, the priority of the security interest continues for a reasonable time.

(6) Notwithstanding paragraph (a) of subsection (4) but otherwise subject to subsections (4) and (5), a security interest in fixtures is subordinate to a construction

mortgage recorded before the goods become fixtures if the goods become fixtures before the completion of the construction. To the extent that it is given to refinance a construction mortgage, a mortgage has this priority to the same extent as the construction mortgage.

(7) In cases not within the preceding subsections, a security interest in fixtures is subordinate to the conflicting interest of an encumbrancer or owner of the related real estate who is not the debtor.

(8) When the secured party has priority over all owners and encumbrancers of the real estate, he may, on default, subject to the provisions of Part 5, remove his collateral from the real estate but he must reimburse any encumbrancer or owner of the real estate who is not the debtor and who has not otherwise agreed for the cost of repair of any physical injury, but not for any diminution in value of the real estate caused by the absence of the goods removed or by any necessity of replacing them. A person entitled to reimbursement may refuse permission to remove until the secured party gives adequate security for the performance of this obligation.

Section 9-314. Accessions.

(1) A security interest in goods which attaches before they are installed in or affixed to other goods takes priority as to the goods installed or affixed (called in this section "accessions") over the claims of all persons to the whole except as stated in subsection (3) and subject to Section 9-315(1).

(2) A security interest which attaches to goods after they become part of a whole is valid against all persons subsequently acquiring interests in the whole except as stated in subsection (3) but is invalid against any person with an interest in the whole at the time the security interest attaches to the goods who has not in writing consented to the security interest or disclaimed an interest in the goods as part of the whole.

(3) The security interests described in subsections (1) and (2) do not take priority over

(a) a subsequent purchaser for value of any interest in the whole; or

(b) a creditor with a lien on the whole subsequently obtained by judicial proceedings; or

(c) a creditor with a prior perfected security interest in the whole to the extent that he makes subsequent advances

if the subsequent purchase is made, the lien by judicial proceedings obtained or the subsequent advance under the prior perfected security interest is made or contracted for without knowledge of the security interest and before it is perfected. A purchaser of the whole at a foreclosure sale other than the holder of a perfected security interest purchasing at his own foreclosure sale is a subsequent purchaser within this section.

(4) When under subsections (1) or (2) and (3) a secured party has an interest in accessions which has priority over the claims of all persons who have interests in the whole, he may on default subject to the provisions of Part 5 remove his collateral from the whole but he must reimburse any encumbrancer or owner of the whole who is not the debtor and who has not otherwise agreed for the cost of repair of any physical injury but not for any diminution in value of the whole caused by the absence of the goods removed or by any necessity for replacing them. A person entitled to reimbursement may refuse permission to remove until the secured party gives adequate security for the performance of this obligation.

Section 9-315. Priority When Goods Are Commingled or Processed.

(1) If a security interest in goods was perfected and subsequently the goods or a part thereof have become part of a product or mass, the security interest continues in the product or mass if

(a) the goods are so manufactured, processed, assembled or commingled that their identity is lost in the product or mass; or

(b) a financing statement covering the original goods also covers the product into which the goods have been manufactured, processed or assembled.

In a case to which paragraph (b) applies, no separate security interest in that part of the original goods which has been manufactured, processed or assembled into the product may be claimed under Section 9-314.

(2) When under subsection (1) more than

one security interest attaches to the product or mass, they rank equally according to the ratio that the cost of the goods to which each interest originally attached bears to the cost of the total product or mass.

Section 9-316. Priority Subject to Subordination. Nothing in this Article prevents subordination by agreement by any person entitled to priority.

Section 9-317. Secured Party Not Obligated on Contract of Debtor. The mere existence of a security interest or authority given to the debtor to dispose of or use collateral does not impose contract or tort liability upon the secured party for the debtor's acts or omissions.

Section 9-318. Defenses Against Assignee; Modification of Contract After Notification of Assignment; Term Prohibiting Assignment Ineffective; Identification and Proof of Assignment.

(1) Unless an account debtor has made an enforceable agreement not to assert defenses or claims arising out of a sale as provided in Section 9-206 the rights of an assignee are subject to

(a) all the terms of the contract between the account debtor and assignor and any defense or claim arising therefrom; and

(b) any other defense or claim of the account debtor against the assignor which accrues before the account debtor receives notification of the assignment.

(2) So far as the right to payment or a part thereof under an assigned contract has not been fully earned by performance, and notwithstanding notification of the assignment, any modification of or substitution for the contract made in good faith and in accordance with reasonable commercial standards is effective against an assignee unless the account debtor has otherwise agreed but the assignee acquires corresponding rights under the modified or substituted contract. The assignment may provide that such modification or substitution is a breach by the assignor.

(3) The account debtor is authorized to pay the assignor until the account debtor receives notification that the amount due or to become due has been assigned and that payment is to be made to the assignee. A notification which does not reasonably identify the rights assigned is ineffective. If requested by the account debtor, the assignee must seasonably furnish reasonable proof that the assignment has been made and unless he does so the account debtor may pay the assignor.

(4) A term in any contract between an account debtor and an assignor is ineffective if it prohibits assignment of an account or prohibits creation of a security interest in a general intangible for money due or to become due or requires the account debtor's consent to such assignment or security interest.

PART 4

FILING

Section 9-401. Place of Filing; Erroneous Filing; Removal of Collateral.

First Alternative Subsection (1)

(1) The proper place to file in order to perfect a security interest is as follows:

(a) when the collateral is timber to be cut or is minerals or the like (including oil and gas) or accounts subject to subsection (5) of Section 9-103, or when the financing statement is filed as a fixture filing (Section 9-313) and the collateral is goods which are or are to become fixtures, then in the office where a mortgage on the real estate would be filed or recorded;

(b) in all other cases, in the office of the [Secretary of State].

Second Alternative Subsection (1)

(1) The proper place to file in order to perfect a security interest is as follows:

(a) when the collateral is equipment used in farming operations, or farm products, or accounts or general intangibles arising from or relating to the sale of farm products by a farmer, or consumer goods, then in the office of the .... in the county of the debtor's residence or if the debtor is not a resident in this state then in the office of the .... in the county where the goods are kept, and in addition when the collateral is crops growing or to be grown in the office of the .... in the county where the land is located;

(b) when the collateral is timber to be cut or is minerals or the like (including oil and gas) or accounts subject to subsection (5) of Section 9-103, or when the financing statement is filed as a fixture filing (Section 9-313) and the collateral is goods which are or are to become fixtures, then in the office where a mortgage on the real estate would be filed or recorded;

(c) in all other cases, in the office of the [Secretary of State].

Third Alternative Subsection (1)

(1) The proper place to file in order to perfect a security interest is as follows:

(a) when the collateral is equipment used in farming operations, or farm products, or accounts or general intangibles arising from or relating to the sale of farm products by a farmer, or consumer goods, then in the office of the .... in the county of the debtor's residence or if the debtor is not a resident of this state then in the office of the .... in the county where the goods are kept, and in addition when the collateral is crops growing or to be grown in the office of the .... in the county where the land is located;

(b) when the collateral is timber to be cut or is minerals or the like (including oil and gas) or accounts subject to subsection (5) of Section 9-103, or when the financing statement is filed as a fixture filing (Section 9-313) and the collateral is goods which are or are to become fixtures, then in the office where a mortgage on the real estate would be filed or recorded;

(c) in all other cases, in the office of the [Secretary of State] and in addition, if the debtor has a place of business in only one county of this state, also in the office of .... of such county, or, if the debtor has no place of business in this state, but resides in the state, also in the office of .... of the county in which he resides.

NOTE: *One of the three alternatives should be selected as subsection (1).*

(2) A filing which is made in good faith in an improper place or not in all of the places required by this section is nevertheless effective with regard to any collateral as to which the filing complied with the requirements of this Article and is also effective with regard to collateral covered by the financing statement against any person who has knowledge of the contents of such financing statement.

(3) A filing which is made in the proper place in this state continues effective even though the debtor's residence or place of business or the location of the collateral or its use, whichever controlled the original filing, is thereafter changed.

Alternative Subsection (3)

[(3) A filing which is made in the proper county continues effective for four months after a change to another county of the debtor's residence or place of business or the location of the collateral, whichever controlled the original filing. It becomes ineffective thereafter unless a copy of the financing statement signed by the secured party is filed in the new county within said period. The security interest may also be perfected in the new county after the expiration of the four-month period; in such case perfection dates from the time of perfection in the new county. A change in the use of the collateral does not impair the effectiveness of the original filing.]

(4) The rules stated in Section 9-103 determine whether filing is necessary in this state.

(5) Notwithstanding the preceding subsections, and subject to subsection (3) of Section 9-302, the proper place to file in order to perfect a security interest in collateral, including fixtures, of a transmitting utility is the office of the [Secretary of State]. This filing constitutes a fixture filing (Section 9-313) as to the collateral described

therein which is or is to become fixtures.

(6) For the purposes of this section, the residence of an organization is its place of business if it has one or its chief executive office if it has more than one place of business.

Section 9-402. Formal Requisites of Financing Statement; Amendments; Mortgage as Financing Statement.

(1) A financing statement is sufficient if it gives the names of the debtor and the secured party, is signed by the debtor, gives an address of the secured party from which information concerning the security interest may be obtained, gives a mailing address of the debtor and contains a statement indicating the types, or describing the items, of collateral. A financing statement may be filed before the security agreement is made or a security interest otherwise attaches. When the financing statement covers crops growing or to be grown, the statement must also contain a description of the real estate concerned. When the financing statement covers timber to be cut or covers minerals, or the like, (including oil and gas) or accounts subject to subsection (5) of Section 9-103, or when the financial statement is filed as a fixture filing (Section 9-313) and the collateral is goods which are or are to become fixtures, the statement must also comply with subsection (5). A copy of the security agreement is sufficient as a financing statement if it contains the above information and is signed by the debtor. A carbon, photographic or other reproduction of a security agreement or a financing statement is sufficient as a financing statement if the security agreement so provides or if the original has been filed in this state.

(2) A financing statement which otherwise complies with subsection (1) is sufficient when it is signed by the secured party instead of the debtor if it is filed to perfect a security interest in

(a) collateral already subject to a security interest in another jurisdiction when it is brought into this state, or when the debtor's location is changed to this state. Such a financing statement must state that the collateral was brought into this state or that the debtor's location was changed to this state under such circumstances; or

(b) proceeds under Section 9-306 if the security interest in the original collateral was perfected. Such a financing statement must describe the original collateral; or

(c) collateral as to which the filing has lapsed; or

(d) collateral acquired after a change of name, identity or corporate structure of the debtor (subsection (7)).

(3) A form substantially as follows is sufficient to comply with subsection (1):

Name of debtor (or assignor) . . . .
Address . . . .
Name of secured party (or assignee) . . . .
Address . . . .

1. This financing statement covers the following types (or items) of property:
   (Describe) . . . .

2. (If collateral is crops) The above crops are growing or are to be grown on:
   (Describe Real Estate) . . . .

3. (If applicable) The above goods are to become fixtures on*
   (Describe Real Estate) . . . .
   and this financing statement is to be filed [for record] in the real estate records. (If the debtor does not have an interest of record) The name of a record owner is . . . .

4. (If products of collateral are claimed) Products of the collateral are also covered. Signature of Debtor (or Assignor) . . . .
   Signature of Secured Party (or Assignee) . . . .

(use whichever is applicable)

(4) A financing statement may be amended by filing a writing signed by both the debtor and the secured party. An amendment does not extend the period of effectiveness of a financing statement. If any amendment adds collateral, it is effective as to the added collateral only from the filing date of the amendment. In this Article, unless the context otherwise requires, the term "financial statement" means the original financing statement and any amendments.

(5) A financing statement covering timber

---

*Where appropriate substitute either "The above timber is standing on . . . ." or "The above minerals or the like (including oil and gas) or accounts will be financed at the wellhead or minehead of the well or mine located on . . . ."

to be cut or covering minerals or the like (including oil and gas) or accounts subject to subsection (5) of Section 9-103, or a financing statement filed as a fixture filing (Section 9-313) where the debtor is not a transmitting utility, must show that it covers this type of collateral, must recite that it is to be filed [for record] in the real estate records, and the financing statement must contain a description of the real estate [sufficient if it were contained in a mortgage of the real estate to give constructive notice of the mortgage under the law of this state]. If the debtor does not have an interest of record in the real estate, the financing statement must show the name of a record owner.

(6) A mortgage is effective as a financing statement filed as a fixture filing from the date of its recording if

(a) the goods are described in the mortgage by item or type; and

(b) the goods are or are to become fixtures related to the real estate described in the mortgage; and

(c) the mortgage complies with the requirements for a financing statement in this section other than a recital that it is to be filed in the real estate records; and

(d) the mortgage is duly recorded.

No fee with reference to the financing statement is required other than the regular recording and satisfaction fees with respect to the mortgage.

(7) A financing statement sufficiently shows the name of the debtor if it gives the individual, partnership or corporate name of the debtor, whether or not it adds other trade names or names of partners. Where the debtor so changes his name or in the case of an organization its name, identity or corporate structure that a filed financing statement becomes seriously misleading, the filing is not effective to perfect a security interest in collateral acquired by the debtor more than four months after the change, unless a new appropriate financing statement is filed before the expiration of that time. A filed financing statement remains effective with respect to collateral transferred by the debtor even though the secured party knows of or consents to the transfer.

(8) A financing statement substantially complying with the requirements of this section is effective even though it contains minor errors which are not seriously misleading.

Section 9-403. What Constitutes Filing; Duration of Filing; Effect of Lapsed Filing; Duties of Filing Officer.

(1) Presentation for filing of a financing statement and tender of the filing fee or acceptance of the statement by the filing officer constitutes filing under this Article.

(2) Except as provided in subsection (6) a filed financing statement is effective for a period of five years from the date of filing. The effectiveness of a filed financing statement lapses on the expiration of the five year period unless a continuation statement is filed prior to the lapse. If a security interest perfected by filing exists at the time insolvency proceedings are commenced by or against the debtor, the security interest remains perfected until termination of the insolvency proceedings and thereafter for a period of sixty days or until the expiration of the five year period, whichever occurs later. Upon lapse the security interest becomes unperfected, unless it is perfected without filing. If the security interest becomes unperfected upon lapse, it is deemed to have been unperfected as against a person who became a purchaser or lien creditor before lapse.

(3) A continuation statement may be filed by the secured party within six months prior to the expiration of the five year period specified in subsection (2). Any such continuation statement must be signed by the secured party, identify the original statement by file number and state that the original statement is still effective. A continuation statement signed by a person other than the secured party of record must be accompanied by a separate written statement of assignment signed by the secured party of record and complying with subsection (2) of Section 9-405, including payment of the required fee. Upon timely filing of the continuation statement, the effectiveness of the original statement is continued for five years after the last date to which the filing was effective whereupon it lapses in the same manner as provided in subsection (2) unless another continuation statement is filed prior to such lapse. Succeeding continuation statements may be filed in the same

manner to continue the effectiveness of the original statement. Unless a statute on disposition of public records provides otherwise, the filing officer may remove a lapsed statement from the files and destroy it immediately if he has retained a microfilm or other photographic record, or in other cases after one year after the lapse. The filing officer shall so arrange matters by physical annexation of financing statements to continuation statements or other related filings, or by other means, that if he physically destroys the financing statements of a period more than five years past, those which have been continued by a continuation statement or which are still effective under subsection (6) shall be retained.

(4) Except as provided in subsection (7) a filing officer shall mark each statement with a file number and with the date and hour of filing and shall hold the statement or a microfilm or other photographic copy thereof for public inspection. In addition the filing officer shall index the statement according to the name of the debtor and shall note in the index the file number and the address of the debtor given in the statement.

(5) The uniform fee for filing and indexing and for stamping a copy furnished by the secured party to show the date and place of filing for an original financing statement or for a continuation statement shall be $.... if the statement is in the standard form prescribed by the [Secretary of State] and otherwise shall be $....., plus in each case, if the financing statement is subject to subsection (5) of Section 9-402, $..... The uniform fee for each name more than one required to be indexed shall be $..... The secured party may at his option show a trade name for any person and an extra uniform indexing fee of $..... shall be paid with respect thereto.

(6) If the debtor is a transmitting utility (subsection (5) of Section 9-401) and a filed financing statement so states, it is effective until a termination statement is filed. A real estate mortgage which is effective as a fixture filing under subsection (6) of Section 9-402 remains effective as a fixture filing until the mortgage is released or satisfied of record or its effectiveness otherwise terminates as to the real estate.

(7) When a financing statement covers timber to be cut or covers minerals or the like (including oil and gas) or accounts subject to subsection (5) of Section 9-103, or is filed as a fixture filing, [it shall be filed for record and] the filing officer shall index it under the names of the debtor and any owner of record shown on the financing statement in the same fashion as if they were the mortgagors in a mortgage of the real estate described, and, to the extent that the law of this state provides for indexing of mortgages under the name of the mortgagee, under the name of the secured party as if he were the mortgagee thereunder, or where indexing is by description in the same fashion as if the financing statement were a mortgage of the real estate described.

Section 9-404. Termination Statement.

(1) If a financing statement covering consumer goods is filed on or after......., then within one month or within ten days following written demand by the debtor after there is no outstanding secured obligation and no commitment to make advances, incur obligations or otherwise give value, the secured party must file with each filing officer with whom the financing statement was filed, a termination statement to the effect that he no longer claims a security interest under the financing statement, which shall be identified by file number. In other cases whenever there is no outstanding secured obligation and no commitment to make advances, incur obligations or otherwise give value, the secured party must on written demand by the debtor send the debtor, for each filing officer with whom the financing statement was filed, a termination statement to the effect that he no longer claims a security interest under the financing statement, which shall be identified by file number. A termination statement signed by a person other than the secured party of record must be accompanied by a separate written statement of assignment signed by the secured party of record and complying with subsection (2) of Section 9-405, including payment of the required fee. If the affected secured party fails to file such a termination statement within ten days after proper demand therefor, he shall be liable to the debtor for one hundred dollars, and in

addition for any loss caused to the debtor by such failure.

(2) On presentation to the filing officer of such a termination statement he must note it in the index. If he has received the termination statement in duplicate, he shall return one copy of the termination statement to the secured party stamped to show the time of receipt thereof. If the filing officer has a microfilm or other photographic record of the financing statement, and of any related continuation statement, statement of assignment and statement of release, he may remove the originals from the files at any time after receipt of the termination statement, or if he has no such record, he may remove them from the files at any time after one year after receipt of the termination statement.

(3) If the termination statement is in the standard form prescribed by the [Secretary of State], the uniform fee for filing and indexing the termination statement shall be $. . . . . and otherwise shall be $. . . . . , plus in each case an additional fee of $. . . . . for each name more than one against which the termination statement is required to be indexed.

Section 9-405. Assignment of Security Interest; Duties of Filing Officer; Fees.

(1) A financing statement may disclose an assignment of a security interest in the collateral described in the financing statement by indication in the financing statement of the name and address of the assignee or by an assignment itself or a copy thereof on the face or back of the statement. On presentation to the filing officer of such a financing statement the filing officer shall mark the same as provided in Section 9-403(4). The uniform fee for filing, indexing and furnishing filing data for a financing statement so indicating an assignment shall be $. . . . . if the statement is in the standard form prescribed by the [Secretary of State] and otherwise shall be $. . . . . , plus in each case an additional fee of $. . . . . for each name more than one against which the financing statement is required to be indexed.

(2) A secured party may assign of record all or part of his rights under a financing statement by the filing in the place where

the original financing statement was filed of a separate written statement of assignment signed by the secured party of record and setting forth the name of the secured party of record and the debtor, the file number and the date of filing of the financing statement and the name and address of the assignee and containing a description of the collateral assigned. A copy of the assignment is sufficient as a separate statement if it complies with the preceding sentence. On presentation to the filing officer of such a separate statement, the filing officer shall mark such separate statement with the date and hour of the filing. He shall note the assignment on the index of the financing statement, or in the case of a fixture filing, or a filing covering timber to be cut, or covering minerals or the like (including oil and gas) or accounts subject to subsection (5) of Section 9-103, he shall index the assignment under the name of the assignor as grantor and, to the extent that the law of this state provides for indexing the assignment of a mortgage under the name of the assignee, he shall index the assignment of the financing statement under the name of the assignee. The uniform fee for filing, indexing and furnishing filing data about such a separate statement of assignment shall be $. . . . . if the statement is in the standard form prescribed by the [Secretary of State] and otherwise shall be $. . . . . , plus in each case an additional fee of $. . . . . for each name more than one against which the statement of assignment is required to be indexed. Notwithstanding the provisions of this subsection, an assignment of record of a security interest in a fixture contained in a mortgage effective as a fixture filing (subsection (6) of Section 9-402) may be made only by an assignment of the mortgage in the manner provided by the law of the state other than this Act.

(3) After the disclosure of filing of an assignment under this section, the assignee is the secured party of record.

Section 9-406. Release of Collateral; Duties of Filing Officer; Fees. A secured party of record may by his signed statement release all or a part of any collateral described in a filed financing statement. The statement of release is sufficient if it contains a description of the collateral being released, the name and address of the debtor, the name and address of the secured party, and the file number of the financing statement. A statement of release signed by a person other than the secured party of record must be accompanied by a separate written statement of assignment signed by the secured party of record and complying with subsection (2) of Section 9-405, including payment of the required fee. Upon presentation of such a statement of release to the filing officer he shall mark the statement with the hour and date of filing and shall note the same upon the margin of the index of the filing of the financing statement. The uniform fee for filing and noting such a statement of release shall be $. . . . if the statement is in the standard form prescribed by the [Secretary of State] and otherwise shall be $. . . . . , plus in each case an additional fee of $. . . . for each name more than one against which the statement of release is required to be indexed.

[Section 9-407. Information From Filing Officer].

[(1) If the person filing any financing statement, termination statement, statement of assignment, or statement of release, furnishes the filing officer a copy thereof, the filing officer shall upon request note upon the copy the file number and date and hour of the filing of the original and deliver or send the copy to such person.]

[(2) Upon request of any person, the filing officer shall issue his certificate showing whether there is on file on the date and hour stated therein, any presently effective financing statement naming a particular debtor and any statement of assignment thereof and if there is, giving the date and hour of filing of each such statement and the names and addresses of each secured party therein. The uniform fee for such a certificate shall be $. . . . if the request for the certificate is in the standard form prescribed by the [Secretary of State] and otherwise shall be $. . . . . Upon request the filing officer shall furnish a copy of any filed financing statement or statement of assignment for a uniform fee of $. . . . per page.]

Section 9-408. Financing Statements Covering Consigned or Leased Goods. A consignor or lessor of goods may file a financing statement using the terms "consignor," "consignee," "lessor," "lessee" or the like instead of the terms specified in Section 9-402. The provisions of this Part shall apply as appropriate to such a financing statement but its filing shall not of itself be a factor in determining whether or not the consignment or lease is intended as security (Section 1-201(37)). However, if it is determined for other reasons that the consignment or lease is so intended, a security interest of the consignor or lessor which attaches to the consigned or leased goods is perfected by such filing.

Added in 1972.

PART 5

DEFAULT

Section 9-501. Default; Procedure When Security Agreement Covers Both Real and Personal Property.

(1) When a debtor is in default under a security agreement, a secured party has the rights and remedies provided in this Part and except as limited by subsection (3) those provided in the security agreement. He may reduce his claim to judgment, foreclose or otherwise enforce the security interest by any available judicial procedure. If the collateral is documents the secured party may proceed either as to the documents or as to the goods covered thereby. A secured party in possession has the rights, remedies and duties provided in Section 9-207. The rights and remedies referred to in this subsection are cumulative.

(2) After default, the debtor has the rights and remedies provided in this Part, those provided in the security agreement and those provided in Section 9-207.

(3) To the extent that they give rights to the debtor and impose duties on the secured party, the rules stated in the subsections referred to below may not be waived or varied except as provided with respect to compulsory disposition of collateral (subsection (3) of Section 9-504 and Section 9-505) and with respect to redemption of collateral

(Section 9-506) but the parties may by agreement determine the standards by which the fulfillment of these rights and duties is to be measured if such standards are not manifestly unreasonable:

(a) subsection (2) of Section 9-502 and subsection (2) of Section 9-504 insofar as they require accounting for surplus proceeds of collateral;

(b) subsection (3) of Section 9-504 and subsection (1) of Section 9-505 which deal with disposition of collateral;

(c) subsection (2) of Section 9-505 which deals with acceptance of collateral as discharge of obligation;

(d) Section 9-506 which deals with redemption of collateral; and

(e) subsection (1) of Section 9-507 which deals with the secured party's liability for failure to comply with this Part.

(4) If the security agreement covers both real and personal property, the secured party may proceed under this Part as to the personal property or he may proceed as to both the real and the personal property in accordance with his rights and remedies in respect of the real property in which case the provisions of this Part do not apply.

(5) When a secured party has reduced his claim to judgment the lien of any levy which may be made upon his collateral by virtue of any execution based upon the judgment shall relate back to the date of the perfection of the security interest in such collateral. A judicial sale, pursuant to such execution, is a foreclosure of the security interest by judicial procedure within the meaning of this section, and the secured party may purchase at the sale and thereafter hold the collateral free of any other requirements of this Article.

Section 9-502. Collection Rights of Secured Party.

(1) When so agreed and in any event on default the secured party is entitled to notify an account debtor or the obligor on an instrument to make payment to him whether or not the assignor was theretofore making collections on the collateral, and also to take control of any proceeds to which he is entitled under Section 9-306.

(2) A secured party who by agreement is entitled to charge back uncollected collateral or otherwise to full or limited recourse against the debtor and who undertakes to collect from the account debtors or obligors must proceed in a commercially reasonable manner and may deduct his reasonable expenses of realization from the collections. If the security agreement secures an indebtedness, the secured party must account to the debtor for any surplus, and unless otherwise agreed, the debtor is liable for any deficiency. But, if the underlying transaction was a sale of accounts or chattel paper, the debtor is entitled to any surplus or is liable for any deficiency only if the security agreement so provides.

Section 9-503. Secured Party's Right to Take Possession After Default. Unless otherwise agreed a secured party has on default the right to take possession of the collateral. In taking possession a secured party may proceed without judicial process if this can be done without breach of the peace or may proceed by action. If the security agreement so provides the secured party may require the debtor to assemble the collateral and make it available to the secured party at a place to be designated by the secured party which is reasonably convenient to both parties. Without removal a secured party may render equipment unusable, and may dispose of collateral on the debtor's premises under Section 9-504.

Section 9-504. Secured Party's Right to Dispose of Collateral After Default; Effect of Disposition.

(1) A secured party after default may sell, lease or otherwise dispose of any or all of the collateral in its then condition or following any commercially reasonable preparation or processing. Any sale of goods is subject to the Article on Sales (Article 2). The proceeds of disposition shall be applied in the order following to

(a) the reasonable expenses of retaking, holding, preparing for sale or lease, selling, leasing and the like and, to the extent provided for in the agreement and not prohibited by law, the reasonable attorneys' fees and legal expenses incurred by the secured party;

(b) the satisfaction of indebtedness secured by the security interest under which the disposition is made;

(c) the satisfaction of indebtedness secured by any subordinate security interest in the collateral if written notification of demand therefor is received before distribution of the proceeds is completed. If requested by the secured party, the holder of a subordinate security interest must seasonably furnish reasonable proof of his interest, and unless he does so, the secured party need not comply with his demand.

(2) If the security interest secured an indebtedness, the secured party must account to the debtor for any surplus, and, unless otherwise agreed, the debtor is liable for any deficiency. But if the underlying transaction was a sale of accounts or chattel paper, the debtor is entitled to any surplus or is liable for any deficiency only if the security agreement so provides.

(3) Disposition of the collateral may be by public or private proceedings and may be made by way of one or more contracts. Sale or other disposition may be as a unit or in parcels and at any time and place and on any terms but every aspect of the disposition including the method, manner, time, place and terms must be commercially reasonable. Unless collateral is perishable or threatens to decline speedily in value or is of a type customarily sold on a recognized market, reasonable notification of the time and place of any public sale or reasonable notification of the time after which any private sale or other intended disposition is to be made shall be sent by the secured party to the debtor, if he has not signed after default a statement renouncing or modifying his right to notification of sale. In the case of consumer goods no other notification need be sent. In other cases notification shall be sent to any other secured party from whom the secured party has received (before sending his notification to the debtor or before the debtor's renunciation of his rights) written notice of a claim of an interest in the collateral. The secured party may buy at any public sale and if the collateral is of a type customarily sold in a recognized market or is of a type which is the subject of widely distributed standard price quotations he may

buy at private sale.

(4) When collateral is disposed of by a secured party after default, the disposition transfers to a purchaser for value all of the debtor's rights therein, discharges the security interest under which it is made and any security interest or lien subordinate or lien subordinate thereto. The purchaser takes free of all such rights and interests even though the secured party fails to comply with the requirements of this Part or of any judicial proceedings.

(a) in the case of a public sale, if the purchaser has no knowledge of any defects in the sale and if he does not buy in collusion with the secured party, other bidders or the person conducting the sale; or

(b) in any other case, if the purchaser acts in good faith.

(5) A person who is liable to a secured party under a guaranty, indorsement, repurchase agreement or the like and who receives a transfer of collateral from the secured party or is subrogated to his rights has thereafter the rights and duties of the secured party. Such a transfer of collateral is not a sale or disposition of the collateral under this Article.

Section 9-505. Compulsory Disposition of Collateral; Acceptance of the Collateral as Discharge of Obligation.

(1) If the debtor has paid sixty per cent of the cash price in the case of a purchase money security interest in consumer goods, and has not signed after default at statement renouncing or modifying his rights under this Part a secured party who has taken possession of collateral must dispose of it under Section 9-504 and if he fails to do so within ninety days after he takes possession the debtor at his option may recover in conversion or under Section 9-507(1) on secured party's liability.

(2) In any other case involving consumer goods or any other collateral a secured party in possession may, after default, propose to retain the collateral in satisfaction of the obligation. Written notice of such proposal shall be sent to the debtor if he has not signed after default a statement renouncing or modifying his rights under this subsec-

tion. In the case of consumer goods no other notice need be given. In other cases notice shall be sent to any other secured party from whom the secured party has received (before sending his notice to the debtor or before the debtor's renunciation of his rights) written notice of a claim of an interest in the collateral. If the secured party receives objection in writing from a person entitled to receive notification within twenty-one days after the notice was sent, the secured party must dispose of the collateral under Section 9-504. In the absence of such written objection the secured party may retain the collateral in satisfaction of the debtor's obligation.

Section 9-506. Debtor's Right to Redeem Collateral. At any time before the secured party has disposed of collateral or entered into a contract for its disposition under Section 9-504 or before the obligation has been discharged under Section 9-505(2) the debtor or any other secured party may unless otherwise agreed in writing after default redeem the collateral by tendering fulfillment of all obligations secured by the collateral as well as the expenses reasonably incurred by the secured party in retaking, holding and preparing the collateral for disposition, in arranging for the sale, and to the extent provided in the agreement and not prohibited by law, his reasonable attorneys' fees and legal expenses.

Section 9-507. Secured Party's Liability for Failure to Comply With This Part.

(1) If it is established that the secured party is not proceeding in accordance with the provisions of this Part disposition may be ordered or restrained on appropriate terms and conditions. If the disposition has oc-

curred the debtor or any person entitled to notification or whose security interest has been made known to the secured party prior to the disposition has a right to recover from the secured party any loss caused by a failure to comply with the provisions of this Part. If the collateral is consumer goods, the debtor has a right to recover in any event an amount not less than the credit service charge plus ten per cent of the principal amount of the debt or the time price differential plus ten per cent of the cash price.

(2) The fact that a better price could have been obtained by a sale at a different time or in a different method from that selected by the secured party is not of itself sufficient to establish that the sale was not made in a commercially reasonable manner. If the secured party either sells the collateral in the usual manner in any recognized market therefor or if he sells at the price current in such market at the time of his sale or if he has otherwise sold in conformity with reasonable commercial practices among dealers in the type of property sold he has sold in a commercially reasonable manner. The principles stated in the two preceding sentences with respect to sales also apply as may be appropriate to other types of disposition. A disposition which has been approved in any judicial proceeding or by any bona fide creditors' committee or representative of creditors shall conclusively be deemed to be commercially reasonable, but this sentence does not indicate that any such approval must be obtained in any case nor does it indicate that any disposition not so approved is not commercially reasonable.

UNIFORM PARTNERSHIP ACT

An Act to make uniform the Law of Partnerships
Be it enacted, etc.:

PART I

PRELIMINARY PROVISIONS

Sec. 1. (Name of Act.) This act may be cited as Uniform Partnership Act.

Sec. 2. (Definition of Terms.) In this act, "Court" includes every court and judge having jurisdiction in the case.

"Business" includes every trade, occupation, or profession.

"Person" includes individuals, partnerships, corporations, and other associations.

"Bankrupt" includes bankrupt under the Federal Bankruptcy Act or insolvent under any state insolvent act.

"Conveyance" includes every assignment, lease, mortgage, or encumbrance.

"Real property" includes land and any interest or estate in land.

Sec. 3. (Interpretation of Knowledge and Notice.) (1) A person has "knowledge" of a fact within the meaning of this act not only when he has actual knowledge thereof, but also when he has knowledge of such other facts as in the circumstances shows bad faith.

(2) A person has "notice" of a fact within the meaning of this act when the person who claims the benefit of the notice

(a) States the fact to such person, or

(b) Delivers through the mail, or by other means of communication, a written statement of the fact to such person or to a proper person at his place of business or residence.

Sec. 4. (Rules of Construction.) (1) The rule that statutes in derogation of the common law are to be strictly construed shall have no application to this act.

(2) The law of estoppel shall apply under this act.

(3) The law of agency shall apply under this act.

(4) This act shall be so interpreted and construed as to effect its general purpose to make uniform the law of those states which enact it.

(5) This act shall not be construed so as to impair the obligations of any contract existing when the act goes into effect, nor to affect any action or proceedings begun or right accrued before this act takes effect.

Sec. 5. (Rules for Cases Not Provided for in this Act.) In any case not provided for in this act the rules of law and equity, including the law merchant, shall govern.

PART II

NATURE OF PARTNERSHIP

Sec. 6. (Partnership Defined.) (1) A partnership is an association of two or more persons to carry on as co-owners a business for profit.

(2) But any association formed under any other statute of this state, or any statute adopted by authority, other than the authority of this state, is not a partnership under this act, unless such association would have been a partnership in this state prior to the adoption of this act; but this act shall apply to limited partnerships except in so far as the statutes relating to such partnerships are inconsistent herewith.

Sec. 7. (Rules for Determining the Existence of a Partnership.) In determining whether a partnership exists, these rules shall apply:

(1) Except as provided by Section 16 persons who are not partners as to each other are not partners as to third persons.

(2) Joint tenancy, tenancy in common, tenancy by the entireties, joint property, common property, or part ownership does not of itself establish a partnership, whether such co-owners do or do not share any profits made by the use of the property.

(3) The sharing of gross returns does not of itself establish a partnership, whether or not the persons sharing them have a joint or common right or interest in any property from which the returns are derived.

(4) The receipt by a person of a share of the profits of a business is prima facie evidence that he is a partner in the business, but no such inference shall be drawn if such profits were received in payment:

(a) As a debt by installments or otherwise,

(b) As wages of an employee or rent to a landlord,

(c) As an annuity to a widow or representative of a deceased partner,

(d) As interest on a loan, though the amount of payment vary with the profits of the business.

(e) As the consideration for the sale of a goodwill of a business or other property by installments or otherwise.

Sec. 8. (Partnership Property.) (1) All property originally brought into the partnership stock or subsequently acquired by purchase or otherwise, on account of the partnership, is partnership property.

(2) Unless the contrary intention appears, property acquired with partnership funds is partnership property.

(3) Any estate in real property may be acquired in the partnership name. Title so acquired can be conveyed only in the partnership name.

(4) A conveyance to a partnership in the partnership name, though without words of inheritance, passes the entire estate of the grantor unless a contrary intent appears.

PART III

RELATIONS OF PARTNERS TO PERSONS DEALING WITH THE PARTNERSHIP

Sec. 9. (Partner Agent of Partnership as to Partnership Business.) (1) Every partner is an agent of the partnership for the purpose of its business, and the act of every partner, including the execution in the partnership name of any instrument, for apparently carrying on in the usual way the business of the partnership of which he is a member binds the partnership, unless the partner so acting has in fact no authority to act for the partnership in the particular matter, and the person with whom he is dealing has knowledge of the fact that he has no such authority.

(2) An act of a partner which is not apparently for the carrying on of the business of the partnership in the usual way does not bind the partnership unless authorized by the other partners.

(3) Unless authorized by the other partners or unless they have abandoned the business, one or more but less than all the partners have no authority to:

(a) Assign the partnership property in trust for creditors or on the assignee's promise to pay the debts of the partnership,

(b) Dispose of the goodwill of the business,

(c) Do any other act which would make it impossible to carry on the ordinary business of a partnership,

(d) Confess a judgment,

(e) Submit a partnership claim or liability to arbitration or reference.

(4) No act of a partner in contravention of a restriction on authority shall bind the partnership to persons having knowledge of the restriction.

Sec. 10. (Conveyance of Real Property of the Partnership.)

(1) Where title to real property is in the partnership name, any partner may convey title to such property by a conveyance executed in the partnership name; but the partnership may recover such property unless the partner's act binds the partnership under the provisions of paragraph (1) of section 9 or unless such property has been conveyed by the grantee or a person claiming through such grantee to a holder for value without knowledge that the partner, in making the conveyance, has exceeded his authority.

(2) Where title to real property is in the name of the partnership, a conveyance executed by a partner, in his own name, passes the equitable interest of the partnership, provided the act is one within the authority of the partner under the provisions of paragraph (1) of section 9.

(3) Where title to real property is in the name of one or more but not all the partners, and the record does not disclose the right of the partnership, the partners in whose name the title stands may convey title to such property, but the partnership may recover such property if the partners' act does not bind the partnership under the provisions of paragraph (1) of section 9, unless the purchaser or his assignee, is a holder for value, without knowledge.

(4) Where the title to real property is in the name of one or more or all the partners, or in a third person in trust for the partnership, a conveyance executed by a partner in the partnership name, or in his own name, passes the equitable interest of the partnership, provided the act is one within the authority of the partner under the provisions of paragraph (1) of section 9.

(5) Where the title to real property is in the names of all the partners a conveyance executed by all the partners passes all their rights in such property.

Sec. 11. (Partnership Bound by Admission of Partner.)

An admission or representation made by any partner concerning partnership affairs within the scope of his authority as conferred by this act is evidence against the partnership.

Sec. 12. (Partnership Charged with Knowledge of or Notice to Partner.)

Notice to any partner of any matter relating to partnership affairs, and the knowledge of the partner acting in the particular matter, acquired while a partner or then present to his mind, and the knowledge of any other partner who reasonably could and should have communicated it to the acting partner, operate as notice to or knowledge of the partnership, except in the case of a fraud on the partnership committed by or with the consent of that partner.

Sec. 13. (Partnership Bound by Partner's Wrongful Act.)

Where, by any wrongful act or omission of any partner acting in the ordinary course of the business of the partnership or with the authority of his co-partners, loss or injury is caused to any person, not being a partner in the partnership, or any penalty is incurred, the partnership is liable therefor to the same extent as the partner so acting or omitting to act.

Sec. 14. (Partnership Bound by Partner's Breach of Trust.) The partnership is bound to make good the loss:

(a) Where one partner acting within the scope of his apparent authority receives money or property of a third person and misapplies it; and

(b) Where the partnership in the course of its business receives money or property of a third person and the money or property so received is misapplied by any partner while it is in the custody of the partnership.

Sec. 15. (Nature of Partner's Liability.) All partners are liable

(a) Jointly and severally for everything chargeable to the partnership under sections 13 and 14.

(b) Jointly for all other debts and obligations of the partnership; but any partner may enter into a separate obligation to perform a partnership contract.

Sec. 16. (Partner by Estoppel.) (1) When a person, by words spoken or written or by conduct, represents himself, or consents to another representing him to any one, as a partner in an existing partnership or with one or more persons not actual partners, he is liable to any such person to whom such representation has been made, who has, on the faith of such representation, given credit to the actual or apparent partnership, and if he has made such representation or consented to its being made in a public manner he is liable to such person, whether the representation has or has not been made or communicated to such person so giving credit by or with the knowledge of the apparent partner making the representation or consenting to its being made.

(a) When a partnership liability results, he is liable as though he were an actual member of the partnership.

(b) When no partnership liability results, he is liable jointly with the other persons, if any, so consenting to the contract or representation as to incur liability, otherwise separately.

(2) When a person has been thus represented to be a partner in an existing partnership, or with one or more persons not actual partners, he is an agent of the persons consenting to such representation to bind them to the same extent and in the same manner as though he were a partner in fact, with respect to persons who rely upon the representation. Where all the members of the existing partnership consent to the representation, a partnership act or obligation results; but in all other cases it is the joint act or obligation of the person acting and the persons consenting to the representation.

Sec. 17. (Liability of Incoming Partner.) A person admitted as a partner into an existing partnership is liable for all the obligations of the partnership arising before his admission as though he had been a partner when such obligations were incurred, except that this liability shall be satisfied only out of partnership property.

PART IV

RELATIONS OF PARTNERS TO ONE ANOTHER

Sec. 18. (Rules Determining Rights and Duties of Partners.) The rights and duties of the partners in relation to the partnership shall be determined, subject to any agreement between them, by the following rules:

(a) Each partner shall be repaid his contributions, whether by way of capital or advances to the partnership property and share equally in the profits and surplus remaining after all liabilities, including those to partners, are satisfied; and must contribute toward the losses, whether of capital or otherwise, sustained by the partnership according to his share in the profits.

(b) The partnership must indemnify every partner in respect of payments made and personal liabilities reasonably incurred by him in the ordinary and proper conduct of its business, or for the preservation of its business or property.

(c) A partner, who in aid of the partnership makes any payment or advance beyond the amount of capital which he agreed to contribute, shall be paid interest from the date of the payment or advance.

(d) A partner shall receive interest on the capital contributed by him only from the date when repayment should be made.

(e) All partners have equal rights in the management and conduct of the partnership business.

(f) No partner is entitled to remuneration for acting in the partnership business, except that a surviving partner is entitled to reasonable compensation for his services in winding up the partnership affairs.

(g) No person can become a member of a partnership without the consent of all the partners.

(h) Any difference arising as to ordinary matters connected with the partnership business may be decided by a majority of the partners; but no act in contravention of any agreement between the partners may be done rightfully without the consent of all the partners.

Sec. 19. (Partnership Books.) The partnership books shall be kept, subject to any agreement between the partners, at the principal place of business of the partnership, and every partner shall at all times have access to and may inspect and copy any of them.

Sec. 20. (Duty of Partners to Render Information.) Partners shall render on demand true and full information of all things affecting the partnership to any partner or the legal representative of any deceased partner or partner under legal disability.

Sec. 21. (Partner Accountable as a Fiduciary.) (1) Every partner must account to the partnership for any benefit, and hold as trustee for it any profits derived by him without the consent of the other partners from any transaction connected with the formation, conduct, or liquidation of the partnership or from any use by him of its property.

(2) This section applies also to the representatives of a deceased partner engaged in the liquidation of the affairs of the partnership as the personal representatives of the last surviving partner.

Sec. 22. (Right to an Account.) Any partner shall have the right to a formal account as to partnership affairs:

(a) If he is wrongfully excluded from the partnership business or possession of its property by his co-partners,

(b) If the right exists under the terms of any agreement,

(c) As provided by Section 21,

(d) Whenever other circumstances render it just and reasonable.

Sec. 23. (Continuation of Partnership Beyond Fixed Term.) (1) When a partnership for a fixed term or particular undertaking is continued after the termination of such term or particular undertaking without any express agreement, the rights and duties of the partners remain the same as they were at such termination, so far as is consistent with a partnership at will.

(2) A continuation of the business by the partners or such of them as habitually acted therein during the term, without any settlement or liquidation of the partnership affairs, is prima facie evidence of a continuation of the partnership.

PART V

PROPERTY RIGHTS OF A PARTNER

Sec. 24. (Extent of Property Rights of a Partner.) The property rights of a partner are (1) his rights in specific partnership property, (2) his interest in the partnership, and (3) his right to participate in the management.

Sec. 25. (Nature of a Partner's Right in Specific Partnership Property.) (1) A partner is co-owner with his partners of specific partnership property holding as a tenant in partnership.

(2) The incidents of this tenancy are such that:

(a) A partner, subject to the provisions of this act and to any agreement between the partners, has an equal right with his partners to possess specific partnership property for partnership purposes; but he has no right to possess such property for any other purpose without the consent of his partners.

(b) A partner's right in specific partnership property is not assignable except in connection with the assignment of rights of all the partners in the same property.

(c) A partner's right in specific partnership property is not subject to attachment or execution, except on a claim against the partnership. When partnership property is attached for a partnership debt the partners, or any of them, or the representatives of a deceased partner, cannot claim any right under the homestead or exemption laws.

(d) On the death of a partner his right in specific partnership property vests in the surviving partner or partners, except where the deceased was the last surviving partner, when his right in such property vests in his legal representative. Such surviving partner or partners, or the legal representative of the last surviving partner, has no right to possess the partnership property for any but a partnership purpose.

(e) A partner's right in specific partnership property is not subject to dower, courtesy, or allowances to widows, heirs, or next of kin.

Sec. 26. (Nature of Partner's Interest in the Partnership.)
A partner's interest in the partnership is his share of the profits and surplus, and the same is personal property.

Sec. 27. (Assignment of Partner's Interest.)
(1) A conveyance by a partner of his interest in the partnership does not of itself dissolve the partnership, nor, as against the other partners in the absence of agreement, entitle the assignee, during the continuance of the partnership to interfere in the management or administration of the partnership business or affairs, or to require any information or account of partnership transactions, or to inspect the partnership books; but it merely entitles the assignee to receive in accordance with his contract the profits to which the assigning partner would otherwise be entitled.

(2) In case of a dissolution of the partnership, the assignee is entitled to receive his assignor's interest and may require an account from the date only of the last account agreed to by all the partners.

Sec. 28. (Partner's Interest Subject to Charging Order.)
(1) On due application to a competent court by any judgment creditor of a partner, the court which entered the judgment, order, or decree, or any other court, may charge the interest of the debtor partner with payment of the unsatisfied amount of such judgment debt with interest thereon; and may then or later appoint a receiver of his share of the profits, and of any other money due or to fall due to him in respect of the partnership, and make all other orders, directions, accounts and inquiries which the debtor partner might have made, or which the circumstances of the case may require.

(2) The interest charged may be redeemed at any time before foreclosure, or in case of a sale being directed by the court may be purchased without thereby causing a dissolution:

(a) With separate property, by any one or more of the partners, or

(b) With partnership property, by any one or more of the partners with the consent of all the partners whose interests are not so charged or sold.

(3) Nothing in this act shall be held to deprive a partner of his right, if any, under the exemption laws, as regards his interest in the partnership.

PART VI

DISSOLUTION AND WINDING UP

Sec. 29. (Dissolution Defined.) The dissolution of a partnership is the change in the relation of the partners caused by any partner ceasing to be associated in the carrying on as distinguished from the winding up of the business.

Sec. 30. (Partnership Not Terminated by Dissolution.) On dissolution the partnership is not terminated, but continues until the winding up of partnership affairs is completed.

Sec. 31. (Causes of Dissolution.)

Dissolution is caused: (1) Without violation of the agreement between the partners,

(a) By the termination of the definite term or particular undertaking specified in the agreement,

(b) By the express will of any partner when no definite term or particular undertaking is specified,

(c) By the express will of all the partners who have not assigned their interests or suffered them to be charged for their separate debts, either before or after the termination of any specified term or particular undertaking,

(d) By the expulsion of any partner from the business bona fide in accordance with such a power conferred by the agreement between the partners;

(2) In contravention of the agreement between the partners, where the circumstances do not permit a dissolution under any other provision of this section, by the express will of any partner at any time;

(3) By any event which makes it unlawful for the business of the partnership to be carried on or for the members to carry it on in partnership;

(4) By the death of any partner;

(5) By the bankruptcy of any partner or the partnership;

(6) By decree of court under Section 32.

Sec. 32. (Dissolution by Decree of Court.)

(1) On application by or for a partner the court shall decree a dissolution whenever:

(a) A partner has been declared a lunatic in any judicial proceeding or is shown to be of unsound mind,

(b) A partner becomes in any other way incapable of performing his part of the partnership contract,

(c) A partner has been guilty of such conduct as tends to affect prejudicially the carrying on of the business,

(d) A partner wilfully or persistently commits a breach of the partnership agreement, or otherwise so conducts himself in matters relating to the partnership business that it is not reasonably practicable to carry on the business in partnership with him,

(e) The business of the partnership can only be carried on at a loss,

(f) Other circumstances render a dissolution equitable.

(2) On the application of the purchaser of a partner's interest under Sections 27 or 28:

(a) After the termination of the specified term or particular undertaking,

(b) At any time if the partnership was a partnership at will when the interest was assigned or when the charging order was issued.

Sec. 33. (General Effect of Dissolution on Authority of Partner.)

Except so far as may be necessary to wind up partnership affairs or to complete transactions begun but not then finished, dissolution terminates all authority of any partner to act for the partnership,

(1) With respect to the partners,

(a) When the dissolution is not by the act, bankruptcy or death of a partner; or

(b) When the dissolution is by such act, bankruptcy or death of a partner, in cases where Section 34 so requires.

(2) With respect to persons not partners, as declared in Section 35.

Sec. 34. (Right of Partner to Contribution from Copartners After Dissolution.)

Where the dissolution is caused by the act, death or bankruptcy of a partner, each partner is liable to his copartners for his share of any liability created by any partner acting for the partnership as if the partnership had not been dissolved unless

(a) The dissolution being by act of any partner, the partner acting for the partnership had knowledge of the dissolution, or

(b) The dissolution being by the death or bankruptcy of a partner, the partner acting for the partnership had knowledge or notice of the death or bankruptcy.

Sec. 35. (Power of Partner to Bind Partnership to Third Persons After Dissolution.)

(1) After dissolution a partner can bind the partnership except as provided in Paragraph (3)

(a) By any act appropriate for winding up partnership affairs or completing transactions unfinished at dissolution;

(b) By any transaction which would bind the partnership if dissolution had not taken place, provided the other party to the transaction

(I) Had extended credit to the partnership prior to dissolution and had no knowledge or notice of the dissolution; or

(II) Though he had not so extended credit, had nevertheless known of the partnership prior to dissolution, and, having no knowledge or notice of dissolution, the fact of dissolution had not been advertised in a newspaper of general circulation in the place (or in each place if more than one) at which the partnership business was regularly carried on.

(2) The liability of a partner under paragraph (1b) shall be satisfied out of partnership assets alone when such partner had been prior to dissolution.

(a) Unknown as a partner to the person with whom the contract is made; and

(b) So far unknown and inactive in partnership affairs that the business reputation of the partnership could not be said to have been in any degree due to his connection with it.

(3) The partnership is in no case bound by any act of a partner after dissolution

(a) Where the partnership is dissolved because it is unlawful to carry on the business, unless the act is appropriate for winding up partnership affairs; or

(b) Where the partner has become bankrupt; or

(c) Where the partner has no authority to wind up partnership affairs; except by a transaction with one who

(I) Had extended credit to the partnership prior to dissolution and had no knowledge or notice of his want of authority; or

(II) Had not extended credit to the partnership prior to dissolution, and, having no knowledge or notice of his want of authority, the fact of his want of authority has not been advertised in the manner provided for advertising the fact of dissolution in paragraph (1bII).

(4) Nothing in this section shall affect the liability under section 16 of any person who after dissolution represents himself or consents to another representing him as a partner in a partnership engaged in carrying on business.

Sec. 36. (Effect of Dissolution on Partner's Existing Liability.) (1) The dissolution of the partnership does not of itself discharge the existing liability of any partner.

(2) A partner is discharged from any existing liability upon dissolution of the partnership by an agreement to that effect between himself, the partnership creditor and the person or partnership continuing the business; and such agreement may be inferred from the course of dealing between the creditor having knowledge of the dissolution and the person or partnership continuing the business.

(3) Where a person agrees to assume the existing obligations of a dissolved partnership, the partners whose obligations have been assumed shall be discharged from any liability to any creditor of the partnership who, knowing of the agreement, consents to a material alteration in the nature or time of payment of such obligations.

(4) The individual property of a deceased partner shall be liable for all obligations of the partnership incurred while he was a partner but subject to the prior payment of his separate debts.

Sec. 37. (Right to Wind Up.) Unless otherwise agreed the partners who have not wrongfully dissolved the partnership or the legal representative of the last surviving partner, not bankrupt, has the right to wind up the partnership affairs; provided, however, that any partner, his legal representative or his assignee, upon cause shown, may obtain winding up by the court.

Sec. 38. (Rights of Partners to Application of Partnership Property.) (1) When dissolution is caused in any way, except in contravention of the partnership agreement, each partner as against his co-partners and all persons claiming through them in respect of their interests in the partnership, unless otherwise agreed, may have the partnership property applied to discharge its liabilities, and the surplus applied to pay in cash the net amount owing to the respective partners. But if dissolution is caused by expulsion of a partner, bona fide under the partnership agreement and if the expelled partner is discharged from all partnership liabilities, either by payment or agreement under Section 36(2), he shall receive in cash only the net amount due him from the partnership.

(2) When dissolution is caused in contravention of the partnership agreement the rights of the partners shall be as follows:

(a) Each partner who has not caused dissolution wrongfully shall have,

(I) All the rights specified in paragraph (1) of this section, and

(II) The right, as against each partner who has caused the dissolution wrongfully, to damages for breach of the agreement.

(b) The partners who have not caused the dissolution wrongfully, if they all desire to continue the business in the same name, either by themselves or jointly with others, may do so, during the agreed term for the partnership and for that purpose may possess the partnership property, provided they secure the payment by bond approved by the court, or pay to any partner who has caused the dissolution wrongfully, the value of his interest in the partnership at the dissolution, less any damages recoverable under clause (2aII) of the section, and in like manner indemnify him against all present or future partnership liabilities.

(c) A partner who has caused the dissolution wrongfully shall have:

(1) If the business is not continued under the provisions of paragraph (2b) all the rights of a partner under paragraph (1), subject to clause (2aII), of this section,

(II) If the business is continued under paragraph (2b) of this section the right as against his co-partners and all claiming through them in respect of their interests in the partnership, to have the value of his interests in the partnership, less any damages caused to his co-partners by the dissolution, ascertained and paid to him in cash, or the payment secured by bond approved by the court, and to be released from all existing liabilities of the partnership; but in ascertaining the value of the partner's interest the value of the goodwill of the business shall not be considered.

Sec. 39. (Rights Where Partnership Is Dissolved for Fraud or Misrepresentation.) Where a partnership contract is rescinded on the ground of the fraud or misrepresentation of one of the parties thereto, the party entitled to rescind is, without prejudice to any other right, entitled,

(a) To a lien on, or right of retention of, the surplus of the partnership property after satisfying the partnership liabilities to third persons for any sum of money paid by him for the purchase of an interest in the partnership and for any capital or advances contributed by him; and

(b) To stand, after all liabilities to third persons have been satisfied, in the place of the creditors of the partnership for any payments made by him in respect of the partnership liabilities; and

(c) To be indemnified by the person guilty of the fraud or making the representation against all debts and liabilities of the partnership.

Sec. 40. (Rules for Distribution.) In settling accounts between the partners after dissolution, the following rules shall be observed, subject to any agreement to the contrary:

(a) The assets of the partnership are;

(I) The partnership property,

(II) The contributions of the partners necessary for the payment of all the liabilities specified in clause (b) of this paragraph.

(b) The liabilities of the partnership shall rank in order of payment, as follows:

(I) Those owing to creditors other than partners,

(II) Those owing to partners other than for capital and profits,

(III) Those owing to partners in respect of capital,

(IV) Those owing to partners in respect of profits.

(c) The assets shall be applied in the order of their declaration in clause (a) of this paragraph to the satisfaction of the liabilities.

(d) The partners shall contribute, as provided by Section 18(a) the amount necessary to satisfy the liabilities; but if any, but not all, of the partners are insolvent, or, not being subject to process, refuse to contribute, the other parties shall contribute their share of the liabilities, and, in the relative proportions in which they share the profits, the additional amount necessary to pay the liabilities.

(e) An assignee for the benefit of creditors or any person appointed by the court shall have the right to enforce the contributions specified in clause (d) of this paragraph.

(f) Any partner or his legal representative shall have the right to enforce the contributions specified in clause (d) of this paragraph, to the extent of the amount which he has paid in excess of his share of the liability.

(g) The individual property of a deceased partner shall be liable for the contributions specified in clause (d) of this paragraph.

(h) When partnership property and the individual properties of the partners are in possession of a court for distribution, partnership creditors shall have priority on partnership property and separate creditors on individual property, saving the rights of lien or secured creditors as heretofore.

(i) Where a partner has become bankrupt or his estate is insolvent the claims against his separate property shall rank in the following order:

(I) Those owing to separate creditors,

(II) Those owing to partnership creditors,

(III) Those owing to partners by way of contribution.

Sec. 41. (Liability of Persons Continuing the Business in Certain Cases.) (1) When any new partner is admitted into an existing partnership, or when any partner retires and assigns (or the representative of the deceased partner assigns) his rights in partnership property to two or more of the partners, or to one or more of the partners and one or more third persons, if the business is continued without liquidation of the partnership affairs, creditors of the first or dissolved partnership are also creditors of the partnership so continuing the business.

(2) When all but one partner retire and assign (or the representative of a deceased partner assigns) their rights in partnership property to the remaining partner, who continues the business without liquidation of partnership affairs, either alone or with others, creditors of the dissolved partnership are also creditors of the person or partnership so continuing the business.

(3) When any partner retires or dies and the business of the dissolved partnership is continued as set forth in paragraphs (1) and (2) of this section, with the consent of the retired partners or the representative of the deceased partner, but without any assignment of his right in partnership property, rights of creditors of the dissolved partnership and of the creditors of the person or partnership continuing the business shall be as if such assignment had been made.

(4) When all the partners or their representatives assign their rights in partnership property to one or more third persons who promise to pay the debts and who continue the business of the dissolved partnership, creditors of the dissolved partnership are also creditors of the person or partnership continuing the business.

(5) When any partner wrongfully causes a dissolution and the remaining partners continue the business under the provisions of section 38(2b), either alone or with others, and without liquidation of the partnership affairs, creditors of the dissolved partnership are also creditors of the person or partnership continuing the business.

(6) When a partner is expelled and the remaining partners continue the business either alone or with others, without liquidation of the partnership affairs, creditors of the dissolved partnership are also creditors of the person or partnership continuing the business.

(7) The liability of a third person becoming a partner in the partnership continuing the business, under this section, to the creditors of the dissolved partnership shall be satisfied out of partnership property only.

(8) When the business of a partnership after dissolution is continued under any conditions set forth in this section the creditors of the dissolved partnership, as against the separate creditors of the retiring or deceased partner or the representative of the deceased partner, have a prior right to any claim of the retired partner or the representative of the deceased partner against the person or partnership continuing the business, on account of the retired or deceased partner's interest in the dissolved partnership or on account of any consideration promised for such interest or for his right in partnership property.

(9) Nothing in this section shall be held to modify any right of creditors to set aside any assignment on the ground of fraud.

(10) The use by the person or partnership continuing the business of the partnership name, or the name of a deceased partner as

part thereof, shall not of itself make the individual property of the deceased partner liable for any debts contracted by such person or partnership.

Sec. 42.   (Rights of Retiring or Estate of Deceased Partner When the Business Is Continued.)   When any partner retires or dies, and the business is continued under any of the conditions set forth in Section 41(1, 2, 3, 5, 6), or Section 38(2b), without any settlement of accounts as between him or his estate and the person or partnership continuing the business, unless otherwise agreed, he or his legal representative as against such persons or partnership may have the value of his interest at the date of dissolution ascertained, and shall receive as an ordinary creditor an amount equal to the value of his interest in the dissolved partnership with interest, or, at his option or at the option of his legal representative, in lieu of interest, the profits attributable to the use of his right in the property of the dissolved partnership; provided that the creditors of the dissolved partnership as against the separate creditors, or the representative of the retired or deceased partner, shall have priority on any claim arising under this section, as provided by Section 41(8) of this act.

Sec. 43.   (Accrual of Actions.)   The right to an account of his interest shall accrue to any partner, or his legal representative, as against the winding up partners or the surviving partners or the person or partnership continuing the business, at the date of dissolution, in the absence of any agreement to the contrary.

PART VII

MISCELLANEOUS PROVISIONS

Sec. 44.   (When Act Takes Effect.)   This act shall take effect on the ———— day of ———— one thousand nine hundred and ————.

Sec. 45.   (Legislation Repealed.)   All acts or parts of acts inconsistent with this act are hereby repealed.

UNIFORM LIMITED PARTNERSHIP ACT

Be it enacted, etc., as follows:

Sec. 1. **(Limited Partnership Defined.)** A limited partnership is a partnership formed by two or more persons under the provisions of Section 2, having as members one or more general partners and one or more limited partners. The limited partners as such shall not be bound by the obligations of the partnership.

Sec. 2. **(Formation.)** (1) Two or more persons desiring to form a limited partnership shall

(a) Sign and swear to a certificate, which shall state

    I.   The name of the partnership,

    II.   The character of the business,

    III.   The location of the principal place of business,

    IV.   The name and place of residence of each member; general and limited partners being respectively designated,

    V.   The term for which the partnership is to exist,

    VI.   The amount of cash and a description of and the agreed value of the other property contributed by each limited partner,

    VII.   The additional contributions, if any, agreed to be made by each limited partner and the times at which or events on the happening of which they shall be made,

    VIII.   The time, if agreed upon, when the contribution of each limited partner is to be returned,

    IX.   The share of the profits or the other compensation by way of income which each limited partner shall receive by reason of his contribution,

    X.   The right, if given, of a limited partner to substitute an assignee as contributor in his place, and the terms and conditions of the substitution,

    XI.   The right, if given, of the partners to admit additional limited partners,

    XII.   The right, if given, of one or more of the limited partners to priority over other limited partners, as to contributions or as to compensation by way of income, and the nature of such priority,

    XIII.   The right, if given, of the remaining general partner or partners to continue the business on the death, retirement or insanity of a general partner, and

    XIV.   The right, if given, of a limited partner to demand and receive property other than cash in return for his contribution.

(b) File for record the certificate in the office of [here designate the proper office].

(2) A limited partnership is formed if there has been substantial compliance in good faith with the requirements of paragraph (1).

Sec. 3. (Business Which may Be Carried On.) A limited partnership may carry on any business which a partnership without limited partners may carry on, except [here designate the business to be prohibited].

Sec. 4. (Character of Limited Partner's Contribution.) The contributions of a limited partner may be cash or other property, but not services.

Sec. 5. (A Name Not to Contain Surname of Limited Partner; Exceptions.) (1) The surname of a limited partner shall not appear in the partnership name, unless

(a) It is also the surname of a general partner, or

(b) Prior to the time when the limited partner became such the business had been carried on under a name in which his surname appeared.

(2) A limited partner whose name appears in a partnership name contrary to the provisions of paragraph (1) is liable as a general partner to partnership creditors who extend credit to the partnership without actual knowledge that he is not a general partner.

Sec. 6. (Liability for False Statements in Certificate.) If the certificate contains a false statement, one who suffers loss by reliance on such statement may hold liable any party to the certificate who knew the statement to be false.

(a) At the time he signed the certificate, or

(b) Subsequently, but within a sufficient time before the statement was relied upon to enable him to cancel or amend the certificate, or to file a petition for its cancellation or amendment as provided in Section 25(3).

Sec. 7. (Limited Partner Not Liable to Creditors.) A limited partner shall not become liable as a general partner unless, in addition to the exercise of his rights and powers as a limited partner, he takes part in the control of the business.

Sec. 8. (Admission of Additional Limited Partners.) After the formation of a limited partnership, additional limited partners may be admitted upon filing an amendment to the original certificate in accordance with the requirements of Section 25.

Sec. 9. (Rights, Powers and Liabilities of a General Partner.) (1) A general partner shall have all the rights and powers and be subject to all the restrictions and liabilities of a partner in a partnership without limited partners, except that without the written consent or ratification of the specific act by all the limited partners, a general partner or all of the general partners have no authority to

(a) Do any act in contravention of the certificate,

(b) Do any act which would make it impossible to carry on the ordinary business of the partnership,

(c) Confess a judgment against the partnership,

(d) Possess partnership property, or assign their rights in specific partnership property, for other than a partnership purpose,

(e) Admit a person as a general partner,

(f) Admit a person as a limited partner, unless the right to do so is given in the certificate,

(g) Continue the business with partnership property on the death, retirement or insanity of a general partner, unless the right so to do is given in the certificate.

Sec. 10. (Rights of a Limited Partner.) (1) A limited partner shall have the same rights as a general partner to

(a) Have the partnership books kept at the principal place of business of the partnership, and at all times to inspect and copy any of them,

(b) Have on demand true and full information of all things affecting the partnership, and a formal account of partnership affairs, whenever circumstances render it just and reasonable, and

(c) Have dissolution and winding up by decree of court.

(2) A limited partner shall have the right to receive a share of the profits or other compensation by way of income, and to the return of his contribution as provided in Sections 15 and 16.

Sec. 11. (Status of Person Erroneously Believing Himself a Limited Partner.) A person who has contributed to the capital of a business conducted by a person or partnership erroneously believing that he has become a limited partner in a limited partnership, is not, by reason of his exercise of the rights of a limited partner, a general partner with the person or in the partnership carrying on the business, or bound by the obligations of such person or partnership; provided that on ascertaining the mistake he promptly renounces his interest in the profits of the business, or other compensation by way of income.

Sec. 12. (One Person Both General and Limited Partner.) (1) A person may be a general partner and a limited partner in the same partnership at the same time.

(2) A person who is a general, and also at the same time a limited partner, shall have all the rights and powers and be subject to all the restrictions of a general partner; except that, in respect to his contribution, he shall have the rights against the other members which he would have had if he were not also a general partner.

Sec. 13. (Loans and Other Business Transactions with Limited Partner.) (1) A limited partner also may loan money to and transact other business with the partnership, and, unless he is also a general partner, receive on account of resulting claims against the partnership, with general creditors, a pro rata share of the assets. No limited partner shall in respect to any such claim

(a) Receive or hold as collateral security any partnership property, or

(b) Receive from a general partner or the partnership any payment, conveyance, or release from liability, if at the time the assets of the partnership are not sufficient to discharge partnership liabilities to persons not claiming as general or limited partners.

(2) The receiving of collateral security, or a payment, conveyance, or release in violation of the provisions of paragraph (1) is a fraud on the creditors of the partnership.

Sec. 14. (Relation of Limited Partners Inter Se.) Where there are several limited partners the members may agree that one or more of the limited partners shall have a priority over other limited partners as to the return of their contributions, as to their compensation by way of income, or as to any other matter. If such an agreement is made it shall be stated in the certificate, and in the absence of such a statement all the limited partners shall stand upon equal footing.

Sec. 15. (Compensation of Limited Partner.) A limited partner may receive from the partnership the share of the profits or the compensation by way of income stipulated for in the certificate; provided, that after such payment is made, whether from the property of the partnership or that of a general partner, the partnership assets are in excess of all liabilities of the partnership except liabilities to limited partners on account of their contributions and to general partners.

Sec. 16. (Withdrawal or Reduction of Limited Partner's Contribution.) (1) A limited partner shall not receive from a general partner or out of partnership property any part of his contribution until

(a) All liabilities of the partnership, except liabilities to general partners and to limited partners on account of their contributions, have been paid or there remains property of the partnership sufficient to pay them,

(b) The consent of all members is had, unless the return of the contribution may be rightfully demanded under the provisions of paragraph (2), and

(c) The certificate is cancelled or so amended as to set forth the withdrawal or reduction.

(2) Subject to the provisions of paragraph (1) a limited partner may rightfully demand the return of his contribution

(a) On the dissolution of a partnership, or

(b) When the date specified in the certificate for its return has arrived, or

(c) After he has given six months' notice in writing to all other members, if no time is specified in the certificate either for the return of the contribution or for the dissolution of the partnership,

(3) In the absence of any statement in the certificate to the contrary or the consent of all members, a limited partner, irrespective of the nature of his contribution, has only the right to demand and receive cash in return for his contribution.

(4) A limited partner may have the partnership dissolved and its affairs wound up when

(a) He rightfully but unsuccessfully demands the return of his contribution, or

(b) The other liabilities of the partnership have not been paid, or the partnership property is insufficient for their payment as required by paragraph (1a) and the limited partner would otherwise be entitled to the return of his contribution.

Sec. 17. (Liability of Limited Partner to Partnership.) (1) A limited partner is liable to the partnership

(a) For the difference between his contribution as actually made and that stated in the certificate as having been made, and

(b) For any unpaid contribution which he agreed in the certificate to make in the future at the time and on the conditions stated in the certificate.

(2) A limited partner holds as trustee for the partnership

(a) Specific property stated in the certificate as contributed by him, but which was not contributed or which has been wrongfully returned, and

(b) Money or other property wrongfully paid or conveyed to him on account of his contribution.

(3) The liabilities of a limited partner as set forth in this section can be waived or compromised only by the consent of all members; but a waiver or compromise shall not affect the right of a creditor of a partnership, who extended credit or whose claim arose after the filing and before a cancellation or amendment of the certificate, to enforce such liabilities.

(4) When a contributor has rightfully received the return in whole or in part of the capital of his contribution, he is nevertheless liable to the partnership for any sum, not in excess of such return with interest, necessary to discharge its liabilities to all creditors who extended credit or whose claims arose before such return.

Sec. 18. (Nature of Limited Partner's Interest in Partnership.) A limited partner's interest in the partnership is personal property.

Sec. 19. (Assignment of Limited Partner's Interest.) (1) A limited partner's interest is assignable.

(2) A substituted limited partner is a person admitted to all the rights of a limited partner who has died or has assigned his interest in a partnership.

(3) An assignee, who does not become a substituted limited partner, has no right to require any information or account of the partnership transactions or to inspect the partnership books; he is only entitled to receive the share of the profits or other compensation by way of income, or the return of his contribution, to which his assignor would otherwise be entitled.

(4) An assignee shall have the right to become a substituted limited partner if all the members (except the assignor) consent thereto or if the assignor, being thereunto empowered by the certificate, gives the assignee that right.

(5) An assignee becomes a substituted limited partner when the certificate is appropriately amended in accordance with Section 25.

(6) The substituted limited partner has all the rights and powers, and is subject to all the restrictions and liabilities of his assignor, except those liabilities of which he was ignorant at the time he became a limited partner and which could not be ascertained from the certificate.

(7) The substitution of the assignee as a limited partner does not release the assignor from liability to the partnership under Sections 6 and 17.

Sec. 20. (Effect of Retirement, Death or Insanity of a General Partner.) The retirement, death or insanity of a general partner dissolves the partnership, unless the business is continued by the remaining general partners

(a) Under a right so to do stated in the certificate, or

(b) With the consent of all members.

Sec. 21. (Death of Limited Partner.) (1) On the death of a limited partner his executor or administrator shall have all the rights of a limited partner for the purpose of settling his estate, and such power as the deceased had to constitute his assignee a substituted limited partner.

(2) The estate of a deceased limited partner shall be liable for all his liabilities as a limited partner.

Sec. 22. (Rights of Creditors of Limited Partner.) (1) On due application to a court of competent jurisdiction by any judgment creditor of a limited partner, the court may charge the interest of the indebted limited partner with payment of the unsatisfied amount of the judgment debt; and may appoint a receiver, and make all other orders, directions, and inquiries which the circumstances of the case may require.

In those states where a creditor on beginning an action can attach debts due the defendant before he has obtained a judgment against the defendant it is recommended that paragraph (1) of this section read as follows:

On due application to a court of competent jurisdiction by any creditor of a limited partner, the court may charge the interest of the indebted limited partner with payment of the unsatisfied amount of such claim; and may appoint a receiver, and make all other orders, directions, and inquiries which the circumstances of the case may require.

(2) The interest may be redeemed with the separate property of any general partner, but may not be redeemed with partnership property.

(3) The remedies conferred by paragraph (1) shall not be deemed exclusive of others which may exist.

(4) Nothing in this act shall be held to deprive a limited partner of his statutory exemption.

Sec. 23. (Distribution of Assets.) (1) In settling accounts after dissolution the liabilities of the partnership shall be entitled to payment in the following order:

(a) Those to creditors, in the order of priority as provided by law, except those to limited partners on account of their contributions, and to general partners,

(b) Those to limited partners in respect to their share of the profits and other compensa-

tion by way of income on their contributions,

(c) Those to limited partners in respect to the capital of their contributions,

(d) Those to general partners other than for capital and profits,

(e) Those to general partners in respect to profits,

(f) Those to general partners in respect to capital.

(2) Subject to any statement in the certificate or to subsequent agreement, limited partners share in the partnership assets in respect to their claims for capital, and in respect to their claims for profits or for compensation by way of income on their contributions respectively, in proportion to the respective amounts of such claims.

Sec. 24. (When Certificate Shall Be Cancelled or Amended.) (1) The certificate shall be cancelled when the partnership is dissolved or all limited partners cease to be such.

(2) A certificate shall be amended when

(a) There is a change in the name of the partnership or in the amount or character of the contribution of any limited partner,

(b) A person is substituted as a limited partner,

(c) An additional limited partner is admitted,

(d) A person is admitted as a general partner,

(e) A general partner retires, dies or becomes insane, and the business is continued under Section 20,

(f) There is a change in the character of the business of the partnership,

(g) There is a false or erroneous statement in the certificate,

(h) There is a change in the time as stated in the certificate for the dissolution of the partnership or for the return of a contribution,

(i) A time is fixed for the dissolution of the partnership, or the return of a contribution, no time having been specified in the certificate, or

(j) The members desire to make a change in any other statement in the certificate in order that it shall accurately represent the agreement between them.

Sec. 25. (Requirements for Amendment and for Cancellation of Certificate.) (1) The writing to amend a certificate shall

(a) Conform to the requirements of Section 2(1a) as far as necessary to set forth clearly the change in the certificate which it is desired to make, and

(b) Be signed and sworn to by all members, and an amendment substituting a limited partner or adding a limited or general partner shall be signed also by the member to be substituted or added, and when a limited partner is to be substituted, the amendment shall also be signed by the assigning limited partner.

(2) The writing to cancel a certificate shall be signed by all members.

(3) A person desiring the cancellation or amendment of a certificate, if any person designated in paragraphs (1) and (2) as a person who must execute the writing refuses to do so, may petition the [here designate the proper court] to direct a cancellation or amendment thereof.

(4) If the court finds that the petitioner has a right to have the writing executed by a person who refuses to do so, it shall order the [here designate the responsible official in the office designated in Section 2] in the office where the certificate is recorded to record the cancellation or amendment of the certificate; and where the certificate is to be amended, the court also cause to be filed for record in said office a certified copy of its decree setting forth the amendment.

(5) A certificate is amended or cancelled when there is filed for record in the office [here designate the office designated in Section 2] where the certificate is recorded

(a) A writing in accordance with the provisions of paragraph (1), or (2) or

(b) A certified copy of the order of court in accordance with the provisions of paragraph (4).

(6) After the certificate is duly amended in accordance with this section, the amended certificate shall thereafter be for all purposes the certificate provided for by this act.

Sec. 26. (Parties to Actions.) A contributor, unless he is a general partner, is not a proper party to proceedings by or against a partnership, except where the object is to enforce a limited partner's right against or liability to the partnership.

Sec. 27. (Name of Act.) This act may be cited as The Uniform Limited Partnership Act.

Sec. 28. (Rules of Construction.) (1) The rule that statutes in derogation of the common law are to be strictly construed shall have no application to this act.

(2) This act shall be so interpreted and construed as to effect its general purpose to make uniform the law of those states which enact it.

(3) This act shall not be so construed as to impair the obligations of any contract existing when the act goes into effect, nor to affect any action on proceedings begun or right accrued before this act takes effect.

Sec. 29. (Rules for Cases Not Provided for in this Act.) In any case not provided for in this act the rules of law and equity, including the law merchant, shall govern.

Sec. 30.[1] (Provisions for Existing Limited Partnerships.) (1) A limited partnership formed under any statute of this state prior to the adoption of this act, may become a limited partnership under this act by complying with the provisions of Section 2; provided the certificate sets forth

(a) The amount of the original contribution of each limited partner, and the time when the contribution was made, and

(b) That the property of the partnership exceeds the amount sufficient to discharge its liabilities to persons not claiming as general or limited partners by an amount greater than the sum of the contributions of its limited partners.

(2) A limited partnership formed under any statute of this state prior to the adoption of this act, until or unless it becomes a limited partnership under this act, shall continue to be governed by the provisions of [here insert proper reference to the existing limited partnership act or acts], except that such partnership shall not be renewed unless so provided in the original agreement.

Sec. 31.[1] (Act [Acts] Repealed.) Except as affecting existing limited partnerships to the extent set forth in Section 30, the act (acts) of [here designate the existing limited partnership act or acts] is (are) hereby repealed.

[1] Sections 30, 31, will be omitted in any state which has not a limited partnership act.

REVISED UNIFORM LIMITED PARTNERSHIP ACT

ARTICLE 1

GENERAL PROVISIONS

Sec. 101. (Definitions.) As used in this Act:

(1) "Certificate of limited partnership" means the certificate referred to in Section 201, as that certificate is amended from time to time.

(2) "Contribution" means any cash, property, or services rendered, or a promissory note or other binding obligation to contribute cash or property or to perform services, which a partner contributes to a limited partnership in his capacity as a partner.

(3) "Event of withdrawal of a general partner" means an event that causes a person to cease to be a general partner as provided in Section 402.

(4) "Foreign limited partnership" means a partnership formed under the laws of any state other than this State and having as partners one or more general partners and one or more limited partners.

(5) "General partner" means a person who has been admitted to a limited partnership as a general partner in accordance with the partnership agreement and who is named in the certifi-cate of limited partnership as a general partner.

(6) "Limited partner" means a person who has been admitted to a limited partnership as a limited partner in accordance with the partnership agreement and who is named in the certifi-limited partner in accordance with the partner-

(7) "Limited partnership" and "domestic limited partnership" mean a partnership formed by 2 or more persons under the laws of this State and having one or more general partners and one or more limited partners.

(8) "Partner" means any limited partner or general partner.

(9) "Partnership agreement" means the agreement, written or, to the extent not prohibited by law, oral or both, of the partners as to the affairs of a limited partnership and the conduct of its business.

(10) "Partnership interest" has the meaning specified in Section 701.

(11) "Person" means a natural person, partnership, limited partnership (domestic or foreign), trust, estate, association, or corporation.

(12) "State" means a state, territory, or possession of the United States, the District of Columbia, or the Commonwealth of Puerto Rico.

Sec. 102. (Name.) The name of each limited partnership as set forth in its certificate of limited partnership:

(1) shall contain the words "limited partnership" in full;

(2) may not contain the name of a limited partner unless (i) it is also the name of a general partner or (ii) the business of the limited partnership had been carried on under that name before the admission of that limited partner;

(3) may not contain any word or phrase indicating or implying that it is organized other than for a purpose stated in its certificate of limited partnership;

(4) may not be the same as, or deceptively similar to, the name of any corporation or limited partnership organized under the laws of this State or licensed or registered as a foreign corporation or limited partnership in this State; and

(5) may not contain the following words [here insert prohibited words].

Sec. 103. (Reservation of Name.)

(a) The exclusive right to the use of a name may be reserved by:

(1) any person intending to organize a limited partnership under this Act and to adopt that name;

(2) any domestic limited partnership or any foreign limited partnership registered in this State which, in either case, intends to adopt that name;

(3) any foreign limited partnership intending to register in this State and to adopt that name; and

(4) any person intending to organize a foreign limited partnership and intending to have it registered in this State and to adopt that name.

(b) The reservation shall be made by filing with the Secretary of State an application, executed by the applicant, to reserve a specified name. If the Secretary of State finds that the name is available for use by a domestic or foreign limited partnership, he shall reserve the name for the exclusive use of the applicant for a period of 120 days. Once having reserved a name, the same applicant may not again reserve the same name until more than 60 days after the expiration of the last 120-day period for which that applicant had reserved that name. The right to the exclusive use of a name so reserved may be transferred to any other person by filing in the office of the Secretary of State a notice of the transfer, executed by the applicant for whom the name was reserved and specifying the name and address of the transferee.

Sec. 104. (Specified Office and Agent.) Each limited partnership shall continuously maintain in this State:

(1) an office, which may but need not be a place of its business in this State, at which shall be kept the records required to be maintained by Section 105; and

(2) an agent for service of process on the limited partnership, which agent must be an individual resident of this State, a domestic corporation, or a foreign corporation authorized to do business in this State.

Sec. 105. (Records to Be Kept.) Each limited partnership shall keep at the office referred to in Section 104(1) the following: (1) a current list of the full name and last-known business address of each partner set forth in alphabetical order, (2) a copy of the certificate of limited partnership and all certificates of amendment thereto, together with executed copies of any powers of attorney pursuant to which any certificate has been executed, (3) copies of the limited partnership's federal, state, and local income tax returns and reports, if any, for the 3 most recent years, and (4) copies of any then effective written partnership agreements and of any financial statements of the limited partnership for the 3 most recent years. These records shall be available for inspection and copying at the reasonable request, and at the expense, of any partner during ordinary business hours.

Sec. 106. (Nature of Business.) A limited partnership may carry on any business that a partnership without limited partners may carry on except [here designate prohibited activities].

Sec. 107. (Business Transactions of Partner with the Partnership.) Except as otherwise provided in the partnership agreement, a partner may lend money to and transact other business with the limited partnership and, subject to other applicable provisions of law, has the same rights and obligations with respect thereto as a person who is not a partner.

ARTICLE 2

FORMATION; CERTIFICATE OF LIMITED PARTNERSHIP

Sec. 201. (Certificate of Limited Partnership.)

(a) Two or more persons desiring to form a limited partnership shall execute a certificate of limited partnership. The certificate shall be filed in the office of the Secretary of State and shall set forth:

(1) the name of the limited partnership;

(2) the general character of its business;

(3) the address of the office and the name and address of the agent for service of process required to be maintained by Section 104;

(4) the name and the business address of each partner (specifying the general partners and limited partners separately);

(5) the amount of cash and a description and statement of the agreed value of the other property or services contributed by each partner and which each partner has agreed to contribute in the future;

(6) the times at which or events on the happening of which any additional contributions agreed to be made by each partner are to be made;

(7) any power of a limited partner to grant an assignee of any part of his partnership interest the right to become a limited partner, and the terms and conditions of the power;

(8) if agreed upon, the time at which or the events on the happening of which a partner may terminate his membership in the limited partnership and the amount of, or the method of determining, the distribution to which he may be entitled respecting his partnership interest, and the terms and conditions of the termination and distribution;

(9) any right of a partner to receive distributions of property including cash from the limited partnership;

(10) any right of a partner to receive, or of a general partner to make, distributions to a partner which include a return of all or any part of the partner's contribution;

(11) any time at which or events upon the happening of which the limited partnership is to be dissolved and its affairs wound up;

(12) any right of the remaining general partners to continue the business on the happening of an event of withdrawal of a general partner; and

(13) any other matters the partners, in their sole discretion, determine to include therein.

(b) A limited partnership is formed at the time of the filing of the certificate of limited partnership in the office of the Secretary of State or at any later time specified in the certificate of limited partnership if, in each case, there has been substantial compliance with the requirements of this section.

Sec. 202. (Amendments to Certificate.)

(a) A certificate of limited partnership is amended by filing a certificate of amendment thereto in the office of the Secretary of State. The certificate shall set forth:

(1) the name of the limited partnership;

(2) the date of filing of the certificate; and

(3) the amendments to the certificate.

(b) Within 30 days after the happening of any of the following events an amendment to a certificate of limited partnership reflecting the occurrence of the event or events shall be filed:

(1) a change in the amount or character of the contribution of any partner, or in any partner's obligation to make a contribution;

(2) the admission of a new partner;

(3) the withdrawal of a partner; and

(4) the continuation of the business under Section 801 after an event of withdrawal of a general partner.

(c) A certificate of limited partnership must be amended promptly by any general partner upon becoming aware that any statement therein was false when made or that any arrangements or other facts described have changed, making the certificate inaccurate in any respect, but amendments to show changes of addresses of limited partners need be filed only once every 12 months.

(d) A certificate of limited partnership may be amended at any time for any other proper purpose the general partners may determine.

(e) No person shall have any liability because an amendment to a certificate of limited partnership has not been filed to reflect the occurrence of any event referred to in subsection (b) of this section if the amendment is filed within the 30-day period specified in subsection (b).

Sec. 203. (Cancellation of Certificate.)

A certificate of limited partnership shall be cancelled upon the dissolution and the commencement of winding up of the limited partnership and at any other time there are no remaining limited partners. A certificate of cancellation shall be filed in the office of the Secretary of State and shall set forth:

(1) the name of the limited partnership;

(2) the date of filing of its certificate of limited partnership;

(3) the reason for filing the certificate of cancellation;

(4) the effective date (which shall be a date certain) of cancellation if it is not to be effective upon the filing of the certificate; and

(5) any other information the general partners filing the certificate may determine.

Sec. 204. (Execution of Certificates.)

(a) Each certificate required by this Article to be filed in the office of the Secretary of State shall be executed in the following manner:

(1) each original certificate of limited partnership must be signed by each partner named therein;

(2) each certificate of amendment must be signed by at least one general partner and by each other partner who is designated in the certificate as a new partner or whose contribution is described as having been increased; and

(3) each certificate of cancellation must be signed by each general partner.

(b) Any person may sign a certificate by an attorney-in-fact, but any power of attorney to sign a certificate relating to the admission or increased contribution of a partner must specifically describe the admission or increase.

(c) The execution of a certificate by a general partner constitutes an affirmation under the penalties of perjury that the facts stated therein are true.

Sec. 205. (Amendment or Cancellation by Judicial Act.)

If the persons required by Section 204 to execute any certificate of amendment or cancellation fail or refuse to do so, any other partner, and any assignee of a partnership interest, who is adversely affected by the failure or refusal, may petition the [here designate the proper court] to direct the amendment or cancellation. If the court finds that the amendment or cancellation is proper and that the persons so designated have failed or refused to execute the certificate, it shall order the Secretary of State to record an appropriate certificate of amendment or cancellation.

Sec. 206. (Filing in the Office of the Secretary of State.)

(a) Two signed copies of the certificate of limited partnership and of any certificates of amendment or cancellation (or of any judicial decree of amendment or cancellation) shall be delivered to the Secretary of State. A person who executes a certificate as an agent or fiduciary need not exhibit evidence of his authority as a prerequisite to filing. Unless the Secretary of State finds that any certificate does not conform to law, upon receipt of all filing fees required by law the Secretary of State shall:

(1) endorse on each duplicate original the word "Filed" and the day, month, and year of the filing thereof;

(2) file one duplicate original in his office; and

(3) return the other duplicate original to the person who filed it or his representative.

(b) Upon the filing of a certificate of amendment (or judicial decree of amendment) in the office of the Secretary of State, the certificate of limited partnership shall be amended as set forth therein, and upon the effective date of a certificate of cancellation (or a judicial decree thereof), the certificate of limited partnership shall be cancelled.

Sec. 207. (Liability for False Statement in Certificate.)

If any certificate of limited partnership or certificate of amendment or cancellation contains a false statement, one who suffers loss by reliance on the statement may recover damages for the loss from:

(1) any person actually executing, or causing another to execute on his behalf, the certificate who knew, and any general partner who knew or should have known, the statement to be false at the time the certificate was executed; and

(2) any general partner who thereafter knew or should have known that any arrangements or other facts described in the certificate have changed, making the statement inaccurate in any respect, within a sufficient time before the statement was relied upon to have reasonably enabled that general partner to cancel or amend the certificate, or to file a petition for its cancellation or amendment under Section 205.

Sec. 208. (Constructive Notice.) The fact that a certificate of limited partnership is on file in the office of the Secretary of State is constructive notice that the partnership is a limited partnership and that the persons designated therein as limited partners are limited partners, but is not constructive notice of any other fact.

Sec. 209. (Delivery of Certificates to Limited Partners.) Upon the return by the Secretary of State pursuant to Section 206 of any certificate marked "Filed," the general partners shall promptly deliver or mail a copy of the certificate to each limited partner unless the partnership agreement provides otherwise.

ARTICLE 3

LIMITED PARTNERS

Sec. 301 (Admission of Additional Limited Partners.)

(a) After the filing of a limited partnership's original certificate of limited partnership, a person may be admitted as a new limited partner:

(1) in the case of a person acquiring a partnership interest directly from the limited partnership, upon compliance with the partnership agreement or, if the partnership agreement does not so provide, upon the written consent of all partners; and

(2) in the case of an assignee of a partnership interest of a partner who has the power, as provided in Section 704, to grant the assignee the right to become a limited partner, upon the exercise of that power and compliance with any conditions limiting the grant or exercise of the power.

(b) In each case under subsection (a), the person acquiring the partnership interest becomes a limited partner only upon amendment of the certificate of limited partnership reflecting that fact.

Sec. 302. (Voting.) Subject to the provisions of Section 303, the partnership agreement may grant to all or a specified group of the limited partners the right to vote (on a per capita or any other basis) upon any matter.

Sec. 303. (Liability to Third Parties.)

(a) Except as provided in subsection (d), a limited partner as such is not liable for the obligations of a limited partnership unless, in addition to the exercise of his rights and powers as a limited partner, he takes part in the control of the business. But the limited partner's participation in the control of the business is not substantially the same as the exercise of the powers of a general partner, he is liable only to persons who transact business with the limited partnership with actual knowledge of his participation in control.

(b) A limited partner does not participate in the control of the business within the meaning of subsection (a) solely by doing one or more of the following:

(1) being a contractor for or an agent or employee of a limited partnership or of a general partner;

(2) consulting with and advising a general partner with respect to the business of the limited partnership;

(3) acting as surety for the limited partnership;

(4) approving or disapproving an amendment to the partnership agreement; and

(5) voting on one or more of the following matters:

(i) the dissolution and winding up of the limited partnership;

(ii) the sale, exchange, lease, mortgage, pledge, or other transfer of all or substantially all of the assets of the limited partnership other than in the ordinary course of its business;

(iii) the incurrence of indebtedness by the limited partnership other than in the ordinary course of its business;

(iv) a change in the nature of the business; or

(v) the removal of a general partner.

(c) The enumeration in subsection (b) shall not be construed to mean that the possession or exercise of any other powers by a limited partner constitutes participation by him in the business of the limited partnership.

(d) A limited partner who knowingly permits his name to be used in the name of the limited partnership, except under circumstances permitted by Section 102(2)(i), is liable to creditors who extend credit to the limited partnership without actual knowledge that the limited partner is not a general partner.

Sec. 304. (Person Erroneously Believing Himself a Limited Partner.)

(a) Except as provided in subsection (b) a person who makes a contribution to a business enterprise and erroneously and in good faith believes that he has become a limited partner in the enterprise is not a general partner in the enterprise and is not bound by its obligations by reason of making the contribution, receiving distributions from the enterprise, or exercising any rights of a limited partner, if, on ascertaining the mistake, he:

(1) causes an appropriate certificate of limited partnership or a certificate of amendment to be executed and filed; or

(2) withdraws from future equity participation in the enterprise.

(b) Any person who makes a contribution of the kind described in subsection (a) is liable as a general partner to any third party who transacts business with the enterprise (i) before the person withdraws and an appropriate certificate if any is filed to show the withdrawal, or (ii) before an appropriate certificate is filed to show his status as a limited partner and, in the case of an amendment, after expiration of the 30-day period for filing an amendment relating to the person as a limited partner under Section 202, but in each case only if the third party actually believed in good faith that the person was a general partner at the time of the transaction.

Sec. 305. (Information.) Each limited partner has the right to:

(1) inspect and copy any of the partnership records required to be maintained by Section 105; and

(2) obtain from the general partners from time to time upon reasonable demand (i) true and full information regarding the state of the business and financial condition of the limited partnership, (ii) promptly after becoming available, a copy of the limited partnership's federal, state, and local income tax return for each year, and (iii) any other information regarding the affairs of the limited partnership as is just and reasonable.

ARTICLE 4

GENERAL PARTNERS

Sec. 401. (Admission.) After the filing of a limited partnership's original certificate of limited partnership, new general partners may be admitted only with the specific written consent of each partner.

Sec. 402. (Events of Withdrawal.) Except as otherwise approved by the specific written consent at the time of all partners, a person ceases to be a general partner of a limited partnership upon the happening of any of the following events:

(1) the general partner withdraws from the limited partnership as provided in Section 602;

(2) the general partner ceases to be a member of the limited partnership as provided in Section 702;

(3) the general partner is removed as a gen-

eral partner in accordance with the partnership agreement;

(4) unless otherwise provided in the certificate of limited partnership, the general partner: makes an assignment for the benefit of creditors; files a voluntary petition in bankruptcy; is adjudicated a bankrupt or insolvent; files any petition or answer seeking for himself any reorganization, arrangement, composition, readjustment, liquidation, dissolution, or similar relief under any statute, law, or regulation; files any answer or other pleading admitting or failing to contest the material allegations of a petition filed against him in any proceeding of this nature; or seeks, consents to, or acquiesces in the appointment of any trustee, receiver, or liquidator of the general partner or of all or any substantial part of his properties;

(5) unless otherwise provided in the certificate of limited partnership, [120] days after the commencement of any proceeding against the general partner seeking any reorganization, arrangement, composition, readjustment, liquidation, dissolution, or similar relief under any statute, law, or regulation, the proceeding has not been dismissed, or if, within [90] days after the appointment without his consent or acquiescence of any trustee, receiver, or liquidator of the general partner or of all or any substantial part of his properties, the appointment is not vacated or stayed, or if, within [90] days after the expiration of any stay, the appointment is not vacated;

(6) in the case of a general partner who is a natural person

(i) his death; or

(ii) the entry by a court of competent jurisdiction adjudicating him incompetent to manage his person or his property;

(7) in the case of a general partner who is acting as such in the capacity of a trustee of a trust, the termination of the trust (but not merely the substitution of a new trustee);

(8) in the case of a general partner that is a partnership, the dissolution and commencement of winding up of the partnership;

(9) in the case of a general partner that is a corporation, the filing of a certificate of dissolution, or its equivalent, for the corporation or the revocation of its charter; and

(10) in the case of an estate, the distribution by the fiduciary of all of the estate's interest in the partnership.

Sec. 403. (General Powers and Liabilities.) Except as otherwise provided in this Act and in the partnership agreement, a general partner of a limited partnership has all the rights and powers and is subject to all the restrictions and liabilities of a partner in a partnership without limited partners.

Sec. 404. (Contributions by a General Partner.) A general partner may make contributions to a limited partnership and share in the profits and losses of, and in distributions from, the limited partnership as a general partner. A general partner may also make contributions to and share in profits, losses, and distributions as a limited partner. A person who is both a general partner and a limited partner has all the rights and powers, and is subject to all the restrictions and liabilities, of a general partner and also has, except as otherwise provided in the partnership agreement, all powers, and is subject to the restrictions, of a limited partner to the extent he is participating in the partnership as a limited partner.

Sec. 405. (Voting.) The partnership agreement may grant to all or a specified group of general partners the right to vote (on a per capita or any other basis), separately or with all or any class of the limited partners, on any matter.

ARTICLE 5

FINANCE

Sec. 501. (Form of Contributions.) The contribution of a partner may be in cash, property, or services rendered, or a promissory note or other obligation to contribute cash or property or to perform services.

Sec. 502. (Liability for Contributions.)

(a) Except as otherwise provided in the certificate of limited partnership, a partner is obligated to the limited partnership to perform any promise to contribute cash or property or to perform services regardless of whether he is unable to perform because of death, disability or any other reason. If a partner does not make the required contribution of property or services, he is obligated at the option of the limited partnership to contribute cash equal to that portion of the value (as stated in the certificate of limited partnership) of the stated contribution that has not been made.

(b) Unless otherwise provided in the partnership agreement, the obligation of a partner to make a contribution or return money or other property paid or distributed in violation of this Act may be compromised only by consent of all of the partners. Notwithstanding a compromise so authorized, a creditor of a limited partnership who extends credit, or whose claim arises, after the filing of the certificate of limited partnership or an amendment thereto which, in either case, reflects the obligation and before the amendment or cancellation thereof to reflect the compromise may enforce the precompromise obligation.

Sec. 503. (Sharing of Profits and Losses.)

The profits and losses of a limited partnership shall be allocated among the partners, and among classes of partners, in the manner provided in the partnership agreement. If the partnership agreement does not so provide, profits and losses shall be allocated on the basis of the value (as stated in the certificate of limited partnership) of the contributions actually made by each partner to the extent they have not been returned.

Sec. 504. (Sharing of Distributions.)

Distributions of cash or other assets of a limited partnership shall be allocated among the partners, and among classes of partners, in the manner provided in the partnership agreement. If the partnership agreement does not so provide, distributions shall be made on the basis of the value (as stated in the certificate of limited partnership) of the contributions actually made by each partner to the extent they have not been returned.

ARTICLE 6

DISTRIBUTIONS AND WITHDRAWAL

Sec. 601. (Interim Distributions.)

Except as otherwise provided in this Article, a partner is entitled to receive distributions from a limited partnership before his withdrawal from the limited partnership and before the dissolution and winding up thereof:

(1) to the extent and at the times or upon the happening of the events specified in the partnership agreement; and

(2) if any distribution constitutes a return of any part of his contribution under Section 608(b), to the extent and at the times or upon the happening of the events specified in the certificate of limited partnership.

Sec. 602. (Withdrawal of General Partner.)

A general partner may withdraw from a limited partnership at any time by giving written notice to the other partners, but if the withdrawal violates the partnership agreement, the limited partnership may recover from the withdrawing general partner damages for breach of the partnership agreement and offset the damages against the amount otherwise distributable to him.

Sec. 603. (Withdrawal of Limited Partner.)

A limited partner may withdraw from a limited partnership at the time or upon the happening of the events specified in the certificate of limited partnership and in accordance with any procedures provided in the partnership agreement. If the certificate of limited partnership does not specify the time or the events upon the happening of which a limited partner may withdraw from the limited partnership or a definite time for the dissolution and winding up of the limited partnership, a limited partner may withdraw from the limited partnership upon not less than 6 months' prior written notice to each general partner at his address on the books of the limited partnership at its office in this State.

Sec. 604. (Distributions Upon Withdrawal.) Except as provided in this Article, upon withdrawal any withdrawing partner is entitled to receive any distributions to which he is entitled under the partnership agreement and, if not provided, he is entitled to receive, within a reasonable time after withdrawal, the fair value of his interest in the limited partnership as of the date of withdrawal, based upon his right to share in distributions from the limited partnership.

Sec. 605. (Distributions in Kind.) Except as provided in the certificate of limited partnership, a partner, regardless of the nature of his contribution, has no right to demand and receive any distribution from a limited partnership in any form other than cash. Except as provided in the partnership agreement, a partner may not be compelled to accept a distribution of any asset in kind from a limited partnership to the extent that the percentage of the asset distributed to him exceeds a percentage of that asset which is equal to the percentage in which he shares in distributions from the limited partnership.

Sec. 606. (Right to Distributions.) At the time a partner becomes entitled to receive a distribution, he has the status of, and is entitled to all of the remedies available to, a creditor of the limited partnership with respect to the distribution.

Sec. 607. (Limitations on Distributions.) A partner may not receive a distribution from a limited partnership to the extent that, after giving effect to the distribution, all liabilities of the limited partnership other than liabilities to partners on account of their partnership interests, exceed the fair value of the partnership's assets.

Sec. 608. (Liability Upon Return of Contributions.)

(a) If a partner has received the return of any part of his contribution without violation of the partnership agreement or this Act, for a period of one year thereafter he is liable to the limited partnership for the amount of his contribution returned, but only to the extent necessary to discharge the limited partnership's liabilities to creditors who extended credit to the limited partnership during the period the contribution was held by the partnership.

(b) If a partner has received the return of any part of his contribution in violation of the partnership agreement or this Act, for a period of 6 years thereafter he is liable to the limited partnership for the amount of the contribution wrongfully returned.

(c) A partner has received a return of his contribution to the extent that a distribution to him reduces his share of the fair value of the net assets of the limited partnership below the value (as set forth in the certificate of limited partnership) of his contributions which have not theretofore been distributed to him.

ARTICLE 7

ASSIGNMENT OF PARTNERSHIP INTERESTS

Sec. 701. (Nature of Partnership Interest.) A partnership interest is a partner's share of the profits and losses of a limited partnership and the right to receive distributions of partnership assets. A partnership interest is personal property.

Sec. 702. (Assignment of Partnership Interest.) Except as otherwise provided in the partnership agreement, a partnership interest is assignable in whole or in part. An assignment of a partnership interest does not dissolve a limited partnership nor entitle the assignee to become a partner or to exercise any of the rights thereof. An assignment only entitles the assignee to receive, to the extent assigned, any distributions to which the assignor would be entitled. Except as otherwise provided in the partnership agreement, a partner ceases to be a partner upon assignment of all his partnership interest.

Sec. 703. (Rights of Creditors.) On due application to a court of competent jurisdiction by any judgment creditor of a partner, the court may charge the partnership interest of the partner with payment of the unsatisfied amount of the judgment debt with interest thereon. To the extent so charged, the judgment creditor has only the rights of an assignee of the partnership interest. This Act shall not be construed to deprive any partner of the benefit of any exemption laws applicable to his partnership interest.

Sec. 704. (Right of Assignee to Become Limited Partner.)

(a) An assignee of a partnership interest, including an assignee of a general partner, may become a limited partner if and to the extent that (1) the assignor gives the assignee that right in accordance with authority described in the certificate of limited partnership or, (2) in the absence of that authority, all other partners consent.

(b) An assignee who has become a limited partner has, to the extent assigned, all the rights and powers, and is subject to all the restrictions and liabilities, of a limited partner under the partnership agreement and this Act. An assignee who becomes a limited partner is also liable for the obligations of his assignor to make and return contributions as provided in Article 6, but the assignee is not obligated for liabilities unknown to the assignee at the time he became a limited partner and which could not be ascertained from the certificate of limited partnership.

(c) If an assignee of a partnership interest becomes a limited partner, the assignor is not released from the liability to the limited partnership under Sections 207 and 502.

Sec. 705. (Power of Estate of Deceased or Incompetent Partner.) If a partner who is a natural person dies or a court of competent jurisdiction adjudges him to be incompetent to manage his person or his property, the partner's executor, administrator, guardian, conservator, or other legal representative may exercise all of the partner's rights for the purpose of settling his estate or administering his property, including any power the partner had to give an assignee the right to become a limited partner. If a partner that is a corporation, trust, or other entity other than a natural person is dissolved or terminated, those powers may be exercised by the legal representative or successor of the partner.

ARTICLE 8

DISSOLUTION

Sec. 801. (Nonjudicial Dissolution.) A limited partnership is dissolved and its affairs shall be wound up upon the happening of the first to occur of the following:

(1) at the time or upon the happening of the events specified in the certificate of limited partnership;

(2) upon the unanimous written consent of all partners;

(3) upon the happening of an event of withdrawal of a general partner unless at the time there is at least one other general partner and the certificate of limited partnership permits the business of the limited partnership to be carried on by the remaining general partner and he does so, but the limited partnership shall not be dissolved or wound up by reason of any event of withdrawal if, within 90 days after the withdrawal, all partners agree in writing to continue the business of the limited partnership and to the appointment of one or more new general partners if necessary or desired; or

(4) upon entry of a decree of judicial dissolution in accordance with Section 802.

Sec. 802. (Dissolution by Decree of Court.) On application by or for a partner the [here designate the proper court] court may decree a dissolution of a limited partnership whenever it is not reasonably practicable to carry on the business in conformity with the partnership agreement.

Sec. 803. (Winding Up.) Unless otherwise provided in the partnership agreement, the general partners who have not wrongfully dissolved the limited partnership or, if none, the limited partners, may wind up the limited partnership's affairs; but any partner, his legal representative or his assignee, upon cause shown, may obtain winding up by the [here designate the proper court] court.

Sec. 804. (Distribution of Assets.) Upon the winding up of a limited partnership, the assets shall be distributed as follows:

(1) to creditors, including partners who are creditors (to the extent otherwise permitted by law), in satisfaction of liabilities of the limited partnership other than liabilities for distribu-tions to partners pursuant to Section 601 or 604;

(2) except as otherwise provided in the partnership agreement, to partners and ex-partners in satisfaction of liabilities for distri-butions pursuant to Section 601 or 604; and

(3) except as otherwise provided in the partnership agreement, to partners *first* for the return of their contributions and *second* re-specting their partnership interests, in the proportions in which the partners share in dis-tributions.

ARTICLE 9
FOREIGN LIMITED PARTNERSHIPS

Sec. 901. (Law Governing.) Subject to the constitution and public policy of this State, the laws of the state under which a foreign limited partnership is organized govern its organization and internal affairs and the lia-bility of its limited partners, and a foreign limited partnership may not be denied registra-tion by reason of any difference betwen those laws and the laws of this state.

Sec. 902. (Registration.) Before transact-ing business in this State, a foreign limited partnership shall register with the Secretary of State. In order to register, a foreign limited partnership shall submit to the Secretary of State in duplicate an application for registra-tion as a foreign limited partnership, signed and sworn to by a general partner and setting forth:

(1) the name of the foreign limited partner-ship and, if different, the name under which it proposes to transact business and register in this State;

(2) the state and date of its formation;

(3) the general character of the business it proposes to transact in this State;

(4) the name and address of any agent for service of process on the foreign limited part-nership whom the foreign limited partnership desires to appoint, which agent must be an individual resident of this State, a domestic corporation, or a foreign corporation author-ized to do business in this State; and with a place of business in this State;

(5) a statement that the Secretary of State is appointed the agent of the foreign limited partnership for service of process if no agent has been appointed pursuant to paragraph (4) or, if appointed the agent's authority has been revoked or the agent cannot be found or served with the exercise of reasonable diligence;

(6) the address of the office required to be maintained in the state of its organization by the laws of that state or, if not so required, of the principal office of the foreign limited part-nership; and

(7) if the certificate of limited partnership filed in the foreign limited partnerships' state of organization is not required to include the names and business addresses of the partners, or list of the names and addresses.

Sec. 903. (Issuance of Registration.)

(a) If the Secretary of State finds that an application for registration conforms to law and all requisite fees have been paid, he shall:

(1) endorse on the application the word "Filed," and the month, day, and year of the filing thereof;

(2) file in his office one of the duplicate originals of the application; and

(3) issue a certificate of registration to transact business in this State.

(b) The certificate of registration, together with one duplicate original of the application, shall be returned to the person who filed the application or his representative.

Sec. 904. (Name.) A foreign limited part-nership may register with the Secretary of State under any name (whether or not it is the name under which it is registered in its state of organization) that includes the words "limited partnership" and that could be registered by a domestic limited partnership.

Sec. 905. (Changes and Amendments.) If any statement in a foreign limited partnership's application for registration was false when made or any arrangements or other facts described have changed, making the application inaccurate in any respect, the foreign limited partnership shall promptly file in the office of the Secretary of State a certificate, signed and sworn to by a general partner, correcting the statement.

Sec. 906. (Cancellation of Registration.) A foreign limited partnership may cancel its registration by filing with the Secretary of State a certificate of cancellation signed and sworn to by a general partner. A cancellation does not terminate the authority of the Secretary of State to accept service of process on the foreign limited partnership with respect to [claims for relief] [causes of action] arising out of the transaction of business in this State.

Sec. 907. (Transaction of Business Without Registration.) (a) A foreign limited partnership transacting business in this State without registration may not maintain any action, suit, or proceeding in any court of this State until it has registered.

(b) The failure of a foreign limited partnership to register in this State does not impair the validity of any contract or act of the foreign limited partnership, and does not prevent the foreign limited partnership from defending any action, suit, or proceeding in any court of this State.

(c) A limited partner of a foreign limited partnership is not liable as a general partner of the foreign limited partnership solely by reason of the foreign limited partnership's transacting business in this State without registration.

(d) A foreign limited partnership, by transacting business in this State without registration, appoints the Secretary of State as its agent for service of process with respect to [claims for relief] [causes of action] arising out of the transaction of business in this State.

Sec. 908. (Action by [Appropriate Official].) The [appropriate official] may bring an action to restrain a foreign limited partnership from transacting business in this State in violation of this Article.

ARTICLE 10

DERIVATIVE ACTIONS

Sec. 1001. (Right of Action.) A limited partner may bring an action in the right of a limited partnership to recover a judgment in its favor if the general partners having authority to do so have refused to bring the action or an effort to cause those general partners to bring the action is not likely to succeed.

Sec. 1002. (Proper Plaintiff.) In a derivative action, the plaintiff must be a partner at (1) the time of bringing the action, and (2) at the time of the transaction of which he complains or his status as a partner must have devolved upon him by operation of law or pursuant to the terms of the partnership agreement from a person who was a partner at the time of the transaction.

Sec. 1003. (Pleading.) In any derivative action, the complaint shall set forth with particularity the effort of the plaintiff to secure initiation of the action by a general partner having authority to do so or the reasons for not making the effort.

Sec. 1004. (Expenses.) If a derivative action is successful, in whole or in part, or anything is received by the plaintiff as a result of a judgment, compromise, or settlement of an action or claim, the court may award the plaintiff reasonable expenses, including reasonable attorney's fees, and shall direct him to account to the limited partnership for the remainder of the proceeds so received by him.

ARTICLE 11

MISCELLANEOUS

Sec. 1101.   (Savings Clause.)

Sec. 1102.   (Name of Act.)   This Act may be cited as the Uniform Limited Partnership Act.

Sec. 1103.   (Construction and Application.) This Act shall be so construed and applied to effect its general purpose to make uniform the law with respect to the subject of this Act among states enacting it.

Sec. 1104.   (Rules for Cases Not Provided for in This Act.)   In any case not provided for in this Act the provisions of the Uniform Partnership Act govern.

Sec. 1105.   (Act Repealed.) Except as affecting existing limited partnerships to the extent set forth in Section ——, the Act of [here designate the existing limited partnership act or acts] is hereby repealed.

GLOSSARY

Abandonment   Applies to many situations. Abandonment of property is giving up dominion and control over it, with intention to relinquish all claims to it. Losing property is an involuntary act; abandonment is voluntary. When used with duty, the word *abandonment* is synonymous with *repudiation*.

Abatement of a nuisance   An action to end any act detrimental to the public; e.g., suit to enjoin a plant from permitting the escape of noxious vapors.

Acceptance*   Under Article 3—Commercial Paper, this is the drawee's signed engagement to honor a draft as presented. It must be written on the draft and may consist of drawee's signature alone. It becomes operative when completed by delivery or notification.

Accord and satisfaction   An agreement between two persons—one of whom has a right of action against the other—that the latter should do or give, and the former accept, something in satisfaction of the right of action—something different from, and usually less than, what might legally be enforced.

Account*   Any right to payment for goods sold or leased or for services rendered but not evidenced by an instrument or chattel paper. Under Article 4—Bank Deposits and Collections, *account* is any account with a bank and includes a checking, time, interest, or savings account.

Account debtor   The person who is obligated on an account, chattel paper, contract right, or general intangible.

Accretion   Gradual, imperceptible accumulation of land by natural causes, usually next to a stream or river.

Action ex contractu   An action at law to recover damages for the breach of a duty arising out of contract. There are two types of causes of action: those arising out of contract, ex contractu, and those arising out of tort, ex delicto.

Action ex delicto   An action at law to recover damages for the breach of a duty existing by reason of a general law. An action to recover damages for an injury caused by the negligent use of an automobile is an ex delicto action. Tort or wrong is the basis of the action. *See* Action ex contractu.

Adjudicate   The exercise of judicial power by hearing, trying, and determining the claims of litigants before the court.

Administrative law   The branch of public law dealing with the operation of the various agency boards and commissions of government.

Administrator   A person to whom letters of administration have been issued by a probate court, giving such person authority to administer, manage, and close the estate of a deceased person.

Adverse possession   Acquisition of legal title to another's land by being in continuous possession during a period prescribed in the statute. Possession must be actual, visible, known to the world, and with intent to claim title as owner, against the rights of the true owner. Claimant usually must pay taxes and liens lawfully charged against the property. Cutting timber or grass from time to time on the land of another is not the kind of adverse possession that will confer title.

Advising bank*   A bank that gives notification of the issuance of a credit by another bank.

Affidavit   A voluntary statement of facts formally reduced to writing, sworn to, or affirmed before, some officer authorized to administer oaths. The officer is usually a notary public.

Affirmative action program   Active recruitment and advancement of minority workers.

Affirmative defense   A matter that constitutes opposition to the allegations of a complaint, which are assumed to be true.

A fortiori   Latin words meaning "by a stronger reason." Often used in judicial opinions to say that since specific proven facts lead to a certain conclusion, there are for this reason other facts that logically follow and strengthen the argument for the conclusion.

Agency coupled with an interest   When an agent has possession or control over the property of his principal and has a right of action against interference by third parties, an agency with an interest has been created. An agent who advances freight for goods sent him by his principal has an interest in the goods.

Agent   A person authorized to act for another (principal). The term may apply to a person in the service of another; but in the strict sense, an agent is one who stands in place of his principal. A works for B as a gardener and is thus a servant, but he may be an agent. If A sells goods for B, he becomes more than a servant. He acts in the place of B.

Agreement*   The bargain of the parties in fact as found in their language or by implication from other circum-

---

*Terms followed by an asterisk are defined in the Uniform Commercial Code and have significance in connection with Code materials. They are often given a particular meaning in relation to the Code, and their definitions do not necessarily conform with meanings outside the framework of the Code.

stances, including course of dealing or usage of trade or course of performance as provided in the Uniform Commercial Code.

Amicus curiae A friend of the court who participates in litigation, usually on appeal, though not a party to the lawsuit.

Annuity A sum of money paid yearly to a person during his lifetime. The sum arises out of a contract by which the recipient or another had previously deposited sums in whole or in part with the grantor—the grantor to return a designated portion of the principal and interest in periodic payments when the beneficiary attains a designated age.

Appellant The party who takes an appeal from one court or jurisdiction to another.

Appellee The party in a cause against whom an appeal is taken.

A priori A generalization resting on presuppositions, not upon proven facts.

Arbitration The submission for determination of disputed matter to private, unofficial persons selected in a manner provided by law or agreement.

Architect's certificate A formal statement signed by an architect that a contractor has performed under his contract and is entitled to be paid. The construction contract provides when and how such certificates shall be issued.

Artisan's lien One who has expended labor upon, or added to, another's property is entitled to possession of the property as security until reimbursed for the value of labor or material. A repairs B's watch. A may keep the watch in his possession until B pays for the repairs.

Assignee An assign or assignee is one to whom an assignment has been made.

Assignment The transfer by one person to another of a right that usually arises out of a contract. Such rights are called *choses in action.* A sells and assigns to C his contract right to purchase B's house. A is an assignor. C is an assignee. The transfer is an assignment.

Assignment* A transfer of the "contract" or of "all my rights under the contract" or an assignment in similar general terms is an assignment of rights. Unless the language or the circumstances (as in an assignment for security) indicate the contrary, it is a delegation of performance of the duties of the assignor, and its acceptance by the assignee constitutes a promise by him to perform those duties. This promise is enforceable by either the assignor or the other party to the original contract.

Assignment for the benefit of creditors A, a debtor, has many creditors. An assignment of his property to X, a third party, with directions to make distribution of his property to his creditors, is called an assignment for the benefit of creditors. *See* Composition of creditors.

Assignor One who makes an assignment.

Assumption of the risk Negligence doctrine that bars the recovery of damages by an injured party on the ground that such party acted with actual or constructive knowledge of the hazard causing the injury.

Attachment A legal proceeding accompanying an action in court by which a plaintiff may acquire a lien on a defendant's property as a security for the payment of any judgment that the plaintiff may recover. It is provisional

and independent of the court action and is usually provided for by statute. A sues B. Before judgment, A attaches B's automobile, in order to make sure of the payment of any judgment that A may secure.

Attorney at law A person to whom the state grants a license to practice law.

Attorney in fact A person acting for another under a grant of special power created by an instrument in writing. B, in writing, grants special power to A to execute and deliver for B a conveyance of B's land to X.

Bad faith "Actual intent" to mislead or deceive another. It does not mean misleading by an honest, inadvertent, or careless misstatement.

Bail (verb) To set at liberty an arrested or imprisoned person after that person or at least two others have given security to the state that the accused will appear at the proper time and place for trial.

Bailee A person into whose possession personal property is delivered.

Bailee* The person who, by a warehouse receipt, bill of lading, or other document of title, acknowledges possession of goods and contracts to deliver it.

Bailment Delivery of personal property to another for a special purpose. Delivery is made under a contract, either expressed or implied, that upon the completion of the special purpose, the property shall be redelivered to the bailor or placed at his disposal. A loans B his truck. A places his watch with B for repair. A places his furniture in B's warehouse. A places his securities in B Bank's safety deposit vault. In each case, A is a bailor and B is a bailee.

Bailor One who delivers personal property into the possession of another.

Banking day* Under Article 4—Bank Deposits and Collections, this is the part of any day on which a bank is open to the public for carrying on substantially all of its banking functions.

Bearer* The person in possession of an instrument, document of title, or security payable to bearer or indorsed in blank.

Bearer form* A security is in bearer form when it runs to bearer according to its terms and not by reason of any indorsement.

Beneficiary A person (not a promisee) for whose benefit a trust, an insurance policy, a will, or a contract promise is made.

Beneficiary* A person who is entitled under a letter of credit to draw or demand payment.

Bequest In a will, a gift of personal property.

Bid An offering of money in exchange for property placed for sale. At an ordinary auction sale, a bid is an offer to purchase. It may be withdrawn before acceptance is indicated by the fall of the hammer.

Bilateral contract One containing mutual promises, with each party being both a promisor and a promisee.

Bill of lading* A document evidencing the receipt of goods for shipment, issued by a person engaged in the business of transporting or forwarding goods. Includes an airbill, a document that serves air transportation as a bill of lading serves marine or rail transportation. It includes an air consignment note or air waybill.

Bill of particulars In legal practice, a written statement that one party to a lawsuit gives to another, describing in detail the elements upon which the claim of the first party is based.

Bill of sale Written evidence that the title to personal property has been transferred from one person to another. It must contain words of transfer and be more than a receipt.

Blue-sky laws Popular name for acts providing for the regulation and supervision of investment securities.

Bona fide purchaser* A purchaser of a security for value, in good faith, and without notice of any adverse claim, who takes delivery of a security in bearer form or in registered form issued to him or indorsed to him or in blank.

Bond A promise under seal to pay money. The term generally designates the promise made by a corporation, either public or private, to pay money to bearer. E.g., U.S. government bonds or Illinois Central Railroad bonds. Also, an obligation by which one person promises to answer for the debt or default of another—a surety bond.

Broker A person employed to make contracts with third persons on behalf of his principal. The contracts involve trade, commerce, buying and selling for a fee (called brokerage or commission).

Broker* A person engaged full or part time in the business of buying and selling securities, who in the transaction concerned acts for, or buys a security from, or sells a security to, a customer.

Bulk transfer* Transfer made outside the ordinary course of the transferor's business but involving a major part of the materials, supplies, merchandise, or other inventory of an enterprise subject to Article 6.

Buyer* A person who buys or contracts to buy goods.

Buyer in ordinary course of business* A person who, in good faith and without knowledge that the sale to him is in violation of the ownership rights or security interest of a third party in the goods, buys in ordinary course from a person in the business of selling goods of that kind. Does not include a pawnbroker. "Buying" may be for cash or by exchange of other property or on secured or unsecured credit. Includes receiving goods or documents of title under a preexisting contract for sale but does not include a transfer in bulk or as security for, or in total or partial satisfaction of, a money debt.

Bylaws Rules for government of a corporation or other organization. Adopted by members or the board of directors, these rules must not be contrary to the law of the land. They affect the rights and duties of the members of the corporation or organization, only, not third persons.

Call An assessment upon a subscriber for partial or full payment on shares of unpaid stock of a corporation. Also, the power of a corporation to make an assessment, notice of an assessment, or the time when the assessment is to be paid.

Cancellation* Either party puts an end to the contract because of breach by the other. Its effect is the same as that of "termination," except that the canceling party also retains any remedy for breach of the whole contract or any unperformed balance.

Capital The net assets of an individual enterprise, partnership, joint stock company, corporation, or business institution, including not only the original investment but also all gains and profits realized from the continued conduct of the business.

Carrier A natural person or a corporation who receives goods under a contract to transport for a consideration from one place to another. A railroad, truckline, busline, airline.

Cashier's check A bill of exchange drawn by the cashier of a bank, for the bank, upon the bank. After the check is delivered or issued to the payee or holder, the drawer bank cannot put a "stop order" against itself. By delivery of the check, the drawer bank has accepted and thus becomes the primary obligor.

Cause of action When one's legal rights have been invaded either by a breach of a contract or by a breach of a legal duty toward one's person or property, a cause of action has been created.

Caveat Literally, "let him beware." It is used generally to mean a warning.

Caveat emptor An old idea at common law—"let the buyer beware." When a vendor sells goods without an express warranty as to their quality and capacity for a particular use and purpose, the buyer must take the risk of loss due to all defects in the goods.

Caveat venditor "Let the seller beware." Unless the seller, by express language, disclaims any responsibility, he shall be liable to the buyer if the goods delivered are different in kind, quality, use, and purpose from those described in the contract of sale.

Cease and desist order An administrative agency order directing a party to refrain from doing a specified act.

Certiorari An order issuing out of an appellate court to a lower court, at the request of an appellant, directing that the record of a case pending in the lower court be transmitted to the upper court for review.

Cestui que trust A person who is the real or beneficial owner of property held in trust. The trustee holds the legal title to the property for the benefit of the cestui que trust.

Chancery Court of equity.

Charter Referring to a private corporation, *charter* includes the contract between the created corporation and the state, the act creating the corporation, and the articles of association granted to the corporation by authority of the legislative act. Referring to municipal corporations, *charter* does not mean a contract between the legislature and the city created. A city charter is a delegation of powers by a state legislature to the governing body of the city. The term includes the creative act, the powers enumerated, and the organization authorized.

Chattel A very broad term derived from the word *cattle*. Includes every kind of property that is not real property. Movable properties, such as horses, automobiles, choses in action, stock certificates, bills of lading, and all "good wares, and merchandise" are chattels personal. Chattels real concern real property such as a lease for years, in which case the lessee owns a chattel real.

Chattel paper* A writing or writings that evidence both a monetary obligation and a security interest in, or a lease of, specific goods. When a transaction is evidenced both by such a security agreement or a lease and by an instrument or a series of instruments, the group of writings taken together constitutes chattel paper.

Chose in action The "right" one person has to recover

money or property from another by a judicial proceeding. The right arises out of contract, claims for money, debts, and rights against property. Notes, drafts, stock certificates, bills of lading, warehouse receipts, and insurance policies are illustrations of choses in action. They are called tangible choses. Book accounts, simple debts, and obligations not evidenced by formal writing are called intangible choses. Choses in action are transferred by assignment.

Circumstantial evidence If, from certain facts and circumstances, according to the experience of mankind, an ordinary, intelligent person may infer that other connected facts and circumstances must necessarily exist, the latter facts and circumstances are considered proven by circumstantial evidence. Proof of fact A from which fact B may be inferred is proof of fact B by circumstantial evidence.

Civil action A proceeding in a law court or a suit in equity by one person against another for the enforcement or protection of a private right or the prevention of a wrong. It includes actions on contract, ex delicto, and all suits in equity. Civil action is in contradistinction to criminal action, in which the state prosecutes a person for breach of a duty.

Civil law The area of law dealing with rights and duties of private parties as individual entities. To be distinguished from criminal law. Sometimes the phrase refers to the European system of codified law.

Clearinghouse* Under Article 4—Bank Deposits and Collections, clearinghouse is any association of banks or other payors regularly clearing items.

Cloud on title Some evidence of record that shows a third person has some prima facie interest in another's property.

Code A collection or compilation of the statutes passed by the legislative body of a state. Often annotated with citations of cases decided by the state supreme courts. These decisions construe the statutes. Examples: Oregon Compiled Laws Annotated, United States Code Annotated.

Codicil An addition to, or a change in, an executed last will and testament. It is a part of the original will and must be executed with the same formality as the original will.

Coinsurer A term in a fire insurance policy that requires the insured to bear a certain portion of the loss when he fails to carry complete coverage. For example, unless the insured carries insurance that totals 80 percent of the value of the property, the insurer shall be liable for only that portion of the loss that the total insurance carried bears to 80 percent of the value of the property.

Collateral With reference to debts or other obligations, *collateral* means security placed with a creditor to assure the performance of the obligator. If the obligator performs, the collateral is returned by the creditor. A owes B $1,000. To secure the payment, A places with B a $500 certificate of stock in X company. The $500 certificate is called collateral security.

Collateral* The property subject to a security interest. Includes accounts, contract rights, and chattel paper that have been sold.

Collecting bank* Under Article 4—Bank Deposits and Collections, any bank handling the item for collection except the payor bank.

Collective bargaining The process of good-faith negotiation between employer's and employees' representatives, concerning issues of mutual interest.

Commerce clause Article I, Section 8, Clause 3 of the Constitution of the United States, granting Congress the authority to regulate commerce with foreign nations and among the states.

Commercial unit* A unit of goods that, by commercial usage, is a single whole for purposes of sale. Its division would materially impair its character or value on the market or in use. A commercial unit may be a single article (as a machine) or a set of articles (as a suite of furniture or an assortment of sizes) or a quantity (as a bale, gross, or carload) or any other unit treated in use or in the relevant market as a single whole.

Commission The sum of money, interest, brokerage, compensation, or allowance given to a factor or broker for carrying on the business of his principal.

Commission merchant An agent or factor employed to sell "goods, wares, and merchandise" consigned or delivered to him by his principal.

Common carrier One who is engaged in the business of transporting personal property from one place to another for compensation. Such person is bound to carry for all who tender their goods and the price for transportation. A common carrier operates as a public utility and is subject to state and federal regulations.

Common law That body of law deriving from judicial decisions, as opposed to legislatively enacted statutes and administrative regulations.

Community property All property acquired after marriage by husband and wife, other than separate property acquired by devise, bequest, or from the proceeds of non-community property. Community property is a concept of property ownership by husband and wife inherited from the civil law. The husband and wife are somewhat like partners in their ownership of property acquired during marriage.

Complaint The first paper a plaintiff files in a court in a lawsuit. It is called a pleading. It is a statement of the facts upon which the plaintiff rests his cause of action.

Composition of creditors An agreement among creditors and their debtors by which the creditors will take a lesser amount in complete satisfaction of the total debt. A owes B and C $500 each. A agrees to pay B and C $250 each in complete satisfaction of the $500 due each. B and C agree to take $250 in satisfaction.

Compromise An agreement between two or more persons, usually opposing parties in a lawsuit, to settle the matters of the controversy without further resort to hostile litigation. An adjustment of issues in dispute by mutual concessions before resorting to a lawsuit.

Condemnation proceedings An action or proceeding in court authorized by legislation (federal or state) for the purpose of taking private property for public use. It is the exercise by the judiciary of the sovereign power of eminent domain.

Condition A clause in a contract, either expressed or implied, that has the effect of investing or divesting the legal rights and duties of the parties to the contract. In a deed, a condition is a qualification or restriction providing for the happening or nonhappening of events that, on occurrence, will destroy, commence, or enlarge an estate. "A grants Blackacre to B, so long as said land shall be used for church purposes." If it ceases to be used for church purposes, the title to Blackacre will revert to the grantor.

Condition precedent A clause in a contract providing that immediate rights and duties shall vest only upon the happening of some event. Securing an architect's certificate by a contractor before the contractor is entitled to payment is a condition precedent. A condition is not a promise; hence, its breach will not give rise to a cause of action for damages. A breach of a condition is the basis for a defense. If the contractor sues the owner without securing the architect's certificate, the owner has a defense.

Conditions concurrent Conditions concurrent are mutually dependent and must be performed at the same time by the parties to the contract. Payment of money and delivery of goods in a cash sale are conditions concurrent. Failure to perform by one party permits a cause of action upon tender by the other party. If S refuses to deliver goods in a cash sale, B, upon tender but not delivery of the money, places S in default and thus may sue S. B does not part with his money without getting the goods. If S sued B, B would have a defense.

Condition subsequent A clause in a contract providing for the happening of an event that divests legal rights and duties. A clause in a fire insurance policy providing that the policy shall be null and void if combustible material is stored within 10 feet of the building is a condition subsequent. If a fire occurs and combustible material was within 10 feet of the building, the insurance company is excused from its duty to pay for the loss.

Confirming bank A bank that engages either that it will itself honor a credit already issued by another bank or that such a credit will be honored by the issuer or a third bank.

Conforming* Goods or conduct, including any part of a performance, are "conforming" or conform to the contract when they are in accordance with the obligations under contract.

Conglomerate merger Merging of companies that have neither the relationship of competitors nor that of supplier and customer.

Consideration An essential element in the creation of contract obligation. A detriment to the promisee and a benefit to the promisor. One promise is consideration for another promise. They create a bilateral contract. An act is consideration for a promise. This creates a unilateral contract. Performance of the act asked for by the promisee is a legal detriment to the promisee and a benefit to the promisor.

Consignee A person to whom a shipper usually directs a carrier to deliver goods; generally the buyer of goods and called a consignee on a bill of lading.

Consignee* The person named in a bill to whom or to whose order the bill promises delivery.

Consignment The delivery, sending, or transferring of property, "goods, wares, and merchandise" into the possession of another, usually for the purpose of sale. Consignment may be a bailment or an agency for sale.

Consignor The shipper who delivers freight to a carrier for shipment and who directs the bill of lading to be exe-

cuted by the carrier. May be the consignor-consignee if the bill of lading is made to his own order.

Consignor* The person named in a bill as the person from whom the goods have been received for shipment.

Conspicuous* A term or clause is conspicuous when it is written so that a reasonable person against whom it is to operate ought to have noticed it. A printed heading in capitals (as NONNEGOTIABLE BILL OF LADING) is conspicuous. Language in the body of a form is "conspicuous" if it is in larger or other contrasting type or color. But in a telegram, any stated term is "conspicuous." Whether a term or clause is "conspicuous" or not is for decision by the court.

Conspiracy A combination or agreement between two or more persons for the commission of a criminal act.

Constructive delivery Although physical delivery of personal property has not occurred, the conduct of the parties may imply that possession and title has passed between them. S sells large and bulky goods to B. Title and possession may pass by the act and conduct of the parties.

Consumer goods* Goods that are used or bought for use primarily for personal, family, or household purposes.

Contingent fee An arrangement whereby an attorney is compensated for services in a lawsuit according to an agreed percentage of the amount of money recovered.

Contract* The total obligation that results from the parties' agreement as affected by the Code and any other applicable rules of law.

Contract right* Under a contract, any right to payment not yet earned by performance and not evidenced by an instrument or chattel paper.

Contributory negligence In a negligence suit, failure of the plaintiff to use reasonable care.

Conversion* Under Article 3—Commercial Paper, an instrument is converted when a drawee to whom it is delivered for acceptance refuses to return it on demand; or any person to whom it is delivered for payment refuses on demand either to pay or to return it; or it is paid on a forged indorsement.

Conveyance A formal written instrument, usually called a deed, by which the title or other interests in land (real property) are transferred from one person to another. The word expresses also the fact that the title to real property has been transferred from one person to another.

Corporation A collection of individuals created by statute as a legal person, vested with powers and capacity to contract, own, control, convey property, and transact business within the limits of the powers granted.

Corporation de facto If persons have attempted in good faith to organize a corporation under a valid law (statute) and have failed in some minor particular but have thereafter exercised corporate powers, they are a corporation de facto. Failure to notarize incorporators' signatures on applications for charter is an illustration of noncompliance with statutory requirements.

Corporation de jure A corporation that has been formed by complying with the mandatory requirements of the law authorizing such a corporation.

Corporeal Physical; perceptible by the senses. Automobiles, grain, fruit, and horses are corporeal and tangible and are called chattels. *Corporeal* is used in contradistinction to *incorporeal* or *intangible*. A chose in action (such as a check) is corporeal and tangible, or a chose in action may be a simple debt, incorporeal and intangible.

Costs In litigation, an allowance authorized by statute to a party for expenses incurred in prosecuting or defending a lawsuit. The word *costs,* unless specifically designated by statute or contract, does not include attorney's fees.

Counterclaims By cross-action, the defendant claims that he is entitled to recover from the plaintiff. Claim must arise out of the same transaction set forth in the plaintiff's complaint and be connected with the same subject matter. S sues B for the purchase price. B counterclaims that the goods were defective and that he thereby suffered damages.

Course of dealing A sequence of previous conduct between the parties to a particular transaction. The conduct is fairly to be regarded as establishing a common basis of understanding for interpreting their expressions and other conduct.

Covenant A promise in writing under seal. It is often used as a substitute for the word *contract.* There are convenants (promises) in deeds, leases, mortgages, and other instruments under seal. The word is used sometimes to name promises in unsealed instruments such as insurance policies.

Cover* After a breach by a seller, the buyer may "cover" by making in good faith and without unreasonable delay any reasonable purchase of, or contract to purchase, goods in substitution for those due from the seller.

Credit* ("Letter of credit.") An engagement by a bank or other person made at the request of a customer and of a kind within the scope of Article 5—Letters of Credit, that the issuer will honor drafts or other demands for payment upon compliance with the conditions specified in the credit. A credit may be either revocable or irrevocable. The engagement may be either an agreement to honor or a statement that the bank or other person is authorized to honor.

Creditor* Includes a general creditor, a secured creditor, a lien creditor, and any representative of creditors, including an assignee for the benefit of creditors, a trustee in bankruptcy, a receiver in equity, and an executor or administrator of an insolvent debtor's or assignor's estate.

Creditor beneficiary One who, for a consideration, promises to discharge another's duty to a third party. A owes C $100. B, for a consideration, promises A to pay A's debt to C. B is a creditor beneficiary.

Cumulative voting In voting for directors, a stockholder may cast as many votes as he has shares of stock multiplied by the number to be elected. His votes may be all for one candidate or distributed among as many candidates as there are offices to be filled.

Custodian bank* A bank or trust company that acts as custodian for a clearing corporation. It must be supervised and examined by the appropriate state or federal authority.

Custody (personal property) The words *custody* and *possession* are not synonymous. *Custody* means in charge of, to keep and care for under the direction of the true owner, without any interest therein adverse to the true owner. A servant is in custody of his master's goods. *See* Possession.

Customer* Under Article 4—Bank Deposits and Collections, a customer is any person having an account with a bank or for whom a bank has agreed to collect items. It includes a bank carrying an account with another bank. As used in Letters of Credit, a customer is a buyer or other person who causes an issuer to issue a credit. The term also includes a bank that procures insurance or confirmation on behalf of that bank's customer.

Damages A sum of money the court imposes upon a defendant as compensation for the plaintiff because the defendant has injured the plaintiff by breach of a legal duty.

d.b.a. "Doing business as." A person who conducts his business under an assumed name is designated "John Doe d.b.a. Excelsior Co."

Debenture A corporate obligation sold as an investment. Similar to a corporate bond but not secured by a trust deed. It is not like corporate stock.

Debtor* The person who owes payment or other performance of the obligation secured, whether or not he owns, or has rights in, the collateral. Includes the seller of accounts, contract rights, or chattel paper. When the debtor and the owner of the collateral are not the same person, *debtor* means the owner of the collateral in any provision of the Article dealing with the obligation and may include both if the context so requires.

Deceit Conduct in a business transaction by which one person, through fraudulent representations, misleads another who has a right to rely on such representations as the truth or who, by reason of an unequal station in life, has no means of detecting such fraud.

Declaratory judgment A determination by a court on a question of law, the court simply declaring the rights of the parties but not ordering anything to be done.

Decree The judgment of the chancellor (judge) in a suit in equity. Like a judgment at law, it is the determination of the rights between the parties and is in the form of an order that requires the decree to be carried out. An order that a contract be specifically enforced is an example of a decree.

Deed A written instrument in a special form, signed, sealed, delivered, and used to pass the legal title of real property from one person to another. (*See* Conveyance.) In order that the public may know about the title to real property, deeds are recorded in the Deed Record office of the county where the land is situated.

Deed of trust An instrument by which title to real property is conveyed to a trustee to hold as security for the holder of notes or bonds. It is like a mortgage, except the security title is held by a person other than the mortgagee creditor. Most corporate bonds are secured by a deed of trust.

De facto Arising out of, or founded upon, fact, although merely apparent or colorable. A de facto officer is one who assumes to be an officer under some color of right, acts as an officer, but in point of law is not a real officer. *See* Corporation de facto.

Defendant A person who has been sued in a court of law; the person who answers the plaintiff's complaint. The word is applied to the defending party in civil actions. In criminal actions, the defending party is referred to as the accused.

Deficiency judgment If, upon the foreclosure of a mortgage, the mortgaged property does not sell for an amount sufficient to pay the mortgage indebtedness, the difference is called a deficiency and is chargeable to the mortgagor or to any person who has purchased the property and assumed and agreed to pay the mortgage. M borrows $10,000 from B and as security gives a mortgage on Blackacre. At maturity, M does not pay the debt. B forecloses, and at public sale Blackacre sells for $8,000. There is a deficiency of $2,000, chargeable against M. If M had sold Blackacre to C and C had assumed and agreed to pay the mortgage, he would also be liable for the deficiency.

Defraud To deprive one of some right by deceitful means. To cheat; to withhold wrongfully that which belongs to another. Conveying one's property for the purpose of avoiding payment of debts is a transfer to "hinder, delay, or defraud creditors."

Del credere agency When an agent, factor, or broker guarantees to his principal the payment of a debt due from a buyer of goods, that agent, factor, or broker is operating under a del credere commission or agency.

Delivery A voluntary transfer of the possession of property; actual or constructive, from one person to another, with the intention that title vests in the transferee. In the law of sales, delivery contemplates the absolute giving up of control and dominion over the property by the vendor, and the assumption of the same by the vendee.

Delivery* With respect to instruments, documents of title, chattel paper, or securities, delivery means voluntary transfer of possession.

Delivery order* A written order to deliver goods directed to a warehouseman, carrier, or other person who, in the ordinary course of business, issues warehouse receipts or bills of lading.

Demand A request by a party entitled, under a claim of right, to the performance of a particular act. In order to bind an indorser on a negotiable instrument, the holder must first make a demand on the primary party, who must dishonor the instrument. Demand notes mean "due when demanded." The word *demand* is also used to mean a claim or legal obligation.

Demurrage Demurrage is a sum provided for in a contract of shipment, to be paid for the delay or detention of vessels or railroad cars beyond the time agreed upon for loading or unloading.

Demurrer A common-law procedural method by which the defendant admits all the facts alleged in the plaintiff's complaint but denies that such facts state a cause of action. It raises a question of law on the facts, which must be decided by the court.

Dependent covenants (promises) In contracts, covenants are either concurrent or mutual, dependent or independent. Dependent covenants mean the performance of one promise must occur before the performance of the other promise. In a cash sale, the buyer must pay the money before the seller is under a duty to deliver the goods.

Depositary bank* Under Article 4—Bank Deposits and Collections, this means the first bank to which an item is transferred for collection, even though it is also the payor bank.

Descent The transfer of the title of property to the heirs upon the death of the ancestor; heredity succession. If a person dies without making a will, his property will "descend" according to the Statute of Descent of the state wherein the property is located.

Detriment Legal detriment that is sufficient consideration constitutes change of position or acts of forbearance by a promisee at the request of a promisor. *See* Consideration.

Devise A gift, usually of real property, by a last will and testament.

Devisee The person who receives title to real property by will.

Dictum The written opinion of a judge, expressing an idea, argument, or rule that is not essential for the determination of the issues. It lacks the force of a decision in a judgment.

Directed verdict If it is apparent to reasonable men and the court that the plaintiff, by his evidence, has not made out his case, the court may instruct the jury to bring in a verdict for the defendant. If, however, different inferences may be drawn from the evidence by reasonable men, then the court cannot direct a verdict.

Discharge The word has many meanings. An employee, upon being released from employment, is discharged. A guardian or trustee, upon termination of his trust, is discharged by the court. A debtor released from his debts is discharged in bankruptcy. A person who is released from any legal obligation is discharged.

Discovery practice The disclosure by one party of facts, titles, documents, and other things in his knowledge or possession and necessary to the party seeking the discovery as a part of a cause of action pending.

Dishonor A negotiable instrument is dishonored when it is presented for acceptance or payment but acceptance or payment is refused or cannot be obtained.

Distress for rent The taking of personal property of a tenant in payment of rent on real estate.

Divestiture The antitrust remedy that forces a company to get rid of assets acquired through illegal mergers or monopolistic practices.

Dividend A stockholder's pro rata share in the profits of a corporation. Dividends are declared by the board of directors of a corporation. They are paid in cash, script, property, and stock.

Docket A book containing a brief summary of all acts done in court in the conduct of each case.

Documentary draft* Under Article 4—Bank Deposits and Collections, this means any negotiable or nonnegotiable draft with accompanying documents, securities, or other papers to be delivered against honor of the draft. Also called a "documentary demand for payment" (Article 5—Letters of Credit). Honoring is conditioned upon the presentation of a document or documents. "Document" means any paper, including document of title, security, invoice, certificate, notice of default, and the like.

Document of title* Includes bill of lading, dock warrant, dock receipt, warehouse receipt, or order for the delivery of goods, and any other document that in the regular course of business or financing is treated as adequately evidencing that the person in possession of it is entitled to receive, hold, and dispose of the document and the goods it covers. To be a document of title, a document must purport to be issued by, or addressed to, a bailee and purport to cover goods in the bailee's possession that are either identified or are fungible portions of an identified mass.

Domicile The place a person intends as his fixed and permanent home and establishment and to which, if he is absent, he intends to return. A person can have but one domicile. The old one continues until the acquisition of a new one. One can have more than one residence at a time, but only one domicile. The word is not synonymous with *residence*.

Dominion Applied to the delivery of property by one person to another, *dominion* means all control over the possession and ownership of the property being separated from the transferor or donor and endowed upon the transferee or donee. *See* Gift.

Donee Recipient of a gift.

Donee beneficiary If a promisee is under no duty to a third party, but for a consideration secures a promise from a promisor for the purpose of making a gift to a third party, then the third party is a donee beneficiary. A, promisee for a premium paid, secures a promise from the insurance company, the promisor, to pay A's wife $10,000 upon A's death. A's wife is a donee beneficiary.

Donor One that gives, donates, or presents.

Dormant partner A partner who is not known to third persons but is entitled to share in the profits and is subject to the losses. Since credit is not extended upon the strength of the dormant partner's name, he may withdraw without notice and not be subject to debts contracted after his withdrawal.

Double jeopardy A constitutional doctrine that prohibits an individual from being prosecuted twice in the same tribunal for the same criminal offense.

Due process Fundamental fairness. Applied to judicial proceedings, it includes adequate notice of a hearing and an opportunity to appear and defend in an orderly tribunal.

Duress (of person) A threat of bodily injury, criminal prosecution, or imprisonment of a contracting party or his near relative to such extent that the threatened party is unable to exercise free will at the time of entering into or discharging a legal obligation.

Duress (of property) Seizing by force or withholding goods by one not entitled, and such person's demanding something as a condition for the release of the goods.

Duty (in law) A legal obligation imposed by general law or voluntarily imposed by the creation of a binding promise. For every legal duty there is a corresponding legal right. By general law, A is under a legal duty not to injure B's person or property. B has a right that A not injure his person or property. X may voluntarily create a duty in himself to Y by a promise to sell Y a horse for $100. If Y accepts, X is under a legal duty to perform his promise. *See* Right.

Earnest money A term used to describe money that one contracting party gives to another at the time of entering into the contract in order to "bind the bargain" and which will be forfeited by the donor if he fails to carry out the contract. Generally, in real estate contracts such money is used as part payment of the purchase price.

Easement An easement is an interest in land—a right that one person has to some profit, benefit, or use in or over the land of another. Such right is created by a deed, or it may be acquired by prescription (the continued use of another's land for a statutory period).

Ejectment An action to recover the possession of real property. It is now generally defined by statute and is a statutory action. *See* Forcible entry and detainer.

Ejusdem generis "Of the same class." General words taking their meaning from specific words which precede the general words. General words have the same meaning as specific words mentioned.

Embezzlement The fraudulent appropriation by one person, acting in a fiduciary capacity, of the money or property of another. *See* Conversion.

Eminent domain The right that resides in the United States, state, county, city, school, or other public body to take private property for public use upon payment of just compensation.

Enjoin To require performance or abstention from some act through issuance of an injunction.

Entity "In being" or "existing." The artificial person created when a corporation is organized is "in being" or "existing" for legal purposes, thus an entity. It is separate from the stockholders. The estate of a deceased person while in administration is an entity. A partnership for many legal purposes is an entity.

Equal protection A principle of the Fifth and Fourteenth Amendments to the Constitution, ensuring that individuals under like circumstances shall be accorded the same benefits and burdens under the law of the sovereign.

Equipment* Goods that are used or bought for use primarily in business (including farming or a profession) or by a debtor who is a nonprofit organization or a governmental subdivision or agency; or goods not included in the definitions of inventory, farm products, or consumer goods.

Equitable action In Anglo-American law, there have developed two types of courts and procedures for the administration of justice: law courts and equity courts. Law courts give as a remedy money damages only, whereas equity courts give the plaintiff what he bargains for. A suit for specific performance of a contract is an equitable action. In many states these two courts are now merged.

Equitable conversion An equitable principle that, for certain purposes, permits real property to be converted into personalty. Thus, real property owned by a partnership is, for the purpose of the partnership, personal property because to ascertain a partner's interest, the real property must be reduced to cash. This is an application of the equitable maxim, "Equity considers that done which ought to be done."

Equitable mortgage A written agreement to make certain property security for a debt, and upon the faith of which the parties have acted in making advances, loans, and thus creating a debt. Example: an improperly executed mortgage, one without seal where a seal is required. An absolute deed made to the mortgagee and intended for security only is an equitable mortgage.

Equity Because the law courts in early English law did not always give an adequate remedy, an aggrieved party sought redress from the king. Since this appeal was to the king's conscience, he referred the case to his spiritual adviser, the chancellor. The chancellor decided the case according to rules of fairness, honesty, right, and natural justice. From this there developed the rules in equity. The laws of trust, divorce, rescission of contracts for fraud, injunction, and specific performance are enforced in courts of equity.

Equity of redemption The right a mortgagor has to redeem or get back his property after it has been forfeited for nonpayment of the debt it secured. By statute, within a certain time before final foreclosure decree, a mortgagor has the privilege of redeeming his property by paying the amount of the debt, interest, and costs.

Escrow An agreement under which a grantor, promisor, or obligor places the instrument upon which he is bound with a third person called escrow holder, until the performance of a condition or the happening of an event stated in the agreement permits the escrow holder to make delivery or performance to the grantee, promisee, or obligee. A (grantor) places a deed to C (grantee) accompanied by the contract of conveyance with B bank, conditioned upon B bank delivering the deed to C (grantee) when C pays all moneys due under contract. The contract and deed have been placed in "escrow."

Estate All the property of a living, deceased, bankrupt, or insane person. Also applied to the property of a ward. In the law of taxation, wills, and inheritance, *estate* has a broad meaning. Historically, the word was limited to an interest in land: i.e., estate in fee simple, estate for years, estate for life, and so forth.

Estoppel When one ought to speak the truth but does not, and by one's acts, representations, or silence intentionally or through negligence induces another to believe certain facts exist, and the other person acts to his detriment on the belief that such facts are true, the first person is estopped to deny the truth of the facts. B, knowingly having kept and used defective goods delivered by S under a contract of sale, is estopped to deny the goods are defective. X holds out Y as his agent. X is estopped to deny that Y is his agent. Persons are estopped to deny the legal effect of written instruments such as deeds, contracts, bills and notes, court records, and judgments. A man's own acts speak louder than his words.

Et al. "And other persons." Used in pleadings and cases to indicate that persons other than those specifically named are parties to a lawsuit.

Eviction An action to expel a tenant from the estate of the landlord. Interfering with the tenant's right of possession or enjoyment amounts to an eviction. Eviction may be actual or constructive. Premises made uninhabitable because the landlord maintains a nuisance is constructive eviction.

Evidence In law, *evidence* has two meanings. (1) Testimony of witnesses and facts presented to the court and jury by way of writings and exhibits, which impress the minds of the court and jury, to the extent that an allegation has been proven. *Testimony* and *evidence* are not synonymous. Testimony is a broader word and includes all the witness says. *Proof* is distinguished from *evidence*, in that proof is the legal consequence of evidence. (2) The rules of law, called the law of evidence,

that deter what evidence shall be introduced at a trial and what shall not; also, what importance shall be placed upon the evidence.

Ex contractu *See* Action ex contractu.

Exculpatory clause A provision in a contract whereby one of the parties attempts to relieve itself of liability for breach of a legal duty.

Exclusive dealing contract A contract under which a buyer agrees to purchase a certain product exclusively from the seller or in which the seller agrees to sell all his product production to the buyer.

Ex delicto *See* Action ex delicto.

Executed Applied to contracts or other written instruments, *executed* means signed, sealed, and delivered. Effective legal obligations have thus been created. The term is also used to mean that the performances of a contract have been completed. The contract is then at an end. All is done that is to be done.

Execution Execution of a judgment is the process by which the court, through the sheriff, enforces the payment of the judgment received by the successful party. The sheriff, by a "writ," levies upon the unsuccessful party's property and sells it to pay the judgment creditor.

Executor (of an estate) The person whom the testator (the one who makes the will) names or appoints to administer his estate upon his death and to dispose of it according to his intention. The terms *executor* and *administrator* are not synonyms. A person who makes a will appoints an executor to administer his estate. A court appoints an administrator to administer the estate of a person who dies without having made a will. *See* Intestate.

Executory (contract) Until the performance required in a contract is completed, it is said to be executory as to that part not executed. *See* Executed.

Exemplary damages A sum assessed by the jury in a tort action (over and above the compensatory damages) as punishment, in order to make an example of the wrongdoer and to deter like conduct by others. Injuries caused by willful, malicious, wanton, and reckless conduct will subject the wrongdoers to exemplary damages.

Exemption The condition of a person who is free or excused from a duty imposed by some rule of law, statutory or otherwise.

Express warranty When a seller makes some positive representation concerning the nature, quality, character, use, and purpose of goods, which induces the buyer to buy, and the seller intends the buyer to rely thereon, the seller has made an express warranty.

Factor An agent for the sale of merchandise. He may hold possession of the goods in his own name or in the name of his principal. He is authorized to sell and to receive payment for the goods. *See* Agent.

Factor's lien A factor's right to keep goods consigned to him if he may reimburse himself for advances previously made to the consignor.

Farm products* Crops or livestock or supplies used or produced in farming operations; products of crops or livestock in their unmanufactured states (such as ginned cotton, wool-clip, maple syrup, milk, and eggs); and goods in the possession of a debtor engaged in raising, fattening, grazing, or other farming operations. If goods are farm products, they are neither equipment nor inventory.

Featherbedding In labor relations, a demand for the payment of wages for a service not actually rendered.

Fee simple estate The total interest a person may have in land. Such an estate is not qualified by any other interest, and it passes upon the death of the owners to the heirs, free from any conditions.

Fellow servant doctrine Precludes an injured employee from recovering damages from his employer when the injury resulted from the negligent act of another employee.

Felony All criminal offenses that are punishable by death or imprisonment in a penitentiary.

Fiduciary In general, a person is a fiduciary when he occupies a position of trust or confidence in relation to another person or his property. Trustees, guardians, and executors occupy fiduciary positions.

Financing agency* A bank, finance company, or person who, in the ordinary course of business, makes advances against goods or documents of title; or who, by arrangement with either the seller or the buyer, intervenes in ordinary course to make or collect payment due or claimed under the contract for sale, as by purchasing or paying the seller's draft or making advances against it or by merely taking it for collection, whether or not documents of title accompany the draft. "Financing agency" includes a bank or person who similarly intervenes between persons who are in the position of seller and buyer in respect to the goods.

Fine A sum of money collected by a court from a person guilty of some criminal offense. The amount may be fixed by statute or left to the discretion of the court.

Firm offer* An offer by a merchant to buy or sell goods in a signed writing that, by its terms, gives assurance it will be held open.

Forbearance Giving up the right to enforce what one honestly believes to be a valid claim, in return for a promise. It is sufficient "consideration" to make a promise binding.

Forcible entry and detainer A remedy given to a landowner to evict persons unlawfully in possession of his land. A landlord may use such remedy to evict a tenant in default.

Forfeiture Money or property taken as compensation and punishment for injury or damage to the person or property of another or to the state. One may forfeit interest earnings for charging a usurious rate.

Forgery False writing or alteration of an instrument with the fraudulent intent of deceiving and injuring another. Writing another's name upon a check, without his consent, to secure money.

Franchise A right conferred or granted by a legislative body. It is a contract right and cannot be revoked without cause. A franchise is more than a license. A license is only a privilege and may be revoked. A corporation exists by virtue of a "franchise." A corporation secures a franchise from the city council to operate a waterworks within the city. *See* License.

Franchise tax A tax on the right of a corporation to do business under its corporate name.

Fraud An intentional misrepresentation of the truth for the purpose of deceiving another person. The elements of fraud are (1) intentionally false representation of fact, not opinion, (2) intent that the deceived person act thereon, (3) knowledge that such statements would naturally deceive, and (4) that the deceived person acted to his injury.

Fraudulent conveyance A conveyance of property by a debtor for the intent and purpose of defrauding his creditors. It is of no effect, and such property may be reached by the creditors through appropriate legal proceedings.

Freehold An estate in fee or for life. A freeholder is usually a person who has a property right in the title to real estate amounting to an estate of inheritance (in fee), or one who has title for life or an indeterminate period.

Full-line forcing An arrangement in which a manufacturer refuses to supply any portion of the product line unless the retailer agrees to accept the entire line.

Fungible* Goods and securities of which any unit is, by nature or usage of trade, the equivalent of any other like unit.

Fungible goods Fungible goods are those "of which any unit is from its nature of mercantile usage treated as the equivalent of any other unit." Grain, wine, and similar items are examples.

Future goods* Goods that are not both existing and identified.

Futures Contracts for the sale and delivery of commodities in the future, made with the intention that no commodity be delivered or received immediately.

Garnishee A person upon whom a garnishment is served. He is a debtor of a defendant and has money or property that the plaintiff is trying to reach in order to satisfy a debt due from the defendant. Also used as a verb: "to garnishee wages or property."

Garnishment A proceeding by which a plaintiff seeks to reach the credits of the defendant that are in the hands of a third party, the garnishee. A garnishment is distinguished from an attachment in that by an attachment, an officer of the court takes actual possession of property by virtue of his writ. In a garnishment, the property or money is left with the garnishee until final adjudication.

General agent An agent authorized to do all the acts connected with carrying on a particular trade, business, or profession.

General intangibles* Any personal property (including things in action) other than goods, accounts, contract rights, chattel paper, documents, and instruments.

Gift A gift is made when a donor delivers the subject matter of the gift into the donee's hands or places in the donee the means of obtaining possession of the subject matter, accompanied by such acts that show clearly the donor's intentions to divest himself of all dominion and control over the property.

Gift causa mortis A gift made in anticipation of death. The donor must have been in sickness and have died as expected, otherwise no effective gift has been made. If the donor survives, the gift is revocable.

Gift inter vivos An effective gift made during the life of the donor. By a gift inter vivos, property vests immediately in the donee at the time of delivery, whereas a gift causa mortis is made in contemplation of death and is effective only upon the donor's death.

Good faith* Honesty in fact in the conduct or transaction concerned. Referring to a merchant, good faith means honesty in fact and the observance of reasonable commercial standards of fair dealing in the trade.

Goods* All things that are movable at the time of identification to the contract for sale, including specially manufactured goods but not money in which the price is to be paid, investment securities, and things in action. Includes unborn young animals, growing crops, and other identified things attached to realty as described in the section on goods to be severed from realty.

Grant A term used in deeds for the transfer of the title to real property. The words *convey, transfer,* and *grant,* as operative words in a deed to pass title, are equivalent. The words *grant, bargain,* and *sell* in a deed, in absence of statute, mean the grantor promises he has good title to transfer free from incumbrances and warrants it to be such.

Grantee A person to whom a grant is made; one named in a deed to receive title.

Grantor A person who makes a grant. The grantor executes the deed by which he divests himself of title.

Gross negligence The lack of even slight or ordinary care.

Guarantor One who by contract undertakes "to answer for the debt, default, and miscarriage of another." In general, a guarantor undertakes to pay if the principal debtor does not; a surety, on the other hand, joins in the contract of the principal and becomes an original party with the principal.

Guardian A person appointed by the court to look after the property rights and person of minors, the insane, and other incompetents or legally incapacitated persons.

Guardian ad litem A special guardian appointed for the sole purpose of carrying on litigation and preserving the interests of a ward. He exercises no control or power over property.

Habeas corpus A writ issued to a sheriff, warden, or other official having allegedly unlawful custody of a person, directing the official to bring the person before a court, in order to determine the legality of the imprisonment.

Hearsay evidence Evidence that is learned from someone else. It does not derive its value from the credit of the witness testifying but rests upon the veracity of another person. It is not good evidence, because there is no opportunity to cross-examine the person who is the source of the testimony.

Hedging contract A contract of purchase or sale of an equal amount of commodities in the future, by which brokers, dealers, or manufacturers protect themselves against the fluctuations of the market. It is a type of insurance against changing prices. A grain dealer, to protect himself, may contract to sell for future delivery the same amount of grain he has purchased in the present market.

Heirs Persons upon whom the statute of descent casts the title to real property upon the death of the ancestor. Consult Statute of Descent for the appropriate state. *See* Descent.

Holder* A person who is in possession of a document of title or an instrument or an investment security drawn, issued, or indorsed to him or to his order or to bearer or in blank.

Holder in due course One who has acquired possession of a negotiable instrument through proper negotiation for value, in good faith, and without notice of any defenses to it. Such a holder is not subject to personal defenses

that would otherwise defeat the obligation embodied in the instrument.

Holding company A corporation organized for the purpose of owning and holding the stock of other corporations. Shareholders of underlying corporations receive in exchange for their stock, upon an agreed value, the shares in the holding corporation.

Homestead A parcel of land upon which a family dwells or resides, and which to them is home. The statute of the state or federal governments should be consulted to determine the meaning of the term as applied to debtor's exemptions, federal land grants, and so forth.

Honor* To pay or to accept and pay or, where a creditor so engages, to purchase or discount a draft complying with the terms of the instrument.

Horizontal merger Merger of corporations that were competitors prior to the merger.

Hot-cargo contract An agreement between employer and union, whereby an employer agrees to refrain from handling, using, selling, transporting, or otherwise dealing in the products of another employer or agrees to cease doing business with some other person.

Illegal Contrary to public policy and the fundamental principles of law. Illegal conduct includes not only violations of criminal statutes but also the creation of agreements that are prohibited by statute and the common law.

Illusory That which has a false appearance. If that which appears to be a promise is not a promise, it is said to be illusory. "I promise to buy your lunch if I decide to." This equivocal statement would not justify reliance, so it is not a promise.

Immunity Freedom from the legal duties and penalties imposed upon others. The "privileges and immunities" clause of the United States Constitution means no state can deny to the citizens of another state the same rights granted to its own citizens. This does not apply to office holding. *See* Exemption.

Implied The finding of a legal right or duty by inference from facts or circumstances. *See* Warranty.

Implied-in-fact contract A legally enforceable agreement inferred from the circumstances and conduct of the parties.

Imputed negligence Negligence that is not directly attributable to the person himself but is the negligence of a person who is in privity with him and with whose fault he is chargeable.

Incidental beneficiary If the performance of a promise would indirectly benefit a person not a party to a contract, such person is an incidental beneficiary. A promises B, for a consideration, to plant a valuable nut orchard on B's land. Such improvement would increase the value of the adjacent land. C, the owner of the adjacent land, is an incidental beneficiary. He has no remedy if A breaches his promise with B.

Incumbrance A burden on either the title to land or thing or upon the land or thing itself. A mortgage or other lien is an incumbrance upon the title. A right-of-way over the land is an incumbrance upon the land and affects its physical condition.

Indemnify Literally, "to save harmless." Thus, one person agrees to protect another against loss.

Indenture A deed executed by both parties, as distinguished from a deed poll that is executed only by the grantor.

Independent contractor   The following elements are essential to establish the relation of independent contractor, in contradistinction to principal and agent. An independent contractor must (1) exercise his independent judgment on the means used to accomplish the result; (2) be free from control or orders from any other person; (3) be responsible only under his contract for the result obtained.

Indictment   A finding by a grand jury that it has reason to believe the accused is guilty as charged. It informs the accused of the offense with which he is charged, so that he may prepare its defense. It is a pleading in a criminal action.

Indorsement   Writing one's name upon paper for the purpose of transferring the title. When a payee of a negotiable instrument writes his name on the back of the instrument, his writing is an indorsement.

Infringement   Infringement of a patent on a machine is the manufacturing of a machine that produces the same result by the same means and operation as the patented machine. Infringement of a trademark consists in reproduction of a registered trademark and its use upon goods in order to mislead the public to believe that the goods are the genuine, original product.

Inherit   The word is used in contradistinction to acquiring property by will. *See* Descent.

Inheritance   An estate that descends to heirs. *See* Descent.

Injunction   A writ of judicial process issued by a court of equity, by which a party is required to do a particular thing or to refrain from doing a particular thing.

In personam   A legal proceeding, the judgment of which binds the defeated party to a personal liability.

In rem   A legal proceeding, the judgment of which binds, affects, or determines the status of property.

Insolvent*   Refers to a person who either has ceased to pay his debts in the ordinary course of business or cannot pay his debts as they become due or is insolvent within the meaning of the federal bankruptcy law.

Installment contract*   One which requires or authorizes the delivery of goods in separate lots to be separately accepted, even though the contract contains a clause "each delivery is a separate contract" or its equivalent.

Instrument*   A negotiable instrument or a security or any other writing that evidences a right to the payment of money and is not itself a security agreement or lease and is of a type that is in ordinary course of business transferred by delivery with any necessary indorsement or assignment.

Insurable interest   A person has an insurable interest in a person or property if he will be directly and financially affected by the death of the person or the loss of the property.

Insurance   By an insurance contract, one party, for an agreed premium, binds himself to another, called the insured, to pay the insured a sum of money conditioned upon the loss of life or property of the insured.

Intangible property   Something which represents value but has no intrinsic value of its own, such as a note or bond.

Intent   A state of mind that exists prior to, or contemporaneous with, an act. A purpose or design to do or forbear to do an act. It cannot be directly proven but is inferred from known facts.

Interlocutory decree   A decree of a court of equity that does not settle the complete issue but settles only some intervening part, awaiting a final decree.

Intermediary bank*   Under Article 4—Bank Deposits and Collections, it is any bank—except the depositary or payor bank—to which an item is transferred in course of collection.

Interpleader   A procedure whereby a person who has an obligation, e.g., to pay money, but does not know which of two or more claimants are entitled to performance, can bring a suit that requires the contesting parties to litigate between themselves.

Interrogatory   A written question from one party to another in a lawsuit; a type of discovery procedure.

Intestate   The intestate laws are the laws of descent or distribution of the estate of a deceased person. A person who has not made a will dies intestate.

Inventory*   Goods that a person holds for sale or lease or to be—or which have been—furnished under contracts of service, or goods that are raw materials, work in process, or materials used or consumed in a business. Inventory of a person is not to be classified as his equipment.

Irreparable damage or injury   *Irreparable* does not mean injury beyond the possibility of repair, but it does mean that it is so constant and frequent in occurrence that no fair or reasonable redress can be had in a court of law. Thus, the plaintiff must seek a remedy in equity by way of an injunction.

Issue*   Under Article 3—Commercial Paper, *issue* means the first delivery of an instrument to a holder or a remitter.

Issuer*   A bailee who issues a document; but in relation to an unaccepted delivery order, the issuer is the person who orders the possessor of goods to deliver. Issuer includes any person for whom an agent or employee purports to act in issuing a document if the agent or employee has real or apparent authority to issue documents, notwithstanding that the issuer received no goods or that the goods were misdescribed or that in any other respect the agent or employee violated the issuer's instructions.

Item*   Under Article 4—Bank Deposits and Collections, *item* means any instrument for the payment of money, even though it is not negotiable, but does not include money.

Jeopardy   A person is in jeopardy when he is regularly charged with a crime before a court properly organized and competent to try him. If acquitted, he cannot be tried again for the same offense.

Joint and several   Two or more persons have an obligation that binds them individually as well as jointly. The obligation can be enforced either by joint action against all of them or by separate actions against one or more.

Joint ownership   The interest that two or more parties have in property. *See* Joint tenants.

Joint tenants   Two or more persons to whom land is deeded in such manner that they have "one and the same interest, accruing by one and the same conveyance, commencing at one and the same time, and held by one and the same undivided possession." Upon the death of one joint tenant, his property passes to the survivor or survivors.

Joint tortfeasors   When two persons commit an injury with a common intent, they are joint tortfeasors.

Judgment (in law)   The decision, pronouncement, or sentence rendered by a court upon an issue in which it has jurisdiction.

Judgment in personam A judgment against a person, directing the defendant to do or not to do something. *See* In personam.

Judgment in rem A judgment against a thing, as distinguished from a judgment against a person. *See* In rem.

Judicial restraint A judicial philosophy. Those following it believe that the power of judicial review should be exercised with great restraint.

Judicial review The power of courts to declare laws and executive actions unconstitutional.

Judicial sale A sale authorized by a court that has jurisdiction to grant such authority. Such sales are conducted by an officer of the court.

Jurisdiction The authority to try causes and determine cases. Conferred upon a court by the Constitution.

Jury A group of persons, usually twelve, sworn to declare the facts of a case as they are proved from the evidence presented to them and, upon instructions from the court, to find a verdict in the cause before them.

Laches A term used in equity to name conduct that neglects to assert one's rights or to do what, by the law, a person should have done. Failure on the part of one to assert a right will give an equitable defense to another party.

Latent defect A defect in materials not discernible by examination. Used in contradistinction to patent defect, which is discernible.

Lease A contract by which one person divests himself of possession of lands or chattels and grants such possession to another for a period of time. The relationship in which land is involved is called landlord and tenant.

Leasehold The land held by a tenant under a lease.

Legacy Personal property disposed of by a will. Sometimes the term is synonymous with *bequest*. The word *devise* is used in connection with real property distributed by will. *See* Bequest; Devise.

Legatee A person to whom a legacy is given by will.

Liability In its broadest legal sense, *liability* means any obligation one may be under by reason of some rule of law. It includes debt, duty, and responsibility.

Libel Malicious publication of a defamation of a person by printing, writing, signs, or pictures, for the purposes of injuring the reputation and good name of such person. "The exposing of a person to public hatred, contempt, or ridicule."

License (governmental regulation) A license is a privilege granted by a state or city upon the payment of a fee. It confers authority upon the licensee to do some act or series of acts, which otherwise would be illegal. A license is not a contract and may be revoked for cause. It is a method of governmental regulation exercised under the police power.

License (privilege) A mere personal privilege given by the owner to another to do designated acts upon the land of the owner. It is revocable at will and creates no estate in the land. The licensee is not in possession. "It is a mere excuse for what otherwise would be a trespass."

Lien The right of one person, usually a creditor, to keep possession of, or control, the property of another for the purpose of satisfying a debt. There are many kinds of liens: judgment lien, attorney's lien, innkeeper's lien, logger's lien, vendor's lien. Consult statute of state for type of lien. *See* Judgment.

Lien creditor* A creditor who has acquired a lien on property involved by attachment, levy, or the like. Includes an assignee for benefit of creditors from the time of assignment and a trustee in bankruptcy from the date of the filing of the petition or a receiver in equity from the time of appointment. Unless all the creditors represented had knowledge of the security interest, such a representative of creditors is a lien creditor without knowledge even though he personally has knowledge of the security interest.

Limitation of actions Statutes of limitations exist for the purpose of bringing to an end old claims. Because witnesses die, memory fails, papers are lost, and the evidence becomes inadequate, stale claims are barred. Such statutes are called statutes of repose. Within a certain period of time, action on claims must be brought; otherwise, they are barred. The period varies from 6 months to 20 years.

Limited partnership A partnership in which one or more individuals are general partners and one or more individuals are limited partners. The limited partners contribute assets to the partnership without taking part in the conduct of the business. They are liable for the debts of the partnership only to the extent of their contributions.

Liquidated A claim is liquidated when it has been made fixed and certain by the parties concerned.

Liquidated damages A fixed sum agreed upon between the parties to a contract, to be paid as ascertained damages by the party who breaches the contract. If the sum is excessive, the courts will declare it to be a penalty and unenforceable.

Liquidation The process of winding up the affairs of a corporation or firm for the purpose of paying its debts and disposing of its assets. May be done voluntarily or under the orders of a court.

Lis pendens "Pending the suit nothing should be changed." The court, having control of the property involved in the suit, issues notice *lis pendens*, that persons dealing with the defendant regarding the subject matter of the suit do so subject to final determination of the action.

Lot* A parcel or a single article that is the subject matter of a separate sale or delivery, whether or not it is sufficient to perform the contract.

Magistrate A public officer, usually a judge, "who has power to issue a warrant for the arrest of a person charged with a public offense." The word has wide application and includes justices of the peace, notaries public, recorders, and other public officers who have power to issue executive orders.

Malice Describes a wrongful act done intentionally without excuse. It does not necessarily mean ill will, but it indicates a state of mind that is reckless concerning the law and the rights of others. *Malice* is distinguished from *negligence*. With *malice* there is always a purpose to injure, whereas such is not true of the word *negligence*.

Malicious prosecution The prosecution of another at law with malice and without probable cause to believe that such legal action will be successful.

Mandamus A writ issued by a court of law, in the name of the state. Writs of mandamus are directed to inferior courts, officers, corporations, or persons, commanding them to do particular things that appertain to their offices or duties.

Mandatory injunction An injunctive order issued by a court of equity that compels affirmative action by the defendant.

Marketable title A title of such character that no apprehension as to its validity would occur to the mind of a reasonable and intelligent person. The title to goods is not marketable if it is in litigation, subject to incumbrances, in doubt as to a third party's right, or subject to lien.

Marshaling assets A principle in equity for a fair distribution of a debtor's assets among his creditors. For example, a creditor of A, by reason of prior right, has two funds, X and Y, belonging to A, out of which he may satisfy his debt. But another creditor of A also has a right to X fund. The first creditor will be compelled to exhaust Y fund before he will be permitted to participate in X fund.

Master in chancery An officer appointed by the court to assist the court of equity in taking testimony, computing interest, auditing accounts, estimating damages, ascertaining liens, and doing other tasks incidental to a suit, as the court requires. The power of a master is merely advisory, and his tasks are largely fact finding.

Maxim A proposition of law that because of its universal approval needs no proof or argument; the mere statement of which gives it authority. Example: "A principal is bound by the acts of his agent when the agent is acting within the scope of his authority."

Mechanic's lien Created by statute to assist suppliers and laborers in collecting their accounts and wages. Its purpose is to subject the land of an owner to a lien for material and labor expended in the construction of buildings and other improvements.

Merchant A person who deals in goods of the kind involved in a transaction; or one who otherwise, by his occupation, holds himself out as having knowledge or skill peculiar to the practices or goods involved; or one to whom such knowledge or skill may be attributed because he employs an agent or broker or other intermediary who, by his occupation, holds himself out as having such knowledge or skill.

Merger Two corporations are merged when one corporation continues in existence and the other loses its identity by its absorption into the first. *Merger* must be distinguished from *consolidation*. In consolidation, both corporations are dissolved, and a new one is created, the new one taking over the assets of the dissolved corporations.

Metes and bounds The description of the boundaries of real property.

Midnight deadline* Under Article 4—Bank Deposits and Collections, this is midnight on the next banking day following the banking day on which a bank receives the relevant item or notice, or from which the time for taking action commences.to run, whichever is later.

Ministerial duty A prescribed duty that requires little judgment or discretion. A sheriff performs ministerial duties.

Minutes The record of a court or the written transactions of the members or board of directors of a corporation. Under the certificate of the clerk of a court or the secretary of a corporation, the minutes are the official evidence of court or corporate action.

Misdemeanor A criminal offense, less than a felony, that is not punishable by death or imprisonment. Consult the local statute.

Misrepresentation The affirmative statement or affirmation of a fact that is not true; the term does not include concealment of true facts or nondisclosure or the mere expression of opinion.

Mistake of fact The unconscious ignorance or forgetfulness of the existence or nonexistence of a fact, past or present, which is material and important to the creation of a legal obligation.

Mistake of law An erroneous conclusion of the legal effect of known facts.

Mitigation of damages A plaintiff is entitled to recover damages caused by the defendant's breach, but the plaintiff is also under a duty to avoid increasing or enhancing such damages. This duty is called a duty to mitigate damages. If a seller fails to deliver the proper goods on time, the buyer, where possible, must buy other goods, thus mitigating damages.

Monopoly Exclusive control of the supply and price of a commodity. May be acquired by a franchise or patent from the government; or the ownership of the source of a commodity or the control of its distribution.

Mortgage A conveyance or transfer of an interest in property for the purpose of creating a security for a debt. The mortgage becomes void upon payment of the debt, although the recording of a release is necessary to clear the title of the mortgaged property.

Mutual assent In every contract, each party must agree to the same thing. Each must know what the other intends; they must mutually assent or be in agreement.

Mutual mistake A situation in which parties to a contract reach a bargain on the basis of an incorrect assumption common to each party.

Mutuality The binding of both parties in every contract. Each party to the contract must be bound to the other party to do something by virtue of the legal duty created.

Negligence Failure to do that which an ordinary, reasonable, prudent man would do, or the doing of some act that an ordinary, prudent man would not do. Reference must always be made to the situation, the circumstances, and the knowledge of the parties.

Negotiation* Under Article 3—Commercial Paper, this is the transfer of an instrument in such form that the transferee becomes a holder. If the instrument is payable to order, it is negotiated by delivery with any necessary indorsement; if payable to bearer, it is negotiated by delivery.

Net assets Property or effects of a firm, corporation, institution, or estate, remaining after all its obligations have been paid.

Nexus Connection, tie, or link used in the law of taxation to establish a connection between a tax and the activity or person being taxed.

NLRB National Labor Relations Board.

No-fault laws Laws barring tort actions by injured persons against third-party tortfeasors and requiring injured persons to obtain recovery from their own insurers.

Nolo contendere A plea by an accused in a criminal action. It does not admit guilt of the offense charged but does equal a plea of guilty for purpose of sentencing.

Nominal damages A small sum assessed as sufficient to

award the case and cover the costs when no actual damages have been proven.

Nonsuit A judgment given against the plaintiff when he is unable to prove his case or fails to proceed with the trial after the case is at issue.

Noscitur a sociis The meaning of a word is or may be known from the accompanying words.

Notary A public officer authorized to administer oaths by way of affidavits and depositions. Attests deeds and other formal papers, in order that they may be used as evidence and be qualified for recording.

Notice* A person has "notice" of a fact when (a) he has actual knowledge of it; or (b) he has received a notice or notification of it; or (c) from all the facts and circumstances known to him at the time in question, he has reason to know that it exists. A person "knows" or has "knowledge" of a fact when he has actual knowledge of it. "Discover" or "learn" or a word or phrase of similar import refers to knowledge rather than to reason to know.

Novation The substitution of one obligation for another. When debtor A is substituted for debtor B, and by agreement with the creditor C, debtor B is discharged, a novation has occurred.

Nudum pactum A naked promise—one for which no consideration has been given.

Nuisance Generally, any continuous or continued conduct that causes annoyance, inconvenience, and damage to person or property. *Nuisance* usually applies to unreasonable, wrongful use of property, causing material discomfort, hurt, and damage to the person or property of another. Example: fumes from a factory.

Obligee A creditor or promisee.

Obligor A debtor or promisor.

Oligopoly Control of a commodity or service in a given market by a small number of companies or suppliers.

Option A right secured by a contract to accept or reject an offer to purchase property at a fixed price within a fixed time. It is an irrevocable offer sometimes called a "paid-for offer."

Order* Under Article 3—Commercial Paper, *order* is a direction to pay and must be more than an authorization or request. It must, with reasonable certainty, identify the person to pay. It may be addressed to one or more such persons jointly or in the alternative but not in succession.

Ordinance Generally speaking, the legislative act of a municipality. A city council is a legislative body, and it passes ordinances that are the laws of the city.

Ordinary care Care that a prudent man would take under the circumstances of the particular case.

Par value "Face value." The par value of stocks and bonds on the date of issuance is the principal. At a later date, the par value is the principal plus interest.

Pari delicto The fault or blame is shared equally.

Pari materia "Related to the same matter or subject." Statutes and covenants concerning the same subject matter are in pari materia and as a general rule, for the purpose of ascertaining their meaning, are construed together.

Parol evidence Legal proof based on oral statements; with regard to a document, any evidence extrinsic to the document itself.

Partition Court proceedings brought by an interested party's request that the court divide real property among respective owners as their interests appear. If the property cannot be divided in kind, then it is to be sold and the money divided as each interest appears.

Party* A person who has engaged in a transaction or made an agreement within the Uniform Commercial Code.

Patent ambiguity An obvious uncertainty in a written instrument.

Payor bank* Under Article 4—Bank Deposits and Collections, a bank by which an item is payable as drawn or accepted.

Penal bond A bond given by an accused, or by another person in his behalf, for the payment of money if the accused fails to appear in court on a certain day.

Pendente lite "Pending during the progress of a suit at law."

Per curiam A decision by the full court without indicating the author of the decision.

Peremptory challenge An objection raised by a party to a lawsuit who rejects a person serving as a juror. No reason need be given.

Perjury False swearing upon an oath properly administered in some judicial proceedings.

Per se "By itself." Thus, a contract clause may be inherently unconscionable—unconscionable per se.

Personal property The rights, powers, and privileges a person has in movable things, such as chattels and choses in action. Personal property is used in contradistinction to real property.

Personal representative The administrator or executor of a deceased person or the guardian of a child or the conservator of an incompetent.

Personal service The sheriff personally delivers a service of process to the defendant.

Plaintiff In an action at law, the complaining party or the one who commences the action. The person who seeks a remedy in court.

Plea An allegation or answer in a court proceeding.

Pleading Process by which the parties in a lawsuit arrive at an issue.

Pledge Personal property, as security for a debt or other obligation, deposited or placed with a person called a pledgee. The pledgee has the implied power to sell the property if the debt is not paid. If the debt is paid, the right to possession returns to the pledgor.

Polling jury Calling the name of each juror to inquire what his verdict is before it is made a matter of record.

Possession The method recognized by law and used by one's self or by another to hold, detain, or control either personal or real property, thereby excluding others from holding, detaining, or controlling such property.

Power of attorney An instrument authorizing another to act as one's agent or attorney in fact.

Precedent A previously decided case that can serve as an authority to help decide a present controversy. Use of such case is called the doctrine of *stare decisis,* which means to adhere to decided cases and settled principles. Literally, "to stand as decided."

Preference The term is used most generally in bankruptcy law. If a bankrupt pays some creditors a greater percentage of the debts than he pays other creditors in the same class, and if the payments are made within 4 months prior to his filing a bankruptcy petition, those payments constitute illegal and voidable preference. An intention to prefer such creditors must be shown.

Preferred stock   Stock that entitles the holder to dividends from earnings before the owners of common stock can receive a dividend.

Preponderance   Preponderance of the evidence means that evidence, in the judgment of the jurors, is entitled to the greatest weight, appears to be more credible, has greater force, and overcomes not only the opposing presumptions but also the opposing evidence.

Presenting bank*   Under Article 4—Bank Deposits and Collections, this is any bank presenting an item except a payor bank.

Presentment*   Under Article 3—Commercial Paper, presentment is a demand for acceptance or payment made upon the maker, acceptor, drawee, or other payor by, or on behalf of, the holder.

Presumption (presumed)*   The trier of fact must find the existence of the fact presumed unless and until evidence is introduced that would support a finding of its nonexistence.

Prima facie   Literally, "at first view." Thus, that which first appears seems to be true. A prima facie case is one that stands until contrary evidence is produced.

Privilege   A legal idea or concept of lesser significance than a right. An invitee has only a privilege to walk on another's land, because such privilege may be revoked at will; whereas a person who has an easement to go on another's land has a right created by a grant, which is an interest in land and cannot be revoked at will. To be exempt from jury service is a privilege.

Privity   Mutual and successive relationship to the same interest. Offeror and offeree, assignor and assignee, grantor and grantee are in privity. Privity of estate means that one takes title from another. In contract law, privity denotes parties in mutual legal relationship to each other by virtue of being promisees and promisors. At early common law, third-party beneficiaries and assignees were said to be not in "privity."

Probate court   Handles the settlement of estates.

Proceeds*   Whatever is received when collateral or proceeds are sold, exchanged, collected or otherwise disposed of. Includes the account arising when the right to payment is earned under a contract right. Money, checks, and the like are "cash proceeds." All other proceeds are "noncash proceeds."

Process   In a court proceeding, before or during the progress of the trial, an instrument issued by the court in the name of the state and under the seal of the court, directing an officer of the court to do, act, or cause some act to be done incidental to the trial.

Product extension merger   A merger that extends the products of the acquiring company into a similar or related product but one which is not directly in competition with existing products.

Promise*   Under Article 3—Commercial Paper, it is an undertaking to pay, and it must be more than an acknowledgment of an obligation.

Property   All rights, powers, privileges, and immunities that one has concerning tangibles and intangibles. The term includes everything of value subject to ownership.

Proximate cause   The cause that sets other causes in operation. The responsible cause of an injury.

Proxy   Authority to act for another, used by absent stockholders or members of legislative bodies to have their votes cast by others.

Punitive damages   Damages by way of punishment. Allowed for an injury caused by a wrong that is willful and malicious.

Purchase*   Includes taking by sale, discount, negotiation, mortgage, pledge, lien, issue or re-issue, gift, or any other voluntary transaction creating an interest in property.

Purchase-money security interest*   A security interest that is taken or retained by the seller of the collateral to secure all or part of its price; or taken by a person who, by making advances or incurring an obligation, gives value to enable the debtor to acquire rights in, or the use of, collateral if such value is in fact so used.

Quasi contract   A situation in which there arises a legal duty that does not rest upon a promise but does involve the payment of money. In order to do justice by a legal fiction, the court enforces the duty as if a promise in fact exists. Thus, if A gives B money by mistake, A can compel B to return the money by an action in quasi contract.

Quasi-judicial   Administrative actions involving factual determinations and the discretionary application of rules and regulations.

Quid pro quo   The exchange of one thing of value for another.

Quiet title   A suit brought by the owner of real property for the purpose of bringing into court any person who claims an adverse interest in the property, requiring him either to establish his claim or be barred from asserting it thereafter. It may be said that the purpose is to remove "clouds" from the title.

Quitclaim   A deed that releases a right or interest in land but does not include any covenants of warranty. The grantor transfers only that which he has.

Quo warranto   A proceeding in court by which a governmental body tests or inquires into the authority or legality of the claim of any person to a public office, franchise, or privilege.

Ratification   The confirmation of one's own previous act or act of another: e.g., a principal may ratify the previous unauthorized act of his agent. B's agent, without authority, buys goods. B, by keeping the goods and receiving the benefits of the agent's act, ratifies the agency.

Ratio decidendi   Logical basis of judicial decision.

Real property   Land with all its buildings, appurtenances, equitable and legal interests therein. In contradistinction to personal property, which refers to movables or chattels.

Reasonable care   The care that prudent persons would exercise under the same circumstances.

Receiver   An officer of the court appointed on behalf of all parties to the litigation to take possession of, hold, and control the property involved in the suit, for the benefit of the party who will be determined to be entitled thereto.

Recoupment   "A cutting back." A right to deduct from the plaintiff's claim any payment or loss that the defendant has suffered by reason of the plaintiff's wrongful act.

Redemption To buy back. A debtor buys back or redeems his mortgaged property when he pays the debt.

Referee A person to whom a cause pending in a court is referred by the court, to take testimony, hear the parties, and report thereon to the court.

Registered form* A security is in registered form when it specifies a person entitled to the security or to the rights it evidences and when its transfer may be registered upon books maintained for that purpose by, or on behalf of, an issuer, as security states.

Reinsurance In a contract of reinsurance, one insurance company agrees to indemnify another insurance company in whole or in part against risks that the first company has assumed. The original contract of insurance and the reinsurance contract are distinct contracts. There is no privity between the original insured and the reinsurer.

Release The voluntary relinquishing of a right, lien, or any other obligation. A release need not be under seal, nor does it necessarily require consideration. The words *release, remise,* and *discharge* are often used together to mean the same thing.

Remand To send back a case from the appellate court to the lower court, in order that the lower court may comply with the instructions of the appellate court. Also to return a prisoner to jail.

Remedy The word is used to signify the judicial means or court procedures by which legal and equitable rights are enforced.

Remitting bank.* Under Article 4—Bank Deposits and Collections, any payor or intermediary bank remitting for an item.

Replevin A remedy given by statute for the recovery of the possession of a chattel. Only the right to possession can be tried in such action.

Res "Thing."

Res adjudicata A controversy once having been decided or adjudged upon its merits is forever settled so far as the particular parties involved are concerned. Such a doctrine avoids vexatious lawsuits.

Rescind To cancel or annul a contract and return the parties to their original positions.

Rescission An apparently valid act may conceal a defect that will make it null and void if any of the parties demand that it be rescinded.

Respondeat superior "The master is liable for the acts of his agent."

Respondent One who answers another's bill or pleading, particularly in an equity case. Quite similar, in many instances, to a defendant in a law case.

Responsible bidder In the phrase "lowest responsible bidder," *responsible,* as used by most statutes concerning public works, means that such bidder has the requisite skill, judgment, and integrity necessary to perform the contract involved and has the financial resources and ability to carry the task to completion.

Restraining order Issued by a court of equity in aid of a suit, to hold matters in abeyance until parties may be heard. A temporary injunction.

Restraint of trade Monopolies, combinations, and contracts that impede free competition.

Right The phrase "legal right" is a correlative of the phrase "legal duty." One has a legal right if, upon the breach of the correlative legal duty, he can secure a remedy in a court of law.

Right of action Synonymous with *cause of action:* a right to enforce a claim in a court.

Right-to-work law A state statute that outlaws a union shop contract; one by which an employer agrees to require membership in the union sometime after an employee has been hired, as a condition of continued employment.

Riparian A person is a riparian owner if his land is situated beside a stream of water, either flowing over or along the border of the land.

Satisfaction In legal phraseology, the release and discharge of a legal obligation. Satisfaction may be partial or full performance of the obligation. The word is used with *accord,* a promise to give a substituted performance for a contract obligation; *satisfaction* means the acceptance by the obligee of such performance.

Scienter Knowledge by a defrauding party of the falsity of a representation. In a tort action of deceit, knowledge that a representation is false must be proved.

Seal A seal shows that an instrument was executed in a formal manner. At early common law, sealing legal documents was of great legal significance. A promise under seal was binding by virtue of the seal. Today under most statutes, any stamp, wafer, mark, scroll, or impression made, adopted, and affixed, is adequate. The printed word *seal* or the letters *L.S. (locus sigilli,* "the place of the seal") are sufficient.

Seasonably* An action is taken "seasonably" when it is taken at, or within, the time agreed; or if no time is agreed, at or within a reasonable time.

Secondary boycott Conspiracy or combination to cause the customers or suppliers of an employer to cease doing business with that employer.

Secondary party* Under Article 3—Commercial Paper, a drawer or indorser.

Secured party* A lender, seller, or other person in whose favor there is a security interest, including a person to whom accounts, contract rights, or chattel paper have been sold. When the holders of obligations issued under an indenture of trust, equipment trust agreement, or the like are represented by a trustee or other person, the representative is the secured party.

Security May be bonds, stocks, and other property that a debtor places with a creditor, who may sell them if the debt is not paid. The plural, *securities,* is used broadly to mean tangible choses in action, such as promissory notes, bonds, stocks, and other vendible obligations.

Security* An instrument issued in bearer form or registered form; commonly dealt in on securities exchanges or markets or commonly recognized in any area in which it is issued or dealt in as a medium for investment; one of a class or series of instruments; evidences a share, a participation or other interest in property or in an enterprise or evidences an obligation of the issuer.

Security agreement* Creates or provides for a security interest.

Security interest* An interest in personal property or fixtures that secures payment or performance of an obligation.

Sell To negotiate or make arrangement for a sale. A sale is an executed contract, a result of the process of selling.

Separation of powers The doctrine that the legislative, executive, and judicial branches of government function independently of one another and that each branch serves as a check on the others.

Servant A person employed by another and subject to the direction and control of the employer in performance of his duties.

Setoff A matter of defense, called a cross-complaint, used by the defendant for the purpose of making a demand on the plaintiff. It arises out of contract but is independent and unconnected with the cause of action set out in the complaint. *See* Counterclaims and Recoupment.

Settle* Under Article 4—Bank Deposits and Collections, *settle* means to pay in cash, by clearinghouse settlement, in a charge or credit or by remittance or otherwise as instructed. A settlement may be either provisional or final.

Severable contract A contract in which the performance is divisible. Two or more parts may be set over against each other. Items and prices may be apportioned to each other without relation to the full performance of all of its parts.

Share of stock A proportional part of the rights in the management and assets of a corporation. It is a chose in action. The certificate is the evidence of the share.

Situs "Place, situation." The place where a thing is located. The situs of personal property is the domicile of the owner. The situs of land is the state or county where it is located.

Slander An oral utterance that tends to injure the reputation of another. *See* Libel.

Special appearance The appearance in court of a person through his attorney for a limited purpose only. A court does not get jurisdiction over a person by special appearance.

Special verdict The jury finds the facts only, leaving it to the court to apply the law and draw the conclusion as to the proper disposition of the case.

Specific performance A remedy in personam in equity that compels performance of a contract to be substantial enough to do justice among the parties. A person who fails to obey a writ for specific performance may be put in jail by the equity judge for contempt of court. The remedy applies to contracts involving real property. In the absence of unique goods or peculiar circumstances, damages generally are an adequate remedy for breach of contracts involving personal property.

Standing to sue The doctrine that requires the plaintiff in a lawsuit to have a sufficient legal interest in the subject matter of the case.

Stare decisis "Stand by the decision." The law should adhere to decided cases. *See* Precedent.

Statute A law passed by the legislative body of a state.

Status quo The conditions or state of affairs at a given time.

Stock dividend New shares of its own stock issued as a dividend by a corporation to its shareholders, in order to transfer retained earnings to capital stock.

Stockholders Persons whose names appear on the books of a corporation as owners of shares of stock and who are entitled to participate in the management and control of the corporation.

Stock split A readjustment of the financial plan of a corporation, whereby each existing share of stock is split into new shares, usually with a lowering of par value.

Stock warrant A certificate that gives the holder the right to subscribe for and purchase, at a stated price, a given number of shares of stock in a corporation.

Stoppage in transitu Upon learning of the insolvency of a buyer of goods, the seller has the right to stop the goods in transit and hold them as security for the purchase price. The right is an extension of the unpaid seller's lien.

Strict liability The doctrine under which a party may be required to respond in tort damages, without regard to that party's use of due care.

Subordinate In the case of a mortgage or other security interest, the mortgagee may agree to make his mortgage inferior to another mortgage or interest.

Subpoena A process issued out of a court requiring the attendance of a witness at a trial.

Subrogation The substitution of one person in another's place, whether as a creditor or as the possessor of any lawful right, so that the substituted person may succeed to the rights, remedies, or proceeds of the claim. It rests in equity on the theory that a party who is compelled to pay a debt for which another is liable should be vested with all the rights the creditor has against the debtor. For example: an insurance company pays Y for damage to Y's car, caused by Z's negligent act. The insurance company will be subrogated to Y's cause of action against Z.

Subsequent purchaser* A person who takes a security other than by original issue.

Substantial performance The complete performance of all the essential elements of a contract. The only permissible omissions or derivations are those that are trivial, inadvertent, and inconsequential. Such performance will not justify repudiation. Compensation for defects may be substituted for actual performance.

Substantive law Law that regulates and controls the rights and duties of all persons in society. In contradistinction to the term *adjective law,* which means the rules of court procedure or remedial law, which prescribe the methods by which substantive law is enforced.

Succession The transfer by operation of law of all rights and obligations of a deceased person to those who are entitled to them.

Summary judgment A judicial determination that no genuine factual dispute exists and that one party to the lawsuit is entitled to judgment as a matter of law.

Summons A writ issued by a court to the sheriff, directing him to notify the defendant that the plaintiff claims to have a cause of action against the defendant and that he is required to answer. If the defendant does not answer, judgment will be taken by default.

Supremacy Clause Article VI, U.S. Constitution, which states that the Constitution, laws, and treaties of the United States shall be the "supreme law of the land" and shall take precedence over conflicting state laws.

Suspends payments* Under Article 4—Bank Deposits and Collections, with respect to a bank this means that it has been closed by order of the supervisory authorities, that a public officer has been appointed to take it over, or that it ceases or refuses to make payments in the ordinary course of business.

Tangible   Describes property that is physical in character and capable of being moved. A debt is intangible, but a promissory note evidencing such debt is tangible. *See* Chattel, Chose in action.

Tenancy   The interest in property that a tenant acquired from a landlord by a lease. It may be at will or for a term. It is an interest in land.

Tenancy by the entireties   Property acquired by husband and wife whereby upon the death of one, the survivor takes the whole property. The tenancy exists in only a few states. The husband and wife are both vested with the whole estate, so that the survivor takes no new title upon death of the other but remains in possession of the whole as originally granted. For the legal effect of such estate, the state statute should be consulted. *See* Joint tenants.

Tenant   The person to whom a lease is made. A lessee.

Tender   To offer and produce money in satisfaction of a debt or obligation and express to the creditor a willingness to pay.

Tender of delivery*   The seller must put and hold conforming goods at the buyer's disposition and give the buyer any notification reasonably necessary to enable him to take delivery.

Testamentary capacity   A person is said to have testamentary capacity when he understands the nature of his business and the value of his property, knows those persons who are natural objects of his bounty, and comprehends the manner in which he has provided for the distribution of his property.

Testator   A male who has died leaving a will. A female is a testatrix.

Testimony   Statements made by a witness under oath or affirmation in a legal proceeding.

Title   This word has limited or broad meaning. When a person has the exclusive rights, powers, privileges, and immunities to property, real and personal, tangible and intangible, against all other persons, he may be said to have the complete title thereto. The aggregate of legal relations concerning property is the title. The term is used to describe the means by which a person exercises control and dominion over property. A trustee has a limited title. *See* Possession.

Tort   "Twisted" or "wrong." A wrongful act committed by one person against another person or his property. It is the breach of a legal duty imposed by law other than by contract. X assaults Y, thus committing a tort. *See* Duty, Right.

Tortfeasor   One who commits a tort.

Trade fixtures   Personal property placed upon, or annexed to, land leased by a tenant for the purpose of carrying on a trade or business during the term of the lease. Such property is generally to be removed at the end of the term, providing removal will not destroy or injure the premises. Trade fixtures include showcases, shelving, racks, machinery, and the like.

Trademark   No complete definition can be given for a trademark. Generally it is any sign, symbol, mark, word, or arrangement of words in the form of a label adopted and used by a manufacturer or distributor to designate his particular goods, and which no other person has the legal right to use. Originally, the design or trademark indicated origin, but today it is used more as an advertising mechanism.

Transfer   In its broadest sense, the word means the act by which an owner sets over or delivers his right, title, and interest in property to another person. A "bill of sale" to personal property is evidence of a transfer.

Treason   The offense of attempting by overt acts to overthrow the government of the state to which the offender owes allegiance; or of betraying the state into the hands of a foreign power.

Treasury stock   Stock of a corporation that has been issued by the corporation for value but is later returned to the corporation by way of gift or purchase or otherwise. It may be returned to the trustees of a corporation for the purpose of sale.

Treble damages   An award of damages allowable under some statutes equal to three times the amount found by the jury to be a single recovery.

Trespass   An injury to the person, property, or rights of another person committed by actual force and violence or under such circumstances that the law will infer that the injury was caused by force or violence.

Trust   A relationship between persons by which one holds property for the use and benefit of another. The relationship is called fiduciary. Such rights are enforced in a court of equity. The person trusted is called a trustee. The person for whose benefit the property is held is called a beneficiary or "cestui que trust."

Trustee (generally)   A person who is entrusted with the management and control of another's property and estate. A person occupying a fiduciary position. An executor, an administrator, a guardian.

Trustee in bankruptcy   An agent of the court authorized to liquidate the assets of the bankrupt, protect them, and bring them to the court for final distribution for the benefit of the bankrupt and all the creditors.

Truth in lending   A federal law that requires disclosure of total finance charges and the annual percentage rate for credit in order that borrowers may be able to shop for credit.

Tying contract   Ties the sales of one piece of property (real or personal) to the sale or lease of another item of property.

Ultra vires   "Beyond power." The acts of a corporation are ultra vires when they are beyond the power or capacity of the corporations as granted by the state in its charter.

Unauthorized*   Refers to a signature or indorsement made without actual, implied, or apparent authority. Includes a forgery.

Unconscionable   In the law of contracts, provisions that are oppressive, overreaching, or shocking to the conscience.

Unfair competition   The imitation, by design, of the goods of another, for the purpose of palming them off on the public, misleading it, and inducing it to buy goods made by the imitator. Includes misrepresentation and deceit; thus, such conduct is fraudulent not only to competitors but to the public.

Unilateral contract   A promise for an act or an act for a promise, a single enforceable promise. C promises B $10 if B will mow C's lawn. B mows the lawn. C's promise, now binding, is a unilateral contract. *See* Bilateral contract.

Usage of trade* Any practice or method of dealing so regularly observed in a place, vocation, or trade that observance may justly be expected in the transaction in question. The existence and scope of such usage are to be proved as facts. If it is established that such a usage is embodied in a written trade code or similar writing, the interpretation of the writing is for the court.

Usurious A contract is usurious if made for a loan of money at a rate of interest in excess of that permitted by statute.

Utter "Put out" or "pass off." To utter a check is to offer it to another in payment of a debt. To "utter a forged writing" means to put such writing in circulation, knowing of the falsity of the instrument, with the intent to injure another.

Value* Except as otherwise provided with respect to negotiable instruments and bank collections, a person gives "value" for rights if he acquires them (a) in return for a binding commitment to extend credit or for the extension of immediately available credit, whether or not drawn upon and whether or not a chargeback is provided for in the event of difficulties in collection; or (b) as security for, or in, total or partial satisfaction of a preexisting claim; or (c) by accepting delivery pursuant to a preexisting contract for purchase; or (d) generally, in return for any consideration sufficient to support a simple contract.

Vendee A purchaser of property. Generally, the purchaser of real property. A *buyer* is usually a purchaser of chattels.

Vendor The seller of property, usually real property. The word *seller* is used with personal property.

Vendor's lien An unpaid seller's right to hold possession of property until he has recovered the purchase price.

Venire To come into court, a writ used to summon potential jurors.

Venue The geographical area over which a court presides. Venue designates the county in which the action is tried. Change of venue means to move to another county.

Verdict The decision of a jury, reported to the court, on matters properly submitted to the jury for consideration.

Vertical merger A merger of corporations, one corporation being the supplier of the other.

Void Has no legal effect. A contract that is void is a nullity and confers no rights or duties.

Voidable That which is valid until one party, who has the power of avoidance, exercises such power. An infant has the power of avoidance of his contract. A defrauded party has the power to avoid his contract. Such contract is voidable.

Voir dire Preliminary examination of a prospective juror.

Voting trust Two or more persons owning stock with voting powers divorce those voting rights from ownership but retain to all intents and purposes the ownership in themselves and transfer the voting rights to trustees in whom voting rights of all depositors in the trust are pooled.

Wager A relationship between persons by which they agree that a certain sum of money or thing owned by one of them will be paid or delivered to the other upon the happening of an uncertain event, which event is not within the control of the parties and rests upon chance.

Waive (verb) To "waive" at law is to relinquish or give up

intentionally a known right or to do an act that is inconsistent with the claiming of a known right

Waiver (noun) The intentional relinquishment or giving up of a known right. It may be done by express words or conduct that involves any acts inconsistent with an intention to claim the right. Such conduct creates an estoppel on the part of the claimant. *See* Estoppel.

Warehouseman* A person engaged in the business of storing goods for hire.

Warehouse receipt* Issued by a person engaged in the business of storing goods for hire.

Warehouse receipt An instrument showing that the signer has in his possession certain described goods for storage. It obligates the signer, the warehouseman, to deliver the goods to a specified person or to his order or bearer upon the return of the instrument. Consult Uniform Warehouse Receipts Act.

Warrant (noun) An order in writing in the name of the state, signed by a magistrate, directed to an officer, commanding him to arrest a person; (verb) to guarantee, to answer for, to assure that a state of facts exists.

Warranty An undertaking, either expressed or implied, that a certain fact regarding the subject matter of a contract is presently true or will be true. The word has particular application in the law of sales of chattels. It relates to title and quality. *Warranty* should be distinguished from *guaranty*, which means a contract or promise by one person to answer for the performance of another.

Warranty of merchantability A promise implied in a sale of goods by merchants: that the goods are reasonably fit for the general purpose for which they are sold.

Waste Damage to the real property, so that its value as security is impaired.

Watered stock Corporate stock issued by a corporation for property at an overvaluation, or stock issued for which the corporation receives nothing in payment.

Will (testament) The formal instrument by which a person makes disposition of his property, to take effect upon his death.

Working capital The amount of cash necessary for the convenient and safe transaction of present business.

Workers' compensation A plan for compensating employees for occupational disease, accidental injury, and death suffered in connection with employment.

Writ An instrument in writing, under seal in the name of the state, issued out of a court of justice at the commencement of, or during, a legal proceeding; directed to an officer of the court, commanding him to do some act or requiring some person to do or refrain from doing some act pertinent or relative to the cause being tried.

Writ of certiorari A discretionary proceeding by which an appellate court may review the ruling of an inferior tribunal.

Writ of habeas corpus A court order to one holding custody of another, to produce that individual before the court for the purpose of determining whether such custody is proper.

Yellow-dog contract A worker agrees not to join a union and to be discharged if he breaches the contract.

Zoning ordinance Passed by a city council by virtue of police power. Regulates and prescribes the kind of buildings, residences, or businesses that shall be built and used in different parts of a city.

1271

INDEX

Negligence: (cont.)
  liability based on, 57, 65–72
  malpractice, 69–70
  personal defense and, 658, 668
  products liability, 577–78
  trend toward no-fault, 72
Negotiable instruments, 617–33
  negotiability, 599, 622–25
  requirements, 617–21, 628–31
  third person in possession of, 652–53
  types of, 599
Negotiation:
  of document of title, 467–68
  of traditional real estate sales contract, 434
  transfer by, 634–35
Newman v. *City of Indianola,* 117, 126–127
Newmaster v. *Southeast Equipment, Inc.,* 533n, 544–45
New York Family Court Act, 104–6
New York Stock Exchange, 975
New York v. *Quarles,* 99n, 110–11
No. Ill. Gas Co. v. *Energy Co-op, Inc.,* 254n, 269–70
Noble v. *Bonnett,* 701n, 715–16
Norris-LaGuardia Act (1932), 1082
Northeast Petroleum Corporation of New Hampshire, Inc. v. *Agency of Transportation,* 416n, 427–28
Northwestern Bell Telephone Co. v. *Cowger,* 142n, 154–55
Note, defined, 599, 601
Novation, 256, 282, 292
Nuclear Regulatory Commission, 1036
Nuisance, 60, 62, 77–78

Obligation:
  agency coupled with, 371
  moral, 169–70, 179
  mutuality of, 162–68
Obligee and obligor, 783
Occupational Safety and Health Act (OSHA), 350, 1019, 1049, 1053–54
Occupational Safety and Health Review Commission, 1049
Offer and acceptance theory, 952
Offeree and offeror, 134
Offering, circular, 1109
Offering, public, 1110
Offer(s), 135–43
  communication of, 138–39
  definition, 135
  duration of, 139–41
  existence, test of, 135–36, 137
  firm, 142–43, 170
  irrevocable, 142–43
  language used, 136
Officers, liability of corporate, 977–81, 987–90
Old Albany Estates v. *Highland Carpet Mills,* 560n, 568
O. P. Ganjo, Inc. v. *Tri-Urban Realty Co.,* 684
Option contract, 142–44, 154–55, 443–44
Order:
  "charging," 916
  defined, 622
  paper, 622–23
  to pay in negotiable instruments, 618–19
  of relief, defined, 846
Ordinances, 7, 393
Osterholt v. *St. Charles Drilling Co.,* 508n, 522–23
Otto Contracting Co. v. *S. Schinella & Son,*

222n, 234–35
Output contracts, 163–64
Owensboro National Bank v. *Crisp,* 658n, 667–68
Owner, defined, 384
Ownership, multiple, 488–91
Ownership interests, 389–95
  real property, 389–92
  restrictions on, 392–95, 403–6

Pacific Metal Company v. *Northwestern Bank of Helena,* 389n, 400–401
Palmateer v. *International Harvester Co.,* 369n, 378–79
Paradise v. *Nowlin,* 893
Parents, tort liability of, 58–59
Park Cities Corporation v. *Byrd,* 935n, 943
Parker v. *Twentieth Century-Fox Film Corporation,* 120n, 129–30
Parol evidence rule, 220, 228–30, 236, 239, 672, 685
Participation theory, 977
Particular fund doctrine, 619–20
Particular purpose, implied warranty of fitness for, 555–56, 566–68, 576
Partnerships:
  advantages and disadvantages, 879
  defined, 878, 897, 905, 906
  dissolution of, 929–46
  formation of, 897–911
  general, 878–79
  "incorporated," 975
  limited, 880–82, 890–92
  operation of, 912–28
  termination of, 929, 939–40
  trading vs. nontrading, 918–19
  at will, 929–30
Payment:
  balloon, 821
  debtor protection in, 822–26, 841–42
  discharge of contract through, 256–57
  tenders of, 247–48
Payor bank, 638, 640–41
Pension plans, Keogh, 886
People, the, defined, 35
Peremptory challenges, 43
Perez v. *United States,* 1016n, 1026–27
Perfection:
  of mechanic's lien, 763–64
  of security interest, 699–703, 712–16
Performance:
  bond, 785
  of conditions, 247–51
  contract (see Contract)
  course of, 511–12
  impossibility of, 252–54, 268–69
  part, 223, 225–28
  remedy, specific, 10–11, 132
  substantial, 248, 266–67
  surety's right to, 788–89
  time of, 513
Perkins v. *Philbrick,* 318n, 334–35
Perlmutter v. *Beth David Hospital,* 593
Personal defenses, 600, 657, 658, 668
Personal freedom, interference with, 59–60
Personal property:
  acquiring title to, 409–13
  artisan's lien on, 779–80, 800–801
  bailment, 462–66
  contracts for sale of, 224
  defined, 385–86

real property distinctions from, 386–87
Pestana v. *Karinol Corp.,* 517n, 526–27
Peter Principle, 1043
Petition, 40
Petitioner, 36
Petty offenses, defined, 89
Pfliger v. *Peavey Company,* 320n, 335–36
Pick v. *Bartel,* 224n, 236
Pierce v. *Plogger,* 177–78
Pierson v. *Jones,* 954n, 964–65
Plaintiff, 35, 47
Plat, 395, 414–15
Plateq Corp. of North Haven v. *Machlett Lab,* 538n, 547–49
Plea bargaining, 100
Pleadings, 40–42
PMSI (see Purchase-money security interest)
Poletown Neighborhood Council v. *City of Detroit,* 393n, 403–5
Police courts, 22
Police power of states, 1016–17, 1028–29
Pontiacs v. *K. M. S. Investments,* 347n, 359–60
Possession:
  adverse, 418–19, 429–30
  defined, 384
  perfection by, 701–2
  unity of, 489
Post Office Department, 1036
Potter v. *Hatter Farms, Inc.,* 227n, 236–37
Power:
  of attorney, 298, 309
  of directors of corporation, 975–76
  given as security, 370
  of partners, 916–19, 924–27
  of sale, foreclosure by, 760
  taxing, 1013–14, 1017
P. P., Inc. v. *McGuire,* 621n, 630–31
Precedent, 10–12
  conditions, 244–45, 679–80
Presentment, 676–80, 687–88
Press, freedom of, 1018
Prevention, nonperformance and, 251
Preventive detention, 104–6
Price:
  discrimination, 1062–64, 1074–77
  -fixing, 167, 1059–60, 1071–74
  information, exchange of, 1060, 1073–74
  in sales contract, 512
  seller's right to collect purchase, 538–39
  stock, determination in mergers, 998–99, 1006–7
Primary parties, liability to commercial paper, 672, 673
Prince Enterprises, Inc. v. *Griffith Oil Co.,* 147n, 157
Principal:
  -agent relationship (see Agency)
  disclosed, 296, 319–20
  duties of, 302–5, 312–13
  liability of, 317, 319–25, 337
  in suretyship, 783
  third parties' liability to, 327–28
  types of, 296
  undisclosed, 296, 320–21, 337
Priorities:
  in Article 9 transactions, 719–37
  creditor, in bankruptcy, 864–66
  in mechanic's liens, 764–65, 776–77
  to mortgages in foreclosure, 760–61
Privacy, right of, 64–65
Private law, defined, 5